The School Services Sourcebook

Editorial Board

Online Editor

The School Services Sourcebook

Second Edition

Editors

Cynthia Franklin
University of Texas at Austin

Mary Beth Harris
University of Southern California

Paula Allen-Meares
University of Illinois at Chicago

KH

OXFORD
UNIVERSITY PRESS

Oxford University Press is a department of the University of Oxford. It furthers the University's objective of excellence in research, scholarship, and education by publishing worldwide.

Oxford New York
Auckland Cape Town Dar es Salaam Hong Kong Karachi
Kuala Lumpur Madrid Melbourne Mexico City Nairobi
New Delhi Shanghai Taipei Toronto

With offices in
Argentina Austria Brazil Chile Czech Republic France Greece
Guatemala Hungary Italy Japan Poland Portugal Singapore
South Korea Switzerland Thailand Turkey Ukraine Vietnam

Published in the United States of America by
Oxford University Press
198 Madison Avenue, New York, NY 10016

Library of Congress Cataloging-in-Publication Data
The school services sourcebook: a guide for school-based professionals / edited by Cynthia Franklin, Mary Beth Harris, Paula Allen-Meares.—2nd ed.
p. cm.
Includes bibliographical references and index.
ISBN 978-0-19-986175-0 (hardcover: alk. paper)
1. School social work—Handbooks, manuals, etc. 2. School children—Mental health services—Handbooks, manuals, etc. I. Harris, Mary Beth. II. Allen-Meares, Paula, 1948-
LB3013.4.S372 2012
371.4'6—dc23
2012017944

9 8 7 6 5 4 3 2 1
Printed in the United States of America
on acid-free paper

8/28/13

Contents

PART V

Improving Multicultural and Community Relationships, School Accountability, and Resource Development

Section XI

Section XII

Section XIII

Preface

The School Services Sourcebook, Second Edition has been revised to provide best practices to social workers, counselors, and mental health professionals who work in schools or whose practices involve consultations or interventions with school systems. This book addresses effective school-based services for students who are high risk because of psychosocial problems and who may have mental health, neurological, and physical disorders that require responsive interventions to ensure their educational progress. This book covers the mandates of the Individual with Disabilities Education Act (IDEA) and the No Child Left Behind program. In this second edition of the book, we also encouraged each author to address how interventions are used within a Response to Intervention (RTI) framework and included additional content that addresses the empirical support for RTI.

The School Services Sourcebook, Second Edition is written so that diverse professionals may make use of its contents, and for this reason we co-mingle professional terms like school social worker, counselor, mental health practitioner, school services professional, and special education teacher. By co-mingling these professional terms, it is not our intention to mitigate the distinct roles of any professional group. We believe, however, that most professionals providing mental health, health, or social services will find many of these chapters informative and valuable to their work. While the book is addressed specifically to school social workers and other mental health professionals who work in schools, we also believe that other counselors as well as child and family welfare workers will welcome the resources in this volume because it offers effective interventions for working with schools that are also essential to child and adolescent practice.

Contents of the Second Edition

The School Services Sourcebook, Second Edition has 73 chapters divided over five parts with 13 sections and an additional online section that offers six chapters. Part 1 covers methods and frameworks for improving school services such as Response to Intervention, school climate initiatives, functional behavioral assessments, and how to integrate ethics into positive behavioral supports. Part 2 illustrates best practice interventions for students with mental health diagnosis, neurodevelopmental, learning, and physical disabilities. Part 3 offers best practice resources for substance abuse, health, interpersonal, and social problems covering a smorgasbord of essential topics such as substance abuse prevention, sexually transmitted diseases, dropout prevention, violence, bullying and conflict resolution, and child abuse, among other relevant issues. Part 4 covers crisis intervention, group work, and training topics such as suicide prevention, preparing for disasters, in-service training and professional development, and resources for parental and family involvement. Part 5 of the book covers how to improve multicultural practice, community relationships, and accountability and resource development for the school. This section offers resources for improving the education of diverse students and helping school-based practitioners enhance community resources and practice accountability.

Objectives of the Book

This second edition of *The School Services Sourcebook* follows the same objectives as the first edition. First, our objective was for the resource book to be a comprehensive resource for school social workers and other school-based services professionals. Of course, we are cognizant of the fact that we cannot cover every issue that a school-based practitioner needs to know, but we wanted the contents of the resource book to cover the most important and timely information needed for school-based practices. For this reason, the contents of this resource book are expansive (73 chapters), but we believe that a volume that provides school-based practitioners with the knowledge and practice tools that cover their work in the schools is needed. We wrote this book to offer practice briefs that busy school professionals could quickly consult for help in their work. We hope the book will be like a desk reference that provides (in one comprehensive volume) the updated knowledge, tools, and resources that can help practitioners to improve their work in the schools.

The second objective was for this book to communicate evidenced-based knowledge from research to practice, but to do it in a way that practitioners could easily consume this knowledge. Evidenced-based practices are often created and tested in universities and research centers, and it may take years for these practices to trickle down into the hands of school-based practitioners. We imagined that this book would serve as a major source for the trickle down. For this reason, we provide the best practices through easy-to-read practice briefs that provide instructions for carrying out the practices in a school, and also provide additional resources for learning more. As editors, we wanted each chapter to be applied, providing practice examples and tools that can be used in the day-to-day practices of school social workers and other school-based services professionals. In the second edition, each chapter follows a practice-friendly outline that includes the headings *Getting Started*, *What We Know*, *What We Can Do*, *Applying Interventions within a Response to Intervention Framework*, *Tools and Practice Examples*, *and Points to Remember*. It can be a challenge for researchers to communicate to practitioners in brief points and steps that can quickly be assimilated and used in practice. As editors, however, we have given this task our best effort. We hope that the practitioners who read this volume (including students) will give us feedback on how we can do this job better. A third objective was to transform this book into a relevant, research-based practice update that would be extremely useful to practitioners because its contents provided the tools and information they needed. The fact that this book has been so well received in the field and has moved into its second edition suggests that it is serving this function for school social workers and other school mental health professionals who use it. We hope that this second edition will continue to serve as a resource for practice, teaching, and research knowledge. School practitioners have told us that they could use the book daily to guide their practices, prepare their presentations, review needed information, and answer questions about issues that they could not remember or did not know. They also told us that they wished the book was a little more condensed and content was a little easier to find, and for this reason we have continued to include quick reference tables, outlines, practice examples, and Internet resources to consult. We have also worked to make titles and index materials more specific so that practitioners could more easily scan the book for information. Practitioners who reviewed this book for its revision suggested that we give more attention to Response to Intervention and positive behavioral supports, and we have encouraged authors to do so in every chapter of the book.

Why Focus on Evidence-Based Practice?

Evidence-based practice is vital to educational and mental health settings, but nowhere is it more important than in schools, because schools provide the majority of the mental health services to children and families. Evidence-based practice is a here-and-now movement, circumscribing mental health practice in all settings. Since the first edition of this book we have learned a great deal about the implementation and sustainability of practices based on research evidence, and we now know that it takes school-wide modifications and planned efforts to successfully implement and sustain best practices in a school setting. Prevention science and Response to Intervention approaches have taught us much about effective practices and their implementation. Practices based on research evidence cannot be separated from practice-based evidence that shows its practical utility in applied settings. Fortunately, implementation science is growing, and we have tried to make this edition of *The School Services Sourcebook* even more specific for explaining how the research-based practices discussed may be best implemented within a school. This book demonstrates the best evidenced-based practices; however, in some areas where evidence is lacking, experimental and best practice wisdom was also included. We hope that this approach will provide the most promising and practical as well as the best evidence for school-based practitioners and that this second edition will continue to be the practical resource that it has proven to be for school social workers and other professionals.

Who Helped Us Develop This Resource Book

We have received valuable direction and support for *The School Services Sourcebook, Second Edition* from our editorial consultants (listed on the next pages). The consultants comprise leaders in school social work organizations as well as researchers and scholars who contribute to the practice, foundation knowledge, empirical study, and professional literature of school mental health. Throughout the process of developing the second edition, the editorial consultants have contributed chapters, nominated authors, and reviewed chapter manuscripts. Their colossal support and participation has been essential to the manual's development and completion.

Authors of the chapters contained in the second edition are experts in their field, with years of practice experience, research, and publications. They range from practicing school social workers, counselors, and psychologists, to physicians and public health specialists, and finally to researchers and scholars across disciplines whose research provides evidence and practice theory and whose writing informs and guides school-based services.

How We Selected the Chapter Topics

The first edition chapter topics were identified through feedback from school social workers in six regions of the country. Social workers in California, Georgia, Michigan, New Mexico, Oregon, and Texas communicated with us through an email questionnaire, individual interviews, and focus groups. We asked about the overall challenges of working in a school setting. We asked for the most urgent and frequent problems that school social workers and other practitioners encounter with students and families. We asked about the areas of practice that require continually updated training and the sources of such training. We asked about service delivery methods such as groups, home visits, and individual contacts.

School practitioners told us that their practice requires skills in diverse areas. A primary aspect of their work is direct services to individuals (school staff as well as students), to groups, and to families. Within these services, they need continually updated skills in conflict mediation and violence prevention; crisis management; and treating the current epidemics of substance abuse, obesity and other eating disorders, and self-mutilation. They need continual updating on psychotropic drugs and their interaction with child and adolescent development. They need cultural knowledge for engaging with increasing numbers of immigrant and refugee families, and clinical tools for working with other challenging families.Beyond direct services, they offer consultations, design and develop programs and program evaluations, and conduct organizational and interdisciplinary team building. They report that they feel more pressure than ever to produce clear evidence of their effectiveness for multiple stakeholder groups. They are being called upon to secure funding for their own programs and need to know the nuts and bolts of grant writing. *The School Services Sourcebook* covers all these areas, as well as other topics that were solicited from our editorial consultants.

Changes in Second Edition Topics

In preparation for this second edition, Oxford had the first edition book contents reviewed by national experts in the field of school-based services, including practitioners and academicians in the field. The reviews were extraordinarily positive toward most of the current contents but suggested that thorough updates were needed due to the age of the book. The authors including integrations of some chapters with similar content have provided extensive revisions of the chapters. We have also worked to reduce the number of chapters without compromising the comprehensive nature of the book, combining some chapters as suggested by reviewers and reorganizing the contents of the book. The second edition chapters have been reduced from 114 to 73 chapters. We added 15 new chapters that address relevant up-to-date issues such as Response to Intervention, positive behavioral supports, school climate, functional behavioral assessment, the integration of ethics, autism and suicide, school engagement, military families, Latino immigrant families, classroom management, transition planning, and several chapters that speak to assessment and accountability. We also moved six chapters that review marketing issues, school policy updates, confidentiality and electronic records, and other helpful information on how to operate a school-based practice to an online section that will be available to readers. Topics in the second edition of the book continue to serve as resources to help practitioners to be effective, marketable, and accountable.

Acknowledgments

First and foremost, we want to thank Oxford University Press for supporting this work. Our deepest gratitude goes to Joan H. Bossert and the staff. We also are grateful to the previous social work editor, Maura Roessner, who helped us with the first edition and encouraged us to take on this revision, and to the assistant editor, Nicholas Liu, who guided the revision process. We would also like to thank Katherine Montgomery for her editorial assistance in the management of this project and the preparation of the manuscript. We also owe gratitude to our editorial consultants, who provided capable guidance in the planning of the book and quick assistance in reviewing the manuscripts. We give credit to all the school social workers and school mental health professionals who participated in our original survey and the reviews of the first edition text. Finally, we would like to thank our family, friends, and colleagues who endured the process of our work on this revision.

Cynthia Franklin, PhD
University of Texas at Austin
Mary Beth Harris, PhD
University of Southern California
Paula Allen-Meares, PhD
University of Illinois at Chicago

Contributors

Howard S. Adelman
Professor and Center Co-Director
Center for Mental Health in Schools
Department of Psychology
University of California Los Angeles

Chris Ahlman, PhD
Professor
Social Work
Lewis-Clark State College

Paula Allen-Meares, PhD
Vice President
University of Illinois
Chancellor
University of Illinois at Chicago
John Corbally Presidential Professor
School of Public Health
College of Education
Jane Addams School of Social Work
Professor
College of Education
School of Social Work
University of Illinois at Urbana-Champaign
Dean Emeritus
School of Social Work
University of Michigan

Michelle E. Alvarez, EdD, LICSW
Associate Professor
Department of Social Work
Minnesota State University, Mankato

Dawn Anderson-Butcher, PhD
Professor
College of Social Work
The Ohio State University

Ron Avi Astor, PhD
Richard M. and Ann L. Thor Professor in Urban Social Development
School of Social Work and School of Education
University of Southern California

Michelle S. Ballan, PhD
Associate Professor
School of Social Work
Columbia University

Cristina B. Bares, PhD
Assistant Professor
School of Social Work
Virginia Commonwealth University

Concepcion Barrio, PhD
Associate Professor
School of Social Work
University of Southern California

Rami Benbenishty, PhD, MSW
Professor
School of Social Work
Bar Ilan University

Kia J. Bentley, PhD, MSSW
Director
PhD Program
Professor
School of Social Work
Virginia Commonwealth University

Sheena Berry
Doctoral Student
School of Education
University of North Carolina at Chapel Hill

Beverly M. Black, PhD
Jillian Michelle Smith Professor in Family Violence Research
School of Social Work
University of Texas at Arlington

Gary L. Bowen, PhD, ACSW
Kenan Distinguished Professor
School of Social Work
The University of North Carolina at Chapel Hill

Natasha K. Bowen, PhD
Associate Professor
School of Social Work
University of North Carolina at Chapel Hill

Stephen E. Brock, PhD
Professor
Department of Special Education, Rehabilitation, School Psychology, and Deaf Studies
California State University, Sacramento

Jacqueline A. Brown, MA
Counseling, Clinical, and School Psychology
University of California, Santa Barbara

Ruth C. Brown, PhD
Postdoctoral Fellow
Virginia Institute for Psychiatric and Behavioral Genetics
Virginia Commonwealth University

Hilary Bunting
Guidance Counselor
Northmor Junior High
Galion, Ohio
Community Lecturer
School of Social Work
The Ohio State University
Columbus, Ohio

Lynn Bye, PhD
Associate Professor
Social Work
University of Minnesota Duluth

Marilyn Camacho
Department of Psychiatry
Columbia University

Laurie M. Carpenter, MSW
Research Area Specialist
Center for Managing Chronic Disease
University of Michigan

Erin A. Casey, PhD
Associate Professor
School of Social Work
University of Washington, Tacoma

Paul K. Cavanagh, PhD, MSW
Director
Academics and Evaluation
Vocational Independence Program
New York Institute of Technology

Allan R. Chavkin, PhD
Professor
English
Texas State University

Nancy Feyl Chavkin, PhD, ACSW, LMSW-AP
Regents Professor
Social Work
Texas State University

Jenell S. Clarke, PhD, MSW
Program Analyst
Office of Inspector General
Federal Department of Health & Human Services
New York, NY

Allen Hugh Cole, Jr.
Nancy Taylor Williamson Associate Professor of Pastoral Care
Associate Dean for Masters Programs
Austin Presbyterian Theological Seminary

Jose E. Coll, PhD, MSW
Associate Professor
Social Work
Director
Veteran Student Services
School of Education and Social Services
Saint Leo University

Kathryn S. Collins, PhD, MSW
Associate Professor
School of Social Work
University of Maryland

Jonathan S. Comer, PhD
Co-Director of Research
Center for Anxiety and Related Disorders (Child Program)
Research Assistant Professor
Psychology
Boston University

Jacqueline Corcoran, PhD
Professor
School of Social Work
Virginia Commonwealth University

Alan J. Dettlaff, PhD
Assistant Professor
Jane Addams College of Social Work
University of Illinois at Chicago

Nic T. Dibble, MSW
Education Consultant
School Social Work
Wisconsin Department of Public Instruction

Hilary Drew, MSW
Doctoral Candidate
Graduate Student Lecturer
College of Social Work
The Ohio State University

David R. Dupper, PhD
College of Social Work
University of Tennessee, Knoxville

Theresa Early, J. PhD
Director
Doctoral and International Programs
Associate Professor
College of Social Work
The Ohio State University

Chaturi Edrisinha, PhD, BCBA-D
Associate Professor
Counseling and Community Psychology
St. Cloud State University

Timothea M. Elizalde, LMSW
School Social Worker
Albuquerque Public Schools
Adjunct Professor
School of Social Work
New Mexico Highlands University

Diane E. Elze, PhD
Associate Professor and MSW Program Director
School of Social Work
University at Buffalo

Cathy Grover Ely, PhD, LSW
School Social Worker
Reynoldsburg City Schools
Reynoldsburg, OH

Anna G. Escamilla, PhD, LCSW
Assistant Professor of Social Work
School of Behavioral and Social Sciences
St. Edward's University

Steven W. Evans, PhD
Professor of Psychology
Center for Intervention Research in Schools
Ohio University

Kathleen Coulborn Faller, PhD, ACSW
Director
Family Assessment Clinic
Marion Elizabeth Blue Professor of Children and Families
School of Social Work
University of Michigan

Kevin J. Filter, PhD
Associate Professor
Psychology Department
Minnesota State University, Mankato

Rowena Fong, EdD
Ruby Lee Piester Centennial Professor
School of Social Work
University of Texas at Austin

Christina Fragale, MED, BCBA
Graduate Research Assistant
Special Education
Meadows Center for Preventing Educational Risk
University of Texas at Austin

Cynthia Franklin, PhD, LCSW, LMFT
Stiernberg/Spencer Family Professor in Mental Health
School of Social Work
University of Texas at Austin

Pam Franzwa, MSW
Clinical Assistant Professor
School of Social Work
University of Southern California
San Diego, CA

Edith M. Freeman, PhD
Professor Emerita of Social Work
School of Social Welfare
The University of Kansas

Charles D. arvin, PhD
Professor Emeritus of Social Work
School of Social Work
University of Michigan

Beth Gerlach, PhD, LCSW
Research Associate
Child and Family Research Institute
School of Social Work
University of Texas at Austin

Dorie J. Gilbert, PhD
Associate Professor
Social Work and African & African Diaspora Studies
University of Texas at Austin

Kristy Gillispie, MSW
Doctoral Student
School of Social Work
University of Texas at Austin

Linda Goldman
Adjunct Faculty
Graduate School of Counseling
Johns Hopkins University
Graduate School of Counseling
George Washington University

Vanessa A. Green, PhD
Associate Professor
School of Educational Psychology and Pedagogy
Victoria University of Wellington

Allen B. Grove, PhD
Licensed Clinical Psychologist
Hofstra University

Jane Hanvey-Phillips
School of Social Work
University of Texas at Arlington

Mary Beth Harris, PhD
Clinical Associate Professor and Director
San Diego Academic Center
School of Social Work
University of Southern California

Elayne Haymes, PhD
Independent Mental Health Care Professional
Washington, DC

Karen F. Hoban, BCBA
Speech Pathologist
Private Practice

Laura M. Hopson, PhD
Assistant Professor
School of Social Work
University of Alabama

Esther Howe, PhD, LCSW
Professor
Department of Social Work
Southern Connecticut State University

Lisa Hunter-Romanelli, PhD
Executive Director
REACH Institute
New York, NY
Adjunct Assistant Professor of Clinical Psychology
School of Psychiatry
Columbia University

Shane R. Jimerson, PhD
Professor
Counseling, Clinical, and School Psychology
University of California, Santa Barbara

Melissa Jonson-Reid, PhD
Director
Center for Violence Prevention and Injury Prevention
Professor
George Warren Brown School of Social Work
Washington University

Soyon Jung, PhD
Graduate
School of Social Work
University of Texas at Austin

Michael S. Kelly, PhD
Associate Professor
Masters Program Director
School of Social Work
Loyola University Chicago

Isok Kim, PhD, LCSW
Assistant Professor
School of Social Work
University at Buffalo
The State University of New York

Jihye Kim, PhD
Graduate
School of Social Work
University of Texas at Austin

Johnny S. Kim, PhD, LICSW
Associate Professor
Social Welfare
University of Kansas

Karen S. Knox, PhD, LCSW
Professor and Field Coordinator
School of Social Work
Texas State University

Wynne S. Korr, PhD
Dean and Professor
School of Social Work
University of Illinois at Urbana-Champaign

Katina M. Lambros, PhD, BCBA-D
Assistant Professor
Counseling and School Psychology
San Diego State University

Giulio Lancioni, PhD
Professor
Department of Psychology
University of Bari

Russell Lang, PhD, BCBA
Assistant Professor of Special Education
Curriculum and Instruction
Texas State University, San Marcos

Amber Lasseigne
Project Development Specialist
Fort Worth Independent School District
Fort Worth, TX

Julia Graham Lear, PhD
Professor
Department of Prevention & Community Health
Senior Adviser
Center for Health & Health Care in Schools
School of Public Health and Health Services
George Washington University

Craig Winston LeCroy, PhD
Professor
School of Social Work
Tucson Component
Arizona State University

Mo Yee Lee, PhD
Professor
College of Social Work
The Ohio State University

Brenda Coble Lindsey, PhD
BSW Program Director
Clinical Associate Professor
School of Social Work
University of Illinois at Urbana-Champaign

Tammy Linseisen, LCSW
Clinical Associate Professor
School of Social Work
University of Texas at Austin

Courtney J. Lynch, PhD, LCSW
Clinical Social Worker
Department of the Army

Helen Cannella, PhD
Associate Professor
Special Education
The Ohio State University

Roxana Marachi, PhD
Associate Professor
Connie L. Lurie College of Education
San José State University

Mary M. McKay, PhD
Professor
New York University Silver School of Social Work
Director
McSilver Institute of Poverty, Policy, and Research
Professional Lecturer
Mount Sinai School of Medicine

Katherine L. Montgomery, MSSW
PhD Candidate
School of Social Work
University of Texas at Austin

Priya Mudholkar
Masters Student
School of Education
North Carolina State University

Reshma B. Naidoo, PhD
Neuropsychologist
Neuro Outcomes
Austin, TX

Paula S. Nurius, PhD
Director
Prevention Research Training Program
Grace Beals-Ferguson Professor
School of Social Work
University of Washington

Mark O'Reilly, PhD, BCBA-D
Mollie Villeret Davis Professor in Learning Disabilities
Professor of Special Education
College of Education
University of Texas at Austin

David Osher, PhD
Vice President and Co-Director
Human and Social Development
American Institute for Research

Julie S. Owens, PhD
Associate Professor
Psychology
Ohio University

Daphna Oyserman, PhD
Edwin J. Thomas Collegiate Professor
School of Social Work and Department of Psychology
Research Professor
Institute for Social Research
University of Michigan

Donna B. Pincus, PhD
Co-Director of Research
Center for Anxiety and Related Disorders (Child Program)
Associate Professor
Psychology
Boston University

Jeffrey M. Poirier, MA, PMP
PhD Candidate
Senior Researcher
American Institutes for Research

Tara Powell, MSW, MPH
Doctoral Student
School of Social Work
University of Texas at Austin

Lauren Z. Powledge, LMSW
Independent Social Work Consultant
The Beacon Group

Nicole Pyle, PhD
Assistant Professor
Teacher Education and Leadership
Utah State University

James C. Raines, PhD
Professor and Department Chair
Health, Human Services & Public Policy
California State University at Monterey Bay

Gilbert A. Ramirez, LISW, LCSW, LSSW
School Social Worker
Albuquerque Public Schools
Associate Professor
School of Social Work
New Mexico Highlands University
Clinical Consultant
New Mexico Young Fathers Project

Carey E. Reinicke
Inquiry Specialist
School of Continuing and Professional Studies
University of Virginia

Albert R. Roberts, PhD
Posthumous, Professor of Criminal Justice
Faculty of Arts and Sciences
Rutgers University

Eden Hernandez Robles
Doctoral Student
School of Social Work
University of Texas at Austin

Tiffany N. Ryan, MSW
Doctoral Student
School of Social Work
University of Texas at Austin

Hayley Sacks
Student
Psychology
University of Pennsylvania

Matthew D. Selekman, LCSW
Co-Director
Partners for Collaborative Solutions
Evanston, IL

Gary L. Shaffer, PhD
Posthumous, Associate Professor
School of Social Work
University of North Carolina at Chapel Hill

Oren Shtayermman, PhD
Director
Mental Health Counseling Program
Department of Interdisciplinary Health Sciences
New York Institute of Technology

Jeff Sigafoos, PhD
Professor
School of Educational Psychology and Pedagogy
Victoria University of Wellington, New Zealand

Gail H. Sims, PhD, MS, BS, AA
Director
Behavioral Health Department
San Carlos Apache Tribe Wellness Center
San Carlos, AZ

Michael S. Spencer, PhD
Professor and Associate Dean of Educational Programs
School of Social Work
University of Michigan

David W. Springer, PhD, LCSW
Dean and Professor
School of Social Work
Portland State University

Lori K. Holleran Steiker, PhD
Assistant Dean
Undergraduate Programs
Associate Professor
School of Social Work
University of Texas at Austin

Calvin L. Streeter, PhD
Professor
School of Social Work
University of Texas at Austin

Danielle C. Swick, PhD, MSW
Research Assistant Professor
School of Social Work
University of North Carolina at Chapel Hill

Linda Taylor, PhD
Center Co-Director
Center for Mental Health in Schools
Department of Psychology
University of California Los Angeles

Martell Teasley, PhD
Professor and Department Chair
Department of Social Work
College of Public Policy
University of Texas at San Antonio

Tanya Tenor, MSW
Waterbury School District
Waterbury, CT

Miki Tesh, LCSW
Assistant Instructor and Doctoral Student
School of Social Work
University of Texas at Austin

Aaron M. Thompson, PhD
Assistant Professor
School of Social Work
University of Missouri

Sanna J. Thompson, PhD
Associate Professor
School of Social Work
University of Texas at Austin

Meghan Tomb, PhD
Post-Doctoral Research Fellow
New York Presbyterian Hospital
Columbia University Medical Center

Dorian E. Traube, PhD
Assistant Professor
Social Work
University of Southern California

Louisa Triandis, LCSW
Adjunct Faculty
Social Work
University of Southern California

Stephen J. Tripodi, PhD
Assistant Professor
College of Social Work
Florida State University

Gena Truitt, MSW
Research Assistant
School of Social Work
University of Southern California
San Diego Academic Center

Ernst O. VanBergeijk, PhD
Associate Dean & Executive Director
Vocational Independence Program
New York Institute of Technology

Adrienne Villagomez
Doctoral Student
School of Education
University of North Carolina at Chapel Hill

Barbara Hanna Wasik, PhD
William R. Kenan, Jr. Distinguished Professor
School of Education
University of North Carolina at Chapel Hill

Eugenia L. Weiss, PsyD, LCSW
Clinical Assistant Professor
Military Social Work
School of Social Work
University of Southern California

Arlene N. Weisz, PhD
Professor
School of Social Work
Wayne State University

Jade Wexler, PhD
Assistant Professor
Department of Counseling, Higher Education, and Special Education
College of Education
University of Maryland

Margaret White, LCSW
Technical Assistance Coordinator
Illinois PBIS Network
La Grange Park, IL

Debra J. Woody, PhD
Associate Professor
Associate Dean for Academic Affairs
School of Social Work
University of Texas at Arlington

Jessica Wright Marini
Masters Student
Social Work
Southern Connecticut State University

Jennifer D. Yates
School Psychologist
Long Beach Unified School District
Long Beach, CA
PhD Student
Spiritual Care and Counseling
Claremont School of Theology

Kimberly A. Zammitt, PhD, LICSW
Assistant Professor
Department of Social Work
Minnesota State University, Mankato

Farah El Zein
Doctoral Student
Special Education
University of Texas at Austin

PART I

Resources for Improving Student Support Services

SECTION I Methods and Frameworks for Improving School Services

This section introduces school practitioners to important methods and frameworks for improving school services that are related to policy changes, school reform, and the changing environment of education. Over the past decade, the school literature has increasingly discussed Response to Intervention, school climate, and functional behavioral assessment as ways to increase the effectiveness of school services. All of these approaches have emphasized prevention, school-wide initiatives, and the use of evidence-based practices. Ethical situations and social complexities have also increased for schools, making it more important than ever for school professionals to know how to respond to the ethical dilemmas they may face in the delivery of their services. This section examines all of these practices and judiciously critiques the delivery of school services, pointing practitioners toward the best practices.

CHAPTER 1 Implementing Evidence-Based Practices within a Response to Intervention Framework

Michael S. Kelly

Getting Started

The school-based prevention and intervention research has influenced models to guide academic and behavior support services in schools. The Response to Intervention (RTI) and the related positive behavior supports (PBS) models are particularly relevant to understanding the changing landscape in delivering instructional support to students, teachers, and families in American schools today.

Imagine two students (call them Marvin and Paul) who attend schools in neighboring suburbs. Both second graders who are having academic and behavior problems in their classes. In many ways, the two boys are similar: Both came to their schools this year, both are from strong and supportive families, and both are struggling to keep up with the reading and associated tasks in their class. Both also tend to act out in class, disrupting the class and at times becoming aggressive with other students.

In Marvin's school (call it Forest Glen), his teacher schedules a meeting with the principal to share her concerns that Marvin isn't "making it" in second grade and needs additional help. The principal suggests that Marvin's teacher bring him to their special education team to discuss whether or not to pursue a case study evaluation for Marvin. The team meets on Marvin and decides that his academic and behavioral performance indicate that he might be eligible for special education services. They then schedule a meeting with Marvin's parents, who agree that Marvin is struggling and is frustrated with getting in trouble at his new school. After Marvin's parents sign the consent forms, the school team conducts a case study, and the test scores noted by the school psychologist indicate that Marvin is eligible for services under the learning disability (LD) category due to a discrepancy between his ability and achievement. A functional behavior assessment (FBA) is completed by the school social worker and, based on that assessment's findings, a behavior intervention plan (BIP) is written to address Marvin's classroom behavior; social work is added to Marvin's individualized education plan (IEP) as a related service. He enters special education in second grade and makes some progress quickly, though he goes on to receive LD resource support and social work all the way through elementary school and into junior high.

Paul attends an elementary school in a suburb nearby, and his school (Crawford Elementary) has very similar academic/behavioral concerns noted by his teacher. At Crawford, there has been an active and well-implemented RTI program in place since the last reauthorization of the federal special education law, IDEIA, in 2004. In Crawford's RTI program, Paul's teacher brings him up to the RTI team, composed of a school social worker, RTI interventionist, school psychologist, and reading specialist. The RTI team looks at the DIBELS (Dynamic Indicators of Basic Early Literacy Skills) (DIBELS, 2007) scores that Paul's teacher has been collecting since the school year started. Based on these scores, the team helps Paul's teacher to develop some more focused reading instruction as well as giving Paul additional time in reading with the team reading specialist. The RTI team school social worker and school psychologist collaborate with Paul's teacher to do a structured classroom observation of Paul to track possible triggers for his behavior problems and to consult with the teacher on the development of an informal behavior plan to address those issues in consultation with Paul. This entire process takes place at the RTI team meeting, with Paul's parents as full partners in the work. After four months of intensive reading and behavioral intervention, Paul is responding and his DIBELS scores reflect improvement as well as his decreased office discipline referrals (ODRs). The RTI team convenes with Paul and his parents to celebrate his progress and to consider what additional supports Paul might need as he heads into third grade. At no point in the conversation about third grade does the RTI team mention the possibility that Paul will need to have a case study to determine eligibility for special education services.

These scenarios may be fictitious, but they are far from unrealistic. In the early 21st century, despite major special education reforms at the federal and state level, it is entirely possible that neighboring districts might approach nearly identical students with dramatically different intervention strategies. This chapter will describe what we know about RTI, how RTI came to dominate cutting-edge thinking about delivering services to at-risk students, and how much is still unknown about applying RTI to social/emotional/behavioral issues that students have in a school setting.

Because this is a book that is working to link our knowledge about evidence-based practices (EBPs) and the three-tier model common in RTI, this chapter will attempt to specify how the use of data in RTI and EBPs can work hand in hand to improve student academic, behavioral, and mental health outcomes across the variety of topics covered in this second edition of *The School Services Sourcebook*. Finally, this chapter will work to draw meaningful contrasts between the RTI process and the related but distinct intervention model in schools known as positive behavior supports (PBS, sometimes also referred to as PBIS or SWPBS) to assist readers in identifying the similar and distinct ways that RTI and PBS both use the three-tier model of intervention to improve school outcomes for students.

What We Know about RTI

RTI is most commonly known in American schools as a process of early intervention to provide intensive, data-driven interventions for students who are showing signs of academic difficulties, particularly in the area of reading. RTI has been recently expanded to enable educators to also address the process to students who are showing behavioral difficulties in the classroom that are impacting their learning. RTI can involve many different techniques and ideas, but typically RTI in American schools includes the following components:

1. Students who are being considered for RTI are first assessed on local classroom and school assessments to gauge their performance relative to age-peers (this is often referred to in the

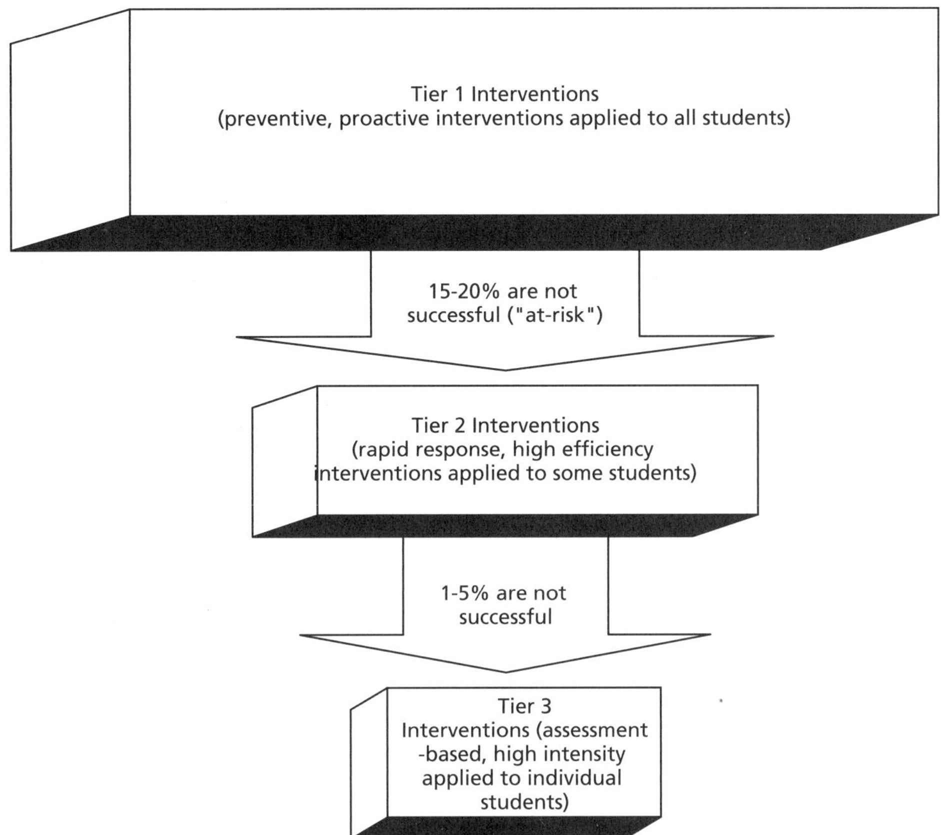

Figure 1.1. Response to Intervention (RTI) as a Basis for Making Intervention Decisions

Source: Reprinted with permission from Frey, A., Lingo, A., & Nelson, C. M. (2009). Positive behavior support and response to intervention in elementary schools. In H. Walker & M. K. Shinn (Eds.), *Interventions for achievement and behavior problems: Preventive and remedial approaches* (3rd ed.). National Association for School Psychologists, Washington, D.C.

literature as being part of the teacher's overall universal screening of their students, and takes place in Tier 1).

2. Teachers bring that data to the RTI team where, in collaboration with the student's parents, a baseline of that student's performance is established, as well as a plan to target progress toward benchmarks that a plan for additional levels of intervention is mapped out, starting with Tier 2 interventions, often involving more intensive learning support that is provided in a small group setting for a specific range of weeks (or months) in the regular education setting.
3. The interventions provided to the student are based on the empirical literature and are considered "research-based."
4. Student progress is continuously monitored by the teacher and the RTI team to inform additional decisions about additional supports or interventions that the student might need.
5. Depending on what the data shows, interventions are adjusted to a more intensive level (Tier 3 support, often involving one-on-one instruction), and eventually a special education referral is considered if the student is still not meeting his or her performance benchmarks in a timely manner (Fuchs & Fuchs, 2006).

As indicated by these components, a key facet of RTI is its use of a three-tier model of intervention to assist RTI teams in helping students. See Figure 1.1 for details on the three-tier model, which is widely used now in American schools, to the point that it is a foundational part of each chapter of this second edition of *The School Services Sourcebook*.

The RTI model is often conflated in school contexts with positive behavior supports. PBS is similar in some key respects to RTI in that it uses a three-tier model to direct intervention strategies and similarly draws on progress monitoring and evidence-informed interventions to change student behavior (Kelly, Raines, Stone, & Frey, 2010). Still, there are key differences between the two, most obviously that RTI is typically designed to be implemented with a specific student who is experiencing academic difficulties, usually in early elementary grades, whereas PBS is meant to be used to transform and improve all students' behavior in a school and can be adapted to fit multiple student populations and grade levels. In this chapter, emphasis will be placed on understanding how the ideas inherent to RTI have been used in pre-referral teams for at-risk students and also how those same ideas have been expanded upon to help schools address whole-school change around student behavior. In the "Practice Examples" section that follows, examples using the three-tier framework in both an RTI and PBS context will be offered.

Similarities between RTI and PBS

Three important similarities between RTI and PBS (Sugai & Horner, 2008) are (1) the multi-tiered system of support, (2) empirically supported interventions, and (3) data-based decision making. These three areas merit closer examination to fully understand how much influence the core ideas of RTI/PBS have begun to influence American schools.

Systems of Support Involving Multiple Tiers

The three-tier system of RTI and PBS is rooted in the U.S. Public Health conceptualization of prevention and intervention strategies. This model addresses primary (Tier 1), secondary (Tier 2), and tertiary (Tier 3) prevention strategies to assist specific populations. Tier 1 involves the application of primary strategies (which can involve literacy or reading curricula, behavior rules, or almost any conceivable school-based program or curriculum), which are applied to an entire population and designed to prevent initial occurrences of problem academic performance or social/emotional/behavioral problems. Tier 2 includes more targeted interventions, which are implemented with student populations who haven't responded to the primary prevention strategy or curriculum, with the goal of forestalling the development or maintenance of academic or social/emotional/behavioral problems. Finally, Tier 3, the "tip" or point on most prevention three-tier triangle frameworks, represents tertiary prevention. These intensive interventions focus on individuals who have serious problems that merit intensive academic support or behavioral health interventions.

Embedded in the three-tiered model are more intensive interventions that should be considered for individual students based on their response (or lack thereof) to interventions at prior levels of prevention.

As shown in Figure 1.1, when Tier 1 strategies are in place and are effective, it may be anticipated that approximately 80% of students will achieve desired outcomes. However, another 20% can be expected to need greater levels of support to meet desired outcomes. Tier 2 strategies, if properly implemented, will allow many of these students (perhaps another 15%) to achieve desired outcomes. Yet, even with primary and secondary prevention supports in place, as many as 5% of students will demonstrate a need for Tier 3 interventions, the highest level of support. While these percentages began as heuristics (Walker et al., 1996), they are beginning to be validated empirically (Horner, Sugai, Todd, & Lewis-Palmer, 2005). It is also important to note that some schools may have relatively higher proportions of students requiring Tier 2 and Tier 3 supports. By monitoring specific outcomes across all students, school personnel can make data-based decisions regarding which students require more intensive levels of intervention.

Empirically Supported Interventions

In addition to the three-tiered approach to delivering services, an important aspect of the RTI model is the notion that interventions should be "evidence-based" or "empirically supported." The term "empirically supported" is still highly controversial in both school practice and the research literature, with several competing classification systems offering scores or ratings regarding the quality of empirical support for intervention or intervention strategies often found in both RTI and PBS programs. Additionally, the very model of RTI appears to argue for a framework that is inclusive of "practice-based evidence" as well as "evidence-based practice"—i.e., students who respond to specific interventions based on systematic data collection points and benchmarks are showing a "response" to the intervention that can be considered "effective," even if there is no published peer-reviewed academic literature supporting it.

Data-Based Decision Making

Another crucial aspect of the RTI model already mentioned is data-based decision making, which typically includes systematic screening for student academic and/or behavioral problems and ongoing progress monitoring at individual and systems levels to inform decisions about implementation and to identify which students might need more intensive levels of support (Kelly et al., 2010).

The Policy Context for RTI

The past half-century has seen a host of federal educational reforms designed to increase access to public education for all American students. The Elementary and Secondary Education Act (ESEA) of 1965, the landmark Individuals with Disabilities Education Act (IDEA) special education law of 1975, and their subsequent reauthorizations and revisions (including the Individuals with Disabilities Education Improvement Act, or IDEIA, in 2004) have deepened American education's commitment to using special education services to attempt to fulfill the legislation's goals of "Free Appropriate Public Education" (FAPE) for all. Recent U.S. Department of Education statistics indicate that 13.2% of American K-12 students are identified as being eligible for special education services under IDEIA's 14 disability categories and to receive a continuum of learning supports designed to increase their access to FAPE (National Center for Education Statistics, 2011).

Despite these policy successes and significant inroads toward providing FAPE to all American students, a number of significant critiques of special education have been levied by parents, policymakers, and special education researchers. This chapter will address three main concerns that relate to the growing use of RTI in American schools, namely:

1. the increasing criticism of the "discrepancy model" as a basis for finding students eligible for LD services
2. the additional critique that special education relies on a "wait to fail" model to get students assessed for special education services, which is inefficient and limits the ability to intervene early for students at risk for academic failure in early elementary grades
3. the growing understanding that special education itself has developed in many school contexts into a setting where minority youth are disproportionately placed, often without trying earlier learning supports that might have prevented the need for any special education referral or assessment (Fuchs & Fuchs, 2006)

Indeed, the movement to increase the use of RTI to address the above critiques has been afoot in the policy world and research literature for more than two decades, culminating in the federal reauthorization of IDEIA in 2004, which gave states and local school districts the ability to target 15% of their special education funds toward establishing RTI procedures and teams to develop RTI further in their states. To date, all 50 states in the U.S. have implemented at least some initial RTI-related programs in their school districts, ranging from training staff in RTI ideas to actual full implementation of RTI within their schools (Hoover, Baca, Wexler-Love, & Saenz, 2008).

Another confusion often heard in discussions of RTI is that it is meant to replace special education or serve as a proxy for identifying students for special education eligibility. The relationship between the RTI process and LD eligibility under IDEIA is a complicated one, with much controversy in the research literature. Some LD researchers claim that the methods and tools of RTI are too vague and unscientific to help diagnose a student's specific learning disability, while some parent advocates and policy analysts worry that the unstated goal of RTI is simply to slowly phase out special education for students with LD altogether, or at least delay the process of special education referral and assessment. Finally, because the RTI process requires that teachers look at their instructional methods and also begin to collect data points systematically on a student who may be academically and behaviorally challenging, some teachers complain about the paperwork and time involved in helping a student using RTI compared to the traditional special education referral model (Reynolds & Shaywitz, 2009).

The (Surprisingly Thin) Evidence Base for RTI

It is ironic that for an approach that emphasizes data-driven decision making, evidence-based practices, and rigorous evaluation, so many doubts remain about the quality and strength of the research base for RTI itself (Hale et al., 2010; Reynolds & Shaywitz, 2009). Components of RTI (curriculum-based measurement, or CBM) have decades of empirical support, as does the notion that early intervention for students with reading difficulties can produce lasting and long-term gains (Fewster & McMillan, 2002). Additionally, though the evidence base for behavior-based RTI is scant, there exists a sizable literature (primarily studies using single-subject designs) for the effectiveness of behavior intervention plans in classroom settings (Kelly et al., 2010). And there is a small but growing empirical literature for the PBS application of the three-tier model in schools. Despite the widespread dissemination of core RTI ideas and related concepts in PBS, the original RTI approach itself so far hasn't been subjected to the kind of rigorous empirical study one might expect of such a data-driven method.

Significant disagreements in the literature persist about whether it is better to conduct RTI with a standard protocol (a set number of weeks) or as a problem-solving model (adjusting intervention and dosage to the specific data indicating how students are responding). Additionally, there is concern about whether RTI methods have been standardized sufficiently to be consistently implemented with fidelity across different learning issues and developmental levels. In a related concern, some scholars have pointed out that there is no consistent definition of what the "R" in RTI is—meaning that there is no clear idea of what a response is and what that response indicates about a student's learning (Hale et al., 2010; Reynolds & Shaywitz).

Finally, despite the focus of this book on school-based mental health services provided by practitioners in schools, there appears to be only a small literature base for the use of RTI as a specific tool to address individual student behavior. While leading RTI scholars such as Gresham (2005) tout RTI as a means to both identify and help students in schools who meet the behavior disorder/emotional disturbance criteria, he acknowledges that this is still a new area of research with limited support for RTI itself. (He and other proponents of RTI as a behavior treatment model argue correctly, however, that though relatively untested as a technique, the actual interventions often used in a three-tier RTI behavior prevention/treatment model do have empirical support and could be expected to help teachers, parents, and students better manage typical behavior problems that occur in school settings.)

Despite these real concerns, there appears to be a growing interest in using RTI as a framework to address both individual student academic and behavioral needs in early grades as well as using the core concepts of RTI to inform PBS programs nationwide. This is likely to continue as the reauthorization of IDEIA is expected from Congress in the next few years, with this reauthorization expected by observers to build on the RTI carve-out in the 2004 IDEIA funds to focus even more dollars and attention on primary prevention and early intervention.

What We Can Do

Because both RTI and PBS are increasingly becoming a part of American public schooling, it is clear that multiple opportunities exist for school-based practitioners to get involved at multiple levels within their schools.

In this chapter, RTI has been shown to focus primarily on something most school-based practitioners don't consider their area of expertise: the importance of helping kids in early grades to learn to read. This remains the focus of RTI nationally, with a focus on using the DIBELS to assess whole-school and individual student progress in reading in early grades (DIBELS, 2007). However, it has also been demonstrated that these same core RTI concepts are being used to address student behavior problems in an RTI context, as well as using overall RTI ideas like multiple tiers of intervention and data-driven decision making to help whole student populations improve their behavior in a PBS framework. It would seem that school-based practitioners might easily gravitate into new roles involving the RTI and PBS processes in their schools, though some empirical data indicates that this hasn't been as easy a transition as hoped for (Kelly & Lueck, 2010).

Given the role that many school-based practitioners already play in the special education referral, diagnosis, and treatment process, it makes sense to think about how they might become part of the RTI process as well. In some schools, the RTI and special education team include the same personnel. Additionally, because RTI is intended to identify and target students quickly and measure impacts of interventions in a systematic and ongoing fashion, the entire process requires additional engagement with students, teachers, and families to make sure that they understand the process underway and are able to make it work smoothly. Finally, as mentioned earlier, a major area of RTI that is still under-researched to this point is how the RTI model can be best used to possibly prevent students with behavior problems from being referred to special education without trying potentially effective behavioral interventions first. All of these areas (case management, parent engagement, group facilitation, and behavioral interventions) are areas where school-based practitioners should have a range of skills that can make them important contributors to RTI and PBS programs in their schools (Kelly, 2008).

Cultural Considerations

This is a new and important area for RTI and PBS implementation and research—namely how to best implement these two models with fidelity while accounting for cultural, gender, linguistic socioeconomic status (SES), and other possible contextual differences across different school settings. One obvious place that is still relatively undeveloped in the literature is how to ensure that culturally responsive and appropriate instruction is being implemented in the classroom for the student(s) who might become part of an RTI process. Another additional new avenue for research is how to best understand "non-responders" to RTI methods and whether their lack of responsiveness indicates something more than learning difficulties and may indicate other possible issues in the classroom or the overall school curricular context (Klinger & Edwards, 2006).

Applying Interventions within a Response to Intervention Framework

The challenge facing the field of school-based mental health doesn't appear to be applying interventions within an RTI/PBS framework as much as it is finding ways around the barriers within school contexts that often prevent these interventions from happening consistently and with fidelity. A number of key barriers presently exist in many school settings (chief among them high caseloads of students getting weekly Tier 3 services, time constraints and high paperwork demands, professional roles that don't permit/encourage primary prevention work, and general resistance within a school context to RTI/PBS itself), and these barriers often prevent school-based practitioners from fully engaging in the kinds of practices associated with RTI (Kelly, et al., 2010). A recent survey of all school-based mental health professions in Illinois revealed that 30% of all school-based practitioners are not on their RTI team at all, or don't know if their school has such an RTI/problem-solving team (Kelly & Lueck, 2010). Addressing these barriers will be crucial to bringing more evidence-informed interventions into school settings for student social/emotional/behavioral problems and applying them across all three tiers of an RTI framework.

Box 1.1 gives an example of how an intervention at Tier 2 in an RTI framework could be evaluated to track whether students with autism were making sufficient progress socially.

Practice Examples

PBS at Crawford Elementary

Let's return to Paul, our second grader at Crawford Elementary. Though he is progressing nicely into third grade, his school is experiencing a lot of frustration around a series of high-profile fights that have taken place on the school playground. The Crawford school social worker, Ms. Jackson, notices that Paul and several of his classmates want to always have lunch with her because they say they don't want to "have any problems" on the playground. She consults with her principal, who suggests that the school PBS team tackle the issue of fighting in their next meeting.

As part of the PBS meeting, the team revisits the school PBS expectations "Be Respectful, Be Responsible, Be Safe" and looks at office discipline referral (ODR) data to learn more about the school fights. They discover that the majority of the fights are concentrated at lunchtime (so Paul and his friends were right about that) and involve boys

Box 1.1 Data Analysis Example for a Tier 2 Group for Adolescents with Autism

Let's say we want to evaluate the social skills group for adolescents with autism. Each participant in the group would have his or her own line. Let's keep track of five factors: grade level, session attendance, pre-test score on the Autism Social Skills Profile (ASSP), post-test score on the ASSP, and improvement (post-test score minus pre-test score).

Excel Spreadsheet

	A	*B*	*C*	*D*	*E*	*F*
1	Group Member	Grade Level	Attendance	ASSP Score 1	ASSP Score 2	Improvement
2	Alice	9	7	105	100	–5
3	Bobby	10	8	110	115	5
4	Carlos	10	9	90	105	15
5	Deon	11	9	115	125	10
6	Edward	9	7	100	105	5
7	Frances	11	8	120	130	10
8	Average	10	8	106.67	113.33	6.67
9	Standard Deviation			10.80	12.11	1.31
10	T-Test (p =)				0.031	
11	Pearson's R					0.82

Based on these results, we can see that the average student is a 10th grader, the average number of sessions attended is eight, and the average improvement was 6.67 points on the ASSP. Standard deviations are important because, if we have a normal distribution, we can expect 68% of students to score within one standard deviation of the average. Those students who are one standard deviation below their peers clearly need more support, and those students who are one standard deviation above their peers can be considered for less support.

When we select the *T*-test from the Insert Function list, it asks us for four pieces of information: Array 1, Array 2, Tails, and Type. Array 1 is the set of cells containing the pre-test data, so we enter D2:D7. Array 2 is the set of cells containing the post-test data, so we input E2:E7. Tails refers to the two ends of a bell-shaped curve. If we have predicted that students will improve, then we have hypothesized that they will move toward one of the tails. Based on this, we input the number 1. Type refers to the type of differences we are trying to determine. Since we are comparing one group to itself, we again enter the number 1. Excel does not return a t value for the t-test; instead it returns a p value, the probability that these results happened by mere chance. Traditionally, researchers have chosen $p < 0.05$ as the standard for statistical significance. Based on these results, we can see that the group did make statistically significant progress!

When we select Pearson's r from the Insert Function list, it asks us for just two pieces of information: Array 1 and Array 2. Array 1 is the set of cells containing the session attendance data, so we input C2:C7. Array 2 is the set of cells containing the improvement calculation, so we enter F2:F7. This time, Excel returns the r value for the correlation between the two sets of values. Correlation values can range from −1 to +1. A correlation of 0.81 indicates a strong positive association between the two variables. In other words, we've determined that the more group sessions our students attended, the more they improved on our outcome measure!

Reprinted with permission from *School Social Work: An Evidence-Informed Framework for Practice* (Kelly, Raines, Stone, & Frey, 2010)

in fourth and fifth grade. They look more closely at the ODR data and see that the most intense fights involve five students, three of whom are new students this year. The PBS team decides to intervene at all three levels with the following interventions:

- Tier 1: The school uses Second Step and an anti-bullying curriculum, and the principal announces at the weekly faculty meeting that the lessons about conflict resolution and working toward peaceful solutions will be revisited over the next month in classrooms. The PBS team also drafts a letter that is sent home and posted on the Crawford School Web site detailing the Tier 1 approaches that will be taken to address conflicts on the playground in the coming months and asking for parental input and support.
- Tier 2: All fourth- and fifth-grade classrooms are visited by the school social worker and principal, who lead a discussion with the classroom teacher and her students about how to stop fights before they start and how to have fun on the playground without arguments and fights.
- Tier 3: Each of the five students who have had more than one fight in the past semester is contacted by the school social worker, who begins an intensive solution-focused/cognitive intervention to teach anger management and conflict resolution.

After two months of applying the interventions at each tier, the PBS team looks again at their ODR data and sees that fights have decreased to only two per month from a high of six per week. They agree to continue working with the five students (who they dubbed their "frequent fliers") on a biweekly basis and to pay monthly visits to the fourth- and fifth-grade classrooms to reinforce the Second Step program lessons.

Key Points to Remember

- RTI is a method, not an intervention itself, and is readily applicable to a range of academic and social/emotional/behavioral issues that present in American K-12 school settings.
- RTI involves screening all students for academic/behavioral problems and then systematically applying data-driven curricular modifications and adaptations to students who don't meet established benchmarks to bring them up to academic and behavioral levels of success in relation to their age-peers. The RTI process involves a high degree of collaboration between teachers, parents, students, and an RTI team.
- RTI is not a new method but has recently taken root in many schools across the country due to concerns about over-identification of students in special education and the growing consensus that academic and social/emotional problems need early, intensive interventions rather than the traditional special education referral and assessment model, which has been characterized by RTI advocates as making schools and parents have to "wait for students to fail" before they can get additional support.
- Federal and state legislation has made RTI and the principles behind it a priority. Despite some controversy in the practice and research communities regarding the long-term impact of moving to a more prevention-oriented model for educating at-risk youth in contrast to the special education model, it appears that RTI is likely to continue to be a policy priority at federal and state levels.
- PBS is a related but distinct concept that seeks to bring the three-tier model of RTI into a whole-school context and use it to focus on improving student behavior and creating positive school climates for all students.
- Despite strong support from many school leaders and solid empirical support for specific interventions embedded at all three tiers of the RTI and PBS frameworks, the actual research showing that RTI and PBS "work" is still in its infancy and has provoked a high level of controversy in the academic community (particularly RTI's claims to provide effective services for students with learning problems).
- Survey data indicate that numerous structural and professional barriers still impact a majority of school-based practitioners in their efforts to work within the three-tier frameworks of RTI and PBS.

Further Learning

Internet sites for more learning:

- http://www.apbs.org/: The home site of the Association for Positive Behavior Support, an international membership organization of researchers, policymakers, and practitioners devoted to disseminating PBS resources

- http://www.interventioncentral.org/home: A helpful site by a veteran school psychologist and administrator that offers lots of practical hands-on RTI materials
- http://www.pbis.org/: A federally funded site from the Office of Special Education Programs (OSEP) offering a range of up-to-date PBIS/PBS materials
- http://www.rtinetwork.org/: A private foundation-funded organization with lots of RTI-related materials to view and download for use in K-12 schools
- http://www.rti4success.org: A site managed by the American Institutes for Research (AIR) and in partnership with Vanderbilt University and the University of Kansas, offering a range of RTI-related tools, with a particular focus on enhancing progress monitoring in the RTI process

References

DIBELS (2007). Introduction to DIBELS. Retrieved from http://dibels.uoregon.edu/index.php

Fewster, S., & McMillan, P. D. (2002). School-based evidence for the validity of curriculum-based measurement of reading and writing. *Remedial and Special Education, 23*(3), 149–156.

Fuchs, D., & Fuchs, L. F. (2006). Introduction to Response to Intervention: What, why, and how valid is it? *Reading Research Quarterly, 41*(1), 93–100.

Gresham, F.M. (2005). Response to Intervention: An alternative means of identifying students as emotionally disturbed. *Education and Treatment of Children, 28*(4), 328–344.

Hale, J., et al. (2010). Critical issues in Response to Intervention, comprehensive evaluation, and specific learning disabilities identification and intervention: An expert white paper consensus. *Learning Disabilities Quarterly, 33*(3), 223–236.

Horner, R. H., Sugai, G., Todd, A. W., & Lewis-Palmer, T. (2005). *Schoolwide positive behavior support. In Individualized supports for students with problem behaviors* (pp. 359–377). New York: The Guilford Press.

Hoover, J. J., Baca, L., Wexler-Love, E., & Saenz, L. (2008). *National implementation of Response to Intervention (RTI): Research summary.* Retrieved from http://www.spannj.org/pti/NationalImplementationofRTI-ResearchSummary.pdf

Kelly, M. S. (2008). *The domains and demands of school social work practice: A guide to working effectively with parents, students, and schools.* New York, NY: Oxford.

Kelly, M. S., Frey, A., Alvarez, M., Berzin, S. C., O'Brien, K., & Shaffer, G. (2010). School social work and Response to Intervention. *Children & Schools, 32*(4), 201–209.

Kelly, M. S., & Lueck, C. (2010, November). *School-based mental health in Illinois.* Retrieved from www.imhp.org

Kelly, M. S., Raines, J. C., Stone, S., & Frey, A. (2010). *School social work: An evidence-informed framework for practice.* New York, NY: Oxford.

Klinger, J. K., & Edwards, P. A. (2006). Cultural considerations with Response to Intervention models. *Reading Research Quarterly, 41*(1), 108–117.

National Center for Education Statistics. (2011). *Fast facts: How many students with disabilities receive services?* Retrieved from http://nces.ed.gov/fastfacts/display.asp?id=64

Reynolds, C. R., & Shaywitz, S. R. (2009). Response to Intervention: Prevention and remediation, perhaps. Diagnosis, no. *Child Development Perspectives, 3*(1), 44–47.

Sugai, G., & Horner, R. H. (2008). What we know and need to know about preventing problem behavior in schools. *Exceptionality, 16*, 67–77.

Walker, H., Horner, R. H., Sugai, G., Bullis, M., Sprauge, J. R., & Bricker, D. (1996). Integrated approaches to preventing antisocial behavior patterns among school-age children and youth. *Journal of Emotional & Behavioral Disorders, 4*, 193–256.

Effective Methods for Improving School Climate

CHAPTER 2

Beth Gerlach Laura M. Hopson

Getting Started

Schools are increasing their attention to school-wide reform, especially to meet the needs of vulnerable populations. With the shift in education toward accountability and the requirements of No Child Left Behind, schools are faced with intense pressure to demonstrate achievement from all students. It has been increasingly important for schools to determine how to meet the needs of at-risk students who are often performing below standard levels. Researchers have investigated variables that contribute to school effectiveness and positive student outcomes, and factors relating to school climate have repeatedly played a significant role as indicators for academic success and healthy youth development (NSCC, 2007). Thus, one of the significant contributions of recent education reform research is the importance of building a positive school climate to improve student outcomes.

School climate is "the learning environment created through the interactions of human relationships, physical setting and psychological atmosphere" (Perkins, 2006, p. 1). School climate is multidimensional and involves many internal and external school factors, even though most people could likely name variables that contribute to (or detract from) feelings of being safe, respected, supported, connected, and engaged in a school environment. Although the study of school climate is not new, recent research sheds light on its importance for all members of the school community. School climates characterized by supportive relationships, emotional and physical safety, and shared goals create the optimal conditions for learning (Cohen & Geier, 2010). In addition, school climate may be important in improving job satisfaction and retention among teachers (Cohen & Geier, 2010). Therefore, working to build a positive school climate is an important way to address a pivotal non-academic barrier to learning. School-based practice models that do not address barriers to learning at multisystem levels are increasingly understood as insufficient. Practice approaches that have shown particular promise in removing barriers to learning are those with a concurrent intervention focus on change at the individual and school levels (Dupper, 2002; Frey & Dupper, 2005).

Creating a positive school climate is an intervention approach that compliments the skills of school social workers, counselors, and school-based mental health professionals. Their skills and expertise in building relationships, collaboration, problem solving, and understanding systems are well suited for improving school climate. Additionally, these skills joined with clinical expertise, cultural competence, leadership, and an emphasis on social justice can play a role in changing school climate. It is also an area where school-based professionals can support a positive school-wide change that is less dependent on particular employment configurations, funding, individual school constraints, or other factors largely beyond the control of practitioners (Gerlach, 2011). Furthermore, with the current trend for accountability and evidence-based practice, it is worth noting that creating a positive school climate has also been linked empirically to improved academic outcomes for students. A positive school climate has been shown to be particularly important for vulnerable students, including minority, economically disadvantaged and GLBT youth, and urban high-poverty schools (Cohen & Geier, 2010; Hopson & Lee, 2011; Woolley, 2006).

What We Know about School Climate

School Climate and Academic Outcomes

The research on school climate is substantial and growing. Many studies have linked dimensions of school climate to student outcomes. For example, research demonstrates that a positive school climate enhances school bonding and results in higher test scores, higher grades, and school completion (Catalano, Haggerty, Oesterle, Fleming, & Hawkins, 2004; Fleming et al., 2005). School climate has been shown to improve student adjustment, behavior, and achievement, especially during times of transition, such as entry into middle school (Haynes, Emmons, & Ben-Avie, 1997; Kuperminc, Leadbeater, Emmons, & Blatt, 1997). Lower levels of student absenteeism and student suspensions have also been associated with a positive student climate (Rumberger, 1987; Wu, Pink, Crain, & Moles, 1982). Finally, a positive school climate is associated with a reduction in risky health behaviors, like smoking, drug use, violence, and early sexual activity (McNeely, Nonnemaker, & Blum, 2002; McNeely & Falci, 2004).

A positive school climate can also be the first step to foster a readiness for systemic change. That is, a school marked by caring, mutual support and a sense of community will be more willing to accept recommendations for change and more adept at implementing new strategies to remove barriers to learning (Adelman & Taylor, 2007). It has also been argued that a positive school climate and effective education reform have complementary effects. That is, schools that have successfully implemented reform strategies report having a more positive school climate, and having a positive school climate has demonstrated an increased likelihood of further success at implementing reform initiatives (Sterbinsky et al., 2006; Desimone, 2002). Thus, even if a school-based professional is not specifically involved in a reform initiative, she can play an important role in setting the stage for change by focusing on aspects of school climate.

Dimensions of School Climate

"Culture" and "climate" are used in the literature to describe the character and quality of the organizational environment. Although these terms are often used interchangeably, much of the research defines organizational culture as how work is done in an organization. Culture encompasses expectations, norms, and values that influence behavior. Organizational climate relates to people's perception of their environment and the psychological impact of those expectations, norms, and values (Glisson et al., 2008). A positive school climate is characterized by a collective perception that individuals within the school are valued, supported, and safe.

School climate encompasses many dimensions of organizational life. Researchers disagree about some of these dimensions and their relative importance. Notwithstanding disagreements, most researchers argue that school climate is shaped by the following characteristics of school life: relationships within the school, school safety, methods of teaching and learning, and the structure of the learning environment. Although no one research study examines the impact of all of these dimensions, the extant research provides solid evidence that they affect learning and academic outcomes (Cohen & Geier, 2010). Furthermore, these are areas that are dynamic within a school environment and, although complex, they can be changed. School climate characteristics can serve as risk or protective factors for students, but they may be more easily changed than other risk factors in a student's life (i.e. poverty or family instability).

Relationships within the School

Relationships among Students

Interactions among students shape their perceptions of physical and emotional safety while they are in school. Loukas and Robinson (2004) examined school climate as a function of interactions among peers in four dimensions: cohesion (positive relationships among students), friction (negative interactions with other students), competition among students, and satisfaction with classes. Each of the school climate dimensions was associated with student adjustment.

Much of the research in the area of peer interactions has focused on bullying. Students often perceive bullying as a more severe problem in their school than teachers and staff do (Cohen, 2006). Recent research indicates that, in addition to negative psychosocial outcomes for bullies and victims, bullying has negative consequences for witnesses as well. Conversely, a positive school climate characterized by positive relationships among students and school personnel is associated with reduced bullying behavior (Flaspohler, Elfstrom, Vanderzee, Sink, & Birchmeier, 2009). Research also suggests that students who feel connected to school are less likely to be involved with bullying (Wilson, 2004).

Relationships between students and school personnel

Students perform better in school when they have a positive relationship with teachers and other school personnel (Crosnoe, 2004). Middle and high school students who feel supported by teachers are more likely to report school engagement and positive behaviors in school (Baker, 1999; Brewster & Bowen, 2004; Powers, Bowen, & Rose, 2005; Rosenfeld, Richman, & Bowen, 2002). Students who feel connected to teachers also perform well academically (Niebuhr & Niebuhr, 1999; Waxman, Anderson, Huang, & Weinstein, 1997). In addition to positive academic outcomes, support from teachers is associated with reduced risk behavior (Erickson, Mattaini, & McGuire, 2004). A positive relationship with a teacher may have the strongest impact on students who have struggled academically in the past (Murray, 2002).

Relationships among School Personnel

School personnel report greater commitment to teaching when they enjoy a supportive, respectful relationship with their principal and colleagues (Cohen & Geier, 2010; Singh & Billingsley, 1998). A positive school climate also reduces feelings of emotional exhaustion (Grayson & Alvarez, 2008). In addition, students perform better academically when school personnel collaborate in decision making, share a common mission, and trust each other (Bowen, Rose, & Ware, 2006; Lee & Smith, 1993; Bryk & Schneider, 2002; Harris & Hopkins, 2000; Hofman, Hofman, & Guldemong, 2001; Keys, Sharp, Greene, & Grayson, 2003).

School-family relationships

Positive, respectful working relationships between parents and school personnel provide a foundation for learning. When parents have positive relationships with school personnel, they are more likely to be involved in their child's academic life. These partnerships also foster school engagement and academic achievement among students (Fraser, Kirby, & Smokowski, 2004).

School Safety

Perceptions of school safety can profoundly affect learning readiness. The relationships among individuals within a school influence whether students and personnel feel emotionally and physically safe in school. Safety concerns affect students' ability to learn. Students may also miss days of school because they fear violent behavior on school grounds (Cohen, 2006).

Although violence is a concern for many students, especially those in urban and economically disadvantaged schools, social and emotional safety is often a greater concern than physical safety. As discussed above, bullying presents a constant threat to students' psychological and emotional well-being. Students who are victimized by bullying are likely to avoid attending school. They may develop long-term psychosocial problems if they experience repeated bullying over time. Bullies often target gender and sexual identity when harassing other students. Students who identify as gay or lesbian are likely to report being bullied at school. Race, ethnicity, and cultural differences may be targets for bullying as well (Cohen & Geier, 2010).

Methods of Teaching and Learning

The methods of teaching and learning within a school also shape students' and personnel's experience of school life. Norms, goals, and values held within the school shape the methods that are used. These methods, then, shape the school climate. The relationship between students and teachers is particularly influential, as a positive student-teacher relationship affects the types of methods that are used. Conversely, teaching methods may shape the quality of the student-teacher relationship (Cohen & Geier, 2010). For example, highly punitive disciplinary policies may have a negative impact on students' connectedness to school and school climate (McNeely, Nonnemaker, & Blum, 2002).

Methods that promote collaborative learning foster a positive climate. Similarly, character education programs and emotional learning programs are associated with positive climates and higher achievement scores. These strategies promote trusting relationships among students and personnel within the school (Cohen & Geier, 2010). Providing students with a voice in decision making is another promising strategy for building a positive climate. This research is important in the current political context shaped by No Child Left

Behind (NCLB) legislation. Some research indicates that teachers perceive a significant decrease in collaborative learning and student-centered teaching practices since the implementation of NCLB. These changes are attributed to teachers' emphasizing test preparation in their teaching methods (Musoleno & White, 2010).

Physical Structure

Small schools, or larger schools that create small learning communities, are associated with better school connectedness and academic achievement. The school's physical appearance also influences how students and teachers experience school life (Tanner, 2008; Uline, Wolsey, Tschannen-Moran, & Lin, 2010). In a study examining the physical environment of 24 elementary schools, Tanner (2008) found that student achievement was influenced significantly by issues of personal space within the school, availability of spaces for large group meetings, and lighting quality. In addition, flexible classroom environments that provide for large group meetings in addition to small group interactions and private spaces or quiet areas for students also play a role. The school's physical structure is a potentially important target for intervention, as a large percentage of schools report problems related to over-enrollment, lighting, air quality, noise pollution, and safety (Tanner, 2008).

What We Can Do

Evidence-based interventions that are multifaceted with some flexibility to be adapted for a specific school environment and that require minimal costs and training are often the best fit for school-based interventions (Franklin & Kelly, 2009; Franklin & Hopson, 2005). Interventions that build a positive school climate include many evidence-based approaches that fit this description. A number of the empirically supported interventions described in other chapters of this book are related to building a positive school climate, including (but not limited to) anti-bullying programs, violence prevention, cultural competency, family support, parental engagement, peer relationships, conflict resolution, and dropout prevention. Therefore, one of the first steps in investigating approaches to intervene with school climate is to examine the many programs highlighted in this sourcebook. School-based professionals can contribute in meaningful ways to a change in school climate through implementing these programs.

It is worth noting that building a positive school climate can incorporate a wide variety of approaches. They can range from implementing a comprehensive school wide redesign to fostering relationships between students and teachers. Therefore, the good news for school-based professionals is that both small-scale and extensive approaches can make a meaningful difference in how students, staff, and families experience the school environment.

On a large scale, some of the most impressive contributions to school climate can be found in full-scale school redesign projects known as comprehensive school reform (CSR) models. CSR models target schools for holistic reform and aim to address all areas of school functioning, from instruction and assessment to parental involvement and student engagement. CSR models are also an integral part of NCLB and aim to raise student achievement using scientifically based research and effective practices by targeting school-wide change. Some examples of highly effective and empirically sound CSR models are the School Development Program, Success for All, and Direct Instruction, all of which have a significant component that addresses school climate (Borman et al., 2003). Although implementation of a CSR model would likely be directed from district administration and require substantial funding, school-based professionals can position themselves as key players by providing important information on non-academic barriers as well as by using their skills to facilitate discussions about school-wide needs (Corbin, 2005).

Positive behavioral interventions and supports (PBIS) is a universal prevention strategy that aims to create a positive school climate that promotes positive behaviors among children and adults within the school (www.pbis.org). It is grounded in principals from behavioral, social learning, and organizational theories and relies on clear expectations and positive reinforcement of desirable behaviors (Bradshaw, Koth, Thornton, & Leaf, 2009). Positive reinforcement includes providing incentives and recognition to students who meet expectations. As of 2008, almost 8,000 schools were using PBIS (Spaulding, Horner, May, & Vincent, 2008).

The school-wide PBIS process is intended to create systems that support the adoption and durable implementation of evidence-based practices and procedures that will improve outcomes for all students, including those considered to be most at risk for academic failure. It is a multi-tiered strategy that creates systems of support at three levels: primary (school-wide/universal), secondary (targeted/selective), and tertiary (individual/indicated). The program relies on ongoing data collection and evaluation to identify students who could benefit from services at each of the three levels and to determine whether outcomes are improving over time.

Bradshaw et al. (2009) conducted a group-randomized trial of PBIS in which 37 elementary schools were randomly assigned to receive PBIS or serve as a comparison site. They examined the impact of PBIS on staff reports of school organizational health. Data from surveys collected from staff in the participating schools revealed that PBIS was associated with significant improvement in organizational health. In particular, PBIS improved three dimensions of organizational health (resource influence, staff affiliation, and academic emphasis), which were characterized by the principal's ability to lobby for resources; collegial relationships among teachers and staff; and respect and cooperation among students (Bradshaw et al., 2009).

In addition, other school-wide reform programs have demonstrated success with school social workers filling key roles. For example, social workers played a key role in a comprehensive school redesign project by creating a solution-building alternative high school drawn from the philosophy and techniques of solution-focused therapy. Social workers were part of the team that facilitated the training of school staff and students in the solution-focused philosophy and techniques. These techniques helped to foster a school climate marked by mutual respect, collaboration, relationship building, trust, and high expectations. The solution-focused school employs three types of intervention teams to facilitate referrals for student success—individual interventions, group interventions, and school culture interventions—and each of these teams has a role for a school practitioner. The solution-focused school has strong indicators of success for student outcomes and for changing the school climate (Franklin, Streeter, Kim, & Tripodi, 2007).

Full-service community schools are also large-scale school redesign projects in which school-based practitioners could play a leadership role. Community schools are comprehensive school-community collaborations that function as a "hub" for comprehensive educational, social, and health services. One of the key goals of community schools is to create a climate that welcomes and supports all members of the school community (Dryfoos et al., 2005; Blank, Melaville, & Shah, 2003). School social workers can be vital in the formation of a community school by assessing the needs of the community, mobilizing resources for the students and families, building relationships and trust with families in the school community, and providing training for school staff.

Certainly, when feasible, school-based professionals can help facilitate broad school restructuring by advocating for comprehensive school reform or by creating a solution-focused school or a community school. However, not all schools are in a position to implement major school-wide reorganization, as it can be expensive and labor intensive. Fortunately, there are a growing number of interventions that demonstrate how school-based professionals can also stimulate a positive change in the school climate by working within their school's existing system, many of which are discussed in other chapters.

In addition, the following are two examples of unique interventions that have shown success in improving school climate with greater feasibility for school-based professionals. Working on What Works (WOWW) is a program piloted in several schools that has shown promise. WOWW places a school social worker in the role of a coach to help teachers and students collaborate and think about strengths and solutions. In particular, the school social worker facilitates a class-wide discussion with students and the teacher about their hopes for and perceived strengths of classroom management and behavior. The goal is to help both teachers and students function better together in the classroom and improve classroom behavior, teacher resilience, and student achievement. Although the results are preliminary, school social workers, teachers, and students have found WOWW to be a program that improved their school climate (Kelly & Bluestone-Miller, 2009).

The School Change Feedback Process (SCFP) is another approach that has exhibited potential for a school-wide change in climate. SCFP provides a means for involving school-based professionals in school-wide change by building relationships with teachers to facilitate discussions about processes that can decrease structural inequalities in schools. For example, school-based professionals can conduct professional training with educators that opens dialogue about how to create equal learning opportunities for all students, regardless of their socioeconomic status (SES) or race. Although these discussions can be challenging on a school campus, an experienced school practitioner can use his or her expertise on issues of social justice and relationship building to facilitate important changes in equity, expectations, and communication on a campus. SCFP has demonstrated that school counselors can use their practice expertise to enhance teacher efficacy and remove system-level barriers to learning (Colbert, Vernon-Jones, & Pransky, 2006).

In addition to utilizing a specific intervention model, school-based practitioners can also employ general practice principles that can be easily translated to each unique school environment. Table 2.1 shows four practice principles that school social workers can use to positively influence school climate.

On a final note, at the heart of many of the programs, interventions, and practice principles related to enhancing aspects of school climate is the importance of fostering positive relationships among all members of a school community. Strong and healthy relationships based on mutual respect are an important foundation for school climate. A positive relationship with a caring adult is a key factor in improved student outcomes and a positive school climate. School-based practitioners can actively facilitate and foster relationships between students and teachers, parents and teachers, the school and the community, and among the school staff. School-based professionals know that relationships can be fostered and changed, and as school climate research has shown, relationships can foster and change the school.

Although working to facilitate relationships on a campus might seem simple, the cumulative effect of building relationships, increasing engagement, and fostering an environment of safety and respect can have a significant impact on school climate. Therefore, in order to affect school climate, school-based professionals can use skills they have already developed through their professional training and practice experience. In fact, preliminary research suggests that many school social workers are actively participating in tasks linked to positively impacting the climate of their school (Gerlach, 2011). Most encouraging, as one of the leading scholars in school climate research writes, "... making even small changes in schools and classrooms can lead to significant improvements in climate" (Freiberg, 1998, p. 22).

Applying Interventions within a Response to Intervention Framework

Response to Intervention (RTI) is a process that aims to match effective interventions to students based on need and requires ongoing monitoring to make decisions about whether goals or interventions need to be changed to improve student outcomes. An RTI framework begins with a thorough assessment of students' academic, social, and behavioral needs (Hawken, Vincent, & Schumann,

Table 2.1 Practice Principals to Influence School Climate

Practice Principles	*Influence on School Climate*
Ongoing Assessment	use formal measures and informal strategies to assess school climate from all members of the school community
Adults are Key	educate, value, and support adults in the school so that they can contribute to a welcoming and supportive environment for students and families
Open and Inclusive Governing Structure	empower all members of the school community to shape the school environment by encouraging collaboration and input from all
Safe and Welcoming	foster relationships among all members of the school community that show mutual respect, emotional and physical safety, cultural competence, trust, and fairness

Source: Adapted from Woolley, M. E. (2006). Advancing a positive school climate for students, families and staff. In C. Franklin, M. B. Harris, & P. Allen-Meares (Eds.), *The school services sourcebook: A guide for school-based professionals* (pp. 777–784). New York, NY: Oxford University Press.

2008). This assessment is designed to help school personnel identify students who may require intervention in order to succeed academically. Ongoing evaluation is used to monitor the progress of students and determine whether the interventions are appropriate and effective (National Center on Response to Intervention, 2010).

RTI employs interventions at the individual, classroom, and school levels to create the conditions for meaningful improvement in student success (National Center on Response to Intervention, 2010). RTI takes into account aspects of the school environment that affect student outcomes. Thus, a positive school climate is an important foundation for achieving the aims of the RTI framework. This work requires clear and consistent expectations for students, parents, and teachers. Achieving these consistent expectations requires that teachers collaborate closely with each other and with school support personnel. A school climate that is characterized by mutual trust and respect is essential for this collaborative work. Teachers and staff will also need to involve students and parents in decision making.

Successful implementation of RTI also requires that students and adults in the school are recognized for adopting effective practices and behaviors. Again, a positive school climate creates a nurturing environment that encourages positive reinforcement, as greater emphasis is placed on rewards and recognition for positive behaviors than discipline.

Many schools have implemented strategies such as PBIS in conjunction with RTI, since a positive school climate is deemed to be a prerequisite for effective implementation of RTI. PBIS, as described earlier, is a process that is consistent with RTI principals in that it offers a range of interventions that are matched to students based on their needs. At the same time, it aims to improve school climate so that the school environment supports healthy, positive behaviors (Sandomierski, Kincaid, & Algozzine, 2007).

Tools and Practice Examples

Assessment of School Climate

The first step for school-based professionals to intervene in building a positive school climate is to understand the multiple perspectives on the current state of the school's climate. There are many instruments for measuring particular domains of school climate, including measures to be completed by students, teachers, parents, and community members. The best measures have empirical support, are comprehensive, are easy to administer and understand, and allow for input from multiple stakeholders (Cohen et al., 2009). Some of these measures include the School as a Caring Community Profile-II (SCCP-II; Lickona & Davidson, 2003), the School Success Profile—Learning Organization survey (SSP-LO; Bowen & Powers, 2003), the Inventory of School Climate—Student survey (ISC-S; Brand et al., 2003), and the Comprehensive School Climate Inventory (CSCI; National School Climate Center, n.d.). School-based professionals can use their leadership and expertise in multidimensional systems to help schools interpret the results of school climate measures and integrate the findings into school improvement plans (Hopson & Lawson, 2011; Hopson & Lee, 2011).

Practice Tasks

School-based professionals can engage in numerous specific practice tasks associated with the domains of school climate as part of their general practice and tailored to suit the individual needs of their school and student population. Some examples include:

- facilitating teacher support groups
- organizing parent coffees or workshops
- modeling strength-based language
- arranging for appropriate translators for non-English-speaking families
- communicating clear rules about violence, harassment, and bullying
- working to raise teacher expectations for at-risk students
- sponsoring a GLBTQ and allies group
- engaging parents and students in school-wide policy and planning teams
- providing anti-bullying and harassment training
- facilitating cultural diversity groups or events
- supporting consistency in school-wide handling of behavioral or discipline issues
- providing opportunities for community involvement and the development of civic responsibility
- recognizing achievements and giving appreciation for students and school staff

- modeling collaboration and mutual respect
- leading staff development in areas of social and emotional learning
- fostering relationships between students and teachers
- developing a school-wide mission statement with input from all members of the school community

Case Study

A high school was experiencing a problem reintegrating students returning from the district's disciplinary alternative school. Students were typically sent to the disciplinary alternative school for fighting on campus or for being in possession or under the influence of illegal substances. Students were assigned to the alternative school for two to six weeks. However, when it was time for the students to return to their home campus, they often showed up unannounced. The lack of communication between the disciplinary alternative school and the home campus had a negative effect on the returning student, the other students, and the teachers.

The returning student often came back to unresolved issues with peers. Since teachers were not expecting his or her return, the student was rarely welcomed back into the classroom. Teachers felt caught off guard by what they perceived as a difficult student's return. No plan was in place for the returning student to successfully integrate back into the classroom or the school community. Students returning from the disciplinary alternative school had a high rate of recidivism and dropping out of school.

In a campus advisory meeting, one of the teachers recognized the problem this was creating on the campus. She asked for assistance in building a plan for better reintegrating students returning from the alternative school. The school social worker, an assistant principal, and a counselor joined the teacher to create the plan. First, the assistant principal asked the administration at the alternative school to notify the home school one week in advance of the student's discharge. The assistant principal then alerted the school social worker, who met with the student prior to his or her return to the home campus. During this meeting, the school social worker assessed any needs the student would have upon return, including academic and peer concerns, and created a joint plan for re-entry into the home school. If unresolved peer issues were a concern, the school social worker scheduled a mediation. The assistant principal also notified the student's teachers so they were prepared for the student's return and encouraged them to welcome the student back into the classroom.

The procedures created to help students successfully integrate back into their home campus led to a transition that felt more welcoming and safe to all students. It also decreased the dropout and reoffense rate for the significantly at-risk students. Teachers reported feeling more supported and prepared for changes in their classroom and, in turn, were better able to meet the needs of the returning student.

Key Points to Remember

- School climate is shaped by the following characteristics of school life: relationships within the school, school safety, methods of teaching and learning, and the structure of the learning environment.
- A positive school climate has been linked empirically to improved academic outcomes and healthy youth development, especially for vulnerable and at-risk students.
- Building a positive school climate can incorporate a wide variety of approaches, including interventions targeted at the individual, family, school, and community level. Large-scale and more specialized interventions can make a meaningful difference in school climate.
- Healthy relationships based on mutual respect are a key factor in school climate. School-based practitioners can use their expertise to foster relationships between all members of the school community.

Further Learning

- National School Climate Center: http://www.schoolclimate.org/
- Center for the Study of School Climate: http://schoolclimatesurvey.com/
- Comer School Development Project: http://childstudycenter.yale.edu/comer/index/index.aspx

- Response to Intervention and School Climate: http://www.cde.state.co.us/RtI/PositiveClimate.htm

References

Adelman, H. S., & Taylor, L. (2007). Systemic change for school improvement. *Journal of Educational & Psychological Consultation, 17*, 55–77.

Baker, J. A. (1999). Teacher-student interaction in urban at-risk classrooms. *Elementary School Journal, 100*(1), 57–70.

Blank, M. J., Melaville, A., & Shah, B. P. (2003). *Making the difference: Research and practice in community schools.* Washington DC: Coalition for Community Schools.

Borman, G. D., Hewes, G., Overman, L.T., Brown, S. (2003). Comprehensive school reform and achievement: A meta-analysis. *Review of Educational Research, 73*(2), 123–230.

Bowen, G. L., & Powers, D. (2003). *School Success Profile—Learning Organization (SSP-LO).* Chapel Hill, NC: University of North Carolina at Chapel Hill, School of Social Work, Jordan Institute for Families.

Bowen, G. L., Rose, R. A., & Ware, W. B . (2006). The reliability and validity of the School Success Profile Learning Organization Measure. *Evaluation and Program Planning, 29*, 97–104.

Bradshaw, C. P., Koth, C.W., Thornton, L. A., & Leaf, P. J. (2009). Altering school climate through school-wide positive behavioral interventions and supports: Findings from a group-randomized effectiveness trial. *Prevention Science, 10*, 100–115.

Brand, S., Felnder, R., Shim, M., Seitsinger, A., & Dumas, T. (2003). Middle school improvement and reform: Development and validation of a school-level assessment of climate, cultural pluralism, and school safety. *Journal of Educational Psychology, 95*(3). 570–588.

Brewster, A. B., & Bowen, G. L. (2004). Teacher support and the school engagement of Latino middle and high school students at risk of school failure. *Child and Adolescent Social Work Journal, 21*, 47–67. doi:10.1023/B:CASW.0000012348.83939.6b

Bryk, A., & Schneider, B. (2002). *Trust in schools: A core resource for improvement.* New York, NY: Russell Sage Foundation.

Catalano, R. F., Haggerty, K. P., Oesterle, S., Fleming, C. B., & Hawkins, J. D. (2004). The importance of bonding to school for healthy development: Findings from the Social Development Research Group. *Journal of School Health, 74*(7), 252–261.

Cohen, J. (2006). Social, emotional, ethical, and academic education: Creating a climate for learning, participation in democracy, and well being. *Harvard Educational Review, 76*(2), 201–237.

Cohen, J., & Geier, V. K. (2010). *School climate research summary: January 2010.* New York, NY: National School Climate Center. Retrieved from www.schoolclimate.org/climate/research.php

Cohen, J., McCabe, L., Michelli, N. M., & Pickeral, T. (2009). School climate: Research, policy, practice, and teacher education. *Teachers College Record, 111*(1), 180–213.

Colbert, R. D., Vernon-Jones, R., & Pransky, K. (2006). The school change feedback process: Creating a new role for counselors in education reform. *Journal of Counseling & Development, 84*(1), 72–82.

Comer, J. P., Joyner, E. T., & Ben-Avie, M. (2004). *Six pathways to healthy child development and academic success: The field guide to Comer Schools in action.* Thousand Oaks, CA: Corwin Press.

Corbin, J. N. (2005). Increasing opportunities for school social work practice resulting from comprehensive school reform. *Children & Schools, 27*, 239–246.

Crosnoe, R. (2004). Social capital and the interplay of families and schools. *Journal of Marriage and Family, 66*, 267–280. doi: 10.1111/j.1741-3737.2004.00019.x

Desimone, L. (2002). How can comprehensive school reform models be successfully implemented? *Review of Educational Research, 72*, 433–480.

Dryfoos, J. G., Quinn, J., & Barkin, C. (2005). *Community schools in action: Lessons from a decade of practice.* New York, NY: Oxford University Press.

Dupper, D. R. (2002). *School social work: Skills and interventions for effective practice.* Hoboken, NJ: John Wiley & Sons.

Erickson, C., Mattaini, M. A., & McGuire, M. S. (2004). Constructing nonviolent cultures in schools: The state of the science. *Children & Schools, 26*, 102–116.

Flaspohler, P., Elfstrom, J., Vanderzee, K., Sink, H., & Birchmeier, Z. (2009). Stand by me: The effects of peer and teacher support in mitigating the impact of bullying on quality of life. *Psychology in the Schools, 46*(7), 636–649.

Fleming, C. B., Haggerty, K. P., Catalano, R. F., Harachi, T.W., Mazza, J. J., & Gruman, D. H. (2005). Do social and behavioral characteristics targeted by preventive interventions predict standardized test scores and grades? *Journal of School Health, 75*, 342–349.

Franklin, C., & Hopson, L. (2005). Into the schools with evidence-based practice. *Children and Schools, 67*, 67–70.

Franklin, C., Streeter, C. L., Kim, J. S., & Tripodi, S. J. (2007). The effectiveness of a solution-focused, public alternative school for dropout prevention and retrieval. *Children & Schools, 29*(3), 133–144.

Franklin, C., & Kelly, M. S. (2009). Becoming evidence-informed in the real world of school social work practice. *Children & Schools, 31*(1), 46–56.

Fraser, M. W., Kirby, L. D., & Smokowski, P. R. (2004). Risk and resilience in childhood. In M. W. Fraser (Ed.), *Risk and resiliency in childhood: An ecological perspective* (pp. 13–66). Washington, DC: NASW Press.

Freiberg, H. J. (1998). Measuring school climate: Let me count the ways. *Educational Leadership, 56*(1), 22–26.

Frey, A. J., & Dupper, D. R. (2005). A broader conceptual approach to clinical practice for the 21st century. *Children & Schools, 27*(1), 33–44.

Gerlach, B. (2011). School social work practice in Texas: Utilization of intervention tasks to enhance school climate (Unpublished doctoral dissertation). The University of Texas at Austin, Austin, TX.

Glisson, C., Landsverk, J., Schoenwald, S. K., Kelleher, K., Hoagwood, K. E., Mayberg, S., & Green, P. (2008). Assessing the Organizational Social Context (OSC) of mental health services: Implications for implementation research and practice. *Administration and Policy in Mental Health and Mental Health Services Research, 35*(1), 98–113. doi: 10.1007/s10488–007–0148–5

Grayson, J. L., & Alvarez, H. K. (2008). School climate factors relating to teacher burnout: A mediator model. *Teaching & Teacher Education, 24*(5), 1349–1363.

Harris, A., & Hopkins, D. (2000). Introduction to special feature: Alternative perspectives on school improvement. *School Leadership and Management, 20*(1), 6–14.

Hawken, L., Vincent, C., & Schumann, J. (2008). Response to intervention for social behavior: Challenges and opportunities. *Journal of Emotional and Behavioral Disorders, 16*, 213–225.

Haynes, N. M., Emmons, C., & Ben-Avie, M. (1997). School climate as a factor in student adjustment and achievement. *Journal of Educational & Psychological Consultation, 8*(3), 321.

Hofman, R. H., Hofman, W. H. A., & Guldemong, H. (2001). The effectiveness of cohesive schools. *International Journal of Leadership in Education, 4*(2), 115–135.

Hopson, L. M., & Lawson, H. (2011). Social workers' leadership for positive school climates via data-informed planning and decision-making. *Children & Schools, 33*(2), 106–118.

Hopson, L. M., & Lee, E. (2011). Mitigating the effect of family poverty on academic and behavioral outcomes: The role of school climate in middle and high school. *Children and Youth Services Review, 33*(11), 2221–2229.

Johnson, W. L., & Johnson, A. M. (1997). Assessing the validity of scores on the Charles F. Kettering Scale for the junior high school. *Educational & Psychological Measurement, 57*(5), 858–869.

Lickona, T., & Davidson, M. (2003). *School as a caring community profile – II*. Center for the 4th and 5th Rs (Respect and Responsibility). Retrieved from http://www2.cortland.edu/centers/character/assessment-instruments.dot

Kelly, M. S., & Bluestone-Miller, R. (2009). Working on What Works (WOWW): Coaching teachers to do more of what's working. *Children & Schools, 31*(1), 35–38.

Keys, W., Sharp, C., Greene, K., & Grayson, H. (2003). *Successful leadership of schools in urban and challenging contexts: A review of the literature*. Retrieved from the National College for School Leadership Web site: www.ncls.org.uk/literaturereviews

Kuperminc, G. P., Leadbeater, B. J., Emmons, C., & Blatt, S. J. (1997). Perceived school climate and difficulties in the social adjustment of middle school students. *Applied Developmental Science, 1*(2), 76.

Lee, V. E., & Smith, J. B. (1993, July). Effects of school restructuring on the achievement and engagement of middle-grade students. *Sociology of Education, 66*(3), 164–187.

Loukas, A., & Robinson, S. (2004). Examining the moderating role of perceived school climate in early adolescent adjustment. *Journal of Research on Adolescence, 14*(2), 209–233. doi:10.1111/j.1532–7795.2004.01402004.x

McNeely, C., & Falci, C. (2004). School connectedness and the transition into and out of health-risk behavior among adolescents: A comparison of social belonging and teacher support. *Journal of School Health, 74*(7), 284–292.

McNeely, C. A., Nonnemaker, J. M., & Blum, R. W. (2002). Promoting school connectedness: Evidence from the National Longitudinal Study of Adolescent Health. *Journal of School Health, 72*(4), 138–147.

Murray, C. (2002). Supportive teacher-student relationships: Promoting the social and emotional health of early adolescents with high incidence disabilities. *Childhood Education, 78*(5), 285–290.

Musoleno, R. R., & White, G. P. (2010). Influences of high-stakes testing on middle school mission and practice. *RMLE Online: Research in Middle Level Education, 34*(3), 1–10.

National Center on Response to Intervention. (2010). *Essential components of RTI—A closer look at Response to Intervention*. Washington, DC: U.S. Department of Education, Office of Special Education Programs, National Center on Response to Intervention.

National School Climate Center. (n.d.). *Measuring school climate*. Retrieved from http://www.schoolclimate.org/climate/practice.php

National School Climate Council (NSCC). (2007). *The School Climate Challenge: Narrowing the gap between school climate research and school climate policy, practice guidelines and teacher education policy*. Retrieved from http://www.ecs.org/school-climate

Niebuhr, K. E., & Niebuhr, R. E. (1999). An empirical study of student relationships and academic achievement. *Education, 119*(4), 679–682.

Perkins, B. (2006). *Where we learn: The CUBE Survey of Urban School Climate*. New Haven, CT: The Urban Student Achievement Task Force.

Powers, J. D., Bowen, G. L., & Rose, R. A. (2005). Using social environment assets to identify intervention strategies for promoting school success. *Children & Schools, 27*, 177–185.

Rosenfeld, L. B., Richman, J. M., & Bowen, G. L. (2000). Social support networks and school outcomes: The centrality of the teacher. *Child and Adolescent Social Work Journal, 17*, 205–226. doi:10.1023/A:1007535930286

Rumberger, R. (1987). High school dropouts: A review of issues and evidence. *Review of Educational Research*, *57*, 1–29.

Sandomierski, T., Kincaid, D., & Algozzine, B. (2007). Response to Intervention and positive behavior support: Brothers with different mothers or sisters with different misters? *PBIS Newsletter*, *24*(2). Retrieved from http://www.pbis.org/pbis_newsletter/volume_4/issue2.aspx

Singh, K., & Billingsley, B. S. (1998). Professional support and its effects on teachers' commitment. *Journal of Educational Research*, *91*(4), 229–239.

Spaulding, S. A., Horner, R. H., May, S. L., & Vincent, C. G. (2008). *Implementation of school-wide PBIS across the United States*. Retrieved from http://www.pbis.org/evaluation/evaluation_briefs/nov_08_(2).aspx

Sterbinsky, A., Ross, S. M., & Redfield, D. (2006). Effects of comprehensive school reform on student achievement and school change: A longitudinal multi-site study. *School Effectiveness and School Improvement*, *17*(3), 367–397.

Tanner, C. K. (2008). Explaining relationships among student outcomes and the school's physical environment. *Journal of Advanced Academics*, *19*(3), 444–471.

Uline, C. L., Wolsey, T. D., Tschannen-Moran, M., & Lin, C.-D. (2010). Improving the physical and social environment of school: A question of equity. *Journal of School Leadership*, *20*(5), 597–632.

Waxman, H. C., Anderson, L., Huang, S. L., & Weinstein, T. (1997). Classroom process differences in inner city elementary schools. *The Journal of Educational Research*, *91*(1), 49–59.

Wilson, D. (2004). The interface of school climate and school connectedness and relationships with aggression and victimization. *Journal of School Health*, *74*(7), 293–299.

Woolley, M. E. (2006). Advancing a positive school climate for students, families and staff. In C. Franklin, M. B. Harris, & P. Allen-Meares (Eds.), *The school services sourcebook: A guide for school-based professionals* (pp. 777–784). New York, NY: Oxford University Press.

Wu, S., Pink, W., Crain, R. L., & Moles, O. (1982). Student suspension: A critical reappraisal. *Urban Review*, *14*(4), 245–303.

Functional Behavioral Assessment in a Three-Tiered Prevention Model

CHAPTER 3

Kevin J. Filter · Michelle E. Alvarez · Kimberly A. Zammitt

Getting Started

Behavior problems in school are a serious issue that is at the forefront of discussions between administrators, school personnel, communities, legislators, families, and students. Physical fights, bullying, and other externalizing behaviors can impact the academic achievement of students and the safety of the school environment (Institute of Educational Sciences, 2011). Key findings from the *Indicators of School Crime and Safety: 2010* report include:

- Of the 38 student, staff, and nonstudent school associated violent deaths[1] occurring between July 1, 2008, and June 30, 2009, 24 were homicides, and 14 were suicides. From July 1, 2008, through June 30, 2009, there were 15 homicides and 7 suicides of school-age youth (ages 5–18) at school *(Indicator 1).*
- Eight percent of students in grades 9–12 reported being threatened or injured with a weapon, such as a gun, knife, or club, on school property in 2009.
- During the 2007–2008 school year, 25% of public schools reported that bullying occurred among students on a daily or weekly basis, and 11% reported that student acts of disrespect for teachers other than verbal abuse took place on a daily or weekly basis.
- With regard to other discipline problems reported as occurring at least once a week, 6% of public schools reported student verbal abuse of teachers, 4% reported widespread disorder in the classroom, 4% reported student racial/ethnic tensions, and 3% reported student sexual harassment of other students *(Indicator 7).* (Institute of Educational Science, 2011, pp. iii–iv)

While some of these incidences are reported to school personnel, many go unreported. Research has demonstrated that a proactive, preventive, and evidence-based approach to curbing disruptive and violent behavior in schools can improve the academic success of students in addition to creating a positive school climate. Functional behavioral assessment (FBA) can serve as the cornerstone for a proactive, preventative, and evidence-based approach to behavior problems.

Although many specialized instructional support personnel such as school social workers and school psychologists associate FBA with special education, research has shown them to be effective in addressing the continuum of student behaviors, from their first occurrence to their chronic presence. When FBAs are conducted in a systematic manner, the function of a behavior is precisely identified, interventions specific to the identified function of a behavior are implemented, and the response to the intervention is tracked; the process follows a single-subject research design methodology. Horner and colleagues (2005) note that "single subject design is a rigorous, scientific methodology used to define basic principles of behavior and establish evidence-based practices"

1. School-associated violent death is defined as "a homicide, suicide, or legal intervention (involving a law enforcement officer), in which the fatal injury occurred on the campus of a functioning elementary or secondary school in the United States." Victims of school-associated violent deaths includedstudents, staff members, and others who are not students.

(p. 165). Use of FBAs in general education is a research-based method to address target behaviors and can be applied to all tiers in a prevention framework.

Therefore, in response to the increased need to address behavior issues in schools, we introduce FBAs across the three tiers of prevention. FBA is a process for identifying the environmental conditions that predict and maintain problem behavior (Filter & Alvarez, 2012; O'Neill et al., 1997). It is based on more than half a century of experimental research (McIntosh, Brown, & Borgmeier, 2008). The process of conducting an FBA includes data interpretation, direct observation, interviews, and record reviews that directly inform interventions. An FBA is complete only when it has been translated into an effective intervention.

What We Know

Key Terms

Before describing a three-tiered model of FBA, it is important to establish the basic concepts behind it. In a simple sense, FBA is a process of "filling in the blanks" for the following four terms: setting events, antecedents, behaviors, and consequences. In other words, if each term were a box, then the assessment process in FBA would be complete when each box had been filled in with the correct information from the individual case. *Behaviors* are any observable acts that are considered to be problematic and in need of change. For example, common behaviors in an FBA would be "disruption" or "aggression." *Consequences* are the events that occur after behaviors. Consequences in FBAs are always reinforcers, which are consequences that maintain a problem behavior. So, when we look for consequences, we are looking for the events that come after and maintain the problem behavior. These are of two types: positive reinforcers (things that are obtained) and negative reinforcers (things that are avoided). Positive reinforcers include obtaining peer attention, obtaining adult attention, obtaining a preferred task, obtaining a tangible, and obtaining sensory stimulation. Negative reinforcers include escaping/avoiding adult attention, escaping/avoiding peer attention, escaping/avoiding a preferred task, escaping/avoiding a tangible, and escaping/avoiding sensory stimulation. *Antecedents* are events that occur before behaviors and predict their occurrence. Examples of antecedents include difficult tasks and corrective adult feedback. *Setting events* are events that occur before behaviors and increase the value of the maintaining consequence. For example, when a student's behavior is maintained by obtaining adult attention, a typical setting event would be a lack of adult attention over an extended period of time.

General Outcomes of FBA

The empirical research on FBA suggests that this systematic method of analyzing the function of a particular behavior in the context of the environment in which the behavior is occurring is an effective method for creating interventions that resolve problem behaviors. The effectiveness of FBA is well documented in both general and special education settings (Blair, Umbreit, & Bos, 1999; Filter & Horner, 2009; Ingram, Lewis-Palmer, & Sugai, 2005; Newcomer & Lewis, 2004). Long-term behavioral changes have also been documented when using FBA as the basis for creating positive support plans (Kern, Gallagher, Starosta, Hickman, & George, 2006). Several reviews on the FBA empirical literature have been conducted (Ervin et al., 2001; Lane, Umbreit, & Beebe-Frankenburger, 1999; Nelson, Roberts, Mathur, & Rutherford, 1999). Ervin et al. (2001) in a review of 100 empirical articles on FBA found that intervention strategies derived from FBA produced behavior change in the desired direction in 146 of 148 intervention cases documented. The literature provides a strong evidence base for using FBA to produce positive outcomes in school settings. Additionally, the literature also suggests that school personnel can successfully implement behavioral interventions based on functional assessments (Kern et al., 2006).

Function-Based Interventions vs. Non-Function-Based Interventions

The literature indicates that behavioral interventions based on functional assessments are more effective than non-function-based interventions (Carter & Horner, 2007; Filter & Horner, 2009; Ingram et al., 2005; Newcomer & Lewis, 2004). Carter and Horner demonstrated that adding FBA to an existing secondary intervention enhanced the effectiveness of the intervention. This study provides support for the efficacy of combining existing manual-based interventions with individualized supports to reduce problem behavior and increase pro-social behaviors. Furthermore, Filter and Horner concluded that function-based academic interventions resulted in significantly fewer problem behaviors than non-function-based interventions for students with low-frequency problem behaviors and without severe disabilities. Function-based interventions appear to have greater effects and more stability than non-function-based interventions (Ingram et al., 2005). The research also indicates that the implementation of non-function-based interventions can result in more "problematic and unpredictable behavior" (Newcomer & Lewis, 2004, p. 179). In reviewing the literature, it has become apparent that implementing interventions without an understanding of the function of the behavior being targeted can lead to well-intended but inadequate interventions that can potentially increase the problem behavior or may not achieve the desired level of behavior change.

FBA Implemented across the Three Tiers

In its simplest form, FBA consists of identifying relationships between factors in the environment and behaviors. FBA is a process that can be applied to all three tiers of a positive behavior support system. FBA is most commonly applied at the tertiary level with individual students that exhibit challenging school behaviors. The literature supports FBA as an effective process for creating successful interventions at the tertiary level (Filter & Horner, 2009; Ingram et al., 2005; Newcomer & Lewis, 2004). There is a growing research base that documents the effectiveness of using FBA on the secondary level with students at risk of failing without additional supports (Carter & Horner, 2007; Todd, Campbell, Meyer, & Horner, 2008; March & Horner, 2002; McIntosh, Campbell, Carter, & Dickey, 2009). The research suggests that the function of problem behavior moderates the response to the intervention (Carter & Horner, 2007; Todd et al., 2008; March & Horner, 2000; McIntosh et al., 2008). This is pertinent information for schools to be mindful of to ensure that selected manual-based secondary interventions are an appropriate match for the function of behavior being observed by the at-risk students. For example, McIntosh et al. found that Check-in/Check-out provides students with high rates of attention for appropriate behavior, thus students whose behavior is maintained by an escape from academic tasks and not an attention-seeking function may not respond to the selected intervention. Lastly, implementing FBA at the primary level with all students school-wide is an emerging phenomenon and is advocated for in the literature (Scott & Eber, 2003). The literature suggests that implementing FBA at the primary level is an effective way to design and implement school-wide behavior programs (Hirsch, Lewis-Palmer, Sugai, & Schnacker, 2004; Luiselli, Putnam, & Sunderland, 2002). Hirsch and colleagues examined bus discipline referrals district-wide and with one elementary school to identify discipline concerns and possible support needs. They concluded that using such school or district-wide transportation information can target factors of behavior and the environment to implement bus behavior remediation programs. Implementing FBA on a school-wide scale helps student support teams to identify problem variables and tailor interventions in an efficient manner, conserving the school's valuable time and resources.

What We Can Do

FBA is a process of identifying the environmental conditions that predict and maintain problem behavior (O'Neill et al., 1997). The details of this process vary as a function of the intensity and breadth of the problem behavior. For problems of narrow scope but high intensity (e.g., a single student with severe problem behavior), the FBA process focuses on highly reliable and time-intensive data sources such as systematic direct observation and structured interviews. For problems of broad scope but low intensity (e.g., school-wide problems with disruptive behavior), the FBA process focuses on existing data that is efficient to collect, such as office discipline referrals. This idea is captured by Figure 3.1, which relates the data collection processes of FBA to the three tiers of prevention.

Regardless of the prevention tier, the definition, outcome, and purpose of FBA remain stable (Filter & Alvarez, 2012). The definition cited above (see O'Neill et al., 1997) emphasizes that FBA is defined by the collection of data about the setting events, antecedents, and consequences

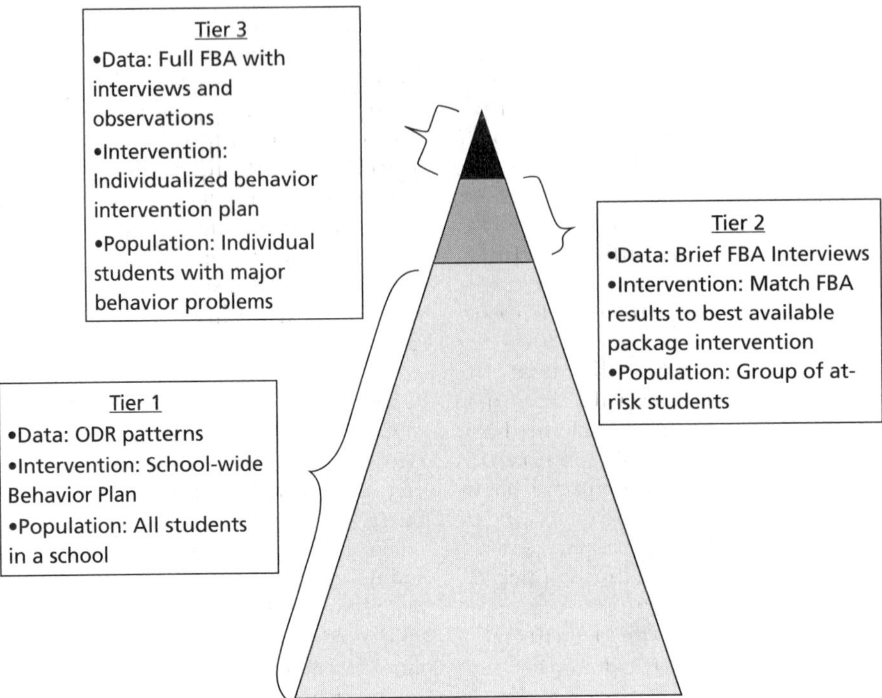

Figure 3.1. Summary of the populations served, data collected, and interventions developed at each tier of the FBA-based prevention model

***Printed with permission from Oxford University Press. Filter and Alvarez (2012), Functional Behavioral Assessment: A Three-Tiered Prevention Model**

of problem behavior. Since this definition applies across tiers, each tier of FBA will involve collecting data about setting events, antecedents, and consequences of problem behavior. The outcome of FBA is the development of a precision hypothesis statement that describes the relationship between the behavior and its setting events, antecedents, and consequences. Therefore, each tier of FBA will result in a precision hypothesis statement. The purpose of FBA is to develop effective interventions. Although the form of the intervention will change across tiers (e.g., school-wide action plan for Tier 1, evidence-based package intervention for Tier 2, and individualized behavior intervention plan for Tier 3), FBA at each tier will be used to develop effective interventions. The remainder of this section will describe the unique FBA processes at each of the three prevention tiers.

In order to implement FBA as a three-tiered process in a school, a team must be convened to manage data collection and interventions. It is recommended that one team manage all tiers because all tiers require someone with behavioral expertise (often the school psychologist or school social worker), someone with the power to allocate money and resources, and someone familiar with general and special education in the school (Anderson & Scott, 2009). Teams should meet as a whole group to review all of the data and make decisions every two weeks. Since the data collection and intervention process can be intense at Tier 3, it is a good idea to create subgroups to manage each individual case in Tier 3. These subgroups should also include the students' primary general education and/or special education teacher. For Tier 2, it is reasonable to assign one or two members of the team the primary responsibility for managing data collection and monitoring interventions. Although some people on the team will be assigned to subgroups or to the management of specific processes, the whole team is responsible for reviewing all of the data and making decisions at biweekly meetings. Further, the FBA team should have a team leader with strong leadership skills, often the school psychologist or school social worker, who is responsible for creating an agenda and ensuring that all team business is completed in an efficient manner.

The remainder of this section will describe the unique FBA processes of identifying setting events, antecedents, behaviors, and consequences at each of the three prevention tiers and developing corresponding interventions.

Tier 1 FBA

Tier 1 FBA addresses the behavior of large groups of students in a school, including those not identified as at risk and those without severe problem behavior. The process described in this chapter emphasizes school-wide applications, but the general idea of Tier 1 FBA could also be applied to other large groups of students in a school, such as a classroom of students or all students in a cafeteria. The process of Tier 1 FBA closely reflects and draws heavily upon the data-based decision-making process employed by schools implementing positive behavior interventions and supports (PBIS; Colvin, Kameenui, & Sugai, 1993; Horner, Sugai, Todd, & Lewis-Palmer, 2005). However, it should be emphasized that PBIS is a broader systems approach to behavior management that involves school-wide teaching of behavior expectations and reinforcement of behavior expectations.

Data collection. The FBA data collected at Tier 1 must reflect the behavior of the broad group of students targeted at this tier while also being efficient to collect. The data that have traditionally characterized FBA for individual students, such as interviews and observations (which will be described later in this chapter as relevant to Tier 2 and Tier 3), will therefore generally not be used because they are inefficient to collect for all students in a school. Instead, data collection should focus on indirect information about the setting events, antecedents, and consequences of problem behavior of all students that is contained in office discipline referrals (ODRs). It is important to qualify, however, that ODRs are useful for FBAs only to the extent that they accurately represent the behavior of students in a school and include information about setting events, antecedents, and consequences of problem behavior. This often requires an initial investment by schools in the modification of ODR forms and the training of faculty and staff in the consistent use of ODRs. For suggestions on how to ensure the quality of ODRs as a data source for FBAs, see Filter and Alvarez (2012).

When using ODRs for Tier 1 FBAs, we recommend reviewing the Big Six. The Big Six are founded on the "Big Five" data used by PBIS teams when reviewing school-wide data (Illinois PBIS network, 2010; Office of Special Education Programs Center on Positive Behavioral Interventions and Supports, 2004) but include the addition of data about perceived motivation (i.e., perceived maintaining consequence). Examples of graphs of the Big Six are presented later in the chapter in the case study example. Graphs of the Big Six data can be easily generated by a school using the *School-Wide Information System* (www.swis.org; May et al., 2010) database. However, any database that includes the appropriate functional information from ODRs can be used to create these graphs for decision making.

The first of the Big Six is *average referrals per day per month*. By reviewing the prevalence of data averaged across time, the team can determine if the level of problem behavior in the school is high enough to warrant the review of further data and development of an FBA-based school-wide action plan. The second of the Big Six is *referrals by problem behavior*. This data indicates what problem behaviors are occurring most frequently in the school and should be the focus of further analysis for the FBA. The third of the Big Six is *referrals by location*. This provides contextual information and can be conceptualized as an antecedent to the problem behavior. The fourth of the Big Six is *referrals by time of day*. This is also antecedent information that indicates when problem behavior is most likely to occur. The fifth of the Big Six is *referrals by students*. This indicates the breadth of the problem. If, for example, more than half of all students in the school have at least one ODR over the past year, then this suggests a school-wide problem. If there are relatively few students with ODRs but each averages five or more referrals, then this suggests that the problem may be better dealt with at Tier 2 or Tier 3 rather than involving all students. The sixth of the Big Six is *referrals by motivation for most frequent problem behavior*. This involves determining which behavior is most frequent using the *referrals by problem behavior* information (the second of the Big Six) and then creating a summary of the motivations reported on the ODRs for these behaviors. For example, it may be that inappropriate language is most often motivated by obtaining teacher attention. In order to determine this, the faculty and staff who complete ODRs must record a perceived motivation for the problem behavior that aligns with the functions of behavior derived from the science of behavior (e.g., attention [from adult or peer], escape [from task or person], and self-stimulation; Filter & Alvarez, 2012; May et al., 2010).

Interventions. For every tier of FBA, an intervention should be developed that follows logically from the results of the FBA. At Tier 1, this involves developing an intervention that will be applied with all students in a large group—most likely the whole school. This should be accomplished by a team that was involved in the FBA data collection and is representative of the faculty and staff in the school. After reviewing the FBA data, the team will think about what would be the most effective intervention that would require the least amount of resources while still being connected to the results of the FBA. For example, if the results from the FBA indicate that disruption is prevalent in the classrooms after transition times (e.g., arrival, lunch, change of rooms) and appears to be motivated by escape from tasks, then several interventions may be indicated. The team could recommend that the school develop a less aversive, more engaging academic curriculum because that may address the motivation to escape tasks, but this is unlikely to be the most efficient option, although it may be something to consider for the long term. Another logical and more efficient option for this problem would be to teach all students appropriate transition behavior (e.g., sit in your seat and get materials out) and reward good classroom behavior with five extra minutes of free time at the end of class (which would address the escape function). The team will then be responsible for developing an action plan to implement the intervention, working with staff to ensure implementation, and monitoring fidelity of implementation and effectiveness. One efficient way to monitor effectiveness is to review the Big Six data after a few weeks of implementation and determine if the rate of the problem behavior in the relevant settings has decreased.

Tier 2 FBA

The FBA and intervention procedures from Tier 1 should reduce the total number of students with behavior problems, but they are highly unlikely to reduce that number to zero. There will likely be some students whose behavioral needs are more intense and whose behaviors serve a different function than was addressed by Tier 1. The FBA process at Tier 2 will focus on identifying the students with at-risk behavior and providing efficient, targeted supports based on the function of their behavior. As with all tiers, we will (a) determine the antecedents, consequences, and setting events of the problem behavior; (b) develop a precision hypothesis statement that summarizes the FBA results; and (c) implement appropriate function-based interventions.

Data collection. The data collection process at Tier 2 involves reviewing existing functional data and collecting efficient indirect information about the function of each at-risk student's problem behavior. The review of existing data begins with ODRs. At-risk students generally have more than one ODR. When this is true, the ODRs provide a useful starting point for determining the most problematic behavior and the antecedents (e.g., time of day, location, others involved) and consequences (e.g., administrative decision, perceived motivation) for that behavior. Other existing functionally relevant information can be determined via a basic review of school records. For example, a student may be taking medications that, depending on whether they are administered or not, may function as setting events for the problem behavior (e.g., attention and anti-anxiety medication).

The new data that should be gathered in Tier 2 FBAs are interviews with one or more adults who are familiar with the students' behavior in school. Since the goal of Tier 2 FBA is not to develop highly individualized and intensive interventions but rather to provide efficient supports for students at risk, the interview process can be relatively brief and simple. This would involve a few minutes of discussion about the problem behavior and its typical antecedents, setting events, and consequences. This will generally require some clinical skills on the part of the interviewer, since many school faculty and staff are not fluent with functional concepts when discussing behavior. The interview should not conclude until the interviewee has indicated that the summary of antecedents, setting events, behaviors, and consequences seems accurate based on the interviewee's knowledge. The Tier 2 FBA data collection process concludes with a team reviewing the findings from the interview and records review and summarizing them into a precision hypothesis statement that specifies the problem behavior and its antecedents, setting events, and consequences.

Interventions. Interventions at Tier 2 of the FBA process are generally package, evidence-based interventions rather than individualized interventions. When a school uses a small number (e.g., two or three) of package, evidence-based interventions at Tier 2, a high degree of fidelity of implementation is possible for the intervention with a high number of students (e.g., 5%–10% of the students in a school). Therefore, the task of the team at Tier 2 is to determine which package, evidence-based intervention currently available in the school best matches the function of each student's behavior. See Filter and Alvarez (2012) for a review of the process of adopting and reviewing Tier 2 package, evidence-based interventions in a school. Examples of interventions that have proven to be effective for this use include Check-in/Check-out (Crone, Hawken, & Horner, 2010) and Check and Connect (Christenson et al., 2008). Check-in/Check-out involves checking in with a program manager each morning, receiving behavior feedback on a behavior point card throughout the day, checking out with a program manager at the end of the day and reviewing performance relative to goals, and sending the behavior point card home to be signed by a guardian and returned the next day, at which point the process repeats (Crone et al., 2010). The program is managed by a team that reviews the behavior point card data on a regular basis for decision making. Check and Connect is a program that establishes a relationship between a student and a mentor who builds a trusting relationship and checks the student's engagement on a regular basis, using the engagement data to facilitate the mentoring process and ensuring connectedness to school (Christenson et al., 2008). Other evidence-based interventions can be found at the National Registry for Evidenced-based Programs and Practices (http://www.nrepp.samhsa.gov/), the Blueprints for Violence Prevention (http://www.colorado.edu/cspv/blueprints/index.html), the What Works Clearinghouse (http://ies.ed.gov/ncee/wwc/), and the Collaborative for Academic, Social, and Emotional Learning (http://www.casel.org/database/index.php).

After students are matched to interventions, it is important for a team to monitor fidelity of implementation and effectiveness. Effectiveness can be monitored with regular direct observation, direct behavior ratings (Chafouleas, Riley-Tillman, & Christ, 2009; see www.directbehavioratings.com for more information), or with the data generated naturally from the intervention (e.g., behavior ratings from Check-in/Check-out; Crone et al., 2010). If the intervention is ineffective even after minor modifications, then it is appropriate to begin a Tier 3 FBA process for a student.

Tier 3 FBA

Tier 3 FBA is the process that has received the most attention in the literature and is therefore the most familiar and established process of the three tiers. Tier 3 FBA targets the students with the most severe and persistent problem behavior who have either failed to respond to Tier 1 and Tier 2 efforts or have dangerous behavior that requires immediate attention. The process of supporting these students involves collecting interview data from multiple sources, conducting direct observations in natural settings, and developing interventions that are highly individualized and resource-intensive (Crone & Horner, 2003).

Data collection. Tier 3 FBA should begin with indirect sources of information that will be compared with direct sources of information gathered later in the Tier 3 process. Indirect sources of information can also be used to streamline the collection of later direct sources of information. Indirect sources of information include the data gathered in previous tiers (e.g., interviews and ODRs) in addition to new interviews. The interviews at Tier 3 are more structured than the interviews at Tier 2 because a higher degree of precision is required to inform a more individualized approach. Structured interviews, such as the Functional Assessment Checklist for Teachers and Staff (FACTS; March et al., 2000), provide more guidance on the process of narrowing information about antecedents, setting events, behaviors, and consequences to inform an accurate hypothesis statement (McIntosh et al., 2008). The best people to interview at Tier 3 are those with the most direct access to the student's behavior (Borgmeier, 2003). This often includes classroom teachers and paraprofessionals.

The direct sources of information for Tier 3 FBAs are systematic direct observations. During these observations, records are kept not only of the occurrence of the problem behaviors as would occur during a more general systematic direct observation, but also of observations of the antecedents and consequences of those behaviors. An example of this is the FBA Observation and Summary Form (FBA-OSF; Filter and Alvarez, 2012; available at www.mnsu.edu/psych/psyd/people/). These observations should occur several times in the student's natural school setting in order to capture a sufficient sample of problem behavior from which to draw functional hypotheses. The information from the interviews and other indirect sources should inform the appropriate times

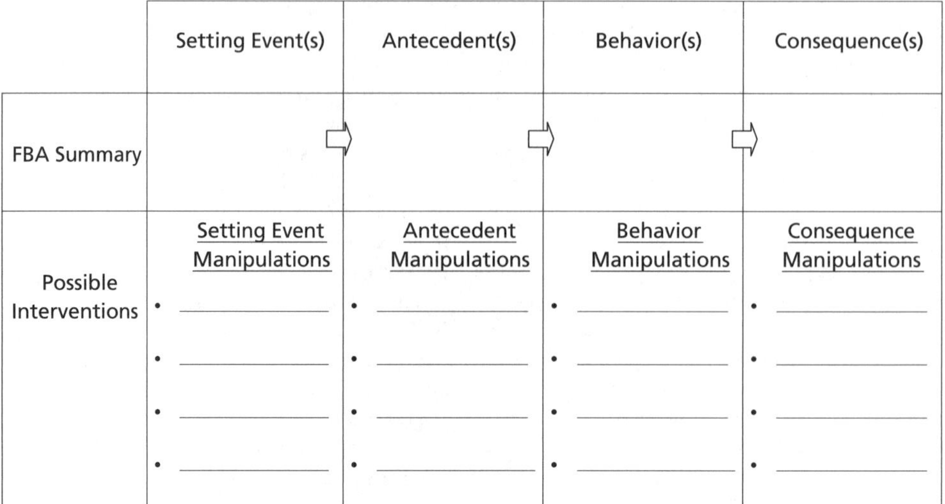

Figure 3.2. Framework for developing interventions for functional behavioral assessment-based behavior interventions plans (FBA-BIPs)

***Printed with permission from Oxford University Press. Filter and Alvarez (2012), Functional Behavioral Assessment: A Three-Tiered Prevention Model**

and locations for these observations to occur. If, for example, the indirect data suggests that behavior is most likely to occur in the classroom during science lessons, then that is the best setting and time to gather representative observations.

After all of the data have been collected, a team will need to organize the data into a precision hypothesis statement that summarizes the antecedents, settings event, problem behavior, and consequences. This can be a difficult task if the data are not all in agreement. The best way to sort through conflicting data is to (a) look for areas of agreement (e.g., antecedents may be consistent across all sources even though consequences are not) and (b) prioritize the most direct and accurate sources of information for decision making. Systematic direction observations would be the most reliable source, interviews would be the second most reliable source, and indirect records would be considered last. After the team comes to consensus on the precision hypothesis statement, then the focus shifts to developing and implementing interventions.

Intervention. The interventions associated with FBAs are generally called behavior intervention plans (Crone & Horner, 2003) or behavior support plans (Sugai, Lewis-Palmer, & Hagan, 1998). We will use the term behavior intervention plan (BIP). Since the purpose of conducting an FBA is to develop an intervention, Tier 3 BIPs should be logically connected to the results of the Tier 3 FBA. The logical connection between the two can be accomplished using the model in Figure 3.2. Teams are encouraged to brainstorm several ideas for how to change the setting events, antecedents, behaviors, and consequences. For example, if the setting event is forgetting to take anxiety medication, then possible ways to change that would include calling the student's family in the morning before school, setting up a routine at home that will ensure that the pills are taken, or having the school nurse dispense the medication. At this point, the team does not need to decide which ideas are best, but simply create a list of at least three ideas for each of the four terms. If the consequence is obtaining adult attention, then ways to change that would include not offering adult attention when the behavior occurs (extinction), offering adult attention only when the student demonstrates a socially acceptable replacement behavior, or having the student place her or his head down on the desk for a time-out from adult attention for 5 minutes each time a behavior occurs. Again, not all of these are the best ideas, but this step is just a brainstorming process, and the selection of interventions will come next based on some basic criteria.

After the competing pathway is developed, the team should select at least one antecedent/setting event strategy, one behavior-teaching strategy, one reinforcement strategy, and one extinction strategy (Filter & Alvarez, 2012). The antecedent/setting event strategy should provide some change that will prevent the behavior from occurring in the first place. For example, if a student's behavior is generally preceded by poorly structured transitions (the antecedent), then a plan can be scripted to make the transitions more predictable. The behavior-teaching strategy should ensure that the student learns how and when to use the socially appropriate replacement behavior that was identified in the competing pathways model. The reinforcement strategy should ensure that the student receives a positive consequence for engaging in the replacement behavior. Finally, the extinction strategy should ensure that the student does not continue to receive the consequence that is maintaining the problem behavior (e.g., adult attention, escape from task) when the problem behavior occurs. It is acceptable to include more interventions than those described above, but it is important not to make the BIP any more complicated than is necessary because complicated BIPs are less likely to be implemented with fidelity. Other things that may be included in a BIP include emergency procedures and brief, low-intensity punishment procedures. Before using punishment or emergency procedures, it is important to review the ethical guidelines affecting these procedures (see Miltenberger, 2004, and any relevant state and federal guidelines related to punishment).

After the intervention components of the BIP have been selected by the team, procedures should be established for monitoring effectiveness and fidelity of implementation. As was noted with Tier 2, the best tools for monitoring effectiveness are direct behavior ratings and systematic direct observation. If regular team reviews of the BIP indicate that it is not effective or not being implemented with fidelity, then the team should develop an action plan to change the procedures or increase fidelity.

Tools and Practice Examples

When working in a three-tiered, FBA-based prevention model, school personnel will be challenged to think in terms beginning in Tier 1 rather than beginning with the most obvious behavior problems at Tier 3. Behavior problems generally come to the attention of school personnel because a referral was submitted for a single student. This is still a viable method of managing some of the behavior problems in a school, but we will briefly review an FBA case beginning in Tier 1 and discuss how the process begins at the school-wide level and concludes at the intensive, individual student level.

The Case of Brandon in a Middle School

Brandon is a student in a middle school located in a suburban area and with an enrollment of about 750 students. A team in the school is responsible for all three tiers of the FBA process in the school. School-wide data that the team reviewed are from the 2010–2011 academic year. The 2011–2012 school year had just begun, and the team was reviewing the data from the previous year to evaluate progress with previous school-wide interventions.

The team began by summarizing their Big Six ODR data. They noted that there was a decrease in disruptive behavior in classrooms over the past year, which was the target of their previous intervention. This was celebrated as a success. However, the overall levels of problem behavior evident in their graph of referrals per day per month indicated that they still had more ODRs than the national average (see www.swis.org for updated national ODR averages). They then reviewed the rest of their Big Six data and determined that bullying was a growing problem. Using the Big Six data, they created the following precision hypothesis statement: "Bullying is occurring at an increasing frequency, and numerous students have been involved. Bullying occurs before and after school in hallways and bathrooms. It appears to be motivated by escape from peer attention." The team then developed a school-wide action plan that involved increased adult supervision in non-classroom settings before and after school, teaching students how to respond to bullying, and more appropriate ways to avoid attention from peers. Within their Big Six data, however, they noted that four students, including Brandon, had been referred for bullying two to four times and were in need of more support than could be offered at the school-wide level. The team then began the Tier 2 FBA process with Brandon and the other three students.

At Tier 2, the team reviewed the existing ODR and school record data for the four at-risk students. They also conducted brief FBA interviews with the students' teachers to determine what antecedents, setting events, and consequences were related to their bullying and related problem behaviors. All students were then matched to existing evidence-based package interventions in the school. Students with attention-maintained behaviors were matched to the Check-in/Check-out program (Crone et al., 2004) and students with escape-maintained behaviors were matched to a modified version of the Check-in/Check-out program. Brandon's brief FBA interviews and ODRs indicated that his bullying and fighting behaviors were maintained by obtaining peer attention, so he was matched to the standard Check-in/Check-out program, during which he received behavior feedback from teachers and was able to earn additional social time with peers based on attaining behavior goals. The Tier 2 interventions were effective in improving the behaviors of three of the students, but Brandon did not demonstrate improvement during his interventions. The three successful students were eventually faded out of the Tier 2 interventions and monitored for continued success. After Brandon showed little progress after his Tier 2 interventions were modified, the team decided that he was in need of Tier 3 FBA-based supports.

At Tier 3, the team conducted an intense, individual FBA of Brandon's behaviors. They reviewed all of the data from Tier 1 and Tier 2 and then conducted structured interviews with all of Brandon's teachers using the FACTS (March et al., 2000). Results from the interviews indicated that his problem behaviors were either maintained by obtaining peer attention or escaping peer attention. Since teachers reported that many of his problem behaviors occurred in the classroom during group activities and in the lunchroom, the team decided to conduct systematic direct observations in those settings using the FBA-OSF (Filter & Alvarez, 2012). The observations clearly indicated that his problem behaviors were maintained by escape from peer attention, contrary to the initial findings from Tier 2. The team created the following precision hypothesis statement of Brandon's behavior: "Brandon engages in fighting and bullying in the classroom during group activities and in the lunchroom. These behaviors are maintained by escape from peer attention and appear to be most likely to occur on days when he is tired."

After creating the precision hypothesis statement, the team then brainstormed intervention ideas using the model in Figure 3.2 and developed an FBA-based BIP for Brandon with the following components:

- Brandon will be taught to politely ask peers to leave him alone when necessary and walk away if they do not respond to his request.
- When Brandon requests to be left alone during group activities, the teacher will allow him to work alone for five minutes.
- The school social worker will talk with Brandon's parents about his sleep schedule and develop a plan with the family to ensure that he attains adequate sleep each night. When he does come to school looking tired, his first period teacher will ask him if he wants to talk with the social worker before class starts to develop a plan to manage his day.
- As an emergency procedure when fighting is observed, teachers will remove the other student and send Brandon to a "partner classroom" to calm down.

It is important to note that an extinction plan was not developed for this case since it would be unethical to require students to continue to interact with Brandon when he is engaging in problem behavior. Brandon's BIP was monitored for effectiveness by collecting direct behavior ratings after training his teachers to use the direct behavior rating forms. Fidelity of implementation was monitored by a school psychologist on the team who checked in with each teacher every two weeks and observed in the classroom once every two weeks. After a few improvements to initial fidelity concerns, the BIP was effective in reducing Brandon's problem behavior, and the team was beginning to discuss plans for adapting more elements of the BIP to include self-management.

Additional Resources

For more information about conducting three-tiered FBAs, we recommend *Functional Behavioral Assessment: A Three-Tiered Prevention Model* by Filter and Alvarez (2012), available from Oxford University Press. Forms and links related to the book and to three-tiered FBA can be found at www.mnsu.edu/psych/psyd/people/filter/book/. Additional information about FBA and three-tiered behavior support in schools can be found at the Web site for the National Technical Assistance Center for Positive Behavior Interventions and Supports (www.pbis.org). Another good book resource for conducting Tier 2 and Tier 3 FBAs in schools is *Building Positive Behavior Support Systems in Schools: Functional Behavioral Assessment* by Crone and Horner (2003), available from Guilford Press.

Key Points to Remember

FBA is a process of identifying the setting events, antecedents, and consequences of problem behavior. The outcome of an FBA is a precision hypothesis statement that specifies the relationship between the behavior and the conditions that predict and maintain it. The purpose of FBA is to develop effective interventions. Although FBA has traditionally been applied only to students with disabilities and students with severe problem behavior, the process is relevant with all students in a school across all tiers of a prevention model. The data collection methods, students served, and scope of interventions differ across tiers, but the definition, outcomes, and purpose of FBA remain the same across tiers. When the FBA and BIP processes are applied with fidelity, problem behaviors are reduced while socially appropriate behaviors are increased.

References

Anderson, C. A., & Scott, T. M. (2009). Implementing function-based support within school-wide positive behavior support. In W. Sailor, G. Dunlap, G. Sugai, & R. H. Horner (Eds.), *Handbook of positive behavior support: Special issues in clinical child psychology* (pp. 705–728). New York, NY: Springer.

Blair, K. C., Umbreit, J., & Bos, C. S. (1999). Using functional assessment and children's preferences to improve the behavior of young children with behavior disorders. *Behavioral Disorders, 24*(2), 151–166.

Borgmeier, C. J. (2003). *An evaluation of informant confidence ratings as a predictive measure of the accuracy of hypotheses from functional assessment interviews* (Doctoral dissertation). Retrieved from ProQuest Information and Learning Company. (UMI No. 3095236)

Carter, D. R., & Horner, R. H. (2007). Adding functional behavioral assessment to First Step to Success. *Journal of Positive Behavior Interventions, 9*(4), 229–238.

Chafouleas, S. M., Riley-Tillman, T. C., & Christ, T. J. (2009). Direct Behavior Rating (DBR): An emerging method for assessing social behavior within a tiered intervention system. *Assessment for Effective Intervention, 34*, 195–200. doi:10.1177/1534508409340391

Christenson, L., Thurlow, M. L., Sinclair, M. F, Lehr, C. A., Kaibel, C. M., Reschly, A., ... Pohl, A. (2008). Check & Connect: A comprehensive student engagement intervention. Retrieved from www.checkandconnect.org

Colvin, G., Kameenui, E. J., & Sugai, G. (1993). Reconceptualizing behavior management and school-wide discipline in general education. *Education and Treatment of Children, 16*(4), 361–382.

Crone, D. A., & Horner, R. H. (2003). *Building positive behavior support systems in schools: Functional behavioral assessment.* New York, NY: Guilford Press.

Crone, D. A., Hawken, L. S., & Horner, R. H. (2010). *Responding to problem behavior in schools* (2nd ed.). New York, NY: Guilford Press.

Ervin, R. A., Radford, P. M., Bertsch, K., Piper, A. L., Ehrhardt, K. E., & Poling, A. (2001). A descriptive analysis and critique of the empirical literature on school-based functional assessment. *School Psychology Review, 30*(2), 193–210.

Filter, K. J., & Horner, R. H. (2009). Function-based academic interventions for problem behavior. *Education and Treatment of Children, 32*(1), 1–19.

Filter, K. J., & Alvarez, M. E. (2012). *Functional behavioral assessment: A three-tiered prevention model.* New York, NY: Oxford University Press.

Hirsch, E. J., Lewis-Palmer, T., Sugai, G., & Schnacker, L. (2004). Using school bus discipline referral data in decision making: Two case studies. *Preventing School Failure, 48*(4), 4–9.

Horner, R. H., Carr, E., Halle, J., McGee, G., Odom, S., & Wolery, M. (2005). The use of single-subject research to identify evidence-based practice in special education. *Exceptional Children, 71*(2), 165–179.

Horner, R. H., Sugai, G., Todd, A. W., & Lewis-Palmer, T. (2005). School-wide positive behavior support: An alternative approach to discipline in schools. In L. Bambara & L. Kern (Eds.), *Individualized supports for students with problem behaviors: Designing positive behavior plans.* New York, NY: Guilford Press.

Illinois PBIS Network. (2010). PBIS glossary of abbreviations and terms. Retrieved from http://community.pbisillinois.org/Home/pbis-glossary

Ingram, K., Lewis-Palmer, T., & Sugai, G. (2005). Function-based intervention planning: Comparing the effectiveness of FBA function-based and non-function-based intervention plans. *Journal of Positive Behavior Interventions, 7*(4), 224–236.

Institute of Educational Sciences, National Center for Education Statistics, Bureau of Justice Statistics. (2011). *Indicators of school crime and safety: 2010* (ECS Publication No. 2011–002). Retrieved from http://nces.ed.gov/pubs2011/2011002.pdf

Kern, L., Gallagher, P., Starosta, K., Hickman, W., & George, M. (2006). Longitudinal outcomes of functional assessment-based interventions. *Journal of Positive Behavior Interventions, 8*(2), 67–78.

Lane, K. L., Umbreit, J., & Beebe-Frankenburger, M. E. (1999). Functional assessment research on students with or at risk for EBD: 1990 to present. *Journal of Positive Behavior Interventions, 1*(2), 101–111.

Luiselli, J. K., Putnam, R. F., & Sunderland, M. (2002). Longitudinal evaluation of behavior support intervention in a public middle school. *Journal of Positive Behavior Interventions, 4*(3), 182–188.

March, R. E., Horner, R. H., Lewis-Palmer, T., Brown, D., Crone, D., Todd, A. W., & Carr, E. (2000). *Functional assessment checklist for teachers and staff.* Eugene, OR: Educational and Community Supports.

March, R. E., & Horner, R. H. (2002). Feasibility and contributions of functional behavioral assessment in schools. *Journal of Emotional and Behavioral Disorders, 10*, 158–170.

May, S., Ard, W., III., Todd, A. W., Horner, R. H., Sugai, G., Glasgow, A., & Sprague, J. R. (2010). School-wide information system. Retrieved from http://www.swis.org

McIntosh, K., Borgmeier, C., Anderson, C. M., Horner, R. H., Rodriguez, B. J., & Tobin, T. J. (2008). Technical adequacy of the functional assessment checklist: Teachers and staff (FACTS) FBA interview measure. *Journal of Positive Behavior Interventions, 10*, 33–45. doi: 10.1177/1098300707311619

McIntosh, K., Brown, J. A., & Borgmeier, C. J. (2008). Validity of functional behavior assessment within a Response to Intervention framework: Evidence, recommended practice, and future directions. *Assessment for Effective Intervention, 34*(1), 6–14. doi: 10.1177/1534508408314096

McIntosh, K., Campbell, A. L., Carter, D. R., & Dickey, C. R. (2009). Differential effects of a tier two behavior intervention based on function of problem behavior. *Journal of Positive Behavior Intervention, 11*(2), 82–93.

Miltenberger, R. G. (2004). *Behavior modification: Principles and procedures* (3rd ed.). Belmont, CA: Wadsworth.

Nelson, J. R., Roberts, M. L., Mathur, S. R., & Rutherford, R. B. (1999). Has public policy exceeded our knowledge base? A review of functional behavioral assessment literature. *Behavioral Disorders, 24*(2), 169–179.

Newcomer, L. L., & Lewis, T. J. (2004). Functional behavioral assessment: An investigation of assessment reliability and effectiveness of function-based interventions. *Journal of Emotional and Behavioral Disorders, 12*(3), 168–181.

Office of Special Education Programs Center on Positive Behavioral Interventions and Supports. (2004). *Implementation blueprint and self-assessment school-wide positive behavioral interventions and supports.* Retrieved from http://www.pbis.org/common/pbisresources/publications/SWPBS_Implementation_Blueprint_v_May_9_2010.pdf

O'Neill, R. E., Horner, R. H., Albin, R. W., Sprague, J. R., Storey, K., & Newton, J. S. (1997). *Functional assessment and program development for problem behavior: A practical handbook* (2nd ed.). Pacific Grove, CA: Brooks Cole.

Scott, T. M., & Eber, L. (2003). Functional assessment and wraparound as systemic school processes: Primary, secondary, and tertiary systems examples. *Journal of Positive Behavior Interventions, 5*(3), 131–143.

Sugai, G., Lewis-Palmer, T., & Hagan, S. (1998). Using functional assessments to develop behavior support plans. *Preventing School Failure, 43*(1), 71–78.

Todd, A. W., Campbell, A. L., Meyer, G. G., & Horner, R. H. (2008). The effects of a targeted intervention to reduce problem behaviors. *Journal of Positive Behavior Interventions, 10*(1), 46–55

Ethical Decision Making in School Mental Health

CHAPTER 4

James C. Raines Nic T. Dibble

Getting Started

This chapter aims to be different from many other works on ethics in three ways. First, instead of focusing on ethical issues (e.g., confidentiality), it focuses on the process of ethical decision making. Second, this chapter references the ethical standards of all four pupil services professions, including the American School Counselor Association (ASCA), the American Nurses Association (ANA), the National Association of School Psychologists (NASP), and the National Association of Social Workers (NASW). Finally, instead of addressing ethics as autonomous ethical agents, readers are encouraged to think as collaborative members of a school-based team.

This process focuses on managing ethical challenges rather than resolving them. The verb "manage" implies active engagement of a situation to seek out the best possible outcomes for a student and stakeholders. The verb "resolve" implies that solutions to ethical predicaments can be found that honor all of the competing ethical standards and other responsibilities and provide satisfactory outcomes for everyone involved. While elegant solutions may sometimes present themselves, some values and responsibilities typically must be given more weight than others.

What We Know

The most recent survey of school-based practitioners found five ethical issues that professionals struggle with most commonly (Bodenhorn, 2006). These were the confidentiality of student disclosures (46%), privacy of student records (36%), intervention related to student dangerousness (33%), parents' rights (22%), and dual relationships with educators (20%). The five most challenging issues were similar: confidentiality of student disclosures (46%), intervention related to student dangerousness (45%), knowledge of a colleague's ethical violation (34%), parents' rights (33%), and dual relationships with educators (19%). Clearly, working as a mental health professional in a host setting results in a host of ethical predicaments.

Ethical Foundations

There are two ethical foundations that undergird this approach to ethics. First, the Golden Rule—treat others as you would have others treat you—is a general precept that has been promoted by all of the major religions (Hick, 1996) as well as many secular moral philosophers from Homer (800 B.C.) to the United Nations' *Declaration of Human Rights* (1948). Gewirth (1978) has provided a rational justification for obeying the Golden Rule, reframing it as "Act in accord with your recipient's rational desires as well as your own" (p. 138). He defines these rational desires as freedom and well-being since they form the basis for all other rights. The U.S. Declaration of Independence takes a similar view of "unalienable rights" in terms of "life, liberty, and the pursuit of happiness." Second, the fiduciary relationship is a common law precept that undergirds all professional-client relationships. *Black's Law Dictionary* defines a fiduciary as "a person who is required to act for the benefit of another person on all matters within the scope of their relationship; one who owes to another the duties of good faith, trust, confidence, and candor" (Garner, 2009, p. 702). Unlike the Golden Rule, which assumes that relationships are both egalitarian and mutually beneficial, the fiduciary relationship assumes that there is a disparity in power that creates a special duty from the professional to the client. Taken together, the Golden Rule and the fiduciary relationship form an excellent foundation for ethical decision making.

What We Can Do: Ethical Decision Making

There are seven recommended steps in the ethical decision-making process. These include (1) knowing yourself and your professional responsibilities, (2) analyzing the predicament, (3) seeking consultation, (4) identifying courses of action, (5) managing the clinical concerns, (6) implementing the decision, and (7) reflecting on the process.

Knowing Yourself and Your Professional Responsibilities

There are two major moral philosophies that form the basis of professional ethics (Congress, 2000). Deontology or duty-based ethics views ethics form a set of prescriptions or proscriptions for professionals working together. These can be justified as either self-evident via logic or jural by way of legislation. Loewenberg, Dolgoff, and Harrington (2000) argue for seven values, including (a) protection of life, (b) equality, (c) autonomy and freedom, (d) least harm, (e) quality of life, (f) privacy and confidentiality, and (g) truthfulness and full-disclosure. For a description of professional values, see Table 4.1. Many of these values are implicit in the four pupil services professions' ethical standards, such as the exception to confidentiality for the protection of life (ANA, §3.2; ASCA, §A2;

Table 4.1 Common Professional Values and Corresponding Ethical Principles

Truthfulness & Full Disclosure	Professionals should be completely honest with their clients.
Dignity & Worth of the Person	Professionals should treat each client in a caring and respectful fashion.
Privacy & Confidentiality	Professionals should seek to acquire only relevant information and should keep that material sacrosanct.
Social Justice	Professionals should pursue social change, particularly with and on behalf of vulnerable and oppressed groups.
Protection of Life	Professionals should seek to protect and prolong a client's biophysical life.
Service	Professionals should seek to help people in need and address social problems above any self-interest.
Equal Treatment	Professionals should treat clients in similar circumstances in a similar manner.
Importance of Human Relationships	Professionals should seek to strengthen relationships among people to enhance the well-being of families, groups, and communities.
Least Harm	When faced with possibly negative outcomes, professionals should choose the least harmful, least permanent, or most reversible option.
Integrity	Professionals should behave in a trustworthy manner, congruent with professional values and ethics.
Quality of Life	Professionals should seek to promote the highest quality of life for both clients and their environments.
Competence	Professionals should practice within their areas of knowledge and skills while constantly striving to improve their expertise.
Autonomy/Freedom	Professionals should respect clients' rights to control or contribute to decisions that affect them.

Adapted from: Raines & Dibble, 2011.

NASP §I.2.4; NASW §1.07). Utilitarianism or consequentialism views ethics by looking at the results of our actions. The best result is the one that leads to the most good for the most people. Most pupil services professionals probably lean toward one moral philosophy or the other in our professional work. In Osmo and Landau's (2006) research, they found that most social workers sided with duty-based ethics in theory, but utilitarian ethics in practice!

There are a great number of similarities among the ethical standards that guide the practice of school counselors, nurses, psychologists, and social workers (Wisconsin Department of Public Instruction, 2010). For instance, all of these professions have ethical standards regarding privacy and confidentiality, conflicts of interest and dual relationships, professional competence, respect for professional colleagues and interdisciplinary collaboration, and consultation. However, each of these professions' ethical standards addresses issues that one or more of the other professions do not. While ethical standards are binding only on professionals from that particular profession, each of these professions can inform the others. Indeed, in the Purpose section, the NASW (2008) Code explicitly recommends that social workers consult other relevant codes of ethics, implying that the NASW Code does not (and cannot) address every practice issue. Some examples of how each of these professions can inform others include the following:

1. The ethical standards for school counselors and school psychologists include guidance on how to involve parents in ways that balance the privacy and confidentiality of students from which school nurses and social workers can learn.
2. School psychologists can obtain guidance from the other three professions regarding self-determination.
3. School nurses can learn more about informed consent from the other three professions.
4. School counselors, nurses, and psychologists can obtain guidance about termination and interruption of services from the NASW Code of Ethics.
5. School social workers can learn more about sharing information with professional colleagues from the other three professions.
6. School counselors and psychologists can obtain guidance about student clients who lack decision-making capacity from the ethical standards of school nurses and social workers.

School counselors, nurses, psychologists, and social workers should be familiar with their respective professions' ethical standards and have a copy readily available for reference. These can be accessed electronically at the Web sites listed below (see Table 4.2). Ethical guidance from the National Association of School Nurses (NASN) is supplemental to the ANA Code of Ethics, and ethical guidance from the School Social Work Association of America is supplemental to the NASW Code of Ethics.

Finally, pupil services professionals should be familiar with the federal and state laws that govern their professional practice. The major federal laws that provide direction for educators in schools are the Family Educational Rights and Privacy Act (FERPA), the Individuals with Disabilities Education Act (IDEA), and the Rehabilitation Act.

Table 4.2 Ethical Guidelines Relevant to Pupil Service Providers

American Nurses Association (ANA)—http://nursingworld.org/MainMenuCategories/EthicsStandards/CodeofEthicsforNurses.aspx
American School Counselor Association (ASCA)—http://asca2.timberlakepublishing.com/files/EthicalStandards2010.pdf
National Association of School Nurses (NASN)—http://www.nasn.org/RoleCareer/CodeofEthics
National Association of School Psychologists (NASP)—http://www.nasponline.org/standards/2010standards/1_%20Ethical%20Principles.pdf
National Association of Social Workers (NASW)—http://www.socialworkers.org/pubs/code/code.asp?print=1
School Social Work Association of America (SSWAA)— http://sswaa.org/displaycommon.cfm?an=1&subarticlenbr=102

Analyzing the Predicament

There are four key questions that must be asked before brainstorming options about an ethical predicament. First, practitioners should ask, "Who is my primary client?" The NASW Code of Ethics explains only who *can* be a client, but it never tells who the client is. Both the ASCA and NASP suggest that the student is generally the primary client. While Kopels and Lindsey (2006) advise that the student should be the *only* client, this is probably too narrow. It is best to view the student as the *primary* client and others as *secondary* or even *tertiary* clients. This helps practitioners prioritize their obligations. Second, practitioners would be wise to inquire, "Who are the non-client stakeholders in this situation?" Most commonly, these include the student's family members, school administrators, other pupil services colleagues (counselors, nurses, psychologists, or social workers), other educators, and community services providers. Because each one of these may have a vested interest in the outcome, they have the potential to influence (for good or bad) the outcomes. Benfari and associates (1986) described eight types of organizational power, including (a) legitimate or positional power, (b) reward power, (c) coercive power, (d) expert power, (e) referent or interpersonal power, (f) information power, (g) affiliation power, and (h) group power. All of these can exist in different combinations within a school system. Pupil services professionals should never make ethical decisions in a social vacuum! Third, practitioners should ask, "What are the key values in conflict in the ethical predicament?" In the preceding section there were many professional values, and any combination of them could be in conflict in a given situation. The NASW (2008) Code of Ethics implies that ranking these values is a common expectation but provides the following caveat: "Reasonable differences of opinion can and do exist among social workers with respect to the ways in which values, ethical principles, and ethical standards should be rank ordered when they conflict" (see Purpose section, p. 2). The final key question is, "Who should I consult about this?" This is a very important question that leads to the next step.

Seeking Consultation

The four pupil services professions' ethical standards all provide explicit direction about seeking consultation in order to provide the best possible services to clients (ASCA §A2b, A4a; ANA §1.5; NASP §II.1.1; NASW §2.05). When obtaining ethical consultation, practitioners have three major responsibilities. First, they should continue to protect the privacy of their clients. There is very seldom any reason to identify the name of client or other identifying information when inquiring about an ethical predicament. Second, they should check the credentials of the consultant. An ethical consultant should be familiar with all of the relevant codes and guidelines discussed above. Finally, they must think critically about the advice being offered. When in doubt, seek a second opinion! When obtaining legal consultation, pupil services professionals should look for someone who is familiar with constitutional issues, federal laws, state statutes, and case law. Kopels (2007) has noted that schools most commonly violate student privileges under three amendments in the Bill of Rights—the 1st, 4th, and 8th Amendments. Respectively, these amendments address freedom of religion, freedom of expression, and freedom to protest; freedom from unreasonable search and seizure; and freedom from harsh punishments. Federal education statutes include the Elementary and Secondary Education Act, also known as No Child Left Behind; the Vocational Rehabilitation Act of 1973; the Family Educational Rights and Privacy Act (FERPA); and the Individuals with Disabilities Education Act (IDEA). Case law includes official judicial decisions in state and federal courts. While cases are binding only for the geographical auspice of the court, they can be very influential even beyond these borders. The *Tarasoff v. Regents of the University of California* (1974, 1976) is a classic example. While the case applied only to the state of California, many state legislatures and state courts have reacted to it (Kopels & Kagle, 1993). A good legal consultant should be able to explain if there is a "duty to protect" in their state. For example, in Texas, therapists only have the "discretion" to warn, but risk civil liability even if they violate confidentiality in good faith (*Thapar v. Zezulka*, 1999).

While pupil services professionals may violate the law as an ethical act of civil disobedience, they would be wise to follow four simple guidelines. First, they should not act alone, but in concert with other professionals. Second, prior to disobeying the law, they should actively advocate for changes through legal channels. Third, they should engage in civil disobedience as a last resort. Fourth, they should not attempt to elude arrest or punishment (Raines & Dibble, 2011).

Pupil services professionals should seek out clinical consultation when they encounter a situation where they believe their clinical knowledge is not sufficient (e.g., the practitioner may never have worked with a student who is embedding objects into her body, a form of self-abuse). Clinical consultation can help determine if a referral is in order, whether the practitioner is able to develop the competence to work with the student, or both.

Identifying Courses of Action

There is a subtle difference between ethical dilemmas and ethical predicaments. *Ethical dilemmas* are framed as either-or problems (e.g., should I disclose client information without consent or risk my client engaging in some kind of risk-taking behavior?). *Ethical predicaments* are more broadly framed as complex problems (e.g., what can done to protect my client and maintain confidentiality to the maximum extent possible?). For any given ethical predicament, it is best to identify at least three possible ways to manage the situation to help avoid either-or thinking. This also helps avoid getting into a tug-of-war with clients or other stakeholders who may take an opposing point of view.

Next, the practitioner projects the outcomes, whether positive, neutral, or negative, to each of the identified possible courses of action. Each alternative is evaluated for its impact on the client and other stakeholders (e.g., parents, other students, professional colleagues, individual practitioner). While the pupil services professional's primary responsibility is to the client, secondary responsibilities to other stakeholders should not be ignored. One way to consider different courses of action is to assess to what degree they are congruent with generally accepted moral principles. McNamara (2008) prioritizes the moral principles of respect for the dignity of persons, responsible caring, integrity of relationships, and responsibility to society, while Stone (2005) identifies the moral principles of autonomy, beneficence, non-maleficence, justice, and loyalty. We can find parallel values in the pupil services professions' ethical standards. For example, the American Nurses Association (2001) Code of Ethics identifies such moral virtues as wisdom, honesty, courage, compassion, and patience as attributes of a good nurse.

Many ethical decision-making models start with the assumption of a single ethical agent. That is, the mental health professional ultimately makes an individual decision as to what course of action will be taken, following consultation (ethical, legal, or clinical) with appropriate professionals and consideration of different courses of action and their impact on the client and stakeholders. While it is important for practitioners to take responsibility for their professional decisions and actions, it is possible to do so while engaging the client and stakeholders in the decision-making process. Inclusion of the client in the decision-making process is consistent with the ethical values of self-determination, autonomy, and respect for human dignity. Since pupil services professionals work primarily with minor students who may make choices that are not in their best interests, it is important to consider a student's age, developmental maturity, cognitive development, and mental health. And while younger children should not be expected to deal with complex problems, it is clear that ethical predicaments can be excellent opportunities for students' learning and growth (e.g., conflict management, problem solving, and coping with crisis) with appropriate adult support. The more challenging the ethical predicament, the less likely there will be a single, readily evident, best course of action. Partnering with students can help to develop greater student commitment to any chosen course of action, which may increase the likelihood of its success. Involving stakeholders in the decision-making process may also increase support and commitment to a chosen course of action, as well as shared responsibility for its outcomes.

Managing Clinical Concerns

Managing clinical concerns is less of a step than a continuous concern throughout the ethical decision-making process. There are three common clinical issues that need attention.

First, practitioners must know how to conduct threat assessments to determine if there is truly a safety concern strong enough to warrant a breach of confidentiality. Generally, we think about both threats against the self (i.e., suicide) and threats against others. It is important to differentiate between risk factors and warning signs. *Risk factors* are demographic characteristics statistically associated with great risk (e.g., males under 25), while *warning signs* are individual indicators that a student's risk level is escalating (e.g., giving away cherished possessions). See Table 4.3 for a list of suicide warning signs. The suicide assessment is best done by a school-based crisis team

Table 4.3 Warning Signs for Suicide

- Direct or indirect threats ("The world would be better off without me.")
- Access to means (e.g., guns, narcotics)
- Prior suicide attempts
- Intense emotional pain
- Extreme sense of hopelessness and helplessness
- Social isolation (often self-induced)
- Prolonged feelings of emptiness, worthlessness, and/or depression
- Sudden improvement in mood after prolonged depression
- Mental confusion (irrational thinking)
- Prior family history of suicide
- Past psychiatric history
- Alcohol or substance abuse
- Anger, aggression, or irritability (esp. in children)
- Childhood history of physical or sexual abuse
- Running away from home
- Sleep or eating disturbances
- Loss of positive motivation (e.g., decline in grades)
- Loss of interest in pleasurable activities (anhedonia)
- Poor personal hygiene or lack of concern about appearance
- Excessive focus on death and dying
- Daring or risk-taking behavior
- Lack of interest in planning for the future (lacking goals)
- Making final arrangements (e.g., giving away prized possessions)

Sources: Brock, Sandoval, & Hart (2006); Poland & Lieberman (2002); Roberts (2006)

(Cornell & Sheras, 2006). This should include a school administrator who is responsible for the school environment, a school resource officer who may need to search for weapons, and pupil services providers who can handle the clinical assessment. When conducting a suicide assessment, the research recommends employing empirical instruments as part of the evaluation for two reasons. First, clinician-only evaluations tend to be subjective and anecdotal, while suicide assessment measures are more objective and comprehensive (Doss, 2005; Jensen & Weisz, 2002). Second, students from some cultural groups will not admit to self-destructive feelings aloud but will admit to such feelings on a written instrument (Eskin, 2003; Morrison & Downey, 2000). See the Tools & Resources section for validated suicide scales.

For threats against others, the FBI report (O'Toole, 2007) recommends an ecological approach that takes four components into consideration. The *personality of the student* addresses issues such as how he or she copes with conflict and expresses anger or degree of emotional dysregulation (Newhill, 2003). The student's *family dynamics* deal with issues such as exposure to child abuse or domestic violence. The *school dynamics* focus on the presence of a social caste system or bullying behavior. The *community milieu* deals with issues such as racism, heterosexism, and the marginalization of kids who are perceived as different. Borum and Verhaagen (2006) recommend using the mnemonic acronym ACTION to identify six warning signs for violence against others (see Table 4.4). The joint report of the

Table 4.4 Warning Signs of Violence against Others

Attitudes that justify violence (e.g., victims are considered subhuman)
Capacity to carry out violence (e.g., possession of weapons and ammunition)
Thresholds or rules broken to further the plan (e.g., stealing a gun or bullets)
Intent or commitment to the plan (e.g., resolute about violent objectives)
Others' reactions or responses to the plan (e.g., fear that student can be lethal)
Noncompliance with risk reduction interventions (e.g., refusal to de-escalate)

U.S. Secret Service and U.S. Department of Education (Fein et al., 2002) recommends combining interview and collateral information into a report that includes the following parts: (1) precipitating events, (2) identifying information about the student, (3) background information, (4) current situation, (5) attack-related preparation, (6) motives, and (7) target selection. Just as there are empirical measures for assessing suicidal risks, there are also scales that measure potential for violence against others (see the Tools & Resources section).

A second major clinical concern is about the student's developmental readiness to participate in ethical decision making. The research is decidedly mixed (Halpern-Felsher, 2009). Most students who are 14 years and older are as capable as adults of understanding medical information and weighing the pros and cons of treatment (Bastiaens, 1995). There are, however, eight risk factors that diminish an adolescent's ability to make good decisions. These include an angry disposition, substance abuse, executive functioning deficits, high levels of testosterone, serious health issues, social skills deficits, mental health problems, and environmental deprivation (Raines & Dibble, 2011). Working in the student's zone of proximal development (Vygotsky, 1934/1978) has five implications for partnering with students about ethical predicaments. First, practitioners should support a student's capacity for understanding the issues with developmentally appropriate explanations (Wolfe, Jaffe, & Crooks, 2006). Second, clinicians should titrate the complexity of the problem so that students get the "gist" of the conundrum (Rivers, Reyna, & Mills, 2008). Third, professionals should role-play key social skills such as assertiveness, conflict resolution, or peer-refusal techniques. Fourth, practitioners should help youth make healthy choices rather than scare them into compliance (Beutler, 2000; Verhulst, 2002). Finally, students need a positive peer culture that protects them from exposure to antisocial events and reinforces prosocial behavior.

The third major clinical issue deals with multicultural sensitivity. There are three general approaches to multiculturalism in ethics. *Absolutism* assumes that the same ethical principles apply across all ethnic groups and minimizes cultural differences. *Relativism* assumes that all moral norms originate from a cultural context and denies that there are any universal standards. *Universalism* assumes that there are transcultural moral principles but allows that these are expressed differently in each culture. For example, the U.N. *Convention on the Rights of the Child* (1989) condemns child abuse but recognizes that abuse may be defined differently. Raines and Dibble (2011) identify six common differences between white, middle-class practitioners and their minority clients. First, family or community may be more highly valued than the individual, so terms such as "self-determination" appear to be an oxymoron (Palmer & Kaufman, 2003). Second, emotional control may be more highly valued than emotional catharsis, so asking about a student's thoughts is preferred over asking about his or her feelings (Jue & Lewis, 2001). Third, cultural mandates about reciprocity may conflict with the professional's refusal of gifts, so expressions of gratitude may need to be redirected as a thank-you note to school administrators (Brown & Trangsrud, 2008). Fourth, cultural inclusion of the professional into the family may conflict with professional detachment and distance, so clinicians may need to rethink rigid ideas about "boundaries" (Ridley, Liddle, Hill, & Li, 2001). Fifth, cultural expectations of mutual self-disclosure may conflict with professional reserve, so practitioners may need to find some middle ground (Burkard et al., 2006). Finally, certain ethnic practices engender concerns about possible child abuse, requiring professionals to critically think about cultural explanations (see Table 4.5).

Table 4.5 Critical Questions about Cultural Practices and Child Abuse

1. Is the intent of the parent to harm or to help?
2. What is the effect on the child—both physically and psychologically?
3. How normative or common is the practice in the minority culture?
4. Do the parent's actions conform to acceptable cultural practices?

Source: Fontes (2005)

Implementing the Decision

The next step in the ethical decision-making process is to implement the selected course of action. Care can be taken to ensure that the chosen method to manage the ethical predicament is the best one available by pupil services professionals asking themselves a series of "test questions":

1. "Golden Rule"—If I was the client, would I want someone to handle this situation with this same course of action?
2. Fiduciary responsibility—If I proceed with this course of action, will I have faithfully discharged my fiduciary responsibility to my client?
3. Justice and generalizability—Would I treat another student the same way in the same situation? If the answer is no, are there legitimate reasons for different treatment?
4. Publicity—Would I feel comfortable if the details of this case were somehow made public (e.g., keeping the identities of students and stakeholders confidential, sharing the case details with a group of colleagues as part of an in-service on ethics)?
5. Universality—If a professional colleague sought me out for consultation on this ethical predicament, would I suggest this course of action?

Negative responses to any of these questions may suggest the need to further review the ethical predicament prior to implementing the selected course of action (e.g., seek out additional consultation).

The more challenging the ethical predicament, the more likely there may be some people who are not satisfied with how the situation was managed. A student might blame you for unanticipated negative outcomes. A parent may be critical because she wanted to be more involved in the decision-making process. A building principal may feel that your choice provided too much autonomy to the student at the expense of the student's safety. By preparing to justify the decision, a practitioner can help to manage and mediate criticism. Raines (2009) suggests focusing on three issues: protection, the present, and positive outcomes. Clearly, to the extent that the course of action protected people (client and stakeholders) from harm, that is an important outcome to stress in the face of criticism. The federal Family Educational Rights and Privacy Act (FERPA) specifically authorizes disclosure of education records to deal with health and safety emergencies. Some people's criticism may highlight the past, which cannot be changed, or the future, which may not come to pass. Future considerations should not be ignored, but at the same time they should not take precedence over current challenges that require immediate attention. If necessary, the situation can be re-engaged in the future. Critics may choose to focus on negative outcomes of the implemented course of action. Being prepared to share the positive outcomes and how the situation had no ideal alternatives available may help them understand the challenges of the ethical predicament. Indeed, the other available alternatives may have had even more negative outcomes than the selected course of action.

Pupil services professionals may use this decision-making process as a template to document what they did and why (i.e., summarize the analysis of the situation, who was consulted with and what they recommended, why some consultative advice was accepted and some rejected, what possible courses of action were generated, what the outcomes of each course of action were, what the impacts on the client and stakeholders were, why a particular course of action was chosen).

Established parameters (e.g., laws, school board policies) can be used to help justify your decision. Was the selected course of action required or allowed by law? Was the action in compliance with school board policy or administrative procedure? Was the situation handled consistently with a group practice decision (e.g., following an established protocol that all pupil services professionals in the school have agreed upon)? To the extent that your actions are consistent with established parameters, the focus of any criticism can be redirected away from the practitioner's individual decision.

Reflecting on the Process

Some ethical decision-making models conclude with the practitioner implementing the selected course of action, but there are important practical and ethical reasons to extend the process to include reflection. The more challenging the ethical aspects of any given situation, the greater the likelihood that there may be unanticipated outcomes that require additional intervention from the practitioner. In addition, there may be criticism from stakeholders (e.g., school administrators or parents) who, in hindsight, believe that a different course of action may have had better outcomes. Further, reflecting upon the decision-making process can be a form of professional development that is embedded within the practitioner's daily work.

There are a number of questions pupil services professionals may use to reflect upon how they have managed a particular ethical predicament. Hindsight can be a valuable "lens" through which to retroactively analyze an ethical predicament and how it was managed. The practitioner has additional information that may not have been available (or perhaps was not sought out) before the selected course of action was implemented.

1. To what extent did my personal values influence the decision? It may be harder for pupil services professionals to give greater weight to the ethical standard of client self-determination when working with young children who need adults to protect them or with adolescents who may be prone to making decisions that endanger their personal safety. However, acting in the best interest of a client should not be influenced by the personal value system of the practitioner.
2. To what extent and how did other participants influence the decision? How was the decision-making process collaborative with the student and other stakeholders? Was the student "herded" toward a decision he or she was not satisfied with? This chapter argues for a collaborative decision-making model that includes the student client and other stakeholders who will be affected by the selected course of action in the decision-making process. That inclusion should be sincere and genuine and allow for potential disagreement with the practitioner.
3. How was the student's self-determination balanced with concerns for safety and well-being? It can be challenging for a practitioner to determine what level of autonomy any given student should be allowed in any given situation. The student's age, developmental maturity, cognitive ability, and mental health are all considerations, as well as the potential risk for harm to the student or others in the current situation.
4. What administrative pressures were exerted in the situation? Administrators have a fundamental responsibility to keep their schools and the people in them safe. In addition, they may lack an understanding of privacy, confidentiality, and self-determination as important student rights.
5. How was the advice of consultants considered? Should other consultants have been approached for advice? Consultation is voluntary, and the practitioner must weigh the advice and decide whether it will help or hinder the management of a particular ethical predicament.
6. Were there any clinical concerns that were missed or not considered appropriately? Even if an ethical predicament is managed well ethically, lack of attention to clinical concerns can still result in unacceptable outcomes for student clients or stakeholders.
7. Were there areas of competence that needed improvement to better serve the student? Should a referral to another practitioner have been made? All four professions stress the importance of professional competence (ASCA, §E1; ANA, §4.3, 4.2; NASP, §II.1; NASW, §1.04, 4.01). The expectation is that the practitioner will not provide any professional services that the individual is not professionally prepared to deliver.
8. Could more knowledge of the law, school board policies, and administrative rules have better served the student? Greater knowledge of the law might reveal specific legal rights to which a minor student is entitled. A better understanding of school board policies or administrative rules may have better prevented and managed criticism of the selected course or action.
9. In hindsight, was the selected course of action the best one available? It may be that a different course of action may have had better outcomes. If so, the practitioner should examine the decision-making process and try to determine if some part of the process was overlooked or could have been better followed.

Any of these nine questions may reveal that the school-based practitioner may have made a mistake. Reamer (2008) identifies three kinds of errors: (1) inadvertent mistakes, (2) well-intentioned mistakes, and (3) deliberate deviances from ethical standards. There are two main goals in managing a mistake. First, we want to mitigate any potential harm. Second, we want to ensure that we do not repeat the mistake in the future. Gutheil (2006) posits that clients who suffer from professional misjudgments need acknowledgment, remorse, and remedy. *Acknowledgment* means that practitioners must admit their mistakes. There is some research that such admissions actually reduce one's risk of being sued or being brought before a licensing board (Mazor et al., 2004; Pelt & Faldmo, 2008). *Remorse* means that clinicians should apologize for their mistakes. Luce (2006) argues that sincere contrition reduces practitioner guilt, facilitates client forgiveness, and restores confidence in the professional's integrity. *Remedy* implies that if the client has experienced adverse consequences (e.g., school expulsion), the professional should take every possible means to rectify the situation (Berlinger, 2004).

Ethics in Response to Intervention

It has become common for schools to consider behavioral screening as part of a positive behavioral intervention and support framework. Chafouleas and colleagues (2010) have identified four ethical issues involved in this practice. First, communities that still view mental health concerns with social stigma may object to such programs as Columbia Teen Screen, a suicide prevention program. It is best to frame behavioral screens as "barriers to school success" in order to gain community acceptance. Second, parents may object to even routine mental health screenings without their express permission. Contrary to Chafouleas and colleagues, the National Research Council and the Institute of Medicine (2009) advise that schools provide clear information and obtain written consent prior to all behavioral screenings. The idea of "passive consent" should be an oxymoron to school-based practitioners regarding behavioral health issues. Neither federal law (i.e., the Protection of Pupil Rights Amendment, 34 C.F.R. §98) nor case law (i.e., *Merriken v. Cressman*, 1973) supports such an interpretation. Third, all screening measures strive for a delicate balance between false negatives (those who have a problem the instrument does not find) and false positives (those who do not have a problem the instrument does find). Even more disconcerting is the possibility that such scales disproportionally identify minority students (Donovan & Cross, 2002). Finally, once behavioral screening locates students at risk, schools may be ill-prepared to provide services for all of the students indicated (Levitt, Saka, Romanelli, & Hoagwood, 2007). While community referrals may be ideal, the evidence suggests that schools have become the default mental health service providers in U.S. society (Rones & Hoagwood, 2000).

Conclusion

This chapter shares a decision-making process that pupil services professionals may use to help manage ethical challenges that may arise in professional practice. It argues for a collaborative approach that involves the student client and other stakeholders who may be affected by how an ethical predicament is managed.

Tools & Resources

There are four validated scales that aim to predict future suicidal behavior for youth:

1. Cull, J. G., & Gill, W. S. (1988). *Suicide Probability Scale (SPS) manual.* Los Angeles, CA: Western Psychological Services.
2. Orbach, I., Milstein, I., Har-Even, D., Apter, A., Tiano, S., & Elizur, A. (1991). A Multi-Attitude Suicide Tendency Scale for adolescents. *Psychological Assessment, 3*(3), 398–404.
3. Reynolds, W. M. (1987). *The Suicidal Ideation Questionnaire: SIQ form HS.* Odessa, FL: Psychological Assessment Resources.
4. Shaffer, D., Scott, M., Wilcox, H., Maslow, C., Hicks, R., Lucas, C. P., ... Greenwald, S. (2004). The Columbia Suicide screen: Validity and reliability of a screen for youth suicide and depression. *Journal of the American Academy of Child & Adolescent Psychiatry, 43*(1), 71–79.

There are also six validated risk assessment measures for violence specifically for youth:

1. Augimeri, L. K., Webster, C. D., Koegl, C. J., & Levene, K. S. (2001). *Early Assessment Risk List for Boys (EARL-20B). Version 2.* Toronto, Canada: Earlscourt Child & Family Centre.
2. Bartel, P., Borum, R., & Forth, A. (2000). *Structured Assessment for Violence Risk in Youth (SAVRY), Consultation ed.* Tampa, FL: University of South Florida.
3. Grinberg, I., Dawkins, M., Dawkins, M. P., & Fullilove, C. (2005). Adolescents at risk for violence: An initial validation of the Life Challenges Questionnaire and Risk Assessment Index. *Adolescence, 40*(159), 573–599.

4. Hoge, R. D., & Andrews, D. A. (2002). *Youth Level of Service/Case Management Inventory (YLS/CMI). Users manual.* North Tonowanda, NY: Multi-Health Systems.
5. Seifert, K., Phillips, S., & Parker, S. (2001). Child and Adolescent Risk for Violence (CARV): A tool to assess juvenile risk. *Journal of Psychiatry & Law, 29*(3), 329–346.
6. Wong, S. C. P., & Gordon, A. (2006). The validity and reliability of the Violence Risk Scale: A treatment-friendly violence risk assessment tool. *Psychology, Public Policy, & Law, 12*(3), 279–309.

Key Points to Remember

- Use a comprehensive process of ethical decision making and avoid shortchanging any of the steps to produce the best possible result in difficult circumstances.
- Become familiar with multiple ethical guidelines to increase the likelihood of locating specific guidance for your ethical predicament.
- Collaborate with others about ethical decisions. These others should include the client, colleagues, and consultants.
- Manage the clinical concerns throughout the process. Every ethical predicament is both an ethical problem and a people problem.
- Be thoughtful and reflective before, during, and after making the ethical decision. Mistakes are bound to occur, but they should become fewer with moral maturity.

Further Learning

Raines, J. C., & Dibble, N. T. (2011). *Ethical decision making in school mental health.* New York, NY: Oxford University Press.

References

American Nurses Association. (2001). *ANA Code of Ethics for Nurses.* Silver Spring, MD: Author.

American School Counselor Association. (2010). *Ethical standards for school counselors.* Alexandria, VA: Author.

Bastiaens, L. (1995). Compliance with pharmacotherapy in adolescents: Effects of patients' and parents' knowledge and attitudes toward treatment. *Journal of Child & Adolescent Psychopharmacology, 5*(1), 39–48.

Benfari, R. C., Wilkinson, H. E., & Orth, C. D. (May–June, 1986). The effective use of power. *Business Horizons, 29,* 12–16.

Berlinger, N. (2004). Fair compensation without litigation: Addressing patients' financial need in disclosure. *Journal of Healthcare Risk Management, 24*(1), 7–11.

Beutler, L. E. (2000). Empirically-based decision making in clinical practice. *Prevention & Treatment, 3* (Article 27). Retrieved from http://journals.apa.org/prevention/volume3/pre0030027a.html

Bodenhorn, N. (2006). Exploratory study of common and challenging ethical dilemmas experienced by professional school counselors. *Professional School Counseling, 10*(2), 195–202.

Borum, R., & Verhaagen, D. (2006). *Assessing and managing violence risk in juveniles.* New York, NY: Guilford Press.

Brock, S. E., Sandoval, J., & Hart, S. (2006). Suicidal ideation and behaviors. In G. G. Bear & K. M. Minke (Eds.), *Children's needs III: Development, prevention, and intervention* (pp. 225–238). Bethesda, MD: National Association of School Psychologists.

Brown, C., & Trangsrud, H. B. (2008). Factors associated with acceptance and decline of client gift giving. *Professional Psychology: Research & Practice, 39*(5), 505–511.

Burkard, A. W., Knox, S., Groen, M., Perez, M., & Hess, S. A. (2006). European American therapist self-disclosure in cross-cultural counseling. *Journal of Counseling Psychology, 53*(1), 15–25.

Chafouleas, S. M., Kilgus, S. P., & Wallach, N. (2010). Ethical dilemmas in school-based behavioral screening. *Assessment for Effective Intervention, 35*(4), 245–252.

Congress, E. P. (2000). What social workers should know about ethics: Understanding and resolving practice dilemmas. *Advances in Social Work, 1*(1), 1–25.

Cornell, D. G., & Sheras, P. L. (2006). *Guidelines for responding to student threats of violence: A manual for school-based teams to assess and respond effectively to students who threaten violence.* Longmont, CO: Sopris West/Cambium Learning.

Donovan, M. S., & Cross, C. T. (2002). *Minority students in special and gifted education.* Washington, DC: National Academies Press.

Doss, A. J. (2005). Evidence-based diagnosis: Incorporating diagnostic instruments into clinical practice. *Journal of the American Academy of Child & Adolescent Psychiatry, 44*(9), 947–952.

Eskin, M. (2003). A cross-cultural investigation of the communication of suicidal intent in Swedish and Turkish adolescents. *Scandinavian Journal of Psychology, 44*(1), 1–6.

Fein, R. A., Vossekuil, B., Pollack, W. S., Borum, R., Modzeleski, W., & Reddy, M. (2002). *Threat assessment in schools: A guide to managing threatening situations and to creating safe school climates*. Washington, DC: U.S. Secret Service & U.S. Department of Education. Retrieved from http://www.secretservice.gov/ntac/ssi_guide.pdf

Fontes, L. A. (2005). *Child abuse and culture: Working with diverse families*. New York, NY: Guilford Press.

Garner, B. A. (2009). *Black's law dictionary* (9th ed.). St. Paul, MN: Thomson/West.

Gewirth, A. (1978). The Golden Rule rationalized. *Midwest Studies in Philosophy, 3*, 133–147.

Gutheil, T. G. (2006). Commentary: Systems, sensitivity, and "sorry." *Journal of the American Academy of Psychiatry & the Law, 34*(1), 101–102.

Halpern-Felsher, B. (2009). Adolescent decision making: An overview [Special issue on adolescent decision making]. *The Prevention Research, 16*(2), 3–7.

Hick, J. (1996). A pluralist view. In J. Hick, C. H. Pinnock, A. E. McGrath, R. D. Geivett, & W. G. Phillips, *Four views on salvation in a pluralistic world* (pp. 29–59). Grand Rapids, MI: Zondervan.

Jensen, A. L., & Weisz, J. R. (2002). Assessing match and mismatch between practitioner generated and standardized interview-generated diagnoses for clinic-referred children and adolescents. *Journal of Consulting and Clinical Psychology, 70*(1), 158–168.

Jue, S., & Lewis, S. Y. (2001). Cultural considerations in HIV ethical decision making: A guide for mental health practitioners. In J. R. Anderson & B. Barret (Eds.), *Ethics in HIV-related psychotherapy: Clinical decision making in complex cases* (pp. 61–82). Washington, DC: American Psychological Association.

Kopels, S., & Kagle, J. D. (1993). Do social workers have a duty to warn? *Social Service Review, 67*(1), 10–26.

Kopels, S., & Lindsey, B. (2006, Summer). The complexity of confidentiality in schools today: The school social worker context. *School Social Work Journal* (special 100th anniversary issue), 61–78.

Kopels, S. (2007). Student rights and control of behavior. In P. Allen-Meares (Ed.), *Social work services in schools* (5th ed., pp. 108–144). Boston, MA: Pearson/Allyn & Bacon.

Levitt, J. M., Saka, N., Romanelli, L. H., & Hoagwood, K. (2007). Early identification of mental health problems in schools: The status of instrumentation. *Journal of School Psychology, 45*, 163–191.

Loewenberg, F. M., Dolgoff, R., & Harrington, D. (2000). *Ethical decisions for social work practice* (6th ed.). Itasca, IL: Peacock.

Luce, J. M. (2006). Acknowledging our mistakes. *Critical Care Medicine, 34*(5), 1575–1576.

Mazor, K. M., Simon, S. R., Yood, R. A., Martinson, B. C., Gunter, M. J., Reed, G. W., & Gurwitz, J. H. (2004). Health plan members' views about disclosure of medical errors. *Annals of Internal Medicine, 140*(6), 409–423.

McNamara, K. (2008). Best practices in the application of professional ethics. In A. Thomas & J. Grimes (Eds.), *Best practices in school psychology, V* (Vol. 6, pp. 1933–1941). Bethesda, MD: National Association of School Psychologists.

Merriken v. Cressman, 364 F. Supp. 913 (E.D. Pa 1973).

Morrison, L. L., & Downey, D. L. (2000). Racial differences in self-disclosure of suicidal ideation and reasons for living: Implications for training. *Cultural Diversity & Ethnic Minority Psychology, 6*(4), 374–386.

National Association of School Nurses. (2002). *Code of Ethics*. Silver Spring, MD: Author. Retrieved from http://www.nasn.org/Default.aspx?tabid=512

National Association of School Psychologists. (2010). *Professional conduct manual; Principles for professional ethics; Guidelines for the Provision of School Psychological Services*. Bethesda, MD: Author.

National Association of Social Workers. (2008). *Code of Ethics*. Silver Spring, MD: Author.

National Research Council and Institute of Medicine. (2009). *Preventing mental, emotional, and behavioral disorders among young people: Progress and possibilities* (M. E. O'Connell, T. Boat, & K. E. Warner, Eds.). Washington, DC: National Academies Press.

Newhill, C. E. (2003). *Client violence in social work practice: Prevention, intervention, and research*. New York, NY: Guilford Press.

Osmo, R., & Landau, R. (2006). The role of ethical theories in decision making by social workers. *Social Work Education, 25*(8), 863–876.

O'Toole, M. E. (July, 2007). *The school shooter: A threat assessment perspective*. Quantico, VA: U.S. Department of Justice/Federal Bureau of Investigation. Retrieved from http:// http://www.fbi.gov/stats-services/publications/school-shooter

Palmer, N., & Kaufman, M. (2003). The ethics of informed consent: Implications for multicultural practice. *Journal of Ethnic & Cultural Diversity in Social Work, 12*(1), 1–26.

Pelt, J. L., & Faldmo, L. P. (2008). Physician error and disclosure. *Clinical Obstetrics & Gynecology, 51*(4), 700–708.

Poland, S., & Lieberman, R. (2002). Best practices in suicide intervention. In A. Thomas & J. Grimes (Eds.), *Best practices in school psychology, IV* (Vol. 2, pp. 1151–165). Bethesda, MD: National Association of School Psychologists.

Protection of Pupil Rights Amendment, 20 U.S.C. §1232h (2002).

Raines, J. C. (2009). The process of ethical decision making in school social work: Confidentiality. In C. R. Massat, R. Constable, S. McDonald, & J. P. Flynn (Eds.), *School social work: Practice, policy, and research* (pp. 71–94). Chicago, IL: Lyceum Books.

Reamer, F. G. (2008). Social workers' management of error: Ethical and risk management issues. *Families in Society, 89*(1), 61–68.

Ridley, C. R., Liddle, M. C., Hill, C. L., & Li, L. C. (2001). Ethical decision making in multicultural counseling. In J. G. Ponterotto, J. M. Casas, L. A. Suzuki, & C. M. Alexander (Eds.), *Handbook of multicultural counseling* (2nd ed., pp. 165–188). Thousand Oaks, CA: Sage.

Rivers, S. E., Reyna, V. F., & Mills, B. (2008). Risk taking under the influence: A fuzzy-trace theory of emotion in adolescence. *Developmental Review, 28*, 107–144.

Roberts, A. R. (2006). School-based, adolescent suicidality: Lethality assessments and crisis intervention. In C. Franklin, M. B. Harris, & P. Allen-Meares (Eds.), *The school services sourcebook: A guide for school-based professionals* (pp. 3–13). New York, NY: Oxford University Press.

Rones, M., & Hoagwood, K. (2000). School-based mental health services: A research review. *Clinical Child and Family Psychology Review, 3*(4), 223–241.

Stone, C. (2005). *School counseling principles: Ethics and law*. Alexandria, VA: American School Counselor Association.

Tarasoff v. Board of Regents of the University of California, 529 P.2d 553 (1974); 551 P.2d 334 (1976).

Thapar v. Zezulka, 994 S.W.2d 635 (Tex. 1999).

United Nations General Assembly. (1948). *Universal declaration of human rights*. New York, NY: United Nations Department of Public Information.

United Nations General Assembly. (1989). *Convention on the rights of the child*. New York, NY: United Nations Department of Public Information.

Verhulst, F. C. (2002). Editorial. *Journal of Child Psychology and Psychiatry, 43*(6), 693–694.

Vygotsky, L. S. (1978). Thinking and speech. In R. W. & A. S. Carton (Eds.), *The collected works of L.S. Vygotsky: Vol. 1. Problems of general psychology* (pp. 37–285). Trans. N. Minick . New York, NY: Plenum. [Original pub. 1934.]

Wisconsin Department of Public Instruction. (2010). *Collaborative and comprehensive pupil services*. Madison, WI: Author.

Wolfe, D. A., Jaffe, P. G., & Crooks, C.V. (2006). *Adolescent risk behaviors: Why teens experiment and strategies to keep them safe*. New Haven, CT: Yale University Press.

PART II

Resources for Helping Students with Diagnosed Mental Health, Developmental, and Physical Disorders

SECTION II

Effective Services for Students with Mental Health Diagnoses

This section offers important updates on the use of psychopharmacology and effective interventions for children diagnosed with one or more mental disorders. Even though schools do not emphasize mental health diagnoses, they continue to be one of the main institutions to offer services to children with mental illnesses, making it important for school professionals to know how to work with these children in a school setting. This section covers several mental illnesses that may impact the education of children and offers best practices and resources for helping students diagnosed with mental disorders to succeed in schools.

CHAPTER 5

Psychopharmacological Treatment for Child and Adolescent Mental Disorders

Kia J. Bentley   Kathryn S. Collins

Getting Started

Psychopharmacological treatment as an attempt to respond to students' social, emotional, and behavioral issues began during the 1930s and since the 1980s has been rapidly increasing as the treatment of choice by many health and mental health care providers (Olfson, Marcus, Weissman, & Jensen, 2002; Popper, 2002). Of particular interest is that despite the widespread use of psychotropic medications, with a few exceptions, the specific effectiveness of most of these drugs in children and adolescents has not been thoroughly researched, *and* they are most commonly used in ways not yet approved by the Food and Drug Administration (FDA) (Center for Mental Health in Schools at UCLA, 2008). Thus, it seems that proactively treating mental disorders in children and adolescents using knowledge acquired from research and real world experiences with adults is an accepted and understandable approach that seeks to help reduce real pain, distress, and dysfunction in young human lives. The thinking of many practitioners and parents is that the positive impact of medications—or, better said, the hope and promise of it—is sufficiently beneficial to outweigh the potential harm of psychopharmacological agents; therefore the use of a wide variety of psychiatric medications is a viable if not much-needed option.

What We Know

Understanding Common Mental Disorders and Challenges

Obviously, children and adolescents can and do experience the entire range of social, emotional, and behavioral problems, which are associated with significant distress to the students and their families, schools, and communities. Mental health problems are thought to affect 1 in 5 students at any given time, while serious emotional disturbances affect 5%–9% of American children and adolescents (Farmer et al., 2005). High prevalence and detrimental effects "highlight the importance of a clinician's ability to understand, identity and diagnose" (Bell, 2010, p. 3). Specifically, when left undiagnosed and untreated, mental health problems can contribute to school failure, family conflicts, drug and alcohol abuse, violence, and suicide. School social workers and other school-based professionals can help by explaining that epidemiological studies indicate that mental and emotional disorders in children and adolescents, like those in adults, are primarily related to some complex interplay of biological and environmental factors (Rutter, 2000, 2002). It is important to note that mental disorders can remit or endure over the life span. School social workers and school-based professionals can work with each other (e.g., nurses, psychologists, psychiatrists, pharmacists) to develop psychoeducational programs and materials to teach students and parents about common disorders and their treatment. Such education can have an empowering effect, strengthen coping skills, provide emotional support, increase clients' hope, and promote good communication, among other things (Bentley & Walsh, 2014). As discussed in more detail elsewhere in this volume, some common categories of disorders found in childhood include anxiety and mood disorders, attention deficit and disruptive disorders, autism and other pervasive developmental disorders, eating disorders, schizophrenia, and tic disorders (American Psychiatric Association, 2000). Table 5.1 provides a brief case vignette for each category of the major mental disorders. It is noted that the categorical approach to classifying mental illnesses and disorders of children and adolescents has been challenged, most recently by DeJong (2010), who calls for the greater use of a dimensional approach to description and classification. She also calls for doing better in taking into account the abuse and trauma histories of children as well as issues of attachment and comorbidity.

Understanding Medications and Their Specific Use in Children

The five classes of medication are antipsychotic medications, antidepressants, anti-anxiety medications, mood stabilizers, and stimulants. Medications from all five drug classes are used with children and adolescents experiencing mental, emotional, and behavioral disorders. An important trend is that a physician's choice of type of medication may be only in part related to a student's diagnosis. That is, it is overly simplistic to say that depression will be treated with an antidepressant, anxiety with an anti-anxiety (anxiolytic) medication, ADHD with a stimulant, and so on. Instead, the choice may relate to concern over a particularly prominent symptom or the interplay of symptoms, the explicit avoidance of a side effect (in youth, for example, weight gain, acne, tremors, confusion, effects on reproductive system or sexual functioning), and especially the past effectiveness of a specific drug in clinical trials or in real-world practice with adults. Thus, in practice, physicians, for example, might choose a selective serotonin reuptake inhibitor (SSRI) for a wide variety of concerns ranging from depression, obsessive-compulsive disorder, and conduct disorder to eating disorder, anxiety disorder, and ADHD (Magno-Zito et al., 2002). Another example is that while anticonvulsant medications have been used instead of, or in combination with, lithium for the treatment of bipolar disorder, some physicians are now prescribing small doses of an antipsychotic medication for bipolar disorder in youth, often in combination with more traditional mood stabilizers (Wilens & Wozniak, 2003). Lithium, a naturally occurring salt categorized as a mood stabilizer, also has been used to treat a range of disorders from the expected bipolar disorder to posttraumatic stress, aggression, and depression. One of the highest profile drugs currently is Strattera (atomoxetine), approved in November 2002 for the treatment of ADHD in both children and adults. Because it is a nonstimulant, it is thought be safer and have less abuse potential. However, it is known to have other serious side effects, such as hallucinations and liver damage. A summary of key medications currently used with children and adolescents is provided in the "Tools and Practice Examples" section of this chapter (see also National Institute of Mental Health, 2012; PDR Health, 2012).

Controversy About the Use of Psychopharmacological Treatment With Children

Much controversy surrounds the practice of child and adolescent psychopharmacology, and

Table 5.1 Case Vignettes of Common Mental Disorders

Category of Disorder	*Common Symptomatology*	*Vignette*
Anxiety	Excessive fear, worry, or uneasiness; social withdrawal, poor concentration, irritability; terror of certain objects or situations; anxiety and/or panic at being separated from parent or guardian; nightmares, continuous memories of traumatic events	Jana is 8 years old and has extreme separation anxiety. On the days her mother is able to get her to go to school, Jana has bouts of hyperventilating, crying spells, trembling hands, and wanting to sit by herself in the corner of the room. She states she is afraid that something bad will happen to her mother if she is not with her.
Depression	Feelings of sadness, hopelessness, worthlessness, and/or suicide; irritability, somatic complaints, poor concentration; loss of interest in friends and/or play; deterioration of school work; poor sleep and appetite, lack of motivation	Ten-year-old Colin's grades went from A's and B's to failing over the course of 6 weeks. He has lost interest in going to recess and spends most of his time alone. Colin told his school counselor that he was really sad and felt like he would never be good enough to pass fifth grade. His parents state that when he comes home from school, he is irritable and usually just wants to go to bed and doesn't even want to eat with the family.
Oppositional defiant/conduct	Violates rights of others by lying, theft, aggression, truancy, the setting of fires, and vandalism; low self-esteem, depression; running away from home	Sonya is in tenth grade. She had to go to juvenile court twice for truancy this school year. Sonya told the judge she would never amount to anything and didn't care that her parents had to pay fines for school truancy. Recently, Sonya also confided to her friend that she has been stealing her teachers' money over the past year so that she can buy a house for herself. Her friend said that Sonya stated that if she told anyone about what she was doing, she would hurt her friend's little brother.
ADD/ADHD	Inattentive, hyperactive, aggressive and/or defiant, impulsive, easily distracted; difficulty completing tasks, fidgets, cannot sit still; interrupts often, cannot wait turn	Jaime's teacher has noticed that she is constantly out of her chair and walking around the room, talking to the other children. Jaime's parents report that they have difficulty calming her down so that she can focus on her homework. They also say she has been teasing and hitting her younger sister.
Learning and communication	Problems with spoken and written language, coordination, attention, or self-control; struggles to explain feelings and thoughts; difficulty with math, technology, and scientific information; delayed in grade-level progress	Alex's counselor describes him as a bright and articulate 12-year-old. If he hears a story, he can tell it back to his teacher and parents verbatim. Yet, he has difficulty answering questions about the significance of characters or actions of characters in the stories. Alex's written work is poor. He cannot create simple sentences, and because he cannot comprehend short stories, he cannot complete his homework assignments without his parents reading to him. His teacher states that his written work is at a third-grade level instead of a sixth-grade level.

(continued)

Table 5.1 *(Continued)*

Category of Disorder	*Common Symptomatology*	*Vignette*
Autism spectrum (pervasive developmental)	Range of mild to severe problems with interpersonal interactions and communication; difficulty with cognition or thinking; struggles with understanding the feelings of others; becomes attached to one object or situation; poor eye contact, tunes people out, does not react to others (such as saying hello or waving goodbye); prefers to play alone and seems independent for stated age; general difficulty with interpreting the world	Tia just started kindergarten. She has very poor eye contact and does not smile when her teacher smiles at her or praises her. Tia's parents told her teacher that they often have to continuously repeat steps of tasks to her and that she seems "to be in her own world" and "does not hear them." During the first week of school, the teacher noticed that Tia constantly echoes what other children say in class and when she is asked to stop, she begins screaming and then has a tantrum.
Schizophrenia	Delusions, hallucinations; withdrawal from others; loss of contact with reality; catatonic or other bizarre motor behaviors, hyperactive without an apparent stimulus; flat affect, does not show emotion	Brian is 17 years old. He had a flat affect when he told the school social worker that sometimes he feels confused because he hears voices telling him to steal things and to hurt himself. He relayed that the only time he can concentrate is after praying late at night in front of the news correspondent on television. Brian believes that the correspondent is the only person who can hear him and understand what he is going through in his life. He asks the social worker if she believes him.
Tic	Involuntary twitches or movements of muscle groups, such as eye blinking, sneezing, shoulder shrugging; involuntary vocalizations, such as humming, grunting, or actual words that are expressed in a spastic or explosive manner; partial control can be obtained for short periods of time; tic behaviors fluctuate in intensity and frequency	Sam was sitting on his hands and holding his face very rigid when he visited his principal for disrupting the class. The principal told Sam that he could relax, that he just wanted to talk to him. Sam said, "I can't or I will be in trouble again." Promptly, Sam took a deep breath and started holding his breath. After a few moments, he let out his breath and his shoulders began jerking up and down a few times. The principal continued talking to Sam about his school behavior and noticed Sam's rapid eye blinking. Throughout their talk, Sam also grunted and then would hold his breath until the next grunt. The principal realized that Sam was trying to stop his motor and vocal tics due to embarrassment.

the school social worker and mental health counselor sit right in the middle of it, that is, "at the nexus of the systems of home, school and community," as one social worker eloquently noted (Allen-Meares, 1991, p. 5). In embracing expanded roles in medication management, school social workers uphold their professional tradition of striving to keep students safe from harm or distress, in its many forms, and help to keep their schools on the forefront of our changing society's thinking about psychotropic medications for children and adolescents. We argue that school social workers and other mental health consultants have a crucial role of not only providing comprehensive biopsycho-social assessment information to health and mental health care providers and parents so that good decisions can be made around the prescription of psychotropic medications but also in helping to monitor the positive and negative effects of medications on students in the school system. Thus the controversy and uncertainly that surrounds the use of psychiatric medication with children and adolescents sets up an "imperative" for shared decision making and models of informed choice (Hetrick, Simmons, & Merry, 2008), from the initial prescription through the initial phases of care to the maintenance use of medications.

As new psychotropic medicines are introduced, as new methods of administration develop, and even as new philosophies about dosing and polypharmacy emerge, it will be important for school social workers and mental health counselors to expand their knowledge and skill base about the medications so that they may promote the full quality of life and well-being of the students they serve, while helping to deter any negative outcomes. Toward this end, we start with the assumption that children and adolescents are both like adults and not like adults, and these different dimensions affect pharmacological treatment and medication management. For example, the rates of absorption, distribution, and metabolism are quite different in children. Importantly, children and adolescents have different cognitive schema that may effect their descriptions of physiologic or psychological changes (Brown & Sammons, 2002). Yet, as human beings, children and adolescents have the same basic anatomy, functional systems, and all of the same basic emotional needs and psychological dimensions as everyone else. With that principle in mind, this chapter will offer ideas on four basic "how do you help" questions faced by school social workers working with children, adolescents, and their families:

- How do you help students and parents make sense of the controversy and ambiguity in child and adolescent psychopharmacotherapy?
- How do you help students and parents understand common mental disorders and the medications used to treat them?
- How do you help students and parents negotiate the referral processes and pharmacological assessment?
- How do you help students and parents in managing and monitoring medications?

Making Sense of the Controversy and Ambiguity in Child and Adolescent Psychopharmacotherapy

Worries About Physical and Psychological Developmental Impact

Clearly one of the biggest concerns about the use of medication in children and adolescents relates to uncertainties about long-term effects, both physical and psychological. These are important considerations for which some assurances can be provided, but also a place where a healthy skepticism may be appropriate. It is true that most formal clinical drug research, both with children and adults, does not help us to understand the long-term effects of medications because studies tend to focus on initial effects over just a few weeks to a few months. The further bad news is that such a lack of research opens the door to speculation and myth. For example, the early concerns that stimulants were associated with significant levels of stunted growth have been largely abandoned by most reputable providers. However, some Internet sites continue to relay what appears to be misinformation about this and closely related issues.

Another specific concern about children and adolescents who take psychiatric medications relates to the fact that brain and neurotransmitter development is occurring at the same time these drugs are being used (Floersch, 2003; Greenhill & Setterberg, 1993). What are the long-term developmental effects? Another concern: Do we fully understand how medication use should be adjusted to account for the physical development of children's renal functioning, gastrointestinal system, or hepatic enzyme system in their early years?

Another compelling concern has been raised by Floersch (2003, p. 52) about the impact of taking psychiatric medication on the self-identity and psychological development of children and adolescents. Recent research on the meaning of medication in adults also affirmed the notion that medication "incites meaning, influences identity and impacts life" (Bentley, 2010, p. 488) in complex ways. It can be an avenue to feeling better even more fully human and yet also different and more resigned about life. These issues will be especially important as school social workers and mental health counselors listen to how students make sense of their medication experience. The RTI, with its more holistic approach to support and assessment, may allow for more school professionals to take greater opportunities to explore the lived experience of children and adolescents, including, for example, their experiences around stigma, sense of self, and morality (see Singh, 2007; Floersch, Longhofer, Kranke, & Townsend, 2010; Moses, 2010). So, as we have noted, while some argue that children are, after all, human beings and thus clinical research in humans is relevant and useful, others argue that children are still other than and different than little adults; thus, given the intrusiveness of the intervention, extreme caution is called for.

Worries About Pathologizing Human Experience

Of equal concern is that the use of psychiatric medications in children represents an inappropriate "blaming the victim." A number of vocal critics of medication use have noted that massive increases in the use of medication with kids, including children and adolescents in the child welfare and juvenile justice systems (Crisom & Argo, 2009; Moses, 2008) in recent years. This has led to an underemphasis on other potential culprits in the seeming rise of mental, emotional, and behavioral difficulties in children, that is, the larger social context and poor school and community supports. Admittedly, it could be said that dramatic prescription increases and expanded use of medications with children and adolescents are not necessarily problematic signs, but rather represent good news about the accessibility of treatment to those in need. However, there remains a pervasive feeling among many school social workers and others in the field that too many children are being medicated without sufficient cause (see below) and that we are neglecting other environmental influences on behavior, which might have even a more powerful impact. These things might include a lack of tolerance of difference among kids, poor parenting practices, misperceptions about what is develop-mentally "typical" in children and adolescents, the violent media and the tendency to rely on over-stimulation, the drug culture, the cultural value of immediate gratification, or more school system-focused influences like lack of school resources, high student-teacher ratios, lack of teacher training, and low teacher salaries, to name a few. The good news is that the RTI framework explicitly acknowledges environmental factors like these and how they may contribute to children's difficulties, thus rejecting a "within-child deficit" only model (McIntosh et al., 2011).

Backlash About Medication in Schools

Fears about the overmedication of children are reflected in the prohibition on mandatory medication in 20 U.S.C. 1412(a)(25), which was added to the IDEA by the Individuals with Disabilities Education Improvement Act Amendments of 2004 and became effective on July 1, 2005. This prohibition on mandatory medication, which is implemented by the U.S. Department of Education, is one of the conditions that a state must meet in order to be eligible for assistance under Part B of the IDEA. The broad application of this statutory provision ensures that states and their public agencies implement the statutory mandate to make a free, appropriate public education available to all eligible children with disabilities. Further, states that receive federal Department of Education funds for any program or activity to create and implement are governed by specific policies *prohibiting* school personnel from "coercing children to receive, or their parents to administer, a controlled substance in schedule II under the Controlled Substances Act, as a condition of attending school or receiving services." However, it does not prohibit classroom teachers or other school personnel from making *observations* about academic achievement and classroom behavior and relaying the information to parents or recommending evaluation regarding special education or related school and classroom services under the Individuals With Disabilities Education Act (IDEA). It should be noted that an amendment with softer wording prohibiting educational personnel from "requiring" medication for children as a condition for attending school or receiving services was attached to the reauthorization of IDEA (P.L. 108–446), which recently passed Congress. Further, the comptroller general of the Government Accounting Office (GAO) plans to research such issues as the variation of states' definitions of medication use and the extent to which school personnel actively influence parents to pursue medication, the prescription rates of psychotropic drugs used in public schools to treat children diagnosed with mental health disorders (with specific mention of ADD/ADHD), and the identification and prevalence of medications used both under the Controlled Substance Act and otherwise.

Many states are in various stages of enacting legislation specifically on this issue. Some states, such as Georgia, Washington, North Carolina, and Hawaii, have created legislation to investigate the prevalence and effects of psychotropic medications on children and develop recommendations on how to better monitor prescription rates. Other states, such as Alaska, Florida, Connecticut, Maryland, Illinois, Colorado, Minnesota, and Virginia, require school policies strictly prohibiting school personnel from recommending or requiring psychotropic drug use. Further, legislation urges school personnel to use nonmedication alternatives only with students who have difficulty learning and/or who display hyperactivity or other behavioral disruptions. New Hampshire, Connecticut, Minnesota, Utah, and Illinois have legislation prohibiting disciplinary actions, such as reports to child protection services or charges of neglect against parents who refuse to seek a prescription for or administer psychotropic medications. It is crucial for school social workers and other personnel to be aware of legislative activities in their respective states and school districts as well as the values (and fears and concerns) they represent.

Off-Label Use by Physicians

Another issue of some concern is the widespread "off-label" use of medications with children and adolescents. *Off-label use* refers to the use of a specific medication with children in spite of the fact that it has not yet been approved by the FDA for use with children in particular. Parents and teachers should know that this practice is not only very common but obviously also quite legal, as long as the drug has been studied and received approval for use in adults. Physicians know well that the FDA is after all about the development and marketing of drugs, not the regulation of the practice of medicine. While off-label use represents up to three quarters of medication use with children, drug companies are not allowed to target their marketing or advertising of a specific nonapproved drug for use in children until sufficient safety and effectiveness has been established and FDA approval obtained. The lack of FDA approval, then, does not mean a drug is *not* safe or effective.

The Media and Clinical Drug Research with Children

Scholars within and without social work have urged professionals to bring a critical perspective to clinical effectiveness trials, encouraging us to recognize potential bias and threats to research integrity that might seriously undermine positive publicized reports (e.g., Sparks & Duncan, 2008; Hughes & Cohen, 2010; Cohen, 2005). Newspapers and magazines have also been generously covering issues related to the testing and marketing of medications for children. Parents, social workers, and school-based mental health workers cannot help but be curious about them or, more likely, have serious questions and concerns. For example, in 2007, the issue of pediatric drug testing in general made it to the pages of *The Washington Post* (Stein, 2007). At issue was that even after the FDA enticed and at times "forced" pharmaceutical companies to test their adult products on children, two-thirds of the thousands of medications given to children remain untested on them. Many might suggest that pharmaceutical companies seem to have ignored the FDA, stating that requirements overstep the authority of the FDA and that there are no incentives to conduct the research when they already had generic competitors. The rule, instituted mainly due to concerns around psychiatric medication use among children, was thought by most lawmakers, health care providers, and advocates to be a step *forward* in ensuring the safety of children. However, the Competitive Enterprise Institute, a think tank concerned about advancing free markets on numerous fronts, brought a successful lawsuit, which has led to alterations and an emphasis on the voluntary testing of many drugs.

One of the most prominent recent topics has been the concern about suicidal ideation and self-harm among some young (and not so young) users of the most popular type of antidepressant, the selective serotonin reuptake inhibitors (SSRIs).

After a series of public hearings and in a surprise move in early 2004, the FDA asked the manufacturers of 10 different SSRI antidepressants to strengthen or add a suitable warning about the possible connection between drug use and suicide. The hope was that this would stimulate closer monitoring of the effects of these antidepressants. What made this a bold move at the time, and different from past actions, was that the FDA request was not preceded by very clear evidence from clinical research about the connection between the actual medications and harm. Reactions of providers and others to the FDA action (see, for example, Elias, 2004, 2005; "FDA Seeks Warning," 2004; Sood, 2004) ranged from relief (from those who have long thought the use of psychiatric medications among children had become too casual) to anger (from those who described it as an overreaction and completely unwarranted) to worry about the chilling effect it may have on getting treatment to children who may benefit. Gualtieri and Johnson (2006), for example, conducted a retrospective records review to support their argument that suicidality in the real world, while not uncommon, may not approximate levels of those involved in clinical trials. More recently, it should be noted that results of a meta-analysis of pediatric trials conducted between 1988 and 2006 suggested that the benefits of antidepressant medications likely outweigh their risks to children and adolescents with major depression and anxiety disorders (Bridge et al., 2007). However, the FDA still urges all manufacturers of all antidepressant medications to update the existing black box warning on their products' labeling to include warnings about increased risks of suicidal thinking and behavior, known as suicidality, in young adults ages 18 to 24 during initial treatment (generally the first one to two months).

Misuse by Consumers

First noticed in the mid-1990s, little is empirically known about the misuse, diversion, or illegal trading or selling of psychiatric medications among youth. Methylphenidate (Ritalin), known by such street names as "vitamin R" and "Skippy," is especially suspect. One study in the mid-90s examined 116 students in Wisconsin with ADHD and found that 16% reported having been approached at least once to sell, trade, or give away their stimulant medication in the past 5 years (Musser, Ahmann, Mundt, Broste, & Mueller-Rizner, 1998). More recently, the Annual Tracking Study for a Drug Free America (2005) indicated that 1 in 10 youth abuse prescription stimulants. (http://www.drugfree.org/portal/drugissue/features/prescription_medicine_misuse). Also recently, a study by Rabiner et al. (2009) found that 26% of college students had at some time diverted their ADHD medication to peers. They also reported commonly taking more medication than prescribed in order to enhance their academic performance. Setlick et al.'s (2009) study of calls to poison control centers affirms that the abuse of medication by youth is on the rise. Reports from those in the field, including social workers, school administrators, and law enforcement authorities, suggest the problem may be much broader and more widespread. Middle school, high school, and college students, who may be trying to balance employment and academics, use medications to become hyperalert or to give them an extra energy boost to stay up all night studying or even partying. Finally, there are reports that some youth use their medications in combination with other medications or alcohol to make "cocktails" so that they can get better effects from getting stoned or high. This abuse has led to students with ADHD selling or trading their much-needed medications to other students.

In a review, Klein-Schwartz (2002) noted disagreement about the extent of abuse and diversion. While pharmacologically similar to cocaine, some experts note lower than expected misuse of Ritalin in comparison with other drugs. However, Kollins, MacDonald, and Rush (2001) concluded that it is "not benign with respect to abuse potential" (p. 624) and called on school administrators and parents to be aware of the potential for its diversion and misuse. Importantly, they added: "This caution should, of course, be weighed against the well-documented clinical benefits of the drug for many children, adolescents, and adults" (p. 624). Likewise, Musser and colleagues (1998) sensibly called for "monitoring prescription usage, periodic reassessment of efficacy, and continuing education of family and teaching staff."

What We Can Do

Typical Rationales for Physician Referral

School social workers and other school counselors will be in the position to suggest that parents seek a psychopharmacological assessment for their child, as well as to explain to students or parents why others may have suggested following through with such a referral. In either case, there seem to be two overarching reasons for referral: first, that teachers or others are seeing the kind of difficulties in a student's behavior or mood that is thought to respond to medications, or second, that the problematic issues or symptoms in the student that have been of concern have not changed with some sort of intervention by teachers or school care providers (psychologists, social workers). Whether or not medication is conceptualized as a last resort, if a referral is being considered, there is an implication that the problems are of such severity that outside medical/psychiatric attention is warranted and likely to be helpful to all of the stakeholders in the situation. While noting that there has been little empirical attention to referral making in the literature, social workers and others can embrace "best practices" with respect to referrals (Bentley, Walsh, & Farmer, 2005b), which include, among other things, sharing up-to-date information on medications with children and adolescents, helping them and their families manage meaning around the referral itself as well as the implications of treatment, and preparing both kids and parents for seeing prescribers, whether psychiatrists, family physicians, nurse practitioners, physicians assistants, or psychologists.

What to Expect From a Pharmacological Evaluation (Processes and Outcomes)

A solid, comprehensive psychopharmacological assessment in children and adolescents is thought to be a bit more complicated than for adults because of the need for family input, the wide developmental differences in the age group, diagnostic ambiguities, and ethical issues around decision making and the rights of minors. While great variability exists in the processes and procedures used, certain common elements can be expected. The goal is to obtain the most complete, accurate, and rich information possible so that decisions about diagnosis and, if relevant, specific medication type and dosage can be made with appropriate confidence. However, it is likely that conclusions by the physician will be presented as tentative, with disclaimers about how adjustments in diagnosis and treatment may be made in the future.

It may go without saying that the process done right will involve one or more face-to-face interviews with the student and parents. A "quick and dirty" 10- or 15-minute evaluation by a single provider should be considered inadequate. The interviewer(s) may be a stranger to the student and her family, or a family may choose to use its primary care physician. Interviews should consist of one or more long sessions where a series of related questions is asked, often seeking quite detailed information on developmental history (parents) or past and current patterns of behavior, thinking, and feeling (student). Interviewers may also seek information/documentation related to the student's situation from a referral source in the school system. For example, the interviewer may want medical records from the primary care physician. Sessions where psychological tests or checklists are administered may be anticipated. Importantly, anticipating a range of emotional responses to the interview by both parents and student will be helpful. Certainly, a comprehensive psychopharmacological assessment, consistent with the RTI framework, is likely to be anxiety producing for the student and his family, even if it is associated with great hope for positive change in the future. Disclosures by students or parents, if they become known, may shock each other. Students may welcome the opportunity for help with their difficulties, or they may respond by denying problems, attempting to diminish their severity, blaming others, or expressing fears of being different or not good enough. Questions may abound, or silence may rule the day.

Helping Students and Parents to Manage and Monitor Medications

Assessing and Maximizing Therapeutic Effects and Side Effects

School social workers and other school-based professionals are not called on to medically evaluate the impact of medications, as might be the case for physicians or nurses. We do not make final decisions about medication adjustments. Instead, our concern is to collaborate with others to help keep track of the whole picture in terms of effects and side effects, both positive and negative.

Therapeutic effects are those that are desired and represent the positive effects of medications. This could certainly mean a reduction of behavioral problems or psychiatric symptoms or an increase in normal activity, enhanced mood, or a sense of being "more like me," with greater investment in personal interests. Negative or adverse effects, referred to as *side effects* because they are, by definition, unwanted, can be physical (such as drowsiness, weight gain, tremors), psychological (such as feeling controlled or "sick"), or social (such as being rejected by a friend). Some specific challenges in monitoring medications with children and adolescents, summarized in Bentley and Walsh (2014), include the fact that they may experience more marked side effects, like sedation or extrapyramidal symptoms (e.g., neuromuscular slowness, rigidity) with antipsychotics, but talk about them less. Hormonal changes may make measuring the effectiveness of antidepressants more problematic, as is the fact that the placebo effect is so prominent in children. Indeed, causal attributions for clinical improvement should be made with care. While children seem to tolerate long-term treatment with lithium well, there are concerns about the long-term build-up of lithium in the body. More concern is expressed over the possible precipitation of agitation or mania with Tegretol (carbamazepine) or the less common but still serious lowered seizure threshold with antihistamine use in the treatment of anxiety.

A number of authors have summarized lists of existing measurement devices that social workers and school-based mental health counselors could use to help track, for example, the positive and negative symptoms of schizophrenia, dyskinesia, or akathesia; the extent of Parkinsonism symptoms; or the levels of anxiety or depression, mania or impulsivity (e.g., Bentley & Walsh, 2014; Bond & Lader, 1996). It is, however, unclear if social workers in the field regularly use this type of assessment tool. Instead, social workers and school counselors may rely on simple graphs or checklists generated from their idiosyncratic knowledge of clients' responses or rely on charting simple, brief, descriptive statements, like a mini-mental status exam, and comparing them over time.

Direct observation and candid, open dialog are the methods for assessing effects and side effects. Helping students to manage both kinds of effects calls for a range of techniques, including simple exercises (stretching), more education (around time lags, need for patience), concrete changes in behavior (using sunscreen, dieting), problem-solving or skills training (around what to tell people at school, how to talk to the school psychologist), or reflective discussion on meaning or stigma. Obviously, tracking the effectiveness, or lack thereof, of psychiatric medications may also call for additional consultation with the physician for possible reevaluation of dosing or medication type.

Addressing Adherence Issues

Certainly we know that for children and adolescents, poor adherence and early termination of medication undermines treatment efficacy. We also know that parents may in fact overestimate the adherence levels of their children (Pappadopulos et al., 2009). Bentley and Walsh (2014) argue, however, that we need to protect against inappropriately simplistic or unidimensional explanations of medication nonadherence, social workers should be equipped with a comprehensive explanatory model of adherence. They argue that *adherence* is best understood as a complex interplay of factors that relate to the *characteristics of clients* (such as health beliefs, the desire to self-regulate, the meaning of medication, and locus of control), *aspects of treatment* (such as regimen complexity, cost, timing of effects, negative side effects, and friendliness of the aftercare environment), *aspects of the social environment* (such as family beliefs and support, and messages from the media and popular culture), and *aspects of the illness or symptoms* (denial, paranoia, depression, hostility, cognitive impairment). A good grasp of the risk and protective factors associated with nonadherence is helpful. For example, we know that bothersome side effects, a history of substance abuse, ambivalence, anger, therapeutic delays, and a poor relationship with helpers all put people at higher risk for nonadherence. Accepting or believing that one has a mental illness, having adequate preparation for and education about medication, and feeling empathy from others are, on the other hand, protective factors. Although the research that undergirds this admittedly partial list is drawn from adult samples, applying developmental theories of adolescence might help us to hypothesize that students are going to be less concerned, for example, with the impact of medication on later life than they are on the current larger meaning and symbolism (to themselves or others) of having to take a psychiatric medication for personal difficulties. It might tell us that issues of authority and trust may have a powerful impact on nonadherence, as will the parental attitudes and beliefs (Brown & Sammons, 2002).

Categories of interventions to directly affect adherence would seem to be the same for adults as for children and adolescents, in that they are likely to rely on education, cognitive and behavioral strategies, and the assessment and management of meaning. However, opportunities to creatively tailor interventions to students can and should be exploited. For example, in getting children and adolescents to express meaning, that is, the perceived impact of taking medication on their sense of self and identity, school social workers and mental health counselors could encourage storytelling, puppet play, drawing and painting and, with older students, using existing or original contemporary music and poetry. An overarching consideration is that issues of adherence are more complicated with children and adolescents in light of their limited decision-making powers. This issue may be likely to regularly rear its head in work with students.

Maximizing the Power of Collaboration

If school social workers and other school counselors are going to fully embrace their role of being a meaningful resource to students, their families, and others in the school community, close and mutually satisfying relationships with physicians, teachers, and other school-related providers is, obviously, crucial. Some philosophical foundations that may be key include:

- Embrace a client-centered "partnership" perspective around the range of medication-related dilemmas and issues that emerge in real-world practice. This suggests working toward a nonthreatening alliance, a demystification of the helping process, and a mutual sharing of respective expertise.
- Maintain a balanced perspective about psychiatric medication in the face of admittedly complex issues related to human rights and professional roles and the very real costs and benefits of psychiatric medication use.
- Work toward the successful integration of psychosocial interventions, therapeutic services, and psychopharmacology, and recognize the intrinsic power of combined treatments.
- Work toward interdisciplinary relationships characterized by equality, flexibility, decreased professional control, mutual understanding, and shared goals, but also appreciate the ideological and practical challenges that emerge, especially in managing parallel treatments.
- Genuinely appreciate both the strengths and the limits of students and their families. Work should center on students' and families' unique strengths and aspirations and away from pathology, symptoms, or weaknesses. Yet real limits (barriers to progress), such as a lack of skills or inadequate resources, have to be appreciated. (list adapted from Bentley & Walsh, 2002)

A balanced perspective acknowledges the positive impact that medications have on the lives of many, yet is not blind to the sociopolitical dimensions of prescribing, the very real dangers involved, or the negative experiences of some. It also seems to call for a rejection of any professional arrogance that would suggest that we are the only ones who embrace a "holistic perspective," are the only ones to have the "best interest" of the client at heart, or that we alone "get it."

Instead, while social workers should recognize the potential for ideological conflict, rivalry, or awkwardness when working with those who were trained and socialized very differently, we should still strive for greater understanding of the legitimate roles and expertise of others. Indeed, a recent survey of practicing social workers concluded that most social workers get their knowledge about psychiatric medications not from books or school, but from everyday interactions with physicians and clients (Bentley, Walsh, & Farmer, 2005a). Thus, school social workers and other school-based professionals working with physicians and others around medication issues should reject building a professional life around keeping insulated or second-guessing the decisions of others, and instead build one around inquiring exchanges and reciprocity of respect. This is so important because we know that off-label practices, the greater acceptability of poly-pharmacy (the use of multiple medications at one time), and even the use of dosages beyond what the desk references allow for are not uncommon. To automatically conclude malpractice would represent naiveté. That is not to say that seeking greater understanding of others, whether clients or other providers, means being passive or not asking the tough questions when needed: *Tell me more about how you came to choose that one first? Why are you prescribing that medication in addition? What is the purpose of different doses for different times? What are you hoping for with that unusual schedule? What would the signs of overmedication look like? Isn't that drug usually used with someone with different symptoms or diagnoses? Is that more than is typically prescribed? What is your thinking on this?* These questions are consistent with the professional mandate, not only to understand the entire service plan of any case, but to be advocates for clients and be an approachable, consumer-friendly translator of information for students and their families. Thus, social workers' efforts to maximize collaboration and increase our confidence in carrying out these roles may center on maximizing our learning about what others do as well as increasing time spent in interaction (Bentley, Walsh, & Farmer, 2005a). Further suggestions for discussing medications are provided in the next section.

Applying Interventions within a Response to Intervention Framework

The RTI model, which originally emerged to help identify and intervene in learning difficulties in reading and math, has been applied to an expanded list of student problems and challenges, as seen throughout this book. The emphasis on "not waiting"—that is, early identification of difficulties—and a collaborative multi-tiered hierarchy of interventions may be applicable to children and adolescents experiencing mental, emotional, and behavioral issues, including the increasing numbers of those receiving psychiatric medications. Since this chapter relates to how school professionals can be more responsive to the medication-related issues that parents and children bring, we offer potential "tiers of intervention" with respect to those specific concerns. Because mental health problems carry more and different kinds of stigma than reading or math difficulties, admittedly, intervention designers have to be sensitive to issues of disclosure. A Tier 1 intervention, potentially controversial and admittedly bold, might be a school-wide educational assembly for all students on understanding common lived experiences of students around anxiety, depression, and hyperactivity, for example, including open discussion on the range of positive and negative experiences that children and adolescents have with medication. Such a program should attempt to both normalize and de-stigmatize the use of medication without glamorizing it or endorsing its use, as well as intentionally expose myths about medication and present potential consequences of misuse. A Tier 2 intervention, aimed at a smaller subset of students and parents in need, might be to offer individual parent consultation or perhaps an evening Q&A session for families who are considering taking their child to a prescriber for an evaluation. Individualized intervention, or Tier 3 intervention with children and adolescents experiencing difficulty with psychiatric medication, might include counseling around the management of meaning and identity, as well as the expansion of academic and social supports.

Tools and Practice Examples

Table 5.1 provides a summary of common mental disorders that are frequently treated with medication and some case examples. Table 5.2 provides a summary of medications that are frequently provided to children.

How to Talk to Students, Parents, and Teachers about Medication

Talking with students, parents, and teachers about medication can be challenging. Following are some guidelines on how to talk to students, parents, and teachers about medication:

1. Healthy skepticism about the use of psychiatric medication is appropriate.
2. Offer chances for folks to talk about their doubts, fears, hopes, and dreams with respect to psychiatric medication.
3. Acknowledge the multiple forces influencing the use of medication with children and adolescents today.
4. Explain off-label use as both common and legal.
5. Welcome conversation on the public controversies around kids and psychiatric medication.
6. Encourage the reporting of trading or selling of medication.

Table 5.2 Common Psychiatric Medications for Children and Adolescents

Trade Name of Drug (generic name)	*Type/Class of Medication*	*Common Psychiatric Uses*	*Common Side Effects*	*Approved for Children?*
Abilify (aripiprazole)	Antipsychotic (atypical)	Schizophrenia, bipolar, aggression	Dry mouth, weight gain, drowsiness	Age 10 and older for bipolar disorder, manic or mixed episodes; 13 to 17 for schizophrenia and bipolar
Adderall (amphetamine mixed salts)	Stimulant	ADHD	High blood pressure, rapid heart rate, gastrointestinal complaints, somnolence, weight gain, middle-ear infection	Age 3 and older
Anafranil (clomipramine)	Antidepressant	OCD		Age 10 and older for OCD
BuSpar (buspirone)	Anti-anxiety	Anxiety, phobias	Drowsiness or fatigue, dry mouth, increase in nightmares or dreams	No
Catapres (clonidine)	Alpha-adrenergic	Impulsivity, hyperactivity	Dry mouth, sedation, hypotension	Age 12 and older
Cibalith-S (lithium citrate)	Mood stabilizer	Mania, bipolar	Diarrhea, drowsiness, lack of coordination, loss of appetite, muscle weakness, nausea or vomiting, slurred speech, trembling	Age 12 and older
Clozaril (clozapine)	Antipsychotic (atypical)	Schizophrenia	Fast or irregular heart beat, dizziness, constipation	No
Concerta (methylphenidate)	Stimulant	ADHD	Headache, stomach pain, insomnia	Age 6 and older

(continued)

Table 5.2 *(Continued)*

Trade Name of Drug (generic name)	*Type/Class of Medication*	*Common Psychiatric Uses*	*Common Side Effects*	*Approved for Children?*
Cylert (pemoline)	Stimulant	ADHD	Potential for serious side effects affecting the liver	Age 6 and older
Depakote (sodium valproate)	Antiseizure, mood stablizer	Bipolar, mania	Headache, nausea, drowsiness, liver and white cell abnormalities	Not for this use Age 12 and older for seizures
Dexedrine (dextroamphetamine sulfate)	Stimulant	ADHD	Headache, restlessness, diarrhea, drowsiness, weight loss	Age 3 and older
Dextrostat (dextroamphetamine)	Stimulant	ADHD	Headache, restlessness, diarrhea, drowsiness, weight loss	Age 3 and older
Effexor (venlafaxine)	Antidepressant (SSRI)	Depression	Reduced appetite, nausea, constipation	No
Eskalith (lithium)	Mood stabilizer	Bipolar, mania, bulimia	Nausea, frequent urination, hand tremor, mild thirst	Age 12 and older
Haldol (haloperidol)	Antipsychotic	Schizophrenia, Tourette's syndrome, aggression, hyperactivity	Dry mouth, drowsiness, dizziness, confusion, tardive dyskinesia	Age 3 and older
Klonopin (clonazepam)	Anti-anxiety (benzodiazepine)	Anxiety, eating disorders, Tourette's	Drowsiness	No
Lexapro (escitalopram)	Antidepressant (SSRI)	Depression, anxiety	Nausea	Age 12–17 for major depressive disorder
Lithobid (lithium carbonate)	Mood stabilizer	Bipolar, mania	Reduced appetite, hand tremors, blurred vision, constipation, decreased appetite, gastrointestinal problems, nausea	Age 12 and older

(continued)

Table 5.2 *(Continued)*

Trade Name of Drug (generic name)	*Type/Class of Medication*	*Common Psychiatric Uses*	*Common Side Effects*	*Approved for Children?*
Luvox (fluvoxamine)	Antidepressant (SSRI)	OCD		Age 8 and older for OCD
Mellaril (thioridazine)	Antipsychotic	Schizophrenia	Nausea, gastrointestinal problems, drowsiness, tardive dyskinesia	Age 2 and older
Orap (pimozide)	Antipsychotic	Tourette's syndrome	Dizziness, drowsiness, insomnia, nausea, diarrhea or constipation, blurred vision or sensitivity to light	Age 12 and older for Tourette's syndrome
Paxil (paroxetine)	Antidepressant (SSRI)	Depression	Drowsiness, nausea, insomnia	No
Prozac (fluoxetine)	Antidepressant (SSRI)	Depression	Anxiety, weight loss, insomnia, nervousness	Age 8 and older
Risperdal (risperidone)	Antipsychotic (atypical)	Schizophrenia	Nausea, gastrointestinal problems, drowsiness, tardive dyskinesia	Age 13 and older for schizophrenia; 10 and older for bipolar mania and mixed episodes; 5 to 16 for irritability associated with autism
Ritalin (methylphenidate)	Stimulant	ADHD	Headache, stomach pain, insomnia	Age 6 and older
Seroquel (quetiapine)	Antipsychotic (atypical)	Schizophrenia	Nausea, gastrointestinal problems, drowsiness, tardive dyskinesia	Age 13 and older for schizophrenia; Age 10–17 for treatment of manic and mixed episodes of bipolar disorder

(continued)

Table 5.2 *(Continued)*

Trade Name of Drug (generic name)	*Type/Class of Medication*	*Common Psychiatric Uses*	*Common Side Effects*	*Approved for Children?*
Serzone (nefazodone)	Antidepressant (SSRI)	Depression	Blurred or abnormal vision, confusion, constipation, dizziness, dry mouth, light headedness, nausea, sleepiness, weakness	No
Sinequan (doxepin)	Tricyclic antidepressant	Depression, anxiety	Drowsiness, weight gain, dry mouth	Age 12 and older
Strattera (atomoxetine)	Nonstimulant (NRI)	ADHD	Headache, dizziness, abdominal pain, insomnia	Age 6 and older
Tegretol (carbamazepine)	Anticonvulsant, mood stabilizer	Seizure disorders, alcohol withdrawal, cocaine addiction, depression, abnormally aggressive behavior	Dizziness, drowsiness, nausea, unsteadiness, vomiting	Not for this use; any age for seizures
Tofranil (imipramine)	Tricyclic antidepressant	Depression, bed wetting, eating disorders, ADD, OCD, panic disorder	Nervousness, sleep disorders, stomach and intestinal problems, tiredness, convulsions, emotional instability, fainting	Age 6 and older for bed wetting
Wellbutrin (bupropion)	Antidepressant	Major depression	Weight loss, constipation, dizziness, dry mouth, excessive sweating, headache, loss of appetite, sleep disturbance	No
Zoloft (sertraline)	Antidepressant (SSRI)	Depression, OCD, anxiety	Dry mouth, reduced appetite, agitation, stomach distress	Age 6 and older (for OCD only)
Zyprexa (olanzapine)	Antipsychotic (atypical)	Schizophrenia, bipolar, mania, Tourette's	Dry mouth, weight gain, drowsiness, seizures	No

7. Provide examples of the typical rationale underlying referrals to a prescriber for medication assessment.
8. Explain the usual relationship among diagnoses, symptoms, and prescriber choices of drug type and dosage.
9. Anticipate a range of emotional reactions to a referral to a prescriber and the medication assessment process itself.
10. Ask about both the positive and negative effects of medication.
11. Explain the complexity of adherence.
12. Develop easy-to-understand (noncommercial) written psychoeducational materials.
13. Offer to be a resource for information, support, and problem solving around medication-related dilemmas.
14. Give folks a chance to talk about the impact of taking medication in general but especially on their sense of self and personal identity.

Key Points to Remember

Sood (2004) noted that, after looking at all of the scientific data, a case could be made for either the overprescribing or the underprescribing of medications to children and adolescents. Certainly data show staggering increases in the number of prescriptions written and the number of children taking medications. Other data show that many children who suffer are not getting the pharmacological and other treatments that may be helpful. Sood urges us to consider the implications of our own beliefs about mental illness in children (does it exist? where does it come from?) on our attitudes toward medication and strive to deliver evidence-based practices to those in need. For school social workers and others, our goals are to help facilitate access to care, participate in multimodal approaches to service delivery, and provide much-needed supports to students, parents, teachers, and health care providers. Summarized above are the "how to's" of reaching these goals, that is, how to help students, parents, and teachers make sense of the controversy and ambiguity in child and adolescent psychopharmacotherapy, understand mental disorders and the medications used to treat them, negotiate referral processes and pharmacological assessment, and manage and monitor medication in the short and long term.

Further Learning

The following list offers cutting edge Internet resources:

1. **DSM-V issues and disorders related to children:**
   - American Psychiatric Association: DSM-V Development: Disorders Usually First Diagnosed in Infancy, Childhood or Adolescence: http://www.dsm5.org/PROPOSEDREVISIONS/Pages/InfancyChildhoodAdolescence.aspx

2. **Children and psychotropic medication controversies:**
   - University of Medicine and Dentistry of New Jersey: HealthState: Children and Psychotropic Drugs: http://www.umdnj.edu/umcweb/marketing_and_communications/publications/umdnj_magazine/hstate/winter_spring01/features/feature03_psychotropic.htm
   - American Academy of Child and Adolescent Psychiatry: Facts for Families: Psychiatric Medication for Children and Adolescents (Part I): http://aacap.org/page.ww?name=Psychiatric+Medication+For+Children+And+Adolescents+Part+I-How+Medications+Are+Used§ion=Facts+for+Families
   - Center for Health Care Strategies: The Use of Psychotropic Medications for Children Involved in Child Welfare (Webinar): http://www.chcs.org/publications3960/publications_show.htm?doc_id=669183
   - St. Luke's Health Initiatives: Arizona Health Futures: Children, Adolescents and Psychotropic Medications: http://www.slhi.org/pdfs/issue_briefs/ib-2006-August.pdf
   - The Hastings Center: Children and Psychiatric Medications: http://www.thehastingscenter.org/Issues/Default.aspx?v=238

3. **Managing and monitoring medication use in children and adolescents/risk for nonadherence:**
   - American Academy of Child and Adolescent Psychiatry: Facts for Families: Psychiatric Medication for Children and Adolescents

(Part III): http://www.aacap.org/cs/root/facts_for_families/psychiatric_medication_for_children_and_adolescents_part_iiI_questions_to_ask
- National Resource Center on AD/HD: Managing Medication for Children and Adolescents with AD/HD (factsheet): http://www.help4adhd.org/documents/WWK3.pdf
- Children's Mental Health Matters: Facts for Families: Medication Management in Children andAdolescents:http://www.childrensmentalhealthmatters.org/Family%20Resource%20Kits/Medication%20Management%20Families.pdf

4. **State and school policies/legislation on recommending or requiring psychotropic drug use:**
   - George Washington University:The Center for Health and Health Care in Schools: Psychotropic Drugs and Children: http://www.healthinschools.org/~/media/Files/psychotropic07.ashx
   - Fight for Kids: Bills and Resolutions: http://www.fightforkids.org/bills_and_resolutions.php AND Able Child: State Legislation: http://www.ablechild.org/slegislation.htm

5. **Clinical drug research/trials with children:**
   - Oregon State University College of Pharmacy: Psychotropic Medication Management in Children and Adolescents: http://pharmacy.oregonstate.edu/drug_policy/pages/ur_board/reviews/articles/PedPsychReview.pdf

6. **Suicide ideation and self-harm among children on SSRIs:**
   - National Institute for Mental Health: Antidepressant Medications for Children and Adolescents: Information for Parents and Caregivers: http://www.nimh.nih.gov/health/topics/child-and-adolescent-mental-health/antidepressant-medications-for-children-and-adolescents-information-for-parents-and-caregivers.shtml
   - Mayo Clinic: Antidepressants for children: Explore the pros and cons: http://www.mayoclinic.com/health/antidepressants/MH00059
   - AACAP: Report 10 of the Council on Scientific Affairs: Safety and Efficacy of Selective Serotonin Reuptake Inhibitors (SSRIs) in Children and Adolescents: http://www.aacap.org/galleries/PsychiatricMedication/CSA_Report_10_final.pdf
   - AACAP: Children and SSRI Antidepressants: Information for Parents by David Fassler, M.D.: http://www.aacap.org/cs/root/resources_for_families/psychiatric_medication/children_and_ssrI_antidepressants_information_for_parents_by_david_fassler_md

7. **Abuse and sale of psychotropic medications (stimulants):**
   - Office of National Drug Control Policy, 2008: Prescription for danger: A report on prescription and over-the-counter drug abuse among the nation's teens: http://theantidrug.com/pdfs/prescription_report.pdf
   - SAMHSA: National Survey on Drug Use and Health: Nonmedical Use of Adderall among Full-Time College Students: http://oas.samhsa.gov/2k9/adderall/adderall.pdf
   - UCLA School Mental Health Project: Hot Topics: Prescription Drug Abuse Among Youth: http://smhp.psych.ucla.edu/hottopic/hottopic%28drugabuse%29.htm
   - NIDA for Teens: Prescription Drug Abuse: http://teens.drugabuse.gov/facts/facts_rx1.php

References

Allen-Meares, P. (1991). The contribution of social workers to schooling. In R. Constable, J. P. Flynn, & S. McDonald (Eds.), *School social work*. Chicago: Lyceum.

American Psychiatric Association. (2000). *Diagnostic and statistical manual of mental disorders* (4th ed., text revision). Washington, DC: Author.

Bell, A. S. (2010). A critical review of ADHD diagnostic criteria: What to address in the DSM-V. *Journal of Attention Disorders*, *15*(1), 3–10.

Bentley, K. J., & Walsh, J. (2002). Social workers' roles in psychopharmacotherapy. In A. R. Roberts and G. J. Greene (Eds.), *Social workers' desk reference* (pp. 643–645). New York: Oxford University Press.

Bentley, K. J., Walsh, J., & Farmer, R. (2005a). Roles and activities of clinical social workers in psychopharmacotherapy: Results of a national survey. *Social Work, 50*(2), 295–303.

Bentley, K. J., Walsh, J., & Farmer, R. (2005b). Referring clients for psychiatric medication: Best practices for social workers. *Best Practices in Mental Health, 1*(1), 59–71.

Bentley, K.J., & Walsh, J. (2014). *The social worker & psychotropic medication: Toward effective collaboration with clients, families and providers* (4th ed.). Pacific Grove, CA: Cengage.

Bentley, K. J. (2010). The meaning of psychiatric medication in a residential program for adults with serious mental illness. *Qualitative Social Work, 9*(4), 479–499.

Bond, A. L., & Lader, M. H. (1996). *Understanding drug treatment in mental health care.* West Sussex, England: John Wiley.

Bridge, J. A., Iyengar, S., Salary, C. B., Barbe, R. P., Birmaher, B., Pincus, H. A., Ren, L., & Brent, D. A. (2007). Clinical response and risk for reported suicidal ideation and suicide attempts in pediatric antidepressant treatment: A meta-analysis of randomized controlled trials. *Journal of the American Medical Association, 297*(15), 1683–1696.

Brown, R., & Sammons, M. (2002). Pediatric psychopharmacology: A review of recent developments and recent research. *Professional Psychology, 33*(2), 135–147.

Center for Mental Health in Schools at UCLA. (2008). *A resource aid packet on students and psychotropic medication: The school's role.* Los Angeles: Author.

Cohen, D. (2005). Clinical psychopharmacology trials: "Gold standard" or "fool's gold"? In S. Kirk (Ed.), *Mental disorders in the social environment: Perspectives from social work* (pp. 247–267). New York, NY: Columbia University.

Crisom, M. L., & Argo, T. (2009). The use of psychotropic medication for children in foster care. *Child Welfare, 88*(1), 71–100.

DeJong, M. (2010). Some reflections on the use of psychiatric diagnosis in the looked after or "in care" population. *Clinical Child Psychology and Psychiatry, 15*(4), 589–599.

Elias, M. (January 22, 2004). Antidepressants and suicide. *USA Today*, p. 7D.

Elias, M. (February 5, 2005). Suicide alert has parents rethinking antidepressants. *USA Today*, p. 1A.

Farmer, E. M. Z., Mustillo, S., Burns, B. J., & Costello, E. J. (2005). The epidemiology of mental health programs and service use in youth: Results from the Great Smoky Mountains Study. In M. H. Epstein, K. Kutash, & A. Duchnowski, (Eds.), *Outcomes for children and youth with behavioral and emotional disorders and their families: Programs and evaluation best practices* (2nd ed., pp. 23–44). Austin, TX: Pro-Ed.

FDA seeks warning for depression drugs. (March 22, 2004). *Richmond Times Dispatch,* p. A1.

Floersch, J. (2003). The subjective experience of youth psychotropic treatment. *Social Work in Mental Health, 1*(4), 51–69.

Floersch, J., Longhofer, J., Kranke, D., & Townsend, L. (2010). Integrating thematic grounded theory and narrative analysis: A case study of adolescent psychotropic treatment. *Qualitative Social Work, 9*(3), 407–435.

Greenhill, L. L., & Setterberg, S. (1993). Pharmacotherapy of disorders of adolescents. *Psychiatric Clinics of North America, 16*(4), 793–814.

Gualtieri, C. G., & Johnson, L. G. (2006). Antidepressant side effects in children and adolescents. *Journal of Child and Adolescent Psychopharmacology, 16*(1–2), 147–157.

Hetrick, S., Simmons, M., and Merry, S. (2008). SSRIs and depression in children and adolescents: The imperative for shared decision-making. *Australasian Psychiatry, 16*(5), 354–358.

Hughes, S., & Cohen, D. (2010). Understanding the assessment of psychotropic drug harms in clinical trials to improve social workers' role in medication monitoring. *Social Work, 55*(2), 105–115.

Klein-Schwartz, W. (2002). Abuse and toxicity of methylphenidate. *Current Opinions in Pediatrics, 14*(2), 219–223.

Kollins, S. H., MacDonald, E. K., & Rush, C. R. (2001). Assessing abuse potential of methylphenidate in human and non-human subjects. *Pharmacology, Biochemistry and Behavior, 68*(3), 611–627.

McIntosh, K., MacKay, L. D., Andreou, T., Brown, J. A., Mathews, S., Gietz, C., & Bennett, J. (2011). Response to Intervention in Canada: Definitions, the evidence base and future directions. *Canadian Journal of School Psychology, 26*(1), 18–43.

Moses, T. (2008). Psychotropic medication practices for youth in systems of care. *Journal of Child and Family Studies, 17*, 567–581.

Moses, T. (2010). Being treated differently: Stigma experiences with family, peers, and school staff among adolescents with mental health disorders. *Social Science & Medicine, 70*, 985–993.

Magno-Zito, J., Safer, D. J., DosReis, S., Gardner, J. F., Soeken, K., Boles, M., & Lynch, F. (2002). Rising prevalence of antidepressants among US youth. *Pediatrics, 108(5),* 721–727.

Musser, C. J., Ahmann, F. W., Mundt, P., Broste, S. K., & Mueller-Rizner, N. (1998). Stimulant use and the potential for abuse in Wisconsin. *Journal of Developmental and Behavioral Pediatrics, 19*(3), 187–192.

National Institute of Mental Health. (September 4, 2012). *Treatment of children with mental disorders.* (NIH Publication No. NIH-04–4702). Retrived from http://www.nimh.nih.gov/health/publications/treatment-of-children-with-mental-illness-fact-sheet/index.shtml.

Olfson, M., Marcus, S. C., Weissman, M. M., & Jensen, J. S. (2002). National trends in the use of psychotropic medications by children. *Journal of the American Academy of Child & Adolescent Psychiatry, 41*(5), 514–521.

Pappadopulos, E., Jensen, P. S., Chait, A. R., Arnold, E., Swanson, J., Greenhill, L. L., Hechtman, L., Chuang, S., Wells, K. C., Pelham, W., Cooper, T., Elliot, G., & Newcorn, J. H. (2009). Medication adherence in the MTA: Saliva methylphenidate samples versus parent report and mediating effect of concomitant behavioral treatment. *Journal of the American Academy of Child and Adolescent Psychiatry, 48*(5), 501–510.

PDR Network. (2012). *PDR health*. Retrieved from http://www.pdrhealth.com/.

Popper, C. W. (2002). Child and adolescent psychopharmacology at the turn of the millennium In S. Kutcher (Ed.), *Practical child and child psychopharmacology* (p. 137). Cambridge: Cambridge University Press.

Rutter, M. (2000). Psychosocial influences: critiques, findings, and research needs. *Developmental Psychopathology, 12*(3), 375–405.

Rutter, M. (2002). The interplay of nature, nurture, and developmental influences. *Archives of General Psychiatry, 59*(11), 996–1000.

Setlick, J., Bond, G. R., & Ho, M. (2009). Adolescent prescription ADHD medication abuse is rising along with prescriptions for these medications. *Pediatrics, 124*(3), 875–880.

Singh, I. (2007). Clinical implications of ethical concepts: Moral self-understandings in children taking methylphenidate for ADHD. *Clinical Child Psychology and Psychiatry, 12*(2), 167–182.

Sood, A. B. (May 14, 2004). *Controversy of the millennium: Drugging of America's children or catalysts for healthy minds*. Keynote address, 42nd Annual Child Psychiatry Spring Forum, Virginia Commonwealth University, Richmond, VA.

Sparks, J. A., & Duncan, B. L. (2008). Do no harm: A critical risk/benefit analysis of child psychotropic medication. *Journal of Family Psychotherapy, 19*(1).

Stein, R. (2007, November 23). A gap in knowledge about kids, medication. *The Washington Post*, p. A1.

Why give kids drugs without pediatric testing? (April 8, 2002). *USA Today*, p. 12A.

Wilens, T. E., & Wozniak, J. (2003). Bipolar disorder in children and adolescents: Diagnostic and therapeutic issues, *Psychiatric Times, 20*(8). Retrieved from http://www.psychiatrictimes.com/p030855.html

CHAPTER 6

Effective Interventions for Students with Conduct Disorder

David W. Springer Courtney J. Lynch Katherine L. Montgomery

Getting Started

School-aged children and adolescents with externalizing disorders are a challenging, yet rewarding, population to help. Many school-based practitioners, teachers, and administrators may be all too familiar with the behaviors associated with a diagnosis of conduct disorder (CD), such as aggressive behavior toward others, using a weapon, fire setting, cruelty to animals or persons, vandalism, lying, truancy, running away, and theft (American Psychiatric Association, 2000). The *DSM-IV-TR* allows for coding a client with one of two subtypes of CD: childhood-onset type (at least one criterion characteristic occurs prior to age 10) and adolescent-onset type (absence of any criteria prior to age 10). A youth must be engaged in a pattern of behavior over an extended period of time (at least 6 months) that consistently violates the rights of others and societal norms.

The prevalence of conduct disorder is found to be higher among male youth with estimates of approximately 12.0% in males and 7.1% in females (Nock, Kazdin, & Kessler, 2006). While the focus of this chapter is on students with a diagnosis of conduct disorder, there is some indication that disruptive behavior disorders in general are on the rise (Loeber, Farrington, & Waschbusch, 1998) and that the prevalence of school-based conduct disturbance, such as bullying or fighting, is also high.

Part of what makes helping school-aged youth with conduct disorder so challenging is the multifaceted nature of their problems. Indeed, students with conduct disorder are often viewed by their teachers as experiencing a wide range of additional types of school adjustment difficulties (comorbidity) (Pullis, 1991). Fortunately, in recent years, significant advances in psychosocial treatments have been made to treat children and adolescents with disruptive behavior disorders. Unfortunately, some states operate with policies that exclude conduct-disordered students from eligibility for services in schools. Nevertheless, in keeping with a recent U.S. surgeon general's report (U.S. Department of Health and Human Services, 2001), this chapter is grounded in the assumption that conduct-disordered youth can be helped using innovative and research-based interventions. Some of these evidence-based practices are applied to the case example of Alex below. For purposes here, Rosen and Proctor's (2002) definition of evidence-based practice (EBP) has been adopted, whereby "practitioners will select interventions on the basis of their empirically demonstrated links to the desired outcomes" (p. 743).

What We Know

The development of conduct disorder is usually preceded by a number of accumulating risk factors over the course of a child's life (Holmes, Slaughter, & Kashani, 2001). Prevention researchers assert that by early identification and treatment of specific risk factors, an at-risk youth has a decreased likelihood of encountering problematic trajectories associated with conduct disorder, such as delinquency, substance use, and school dropout (Catalano & Hawkins, 1996). Research on risk factors is typically categorized by the following domains: individual, family, peer, school, and community (Hawkins, Catalano, & Miller, 1992). Some of the most common risk factors for conduct disorder are the presence of another mental illness (such as attention deficit hyperactivity disorder, depression, anxiety, and/or oppositional defiant disorder), impulsivity, aggression, academic underachievement, substance use, association with deviant peers, peer rejection, inconsistent or overly harsh parenting, large family size, parental rejection, parental substance use, parental conflict, physical abuse, neglect, and fetal exposure to alcohol and/or drugs (Holmes, Slaughter, & Kashani, 2001).

The most efficacious interventions for youth with conduct disorder are primarily delivered as community- or family-based interventions. To date, there are no identified rigorously evaluated evidence-based practices (EBP) for intervening with students with conduct disorder in the classroom. However, prevention interventions designed to prevent delinquency, substance use, and school dropout are primarily delivered in the school setting and address the same risk factors that place a youth at risk of developing conduct disorder. These interventions have been labeled as EBPs and are shown to be effective under the strongest research design rigor. Some of these school-based interventions will be highlighted below.

There are also some general factors that are associated with lower levels of problem behaviors in schools, including strong positive leadership; high pupil expectations; close monitoring of pupils; good opportunities to engage in school life and take on responsibility; well-functioning incentive, reward, and punishment systems; high levels of parental involvement; an academic emphasis; and a focus on learning (Mortimore, 1995; Reynolds, Sammons, Stoll, Barber, & Hillman, 1996; cited in Fonagy & Kurtz, 2002). All of these factors have an overall positive influence on youth development, learning, and behavior management and are explored in more detail in subsequent chapters of this book.

What We Can Do

Conduct Disorder Prevention

In preventing problematic life trajectories for at-risk youth, such as conduct disorder, delinquency, substance use, or school dropout, researchers turn primarily to school-based prevention interventions that target the previously mentioned risk factors. Several school-based programs have been identified as effective in impacting risk factors at the individual, peer, family, and school level. In this chapter, we are going to highlight a few of these interventions that have shown efficacy under the most rigorous types of research designs, randomized controlled trials (RCT). These programs have been given some of the highest ratings from the Office of Juvenile Justice and Delinquency Prevention (OJJDP) and/or the Substance Abuse and Mental Health Services Administration's (SAMHSA) national evidence-based registry.

Coping Power Program

Given an "exemplary" rating by OJJDP, the Coping Power Program (Lochman et al., 2009) was designed to prevent aggression, violence, and delinquency among late elementary- and early middle school-aged male youth. The program is approximately 15 months in duration and has both child and parent intervention components. Thirty-three 40- to 60-minute group sessions addressing several socio-cognitive components are delivered to the students by a school counselor, psychologist, or social worker. The 16-group-session parent component is delivered to groups of approximately four to six couples and addresses effective parenting training techniques with at-risk children. Over time, two RCTs have been conducted on the Coping Power Program and have revealed significantly fewer school problem behaviors, delinquent acts (Lochman & Wells, 2002; Peterson, Hamilton, & Russell, 2009), learning problems, and improvement in social and adaptive skills (Peterson et al., 2009). Although originally designed for intervention with males, the Peterson and colleagues (2009) study included females, suggesting this program is effective for both males and females at risk of conduct disorder. For more information on the Coping Power Program, see http://www.copingpower.com/.

Fast Track

Fast Track is a comprehensive partially school-based prevention program with several components designed to develop social skills and regulate behavior. The Fast Track intervention consists of five approaches to intervention: (1) parent training groups, (2) home visits, (3) social skills training groups, (4) reading tutoring, and (5) classroom-based friendship enhancement. This is one of the only school-based programs that has been shown to effectively prevent conduct disorder (as opposed to being linked to risk factors associated with conduct disorder; Conduct Problems Prevention Research Group, 2010).

LifeSkills Training

Next to the Good Behavior Game (see chapter 27 on juvenile justice prevention), LifeSkills Training (LST; Botvin, Mahalic, & Grotpeter, 1998) is a school-based program with the largest amount of rigorous research support. While most RCTs have been conducted with middle school-aged youth, LST has been manualized for school-aged youth ranging from third through tenth grade. Classroom teachers deliver anywhere from 10 to 24 sessions, delivering one 45-minute session per week. Driven by a risk and protective factor model, LST sessions promote an acquisition of skills through discussion, group activities, and role-play (SAMHSA, 2008). Recent RCTs have found that students receiving LST have had significantly lower levels of delinquency, fighting, physical and verbal aggression, and violence (Botvin, Griffin, & Nichols, 2006); had a decreased risk for HIV (Griffin, Botvin, & Nichols, 2006); and were significantly less likely to use substances (Spoth, Clair, Shin, & Redmond, 2006), particularly among high-risk youth (Spoth, Randall, Trudeau, Shin, & Redmond, 2008). For more information on LST, see http://www.lifeskillstraining.com/.

Promoting Alternative THinking Strategies

Promoting Alternative THinking Strategies (PATHS; Kusche, 2002) is a school-based prevention program designed for elementary- and preschool-aged youth. The elementary-aged intervention is delivered over the course of one academic school year and totals approximately 121 20-minutes sessions. PATHS is delivered three times a week by the teacher in a classroom setting with lessons that include a combination of instruction, modeling, storytelling, role-play, discussion, and videos (SAMHSA, 2007). Recent RCTs have revealed that students receiving this intervention have significantly reduced levels of aggression (Bierman et al., 2010) and internalizing and externalizing behaviors (Riggs, Greenberg, Kusché, & Pentz, 2006). Studies have also found a significant level of improvement in prosocial behavior, academic engagement (Beirman et al., 2010), emotional knowledge, self-regulation, social interaction, and social skills (Domitrovich, Cortes, & Greenberg, 2007). For more information on PATHS, see http://www.pathstraining.com/.

Positive Action

Positive Action (PA) is a school-based prevention program with grade-specific intervention manuals available for kindergarten through 12th-grade intervention. Classroom teachers deliver the main intervention component, which targets improving school achievement and attendance, as well as addressing problem behaviors such as substance use, poor classroom behavior, and sexually risky behavior. PA is also designed to impact relationships between the parent(s) and student, family conflict, and family cohesion (SAMHSA, 2006a). PA is a multiyear program where approximately 140 lessons are delivered over the course of one academic year. Recent research reporting on the efficacy of PA has shown that elementary students who received the intervention were less likely to engage in substance use, violent behavior (Beets et al., 2009; Li et al., 2011), sexually risky activity (Beets et al., 2009), and bullying behavior (Li et al., 2011); were less likely to be suspended; and had significantly higher school attendance and reading and math scores (Snyder et al., 2010). For more information on PA, see http://www.positiveaction.net/research/.

Second Step

Second Step is a school-based violence prevention program. Although this program is relatively newer and has a smaller body of empirical support (Alvarez & Anderson-Ketchmark, 2009), both OJJDP and SAMHSA have highlighted Second Step as efficacious with at-risk youth (OJJDP, n.d.; SAMHSA, 2006c). Similar to previously described programs, Second Step is delivered by teachers in the classroom. This intervention has been manualized to intervene with students 4 to 14 years of age, and two age-specific curriculums have been developed (preschool through fifth grade and sixth through ninth grade). Heavily influenced by theory, this two-year program targets change by teaching socioemotional skills aimed at increasing social competence and reducing impulsive and aggressive behavior through 8 to 25 lessons (dependent upon the grade and year in the program) offered in an academic school year. Specific lessons include developmentally appropriate topics such as anger management, empathy training, and impulse control (SAMHSA, 2006c). To date, only one RCT has been conducted that implemented Second Step with at-risk students (Frey, Nolen, Edstrom, & Hirschstein, 2005). This study included 1253 primarily white second-grade students who remained in the study for approximately two years. Moderate levels of attrition and no follow-up data warrant cautious interpretation of the results. That noted, students receiving the Second Step intervention displayed significantly lower levels of aggression, had less need for adult conflict intervention, and were more likely to choose positive social goals than those in the control group (Frey et al., 2005). For more information on Second Step, see http://www.secondstep.org/.

Project Towards No Drug Abuse

Project Towards No Drug Abuse (TND) is a school-based drug use prevention program designed for high school students. The curriculum was specifically designed for high-risk students enrolled in an alternative education program and targets change by improving self-control, communication skills, drug use resistance, and decision-making strategies (SAMHSA, 2006b). Taught by teachers or health educators, TND contains 12 40-minutes lessons. Recent RCTs conducted on TND found that the intervention significantly reduced the use of hard drugs; however, there was no statistical difference in alcohol, marijuana, or cigarette use (Sun, Sussman, Dent, & Rohrbach, 2008; Sun, Skara, Sun, Dent, & Sussman, 2006). Although this intervention does not have strong research support for impacting some types of substance use, impacting hard drug use among high-risk high school youth is difficult to do, and this specific school-based intervention should be considered when wanting to impact this specific population at risk of developing conduct disorder. For more information on TND, see http://tnd.usc.edu/.

Conduct Disorder Treatment

Among the effective interventions for children with conduct problems, two were found to be well-established, according to the Division 12 (Clinical Psychology) Task Force on Promotion and Dissemination of Psychological Procedures (Brestan & Eyberg, 1998). One of these is the Incredible Years Parents, Teachers and Children's Training series developed by Webster-Stratton and based on a trained leader using videotape modeling to trigger group discussion. Supporting randomized control group studies using the program as a treatment program for parents of children ages 3 to 8 years with conduct problems and as a prevention program for high-risk families include those by Reid, Webster-Stratton, and Baydar (2004); Reid, Webster-Stratton, and Hammond (2003); Spaccarelli, Cotler, and Penman (1992); Webster-Stratton (1984, 1990, 1994, 1998); Webster-Stratton, Kolpacoff, and Hollinsworth (1988); and Webster-Stratton, Reid, and Hammond (2001a). The second well-established approach is parent-training programs based on Patterson and Gullion's (1968) manual *Living With Children* (Alexander & Parsons, 1973; Bernal, Klinnert, & Schultz, 1980; Wiltz & Patterson, 1974). See Table 6.1 for supporting studies. In short, parent management training (PMT) is the only intervention that is considered well established for the treatment of conduct disorder.

Table 6.1 Well-Established Treatments and Supporting Studies

Best-Supported (Well-Established) Treatments	*Supporting Studies*
Videotape Modeling Parent Training	Reid, Webster-Stratton, & Hammond (2003); Spaccarelli, Cotler, & Penman (1992); Webster-Stratton (1984, 1990, 1994, 1998); Webster-Stratton, Kolpacoff, & Hollinsworth (1988); Webster-Stratton, Reid, & Hammond (2001b)
Parent Training Based on Living With Children	Alexander & Parsons (1973); Bernal, Klinnert, & Schultz (1980); Wiltz & Patterson (1974)

Several treatments for children with conduct problems were found to be probably efficacious, according to the same criteria (Brestan & Eyberg, 1998). Probably efficacious treatments for preschool-age children include parent—child interaction therapy, time out plus signal seat treatment, delinquency prevention program, and parent training program. Two treatments meeting the probably efficacious criteria designed for use with school-age children are problem-solving skills training and anger coping therapy. Finally, four treatments for adolescents with conduct problems were found to be probably efficacious: multisystemic therapy, assertiveness training, rational-emotive therapy, and anger control training with stress inoculation. See Table 6.2 for supporting studies.

Parent Management Training

Parent management training (PMT) is a summary term that describes a therapeutic strategy in which parents are trained to use skills for managing their child's problem behavior (Kazdin, 2004), such as effective command giving, setting up reinforcement systems, and using punishment, including taking away privileges and assigning extra chores. While PMT programs may differ in focus and therapeutic strategies used, they all share the common goal of enhancing parental control over children's behavior (Barkley, 1987; Cavell, 2000; Eyberg, 1988; Forehand & McMahon, 1981; Patterson, Reid, Jones, & Conger, 1975; Webster-Stratton, 1998).

Table 6.2 Probably Efficacious Treatments and Supporting Studies

Promising (Probably Efficacious) Treatments for Preschool-Aged Children	*Supporting Studies*
Parent-Child Interaction Therapy	Eyberg, Boggs, & Algina (1995); McNeil, Eyberg, Eisenstadt, Newcomb, & Funderburk (1991);Zangwill (1983)
Time-Out Plus Signal Seat Treatment	Hamilton & MacQuiddy (1984)
Delinquency Prevention Program	Tremblay, Pagani-Kurtz, Masse, Vitaro, & Phil (1995); Vitaro & Tremblay (1994)
Parent Training Program for School-Aged Children	Peed, Roberts, & Forehand (1977); Wells & Egan (1988)
For School-Aged Children	
Problem-Solving Skills Training	Kazdin, Esveldt-Dawson, French, & Unis (1987a, 1987b); Kazdin, Siegel, & Bass (1992)
Anger Coping Therapy	Lochman, Burch, Curry, & Lampron (1984); Lochman, Lampron, Gemmer, & Harris (1989)
For Adolescents	
Multisystemic Therapy	Borduin, Mann, Cone, Henggeler, Fucci, Blaske, & Williams (1995); Henggeler, Melton, & Smith (1992); Henggeler, Rodick, Bourdin, Hanson, Watson, & Urey (1986)
Assertiveness Training	Huey & Rank (1984)
Rational-Emotive Therapy	Block (1978)
Anger Control Training With Stress Inoculation	Feindler, Marriott, & Iwata (1984); Schlichter & Horan (1981)

Source: This table was compiled by synthesizing information from the following: Brestan, E.V., & Eyberg, S. M. (1998). Effective psychosocial treatments of conduct-disordered children and adolescents: 29 years, 82 studies, and 5, 272 kids. *Journal of Clinical Child Psychology, 27*(2), 180–189; www.effectivechildtherapy.com.

While PMT approaches are typically used for parents with younger children (Serketich & Dumas, 1996), they have been successfully adapted for parents with adolescents (cf. Bank, Marlowe, Reid, Patterson, & Weinrott, 1991; Barkley, Edwards, Laneri, Fletcher, & Metevia, 2001;Barkley, Guevremont, Anastopoulos, & Fletcher, 1992). The effectiveness of parent training is well documented and, in many respects, impressive. Still, school practitioners should be aware that studies examining the effectiveness of PMT with adolescents are equivocal, with some studies suggesting that adolescents respond less well to PMT than do their younger counterparts (Dishion & Patterson, 1992; Kazdin, 2002). In much of the outcome research, PMT has been administered to individual families in clinic settings, while group administration has been facilitated primarily through videotaped materials. PMT has been effective in reducing conduct problems and increasing positive parenting behaviors when implemented on a large scale as part of early school intervention (Head Start) programs (Webster-Stratton, 1998; cited in Kazdin, 2004).

Problem-Solving Skills Training

Problem-solving skills training (PSST) is a cognitively based intervention that has been used to treat aggressive and antisocial youth (Kazdin, 1994). The problem-solving process involves helping clients learn how to produce a variety of potentially effective responses when faced with problem situations (D'Zurilla & Nezu, 2001). Regardless of the specific problem-solving model used, the primary focus is on addressing the thought process to help adolescents address deficiencies and distortions in their approach to interpersonal situations (Kazdin, 1994). A variety of techniques are used, including didactic teaching, practice, modeling, role playing, feedback, social reinforcement, and therapeutic games (Kronenberger & Meyer, 2001).

The problem-solving approach includes five steps for the practitioner and client to address: (1) defining the problem; (2) brainstorming; (3) evaluating the alternatives; (4) choosing and implementing an alternative; and (5) evaluating the implemented option. Several randomized clinical trials (Type 1 and 2 studies) have demonstrated the effectiveness of PSST with impulsive, aggressive, and conduct-disordered children and adolescents (cf. Baer & Nietzel, 1991; Durlak, Fuhrman, & Lampman, 1991; Kazdin, 2000; cited in Kazdin, 2002). Webster-Stratton and colleagues have developed a small-group treatment program that teaches problem solving, anger management, and social skills for children ages 4 to 8 years, and two randomized control group studies demonstrate the efficacy of this treatment program (Webster-Stratton & Hammond, 1997; Webster-Stratton & Reid, 2003a; Webster-Stratton, Reid, & Hammond, 2001b; Webster-Stratton, Reid, & Hammond, 2004). Problem-solving training produces significant reductions in conduct symptoms and improvements in prosocial behavior among antisocial youth.

Videotape Modeling Parent Program

Webster-Stratton's Videotape Modeling Parent Program, part of the Incredible Years training series, was developed to address parent, family, child, and school risk factors related to childhood conduct disorders. The series is a result of Webster-Stratton's own research, which suggested that comprehensive videotape training methods are effective treatments for early-onset ODD/CD. The training series includes the Incredible Years Parent Interventions, the Incredible Years Teacher Training Intervention, and the Incredible Years Child Training Intervention, each of which relies on performance training methods, including videotape modeling, role play, practice activities, and live therapist feedback (Webster-Stratton & Reid, 2003b).

The parent component aims to promote competencies and strengthen families by increasing positive parenting skills, teaching positive discipline strategies, improving problem solving, and increasing family supports and collaboration, to name a few. The teacher component of the training series aims to promote teacher competencies and strengthen home-school relationships by increasing effective classroom management skills, increasing teachers' use of effective discipline and collaboration with parents, and increasing teachers' abilities in the areas of social skills, anger management, and problem solving. The child component aims to strengthen children's social and play skills, increase effective problem-solving strategies and emotional awareness, boost academic success, reduce defiance and aggression, and increase self-esteem.

Webster-Stratton and Reid (2003b) assert that the most proactive and powerful approach to the problem of escalating aggression in young children is to offer their programs using a school-based prevention/early intervention model designed to strengthen *all* children's social and emotional competence. Their reasons are threefold: (1) Offering interventions in schools makes programs more accessible to families and eliminates some of the barriers (i.e., transportation) typically encountered with services offered in traditional mental health settings; (2) offering interventions in schools integrates programs before children's common behavior problems escalate to the point of needing intense clinical intervention; and (3) offering a social and emotional curriculum such as the Dinosaur School program to an entire class is less stigmatizing than a "pullout" group and is more likely to produce sustained effects across settings and time.

For more information about the Incredible Years Parent, Teacher, and Child Programs, the reader is encouraged to visit the Web site http://www.incredibleyears.com.

Applying Interventions within a Response to Intervention Framework

If you are currently working in American public schools, there is a good chance that you have heard of Response to Intervention (RTI). As many others did, you also probably have seen how the well-intentioned individualized education plans (IEPs) have fallen short of providing the services to some students who need it most. Out of this necessity to most adequately serve students in the school system, RTI was created (Brown-Chidsey & Steege, 2005). If you are unfamiliar with RTI, there are two good resources available:

1. Visit the National Center on Response to Intervention at the following link: http://www.rti4success.org/.
2. Purchase the book *Response to Intervention: Principles and Strategies for Effective Practice (2nd Edition)* by Rachel Brown-Chidsey and Mark W. Steege.

Conduct disorder prevention interventions described in this chapter may prove helpful resources for the school practitioner working within an RTI framework. For example, programs like the Good Behavior Game, LifeSkills Training, Promoting Alternative THinking Strategies, Positive Action, and Second Step are universal programs that can be delivered as a Tier 1 intervention to aid the school in preventing conduct disorder, among other problems. More intense programs, like Coping Cat Power Program and Project Towards No Drug Abuse, might be relevant evidence-based alternatives for the student in need of Tier 2 or Tier 3 services.

Tools and Practice Example

Practice Example

Alex is a 12-year-old White male who was recently arrested at school for stealing several items from his teacher, including a cell phone, $200, a watch, a lighter, and some pocket-sized school supplies. At the time of the arrest, Alex was found to be in possession of marijuana. For these offenses, Alex was placed on probation and ordered to receive mental health counseling for the length of his probation. Alex has always had minor behavior problems, but over the last year his behavior problems have escalated considerably. He lives with his parents and three siblings in a rural farming community. Though it was never confirmed, Alex's parents suspect that he was responsible for setting a small grass fire in a field behind their home last month. Alex frequently returns home from school with items that do not belong to him, and he engages in physical fights on the school bus at least once a week. Witnesses to these altercations report that Alex instigates fights with no apparent provocation. Although he tests above grade level in most subjects and his IQ falls within the normal range, Alex's teachers report that he is in danger of failing the sixth grade because he does not complete class or homework assignments. When his parents gave a blank check to his sibling for a school project, Alex stole the check, forged his parent's signature, and attempted to cash the check for $50. At home, his siblings complain that Alex steals things from them, bullies them into doing things his way, and breaks their belongings. Last month, he denied carving his initials into the bathroom wall and breaking his bedroom window with a baseball.

Among the various interventions available for use with Alex and his family, his school social worker chose to use interventions that had a solid evidence base in an effort to maximize the possibility for a successful outcome. As the first active phase of treatment, a thorough assessment is the cornerstone of a solid treatment plan (Springer, 2002). During their initial session together, the school social worker conducted a complete biopsychosocial assessment with Alex and his parents, which resulted in the following diagnoses:

- Axis I 312.81: Conduct disorder, childhood onset type, moderate
- Axis II V71.09: No diagnosis
- Axis III: None
- Axis IV V61.8: Sibling relational problem
- V62.3: Academic problem
- V61.20: Parent—child relational problem/ Involvement with juvenile justice system
- Axis V GAF = 45

In light of Alex's diagnosis, his age (12 years), the evidence supporting the use of PMT and PSST as probably efficacious approaches, and the availability of Alex's parents to participate in his treatment, the school social worker chose to utilize parent management training (PMT) and problem-solving skills training (PSST) with Alex and his parents. Using a combination of PMT and PSST together tends to be more effective than using either treatment alone (Kazdin, 2003). Both treatments are manualized and have core sets of themes and skills domains for treatment sessions.

PMT With Alex

One core session of PMT teaches parents to use positive reinforcement to change behavior (see step 3 in Table 6.3). Alex's social worker first spent some time training his parents to pinpoint, define, and observe problematic behavior in new ways, focusing on careful inspection of the problems. She then worked with the family to develop a token system to be implemented in their home, which would provide them a structured, consistent way to reinforce Alex's behavior. Rather than creating an exhaustive list of behaviors that would likely be difficult to track, Alex's parents began with three target behaviors/goals that they believed would be easier to manage and accomplish: respecting others' property and belongings, completing and turning in homework, and riding the school bus without fighting. In reviewing Alex's behavior, his father realized that Alex experienced very few behavior problems when he worked on outdoor projects with him. Spending time outdoors with his father, extra recreation/video game time, and an extra trip to the corner store to spend his money were the main incentives integrated into the token system. The tokens, paired with praise, were contingent on Alex's behavior specific to the targeted behaviors/goals. The social worker spent the bulk of this treatment session modeling and role playing the implementation of this token system, developing the parents' proficiency in prompting, praising behavior, and delivering consequences. The social worker reviewed the previous week's events in each subsequent session, reenacting and rehearsing problems or difficulties as needed.

The following exchange among Alex, his family, and his social worker illustrates positive reinforcement and developing effective discipline strategies:

Social worker [to parents]: You've stated that Alex's fighting is a big problem that seems to remain no matter what you do. You said that you tried time out, but that did not work. What reward do you give Alex when he does not get into fights?

Mother: I don't want to give him toys or money because it's too expensive and usually just starts more fights with his brother and sisters.

Social worker: Your husband said that Alex behaves well when he works outside with him. Is that something you would consider giving him for a reward?

Alex: I'd rather be with Dad than at home with people who pick on me and accuse me of stealing their stuff anyway!

Mother [following social worker's earlier suggestion to avoid "proving" Alex's misbehavior]: Absolutely, and if he can make it through one dinner without a fight, he can go with his father to do the evening chores outside.

The dialog continued in this vein until the family agreed on two more problems, rewards, and consequences. The social worker met with Alex's parents to review the purpose and effective use of time out as an intervention. The last time he was in time out, Alex threw a baseball through his bedroom window. They discussed finding a safer timeout area in the house where Alex could be directly monitored and removing possibly dangerous items from his bedroom. The social worker cautioned Alex's parents that his behaviors might escalate as they begin to implement

Table 6.3 Parent Management Training Sessions: Overview of the Core Sessions

1.	*Introduction and overview.* This session provides the parents with an overview of the program and outlines the demands placed on them and the focus of the intervention.
2.	*Defining and observing.* This session trains parents to pinpoint, define, and observe behavior. The parents and trainer define specific problems that can be observed and develop a specific plan to begin observations.
3.	*Positive reinforcement (point chart and praise).* This session focuses on learning the concept of positive reinforcement, factors that contribute to the effective application, and rehearsal of applications in relation to the target child. Specific programs are outlined where praise and points are to be provided for the behaviors observed during the week. An incentive (token/point) chart is devised, and the delivery praise of the parent is developed through modeling, prompting, feedback, and praise by the therapist.
4.	*Time-out form reinforcement.* Parents learn about time out and the factors related to its effective application. Delivery of time out is extensively role played and practiced. The use of time out is planned for the next week for specific behaviors.
5.	*Attending and ignoring.* In this session, parents learn about attending and ignoring and choose an undesirable behavior that they will ignore and a positive behavior to which they will attend. These procedures are practiced within the session. Attention and praise for positive behaviors are key components of this session and are practiced.
6.	*Shaping and school intervention.* Parents are trained to develop behaviors by reinforcement of successive approximations and to use prompts and fading of prompts to develop terminal behaviors. Also, in this session, plans are made to implement a home-based reinforcement program to develop school-related behaviors. These behaviors include individually targeted academic domains, classroom deportment, and other tasks (e.g., homework completion). Prior to the session, the therapist identifies domains of functioning, specific goals, and concrete opportunities to implement procedures at school. The specific behaviors are incorporated into the home-based reinforcement program. After this session, the school-based program continues to be developed and monitored over the course of treatment, with changes in foci as needed in discussion with the teachers and parents.
7.	*Review of the program.* Observations of the previous week as well as application of the reinforcement program are reviewed. Details about the administration of praise, points, and back-up reinforcers are discussed and enacted so the therapist can identify how to improve parent performance. Changes are made in the program as needed. The parent practices designing programs for a set of hypothetical problems. The purpose is to develop skills that extend beyond implementing programs devised with the therapist.
8.	*Family meeting.* At this meeting, the child and parent(s) are bought into the session. The programs are discussed along with any problems. Revisions are made as needed to correct misunderstandings or to alter facets that may not be implemented in a way that is likely to be effective. The programs are practiced (role played) to see how they are implemented and to make refinements.
9–10.	*Negotiating, contracting, and compromising.* The child and parent meet together to negotiate new behavioral programs and to place these in contractual form. In the first of these sessions, negotiating and contracting are introduced, and the parent and child practice with each other on a problem/issue in the home and develop a contract that will be used as part of the program. Over the course of the sessions, the therapist shapes negotiating skills in the parent and child, reinforces compromise, and provides less and less guidance (e.g., prompts) as more difficult situations are presented.

(continued)

Table 6.3 *(continued)*

11.	*Reprimands and consequences for low-rate behaviors.* Parents are trained in effective use of reprimands and how to deal with low-rate behaviors, such as setting fires, stealing, or truancy. Specific punishment programs (usually chores) are planned and presented to the child, as needed, for low-rate behaviors.
12–13.	*Review, problem solving, and practice.* Material from other sessions is reviewed in theory and practice. Special emphasis is given to role playing the application of individual principles as they are enacted with the trainer. Parents practice designing new programs, revising ailing programs, and responding to a complex array of situations in which principles and practices discussed in prior sessions are reviewed.

Source: From Kazdin, A. E. (2003). Problem-solving skills training and parent management training for conduct disorder. In A. E. Kazdin & J. R. Weisz (Eds.), *Evidence-based psychotherapies for children and adolescents* (pp. 241–262). New York: Guilford. Copyright 2003 by Guilford Press. Reprinted with permission.

these new interventions. She encouraged them to have back-up plans in the event that their first attempt to intervene did not work. Together, they role played some possible scenarios and practiced back-up plans, alternating roles to develop proficiency. See Sells (1998) for step-by-step and detailed descriptions on developing creative and proactive interventions with parents who have challenging adolescents.

PSST With Alex

Since Alex's parents were actively participating in his treatment, the first few sessions with Alex were spent not only introducing steps in problem solving, but discussing the token system and how consequences (positive or negative) were contingent on his behavior (see steps 1–4 in Table 6.4). Alex was initially very confident in his ability but anticipated that his siblings would sabotage his efforts with their constant provocations and false accusations of stealing. Hearing this, the social worker introduced the following self-statements in problem solving in order to guide Alex's behavior and lead to developing effective solutions (Kazdin, 2003):

1. What am I supposed to do?
2. I have to look at all my possibilities.
3. I'd better concentrate and focus in.
4. I need to make a choice.
5. I did a good job (or) Oh, I made a mistake.

Alex reported that he often fought with his siblings because they provoked him, so the social worker engaged Alex in multiple role plays, repeatedly practicing how he might respond to perceived provocation. The social worker effusively praised Alex's quick recall of the self-statements and his efforts to use a "stop and think" technique that she modeled and prompted. Additionally, they practiced how to respond to mistakes and failures without exploding at others or destroying property. Alex's parents were instructed to praise and reward his efforts to avoid conflicts and employ the problem-solving steps in everyday situations at home. Subsequent treatment sessions would require Alex to use the steps in increasingly more difficult and clinically relevant, real-life situations (Kazdin, 2003).

It is important to note that medication management was not part of Alex's treatment plan. While there is survey evidence for the significant use of polypharmacy in the treatment of children with CD in the United States, "medication cannot be justified as the first line of treatment for conduct problems. A diagnosis-based approach, which defines primary or comorbid psychiatric disorders associated with aggression, should guide the pharmacological treatment of CD" (Fonagy & Kurtz, 2002, p. 192).

Had Alex been younger (ages 4 to 8 years), the social worker could have selected from the range of interventions available under the Incredible Years Training Series developed by Webster-Stratton and colleagues at the University of Washington's Parenting Clinic. One of the appealing qualities of this approach is that it has been tailored for work with youth in school settings.

Key Points to Remember

Some of the key points from this chapter are as follows:

- Conduct disorder among youth in schools can be effectively prevented through interventions designed around risk factors.

Table 6.4 Problem-Solving Skills Training: Overview of the Core Sessions

1.	*Introduction and learning the steps.* The purpose of this initial session is to establish rapport with the child, to teach the problem-solving steps, and to explain the procedures of the cognitively based treatment program. The child is acquainted with the use of tokens (chips), reward menus for exchange of the chips, and response-cost contingencies. The child is trained to use the problem-solving steps in a game-like fashion in which the therapist and child take turns learning the individual steps and placing them together in a sequence.
2–3.	*Applying the steps.* The second session reviews and continues to teach the steps as needed. The child is taught to employ the problem-solving steps to complete a relatively simple game. The child applies the steps to simple problem situations presented in a board-game fashion in which the therapist and child alternate turns. During the session, the therapist demonstrates how to use the problem-solving steps in decision making, how to provide self-reinforcement for successful performance, and how to cope with mistakes and failure. One of the goals of this session is to illustrate how the self-statements can be used to help "stop and think" rather than respond impulsively when confronted with a problem. The third session includes another game that leads to selection of hypothetical situations to which the child applies the steps. The therapist and child take turns, and further practice is provided using prompts, modeling, shaping, and reinforcement to help the child be facile and fluid in applying the steps. The therapist fades prompts and assistance to shape proficient use and application of the steps. A series of "supersolvers" (homework assignments) begins at this point, in which the child is asked to identify when the steps could be used, then to use the steps in increasingly more difficult and clinically relevant situations as treatment continues.
4.	*Applying the steps and role playing.* The child applies the steps to real-life situations. The steps are applied to the situation to identify solutions and consequences. Then, the preferred solution, based on the likely consequences, is selected and then enacted through repeated role plays. Practice and role play are continued to develop the child's application of the steps. Multiple situations are presented and practiced in this way.
5.	*Parent-child contact. The* parent(s), therapist, and child are all present in the session. The child enacts the steps to solve problems. The parents learn more about the steps and are trained to provide attention and contingent praise for the child's use of the steps and selecting and enacting prosocial solutions. The primary goal is to develop the repertoire in the parent to encourage (prompt) use of the steps and to praise applications in a way that will influence child behavior (i.e., contingent, enthusiastic, continuous, verbal, and nonverbal praise). Further contacts with the parents at the end of later sessions continue this aspect of treatment as needed.
6–11.	*Continued applications to real-life situations.* In these sessions, the child uses the problem-solving steps to generate prosocial solutions to provocative interpersonal problems or situations. Each session concentrates on a different category of social interaction that the child might realistically encounter (peers, parents, siblings, teachers, etc.). Real-life situations, generated by the child or parent or from contacts with teachers and others, are enacted; hypothetical situations are also presented to elaborate themes and problem areas of the child (e.g., responding to provocation, fighting, being excluded socially, and being encouraged by peers to engage in antisocial behavior). The child's supersolvers also become a more integral part of each session; they are reenacted with the therapist beginning in session in order to better evaluate how the child is transferring skills to the daily environment.

(continued)

Table 6.4 *(Continued)*

12.	*Wrap-up and role reversal.* This wrap-up session is included (1) to help the therapist generally assess what the child has learned in the session, (2) to clear up any remaining confusions the child may have concerning use of the steps, and (3) to provide a final summary for the child of what has been covered in the meetings. The final session is based on role reversal in which the child plays the role of the therapist and the therapist plays the role of the child learning and applying the steps. The purpose of this session is to have the child teach and benefit from the learning that teaching provides, to allow for any unfinished business of the treatment ("spending" remaining chips, completing final supersolvers), and to provide closure for the therapy.
13.	*Optional sessions.* During the course of therapy, additional sessions are provided to the child as needed, if the child has special difficulty in grasping any features of the problem-solving steps or their application. For example, the child may have difficulty in applying the steps, learning to state them covertly, and so on. An additional session may be applied to repeat material of a previous session, so that the child has a solid grasp of the approach. Optional sessions may be implemented at any point that the child's progress lags behind the level appropriate to the session that has been completed. For example, if a facet of treatment has not been learned (e.g., memorization of steps and fading of steps), which is associated with the particular session that has been completed, an optional session may be implemented. Also, if there is a problem or issue of the child's or parent's participation in supersolvers, a session will be scheduled with the parent and child to shape the requisite behaviors in the session and to make assignments to ensure that this aspect of treatment is carried out.

Source: From Kazdin, A. E. (2003). Problem-solving skills training and parent management training for conduct disorder. In A. E. Kazdin & J. R. Weisz (Eds.), *Evidence-based psychotherapies for children and adolescents* (pp. 241–262). New York: Guilford. Copyright 2003 by Guilford Press. Reprinted with permission.

- There are two well-established and a range of probably efficacious treatment approaches from which to select when working with conduct-disordered youth.
- Using a combination of PMT and PSST together tends to be more effective than using either treatment alone (Kazdin, 2003). Both treatments are manualized and have core sets of themes and skills domains for treatment sessions.
- Medication cannot be justified as the first line of treatment for conduct problems.
- One of the well-established approaches, Webster-Stratton's videotape modeling parent program, the Incredible Years Training Series, was developed to address parent, family, child, and school risk factors related to childhood conduct disorders.
- The most proactive and powerful approach to the problem of escalating aggression in young children is to offer their programs using a school-based prevention/early intervention model designed to strengthen all children's social and emotional competence.

Despite the promising treatment effects produced by the interventions reviewed above, existing treatments need to be refined and new ones developed. We cannot yet determine the short- and long-term impact of evidence-based treatments on conduct-disordered youths, and it is sometimes unclear what part of the therapeutic process produces change. A child's eventual outcome is most likely dependent on the interrelationship among child, parent, teacher, and peer risk factors; accordingly, the most effective interventions should be those that assess these risk factors and determine which programs are needed for a particular family and child (Webster-Stratton & Reid, 2003b).

The focus in this chapter has been geared toward school social workers and other mental health practitioners working with individual students in school settings. We cannot emphasize enough that contextual issues should not be ignored. Equally important in sustaining therapeutic change with conduct-disordered youth are issues surrounding classroom management and strategies that promote positive behavior through school-wide interventions. Accordingly, practitioners must work collaboratively with parents, teachers, peers, and school administrators to sustain change across settings. For a detailed exposition on best practice models for schoolwide interventions, the reader is referred to Bloomquist and Schnell (2002), which is an excellent source.

Additional Resources

American Academy of Child and Adolescent Psychiatry: http://aacap.org.

Barkley, R.A. (1987). *Defiant children: A clinician's manual for parent training.* New York: Guilford.

Bloomquist, M. L., & Schnell, S. V. (2002). *Helping children with aggression and conduct problems: Best practices for intervention.* New York: Guilford.

Blueprints. Developed by the Center for the Study and Prevention of Violence at the University of Colorado at Boulder: http://www.colorado.edu/cspv/blueprints.

Catalano, R. F., & Hawkins, J. D. (1996). The social development model: A theory of antisocial behavior. In J. D. Hawkins (Ed.), *Delinquency and crime: Current theories.* New York: Cambridge University Press.

Cavell, T. A. (2000). *Working with parents of aggressive children: A practitioner's guide.* Washington, DC: American Psychological Association.

Cavell, T. A. (2001). Updating our approach to parent training. I: The case against targeting noncompliance. *Clinical Psychology: Science and Practice,* 8, 299–318. doi:10.1093/clipsy.8.3.299

Centers for Disease Control and Prevention: http://www.cdc.gov.

Evidence-Based Treatment for Children and Adolescents: http://www.effectivechildtherapy.com.

Fonagy, P., & Kurtz, A. (2002). Disturbance of conduct. In P. Fonagy, M. Target, D. Cottrell, J. Phillips, & Z. Kurtz (Eds.), *What works for whom? A critical review of treatments for children and adolescents* (pp. 106–192). New York: Guilford.

Forehand, R. L., & McMahon, R. J. (1981). *Helping the noncompliant child: A clinician's guide to parent training.* New York: Guilford.

Henggeler, S.W., Schoenwald, S. K., Rowland, M. D., & Cunningham, P. B. (2002). *Serious emotional disturbance in children and adolescents: Multisystemic therapy.* New York: Guilford.

Incredible Years Parent, Teacher, and Child Programs: http://www.incredibleyears.com.

Lochman, J. E., Barry, T. D., & Pardini, D. A. (2003). Anger control training for aggressive youth. In A. E. Kazdin & J. R. Weisz (Eds.), *Evidence-based psychotherapies for children and adolescents* (pp. 263–281). New York: Guilford.

McMahon, R. J., & Forehand, R. L. (2003). *Helping the noncompliant child: Family-based treatment for oppositional behavior* (2nd ed.). New York, NY: Guilford Press.

National Institute of Mental Health: http://www.nimh.nih.gov/index.shtml.

Parenting Clinic, University of Washington: http://www.son.washington.edu/centers/parentingclinic/bibligraphy.asp.

Sells, S. P. (1998). *Treating the tough adolescent: A family-based, step-by-step guide.* New York: Guilford.

Substance Abuse and Mental Health Services Administration: http://www.mentalhealth.samhsa.gov.

UCLA School Mental Health Project, Center for Mental Health in Schools: http://smhp.psych.ucla.edu.

U.S. Department of Health and Human Services, Administration for Children and Families: http://www.acf.hhs.gov/.

U.S. Department of Justice, Office of Juvenile Justice and Delinquency Prevention: http://www.ojjdp.gov/.

Yale Parenting Center and Child Conduct Clinic: http://childconductclinic.yale.edu/.

References

Alexander, J. F., & Parsons, B. V. (1973). Short-term behavioral intervention with delinquents: Impact on family process and recidivism. *Journal of Abnormal Psychology, 81,* 219–225.

Alvarez, M., & Anderson-Ketchmark, C. (2009). Review of an evidence-based school social work intervention: Second Step. *Children & Schools, 31*(4), 247–250.

American Psychiatric Association. (2000). *Diagnostic and statistical manual of mental disorders* (4th ed., text revision). Washington, DC: Author.

Baer, R. A., & Nietzel, M. T. (1991). Cognitive and behavioral treatment of impulsivity in children: A meta analytic review of the outcome literature. *Journal of Clinical Child Psychology, 20,* 400-412.

Bank, L., Marlowe, J. H., Reid, J. B., Patterson, G. R., & Weinrott, M. R. (1991). A comparative evaluation of parent training interventions for families of chronic delinquents. *Journal of Abnormal Child Psychology, 19,* 15–33.

Barkley, R., Edwards, G., Laneri, M., Fletcher, K., & Metevia, L. (2001). The efficacy of problem-solving communication training alone, behavior management training alone, and their combination for parent-adolescent conflict in teenagers with ADHD and ODD. *Journal of Consulting & Clinical Psychology, 69,* 926–941.

Barkley, R. A. (1987). *Defiant children: A clinician's manual for parent training.* New York: Guilford.

Barkley, R. A., Guevremont, D. C., Anastopoulos, A. D., & Fletcher, K. E. (1992). A comparison of three family therapy programs for treating family conflicts in adolescents with attention-deficit hyperactivity disorder. *Journal of Consulting and Clinical Psychology, 60*, 450–462.

Beets, M. W., Flay, B. R., Vuchinich, S., Snyder, F. J., Acock, A., Li, K.-K., ... Durlak, J. A. (2009). Use of a social and character development program to prevent substance use, violent behaviors, and sexual activity among elementary students in Hawai'i. *American Journal of Public Health, 99*, 1438–1445. doi:10.2105/AJPH.2008.142919

Bernal, M. E., Klinnert, M. D., & Schultz, L. A. (1980). Outcome evaluation of behavioral parent training and client-centered parent counseling for children with conduct problems. *Journal of Applied Behavior Analysis, 13*, 677–691.

Bierman, K. L., Coie, J. D., Dodge, K. A., Greenberg, M. T., Lochman, J. E., McMahon, R. J., & Pinderhughes, E. (2010). The effects of a multiyear universal social–emotional learning program: The role of student and school characteristics. *Journal of Consulting and Clinical Psychology, 78*(2), 156–168. doi:10.1037/a0018607

Block, J. (1978). Effects of a rational-emotive mental health program on poorly achieving disruptive high school students. *Journal of Counseling Psychology, 25*, 61–65.

Bloomquist, M. L., & Schnell, S. V. (2002). *Helping children with aggression and conduct problems: Best practices for intervention.* New York: Guilford.

Borduin, C. M., Mann, B. J., Cone, L. T., Henggeler, S. W., Fucci, B. R., Blaske, D. M., & Williams, R. A. (1995). Multisystemic treatment of serious juvenile offenders: Long-term prevention of criminality and violence. *Journal of Consulting and Clinical Psychology, 63*, 569–578.

Botvin, G. J., Griffin, K. W., & Nichols, T. R. (2006). Preventing youth violence and delinquency through a universal school-based prevention approach. *Prevention Science*, 7, 403–408.

Botvin, G. J., Mahalic, S. F., & Grotpeter, J. (1998). *Life skills training: Book 5 of blueprints for violence prevention.* Center for the Study of Prevention ofViolence, Institute of Behavioral Science, University of Colorado at Boulder.

Brestan, E. V., & Eyberg, S. M. (1998). Effective psychosocial treatments of conduct-disordered children and adolescents: 29 years, 82 studies, and 5,272 kids. *Journal of Clinical Child Psychology, 27*(2), 180–189.

Brown-Chidsey, R., & Steege, M. W. (2005). *Response to Intervention: Principles and strategies for effective practice* (2nd ed.). New York, NY: Guildford Press.

Cavell, T. A. (2000). *Working with parents of aggressive children: A practitioner's guide.* Washington, DC: American Psychological Association.

Conduct Problems Prevention Research Group. (2010). The Fast Track Project: Preventing severe conduct problems in school-age youth. In R. C. Murrihy, A. D. Kidman, & T. H. Ollendick (Eds.), *Handbook of clinical assessment and treatment of conduct problems in youth* (407–433). New York, NY: Springer.

Dishion, T. J., & Patterson, G. R. (1992). Age effects in parent training outcomes. *Behavior Therapy, 23*, 719–729.

Domitrovich, C. E., Cortes, R. C., & Greenberg, M. T. (2007). Improving young children's social and emotional competence: A randomized trial of the preschool 'PATHS' curriculum. *The Journal of Primary Prevention, 28*(2), 67–91. doi:10.1007/s10935-007-0081-0

Durlak, J., Fuhrman, T., & Lampman, C. (1991). Effectiveness of cognitive-behavior therapy for maladapting children: A meta-analysis. *Psychological Bulletin, 110*, 204–214.

D'Zurilla, T., & Nezu, A. (2001). Problem-solving therapies. In K. Dobson & S. Keith (Eds.), *Handbook of cognitive-behavioral therapies* (2nd ed., pp. 211–245). New York: Guilford.

Eyberg, S. (1988). Parent-child interaction therapy: Integration of traditional and behavioral concerns. *Child and Family Behavior Therapy, 10*, 33–45.

Eyberg, S. M., Boggs, S., & Algina, J. (1995). Parent–child interaction therapy: A psychosocial model for the treatment of young children with conduct problem behavior and their families. *Psychopharmacology Bulletin, 110*, 204–214.

Feindler, D. L., Marriott, S. A. A., & Iwata, M. (1984). Group anger control training for junior high school delinquents. *Cognitive Therapyand Research, 8*, 299–311.

Fonagy, P., & Kurtz, A. (2002). Disturbance of conduct. In P. Fonagy, M. Target, D. Cottrell, J. Phillips, & Z. Kurtz (Eds.), *What works for whom? A critical review of treatments for children and adolescents* (pp. 106–192). New York: Guilford.

Forehand, R. L., & McMahon, R. J. (1981). *Helping the noncompliant child: A clinician's guide to present training.* New York: Guilford.

Frey, K. S., Nolen, S. B., Edstrom, L.V., & Hirschstein, M. K. (2005). Effects of a school-based social-emotional competence program: Linking children's goals, attributions, and behavior. *Journal ofApplied Developmental Psychology, 26*, 171–200.

Griffin, K. W., Botvin, G. J., & Nichols, T. R. (2006). Effects of a school-based drug abuse prevention program for adolescents on HIV risk behaviors in young adulthood. *Prevention Science*, 7, 103–112.

Hamilton, S. B., & MacQuiddy, S. L. (1984). Self-administered behavioral parent training: Enhancement of treatment efficacy using a time-out signal seat. *Journal of Clinical Child Psychology, 13*, 61–69.

Hawkins, J. D., Catalano, R. F., & Miller, J. Y. (1992). Risk and protective factors for alcohol and other drug problems in adolescence and early adulthood: Implications for substance abuse prevention. *Psychological Bulletin, 112*, 64–105.

Henggeler, S. W., Rodick, J. D., Bourdin, C. M., Hanson, C. L., Watson, S. M., & Urey, J. R. (1986). Multisystemic treatment of juvenile offenders: Effects on adolescent behavior and family interaction. *Developmental Psychology, 22,* 132–141.

Henggeler, S. W., Melton, G. B., & Smith, L. A. (1992). Family preservation using multisystemic therapy: An effective alternative to incarcerating serious juvenile offenders. *Journal of Consulting and Clinical Psychology, 60,* 953–961.

Holmes, S. E., Slaughter, J. R., & Kashani, J. (2001). Risk factors in childhood that lead to the development of conduct disorder and antisocial personality disorder. *Child Psychiatry and Human Development, 31,* 183-193.

Huey, W. C., & Rank, R. C. (1984). Effects of counselor and peer-led group assertiveness training on black adolescent aggression. *Journal of Counseling Psychology, 31,* 95–98.

Kazdin, A. E., Esveldt-Dawson, K., French, N. H., & Unis, A. S. (1987a). Effect of parent management training and problem-solving skills training combined in the treatment of antisocial child behavior. *Journal of the American Academy of Child and Adolescent Psychiatry, 26,* 416–424

Kazdin, A. E., Esveldt-Dawson, K., French, N. H., & Unis, A. S. (1987b). Problem-solving skills training and relationship therapy in the treatment of antisocial child behavior. *Journal of Consulting and Clinical Psychology, 55,* 76–85.

Kazdin, A. E., Siegel, T. C., & Bass, D. (1992). Cognitive problem-solving skills training and parent management training in the treatment of antisocial behavior in children. *Journal of Consulting and Clinical Psychology, 60,* 733–747.

Kazdin, A. E. (1994). Psychotherapy for children and adolescents. In A. E. Bergin, & S. L. Garfield (Eds.), *Handbook of psychotherapy and behavior change* (4th ed., pp. 543–594). New York: Wiley.

Kazdin, A. E. (2000). *Psychotherapy for children and adolescents: Directions for research and practice.* New York: Oxford University Press.

Kazdin, A. E. (2002). Psychosocial treatments for conduct disorder in children and adolescents. In P. E. Nathan & J. M. Gorman (Eds.), *A guide to treatments that work* (2nd ed., pp. 57–85). New York: Oxford University Press.

Kazdin, A. E. (2003). Problem-solving skills training and parent management training for conduct disorder. In A. E. Kazdin & J. R. Weisz (Eds.), *Evidence-based psychotherapies for children and adolescents* (pp. 241–262). New York: Guilford.

Kazdin, A. E. (2004). Psychotherapy for children and adolescents. In M. J. Lambert (Ed.), *Bergin and Garfield's handbook of psychotherapy and behavior change* (5th ed., pp. 543–589). New York: Wiley.

Kronenberger, W. S., & Meyer, R. G. (2001). *The child clinician's handbook* (2nd ed.). Needham Heights, MA: Allyn & Bacon.

Kusche, C. A. (2002). Psychoanalysis as prevention: Using PATHS to enhance ego development, object relationships, and cortical integration in children. *Journal of Applied Psychoanalytic Studies, 4,* 283–301.

Li, K.-K., Washburn, I., DuBois, D. L., Vuchinich, S., Ji, P., Brechling, V., ... Flay, B. R. (2011). Effects of the *Positive Action* programme on problem behaviors in elementary school students: A matched-pair, randomized control trial in Chicago. *Psychology & Health, 26,* 187–204. doi:10.1080/08870446.2011.531574

Lochman, J., Boxmeyer, C., Powell, N., Qu, L., Wells, K., & Windle, M. (2009). Dissemination of the Coping Power Program: Importance of intensity of counselor training. *Journal of Consulting and Clinical Psychology,* 77(3), 397–409.

Lochman, J., & Wells, K. (2002). The Coping Power Program at the middle-school transition: Universal and indicated prevention effects. *Psychology of Addictive Behaviors, 1,* S40–S54. doi:10.1037/0893-164X.16.4S.S40

Lochman, J. E., Burch, P. R., Curry, J. F., & Lampron, L. B. (1984). Treatment and generalization effects of cognitive-behavioral and goal-setting interventions with aggressive boys. *Journal of Consulting and Clinical Psychology, 52,* 915–916.

Lochman, J. E., Lampron, L. B., Gemmer, T. C., & Harris, S. R. (1989). Teacher consultation and cognitive-behavioral interventions with aggressive boys. *Psychology in the Schools, 26,* 179–188.

Loeber, R., Farrington, D. P., & Waschbusch, D. A. (1998). Serious and violent juvenile offenders. In R. Loeber & D. P. Farrington (Eds.), *Serious and violent juvenile offenders: Risk factors and successful interventions* (pp. 13–29). Thousand Oaks, CA: Sage.

McNeil, C. B., Eyberg, S., Eisenstadt, T. H., Newcomb, K., & Funderburk, B. W. (1991). Parent-child interaction therapy with behavior problem children: Generalization of treatment effects to the school setting. *Journal of Clinical Child Psychology, 20,* 140–151.

Mortimore, P. (1995). The positive effects of schooling. In M. Rutter (Ed.), *Psychosocial disturbances in young people: Challenges for prevention* (pp. 333–363). Cambridge: Cambridge University Press.

Nock, M. K., Kazdin, A. E., & Kessler, R. C. (2006). Prevalence, subtypes, and correlates of DSM-IV conduct disorder in the national comorbidity survey replication. *Psychological Medicine, 36,* 699-710.

OJJDP (n.d.). *Second step: A violence prevention program.* Retrieved from http://www.ojjdp.gov/mpg/mpg-ProgramDetails.aspx

Patterson, G. R., & Gullion, M. E. (1968). *Living with children: New methods for parents and teachers.* Champaign, IL: Research Press.

Patterson, G. R., Reid, J. B., Jones, R. R., & Conger, R. E. (1975). *A social learning approach to family interven-*

tion: Vol. 1. Families with aggressive children. Eugene, OR: Castalia.

Peed, S., Roberts, M., & Forehand, R. (1977). Evaluation of the effectiveness of a standardized parent training program in altering the interaction of mothers and their noncompliant children. *Behavior Modification, 1*, 323–350.

Peterson, M., Hamilton, E., & Russell, A. (2009). Starting well: Facilitating the middle school transition. *Journal of Applied School Psychology, 25*(3), 286–304.

Pullis, M. (1991). Practical considerations of excluding conduct disordered students: An empirical analysis. *Behavioral Disorders, 17*(1), 9–22.

Reid, M. J., Webster-Stratton, C., & Hammond, M. (2003). Follow-up of children who received the incredible years intervention for oppositional defiant disorder: Maintenance and prediction of 2-year outcome. *Behavior Therapy, 34*(4), 471–491.

Reid, M. J., Webster-Stratton, C., & Baydar, N. (2004). Halting the development of conduct problems in Head Start children: The effects of parent training. *Journal of Clinical Child and Adolescent Psychology, 33*(2), 279–291.

Riggs, N. R., Greenberg, M. T., Kusché, C. A., & Pentz, M. (2006). The mediational role of neurocognition in the behavioral outcomes of a social-emotional prevention program in elementary school students: Effects of the PATHS curriculum. *Prevention Science*, 7(1), 91–102. doi:10.1007/s11121-005-0022-1.

Reynolds, D., Sammons, P., Stoll, L., Barber, M., & Hillman, J. (1996). School effectiveness and school improvement in the United Kingdom. *School Effectiveness and School Improvement*, 7, 133–158.

Rosen, A., & Proctor, E. K. (2002). Standards for evidence-based social work practice: The role of replicable and appropriate interventions, outcomes, and practice guidelines. In A. R. Roberts & G. J. Greene (Eds.), *Social workers' desk reference* (pp. 743–747). New York: Oxford University Press.

SAMHSA . (2006a). *Positive Action*. Retrieved from http://www.nrepp.samhsa.gov/ViewIntervention.aspx?id=78

SAMHSA . (2006b). *Project Towards No Drug Abuse*. Retrieved from http://nrepp.samhsa.gov/ViewIntervention.aspx?id=21

SAMHSA . (2006c). *Second Step*. Retrieved from http://nrepp.samhsa.gov/ViewIntervention.aspx?id=66

SAMHSA . (2007). *Promoting alternative thinking strategies (PATHS), PATHS preschool*. Retrieved from http://www.nrepp.samhsa.gov/ViewIntervention.aspx?id=20

SAMHSA . (2008). *LifeSkills training (LST)*. Retrieved from http://www.nrepp.samhsa.gov/ViewIntervention.aspx?id=109

Schlichter, K. J., & Horan, J. J. (1981). Effects of stress inoculation on the anger and aggression management skills of institutionalized juvenile delinquents. *Cognitive Therapy and Research, 5*, 359–365.

Sells, S. P. (1998). *Treating the tough adolescent: A family-based, step-by-step guide*. New York: Guilford.

Serketich, W. J., & Dumas, J. E. (1996). The effectiveness of behavioral parent training to modify antisocial behavior in children: A meta analysis. *Behavior Therapy, 27*, 171–186.

Spaccarelli, S., Cotler, S., & Penman, D. (1992). Problem-solving skills training as a supplement to behavioral parent training. *Cognitive Therapy and Research, 16*, 1–18.

Springer, D. W. (2002). Assessment protocols and rapid assessment instruments with troubled adolescents. In A. R. Roberts & G. J. Greene (Eds.), *Social workers' desk reference* (pp. 217–221). New York: Oxford University Press.

Spoth, R. L., Clair, S., Shin, C., & Redmond, C. (2006). Long-term effects of universal preventative interventions on methamphetamine use among adolescents. *Archives of Pediatric & Adolescent Medicine, 160*, 876–882.

Spoth, R. L., Randall, G., Trudeau, L., Shin, C., Redmond, C. (2008). Substance use outcomes 5-1/2 years past baseline for partnership-based, family school preventive interventions. *Drug and Alcohol Dependence, 96*, 57-68.

Snyder, F. J., Flay, B. R., Vuchinich, S., Acock, A., Washburn, I. J., Beets, & Li, K.-K. (2010). Impact of a social-emotional and character development program on school-level indicators of academic achievement, absenteeism, and disciplinary outcomes: A matched-pair, cluster randomized, controlled trial. *Journal of Research on Educational Effectiveness, 3*, 26–55.

Sun, P., Sussman, S., Dent, C., & Rohrbach, L. (2008). One-year follow-up evaluation of Project Towards No Drug Abuse (TND-4). *Preventive Medicine, 47*(4), 438–442.

Sun, W., Skara, S., Sun, P., Dent, C. W., & Sussman, S. (2006). Project Towards No Drug Abuse: Long-term substance use outcomes evaluation. *Preventive Medicine, 42*(3), 188–192. doi:10.1016/j.ypmed.2005.11.011

Tremblay, R. E., Pagani-Kurtz, L., Masse, L. C., Vitaro, F., & Phil, R. (1995). A bimodal preventive intervention for disruptive kindergarten boys: Its impact through mid-adolescence. *Journal of Consulting and Clinical Psychology, 63*, 560–568.

U.S. Department of Health and Human Services. (2001). *Youth violence: A report of the Surgeon General*. Rockville, MD: Author.

Vitaro, F., & Tremblay, R. E. (1994). Impact of a prevention program on aggressive children's friendships and social adjustment. *Journal of Abnormal Child Psychology, 22*, 457–475.

Webster-Stratton, C. (1984). Randomized trial of two parent-training programs for families with conduct-disordered children. *Journal of Consulting and Clinical Psychology, 52*, 666–678.

Webster-Stratton, C., Kolpacoff, M., & Hollinsworth, T. (1988). Self-administered videotape therapy for families with conduct-problem children: Comparison with two cost effective treatments and a control group. *Journal of Consulting and Clinical Psychology, 56*, 558–566.

Webster-Stratton, C. (1990). Enhancing the effectiveness of self-administered videotape parent training for families with conduct-problem children. *Journal of Abnormal Child Psychology, 18*, 479–492.

Webster-Stratton, C. (1994). Advancing videotape parent training: A comparison study. *Journal of Consulting and Clinical Psychology, 62*, 583–593.

Webster-Stratton, C., & Hammond, M. (1997). Treating children with early-onset conduct problems: A comparison of child and parent training interventions. *Journal of Consulting and Clinical Psychology, 65*(1), 93–109.

Webster-Stratton, C. (1998). Preventing conduct problems in Head Start children: Strengthening parenting competencies. *Journal of Consulting and Clinical Psychology, 66*(5), 715–730.

Webster-Stratton, C., Reid, M. J., & Hammond, M. (2001a). Preventing conduct problems, promoting social competence: A parent and teacher training partnership in Head Start. *Journal of Clinical Child Psychology, 30*(3), 283–302.

Webster-Stratton, C., Reid, M. J., & Hammond, M. (2001b). Social skills and problem solving training for children with early-onset conduct problems: Who benefits? *Journal of Child Psychology and Psychiatry, 42*(7), 943–952.

Webster-Stratton, C., & Reid, M. J. (2003a). Treating conduct problems and strengthening social emotional competence in young children (ages 4–8 years): The Dina Dinosaur treatment program. *Journal of Emotional and Behavioral Disorders, 11* (3), 130–143.

Webster-Stratton, C., & Reid, M. J. (2003b). The incredible years parents, teachers, and children training series: A multifaceted treatment approach for young children with conduct problems. In A. E. Kazdin & J. R. Weisz (Eds.), *Evidence-based psychotherapies for children and adolescents* (pp. 224–240). New York: Guilford.

Webster-Stratton, C., Reid, M. J., & Hammond, M. (2004). Treating children with early onset conduct problems: Intervention outcomes for parent, child, and teacher training. *Journal of Clinical Child and Adolescent Psychology, 33*(1), 105–124.

Wells, K. C., & Egan, J. (1988). Social learning and systems family therapy for childhood oppositional disorder: Comparative treatment outcome. *Comprehensive Psychiatry, 29*, 138–146

Wiltz, N. A., & Patterson, G. R. (1974). An evaluation of parent training procedures designed to alter inappropriate aggressive behavior of boys. *Behavior Therapy, 5*, 215–221.

Zangwill, W. M. (1983). An evaluation of a parent training program. *Child and Family Behavior Therapy, 5*, 1–6.

CHAPTER 7

Effective Interventions for Youth with Oppositional Defiant Disorder

Tammy Linseisen

Getting Started

"Disruptive," "mad all the time," "can't handle frustration," "touchy," "annoying," "driving me crazy," "emotionally disturbed," "passive-aggressive," "blames everyone for everything," "never takes responsibility," "doesn't listen," "noncompliant," "rude," "pushy," "oppositional," "defiant"—do any of these words or descriptions sound familiar? These are some of the terms and phrases used when parents and professionals are describing their observations of and reactions to children and adolescents who exhibit symptoms consistent with the diagnosis of oppositional defiant disorder (ODD). The prevalence of children with symptoms and/or actual diagnoses of oppositional defiant disorder has been documented in a number of publications (Eamon & Altshuler, 2004; Freeman, Franklin, Fong, Shaffer, & Timberlake, 1998; Markward & Bride, 2001; Sprague & Thyer, 2002). In fact, in the early school years, more than one half and maybe as many as two thirds of referrals made for clinical purposes are for behaviors consistent with this diagnosis (Fisher & Fagot, 1996). This diagnosis is not relegated to young children only. The following are facts about this disorder as listed in the *Diagnostic and Statistical Manual of Mental Disorders* (American Psychiatric Association, 2000):

- Evidence of the disorder is usually shown before the child is age 8.
- Evidence of the disorder will usually be shown by early adolescence.
- It is more common in families where marital difficulties exist.
- It appears more in families where at least one parent has a history of one of the following psychiatric diagnoses: mood disorder, ODD, conduct disorder, attention deficit/hyperactivity disorder, antisocial personality disorder, or a substance-related disorder.
- Amount of oppositional symptoms seems to increase with age.
- ODD is found more often in males than in females until puberty.
- After puberty, ODD is found in both males and females at equal rates.

Disruptive behavior disorders such as ODD have a number of contributing or causal factors related to family, genetics, and environment. The American Psychiatric Association (2000) notes in its diagnostic manual that ODD is found more commonly in families with significant marital problems. The manual also indicates that ODD is found more frequently in families in which one parent has a history of mood disorders, disruptive behavior disorder, antisocial personality disorder, or a substance-related disorder. McKinney & Renk (2007) cite many risk factors in the etiology of ODD. Some of these include low socioeconomic status (SES), gender socialization, parental stress levels, and lack of parental problem-solving skill (McKinney & Renk, 2007).

A critical responsibility of the school mental health professional is to accurately assess a youth's level of functioning in the school setting, although the provision of a diagnosis is not always helpful or necessary. For the orderly classification of symptoms, though, it is beneficial to work from one set of criteria. Utilizing set criteria can minimize misdiagnosis as well as pinpoint particular data when observing children or adolescents with behavioral difficulties. Not only are these behaviors disruptive to learning and the school setting in general, but the literature indicates that children with these kinds of behaviors are more prone to dropping out of school, substance use, peer rejection, adolescent-onset psychiatric disorders, and later antisocial behavior (Coie, Lochman, Terry, & Hyman, 1992; Kupersmidt & Coie, 1990; Kupersmidt & Patterson, 1991; Loeber, 1990). The *DSM-IV-TR* (2000) further states that significant impairment in social, academic, or occupational functioning must be caused by these behavioral disturbances. ODD should not be considered to be an accurate diagnosis if the criteria for the diagnosis of conduct disorder are met, and the same holds true if the individual is 18 years of age or older and the criteria for antisocial personality disorder are met. Even though conduct disorder and ODD are considered to be distinct, they do appear to exist on a spectrum of related disruptive behavior disorders. For this reason, the effective treatments of the two are similar.

Box 7.1

According to the *DSM-IV-TR* (2000), a youth can be diagnosed with ODD if he or she shows "a pattern of negativistic, hostile, and defiant behavior lasting at least 6 months, during which four (or more) of the following are present:

1. often loses temper;
2. often argues with adults;
3. often actively defies or refuses to comply with adults' requests or rules;
4. often deliberately annoys people;
5. often blames others for his or her mistakes or misbehavior;
6. is often touchy or easily annoyed by others;
7. is often angry and resentful;
8. is often spiteful or vindictive" (p. 102).

What We Know

A literature review of evidence-based interventions for ODD has revealed minimal results for individual practice but more promising results for group methods. Also, parent-training interventions have shown some promise, but no pharmacological treatment has been shown to be successful for the treatment of ODD in current studies. Practice wisdom as well as resiliency theory have informed the examples provided in this chapter, and information highlighting the resources not addressed in detail are located at the chapter's end.

If evidence-based programs or interventions discussed in the literature targeted youth with aggressive behaviors only, the information is not included here because two defining differences between ODD and conduct disorder, according to the *DSM-IV-TR* (2000), are that disruptive behaviors of individuals with ODD do not ordinarily involve aggression toward animals or people or the destruction of property. In the upcoming edition of the *Diagnostic and Statistical Manual of Mental Disorders*, the DSM-V, only minor changes to the diagnosis of ODD are expected (American Psychiatric Association, 2010). The disorder will be defined using three criteria areas: angry/irritable mood; defiant/headstrong behavior; and vindictiveness. Symptoms will be evaluated using persistence and frequency designations that will help to determine the severity of the disorder. Especially relevant for school personnel is that students might demonstrate symptoms of ODD at school only and qualify for this diagnosis, as the DSM-V criteria indicate that behavior might be confined to only one setting.

The language used in research-based literature is variable when discussing behavioral problems of youth. Phrases like "disruptive school behavior," "conduct problems," "bullying and/or violent behaviors," "attachment disorders," and "emotional and/or behavioral disorders" are common when evidence-based interventions are being mentioned. This offers a challenge to determine which of the studies is speaking to treatment of ODD specifically. Additionally, few studies have been conducted which involve youth who meet only the criteria for ODD without symptoms of other disorders or related conditions (Sprague & Thyer, 2002). This confounds the ability to define effective treatments for specified disorders, such as ODD by itself.

Certain evidence-based specifics might prove helpful to school social workers and mental health workers in their attempts to affect students via multiple systems. The following information might be useful when planning and facilitating groups with youth who meet the diagnostic criteria for ODD; when consulting with teachers who are managing students with ODD in their classrooms; or when attempting to provide effective interventions with an individual youth displaying oppositional and/or defiant behavior.

- Interventions that succeed in helping students to comply with adult directives usually lead to a decrease in disruptive behaviors (Musser, Bray, Kehle, & Jenson, 2001).
- Training parents and teachers to give commands and provide consequences effectively has been shown to improve compliance with adult requests (Musser et al., 2001).
- Delivery of requests for compliance in a firm but quiet tone of voice and also in statement form increased one program's effectiveness (O'Leary, Kaufman, Kass, & Drabman, 1970).
- Requests for compliance are more effective if specific and delivered within approximately 3 feet from the student (Van Houten, Nau, MacKenzie-Keating, Sameoto, & Colavecchia, 1982) and only once eye contact is established (Hamlet, Axelrod, & Kuerschner, 1984).
- Improving rates of students' compliance with adult requests can be achieved by obvious posting of four or five positively and behaviorally stated rules (Osenton & Chang, 1999; Rosenberg, 1986).
- Teacher movement in the classroom provides more supervision, earlier detection of potential problem situations, and increased opportunity to reward positive and prosocial behaviors (Rhode, Jenson, & Reavis, 1993).
- The use of mystery motivators can promote requests for compliance (Rhode et al., 1993). Mystery motivators are positive reinforcers that are not made known to the child, and they have been shown to help with the improvement of inappropriate behaviors (Kehle, Madaus, Baratta, & Bray, 1998).

What We Can Do

Assessment

In order to use evidence-based interventions most effectively, an accurate assessment must be conducted in order to ensure that the youth meets the diagnostic criteria for ODD. Eamon and Altshuler (2004) highlighted the "multilayered and reciprocal nature of child, family, peer, neighborhood, and school factors in development" (p. 24). For this reason, it can be beneficial to observe children in different settings within school during a school day or week, obtain data from others in the school environment, read and review school files and referral materials, obtain data from parents regarding the youth's behavior in the home environment, as well as conduct individual interviews with the youth. The Eyberg Child Behavior Inventory (ECBI) and the Sutter-Eyberg Student Behavior Inventory (SESBI) are two of the instruments outlined in the literature that might offer some information regarding the child's behavioral functioning in the schools (Burns & Patterson, 2001). The Achenbach Child Behavior Checklist is another assessment tool utilized for home and school data, although the evidence base is not strong regarding its accuracy for diagnosis of ODD (Abolt & Thyer, 2002).

Individual Interventions

Currently, no individual interventions have been shown to be effective in producing clinically significant changes in children or adolescents who meet the criteria of ODD (Hemphill & Littlefield, 2001).

Relational and attachment theories subscribe to the notion that change can occur based on the healing power of the relationship. Oppositional and defiant children have difficulties regulating emotions and behaviors. Because advanced capabilities now exist for studying the brain, a significant interest in the theory of attachment has reemerged. The attachment process between parent and child forms the child's self-regulatory mechanisms within the brain (Schore, 2001). Children who are securely attached to a significant caregiver have a "learned" capacity, via consistent and responsive caregiving, to regulate their emotions and behaviors. Given this knowledge about attachment theory, there are implications for the school environment. In school settings, relational approaches may be integrated with evidence-based practices, such as problem-solving skills training, anger control training, and cognitive-behavioral therapies.

One of the most important components of work with oppositional youth is often overlooked. In order to engage most effectively with behaviorally disrupted youth, school workers must manage their own reactions to the challenges these youth present. Increasing a school worker's self-awareness is critical because these youth are sensitive to emotional and behavioral reactions of those who work with them. If a worker can respond consciously to the youth, rather than react to the youth without self-awareness, the youth often will begin to respond in a calmer manner.

Resiliency

Garbarino (1999) identifies certain characteristics and conditions as directly relevant to making an impact on behaviorally disordered boys and their futures. Some of these are particularly relevant to the school environment: a stable positive emotional relationship with at least one person; actively coping with stress by finding meaning in it or making something positive out of it; an intelligence quotient (IQ) in the average range (but IQ scores can be misleading; a child's emotional intelligence is not scored on standard IQ measures); awareness of the student's own strengths and possession of a real concept of self; and positive social support from persons or institutions outside of the family (p. 168). Garbarino (1999) goes on to say that there are a number of "psychological anchors of resilience" that "are important in generating ideas for programs to save boys before they become troubled and violent" (p. 170). He defines social anchors as "the characteristics of a healthy community that holds and protects boys as they grow" (p. 170). Some of these social anchors are particularly relevant to schools and their communities:

1. Youth need some level of predictability and routine in their lives, and they thrive when this stability is present for them (the concept of stability).
2. All children need to be affirmed, which means "receiving messages of one's value and worth" (p. 171).
3. An environment that provides a sense of security allows for active exploration of the environment without fear of abandonment or danger.
4. Adults need to invest time and be physically and psychologically present with the youth.

Schools can create environments which will act as social anchors for the students, enhancing their resiliency and making a systemic impact on their overall functioning in constructive ways.

Relationship-Based Interventions

Although no efficacious individual interventions are presently documented, skilled practitioners discuss the positive effects of relational, cognitive-behavioral, and supportive individual work with children and adolescents who meet the criteria for the diagnosis of ODD. So often, these youth are disliked or disregarded by adults, and this is understandable in schools, given the challenges they can present in a classroom and with authority. Relationships with these youngsters, identified in the system as "problematic" or "defiant" can sometimes take time and require great patience from the school mental health worker or social worker. It is likely that the older the youth, the more challenging the relationship is to develop. The worker must meet the youth where he is, without pushing him to make changes in his behavior or to connect with the worker faster or more intimately than the youth can manage. By working with the youth at his own pace, the worker can gain trust and promote security and stability in the relationship. Once a relationship is established, infusion of problem-solving skill curricula or social skills training can occur, although modeling of prosocial behaviors is occurring all along within the relationship-building process. As part of the modeling process, games can be played with the youth that emphasize turn taking, promote problem solving, and de-emphasize competition.

Play Therapy

For children ages 12 and under, individual, child-centered play therapy is supported by practice wisdom to be an effective option, although adequate evaluative research does not exist to support this model. Briefly, then, the basic skills of child-centered play therapy lend themselves to creating an atmosphere that encourages the development of "necessary coping skills within safe boundaries" (Mader, 2000, p. 57). Play therapy is based on the premise that children express themselves via play, as adults express themselves via talking. Mader (2000) suggests "a framework within which one can work with the principal, teaching colleagues, and parents to develop an action plan that includes play counseling as a viable approach to changing behavior in disruptive students" (p. 56).

Group Interventions

Problem-Solving and Social Skills Training in Groups

Problem-solving training and social skills training have evidence bases in the literature for affecting younger children who show symptoms of ODD (Bierman, Miller, & Stabb, 1987; Kazdin, 1997).

Dodge and Price (1994) relate that children who accurately perceive and effectively solve interpersonal problems use a five-stage, sequential, problem-solving decision-making process. Group settings are ideal for teaching and practicing social problem-solving skills in the school setting. One problem-solving method using these highlighted steps is Second Step, "a violence-prevention curriculum created with the dual goals of reducing development of social, emotional, and behavioral problems and promoting the development of core competencies" (Frey, Hirschstein, & Guzzo, 2000, p. 103).

Using the group process, students practice this problem-solving model with hypothetical situations. Providing role plays and dramatic and comedic scenes for the youth to practice sometimes offers emotional distance when skills teaching and practicing begins in the group. Video clips are also useful for this purpose. Shorter role plays, scenes, and video clips might be utilized with younger children, and puppets or doll play might also benefit this age group.

Meichenbaum (1977) discusses the use of verbal mediation, or "self-talk," as a strategy, in this case, for youth to remember to manage impulses and to think about consequences of behavior or solutions. Self-talk can also be used to reward the children and adolescents for their own positive or successful behaviors. The third step of the problem-solving process is particularly important because it "establishes four basic values or norms for behavior: safety, fairness, people's feelings, and effectiveness" (Frey, Hirschstein, & Guzzo, 2000, p. 105). Values clarification is considered relevant when teaching children to problem solve, as children's problem-solving skills are improved once they are able to establish their own positive norms (Lochman, Coie, Underwood, & Terry, 1993).

Box 7.2 Problem-Solving Method

1. Identify the problem.
2. Brainstorm solutions.
3. Evaluate solutions by asking, "Is it safe? Is it fair? How might people feel? Will it work?"
4. Select, plan, and try the solution.
5. Evaluate if the solution worked and what to do next. (Frey, Hirschstein, & Guzzo, 2002, p. 105)

Anger Control and Stress Inoculation Training

Because the peer group is such an important part of adolescent development and because schools tend to have limited resources to provide mental health services to greater numbers of students in need, group treatment can be an effective modality for the youth and for the school. Anger control groups have been shown to be efficacious in treating ODD youngsters (Sprague & Thyer, 2002).

The following steps might be helpful to make the group work:

Preparation

- Review the files and referral materials of those youth indicated to be showing symptoms of ODD.
- Complete assessments of the youth by interviewing them individually and speaking with their various teachers directly about their behaviors.
- Using the written materials and the interviews, determine if the referred youth meet the criteria for ODD as indicated by the *DSM-IV-TR*.
- Consider limiting the group to no more than six to eight members if the facilitator's group experience with this type of adolescent is minimal or if the acuity of the collective behaviors is intense. The group can be limited to as few as four students, but it can be quite small then when students are absent or unable to attend.
- In this age group, it is suggested that same-sex membership might be more effective in order to minimize the heterosexual peer issues inherent in early adolescence.
- A cofacilitator is a helpful resource when working with youth who require a higher level of supervision and subsequent intervention. With cofacilitation, though, much work must be done to ensure active and open communication between facilitators in order to minimize splitting by the group members and other potential downfalls.
- Determine a plan for effective evaluation of the group treatment intervention. One might use disciplinary referrals to the office, teacher reports of in-class behavioral problems/consequences, and in-school suspensions to evaluate pre- and posttreatment outcomes. A pretest can

be administered to the group members as well, determining their own views of their behaviors or their responses to conflictual situations.

- The group meets two times per week for 5 weeks, and it would consist of 10 50-minute training sessions. This might be modified to a 9-week session of one group session per week if necessary.
- Individual meetings occur again with the group members chosen for the group, and relationship development begins between the facilitator and the student. The facilitator begins to learn more about the student and his view of the world.

Group Process

- Group 1 establishes a group contract about participation and rules for the group. The group leader will discuss behavioral rewards for participation and homework completion. Some programs use snacks and soft drinks. Others use a point system that can accumulate into rewards at the end of a session. With this age group, using rewards more quickly can provide the short-term reinforcement necessary to promote compliance and participation. Group 1 should engage group members to keep their interests and to whet their appetites for future groups. At the end of the first group session, it might be beneficial to review with the group the goals that might be accomplished in this group. If there is resistance, this question can wait until later or be asked individually of group members in separate sessions between the group meetings.
    - It is critical that the group leader use skills to prevent power struggles from occurring with these group members. Other than issues of safety, few reasons exist which warrant a struggle with the youth over power.
    - Put a structure into place in the group that offers clear and direct guidelines and expectations for behavior. Determine what will happen if a group member is not following directions or is violating any other group rule.
    - Find ways to reward group members for following the rules but also for the prosocial behavior of helping their peers to follow the rules.
    - Use group process to help in sticky situations. For example: "What do you think we need to do about Joey's behavior, guys?" "What do you think our choices are?" "If Joey continues to break Rule #2, our group can't [pick something positive that is planned or a group reward that could be given]. I'm wondering how the group can help?" Give verbal praise to the suggestions that are beneficial, while trying to ignore or minimize the negative or threatening comments.
    - It is sometimes helpful to use humor to defuse negative comments as well. "Well, Freddy, punching Joey in the face is an option. However, then, you would be in even more trouble with the group than Joey is. Great idea?"
- Group Two would teach the group about the cycle of provocation, which includes how to identify one's own cues of anger and one's own aggressive or inappropriate responses and then the consequences of these types of events. Movie clips can again be shown to demonstrate this cycle, and group members can use these to understand the way the cycle works with others. Depending on the group's willingness at this point, role plays can begin to demonstrate either predetermined situations provided on index cards to the players, or if the group is engaging more readily, they can provide their own scenarios. Inside-the-group reinforcements happen when certain students are shown how to work and commandeer the video player or they are chosen as the director of a scene (Sprague & Thyer, 2002).
- Future groups can focus on common self-control strategies as well as assertiveness versus aggression. Specific microskills must be defined for each strategy in order to teach it in a step-by-step way. Videotaping role plays of the youth engaging in a problematic situation can be extremely helpful. The group can review the tape together, with individual input from group members about what details led to the problems in the situation. They might identify details such as voice tones, facial expressions, hand gestures, defensiveness, hostile posturing, and angry eye contact. The scenes can be rehearsed then, using different types of coping and self-control strategies, and videotapes can be reviewed again during the course of the group. Voice tone, eye contact, the broken-record technique, problem solving, choosing battles, taking time outs, and other forms of relaxation for deescalation are all suitable for the self-control strategy curricula.

- Rehearsal is a critical component of this type of program. Practice! Practice! Practice! Have different kids role play alternative responses for other kids. Practice the new skills as much as possible, and provide homework to the youth to try these new skills in other situations. Have them write about their experiences and bring this information back to the group. Reward them for completing assignments and bringing them back to the group

Box 7.3 Idea for Group One

Show video clips of popular movies where characters are exhibiting both negative and positive behaviors. Group discussions can occur after these video clips with specific questions offered, such as "What set the character off?" "What did you see happen?" "What were the consequences?"

Often, ODD youth do not see all of the consequences of their actions, particularly the consequences that involve their peer relationships and issues of respect or trust. This is an opportunity to point these things out without stepping on anyone's toes personally in the first meeting.

Box 7.4 Four Methods to Teach Alternative Responses to Conflict or Provocation

1. Self-Instruction: This is also called self-talk. The student might remind himself to keep cool or to ignore a situation.
2. Covert Modification of the Participant's Understanding of the Aggression-Causing Conditions: This is the "you're just jealous" reaction. The student uses self-talk to reframe the reason for the person's provocative behavior.
3. Self-Evaluation of Behavior During a Conflict and of Efficient Goal Accomplishment: This is a technique that asks the student to evaluate his own reactions as they are happening: "How am I doing here?" or "How did I handle that?"
4. Cognitive Control Technique of Thinking Ahead: This method focuses on changing faulty thinking skills inherent in many troubled youth.

Sources: Feindler, Marriott, & Iwata, 1984; Sprague & Thyer, 2002.

Termination

- Begin preparing the group for termination several sessions prior to the last one. Remind them of the number of group meetings left. Anticipate that the group members might regress some or even miss a group or two while they begin the process of preparing for termination. Youth with ODD sometimes have issues with attachment and intimacy, and termination might trigger these issues. Encourage the group members to talk about termination and how endings have happened for them in the past. If the group is unable to do this as a whole, provide one more individual session to each student and discuss his progress in the group, strengths, and areas for growth. Offer the opportunity for more discussion about termination in this one-to-one meeting.
- Provide an ending to remember! Offer certificates for completion of the training, and it might even be worthwhile to frame them so that the youth are less likely to throw them away or misplace them. Provide a letter to the youth outlining the things discussed at the individual meetings, particularly the issues where growth has taken place and where strengths have been shown. If possible, this ending session might even involve a party where teachers and others are invited to celebrate the program's completion. This will depend on resources as well as the group's functioning and state of cohesion at the time of termination. Have the group members talk to each other about what they learned from each other specifically and ask what they will take with them from the group.
- Conduct a posttest to review the students' evaluation of their behaviors now that the group intervention has occurred. Review the post-treatment data to determine if changes have occurred in the students' school behavior and problem-solving abilities.

Group Assertiveness Training

Huey and Rank (1984) provided group assertiveness training to African American boys who were identified as demonstrating aggression in the classroom. The following definitions were provided to distinguish assertive, passive, or aggressive responses:

"A response that was forthright and honest without being threatening or abusive was considered an assertive response" (Sprague & Thyer, 2002, p. 68). A passive response was one that showed unwillingness for the student to stand up for his rights (Sprague & Thyer, 2002). An aggressive response was when the student "used sarcasm, insults, threats, and tried to reach his goals in an abusive way" (Sprague & Thyer, 2002, p. 68). The boys receiving assertiveness training showed significant improvement posttreatment with their aggressiveness and anger in the classroom, more so than those assigned to group discussion only or to no treatment at all (Sprague & Thyer, 2002). This provides another intervention option, then, using the group formation and implementation suggestions above.

Rational-Emotive Therapy

Finally, Block (1978) reviewed a mental health program utilized with African American and Latino youth in the 11th and 12th grades. These youth were "prone to misconduct" and were also at risk of school failure. The program was one of rational-emotive therapy (RET), which is based on cognitive theory and which was made famous by Albert Ellis, a psychologist. Barker (1999) writes that the therapy is one in which the "client is encouraged to make distinctions between what is objective fact in the environment and the inaccurate, negative, and self-limiting interpretations made of one's own behavior and life" (p. 400). The group leaders used a task-oriented approach, and they maintained a more directive stance in the group. The process used much role play, small-group directed discussion, and homework assignments. Exercises involved direct confrontations and taking risks, and the youth were asked to discuss openly their feelings and reactions to the homework and the assignments in the group (Sprague & Thyer, 2002). With more information about the RET method and more study about the processes underlying this model, group interventions could be developed in schools which utilize this evidence-based approach.

School mental health professionals starting groups should consider this important caution. Although particular cognitive-behavioral interventions have shown some promise with improving problematic behavior in adolescents, it is always a challenging practice to bring together a group of youth, especially of adolescent age, who demonstrate the same types of ego limitations or acting-out defenses. Ideally, prosocial and cognitive restructuring opportunities might happen in a group carefully selected with a balance of personality types and varied strengths. Who decided to put all the kids with behavior problems in the same class anyway, expecting them to be educated? Balancing a group with students who have various issues or varying degrees of symptoms could be beneficial for all involved.

Parent Training

Parent–child interaction therapy (PCIT) is a family therapy approach to the treatment of psychological problems of preschool children that integrates both traditional and behavioral methods (Brinkmeyer & Eyberg, 2003). Treatment is conducted in two phases, labeled child-directed interaction (CDI) and parent-directed interaction (PDI). In CDI, the parents are taught to allow their child to lead the play activity. Parents are taught to describe, imitate, and praise the child's appropriate behavior, and they are also taught not to criticize the child. In PDI, the parents are taught how to direct and redirect their child's activity. Parents are taught to use clear and positive statements and direct commands as well as consistent consequences, both positive and negative, for behavior. Quite a bit of evidence base exists for the use of parent training models with oppositional defiant children.

Some of the training utilized in PCIT focuses on how to make effective commands (Zisser & Eyberg, 2010). Because these skills have been shown effective, teaching these skills to teachers and other school personnel might improve relationships and interactions with oppositional youth. Examples include:

1. Make commands direct rather than indirect.
2. State commands positively, politely, and respectfully.
3. Give commands one at a time.
4. Use age-appropriate and specific, not vague, commands.
5. Explain commands before given and after obeyed, ignoring attempts to distract or disobey. (Zisser & Eyberg, 2010)

Kazdin (2010) reports of two evidence-based treatments for youth (ages 5–12): cognitive problem-solving skills training (PSST) and parent management training (PMT). PSST has similarities to the problem-solving therapies discussed earlier in this chapter. This therapy teaches youth alternative ways to manage interpersonal problems and social situations as well as the consequences of particular actions (Kazdin, 2010). PMT focuses on interactions between parent and child and provides alternative solutions for difficulties in this relationship. See the Resources section later in the chapter in order to obtain more specific information about these treatments.

Helping the Noncompliant Child, the Forehand and McMahon program (Forehand & McMahon, 1981) is an efficacious individual family-based, structured intervention that emphasizes socially appropriate behavior and compliance. A number of studies exist "that demonstrate progress made during the program is maintained" (Fonagy & Kurtz, 2005, p. 118).

Pharmacological Interventions

No one type of medication is usually prescribed for ODD because no particular medication or class of medication has been shown to be beneficial. There is no evidence base for effective use of psychotropic medications to treat ODD (Hoagwood, Burns, Kiser, Ringeisen, & Schoenwald, 2001). This finding highlights the importance of accurate assessment of the child diagnosed with ODD, as there can be co-occurring disorders that might respond to pharmacological treatment (e.g., depression). It is the ethical responsibility of the school social worker or mental health worker to refer the student for psychiatric consultation should any information from the youth's assessment indicate the need for further medical intervention.

Applying Interventions within a Response to Intervention Framework

All of the listed interventions can work effectively within a Response to Intervention (RTI) framework. Conducting a thorough assessment of each child's specific needs is important to determine what interventions might be needed to improve behavioral outcomes. Whether an intervention is offered at a primary, secondary, or tertiary level is determined by the assessment process, and ongoing assessment of each student's response to the intervention is critical. This ensures that the least restrictive behavioral intervention is in place for each student, either in the classroom, in small groups, or individually.

Training provided to teachers and/or parents to improve their abilities to reward prosocial behaviors, increase student compliance with adult requests, and increase skills in giving commands and providing effective consequences are examples of Tier 1 interventions. These interventions are provided to impact classrooms and groups of youth, while these skills are known to decrease disruptive behavior exhibited by children meeting the criteria for ODD as well. Playing games such as the Good Behavior Game or games with mystery motivators are Tier 1 interventions that can be offered in the classroom. If particular students respond less to these interventions or if disruptive behavior continues to escalate, Tier 2 interventions can be implemented. Examples of these types of interventions might include educational skill groups focused on anger control, social skills, stress management, assertiveness, and problem solving. Tier 3 interventions are the most intensive and might include more specialized therapy with a child or adolescent individually or with a parent and child together. School-based mental health professionals might provide these services or might consult with agencies or professionals in the community for referral purposes. Multisystemic therapy is an example of a Tier 3 intervention, as it is a more specialized, intensive therapeutic modality that might support school services while providing intervention and case management to the youth and his or her family outside of the school.

Tools and Practice Examples

Practice Example

A 13-year-old, Latino male student (Rico) was referred to a 27-year-old, Caucasian female social work intern (Polly) because of his school-based acting-out behavior, which included angry outbursts in the classroom and truancy. Rico told Polly that he did not have any problems, and when she asked specifically about why he thought he might have been referred to her, he replied, "I don't know, Miss." Polly established a consistent date and time to see Rico, and she met with him in the same office for several sessions, even though both of these issues were very difficult to achieve in her schedule and in this school setting. His attention span was reported to be short, so Polly started sessions at 30 minutes each.

Polly played cards with Rico and engaged him in discussions about things that he liked, disliked, enjoyed, and did not enjoy (his favorite movies, favorite foods, favorite sports, important people in his life, people he admired, people he did not, and so on). Polly raised questions about this in her supervision, questioning her effectiveness and purpose if this were the extent of her intervention with this young male. If Rico were absent on a day when a session was supposed to occur, Polly would call his home and leave a message and follow up on a subsequent day to see him in the school environment. She would not offer him a full session, but instead, she would notice his absence from their session and express her hope that he would be there for the next one.

Polly challenged Rico to think before he answered and to use different words to express himself, rather than "I don't know." She countered his potential resistance to engaging in the intervention by saying, "This probably won't work, or you might choose not to do it, but it might be interesting to see what happens." Rico eventually began to stop himself from answering with "I don't know" without any prompting, but Polly had to wait for him to do this in his own time frame. There were days that he did not seem interested, most often due to a problem he had in school prior to the session or to a health issue, and Polly did not pressure Rico to perform. Any outside pressure can regress the relationship to an earlier stage or push the child to cope ineffectively, as in previous times.

Polly walked around the school track and played basketball with Rico during some sessions. She worked with Rico's teachers, assisting them to manage their own impatience regarding his change process. Work with teachers is critical for the youth's success, as the youth often experiences negativity from school professionals about the rate of his progress. This allows the teachers to express their frustrations appropriately to the worker, while also gaining wisdom about the youth's progress. Providing support to teachers can infuse energy into their work as well, and this might be demonstrated via more patience with the youth or by employing alternative techniques, such as humor or planned ignoring, to manage behavioral difficulties.

Polly implemented more one-on-one problem-solving skills training. She and Rico practiced the skills and videotaped the role plays, showing all types of responses. Polly brought professional movie clips into her sessions with Rico also and discussed what worked and what did not work for the characters in the movies. At year's end, Rico tolerated 50-minute sessions. Truancy was no longer a problem, and his classroom behavior showed significant improvement.

Resources

The following list offers resources to locate further information as needed about other relevant research.

Social Skills Training Program for Peer-Rejected Boys

Bierman, K. L., Miller, C. M., & Stabb, S. (1987). Improving the social behavior and peer acceptance of rejected boys: Effects of social skill training with instructions and prohibitions. *Journal of Consulting and Clinical Psychology, 55,* 194–200.

Webster-Stratton, C., & Reid, M. (2003). *The incredible years parents, teachers, and children training series: A multifaceted treatment approach for young children with conduct problems.* http://www.incredibleyears.com.

Community-Based Collaboration With School Professionals

Multisystemic Therapy: http://www.mstservices.com. (This evidence-based approach requires interventions outside of school with professionals trained specifically in this area. Schools will often collaborate with this type of treatment as part of a team. This treatment is appropriate for adolescent youth who engage in severe willful misconduct that places them at risk for out-of-home placement.)

Anger Management Curriculum for 8–12-Year-Olds

Larson, J., & Lochman, J. (2002). *Helping schoolchildren cope with anger: A cognitive-behavioral intervention*. New York: Guilford. (The Anger Coping Program, an empirically supported group intervention for 8–12-year-olds with anger and aggression problems, is offered in this manual. This program is supported by research to reduce teacher- and parent-directed aggression; improve on-task behavior in the classroom; and improve participants' verbal assertiveness and compromise skills, social competence, and academic achievement.)

The Parent Management Training (PMT) manual with supporting materials for each session is available for professionals (Kazdin, 2005; www.oup.com/us/pmt).

The Kazdin Method for Parenting the Defiant Child (Kazdin & Rotella, 2008) is another resource that can help parents deal with many problems of young, latency, and teenaged children, and there is also a DVD available (www.alankazdin.com).

Manuals also exist for Problem-Solving Skills Training (PSST). See the following resource: Larson & Lochman, 2002.

Mystery Motivators

Rhode, G., Jenson, W., & Reavis, H. (1993). *The tough kid book: Practical classroom management strategies*. Longmont, CO: Sopris West. (This book offers further information about mystery motivators, mentioned above.)

Classroom Behavior Management

Harris, V. W., & Sherman, J. A. (1973). Use and analysis of the "good behavior game" to reduce disruptive classroom behavior. *Journal of Applied Behavior Analysis, 6,* 405–417. (The good behavior game is a school-based prevention program which has an evidence base for reducing problem behaviors in children.) http://www.interventioncentral.org/index.php/challenging-students/162-school-wide-strategies-for-managing-defiance-non-compliance (This Web site offers several classroom behavioral interventions that might be helpful for classroom behavioral management.)

Hops & Walker (1988) designed programs to decrease disruptive behavior (CLASS) and to reduce aggression with peers (RECESS), based on social learning principles. Some evidence exists that change from the CLASS program in both rural and urban settings is maintained at a 1-year follow-up. Data exists that support the success of RECESS while it is in place, although no evidence exists regarding the maintenance of its positive effects over time.

General Behavioral Management for Difficult Behaviors

Post, B. (2009). *The great behavior breakdown*. Palmyra, VA: Post Institutes & Associates. Retrieved from www.postinstitute.com (This book offers valuable information for people working with traumatized youth with challenging behaviors. The interventions included originate from an attachment-oriented framework.)

Key Points to Remember

Given the prevalence of children and adolescents with oppositional defiant disorder, it is somewhat surprising the limited number of evidence-based treatments documented to be effective with this population. Within a school setting, particular group interventions and parent training modules have been shown to be effective in treating ODD, but presently no pharmacological or individual interventions have shown clinical effectiveness. Advanced brain research and the re-emergence of interest in attachment theory as a result offers promising possibilities for school-based relational interventions. In order for oppositional behavior and emotional upheaval to be managed, the brain must create regulatory functions. Through consistent and responsive interventions, these changes can be promoted in the school environment, especially when school personnel increase their self-awareness and decrease their own reactivity. Students will respond to the calm, consistent, and clear communication from mindful staff members over time.

Practice wisdom gains support from the concept of resiliency, offering that certain relational therapies can be effective in ameliorating the symptoms of ODD in youth, even though current research does not exist which demonstrates evidence-based effectiveness. Clearly, further research is necessary to expand the list of what works with these youth, and it is hoped that this research can focus specifically on the symptoms of ODD, rather than grouping it together with other disorders and, consequently, creating confounds about what really works with ODD youth.

Within the school setting, though, a number of the evidence-based interventions are appropriate for implementation. Groups targeting social skills training, problem solving, assertiveness, and anger management can be offered in the schools, and consultation regarding these issues can be provided to educators by school social workers and mental health workers. Individual relationship building seems relevant in order to model prosocial behaviors as well as build resiliency in the youth. Parent training is another possibility. From a systems perspective, a model of intervention for youth with ODD which targets multiple layers of the system is likely to offer the most chances for youth to gain the skills necessary for optimum functioning within the school environment.

References

Abolt, T., & Thyer, B. A. (2002). Social work assessment of children with oppositional defiant disorder: Reliability and validity of the Child Behavior Checklist. *Social Work in Mental Health, 1*, 73–84.

American Psychiatric Association. (2000). *Diagnostic and statistical manual of mental disorders* (4th ed., text revision). Washington, DC: Author.

American Psychiatric Association. (2010). *DSM-5: The future of psychiatric diagnosis.* Retrieved from the American Psychiatric Association Web site: http://www.dsm5.org

Barker, P. (1999). *Talking cures: An introduction to the psychotherapies for health care professionals.* London: NT Books.

Bierman, K. L., Miller, C. M., & Stabb, S. (1987). Improving the social behavior and peer acceptance of rejected boys: Effects of social skill training with instructions and prohibitions. *Journal of Consulting and Clinical Psychology, 55*, 194–200.

Block, J. (1978). Effects of a rational emotive mental health program on poorly achieving, disrupting high school students. *Journal of Counseling Psychology, 25*, 61–65.

Brinkmeyer, M., & Eyberg, S. M. (2003). Parent–child interaction therapy for oppositional children. In A. E. Kazdin & J. R. Weisz (Eds.), *Evidence-based psychotherapies for children and adolescents* (pp. 204–223). New York: Guilford.

Burns, G., & Patterson, D. (2001). Normative data on the Eyberg Child Behavior Inventory and Sutter-Eyberg Student Behavior Inventory: Parent and teacher rating scales of disruptive behavior problems in children and adolescents. *Child and Family Behavior Therapy, 23*, 15–28.

Coie, J., Lochman, J., Terry, R., & Hyman, C. (1992). Predicting early adolescent disorder from childhood aggression and peer rejection. *Journal of Consulting and Clinical Psychology, 60*, 783–792.

Dodge, K. A., & Price, J. M. (1994). On the relation between social information processing and socially competent behavior in early school-aged children. *Child Development, 65*, 1385–1397.

Eamon, M. K., & Altshuler, S. J. (2004). Can we predict disruptive school behavior? *Children & Schools, 26*, 23–37.

Feindler, E. L., Marriott, S., & Iwata, M. (1984). Group anger-control training for junior high school delinquents. *Cognitive Therapy and Research, 8*, 299–311.

Fisher, P. A., & Fagot, B. I. (1996). Development of consensus about child oppositional behavior: Increased convergence with entry into school. *Journal of Applied Developmental Psychology, 17*, 519–534.

Fonagy, P., & Kurtz, A. (2005). Disturbance of conduct. In P. Fonagy, M. Target, D. Cóttrell, J. Phillips, & Z. Kurtz (Eds.), *What works for whom? A critical review of treatments for children and adolescents* (2nd ed., pp. 106–192). New York, NY: Guilford Press.

Forehand, R. L., & McMahon, R. J. (1981). *Helping the noncompliant child: A clinician's guide to parent training.* New York, New York: Guilford Press.

Freeman, E. M., Franklin, C. G., Fong, R., Shaffer, G. L., and Timberlake, E. M. (Eds.). (1998). *Multisystem skills and interventions in school social work practice.* Washington, DC: NASW Press.

Frey, K. S., Hirschstein, M. K., & Guzzo, B. A. (2000). Second step: Preventing aggression by promoting social competence. *Journal of Emotional and Behavioral Disorders, 8*(2), 102–112.

Garbarino, J. (1999). *Lost boys.* New York: Free Press.

Hamlet, C., Axelrod, S., & Kuerschner, S. (1984). Eye contact as an antecedent to compliant behavior. *Journal of Applied Behavior Analysis, 17*, 553–557.

Harris, V.W., & Sherman, J. A. (1973). Use and analysis of the "good behavior game" to reduce disruptive classroom behavior. *Journal of Applied Behavior Analysis, 6*, 405–417.

Hemphill, S., & Littlefield, L. (2001). Evaluation of a community-based group therapy program for children with behavior problems and their parents. *Behaviour Research and Therapy, 39*, 823–841.

Hoagwood, K., Burns, B., Kiser, L., Ringeisen, H., & Schoenwald, S. (2001). Evidence-based practice in child and adolescent mental health services. *Psychiatric Services, 52*(9), 1179–1189.

Hops, H., & Walker, H. M. (1988). *CLASS: Contingencies for learning academic and social skills.* Seattle, WA: Educational Achievement Systems.

Huey, W. C., & Rank, R. C. (1984). Effects of counselor-and peer-led group assertive training on black adolescent aggression. *Journal of Counseling Psychology, 31*(1), 95–98.

Kazdin, A. E. (1997). Practitioner review: Psychosocial treatments for conduct disorder in children. *Journal of Child Psychology and Psychiatry, 38*, 161–178.

Kazdin, A. E. (2005). *Parent management training: Treatment for oppositional, aggressive, and antisocial behavior in children and adolescents*. New York, NY: Oxford University Press.

Kazdin, A. E. (2010). Problem-solving skills training and parent management training for oppositional defiant disorder and conduct disorder. In J. R. Weisz & A. E. Kazdin (Eds.), *Evidence-based psychotherapies for children and adolescents* (2nd ed., pp. 211–226). New York, NY: Guilford Press.

Kazdin, A. E., & Rotella, C. (2008). *The Kazdin method for parenting the defiant child: With no pills, no therapy, no contest of wills*. Boston, MA: Houghton Mifflin.

Kehle, T. J., Madaus, M. R., Baratta, V. S., & Bray, M. A. (1998). Employing self-modeling with children with selective mutism. *Journal of School Psychology, 36*, 247–260.

Kupersmidt, J. B., & Coie, J. D. (1990). Preadolescent peer status, aggression, and school adjustment as predictors of externalizing problems in adolescence. *Child Development, 61*, 1350–1362.

Kupersmidt, J. B., & Patterson, C. J. (1991). Childhood peer rejection, aggression, withdrawal, and perceived competence as predictors of self-reported behavior problems in preadolescence. *Journal of Abnormal Child Psychology, 19*, 427–503.

Lochman, J., Coie, J., Underwood, M., & Terry, R. (1993). Effectiveness of a social relations intervention program for aggressive and nonaggressive, rejected children. *Journal of Consulting and Clinical Psychology, 61*, 1053–1058.

Loeber, R. (1990). Development and risk factors of juvenile antisocial behavior and delinquency. *Clinical Psychology Review, 10*, 1–42.

Mader, C. (2000). Child-centered play therapy with disruptive school students. In H. G. Kaduson & C. E. Schaffer (Eds.), *Short-term play therapy for children* (pp. 53–68). New York: Guilford.

Markward, M. J., & Bride, B. E. (2001). Oppositional defiant disorder and the need for family-centered practice in schools. *Children & Schools, 23*(2), 73–83.

McKinney, C., & Renk, K. (2007). Emerging research and theory in the etiology of oppositional defiant disorder: Current concerns and future directions. *International Journal of Behavioral Consultation and Therapy, 3*(3), 349–371.

Meichenbaum, D. H. (1977). *Cognitive-behavior modification: An integrative approach*. New York: Plenum.

Musser, E. H., Bray, M. A., Kehle, T. J., & Jenson, W. R. (2001). Reducing disruptive behaviors in students with serious emotional disturbance. *School Psychology Review, 30*, 294–305.

O'Leary, K. D., Kaufman, K. F., Kass, R., & Drabman, R. (1970). The effects of loud and soft reprimands on the behavior of disruptive students. *Exceptional Children, 37*(2), 145–155.

Osenton, T., & Chang, J. (1999). Solution-oriented classroom management: Application with young children. *Journal of Systemic Therapies, 18*(2), 65–76.

Post, B. B. (2009). *The great behavior breakdown*. Palmyra, VA: Post Institutes & Associates.

Rhode, G., Jenson, W. R., & Reavis, H. K. (1993). *The tough kid book: Practical classroom management strategies*. Longmont, CO: Sopris West.

Rosenberg, M. S. (1986). Maximizing the effectiveness of structured classroom management programs: Implementing rule-review procedures with disruptive and distractible students. *Behavioral Disorders, 11*, 239–248.

Schore, A. (2001). Effects of a secure attachment relationship on right brain development, affect regulation, and infant mental health. *Infant Mental Health Journal, 22*, 7–66.

Sprague, A., & Thyer, B. A. (2002). Psychosocial treatment of oppositional defiant disorder: A review of empirical outcome studies. *Social Work in Mental Health, 1*, 63–72.

Van Houten, R., Nau, P., MacKenzie-Keating, S., Sameoto, D., & Colavecchia, B. (1982). An analysis of some variables influencing the effectiveness of reprimands. *Journal of Applied Behavior Analysis, 15*, 65–83.

Zisser, A., & Eyberg, S. M. (2010). Parent-child interaction therapy and the treatment of disruptive behavior disorders. In J. R. Weisz & A. E. Kazdin (Eds.), *Evidence-based psychotherapies for children and adolescents* (2nd ed., pp. 179–193). New York, NY: Guilford Press.

CHAPTER 8

Effective Interventions for Students with Separation Anxiety Disorder

Hayley Sacks ▪ Jonathan S. Comer ▪ Donna B. Pincus ▪ Marilyn Camacho ▪ Lisa Hunter-Romanelli

Getting Started

Children experiencing separation anxiety display signs of distress when separated from their parents or primary caregivers. Separation anxiety is a normal phase of development typically evident between 10 and 18 months, and symptoms tend to dissipate by the time the child reaches the age of 2 or 3 years (Carruth, 2000). Separation anxiety becomes a disorder when "the expected developmental levels are exceeded, resulting in significant distress and impairment at home, school, and in social contexts" (Albano & Kendall, 2002, p. 130). The detrimental effects of separation anxiety disorder (SAD) are particularly noticeable in schools given that they are the setting where children are separated from their parents for the longest period of time. As such, school-based practitioners are in the unique position to identify and treat SAD. Their access to students, parents, and school staff facilitates the identification of the disorder and the implementation of appropriate interventions. In this chapter, we will briefly review the diagnostic criteria and epidemiology of SAD, describe the Coping Cat program (Kendall & Hedtke, 2006), the intervention of choice for this disorder, and discuss how it can be implemented in a school setting. We also briefly present recent work on the treatment of early-onset SAD (i.e., < age 7).

What We Know

Diagnosis and Prevalence of Separation Anxiety Disorder (SAD)

According to the American Psychiatric Association's Diagnostic and Statistical Manual of Mental *Disorders (DSM-IV-TR), separation* anxiety disorder in children and young adolescents is marked by "developmentally inappropriate and excessive anxiety concerning separation from the home or from those to whom the person is attached" (American Psychiatric Association, 2000, p. 125). The DSM-IV-TR diagnostic criteria for SAD are listed in Table 8.1.

The prevalence rate for SAD is 4% (American Psychiatric Association, 2000). Children with SAD typically range in age from 8 to 12 years old (Compton et al., 2000) with age of onset being 9 years old in clinical samples (Tonge, 1994). SAD is more common in children from lower socioeconomic backgrounds (Saavedra & Silverman, 2002) and is more prevalent in girls than boys (Last, Hersen, Kazdin, Finkelstein, & Strauss, 1987), although there is increasing recognition that the disorder can affect adults as well. In fact, roughly one-third of child SAD cases persist into adulthood (Shear et al., 2006). Overall, there is no evidence that SAD is more prevalent in any particular culture (Albano & Kendall, 2002).

Children with SAD often have other psychiatric disorders as well. Disorders that most commonly occur with SAD include generalized anxiety disorder (GAD) and social phobia (SoP) (Velting, Setzer, & Albano, 2004). There is also evidence of comorbidity between SAD and depression, obsessive-compulsive disorder, and gender identity disorder (Silverman & Dick-Niederhauser, 2004).

What Does SAD Look Like?

There are some developmental variations in the presentation of SAD among children. Younger children tend to report more symptoms than their older counterparts (Francis, Last, & Strauss,

Table 8.1 DSM-IV-TR Diagnostic Criteria for Separation Anxiety Disorder

Criterion A: Developmentally inappropriate and excessive anxiety concerning separation from home or from those to whom the individual is attached, as shown by at least three of the following:

- Recurrent excessive distress when separation from home or major attachment figures occurs or is anticipated
- Persistent and excessive worry about losing, or about possible harm befalling, major attachment figures
- Persistent and excessive worry that an untoward event will lead to separation from a major attachment figure
- Persistent reluctance or refusal to go to school or elsewhere because of fear of separation
- Persistently and excessively fearful or reluctant to be alone or without major attachment figures at home or without significant adults in other settings
- Persistent reluctance or refusal to go to sleep without being near a major attachment figure or to sleep away from home
- Repeated nightmares involving the theme of separation
- Repeated complaints of physical symptoms (such as headaches, stomachaches, nausea, or vomiting) when separation from major attachment figures occurs or is anticipated

Criterion B: Duration of disturbance is at least 4 weeks

Criterion C: Age of onset is before 18 years (specify if early onset occurs before age 6 years)

Criterion D: Disturbance causes clinically significant distress or impairment in social, academic (occupational), or other important areas of functioning

Criterion E: Disturbance does not occur exclusively during the course of a pervasive developmental disorder, or other psychotic disorder and, in adolescents, is not better accounted for by panic disorder with agoraphobia

Source: Reprinted with permission from the Diagnostic and Statistical Manual of Mental Disorders, Copyright 2000, American Psychiatric Association.

1987). Additionally, the presentation of SAD in younger children has been described as "amorphous" while older children present more explicit concerns relating to separation (Perwien & Berstein, 2004).

Young children may express SAD by closely shadowing their parents throughout the day and checking on their whereabouts for fear that they or their parents may become harmed (Fischer, Himle, & Thyer, 1999). In a school-aged child, symptoms associated with school refusal are most evident (Fischer et al., 1999). Some of these symptoms may include somatic complaints accompanied by frequent visits to the school nurse (Walkup & Ginsburg, 2002), tantrums, terror outbursts, attempts to leave the school to go home (Fischer et al., 1999), and high rates of school absence (Walkup & Ginsburg, 2002). It is important to note that although school refusal is a common symptom of SAD, it is not unique to the disorder and can be attributed to other disorders, such as specific phobia, social phobia, mood disorder, disruptive behavior disorder, or family conflict (Silverman & Dick-Niederhauser, 2004). Additional symptoms associated with SAD among school-aged children include frequent nightmares depicting threats to or separation from parents (Francis et al., 1987), refusal to participate in social activities that involve separation from parents, and a tendency to sleep with parents (Fischer et al., 1999).

Importance of Treating SAD in Schools

School personnel may not view SAD as a problem in need of immediate attention since externalizing disorders are so much more disruptive. This lack of attention may contribute to the under-recognition of SAD, leaving children suffering from the disorder significantly impaired and never referred for treatment. Left untreated, SAD may contribute to limited academic achievement, substance abuse, development of additional psychiatric disorders, and minimal social supports (Velting et al., 2004). Additionally, there may be a relationship between SAD in childhood and panic disorder in adulthood (Gittelman & Klein, 1984), although the specificity of this relationship continues to generate debate

(Aschenbrand et al., 2003). Given these possibilities, it is imperative that school staff, particularly teachers, learn how to identify children with SAD. School-based practitioners can provide teachers with informational sessions on how to identify SAD behaviors and guidance on when and how to make referrals to the school-based mental health clinic.

What We Can Do

Assessing Separation Anxiety Disorder

Clinical judgment is necessary to distinguish "developmentally appropriate levels of separation anxiety from the clinically significant concerns about separation seen in SAD" (American Psychiatric Association, 2000, p. 124). Diagnostic interviews have been developed to augment clinical judgment by providing systematic means of establishing the primary diagnosis and aid in the differential diagnosis of comorbid disorders (Langley, Bergman, & Piacentini, 2002). This is especially helpful in diagnosing anxiety disorders given the high incidence of comorbidity associated with these disorders. Additionally, the use of self-report scales for anxiety disorders has proven to be useful in collecting information on patients' symptomology through multiple informants (Albano, 2003). These assessment measures may be administered in the beginning, middle, and termination phases of treatment in order to track changes in symptoms.

Clinical Interviews

There are two types of clinical interviews—structured and unstructured—that can be used to assess for anxiety disorders in children. The structured interview can be used flexibly and by clinicians with "limited clinical judgment" (Albano, 2003). Semistructured interviews "provide guidelines for adapting inquiries to the age or developmental level of the child, and also allow for some flexibility in probing for clarification and further information" (Albano, 2003, p. 134). Although there are no diagnostic interviews designed exclusively to assess SAD, there are several interviews with a SAD module. Some examples of clinical interviews with specific subscales for assessing SAD include the Anxiety Disorders Interview Schedule for DSM-IV (ADIS; Silverman & Albano, 1996), the Diagnostic Interview Schedule for Children (DISC-IV; Shaffer, Fisher, Lucas, Dulcan, & Schwab-Stone, 2000), the Diagnostic Interview for Children and Adolescents (DICA; Reich, 2000), the Child and Adolescent Psychiatric Assessment (CAPA; Angold & Costello, 2000), and the Children's Interview for Psychiatric Symptoms (ChIPS; Weller, Weller, Fristad, Rooney, & Schecter, 2000). Table 8.2 provides brief descriptions of these instruments.

Although clinical interviews such as those listed in Table 8.2 are useful tools for assessing SAD, they are most frequently used in research settings, can be time consuming to administer (2–3 hours), and may require clinician training. As such, they may not be practical for use in a school setting. The school-based practitioner, however, may find it useful to review these interviews to learn how to ask questions about SAD. Table 8.3 provides some sample questions that school-based clinicians can use when assessing for SAD.

Self-Report Measures

A number of self-report anxiety rating scales can be completed by children, as well as by parents. Although there is no established self-report measure for SAD, there are several assessment measures with items relevant to SAD that can be used to assess the disorder. These include the Multidimensional Anxiety Scale for Children (MASC; March, Parker, Sullivan, Stallings, & Conners, 1997), Screen for Child Anxiety Related Emotional Disorders (SCARED; Birmaher et al., 1997), and Spence Children's Anxiety Scale (SCAS; Spence, 1997). Table 8.4 describes the above-mentioned self-report measures. Additionally, the School Refusal Assessment Scale (SRAS; Kearney & Silverman, 1993) may be particularly useful for SAD in order to establish whether symptoms of school refusal are indeed a feature of SAD and not other disorders, such as school phobia. These measures are particularly useful in school settings given that they require little time to administer (10–15 minutes), do not require special equipment, and are of minimal cost (James, Reynolds, & Dunbar, 1994).

Teacher Reports

In addition to parents, teachers are also valuable informants in the assessment of SAD symptoms.

Table 8.2 Clinical Interviews With Separation Anxiety Disorder Subscales

		Characteristic Features of Interview			
Clinical Interview	*Age*	*Informant*	*Format*	*Administration*	*Source*
Diagnostic Interview Schedule for Children (DISC-IV; Shaffer et al., 2000)	6–17	Child & Parent	Highly Structured	90–120 minutes	DISC Development Group Division of Child Psychiatry 1051 Riverside Drive, Box 78 New York, NY 10032
Diagnostic Interview for Children and Adolescents (DICA; Reich, 2000)	6–17	Child, Parent	Structured & Semi-structured	60 minutes	Wendy Reich, PhD Division of Child Psychiatry Washington Univertsity 660 S. Euclid, Box 8134 St. Louis, MO 63110 314–286–2263 Wendyr@twins.wustl.edu
Child and Adolescent Psychiatric Assessment (CAPA;Angold & Costello, 2000)	9–17	Child & Parent	Structured	60–150 minutes	Adrian Angold, MD Department of Psychiatry & Behavioral Sciences Duke University Center, Box 3454 Durham, NC 277710 919–687–4686 Adrian.angold@duke.edu
Preschool Age Psychiatric Assessment (PAPA; Egger & Angold, 2004)	2–5	Parent	Structured	approx. 120 minutes	Same as CAPA (Adrian Angold)
Anxiety Disorders Interview Schedule for DSM-IV (ADIS; Silverman & Albano, 1996)	6–17	Child & Parent	Semi-structured	60 minutes	Wendy Silverman, PhD Department of Psychology Florida International University University Park Miami, FL 33199 305–348–2064 Wendy.Silverman@fiu.edu
Children's Interview for Psychiatric Symptoms (ChIPS;Weller et al., 2000)	6–18	Child & Parent	Highly Structured	40 minutes	American Psychiatric Publishing, Inc. 800–368–5777 1000 Wilson Boulevard Suite 1825 Arlington,VA 22209 http://www.appi.org appi@psych.org

Table 8.3 Sample Questions for Assessing Separation Anxiety Disorder in School-Aged Children*

- Are there times when you don't want to be in places without your mother like school or at a relative's house?
- Sometimes you may know ahead of time if you are going to a place without your mother. Do you ever start feeling sick when thinking about not being with your mother?
- Do you ever feel sick (e.g., headaches or stomachaches) when you are someplace without your mother?
- Do you worry that something bad will happen to your mother? What do you worry may happen to her?
- Has your mother ever been very sick, or hurt by someone, or been in a bad situation, like a car accident or robbery?
- Does your mother complain that you follow her around too much?
- Does your mother get upset with you when you worry about being away from her?
- Do you know anyone in your family or any of your friends who is very ill?
- Do you remember a time that you were not with your mother for a long time? When was that time and why were you not with her?
- At bedtime, do you sleep by yourself or with your mother?
- Does your mother ever ask you to sleep by yourself? How often does she ask you to sleep on your own?
- Do you ever have nightmares about someone in your family getting sick, or that you get lost, or even about something happening that stops you from being with your family? How often do you have these dreams?
- Do you like sleeping over at a friend's or relative's home? How did you feel the last time you slept over at someone's home?
- Do you have trouble getting to school in the morning?
- How often are you absent from school?
- How often do you visit the school nurse's office?
- Do you often want to leave school during the day and go home to be with your mother?
- Do you think about your mother often during the day while you are in school?
- Does thinking about your mother make it difficult for you to concentrate on your schoolwork?
- When you are at home, do you get dressed or shower by yourself?
- When you are at home without your mother, who takes care of you? Do you like spending time with him or her when your mother is away?

* The term "mother" should be replaced with "father" or "caregiver" as indicated.

Teachers are often the first to witness SAD, particularly when school refusal is one of the more prominent features. They can report on the frequency of a child's absences, presentation of symptoms, and degree to which symptoms are manifested. Although there are currently no SAD-specific teacher report measures, the Teacher Report Form (TRF; Achenbach, 1991) has been recommended when working with SAD (Perwien & Berstein, 2004).

Interventions

Once SAD has been assessed and diagnosed, the school-based practitioner has sufficient information to decide what intervention will best meet the child's needs. When selecting a treatment, practitioners should consider life stressors (e.g., death in family), time constraints (e.g., school setting), level of family involvement, and child's level of functioning. In the following section, we will present a cognitive-behavioral approach for treating SAD and its applicability in the school setting.

The Coping Cat Program: A Cognitive-Behavioral Approach for Treating SAD (Ages 7–17)

Cognitive-behavioral therapy (CBT) for the treatment of anxiety involves both working with the child's external environment through the use of

Table 8.4 Self-Report Measures With Separation Anxiety Disorder Subscales

	Characteristic Features of Interview				
Interview	*Age*	*Informant*	*Length*	*Assessment*	*Source*
Multidimensional Anxiety Scale for Children (MASC; March et al., 1997)	8–19	Child	39 items	Four subscales: physical anxiety; harm avoidance; social anxiety; and separation anxiety	John S. March, MD Duke University Medical Center Department of Psychiatry, Box 3527 Durham, NC 27710 919–416–2404 jsmarch@acpub.duke.edu
Screen for Anxiety and Related Emotional Disorders (SCARED; Birmaher et al., 1997)	8–18	Child & Parent	41 items	Five subscales: separation anxiety; school phobia; panic/somatic symptoms, generalized anxiety; social phobia	Boris Birmaher, MD Western Psychiatric Institute & Clinic Department of Child Psychology 3811 O'Hara Street Pittsburgh, PA 15213 412–246–5788 birmaherb@upmc.edu
Spence Children's Anxiety Scale (SCAS; Spence, 1997)	8–12	Child	44 items	Six scales: separation anxiety; social phobia; obsessive-compulsive disorder; panic/agoraphobia; generalized anxiety	Susan H. Spence, PhD Griffith University Nathan, QLD 4111, Australia (07) 373 55447 s.spence@griffith.edu.au
Preschool Anxiety Scale (PAS; Spence & Rapee, 1999)	3–5	Parent	28 items	Six subscales: generalized anxiety; social anxiety; obsessive-compulsive disorder; physical injury fears; separation anxiety	Susan H. Spence, PhD Griffith University Nathan, QLD 4111, Australia (07) 373 55447 s.spence@griffith.edu.au

behavioral techniques, such as practice and exposure tasks, and working with the child's internal environment through the mastery of cognitive techniques, such as adaptive self-talk and problem solving (Kendall, 2005).

Although there have been no randomized clinical trials exclusively for SAD (Silverman & Dick-Niederhauser, 2004), the efficacy of using cognitive-behavioral methods for the treatment of SAD has been well documented in case studies (Hagopian & Slifer, 1993; Ollendick, Hagopian, & Huntzinger, 1991; Thyer & Sowers-Hoag, 1988). In the landmark multisite Child and Adolescent Anxiety Multimodal Study (CAMS), a combination of cognitive-behavioral therapy and antidepressant medication was shown to be most effective—relative to either intervention alone or pill placebo—in treating childhood SAD and other childhood anxiety disorders (Walkup et al., 2008). As such, medication is not recommended as a "front-line intervention" but rather should be used with patients who experience severe SAD symptoms (Silverman & Dick-Niederhauser, 2004, p. 179), or with patients who have not responded to an adequate trial of cognitive-behavioral therapy.

The Coping Cat treatment program developed by Kendall and colleagues (1990) is the most evaluated treatment specifically designed to treat children with SAD in addition to related anxiety disorders (Kendall, Aschenbrand, & Hudson, 2003). Coping Cat is an individual, short-term, manualized treatment for children and young adolescents ranging in age from 7 to 17 years old with a principal diagnosis of SAD, GAD, or SoP (Kendall et al., 1994.The program uses a combination of behavioral strategies to achieve the following treatment goals (Kendall & Southam-Gerow, 1995):

- Identifying anxious feelings and the body's response to the anxiety
- Understanding the role that self-talk plays in worsening the anxiety
- Increasing the capability to deal with anxiety by utilizing problem-solving and coping techniques
- Evaluating one's use of coping strategies and provision of appropriate rewards

Empirical Support for Coping Cat

The efficacy of the Coping Cat program has been well documented in the literature (Kendall, 1994; Kendall et al., 1997; Kendall & Southam-Gerow, 1996). It is identified as the "most widely disseminated CBT protocol for childhood anxiety" (Velting et al., 2004, p. 48) and has been used with success in the United States (Kendall, 1994), Australia (Barrett, Dadds, & Rapee, 1996), and Canada (Mendlowitz et al., 1999). Cognitive-behavioral therapy for child anxiety is highly adaptable and has proven effective when used in a group format (Barrett, 1998; Cobham et al., 1998; Flannery-Schroeder & Kendall, 2000; Silverman et al., 1999) and in conjunction with family anxiety management (Barrett et al., 1996). Additionally, the Coping Cat program is efficacious across different ethnic groups and genders (Treadwell, Flannery-Schroeder, & Kendall, 1995).

Implementing the Coping Cat Program

Detailed guidelines for implementing the Coping Cat program are found in *Cognitive-Behavioral Therapy for Anxious Children: Therapist Manual* (Kendall, 2000). Information about purchasing this manual is available at www.WorkbookPublishing.com. In addition to the *Therapist Manual, a Coping Cat Workbook* (Kendall, 1992) is available for children to use throughout treatment. The workbook facilitates the implementation of the treatment manual by providing child-friendly tasks that help the child to understand and apply treatment concepts more easily. The accompanying notebook allows the child to record homework assignments (Show-That-I-Can tasks) that reinforce strategies learned during the session. In the next section we will describe the Coping Cat program for anxious youth ages 7–13. A version for older adolescents also exists: the C.A.T. program (Kendall, Choudhury, Hudson, & Webb, 2002a, 2002b).

Training and Supervision

Coping Cat requires proper training and supervision for successful program implementation. Although there is no set protocol for training clinicians in the use of Coping Cat, training in a manualized treatment generally involves introduction to the manual, reading and learning the manual through seminars and/or workshops, and group or individual supervision (Miller & Binder, 2002). Computer-based training in the administration of the Coping Cat, including video clips of various therapy sessions, is also available (Kendall & Khanna, 2008). Supervision addresses the extent to which session goals were met by the clinician and the degree to which the treatment meets individual patient needs while maintaining the integrity of the protocol (Kendall & Southam-Gerow, 1995). As mentioned previously, this chapter will provide an overview of the Coping Cat program and offer specific suggestions for using it in a school setting for the treatment of SAD. This chapter is not meant to replace the treatment manual or appropriate training and supervision from a clinician knowledgeable in the Coping Cat program. It is highly recommended that school-based practitioners interested in using the Coping Cat program with their clients read the manual and receive proper supervision before doing so.

Flexibility with the Manual

Research indicates that flexible application of the Coping Cat manual does not lead to poor treatment outcomes (Kendall & Chu, 2000). It is likely that school-based practitioners will have to make modifications to the manual in order to use it effectively in a school setting. For example, practitioners may need to cover less material in a given session in order to fit sessions into a school schedule. This type of flexibility is acceptable and encouraged.

Computer-Assisted Coping Cat

New technologies may offer an important alternative to traditional anxiety treatment formats, overcoming systematic barriers to care and potentially reaching a broader population of affected youth. Building on the empirical support for the Coping Cat program, researchers have worked to establish cost-effective and transportable adaptations through the use of computer-assisted treatments. Camp Cope-A-Lot, based on the Coping Cat treatment, is a computer-assisted 12-week program comprising 6 weeks of independent "levels" (sessions) and 6 weeks of sessions with the therapist to assist in exposures (Kendall et al., 2011). The program uses a diversity of characters and animation to stimulate the child's interest, and the computer's standardization makes it easy for minimally trained therapists to administer. The Camp Cope-A-Lot format has been found to produce comparable gains relative to individual cognitive-behavioral therapy in reducing symptoms of child anxiety, and has been shown to be more effective than an education, support, and attention control intervention (Khanna & Kendall, 2010).

Role of the Family in Implementation

Family involvement is essential when implementing the Coping Cat program. It is important that the family be involved in the assessment, planning, and execution of treatment goals. This is especially the case for children with SAD given that their fears are directly related to separation from their parents. Parents are involved during the assessment phase of treatment by providing valuable information on the manifestation of symptoms and history through verbal reports and completion of parent assessment scales. In some cases, the assessment phase may be the first interaction with the family and serves as an opportunity to establish rapport with the family (Kendall & Gosch, 1994). Parent sessions are integrated into the course of treatment in order to provide additional opportunities for open dialog between therapist and family, to allow therapists to get feedback from parents and track the progress of treatment, and to coach parents on how to help their child cope with anxiety (Kendall & Gosch, 1994). It has been suggested that CBT that includes the parent(s) as a co-client can be more efficacious than individual child CBT, but only when the child's parents also struggle with anxiety (Barmish & Kendall, 2005). For such cases, including anxious parents in treatment allows affected parents to apply skills to manage their own anxiety and to limit inadvertent reinforcement of their child's avoidance behavior.

Role of Teachers in Implementation

Not only can teachers play an active role in the identification of SAD behaviors, they can also provide valuable information on the course of SAD symptoms and aid in the implementation of treatment. Given their everyday contact with the child, they are highly likely to notice fluctuations in behavior throughout treatment and should be encouraged to share these observations with the school-based practitioner. Additionally, teachers can facilitate treatment by participating in exposure exercises when appropriate, monitoring a child's visits to the school-based medical clinic in response to somatic symptoms associated with SAD, limiting these visits, and restricting the child's contact with parents throughout the school day (Perwien & Berstein, 2004).

The Coping Cat Program: Sequence and Content of Child Sessions

The main goal of the Coping Cat program is to teach children and young adolescents how to "recognize signs of unwanted anxious arousal and to let these signs serve as cues for the use of the strategies the child has learned" (Kendall et al., 2003, p. 84). The treatment involves 14–18 sessions completed over the course of 12–16 weeks. However, the program may need to be adapted to a shorter number of sessions in order to fit into the academic calendar. Additionally, the length of each session may need to be shortened to 40–45 minutes in order to better fit the scheduling demands of school settings.

Scheduling treatment sessions during school hours may prove to be challenging. Teachers may be reluctant to allow the child to leave the classroom to meet with the therapist during class time. As such, it is recommended that sessions be scheduled flexibly around school periods that involve elective classes (e.g., gym, music) or any free periods (e.g., study hall). It also may be difficult to schedule parent sessions during school hours. In some cases, it may be necessary for school practitioners to involve parents in treatment through telephone rather than face-to-face sessions.

Treatment includes a training phase and a practice phase. During the training phase (sessions 1–8), the child learns different techniques to cope with anxiety-provoking situations. In the practice phase, the child begins to practice learned coping techniques within the session or in vivo (sessions 9–18) (Kendall, 2000a). Show-That-I-Can (STIC) homework tasks are introduced during each session. STIC tasks give the child an opportunity to recap what is learned in the session and apply it in the form of an at-home assignment. Each session begins with a review of the assignment and positive reinforcement from the therapist for completed tasks. The following section summarizes the Coping Cat sessions while highlighting the key tasks for each. The session summaries are not meant to replace the manual but to introduce the session content to school-based practitioners.

The Coping Cat Training Phase (Sessions 1–8)

During the training phase, ideas and tasks are introduced to the child in order from simplest to more complex. The segment begins with the child's awareness of how the body reacts to anxious situations and learning to use these reactions as internal cues that anxiety is present. These concepts are presented in a child-friendly four-step plan with the acronym FEAR (**F**eeling frightened? **E**xpecting bad things to happen? **A**ttitudes and actions that will help? **R**esults and rewards?).

Session 1: Program Orientation

The training phase begins with the therapist establishing rapport with the child. The therapist assumes the role of a "coach" as she works together with the child throughout the Coping Cat program. In this first session, the therapist provides the child with an overview of what treatment entails while at the same time collecting information about what situations make the child anxious. Together, the therapist and child identify those situations that trigger the child's anxious reactions (e.g., when child is dropped off at school; when parent goes to bed and leaves child alone in bedroom; when parent goes away on vacation). Treatment goals are introduced as well as the utility of the *Coping Cat Workbook* and *Coping Cat Notebook* in meeting these goals.

Session 2: Identifying Anxious Feelings

The second session focuses on the link between anxious feelings and how different feelings manifest themselves in physical expressions. One of the goals of this session is to normalize the experience of fears and explain that the program is to help cope with these feelings. The therapist models having experienced anxiety-provoking situations and overcoming them. Additionally, role play ("feelings charades") is used to facilitate the child's understanding that different feelings have different physical expressions. A "feelings dictionary" is then created to help the child identify the associated feelings.

As the child identifies the somatic feelings he experiences when feeling anxious, he begins to construct a fear hierarchy that ranks these feelings from least to most anxiety provoking. The fear hierarchy is developed over time beginning with the identification of low anxiety-provoking situations during the first sessions and then medium and high anxiety-provoking situations in subsequent sessions. For the SAD child, a low-anxiety situation may involve the mother cooking in the kitchen while the child is watching television in the living room. A medium anxiety-provoking situation may be staying home with a babysitter for a few hours while a high-anxiety situation may involve the mother leaving the home for business travel.

In the case of the school refuser, it is important to assess whether refusal is due to a phobia or to separation. Other low-stress situations that are not necessarily related to school or separation from parents are explored. Showing empathy is particularly important at this stage, given that children with SAD often experience a lot of anger from parents and teachers about missing school. Specific strategies, like making a "survival pack" (e.g., stickers, helpful positive thoughts, or coping strategies that can be brought to school), are implemented to remind the child of the learned coping strategies. Additionally, an in-school reward, such as making contact with a favorite teacher or counselor, is recommended.

Session 3: Recognizing Somatic Responses to Anxiety

Here, the child learns about the different somatic responses that are felt when in anxiety-provoking situations and how these responses serve as internal cues that anxiety is present. During this session, the first step of the coping plan—"F" (**F**eeling **F**rightened?)—is introduced. The therapist and child review specific somatic reactions to anxiety (e.g., stomach pains, nausea, headaches) and the differences between low and high anxiety. Imagery, modeling, and role-play strategies are used to help the child verbalize somatic feelings during an identified low-anxiety situation. Although the therapist will often take the lead in initiating these exercises, the child is encouraged to "tag along" by adding his feelings to the role play. Throughout the session, the child practices using his somatic responses as cues with higher anxiety situations (via modeling and role-play exercises). The coping concept of "freeze frame" is introduced to allow the child to stop the anxiety-provoking situation, take a deep breath, and re-group.

Parent Session 1: Engaging the Parent

The primary purpose of the first parent session is to encourage parental cooperation in treatment. During this session, the therapist provides the parent with information about the treatment and discusses the child's progress in treatment. The parent is encouraged to ask questions regarding the treatment and to provide additional information about the child's anxiety (i.e., identify troublesome situations and somatic/cognitive reactions).

Parents often need to be reminded that the beginning sessions are only training and that reductions in symptoms will not be seen until later when the skills learned during the training are applied and practiced. During the first parent session, the therapist should also discuss with parents the active role they will be required to take in treatment (e.g., practice the relaxation techniques to be learned in session 4 at home with their child, help their child with STIC tasks).

When working with SAD children who refuse to go to school, it is important to assess stressors in the home or community that may potentially interfere with the course of treatment. The therapist should explore whether the parent is facilitating the behavior through their fears or inability to cope with disruptive behaviors (e.g., tantrums, crying). It is also important to address parental concerns and to provide strategies the parents can use to cope with their child's illness. Also, parents should be strongly encouraged to reward any attempts by the child to go to school as a means of reinforcing the behavior.

Session 4: Relaxation Training

During the fourth session, the therapist teaches the child relaxation techniques that can be used to alleviate symptoms of anxiety. Here, the child identifies the connection between anxiety and muscle tension. The therapist introduces the concept of relaxation by differentiating how the body feels when relaxed versus tense (e.g., have child lift shoulders as high as possible and then release) and by introducing relaxation procedures, such as deep breathing, visualization, and deep muscle tension and relaxation. (This exercise takes approximately 15 minutes.) Together, the therapist and child tape-record a relaxation script and practice using relaxation, coping modeling, and role playing in anxious situations.

Session 5: Identifying Anxious Self-Talk

As the child becomes aware of his bodily responses, he is also taught to become aware of his thoughts during anxiety-provoking situations. In the fifth session, the child begins to identify his self-talk during anxiety-provoking situations with the goal of reducing anxiety-provoking self-talk and using more coping self-talk. Here, the "E" step (**E**xpecting bad things to happen?) is introduced to help the child identify thoughts associated with anxiety and the differences between anxious thoughts and coping thoughts. The child can use cartoon bubbles to identify thoughts that reduce stress and thoughts that might induce stress (see workbook). Through modeling and role play, the child practices coping self-talk, detecting possible thinking traps, and coping in more anxiety-provoking situations.

Session 6: Identifying Coping Thoughts and Actions

During this session, the child is taught how to cope in an anxiety-provoking situation. The therapist introduces the "**A**" step (**A**ttitudes and Actions that will help?). In this sixth session, problem solving is introduced and an action plan is developed to help the child cope in anxious situations. Both the therapist and the child practice problem solving with low- and moderate-stress situations and then practice with increasingly higher-anxiety situations.

Session 7: Self-Evaluation and Rewards

In the seventh session, self-rating and rewards are introduced as the final step ("R": *R*esults and *R*ewards) of the coping plan. Here, the child learns how to evaluate his own work and reward successes. The child uses a "feelings barometer" to rate his performance and is encouraged to practice self-rating and -rewarding in stressful situations (e.g., how well did I handle the situation?).

Session 8: FEAR Plan Review

By the eighth session, the child has already learned the main anxiety coping skills covered in the Coping Cat program. To help facilitate recall of these strategies, they are conceptualized in a child-friendly four-step plan called the FEAR plan. During this session, the child creates a FEAR plan poster to illustrate the strategies learned. Additionally, a wallet-sized FEAR card is created for the child to help remember the strategies learned and to use as an anchor during anxiety-provoking situations. The FEAR plan is practiced (via modeling/role play) during the session beginning with nonstressful situations and continuing with increasingly anxious situations.

The Coping Cat Practice Phase (Sessions 9–16)

The second half of treatment is the practice phase. During this phase, the child applies the skills learned during the training phase to situations that elicit anxiety. The child is exposed to anxiety-provoking situations gradually, moving along a continuum from low-grade anxiety to higher grades of anxiety. The practice phase of treatment begins with a parent session.

Parent Session 2: Introduction to Practice Phase of Treatment

A second parent meeting is planned to introduce the parent to the practice phase of treatment. The therapist explains to the parent that the child will begin to practice the learned coping skills, and this will most probably make him appear to be more anxious. The exposure and practice goals of treatment are reviewed with the parent as well as ways in which the parent can support the child in what has been learned and continue to encourage the child's efforts.

Sessions 9–10: Exposure to Low-Anxiety Scenarios

In the 9th and 10th treatment sessions, the therapist initiates and continues to practice the FEAR plan with low-anxiety-provoking situations using exposure strategies in both imaginal and in vivo scenarios. It is important to "acknowledge that this portion of treatment will provoke greater anxiety" (Kendall et al., 2003, p. 85).

The ninth session begins with a shift from learning skills to practicing the learned skills in real situations (the fear hierarchy is reviewed).

Imaginal exposure exercises are implemented using the FEAR plan with low-anxiety situations (coping modeling) followed by in-session exposure exercises (e.g., for students with SAD, naturally occurring scenarios can be created in schools with the help of teachers and guidance counselors). In order to assess the extent to which the child experiences distress during exposure exercises, the subjective units of distress scale (SUDS) may be used. The therapist and child plan for additional exposure exercises to be implemented at home with the parents.

Imaginal and in-session exposure exercises with low-anxiety-provoking situations (implementation of FEAR plan through coping modeling) are continued through the 10th session. One anxiety-provoking scenario may have several anxiety-provoking elements, which should be tackled one at a time. It is important that the therapist collaborate with the child in planning more challenging situations to practice during the following treatment session.

Sessions 11–12: Exposure to Moderate-Anxiety Scenarios

During these sessions, the child practices the FEAR coping plan in situations that produce moderate anxiety. In addition to using imaginal and in-session exposure to practice the FEAR plan, the therapist may want to initiate the child's first out-of-office exposure.

Sessions 13–14: Exposure to High-Anxiety Scenarios

Sessions 13 and 14 focus on the application of the FEAR plan to situations that produce high anxiety. Imaginal exposure exercises with high-anxiety-provoking situations are implemented via modeling and role-play exercises. Throughout these two sessions, the child is reminded to use relaxation exercises to help control anxiety levels. As the child masters the imaginal exposure exercises, in-session exposure exercises are implemented with high-anxiety-provoking situations.

The idea of a commercial is introduced in session 14 as an informational piece, created by the child, to tell children how to manage anxiety. Producing a commercial will allow the child to act and feel like an expert on his own treatment and will provide a venue for the practitioner to observe what the child has learned over the course of therapy. The commercial can also be shared with others as evidence of the child's accomplishments.

Sessions 15–16: Making the Commercial

During sessions 15 and 16, the child continues to engage in in-vivo exposures in high-stress situations and to practice the FEAR plan. The therapist also begins to address anticipated concerns with termination while reinforcing the therapist's confidence in the child's ability to continue to progress on his own. Time is allotted in between sessions to allow the child to practice the FEAR coping skills on his own. As such, telephone check-ins are scheduled in between sessions as a means of providing more distanced support from the therapist.

The child, together with the therapist, begins to more actively plan the commercial. By session 16, the therapist reviews and summarizes the Coping Cat program. The commercial or audiotape "testimonial" is made, and the child's family is invited to view the commercial with the child and therapist.

Termination Session

The termination session, scheduled one week following the 16th session, is an opportunity for the therapist to provide feedback to the child and family on the child's overall progress in treatment and to comment on the child's strengths and weaknesses.

During this session, the child is presented with a certificate of completion ("goodbye ritual"), and the therapist establishes posttreatment plans with the parent that focus on helping the child to maintain and generalize his newly acquired skills. A check-in call is scheduled in 4 weeks, and future booster sessions are offered thereafter if needed.

Treating Early Childhood Separation Anxiety Disorder

Importantly, younger children (i.e., < 7 years) may benefit less from traditional CBT for child anxiety, as such methods rely heavily on strategies and tasks that are beyond the developmental capacities of younger children. In recent years, a small handful of research groups have begun to show support for the use of developmentally sensitive downward extensions of treatments found to work with older youth in controlled trials with early-onset separation anxiety disorder (e.g., Hirshfeld-Becker, Masek, Henin, Blakely, Pollock-Wurman et al., 2010; Pincus, Santucci, Ehrenreich, & Eyberg, 2008; Puliafico, Comer, & Albano, 2008). In particular, Pincus and colleagues (2008) have modified Parent Child Interaction Therapy (PCIT; Brinkmeyer & Eyeberg, 2003)—an empirically supported treatment originally developed for the treatment of early disruptive behavior disorders—to treat early-onset SAD. As in traditional PCIT, parents receive live coaching from a therapist observing parent-child interactions from behind a one-way mirror via a bug-in-the-ear device. In addition, Pincus and colleagues have introduced an anxiety-based module (Bravery Directed Interaction, or BDI), in which parents are taught about anxiety and how to facilitate exposures to separation situations. Recent modifications incorporate live parent-coaching during *in vivo* exposures for SAD, as in the CALM Program (**C**oaching **A**pproach behavior and **L**eading by **M**odeling; Puliafico, Comer, & Albano, 2008).

Applying Interventions within a Response to Intervention Framework

The state of science for treating SAD affords consistency with the RTI framework, in which school officials implement assessment, monitoring, and intervention programs across primary, secondary, and tertiary prevention levels. In the primary prevention level, the school is sensitive to the needs of separation anxious youth. At the secondary prevention level, school officials effectively screen for separation anxious youth by means of the MASC and/or ADIS (see Table 6.2), and treat the majority of separation anxiety disorder cases with school-based mental health resources. For those children not responding to secondary-level support, tertiary support is necessary, which may include seeking a comprehensive and interdisciplinary approach to treatment by clinicians with specific expertise in separation anxiety disorder, in order to return the child to normal functioning.

Tools and Practice Example

Practice Example

Diego is an 8-year-old boy in the third grade, living in a single-parent home with his mother, Ms. Peña. His teacher, Miss Phillips, referred him to the school-based mental health clinic (SBMHC). Miss Phillips reported that Diego has been excessively absent in the last couple of months. When he does attend class, he arrives late, tearful, and in an irritable mood. When questioned about his tearfulness, he tells Miss Phillips that he feels sick and wants to go home. Attempts to go home are often unsuccessful. On these days, he seems distracted for most of the day and refuses to engage in school tasks. Miss Phillips reported that his behavior is worsening and is beginning to disrupt his learning.

The school-based therapist contacted Diego's mother following the teacher's referral. Ms. Peña recently started working in a perfume factory where she puts in long work hours and has an erratic work schedule. Although she acknowledged Miss Phillips's report of Diego's symptoms, she expressed that this is just a phase he is going through. Ms. Peña assured the therapist that she tries her best to bring Diego to school in order to force him to "get over it" but admits that she often gives in because "he acts up way too much." Additionally, Ms. Peña expressed disappointment with the school staff for being so impatient with Diego and not understanding that his refusal to go to school is just a phase. In the spirit of building rapport with Ms. Peña, the therapist acknowledged Ms. Peña's frustrations in dealing with Diego's behaviors and invited her to come to the SBMHC with Diego for a preliminary assessment.

Assessing for Separation Anxiety Disorder

The therapist met with Diego and Ms. Peña to get some information about Diego's symptoms and to assess the extent of impairment they may be causing. Ms. Peña reported that Diego has been refusing to go to school for more than 3 months. His school avoidance leaves Ms. Peña feeling distressed given that it interferes with her work and social life. On the days she is unable to get Diego to school, she calls in sick to stay home and take care of him. On the days she does get to work, his morning tantrums make her late and his somatic symptoms require her to leave work early to pick him up from school. She also finds that she has little time for herself given his refusal to go anywhere outside the home without her. Additionally, Diego has been sleeping with Ms. Peña for the past 2 months because of recurrent nightmares that something "bad" is going to happen to her. Ms. Peña reported no other psychosocial stressors.

When it was Diego's turn to meet with the therapist alone, Diego appeared quite distressed about his mother leaving the room. Throughout the session, Diego consistently sought reassurance of his mother's whereabouts by opening the door of the therapist's office to see if she was still in the waiting room. The therapist used the SAD section of the Anxiety Disorders Interview Scale (ADIS; Silverman & Nelles, 1988) as a guide while interviewing Diego regarding his SAD symptoms. During the interview, Diego shared that when he thinks of something bad happening to his mother (e.g., car accident) his "tummy hurts real bad." Although Diego identified a few friends with whom he enjoys spending time, most of his social activities are limited to home since he refuses to go to a friend's home unless his mother accompanies him.

The assessment concluded with completion of the Screen for Anxiety and Related Emotional Disorders (SCARED; Birmaher et al., 1997) measure by both Diego and his mother. The therapist explained that the SCARED would be useful for assessing the severity of Diego's symptoms and monitoring his progress throughout treatment. Scores on the SAD subscale of the SCARED reflected significant impairment. After a careful review of Diego's symptoms, the therapist concluded that Diego met DSM-IV-TR diagnostic criteria for SAD and decided to use the Coping Cat program as the intervention of choice.

Implementing a 12-Week Coping Cat Program

Setting Up the FEAR Plan

The primary focus of the first phase of treatment was to help Diego learn the coping strategies of the FEAR plan. In order to help Diego link his bodily reactions to an emotion, the therapist and Diego played "feelings charades." Diego enjoyed playing the game and was able to identify feelings and their associated physical expressions. Diego then worked with the therapist to construct a fear hierarchy in which a low-anxiety situation was identified as sitting in the therapist's office alone while his mother stayed in the waiting area; a medium-anxiety-provoking situation was identified as going to sleep by himself in his room; and a high-anxiety situation was spending a night at his grandma's house without contacting his mother. Beginning with the situation that caused the least stress, the therapist modeled the first step of the FEAR plan (F: Feeling Frightened?). Diego role played a low-anxiety scenario where he recognized that the tightening of his chest was a clue that he was feeling anxious about not being able to check and see if his mother was still in the waiting room.

Mastering the second step in the FEAR plan (E: Expecting bad things to happen?) was not so easy. The therapist used the cartoons and empty thought bubbles in the Coping Cat workbook to help Diego master this concept. After much practice, Diego gradually was able to identify what thoughts made him anxious during his day-to-day experiences. The therapist coached Diego to use thoughts that reduce stress (coping self-talk) instead of those that induce it (anxious self-talk). The therapist and Diego practiced using coping self-talk when imagining Diego's fears of sleeping alone in his room. Diego repeated this exercise several times with different anxiety-provoking scenarios.

In the following sessions, the therapist and Diego explored some ideas about what he can do when he is anxious. During this problem-solving exercise (FEAR step A: Attitudes and Actions that will help?), Diego listed actions he could take, such as using deep-breathing exercises when alone in his room. The therapist referred to Diego's hierarchy of anxiety and modeled problem solving at bedtime. Diego recognized his anxious feelings and thoughts while getting ready to go to bed, joined in the role play, and acted out how he would listen to his favorite audio book while in bed.

Implementing the final coping step (R: Results and Rewards?) was challenging given the constant negative feedback Diego received from school staff and his mother in response to his SAD symptoms. Diego felt "bad" and undeserving of anything "good." His low self-esteem hindered his ability to evaluate his performance. The therapist worked with Diego on how to rate his own performance and praise his efforts even if the end result was not what he wanted. The therapist used Diego's past successes during session practices as examples of how Diego could rate himself positively. Diego enjoyed planning for potential rewards for successful efforts. When the therapist checked in with Ms. Peña, she expressed reluctance to reward Diego for behaviors such as going to school. She believed that Diego's attendance was to be expected and did not merit a reward. The therapist educated Ms. Peña on the importance of reinforcing positive behavior to sustain those behaviors that are desirable (i.e., going to school). Ms. Peña was receptive to the therapist's suggestions and rewarded Diego's efforts more consistently as she became comfortable with the concept of rewards.

By the end of the training phase, the therapist and Diego worked on creating a poster that illustrated the FEAR plan. Diego used bright-colored markers to detail each of the four steps to the FEAR plan while adding cut-outs from magazines that had phrases to help him recall different aspects of the plan. Diego then created a wallet-sized card and wrote the FEAR acronym on it. The FEAR card was in Diego's possession at all times and served as an anchor for him to refer to when confronting an anxiety-provoking situation.

Coping Cat Practice Phase

The main treatment goals of the second phase of treatment were to practice the FEAR plan in actual anxiety-provoking situations. Exposure to these situations was gradual, beginning with exposure to low-level situations and gradually progressing to higher-level situations.

During the beginning of the practice phase, the therapist met with Ms. Peña to review this phase of treatment. Ms. Peña was forewarned that Diego might appear more anxious in the next couple of weeks given his repeated exposure to anxiety-provoking situations. Ms. Peña was reminded of the importance of being a support for Diego and to continue praising his efforts and providing rewards for successes.

The first series of exposure sessions began with low-anxiety situations using both imaginal and in vivo exposure. For the imaginal exposure, the goal was for Diego to stay in his bedroom for 1 hour while his mother was cooking dinner in the kitchen. The therapist set up the situation as realistically as possible by hiding behind a bookcase in the office to represent the wall that separates Diego's room from the kitchen. Diego identified the stressor, used the feeling barometer to rate his anxiety, and problem solved how he would cope. The therapist later identified an anxiety-producing situation to be practiced in the office. Diego's goal was to stay in the therapist's office for the entire session without checking (e.g., opening the office door, calling out to his mother) to see if his mother was still in the waiting room. Additional in vivo exercises were practiced using low-level anxiety-provoking situations.

During the second series of exposures, the therapist referred to Diego's hierarchy of anxiety to select a situation of moderate anxiety for imaginal exposure. The first situation required Diego to imagine going to his cousin Jimmy's house to watch a movie without his mother. His mother would take him to Jimmy's home and pick him up when the movie was over. Through modeling and role play, Diego implemented the FEAR plan in this situation.

For the in vivo exposure, the goal was to implement the FEAR plan in the classroom upon arrival at school. The session was scheduled in the early morning and required collaboration between the therapist and Miss Phillips. On this day, Diego verbalized that he was feeling a bit queasy and recognized it was a signal that he was anxious because his mother had just dropped him off. Miss Phillips facilitated the exposure by reminding Diego to pull out his FEAR card. Diego sat through first period without requesting to go to the nurse's office. He was very proud of himself for his success and asked for his stickers as promised by Miss Phillips. Additional in vivo exposures for moderate-anxiety-provoking situations were practiced in subsequent sessions.

The third in vivo exposure involved a high-anxiety situation. For Diego, this involved a one-night stay at his grandma's house without calling his mother. The therapist helped Diego to practice this situation in session by inviting his grandma to the office. The therapist coached his grandma on how to support Diego through the exercise. Diego identified the somatic cues (e.g., feeling sick) he experiences at grandma's house. He also identified for both his grandma and therapist his anxious thoughts about sleeping over without his mother (e.g., Mom will never come back to get me!) and how he would use coping thoughts instead (e.g., Mom has shown that she loves me very much and would not leave me at grandma's). Diego planned to evaluate his efforts the next morning and reward his successes. Grandma, armed with an understanding of Diego's action plan, detailed how she would support Diego by giving him reminders of the FEAR strategy, offering to participate in relaxation techniques, and praising his efforts throughout his stay. For additional support, the therapist arranged to conduct a telephone check that night to reassure Diego that she was confident he could do it on his own.

Termination

Diego was fully aware of the progress he had made throughout the course of treatment and was looking forward to sharing what he learned with other kids. Given the limited resources at the school, the therapist and Diego opted for creating a brochure to present his message to other children rather than filming a commercial. Multiple copies of the brochure were made so that he could distribute it to family and friends.

The therapist met with Ms. Peña and devised a maintenance plan for Diego's learned coping skills. Ms. Peña reported a reduction in Diego's symptoms and seemed quite pleased with his progression throughout treatment. This was corroborated by the low SAD score on the SCARED measure completed by Ms. Peña and Diego. As a final reward for Diego's successful efforts, the therapist and Diego played basketball (Diego's favorite sport) in the school gym. The session ended with a goodbye ritual during which Diego was presented with a certificate of completion by the therapist in recognition of his participation in and successful completion of the Coping Cat program.

Resources

Coping Cat Program: Cognitive-Behavioral Intervention for Anxious Youth (Ages 7–13)

Philip C. Kendall, Cognitive-Behavioral Therapy for Anxious Children: Therapist Manual (3rd ed.). Temple University. www.workbookpublishing.com

Philip C. Kendall, Coping Cat Workbook. Temple University. www.workbookpublishing.com

Ellen Flannery-Schroeder & Philip C. Kendall, Cognitive-Behavioral Therapy for Anxious Children: Therapist Manual for Group Treatment. Temple University. www.workbookpublishing.com

Bonnie Howard, Brian C. Chu, Amy L. Krain, Abbe L. Marrs-Garcia, & Philip C. Kendall, Cognitive-Behavioral Family Therapy for Anxious Children: Therapist Manual (2nd ed.). Temple University. www.workbookpublishing.com

Philip C. Kendall & W. Michael Nelson III, Managing Anxiety in Youth: The "Coping Cat" Video. Xavier University. www.workbookpublishing.com

Phillip C. Kendall & W. Michael Nelson III, Managing Anxiety in Youth: The "Coping Cat" DVD. Temple University and Xavier University. www.workbookpublishing.com

W. Michael Nelson III & Phillip C. Kendall, The Coping Cat Therapist: Session-By-Session Guide [Video]. Xavier University and Temple University. www.workbookpublishing.com

W. Michael Nelson III & Phillip C. Kendall, The Coping Cat Therapist: Session-by-Session Guide [DVD]. Xavier University and Temple University. www.workbookpublishing.com

Phillip C. Kendall & Muniya Khanna, CBT4CBT: Computer-Based Training to be a Cognitive Behavioral Therapist. Temple University and University of Pennsylvania. www.workbookpublishing.com

Phillip C. Kendall & Muniya Khanna, Camp Cope-A-Lot. Temple University and University of Pennsylvania. www.workbookpublishing.com

The C.A.T. Project: Cognitive-Behavioral Intervention for Anxious Older Youth (Ages 14–17)

Philip C. Kendall, Muniya Choudhury, Jennifer Hudson, & Alicia Webb, The C.A.T. Project Workbook for the Cognitive-Behavioral Treatment of Anxious Adolescents. Temple University. www.workbookpublishing.com

Philip C. Kendall, Muniya Choudhury, Jennifer Hudson, & Alicia Webb, The C.A.T. Project Manual for the Cognitive Behavioral Treatment of Anxious Adolescents. Temple University. www.workbookpublishing.com

Children's Books on Separation Anxiety

Elizabeth Crary & Marina Megale, Mommy, Don't Go. Reading level: Ages 4–8.

Irene Wineman Marcus, Paul Marcus, & Susan Jeschke, Into the Great Forest: A Story for Children Away From Parents for the First Time. Reading level: Ages 4–8

Judith Viorst, The Good-Bye Book. Reading level: Ages 4–8

Pincus, D.B. (2012), Growing up brave: Expert strategies for helping your child overcome fear, stress, and anxiety. New York, NY: Little, Brown and Company.

Anxiety Organizations

Child & Adolescent Anxiety Disorders Clinic (CAADC). Temple University. 13th Street & Cecil B. Moore

Avenue (Weiss Hall, Ground Level), Philadelphia, PA 19122. www.childanxiety.org

The Child Anxiety Network, Child and Adolescent Fear and Anxiety Treatment Program. 648 Beacon Street, 6th floor, Kenmore Square, Boston, MA 02215.617–353–9610.www.childanxiety.net

Anxiety Disorder Association of America. 8730 Georgia Avenue, Suite 600, Silver Spring, MD 20910. 240-485-1001. www.adaa.org

Key Points to Remember

SAD is one of the most frequently reported disorders in the school setting. The literature on treating SAD indicates that cognitive-behavioral therapy (CBT) is the intervention of choice for treating the disorder. The Coping Cat program is particularly useful in treating SAD in schools given its demonstrated effectiveness, transportability, and adaptability across diverse settings.

Implementing the Coping Cat program in the school setting requires some flexibility on the part of the school-based practitioner. Some of the factors that school-based therapists should keep in mind when implementing Coping Cat are summarized as follows:

- High comorbidity of SAD with other anxiety disorders requires that differential diagnoses be assessed thoroughly. This is especially true for children presenting with school refusal, given its similarity to school or social phobia.
- Teachers are instrumental in identifying SAD kids when provided with the resources to do so.
- Assessment of SAD is most comprehensive when multiple informants provide information on the manifestation of symptoms. Clinical interviews, self-reports (including parent versions), and teacher reports are strongly encouraged.
- The Coping Cat manual and accompanying workbook and notebook are essential tools for the delivery of CBT for SAD but must be used flexibly. Readers should obtain and read the manual prior to administering the treatment.
- Appropriate training and supervision are necessary for implementing Coping Cat.
- Family involvement throughout treatment will greatly enhance treatment effects. Parents are not only in the best position for reporting SAD symptoms but should participate actively in facilitating and reinforcing the strategies learned throughout treatment.

References

Achenbach, T. (1991). *Manual for the teacher's report form and 1991 profile*. Burlington: University of Vermont, Department of Psychiatry.

Albano, A. M., & Kendall, P. C. (2002). Cognitive behavioral therapy for children and adolescents with anxiety disorders: Clinical research advances. *International Review of Psychiatry, 14*(2), 129–134.

Albano, A. M. (2003). Treatment of social anxiety disorder. In M. A. Reinecke & F. M. Dattilio (Eds.), *Cognitive therapy with children and adolescents: A casebook for clinical practice* (2nd ed., pp. 128–161). New York: Guilford.

American Psychiatric Association. (2000). *Diagnostic and statistical manual of mental disorders* (4th ed., text revision). Washington, DC: Author.

Angold, A., & Costello, E. J. (2000). The Child and Adolescent Psychiatric Assessment (CAPA). *Journal of the American Academy of Child & Adolescent Psychiatry, 39*(1), 39–48.

Barrett, P. M., Dadds, M. R., & Rapee, R. M. (1996). Family treatment of childhood anxiety: A controlled trial. *Journal of Consulting & Clinical Psychology, 64*(2), 333–342.

Barrett, P. M. (1998). Evaluation of cognitive-behavioral group treatments for childhood anxiety disorders. *Journal of Clinical Child Psychology, 27*(4), 459–468.

Birmaher, B., Khetarpal, S., Brent, D., Cully, M., Balach, L., Kaufman, J., & Neer, S. M. (1997). The Screen for Child Anxiety Related Emotional Disorders (SCARED): Scale construction and psychometric characteristics. *Journal of the American Academy of Child & Adolescent Psychiatry, 36*(4), 545–553.

Brinkmeyer, M., & Eyeberg, S. M. (2003). Parent-child interaction therapy for oppositional children. In A. E. Kazdin & J. R. Weisz (Eds.), *Evidence-based psychotherapies for children and adolescents* (pp. 204–223). New York: Guilford.

Carruth, S. G. (2000). Separation anxiety disorder: Planning treatment. *Pediatrics in Review, 21*(7), 248.

Cobham, V. E., Dadds, M. R., & Spence, S. H. (1998). The role of parental anxiety in the treatment of childhood anxiety. *Journal of Consulting & Clinical Psychology, 66*(6), 893–905.

Compton, S. N., Nelson, A. H., & March, J. S. (2000). Social phobia and separation anxiety symptoms in community and clinical samples of children and adolescents. *Journal of the American Academy of Child & Adolescent Psychiatry, 39*(8), 1040–1046.

Egger, H.L., & Angold, A. (2004). The Preschool Age Psychiatric Assessment (PAPA); A structured parent interview for diagnosing psychiatric disorders in pre-school children. In R. Delcarmen-Wiggens & A. Carter (Eds.), *A handbook of infant, toddler, and preschool mental health assessment* (pp. 224–243). New York: Oxford University Press.

Fischer, D. J., Himle, J. A., & Thyer, B. A. (1999). Separation anxiety disorder. In R. T. Ammerman, M. Hersen, & C. G. Last (Eds.), *Handbook of prescriptive treatments for children and adolescents* (2nd ed., pp. 141–154). Needham Heights,MA: Allyn & Bacon.

Flannery-Schroeder, E. C., & Kendall, P. C. (2000). Group and individual cognitive-behavioral treatments for youth with anxiety disorders: A randomized clinical trial. *Cognitive Therapy & Research, 24*(3), 251–278.

Francis, G., Last, C. G., & Strauss, C. C. (1987). Expression of separation anxiety disorder: The roles of age and gender. *Child Psychiatry & Human Development, 18*(2), 82–89.

Gittelman, R., & Klein, D. F. (1984). Relationship between separation anxiety and panic and agoraphobic disorders. *Psychopathology, 17*(Suppl. 1), 56–65.

Hagopian, L. P., & Slifer, K. J. (1993). Treatment of separation anxiety disorder with graduated exposure and reinforcement targeting school attendance: A controlled case study. *Journal of Anxiety Disorders*, 7(3), 271–280.

Hirshfeld-Becker, D., Masek, B., Henin, A., Blakely, L., Pollock-Wurman, R., et al. (2010) Cognitive behavioral therapy for 4- to 7-year-old children with anxiety disorders: a randomized clinical trial. *Journal of Consulting and Clinical Psychology, 78(4),* 498–510.

James, E. M., Reynolds, C. R., & Dunbar, J. (1994). Self-report instruments. In T. H. Ollendick, N. J. King, & W. Yule (Eds.), *International handbook of phobic and anxiety disorders in children and adolescents* (pp. 317–329). New York: Plenum.

Kearney, C. A., & Silverman, W. K. (1993). Measuring the function of school refusal behavior: The School Assessment Scale. *Journal of Clinical Child Psychology, 22*(1), 85–96.

Kendall, P. C. (1990). *Coping Cat workbook*. Ardmore, PA: Workbook Publishing.

Kendall, P. C. (1994). Treating anxiety disorders in children: Results of a randomized clinical trial. *Journal of Consulting & Clinical Psychology, 62*(1), 100–110.

Kendall, P. C., & Gosch, E. A. (1994). Cognitive-behavioral interventions In T. H. Ollendick, N. J. King, & W. Yule (Eds.), *International handbook of phobic and anxiety disorders in children and adolescents* (pp. 415–438). New York: Plenum.

Kendall, P. C., & Southam-Gerow, M. A. (1995). Issues in the transportability of treatment: The case of anxiety disorders in youths. *Journal of Consulting & Clinical Psychology, 63*(5), 702–708.

Kendall, P. C., & Southam-Gerow, M. A. (1996). Long-term follow-up of a cognitive-behavioral therapy for anxiety-disordered youth. *Journal of Consulting & Clinical Psychology, 64*(4), 724–730.

Kendall, P. C., Flannery-Schroeder, E., Panichelli-Mindel, S. M., Southam-Gerow, M., Henin, A., & Warman, M. (1997). Therapy for youths with anxiety disorders: A second randomized clinical trial. *Journal of Consulting & Clinical Psychology, 65*(3), 366–380.

Kendall, P. C. (2000). *Cognitive-behavioral therapy for anxious children: Therapist manual* (3rd ed.). Ardmore, PA: Workbook Publishing.

Kendall, P. C., & Chu, B. C. (2000). Retrospective self-reports of therapist flexibility in a manual-based treatment for youths with anxiety disorders. *Journal of Clinical Child Psychology, 29*(2), 209–220.

Kendall, P. C., Choudhury, M., Hudson, J ., & Webb, A. (2002a). *The C.A.T. project therapist manual*. Ardmore, PA: Workbook Publishing.

Kendall, P. C., Choudhury, M., Hudson, J., & Webb, A. (2002b). *The C.A.T. project workbook for the cognitive-behavioral treatment of anxious adolescents*. Ardmore, PA: Workbook Publishing.

Kendall, P. C. (2005). Guiding theory for therapy with children and adolescents. In P. C. Kendall (Ed.), *Child and adolescent therapy: Cognitive-behavioral procedures* (3rd ed., pp. 3–27). New York: Guilford.

Kendall, P. C., & Hedtke, K. A. (2006). *Cognitive-behavioral treatment of anxious children: Treatment manual*. (Available from P. C. Kendall, Department of Psychology, Temple University, Philadelphia, PA 19122)

Kendall, P.C. & Khanna, M.S. (2008). *Camp Cope-A-Lot: The Coping Cat CD Rom*, Ardmore, PA: Workbook Publishing Inc.

Kendall, P.C., Khanna, M.S., Edson, A., Cummings, C., et al. (2011). Computers and psychosocial treatment for child anxiety: Recent advances and ongoing efforts. *Depression and Anxiety, 28*, 58–66.

Khanna, M.S., & Kendall, P.C. (2010). Computer-assisted cognitive-behavioral therapy for child anxiety: Results of a randomized clinical trial, *Journal of Consulting and Clinical Psychology, 78(5),* 737–745.

Langley, A. K., Bergman, R. L., & Piacentini, J. C. (2002). Assessment of childhood anxiety. *International Review of Psychiatry, 14*(2), 102–113.

Last, C. G., Hersen, M., Kazdin, A. E., Finkelstein, R., & Strauss, C. C. (1987). Comparison of DSM-III separation anxiety and overanxious disorders: Demographic characteristics and patterns of comorbidity. *Journal of the American Academy of Child & Adolescent Psychiatry, 26*(4), 527–531.

March, J. S., Parker, J. D. A., Sullivan, K., Stallings, P., & Conners, C. K. (1997). The Multidimensional Anxiety Scale for Children (MASC): Factor structure, reliability, and validity. *Journal of the American Academy of Child & Adolescent Psychiatry, 36*(4), 554–565.

Mendlowitz, S. L., Manassis, K., Bradley, S., Scapillato, D., Miezitis, S., & Shaw, B. F. (1999). Cognitive-behavioral group treatments in childhood anxiety disorders: The role of parental involvement. *Journal of the American Academy of Child & Adolescent Psychiatry, 38*(10), 1223–1229.

Miller, S.J., & Binder, J. L. (2002). The effects of manual-based training on treatment fidelity and outcome: A review of the literature on adult individual psychotherapy. *Psychotherapy: Theory, Research, Practice, Training, 39*(2), 184–198.

Ollendick, T. H., Hagopian, L. P., & Huntzinger, R. M. (1991). Cognitive-behavior therapy with nighttime fearful children. *Journal of Behavior Therapy & Experimental Psychiatry, 22*(2), 113–121.

Perwien, A. R., & Berstein, G. A. (2004). Separation anxiety disorder. In T. H. Ollendick & J. S. March (Eds.), *Phobic and anxiety disorders in children and adolescents* (pp. 272–305). New York: Oxford University Press.

Pincus, D.B., Santucci, L. C., Ehrenreich, J. T., Eyeberg, S. M. (2008). The implementation of modified parent-child interaction therapy for youth with Separation Anxiety Disorder. *Cognitive and Behavioral Practice, 15*(2), 118–125.

Puliafico, A.C., Comer, J.S., & Albano, A.M. (2008). *Coaching Approach behavior and Leading by Modeling: The CALM Program for anxious preschoolers.* New York, NY: Columbia University.

Reich, W. (2000). Diagnostic interview for children and adolescents (DICA). *Journal of the American Academy of Child & Adolescent Psychiatry, 39*(1), 59–66.

Saavedra, L.M., & Silverman, W. K. (2002). Classification of anxiety disorders in children: What a difference two decades make. *International Review of Psychiatry, 14*(2), 87–101.

Shaffer, D., Fisher, P., Lucas, C. P., Dulcan, M. K., & Schwab-Stone, M. E. (2000). NIMH diagnostic interview schedule for children version IV (NIMH DISC-IV): Description, differences from previous versions, and reliability of some common diagnoses. *Journal of the American Academy of Child & Adolescent Psychiatry, 39*(1), 28–38.

Shear, K., Jin, R., Ruscio, A.M., Walters, E.E., & Kessler, R. C. (2006). Prevalence and correlates of estimated DSM-IV child and adult Separation Anxiety Disorder in the national comorbidity survey replication. *The American Journal of Psychiatry, 163*(6), 1074–1083.

Silverman, W. K., & Nelles, W. B. (1988). The anxiety disorders interview schedule for children. *Journal of the American Academy of Child & Adolescent Psychiatry, 27*(6), 772–778.

Silverman, W.K., & Albano, A.M. (1996). *The Anxiety Disorders Interview Schedule for DSM-IV-Child and Parent Versions*, London: Oxford University Press.

Silverman, W. K., Kurtines, W. M., Ginsburg, G. S., Weems, C. F., Lumpkin, P. W., & Carmichael, D. H. (1999). Treating anxiety disorders in children with group cognitive-behavioral therapy: A randomized clinical trial. *Journal of Consulting & Clinical Psychology, 67*(6), 995–1003.

Silverman, W. K., & Dick-Niederhauser, A. (2004). Separation anxiety disorder. In T. L. Morris & J. S. March (Eds.), *Anxiety disorders in children and adolescents* (2nd ed., pp. 164–188). New York: Guilford.

Spence, S. H. (1997). A measure of anxiety symptoms among children. *Behaviour Research & Therapy, 36*(5), 545–566.

Spence, S. H., & Rapee, R. (1999). *Preschool Anxiety Scale (Parent Report), Brisbane,* Australia: University of Queensland.

Thyer, B. A., & Sowers-Hoag, K. M. (1988). Behavior therapy for separation anxiety disorder. *Behavior Modification, 12*(2), 205–233.

Tonge, B. (1994). Separation anxiety disorder. In T. H. Ollendick, N. J. King, & W. Yule (Eds.), *International handbook of phobic and anxiety disorders in children and adolescents* (pp. 145–167). New York: Plenum.

Treadwell, K. R. H., Flannery-Schroeder, E. C., & Kendall, P. C. (1995). Ethnicity and gender in relation to adaptive functioning, diagnostic status, and treatment outcome in children from an anxiety clinic. *Journal of Anxiety Disorders, 9*(5), 373–384.

Velting, O. N., Setzer, N. J., & Albano, A. M. (2004). Update on and advances in assessment and cognitive-behavioral treatment of anxiety disorders in children and adolescents. *Professional Psychology: Research & Practice, 35*(1), 42–54.

Walkup, J. T., Albano, A. M., Piacentini, J., Birmaher, B., Compton, S. N., et al. (2008). Cognitive behavioral therapy, sertraline, or a combination in childhood anxiety. *New England Journal of Medicine, 359*(26), 2753–2766.

Walkup, J. T., & Ginsburg, G. S. (2002). Anxiety disorders in children and adolescents. *International Review of Psychiatry, 14*(2), 85–86.

Weller, E. B., Weller, R. A., Fristad, M. A., Rooney, M. T., & Schecter, J. (2000). Children's interview for psychiatric syndromes (ChIPS). *Journal of the American Academy of Child & Adolescent Psychiatry, 39*(1), 76–84.

Effective Interventions for Students with Obsessive-Compulsive Disorder

CHAPTER 9

Jonathan S. Comer • Meghan Tomb • Lisa Hunter-Romanelli

Getting Started

Obsessive-compulsive disorder (OCD) is characterized by recurrent obsessions (which cause marked anxiety or distress) and by compulsions (which serve to neutralize anxiety) that are severe enough to be time consuming (i.e., take more than 1 hour a day) or cause marked distress or impairment in functioning (American Psychiatric Association, 2000). Obsessions are "recurrent, persistent ideas, thoughts, images, or impulses, which are ego-dystonic, and experienced as senseless or repugnant." Compulsions are "repetitive and seemingly purposeful actions which are performed according to certain rules, or in a stereotyped fashion" (Thomsen, 1998, p. 2). Compulsions act to neutralize the threat stemming from an obsession (Clark, 2000). OCD is not an exclusionary disorder and is often associated with major depressive disorder, other anxiety disorders (e.g., specific phobia, social phobia, panic disorder), eating disorders, generalized anxiety disorder, and obsessive-compulsive personality disorder (American Psychiatric Association, 2000; Comer et al., 2004; Langley et al., 2010; March & Mulle, 1998). Symptomatology is similar in adults and children/adolescents with OCD; however, children may not recognize the obsessions and compulsions as excessive or unreasonable (American Psychiatric Association, 2000; Foster & Eisler, 2001; Wagner, 2003a). Table 9.2 (p. 102) shows the complete diagnostic criteria for OCD (American Psychiatric Association, 2000).

It is important to note that some behaviors associated with OCD are common in the normal development of children. For instance, many children go through phases where they maintain superstitious beliefs, carry out certain rituals, such as bedtime rituals, or become fixed on a favorite number (Thomsen, 1998). However, these "normal" rituals typically dissipate by 8 years old, while children with OCD generally show an onset of the disorder after age 7. Nonetheless, early-onset OCD (i.e., onset before age 8) has been observed. Early-onset OCD is typically comparable in severity to later-onset OCD but is accompanied by lower rates of comorbid depressive disorders (Garcia et al., 2009). Only when rituals begin to interfere with daily life or cause marked distress should a diagnosis of OCD be considered. Washing, checking, and ordering rituals (see Table 9.1 for definitions) are particularly common, seen in about half the children with OCD (March & Mulle, 1998; Thomsen, 1998). However, these symptoms in children may not be ego-dystonic (disturbing to the self), and children do not frequently seek help. More commonly, parents will identify the problem and bring the child in for treatment. Like adults, children are more prone to engage in rituals at home than in front of peers, teachers, or strangers. This may make it difficult for school-based personnel (staff, practitioners) to identify children who are suffering quietly from OCD during school hours. Relatedly, gradual declines in schoolwork secondary to impaired concentration capabilities have been reported (American Psychiatric Association, 2000). Some of the common symptoms of OCD and ways these symptoms may be exhibited in the school setting are shown in Table 9.1.

What We Know

According to the APA (2000), community studies show that the estimated lifetime prevalence for OCD ranges from 1.6–2.5% (Comer & Olfson,

Table 9.1 Symptoms and Behavioral Manifestations of Obsessive-Compulsive Disorder

Symptom	*Behavioral Manifestations*	*Examples in School Setting*
Obsessions		
	Students may get "stuck," or fixated, on certain points and lose the need or ability to go on. Fixation on an obsessional thought may appear to be and is often mistaken for an attention problem, daydreaming, laziness, or poor motivation.	• Fixation on a thought may cause distraction from the task at hand, which delays students in completing schoolwork or following directions and can lead to a decrease in work production and low grades • Fear of contamination, number obsessions ("safe" versus "bad" numbers), fear of harm or death
Compulsions		
Washing/ cleaning rituals	These students may feel obligated to wash extensively and according to a self-prescribed manner for minutes to hours at a time. Others may be less thorough about washing or cleaning but may engage in the act frequently each day.	• May appear as subtle behaviors not obviously related to washing or cleaning (i.e., going to the bathroom) • Students may frequently leave the classroom to go to the bathroom in order to privately carry out cleaning rituals • A physical sign of excessive washing is the presence of dry, red, chapped, cracked, or bleeding hands
Checking rituals	The student may unnecessarily check specific things over and over again.	• Getting ready for school, the student may check books over and over again to see if all the necessary books are there, sometimes causing lateness • At school, the student may want to call or return home to check something yet another time • The student may check and recheck answers on assignments to the point that they are submitted late or not at all • Repeatedly checking a locker to see if it is locked • Checking rituals may interfere with the completion of homework, can cause a student to work late into the night on assignments that should have taken 2 or 3 hours to complete
Repeating rituals	The student repeats a behavior or task over and over again (often connected with counting rituals)	• Repetitious questioning • Reading and rereading sentences or paragraphs in a book
Symptom	Behavioral Manifestations	Examples in School Setting
		• Sharpening pencils several times in a row • Repeatedly crossing out, tracing, or rewriting letters or words, erasing and re-erasing words • May interfere with student's ability to take notes, complete computer-scored tests, and open locker

(Continued)

Symptom Obsessions	*Behavioral Manifestations*	*Examples in School Setting*
Symmetry/ exactness rituals	Obsessions revolving around a need for symmetry	• Student may compulsively arrange objects in the classroom (e.g., books on a shelf, items on a page, pencils on a desk) • Student may feel the need to have both sides of the body identical (e.g., laces on shoes), take steps that are identical in length, or place equal emphasis on each syllable of a word
Other Compulsive behaviors	Obsessional thoughts that lead to compulsive avoidance; individuals may go to great lengths to avoid objects, substances, or situations that are capable of triggering fear or discomfort	• Fear of contamination may cause avoidance of objects in classroom (paint, glue, paste, clay, tape, ink) • Inappropriately covering the hands with clothing or gloves or using shirttails or cuffs to open doors or turn on faucets • If an obsessive fear of harm, may avoid using scissors or other sharp tools in the classroom • Student may avoid using a particular doorway because passage through it may trigger a repeating ritual
	Compulsive reassurance seeking	• May continually ask teachers for reassurance that there are no germs on the drinking fountain or that there are no errors on a page
	Obsessions concerning fear	• Fear of cheating may cause students to compulsively seek reassurance, avoid looking at other children, and sometimes even to give wrong answers intentionally

2010; Franklin et al., 1998; Kessler et al., 2005) and the 1-year prevalence is 0.5–2.1% in adults and 0.7% in children. More-recent reviews have reported lifetime prevalence rates of up to 4% (Foster & Eisler, 2001), with as many as 33–50% of adults with OCD reporting onset of the disorder during childhood or adolescence (Franklin et al., 1998). There are not any differences in prevalence rates across different cultures (American Psychiatric Association, 2000). It is estimated that 1 in 200 children and adolescents has obsessive-compulsive disorder (Adams et al., 1994). Given this approximation, there may be 3–4 youths with OCD in an average-sized elementary school and possibly 20–30 in a large urban high school (Adams et al., 1994; March & Mulle, 1998). When left untreated, OCD can severely disrupt academic, home, social, and vocational functioning (Geller, Biederman, et al., 2001; March & Mulle, 1998; Piacentini et al., 2003). Without proper identification and treatment, these children and adolescents are at risk for significant difficulty in school.

Implications for School Social Workers and Other School-Based Practitioners and Staff

Classroom teachers and other school staff observe and interact with students on a daily basis for consistent periods of time and therefore have a unique opportunity to notice and identify OCD symptoms in children and adolescents (Adams et al., 1994). In some instances, school personnel may be the first adults in a child's life to identify potential OCD symptoms. It is essential, therefore, that "classroom teachers, school social workers, school psychologists, counselors, nurses, and administrators learn to identify OCD symptoms in the school setting, help make appropriate referrals, and assist, as appropriate, in the treatment of childhood OCD" (March & Mulle, 1998, p. 197).

School-based practitioners, like school social workers and counselors, play an important part in identifying children and adolescents who are

Table 9.2 Diagnostic Criteria for 300.3 Obsessive-Compulsive Disorder

A. Either obsessions or compulsions:

Obsessions as defined by (1), (2), (3), and (4):

(1) recurrent and persistent thoughts, impulses, or images that are experienced, at some time during the disturbance, as intrusive and inappropriate and that cause marked anxiety or distress

(2) the thoughts, impulses, or images are not simply excessive worries about real-life problems

(3) the person attempts to ignore or suppress such thoughts, impulses, or images, or to neutralize them with some other thought or action

(4) the person recognizes that the obsessional thoughts, impulses, or images are a product of his or her own mind (not imposed from without as in thought insertion)

Compulsions as defined by (1) and (2):

(1) repetitive behaviors (e.g., hand washing, ordering, checking) or mental acts (e.g., praying, counting, repeating words silently) that the person feels driven to perform in response to an obsession, or according to rules that must be applied rigidly

(2) the behaviors or mental acts are aimed at preventing or reducing distress or preventing some dreaded event or situation; however, these behaviors or mental acts either are not connected in a realistic way with what they are designed to neutralize or prevent or are clearly excessive

B. At some point during the course of the disorder, the person has recognized that the obsessions or compulsions are excessive or unreasonable. Note: This does not apply to children.

C. The obsessions or compulsions cause marked distress, are time consuming (take more than 1 hour a day), or significantly interfere with the person's normal routine, occupational (or academic) functioning, or usual social activities or relationships.

D. If another Axis I disorder is present, the content of the obsessions or compulsions is not restricted to it (e.g., preoccupation with food in the presence of an eating disorder; hair pulling in the presence of trichotillomania; concern with appearance in the presence of body dysmorphic disorder; preoccupation with drugs in the presence of a substance use disorder; preoccupation with having a serious illness in the presence of hypochondriasis; preoccupation with sexual urges or fantasies in the presence of a paraphilia; or guilty ruminations in the presence of major depressive disorder).

E. The disturbance is not due to the direct physiological effects of a substance (e.g., a drug or abuse of a medication) or a general medical condition.

Specify if:

With poor insight: if, for most of the time during the current episode, the person does not recognize that the obsessions and compulsions are excessive or unreasonable.

Source: Reprinted with permission from the Diagnostic and Statistical Manual of Mental Disorders, Copyright 2000, American Psychiatric Association.

suffering from OCD symptoms and in educating school personnel about OCD. When a child with OCD is properly identified and referred for services, the symptoms can be addressed, treated, and managed. If classroom teachers do not have the knowledge and tools to do this, symptoms may continue to impair the child's functioning on a greater scale and eventually cause the child to be unable to attend school (March & Mulle, 1998). One way that school-based practitioners can help this process is by educating school personnel on the specific ways that OCD symptoms can manifest themselves in the school setting. Information on OCD can be disseminated through teacher in-service trainings and seminars. These should include information on proper identification of OCD symptoms, referral options, and a description of available treatments for OCD. School-based practitioners may want to consult various resources in order to obtain the most up-to-date information on OCD and its treatment (Freeman et al., 2006; Leonard et al., 2005).

Teachers can be a valuable asset to school-based practitioners treating children with OCD. Teachers are in a position to report their own observations of the child in treatment as well as those of the child's peers in the classroom. Establishing a relationship with the teacher is imperative for this process. Teachers can also provide written records of social and academic problems the student is having (March & Mulle, 1998), as well as complete assessment measures. School-based practitioners should keep in mind that teachers may be more compliant in completing assessment measures for a referred student when the burden is kept low by short-form assessment measures (Velting et al., 2004).

What We Can Do

Cognitive-Behavioral Therapy as the First-Line Psychotherapy for OCD

After a school-based mental health practitioner diagnoses a child as having OCD, one of several different interventions may be implemented. Cognitive-behavioral therapy (CBT), alone or in combination with medication, represents the foundation of treatment for children and adolescents with OCD (American Academy of Child and Adolescent Psychiatry, 1998; Franklin, Freeman, & March, 2010; March & Mulle, 1998) and is the basis for effective treatments for all anxiety disorders (Velting et al., 2004). For a complete review of the research literature supporting the efficacy of CBT for children and adolescents with anxiety disorders, see Silverman and colleagues (2008), and Albano and Kendall (2002). CBT programs for OCD utilize a combination of behavioral and cognitive information-processing approaches to alter symptoms. CBT aims to help the child with OCD to restructure unhealthy thoughts associated with the disorder in order to generate changes in the maladaptive behaviors that impair the child's daily home, school, and social functioning. The child learns specific strategies for coping with the disorder and, most important, for managing situations that may trigger certain thoughts and behavioral responses related to OCD.

The efficacy of CBT involving exposure and response prevention (EX/RP) and pharmacotherapy with serotonin reuptake inhibitors (SRIs) is well established for adults and youth (Franklin et al., 2002; Franklin et al., 2003; Kampman et al., 2002; POTS Team, 2004). In an open trial, March et al. (1994) used an adapted version of CBT to treat 15 children and adolescents (6–18 years old) with OCD, most of whom had been previously stabilized on medication. The authors reported significant benefit immediately following treatment and at 6-month follow-up. At post-treatment, results demonstrated a mean reduction of 50% in OCD symptomatology on the Yale-Brown Obsessive Compulsive Scale (Y-BOCS) and clinically asymptomatic ratings on the NIMH Global OC Scale (March et al., 1994). Eighty percent of patients were defined as responders to treatment. No patients relapsed after symptoms recurred, and booster sessions enabled 6 of the 9 asymptomatic patients to stop taking medication without relapse (March & Mulle, 1998). In another open trial, Franklin et al. (1998), found CBT to be effective in reducing OCD symptoms. Twelve of 14 patients (10 to 17 years old) in this trial showed at least 50% improvement over their pretreatment Y-BOCS severity scores, and 83% remained improved in severity at follow-up. The results of both of these trials are comparable to treatment studies using pharmacotherapy only (Southam-Gerow & Kendall, 2000).

The Pediatric Obsessive-Compulsive Disorder Treatment Study (POTS, 2004) was a large multisite randomized controlled trial comparing EX/RP, antidepressant medication, and their combination, relative to a pill placebo, in the treatment of 7- to 17-year-olds with obsessive-compulsive disorder. Results showed EX/RP, antidepressant medication, and their combination yielded significantly better outcomes than pill placebo (which showed only a 4% response rate). Among these three supported treatments, combination EX/RP and antidepressant medication resulted in the most favorable outcomes (54% response rate), followed by EX/RP alone (39%), and then antidepressant medication alone (21%). Follow-up analyses showed that children with lower baseline severity and impairment, and with greater insight, showed the most favorable responses across the treatments, and children with a positive family history of OCD, relative to those without a family history, showed considerably less favorable response to EX/RP alone (Garcia et al., 2010). The current acceptance of CBT as the preferred treatment for OCD may be explained by the fact that exposure and response prevention (EX/RP) is an integral part of any CBT protocol for OCD (Rowa et al., 2000). EX/RP specifically has been shown to be an effective treatment for OCD (for reviews, see Franklin, Freeman, & March, 2010). Additionally, studies measuring the effectiveness and transportability of cognitive-behavioral therapy from research-based randomized controlled trials (RCTs) to clinical and school practice are being seen in the literature (Warren & Thomas, 2001). In addition, Piacentini and colleagues' (2007) CBT treatment protocol offers another well-researched, developmentally sensitive program. Pinto Wagner's CBT protocol for children with OCD (see Wagner [2003a] for a review of this treatment protocol). Wagner's protocol, named RIDE Up and Down the Worry Hill (Wagner, 2002; 2003b), is a developmentally sensitive protocol designed as a flexible and feasible approach for clinicians in clinical settings treating children with OCD. Although comparative data do not exist for this protocol versus the protocol described in this chapter, both share many common features (Wagner, 2003a).

Pharmacotherapy

The literature on pharmacotherapy for pediatric OCD is more extensive than that of cognitive-behavioral treatment for OCD in children (Franklin et al., 2003). The medications most frequently used to treat OCD in children are SRIs. These include the tricyclic antidepressant (TCA) clomipramine, which is an SRI, and the selective serotonin reuptake inhibitors (SSRIs) fluoxetine, fluvoxamine, paroxetine, and sertraline. The majority of studies on psychopharmacology in pediatric OCD have focused on clomipramine (Franklin et al., 1998), which was approved by the FDA in 1989 for the treatment of OCD in children and adolescents aged 10 and older (March & Mulle, 1998

Though there have been fewer trials with the other medications listed above, all of the SSRIs are likely to be effective treatments for OCD in children and adolescents (Franklin et al., 2003; March & Mulle, 1998). Fluoxetine and fluvoxamine have shown benefit in smaller trials but await further study on a larger scale. In a 12-week, double-blind, placebo-controlled trial, sertraline was found to be effective for pediatric OCD treatment, with 42% of patients rated as improved (March et al., 1998). Sertraline also showed significantly greater response, relative to placebo, per the previously mentioned POTS trial (POTS Team, 2004). Geller, Hoog, et al. (2001) reported the efficacy and safety of fluoxetine in the treatment of pediatric OCD after a 13-week double-blind, placebo-controlled clinical trial resulted in 55% of patients (7–18 years old) randomized to the medication being rated as improved. A more complete review of the research base for these medications is beyond the scope of this chapter. For additional information on recommended psychopharmacological treatment for OCD, see March et al., *The Expert Consensus Guideline Series: Treatment of Obsessive-Compulsive Disorder* (1997). The off-label prescribing of polypharmacy combinations, and the use of off-label antipsychotic medications for anxiety, are becoming increasingly common practices in community psychiatry (Comer, Olfson, & Mojtabai, 2010; Comer, Mojtabai, & Olfson, 2011).

Although school-based practitioners are not responsible for prescribing medication to a child with OCD, they should be aware of the medications the child is taking. Practitioners should note any change in behavior, either improvement or otherwise since the start of medication treatment. Practitioners providing psychotherapy to a child should be in close contact with the child's prescribing primary physician and/or psychiatrist. Keeping these lines of communication open is essential for ensuring the best possible treatment outcome for the child.

Assessment and Initial Evaluation

Proper assessment and evaluation is critical in the treatment of OCD. This assessment process should include an initial screening, telephone contact with parents, pretreatment evaluation (including a behavioral analysis), and referral. There are a number of assessment tools that school social workers and other school-based practitioners can use. For a list and description of assessment tools, see Table 9.3 (p. 103). After these preliminary measures, a first appointment is scheduled. Following this first meeting, the practitioner should provide feedback to the child, parent(s), and teacher(s) involved. Once a treatment program has been established, the student's services team should meet with the mental health practitioners involved to decide on school-based interventions. It is also important at this stage to devise a plan for keeping the lines of communication open among the student, the parents, and the school. This component will be essential for developing and implementing the treatment intervention that provides the greatest benefit to the student with OCD (March & Mulle, 1998).

Overview of Cognitive-Behavioral Therapy for OCD

Cognitive-behavioral therapy is the most effective psychosocial treatment for OCD (March & Mulle, 1998). However, there is a lack of studies examining whether CBT protocols can be delivered by practitioners of all theoretical and clinical backgrounds with the same level of efficacy found in research trials (Velting et al., 2004). Similarly, the transportability of these treatments to nonresearch settings, such as schools, has not been examined extensively, though studies designed for this purpose are in progress (Albano & Kendall, 2002). When delivering CBT as treatment for anxious youth, school social workers and other practitioners are encouraged to be flexible, clinically sensitive, and developmentally appropriate (Albano & Kendall, 2002; Kendall & Chu, 2000). Keeping this in mind, practitioners in all settings seeking to use CBT must receive appropriate training and supervision (Velting et al., 2004). Below, the reader will find an overview of cognitive-behavioral therapy, as well as a more detailed description of a CBT protocol for OCD, developed by March and Mulle (1998). This description is not meant to replace the comprehensive protocol in *OCD in Children and Adolescents: A Cognitive-Behavioral Treatment Manual* (March & Mulle, 1998), and school social workers and other practitioners should not use it as such. At the end of this chapter, the reader will find a list of resources and information on how to obtain materials for use in the treatment of OCD, including the *CBT Manual for Children and Adolescents with OCD.*

The Treatment Process

Typically, CBT takes place over 12–20 sessions, depending on the severity and complexity of the case (March & Mulle, 1998). At the beginning of treatment, it is expected that the child has been through a pretreatment evaluation and assessment procedures. Though each session has its own specific goals, there are a few general themes consistent throughout treatment. Each time the practitioner meets with the child, he or she should:

- Check in with parents.
- Review the goals for that session.
- Review topics covered the previous session and any lingering questions or concerns the child may have.
- Introduce new material for the current session.
- Practice/role play new tasks.
- Explain and administer homework for the coming week.
- Provide any fact sheets pertinent to the topics covered at the end of the session. (March & Mulle, 1998)

Keeping these common themes in mind, the CBT treatment process for OCD can be broken into two phases: the acute treatment phase and the maintenance treatment phase. In the acute phase, treatment is geared toward ending the current episode of OCD. In the maintenance phase, treatment focuses on preventing any possible future episodes of OCD. These two phases are marked by the following components of treatment:

- Education: Education is crucial in helping patients and families learn how best to manage OCD and prevent its complications.
- Psychotherapy: Cognitive-behavioral psychotherapy is the key element of treatment for most patients with OCD. (This treatment may either be delivered in school or referred out to community-based programs depending on the available resources.)
- Medication: Medication with a serotonin reuptake inhibitor is helpful for many patients. (March & Mulle, 1998)

Within these two phases, treatment is broken up into four general steps over the course of 12–20 sessions. The following steps are fully described in the next section:

- Psychoeducation (sessions 1–2, week 1)
- Cognitive training (sessions 2–3, weeks 1–2)
- Mapping OCD (sessions 3–4, week 2)
- Exposure/response prevention (sessions 5–20, weeks 3–18) (March & Mulle, 1998)

The length of each session may vary slightly and can depend on the schedules of the parent and child as well as the location of treatment. Ideally, each session should allow 50–60 minutes to cover all of the goals and any additional concerns raised by the child and/or parent. In a school setting, it may be difficult to schedule sessions for this length of time. Some school-based practitioners have modified this type of treatment to fit within one class period to avoid taking the child out of more than one class at a time. Generally the time of each treatment session is arranged as follows:

- Check in (5 minutes)
- Homework review (5 minutes)

- Instruction of new task (20 minutes)
- Discussion of new homework (10 minutes)
- Review of session and homework with parents (10 minutes) (March & Mulle, 1998)

Step 1: Psychoeducation (Session 1)

During the first step of treatment, the practitioner is primarily focusing on establishing rapport with the child and parent as well as educating the family about OCD. This includes talking about OCD as a medical illness and giving the family a comprehensive knowledge base on treatment for the disorder.

Session 1 Goals

1. Establish rapport (initial interview). Treatment begins with the practitioner working to make the child feel safe and comfortable about being in therapy. One or both of the parents should be included in this first part of treatment, and initial conversation should be focused around the child's life apart from OCD. Once the practitioner begins to discuss OCD and how he or she will be working with the child and parent to establish the goals of treatment, the practitioner may be able to assess the level of understanding the family has of OCD and its treatment.
2. Establish a neurobehavioral framework.
    - As a first step in discussing OCD as a disorder, the practitioner provides a neurobehavioral framework around OCD for the child. This is extremely important during the onset of treatment in that it connects the disorder, OCD, and its symptoms with specific behavioral treatments and symptom reduction.
    - Within this discussion, the practitioner should use the neurobehavioral framework to compare OCD to medical illnesses, such as asthma or diabetes.
    - The practitioner should explain how OCD affects the brain and how it works to alter thoughts and behaviors. Symptoms of OCD, such as obsessions, can be described to the child as "brain hiccups."
    - The practitioner can use other illnesses to explain how treatment for OCD will work. Similar to insulin treatment for diabetes, the treatment of OCD may involve medication (SSRIs), and in both disorders, psychosocial interventions are used (i.e., diet and exercise for diabetes, CBT for OCD). Also in both situations, not everyone completely recovers, so additional interventions are used to address any residual symptoms.
    - The practitioner may take this opportunity to use information from the child's psychiatric evaluation to answer questions about and discuss OCD. When working with children who are on medication for OCD, the practitioner may want to stress how medication and CBT can work together to provide an effective treatment for the child.
3. Explain the treatment process. During the first two sessions, CBT as a treatment is explained and discussed in detail, including the following key points:
    - The practitioner should review risks and benefits of behavioral treatment for OCD.
    - Components, expectations, and goals of the treatment are reviewed. This can be a time for questions from the parents and the child about all three of these things. The practitioner should make sure the child understands each of the goals and what the different stages and components of treatment entail. Specifically, the child should have a grasp on EX/RP and how they are connected. The child may be reassured that he or she will not have to do these things on his or her own but will have allies throughout treatment (practitioner, parents) and will be aided with a "tool kit" of coping strategies to use during these exercises.
    - The practitioner lays out an expected time frame for treatment, which can be revisited throughout treatment and altered, based on the child's progress. The practitioner may want to use visual handouts to show what the timeline will look like.
4. Externalize OCD.
    - Practitioners may want to encourage younger children to give OCD an unfavorable nickname, putting OCD on the "other side" of the child. This allows the child to view OCD as something that can be fought rather than something associated with a bad habit or a bad part of his or her personality.
    - Discuss the concept of "bossing back" OCD.

5. Homework. The concept of homework is introduced and discussed. The practitioner should make it clear that the child will always have a collaborative say in what the homework will be.
   - The child should pay attention to where OCD wins and where the child wins in preparation for session 2.
   - If the child has not already done so, he or she should think about a nickname to be used for OCD.
   - The child and parents should review any materials given them from the practitioner and generate any lingering questions they may have for the next session.
   - Parents should work on redirecting their attention toward those things the child does well and away from OCD-related behaviors.
   - When in a school setting, the practitioner may want to spend some time with the parents working on communicating with teachers about their child's OCD. The practitioner may also suggest ways in which teachers can use strategies in the classroom to help the child combat OCD.
   - The child is asked to practice the technique of bossing back OCD for homework.

Step 2: Cognitive Training (CT): Introducing the Tool Kit (Sessions 2–3)

During the second step of treatment, the practitioner introduces cognitive training (CT), which is training in cognitive tactics for resisting OCD (March & Mulle, 1998). This can be distinguished from response prevention for mental rituals. Using CT will work to increase a sense of self-efficacy, controllability, and predictability of a positive outcome for EX/RP tasks.

Session 2 Goals

1. Reinforce information around OCD and its treatment (may be introduced in session 1).
2. Make OCD the problem.
   - Introduce cognitive resistance (bossing back OCD) to reinforce the concept that OCD is external to the child.
   - The practitioner should begin by asking some general questions around how OCD has been bossing the child around since the last session and how the child has successfully bossed OCD back. Some of the settings the practitioner may want to address include home, playing with friends, school, etc. When talking about school, the practitioner may want to ask questions around specific places and times in school and when the child is with specific people.
   - It is imperative during this time to frame EX/RP as the strategy used in the child's "fight" against OCD and the practitioner and parents as the child's allies in this fight.
3. Begin mapping OCD.
   - Introduce the concept of a transition zone between territory controlled by OCD and territory under the child's control.
   - March and Mulle (1998) suggest using the CY-BOCS (Goodman et al., 1989a, 1989b) Symptom Checklist and the patient's history to inventory the child's OCD symptoms. The fear thermometer, introduced in step 4 below, is used as a guide to generate subjective units of discomfort scores (SUDS) for each item on the stimulus hierarchy formulated in session.
   - The child generates the stimulus hierarchy by ranking the OCD symptoms from the easiest to the hardest to boss back. After the child has ranked his or her OCD symptoms on the stimulus hierarchy, areas where the child's life territory is free from OCD, where OCD and the child each "win" some of the time, and where the child cedes control to OCD will become apparent.
   - The transition zone will become obvious as the symptoms are ranked.
4. Introduce the fear thermometer, which encompasses the concepts of talking back to OCD and EX/RP.
5. Using the tool kit. Once the child learns self-talk (bossing back OCD) and how to use positive coping strategies, introduce the cognitive tool kit for use during exposure and response prevention (EX/RP) tasks, which will ease the process as well as support its effectiveness for the child.
6. Homework.
   - The child should pay attention to any OCD triggers he or she can detect and build a symptom list.
   - The CY-BOCS checklist can aid as a guide.

Step 3: Mapping OCD: Completing the Tool Kit (Sessions 3–4)

By the third step of treatment, the child has developed a knowledge base of OCD and a preliminary tool kit of strategies to fight OCD. At this point, the child can begin to work within his or her own experience with OCD, identifying specific obsessions, compulsions, triggers, avoidance behaviors, and consequences (March & Mulle, 1998).

Session 3 Goals

1. Begin cognitive training (CT). The purpose of CT is to provide the child with a cognitive strategy for bossing back OCD. By learning these strategies, the child further solidifies his or her knowledge base of OCD and its treatment, cognitive resistance to OCD, and self-administered positive reinforcement.

- Child reinforcement.
    - Constructive self-talk: The practitioner should identify and help correct negative self-talk.
    - Cognitive restructuring: The practitioner helps the child directly to address any negative assumptions (e.g., risk of getting sick from touching a doorknob) feeding into the child's obsessions. This will help the child's willingness to participate in exposure tasks in later sessions.
    - Separation from OCD: Continue to externalize OCD by separating OCD from the child as something that just comes and goes.
    - Short-form cognitive training: The practitioner may help the child to review and keep these concepts separate by giving repeated examples or writing the concepts down on separate cards the child may take home.

2. Continue mapping OCD and review the symptom list (trigger, obsession, compulsion, fear thermometer).
    - Complete the symptom list (stimulus hierarchy) begun in session 1.
    - Identify obsessions and compulsions using the CY-BOCS Symptom Checklist as a guide.
    - Link obsessions and compulsions with the child's specific triggers.
    - Then rank each trigger, obsession, and compulsion according to fear temperature on a hierarchy (with the highest fear temperature on the top and the lowest on the bottom). The practitioner should be sure to get all of the details around each of these components from the child using specific questions aimed at alleviating any embarrassment the child may have around these behaviors.
3. Learn to use rewards as a strategy. Verbal praise, small prizes, and certificates can be used as positive reinforcement to the child for bossing back OCD successfully and for making progress from session to session. These should be discussed with the child from the beginning of treatment.
4. Homework.
    - Have the child try to identify when OCD wins and when he/she wins as a lead-in to exposure and response prevention.
    - The child should practice cognitive interventions learned in session.

Session 4 Goals

1. Finalize the transition zone.
    - The child generates a stimulus hierarchy with the practitioner on paper which shows where the child is completely free from OCD, where the child and OCD each win the fight some of the time, and where the child feels helpless against OCD.
    - The transition zone lies in the central region and is the point where the child has some success against OCD. Essentially, the transition zone can be identified where the child and OCD overlap.
    - The practitioner should express to the child that she or he is on the child's side as an ally in the area of the hierarchy where the child is free from OCD.
    - Throughout this exercise, the practitioner will help the child work within the transition zone, recognizing and using aspects of the transition zone that will help to guide graded exposure throughout later treatment. The transition zone is recognized as being at the lower end of the stimulus hierarchy, where the high end includes those areas in which the child feels helpless against OCD.
2. Finalize the tool kit in preparation for EX/RP.
    - Solidify a method for selecting EX/RP targets in the transition zone.
    - Review and use the fear thermometer with specifics from the child's symptom hierarchy.

- Review and discuss additional cognitive strategies.
- Review the rewards discussed as a strategy to fight OCD and identify any other rewards for bossing back OCD.

3. Assign trial exposure tasks.
    - Before moving on to the final and longest phase of treatment, some initial exposure and response prevention tasks may be introduced to determine the child's levels of anxiety, understanding of concepts and tasks, and compliance and/or ability to participate in this area of treatment.
    - Some introduction to these tasks reinforces the notion that the child can successfully resist and win the fight against OCD.
    - During this trial period, the practitioner should pay particular attention to the transition zone and whether targets within this zone have been placed correctly. Identifying mistakes in this area at this point in treatment will reduce the chance for hang-ups or misdirection later in treatment.
    - Practice trial EX/RP task in session.
4. Homework. The child should practice a trial exposure every day and pay attention to the level of anxiety felt during each exercise.

Step 4: Exposure and Response Prevention: Implement EX/RP (Sessions 5–20, Weeks 3–18)

During the remaining sessions of treatment, graded EX/RP is implemented. Some children may not need all of the additional 16 sessions. The practitioner also assists in imaginal and in vivo EX/RP practice, which is actively associated with weekly homework assignments. *Exposure* occurs when the child exposes him- or herself to the feared object, action, or thought. *Response prevention* follows and is the process of blocking rituals triggered by the exposure to the feared stimulus and/or reducing avoidance behaviors (March & Mulle, 1998). The practitioner should continue to frame OCD as the enemy, with the child, parents, and practitioner all on the same side, fighting against OCD. Within this framework, the child may use the allies and the tool kit (from CT and EX/RP) developed with the help of the practitioner to resist OCD. This resistance is practiced at home, in school, and throughout therapy. At the beginning of each EX/RP session, the transition zone should be revisited and altered when appropriate. Throughout this process, the child should become more skillful and successful at resisting OCD. Relapse prevention should also be covered, usually in the last one or two sessions of treatment. Additionally, within the main course of treatment, at least two sessions (besides the first one) should include the parents. Finally, one or more booster sessions should be scheduled after treatment is terminated. The first booster session should occur approximately 1 month after the end of treatment (i.e., week 24).

Session 5 Goals

1. Identify OCD's influence with family members.
    - The practitioner should discuss the impact that OCD may have on the child's parents and other family members.
    - OCD symptoms involving the child's parents may be identified and placed on the hierarchy with their own fear temperature.
2. Update symptom hierarchy.
    - At the beginning of each session using exposure and response prevention, it is essential to go back to the symptom hierarchy and make any changes and/or additions necessary.
    - The fear thermometer will also change when the transition zone moves up the hierarchy as the child becomes more and more successful at bossing back OCD at different stages.
3. Continue imaginal and/or in vivo EX/RP. There are a number of different components to consider when using exposure techniques.
    - *Contrived exposure* is shown when the child chooses to face a feared stimulus while *uncontrived exposure* is shown when the child comes into contact with the stimulus unavoidably. With contrived exposure the child is working to end avoidance while uncontrived exposure will force the child to pick RP targets.
    - The practitioner can also introduce the child to exposure for obsessions and/or mental rituals where the child allows him or herself time for obsessions.
    - After the exposure here, the practitioner helps the child to break the rules that OCD usually sets. Some ways to break these rules include:
        - delay the ritual
        - shorten the ritual
        - do the ritual differently
        - do the ritual slowly

- The practitioner should assist EX/RP by modeling the exposure task with and without telling the child.

4. Homework. The child should practice the chosen exposure or response prevention tasks daily. The practitioner should make sure the child has chosen an exposure that will be relatively easy as this will be the first time the child practices on his or her own. The child should be reminded to use all of the strategies in the tool kit.

Session 6 Goals

1. Identify areas of difficulty with EX/RP.
   - Since the last session involved actually doing exposure and response prevention for the first time, the practitioner should try to identify any areas of difficulty or frustration the child is having with EX/RP.
   - The practitioner should pay close attention to the child's levels of anxiety and how he or she manages the anxiety during the exposure task.
2. Continue therapist-assisted EX/RP.
   - After any questions or concerns have been addressed, the practitioner should continue with assisted EX/RP.
   - The tasks that are practiced in session should be among those chosen for homework.
3. Homework. The child should choose one exposure task to practice.

Family Session 1 (Session 7)

At this point in treatment, the practitioner should encourage the parents and/or family to participate in a family session.

Session 7 Goals

1. Include parents in treatment.
   - The primary goal of the family session is to make sure that the parents feel they are included in the treatment. The practitioner may need to review the purpose of treatment at the outset.
   - Discuss the role of parents in treatment as a supportive force for the child and completely separate from OCD itself. The practitioner should discuss with the parents the various roles they may play in the child's treatment and how to carefully manage their own behavior around the child, OCD, and treatment.
   - The practitioner should discuss with the child and parents ways in which the parents can engage in extinction strategies. Extinction procedures should always be discussed and approved by the child.
   - Discuss the possibility of family therapy.
2. Positive reinforcement. Make a plan for special occasions to recognize the child's success (ceremonies) and to inform significant others of the child's success (notifications).
3. Continue EX/RP. The practitioner should continue with an exposure task in session with the child. Based on the discussion with the parents, the exposure task may involve them.
4. Homework. The child should choose an exposure task to practice at home. If the parents are involved in corresponding rituals, the homework may include practice around the parents.

Moving Up the Stimulus Hierarchy (Sessions 8–11)

These four sessions over 4 weeks cover similar material, each session building on the last.

Sessions 8–11 Goals

1. Arrange rewards, ceremonies, and notifications.
   - The practitioner should review these three topics and decisions from the last session.
   - The practitioner should monitor how the child is responding to these reinforcements and whether they are a positive reinforcement to treatment. The practitioner may work with the child and parents to identify points where a ceremony is warranted and how to plan a party around accomplishments.
2. Address comorbidity and therapy needs. The reader is directed to the original treatment manual (March & Mulle, 1998) as well as *The Expert Consensus Guideline Series: Treatment of Obsessive-Compulsive Disorder* (March et al., 1997), for recommendations and references on treatment for comorbidity.
   - Any comorbidity that is present should be addressed, as well as any other therapy needs.
   - Comorbid symptoms should be separated from OCD and treated as such.

3. Continue practitioner-assisted EX/RP.
   - Practitioner-assisted EX/RP is continued with special attention to developmental considerations.
   - The practitioner should continue to encourage the child to move up the symptom hierarchy, practicing harder exposure tasks as treatment continues.
4. Homework. Homework for each session should involve practice of skills learned within the session.

Family Session 2 (Session 12)

Session 12 Goals

1. Remap OCD.
   - The practitioner should revisit how OCD involves and influences the parents and family of the child with OCD.
   - The practitioner should remap OCD with the child and family and make any changes to the symptom hierarchy that has developed over the last four sessions of EX/RP.
2. Implement extinction tasks. With the child's permission, the practitioner should implement extinction tasks with the parents working as co-therapists.
3. Continue EX/RP.
   - The child and parents may practice extinction tasks in session with the practitioner for those tasks in which the parents are enmeshed with OCD.
   - For parents who are not involved directly with the child's OCD, the practitioner may begin to transfer some of the management decisions around choosing exposure tasks to the parents. With the child's permission, the parents may act as co-therapists in this sense. This decision may be influenced by the relationship between the parents and child as well as the parents' understanding of OCD and willingness to be involved in treatment.
4. Homework. The child may choose a new EX/RP task to practice. Additionally, an extinction procedure for the parents to practice for homework is chosen.

Completing EX/RP (Sessions 13–18)

Sessions 13–18 Goals

1. Review child's overall progress. The practitioner should review the child's progress in treatment thus far.
2. Address plateaus.
   - The practitioner should address any areas where the child has exhibited a plateau point between easy and harder EX/RP and the reasons for this.
   - If the child is having a particularly hard time moving to the next stage in the hierarchy, the practitioner may want to schedule a ceremony to officially congratulate the child on completing one stage and moving on to the beginning of another.
3. Choose harder EX/RP tasks. The practitioner can move forward by considering harder EX/RP tasks for the child to practice, with an especially hard EX/RP for the following weekly session.
4. Address comorbidity. The practitioner should be aware at this point in treatment of any comorbidity the child is exhibiting. This should be addressed in treatment and discussed with the parents.
5. Homework.
   - The child should practice an EX/RP task based on the updated stimulus hierarchy.
   - The child may want to ask a friend or family member for help in working on a difficult exposure task at home.

Relapse Prevention (Session 19)

Relapse prevention can be covered in one session but may extend to two or more depending on the needs of the child. The practitioner may assess how the child feels about possible relapse or even "slips" after ending treatment. During these sessions, the practitioner may set up imaginal exposures for the child to practice how he or she would react if a slip were to occur.

Session 19 Goals

1. Explain concept of relapse prevention.
   - Primarily, the child should understand that slips are not a loss of efforts up to this point.
   - The practitioner may openly discuss and address any fears and/or misconceptions the child has of relapse.
2. Provide opportunity for imaginal exposure of relapse. The practitioner may ask the child to think of an example in which he or she may slip and then successfully use the tool kit to boss back OCD. The child should express his or her anxiety levels throughout the exposure, and the practitioner may help by suggesting specific tools to use (e.g., self-talk) in working through the exposure.

3. Address questions or concerns regarding the treatment. Since this session marks the last true treatment session, the child may have questions or concerns regarding the treatment and what happens after treatment.
4. Homework.The child should practice a relapse prevention task either imaginal or in vivo.

Graduation (Session 20)

The main purpose of this "graduation" session is to have a celebration for the child upon completion of treatment.

Session 20 Goals

1. Celebrate the child's accomplishments. During this final session, the main focus is on celebration of the child's accomplishments during treatment.
2. The practitioner should present the child with a certificate of achievement.
3. Notify friends and family members. The child is encouraged to share his or her success with friends and family members.
4. Parents check in. The practitioner should check in with the parents at the end of this last session to address any lingering concerns regarding treatment and OCD.
5. Homework. Homework for the child should be simply to share his or her success with friends and family and to frame the certificate of achievement.

Booster Session (Session 21)

A booster session is scheduled at 4 weeks to reinforce the strategies learned throughout treatment.

Session 21 Goals

1. Celebrate the child's accomplishments since graduation.
2. Review the tool kit.
3. Reinforce relapse prevention.
4. Plan further notifications regarding the end of treatment

Applying Interventions within a Response to Intervention Framework

The state of science for treating OCD affords consistency with the Response to Intervention (RTI) framework, in which school officials implement assessment, monitoring, and intervention programs across primary, secondary, and tertiary prevention levels. In the primary prevention level, the school is sensitive to the needs of youth with OCD. At the secondary prevention level, trained school officials effectively screen for obsessive-compulsive disorder by means of the CY-BOCS, C-FOCI, ChOCI, OCI-CV, and/or ADIS (see Table 9.3), and treat the majority of obsessive-compulsive disorder cases with school-based mental health resources. For those children not responding to secondary-level support, tertiary support is necessary, which may include seeking a comprehensive and interdisciplinary approach to treatment by clinicians with specific expertise in obsessive-compulsive disorder, in order to return the child to normal functioning.

Tools and Practice Examples

Assessment Instruments

In order to make a diagnosis of OCD in children and adolescents, a thorough review of the patient's behavior must be coupled with psychiatric interviews that are specific to an OCD diagnosis (Thomsen, 1998). Table 9.3 lists several assessment tools that may be helpful in the process of diagnosing OCD.

Resources

International Obsessive Compulsive Disorder Foundation (IOCDF)

PO Box 961029
Boston, MA 02196
617–973–5801,
http://www.ocfoundation.org/

- Videotapes on OCD in school-age children
- Reading materials
  - Treatment
  - Symptoms
  - Comorbidity
- List of other resources and Web sites on OCD

Table 9.3 Recommended Assessment Tools

Assessment	*Source*	*Description*
Children's Florida Obsessive Compulsive Inventory (C-FOCI)	Storch et al., 2009	This brief child self-report measure of OCD symptoms for use in clinical and non-clinical settings assesses symptoms and severity along two separate scales. The scale collapses obsessions and compulsions in order to minimize the impact of differing obsession and compulsion severities on a scale total score.
Children's Obsessional Compulsive Inventory (ChOCI)	Shafran et al., 2003	This scale is a child self-report measure used to measure symptoms of compulsions, impairment associated with compulsions, obsessional symptoms, impairment associated with obsessions, and an overall impairment scale. The ChOCI is a downward extension of the adult Maudsley Obsessional Compulsive Inventory. Items are rated on a three-point scale of 1–3, corresponding to "not at all," "somewhat," and "a lot."
Obsessive Compulsive Inventory-Child Version (OCI-CV)	Foa et al., 2009	This 21-item self-report measure of OCD symptoms is a downward extension of the Obsessive Compulsive Inventory for adults. Items are rated on 3-point scales and assess severity across six OCD domains (e.g., hoarding, ordering, washing).
NIMH Global Obsessive-Compulsive Scale	National Institute of Mental Health (public domain)	The scale is clinician-rated and used to generate a global rating from 1 to 15 that represents a description of the present clinical state of the patient. This rating is based on guidelines provided on the scale ranging from "minimal within range of normal or very mild symptoms" to "very severe obsessive-compulsive behavior."
Clinical Global Impairment Scale	National Institute of Mental Health (public domain)	This scale is clinician-rated and used to generate a global rating from 1 to 7 that represents how mentally ill the patient is at the current time, based on the therapist's clinical experience. The descriptions range from "normal, not at all ill" to "among the most extremely ill."
Clinical Global Improvement Scale	National Institute of Mental Health (public domain)	This scale is clinician-rated and used to generate a global rating from 1 to 7 that represents how the patient's condition has changed since the beginning of treatment. The descriptions range from "very much improved" to "very much worse."

(continued)

Table 9.3 (*Countinued*)

Assessment	*Source*	*Description*
Children's Yale-Brown Obsessive-Compulsive Scale*	Developed by Wayne K. Goodman, Lawrence H. Price, Steven A. Rasmussen, Mark A. Riddle, & Judith L. Rapoport Department of Psychiatry Child Study Center, Yale University School of Medicine; Department of Psychiatry, Brown University School of Medicine; Child Psychiatry Branch, National Institute of Mental Health	The CY-BOCS is the most useful and widely used instrument, both clinically and in research. This scale is designed to rate the severity of obsessive and compulsive symptoms in children and adolescents, ages 6 to 17 years old. A clinician or a trained interviewer can administer the scale in a semistructured fashion. Ratings are generated from the parent's and child's reports, who are interviewed together, and the final rating is determined from the clinical judgment of the interviewer. In total, 19 items are rated, and items 1–10 are scored for the total score, with 5 questions pertaining to obsessions and compulsions, respectively. Revised from an adult version, the interview contains questions regarding phenomenology of obsessions and compulsions, distress caused by the symptoms, control over OCD, avoidant behavior, pathological doubting, and obsessive slowness. The instrument is applicable for clinical use, particularly in describing symptoms and measuring any change in treatment (Thomsen, 1998).
Leyton Obsessional Inventory-Child Version	Berg, Whitaker, Davies, Flament, & Rapoport, 1988. © 1988 by Williams and Wilkins.	Transformed from a 65-item questionnaire (or card-sorting test) for adults, to a 20-item test for children and adolescents, this instrument can be used when screening for obsessive-compulsive symptoms, but does not specifically differentiate between obsessive traits and ego-dystonic symptoms (Thomsen, 1998).
Anxiety Disorders Interview Schedule for Children (ADIS-C)	Silverman & Albano, 1996 (available through Oxford University Press)	Semi structured clinical interview for 6–17-year-olds, with child and parent as informants.
Multidimensional Anxiety Scale for Children (MASC)	March, Parker, et al., 1997	Self-report measure for 8–19-year-olds; child informant, 39 items total (10-item short form available), four subscales: physical anxiety, harm avoidance, social anxiety, separation anxiety

*Investigators interested in using this rating scale should contact Wayne Goodman at the Clinical Neuroscience Research Unit, Connecticut Mental Health Center, 34 Park Street, New Haven, CT 06508 or Mark Riddle at the Yale Child Study Center, P.O. Box 3333, New Haven, CT 06510

Pincus, D. B. (2012). *Growing up brave: Expert strategies for helping your child overcome fear, stress, and anxiety*. New York, NY: Little, Brown and Company.

Anxiety-Specific Organizations

Anxiety Disorders Association of America (ADAA)
8730 Georgia Ave.
Silver Spring, MD 20910
240–485–1001

Child & Adolescent Anxiety Disorders Clinic (CAADC)
Temple University
13th Street & Cecil B. Moore Avenue (Weiss Hall, Ground Level)

Philadelphia, PA 19122
www.childanxiety.org

Child and Adolescent Fear and Anxiety Treatment Program
648 Beacon Street, 6th Floor, Kenmore Square
Boston, MA 02215
617–353–9610
http://www.bu.edu/card/

Child Anxiety Network
www.childanxiety.net

Columbia University Clinic for Anxiety and Related Disorders (CUCARD)
3 Columbus Circle, Suite 601
New York, NY 10019
212–246–5740
www.anxietytreatmentnyc.org

Chanskey, T. E. (2001). *Freeing your child from obsessive-compulsive disorder.* New York, NY: Three Rivers Press.

Freeman, J. B., & Garcia, A. M. (2008). *Family-based treatment for young children with OCD: Therapist guide.* New York, NY: Oxford University Press.

March, J. S., & Mulle, K. (1998). *OCD in children and adolescents: A cognitive-behavioral treatment manual.* New York, NY: Guilford Press. Retrieved from www.guilford.com

March, J. S. (2006). Talking back to OCD: The program that helps kids say "no way"—and parents say "way to go." New York, NY: Guilford Press.

Piacentini, J., Langley, A., & Roblek, T. (2007). *Cognitive behavioral treatment of childhood OCD: It's only a false alarm.* New York, NY: Oxford University Press.

Rapoport, J. (1991). *The boy who couldn't stop washing.* New York, NY: Penguin.

Wagner, A. P. (2000). *Up and down the worry hill: A children's book about obsessive-compulsive disorder.* Rochester, NY: Lighthouse Press.

Wagner, A. P. (2002). *Worried no more: Help and hope for anxious children.* Rochester, NY: Lighthouse Press.

Handouts, Tips for Parents, and Guidelines

Expert Knowledge Systems
P.O. Box 917
Independence, VA 24348
www.psychguides.com

OCD Support Groups

http://groups.yahoo.com/group/OCDSupportGroups/links

Practice Example: Background and Reason for Referral

Maria is a 10-year-old Hispanic female in the fifth grade, living with her mother and two older brothers. Her two brothers are significantly older and do not spend a lot of time with Maria. Maria's mother, Ms. Alba, works two jobs, and Maria is often at home by herself. Maria was initially referred to the school-based health clinic at the beginning of the school year by her teacher, who was concerned because he noticed that she was leaving to go to the bathroom a lot and had very red, chapped hands. Maria was assessed by the health clinic and referred to the partnering school-based mental health clinic for further assessment when it became apparent she had underlying symptoms in addition to those exhibited physically.

Jennifer, a social worker at the clinic, contacted Ms. Alba and obtained a verbal report over the phone of Maria's behavior at home. At home, Ms. Alba reported, Maria was very concerned with cleanliness and often spent hours rearranging her room, placing and replacing toys and books on her shelves. Ms. Alba also continually had trouble getting Maria out of the apartment on time for school because Maria would insist on checking to make sure her bed was made correctly and to make sure she had all of her school books in her bag. This could sometimes go on for 30 minutes to an hour and caused Ms. Alba to be late to work on a regular basis. Around meal times, Maria would insist on washing her plate, glass, and hands numerous times before and after her meal. Ms. Alba also noticed Maria had been staying up much later than usual since the start of the school year, completing her homework. Ms. Alba hadn't worried too much about this because she assumed that Maria had more challenging homework to do since she had moved into the fifth grade. Ms. Alba agreed to come into the school-based mental health clinic with Maria to meet with Jennifer for an initial screening and evaluation.

Jennifer also met with Maria's teacher to get a better sense of how Maria behaved in the classroom. Maria's teacher had noticed that Maria seemed extremely anxious when working in certain areas of the classroom and tended to go to the bathroom following activities in other areas of the classroom, including the reading circle and arts and crafts corner. When working at her desk independently or in a group, Maria always seemed to be falling behind, and her teacher would often catch her retracing one word or sentence over and over. When working on writing assignments or math problems, Maria would sometimes get stuck on the first sentence or problem, erasing and rewriting the same thing over and over. Maria seldom finished an assignment and would often be blamed or teased when working in a group for incomplete work.

Assessment

Given the information provided by the mother, teacher, Maria, and intake evaluation, Maria was diagnosed with OCD according to the *DSM-IV-TR* (American Psychiatric Association, 2000).

Other than OCD-related symptoms, Maria did not exhibit any impairment or symptoms for any other Axis I or II *DSM-IV-TR* diagnoses. She had had no previous psychiatric history, and her medical and developmental histories were normal. Nothing remarkable or traumatic had occurred in Maria's life at home or at school recently other than the reported symptoms. Jennifer scheduled a first session with Maria and her mother to begin cognitive-behavioral therapy for OCD. After the initial screening following standard clinic procedures, Jennifer completed an intake evaluation with Maria. Jennifer administered the symptom checklist from the Children's Yale-Brown Obsessive Compulsive Scale (CYBOCS) to determine if specific OCD symptoms were present. Jennifer assigned a baseline score on the CYBOCS showing significant impairment and gave a global rating using the NIMH Global Obsessive-Compulsive Scale. Jennifer also rated Maria's global symptom severity and functional impairment using the Clinical Global Impairment Scale. Jennifer continued to give global ratings after each session using these two scales. Beginning with session two of Maria's treatment, Jennifer assigned a global rating after each session using the NIMH Global Improvement Scale, to monitor functioning and improvement across sessions. Jennifer also checked in with Ms. Alba after each session to address any lingering questions and discuss what she and Maria covered in session.

Implementing the CBT for OCD in Children and Adolescents Treatment Program

Step 1: Psychoeducation and Building Rapport

At the beginning of treatment, Jennifer took some time to talk to Maria about what she likes to do in and out of school, with her friends and family. Maria reported that she likes to spend time with her mother when she is not working. She does not have many friends her own age and does not really like to play games with other children because they get annoyed at her for "ruining" the game by repeating certain steps and movements. Jennifer made an effort to also establish rapport with Ms. Alba by empathizing with her frustrations around struggling in the morning with Maria to get out of the house, as well as dealing with Maria's other behaviors associated with OCD.

Next, Jennifer explained OCD as a type of "hiccup" in Maria's brain that sometimes tells Maria what to think and how to act. While describing the treatment process to Maria and Ms. Alba, Jennifer explained how they will be working together to help Maria "boss back" her OCD. She asked Maria to think of a nickname to give her OCD. Maria chose to call her OCD "Weird Worry" and identified some of her "weird worries" as staying clean; not getting germs from food, other kids, or things in the classroom; keeping her room and desk neat; getting her homework right; and making sure she hasn't forgotten anything when she leaves her apartment. She explained that she makes sure these things don't happen by always washing her hands when she does something new, making sure she cleans and tidies her room before she goes to bed and to school, and checking her assignments over and over again to make sure they are the right answers, at home and at school.

At the end of the first session, Jennifer explained how "homework" would be used during treatment. Jennifer assured Maria that she wouldn't have to write anything for homework outside of treatment, but that treatment homework would involve practicing and thinking about things they talked about and did in session. Maria agreed to this, and after the first session, Jennifer asked her to think about Weird Worry until the next session and look out for where, when, and how Weird Worry bothers her.

Steps 2 and 3: Mapping OCD and Cognitive Training

Over the next three sessions, Jennifer continued to work on showing Maria that OCD is the problem and that Maria can develop skills to boss back and control Weird Worry. Maria practiced resisting her OCD and reported that she had tried to resist copying over her work by telling Weird Worry to go away. During these reports, Jennifer asked Maria about her level of anxiety when resisting Weird Worry. Jennifer explained to Maria that they would begin "mapping" her OCD by labeling the degree of anxiety she experiences over different obsessions and compulsions. Jennifer introduced Maria to the concept of the "fear thermometer" and explained how it would be used to rate her anxiety. Jennifer explained that Maria will rank her specific OCD symptoms/triggers on a scale of 1 to 10. Jennifer helped Maria to write down her specific triggers, obsessions, compulsions, and fear ratings on a chart and labeled this symptom hierarchy as the "Weird Worry List." Jennifer explained she would be helping to coach Maria through this list from the lowest to the highest point, and they would only move on to the next level when Maria was comfortable.

After the symptom hierarchy was complete, Jennifer and Maria determined where in Maria's life she was free from OCD, where she shared control with Weird Worry, and where Weird Worry had complete control over her. Jennifer explained they would be working primarily in the middle area, the transition zone, and would slowly move the transition zone up the hierarchy until Weird Worry did not have any areas of control. Through cognitive training instruction, Jennifer reassured Maria that she could do this by using her tool kit of strategies created in treatment, including bossing back OCD, remembering that her worries/obsessions are just OCD, or Weird Worry, and are separate from her compulsions, and that she didn't have to pay attention to Weird Worry. Jennifer wrote these steps on a card for Maria to carry around with her. Maria continued to think about her symptom hierarchy for homework and began practicing the cognitive strategies she had learned.

At the end of session four, Maria had finalized her symptom hierarchy, including the transition zone, and had a complete tool kit of strategies she was comfortable using in fighting Weird Worry. Jennifer also set up a variety of appropriate rewards for levels of achievement upon which Maria had agreed, including small prizes and certificates.

Step 4: Exposure and Response Prevention (EX/RP)

At the beginning of this step of treatment, Jennifer explained to Maria that they would be moving on to put EX/RP into action. Maria had been practicing not erasing and rewriting her answers so many times and reported her anxiety was much lower when she only copied her answers 5 times instead of 10. Since this symptom target was low on the symptom hierarchy, Jennifer suggested they try practicing the exposure in vivo so Jennifer could help coach Maria through it. Jennifer reminded Maria of her tool kit, and by the end of the exercise Maria had done a few math problems without copying over the numbers. Maria expressed confidence that she could work on this over the next week using her classroom homework as the exposure.

Over the next couple of sessions, Maria reported to Jennifer that she was able to practice resisting Weird Worry by not copying over her answers for classroom homework. She practiced the EX/RP at home and was able to reduce her anxiety so she did not copy some of the questions in her homework and, finally, her entire homework. Jennifer rewarded these accomplishments with praise and asked Maria to identify some new targets from higher up on the symptom hierarchy.

As a higher-anxiety exposure, Maria thought that she might be able to try getting through an activity in the classroom without washing her hands repeatedly afterward. Jennifer suggested trying this as an imaginal exposure first, asking Maria to imagine how she would feel if she participated in this activity and then did not wash her hands before moving on to the next activity. Maria used examples of self-talk to explain how she would lower the anxiety she would feel resisting Weird Worry. Jennifer then set up an in vivo exposure where Maria read her a story and then bossed back OCD by not washing her hands afterward. Jennifer coached Maria through the process of self-talk and pushing away Weird Worry and the urges to wash her hands. Although Maria did not make it through the response prevention the first time without washing her hands, she limited the time spent on scrubbing her hands with soap. After a few sessions of practice, Maria's anxiety around this target had diminished. Jennifer rewarded Maria for her efforts throughout her attempts and Maria agreed to practice resisting this urge in class.

Family Sessions

During the EX/RP step in treatment, Jennifer scheduled two family sessions with Maria and Ms. Alba. Jennifer began the sessions by reviewing Maria's homework and answering any questions Ms. Alba had. Jennifer asked how Weird Worry might affect members of Maria's family. Maria talked about how Weird Worry bosses around her mom and what the fear temperature would be for her if Ms. Alba didn't listen to Weird Worry. Ms. Alba had noticed that Maria was working on practicing the exposures at home but still expressed some frustration with the time she had to take to accommodate Maria's anxiety over dirtiness in the apartment. Ms. Alba had to wash Maria's bed sheets almost every day and wash the dishes multiple times a day or else Maria would not eat off them. Jennifer reiterated the importance of Ms. Alba as a cheerleader for Maria and helped her to think of ways she could help Maria complete an exposure task at home. At first, Ms. Alba was reluctant to reward Maria for eating her dinner without washing the dishes so many times because Ms. Alba believed this was something Maria should be doing anyway. After Jennifer explained the importance of positive reinforcement from her, Ms. Alba agreed to try giving Maria small rewards for accomplishing exposure tasks such as this. Jennifer set up an in vivo exposure with Ms. Alba and Maria where Maria completed a task on her hierarchy with which she was comfortable (writing without retracing), and Ms. Alba practiced encouraging and praising her efforts. At the end of the session, Maria agreed to try sitting down to dinner without having Ms. Alba wash her dishes and glass so many times beforehand.

Throughout the EX/RP step in treatment, which took place over 13 sessions in 14 weeks, Maria continued to practice in vivo EX/RP as well as practicing at home and in the classroom. Jennifer continued to monitor Maria's progress through global ratings and check ins with Ms. Alba. She also held conferences with Maria's teacher to discuss any progress or possible regression in the classroom, but the teacher reported only positive results. Jennifer worked with the teacher to come up with some small rewards and examples of praise the teacher could use without singling Maria out from the rest of the class.

Relapse Prevention

After the EX/RP sessions were complete and Maria felt that Weird Worry had been won over, one session was devoted to discussing relapse prevention. Jennifer distinguished the concept of "relapse" from a "slip" in which Maria may feel some of her OCD symptoms coming back. Jennifer assured Maria that she should not think of possible slips as failure on her part but that they are normal occurrences that may come and go, which she can manage using the strategies learned and practiced while in treatment. Jennifer coached Maria through an imaginal exposure where she pictured herself having a slip in which she felt the urge to scrub her hands after sharing in an art project with classmates. Maria successfully used self-talk to extinguish the anxiety she felt during the exposure and felt confident she would be able to manage the same situation if it happened for real. Jennifer walked Maria through her symptom hierarchy and discussed ways in which Maria could handle various slips for each symptom. Jennifer checked in with Ms. Alba and discussed the upcoming graduation with her and Maria as well as the process for booster sessions in the future if Maria or Ms. Alba felt they were needed.

Graduation

This final session of treatment focused solely on Maria's accomplishments since first coming to the mental health clinic. Maria reflected on the treatment process and recalled specific advances she had made up the symptom hierarchy as well as all of the times she won and gained control over OCD. Jennifer supported this realization by sharing the declining scores on the CY-BOCS and the increase in global ratings over the course of Maria's treatment. Jennifer presented Maria with a certificate of achievement and encouraged Maria to share her certificate as well as her success with her friends and family members. Jennifer checked in with Ms. Alba as well to address any remaining questions she had about the treatment and what would happen now that Maria was not in treatment. Ms. Alba seemed confident that Maria had the tools to manage her OCD on her own with Ms. Alba as the primary cheerleader. Jennifer scheduled one booster session for the following month and reminded Maria that she could always come speak to her if she felt the need for additional booster sessions.

Key Points to Remember

Obsessive-compulsive disorder poses a significant risk to children and adolescents, with estimates of 1 in 200 children suffering from the disorder (Adams et al., 1994). School-based practitioners can play a valuable role in identifying, assessing, and treating children with OCD. Cognitive-behavior therapy, often in conjunction with pharmacotherapy, is the intervention most commonly used to treat OCD.

Though not thoroughly tested in school-based settings, CBT is an effective and useful treatment for school-based practitioners, given the brevity of treatment, flexibility, and transportability across settings and age groups. The school-based setting poses multiple challenges, however, and school-based practitioners should keep the following key points in mind:

- Training and supervision are crucial in learning and implementing cognitive-behavioral therapy.
- The *CBT Treatment Manual* for children and adolescents with OCD (March & Mulle, 1998) and the helpful handouts and tips within the manual are essential tools when providing this intervention.
- Teachers and parents can be a valuable asset to the school-based practitioner in identifying, assessing, and treating the child. Practitioners are encouraged to provide teachers and parents in the school and community with information about OCD as an educational and preventive measure.
- Asking parents, teachers, and other informants to complete assessments about the child in treatment can help the practitioner to obtain a comprehensive picture of the child's behavior at the outset as well as the child's improvement throughout treatment. Practitioners should be aware of the time constraints on teachers' schedules and use appropriate assessment instruments (e.g., short version self-report assessments).
- Because OCD can be exhibited differently at home and school, ongoing communication among teachers, parents, and the practitioner is instrumental in the success of the treatment. School-based practitioners should collaborate with teachers and parents on scheduling sessions and sharing information so as to best fit the needs of all parties involved.

References

Adams, G. B., Waas, G. A., March, J. S., & Smith, M. C. (1994). Obsessive-compulsive disorder in children and adolescents: The role of the school psychologist in identification, assessment, and treatment. *School Psychology Quarterly, 9*(4), 274–294.

Albano, A. M., & Kendall, P. C. (2002). Cognitive behavioural therapy for children and adolescents with anxiety disorders: Clinical research advances. *International Review of Psychiatry, 14*, 129–134.

American Academy of Child and Adolescent Psychiatry. (1998). Practice parameters for the assessment and treatment of children and adolescents with obsessive-compulsive disorder. *Journal of the American Academy of Child and Adolescent Psychiatry, 37*, 27S–45S.

American Psychiatric Association. (2000). *Diagnostic and statistical manual of mental disorders* (4th ed., text revision). Washington, DC: Author.

Berg, C. Z., Whitaker, A., Davies, M., Flament, M. F., & Rapoport, J. L. (1988). The survey form of the Leyton Obsessional Inventory-child version: Norms from an epidemiological study. *Journal of the American Academy of Child and Adolescent Psychiatry, 27*(6), 759–763.

Chansky, T. E. (2001). *Freeing your child from obsessive-compulsive disorder: A powerful, practical program for parents of children and adolescents.* New York, NY: Three Rivers Press.

Clark, D. A. (2000). Cognitive behavior therapy for obsessions and compulsions: New applications and emerging trends. *Journal of Contemporary Psychotherapy, 30*(2), 129–147.

Comer, J. S., Kendall, P. C., Franklin, M. E., Hudson, J. L., & Pimentel, S. S. (2004). Obsessing/worrying about the overlap between obsessive-compulsive disorder and generalized anxiety disorder in youth. *Clinical Psychology Review, 24*, 663–683.

Comer, J. S., Mojtabai, R., & Olfson, M. (2011). National trends in the antipsychotic treatment of psychiatric outpatients with anxiety disorders. *American Journal of Psychiatry, 168*, 1057–1065.

Comer, J. S., & Olfson, M. (2010). The epidemiology of anxiety disorders. In H. B. Simpson, F. Schneier, Y. Neria, & R. Lewis-Fernandez (Eds.), *Anxiety disorders: Theory, research, and clinical perspectives* (pp. 6–19). New York, NY: Cambridge University Press.

Comer, J. S., Olfson, M., & Mojtabai, R. (2010). National trends in child and adolescent psychotropic polypharmacy in office-based practice, 1996–2007. *Journal of the American Academy of Child and Adolescent Psychiatry, 49*, 1001–1010.

Foa, E. B., Coles, M. E., Huppert, J. D., Pasupuleti, R., Franklin, M. E., & March, J. S. (2009). Development and validation of a child version of the Obsessive Compulsive Inventory. *Behavior Therapy, 41*, 121–132.

Foa, E. B., Franklin, M. E., & Kozak, M. J. (1998). Psychosocial treatments for obsessive-compulsive disorder. In R. P. Swinson, M. M. Antony, et al. (Eds.), *Obsessive-compulsive disorder: Theory, research, and treatment* (pp. 258–276). New York: Guilford.

Foster, P. S., & Eisler, R. M. (2001). An integrative approach to the treatment of obsessive-compulsive disorder. *Comprehensive Psychiatry, 42*(1), 24–31.

Franklin, M. E., Kozak, M. J., Cashman, L. A., Coles, M. E., Rheingold, A. A., & Foa, E. B. (1998). Cognitive-behavioral treatment of pediatric obsessive-compulsive disorder: An open clinical trial. *Journal of the American Academy of Child and Adolescent Psychiatry, 37*(4), 412–419.

Franklin, M. E., Abramowitz, J. S., Bux, Jr., D. A., Zoellner, L. A., & Feeny, N. C. (2002). Cognitive-behavioral therapy with and without medication in the treatment of obsessive-compulsive disorder. *Professional Psychology, 33*(2), 162–168.

Franklin, M. E., Rynn, M., Foa, E. B., & March, J. S. (2003). Treatment of obsessive-compulsive disorder. In M. A. Reinecke, M. F. Dattilio, et al. (Eds.), *Cognitive therapy with children and adolescents: A casebook for clinical practice* (2nd ed., pp. 162–184). New York: Guilford.

Franklin, M. E., Freeman, J., & March, J. S. (2010). Treating pediatric obsessive-compulsive disorder using exposure-based cognitive-behavioral therapy. In J. R. Weisz & A. E. Kazdin (Eds.), *Evidence-based psychotherapies for children and adolescents* (2nd ed.). New York, NY: Guilford.

Freeman, J. M., & Garcia, A. M. (2008). *Family-based treatment for young children with OCD: Therapist guide*. New York, NY: Oxford University Press.

Freeman, J. M., Garcia, A. M., Swedo, S. E., Rapoport, J. L., Ng, J. S., & Leonard, H. L. (2006). Obsessive-compulsive disorder. In M. K. Dulcan & J. M. Weinerm (Eds.), *Essentials of child and adolescent psychiatry* (pp. 441–454). Arlington, VA: American Psychiatric Publishing.

Garcia, A. M., Freeman, J. B., Himle, M. B., Berman, N., Ogata, A. K., Ng, J., Choate-Summers, M. L., Leonard, H. et al. (2009). Phenomenology of early childhood onset obsessive-compulsive disorder. *Journal of Psychopathology and Behavioral Assessment, 31*, 104–111.

Garcia, A. M., Sapyta, J. J., Moore, P. S., Freeman, J. B., Franklin, M. E., March, J. S., & Foa, E. B. (2010). Predictors and moderators of treatment outcome in the Pediatric Obsessive Compulsive Treatment Study (POTS I). *Journal of the American Academy of Child and Adolescent Psychiatry, 49*, 1024–1033.

Geller, D. A., Biederman, J., Faraone, S., Agranat, A., Cradock, K., Hagermoser, L., Kim, G., Frazier, J., & Coffey, B. J. (2001). Developmental aspects of obsessive-compulsive disorder: Findings in children, adolescents, and adults. *Journal of Nervous and Mental Disease, 189*(7), 471–477.

Geller, D. A., Hoog, S. L., Heiligenstein, J. H., Ricardi, R. K., Tamura, R., Kluszynski, S., Jacobson, J. G., & Fluoxetine Pediatric OCD Study Team. (2001). Fluoxetine treatment for obsessive-compulsive disorder in children and adolescents: A placebo-controlled clinical trial. *Journal of the American Academy of Child and Adolescent Psychiatry, 40*(7), 773–779.

Goodman, W., Price, L., Rasmussen, S., Mazure, C., Delgado, P., Heninger, G. R., & Charney, D. S. (1989a). The Yale-Brown Obsessive Compulsive Scale: II. Validity. *Archives of General Psychiatry, 46*(11), 1012–1016.

Goodman, W., Price, L., Rasmussen, S., Mazure, C., Fleischmann, R. L., Hill, C. L., Heninger, G. R., & Charney, D. S. (1989b). The Yale-Brown Obsessive Compulsive Scale: I. Development, use, and reliability. *Archives of General Psychiatry, 46*(11), 1006–1011.

Kampman, M., Keijsers, G. P. J., Hoogduin, C. A. L., & Verbraak, M. J. P. M. (2002). Addition of cognitive-behaviour therapy for obsessive-compulsive disorder patients non-responding to fluoxetine. *Acta Psychiatrica Scandinavica, 106*, 314–319.

Kendall, P. C., & Chu, B. C. (2000). Retrospective self-reports of therapist flexibility in a manual-based treatment for youth with anxiety disorders. *Journal of Clinical Child Psychology, 29*(2), 209–220.

Kessler, R. C., Berglund, P., Demler, O., et al. (2005). Lifetime prevalence and age-of-onset distributions of DSM-IV disorders in the National Comorbidity Survey Replication. *Archives of General Psychiatry, 62*, 593–602.

Langley, A. K., Lewin, A. B., Bergman, R. L., Lee, J. C., & Piacentini, J. (2010). Correlates of comorbid anxiety and externalizing disorders in childhood obsessive-compulsive disorder. *European Child and Adolescent Psychiatry, 19*, 637–645.

Leonard, H. L., Ale, C. M., Freeman, J. B., Garcia, A. M., & Ng, J. S. (2005). Obsessive-compulsive disorder. *Child and Adolescent Psychiatric Clinics of North America, 14*, 727–743.

March, J., Frances, A., Kahn, D., & Carpenter, D. (1997). The expert consensus guidelines series: Treatment of obsessive-compulsive disorder. *Journal of Clinical Psychiatry, 58*(Suppl. 4), 1–72.

March, J. S., Mulle, K., & Herbel, B. (1994). Behavioral psychotherapy for children and adolescents with obsessive-compulsive disorder: An open trial of a new protocol-driven treatment package. *Journal of the American Academy of Child & Adolescent Psychiatry, 33*(3), 333–341.

March, J. S., Parker, J. D. A., Sullivan, K., Stallings, P., & Conners, C. K. (1997). The Multidimensional Anxiety Scale for Children (MASC): Factor structure, reliability, and validity. *Journal of the American Academy of Child & Adolescent Psychiatry, 36*(4), 554–565.

March, J. S., Biederman, J., Wolkow, R., Safferman, A., Mardekian, J., Cook, E. H., Cutler, N. R., Dominguez, R., Ferguson, J., Muller, B., Riesenberg, R., Rosenthal, M., Sallee, F. R., & Wagner, K. D. (1998). Sertraline in children and adolescents with obsessive-compulsive disorder: A multicenter randomized controlled trial. *Journal of the American Medical Association, 280*(20), 1752–1757.

March, J. S., & Mulle, K. (1998). *OCD in children and adolescents: A cognitive-behavioral treatment manual.* New York: Guilford.

Pediatric OCD Treatment Study (POTS) Team. Cognitive-behavior therapy, sertraline, and their combination for children and adolescents with obsessive-compulsive disorder: The Pediatric OCD Treatment Study (POTS) randomized controlled trial. *Journal of the American Medical Association, 27,* 1969–1976.

Piacentini, J., Bergman, L., Keller, M., & McCracken, J. (2003). Functional impairment in children and adolescents with obsessive-compulsive disorder. *Journal of Child and Adolescent Psychopharmacology, 13*(1), S61–S69.

Piacentini, J., Langley, A., & Roblek, T. (2007). Cognitive behavioral treatment of childhood OCD: It's only a false alarm. New York, NY: Oxford University Press.

Rowa, K., Antony, M. M., & Swinson, R. P. (2000). Behavioral treatment of obsessive-compulsive disorder. *Behavioural and Cognitive Psychotherapy, 28,* 353–360.

Scahill, L., Riddle, M., McSwiggin-Hardin, M., Ort, S., King, R., Goodman, W., et al. (1997). Children's Yale-Brown Obsessive-Compulsive Scale: Reliability and validity. *Journal of Child and Adolescent Psychiatry, 36,* 844–852.

Shafran, R., Frampton, I., Heyman, I., Reynolds, M., Teachman, B., & Rachman, S. (2003). The preliminary development of a new self-report measure for OCD in young people. *Journal of Adolescence, 26,* 137–142.

Silverman, W. K., & Albano, A. M. (1996). *Anxiety Disorders Interview Schedule for DSM-IV: Child and parent versions.* San Antonio, TX: The Psychological Corporation.

Silverman, W. K., Pina, A. A., & Viswesvaran, C. (2008). Evidence-based psychosocial treatments for phobic and anxiety disorders in children and adolescents. *Journal of Clinical Child and Adolescent Psychology, 37,* 105–130.

Southam-Gerow, M. A., & Kendall, P. C. (2000). Cognitive-behavioral therapy with youth: Advances, challenges, and future directions. *Clinical Psychology and Psychotherapy,* 7, 343–366.

Storch, E. A., Khanna, M., Merlo, L. J., Loew, B. A., Franklin, M., Reid, J. M., Goodman, W. K., & Murphy, T. K. (2009). Children's Florida Obsessive Compulsive Inventory: Psychometric properties and feasibility of a self-report measure of obsessive-compulsive symptoms in youth. *Child Psychiatric and Human Development, 40,* 467–483.

Thomsen, P. H. (1998). Obsessive-compulsive disorder in children and adolescent: Clinical guidelines. *European Child and Adolescent Psychiatry,* 7, 1–11.

Velting, O. N., Setzer, N. J., & Albano, A. M. (2004). Update on and advances in assessment and cognitive-behavioral treatment of anxiety disorders in children and adolescents. *Professional Psychology, 35*(1), 42–54.

Wagner, A. P. (2002). *What to do when your child has obsessive-compulsive disorder: Strategies and solutions.* Rochester, NY: Lighthouse Press.

Wagner, A. P. (2003a). Cognitive-behavioral therapy for children and adolescents with obsessive-compulsive disorder. *Brief Treatment and Crisis Intervention, 3*(3), 291–306.

Wagner, A. P. (2003b). *Treatment of OCD in children and adolescents: A cognitive-behavioral therapy manual.* Rochester, NY: Lighthouse Press.

Warren, R., & Thomas, J.C. (2001). Cognitive-behavior therapy of obsessive-compulsive disorder in private practice: An effectiveness study. *Anxiety Disorders, 15,* 277–285.

CHAPTER 10

Effective Interventions for Adolescents with Depression

Jacqueline Corcoran ■ Jane Hanvey-Phillips

Getting Started

A *major depression* is a period of two weeks or longer during which a person experiences a depressed mood or loss of interest in nearly all life activities (APA, 2000). *Dysthymic disorder* represents a general personality style featuring symptoms that are similar to, but less intense than, those of major depression. Depression occurs in about 2.8% of elementary-age children, but in adolescents rates increase to 5.7% (Costello, Erkanli, & Angold, 2006), making depression for this age group a significant mental health issue. For this reason the focus of this chapter will be on depression in adolescence. Adolescent depression is a major risk factor for suicidal ideation, suicide attempts, and completed suicides (Cottrell et al., 2002; Waslick, Kandel, & Kakouros, 2002). See chapter 1 on how to identify and prevent suicide in adolescents. Finally, adolescent depression presents risk for the continuation of depression into adulthood (Klein, Dougherty, & Olino, 2005). For these reasons, school social workers should demonstrate the knowledge and competence to assess for depression in teenagers and offer appropriate treatment and referrals.

What We Know

Intervention research has tended to focus on cognitive-behavioral models. *Behavioral* models focus on the development of coping skills, especially in the domain of social skills and choosing pleasant daily activities, so that the youth receive more reinforcement from their environments. *Cognitive* models include assessing and changing the distorted thinking that people with depression exhibit, in which they cast everyday experiences in a negative light. Interventions based on cognitive-behavioral models include the following components:

- the identification and restructuring of depressive thinking
- social skills training (how to make and maintain friendships)
- communication and social problem solving (how to share feelings and resolve conflicts without alienating others)
- developing aptitudes pertaining to self-esteem (establishing performance goals)
- progressive relaxation training to ease the stress and tension that can undercut enjoyment of activities
- structuring mood-boosting activities into daily life

A representative cognitive-behavioral model for teens involves the Coping with Depression for Adolescents course (Clarke et al., 1995; Lewinsohn, Clarke, Hops, & Andrews, 1990). Although modified over time, versions include the following components delivered over 15–16 sessions: (1) cognitive restructuring, (2) social skills training (how to make and maintain friendships), (3) communication and social problem solving (how to share feelings and resolve conflict without alienating others), (4) progressive relaxation training (to ease stress and tension), and (5) structuring mood-boosting activities into daily life. Some versions involve concurrent parent groups that involve sharing information about the topics and skills being taught in the adolescent group.

Several reviews—both meta-analyses and reviews according to the American Psychological Association (APA) Division 12 Task Force—have been conducted on the youth depression treatment outcome studies. Two meta-analyses will be reviewed here, Weisz et al. (2006) and Watanabe, Hunot, Omori, Churchill, and Furukawa (2007), as earlier meta-analyses (Lewinsohn & Clarke, 1999; Michael & Crowley, 2002; Reinecke, Ryan, & DuBois, 1998) possessed certain limitations (Weisz et al., 2006). The Weisz et al. (2006) meta-analysis targeted psychotherapy of child and adolescent depression and included dissertations, along with the published research. Weisz et al. (2006) located 35 studies and found an overall effect size of 0.34 with regard to improvement of depression. At follow-up, the effects diminished still further.

Another systematic review was published on child and adolescent psychotherapy that manualized treatment of depression excluding family therapy (Watanabe et al., 2007). Twenty-seven studies were included; psychotherapy was found to be significantly superior to wait-list or attention-placebo, but not to treatment as usual. In sum, these two reviews indicate that treatment appears to result in a small effect on depression symptoms, and findings dissipate over time. However, Vitiello (2009) states that "The overall small effect size of these treatments should not be misinterpreted as a sign of weak therapeutic value. For about one third of depressed youths treatment does make a substantial difference, alleviating depression and returning them to normal functioning. Another third, however, improve on nonspecific clinical contact (placebo condition) ... The small effect size of treatments of adolescent depression is in good part a consequence of the large placebo effect" (p. 394).

Two APA Division 12 Task Force Criteria reviews have also recently been conducted (David-Ferdon & Kaslow, 2008; Verdeli et al., 2006). For adolescents, if all the different CBT manuals offered for adolescent depression are considered as an aggregate, then they meet the criteria for "well-established" (Verdeli et al., 2006). However, when the manualized treatments are covered separately, only the work of the research team of Lewinsohn and colleagues, Coping with Depression for Adolescents (Clarke et al., 1995; Lewinsohn et al., 1990), merited the standard of "probably efficacious treatment" for adolescents. In studies, client characteristics were provided, treatment was manualized, and more than two group design studies performed better than alternative treatment or no-treatment control for reducing depression. It is prevented from having the status of "well-established" because only one research team has been involved in its study (David-Ferdon & Kaslow, 2008). However, the Coping with Depression for Adolescents course is particularly relevant for the school setting since some of its studies have been located in school systems.

What We Can Do

Intervention in the school system for depression could include primary prevention (for all teens in a particular school), secondary prevention (targeting teens of parents who are depressed, as these teens have a high risk of becoming depressed themselves), or tertiary prevention (targeting teens who test positive when screened for depression). It is highly recommended that the social worker and mental health counselors screen for depression in the school; unlike externalizing problems (aggression, acting-out behaviors), which are better identified by a teacher or parent, internalizing problems, such as depression, are more accurately reported by the adolescent (Cottrell et al., 2002; Mufson & Moreau, 1997). As a result, we recommend that school social workers and mental health counselors use measures of proven standardization to screen for depression. A review of this literature was drawn from Myers and Winters (2002). The interested reader may also consult Klein et al. (2005). Please see Table 10.1 for information on these measurement instruments.

Empirically tested cognitive-behavioral treatment models are available for public use. Specifically, the Clarke, Lewinsohn, and Hops (1990) curriculum, the Adolescent Coping with Depression course, is available on the Internet (http://www.kpchr.org/public/acwd/acwd.html). A shortened version of this curriculum will be described in this chapter and is available from the second author. (For some other empirically validated manuals, please see the list at the end of the chapter.)

The present intervention uses a group format consisting of six one-hour sessions offered once a week. A variety of techniques are employed, including education, group discussion, role-play, and behavior rehearsal. Homework is emphasized as an important component of the intervention, with students being told that the amount of effort they invest in homework is associated with the amount of improvement they will feel. Given that teenagers may have difficulty with written assignments, participants are given credit even if they try to do tasks and report the results of their attempts to the group. Reinforcement may involve candy or small novelty

Table 10.1 Measures for Youth Depression

Children's Depression Inventory (Kovacs, 1992)	• 27-item, self-report inventory for children from ages 8 to 13 • measures severity (0 to 2) of overt symptoms of depression such as sadness, sleep and eating disturbances, anhedonia, and suicidal ideation • modified from the Beck Depression Inventory for adults • translated into several languages	Multi-Health Systems 908 Niagra Falls Blvd. North Tonawanda, NY 14120–2060 800–456–3003 www.mhs.com
Reynolds Adolescent Depression Scale (Reynolds, 1987)	• measures *DSM-III* criteria for depression over the past two weeks • has primarily been developed and used with school samples • recommended for screening rather than outcome	Psychological Assessment Resources, Inc. P.O. Box 998 Odessa, FL 33549 800–383–6595 800–331–8378 www.parine.com
Center for Epidemiologic Studies Depression Scale for Children (Weissman, Orvaschel, & Padian, 1980)	• comprises items empirically derived from adult depression scales • assesses symptoms over the past week • widely employed with adolescents	www. depressedchild.org/ Tests/Depression %20Test.htm
Beck Depression Inventory II (Beck, Brown, & Steer, 1996)	• self-report measure with 21 items, each having four answer options • targeted audience includes depressed adults, adolescents, elderly individuals, inpatients, outpatients, primary care patients, patients with medical conditions • works well with a wide range of ages and cultures, both males and females	Harcourt Assessment 19500 Bulverde Road San Antonio, TX 78259

items that teens find desirable. It often helps to ask the students what they find rewarding.

To make the intervention generally available to a wide variety of students, inclusion and exclusion criteria are kept to a minimum. The primary inclusion criteria for prospective participants include clinically significant depression as shown by scores on standardized measures that suggest depression (for example, a score of 10 or greater on the Beck Depression Inventory [BDI]). Exclusion criteria also include unwillingness to consent to the intervention and students who do not speak or understand English (unless the group is composed entirely of students who speak another language and a facilitator is available to speak the language effectively). Students who report suicidality or who are determined to be suicidal are referred for evaluation and additional intervention outside the school setting.

Session 1: Introduction to the Group and Social Skills

The purpose of the group is shared with the students; it is to help them learn skills for controlling their moods. The following introduces the connections among feelings, thoughts, and actions.

Students learn that the way they feel influences how they think and behave, which then influences their feelings and thoughts, and so on. They are told that when people "feel bad," they're less likely to engage in enjoyable activities, and they doubt their ability to be successful at those things (for example, making new friends). When people are successful at some effort, they feel positive and gain self-confidence.

The facilitator then explains that they will work on changing *actions* by increasing pleasant activities, improving social skills, and developing effective communication and problem-solving skills. They will work on changing *thoughts* by stopping negative thoughts and increasing positive thoughts. They will work on changing *feelings* by changing their thoughts, changing their actions, and learning relaxation skills.

Rules for the group are then formulated. Although group members are encouraged to come up with their own rules, the following should be included:

- Avoid depressive talk.
- Allow each person to have equal time.
- Maintain confidentiality.
- Offer support that is constructive, caring, and non-pressuring.

The first topic for the group is social skills, which are discussed as important for positive interactions to occur and to build or improve relationships. Students are taught to make eye contact, to smile, to say something positive about other people, to reveal information about themselves, when to start a conversation and what to say, and how to leave a conversation.

For the first session's homework, students are asked to practice their newly acquired skills at least twice in the upcoming week.

Session 2: Pleasant Activities

The session begins by asking students to report on their homework efforts from session 1. As an introduction to the topic for the day, students are told that pleasant activities are important for feelings of well-being. Teens are then given a list of possible activities to engage in during the upcoming week, including listening to music, hanging out with friends, and driving a car. It is recommended that co-facilitators brainstorm with the group about ideas for activities. Homework assigned for this session involves setting a reasonable goal for increasing the number of pleasant activities and then engaging in this number of activities during the upcoming week.

Session 3: Relaxation Training

Students are informed about the role of stress and tension in depression. They are then informed that relaxation is likely to contribute to a reduction in both anxiety and depression. The facilitators guide the students through two different relaxation techniques: the Jacobson technique (progressive muscle relaxation) and the Benson technique (focusing on a word or phrase while doing progressive muscle relaxation). Homework for this session is to practice the Benson relaxation technique three times and to practice the Jacobson relaxation technique at least three times. The recommendation is made to do at least one of these techniques *every day* at a quiet time.

Session 4: Cognitive Restructuring

This session begins by educating students about the effects of decreasing negative thoughts and increasing positive thoughts. They are then taught how to replace negative thoughts with positive counter-thoughts. Students are given instructions on how to use the A-B-C (activating event, belief, and consequences) technique to change their thoughts, and thus their moods.

To interrupt or stop negative thoughts, three techniques are taught:

1. *Thought stopping.* When alone and thinking negatively, students are instructed to yell "STOP" as loudly as possible and to then say, "I won't think about that any more." Students are told to gradually change from yelling to thinking "Stop," so the technique can be used in public.
2. *The rubber band technique.* Students are told to wear a rubber band on their wrists and snap it every time they catch themselves thinking negatively. This technique should reduce negative thoughts.
3. *Set aside worrying time.* This involves scheduling a time each day to focus on troubling issues. The idea is to make an appointment with oneself for worrying; 15 minutes should be plenty.

Homework for this session is to use at least one thought-stopping technique at least twice during the week when negative thoughts cause problems.

Session 5: Communication Skills

This session involves a great deal of active participation from group members. Group members learn about appropriate responses that emphasize reflective, or active, listening with the facilitators modeling appropriate reflective listening techniques following a didactic presentation. Students are taught the difference between *understanding* and *judgmental* responses and are told that *understanding* responses promote healthier communication. Next, self-disclosure and the appropriateness of self-disclosure in given situations are addressed. Students are taught that appropriate self-disclosure includes talking about feelings related to events: "I feel _________ when you _________. I would prefer _________." They then practice this technique with their peers.

It is important to note that teens often have difficulty expressing negative feelings; therefore, in this session, they are educated about helpful ways to do this. Three possible situations are addressed: resisting peer pressure, telling a friend about something that person did that bothered them, and declining a friend's request for something. Students are assisted in identifying appropriate ways to express their feelings in these situations. For homework, group members are asked to use the self-disclosing format ("I feel ...") two times in the coming week.

Session 6: Problem Solving/ Negotiation and Maintaining Gains

The problem-solving process is taught in order to work out situations with others that are bothersome. The process includes defining the problem, brainstorming, examining possible options, deciding on an option, implementing an option, and evaluating the implementation. The co-facilitators model the techniques in a role-play, and group members practice.

During this final session, students are asked to "change gears" and prepare for the group's termination. They are told that, not uncommonly, group members feel a void when the group disbands. They are assisted in preparing for termination by reminding them to use the cognitive-behavioral coping skills they have been learning throughout the course. Students are given a "life plan" worksheet to identify potentially stressful life situations—both positive and negative—and the plans they can make to cope with these. They are also given information on the symptoms of depression and are strongly encouraged to contact a physician, school social worker, or therapist if they notice symptoms persisting for a period of two weeks. They are reminded that putting off the help they need won't make the depression go away. Finally, students are asked to complete a posttest measure of depression to determine their level of improvement (or decline) since the beginning of treatment. If appropriate and feasible, the measure could be used weekly to evaluate results via a single system design approach.

Use of Medications

For adolescent depression, selective serotonin reuptake inhibitors (SSRIs) (i.e., Prozac, Paxil, Celexa, Zoloft), as compared to tricyclic antidepressants, have shown greater therapeutic effectiveness and fewer adverse effects. Indeed, the tricyclic antidepressants are not recommended for children given the lack of evidence to support their use (Hazell, O'Connell, Heathcote, & Henryk, 2003). In examining the SSRI treatment outcome studies in youth overall, Hetrick et al. (2007) found significant improvement in depression compared to placebo but also an 80% greater risk of a suicide event. Separate results for the different SSRIs have also been aggregated. Prozac and Zoloft have shown sufficient efficacy for adolescents, but only Prozac has received sufficient support for children (Bridge et al., 2007; Usala, Clavenna, Zuddas, & Bonati, 2008; Whittington et al., 2004). The reason why depressed children respond better to fluoxetine compared with other agents is unclear but could be due to study quality, location, or properties of the medication itself, such as its long half-life (Bridge et al., 2007). From the findings on the risk of suicide with SSRIs, practitioners should educate the youth and the family on the potential benefits and risks of SSRIs and help them consider the various options for treatment. The risk of suicide should be assessed and, if medication is used, it should be monitored regularly.

Often, medication must be administered in the school setting. This may be the case because the student has a dosing schedule requiring administration during the time he or she is at school, or may occur if a child forgets to take medication at home. As McCarthy, Kelly, and Reed (2000) note, budget cuts in a time of increasing demand for school-based health services require more unlicensed assistive personnel (UAP) or students themselves to administer medication at school. Controversy concerns the administration of medication by nonmedical personnel and their ability to read health care provider orders, to properly store medications, to monitor students for side effects, and to dispense medications accurately. An additional area of concern is the need to have parental permission to dispense needed medications at school (McCarthy et al., 2000). For parents who do not realize the importance of medication compliance, obtaining permission to dispense medication at school may be difficult. Additionally, it may be necessary for students to keep medication at home *and* at school, creating a financial burden for the family. Finally, there is the potential for students to abuse medication at school if proper monitoring is not in place. This might include selling or trading medication with other students or taking the wrong dose of their own medication. Clearly, medication issues create a dilemma for effective management in the school setting.

Challenges with School-Based Interventions

Although school-based interventions provide access to services that might otherwise be unavailable to depressed teens, they are not without challenges. Confidentiality remains one of the chief concerns in the implementation of interventions in the school setting, both in terms of identifying those at risk and in providing a confidential environment for provision of interventions (Atkins, Graczyk, Frazier, & Abdul-Adil, 2003; Satcher, 2004). Additional difficulties include integration of services with other providers outside the school and obtaining support from school personnel to facilitate interventions (Satcher, 2004). Parents also play a significant role in the success of school-based interventions. Without their consent, interventions may be prohibited for students; therefore it is necessary to educate parents, as well as students, about the intended outcomes of participation in school-based interventions. Despite these challenges, the benefits of providing interventions are likely to outweigh the difficulties of implementation.

Applying Interventions within a Response to Intervention Framework

Although cost-benefit studies may still need to be addressed, universal interventions for the prevention of adolescent depression, based on the available evidence, may not be indicated (Merry et al., 2004; Sawyer et al., 2007). However, an RTI approach might involve the school professional administering one of the screening instruments (like the ones reviewed above) school-wide to identify youth with elevated scores. Then, based on the scores, the most appropriate level of intervention can be determined. For example, group CBT intervention might then be offered to youth at Tier 3. Youth at high risk for depression, such as those whose parent is depressed or divorcing or those who have recently lost a family member, could also be offered group CBT as a Tier 2 approach. Selective programs offered to these types of high-risk youth seem to produce larger intervention effects than universal programs, at both posttest and follow-up (Horowitz & Garber, 2006; Merry et al., 2004; Stice et al., 2009).

Tools and Practice Examples

The following list provides an overview of interventions used with depressed students in the school setting.

Manuals

Clarke, G., Lewinsohn, P., & Hops, H. (1990). The adolescent coping with depression course. Available from http://www.kpchr.org/public/acwd/acwd.html

Gilham, J., Reivich, K., & Jaycox, L. (2008). *The Penn Resiliency Program*. Unpublished manuscript. University of Pennsylvania.

Mufson, L., Dorta, K. P., Moreau, D., & Weissman, M. M. (2004). *Interpersonal psychotherapy for depressed adolescents* (2nd ed.). New York, NY: Guilford Press.

Stark, K. (1990). *Childhood depression: School-based intervention*. New York, NY: Guilford Press.

Stark, K., & Kendall, P. (1996a). *Taking action: A workbook for overcoming depression*. Available from www.workbookpublishing.com

Stark, K., & Kendall, P. (1996b). *Treating depressed children: Therapist manual for "Taking action."* Available from www.workbookpublishing.com

Weisz, J. R., Weersing, V. R., Valeri, S. M., & McCarty, C. A. (1999a). *Therapist's manual for PASCET: Primary and secondary control enhancement training program*. Los Angeles, CA: University of California.

Weisz, J. R., Weersing, V. R., Valeri, S. M., & McCarty, C. A. (1999b). *Act and think: Youth practice book for PASCET.* Los Angeles, CA: University of California.

Case Example

Leah Hernandez was a 15-year-old Hispanic female who lived with her mother, stepfather, and older brother. There were economic difficulties, and the level of tension in the household was high. Leah's grades had begun to decline in the past few months; she was irritable and spent most of her free time sitting alone in her room or sleeping. At her school, social workers began screening students for depression, using the Beck Depression Inventory (BDI), to identify students who could benefit from participation in a cognitive-behavioral intervention. Leah participated in the screening and obtained a score of 23, which is considered a moderate level of depression.

The social worker met with Leah privately to explain that a training course was being offered to help students manage their moods. Leah was agreeable to participating, but since she was a minor, the social worker had to contact Leah's mother, Gloria Perez, and described the program to her. Mrs. Perez agreed to allow Leah to participate.

The course began one week after the conversation with Leah's mother. Arrangements had been made for the students to be excused from class for an hour, and they were welcomed with doughnuts and soft drinks. Two social workers introduced themselves as the group facilitators, then explained the format of the course and the rules for participation. Leah was shy about role-playing in front of the other students, but said that having practiced starting a new conversation, it would probably be easier for her to do so on her own that week as homework.

During the session on pleasant activities, Leah reported that she rarely engaged in any activities she enjoyed. She told the group that her mother and stepfather would tell her she should be working rather than having fun. The social workers addressed this issue and encouraged Leah to identify activities that would not disrupt the household, such as listening to relaxing music in her room, writing poetry (which Leah said she used to enjoy), or taking bubble baths.

During the session on relaxation, the students were given the opportunity to practice progressive muscle relaxation skills. At first, Leah reported that she felt awkward trying to relax with other people in the room, but found she was able to follow instructions easily after the social worker told all of the students to close their eyes so nobody was looking. Leah reported feeling calm and comfortable at the end of the session and willingly practiced the relaxation skills at home during the week.

Leah realized during the session on cognitive restructuring that she usually exaggerated negative experiences and minimized positive experiences. During the time Leah was participating in the group, she failed a math test and told one of the social workers, "I'm just stupid. That's why I failed." The social worker pointed out that Leah usually passed tests and, in fact, her grades had been improving recently. Leah was able to acknowledge this and stated that she would ask for help before the next math test and believed she could pass it then.

The session on communication skills focused on reflective listening and the use of "I feel ..." messages. Leah had difficulty, at first, using "I feel" statements but eventually was able to understand the concept and was encouraged to practice at home. Leah reported that during the week, she and her mother had several positive conversations and that Leah's mood had improved as a result of them.

Leah was quiet during the session on conflict resolution. She appeared to attend to the discussion but did not participate. At the end of the group time, the social workers asked if she understood the concepts of brainstorming and problem solving as ways to reduce conflict. Leah replied that they seemed like good ideas, but she didn't think they would work with her family. The social workers encouraged Leah to present the material to her parents and ask them to try the strategies. She agreed to do so. When she returned the following week, she reported that her mother tried to use brainstorming with her, but her stepfather told her he wasn't going to negotiate anything with her; she would have to do things his way. The social workers helped Leah to identify cognitive coping strategies she could use when faced with her stepfather's unwillingness to change.

As part of the final group session, students identified gains made in treatment and planned for the future. During this session, Leah reported feeling a sense of contentment: Her grades had improved, conflict with her mother was greatly reduced, and she had found pleasant activities to do that did not upset the family.

Key Points to Remember

- Depressed adolescents are at risk for serious negative outcomes and can benefit from school-based interventions.
- Cognitive-behavioral group interventions have been shown to be effective and are recommended in the school setting.
- The recommended intervention includes attention to social skills, pleasant activities, relaxation, cognitive restructuring, communication, and problem-solving and negotiation skills.
- Assessment before and after the intervention is recommended.
- For adolescents with severe depression and/or suicidal ideation, adjunctive interventions may also be recommended.

Notes

1. A *major depressive episode* is a period of at least two weeks during which a person experiences a depressed mood or loss of interest in nearly all life activities.
2. *Dysthymic disorder* represents a general personality style featuring symptoms that are similar to, but less intense than, those of major depression. This diagnosis requires two years of a continuously depressed mood (one year for children and adolescents). It generally has an early age of onset (childhood through early adulthood) and produces impairments in school, work, and social life.
3. *Dysphoria* is depression that is subclinical in nature—when teens do not meet full criteria for either dysthymia or major depression.

References

American Psychiatric Association. (2000). *Diagnostic and statistical manual of mental disorders* (4th ed., text rev.). Washington, DC: Author.

Atkins, M. S., Graczyk, P. A., Frazier, S. L., & Abdul-Adil, J. (2003). Toward a new model for promoting urban children's mental health: Accessible, effective, and sustainable school-based mental health services. *School Psychology Review, 35*, 525–529.

Beck, A. T., Brown, G., & Steer, R. A. (1996). *Beck Depression Inventory II manual.* San Antonio, TX: Psychological Corporation.

Bridge, J. A., Iyengar, S., Salary, C. B., Barbe, R. P., Birmaher, B., Pincus, H. A., ... Brent, D. A. (2007). Clinical response and risk for reported suicidal ideation and suicide attempts in pediatric antidepressant treatment: A meta-analysis of randomized controlled trials. *The Journal of the American Medical Association, 297*, 1683–1696.

Clarke, G., Hawkins, W., Murphy, M., Sheeber, L., Lewinsohn, P., & Seeley J. (1995). Targeted prevention of unipolar depressive disorder in an at-risk sample of high school adolescents: A randomized trial of a group cognitive intervention. *Journal of the American Academy of Child and Adolescent Psychiatry, 34*, 312–321.

Clarke, G., Lewinsohn, P., & Hops, H. (1990). *The adolescent coping with depression course.* Retrieved from http://www.kpchr.org/public/acwd/acwd.html

Costello, E. J., Erkanli, A., & Angold, A. (2006). Is there an epidemic of child or adolescent depression? *Journal of Child Psychology and Psychiatry and Allied Disciplines, 47*, 1263–1271.

Cottrell, D., Fonagy, P., Kurtz, Z., Phillips, J., & Target, M. (2002). What works for whom? A critical review of treatments for children and adolescents. In P. Fonagy, M. Target, D. Cottrell, J. Phillips, & Z. Kurtz (Eds.), *Depressive disorders* (pp. 89–105). New York, NY: Guilford Press.

David-Ferdon, C., & Kaslow, N. J. (2008). Evidence-based psychosocial treatments for child and adolescent depression. *Journal of Clinical Child and Adolescent Psychology, 37*(1), 62–104.

Hazell, P., O'Connell, D., Heathcote, D., & Henryk, D. (2003). Tricyclic drugs for depression in children and adolescents (Cochrane Review). In *The Cochrane Library*, Issue 1. Oxford: Update Software.

Hetrick, S. E., Merry, S. N., McKenzie, J., Sindahl, P., & Proctor, M. (2007). Selective serotonin reuptake inhibitors (SSRIs) for depressive disorders in children and adolescents. *Cochrane Database of Systematic Reviews*, Issue *3*, CD004851.

Horowitz, J. L., & Garber, J. (2006). The prevention of depressive symptoms in children and adolescents: A meta-analytic review. *Journal of Consulting and Clinical Psychology, 74*, 401–415.

Klein, D., Dougherty, L., & Olino, T. (2005). Toward guidelines for evidence-based assessment of depression in children and adolescents. *Journal of Clinical Child and Adolescent Psychology, 34*, 412–432.

Kovacs, M. (1992). *Children's Depression Inventory manual.* (Available from Multi-Health Systems, 908 Niagara Falls Blvd., North Tonawanda, NY 14120–2060; (800) 456–3003; www.mhs.com)

Lewinsohn, P., Clarke, G., Hops, H., & Andrews, J. (1990). Cognitive-behavioral treatment for depressed adolescents. *Behavior Therapy, 21*, 385–401.

Lewinsohn, P., & Clarke, G. (1999). Psychosocial treatments for adolescent depression. *Clinical Psychology Review, 19*(3), 329–342.

McCarthy, A. M., Kelly, M. W., & Reed, D. (2000). Medication administration practices of school nurses. *Journal of School Health, 70*(9), 371–376.

Merry, S., McDowell, H., Hetrick, S., Bir, J., & Muller, N. (2004). Psychological and/or educational interventions for the prevention of depression in children and adolescents (Cochrane Review). In *The Cochrane Library* (Issue 2). Chichester, England: John Wiley & Sons.

Michael, K. D., & Crowley, S. L. (2002). How effective are treatments for child and adolescent depression? A meta-analytic review. *Clinical Psychology Review, 22*, 247–269.

Mufson, L., & Moreau, D. (1997). Depressive disorders. In R. T Ammerman & M. Hersen (Eds.), *Handbook of prevention and treatment with children and adolescents: Intervention in the real world context* (pp. 403–430). New York, NY: John Wiley.

Myers, K., & Winters, N. C. (2002). Ten-year review of rating scales: II. Scales for internalizing disorders. *Journal of the American Academy of Child and Adolescent Psychiatry, 41*, 634–660.

Reinecke, M., Ryan, N., & Dubois, D. (1998). Cognitive-behavioral therapy of depression and depressive symptoms during adolescence: A review and meta-analysis. *Journal of the American Academy of Child and Adolescent Psychiatry, 37*, 26–34.

Reynolds, W. (1987). *Reynolds Adolescent Depression Scale (RADS).* Odessa, FL: Psychological Assessment Resources.

Satcher, D. (2004). School-based mental health services (policy statement). *Pediatrics, 113*, 1839–1845.

Sawyer, M., Harchak, T., Spence, S., Bond, S., Graetz, B., Kay, D., ... Sheffield, J. (2010). School-based prevention of depression: A 2 year follow-up of a randomized controlled trial of the beyondblue schools research initiative. *Journal of Adolescent Health, 47*, 297–304.

Stice, E., Shaw, H., Bohon, C., Marti, C., & Rohde, P. (2009). A meta-analytic review of depression prevention programs for children and adolescents: Factors that predict magnitude of intervention effects. *Journal of Consulting and Clinical Psychology, 77*, 486–503.

Verdeli, H., Mufson, L., Lee, L., & Keith, J. A. (2006). Review of evidence-based psychotherapies for pediatric mood and anxiety disorders. *Current Psychiatry Reviews, 2*(3), 395–421.

Usala, T., Clavenna, A., Zuddas, A., & Bonati, M. (2008). Randomized controlled trials of selective serotonin reuptake inhibitors in treating depression in children and adolescents: Systematic review and meta-analysis. *European Neuropsychopharmacology, 18*, 62–73.

Vitiello, B. (2009). Treatment of adolescent depression: What we have come to know. *Depression & Anxiety, 26*, 393–395.

Waslick, B. D., Kandel, B. A., & Kakouros, B. S. (2002). Depression in children and adolescents: An overview. In D. Shaffer & B. D. Waslick (Eds.), *The many faces of depression in children and adolescents* (pp. 1–36). Washington, DC: American Psychiatric Association.

Watanabe, N., Hunot, V., Omori, I. M., Churchill, R., & Furukawa, T. A. (2007). Psychotherapy for depression among children and adolescents: A systematic review. *Acta Psychiatrica Scandinavica, 116*, 84–95.

Weissman, M. M., Orvaschel, H., & Padian, N. (1980). Children's symptom and social functioning self-report scales: Comparison of mothers' and children's reports. *The Journal of Nervous and Mental Disease, 168*, 736–740

Weisz, J., Jensen-Doss, A., & Hawley, K. (2006). Evidence-based youth psychotherapies versus usual clinical care. *American Psychologist, 61*(7), 671–689.

Whittington, C. J., Kendall, T., Fonagy, P., Cottrell, D., Cotgrove, A., & Boddington, E. (2004). Selective serotonin reuptake inhibitors in childhood depression: Systematic review of published versus unpublished data. *Lancet, 363*, 1341–1345.

CHAPTER 11

Collaborative Strengths-Based Brief Therapy with Self-Harming Students

Matthew D. Selekman

Getting Started

Adolescents today are growing up in a highly toxic, media-driven, consumerist culture and struggling to cope with high levels of stress in all areas of their lives. Like a fast-acting pain killer, many adolescents report that self-harming behavior can offer them quick relief from emotional distress and other stressors in their lives. Several of my students have identified trying to fit in and keep up with their peers as the number one stressor they struggle with. Adolescents are plagued by "too-muchness," too many consumer choices, too many activities, too much homework, too many colleges to choose from, and so forth (Schwartz, 2004). Many of these youth are being hurried along into adulthood long before they are ready to assume these responsibilities. Their parents have overscheduled them in too many extracurricular activities and put a lot of pressure on them to pull in those high grades so that they can get into the *best* colleges possible!

Thanks to the power of media advertisements and the blatant biases of some of the major TV networks, teenagers are regularly seduced into believing that quick-fix solutions are the best way to manage stress and problems. Pharmaceutical companies are buying up more advertising time on major television network stations to market their wonder drugs for depression, anxiety, and attention deficit disorder. Several times a day young people are being bombarded by violent images and receiving messages that the way to solve problems is to respond with aggression. In other forms of the media, teenagers see images of how certain alcoholic beverages can make them more "sexy," "social," and look "cool." They may observe their parents chain smoking or misusing alcohol and other drugs to relieve stress or to manage difficulties in their lives. Today's teenagers have learned a number of shortcuts for numbing away emotional distress and escaping from the demands of life, such as self-harming behavior. When adolescents cut or burn themselves, their bodies' immediately secrete endorphins into their bloodstream to quickly numb away the pain. Self-harming adolescents and adults learn that they can manipulate their brain chemistry into serving as a 24-hour pharmacy for an endogenous opiate fix whenever they need quick emotional relief. Two other commonalities that self-harming adolescents and adults share is that close to 70% of the students tend to experience relief from emotional distress after engaging in this behavior and tend to feel guilty and ashamed, and experience a downward swing in mood a few hours later (Favazza & Selekman, 2003). This, in turn, will often lead to thoughts of wanting to self-harm again to alleviate the emotional distress. Favazza (1998) has also found that 50% of his students had concurrent difficulties with bulimia.

Many self-harming students report feeling emotionally disconnected and invalidated by their parents and, in some cases, their peers. One major cause of the family emotional disconnection process is high technology. Today, it is more important for adolescents to spend most of their free time on Facebook, texting, and playing computer games than being in the offline world with family and friends. Screens do not help develop or strengthen adolescents' social skills, uphold family values, and make them more compassionate people. Many parents do not provide any guidelines around screen usage and then get upset with their kids for not wanting to spend time together as a family. In some cases, the parents are emotionally spent from their stressful jobs or are experiencing the perils of long-term unemployment and are just not available to provide emotional support to their kids. Unfortunately, this disconnection process may lead to the adolescent seeking refuge in a second *family* outside the home of unsavory peers who may be engaging in self-harming, substance-abusing, eating-distressed, and other problematic behaviors (Selekman, 2006; Taffel & Blau, 2001). As school social workers and school-based professionals, we need to be sensitive to the role the above aggravating factors have played in the development and maintenance of a student's self-harming behavior.

What We Know

The collaborative strengths-based brief therapy approach to resolving adolescent self-harming and other closely related self-destructive behaviors has shown good clinical results. This integrative and eco-systemic model combines the best elements of solution-focused (De Shazer, 1991, 1988; Berg & Miller, 1992; De Shazer et al., 2007); positive psychology (Czikszentmihalyi, 1997; Fredrickson, 2009; Peterson, 2006; Peterson & Seligman, 2004; Seligman, 2011); MRI brief strategic (Fisch & Schlanger, 1999; Fisch, Weakland, & Segal, 1982; Watzlawick, Fisch, & Weakland, 1974); narrative (White, 2007; Epston, 1998; White & Epston, 1990; Durrant & Coles, 1991); collaborative language systems (Anderson, 1997; Anderson & Goolishian, 1988); Buddhist psychology (Hanh, 2003, 2001; Bennett-Goleman, 2001); cognitive therapy (Seligman, Reivich, Jaycox, & Gillham, 1995); art therapy (Selekman, 2010, 2009); and expressive writing (Pennebaker, 2004) approaches. In a qualitative study, 20 high-school-aged female and male self-harming adolescents who had concurrent difficulties with bulimia, substance abuse, and engaging in sexually risky behaviors and also had had multiple treatment experiences in a variety of treatment settings were interviewed while receiving collaborative strengths-based brief family therapy and up to two years follow-up. What we found was that all the participants, both adolescents and parents alike, reported that they liked the "positive emphasis on strengths," "the optimistic nature," and "feeling empowered and more hopeful" about their situations after just one collaborative strengths-based brief family therapy session. They also reported that this approach increased their awareness levels of "the tools built into them," both past and present positive problem-solving and coping strategies, and creative ideas and insights. Finally, in spite of intense conflicts with their parents, the majority of the adolescents in the study wanted to "grow into" their relationships with their parents and wanted them to know that they appreciated and loved them (Selekman, 2009; Selekman & Schulem, 2007).

The only other major family research study that could be found in the literature with self-harming adolescents was conducted by Santisteban and colleagues (2003). They developed an integrative family therapy approach, which they tested out in a study with self-harming adolescents who were diagnosed with borderline personality disorder. The researchers found that 70% of their sample was retained in therapy, and the clients rated their treatment experiences highly on alliance and satisfaction measures. This study was one of the first attempts to study the effectiveness of family interventions with self-harming adolescents. Unfortunately, most of the other studies conducted with self-harming individuals combined adolescents and adults in their samples, so it is difficult to determine who responded best to the interventions employed.

What We Can Do

Since many self-harming adolescents have difficulties with mood management, using therapeutic approaches like collaborative strengths-based brief therapy can trigger positive emotion, decrease negative mood states, and increase happiness, hope, and optimism levels. Fredrickson (2009) has found in numerous studies that when individuals are living and working in climates with high levels of positive emotion, they tend to be more focused and perform at a higher level with their creative problem-solving abilities. Another important dimension of the collaborative strengths-based brief therapy approach is strengthening self-harming adolescents' self-soothing capacities. In addition to teaching them disputation skills for disrupting negative thought processes (Seligman, 2011; Seligman et al., 1995), teaching adolescents mindfulness meditation and visualization strategies can help them to quiet their minds and center them (Selekman, 2010, 2009; Hanh, 2003, 2001; Bennett-Goleman, 2001). Finally, because adolescent self-harming difficulties can be multifaceted and quite complex, I have found it necessary to intervene on multiple levels in their social ecologies. This includes intervening with their families, with their peer groups, with concerned school staff and/or adult inspirational others, with other involved larger systems professionals, and with other key members from their social networks. In school settings, it may not always be possible to get parents and key members from the adolescents' social networks to come for meetings there because of conflicting work schedules, child care responsibilities, transportation difficulties, and so forth. In these situations, family sessions can be conducted telephonically, or a one-person family therapy approach can be employed (Szapocznik, Hervis, & Schwartz, 2003). On a flip chart or whiteboard, the adolescents can identify particular relationships they wish to change in their family and map out the key destructive problem-maintaining patterns of interaction that they would like to see changed in these relationships. The school-based professional can offer pattern intervention strategies for the adolescent to experiment with in an attempt to disrupt the destructive patterns of interaction in the relationship. It is important to let the adolescent know that in spite of his or her best efforts, the proposed experiments do not always work, and it is helpful to come up with a plan b, c, and d as backup options to pursue, in case what he or she has attempted is not producing the kind of changes desired.

Major Collaborative Strengths-Based Brief Therapy Strategies and Experiments

In this section of the chapter, I present some of the major collaborative strengths-based brief therapy strategies and experiments I regularly use with self-harming adolescents to empower them to achieve their treatment goals and resolve their difficulties. Since most school social workers and mental health counselors do not have access to students' parents due to their work schedules or have the luxury of doing family therapy sessions, I present only interventions that can be used with individual students.

Interviewing for Possibilities: Creating a Climate Ripe for Change in the First Session

When beginning the counseling process with self-harming students, it is critical to take the time to elicit from them information regarding their self-generated pretreatment changes, key strengths and resources, theories of change, and what their best hopes from the counseling experience are. The students' strengths and resources can be channeled into their identified problem and goal areas to co-construct solutions. In our therapeutic conversations and with therapeutic experiment design and selection, we should use the clients' strengths, key words, beliefs, and metaphors connected to their major skill areas as much as possible to help foster a cooperative relationship with them. In addition, having the client talk about his or her strengths and resources triggers positive emotion, which can enhance his or her problem-solving capacities (Fredrickson, 2002).

In order to gain a better understanding of why students gravitated toward self-harming behavior as a coping strategy, it is important to invite students to share their self-harming story about how they discovered it, what the benefits and various specific functions it serves for them are, when and where it is most likely to occur, and what effect this behavior has on key relationships within their family and in their social network. The students take the lead in determining the treatment goals they wish to work on, even if it has nothing to do with their self-harming behavior. Our job is to closely collaborate with them in negotiating small and doable behavioral goals.

The Solution-Enhancement and Positive Trigger Log Experiments

The solution-enhancement and positive trigger log experiments complement one another and are specifically designed to reduce the frequency of self-harming episodes and for relapse prevention purposes. Adolescents are instructed to pay close attention to useful self-talk, problem-solving and coping strategies, and involvement in specific hobbies and activities that help them not cave into hurting themselves (Selekman, 2009, 2006, 2005; De Shazer, 1985).

The positive trigger log encourages self-harming students to keep track of and write down daily what specifically their parents and siblings, closest friends, adult inspirational others, and other important people from their social network do that help them to not cave in to hurting themselves and trigger positive emotions for them. After one week of adding entries to the log and reviewing it with adolescents, I make a copy of it and they can carry it around with them and refer to it in a high-risk and stressful situations when in need of useful coping strategies (Selekman, 2009, 2006).

Plan Out Your Perfect Day

One highly effective therapeutic experiment for helping self-harming adolescents be less reactive to their negative triggers and avoid toxic people and places is having them write down the night before what specifically they would need to do or accomplish that would make the next day a perfect one (Selekman, 2009; Peterson, 2006). This includes certain tasks they would need to complete or master, certain positive and supportive people they would be associating with, and living and performing in certain contexts that tend to be positive and uplifting environments for them. At the end of each day, they are to rate the day on a scale from 10 to 1, with 10 being the best day of their life and 1 being the worst. It is best to have students do this experiment over a two-week period so that clear patterns will emerge of what works best to prevent self-harming and other self-destructive behaviors from occurring and triggers positive emotion for them. They also learn what specifically they need to make happen to have 6 (good days) or better days. Conversely, they learn what tasks or activities to not slip up with or to steer clear of and toxic people and places they need to avoid at all costs that could lead to 4 (sub-par days) or lower. With the help of this highly practical experiment, both the clients and school social workers gain valuable insight about what to increase doing that works.

Pretend the Miracle Happened

When the student cannot identify any pretreatment changes or presently occurring exceptions (non-problem behaviors, thoughts, or feelings), I like to offer the student the *pretend the miracle happened* experiment. For example, if the student has conflict with two of her teachers and she is failing those classes, I may have her pick 2 days over the next week to pretend to engage in the miracle-like behaviors she thinks they would like to see from her. While pretending to engage in the teachers' miracle behaviors for the student, she is to carefully notice how they respond to her. Oftentimes students are pleasantly surprised to see how people dramatically change when they alter their behavior. I have used this experiment with students who are experiencing peer difficulties as well.

Do Something Different

This experiment can be used in multiple ways in school settings. I offer it to students who are stuck engaging in unproductive ways of thinking or behaving that are further exacerbating their problem situations. For example, one of my former clients associated with a group of peers that she would be more than likely to share a razor blade with. These peers were her best friends, and she was not ready or willing to sever her ties with them. As an experiment, I had her respond differently to them whenever they would encourage her to or begin to cut themselves around her. The client came up with three useful different ways of responding to them: leave the room in which the group self-harming behavior was occurring, change the topic when the idea of cutting was brought up, and raise the volume on the stereo and start dancing. According to my client, these creative strategies helped her to successfully avoid the temptation to cut herself and at times would change her friends' behaviors as well. Similar to the pretend the miracle happened experiment, this change strategy can be used with clients who are experiencing difficulties with particular teachers.

Imaginary Feelings X-Ray Machine

When working with self-harming students who appear to have grave difficulty expressing their thoughts and feelings or have somatic complaints, I offer them the *imaginary feelings X-ray machine experiment* (Selekman, 2005, 2006, 2009, 2010). I have the student lie down on a long sheet of paper that has the durability of meat wrapping paper. The next step is to draw the outline of his or her body. I share with the adolescent to pretend that I have turned the X-ray machine on so we can see inside them what their feelings look like. The student is to draw pictures of what he or she thinks his or her feelings look like. The feelings can be depicted in scenarios from his or her life or in symbol form. On a cautionary note, try to refrain from making interpretations of the symbols, images, or scenes depicted in the self-harming student's drawings. Instead, use curiosity and ask open-ended questions, like a cultural anthropologist visiting an indigenous native's village for the first time and asking, "What does that symbol mean to you?" This art experiment is a wonderful exercise to use in adolescent groups.

Famous Guest Consultant Experiment

This playful thinking-out-of-the-box experiment taps clients' imagination powers to generate solutions for their difficulties (Selekman, 2005, 2006). I have students generate the list of three famous people that they have always admired or have been inspired by. These famous people can be historic figures, TV and movie celebrities, singers and groups, star athletes, artists, authors, and characters from popular books. I ask the students to pretend to put themselves in the heads of their selected famous people and think about how they would solve their problem or achieve their goal. Adolescents have a lot of fun with this experiment and often generate some very creative solutions with the help of their famous consultants.

Visualizing Movies of Success

This highly effective visualization tool can help disrupt the student's self-harming pattern of behavior (Selekman, 2005, 2006). The student is to close her eyes and capture a sparkling moment in her past where she had achieved or accomplished something that made her very proud of herself. She is to apply all of her senses to the experience, including color and motion. I have the client project this movie of success onto a screen in her head and watch it for 10–15 minutes with her eyes remaining closed. In order to get good at accessing their movies of success, I have students practice this visualization twice a day. What is interesting to note is that this exercise generates positive emotion in the person, which has been found to create a climate ripe for high-quality creative problem solving (Fredrickson, 2009).

Mindfulness Meditation

Many self-harming students lack the capacity to soothe themselves when experiencing emotional distress. One effective tool we can teach them is mindfulness meditation (Hanh, 2003, 2001; Bennett-Goleman, 2001). There are many types of *mindfulness meditations*. Being mindful is one's ability to focus on one specific word, bodily sensation, or object and yet embrace or label everything that enters your mind. I teach students about *mantras*, that is, a word or a line they can say to themselves for a designated period of time. If the word *mantra* is objectionable to the school or the client, another word can be used to describe the process. I also like to teach them food and sound meditation. Like the visualizing movies of success tool, it is helpful to practice meditating twice a day for 10–15 minutes at a time. Research indicates that mindfulness meditation can lower our breathing and heart rates, reduce our emotional reactivity when experiencing stress, and strengthen our self-awareness and concentration abilities (Selekman, 2009, 2010; Bennett-Goleman, 2001).

Interviewing the Problem

This very creative narrative therapy experiment (Selekman, 2006; Epston, 1998) can be used with students who have been oppressed by their self-harming behavior or other chronic difficulties for a long time. The social worker or counselor is to pretend to be a reporter for the *New York Times* newspaper covering a story on the student's identified problem (cutting, the attitude, bulimia, etc.). The student is to pretend to put herself into the shoes of the problem and gain an inside-looking-out-perspective through its eyes and mind. Like a good reporter, the social worker or counselor needs to secure as many details as possible from the problem regarding its decision to enter the student's life; whether it is a friend or foe; how it has been helpful to the student; how it has wreaked havoc in the student's life; how it brainwashes the student; and what effect it has on family members, peers, teachers, and other significant people in her life. The reporter can also ask the problem what the student and significant others do to thwart or frustrate it and what they do that works the most to undermine it when it is up to its tricks.

The power of this therapeutic experiment is that helps liberate the student from the clutches of the problem and it can help her become more aware of the problem's tricks, so she can outsmart it when it is up to no good. Most adolescents like drama and find this experiment to be fun and insightful.

Habit Control Ritual

The habit control ritual was developed by Durrant and Coles (1991) to help empower the client, his or her parents, and involved helping professionals to conquer the externalized tyrannical problem. Once the student, the parents, the social worker, and concerned school staff have externalized the problem based on the client's description of it or belief about it, as a team they can keep track on a daily basis of what they do to stand up to the problem and not allow it to get the best of them. They are also to keep track of the problem's victories over them. On a chart in the social worker's or school-based professional's office, they can write down their effective coping and problem-solving strategies as well as the various ways the problem undermines their efforts by dividing them and promoting behavioral slips with the client. Like the interviewing the problem experiment, the client is liberated from the shackles of the problem and free to pursue a new direction with his or her life. The parents' and school staff's original way of viewing the problem situation and interactions with the client can dramatically change as well.

Bringing in Peers and Inspirational Others

Some of the self-harming students we work with are struggling to cope with very stressful home situations. There may be destructive invalidating family interactions, or the parents may be emotionally disconnected from the student. They may have a few close and concerned friends at school that can be mobilized to provide added support for them. In addition, there may be a teacher or a coach who has taken a special interest in your client and is already providing advice and support to him or her. In fact, this *inspirational other* (Selekman, 2006; Anthony, 1984) may have a lot of creative ideas for helping your client. Bringing the concerned peers and the inspirational other into sessions as resources can help put in place a strong support system to help the client get to a better place. For example, Billy had a tendency to brutalize his body with pens and sharp items when peers at school would bully or tease him. For years, his older brother treated him the same way that the peers did at school. Billy's closest friend at school was Stacy and his inspirational other was his computer teacher Mr. Simon. With the permission of the school dean and Billy's parents, I was able to set up a crisis support team composed of the school social worker or school-based professional, Mr. Simon, Stacy, and his friend Phil. Whenever Billy would come to school emotionally distraught or he had been verbally abused by the bullies at school, an impromptu meeting would be arranged in the or school-based professional's office with the other crisis support team members to provide support and brainstorm solutions. With the help of the crisis support team, we completely eliminated Billy's self-harming behavior at school.

Constructive Management of Slips and Goal Maintenance

Self-harming students will experience inevitable slips throughout the course of intervention. Therefore, it is imperative that we prepare our students for how to constructively manage slips so that they do not escalate into prolonged relapsing and demoralizing crisis situations. First off, I like to normalize slips as signs that progress has already occurred, teachers of wisdom, and a sign that more structure is needed during leisure times. It is important in second and subsequent sessions to ask consolidating questions (Selekman, 2006; O'Hanlon & Weiner-Davis, 1989) to help solidify the gains the student is making and how to quickly get back on track when slips occur. Some examples of consolidating questions are as follows:

- "In what ways has cutting been helpful to you?"
- "How else has it benefited you?"
- "What does cutting mean to you and how does it fit into your life story?"
- "Do you experience any specific thoughts, feelings, or bodily sensations prior to cutting yourself?"
- "What are other triggers for you?"
- "If you could put a voice to that fresh cut mark or your most meaningful scar, what would it say about you or your situation?"

- "What is different during the times that you don't cave in to cutting yourself; what do you tell yourself or do that seems to really work?"
- "What effect has your cutting had on your relationships with your parents?"
- "Have any of your friends voiced any concerns about your cutting?"
- "This is a routine question I typically ask, 'Have you ever thought about or attempted to take your life in the past?'"
- "This is another routine question I typically ask, and please know that if it feels uncomfortable to respond to it that is absolutely okay. 'Has anybody in the past ever hurt you emotionally or physically?'"

Finally, we need to address any student concerns or intervene as early as possible if he or she reports that the goal maintenance situation is beginning to unravel. Otherwise, the student will feel like he or she has returned back to square one.

Applying Interventions within a Response to Intervention Framework

The collaborative strengths-based brief therapy approach described in this chapter is very compatible with the Response to Intervention (RTI) framework and can help prevent out of regular classroom placements into more restrictive school settings. This highly pragmatic counseling approach is governed by core assumptions that change is always happening; the temporal focus of treatment is in the here and now; and together with students, teachers, and other involved school staff, a compelling and successful future reality can be co-created. Through training and collaborative partnerships, school social workers can empower teachers to identify and utilize at-risk self-harming students' strengths, resources, and unique passions to disrupt negative problem-maintaining behavior patterns and bring out the best in their behaviors as they occur in the classroom. Teachers also can learn how to become better solution detectives and focus most of their attention on what is working with particular at-risk self-harming students; that is, how to become more keenly aware of what they are doing during those times when students are behaving well in class that is contributing to these students' better behavior and improved academic performances.

In situations where particular at-risk self-harming students are not responding well to the positive approach described above and the problem of concern seemingly has a life of its own, it may be useful as a school team (the student, parents who can attend school meetings, concerned teachers, dean and/or principal) to externalize the problem and employ the habit control ritual (Selekman, 2005, 2009, 2010; Durrant & Coles, 1991) to try and conquer it. This can be a playful and powerful way to prevent out-of-classroom placements for self-harming at-risk students as well.

Tools and Practice Examples

Key Assessment Questions to Ask Self-Harming Adolescents

- Where did you learn to cut or burn yourself?
- Has anyone significant in your past ever hurt you?
- What does the cutting/burning do for you?
- Are there any particular things that happen to you or thoughts experience when you are more likely to cut/burn yourself?
- Are there any particular things that happen to you or thoughts and feelings that you experience when you are more likely to cut/burn yourself?
- What effect does your cutting/burning have on your relationship with your parents and/or siblings?
- How do your friends feel about your cutting/burning yourself?
- If you could put a voice to your cutting/burning habit, what would it say about you as a person and your situation?
- When you avoid the urge to cut/burn yourself, what do you tell yourself or do that works?

Quieting the Mind: The Power of Mindfulness Meditation

The following techniques are effective in reducing self-harming behaviors among adolescents.

The Mantra

A mantra can be a word or a line that is meaningful to the adolescent. The word or line can be taken from one of their favorite tunes, books, or from their own unique self-generated self-talk tapes. The adolescent is to become so well acquainted with their mantra that it becomes a part of them. Adolescents should practice 10–12 minutes twice a day silently saying to themselves their mantras. The mantra can help center and sooth them when faced with stressors at home and at school.

Taking a Trip to Popcorn Land Food Meditation

I like to use a piece of popcorn when doing this simple food meditation. A single piece of popcorn is placed in the adolescent's left palm. He or she is to carefully study its coloring, indentations, and the shadowing around it for a few minutes. Then he or she is to slowly pick it up and roll it around on his or her fingertips, feeling its texture for a few minutes. Next, he or she is to place the piece of popcorn in his or her mouth without biting down on it. The adolescent should roll it around with his or her teeth and tongue. After doing this for a few minutes, he or she is to bite down on it, which will access the taste sensation. In his or her mind, the adolescent should describe its taste (salty and/or buttery). The adolescent is to finely chew the piece of popcorn, paying close attention to whatever sensations he or she experiences as it travels down his or her esophagus and eventually reaches his or her stomach. For approximately 10–12 minutes, the adolescent has been totally immersed in the popcorn-eating experience.

Sound Meditation

The adolescent is to find a nice quiet place to do this meditation. He or she is to sit comfortably in a chair or lie down on the floor. With eyes closed, the adolescent is to tune into all the various sounds he or she hears around him or her. While listening to each sound, the adolescent is not to get too attached to what he or she hears, just simply label it in his or her mind. This meditation should be done for 10–12 minutes.

Key Points to Remember

Self-harming students can be a challenge to work with. Their behavior can be quite intimidating for even the most seasoned of school social workers, counselors, and teachers. To further complicate matters, some of these adolescents' symptoms switch to bulimia, substance abuse, and sexual promiscuity as well. By following the guidelines below, social workers and other school professionals will be able to foster a cooperative relationship and create a context for change with self-harming students:

- Take the time to build a safe and trusting relationship.
- Provide plenty of room for the student to share his or her self-harming story.
- Go with whatever the student wishes to work on changing first.
- Utilize the student's key strengths and resources in presenting problem areas.
- Carefully match your intervention questions and experiments with the student's cooperative response patterns, strengths and resources, and treatment goals.
- Actively collaborate with concerned school staff.
- Involve the student's closest friends and inspirational others as resources in the counseling process.
- Normalize for the student the inevitability of future slips and teach tools for constructively managing them.

References

Anderson, H., & Goolishian, H. (1988). Human systems as linguistic systems: Evolving ideas about the implications for theory and practice. *Family Process, 27*, 371–393.

Anderson, H. (1997). *Conversation, language, and possibilities: A postmodern approach to therapy.* New York: Basic.

Anthony, E. J. (1984). The St. Louis risk research project. In N. F. Watt, E. J. Anthony, L. C. Wynne, & J. Roth (Eds.), *Children at risk for schizophrenia: A longitudinal perspective* (pp. 105–148). Cambridge, UK: Cambridge University Press.

Bennett-Goleman, T. (2001). *Emotional alchemy: How the mind can heal the heart.* New York: Harmony.

Berg, I. K., & Miller, S. D. (1992). *Working with the problem drinker: A solution-focused approach.* New York: Norton.

Czikszentmihalyi, M. (1997). *Finding flow.* New York: Basic.

De Shazer, S. (1985). Keys to solution in brief therapy. New York: Norton.

De Shazer, S. (1988). *Clues: Investigating solutions in brief therapy.* New York: Norton.

De Shazer, S. (1991). *Putting difference to work.* New York: Norton.

De Shazer, S., Dolan, Y., Korman, H., Trepper, T., McCollum, E ., & Berg, I. K. (2007). *More than miracles: The state of the art of solution-focused brief therapy.* Binghamton, NY: Haworth.

Durrant, M., & Coles, D. (1991). Michael White's cybernetic approach. In T. C. Todd & M. D. Selekman (Eds.), *Family therapy approaches with adolescent substance abusers* (pp. 135–174). Needham Heights, MA: Allyn & Bacon.

Epston, D. (1998). *Catching up with David Epston: Collection of narrative-based papers 1991–1996.* Adelaide, South Australia: Dulwich Centre Publications.

Favazza, A. R. (1998). *Bodies under siege: Self-mutilation and body modification in culture and psychiatry* (2nd ed.). Baltimore, MD: Johns Hopkins University Press.

Favazza, A. R., & Selekman, M. (2003/April). *Self-injury in adolescents.* Annual Spring Conference of the Child and Adolescent Centre, London, Ontario, Canada.

Fisch, R., Weakland, J., Segal, L. (1982). *The tactics of change.* San Francisco, CA: Jossey-Bass.

Fisch, R., & Schlanger, K. (1999). *Brief therapy with intimidating cases.* San Francisco, CA: Jossey-Bass.

Fredrickson, B. (2002). Positive emotion. In C. R. Snyder & S. J. Lopez (Eds.), *Handbook of positive psychology* (pp. 120–135). New York: Oxford University Press.

Fredrickson, B. L. (2009). *Positivity: Groundbreaking research reveals how to embrace the hidden strength of positive emotions, overcome negativity, and thrive.* New York, NY: Crown Books.

Hanh, T. N. (2001). *Anger.* New York: Riverhead.

Hanh, T. N. (2003). *Creating true peace: Ending violence in yourself, your family, your community, and the world.* New York: Free Press.

O'Hanlon, W. H., & Weiner-Davis, M. (1989). *In search of solutions: A new direction in psychotherapy.* New York, NY: Norton.

Pennebaker, J. W. (2004). *Writing to heal: A guided journal for recovering from trauma and emotional upheaval.* Oakland, CA: New Harbinger.

Peterson, C. (2006). *A primer in positive psychology.* New York: Oxford University.

Peterson, C., & Seligman, M. E. P. (2004). *Character strengths and virtues: Handbook and classification.* New York: Oxford University Press.

Santisteban, D. A., Muir, J. A., Mena, M. P., & Mitrani, V. B. (2003). Integrated borderline family therapy: Meeting the challenge of treating adolescents with borderline personality disorder. *Psychotherapy: Theory, Research, Practice, & Training, 40,* 251–264.

Schwartz, B. (2004). *The paradox of choice: Why more is less.* New York: HarperCollins.

Selekman, M. D. (2005). *Pathways to change: Brief therapy solutions with difficult adolescents* (2nd ed.). New York: Guilford.

Selekman, M.D. (2006). *Working with self-harming adolescents. A collaborative, strengths-based therapy approach.* New York: Norton.

Selekman, M. D., & Schulem, H. (2007). *The self-harming adolescents and their families expert consultants project: A qualitative study.* Unpublished manuscript.

Selekman, M. D. (2009). *The adolescent and young adult self-harming treatment manual: A collaborative strengths-based brief therapy approach.* New York, NY: Norton.

Selekman, M. D. (2010). *Collaborative brief therapy with children.* New York, NY: Guilford.

Seligman, M. E. P., Reivich, K., Jaycox, J., & Gillham, J. (1995). *The optimistic child.* New York: Houghton-Mifflin.

Seligman, M. E. P. (2011). *Flourish: A visionary new understanding of happiness and well-being.* New York, NY: The Free Press.

Szapocznik, J., Hervis, O., & Schwartz, S. (2003). *Brief strategic family therapy for adolescent drug abuse. Therapy manuals for drug addiction, Manual 5.* Bethesda, MD: U.S. Department of Health and Human Services and National Institutes of Health.

Taffel, R., & Blau, M. (2001). *The second family: How adolescent power is challenging the American family.* New York: St. Martin's.

Watzlawick, P., Fisch, R., & Weakland, J. (1974). *Change: Principles of problem formation and problem resolution.* New York, NY: Norton.

White, M., & Epston, D. (1990). *Narrative means to therapeutic ends.* New York: Norton.

White, M. (2007). *Maps in narrative practice.* New York, NY: Norton.

CHAPTER 12

Positive Behavior Supports for Children with Major Mental Illness: Working with Teachers and Parents

Chris Ahlman

Getting Started

This chapter is written for those school-based practitioners who are called upon by parents and teachers to help them, often the frontline workers, to assess, intervene, and evaluate the educational needs and progress of their children or students who have major mental health disorders. A major mental health disorder is defined here as a disorder that is pervasive, chronic, and a lifelong condition.

To accomplish the mandates of Response to Intervention (RTI) (NCRTI, n.d.), it is necessary to have a workable understanding of the issues facing students, teachers, and parents regarding major mental health disorders. The school-based practitioner is required to not only have some expertise on these disorders but also to support and inform parents and teachers so they are also equipped to be part of the educational team. Research shows us that parents' participation in their child's social, emotional, and academic growth is important for academic achievement (Taylor & Adelman, 2001). Research also informs us that trained, skilled, and committed teachers are essential to the success of evidence-based interventions (Lewis, Jones, Horner, & Sugai, 2010).

While this chapter will focus on children labeled with childhood bipolar disorder and childhood schizophrenia, many of the resources and intervention strategies could be useful in working with other major disorders. Research on positive behavior supports (PBS) reinforces the notion that all members of the team (student, parents, teachers, social workers, administrators) need to be able to understand the student's educational needs and be able to implement programming in an environment that supports these interventions (Lewis et al, 2010).

This chapter will first give context for identification and interventions with children with major mental health diagnoses by reviewing specific information on the identification of childhood bipolar disorder and childhood schizophrenia and new research on children exhibiting similar symptoms. Also covered here will be some specific suggestions for developing interventions. There are resources for sample individual education plans (IEPs). Included as well is a discussion of how these strategies might be useful for working with children with other major mental health issues. Finally, there will be a list of resources where all team members can learn more about issues important to them in their attempts to support the education of these students.

What We Know about the Major Mental Health Disorders in Children

As with any diagnosis or label, it is crucial to have experts in the field making the determination; however, with conditions such as pediatric bipolar disorder (PBD), childhood bipolar disorder (CBD), and early onset bipolar disorder (EOBD), childhood schizophrenia (COS—before age 13), or early onset schizophrenia (EOS—age 13 to 21), there are confusing and sometimes contradictory beliefs about the disorders and their symptoms (Gonthier & Lyon, 2004; Youngstrom, Findling, Youngstrom, & Calabrese, 2005). The DSM-IV-TR (APA, 2000) is still the standard in the mental health field for listing symptoms for mental illnesses (Olson & Pacheco, 2005). However, the manual does not differentiate between childhood and adult versions of either bipolar disorder or schizophrenia, while there is substantial literature noting that there are differences (Gonthier & Lyon, 2004; Killu & Crundwell, 2008; Lofthouse & Fristad, 2004). Both bipolar disorders and schizophrenia have been labeled as brain disorders (NIMH, n.d.) due to differences in brain structure and chemistry from the general population.

For the school-based practitioner who works with parents, it is most important to identify behaviors and symptoms that might point toward a diagnosis of either of these conditions or the proposed diagnosis of severe mood dysregulation or temper dysregulation disorder with dysphoria (TDD; Brotman et al., 2007; Lopez-Duran, 2010) to help them be informed as they work with their doctor or psychiatrist who will decide on a diagnosis. However, when working with parents and teachers attempting to address behaviors and symptoms in the school setting, it is also important to have a good understanding of each condition in order to set appropriate and achievable goals.

The reported incidence of bipolar disorder in children has increased by 40 times in the decade prior to a 2007 NIH study (NIMH, 2011). The symptoms that are associated with bipolar disorders in children are episodes of mania, depression, or both when children might feel an elevated mood or euphoria and act silly or giddy, especially in an inappropriate setting like church; they may have grandiose ideas that are not in touch with reality, as in their ability to teach better than the teacher; they might have racing and competing thoughts that can lead to them being very talkative, talking very fast, and talking for long periods of time; they are often irritable and become hostile and demanding; they are much more distractible than same-aged peers; they can go without sleep and still have energy; they can engage in high-risk (dangerous and/or sexual) activities that they find pleasant; they exhibit poor judgment; and they can have hallucinations or other psychotic experiences. During depressive episodes, children may show no enjoyment; they may stop participating in activities that they formerly liked; they may be easily agitated; they may cry often and for long periods of time; their normal sleep patterns may be either increased or decreased; their grades may go down as they have difficulty concentrating and are tired; their weight may go up or down; and they can express feelings of being worthless or even have suicidal ideations (Child and Adolescent Bipolar Foundation, or CABF, 2010). Because many children, while having a fair number of the above symptoms, do not have them in the episodic timing required by the diagnosis or do not have a distinct mania phase (APA, 2000), the American Psychological Association is researching the possibility of a new diagnosis of temper dysregulation disorder with dysphoria (TDD) to be included in the new DSM-V (Lopez-Duran, 2010). Here the symptoms focus on tantrum-like behaviors when responding to stressors in the environment. The "temper outbursts" or rages can be physical or verbal and out of proportion in frequency and intensity to the stimulus and are different than same-aged peers. Part of the criteria for this proposed diagnosis also includes timing—these tantrum behaviors need to be seen three or more times a week. Between the episodes the child is negative, pessimistic, irritable, and angry, and may or may not be sad. These behaviors are observed in multiple settings by a number of individuals and have been occurring for at least 12 months with no more than a three-month break; symptoms begin before age 10, but diagnosis begins on or after age 6. Also, if there are manic episodes of more than a day, the diagnosis is ruled out. Other diagnoses also need to be ruled out before TDD can be considered (NAMI, 2010b).

Schizophrenia in children also presents in some ways differently than in adults (Gonthier & Lyon, 2004). Childhood schizophrenia (onset before age 13) is quite rare and reportedly very severe (Dulmus & Smyth, 2000). Dulmus and Smyth go on to say that only 1 out of 10,000 children will develop COS, and with early onset comes a poor prognosis. They reviewed the literature to note that there is a strong genetic link as well as links with environmental factors. COS may result in compounding factors in genetics and/or environment.

School practitioners must always remain sensitive when genetic factors are associated with a child's diagnosis, as the parent with whom they are engaged could be the parent with the genetic markers either presenting or non-presenting. While it is important to understand etiology of disorders, work with parents and teachers requires starting "where the child is" and moving forward. For the child with COS, this means that there is a slightly higher percentage of boys; they often have low-average to average intelligence with attention and conduct problems; they have poor working memory and executive function; they are often shy, inhibited, and sensitive; and they are usually at least 5 years old with about 80% having auditory hallucinations and 50% having delusional beliefs. These children and students often have other mental health conditions such as learning disabilities, mental retardation, and autism; language and motor abnormalities are seen in over half the children, as well as social problems (Yates, 2001). In fact, interest in friendships is considered a disqualifier for COS (NIMH, 2003).

These symptoms are what we can see through observation. With brain scan technology, changes in brain structure and brain chemistry are also tracked, with greater change occurring in children with COS often associated with changes in developmental stages (NIMH, 2003). Due to the physiological conditions of this disorder, a variety of medications including mood stabilizers, stimulants, antipsychotic medication, and selective serotonin reuptake inhibitors have been successful in reducing symptoms of children with bipolar disorder (Bhangoo, 2003). It is often necessary to first treat the condition with pharmacological interventions before the child is stable enough to be included in the classroom (Gonthier & Lyon, 2004). The Child and Adolescent Bipolar Foundation (CABF, 2007) makes the suggestion regarding the special education classification for children with bipolar disorder that the OHI (other health impaired) classification be used, as bipolar disorder, as noted earlier, is a brain disorder, and much of what the child experiences is out of his or her control.

All major mental health disorders can come in combinations or with comorbid conditions. Youngstrom, Findling, Youngstrom, and Calabrese (2005) state that it is estimated that children with bipolar disorder often meet the criteria for one or more other Axis I diagnoses. The most common comorbid conditions are ADHD, oppositional defiant disorder, conduct disorder, and learning disorders. They go on to say that there are also increases in anxiety disorders, and substance abuse appears significantly elevated in adolescents and young adults with bipolar disorder. For children with bipolar disorder, accurate diagnosing is crucial, as many are misdiagnosed with ADHD, and the stimulant medication can exacerbate or precipitate the bipolar disorder (Olson & Pacheco, 2005). It is difficult for the best of physicians to treat several comorbid conditions at the same time, and it is recommended (CABF, 2007) that the bipolar disorder be addressed first and the comorbid conditions treated when moods are stabilized. However, we understand that all children react differently, so continuous observation and assessment of moods and behaviors is extremely important to treatment.

In addition to the behaviors and challenges associated with major mental health disorders is the reality that the regular education environment is underequipped to provide extensive services to these students along with educating their nondisabled peers (Killu & Crundwell, 2008). Much of what will be offered in this section is based on best practices in optimal environments; however, school-based practitioners act as advocates and resource developers. Some suggestions for how they might help bring resources to the regular education setting will also be covered.

What We Can Do

While these major mental health disorders are complex and present with a large number of symptoms, there is a fairly large body of literature that addresses interventions. As stated earlier, these interventions housed in positive behavior supports (PBS) can be appropriate for students who are undiagnosed as well as those with a diagnosis. So while it is useful to know exactly which diagnosis and accompanying symptoms a student has, it is also important to provide interventions that address his or her behaviors and capacities. This section will introduce interventions and resources specific to children with bipolar disorder and schizophrenia; however, as noted earlier, these suggestions can benefit children and students with other major mental health disorders.

The first course of intervention for both bipolar disorder and schizophrenia should begin with medication to stabilize moods and symptoms (Gonthier & Lyon, 2004; NAMI, 2010ba). Then, educational and social interventions need to follow for these children to attain their maximum functioning. Medication alone will not overcome the gaps in learning and social skills experienced by these children. Chesno Grier, Wilkins, and Stirling Pender (2007) reviewed the literature for evidenced-based intervention and share the following: "... cognitive restructuring for depressive symptoms, problem-solving strategies to intervene with emotional dysregulation, and behavior management techniques to establish routine and consistency. Family psycho-education (providing information and guidance to families in a teaching format) has also proven to decrease symptom expression and increase parental knowledge and positive family interactions" (p. 13).

Positive behavior supports (PBS) in the school setting require a team mentality. Interventions, accommodations, and modifications do not happen in a vacuum. Lewis et al. (2010) stress the need for educating the school personnel in an effort to educate the student. According to the authors, evidence-based interventions often are not carried out on behalf of students because school personnel are lacking the specific knowledge and skills to do so. Therefore, best practice begins with adequate training and ongoing support of team members. Lewis et al. go on to suggest that when interventions are developed and implemented in a school-wide positive behavior support system, the likelihood of maintaining intervention fidelity increases; for example, if all students and personnel practice respect, teaching a student with a major mental health disorder to wait his or her turn is more likely to be carried out consistently. Whether school systems choose school-wide positive behavior supports or whether the supports are more targeted, team members need knowledge and skills for providing services to students with major mental health disorders.

Killu and Crundwell (2008) offer a comprehensive table titled "Characteristics of Bipolar Disorder in the Classroom Across the Dimensions of Social/Behavioral, Cognitive/Academic, and Affect/Mood" (p. 246). A glance at this table can overwhelm the team members who are attempting to accommodate education to meet these varied and constantly changing conditions as the student's mood swings from mania to depression. However, they go on to offer four more tables with exquisite detail and citations for making adjustments in the classroom and school environment that can benefit the student as he or she cycles through the episodes associated with bipolar disorder.

Killu and Crundwell's (2008) tables include a list of environmental, behavioral, and medical issues matched with evidenced-based accommodations and interventions. This must-read article acknowledges both the research community and organizations dedicated to education and support for families of children with bipolar disorder, like the Child and Adolescent Bipolar Foundation (CABF). The information offered by them is easy to decipher, as most of the pertinent material is found in tables.

The Center for Mental Health in Schools (2008) offers a packet tilted "Affect and Mood Problems Related to School Aged Youth." This 120-page downloadable document is written for parents, teachers, and other school personnel working on behalf of children with issues related to affect and mood. It covers a variety of topics, including how to recognize these issues, what can be done to prevent or relieve them, and how can they be addressed either at home or in school. A sample IEP is offered that includes academic and social goals, modifications needed, and a behavior plan.

The Child and Adolescent Bipolar Foundation has available online (CABF, 2007) a brochure directed toward parents and teachers explaining the issues a child with bipolar disorder faces in the school setting. The brochure includes very specific suggestions for helping the child benefit from the educational environment. Their list of modifications and interventions are strongly aligned with Killu and Crundwell (2008) and the Center for Mental Health in Schools (2008). A summary is presented below in Key Points to Remember.

A new application for the time-honored practice of meditation—in the unique form of mindfulness training or its clinical application of mindfulness-based cognitive therapy (MBCT)—has been found to be very successful in reducing anxiety in adults (Kabat-Zin, 2003; Weber et al., 2010). In more recent research, it has been shown to be effective in reducing anxiety in adults both with bipolar disorder and with schizophrenia (Davis, Strasburger, & Brown, 2007; Williams et al., 2008). Mindfulness is defined as "the awareness that emerges through paying attention on purpose, in the present moment, and nonjudgmentally to the unfolding of experiences moment by moment" (Kabat-Zin, 2003, p. 145). Mindfulness training develops a set of skills whereby the individual is able to attend to exactly what is happening to the mind and body at any given moment. And mindfulness training has also been found to be very effective with children (Hooker & Fodor, 2008; Thompson & Gauntlett-Gilbert, 2008). The authors of both of these articles provide context for mindfulness intervention by sharing extensive literature reviews and explaining how it applies to interventions with children, as well as offering several exercises to be used in the school setting.

Applying Interventions within a Response to Intervention Framework

A recent report produced by the Center for Mental Health in Schools, a federally funded organization housed at UCLA, addressed the issue of implementation of Response to Intervention (RTI) and positive behavior interventions and support (PBIS) since they were mandated in 2004 (Center, 2011b). This report notes that most schools interpreted the multilevel stipulation in the law as the popular three-tiered pyramid of interventions, with about 80% of students served by core interventions (PBIS and engaging curriculum), 15% of students needing more intensive short-term supports, and the remaining 5% of students needing ongoing, intense supports and services. While RTI was conceived as a preventive and proactive process to avoid school failure (Sugai & Horner, 2009), it has developed some core components that are beneficial to serving students with major mental health disorders. Those components are:

1. interventions that are supported by scientifically based research
2. interventions that are organized along a tiered continuum that increases in intensity (e.g., frequency, duration, individualization, specialized supports, etc.)
3. standardized problem-solving protocol for assessment and instructional decision making
4. explicit data-based decision rules for assessing student progress and making instructional and intervention adjustments
5. emphasis on assessing and ensuring implementation integrity
6. regular and systematic screening for early identification of students whose performance is not responsive to instruction (Sugai & Horner, 2009, p. 226)

However, when RTI and PBIS are interpreted strictly within the multi-tiered system that is focused mostly on a way to provide effective instruction, and PBIS is implemented to address negative behaviors, the interventions will not be effective over time for a large number of students (Center for Mental Health in Schools, 2011b). Another report produced by the Center (Center for Mental Health in Schools, 2011a) suggests that for RTI to be effective, more attention needs to be paid to supports in the classroom and school-wide supports. It suggests that supports are implemented to "overcome barriers to learning," and classroom interventions are to be a personalized version of the school-wide plan. This report also strongly suggests that if the teachers are to be able to accomplish personalized, engaging, supportive instruction, they need help in the way of trained volunteers and aides. Very specific suggestions on how to use the extra help and how this help will increase the effectiveness of RTI in a school system are given. Finally, the idea of bringing help into the classroom from community resources is familiar to school social work practitioners who have served as a liaison between home, school, and community (Rippey Massat, Constable, McDonald, & Flynn, 2008), but different school mental health professionals may not have as much experience in community roles and may need to increase their expertise in this area to be effective with students with persistent mental illnesses.

Tools and Practice Examples

A screening tool that has been used in schools and mental health agencies is the Pediatric Symptom Checklist (Murphy et al., 1996). It is meant to be used as a screening tool only. Parents are asked to rate their child's behavior on a frequency scale of never, sometimes, or often. The behaviors are described in very easily understandable terms that tend to be descriptive, e.g., "fidgety, unable to sit still" or "irritable, angry." The instrument has a 68% positive predictability (it is accurate in identifying children with mental health disorders), and it is 95% accurate in ruling out disorders. As this instrument is available online from its authors, Michael Jellinek, M.D., and Michael Murphy, Ed.D., school personnel with the appropriate credentials (see Web site: http://psc.partners.org/psc_order.htm) can use it free of charge. One of the benefits of using this instrument is that it comes in a variety of versions: parent versions (English, Spanish, Japanese) and youth self-report versions (English, Spanish). Whether a child is found to be clinically at risk for mental health disorders, the instrument can be used to plan interventions and positive behavior supports for those behaviors that interfere with the child's education and relationships both at home and in school.

The Bipolar Child Questionnaire (Papolos & Papolos, 2002) is a diagnosis-specific assessment completed by parents to identify behavioral symptoms of BPD. This instrument also gathers information on family history of mental illness and the course and effectiveness of attempted interventions. Although these tools are useful in identifying behavioral patterns, Response to Intervention (RTI) requires that progress toward goals is monitored

(U.S. Dept. of Education, 2004). The tools offered by the government-funded Web site, the National Center on Response to Intervention (NCRTI), are focused on math, reading, and other academic goals. For monitoring progress of interventions or positive behavior supports that address behaviors, school personnel need to find other sources. One such resource is a mood chart. Because of the continual mood changes in children with bipolar disorders and schizophrenia, it is important to keep track of their daily moods to make appropriate accommodations (Senokossoff & Stoddard, 2009). Most mood charts need to be purchased or are "free" from organizations like the Child and Adolescent Bipolar Foundation (http://www.bpkids.org/sites/default/files/nimh_mood_chart_1.pdf).

Another type of tool for parents and teachers is the personal account in the form of case studies, personal stories, and autobiographies. These personal experiences with major mental health disorders help parents especially to normalize their experience. They help teachers by providing some insights into the parents' experience. While there are some sensational reports in the news, it is best to use more professional resources to reduce misinformation. Gwyn W. Senokossoff is a university instructor in childhood education and literacy and shares her personal experience with her child's bipolar disorder (Senokossoff & Stoddard, 2009) while offering strategies for working with the child at home and in school. Demitri Papolos, M.D., and his wife Janice, founders of the Child and Adolescent Bipolar Foundation and the Juvenile Bipolar Research Foundation, have developed a presentation titled "24: A Day in the Life of Bipolar Children and Their Families" (DVD or CD) that is based on their extensive research on the condition of childhood bipolar disorder. Several children and their families are presented to show how the disorder can vary from child to child. Finally, there is a series of books published by Oxford University Press through the Adolescent Mental Health Initiative. The books are written from the perspective of a child who has a particular disorder (bipolar disorder, schizophrenia, major depression, anxiety disorders, and others). In addition to the personal stories, the books contain information on the courses and treatments for the disorders. The two related to childhood bipolar disorder and childhood schizophrenia are located in the references below (Gur & Wasmer, 2007; Jamieson & Rynn, 2006).

Since many children with major mental health disorders have difficulty with transitions either in their daily lives or in transitioning from one grade level to the next or one school to the next, it has been suggested that interventions like the Carol Gray social stories (used for many years with children with autism spectrum disorder) be used to help students prepare and cope (CABF, 2007). Education and support for parents, teachers, and social work practitioners to learn how to develop social stories for children with major mental health disorders can be found online at The Gray Center (www.thegraycenter.org).

Key Points to Remember

- Proper diagnosis is important to understand the child/student's capacities.
- Proper diagnosis is required for proper treatment and interventions.
- Treatments will address biopsychosocial issues for child and family.
- All treatment and interventions should include input from all team members.
- Medication will be the first step in treatment and intervention:
    - Requires constant monitoring:
        - side effects
        - changing moods
- Symptoms of major mental health disorders are complex and varied.
- Use positive behavior supports: school-wide and individual student.
    - Flexibility:
        - in how instruction is delivered, what is delivered, when it is delivered
        - in how performance is expected, when it is expected
    - Minimize distractions and unplanned change.
    - Control physical environment to reduce distractions.
    - Maintain a stable, structured, predictable environment.
    - Notify before a change (scheduled or unscheduled) occurs.
    - Plan for times when student is tired, agitated, frustrated, disinterested:
        - more time to complete or practice work
        - less interaction with classmates
        - need for "a break"
- Use Carol Gray's social stories to plan daily activities.

- Give feedback and provide continuous support to acquire skills:
    - especially during manic or emotional periods
- Schedule homework with student's present mood/behavior in mind.
- Help student to develop goals while understanding that he or she is susceptible to change with swings in moods or emotions.
- Help student to organize with calendars, daily planners, checklists.
- Work with parents to ensure consistency and structure between school and home.
- Be patient and ignore minor negative behaviors.
- Encourage positive behaviors and provide positive behavioral choices.
- Maintain positive, calm, firm, patient, consistent, and encouraging interactions.
- Provide ongoing education to school personnel regarding the disorder.
- Build teams to work with students.
- Use standardized assessment to understand the student's behavior.
- Develop more proactive and preventive strategies.
- Develop positive behavioral supports:
    - affective supports
    - schedule and activity supports
    - peer supports
- Promote positive support and positive discipline.
- Avoid negative consequences, as these may in fact escalate undesirable behaviors.
- Establish a "safe" adult and place that the student may seek out.
- Teach social skills.
- Provide supervision during unstructured times. (CABF, 2007; Killu & Crundwell, 2008)

• There is a substantial amount of information on the Internet.

Further Learning: References and Resources for Parents and Teachers

24: A Day in the Life of Bipolar Children and Their Families (There is a charge for DVD or CDs.): http://www.bipolarchild.com/24/

Bipolar Disorder (Easy to Read): http://www.nimh.nih.gov/health/publications/bipolar-disorder-easy-to-read/index.shtml

Bipolar Disorder in Children and Adolescents (Fact Sheet): http://www.nimh.nih.gov/health/publications/bipolar-disorder-in-children-and-adolescents/index.shtml

Bipolar Disorder in Children and Teens (Easy to Read), also in Spanish: http://www.nimh.nih.gov/health/publications/bipolar-disorder-in-children-and-teens-easy-to-read/index.shtml

Bipolar Disorder in Children and Teens: A Parent's Guide: http://www.nimh.nih.gov/health/publications/bipolar-disorder-in-children-and-teens-a-parents-guide/index.shtml

Bipolar Significant Others (BPSO): Extensive list of resources: http://www.bpso.org/showinfo.php?topic=children

Books for Parents and Children: http://bipolar.about.com/od/childrensbooks/Childrens_Books.htm

Center for Mental Health in Schools—Affect and Mood Problems Related to School Aged Youth:

http://smhp.psych.ucla.edu/pdfdocs/Affect/affect.pdf

Child & Adolescent Bipolar Foundation: http://www.bpkids.org/learn/library/about-pediatric-bipolar-disorder

Childhood Schizophrenia: National Institute of Mental Health: http://www.nimh.nih.gov/science-news/2008/brains-wiring-stunted-lopsided-in-childhood-onset-schizophrenia.shtml

Developing an IEP for Children with Bipolar Disorder: http://bipolar.about.com/cs/kids_parents/a/9808_schooltool.htm

Educating the Child with Bipolar Disorder Brochure: http://www.bpkids.org/sites/default/files/edbrochure.pdf

Emotionally Disturbed Students, by Dr. A. Ogonosky, School Psychologist (good general suggestions): http://www.atpe.org/resources/student&parentissues/emodisturb.asp

Feeling Charts for Young Children (free): http://www.child-behavior-guide.com/feelings-chart.html

General Information about Childhood Schizophrenia: Mayo Clinic: http://www.mayoclinic.com/health/childhood-schizophrenia/DS00868

IEP Example for Elementary School: http://www.bipolarchild.com/IEP/

Juvenile Bipolar Research Foundation: Educational Issues (504 and IEP): http://www.jbrf.org/edu_forums/issues.html

Mood Charting Resources (Note: To access some of the charts on this site, you need to do a Google search on the name of the chart.): http://bipolar.about.com/od/moodchartingforchildren/Mood_Charting_for_Children.htm

National Alliance on Mental Illness (NAMI): Child and Adolescent Bipolar Disorder: http://www.nami.org/Template.cfm?Section=By_Illness&template=/ContentManagement/ContentDisplay.cfm&ContentID=102859

National Center on Response to Intervention (NCRTI): http://www.rti4success.org/resourceslanding

National Institute of Mental Health: Bipolar Disorder in Children and Teens: http://www.nimh.nih.gov/health/publications/bipolar-disorder-in-children-and-teens-easy-to-read/index.shtml

National Institute of Mental Health: Information on CS: http://www.nimh.nih.gov/science-news/2008/brains-wiring-stunted-lopsided-in-childhood-onset-schizophrenia.shtml

The Rise of Bipolar Disorder in Children—Bipolar Disorder Webcast (60 min. audio; good overall discussion about labeling and characteristics): http://www.everydayhealth.com/bipolar/webcasts/the-rise-of-bipolar-disorder-in-children-listen.aspx

Schizophrenia.com: A Non-Profit Source of Information, Support, and Education: http://www.schizophrenia.com/family/childsz.htm

School Information Regarding Educating Child with Bipolar Disorder: http://bipolar.about.com/od/schoolissues/School_Issues.htm

Temper dysregulation disorder with dysphoria: http://www.child-psych.org/2010/02/childhood-bipolar-disorder-is-not-bipolar-dsm-v-and-the-new-temper-dysregulation-disorder-with-dysphoria.html

Treatment Guidelines for Children and Adolescents with Bipolar Disorder Brochure: http://www.bpkids.org/learn/library/treatment-guidelines-for-children-and-adolescents-with-bipolar-disorder

Treatment Guidelines: Article in the *Journal of American Academy of Child and Adolescent Psychiatry*: http://www.bpchildren.org/files/Download/TreatmentGuidelines.pdf

References

American Psychiatric Association. (2000). *Diagnostic and statistical manual of mental disorders-text revision* (4th ed.). Washington, DC: Author.

Bhangoo, R., Lowe, C., Myers, F., Treland, J., Curran, J., Towbin, K., & Leibenluft, E. (2003). Medication use in children and adolescents treated in the community for bipolar disorder. *Journal of Child and Adolescent Psychopharmacology, 13*(4), 515–522. doi:10.1089/104454603322724904

Brotman, M., Kassem, L., Reising, M., Guyer, A., Dickstein, D., Rich, B., et al. (2007). Parental diagnoses in youth with narrow phenotype bipolar disorder or severe mood dysregulation. *American Journal of Psychiatry, 164*, 1238–1241

Child and Adolescent Bipolar Foundation (CABF). (2007). *Educating the child with bipolar disorder.* Retrieved from http://www.bpkids.org/sites/default/files/edbrochure.pdf

Child and Adolescent Bipolar Foundation. (CABF). (2010). *About pediatric bipolar disorder.* Retrieved from http://www.bpkids.org/learn/library/about-pediatric-bipolar-disorder

Center for Mental Health in Schools. (2008). *Affect and mood problems related to school aged youth.* Los Angeles, CA: Author.

Center for Mental Health in Schools. (2011a). *Implementing Response to Intervention in context.* Los Angeles, CA: Author.

Center for Mental Health in Schools. (2011b). *Moving beyond the three tiered intervention pyramid toward a comprehensive framework for student and learning supports.* Los Angeles, CA: Author.

Chesno Grier, E., Wilkins, M., & Stirling Pender, C. (2007). Bipolar disorder: Educational implications for secondary students. *Student Services,* 12–15. Retreived from http://www.nasponline.org/resources/principals/bipolar.pdf

Davis, L., Strasburger, A., & Brown, L. (2007). Mindfulness: An intervention for anxiety in schizophrenia. *Journal of Psychosocial Nursing & Mental Health Services, 45*(11), 23–29. Retrieved from http://www.ncbi.nlm.nih.gov/pubmed/18041355

Dulmus, C., & Smyth, N. (2000). Early-onset schizophrenia: A literature review of empirically based interventions. *Child & Adolescent Social Work Journal, 17*(1), 55–69.

Gonthier, M., & Lyon, M. (2004). Childhood-onset schizophrenia: An overview. *Psychology in the Schools, 41*(7), 803–811.

Gur, R., & Wasmer Andrews, L. (2007). *Me, myself, and them: A firsthand account of one young person's experience with schizophrenia (Adolescent Mental Health Initiative).* New York, NY: Oxford University Press.

Hooker, K., & Fodor, I. (2008). Teaching mindfulness to children. *Gestalt Review, 12*(1), 75–91. Retrieved from http://www.gestaltreview.com/Portals/0/GR1201Hooker&Fodor.pdf

Jamieson, P., & Rynn, M. (2006). *Mind race: A firsthand account of one teenager's experience with bipolar disorder (Adolescent Mental Health Initiative).* New York, NY: Oxford University Press.

Kabat-Zin, J. (2003). Mindfulness-based interventions in context: Past, present, and future. *Clinical Psychology: Science and Practice, 10*(2), 144–156.

Killu, K., & Crundwell, R. M. (2008). Understanding and developing academic and behavioral interventions for students with bipolar disorder. *Interventions in School and Clinic, 43*(4), 244–251.

Lewis, T., Jones, S., Horner, R., & Sugai, G. (2010). School-wide positive behavior support and students with emotional/behavioral disorders: Implications for prevention, identification and intervention. *Exceptionality, 18*, 82–93.

Lofthouse, N., & Fristad, M. (2004). Psychosocial interventions for children with early-onset bipolar spectrum disorder. *Clinical Child and Family Psychology Review*, 7(0), 71–88.

Lopez-Duran, N. (2010). *Childhood bipolar disorder is not bipolar? DSM-V and the new temper dysregulation disorder with dysphoria.* Retrieved from http://www.child-psych.org/2010/02/childhood-bipolar-disorder-is-not-bipolar-dsm-v-and-the-new-temper-dysregulation-disorder-with-dysphoria.html

Murphy, J., Ichinose, C., Hicks, R., Kingdon, D., Crist-Whitzel, J., Jordan, P ., ... Jellinek, M. (1996). Utility of the Pediatric Symptom Checklist as a psychosocial screen in EPSDT. *Journal of Pediatrics, 129*, 864–869.

National Alliance of Mental Illness (NAMI). (2010a). *Early onset schizophrenia.* Retrieved from http://www.nami.org/Content/ContentGroups/Helpline1/Early_Onset_Schizophrenia.htm

National Alliance of Mental Illness (NAMI). (2010b). *NAMI comments on the APA's draft revision of the DSM-V proposed new diagnosis: Temper dysregulation disorder with dysphoria.* Retrieved from http://www.nami.org/Content/ContentGroups/Policy/Issues_Spotlights/DSM5/TDD_Paper_4_13_2010.pdf

National Center on Response to Intervention (NCRTI). *Resources.* Retrieved from http://www.rti4success.org/resourceslanding

National Institute of Mental Health (NIMH). (2003). *Childhood-onset schizophrenia: An update from the National Institute of Mental Health* (NIH Publication No. 04–5124). Retrieved from http://www.nimh.nih.gov/health/publications/index.shtml

National Institute of Mental Health (NIMH). (2011). *Bipolar disorder in children and teens (easy to read).* Retrieved from http://www.nimh.nih.gov/health/publications/bipolar-disorder-in-children-and-teens-easy-to-read/index.shtml#What-is-bipolar-disorder?

Olson, P., & Pacheco, M. (2005). Bipolar disorder in school age children. *Journal of School Nursing, 21*(3), 152–157.

Papolos, D., & Papolos, J. (2002). *The bipolar child: The definitive and reassuring guide to childhood's most misunderstood disorder. New York, NY: Broadway Books.*

Rippey Massat, C., Constable, R., McDonald, S., & Flynn, J. (2008). *School social work: Practice, policy, and research.* Itasca, IL: Lyceum.

Senokossoff, G., & Stoddard, K. (2009). Swimming in deep water: Childhood bipolar disorder. *Preventing School Failure, 53*(2), 89–93.

Sugai, G., & Horner, R. (2009). Responsiveness-to-intervention and school-wide positive behavior supports: Integration of multi-tiered system approaches. *Exceptionality, 17*, 223–237. doi:10.1080/09362830903235375

Taylor, L., & Adelman, H. (2001). Enlisting appropriate parental cooperation and involvement in children's mental health treatment. In E. Welfel & R. Ingersoll (Eds.), *The mental health desk reference* (pp. 219–224). New York, NY: Wiley.

Thompson, M., & Gauntlett-Gilbert, J. (2008). Mindfulness with children and adolescents: Effective clinical application. *Clinical Child Psychology & Psychiatry, 13*, 395–408. doi:10.1177/1359104508090603

U.S. Department of Education. (2004). *Individuals with Disabilities Education Act (IDEA).* Retrieved from http://idea.ed.gov/explore/view/p/%2Croot%2Cstatute%2C

Weber, B., Jermann, F., Gex-Fabry, M., Nallet, A., Bondolfi, G., & Aurbry, J. (2010). Mindfulness-based cognitive therapy for bipolar disorder: A feasibility trial. *European Psychiatry, 6*, 334–337. Retrieved from http://www.ncbi.nlm.nih.gov/pubmed/20561769

Williams, J., Alatiq, C., Crane, T., Barnhofer, M., Fennell, D., Duggan, S., ... Goodwin, G. (2008). Mindfulness-based cognitive therapy (MBCT) in bipolar disorder: Preliminary evaluation of immediate effects on between-episode functioning. *Journal of Affect Disorders, 107*(1–3), 275–279.

Yates, M. (2001). *Childhood schizophrenia summary.* Retrieved from http://www.childadvocate.net/childhood_schizophrenia_summary.htm

CHAPTER 13

Effective Interventions for Students with Eating Disorders

Theresa J. Early ■ Hilary Drew

Getting Started

From weight loss success by a diet plan celebrity spokesperson to reality television, losing weight has never been more present in the media. At the same time, obesity rates continue to rise among children as well as adults. Media images of the "ideal" body are unrealistically thin. Many people, including children and youth, are dissatisfied with the size or shape of their bodies, and a small percentage of people develop eating disorders. Eating disorders are characterized by extreme obsessions with shape, weight, and eating, along with disordered behaviors around eating and weight control. Eating disorders are an important concern for school social workers and mental health personnel because these disorders often begin in adolescence. Within a Response to Intervention (RTI) framework, Tier 1 includes school-based interventions aimed at prevention. In addition, professionals in the schools are in a position to notice eating disorders and assist with interventions, either through providing treatment (Tier 3 interventions) or through supporting students who are participating in treatment in another setting. In this chapter, we will discuss two types of eating disorders that are diagnosed in youth, anorexia nervosa and bulimia nervosa, and strategies of effective intervention based on the small amount of existing empirical evidence.

What We Know

Anorexia nervosa frequently begins during early adolescence, and bulimia nervosa usually affects older adolescents and young adults, so both disorders may be seen in schools. Effective interventions have been identified for both bulimia nervosa and anorexia nervosa, but there is less empirical evidence regarding effective treatments for anorexia nervosa. Cognitive-behavioral therapy (CBT) has been identified as an effective treatment for bulimia nervosa through several randomized clinical trials (see, for example, a review of 10 studies in Fairburn, Agras, & Wilson, 1992). Unfortunately, many of the studies of treatment effectiveness have been conducted with adults rather than among school-aged populations. However, several authors in the eating disorders field have described promising approaches that take into account adolescent development and the differences between anorexia nervosa and bulimia nervosa (Agras & Apple, 2002; Bowers, Evans, & Van Cleve, 1996; Gowers & Green, 2009; Lock, Le Grange, Agras, & Dare, 2001; Nicholls & Bryant-Waugh, 2003; Schmidt, 1998; Treasure, Schmidt, & Macdonald, 2010). In particular, Cooper and Stewart (2008) have described an enhanced CBT for use with adolescents, and Lock and colleagues (2001) have described a manualized family-based therapy approach for treatment of anorexia nervosa, which has evidence of effectiveness both as a primary treatment approach (Eisler, Dare, Hodes, Russell, Dodge, & Le Grange, 2000) and following failure of other treatments (Sim, Sadowski, Whiteside, & Wells, 2004). A general criticism of the literature pertaining to treatment and treatment effectiveness is the lack of attention to racial and ethnic diversity.

According to the standard diagnostic criteria used in mental health practice, anorexia nervosa is the refusal to maintain a (minimal) normal body weight along with intense fear of gaining weight or becoming fat (American Psychiatric Association, 2000). People with anorexia nervosa also have a distorted body image, including an unrealistic appraisal of body weight/shape and an overemphasis on body weight and shape for self-evaluation. Thus, individuals with anorexia nervosa may be dangerously underweight but believe themselves to be fat. In addition, they believe that their shape and weight are the most important aspects of themselves. Some individuals with anorexia nervosa also engage in binge-eating and/or purging behavior. Weight loss is achieved through some combination of extreme restriction in the amount and type of food eaten, excessive exercise, and purging (vomiting, using laxatives or diuretics). In females who have reached puberty, menstrual cycles may cease (amenorrhea).

Bulimia nervosa, on the other hand, is indicated by recurrent binge eating—eating a larger amount of food in a specific period of time than most people would eat and feeling a lack of control over eating during the binge episode. Individuals with bulimia nervosa usually weigh in a normal range because they also engage in behaviors to compensate for their overeating, such as purging, fasting, or excessive exercise. Bulimia nervosa shares with anorexia nervosa an overemphasis on body shape in evaluation of the self and extreme dissatisfaction with body weight and shape.

Anorexia nervosa is relatively rare, with an average prevalence rate of 0.3% in young females (Hoek & van Hoeken, 2003). Bulimia nervosa, although still rare, is more common than anorexia nervosa, having a prevalence of about 1% in young women (Hoek & van Hoeken, 2003). Although females are at much higher risk, these disorders do also occur in young males. Although rates of eating disorders vary cross-culturally, they do occur on every continent. Among racial/ethnic groups in the United States, anorexia nervosa is rare among African Americans, who also report the lowest body dissatisfaction, and bulimia nervosa is seen less frequently among African-American than Caucasian populations. Prevalence among Latino/a and Asian-American populations is also lower than among Caucasians and follows the same pattern of anorexia nervosa being more rare (Levine & Smolak, 2010). The most frequently occurring eating disorder (prevalence estimates ranging from 5%–15%) is a catch-all called "eating disorder not otherwise specified," which includes eating disorders that meet many but not all of the criteria of anorexia or bulimia disorder.

Further, even though only a small number of young people with eating problems would meet the strict diagnostic criteria set out in the *DSM-IV-TR* (American Psychiatric Association, 2000), a greater number of youth experience many of the same obsessions with food and body image. These youth are at risk of developing eating disorders. Among young women who are dieting, already having a low body mass index and frequently eating in secret are risk factors for developing an eating disorder (Fairburn, Cooper, Doll, & Davies, 2005). In summary, risk factors include:

- perceived pressure to be thin
- weight concerns and body dissatisfaction
- dieting, especially repeated, unsuccessful dieting (for bulimia nervosa)
- perfectionism
- family history of eating disorder
- parental problems such as obesity or alcohol abuse
- critical comments by family members about the student's body weight or eating
- competitive involvement in gymnastics, swimming, wrestling, or ballet

The consequences of eating disorders in youth are serious and include dental problems, bone loss, osteoporosis, stunted growth, suicide, or death from excessive weight loss in extreme cases of anorexia nervosa. A number of other emotional disorders may also occur along with either anorexia or bulimia nervosa, including depression, anxiety disorders, obsessive-compulsive disorder, and personality disorders.

Although the cause of eating disorders is not conclusively known, one theory of causation is that a young person's insecurity, perhaps related to a crisis such as moving or parental job loss, becomes focused on her or his weight and shape. The energy of the person is directed toward strictly controlling food intake and weight. In anorexia nervosa, successful efforts at restricting food and losing weight may initially result in positive feedback from parents, teachers, or others whose opinions the youth values. The youth wants to continue to experience success, and control becomes its own reward. The young person continues to believe she or he is still too fat, even though the amount of weight lost may have been dramatic and dangerous. In bulimia nervosa, efforts to restrict food backfire into binge-eating episodes. The youth may try to control eating through restricting herself from certain foods (e.g., chocolate) or for most of the day. The resulting guilt and shame at the loss of control, as well as intense fear of gaining weight, lead to attempts to compensate for the excess food, often through vomiting or taking large amounts of laxatives.

What We Can Do

Tasks of the school social worker/counselor in relation to eating disorders include:

- offering effective prevention programs
- identification of youth with eating disorders
- assessment of the seriousness of a student's physical condition and enlisting the aid of parents
- if physical condition warrants, referring the student for medical treatment
- participating in cognitive-behavioral care after medical treatment *or* carrying out cognitive-behavioral intervention if medical treatment is not indicated
- assisting in monitoring medication effectiveness and side effects, if pharmacological treatment is occurring
- providing support for students who are receiving treatment in other settings

Identifying Youth with Eating Disorders

- Physical signs include significant changes in weight, especially weight loss; failure to gain weight or height expected for age and stage of development; and delayed or disrupted puberty. In anorexia, abnormal hair growth (soft, downy) may be present on the face or back.
- Behavioral signs include limited food intake, either in terms of energy quality or nutrient range; excessive or irregular food intake.
- Social signs may include social isolation, withdrawal from friends and activities, and a general regression in development.

Other school personnel also are in a position to identify youth with eating disorders. Teachers and coaches, in particular, may have more regular, ongoing contact with students than do school social workers or counselors. Therefore, it is important for the school mental health professional to be a resource for other school personnel in regard to identifying and responding to signs of eating disorders in students.

Assessing Seriousness of Physical Condition

A diagnosis of anorexia nervosa requires that weight be 85% of normal weight for height and developmental stage (or less) and in postmenarche females, amenorrhea of at least three cycles. If a student meets these criteria, the school social worker should refer the youth for a medical checkup. Hospitalization may be necessary if the youth is 75–80% of expected body weight. Bulimia nervosa has fewer potential medical complications unless the youth is heavily abusing laxatives or diuretics, in which case electrolytes may become out of balance and cause rapid changes in blood pressure and/or pulse rate. If in doubt, the social worker should refer the student for a medical checkup.

Enlisting the Aid of Parents

The involvement and support of parents is important in treating many emotional and behavioral disorders in children and youth. In treating eating disorders, family support is critical. Although there may be family dynamics that play into a youth's eating disorder, it is important to avoid blaming parents for their child's eating disorder. Family therapy to lessen over-expression of emotions and improve general communication may be helpful in treating a youth's eating disorder. In family-based therapy for eating disorders, parents are specifically put in charge of refeeding their child; family relationships are renegotiated to increase parental monitoring for prevention of binge/purge behaviors; and youth are assisted with normal adolescent development (separation and individuation) (Lock et al., 2001).

Steps in Cognitive-Behavioral Intervention for Eating Disorders

The primary targets of CBT intervention for bulimia nervosa and anorexia nervosa are (1) modifying the beliefs and attitudes that support the importance of body shape and weight; and (2) normalizing eating. CBT for eating disorders relies on a variety of behavioral and cognitive strategies. The treatment is problem-oriented, focused on the present and future, and proceeds (for bulimia nervosa) over 19 sessions in three stages.

Stage 1. The goal of the first stage is to normalize eating. During the first session, the mental health professional orients the student to the goals and processes of therapy. The youth must be willing to play an active role in therapy and must develop confidence in the mental health professional and the cognitive-behavioral approach. Illustrating the cognitive model of eating disorders, the mental health professional helps the student to draw connections between her own situation and the links among emotions, dietary restrictions, binge eating, and purging. The mental health professional emphasizes the importance of regular meals—three meals and two snacks daily, going no more than 3–4 hours (while awake) without eating—highlighting how hunger and cravings from strict dieting lead to binge eating and purging. Accurate information about food, nutrition, and weight regulation is provided. The mental health professional will ask the youth to make one change (e.g., eat something in the morning if breakfast is usually skipped).

Self-monitoring is an important strategy in cognitive-behavioral interventions. During the first session, the mental health professional teaches the youth to use the Daily Food Diary (see Figure 13.1). This form is used to track what the youth eats, when, how much, and various aspects of the context of eating, such as the location and associated thoughts and feelings about each episode of eating. The youth also classifies each episode as a meal, snack, or binge and records purging behavior. The purpose of keeping the food record is to identify eating episodes that are handled appropriately as well as patterns of problems and the factors that contribute to them. The record also can be used to track progress over time.

Stage 2. Once the student is eating more regularly and having fewer episodes of binge eating and purging, the treatment moves on to more cognitive aspects. The Daily Food Diary has probably already turned up some of the triggers of problematic situations, thoughts, and emotions. One of the basic tenets of cognitive-behavioral therapy is that individuals commit thinking errors, using faulty logic. The interpretation of events resulting from these errors causes negative emotions. To relieve negative emotions, then, the youth engages in binge eating, purging, or other control mechanisms in order to feel better (less anxious, for example). The mental health professional now teaches the student to identify and challenge the dysfunctional thoughts that are influencing both her emotions and behavior. A method for challenging dysfunctional thoughts involves using the Daily Record of Dysfunctional Thoughts (see Figure 13.2). From the first session on, the mental health professional should help the student to clarify the difference between thoughts and emotions to model the identification of emotions and the uncovering of automatic thoughts. The mental health professional then helps the student to identify more rational thoughts to substitute for the dysfunctional thoughts.

This stage also includes behavioral experiments through which the student actively challenges her dysfunctional thoughts. Usually the youth is convinced that there are certain foods that she just cannot eat because to have even a small amount would have a disastrous effect on her weight or shape. The intervention uses the Feared Foods List (see Figure 13.3) to identify these foods and rank them in terms of difficulty on a scale of 1–4, with 1 being the easiest to handle. The goal here is to experiment with adding a moderately-sized portion of one or more of these foods, starting with the easiest ones, to the eating plan once per week or every other week. The youth should record her reactions to consuming the feared food in her Daily Food Diary and process dysfunctional thoughts that arise.

Stage 3. The final stage of treatment is to create a maintenance plan. The mental health professional and student should brainstorm and problem solve about upcoming events and situations that are high risk for the student. The student should be prepared for a relapse of some of the disordered eating behaviors and have plans in place for what she will do. The student should write out plans of what she will do if/when relapse occurs. The plan should be specific, including making reframing statements to herself ("I have binged on fatty food today, but that does not mean that I am back to having an eating disorder") and returning to practicing the cognitive and behavioral strategies that were effective. The goal is for the student to be able to apply the tools she has learned before a short-term relapse gets out of hand and becomes a longer-term problem.

Monitoring Medication Effects and Side Effects

Table 13.1 lists some medications that are used in treatment of anorexia nervosa and bulimia

Name____________________ Day ____________________ Date____________________

Time	*Type & Amount Food/Beverage*	*Place*	*Snack (S) Meal (M) Binge (B)*	*Purge (V/L)*	*Situation*

Figure 13.1. Daily Food Diary

Name__________________ Day__________________ Date__________________

Situation	*Emotions*	*Automatic Thoughts*	*Rational Response*

Figure 13.2. Daily Record of Dysfunctional Thoughts

1. Food or beverage	*Rank Difficulty (1 easiest to deal with)*
____________________	*1 2 3 4*
____________________	*1 2 3 4*
____________________	*1 2 3 4*
____________________	*1 2 3 4*
____________________	*1 2 3 4*
____________________	*1 2 3 4*
____________________	*1 2 3 4*
____________________	*1 2 3 4*
____________________	*1 2 3 4*
____________________	*1 2 3 4*
____________________	*1 2 3 4*

2. Select one or more of the food items rated "1." Describe a plan for consuming moderately-sized portions each week or every other week.Describe your reaction in your Daily Food Diary.

Food/Beverage	*Amount in a Moderate Portion*	*How Often to Consume*

Figure 13.3. Feared Foods List

nervosa. Medications usually would be used in conjunction with therapy. Antidepressant medications combined with CBT seem to be an effective combination (Halmi, 2003). Fluoxetine (Prozac) and olanzapine (Zyprexa) have been found to be the most commonly prescribed drugs for eating disorders in children and adolescents (Gowers et al., 2010).

Non-specialists, particularly primary care physicians, may prescribe psychotropic medication to youth with eating disorders without referring the youth to a specialist (Gowers et al., 2010). If a student is receiving treatment for an eating disorder that includes medication, the school social worker or mental health professional should watch for the intended effects and side effects, as listed in

Table 13.1 Medications Used in Treatment of Eating Disorders

Medication/Source	*Disorder*	*When Used*	*Symptoms Targeted*	*Side Effects*
Fluoxetine (Prozac) or other SSRIs (Halmi, 2003)	Anorexia nervosa	Following some weight restoration	Prevent relapse; reduce depression, anxiety, and obsessive-compulsive symptoms	Nervousness, difficulty falling asleep or staying asleep, upset stomach, dry mouth, sore throat, drowsiness, weakness, shaking of hands
Olanzapine (Zyprexa) (Boachie et al., 2003)	Anorexia nervosa	During treatment	Dysfunctional thinking, weight loss	Drowsiness, increased appetite, weight gain
Fluoxetine (Prozac) or other SSRIs (Halmi, 2003)	Bulimia nervosa	During treatment	Reduce binge eating; improve mood; reduce preoccupation with shape and weight	See above
		Aftercare	Prevent relapse	
Topiramate (anticonvulsant) (Kotwal, McElroy, & Malhotra, 2003)	Bulimia nervosa	During treatment	Reduce binge eating and purging	Fatigue, flu-like symptoms, prickling or tingling or decreased tactile sensations of the skin, rare but serious side effects include kidney problems, eye problems (acute myopia and acute angle-closure glaucoma)

Table 13.1, and communicate these observations to parents and/or medical personnel treating the student.

Applying Interventions within a Response to Intervention Framework

In an RTI framework, the CBT treatment for eating disorders described in this chapter would be a Tier 3 intervention. Tier 1 interventions might consist of prevention information in the curriculum for the school population at large. The curriculum could be focused on topics such as nutrition, healthy bodies, healthy self-esteem, and the role of the media in promoting unrealistic body and shape ideals. Other school-wide prevention efforts may include creating a safe school environment that does not tolerate bullying of any type and disciplines students who harass others on the basis of size, physical education focused on skills building and establishing healthy habits, and evaluating schools' lunches and vending machine options (Keca & Cook-Cottone, 2005). For students at elevated risk of developing an eating disorder, such as those who engage in dieting, bingeing, or purging, Tier 2 interventions might consist of psychoeducation in a group setting such as the Girls' Group, which addresses factors related to body dissatisfaction and eating-disordered behavior (Keca & Cook-Cottone, 2005). At-risk youth may be screened for disordered eating using the dietary restraint subscale of the Eating Disorder Examination Questionnaire, which consists of five questions about behaviors in the previous 28 days (Fairburn & Beglin, 1994). If the school participates in routine screening for depression and suicidality, the dietary restraint subscale could be added, as eating disorders are often accompanied by disorders of mood or anxiety.

Practice Example

Tina was referred to the school social worker when her homeroom teacher noticed that Tina was throwing up in the bathroom after lunch. The teacher asked Tina if she were sick and needed to go home, and Tina's hesitation led the teacher to walk Tina to the social worker's office. In tears, Tina admitted to the social worker that she made herself vomit because she didn't want to gain weight. After a conference later in the week with Tina's mother, the social worker began meeting with Tina during a free period.

The social worker learned that Tina was the youngest child of four in the family. Growing up, she idolized her older sister, Judy. Tina had medical problems from birth and was babied a great deal by her parents and her older siblings. One day when Tina was about 13 years old, Judy remarked on Tina's shape, saying teasingly that she was "getting to be a little fatty." Tina was hurt—and enraged—and vowed to herself to "show her!" Although she was actually a normal weight, Tina began a diet immediately. For the next several weeks, she followed a pattern of eating little but thinking about food all the time. Initially she lost weight, but after a couple of months, one day she was so hungry after school that she stopped on the way home and bought a box of chocolate-covered doughnuts. She meant to eat one, but soon realized she had eaten the whole box. Then she stopped at another store and bought a quart of milk. She drank the whole quart and then felt sick. This pattern continued for several days. Tina grew more and more concerned about her weight and began to make herself vomit after the doughnuts and milk.

Stage 1. The social worker got Tina to describe her eating pattern, which consisted of no breakfast, plain lettuce at lunch, then a binge on doughnuts, milk, roasted chicken, ice cream, and other foods on the way home. Tina would vomit after the binge, then eat dinner in her room, and vomit again before bed. The social worker explained the food record and the goal of eating something every 3–4 hours. Tina was alarmed that eating this much would make her weight go up. The social worker explained that eating a normal amount of food spread out over the day should result in a stable weight and that Tina's pattern, even though her intent is to lose weight through purging the food she eats, actually may be resulting in weight gain. Her strict restriction of food during the day leads to the cravings she experiences and gives in to on the way home. She feels guilty until she purges. The social worker explained that even though Tina is vomiting, it is likely that she is not able to get rid of all of the calories in the food she has consumed. Tina agreed to try to eat a small bowl of cereal with milk and half of a banana for breakfast.

The next week, Tina reported eating breakfast as planned and adding two crackers to her salad at lunch. However, she was still binge eating on doughnuts and/or roasted chicken on the way home and purging. She reported that she meant to eat only half of the doughnuts, but was unable to stop. She was able to then eat a normal amount for dinner and not purge. She worried about her weight, which was up 2 pounds from last week. The social worker explained that weight fluctuates as much as several pounds up or down per day, often depending on water retention (e.g., from where she is in her menstrual cycle or from eating a great deal of salty food). Pointing out to Tina that it is a long time between breakfast and the end of the school day, with only a small amount of food that amounts to anything in between, she suggested that Tina add to her lunch. Tina agreed to add cheese and crackers and tomato to her plain lettuce.

Stage 2. As Tina adopted a more regular meal and snack schedule, she was able to avoid binge eating on the way home most days. When she got a bad grade on a test, though, she binged on doughnuts once again. At this point, the intervention moved on to the thoughts and emotions that are associated with her eating disorder. All along, the social worker had tried to help Tina to recognize her emotions. Like many other people, Tina is not always able to label how she is feeling, confusing thoughts and feelings. In discussing the test grade, Tina said, "I feel like I'll never be able to get into a good college with these grades." The social worker responded, "You think your grades may keep you from getting into a good college, and you feel scared or sad about that." Tina acknowledged that she feels scared; she is afraid she will disappoint her parents. The social worker introduced the Daily Record of Dysfunctional Thoughts (Figure 13.3) and helped Tina to fill it out with this example:

SW: The situation is getting a bad grade on a test. Your emotions—how you feel—is scared. What is it that you think automatically about this?
Tina: My parents will think I'm not smart enough to go to a good college.
SW: Okay, let's come up with a more rational thought. Do you really think that one test grade will keep you out of a good college?
Tina: No, I guess not.
SW: Is this bad grade what you usually get on tests?
Tina: No, I usually do much better.
SW: What was the grade?
Tina: I only got 85%.
SW: Aha, now I see. How about this for a more rational response: "Even though I got a B on the test, it is just one test. A few B's won't hurt my overall GPA anyway."
Tina: Okay, but my parents are still going to be upset.
SW: What will happen because they are upset about the grade?
Tina: I guess they will still love me.

Stage 3. Tina accomplished a great deal in treatment. She was eating regular meals and snacks, rarely binge eating, knew what was likely to trigger a binge-eating episode, and had begun to exercise more regularly. There were only a couple of sessions left, and school would be out soon for summer. Tina and the social worker were thinking about high-risk situations that might come up for Tina in the near future. Tina would be going away to band camp in July and had identified that as a potentially risky time. Tina decided to begin keeping the food diary again a week before she leaves for camp. In this way, she will be able to monitor her emotions and eating while she is away. If she begins to have problems sticking to a regular meal schedule or is tempted to binge, she will work on a more rational response to what she is feeling and thinking. If she does binge and/or purge while she is away, she will remind herself that she can stop again when she gets home.

Key Points to Remember

- Eating disorders (meeting full diagnostic criteria) are fairly rare but may have serious consequences. School personnel should be attuned to extreme weight loss and other signs of disordered eating behavior. A greater number of students may have disturbed eating behaviors that may later lead to a full-blown eating disorder.
- Individuals with anorexia nervosa are more likely to have medical complications. If anorexia nervosa is suspected, there should probably be a referral for a medical examination.
- Bulimia nervosa in particular is amenable to treatment with a cognitive-behavioral intervention. The treatment that is described here and in the treatment manuals referenced consists of 19 sessions in three stages.
- The first stage of treatment emphasizes restoring a normal eating pattern of three meals and two snacks per day.
- Stage 2 of treatment addresses the distorted thinking and emotions that lead to and maintain eating disorders.
- Stage 3 plans for relapse prevention.
- Medications are sometimes used along with therapy during treatment or afterward for relapse prevention.

Further Learning

National Eating Disorders Association—resources including toolkits for coaches/athletic trainers, educators and parents: http://www.nationaleatingdisorders.org

Academy for Eating Disorders—professional association committed to leadership in eating disorders research, education, treatment and prevention: http://www.aedweb.org

Eating Disorder HOPE—information and resources for treatment and recovery: http://www.eatingdisorderhope.com

References

Agras, W. S., & Apple, R. F. (2002). Understanding and treating eating disorders. In F. W. Kaslow & T. Patterson (Eds.), *Comprehensive handbook of psychotherapy: Vol. 2. Cognitive behavioral approaches* (pp. 189–212). New York: Wiley.

American Psychiatric Association. (2000). *Diagnostic and statistical manual of mental disorders* (4th ed., text revision). Washington, DC: Author.

Boachie, A., Goldfield, G. S., & Spettigue, W. (2003). Olanzapine use as an adjunctive treatment for hospitalized children with anorexia nervosa: Case reports. *International Journal of Eating Disorders, 33*(1), 98–103.

Bowers, W. A., Evans, K., & Van Cleve, L. (1996). Treatment of adolescent eating disorders. In M. A. Reineke, F. M. Dattilio, & A. Freeman (Eds.), *Cognitive therapy with children and adolescents: A casebook for clinical practice* (pp. 227–250). New York: Guilford.

Cooper, Z., & Stewart, A. (2008). CBT-E and the younger patient. In C. G. Fairburn (Ed.), *Cognitive behavior therapy and eating disorders* (pp. 221–230). New York, NY: Guilford Press.

Eisler, I., Dare, C., Hodes, M., Russell, G., Dodge, E., & Le Grange, D. (2000). Family therapy for adolescent anorexia nervosa: The results of a controlled comparison of two family interventions. *Journal of Child Psychology and Psychiatry, 41*, 727–736.

Fairburn, C. G., Agras, W. S., & Wilson, G. T. (1992). The research on the treatment of bulimia nervosa: Practical and theoretical implications. In G. H. Anderson & S. H. Kennedy (Eds.), *The biology of feast and famine: Relevance to eating disorders* (pp. 318–340). New York: Academic.

Fairburn, C. G., & Beglin, S. J. (1994). Assessment of eating disorders: Interview or self-report questionnaire? *International Journal of Eating Disorders, 16*, 363–370.

Fairburn, C. G., Cooper, Z., Doll, H. A., & Davies, B. A. (2005). Identifying dieters who will develop an eating disorder: A prospective, population-based study. *American Journal of Psychiatry, 162*, 2249–2255.

Gowers, S. G., & Green, L. (2009). *Eating disorders: Cognitive behaviour therapy with children and young people*. London, England: Routledge.

Gowers, S., Claxton, M., Rowlands, L., Inbasagaran, A., Wood, D., et al. (2010). Drug prescribing in child and adolescent eating disorder services. *Child and Adolescent Mental Health, 15*(1), 18–22.

Halmi, K. (2003). Eating disorders. In A. Martin, L. Scahill, D. Charney, & J. Leckman (Eds.), *Pediatric psychopharmacology* (pp. 592–602). New York: Oxford University Press.

Hoek, H. W., & van Hoeken, D. (2003). Review of the prevalence and incidence of eating disorders. *International Journal of Eating Disorders, 34*, 383–396.

Keca, J., & Cook-Cottone, C. (2005). eating disorders: prevention is worth every ounce. *Principal Leadership: High School Edition, 5*(9), 11–15.

Kotwal, R., McElroy, S., & Malhotra, S. (2003). What treatment data support Topiramate in bulimia nervosa and binge eating disorder? What is the drug's safety profile? How is it used in these conditions? *Eating Disorders, 11*, 71–75.

Levine, M. P., & Smolak, L. (2010). Cultural influences on body image and the eating disorders. In W. S. Agras (Ed.), *The Oxford handbook of eating disorders* (pp. 223–246). New York, NY: Oxford University Press.

Lock, J., Le Grange, D., Agras, W. S., & Dare, C. (2001). *Treatment manual for anorexia nervosa: A family-based approach*. New York: Guilford.

Nicholls, D., & Bryant-Waugh, R. (2003). Children and young adolescents. In J. Treasure, U. Schmidt, & E. van Furth (Eds.), *Handbook of eating disorders* (pp. 415–433). New York: Wiley.

Schmidt, U. (1998). Eating disorders and obesity. In P. Graham (Ed.), *Cognitive-behaviour therapy for children and families* (pp. 262–281). Cambridge: Cambridge University Press.

Sim, L., Sadowski, C., Whiteside, S., & Wells, L. (2004). Family-based therapy for adolescents with anorexia nervosa. *Mayo Clinic Proceedings, 79*, 1305–1308.

Treasure, J., Schmidt, U., & Macdonald, P. (2010). *The clinician's guide to collaborative caring in eating disorders*. London, England: Routledge.

SECTION III

Effective Interventions for Students with Neurodevelopmental, Learning, and Physical Disorders

Neurodevelopmental issues such as ADHD, autism spectrum disorders, learning disorders, and physical challenges require knowledge of evidence-based practices for school professionals to be effective with these students. The chapters in this section discuss timely updates and information on how to best help these children, along with many resources for designing effective school programs.

CHAPTER 14

Effective Interventions for Students with ADHD

Martell Teasley

Getting Started

This chapter provides an overview of evidence-based practice methods for school social workers and other school counselors in the assessment and treatment of attention deficit/hyperactivity disorder (ADHD) (DuPaul & Eckert, 1997; DuPaul, Eckert, & McGoey, 1997; Erk, 1995, 2000; Hoagwood, Kelleher, Feil, & Comer, 2000; Jensen, 2000; Jensen et al., 1999; McGoey, Eckert, & DuPaul, 2002; Olfson, Gameroff, Marcus, & Jensen, 2003; Perrin et al., 2001; Richters et al., 1995; Thomas & Corcoran, 2000). Concurrently, this chapter places an emphasis on culturally competent practice with minority schoolchildren and families. "Cultural and linguistic competence is a set of congruent behaviors, attitudes, and policies that come together in a system, agency, or among professionals that enables effective work in cross-cultural situations" (U.S. Department of Health & Human Services, 2005). There is growing diversification of children attending our public school systems and known challenges identified within research literature for minority populations diagnosed with ADHD (Eirldi, 2006;Gerdes & Schneider, 2008; Hervey-Jumper, Douyon, Falcone, & Franco, 2009; Jones et al., 2009; Kendall, & Hatton, 2002). The Latino population is one of the fastest growing within the country. Findings from the 2010 Census revealed that while just 3 million Anglo-American babies were born in the last decade, there were 15 million babies of Hispanic decent born in the U.S. during the same time period. Yet, little evidence-based information exists on school-based services in working with Latino children and youth with ADHD (Gerdes & Schneider, 2009). Step-by-step procedures and guidelines for assessment and treatment interventions are discussed. Resources that will assist school social workers with specific intervention procedures and methods are cited. These resources contain in-depth information supported by evidence-based research and intervention methods that are cited in the reference list for this chapter. Some examples and one case scenario that will assist school social workers with the development of a framework for understanding how to develop an intervention plan for school children diagnosed with ADHD are provided.

What We Know

Attention deficit/hyperactivity disorder is a complicated neurobiological disorder caused by malfunctioning neurotransmitters within the central nervous system (Litner, 2003). It is usually an inherited disorder "typically beginning in childhood and continuing throughout the lifespan.... it has been estimated that nearly 70% of children diagnosed with ADHD continue [to experience] ongoing problems as adolescents" (Litner, 2003, p. 138). With ratios varying across all racial and ethnic groups, more males are diagnosed with ADHD than females (Bussing, Gary, Mills, & Garvan, 2003). Individuals with ADHD experience a host of psychological, behavioral, and cognitive problems that present them with specific challenges in their activities of daily living and interactions with their families, peers, and communities. Complications include inconsistency in sustaining attention, poor organization and planning, lack of forethought, low energy, mood swings, poor memory, overactive behavior, and impulsivity (DuPaul, Eckert, & McGoey, 1997; Erk, 2000). While coexisting learning disorders, such as conduct or oppositional disorder, are common in children diagnosed with ADHD, prevalence rates vary in research findings (Richters et al., 1995).

Minority children and youth, particularly African Americans, are overdiagnosed with learning disorders and have higher rates of comorbid disorders when diagnosed with ADHD. African-American and Hispanic children statistically experience 2 to 4 times more physical or mental health problems than do the general public (Hervey-Jumper et al., 2008). For example, in each year since 1968, government education data revealed overrepresentation of African-American students in categories of emotional disturbance and mental retardation (Hosterman, DuPaul, & Jitendra, 2008).

Attention deficit/hyperactivity disorder has multiple consequences in the school setting and presents a host of challenges for students, their families, educators, and related school services personnel. Many students diagnosed with ADHD exhibit higher than average rates of interrupting classroom activities, calling out answers or asking questions without raising their hand, getting out of an assigned seat without permission, and failing to complete assigned tasks in the classroom as well as at home. For the ADHD student, a great deal of energy and behavior in the classroom is often aimed at avoiding the completion of tasks (DuPaul et al., 1997). As a result, there is an association between individuals with ADHD and academic underachievement, school suspension, dropping out, peer rejection, the development of antisocial patterns, low self-esteem, and depression (DuPaul et al., 1997). School disciplinary problems, such as suspension and expulsion, are more characteristic of those diagnosed as hyperactive (Richters et al., 1995). Moreover, students with ADHD often do not develop the academic skills necessary for college. The bulk of studies on racial and ethnic minority students diagnosed with ADHD focus on African-American and Hispanic children and youth (Hervey-Jumper et al., 2008; Jones et al., 2009; Miller, Nigg, & Miller, 2009). Yet, although prevalence rates are believed to be similar or slightly higher for minority children, African-American and Latino children are underdiagnosed with ADHD, particularly at an early age when initial signs are present (Gerdes & Schneider, 2009; Miller et al., 2009). Conversely, black and Latino children are more likely to be diagnosed with learning disorders, which confounds both diagnosis and treatment (Hervey-Jumper et al., 2008).

Despite greater efforts to reduce the discrepancies in diagnosis and treatment of ADHD, disparities still exist. A study of a North Carolina county among 6,000 elementary school students revealed that when compared to their white and black counterparts, Latino children are much less likely to be diagnosed with ADHD. Considering gains in early identification and treatment in the past decade, minority children are still less likely to be treated for ADHD and other mental health disorders (Eiraldi et al., 2006). Identified disparities are explained in the form of cultural factors, rater bias and discrimination, language barriers, health care access and fragmentation, lack of knowledge among minority parents (Jones et al., 2009), inexperienced teachers (Hosterman et al., 2008; Wood, Heiskell, Delay, Jongeling, & Perry, 2009), and mistrust of the mental health system and are commonly cited explanations for continued diagnostic and treatment disparities among racial and ethnic groups (Eiraldi et al., 2006; Haack, Gerdes, Schneider, & Hurtado, 2011; Miller et al., 2009). Once identified, treatment disparities continue. "Minority children are also much less likely than non-minority children to be treated for this [ADHD] or other mental health disorders" (Eiraldi et al., 2006, p. 3).

What We Can Do

Assessment and Diagnosis of ADHD in Children

The *Diagnostic and Statistical Manual of Mental Disorders (DSM-IV-TR)* defines ADHD as a multidimensional disorder identified by subtypes: "Diagnosis is based on a collaborative process that involves children and adolescent psychiatrists or other physicians, the child, and the child's family, and school-based or other health care professionals as appropriate" (American Psychiatric Association, 2000, p. 1). School social workers and other mental health counselors should become familiar with the diagnostic criteria for ADHD as stated in the *DSM-IV-TR*. There are several psychometric instruments with which school social workers should become knowledgeable (Table 14.1) that are frequently used in the diagnosis of ADHD. It is

Table 14.1 Instrumentation Used in the Assessment and Diagnosis of ADHD

1. *Child Attention Profile* (DuPaul & Kern, 2011). A 12-item scale taken from Child Behavior Checklist Teacher Report that measures rate and severity of undesirable behaviors.	Ages 6–16
2. *Child Behavior Checklist* (CBCL). Used to measure behavioral problems in children and adolescents. It relies on parent and caregiver reports and provides a total problem score in the assessment of depression, social problems, attention problems, and withdrawn, delinquent, and aggressive behavior.	Ages 3 years and older
3. *Conners's Teacher Rating Scale.* A 28-item questionnaire designed to measure various types of clinical and research applications with children. It contains four indexes including for assessment of hyperactivity and for assessment of inattention.	Ages 2–18
4. *Caregiver—Teacher Report Form.* Adapted from items in the CBCL, it replaces problems more likely observed at home with those more likely observed in daycare and preschool settings.	Ages 2–5
5. *Teacher Report Form.* Contains many of the problem items found in the CBCL but substitutes the assessment of home-specific items with school-specific behaviors and provides a standardized description of problem behaviors, academic functioning, and adaptive behaviors.	Ages 5–18
6. *Youth Self-Report for Age.* Contains specific components of the CBCL as they relate to adolescents and many items that youth may not report about themselves. Using this instrument in an interview may be the best method.	Ages 11–18
7. *ADHD Rating Scale* (DuPaul, 1990). This is a scale using 14 items from the *DSM-III-R* on ADHD.	Ages 5–18

important to note that one of the more frequent complications in objective measurement for diagnosing AHDH is the recurrence of scales that are ethnically insensitive and that vary in measurement across cultures (Jones et al., 2009). For example, "the lack of available Spanish versions of assessment measures contributes to insufficient research and underutilization of mental health services for Latino children with [ADHD]" (Haack et al., 2010, p. 33). Greater information on clinical practice guidelines and the evaluation of ADHD in children (Perrin et al., 2001) can be found on the American Academy of Pediatrics Web site: www.help4adhd.org.

Research in Support of Treatment Interventions

Nationwide estimates of the prevalence of ADHD suggest that between 3% and 9% of children are afflicted (Richters et al., 1995). However, it is estimated that 3.4% of children ages 3 to 18 receive treatment for ADHD (Erk, 2000). There is also a high comorbidity with other mental disorders, such as conduct disorder, depression, and anxiety disorders. Although ADHD is arguably one of the most common mental health disorders challenging schools, it is also the most treatable. The most successful interventions for ADHD in school settings have been with the use of the multimodal approach consisting of pharmaceutical intervention, cognitive-behavioral training, parent training, and teacher training in classroom management techniques and special education methods. This was confirmed in separate investigations of evidence-based best practice research findings from the National Institute of Mental Health's Collaborative Multisite Multimodal Treatment Study of Children with ADHD and the American Academy of Pediatrics Committee on Quality Improvement's Subcommittee on Attention Deficit/Hyperactivity Disorder (Perrin et al., 2001). Intervention strategies suggested in this chapter are consistent with research findings from these investigations.

Approximately 70–80% of children with ADHD are treated with pharmacological intervention. A review of research among ethnic and racial groups indicates that while nearly 80% of white children diagnosed with ADHD take medication, less than 60% of African Americans and 55% of Latinos similarly diagnosed take medication (Eiraldi et al., 2006). In general, stimulants assist in the connection of neurotransmissions, which may help to diminish motor activity and impulsive behaviors characteristic of those diagnosed with ADHD. The clinical use of stimulant drugs has demonstrated short-term efficacy in the reduction of a range of core symptoms of ADHD, such as fidgetiness, finger tapping, fine motor movement, and classroom disturbances (Richters et al., 1995). "Stimulants have been found to enhance the sustained attention, impulse control, interpersonal behavior, and academic productivity of 70% to 80% of children with ADHD" (DuPaul & Eckert, 1997, p. 5). Additionally, stimulants have been shown to have positive effects on problem solving with peers, parent-child interactions, and a variety of controlled laboratory tasks, such as auditory and reading comprehension, spelling recall, continuous performance tasks, cue and free recall, and arithmetic computation (Richters et al., 1995). For discussion of the common medication used, see Bentley and Collins (in press).

Compliance with prescription medication protocols in the treatment of ADHD varies due to the possibility of complications from side effects (e.g., appetite reduction, insomnia, nervousness, etc.), possible addiction, or differences in environmental (home, school, or control settings) treatment reinforcement (DuPaul & Eckert, 1997). Comprehensive research studies have found that among the estimated 90% of children and adolescents with ADHD who receive prescription medication to treat ADHD, only 12–25% regularly take their medication (Smith, Waschbusch, Willoughby, & Evans, 2000). However, research on samples of children using pharmaceutical interventions in the treatment of ADHD (DuPaul & Eckert, 1997; Jensen et al., 1999; Richters et al., 1995) suggest that side effects of medication treatments may be unpleasant in the short run but are usually reversible and often dose dependent (Smith et al., 2000).

Unfortunately, previous studies are often inconsistent regarding the efficacy of pharmacological intervention in differential settings (e.g., home, school, and peer groups). The use of stimulants has demonstrated greater success in the treatment of hyperactivity than in curbing challenges with academic achievement and inattention. There is also evidence that the magnitude of stimulant benefits is not consistent across age groups. Likewise, the impact of comorbidity diagnoses in individuals with ADHD may produce differential effectiveness in the use of stimulants. Research studies have demonstrated that stabilization of treatment through pharmaceutical intervention takes approximately 14 months for school-aged children (Perrin et al., 2001). Medication regimens should be monitored closely for possible side effects (Table 14.3). Most medication side effects occur early during treatment, tend to be mild, and are short-lived. Conversely, for some children, side effects from medication have a greater effect than the reduction of problem behaviors or an increase in cognitive performance. Although rare, with high doses, some children experience mood disturbances, psychotic reactions, or hallucinations. Medication adjustments (lowering dosage or switching medication) may curb side effects. Many clinicians and physicians recommend "drug holidays"—no prescription ADHD medication on the weekends during the school year and/or during the entire summer—as a way of reducing the impact of side effects and potential long-term medical complications (Perrin et al., 2001). Overall, the use of stimulants for the treatment of ADHD may have minimal benefits in some clients, become contraindicated in others, and may be expected to yield gains beyond reduction of inattention and impulsivity in others (Richters et al., 1995).

An essential component of behavior management for school children diagnosed with ADHD is home-based treatment, with parental involvement that is coordinated with school-based interventions. Parent training in behavior modification techniques and stress management has shown improvement in school behavior and home behavior for hyperactive children and has demonstrated improvements in parent, child, and family relations (see Thomas & Corcoran, 2000, for a review of literature on family-centered approaches to ADHD). Cognitive-behavioral interventions, such as the use of token reinforcement as a reward for desired classroom behaviors, have demonstrated positive results. Successful use of behavioral therapy in the classroom must include teacher training in classroom management techniques and individualized strategies to combat behavioral maladaptation. Techniques that encourage and accommodate students with ADHD should be at the core of a teacher's class management interventions.

Teachers are actually the most valuable informant in the course of diagnoses, as they are able to compare and contrast a student's behavior to either all the other students in general or specifically other students of the same cultural background at the same developmental level (Busse & Beaver, 2000). Teacher bias in the assessment of minority ADHD has been demonstrated in numerous studies (Epstein et al., 2005; Wood, Heiskell, Joungeling, & Perry, 2009). Therefore, school social workers must understand the dynamics that surround the referral and assessment of schoolchildren and youth for mental health diagnosis.

Based on subgroup differences in comorbidity, age, cognitive ability, and the varied impact of pharmaceutical interventions, researchers have become increasingly interested in combined forms of treatment, or multimodal treatment strategies. *Multimodal treatment strategies* are those that tailor specific pharmaceutical and behavioral interventions to suit a client's particular needs in a given setting (e.g., home, school, and social). Treatment interventions outlined below are consistent with the multimodal approach.

Multimodal treatment interventions have demonstrated success with African-American and Latino children diagnosed with ADHD (Eiraldi et al., 2006; Jones et al., 2009; Miller et al., 2009). Yet, studies demonstrate that if the integrity of services cannot be maintained, then minority families are less likely to invest in participation in multimodal treatment strategies (Lillie-Blanton, Brodie, Rowland, Altman, & McIntosh, 2000). Concurrently, economic factors are likely to influence whether or not minority families can receive treatment (Bailey & Owens, 2005; Eiraldi et al., 2006). Black and Latino Americans have inadequate access to behavioral intervention plans due mainly to inadequate financial support (Hervey-Jumper et al., 2008). Even when there is access to behavioral health intervention, poor knowledge of best practices by school-based social service professionals and teachers hinders intervention with minority clients (Epstein et al., 2005; Hosterman et al., 2008).

Treatment Interventions

Figure 14.1 contains an evidence-based treatment algorithm developed by the American Academy of Pediatrics for children diagnosed with ADHD. Primary care clinicians should establish a management program that recognizes ADHD as a chronic condition. Prior to engaging in treatment intervention, social workers must determine the source of the ADHD diagnosis and review all accessible documentation, including those completed by psychologists, psychiatrists, and parents and teachers' evaluations of the student's classroom behavior and grades. Evidence-based treatment intervention

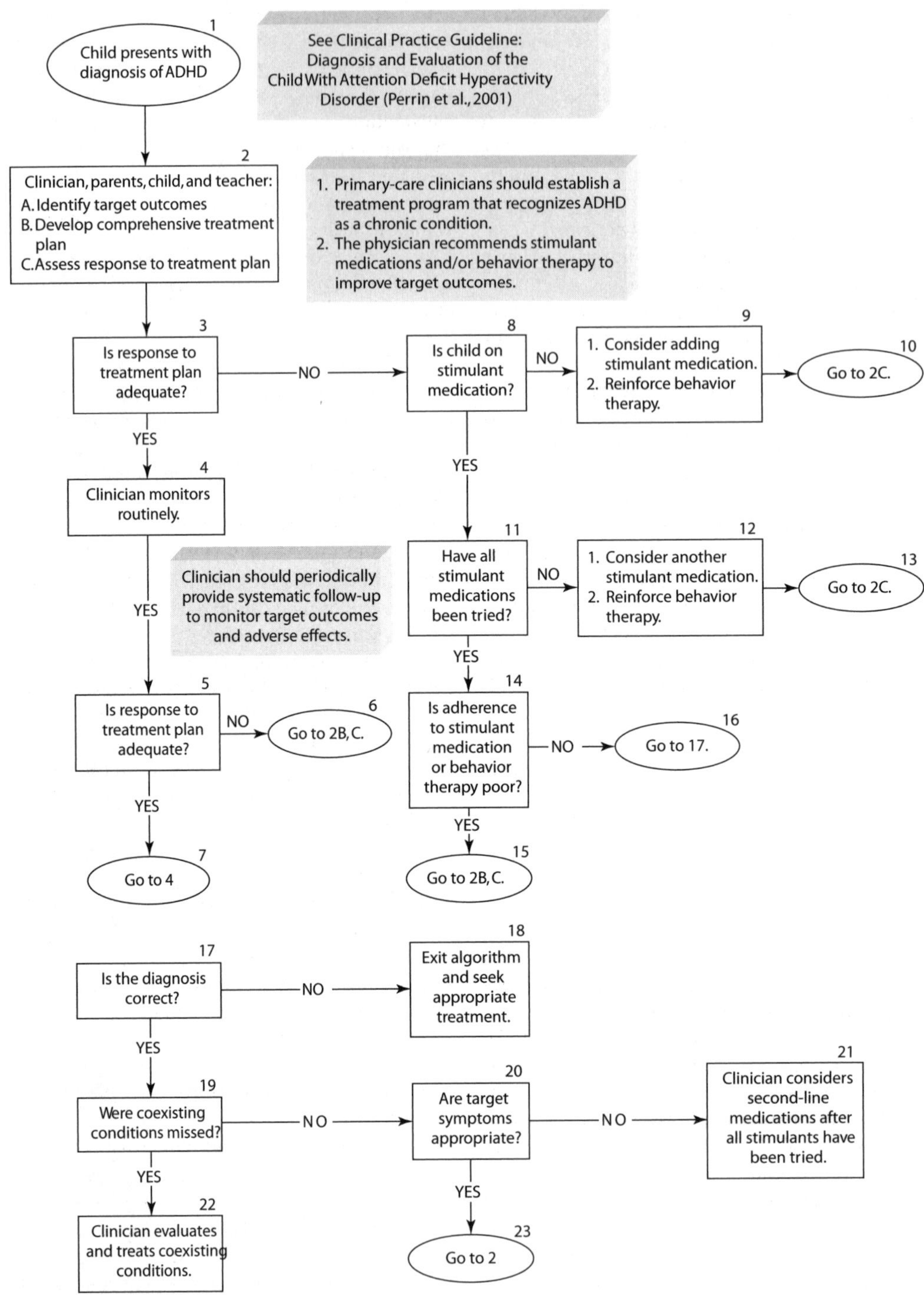

Figure 14.1. Algorithm for the Treatment of School-Aged Children with Attention Deficit/Hyperactivity Disorder

Source: Reproduced with permission from *Pediatrics, 108*, 1033–1044. Copyright 2001.

guidelines identified from a review of the literature are outlined below.

Development of Intervention Plan

- Determine target outcomes. Desired results may include:
    - decrease in disruptive behaviors
    - improvements in relationships with parents, siblings, teachers, and peers
    - improved academic performance, particularly in completion of work, volume of work, efficiency, and accuracy
    - increased independence and self-direction
    - enhanced safety in the community, such as riding a bicycle or crossing the street without incident
    - improved self-esteem
- Treatment plan must include:
    - collaboration with other school-based professionals (e.g., school psychologists, counselors, nurses) for special education services
    - coordination of services exterior to the school system (e.g., primary care, psychological, support groups)
    - parental and home-based intervention
    - specific cognitive-behavioral interventions
    - educational services (teachers and other faculty)
    - ongoing and outcome evaluation

Collaborative Practice

- "Collaboration between service providers and teachers is an important tool for optimizing ADHD treatment intervention" (LeFever, Villers, Morrow, & Vaughn, 2002, p. 68). An individualized approach to treatment intervention is necessary.
- Discuss findings from psychometric instrumentation used in assessment and diagnosis with the treatment team.
- Assist treatment team in the development of a functional behavioral assessment. Assist teachers with the development of a classroom individualized education program (IEP).

Medication

School social workers and mental health counselors should have a working knowledge of the most commonly used medications in the treatment of ADHD. Culturally competent school-based professionals who work with minority students diagnosed with ADHD must understand the multiple challenges that medication compliance can present. Advocacy in the form of coordinating services and identifying gaps in services to obtain medication are of paramount importance. While stimulants have proven to be beneficial to African-American and Latino children diagnosed with ADHD, greater attention should be given to increased medication side effects for both groups (Gerdes & Schneider, 2009; Miller et al., 2009). Many Spanish-speaking Latino parents are resistant to medication as a treatment option (Gerdes & Schneider, 2009). Similarly, African-American families "may be averse to the ideal of medication treatment for ADHD" (Miller et al., 2009, p. 83). Hence, client and family education is extremely important in order to gain medication compliance with Latino and African-American families. The NIMH has developed a list of stimulants for the treatment of ADHD approved by the federal Food and Drug Administration (Table 14.2). The most common potential side effects of these medications are listed in Table 14.3; however, for more detailed information see nlm.nih.gov/medlineplus.

- Monitor medication compliance: Is the individual taking medication as prescribed by physician/psychiatrist?
- Monitor bodily movement pre- and postmedication interventions.
- Determine when medication is most beneficial (e.g., time of day, duration of effects, differences in body movement).
- Monitor side effects of medication.
- Assess parents' knowledge of medication and attitude toward use of medications.
- If necessary, provide information to parents:
    - See Medline at www.ncbi.nlm.nih.gov.
    - Provide handouts, videotapes, Internet Web sites, and support group information.

Behavioral Therapy

- Set specific goals: Develop and set clear goals; set small, reachable goals; and make certain that the child understands the goals. For example, require the child to stay focused on homework for a specified period of time or to share a toy while playing with a friend. For students with ADHD, behavioral therapy is

Table 14.2 List of Medications for the Treatment of Children with ADHD

Medication	*Approved Age*
Adderall (amphetamine)	3 and older
Concerta (methylphenidate)	6 and older
Cylert (pemoline)	6 and older
Dexedrine (dextroamphetamine)	3 and older
Dextrostat (dextroamphetamine)	3 and older
Focalin (dexmethylphenidate)	6 and older
Metadate ER (Methylphenidate, extended release)	6 and older
Metadate CD (Methylphenidate, extended release)	6 and older
Ritalin (methylphenidate, extended release)	6 and older
Ritalin SR (Methylphenidate, extended release)	6 and older
Ritalin LA (methylphenidate, extended release)	6 and older

the preferred intervention (Miller et al., 2009; Jones et al., 2009). Although few in number, studies have demonstrated its effectiveness with African-American and Latino children and youth (Gerdes & Schneider, 2009; Miller et al., 2009). Language and acculturation can be important factors for Spanish-speaking Latino families. In general, when linguistic barriers are reduced, intervention compliance increases. Behavioral therapy with minority youth has been found to be effective, with improvements in a variety of areas including a decrease in hyperactivity and an increase in child compliance, resulting in improved parent-child interactions as well as decreased parental stress (Gerdes & Schneider, 2009; Miller et al., 2009).

- Provide rewards and consequences:
  - Positive reinforcement: Provide privileges and rewards as responses to desired behavior. Instruct parents to give their child rewards when desired behavior is demonstrated or

Table 14.3 Common Side Effects of Medications Prescribed for Children with ADHD

Generic Names	*Possible Side Effects*
Amphetamine	restlessness or tremors, anxiety, nervousness, headaches, dizziness, insomnia, diarrhea, constipation, dryness of the mouth, unpleasant taste in the mouth
Dexmethylphenidate	stomach pain, fever, loss of appetite, upset stomach, vomiting, difficulty falling asleep or staying asleep, dizziness, nervousness, weight loss, skin rash, headache
Dextroamphetamine	nervousness, restlessness, difficulty falling or staying asleep, false feeling of well-being, feeling of unpleasantness, dizziness, tremor, difficulty coordinating movements, headache, dry mouth, diarrhea, constipation, loss of appetite, weight loss, bad taste in mouth
Methylphenidate	nervousness, difficulty falling asleep or staying asleep, dizziness, drowsiness, upset stomach, vomiting, headache, loss of appetite
Pemoline	loss of appetite, trouble sleeping, weight loss, dizziness, drowsiness, headache, increased irritability, mental depression, stomach ache

request that teachers give points for appropriate behavior in the classroom. For example, after the completion of homework, a parent might provide free time for a desired activity, such as bike riding or playing computer games.
- Time out: Remove access to desired activities when undesirable behavior occurs. For example, a teacher might decrease recess time for inappropriate classroom behavior, or a parent might require the child to sit in the corner of a room for hitting a sibling.
- Response cost: Withdraw privileges or rewards due to unwanted behavior, for example, the loss of free time or other desired activities because homework has not been completed.
- Token economy: Combine rewards and consequences for behavior, in which the child is given a reward for desired behavior and loses privileges and rewards for unwanted behavior: (1) A teacher might give points for not daydreaming and take points away for missing assignments. (2) A teacher might give points for turning in completed assignments but deduct points if the child gets out of an assigned seat at an inappropriate time.

- The child cashes in the sum total of points daily and weekly for assessment of behavior and a possible prize if set goals are obtained.
- Maintain rewards and consequences: The benefit of constant, long-term use of rewards and consequences is the eventual shaping of the child's behavior.

Interventions with Parents

Culturally competent school-based professionals are those who seek knowledge and understanding of how minority families perceive mental health issues, cope with diagnosis, and exhibit health-seeking behaviors. This includes *barriers* (bias and discriminatory practices, language, inadequate insurance, low parental knowledge) and *facilitators* (community access to services, collaboration, helpful extended family networks, culturally sensitive professionals and paraprofessionals, etc.) to meaningful and sustained treatment intervention (Kendall & Hatton, 2002; Pham, Carlson, & Kosiulek, 2010). Family dynamics are a key factor to understand in any attempt to gain treatment compliance among minority populations. Latino families often involve extended family in the treatment of a family member with ADHD. The fact that the majority of minority children are now born into single-parent families can complicate treatment adherence. For example, African-American parents are more likely to return for treatment when there is high parent stress, the presence of a second parent, and frustration from attempts to curb undesirable behaviors and gain compliance (Hervey-Jumper et al., 2008).

Assist parents in monitoring school assignments and require that they:

- Create a routine environment in the home:
  - Organize home: Provide specific and logical places to place the child's schoolwork and supplies.
  - Make a daily/weekly schedule.
  - Insist that the child prepare for school each evening.
  - Help the child stay on task: Make use of charts and checklists to track progress in school and with chores in the home.
  - Place items for school in highly visible areas.
  - Reduce distractions during homework and meal times, such as loud music, television, and computer games, as such distractions can overstimulate children with ADHD.
  - Engage in daily/weekly discussion of schoolwork and behavior:
    - Discuss ways to improve problem behaviors.
    - Role play and demonstrate desired behaviors and require the child to role play problem behaviors as well as desired behaviors.
    - If multiple problems persist, partialize role-playing sessions.
    - Do not use time for behavior training as a punitive measure.
  - Give the child praise for completion of tasks.
  - Do not overemphasize failures.
- Assist parents in the development of positive reinforcement measures.
- Obtain support and seek counseling if necessary.

Interventions with Teachers

- Assist teachers with the development of classroom management techniques:
  - Require the student to sit in the front of the classroom near the teacher.

- Make sure that the student is away from other students who may provoke him or her.
- Give the student classroom tasks, such as collecting books or homework.
- Develop a plan for the student to release energy (e.g., stretching, classroom activities, educational games that require movement).

- Determine the student's ability to take notes and assist as necessary with classroom note-taking strategies.
- Assist teachers in setting up behavioral monitoring mechanisms in the classroom, including positive reinforcement measures, token economy, and time outs.
- If possible, the student should receive a copy of notes prior to class.
- Review and outline all lesson plans.
- Provide the student with written and oral instructions on homework assignments.
- Break down homework instructions into simple components.
- If available, make use of study carrel for assignment completion.
- Assist the student in the development of organizational skills.
  - Provide positive reinforcement for organizational milestones (e.g., not forgetting homework for one week, completion of all homework assignments, neatness of work, preparation for class).
  - Make checklist of school supplies and review with child.
- Give short but frequent assignments rather than one large assignment.
- Prepare daily or weekly report cards for home discussion.
- Assist with test taking:
  - Provide clear instructions on materials to be covered during the test.
  - Allow for additional time.
  - Consider giving verbal tests if there is no success with written tests.
  - Provide retesting on the same materials until student scores well.
  - Communicate with parents about upcoming tests.
- When possible, make use of word processors, recorded books, calculators, videotapes, and cassette recorders.
- It is important to emphasize to teachers that behavioral intervention techniques should be sustained over time.
- Schedule regular meetings with teachers.

Homework Assignments

- Make sure homework assignments are given verbally as well as in writing.
- If possible, have the student repeat and acknowledge understanding of homework assignments.
- If possible, have pre- and post-classroom group sessions in which assignments are reviewed:
  - Closely monitor students in group dynamics.
  - Anticipate problems with group dynamics, and implement changes as necessary.
- Pair the student with another student who is more patient or younger.
- Assist the student in the development of a homework log book. Parents and teachers should review the homework log with the student weekly.
- Assist parents in establishing a consistent homework protocol. Parents should personally check and verify completion of homework.

Assess Response to Treatment Plan

Develop routine monitoring to evaluate the following:

- individual and combined effects of medication and behavioral therapy
- effectiveness of behavioral interventions and any necessary revisions
- adequacy of treatment plan toward accomplishing set goals:
  - Determine cause-and-effect relationship between treatment plan and specific goals.
  - Revise treatment plan as necessary.

Base the assessment on collaborative findings using information from the IEP.

Applying Interventions within a Response to Intervention Framework

Response to Intervention (RTI) is as a comprehensive model of instruction for both regular and special education students. It allows for intense intervention based on a child's learning characteristics. As a three-tiered model, it is an approach to the identification of academic challenges in the classroom without the formal evaluation of a student's cognitive abilities. "The major premise of RTI is that early intervening services can both prevent academic problems for many students who experience learning difficulties and determine which students actually have learning disabilities, as distinct from those whose underachievement can be attributed to other factors such as inadequate instruction" (Coleman, Buysse, & Neitzel, 2006, p. 3). From this perspective, students are mainstreamed in the classroom with the intent to not stimulate special education services. In essence, appropriate treatment is provided for an underlying cognitive issue without the diagnosis of a learning disability. This is provided that the intervention has been consistently utilized and based on proven research methods using sound scientific principle in its application.

Part of RTI is aimed at reducing the disproportionate numbers of minority students diagnosed with learning disorders. RTI is considered a "non-deficit" approach to intervention in that identification can occur prior to a student failing academically. It can be applied to all age groups, and its central focus is to be proactive in providing appropriate and scientifically sound intervention. A problem-solving approach is used to evaluate instructional strategies and students' particular educational challenges to determine the specialized intervention needed (Coleman, Buyee, & Neitzel, 2006).

Although there is an emerging body of literature on RTI, there are few studies that focus on issues related to cultural diversity. Yet, studies have demonstrated effectiveness in work with children with learning disabilities using RTI methods. Monitoring and evaluation of outcomes for the purpose of corrective actions are important. Using RTI in working cross culturally with students diagnosed with ADHD, there are several factors that should be considered:

- Build on cultural strengths (including the home culture) in the learning and intervention process.
- Identify each student's individual learning style.
- Ensure bilingual competence in teaching and tutoring students with English as a second language.
- Monitor and evaluate outcomes.
- Support increasing intensity of intervention methods to fit the needs of students.
- Use extensive reading programs.
- Make use of small groups and visual aids.
- Use intense instructional practices for phonics and word recognition.
- Aim at higher-order thinking.

Tools and Practice Example

Case Scenario: ADHD, Predominantly Inattentive Type

Michelle is a 9-year-old girl who just started the fourth grade. Her teacher has referred her to social work services because she believes that Michelle needs special education testing. Michelle's teacher has based this request on several behavioral patterns that she has noticed during the first month of the school year. First, although homework assignments are printed on the blackboard daily, Michelle often forgets to write them down, as instructed. Second, Michelle has had poor scores on all of her tests and fails to complete her reading assignments. The teacher states that she has to call Michelle several times before getting a response. "It often appears as if she is daydreaming or mentally somewhere else," she states. During recess, the teacher also has noticed that Michelle does not play with her fourth-grade classmates but with children from the second grade instead.

In your discussion with Michelle, you record the following: She says that she does not like her sisters because they are always teasing her and that her mother treats her like a baby. When asked about her reading and her homework, Michelle states that she does not like reading because it takes too long. She states that she forgets to do her homework sometimes, and on other occasions, she gets sleepy while doing it and does not finish.

In your interview with Michelle's mother, she informs you of the following: "Michelle reminds me of my brother. He was always tripping over things, and he got into fights at school because the other kids called him goofy." Michelle's mother only lets her ride her bicycle in the backyard because Michelle was almost struck by a car twice. "Both times, Michelle stated that she thought that she could beat the car going across the street," her mother says. Michelle is also very untidy around the house: "She really makes a mess in the bathroom, so I tend to supervise her in order to avoid

Table 14.4 Internet Resources on ADHD

Resource	*Description*	*Web Site*
National Resource Center on ADHD	Clearinghouse for evidence-based information on ADHD symptoms, diagnosis, and treatment	www.help4adhd.org
Children and Adults with ADHD (CHADD)	Major advocate for those with ADHD; contains educational resources, newsletters, conference information, membership opportunity, prescription discount card, and links to local and online support communities	www.chadd.org
National Institute of Mental Health	ADHD fact sheets and publications that contain information on signs and symptoms of ADHD, causes, coexisting disorders, family treatment strategies, diagnostic and treatment information, behavioral therapy, and information on help with coping	www.nimh.nih.gov/health/publications/adhd-listing.shtml
MEDLINE's PubMed	Contains the latest research publication on ADHD funded by the National Institutes of Health	www.ncbi.nlm.nih.gov/pubmed
ADHD Parents Medication Guide	Contains information on pharmaceutical medications as well as alternative treatment options	http://www.parentsmedguide.org/ParentGuide_English.pdf
KidsHealth	Internet Web site that explains ADHD in terms that children can understand	www.kidshealth.org/kid/health_problems/learning_problem/adhdkid.html#
PSEP Technical Assistance Center on Positive Behavioral Interventions & Supports	Contains information on behavioral interventions for unwanted behavior in the school, home, and community	www.pbis.org
Healthy Children	Parenting Web site powered by the American Academy of Pediatrics; contains information on all aspects of ADHD	www.healthychildren.org/English/health-issues/conditions/adhd/Pages/default.aspx
American Academy of Child and Adolescent Psychiatry	Contains answers to frequently asked questions about ADHD, video clips, clinical resources, information about research and training	www.aacap.org/cs/ADHD.ResourceCenter
Centers for Disease Control and Prevention	Contains information on ADHD symptoms, diagnosis, and treatment as well as common coexisting conditions, evaluation methods, and statistics. Free materials and access to articles are also provided.	www.cdc.gov/ncbddd/adhd

extra cleaning, but I don't always have time to do this." Because she makes such a mess, neither of her siblings wants to go in the bathroom after her. This sometimes starts arguments and confrontations in the mornings, when the family is preparing for the day. Her sisters, Elizabeth (age 12) and Kelly (age 8), complain that Michelle has poor cleaning habits in their room. When asked about Michelle's homework routine, her mother remarks, "It's the strangest thing. Sometimes Michelle completes her homework and forgets to take it to school or forgets that she has taken it with her and does not turn it in. I have scolded her several times for this, but nothing I do has really done much good." Sometimes, she plays too much and starts her homework late, then falls asleep; she also claims that her stomach hurts when it is time to do homework.

Assessment and Diagnosis

You suspect that Michelle is exhibiting signs of ADHD, predominantly inattentive. Follow the protocol as suggested by the American Academy of Pediatrics:

- Verify the appropriate social work protocols specific to your particular school system.
- Suggest that parents refer the ADHD child to a primary care physician for a standard history and physical.
- Coordinate school-based services in assessing a child's behavior.
- Gather evidence and make use of assessment tools.
- Document individual observations, including report cards and written comments from teachers.
- Document specific elements of behavior, including age of onset, duration of symptoms, multiple settings, and degree of functional impairment.
- Conduct a family assessment.
- Develop an individual treatment program (ITP) with the assistance of other school-based professionals (e.g., schoolteacher, counselor, psychologist, nurse).

Numerous resources exist to help school social workers and other school counselors work with youth with ADHD. Internet Web sites that are useful in the understanding and treatment of ADHD can be found in Table 14.4.

Key Points to Remember

- The diagnosis of ADHD should be made only after reliable diagnostic interviewing methods.
- Diagnosis is based on history and observable behaviors in multiple settings (e.g., home, school, play).
- Therapists should develop a comprehensive treatment plan through collaborative efforts with other school-based professionals and community service providers.
- Culturally competent school social workers and other related service professionals are those who are knowledgeable of best practices and culturally sensitive methods for mental health assessment and diagnosis. They are aware of minority community health issues within their service areas and have developed skills and strategies for addressing client needs and gaps in services (Eiraldi et al., 2006; Lillie-Blanton et al., 2000).
- The most successful treatment of ADHD for the context of the school setting has been with the use of the multimodal approach, consisting of pharmaceutical intervention, cognitive-behavioral training, parent training, and teacher training in classroom management techniques and special education methods.
- Provide teacher and parental support, and develop a supportive network for the client.
- Provide ongoing assessment, reassessment, and evaluation of treatment regimen.
- Follow the treatment algorithm as stated in Figure 14.1.

I would like to thank Angela Moore for her excellent work in editing this chapter.

References

American Psychiatric Association. (2000). *Diagnostic and statistical manual of mental disorders* (4th ed., text revision). Washington, DC: Author.

Bailey, R. K., & Owens, D. L. (2005). Overcoming challenges in the diagnosis and treatment of attention-deficit hyperactivity disorder in African-Americans. *Journal of the National Medical Association, 97*(10 Suppl.), 55–105.

Bentley, K., & Collins, K. (in press). Psychopharmacological treatments for children & adolescents. In C. F.

Franklin et al., *Social workers and mental health workers training and resource manual.* New York: Oxford University Press.

Busse, R. T., & Beaver, B. R. (2000). Informant report: Parent and teacher interviews. In E. S. Shapiro & T. R. Kratochwill (Eds.), *Conducting school-based assessments of child and adolescent behavior* (pp. 235–273). New York, NY: Guilford Press.

Bussing, R., Gary, F. A., Mills, T. L., & Garvan, C. W. (2003). Parental explanatory models of ADHD: Gender and cultural variations. *Social Psychiatry & Psychiatric Epidemiology, 38*, 563–575.

Coleman, M. R., Buysse, V., & Neitzel, J. (2006). *Recognition and response: An early intervening system for young children at-risk for learning disabilities.* Chapel Hill, NC: The University of North Carolina, FPG Child Development Institute.

DuPaul, G. J., & Eckert, T. L. (1997). The effects of school-based interventions for attention deficit hyperactivity disorder: A meta-analysis. *School Psychology Review, 26*(3), 2–27.

DuPaul, G.J., & Kern, L. (2011). Assessment and identification of attention deficit/hyperactivity disorder. In G. J. DuPaul & L. Kern (Eds.), *Young children with ADHD: Early identification and intervention* (pp. 23-46). Washington, DC, US: American Psychological Association.

DuPaul, G. J., Eckert, T. L., & McGoey, K. E. (1997). Interventions for students with attention-deficit/hyperactivity disorder: One size dose not fit all. *School Psychology Review, 26*(3), 369–381.

Eiraldi, R. B., Mazzuca, L. B., Clarke, A. T., & Power, T. (2006). Service utilization among ethnic minority children with ADHD: A model of help-seeking behavior. *Administration and Policy in Mental Health, 33*, 607–622.

Epstein, J. N., Willoughby, M., Valencia, E. Y., Tonev, S. T., Abikoff, H. B., Arnold, L. E.& Hinshaw, S.P. (2005). The role of children's ethnicity in the relationship between teacher ratings of attention-deficit/hyperactivity disorder and observed classroom behavior. *Journal of Consulting and Clinical Psychology, 73*, 424–434.

Erk, R. R. (1995). A diagnosis of attention deficit disorder: What does it mean for school counselors? *School Counselor, 42*, 292–299.

Erk, R. R (2000). Five frameworks for increasing understanding and effective treatment of attention deficit/hyperactivity disorder: Predominately inattentive type. *Journal of Counseling and Development, 78*(4), 389–399.

Gerdes, A. C., & Schneider, B.W. (2009). Evidence-based ADHD treatment with a Spanish-speaking Latino family. *Clinical Case Studies, 8*(3), 174–192.

Haack, L. M., Gerdes, A. C., Schneider, B.W., & Hurtado, G. D. (2011). Advancing our knowledge of ADHD in Latino children: Psychometric and cultural properties of Spanish-versions of parental/family functioning measures. *Journal of Abnormal Child Psychology, 39*, 33–43.

Hervey-Jumper, H., Douyon, K., Falcone, T. F., & Franco, K. N. (2008). Identifying, evaluating, diagnosing, and treating ADHD in minority youth. *Journal of Attention Disorders, 11*(5), 522–528.

Hoagwood, K., Kelleher, K. J., Feil, M., & Comer, D. (2000). Treatment services for children with ADHD: A national perspective. *Journal of the American Academy of Child and Adolescent Psychiatry, 38*(7), 797–804.

Hosterman, S. J., DuPaul, G. J., & Jitendra, A. K. (2008). Teacher rating of ADHD symptoms in ethnic minority students: Bias or behavioral difference? *School Psychology Quarterly, 23*(3), 418–435.

Jensen, P. S., Kettle, L., Roper, M. T., Sloan, M. T., Dulcan, M. K., Hoven, C., Bird, H., Bauermeister, J., & Panye, J. (1999). Are stimulants overprescribed? Treatment of ADHD in four U. S. communities. *Journal of the American Academy of Child and Adolescent Psychiatry, 38*(7), 797–804.

Jensen, P. S. (2000). The National Institutes of Health attention-deficit/hyperactivity disorder consensus statement: Implications for practitioners and scientists. *CNS Spectrums, 5*(6), 29–33.

Jones, H. A., Epstein, J. N., Hinshaw, S. P., Owens, E. B., Chi, T.C., Arnold, L. E....Wells, K.C. (2009). Ethnicity as a moderator of treatment effects on parent-child interaction for children with ADHD. *Journal of Attention Disorders, 13*(6), 592–600.

Kendall, J., & Hatton, D. (2002). Racism as a source of health disparity in families with children with attention deficit hyperactivity disorder. *Advances in Nursing Science, 25*, 22–39.

LeFever, G. B., Villers, M. S., Morrow, A. L., & Vaughn, E. S. (2002). Parental perceptions of adverse educational outcomes among children diagnosed and treated for ADHD: A call for improved school/provider collaboration. *Psychology in the Schools, 39*(1), 63–71.

Lillie-Blanton, M., Brodie, M., Rowland, D., Altman, D., & McIntosh, M. (2000). Race, ethnicity, and the health care system: Public perceptions and experiences. *Medical Care Research and Review, 57*, 218–235.

Litner, B. (2003). Teens with ADHD: The challenge of high school. *Children and Youth Care Forum, 32*(3), 137–158.

McGoey, K., Eckert, T. L., & DuPaul, G. J. (2002). Early intervention for preschool-age children with ADHD: A literature review. *Journal of Emotional and Behavioral Disorders, 10*(1), 14–28.

Miller, T.W., Nigg, J.T., & Miller, R. L. (2009). Attention deficit hyperactivity disorder in African Americans: What can be concluded from the past ten years? *Clinical Psychology Review, 29*, 77–86.

Olfson, M., Gameroff, M. J., Marcus, S. C., & Jensen, P. S. (2003). National trends in the treatment of attention deficit hyperactivity disorder. *American Journal of Psychiatry, 160*(6), 1071–1077.

Perrin, J. M., Stein, M. T., Amler, R. W., Blondis, T. A., Feldman, H. M., Meyer, B. P., Shaywitz, A. B., & Wolraich, M. L. (2001). Clinical practice guideline: Treatment of the school-aged child with attention-deficit/hyperactivity disorder. *Pediatrics, 108*(4), 1033–1042.

Pham, A. V., Carlson, J. S., & Kosiulek, J. F. (2010). Ethnic differences in parental beliefs of attention-deficit/hyperactivity disorder and treatment. *Journal of Attention Disorders, 13*(6), 584–591.

Richters, J. E., Arnold, L. E., Jensen, P. S., Abikoff, H., Conners, C. K., Greenhill, L. L., Laurence, L., Hechtman, L., Hinshaw, S. P., Pelham, W. E., & Swanson, J. M. (1995). NIMH collaborative multisite multimodal treatment study of children with ADHD: I. Background and rationale. *Journal of the American Academy of Child and Adolescent Psychiatry, 34*(8), 987–1000.

Smith, B. H., Waschbusch, D. A., Willoughby, M. T., & Evans, S. (2000). The efficacy, safety, and practicality of treatments for adolescents withattention-deficit/hyperactivity disorder. *Clinical Child and Family Psychology Review, 3*(4), 243–247.

Thomas, C., & Corcoran, J. (2000). Family approaches to attention deficit hyperactivity disorder: Review of guide school social work practice. *Children & Schools, 25*(1), 19–34.

U.S. Department of Health and Human Services. (2005). The Office of Minority Health. *What is cultural competency?* Retrieved July 11, 2011, from http://minorityhealth.hhs.gov/templates/browse.aspx?lvl=2&lvlID=11

Wood, J. C., Heiskell, K. D., Delay, D. M., Jongeling, J. S., & Perry, D. (2009). Teachers' preferences for interventions for ethnically diverse learners with attention-deficit hyperactivity disorder. *Adolescence, 44*(174), 273–288.

CHAPTER 15

Effective Interventions for Students with Autism and Asperger's Syndrome

Michelle S. Ballan · Lauren Z. Powledge · Karen F. Hoban

Getting Started

Autism is a complex disorder defined by numerous developmental and behavioral features. The canopy of the autism spectrum is far reaching, with school-aged children and adolescents ranging from nonverbal with multiple developmental disabilities to mild Asperger's syndrome with advanced capabilities for mathematics and science. Autism spectrum disorders (ASDs), termed pervasive developmental disorders (PDDs) in the *Diagnostic and Statistical Manual of Mental Disorders* (DSM-IV-TR; American Psychiatric Association, 2000) and in the *International Classification of Diseases (ICD-10;* World Health Organization, 1992), is a term often used in educational and clinical settings to refer to various disorders spanning a severe form known as autistic disorder (AD), to a milder form called Asperger's syndrome or disorder (AS). If a child exhibits symptoms of AD or AS, but does not meet the specific criteria for either disorder, the child is diagnosed with an ASD identified as pervasive developmental disorder not otherwise specified (PDD-NOS) (American Psychiatric Association, 2000; Strock, 2004). Less common are two additional acute ASDs known as Rett's syndrome or disorder (RS) and childhood disintegrative disorder (CDD).

Students identified as having an ASD exhibit a tremendous range in symptoms and characteristics due to developmental maturity and varying degrees of associated cognitive limitations (Filipek et al., 1999). Many school social workers, psychologists, and special educators are familiar with the primary clinical symptomatology of the majority of ASDs, which typically falls within three major categories: (1) qualitative impairment in social interaction, such as gaze aversion or the absence of communication; (2) impairments in communication, such as mutism and lack of pretend play; and (3) restricted, repetitive, stereotyped behavior, interests, and activities, such as retentive motor mannerisms (American Psychiatric Association, 2000; Bregman, 2005). Autism spectrum disorders vary with respect to age of onset and associations with other disorders. Differences among ASDs appear to be linked to intelligence, level of adaptive functioning, and number of autistic symptoms rather than to the presence of distinct symptoms (Hollander & Nowinski, 2003, p. 17).

Since the 1990s, research has revealed an upward trend in the prevalence rate for ASDs (CDC, 2007; CDC, 2009; Fombonne, 2009) due largely in part to issues regarding diagnosis. However, clinical bias contributes to under-identification of ASDs in children who are racial minorities. This disparity is most notable among Latino and Asian children with intellectual disabilities (Mandell et al., 2009). An increase in the prevalence rate may be attributable to a diverse range of factors, such as the broadening of diagnostic concepts to include milder and more atypical variants (Bregman, 2005), greater awareness among parents and professionals, the prospect of securing specialized services or benefits for children due to educational funding formulas, and the extent to which families advocate for the diagnosis during assessment (Volkmar & Weisner, 2009). Fombonne (2009) reported an estimate of 60 to 70 out of 10,000 for the prevalence of all ASDs. The majority of studies report that ASDs are three to more than five times more common in boys than girls (CDC, 2009), and approximately 50% of all individuals classified with autism have measured intelligence in the range of mental retardation (Volkmar & Weisner, 2009). Autism spectrum disorders are often accompanied by a range of abnormalities within cognitive, adaptive, affective, and behavioral domains of development, deficits in executive functions, limitations in adaptive skills, learning disabilities, mood instability, stereotypic and self-injurious behaviors, anxiety disorders, and aggression (Bregman, 2005). One in three children with an ASD develops seizures, often beginning in either early childhood or adolescence (Jeste, 2011), and approximately 2 to 4% of children with ASDs present with tuberous sclerosis (Semrud-Clikeman & Ellison, 2009). Additionally, macrocephaly occurs in 20% of children with ASDs (Levy, Mandell, & Schultz, 2009).

Children of racial and ethnic minority groups are less likely to be screened for ASDs. In addition to factors such as maternal education (Mandell et al., 2009), socioeconomic status, and geographical location (Rodriguez, 2009), an increase or variation in prevalence rates may also be due largely in part to the utilization of different diagnostic criteria for ASDs across research studies. There are varying diagnostic groups within ASDs and varying diagnostic criteria for assessment. However, the DSM-IV-TR (2000) and the ICD-10 (1992) share general agreement regarding the almost identical criteria for the diagnosis of the five subtypes of PDDs or ASDs (AD, AS, PDD-NOS, RS, and CDD).[1] For the purpose of this chapter, two of the more common ASDs (AD and AS) seen among school-aged children and adolescents will be the focus. The DSM-IV-TR (2000) outlines specific criteria for AD (see Table 15.1) and AS (see Table 15.2).

Table 15.1 *DSM-IV* Diagnostic Criteria for Autistic Disorder

A. A total of six (or more) items from (1), (2), and (3), with at least two from (1), and one each from (2) and (3):
   (1) qualitative impairment in social interaction, as manifested by at least two of the following:
      (a) marked impairment in the use of multiple nonverbal behaviors such as eye-to-eye gaze, facial expression, body postures, and gestures to regulate social interaction
      (b) failure to develop peer relationships appropriate to developmental level
      (c) a lack of spontaneous seeking to share enjoyment, interests, or achievements with other people (e.g., by a lack of showing, bringing, or pointing out objects of interest)
      (d) lack of social or emotional reciprocity
   (2) qualitative impairments in communication as manifested by at least one of the following:
      (a) delay in, or total lack of, the development of spoken language (not accompanied by an attempt to compensate through alternative modes of communication such as gesture or mime)
      (b) in individuals with adequate speech, marked impairment in the ability to initiate or sustain a conversation with others
      (c) stereotyped and repetitive use of language or idiosyncratic language
      (d) lack of varied, spontaneous make-believe play or social imitative play appropriate to developmental level
   (3) restricted, repetitive, and stereotyped patterns of behavior, interests, and activities, as manifested by at least one of the following:
      (a) encompassing preoccupation with one or more stereotyped and restricted patterns of interest that is abnormal either in intensity or focus
      (b) apparently inflexible adherence to specific, nonfunctional routines or rituals
      (c) stereotyped and repetitive motor mannerisms (e.g., hand or finger flapping or twisting, or complex whole-body movements)
      (d) persistent preoccupation with parts of objects

B. Delays or abnormal functioning in at least one of the following areas, with onset prior to age 3 years: (1) social interaction, (2) language as used in social communication, or (3) symbolic or imaginative play

C. The disturbance is not better accounted for by Rett's disorder or childhood disintegrative disorder.

Source: Reprinted with permission from the *Diagnostic and Statistical Manual of Mental Disorders.* Copyright 2000. American Psychiatric Association.

Table 15.2 *DSM-IV-TR* Diagnostic Criteria for Asperger's Syndrome

A. Qualitative impairment in social interaction, as manifested by at least two of the following:
   (1) marked impairment in the use of multiple nonverbal behaviors such as eye-to-eye gaze, facial expression, body postures, and gestures to regulate social interaction
   (2) failure to develop peer relationships appropriate to developmental level
   (3) a lack of spontaneous seeking to share enjoyment, interests, or achievements with other people (e.g., by a lack of showing, bringing, or pointing out objects of interest to other people)
   (4) lack of social or emotional reciprocity

B. Restricted, repetitive, and stereotyped patterns of behavior, interests, and activities, as manifested by at least one of the following:
   (1) encompassing preoccupation with one or more stereotyped and restricted patterns of interest that is abnormal either in intensity or focus
   (2) apparently inflexible adherence to specific, nonfunctional routines or rituals
   (3) stereotyped and repetitive motor mannerisms (e.g., hand or finger flapping or twisting, or complex whole-body movements)
   (4) persistent preoccupation with parts of objects

C. The disturbance causes clinically significant impairment in social, occupational, or other important areas of functioning.

D. There is no clinically significant general delay in language (e.g., single words used by age 2 years, communicative phrases used by age 3 years).

E. There is no clinically significant delay in cognitive development or in the development of age-appropriate self-help skills, adaptive behavior (other than in social interaction), and curiosity about the environment in childhood.

F. Criteria are not met for another specific pervasive developmental disorder or schizophrenia.

Source: Reprinted with permission from the *Diagnostic and Statistical Manual of Mental Disorders.* Copyright 2000. American Psychiatric Association.

The most notable difference between AD and AS involves age-appropriate communication skills. Communication is presumed to be within normal limits in children with AS, although as one might expect of a school-aged youth with severe limitations in recognizing and interpreting social messages, pragmatic deficits are frequent (Scott et al., 2000). Because pragmatic deficits constitute a core area of communication functioning, this minimizes the true differences between children diagnosed with AS and AD (Chevallier, Wilson, Happé, & Noveck, 2010; Scott et al., 2000). For children whose native language differs from the dominant language, problems with communication may be misattributed difficulties with acquiring a second language, rather than pragmatic deficits characteristic of ASDs (Begeer, El Bouk, Boussaid, Terwogt, & Koot, 2009).

The *DSM IV-TR* (2000) specifies a set of criteria for AS and AD that might lead one to believe that diagnosis of such disorders is made with ease. However, diagnosis can be difficult due in part to the lack of definitive diagnostic tests for AD or AS. There are currently no reliable physiological markers for diagnosis as there are in some other disabilities (i.e., the genetic markers associated with Fragile X syndrome). To make a diagnosis, clinicians frequently rely heavily on behavioral characteristics, which may be apparent in the first few months of a child's life or appear during the early years. Throughout screening and diagnosis of ASDs, it is essential to discern the moderating impacts of child and family characteristics. Demographic and clinical factors, such as gender and IQ, may influence clinical judgment based on prevalence rates of ASDs (Mandell et al., 2009). Furthermore, professionals are not impervious to personal biases toward race and ethnicity. Research indicates that among children with ASDs, black children are disproportionately misdiagnosed with conduct disorder or attention deficit hyperactivity disorder (Mandell, Ittenbach, Levy, & Pinto-Martin, 2007).

The diagnosis of AD or AS necessitates a two-stage process composed of a broad developmental screening during "well child" checkups and a comprehensive evaluation by a multidisciplinary team (Volkmar & Weisner, 2009, p. 49, 53). If children experienced preterm complications, were born with low birth weight, or have a sibling with an ASD, they are considered high risk for ASDs and may undergo screenings at younger ages (Lord et al., 2006). Among the most promising first- and second-degree screening tools for AD are the Modified Checklist for Autism in Toddlers (M-CHAT; Robins, Fein, Barton, & Green, 2001) with the follow-up interview (Kleinman et al., 2008; Kleinman et al., 2008a) and the PDDST-II PCS (Siegel, 2004). Children who meet threshold criteria for the M-CHAT and the PDDST-II PCS can receive further assessment with the Screening Tool for Autism in Two-Year-Olds (STAT; Stone, Coonrod, & Ousley, 2000) and the ASQ-3. The STAT has been recommended in children as young as 14 months (Stone, McMahon, & Henderson, 2008) and has demonstrated consistency across race, gender, and maternal education (Stone, Coonrod, Turner, & Pozdol, 2004), and the ASQ-3 has been validated in children as young as 4 months old and is also supported for screening in ASDs (Squires & Bricker, 2009). For AS, the tools are the Autism Spectrum Screening Questionnaire (ASSQ; Ehlers, Gillberg, & Wing, 1999) and the Childhood Asperger Syndrome Test (CAST; Scott, Baron-Cohen, Bolton, & Brayne, 2002) for the first stage of screening and the Krug's Asperger's Disorder Index (KADI; Krug & Arick, 2003)[2] (see Table 15.3) for the second stage of screening. Assessment and diagnostic tools for ASDs have not be utilized in culturally and ethnically diverse populations, thus additional importance may be placed on

Table 15.3 Screening Instruments for Autistic Disorder and Asperger's Syndrome

Instrument	*Type of Screening*	*Age Level*	*Informant*	*Characteristics*
Autistic Disorder				
M-CHAT (Kleinman et al., 2008)	Level 1	16–30 months	Parent	23-item checklist to examine child's developmental milestones
STAT (Stone et al., 2008)	Level 2	14 months	Clinician	12 activities for observing child's early social/ communicative behaviors
PDDST-II PCS (Siegel, 2004)	Level 1	18–48 months	Parent	22-item questionnaire to assess child's developmental milestones
ASQ3 (Squires & Bricker, 2009)	Level 1	1 month–5.5 years	Parent	21-item questionnaire assessing communication, gross motor, fine motor, problem solving, and personal-social skills
Asperger's Syndrome				
ASSQ (Ehlers et al., 1999)	Level 1	> 6 years	Parent/Teacher	27-item checklist for assessing symptoms characteristic of Asperger's syndrome
KADI (Krug & Arick, 2003)	Levels 1 & 2	> 6 years	Individual with daily and regular contact with child for at least a few weeks	32-item norm-referenced rating scale for presence or absence of behaviors indicative of Asperger's syndrome

parent report and informed clinical opinion. Furthermore, these screening instruments do not provide a diagnosis; instead they aim to assess the need for referral for possible diagnosis of AS or AD.

Inherent in a multidisciplinary evaluation are standards of assessment that are both culturally and linguistically accessible. Thus, an accurate diagnosis necessitates assessment in the client's native language and through a medium that reflects cultural values (National Association of Social Workers, 2007; Williams, Atkins, & Soles, 2009).

Autistic disorder and AS often involve other neurological or genetic problems, thereby necessitating a first-line comprehensive assessment of medical conditions (Filipek et al., 2000). The diagnosis of AD or AS often entails a school-based social worker gathering information on developmental history, medical background, psychiatric or health disorders of family members, and psychosocial factors. Additionally, a social worker typically conducts a social family history by assessing the child's parents, caregivers, and environmental setting (McCarton, 2003). Culturally normative behaviors may overlap with prominent symptoms of ASDs. Thus, attention to individual, familial, and cultural conceptions of ASD symptoms is necessary to inform diagnosis, lest typical behaviors be misconstrued as atypical development (Rodriguez, 2009). Psychological assessment and communicative assessment via testing, direct observation, and interviews should also inform the diagnosis. The psychological assessment helps to develop an understanding of the cognitive functioning and should address adaptive functioning, motor and visual skills, play, and social cognition (National Research Council, 2001). Communicative assessment should address communication skills in the context of a child's development (Lord & Paul, 1997), native language, and culture (Begeer et al., 2009), and assess expressive language and language comprehension.

Additionally, diagnostic instruments can be used to help structure and quantify clinical observations. The Childhood Autism Rating Scale (CARS; Schopler, Reichler, & Renner, 1986) is the strongest, best-documented, and most widely used clinical rating scale for behaviors associated with autism (Lord & Cosello, 2005, p. 748) with no significant differences across gender or ethnicity (Chlebowski, Green, Barton, & Fein, 2010). Other instruments with strong psychometric data to support their use as a component of the diagnostic process include the Autism Diagnostic Interview-Revised (ADI-R; Lord, Rutter, & Le Couteur, 1994), the Autism Diagnostic Observation Schedule (ADOS; Lord, Rutter, DiLavore, & Risi, 1999), and the Autism Diagnostic Observation Schedule-Generic (ADOS-G; Lord et al., 2000). The ADOS-G subsumed ADOS and was created in response to the need for a measure appropriate for observing behavior among a broader range of ages and developmental and language abilities (Lord et al.,

Table 15.4 Diagnostic Instruments for Autistic Disorder

Instrument	*Characteristics*
CARS (Schopler et al., 1986)	15-item rating scale covering a particular characteristic, ability, or behavior on which children are rated after observation; can be administered by clinician or educator, and some studies have demonstrated use by parents
ADI-R (Lord et al., 1994)	93-item semistructured interview composed of three subscales (social reciprocity, communication, and restricted, repetitive behaviors); administered by a clinician to caregivers
ADOS (Lord et al., 1999)	Standardized protocol for the observation of social and communicative behavior of children who may have an ASD; administered by a clinician
ADOS-G (Lord et al., 2000)	Standardized assessment of social interaction, communication, play, and imaginative use of materials for individuals who may have an ASD; administered by a clinician

2000). An instrument for measuring symptom severity is the Social Responsiveness Scale (SRS; Constantino, 2002). The SRS is unique in its capacity to measure degrees of impairment in social reciprocity, thus informing specific treatment goals and measuring progress over time (Booker & Starling, 2011). No diagnosis would be complete without documentation of a child's unique strengths and weaknesses, as this component is critical to designing an effective intervention program since unusual developmental profiles are typical (National Research Council, 2001).

Although several instruments have been proposed to formally substantiate a diagnosis of AS,[3] these instruments have little relationship to each other and have not been found to be reliable (Lord & Cosello, 2005). In addition to the aforementioned categories, when diagnosing AS, joint attention (Schietecatte, Roeyers, & Warreyn, 2011), auditory and visual perception, and memory should be assessed (DuCharme & McGrady, 2003). Additional observations may address components of topic management and conversational ability, ability to deal with nonliteral language, and language flexibility (Volkmar & Weisner, 2009).

In regard to diagnosis, parents and professionals should serve as partners in reaching the best possible understanding of the child. The developmental, medical, and family histories that parents provide are crucial components of a diagnosis. Their description of their child's behavior across multiple settings is essential. Few screening tools have been adapted to multiple languages with demonstrated reliability and validity (Dababnah et al., 2011). Thus, obtaining a parent's informed report of child characteristics is vital to an appropriate diagnosis. The role of the professionals on the multidisciplinary team is to interpret the information that parents provide. Parents know their child better than anyone, but professionals can offer a broad view of what is typical and where the child might differ from the norm (Wagner & McGrady, 2003).

Once a diagnosis of AD or AS is provided, parent attention is often consumed by a variety of concerns, such as uncertainty of long-term outcomes, fluctuating behaviors of the child that impact family dynamics, and concern over fostering and maintaining significant familial relationships (O'Brien, 2007, p. 136). Consequently, parents of newly diagnosed children report increased levels of stress (O'Brien, 2007). Parent stress has been shown to produce deleterious effects on children with ASDs (Levy et al., 2009), which may be further exacerbated in children from culturally diverse backgrounds. Thus, designing an intervention plan that is both culturally and linguistically consonant is essential to favorable outcomes.

Although early intervention has been shown to have a dramatic impact on reducing symptoms and increasing a child's ability to develop and gain new skills,[4] it is estimated that only 50% of children are diagnosed with an ASD before kindergarten (American Autism Society, 2011). Furthermore, children with ASDs of minority race and ethnicity disproportionately receive early intervention services at later ages (Mandell, Listerud, Levy, & Pinto-Martin, 2002). Thus, upon diagnosis, school-based interventions for youth with AD or AS often become the immediate focus of parents. Family education on ASDs, implications for individual outcomes, and effective interventions are critical to fostering a positive outcome (Elder, Valcante, Won, & Zylis, 2003). Unfortunately, parents from multicultural backgrounds that occupy a minority status risk alienation from intervention planning and participation due to cultural and linguistic barriers (Rodriguez, 2009). Parents are soon faced with a prolific body of literature and disparate professional advice composed to some extent of ineffective approaches and treatment fads. Accordingly, it is incumbent on professionals to communicate information in an appropriate and accessible manner so that parents can navigate the multitude of evidence-based and unsupported approaches. Among the recommended treatments are facilitated communication, holding therapy, auditory integration training, gentle teaching, and hormone therapies, such as secretin, which are not adequately supported by scientific evidence for practice, and research has actually demonstrated some of these treatments to be harmful (Jacobson, Foxx, & Mulick, 2005; Mesibov & Shea, 2011; Simpson et al., 2004; Smith, 1996). Part of the problem of resulting treatment fads is that research has not demonstrated a single best treatment program for children with ASDs. Per Rogers and Vismara (2008), the limited number of randomized control trial (RCT) studies, lack of diverse ethnic and cultural considerations, and absence of peer-reviewed data have contributed to the minimum of evidence-based interventions for ASDs.

What We Know

School-aged children with ASDs face transitions to a new learning environment, socialization with new peers and adults, and departures from familiar routines and settings. This process may be compounded in children who have immigrated into a vastly different culture with demands for alternative social norms and a new primary language (Jegatheesan, Fowler, & Miller, 2010). Thus, many professionals agree that a highly structured, specialized program is optimal for this transition to an individualized learning environment. Among the many methods available for treatment and education of school-aged children with AD or AS, behaviorally based interventions continue to be the most widely supported in the research.

Recently, the National Autism Center's National Standards Project (2009) conducted an evaluation of the extant literature on available treatments for individuals with ASDs who are under 22 years of age. A panel of experts culled 11 interventions meeting the standards of rigor and beneficial outcome to qualify as "Established Treatments": Antecedent Package, Behavioral Package, Comprehensive Behavioral Treatment for Young Children, Joint Attention, Modeling, Naturalistic Teaching Strategies, Peer Training, Pivotal Response Training, Schedules, Self-management, and Story-based. Although newer treatments such as the Story-based Intervention Package were included, two-thirds of Established Treatments originated from a behavioral orientation, such as applied behavioral analysis (ABA), behavioral psychology, and positive behavioral supports (National Autism Center, 2009). Furthermore, the remaining one-third of treatments is overwhelmingly supported in the behavioral literature. Other contributing fields include speech-language pathology and special education.

Established Treatments specifically target skills to be increased or behaviors to be decreased. Among skills to be increased, academic performance, communication, higher cognitive functions, interpersonal skills, learning readiness, motor skills, personal responsibility, placement, play, and self-regulation have all been targeted with favorable outcomes. Among behaviors to be decreased, general problem behaviors, restricted or repetitive interests or activities, emotional regulation, and general symptoms connected to ASDs have all been successfully addressed by Established Treatments. Of the 11 Established Treatments, two are supported for use with children with AS. All 11 treatments are supported for use with children with AD at various ages.

What We Can Do

Antecedent Package interventions aim to increase an identified behavior by modifying individuals and environmental elements that typically occur prior to the target behavior, such as cueing, priming, behavior chain interruption, and environmental modification of task demands, all of which are founded on ABA.

Applied Behavior Analysis

Applied behavior analysis (ABA) is a discipline devoted to understanding the function behind human behavior and finding ways of altering or improving behaviors (Cooper, Heron, & Heward, 1987). Applied behavior analysis involves systematically applying learning theory—based interventions to improve socially significant observable behaviors to a meaningful degree and seeks to demonstrate that the improvement in behavior stems directly from the interventions that are utilized (Anderson, Taras, & Cannon, 1996; Baer, Wolf, & Risley, 1968; Sulzer-Azaroff & Mayer, 1991). The emphasis is on teaching the student how to learn from the environment and how to act on the environment in order to produce positive outcomes for himself and those around him (Harris & Handleman, 1994; Koegel & Koegel, 1995; Lovaas, 1993, 1981; Lovaas & Smith, 1989; Maurice, Green, & Luce, 1996; Schreibman, Charlop, & Milstein, 1993).

Behavior analytic treatment systematically teaches measurable units of a behavior or skill. Skills that a student with autism needs to learn are broken down into small steps. This form of teaching can be utilized for simple skills, such as making eye contact, to complex skills, like social interactions. Each step is initially taught by using a specific cue and pairing that cue with a prompt. Prompts range from physical guidance to verbal cues to very discrete gestures. Prompts should be faded out systematically by decreasing the level of prompt needed for the student to perform the target skill until, ideally, the student can perform the skill independently. In addition, skills should be taught by a variety of individuals, including teachers, aides, social workers, speech pathologists, and parents. There is strong evidence that parents can learn to employ ABA techniques and that doing so helps them to feel better in general and more satisfied and confident in their parenting role (Ozonoff & Cathcart, 1998; Schreibman, 1997; Sofronoff & Farbotko, 2002, as cited in Wagner & McGrady, 2003). However, students should not become dependent on a particular individual or prompt. The student should be reinforced immediately after responding appropriately. The reinforcement should be a consequence that has been shown to increase the likelihood of the student responding appropriately again (Cooper et al., 1987). Reinforcements will vary from student to student. Inappropriate behavioral responses (such as tantrums, aggressive acts, screaming/yelling, stereotypic behaviors) are purposely not reinforced. Often, a functional analysis of antecedents and consequences is performed to determine what environmental reactions are reinforcing such behaviors (Cooper et al., 1987).

Applied behavior analysis has been proven effective across different providers (parents, teachers, therapists), different settings (schools, homes, hospitals, recreational areas), and behaviors (social, academic, and functional life skills; language; self-stimulatory, aggressive, and oppositional behaviors). Professionals who use ABA systematically and regularly measure progress on behavioral targets, leading to numerous studies of the effectiveness of ABA approaches. However, as Green (1996) pointed out, it is still unclear what variables are critical to intervention intensity (number of hours, length of the intervention, proportion of one-to-one to group instruction) and what are the expected outcomes when intervention intensity varies. It is also unclear what particular behavioral techniques (discrete trials, incidental teaching, pivotal response training) are most likely to be successful for a given child with an ASD and in what proportions particular techniques should be used (Anderson & Romanczyk, 1999). The current research is limited in that it does not allow us to draw comparisons across studies. For a review of the effectiveness of more broadly defined ABA intervention studies, see Anderson and Romanczyk (1999); Matson, Benavidez, Compton, Paclawskyj, and Baglio (1996); National Research Council (2001); New York State Department of Health (1999a); and Simpson et al. (2004).

Also drawing upon ABA are Behavioral Package interventions. Counter to Antecedent Packages, this array of interventions is intended to reduce or extinguish target behaviors through the learning and replacement of alternate skills. Diverse in focus and modality, interventions address behaviors related to sleep, toilet training, and functional communication, among others, and include mediums such as scheduled awakenings, successive approximation, task analysis, token economy, and discrete trial training.

Discrete Trial Training

It is important to understand that ABA is a framework for the practice of a science and not a specific program. Programs using ABA often utilize discrete trial training or teaching (DTT), which represents a specific type of presentation of opportunities to respond. Discrete trial training is a specialized teaching technique or process used to develop many new forms of behavior (Smith, 2001) and skills, including cognitive, communication, play, social, readiness, receptive-language, and self-help skills (Newsome, 1998). In addition, DTT can be used to reduce self-stimulatory responses and aggressive behaviors (Lovaas, 1981; Smith, 2001).

Discrete trial training involves breaking skills into the smallest steps, teaching each step of the skill until mastery, providing lots of repetition, prompting the correct response and fading the prompts as soon as possible, and using positive reinforcement procedures. Each discrete trial has five separate parts: (1) cue: the social worker presents a brief clear instruction or question; (2) prompt: at the same time as the cue or immediately thereafter, the social worker assists the child in responding correctly to the cue; (3) response: the child gives a correct or incorrect answer to the social worker's cue; (4) consequence: if the child has given a correct response, the social worker immediately reinforces the response with praise, access to toys, or other activities that the child enjoys. If the child has given an incorrect response, the social worker says "no," looks away, removes teaching materials, or otherwise signals that the response was incorrect; and (5) inter-trial interval: after giving the consequence, the social worker pauses briefly (1–5 seconds) before presenting the cue for the next trial (Smith, 2001, p. 86). The following is an example of DTT:

The social worker says, "Touch your nose." (verbal cue)
The student does not respond (response).
After a few seconds, the social worker places her hand on the student's hand. (prompt)
The child extends his index finger himself, and the social worker helps the child to touch his nose. (response)
The social worker says, "Yes, that is your nose. Good job touching your nose." (consequence)

This is an example of one trial. The correct response is considered a measurable unit of a skill. Data can be collected on the number of correct versus incorrect responses to chart a student's progress. This trial would be repeated approximately five times, as repetition of skills is a component of discrete trial teaching.

The social worker says, "What's your address?" (verbal cue)
The student says, "My address is 123 House Street, Maywood, New Jersey." (response)
The instructor gives the student behavior-descriptive praise (i.e., "Good, you said your address correctly") and 30 seconds to play with a toy of his choice. (consequence)

As one can see from the examples above, DTT can be used to teach the most basic information up to slightly more advanced knowledge. Discrete trial teaching affords children with AS and AD opportunities to respond which have been linked with improved performance on measures of academic achievement (Delquadri, Greenwood, Stretton, & Hall, 1983). This approach has also been credited with impressive gains in children with otherwise poor prognoses (Lovaas, 1987) and in accelerated skill acquisition (Miranda-Linne & Melin, 1992). An effective school-based intervention should prioritize discrimination issues by using DTT strategies that (1) carefully present stimuli in a systematic manner and with planned repetition; (2) provide a planned process for teaching the relationship of words to functional objects, people, and other important concepts; and (3) use systematic visual stimuli to teach important functional auditory discriminations (Arick et al., 2005, p. 1007). For studies documenting the effectiveness of DTT, see Cummings and Williams (2000); Dawson and Osterling (1997); Goldstein (2002); National Research Council (2001); Odom et al. (2003); Simpson et al. (2004); and Smith (2001).

Parents are encouraged to participate in intervention delivery and practice skill development with children in natural settings in order to globalize developmental gains. While DTT targets new behaviors to learn, other techniques such as Pivotal Response Training are utilized to integrate skills between fundamental domains.

Pivotal Response Training

Pivotal response training (PRT) is a model that aims to apply educational techniques in pivotal areas that affect target behaviors (Koegel, Koegel, Harrower, & Carter, 1999). Pivotal areas when effectively targeted result in substantial collateral gains in numerous developmental domains. Pivotal areas of primary focus include (a) responding to multiple cues and stimuli (i.e., decreasing over-selectivity by distinguishing relevant features); (b) improving child motivation (i.e., increasing appropriate responses, decreasing response latency, and improving affect); (c) increasing self-management capacity (i.e., teaching children to be aware of their aberrant behaviors to self-monitor and to self-reinforce); and (d) increasing self-initiations (i.e., teaching children to respond to natural cues in the environment) (Simpson et al., 2004, pp. 114–115).

The goals of intervention in pivotal areas are "(1) to teach the child to be responsive to the many learning opportunities and social interactions that occur in the natural environment, (2) to decrease the need for constant supervision by an intervention provider, and (3) to decrease the number of services that remove the child from the natural environment" (Koegel et al., 1999, p. 174). Thus the primary purpose of PRT is to provide children with the social and educational proficiency to participate in inclusive settings.

Designed based on a series of studies identifying important treatment components, PRT in its fledgling stages used a discrete trial, applied behavior analysis approach. Currently, PRT uses the principles of applied behavior analysis (ABA) in a manner that excludes negative interactions, reduces dependence on artificial prompts, and is family centered (Simpson et al., 2004, p. 114). Utilizing the strategies of PRT, target behaviors are taught in natural settings with items that are age-appropriate and meaningful as well as reinforcing to the child. Pivotal response training involves specific strategies such as (1) clear instructions and questions presented by the social worker, (2) child choice of stimuli (based on choices offered by the social worker), (3) integration of maintenance tasks (previously mastered tasks) (Dunlap, 1984), (4) direct reinforcement (the chosen stimuli is the reinforcer) (Koegel & Williams, 1980), (5) reinforcement of reasonable purposeful attempts at correct responding (Koegel, O'Dell, & Dunlap, 1988), and (6) turn taking to allow modeling and appropriate pace of interaction (Stahmer, Ingersoll, & Carter, 2003, p. 404). An example of using the specific steps of PRT to teach symbolic play might be as follows:

A child may choose to play with a doll. (choice)
The child is then given an empty cup and saucer, and asked, "What can we do with these toys?" (acquisition task)
The child is expected to use the teacup in some symbolic manner, such as having a tea party.
If the child does not respond, the social worker would model the symbolic behavior. (turn taking)
The teacup would then be returned to the child. If the child still does not respond, a new toy would be selected, or the social worker could assist the child.
When the child does respond, many of the child's dolls would be given to him to play with in any manner chosen, thus reinforcing the new behavior.

A more detailed description of using PRT to teach complex skills can be found in Stahmer (1999) and in *How to Teach Pivotal Behaviors to Children With Autism: A Training Manual* (Koegel et al., n.d.).

PRT has been adapted to teach a variety of skills, including social skills (Koegel & Frea, 1993), symbolic (Stahmer, 1995) and sociodramatic play (Thorpe, Stahmer, & Schreibman, 1995), and joint attention (Whalen & Schreibman, 2003). Parents have been trained to successfully implement PRT. Schreibman, Kaneko, and Koegel (1991) found that parents appeared happier and more relaxed when they used PRT methods with their children than when they used more structured teaching techniques (Bregman, Zager, & Gerdtz, 2005). For studies documenting the effectiveness of PRT, see Koegel, Koegel, Shoshan, and McNerney (1999); the National Research Council (2001); Simpson et al. (2004); and the National Autism Center (2009).

The core area of social skills has received considerable attention, supported by gainful outcomes. While PRT is utilized in shaping social skills, other approaches have produced favorable outcomes specific to social communication. Specifically, Joint Attention Intervention or Joint Attention Training has been emphasized in the development of social communication skills.

Joint Attention Intervention

Joint attention (JA) is "a social communicative behavior that is generally defined as a child's ability to use gestures and eye contact to coordinate attention with another person to share the experience of an interesting object or event" (Ferraioli & Harris, 2011, p. 172). JA is a pivotal skill, and children across the autism spectrum exhibit impairment in social skills, such as a preference for social stimuli like faces and voices over nonsocial stimuli, the ability to disengage and shift attention, and the capacity to understand the intentions of others (Schietecatte et al., 2011), regardless of developmental level. Thus, development of social skills that enable children with ASDs to participate in socio-typical ways is vital to inclusion in mainstream settings. Derived from Discrete Trial Training (DTT) and Pivotal Response Training (PRT), JA Training is a naturalistic behavior modification technique (Whalen & Schreibman, 2003). Due to the relationship between JA and language development, outcomes of JA interventions may vary as a result of differing verbal abilities among children. Deficits in JA manifest through response and initiation and are both integral in development (Schietecatte et al., 2011). Responding to joint attention (RJA) requires the ability to respond to or follow another individual's gaze or gesture in order to coordinate attention. Conversely, a child initiates joint attention (IJA) by directing the attention of another individual through eye gaze or gesture for the goal of coordinating attention (Ferraioli & Harris, 2011).

The following is an example of RJA:

A child and schoolmate are sitting in close proximity to one another on the floor.
The schoolmate picks up a puzzle piece, points to it, and says, "Look at this!"
The child responds by following the schoolmate's gaze and point, so that the child looks at the puzzle piece.

While RJA and IJA are both forms of joint attention, they require different skills and instruction, accordingly. Learning RJA first may facilitate the acquisition of IJA skills (Meindi & Cannella-Malone, 2011). The following is an example of IJA:

A child holds a toy car.
The child uses gestures (points to the car, holds up the toy car) and vocalizes (speaks the peer's name or calls "hello") in addition to gazing (looks at peer and then back at the toy car) in order to get the peer to look at the toy car as well.
Because RJA and IJA require different behaviors, interventions are designed to specifically address the target behaviors of both.

Observational skills are integral to learning social skills, such as sharing, playing, and initiating and engaging in conversations. The significance of observational learning has also been linked to JA, reciprocity, and descriptive gestures (Ferraioli & Harris, 2011, p. 174). One way to garner an understanding of reciprocity is through modeling. In vivo modeling and video modeling are two interventions that target imitation skills in children with ASDs. Comparative studies have asserted that both interventions are equally efficacious (Gena et al., 2005).

Modeling

In vivo modeling utilizes observational learning to instruct cues, target behaviors, and behavior consequences. Due to its applicability in real-time social situations and use of peers as effective models, in vivo modeling is generalizable across contexts. The following is an example of in vivo modeling:

Target behavior: Expressive labeling of the emotions happy and sad

In a slow, exaggerated manner, the social worker holds up a picture of a boy with a big smile and asks, "What is he feeling?" (The child is allotted 10 seconds to respond). If the child does not respond, the social worker offers a prompt accordingly.

Success with targeted behaviors in video modeling include social initiation, reciprocal play, peer imitation, and less isolated object manipulation (Ferraioli & Harris, 2011, p. 177). Furthermore, research on the use of video modeling to encourage attention understanding as a component of joint attention is promising (Schietecatte et al., 2011). In video modeling, a child is repeatedly shown a video clip depicting a targeted skill. The recorded video medium allows for ease of repetition and is often enjoyed by children with ASDs. In order to direct the focus of the skill, the model emphasizes the task's important features. The child is then encouraged to perform the skill in a natural setting. The following is an example of video modeling:

Target behavior: ADL skill, brushing teeth

The social worker shows the child a video depicting the social worker brushing her teeth. The task is broken down so that each step is differentiated and specified. Opening the cap of the toothpaste, placing toothpaste on the head of the toothbrush, placing the toothbrush in the mouth, brushing in a circular motion on all sides, spitting, and rinsing are all demonstrated in sequence. After the video is shown a second time, the social worker invites the child to try, "Just like on TV." When steps are performed out of sequence or incorrectly, the social worker encourages corrections as appropriate.

Research suggests that in vivo and video modeling are effective techniques for teaching and generalizing a wide variety of behavior to children with ASD, such as expressive labeling, independent play, spontaneous greetings, oral comprehension, conversational speech, cooperative and social play, and self-help skills.

Last, due to the widespread use of various medications for symptoms associated with autism, a review of interventions for school-aged children would not be complete without a brief discussion of psychopharmacology.

Psychopharmacology

Psychopharmacological treatment of children with ASDs appears to be common in clinical practice via the use of atypical antipsychotics, serotonin reuptake inhibitors, stimulants, and mood stabilizers (Aman, Collier-Crespin, & Lindsay, 2000; Floyd & McIntosh, 2009; Martin, Scahill, Klin, & Volkmar, 1999). Currently, psychopharmacology for individuals with ASDs is not primarily directed at the social and communication components and is thus considered relatively aspecific (West, Waldrop, & Brunssen, 2009).

The pharmacological approach is aimed mostly at reducing the frequency of problematic behaviors such as stereotypes, self-injurious behavior, and aggressive behavior (McDougle, Stigler, Erickson, & Posey, 2008; Posey, Erickson, & McDougle, 2008). It is estimated that as many as half of all individuals with a diagnosis of an ASD are treated with one or more psychotropic medications (Martin et al., 1999). However, with the sole exception of risperidone, the U.S. Food and Drug Administration has not approved any pharmacologic drug for use in the treatment of children with ASDs (Floyd & McIntosh, 2009). Risperidone is known as an atypical antipsychotic and is frequently used for treating severe maladaptive behavior and symptoms associated with AD (McDougle et al., 2000), such as aggression, self-injury, property destruction, irritability, self-injury, or severe tantrums. Few studies specifically targeting a sample of children with ASDs and adhering to conventional standards of research design and methodology with efficacious results were found. The Research Units on Pediatric Psychopharmacology Autism Network (2002) and Shea et al. (2004) completed large-scale multisite, randomized, double-blind, placebo-controlled clinical trials of risperidone in children with autism. The studies provided convincing evidence that risperidone is safe and effective for the short-term treatment of severe behavioral problems. The focus on severe behavior problems leaves an open question about possible additive effects of medication and applied behavioral interventions (Scahill & Martin, 2005). For example, the improvement in serious behavior problems associated with risperidone may enable a child to participate in an inclusive setting with DTT techniques employed.

For a complete list of randomized controlled trials carried out in 2001–2010 using standardized outcome measures with clinical samples of children and adolescents with ASDs, see Canitano and Scandurra (2011). Additional randomized, double-blind, placebo-controlled clinical trials have been conducted to test the effects of liquid fluoxetine, donepezil hydrochloride, and amantadine. All three had efficacious findings to some extent. The clinical trial conducted to examine the selective serotonin reuptake inhibitor liquid fluoxetine yielded results that indicate that a low dose is more effective than a placebo in the treatment of repetitive behaviors in childhood and adolescents with ASDs (Hollander et al., 2005). The study of donepezil hydrochloride found expressive and receptive speech gains, as well as decreases in the severity of overall autistic behavior after six weeks for the treatment group (Chez et al., 2003). Last, a randomized control trial of amantadine for childhood autism reported clinician-rated improvements on behavioral ratings but showed no difference between the placebo and the active drug for parent ratings (King et al., 2001). However, a large placebo response was also found in this group. There is some evidence to support the usefulness of the SSRIs fluvoxamine and escitalopram in addressing anxious and repetitive behaviors associated with ASDs (Sugie et al., 2005; West, Waldrop, & Brunssen, 2009). Anticonvulsants are often used in children with ASDs for treating mood disorders and maladaptive behaviors (Ettinger, 2006), and they have been progressively used to attenuate mood instability, anxiety, and impulsivity (Di Martino & Tuchman, 2001; Tuchman, 2004). Valproate has also been demonstrated as effective in controlling the domain of the repetitive behaviors, yet more trials are needed to replicate encouraging findings (Canitano & Scandurra, 2011). It is important to strongly caution professionals and family members that there are no medications specifically targeting the core symptoms of social and language impairments of autism in children.

Tools and Practice Example

Increasingly, school-based social workers and other mental health professionals are providing collaborative consultation (Idol, 1988; Idol, Paolucci-Whitcomb, & Nevin, 1986) to general education teachers of students with disabilities, focused on problem-solving efforts to identify students' behavioral difficulties and to devise strategies to reduce the problems (Curtis & Myers, 1988, as cited in Pryor, Kent, McGunn, & LeRoy, 1996). The following case example illustrates a school social worker employing ABA and DTT to address the classroom behavior of a child with AD in an inclusive setting.

Applying Interventions within a Response to Intervention Framework

Addressing symptoms of ASDs requires a dynamic approach, replete with a means of systematic, ongoing evaluation. Response to Intervention (RTI) is a framework for early screening and multi-tiered intervention for young students with learning needs. Children with ASDs commonly exhibit early signs of atypical development by school age. Furthermore, evidence concludes that early intervention in an interdisciplinary team framework with family, teacher, and therapeutic intervention yields the most favorable outcomes. Thus, an RTI approach provides the comprehensiveness and continuity necessary to support children with ASDs.

As mentioned earlier in this chapter, a variety of screening tools are utilized in the initial and second stages in order to identify symptoms of ASDs. Through an RTI approach, necessary screening information is obtained during well-child visits, via parent-reported indicators of risk, teacher reports of academic performance and observation of behaviors, and findings from empirically supported clinical tools, such as the M-CHAT, STAT, ASSQ, and KADI. Findings from screening tools are then substantiated, accordingly, by diagnostic instruments.

Upon diagnosis, a package of empirically supported interventions is designed at the family, school, and clinical levels. Due to the heterogeneous presentation of behaviors and intellectual and social abilities among children with ASDs, combinations of intervention packages vary for each individual. Thus, objectives may aim to cultivate and increase targeted behaviors and reduce or eliminate maladaptive ones. Foci of interventions will change as children acquire new skills and are influenced by other life factors, such as development due to aging, hence the crucial component of ongoing evaluation is a cornerstone of an RTI approach.

Evaluating the efficacy of an intervention requires that the outcomes directly result from the intervention and not as a result of extraneous influencing factors. The aforementioned complexities inherent to diagnosing ASDs pose similar challenges in assessing RTI. Responsiveness is measured through the demonstration of adaptive behaviors and the extinction of maladaptive behaviors. However, the cadre of psychopharmacological and therapeutic interventions and co-occurring development due to aging present a host of necessary considerations in differentiating between behaviors as a result of treatment effects, concomitant child development, and interplay of intended and unintended factors.

The Pervasive Developmental Disorder Behavior Inventory (PDDBI; Cohen & Sudhalter, 2005) is a tool for measuring RTI and assesses individuals across an array of dimensions, including both adaptive and maladaptive verbal and nonverbal competencies. Unique to the PDDBI, a child's adaptive abilities can be referenced by age and evaluated among a cohort of children diagnosed with ASD. Additionally, resulting behaviors are evaluated in relation to co-occurring increasing and decreasing maladaptive and adaptive behaviors and within the context of expected developmental changes. Furthermore, the inclusion of both parent and teacher observations provides a means to reference behaviors across settings and assess the full response to the intervention. Thus, the PDDBI is an essential tool for evaluating efficacy over time and crafting an intervention to best support a child across settings and at multiple points in his or her schooling.

Practice Example

John is an 11-year-old Caucasian male currently enrolled in a public middle school in a blue-ribbon school district on the East Coast. John comes from an upper-middle-class family. Though John has no siblings, he has many relatives, including cousins in his peer group, with whom he interacts frequently. Between the ages of 2 and 2½ years old, John's language development regressed significantly. His parents noticed that he was not utilizing his functional language at the same level he had in the past, and he began to consistently make syntactic and pragmatic errors, such as pronoun reversal, and experienced difficulty answering simple what, where, when, and why questions. In addition, John began to exhibit strange behaviors, such as placing his toys in perfectly straight lines and verbally repeating television shows and commercials out of context. He exhibited additional impairments in his social interactions, including difficulty making and maintaining eye contact and an inability to understand nonverbal social cues, such as the curling of one's finger to mean "come here." John also exhibited a lack of social reciprocity. For example, when adults or peers would offer social greetings ("Hi John. How are you?"), John would not reply. At this time, John's parents consulted a myriad of specialists to search for an explanation for their son's changes in behavior and speech. John was eventually assessed by a multidisciplinary team of professionals, which resulted in an Axis I diagnosis of 299.00 Autistic Disorder.

In concert with the parents' preference, John's school district enrolled him in a school that specialized in educating young children with autism. Due to the research evidence demonstrating the effectiveness of ABA methods with young children with AD in preschool settings, the school he attended utilized this systematic approach to teach students a continuum of skills and behaviors. A school social worker was assigned to support John in the school and home, guiding him in the areas of social interaction, functional language, academic skills, and decreasing inappropriate behaviors. She worked closely with the parents to further reinforce their instruction of the structured approach in an effort to incorporate ABA techniques into their everyday routine, thereby reinforcing John's skill set across persons and settings.

During his kindergarten year, John was enrolled part time in a regular public school. He went to his specialized school for children with autism in the morning, where he received intensive skill training through discrete trial teaching. In the afternoon, John was integrated into a regular kindergarten class in a public school. The school social worker stayed in this class with John for 1 hour per day to aid in generalization of the skills taught in his specialized school and in the home setting. Generalization of skills has been defined as an important aspect to consider in designing any intervention for children with autism (Prizant & Wetherby, 1998; Smith, 2001).

Two advantages to John's social worker shadowing him in the public school class were the opportunity to train the school staff in ABA principles and instruction and to gather data on John's behaviors and skill level in the school setting. For example, the social worker took occurrence/nonoccurrence data on John's "TV talk" (verbal repetition of lines from his favorite television shows). On a data sheet, she divided the school day into 5-minute intervals and took data on whether John exhibited TV talk or did not. The social worker marked each 5-minute interval with a "+" if John demonstrated TV talk or a "–" if no TV talk occurred. This type of data was collected over a 3-day period during a 1-week interval. After the data collection was completed and the frequency of the behavior was established, the social worker performed a functional analysis of the behavior. The purpose of a functional analysis is to determine what environmental element is encouraging the student to engage in a particular behavior. To perform a functional analysis, the social worker took "ABC data." At each instance of the behavior, the social worker wrote down the (A) antecedent to the behavior: what occurred in the environment directly prior to the behavior being exhibited; the (B) behavior itself: exactly how the behavior was manifested, what the student said and did while participating in the behavior; and the (C) consequence(s) to the behavior: how the individuals in the environment responded to the behavior. Did the student receive attention? Was the student removed from a demanding task? After a functional analysis was performed on John's TV talk, the social worker established that John participated in the behavior to "escape" demanding social situations.

At this time, John was exhibiting noncontextual speech in the form of TV talk habitually throughout the day. The educator requested that the school social worker assist with the reduction of this behavior as it prevented John from interacting in a reciprocal way with his peers and caused many distractions for both John and his peers in relation to their learning. His social worker wrote a behavior modification plan to target this behavior. The plan was a differential reinforcement of appropriate behaviors (DRA) with a social skills training component to teach appropriate replacement behaviors. The DRA was selected as a treatment strategy as it enabled other school staff to be trained in the intervention techniques and built upon John's strengths by encouraging his appropriate behaviors. The DRA was executed throughout his day. When John would engage in appropriate activities without exhibiting TV talk, the social worker (or whoever was with him at the time) would sporadically give him a happy-face token, paired with social praise ("You're doing a nice job working on the puzzle"). When John would engage in TV talk, the social worker would give him a sad-face token paired with the verbal cue, "Tell me what you're doing now." This verbal cue taught John to comment on a present task rather than to perseverate on television shows. When John earned five happy-face tokens, he was able to choose a preferred activity (e.g., working on the computer) to engage in for a 3-minute period. If John received five sad-face tokens before earning five happy-face tokens, he was given a verbal prompt, "You need to talk about what is going on in the [classroom], not about TV" The staff of both his specialized and inclusive schools was trained to implement the plan, as were his parents. John exhibited this behavior very frequently (some instance of TV talk occurred in 80% of the 5-minute intervals during baseline data collection) when the behavior plan was initially implemented. With the consistency of the implementation, the behavior was reduced to one or two instances a day after 6 months and was eventually eliminated by the end of the school year.

John was mainstreamed into the public school, full time, with a one-to-one aide at the start of his first-grade year. He was able to complete the full curriculum with the help of the school staff, who worked with the school social worker to learn how to break down John's assignments into manageable steps. For example, stories read in class were broken down into "chunks" and paired with visual cues to aid in comprehension. He continued to receive ABA instruction and DTT after school with the social worker. The social worker utilized role-play techniques to teach social skills, breaking down the skills into manageable steps:

SW: I'm going to pretend to be Kyle. I'm on the playground with a soccer ball. You're going to walk up to me, tap me on the shoulder, look in my eyes and say, "Can I play soccer with you?" Get ready. Go!

John: [walks up, taps the social worker on the shoulder, looks in her eyes, but says nothing]

SW: Say, "Can I play soccer with you?" (verbal cue)

John: Can I play soccer with you?

SW: That was great! Let's try it again. (social praise used as positive reinforcement)

In the example, the social worker is breaking down a social interaction into small, teachable steps. After John mastered this first step of playground interaction (initiating play) in several different play scenarios, the social worker expanded the recess role-play scenes to teach John how to maintain extended play periods. During lunch time and recess at the school, John's social worker would shadow him and deliver verbal cues such as "Ask Kyle, 'Can I play with you?'" or gestural prompts (i.e., point at a peer with whom he can play). The verbal cue was also paired with the gestural prompt: pointing at the peer while modeling "Can I play with you?" These strategies aimed to help John generalize the skills he learned during his therapy sessions. Again, the school staff was also taught these prompts to assist with John's socialization throughout the school day. All team members were also instructed to fade the verbal prompts over time as John's social skills became stronger. For a child with AD to be included in a mainstream setting, he needs to be able to manage social experiences (National Research Council, 2001).

John's social worker continued to consult in the school setting. John was taught to respond to discrete hand gestures to help him to refocus on the teacher when environmental distractions would impede his concentration. If John would look out the window when his teacher was speaking, the social worker would touch his shoulder, and when John looked up, she would tap her ear twice and point to the teacher. John was taught that this gesture meant "listen to the teacher." The school staff was taught to utilize these hand gestures as well. These discrete gestures kept John from standing out too much from his peers, as verbal redirecting would draw attention to him. Through the use of such gestures by various staff members, John's classmates also began to respond to the gestures when they became unfocused.

John is currently enrolled in a public middle school. He continues to complete the full curriculum and plays on his town soccer and basketball teams. John does continue to experience difficulty in the area of reading comprehension and in assessing social cues at times. However, the progress John has made is quite noteworthy. He is a friendly and empathic boy who excels in math and enjoys athletic activities. John's success could not have been accomplished without the support of a multidisciplinary team effort. John's school social worker, teachers, speech therapist, and occupational therapist all collaborated through the years to utilize similar strategies and target compatible goals. John's parents employed reinforcement strategies in the home by carrying over the skills targeted in therapy and at school.

Resources

Overview of AD and AS

http://www.autism-society.org
http://www.myautisminfo.com
http://www.nichcy.org
http://www.aspergers.com
http://www.udel.edu/bkirby/asperger/aslink.html
http://www.autism-pdd.net/autism.htm
http://www.autism.com

Educational and Therapeutic Interventions

http://www.teacch.com
http://www.autism.org
http://www.verbalbehaviournetwork.com
http://www.abatoolchest.com
http://www.nationalautismcenter.org/about/

Treatment Centers

http://www.pcdi.org
http://gsappweb.rutgers.edu/DDDC
http://info.med.yale.edu/chldstdy/autism
http://www.behavior.org
http://www.son-rise.org
http://alpinelearninggroup.org

Training Materials

Arick, J. R., Loos, L., Falco, R., & Krug, D. A. (2004). *Strategies for teaching based on autism research: STAR*. Austin, TX: Pro-Ed.

Barbera, M., & Rasmussen, T. (2007). *The verbal behavior approach: How to teach children with autism and related disorders*. London, England: Jessica Kingsley Publishers. www.socialskillstraining.org; www.behavioraldirections.com/videos-training.html

Freeman, S., & Dake, L. (1997). *Teach me language*. Langley, BC: SKF Books.

Koegel, R. L., Koegel, L. K., & Parks, D. R. (1990). *How to teach self-management skills to people with severe disabilities: A training manual*. Santa Barbara, CA: University of California.

Leaf, R., & McEachin, J. (1999). *A work in progress*. New York, NY: DRL Books.

McClannahan, L. E., & Krantz, P. J. (1999). *Activity schedules for children with autism: Teaching independent behavior.* Bethesda, MD: Woodbine. http://www.dttrainer.com/pi_overview.htm; http://www.nationalspeech.com; http://rsaffran.tripod.com; http://www.users.qwest.net/~tbharris/prt.htm; http://www.education.ucsb.edu/autism/behaviormanuals.html

Suggested Practice Exercise Related to Intervention

Consider that a parent has received a diagnosis of AD for his 5-year-old son. How would you begin to present the options for intervention? Describe your role as a social worker in providing the information.

Key Points to Remember

- Autism spectrum disorders are defined by clinical symptomatology, which typically falls within three major categories: (1) qualitative impairment in social interaction; (2) impairments in communication; and (3) restricted, repetitive, stereotyped behavior, interests, and activities.
- One of the important characteristics of children with ASDs is uneven learning ability and skill levels, and as such, individualization of intervention is necessary.
- Applied behavior analysis is the most widely accepted effective intervention model for children and adolescents with AD and AS.
- Discrete trial training is a specialized teaching technique or process used to develop new forms of behavior and skills, including cognitive, communication, play, social, readiness, receptive-language, and self-help skills, as well as reducing self-stimulatory responses and aggressive behaviors.
- The primary purpose of pivotal response training is to provide children with the social and educational proficiency to participate in inclusive settings.
- Joint attention training, in vivo modeling, and video modeling are effective techniques to enhance social and communication skills.
- Medication cannot be justified as the first line of treatment for AD, AS, or the associated symptoms.
- Behavioral treatments are most successful when applied across settings and persons in the child's life.
- Evidence-based practice requires assessment and intervention in accessible and culturally sensitive mediums.

Despite the promising treatment effects produced by the interventions reviewed above, existing treatments need to be refined and evaluated with rigorous testing procedures to establish efficacy. A primary goal of the research should be to determine the types of interventions that are most effective for children with different subtypes of ASDs and with specific characteristics, across cultures, since the characteristics of children with ASDs and their life circumstances are exceedingly heterogeneous in nature (National Research Council, 2001). Regardless of the intervention selected, it is essential that strategies be devised to take advantage of the unique constellation of strengths and characteristics of the learner with AS or AD and to modify contexts to support the learning and behavioral style of the individual student (Klin, McPartland, & Volkmar, 2005).

The focus in this chapter has been geared toward the school social worker and mental health practitioner working with individual students in school settings. Equally important in sustaining gains in behavior and skill acquisition with school-aged children and adolescents with AD and AS are issues surrounding classroom management, group skill-based interventions, especially for students with AS, and working collaboratively with parents, teachers, peers, and school administrators to promote skill generalization across settings and persons in addition to sustaining change.

Notes

1. It should be noted that in addition to the diagnostic criteria for AS delineated in the *DSM-IV-TR* (2000) and the *ICD-10* (1992), there are at least five very different conceptualizations of AS (Ghaziuddin, Tsai, & Ghaziuddin, 1992; Klin & Volkmar, 1997; Leekam, Libby, Wing, Gould, & Gillberg, 2000; Szatmari, Bryson, Boyle, Streiner, & Duku, 2003), which represent to some extent the major differences in the conceptualization of this disorder (e.g., Asperger's syndrome as a milder form of autism, different conceptions of the timing when motor skills should be taken into account, etc.).

2. Level-one screening measures for autism are used to identify children at risk for autism from the general population, while level-two screening involves the identification of children at risk for autism from a population of children demonstrating a broad range of developmental concerns (Stone, Coonrod, Turner, & Pozdol, 2004).

3. There are two instruments specifically designed as diagnostic tools for Asperger's syndrome: the Asperger's Syndrome Diagnostic Interview and the Australian Scale for Asperger's Syndrome. Both require further testing to determine their reliability and validity prior to use as diagnostic instruments.

4. See Rogers (1998); National Research Council (2001); and New York State Department of Health (1999b) for a complete review of evidence-based early intervention programs.

References

Aman, M. G., Collier-Crespin, A., & Lindsay, R. L. (2000). Pharmacotherapy of disorders in mental retardation. *European Child and Adolescent Psychiatry, Sup. 1,* I98–I107.

American Autism Society. *Can children be diagnosed as toddlers?* Retrieved July 12, 2011, from http://www.americanautismsociety.org/autism-diagnosis-can-children-be-diagnosed-as-toddlers/

American Psychiatric Association. (2000). *Diagnostic and statistical manual of mental disorders* (4th ed., text revision). Washington, DC: Author.

Anderson, S. R., Taras, M., & Cannon, B. O. (1996). Teaching new skills to young children with autism. In C. Maurice, G. Green, & S. C. Luce (Eds.), *Behavioral intervention for young children with autism: A manual for parents and professionals* (pp. 181–194). Austin, TX: Pro-Ed.

Anderson, S. R., & Romanczyk, R. G. (1999). Early intervention for young children with autism: Continuum-based behavioral models. *Journal of the Association for Persons with Severe Handicaps, 24*(3), 162–173.

Arick, J. R., Krug, D. A., Fullerton, A., Loos, L., & Falco, R. (2005). School-based programs. In D. J. Cohen & F. R. Volkmar (Eds.), *Handbook of autism and pervasive developmental disorders: Vol. 2, Assessment, interventions, and policy* (3rd ed., pp. 1003–1028). New York, NY: Wiley.

Baer, D., Wolf, M., & Risley, R. (1968). Some current dimensions of applied behavior analysis. *Journal of Applied Behavior Analysis, 1,* 91–97.

Begeer, S., El Bouk, S., Boussaid, W., Terwogt, M. M., & Koot, H. M. (2009). Underdiagnosis and referral bias of autism in ethnic minorities. *Journal of Autism and Developmental Disorders, 39*(1), 142–148.

Booker, K. W., & Starling, L. (2011). Test review: Social responsiveness scale by J. N. Constantino and C. P. Gruber. *Assessment for Effective Intervention, 36,* 192–194.

Bregman, J. (2005). Definitions and characteristics of the spectrum. In D. Zager (Ed.), *Autism spectrum disorders: Identification, education and treatment* (3rd ed., pp. 3–46). Mahwah, NJ: Erlbaum.

Bregman, J. D., Zager, D., & Gerdtz, J. (2005). Behavioral interventions. In F. Volkmar et al. (Eds.), *Handbook of autism and pervasive developmental disorders* (pp. 897–924). Hoboken, NJ: John Wiley & Sons.

Canitano, R., & Scandurra, V. (2011). Psychopharmacology in autism: An update. *Progress in Neuro-Psychopharmacology & Biological Psychiatry, 35,* 18–28.

Centers for Disease Control and Prevention. (2007). Prevalence of autism spectrum disorders—Autism and developmental disabilities monitoring network, 14 sites, United States, 2002. *Morbidity and Mortality Weekly Report, 56*(SS-1), 12–28.

Centers for Disease Control and Prevention. (2009). Prevalence of autism spectrum disorders—Autism and developmental disabilities monitoring network, 14 sites, United States, 2006. *Morbidity and Mortality Weekly Report, 58*(SS-10), 1–20.

Chevallier, C., Wilson, D., Happé, F., & Noveck, I. (2010). Scalar inferences in autism spectrum disorders. *Journal of Autism and Developmental Disorders, 40,* 1104–1117.

Chez, M. G., Buchanan, T. M., Becker, M., Kessler, J., Aimonovitch, M. C., & Mrazek, S. R. (2003). Donepezil hydrochloride: A double-blind study in autistic children. *Journal of Pediatric Neurology, 1*(2), 83–88.

Chlebowski, C., Green, J. A., Barton, M. L., & Fein, D. (2010). Using childhood autism rating scale to diagnose autism spectrum disorders. *Journal of Autism and Developmental Disorders, 40,* 787–799.

Cohen, I. L., & Sudhalter, V. (2005). *The PDD behavior inventory*. Lutz, FL: Psychological Assessment Resources.

Constantino, J. N. (2002). *The social-responsiveness scale.* Los Angeles: Western Psychological Services.

Cooper, J. O., Heron, T., & Heward, W. (1987). *Applied behavior analysis.* Columbus, OH: Merrill.

Cummings, A. R., & Williams, W. L. (2000). Visual identity matching and vocal imitation training with children with autism: A surprising finding. *Journal on Developmental Disabilities,* 7(2), 109–122.

Dababnah, S., Parish, S. L., Brown, L. T., & Hooper, S. R. (2011). Early screening for autism spectrum disorders: A primer for social work practice. *Children and Youth Services Review, 33*(2), 265–273.

Dawson, G., & Osterling, J. (1997). Early intervention in autism. In M. Guralnick (Ed.), *The effectiveness of early intervention* (pp. 307–326). Baltimore, MD: Brookes.

Delquadri, J. C., Greenwood, C. R., Stretton, K., & Hall, R. V. (1983). The peer tutoring spelling game: A classroom procedure for increasing opportunity to respond and spelling performance. *Education and Treatment of Children, 6*(3), 225–239.

Di Martino, A., & Tuchman, R. (2001). Antiepileptic drugs: Affective use in autism spectrum disorders. *Pediatric Neurology, 25,* 199–207.

DuCharme, R. W., & McGrady, K. A. (2003). What is Asperger syndrome? In R. W. DuCharme & T. P. Gullotta (Eds.), *Asperger syndrome: A guide for professionals and families* (pp. 1–20). New York, NY: Kluwer Academic/Plenum.

Dunlap, G. (1984). The influence of task variation and maintenance tasks on the learning and affect of autistic children. *Journal of Experimental Child Psychology, 31,* 41–64.

Ehlers, S., Gillberg, C., & Wing, L. (1999). A screening questionnaire for Asperger syndrome and other high-functioning autism spectrum disorders in school-age children. *Journal of Autism and Developmental Disabilities, 29*(2), 129–141.

Elder, J. H., Valcante, G., Won, S., & Zylis, R. (2003). Effects of in-home training for culturally diverse fathers or children with autism. *Issues in Mental Health Nursing, 24,* 273–295.

Ettinger, A. B. (2006). Psychotropic effects of antiepileptic drugs. *Neurology, 67,* 1916–1925.

Ferraioli, S. J., & Harris, S. L. (2011). Evidence-based treatment in communication for children with autism spectrum disorders. In B. Reichow, P. Doehring, D.V. Cicchetti, & F. R. Volkmar (Eds.), *Evidence-based practices and treatment for children with autism.* New York, NY: Springer.

Filipek, P. A., Accardo, P. J., Baranek, G. T., Cook, E. H., Jr., Dawson, G., Gordon, B., ... Volkmar, F. R. (1999). The screening and diagnosis of autism spectrum disorders. *Journal of Autism and Developmental Disorders, 29*(6), 439–484.

Filipek, P. A., Accardo, P. J., Ashwal, S., Baranek, G.T., Cook, E. H., Dawson G., ... Volkmar, F. R. (2000). Practice parameter: Screening and diagnosis of autism. *Neurology, 55,* 468–479.

Floyd, E. F., & McIntosh, D. E. (2009). Current practice in psychopharmacology for children and adolescents with autism spectrum disorders. *Psychology in the Schools, 46*(9), 905–909.

Fombonne, E. (2009). Epidemiology of pervasive developmental disorders. *Pediatric Research, 65*(6), 591–598.

Gena, A., Couloura, S., & Kymissis, E. (2005). Modifying the affective behavior of preschoolers with autism using in-vivo or video modeling and reinforcement contingencies. *Journal of Autism and Developmental Disorders, 35*(5), 545–556.

Ghaziuddin, M., Tsai, L., & Ghaziuddin, N. (1992). Comorbidity of autistic disorder in children and adolescents. *European Child and Adolescent Psychiatry, 1,* 209–213.

Goldstein, H. (2002). Communication intervention for children with autism: A review of treatment efficacy. *Journal of Autism and Developmental Disorders, 35*(2), 373–396.

Green, G. (1996). Early behavioral intervention for autism: What does research tell us? In C. Maurice, G. Green, & S. C. Luce (Eds.), *Behavioral intervention for young children with autism* (pp. 29–44). Austin, TX: Pro-Ed.

Harris, S. L., & Handleman, J. S. (1994). *Preschool education programs for children with autism.* Austin, TX: Pro-Ed.

Hollander, E., & Nowinski, C. V. (2003). Core symptoms, related disorders and course of autism. In E. Hollander (Ed.), *Autism spectrum disorders* (pp. 15–38). New York, NY: Dekker.

Hollander, E., Phillips, A., Chaplin, W., Zagursky, K., Novotny, S. Wasserman, S. & Iyengar, R. (2005). A placebo controlled crossover trial of liquid fluoxetine on repetitive behaviors in childhood and adolescent autism. *Neuropsychopharmacology, 30*(3), 582–589.

Howlin, P. (1998). *Children with autism and Asperger syndrome: A guide for practitioners and carers*. Chichester, England: Wiley.

Idol, L., Paolucci-Whitcomb, P., & Nevin, A. (1986). *Collaborative consultation*. Rockville, MD: Aspen.

Idol, L., West, J. F., & Lloyd, S. R. (1988). Organizing and implementing specialized reading programs: A collaborative approach involving classroom, remedial, and special education teachers. *Remedial and Special Education, 9*(2), 54–61.

Jacobson, J. W., Foxx, R. M., & Mulick, J. A. (Eds.). (2005). *Controversial therapies for developmental disabilities: Fad, fashion and science in professional practice*. Mahwah, NJ: Erlbaum.

Jegatheesan, B., Fowler, S., & Miller, P. J. (2010). From symptom recognition to services: How South Asian Muslim immigrant families navigate autism. *Disability & Society, 25*(7), 797–811.

Jeste, S. S. (2011). The neurology of autism spectrum disorders. *Current Opinion in Neurology, 24*(2), 132–139.

King, B. H., Handen, B. L., Sikich, L., Zimmerman, A. W., McMahon, W., Cantwell, E., ... Cook, E. H. (2001). Double-blind, placebo-controlled study of amantadine hydrochloride in the treatment of children with autistic disorder. *Journal of American Academy of Child and Adolescent Psychiatry, 40*(6), 658–665.

Kleinman, J. M., Robins, D. L., Ventola, P. E., Pandey, J., Boorstein, H. C., Esser, E. L., ... Fein, D. (2008). The modified checklist for autism in toddlers: A follow-up study investigating the early detection of autism spectrum disorders. *Journal of Autism and Developmental Disorders, 38*, 827–839.

Kleinman, J. M., Ventola, P. E., Pandey, J., Verbalis, A. D., Barton, M., Hodgson, S., ... & Fein, D. (2008a). Disability stability in very young children with autism spectrum disorders. *Journal of Autism and Developmental Disorders, 38*(4), 606–615.

Klin, A., & Volkmar, F. R. (1997). Asperger's syndrome. In D. J. Cohen & F. R. Volkmar (Eds.), *Handbook of autism and pervasive developmental disorders* (2nd ed.). New York, NY: Wiley and Sons.

King, B. H., Handen, B. L., Sikich, L., Zimmerman, A. W., McMahon, W., Cantwell, E., ... Cook, E. H. (2001). Double-blind, placebo-controlled study of amantadine hydrochloride in the treatment of children with autistic disorder. *Journal of American Academy of Child and Adolescent Psychiatry, 40*(6), 658–665.

Koegel, L. K., Koegel, R. L., Harrower, J. K., & Carter, C. M. (1999). Pivotal response intervention I: Overview of approach. *Journal of the Association for Persons with Severe Handicaps, 24*(3), 174–185

Koegel, L. K., Koegel, R. L., Shoshan, Y., & McNerney, E. (1999). Pivotal response intervention II: Preliminary long-term outcome data. *Journal of the Association for Persons with Severe Handicaps, 24*(3), 186–198.

Koegel, R. L., & Williams, J.A. (1980). Direct versus indirect response-reinforcer relationships in teaching autistic children. *Journal of Abnormal Child Psychology, 8*, 537–547.

Koegel, R. L., O'Dell, M., & Dunlap, G. (1988). Producing speech use in nonverbal autistic children by reinforcing attempts. *Journal of Autism and Developmental Disorders, 18*, 525–538.

Koegel, R. L., & Frea, W. D. (1993). Treatment of social behavior in autism through the modification of pivotal social skills. *Journal of Applied Behavior Analysis, 26*(3), 369–377.

Koegel, R. L., & Koegel, L. K. (Eds.). (1995). *Teaching children with autism: Strategies for initiating positive interactions and improving learning opportunities*. Baltimore, MD: Brookes.

Koegel, R. L., Schreffirnan, L., Good, A., Cerniglia, L., Murphy, C., & Koegel, L. K. (n.d.). *How to teach pivotal behaviors to children with autism: A training manual*. Retrieved from http://www.users.qwest.net/~tbharris/prt.htm

Krug, D. A., & Arick, J. R. (2003). *Krug Asperger's Disorder Index*. Austin, TX: Pro-Ed.

Leekam, S., Libby, S., Wing, L., Gould, J., & Gillberg C. (2000). Comparison of ICD-10 and Gillberg's criteria for Asperger syndrome. *Autism, 4*, 11–28.

Levy, S. E., Mandell, D. S., & Schultz, R. T. (2009). Autism. *The Lancet, 374*, 1627–1638.

Lord, C., Rutter, M. L., & Le Couteur, A. (1994). The Autism Diagnostic Interview-Revised: A revised version of the diagnostic interview for caregivers of individuals with possible pervasive developmental disorders. *Journal of Autism and Developmental Disorders, 24*(5), 659–685.

Lord, C., & Paul, R. (1997). Language and communication in autism. In D. J. Cohen & F. R. Volkmar (Eds.), *Handbook of autism and pervasive developmental disorders* (2nd ed., pp. 460–483). New York, NY: Wiley.

Lord, C., Rutter, M. L., DiLavore, P. C., & Risi, S. (1999). *Autism Diagnostic Observation Schedule-WPS* (WPS ed.). Los Angeles, CA: Western Psychological Services.

Lord, C., Risi, S., Lambrecht, L., Cook, E. H., Leventhal, B. L., DiLavore, P. C., Pickles, A., & Rutter, M. (2000). The autism diagnostic observation schedule-generic: A standard measure of social and communication deficits associated with the spectrum of autism. *Journal of Autism and Developmental Disorders, 30*(3), 205–223.

Lord, C., & Cosello, C. (2005). Diagnostic instruments in autistic spectrum disorders. In F. R. Volkmar, R. Paul, A. Klin, & D. Cohen (Eds.), *Handbook of autism and pervasive developmental disorders: Vol. 2. Assessment, interventions and policy* (3rd ed., pp. 730–771). Hoboken, NJ: Wiley.

Lord, C., Risi, S., DiLavore, P. S., Schulman, C., Thurm, A., & Pickles, A. (2006). Autism from 2 to 9 years of age. *Archives of General Psychiatry, 63*(6), 694–701.

Lovaas, O. (1993). The development of a treatment research project for developmentally disabled and autistic children. *Journal of Applied Behavior Analysis, 26*(4), 617–630.

Lovaas, O. I. (1981). *Teaching developmentally disabled children: The me book.* Austin, TX: Pro-Ed.

Lovaas, O. I. (1987). Behavioral treatment and normal educational and intellectual functioning in young autistic children. *Journal of Consulting and Clinical Psychology, 55*, 3–9.

Lovaas, O. I., & Smith, T. (1989). A comprehensive behavioral theory of autistic children: Paradigm for research and treatment. *Journal of Behavior Therapy and Experimental Psychology, 20*, 17–29.

Mandell, D. S., Listerud, J., Levy, S. E., & Pinto-Martin, J. A. (2002). Race differences in the age at diagnosis among Medicaid-eligible children with autism. *Journal of the American Academy of Child and Adolescent Psychiatry, 41*(12), 1447–1453.

Mandell, D. S., Ittenbach, R. F., Levy, S. E., & Pinto-Martin, J. A. (2007). Disparities in diagnoses received prior to a diagnosis of autism spectrum disorder. *Journal of Autism and Developmental Disorders, 37*(9), 1795–1802.

Mandell, D. S., Wiggins, L. D., Carpenter, L. A., Daniels, J., & DiGuiseppi, C. (2009). Racial/Ethnic disparities in the identification of children with autism spectrum disorders. *American Journal of Public Health, 99*(3), 493–498.

Martin, A., Scahill, L., Klin, A., & Volkmar, F. R. (1999). Higher-functioning pervasive developmental disorders: Rates and patterns of psychotropic drug use. *Journal of the American Academy of Child and Adolescent Psychiatry, 38*, 923–931.

Matson, J. L., Benavidez, D. A., Compton, L. S., Paclawskyj, T., & Baglio, C. (1996). Behavioral treatment of autistic persons: A review of research from 1980 to the present. *Research in Developmental Disabilities, 17*, 433–465.

Maurice, C., Green, G., & Luce, S. C. (Eds.). (1996). *Behavioral intervention for young children with autism: A manual for parents and professionals.* Austin, TX: Pro-Ed.

McCarton, C. (2003). Assessment and diagnosis of pervasive developmental disorder. In E. Hollander (Ed.), *Autism spectrum disorders* (pp. 101–132). New York, NY: Dekker.

McDougle, C. J., Scahill, L., McCracken, J. T., Aman, M. G., Tierney, E., Arnold, L. E., et al. (2000). Research Units on Pediatric Psychopharmacology (RUPP) Autism Network: Background and rationale for an initial controlled study of risperidone. *Child and Adolescent Psychiatric Clinics of North America, 9*, 201–224.

McDougle, C. J., Stigler, K. A., Erickson, C. A., & Posey, D. (2008). Atypical antipsychotics in children and adolescents with autistic and other pervasive developmental disorders. *Journal of Clinical Psychiatry, 69*(Sup. 4), 15–20.

Meindi, J. N., & Cannella-Malone, H. I. (2011). Initiating and responding to joint attention bids in children with autism: A review of the literature. *Research in Developmental Disabilities, 32*(5), 1441–1454.

Mesibov, G. B., & Shea, V. (2011) Evidence-based practice and autism. *Autism, 15*, 114–133.

Miranda-Linne, F., & Melin, L. (1992). Acquisition, generalization and spontaneous use of color adjectives: A comparison of incidental teaching and traditional discrete-trial procedures for children with autism. *Research in Developmental Disabilities, 13*, 191–210.

National Association of Social Workers. (2007). *Indicators for the achievement of the NASW standards for cultural competence in social work practice.* Retrieved July 12, 2011, from http://www.socialworkers.org/practice/standards/NASWCulturalStandardsIndicators2006.pdf

National Autism Center. (2009). *The National Autism Center's National Standards Project: Findings and Conclusions.* Randolph, MA: Author.

National Research Council. (2001). *Educating children with autism.* Washington, DC: National Academy Press.

New York State Department of Health, Early Intervention Program. (1999a). *Clinical practice guideline: Guideline technical report: Autism/pervasive developmental disorders, assessment and intervention for young children (ages 0–3 years)* (No. 4217). Albany, NY: Author.

New York State Department of Health, Early Intervention Program. (1999b). *Clinical practice guideline: Report of the recommendations: Autism/PDD, assessment and intervention in young children (age 0–3 years)* (No. 4215). Albany, NY: Author.

Newsome, C. B. (1998). Autistic disorder. In E. J. Mash & R. A. Barkley (Eds.), *Treatment of childhood disorders* (2nd ed., pp. 416–467). New York, NY: Guilford.

O'Brien, M. (2007). Ambiguous loss in families of children with autism spectrum disorders. *Family Relations, 56*(2), 135.

Odom, S. L., Brown, W. H., Frey, T., Karasu, N., Smith-Canter, L. L., & Strain, P. S. (2003). Evidence-based practices for young children with autism: Contributions for single-subject design research. *Focus on Autism and Other Developmental Disabilities, 18*(3), 166–175.

Ozonoff, S., & Cathcart, K. (1998). Effectiveness of a home program intervention for young children with autism. *Journal of Autism and Developmental Disorders, 28*(1), 25–32.

Posey, D. J., Erickson, C. A., & McDougle, C. J. (2008). Developing drugs for core social and communication impairment in autism. *Child & Adolescent Psychiatric Clinics of North America, 4*, 787–790.

Prizant, B. M., & Wetherby, A. M. (1998). Understanding the continuum of discrete-trial traditional behavioral to social-pragmatic, developmental approaches in communication enhancement for young children with ASD. *Seminars in Speech and Language, 19*, 329–353.

Pryor, G. B., Kent, C., McGunn, C., & LeRoy, B. (1996). Redesigning social work in inclusive schools. *Social Work, 41*(6), 668–695.

Robins, D. L., Fein, D., Barton, M. L., & Green, J. A. (2001). The Modified Checklist for Autism in Toddlers: An initial study investigating the early detection of autism and pervasive developmental disorders. *Journal of Autism and Developmental Disorders, 31*(2), 131–145.

Rodriguez, D. (2009). Culturally and linguistically diverse students with autism. *Childhood Education, 85*(5) 313–317.

Rogers, S. J. (1998). Empirically supported comprehensive treatments for young children with autism. *Journal of Clinical Child Psychology, 27*, 168–179.

Rogers, S., & Vismara, L. A. (2008). Evidence-based comprehensive treatments for early autism. *Journal of Clinical Child & Adolescent Psychology, 37*(1), 8–38.

Scahill, L., & Martin, A. (2005). Psychopharmacology. In F. R. Volkmar, A. Klin, R. Paul, & D. J. Cohen (Eds.), *Handbook of autism and pervasive developmental disorders* (Vol. 2, pp. 1102–1122). Hoboken, NJ: Wiley.

Schietecatte, I., Roeyers, H., & Warreyn, P. (2012). Exploring the nature of joint attention impairment in young children with autism spectrum disorder: Associated social and cognitive skills. *Journal of Autism and Developmental Disorders, 42*(1), 1–12.

Schopler, E., Reichler, R. J., & Renner, B. R. (1986). *The Childhood Autism Rating Scale (CARS) for diagnostic screening and classification of autism*. New York, NY: Irvington.

Schreibman, L. (1997). Theoretical perspectives on behavioral intervention for individuals with autism. In D.J. Cohen & F.R. Volkmar (Eds.), *Handbook of autism and pervasive developmental disorders* (2nd ed., pp. 920–933). New York, NY: John Wiley & Sons.

Schreibman, L., Kaneko, W. M., & Koegel, R. L. (1991). Positive affect of parents of autistic children: Comparison across two teaching techniques. *Behavior Therapy, 22*, 479–490.

Schreibman, L., Charlop, M. H., & Milstein, J. P. (1993). Autism: Behavioral treatment. In V. P. Van- Hasselt & M. Hersen (Eds.), *Handbook of behavior therapy and pharmacotherapy of children: A comparative analysis* (pp. 149–170). Needham Heights, MA: Allyn & Bacon.

Scott, F., Baron-Cohen, S., Bolton, P., & Brayne, C. (2002). The CAST (Childhood Asperger Syndrome Test): Preliminary development of UK screen for mainstream primary-school children. *Autism, 6*(1), 9–31.

Scott, J., Clark, C., & Brady, M. P. (2000). *Students with autism: Characteristics and instructional programming for special educators*. San Diego, CA: Singular.

Semrud-Clikeman, M., & Ellison, P. A. T. (2009). *Child neuropsychology: Assessment and intervention*. New York, NY: Springer.

Shea, S., Turqay, A., Carroll, A., Schulz, M., Orlik, H., Smith, I., & Dunbar, F. (2004). Risperidone in the treatment of disruptive behavioral symptoms in children with autistic and other pervasive developmental disorders. *Pediatrics, 114*(5), 634–641.

Siegel, B. (2004). *The Pervasive Disorders Screening Test II (PDDST-II)*. San Antonio, TX: Harcourt Assessment.

Simpson, R. L., de Boer-Ott, S. R., Griswold, D. E., Myles, B. S., Byrd, S. E., Ganz, J. B., ... Adams, L. G. (2004). *Autism spectrum disorders: Interventions and treatments for children and youth*. Thousand Oaks, CA: Corwin.

Smith, T. (1996). Are other treatments effective? In C. Maurice, G. Green, & S. C. Luce (Eds.), *Behavioral intervention for young children with autism* (pp. 45–59). Austin, TX: Pro-Ed.

Smith, T. (2001). Discrete trial training in the treatment of autism. *Focus on Autism and Other Developmental Disabilities, 16*(2), 86–92.

Squires, J., & Bricker, D. (2009). *Ages & Stages Questionnaire-Third Edition (ASQ-3)*. Baltimore, MD: Paul H. Brookes.

Stahmer, A. C. (1995). Teaching symbolic play skills to children with autism using pivotal response training. *Journal of Autism and Developmental Disorders, 25*, 123–141.

Stahmer, A. C. (1999). Using pivotal response training to facilitate appropriate play in children with autistic spectrum disorders. *Child Language Teaching and Therapy, 15*(1), 29–40.

Stahmer, A. C., Ingersoll, B., & Carter, C. (2003). Behavioral approaches to promoting play. *Autism, 7*(4), 401–413.

Stone, W. L., Coonrod, E. E., & Ousley, O.Y. (2000). Brief report: Screening tool for autism in two-year-olds (STAT): Development and preliminary data. *Journal of Autism and Developmental Disorders, 30*(6), 607–612.

Stone, W. L., Coonrod, E. E., Turner, L. M., & Pozdol, S. L. (2004). Psychometric properties of the STAT for early autism screening. *Journal of Autism and Developmental Disorders, 34*(6), 691–701.

Stone, W. L., McMahon, C. R., Henderson, L. M. (2008). Use of the screening tool for autism in two-year-olds (STAT) for children under 24 months: An exploratory study. *Autism, 12*, 557–573.

Strock, M. (2004). *Autism spectrum disorders (pervasive developmental disorders)* (NIH Publication No. 04–5511, pp. 1–40). Bethesda, MD: U.S. Department of Health and Human Services.

Sugie, Y., Sugie, H., Fukuda, T., Ito, M., Sasada, Y., Nakabayashi, M., ... Ohzeki, T. (2005). Clinical efficacy of fluvoxamine and functional polymorphism in a serotonin transporter gene on childhood autism. *Journal of Autism and Developmental Disorders, 35*, 377–385.

Sulzer-Azaroff, B., & Mayer, R. (1991). *Behavior analysis for lasting change*. Fort Worth, TX: Holt, Rinehart & Winston.

Szatmari, P., Bryson, S. E., Boyle, M. H., Streiner, D. L., & Duku, E. (2003). Predictors of outcome among high functioning children with autism and Asperger syndrome. *Journal of Child Psychology and Psychiatry, 44*(4), 520–528.

Thorpe, D. M., Stahmer, A. C., & Schreibman, L. (1995). Effects of sociodramatic play training on children with autism. *Journal of Autism and Developmental Disorders, 25*, 265–281.

Tuchman, R. (2004). AEDs and psychotropic drugs in children with autism and epilepsy. *Mental Retardation and Developmental Disabilities Research Review, 10*, 135–138.

Volkmar, F. R. & Weisner, L. A. (2009). *A practical guide to autism: What every parent, family member, and teacher needs to know*. Hoboken, NJ: John Wiley & Sons.

Wagner, A., & McGrady, K. A. (2003). Counseling and other therapeutic strategies for children with Asperger syndrome and their families. In R. W. DuCharme & T. P. Gullotta (Eds.), *Asperger syndrome: A guide for professionals and families* (pp. 83–134). New York, NY: Kluwer Academic/Plenum.

West, L., Waldrop, J., & Brunssen, S. (2009). Pharmacologic treatment for the core deficits and associated symptoms of autism in children. *Journal of Pediatric Health Care, 23*, 75–89.

Whalen, C., & Schreibman, L. (2003). Joint attention training for children with autism using behavior modification procedures. *Journal of Child Psychology & Psychiatry & Allied Disciplines, 44*, 456–468.

Williams, M. E., Atkins, M., & Soles, T. (2009). Assessment of autism in community settings: Discrepancies in classification. *Journal of Autism and Developmental Disorders, 39*, 660–669.

World Health Organization. (1992). *International classification of diseases: Diagnostic criteria for research* (10th ed.). Geneva, Switzerland: Author.

CHAPTER 16

Working with Students with Intellectual Disabilities Who Exhibit Severe Challenging Behavior

Mark O'Reilly ■ Vanessa A. Green ■ Jeff Sigafoos ■ Giulio Lancioni ■ Russell Lang ■ Christina Fragale ■ Farah El Zein ■ Helen Cannella ■ Chaturi Edrisinha

Getting Started

Approximately 5% of the school-age population suffers from intellectual disability. Intellectual disability, a form of disability, is characterized by significantly sub-average functioning both intellectually and in terms of adaptive (or everyday life skills) behavior (Schalock et al., 2010). The causes of intellectual disability vary and include genetic and chromosomal anomalies and injuries or accidents during the developmental period. These students typically require special education support that usually occurs along a continuum of educational placement from the special education classroom to inclusion in a general education classroom with ongoing consultation from a special education teacher. In addition to difficulties in intellectual and adaptive functioning, as many as 20% of these students exhibit challenging behavior (Marchand, Nelson, Marchand-Martella, & O'Reilly, 2012). Challenging behavior is behavior of such intensity or frequency that the safety of the student or fellow students is placed in jeopardy. Challenging behavior can take the form of aggressive outbursts (hitting, screaming, kicking), property destruction (breaking school property and instructional materials), and self-abuse (self-hitting, self-biting). Such behaviors are consistently ranked as one of the biggest problems facing the public schools in the United States (Bushaw & Lopez, 2010).

What We Know

A significant amount of empirical research has been conducted, and the clinical protocol for assessing and treating challenging behavior with this population of students is well established. For comprehensive reviews of the empirical literature on the assessment and treatment of aggression and self-abuse with this population, please study the following: Iwata et al. (1994), Kahng and Iwata (2002), and Matson, Dixon, and Matson (2005). In this chapter we will present the core set of clinical assessment and treatment protocol to be used when a child with such disabilities is referred within the school system. For a comprehensive yet accessible manual on how to assess and treat such behaviors, please see Carr, Levin, McConnachie, Carlson, Kemp, and Smith (1998).

What We Can Do

A Model for Understanding Challenging Behavior

The assessment and treatment protocol outlined below are premised on a particular understanding of the nature of challenging behavior exhibited by individuals with intellectual disability. We believe that challenging behavior is best understood by a comprehensive examination of the context in which it occurs. We are not as much interested in "what" the child does but rather "why" the child is doing it. By understanding the context in which such behavior occurs, we may begin to understand why the child engages in challenging behavior. This model is presented in schematic form in Figure 16.1. We will briefly describe each component of the model here and further elucidate these components as we proceed through the chapter.

Setting events are bio-behavioral or social/ecological events or conditions that predispose the

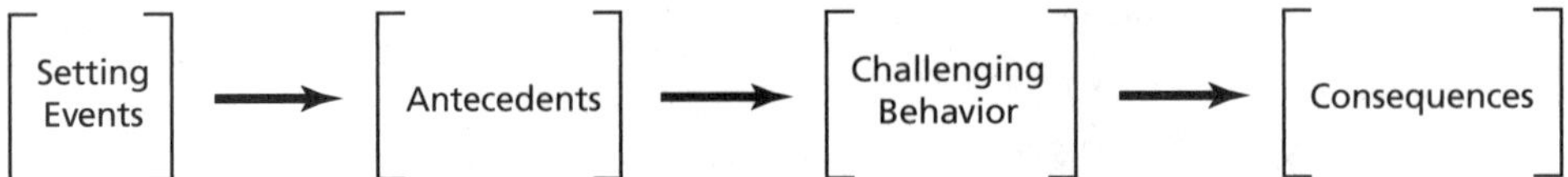

Figure 16.1. A Model for Understanding Challenging Behavior

student to challenging behavior. For example, certain diagnoses may be associated with high levels of challenging behavior under particular contexts. Children with autism, for example, can exhibit extreme levels of aggression and self-injury when there is a change in everyday routines. Routine illnesses among children, such as inner ear infections, can also be associated with increased levels of challenging behavior. Social/ecological conditions describe the influence of environmental factors (e.g., overcrowded classroom, negative social interactions with peers or staff) that can exacerbate challenging behavior. Setting events in themselves do not cause challenging behavior, but they may predispose the student to be grumpy at a given point in time.

Antecedent conditions are those interactions that spark the challenging behavior. Examples of antecedent conditions might be the presentation of a difficult academic task by the teacher or low levels of teacher attention. Antecedent conditions are those interactions that happen immediately prior to the challenging behavior. Antecedent conditions are more likely to evoke challenging behavior for the student if setting events have occurred prior.

Challenging behaviors typically produce some predictable reaction by others such as caregivers, teachers, and fellow students. Some of the typical reactions include removal of instructional materials, removal from a current environment, attention from others in the form of reprimands, restraint, or concerned statements. These social consequences for challenging behavior can be collapsed into two major categories—behaviors that produce escape from situations or people and behaviors that produce attention from others. Researchers have demonstrated that students often use challenging behavior as a form of communication to escape from situations or to access attention from others.

Assessment of Challenging Behavior

A thorough assessment of challenging behavior is necessary prior to putting any interventions in place. In fact the assessment results will dictate the nature of the intervention. In this section we will go through the essential protocols for assessing challenging behavior. These assessment protocols are derived from our model of understanding challenging behavior that was presented in the previous section. There are four essential steps to assessment: identify the challenging behavior, identify when the behavior occurs during the school day, identify any setting events for the challenging behavior, and identify what occurs in the school environment when the student engages in challenging behavior.

Step 1: Identify the Challenging Behavior

At face value this may seem a very easy task. However, challenging behavior is typically described in emotive terms and as personality traits (e.g., "She likes to hurt other students. He is a very stubborn child. He is aggressive"). These initial descriptions are ultimately unhelpful to the assessment process. In our example, the teacher reports that Manuel seems to get upset in class and abuses himself. Such descriptions must be translated into observable behaviors that the teacher perceives to be challenging. You can lead this discussion with the teacher by asking such questions as: "When you say he is abusive (aggressive), can you tell me what he does?" or "What does she do to hurt herself (other children)?" In other words, you must translate the initial descriptions of the student's difficulties into a description of observable behaviors.

This is an essential step in the assessment process for several reasons. First, it clarifies to all stakeholders (that is, the social worker, teacher, parent) the precise nature of the behavior to be changed. If stakeholders disagree with the focus of treatment, then new target behaviors may be selected and unnecessary interventions may be forestalled. Second, it allows for ongoing evaluation of challenging behavior during the intervention process. If desired change is not occurring, then the intervention can be altered.

There are three general guidelines for developing a clear description of challenging behavior.

1. The description should be objective, referring only to observable characteristics of the behavior and translating any inferential terms into more objective ones.
2. The description should be clear and unambiguous so that others could read the description and observe the behavior accurately.
3. The description should be complete, delineating the boundaries of what is to be included as an instance of challenging behavior and what is to be excluded.

An example of a clear description of challenging behavior arising from the statement "This student is aggressive" might be "Striking other students in a forceful manner with an open hand or closed fist, but excluding touching students with tips of fingers or with an open hand in a gentle manner." This description identifies challenging behaviors in objective terms and delineates examples of behavior to be included and excluded. Consider the following descriptions adapted from Iwata et al. (1994, p. 219), which provide clear descriptions of challenging behaviors:

- Head banging: Audible or forceful contact of the head against a stationary object.
- Biting: Closure of upper and lower teeth on any part of the body.
- Scratching: Raking the skin with fingernails or rubbing against objects.
- Pinching: Forceful grasping of skin between fingers.
- Hair pulling: Closure of fingers on hair with a pulling motion.

For our case study we defined Manuel's self-abuse as "hitting his head with a closed fist." We have moved from the global term *self-abuse* to very specific and observable behavior. Once there is agreement between all stakeholders on a description of the student's challenging behavior the next step is to begin to measure the behavior.

Step 2: Identify When the Behavior Occurs During the School Day

In this phase of the assessment process, we want to identify the times during the day when the behavior occurs. Equally important, we want to identify those times of day when the behavior does not occur, as this may provide clues for developing effective interventions. The scatterplot assessment method is probably the easiest method to use for this purpose. We find that teachers have little difficulty using this instrument with minimal instruction from a consultant. This assessment instrument provides information regarding the temporal distribution of the challenging behavior throughout the school day. Once we identify those time periods when the behavior occurs, we can then use more detailed assessment instruments to clarify the antecedents and consequences maintaining challenging behavior during those time periods (see steps 3 and 4 below).

The first step in conducting a scatterplot is to design a grid with time periods on the vertical axis and days on the horizontal axis. See Figure 16.2 for an example of a scatterplot grid. The time intervals used should suit the context. For example, you can design the intervals around a structured curriculum with each interval representing a new lesson or new activity as shown in Figure 16.2. You could also break the day into specific time segments (e.g., 15 min, 30 min, etc.) according to the exigencies of the situation. You can see from the example in Figure 16.2 that the school day (total of 3 hours) is broken into nine segments. Each of these segments represents a distinct curricular activity, and each activity lasts for 20 min. Next a decision needs to be made with regard to how to record the challenging behavior. The scatterplot technique does not require that you record the exact frequency of occurrence of challenging behavior during each time interval. Instead, a more general recording procedure can be used. In Figure 16.2 we have decided to leave the interval empty when no behavior occurs, to place a "\" when one instance of the behavior occurs, and to shade the interval in black if more than one instance of the challenging behavior occurs during that time interval.

You can see from the results of the scatterplot in the figure that Manuel's challenging behavior seems to display a particular pattern. He tends to hit his head when he is engaged in demand or academic-type tasks. Also, his behavior seems to be a lot more severe on Monday and Wednesday during our assessment. Thus the teacher will focus further assessments of Manuel's behavior during those academic periods of the curriculum when Manuel's behavior is most problematic. We will also want to explore why his behavior is more severe on some days than on others.

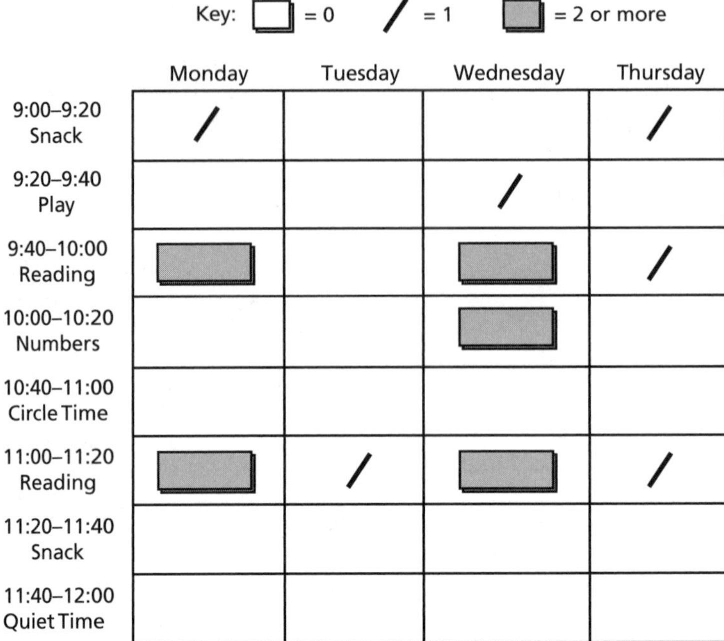

Figure 16.2. Student: Manuel. Challenging Behavior: Hitting His Head with a Closed Fist

Step 3: Identify Any Setting Events for the Challenging Behavior

As described earlier in our model for understanding challenging behavior, setting events are environmental or health conditions that influence the probability or intensity of challenging behavior. Setting events can be idiosyncratic. If the results of a scatterplot assessment demonstrate large variability in challenging behavior within or across days, then it is very important to explore the influence of setting events. In our case example we saw that Manuel engaged in a lot of challenging behavior on some days but not on others. It is best to interview parents and the teacher with regard to the influence of setting events. Using the scatterplot as a springboard for such interviews can be helpful. There is no single interview format available that can tap all possible setting events. We recommend that you explore the influence of the following possibilities: prior negative social interactions, rushed through routines, changes in routines, significant others absent, major changes in living environment, changes in medication, bad mood, illness, and so on. We interviewed Manuel's mother and teacher with regard to setting events. We found that Manuel did not sleep very well on Sunday or Tuesday nights. The severe levels of challenging behavior on Monday and Wednesday might be related to the possibility that Manuel was sleep deprived on those days. Of course sleep deprivation does not explain why he engages in challenging behavior at certain periods of time during the day and not at others. To examine this issue we need to conduct our final step of the assessment process.

Step 4: Identify What Occurs in the School Environment When the Student Engages in the Challenging Behavior

During this phase of the assessment we focus on those periods of time during the day when challenging behavior is most likely. An Antecedent-Behavior-Consequence (ABC) assessment is used to identify what happened immediately before and after each occurrence of challenging behavior. We recommend that an ABC assessment be conducted for approximately 5 school days. A consultant and not the teacher should conduct this assessment, as it is not possible for a teacher to continue with normal duties and accurately implement the ABC. ABC results should provide a reasonably comprehensive picture of the immediate environmental conditions

What Happened Before the Behavior	*Target Behavior*	*What Happened after the Behavior*
Teacher says. "What word is this Manuel?"	✔	Teacher moves away and asks another student
Teacher points to letter and asks, "What letter is this Manuel?"	✔	Teacher moves on to a different topic with the class
Teacher asks Manuel to open his book	✔	Teacher does not persist but moves on to another student

Figure 16.3. Child: Manuel. Date and Time of Observation: April 4, 2004, 9:20–11:20

influencing challenging behavior. Essentially, the ABC assessment is designed to examine those immediate antecedent conditions that spark or evoke the challenging behavior as well as those consequences that follow the behavior. As mentioned in our model for understanding challenging behavior, children with intellectual disability typically engage in challenging behavior for two major consequences—escape a situation or gain attention from another person. So in this phase of the assessment we are trying to identify the antecedent conditions for the challenging behavior and the consequences that occur in the environment when challenging behavior occurs.

To implement an ABC assessment the consultant continuously observes the student during those time periods when challenging behavior is most problematic (these time periods have been identified by the scatterplot assessment). In our example, the consultant will observe Manuel from 9:40 a.m. to 10:20 a.m. and from 11:00 a.m. to 11:20 a.m. for five consecutive days. The consultant will use a data collection sheet similar to the one presented in Figure 16.3. The target behavior, identified in Step 1 of the assessment, is presented in the middle column. Each time the target behavior occurs, a check mark is placed in the target behavior box. The consultant then describes what happened immediately prior to the behavior. In the final column the consultant describes what people did in response to the student's behavior. Three incidents of the target behavior are included in Figure 16.3. You can see from this example that the level of detail requires significant effort on the part of those conducting the assessment. This is why we suggest that a consultant with expertise in conducting such assessments is recruited for this task. We can see from our example that Manuel engaged in head hitting immediately following an instruction from the teacher. When Manuel hits his head, the teacher withdraws the task. We can infer from the results of this assessment that Manuel's challenging behavior is motivated by escape from instructional activities. The results of our setting event assessment would indicate that when he is tired he is more likely to find instructional activities aversive and he therefore engages in more severe challenging behavior when sleep deprived. We will discuss strategies that the teacher can use to decrease such behavior in the next section.

Of course not all assessments produce such clear results as the example that we have presented here in this chapter. Sometimes it can be difficult to interpret the results of these assessments. Unclear results can occur when the student's behavior is motivated by many consequences such as escape and attention or when some unknown factor is influencing the child's behavior. In such cases a more intensive functional analysis may need to be conducted. A functional analysis would require a consultation with a professional who has expertise in behavior analysis. The process of conducting a functional analysis is beyond the scope of this chapter (see Marchand et al., 2011, for a description of how to conduct a functional analysis).

Interventions Based on the Results of the Assessment

The specific intervention selected for a student will be derived from the results of the assessment process outlined in the previous section. Interventions can be highly idiosyncratic depending on the specific setting events that exacerbate challenging behavior, the antecedent conditions that spark such behavior, and the consequences that are produced as a result of this behavior. Other factors are also important to consider, such as student–teacher ratios, level of knowledge of the teacher, and motivation of teaching staff. In this section we will describe general guidelines for intervention selection. These guidelines are inextricably linked to the results of the prior assessment. We will discuss interventions for setting events and attention-motivated and escape-motivated challenging behavior.

Arranging positive consequences for appropriate behavior and eliminating positive consequences for challenging behavior is an important part of any intervention. In addition, other types of corrective consequences may also be necessary. Negative feedback can help the student to learn what is right and what is wrong. In selecting consequences, it is important to consider the use of natural consequences that provide feedback without special intervention. For example, when a child rips up his coloring book, the natural consequence is that he no longer has a coloring book to use. Similarly, when a child spills her juice on the floor, the natural consequence is that she no longer has any juice to drink.

Interventions for Setting Events

As described in our model for understanding challenging behavior, setting events can be divided into two generic categories—social/ecological and bio-behavioral. Social/ecological conditions can include environmental conditions (e.g., cold classroom, cramped environment, low academic stimulation) or interactions with individuals (e.g., disliked teacher's aide, being bullied). Cultural factors may also come into play in such circumstances. For example, if the language in the home is not English, then the student will have difficulties understanding instructions in the classroom. Understandably, such circumstances may evoke challenging behavior on the part of the student. It may be possible to remove or reduce such conditions. For example, the curriculum might be made more stimulating, a more pleasant classroom setting might be arranged, and interactions between the student with challenging behavior and a disliked aide might be minimized. Attempts to include or increase instruction in the child's home language might be attempted by the school. In some circumstances, even when the ecological/social setting event is identified it cannot be eliminated. For example, the student may not like the teacher, but we cannot change the teacher. In such circumstances it may be necessary to focus on alternative strategies, such as teaching communication skills and enriching the current environment to manage challenging behavior.

The second broad category, bio-behavioral setting events, can be subdivided into two conditions: a permanent or temporary influence. An example of a permanent condition would be the medical and behavioral predispositions that accompany various genetic syndromes. For example, students with Williams syndrome often display hypersensitivity to everyday sounds such as those from a vacuum cleaner or lawnmower. This sensitivity can produce aggressive behavior. Students with Prader-Willi syndrome have difficulty controlling their eating patterns and may engage in aggression when denied access to food. The impact of such genetic predispositions can be minimized by altering environmental arrangements or by direct medical monitoring and intervention.

Other bio-behavioral setting events may be temporary in nature. Conditions such as allergies, ear infections, and sleep disturbance are more common among children with intellectual disability than the typical population. Such conditions may predispose students to engage in challenging behavior. These temporary bio-behavioral conditions can be treated directly (through medical/psychological intervention). Additionally, when such conditions are present, it may be advisable to eliminate or at least reduce those immediate antecedents that spark the challenging behavior during the school day. In our case example we saw that sleep disturbance might be influencing Manuel's challenging behavior. A number of strategies might be suggested in this case. A consultation may be suggested for the home to examine his bedtime routine and make suggestions to facilitate better sleep patterns. Following a night of disturbed sleep the curriculum could be modified so that Manuel is exposed to fewer academic requests on those particular days.

Interventions for Attention-Motivated Challenging Behavior

In our model for understanding challenging behavior we noted that many challenging behaviors result in or gain attention from others. That is, the consequence that maintains behavior is attention. Challenging behaviors may emerge as a means of getting attention if the person's repertoire contains few alternative responses that are effective in recruiting attention. In some situations the student's behavior may occur to gain access to items (e.g., toys, food, etc.). The intervention strategies described below would be similar for behavior that is maintained by tangible items as well as attention. We recommend that teachers use all of these techniques in combination when dealing with attention-maintained challenging behavior.

When attention is the maintaining consequence for challenging behavior one way to decrease the behavior is to *increase the overall amount of attention* that the student receives. For example, the teacher could set a kitchen timer at varying intervals of time (e.g., 30 s, 60 s) and when the timer goes off the student receives 10–20 s of positive attention. As the student starts to receive more attention than usual there is likely to be less need for that person to engage in attention-motivated challenging behavior. A variation of this strategy is to *provide attention to the student when challenging behavior is absent*. As the student learns that attention is received without having to resort to challenging behavior, then this behavior is less likely to occur. Along with attention for appropriate behavior, the teacher should *ignore challenging behavior as much as possible*. If the behavior must be attended to, then it should be done as matter-of-factly as possible. If the student has limited communication skills, then it is important to *teach more appropriate ways of gaining attention*. For example, the student might be taught to seek attention ("Will you sit with me?") so that others will come and spend time with them.

Interventions for Escape-Motivated Challenging Behavior

There are a number of interventions for escape-motivated challenging behavior. Teachers may want to use several of these strategies in combination when working with students who exhibit escape-maintained challenging behavior. If challenging behavior is reinforced by escape from nonpreferred activities, then the intervention plan should include some form of *reinforcement for increasing levels of participation*. Potential reinforcers might include praise (e.g., "Good job!"), access to preferred objects, and being allowed to take a break from task. In our example, the teacher could allow Manuel a break from instruction for 1 minute to play with a favorite toy after he correctly follows a direction. Over several weeks Manuel will be required to participate for longer periods of time before receiving a break. In this way the teacher can eventually increase participation and reduce challenging behavior. Another strategy is to *make sure that challenging behavior no longer produces escape from the task*. The teacher must be prepared to persist with instruction even if the challenging behavior escalates. In our example, when Manuel hits his head in response to a teacher direction, then the teacher must follow through with the task until Manuel completes it. In some cases challenging behavior occurs during demands because the demands are too difficult for the student to complete. In such cases *the task should be made easier by breaking it into smaller and more manageable steps or by teaching the student to request help in completing the task*. In our example, when the teacher makes an academic request of Manuel, she could immediately prompt him to ask for help. The teacher could then help Manuel to complete the task and gradually fade this assistance over time. In other cases the task presented may be less preferred than some other activities that may be available. In such a situation the teacher might *eliminate the unpreferred tasks (if possible) and introduce more preferred tasks for instruction*. Likewise, the teacher might also consider *reducing the amount of time spent on unpreferred tasks*. Manuel's teacher might consider reducing reading periods from 20 min to 10 min.

Applying Interventions within a Response to Intervention Framework

Schools are encouraged to use a proactive and preventive model of support that matches the services students receive with their level of need. Response to Intervention (RTI) is an initiative aimed at providing a high-quality continuum of instruction and interventions matched to student need and monitoring progress frequently to evaluate what changes need to be made for students to succeed (Marchand et al., 2011). The strategies outlined in this chapter to support students with severe challenging behavior fit naturally into an RTI framework. The assessment process is highly individualized, identifying antecedent and consequent events that evoke and reinforce challenging behavior. An individualized behavior support plan that removes or minimizes the negative impact of antecedent conditions and teaches alternative skills to the student is developed. Student progress is continuously monitored to evaluate the effectiveness and to change the behavior support plan if needed. In fact, we would go so far as to say that the strategies described in this chapter are a necessary component of RTI in order to provide appropriate supports to this population of students with severe disabilities.

Tools and Practice Examples

For a case study, see the above discussion of how to intervene with Manuel, a 6-year-old boy with a diagnosis of Down syndrome and severe intellectual disability. He attends a regular elementary school in a large urban area. In the mornings Manuel is included in the regular kindergarten class. He is the only student with a diagnosis of intellectual disability in this class of 20. Overall, he seems to be adapting well to the general education setting. However, his general education teacher reports that he has begun to engage in self-abuse in class. The teacher notes that Manuel's self-abuse is beginning to upset many of the other students. The teacher has requested help in dealing with Manuel's self-abuse during class. Steps are detailed on how to help Manual in the classroom setting.

Key Points to Remember

Approximately 5% of the student population is diagnosed with intellectual disability. Of this group, some 20% exhibit severe challenging behavior, such as self-abuse and aggression. Such behaviors typically require clinical assessment and intervention. We presented an empirically validated model of assessment and treatment of challenging behavior for students with intellectual disability. First, the behavior must be carefully defined in observable behavioral terms. Then the periods of time during the school day in which this behavior occurs are plotted. Next, bio-behavioral and ecological/social setting events are identified that may account for fluctuations in intensity or frequency of the behavior. The final part of thorough assessment is to identify the consequences that occur following the challenging behavior. Interventions, then, are multicomponent and are linked to the assessment results. Interventions typically involve some manipulation of setting events, modifications to the curriculum, and changes in how the teacher interacts with the student prior to and following challenging behavior.

References

Bushaw, W. J., & Lopez, S. J. (2010). A time for change: The 42nd annual Phi Delta Kappa/Gallup poll of the public's attitudes toward the public schools. *Kappan, 92*(1), 9–26.

Carr, E., Levin, L., McConnachie, G., Carlson, J., Kemp, D., & Smith, C. (1998). *Communication-based intervention for problem behavior: A user's guide for producing positive change.* Baltimore: Paul H. Brookes Publishing Company.

Iwata, B., Pace, G., Dorsey, M., Zarcone, J., Vollmer, T., Smith, R., Rodgers, T., Lerman, D., Shore, B., Mazaleski, J., Goh, H., Cowdery, G., Kalsher, M., McCosh, K., & Willis, K. (1994). The functions of self-injurious behavior: An experimental-epidemiological analysis. *Journal of Applied Behavior Analysis, 27*, 215–240.

Kahng, S., & Iwata, B. (2002). Behavioral treatment of self-injury, 1964 to 2000. *American Journal on Mental Retardation, 107*, 212–221.

Marchand, R., Nelson, R., Martella, N., & O'Reilly, M. (2012). *Comprehensive behavior management: Individualized, classroom, and school-wide approaches.* Boston, MA: Sage.

Matson, J., Dixon, D., & Matson, M. (2005). Assessing and treating aggression in children and adolescents with developmental disabilities: A 20-year overview. *Educational Psychology, 25*, 151–181.

Schalock, R., Borthwick-Duffy, S., Bradley, V., Buntix, W., Coulter, D., Craig, E., ... Yeager, M. (2010). Intellectual disability: Definition, classification, and systems of support (11th ed.). Washington DC: American Association on Intellectual and Developmental Disabilities.

CHAPTER 17

Improving the Self-Esteem and Social Skills of Students with Learning Disabilities

James C. Raines

Getting Started

Until the Education for All Handicapped Children's Act of 1975 (P.L. 94–142), students with learning disabilities were routinely unidentified (treated as "slow learners") or misidentified (treated as "mentally retarded"). Every mental health professional should be familiar with the federal definition of the term, which still relies on the conceptualization of Samuel Kirk (1962). "Specific learning disability" means:

> a disorder in one or more of the basic psychological processes involved in understanding or in using language, spoken or written, that may manifest itself in an imperfect ability to listen, think, speak, read, write, spell, or to do mathematical calculations, including conditions such as perceptual handicaps, brain injury, minimal brain dysfunction, dyslexia, and developmental aphasia.... The term does not include children who have learning problems that are primarily the result of visual, hearing, or motor handicaps, or mental retardation, or emotional disturbance, or of environmental, cultural, or economic disadvantage. (Assistance to the States, 1999, 34 C.F.R.§300.7(b)(10))

Thus, students with learning disabilities (LD) are a very heterogeneous group (Kavale & Forness, 1995). Since the passage of P.L. 94–142, reauthorized as the Individuals with Disabilities Education Act (IDEA) in 1990, the number of youth found to have learning disabilities has grown from 800,000 students in 1976–1977 to nearly 2.9 million students in 2000–2001. Since 2001, however, the percentage of students diagnosed with a learning disability has steadily declined from 6.1% to 5.2% in 2008, a decrease of 300,000 students (Samuels, 2010). This figure accounts for 50% of all students receiving special education services and is the most common disability across all racial/ethnic groups. Students with learning disabilities have a high school graduation rate of 62.1% compared to 88% for their nondisabled peers (U.S. Dept. of Education, 2002). Furthermore, children do not simply "grow out of" learning disabilities. Their problems continue into adulthood and affect their ability to adapt and achieve in the workplace (Gerber, 2001).

The two primary mental health concerns about students with learning disabilities have been in the related areas of self-concept and social skills. Self-concept is a multidimensional construct that includes a person's perception of him/herself across several categories: academic, emotional, physical, social, and global (Harter, 1999). Social skills are a heterogeneous set of competencies that include initiating, maintaining, repairing, and ending a variety of social relationships. Regardless of the mental health problem faced by a person with learning disabilities, practitioners will want to determine how this student learns best and adapt their interventions accordingly. This chapter will first review the research support for interventions in these two areas, focusing first on general principles and secondly on specific interventions.

What We Know

Research Support for Interventions

The literature on learning disabilities/differences has, however, continued to grow exponentially. PsycINFO lists over 22,000 articles, Medline lists over 10,000 entries, ERIC lists over 21,000 resources, and Social Work Abstracts contains nearly 200 references. Thus, even a conservative estimate would put the combined total at over 50,000 articles.

Fortunately, there have been 115 meta-analyses that have systematically collected, culled, and compared the vast literature to date. Not all meta-analyses have the same methodological rigor, and readers are encouraged to see Swanson's (1996) list of criteria for evaluating syntheses of the research literature. This review will summarize the most pertinent meta-analyses and infer some general principles from them (see Table 17.1).

General Principles

- Learning disabilities place children at greater risk for some self-esteem and social skills deficits, but these are not universal problems, so screening is important.
- Different informants see different aspects of the problem, so it is important to triangulate both baseline and outcome measures by collecting data from teachers, parents, peers, and/or students with LD.
- There is no single cause for self-concept or social skills problems seen in students with LD. Clinicians should assess each student's dynamics individually.
- Students with LD may be more aware of social skills deficits than self-esteem problems. They may be oblivious about their "social self."
- Students who compare themselves with average or high-achieving peers may be at special risk for self-esteem issues.
- There appear to be different cultural meanings about the "LD" label, thus terms like "LD" and "special ed" should be explored with each family.
- Social skills training may improve students' self-concepts more than their social competence as rated by others in the environment.
- Elementary students' self-esteem will benefit most from academic interventions rather than counseling. Strategy instruction and small group instruction are helpful.
- Middle school students' self-esteem will benefit most from counseling interventions. High school students may benefit from counseling.
- Collateral interventions are especially helpful in improved social self-concepts.
- Optimal duration of social skills training is about 10 weeks. Mixed gender groups may be best.

What We Can Do

Best Practices

In order to identify best practices, three methods were used. First, the four databases above were searched for specific programs that have passed methodological rigor. Roans and Hoagwood (2000) define well-established treatments as those subjected to rigorous testing involving (1) a control group (including no-treatment groups, comparative treatment groups, or multiple baseline methods); (2) standardized outcome measures; and (3) outcomes assessed at baseline and postintervention and at (3–, 6–, or 12–month) follow-up. For example, PsycInfo was searched using the following combinations of terms: (learning differences, learning disabilities, or learning disabled) AND (counseling, intervention, program, therapy, training, or treatment) AND (clinical trial, comparative, control group, experiment controls, experimental design, multiple baseline, quasi-experimental, or random sampling) AND ((self-concept, self-esteem, or self-perception) OR (social adjustment, social skills, or social competence)). Second, citations were gleaned from the intervention meta-analyses for those studies that had a large effect size (ES >.80; Cohen, 1988). Finally, recent issues of core journals were hand searched, including *Exceptional Children, Journal of Learning Disabilities, Journal of Special Education, Learning Disability Quarterly,* and *Learning Disabilities Research and Practice.* This process resulted in many promising articles, which were then read to determine which ones possessed a "goodness of fit" with the general principles drawn from the meta-analyses above as well as the seven criteria for systematic eclecticism proposed by Hepworth, Rooney, and Larsen (2002) that techniques should be empirical, efficient, specific, and ethical; use generalist skills; be culturally sensitive; and have a person-in-environment perspective. A final criterion was that the technique be *practical* in a regular education school with no expensive equipment. For a methodological summary of the studies chosen, see Table 17.2. Posttreatment effect size was calculated for studies that included

Table 17.1 Meta-Analyses Regarding Self-Concept or Social Skills of Students with LD

Study	*Problem*	*Sample*	*Results*
Bear, Minke, & Manning (2002)	Self-concepts	61 studies 1986–2000	Students with LD exhibit slightly lower global self-esteem (ES = -.18) than non-LD students and moderately lower intellectual self-esteem (ES = -.66). LD students in inclusive classrooms and resource rooms have lower intellectual self-esteem than LD students in self-contained classrooms.
Elbaum (2002)	Self-concepts across placements	38 studies 1975–1999	There were no significant differences in self-concepts across placements, except that students in self-contained classrooms had moderately lower self-concepts than those in special schools (ES = – .38).
Elbaum & Vaughn (2003)	Self-concept interventions	15 studies 1975–1997	Students w/LD have wide variations in their general self-concept. Students with the lowest self-concept at pretest improved three times as much as their average or high self-concept peers. Young adolescents were more responsive to interventions than either children or older adolescents.
Elbaum & Vaughn (2001)	Self-concept of interventions	64 studies 1975–1997	Average effects were low (ES = .19) across all age groups. Median intervention lasted 10 weeks. Elementary students benefited most from academic interventions. Middle and high school students benefited most from counseling interventions. Collateral interventions made the only impact on students' social self-concept.
Forness & Kavale (1996)	Social skills interventions	53 studies 1980–1994	Average effects were low (ES = .21) across all age groups. Average intervention was 3 hours/ week over 10 weeks. Longer training was not better than brief training. Training improved self-assessment of social status, peers' assessment of communication skills, and teachers' assessment of school adjustment.
Kavale & Forness (1996)	Social skills deficits	152 studies (1980–1994)	Students w/LD demonstrate more social skills deficits (ES = .65) than their non-LD peers. Students with LD rate themselves slightly lower than peers or teachers. Teachers rated students w/LD lowest on academic competence and social interaction. Peers rated students with LD lowest on acceptance. Self-ratings showed lower academic competence, nonverbal communication ability, and social problem solving.
Kavale & Mostert (2004)	Social Skills Interventions	53 studies 1994–2002	Students with LD who receive social skills training receive a small benefit (ES = .211) and improve more than 58% of students with LD who do not receive social skills training.
Ochoa & Olivarez (1995)	Peer ratings	17 studies 1978–1991	Students w/LD have much lower social status than non-LD peers (ES = -.69). Opposite-sex raters were more accepting than same-sex raters.

(continued)

Table 17.1 *(Continued)*

Study	*Problem*	*Sample*	*Results*
Nowicki (2003)	Social competence	32 studies 1990–2000	Students w/LD or low academic achievement are at greater risk for social difficulties than average or high-achieving peers. Students w/ LD or low academic achievement lack accurate self-perceptions of their social acceptance.
Prout, Marcal, & Marcal (1992)	Self-reported problems	34 studies 1966–1990	Students w/LD have moderately lower self-esteem than non-LD peers (ES = .68), more anxiety (ES = .59), and more academic concerns (ES = .71).
Swanson (2001)	Academic interventions for adolescents	58 studies 1963–1997	Adolescents benefit from higher order processing interventions (ES = .82) such as extended practice with feedback, learning new skills, and advance organization of the material. High-discrepancy learners improved less than low-discrepancy learners. Ideas about self-efficacy, effort, and ability were hardest to change.
Swanson & Hoskyn (1998)	Academic interventions	180 studies 1963–1997	Students w/LD generally benefit from intervention (ES = .79). A combined model that uses direct instruction with strategic instruction worked best. Components that helped most included strategy modeling, skill demonstration, and use of small-group instruction. Effects on students' self-concept (ES = .39) and social skills (ES = .41) were low.
Swanson & Malone (1992)	Social skills deficits	117 studies 1974–1990	Students w/LD have lower social acceptance (ES = -.79) and social problem solving (ES = -.80) than their non-LD peers. White students are at higher risk for social rejection than Black students. Students with LD had more problems with nonverbal sensitivity, friendship formation, and conflict resolution.
Zeleke (2004)	Self-concepts (academic, social & general)	41 studies 1987–2003	Students with LD exhibit lower academic self-concepts than non-LD students. Only students with both LD and behavior disorders had lower social self-concepts than non-LD students. Students with LD showed no difference in their general self-concept.

means and standard deviations; otherwise, probability values are provided.

Screening

Because group design studies can only describe groups, not individuals, screening should be done to ensure that those who do not need socioemotional help are not pulled out of academic classes. There are three self-concept scales that surpass the rest in terms of being psychometrically sound. These multidimensional and culturally sensitive scales are the Self-Perception Profile for Children (Harter, 1985), the Self-Description Questionnaire (SDQ-I), and the Perception of Ability Scale for

Table 17.2 Articles Regarding Self-Concept or Social Skills

Study	*Sample*	*Measures*	*Intervention*	*Effect size/ Probability*
Fuchs, Fuchs, Mathes, & Martinez (2002)	156 children, grades 2–6 at 12 Nashville, TN elementary schools	How I Feel Toward Others (Peer rating scale; Agard et al., 1978)	Classroom-wide peer-tutoring program	ES = 1.32
Kuzell, Brassington, & Mahoney (1988)	48 children, ages 7–12 in 3 Ottawa, ON school districts	Psycho-Social Competence Incomplete Stories Test (Mondel, 1980)	Weekly parent education group	p <.025
Lenkowsky, Barowsky, Daybock, Puccio, & Lenkowsky (1987)	96 children, ages 12–14 in 1 New York NY special ed. school	Piers-Harris, Children's Self-concept Scale (1969)	Classroom bibliotherapy combined with group debriefing	1. ES = 1.87 2. ES = 1.80 3. ES = 0.59
Utay & Lampe (1995)	66 children, grades 3–6 in 1 Dallas, TX private special ed. school	alker-McConnell Scale of social competence and school adjustment (1988)	Cognitive-behavioral social skills game used in a small group	1. p <.05 2. p <.05

Students (PASS; Marsh, 1990). Likewise, there are two social skills scales that are psychometrically valid, multidimensional, and culturally sensitive. These are the Social Skills Rating System (SSRS), recently renamed the Social Skills Improvement System (SSIS) and the Interpersonal Competence Scale (ICQ; Buhrmester, Furman, Wittenberg, & Reis, 1988). The Tools and Practice Examples section of this chapter provides lists of the availability and grade level of each scale.

For those practitioners who cannot afford or do not have the proper training to use such scales, they may try scaled questions, such as: "On a scale from 1–10 (1 being the lowest and 10 the highest), how do your feel about yourself in each of the following areas: academic, emotional, physical, social, and overall?" (Sklare, 1997). Another option for students who have difficulty admitting any needs is to have them rank order how they are functioning, for example: "Relationships take a lot of work. Can you rank order (1 being the hardest and 4 being the easiest), which areas of relating to others you find hardest? (e.g., starting, keeping, fixing, and ending relationships)?"

Self-Esteem Interventions

The most effective interventions are ones aimed at the children and their nurturing environment. The first one addresses elementary age children and the second deals with adolescents.

Interventions with Parents

Kuzell, Brassington, and Mahoney (1988) found that a 10-week parenting course was effective in improving the self-esteem of preadolescent children with LD both at the end of the course as well as a year later. The goals of the course include: (1) teaching general parenting skills; (2) exploring how to adapt these skills for children with LD; (3) providing current information on how parents can improve their child's social and daily living skills; and (4) giving parents the chance to share their experiences in a supportive environment. Materials include both a leader's manual and parents' manual (Kuzell & Brassington, 1985). The authors recommend using two co-leaders with the following qualifications: motivation to lead, an understanding of learning disabilities, teaching skills, and knowledge of basic parenting techniques. They also recommend that leaders present the proposal to the following constituencies before implementation: school administrators, related service personnel (i.e., school social workers, psychologists, and special educators), and the parent association to elicit suggestions before beginning the group. Participation by 8–10 families is optimal, so that the larger group can be broken into two subgroups for skills practice. The example in Box 17.1 shows how this can occur.

The group should be held in a central location with convenient parking, a comfortable room (e.g., the teachers' lounge), refreshments, a phone, and nearby washrooms. The course is designed to last 2.5 hours one night/week for 10 consecutive weeks. Ideal seasons to offer the group include September to November or January to March because of the lack of holiday interruptions. Ideal nights are Mondays or Tuesdays so that routine weekdays follow during which to practice the skills learned in the course. A flyer should contain information about sponsors, goals, leaders, time, place, cost, and registration procedures. Each week the course includes multisensory teaching about learning disabilities, some practical parenting concepts, and opportunities for parents to practice these skills in small groups. The course outline shown in Table 17.3 is supplemented by newer readings, since the authors' original book is now out-of-print. The Learning Disabilities Council (2002) also publishes a parent workbook.

Direct Interventions

Lenkowsky et al. (1987) found that bibliotherapy in classroom groups was effective for middle school children (ages 12–14) with learning disabilities. Bibliotherapy involves students in reading a story, identifying with a character, experiencing catharsis, and gaining new insight about their problem (Pardeck, 1998). This approach is especially appealing because it connects an academic means (reading) to a therapeutic end (self-esteem). The students read three age-appropriate books (e.g., Albert, 1976; Swarthout & Swarthout, 1975) about other children with learning difficulties in a "literature" class that met three times per week. They also participated in a weekly discussion group that addressed the feelings, mutual experiences, and school-related problems reflected in the books. This intervention involves collaboration between teachers, practitioners, and the school librarian to create a viable program (Lynn, McKay, & Atkins, 2003). Language arts teachers should ensure that state reading standards are met, practitioners can facilitate the group discussions, and librarians can help determine which books are currently in print and available at a group discount. For students with reading difficulties, it may be best to choose a story that is also available on audiotape. It is important to select age-appropriate books that reflect problems similar to the ones faced by the students. The Tools and Practice Examples section of this chapter provides a grade-level list of recommended bibliotherapy books for students with LD.

Box 17.1 Identifying Strengths in the Student With LD

Preparation: Cook two pizzas with eight different toppings in separate quarters ahead of time (e.g., cheese, sausage, pepperoni, mushroom, olives, spinach, onions, and peppers).

Opening: Ask parents to define the word *pizza*. Ask if there are different kinds of pizza that all qualify under the definition. Ask if they have a favorite type of pizza. Now ask the parents to define the word *smart*. Ask if there are different kinds of smart that all qualify under the definition. Ask if they have a favorite way to learn.

Teaching: Share with the group the basics of multiple intelligences theory (Gardner, 1999), including his definition of an intelligence, the eight intelligences, their aptitudes, and their educational needs (Raines, 2003). Be sure to use visual aids and examples of each one. Armstrong (2000) has a wonderful list of prominent individuals from minority cultures that exemplify each intelligence.

Practicing: In small groups, enable parents to identify which intelligences apply to their children using Armstrong's "Checklist for Assessing Students' Multiple Intelligences" (pp. 24–27). Based on the results, empower parents to identify which tools are needed to help their children learn best. Have parents think of a recent homework assignment and how it could be adapted to fit the strengths of each child. Encourage feedback between parents about their ideas.

Table 17.3 Outline for a Parents' Group

Week	*Content*	*New Resources*
Week 1	Expectations; Philosophy of Course; Group Responsibilities; Introductions	
Week 2	Definition: Learning Disabilities Labeling: Pros and Cons Stages of Acceptance	See definition in text Sternberg & Grigorenko (1999) Higgins et al. (2002)
Week 3	Development and the Child with LD Encouragement of Strengths	Dane (1990) Raines (2003)
Week 4	Structuring the Environment Family Constellation	Cooper & Nye (1994) Dane (1990)
Week 5	Purposes of Behavior Home Activities for Specific Learning Disabilities	Raines (2002) Adelizzi & Goss (2001) Bryan et al. (2001)
Week 6	Communication Skills: Recognizing Feelings & Reflective Listening Social Skills Deficits: Nonverbal	Learning Disabilities Council (2002) Elksnin & Elksnin (2000)
Week 7	Communication Skills: "I" Messages Social Skill Deficits: Verbal	
Week 8	Problem-Solving Steps Applications to Social Situations Consequences for Children with LD	Gammon & Rose (1991) Learning Disabilities Council (2002)
Week 9	Values Clarification Family Council	
Week 10	Using Resources	Adelizzi & Goss (2001)

Sridhar and Vaughn (2002) provide a list of sample questions to be asked before, during, and after reading Polacco's (1998) story. Before reading the book, students are given a brief introduction (from the book's preface) and asked to make hypotheses about the book and the outcome of the story. During the story, students are asked to paraphrase the plot and infer the emotions of the lead characters. After reading the book, students retell the story, recount similar personal experiences, and generate possible solutions to problems shared.

Direct Interventions

Mishna, Muskat, and Wiener (2010) conducted a qualitative evaluation of a support group for students with LD in grades 6–8 for 12 60-minute sessions. The support group had three goals: (1) improve students' understanding of LD, (2) identify their learning strengths and weaknesses, and (3) increase their ability to self-advocate for their needs. Most students reported improvement in their academic self-esteem. Several students were especially surprised that some successful people, like celebrities, had an LD. For a list of topics covered by the current version of Integra's group work manual, see Table 17.4.

Social Skills Interventions

There are two kinds of social behavior problems that may need intervention. Skills deficits refer to a lack of learned behaviors. Performance deficits refer to a lack of motivation to employ skills already learned (Kavale & Mostert, 2004). For social skills deficits, intervention should be aimed at the students. For social performance deficits, intervention should be aimed at parents and teachers who have the ability to cue, shape, and reinforce the execution of social skills. Thus, interventions for social skills can be done both directly and indirectly. Direct interventions aim at the student with LD while indirect interventions aim at changing others in their environment.

Table 17.4 Social Support Group for Students with LD

Session 1	Introductions and orientation to the group
Session 2	What is a learning disability?
Session 3	What are my strengths and interests?
Session 4	What are my learning disabilities?
Session 5	What helps me to learn best?
Session 6	How do I stand up for myself?
Session 7	Practicing what to do if bullied
Session 8	Learning to ask for help with homework
Session 9	Learning to calm down and relax
Session 10	Practicing relaxing and problem-solving

Direct Interventions

Utay and Lampe (1995) found that the Social Skills Game, a cognitive-behavioral group play therapy by Berg, was effective in improving the peer-related social skills and academic-related skills of students with LD. They used the game with two groups of children in grades 3–4 and grades 5–6 for 50-minute sessions over 8 weeks. The game is designed to be used for children ages 8 and up. It includes three inventories to identify the students' specific skill deficits so that game cards can be preselected by the group therapist to address these problems. The cards address four social skill areas: (1) making friends; (2) responding positively to peers; (3) cooperating with peers; and (4) communicating needs. While the game can be played one-to-one, the authors felt that part of the effectiveness of the game was the group process itself. Because students with LD should spend the least amount of time possible away from core academic subjects, clinicians should consider running such groups before school, during recess or lunch, or after school. Use of a "game" may also help these students from feeling like they are missing out on the "fun" if the group is held during nonacademic times.

Interventions with Peers

Fuchs et al. (2002) found that Peer-Assisted Learning Strategies (PALS), a form of peer academic tutoring, improved the social acceptance and social standing of students with LD. This finding is especially interesting in light of Mastropieri et al.'s (2000) meta-analysis, which found that tutors generally gained more from tutoring by students with disabilities than the tutees. PALS creates 12–14 pairs of students in a classroom who work collaboratively on different learning activities, such as reading or math. It may be beneficial for the teachers to be careful not to pair students with similar learning disabilities. The class is also divided into two teams. Students earn points for their team by correct performance and good collaboration. PALS thus uses both competition and cooperation to motivate students. Teachers establish four classroom rules at the beginning: (1) talk only to your partner and only about PALS; (2) keep your voice low; (3) help your partner; and (4) try your best. The teacher gives direct instruction and clarifies understanding of each concept through a choral response (e.g., everyone, boys, or girls). Each member of the pair takes turns being either the Coach (tutor) or the Player (reader). The teacher first gives direct instructions to the Players (e.g., "M sounds like mmm ..."). The instructor then gives strategy hints to the Coaches (e.g., "Point to the letter and say, 'What sound?'") as well as appropriate praise statements (e.g., "You could say, 'good job!'").

There are four PALS reading activities. The first activity is *Partner Reading,* during which the higher performing student reads for 5 minutes and then the lower performing student rereads the same material. As the Player works on the material, the Coach provides strategy hints, for example, "Stop, you missed that word. Can you figure it out?" After both have read, the lower performing student gets two minutes to retell what has happened.

Students earn 1 point for each correctly read sentence and 10 points for the rehearsal. The second PALS activity is *Paragraph Shrinking,* during which the Player reads one paragraph at a time and tries to summarize the story in 10 words or less. If the Coach feels that they made an error, they give feedback, for example, "That's not quite right. Skim the paragraph and try again." Students earn 1 point for correctly identifying the most important idea and 1 point for stating it in 10 words or less. The third PALS activity is *Prediction Relay,* during which the Player makes a guess about what will be found in the next half page. If the Coach thinks the prediction is irrational, they can object, for example, "I don't agree. Think of something better." The Player then reads the half page aloud (with the Coach's help), confirms or contradicts the prediction, and summarizes the main point. Students earn 1 point for each reasonable prediction, 1 point for accurately confirming or contradicting the guess, and 1 point for summarization (Fuchs, Fuchs, & Burish, 2000). The final step is *Story Mapping,* where each pair combines with another pair. Each of the four students takes a turn being the leader, who identifies one part of the story (lead character, setting, problem, and result) and one major event in the story. Each leader must follow a pattern of (1) telling their answer, (2) asking group members their ideas, (3) leading discussion toward a consensus, (4) recording the group's answer on a story map, and (5) reporting the answer to the teacher. Finally, the teacher debriefs the group answers with the entire class. Each pair earns 10 points for collaborating, 2 points for each correct story part, and 1 point for each reasonable, but incorrect story part (Fuchs, Fuchs, Mathes, & Martinez, 2002). During each of these steps, the teacher roams around the class giving extra points for cooperative behavior and good tutoring.

PALS takes approximately 30 minutes three times per week. Most teachers use PALS to replace individual seatwork. Every four weeks, teachers change both pair and team assignments. Materials needed to implement PALS are minimal: teachers need an overhead projector, a folder for each pair, and a manual. Manuals help teachers partialize reading and math tasks and give strategy hints to coaches. The developers assume that beginning teachers will probably use the manual scripts verbatim while more experienced teachers will naturally paraphrase them. All teachers are encouraged to elaborate on the scripts if students do not seem to comprehend the concepts being taught. Students use their regular textbooks or library books. One-day training in PALS is arranged through PALS Outreach in Nashville, TN.

Applying Interventions within a Response to Intervention Framework

The rapid growth of learning disabilities directly led to the change in IDEA, allowing (but not requiring) school districts to use a Response to Intervention (RTI) model to identify children with LD (Raines, 2006). RTI has five essential steps. First, all students are provided with effective instruction with an appropriate curriculum in a supportive environment. Second, student progress is continually monitored to determine how well they are responding. Third, students who do not respond to universal instruction will be provided with evidence-based supplemental strategic interventions. Fourth, struggling students are monitored even more frequently. Finally, students who do not respond to both universal and strategic interventions will receive evidence-based intensive and/or individual interventions (Fuchs, Mock, Morgan, & Young, 2003).

Applying these five steps to the interventions mentioned above has several implications. First, all students with LD should be provided a supportive environment that is strengths-based and reframes the D in LD from "disabilities" to "differences." This helps students to both understand their differences and to advocate for instruction in ways that they learn best. The PALS program is an excellent example of a Tier 1 intervention. Second, it should never be assumed that all students with LD have self-esteem or social skills deficits. A brief screener should be able to identify students at risk for one or both of these problems. Third, those students who are at risk should be provided time-limited and/or group interventions *prior to* more intensive interventions. The parents' group, bibliotherapy group, and social support group are excellent examples of Tier 2 interventions. Fourth, progress monitoring should be a routine part of school-based services. Evidence-based programs inform practitioners only about what works for most students, not all students. This means that some students will not improve even with the most evidence-based programs, and a few students may even get worse. Finally, long-term intensive interventions should be reserved only for those students who do not respond to less invasive procedures. One-to-one use of the Social Skills Game is an excellent example of a Tier 3 intervention. There are few reasons to place a student with LD in special education if he or she can succeed in general education with only supplemental or strategically timed interventions. RTI is effective at reducing the number of students with LD referred for special education (Van der Heyden, 2006). Unfortunately, even with the advent of RTI, disproportionality for minority students with LD persists—probably because many schools have yet to achieve the first step of the RTI model (Bouman, 2011). For schools with high numbers of poor, minority, or English language learners, Tier 1 may look more like Tier 2 at a middle-class school. Two simple rules of thumb illustrate this. First, if more than 20% of students require extra assistance, then the school does not have a Tier 2 problem—it has a Tier 1 problem because it is failing to meet the needs of at least 80% of its students. Second, if a school has more than 5% of students in special education, then the school does not have a Tier 3 problem—it has a Tier 2 problem because it is failing to meet the needs of at least 20% of its at-risk students.

Tools and Practice Examples

As previously discussed, asking students a series of questions is a helpful reading intervention. A generic set of questions has been placed in Table 17.5.

The following measures are helpful to use to assess the emotional functioning of youth with learning disabilities.

Self-Concept Scales

Self-Perception Profile for Children
Susan Harter, Ph.D.,
University of Denver, Department of Psychology
2155 South Race Street,
Denver, CO 80208–0204

Perception of Ability Scale for Children (Grades 3–6)
Western Psychological Services
12031 Wilshire Blvd.
Los Angeles, CA 90025–1251
Phone: 800–648–8857
www.wpspublish.com

Table 17.5 General Questions Before, During, and After Reading

Key Questions	*Predictions: What Might happen?*	*Actuality: What Really Happened?*	*Identification: How Are You Like That? Give an Example*
1. Who are the lead characters in this story?			
2. Which one has a learning difference (LD)?			
3. What are some things that might/have happen(ed)?			
4. How does the person with LD feel about him/herself?			
5. How would this person like to be?			
6. What happens to help this person?			
7. How does this person feel about him/herself in the end?			

Self-Description Questionnaire-I (Grades 2–6)
Self-Description Questionnaire-II (Grades 7–11)
Self Research Centre
University of Western Sydney
Building 1—Bankstown Campus
Penrith South, DC 1797
Australia
Phone: 612–9772–6428
http://www.education.ox.ac.uk/research/self/resources/

Social Skills Scales

Social Skills Improvement System (Grades 3–12)
American Guidance Service
Pearson Assessments
4201 Woodland Rd.
Circle Pines, MN 55014–1796
Phone: 800–328–5999
www.pearsonassessments.com

The following resources provide help for school social workers and school-based practitioners working with youth with learning disabilities.

Peer-Assisted Learning Strategies (PALS) (Grades 2–6)
Kennedy Center
Vanderbilt University
Peabody Box 328
230 Appleton Pl.
Nashville, TN 37203–5701
(615) 343–4782
http://kc.vanderbilt.edu/pals/

Social Skills Game (Grades 3–6)
Creative Therapy Store
Western Psychological Services
12031 Wilshire Blvd.
Los Angeles, CA 90025–1251
Phone: 800–648–8857
www.creativetherapystore.com

Group Therapy Manual for Students with LD
Integra
25 Imperial Street
Toronto, Ontario
Canada M5P 1B9
http://integra.on.ca/index.htm

The following list provides bibliotherapy books that may be useful for school social workers and school-based practitioners working with youth with learning disabilities.

Elementary School (Primary: Grades 1–3)

Aiello, B., & Shulman, J. (1988). *Secrets aren't always for keeps.* Frederick, MD: Twenty-first Century (48 pages).

Daly, N. (2003). *Once upon a time.* New York: Farrar, Strauss and Giroux (picture book).

Gehret, J. (1991). *The don't give up kid and learning differences.* Fairport, NY: Verbal Images (26 pages;parent guide).

Giff, P. R. (1984). *The beast in Ms. Rooney's room.* New York: Delacourte (76 pages; audio, Braille, Spanish).

Kline, S. (1985). *Herbie Jones.* New York: Puffin (95 pages; audio).

Kraus, R. (1971). *Leo, the late bloomer.* New York: Harper Collins (40 pages; audio, French, Spanish, video).

Lewis, M. (1984). *Wrongway Applebaum.* New York: Coward-McCann (63 pages).

Paterson, K. (2001). *Marvin one too many.* New York: Harper Collins (48 pages; audio).

Shreve, S. (1985). *The flunking of Joshua T. Bates.* New York: Knopf (90 pages; audio, Braille, large print).

Sinykin, S. C. (1996). *Allison walks the wire.* Portland, ME: Magic Attic (74 pages).

Elementary School (Intermediate: Grades 4–5)

Banks, J. T. (1995). *Egg drop blues.* Boston: Houghton-Mifflin (120 pages; Braille).

Carris, J. (1990). *Aunt Morbelia & the screaming skulls.* Boston: Little Brown (134 pages; audio).

Cleary, B. (1990). *Muggie Maggie.* New York: Avon (70 pages; audio, Braille, large print, Spanish).

Cutler, J. (1997). *Spaceman.* New York: Dutton (138 pages).

Greenwald, S. (1983). *Will the real Gertrude Hollings please stand up?* New York: Dell (162 pages).

Hansen, J. (1986). *Yellow Bird and me.* New York: Clarion (155 pages).

Martin, A. M. (1988). *Yours turly, Shirley.* New York: Holiday House (133 pages; audio).

McNamee, G. (2002). *Sparks.* New York: Dell/Random House (119 pages).

Polacco, P. (1998). *Thank you, Mr. Falker.* New York: Scholastic Books (unpaged, audio, Korean, Spanish, video).

Sachar, L. (1987). *There's a boy in the girls' bathroom.* New York: Knopf (195 pages; audio, Braille, large print, Spanish).

Middle School (Grades 6–8)

Betancourt, J. (1993). *My name is Brain Brian.* New York: Scholastic (128 pages; large print).

Bunting, E. (1986). *Sixth grade sleepover.* San Diego: Harcourt Brace Jovanovich (96 pages; Braille, large print).

Cassedy, S. (1987). *M. E. and Morton.* New York: Crowell (312 pages; Braille).

DeClements, B. (1985). *Sixth grade can really kill you.* New York: Puffin (146 pages; Braille, large print, teachers guide).

Gilson, J. (1980). *Do bananas chew gum?* New York: Lothrop, Lee, & Shepard (158 pages; Braille).

Janover, C. (1995). *The worst speller in Jr. High.* Minneapolis: Free Spirit (200 pages; audio).

Lowry, L. (1984). *Us and Uncle Fraud.* New York: Dell (148 pages).

Philbrick, W. R. (1993). *Freak the mighty.* New York: Blue Sky (169 pages; audio).

Suzanne, J. (1990). *Danny means trouble.* New York: Bantam (138 pages; Spanish).

Swarthout, G., & Swarthout, K. (1975). *Whales to see the.* Garden City, NY: Doubleday (121 pages).

High School (Grades 9–12)

Adler, C. S. (1986). *Kiss the clown.* New York: Clarion (178 pages).

Albert, L. (1976). *But I'm ready to go.* Scarsdale, NY: Bradbury (230 pages; Braille).

Barrie, B. (1994). *Adam Zigzag.* New York: Delacorte (181 pages; audio).

Bezant, P. (1994). *Angie.* New York: Ballantine (170 pages).

Brown, K. (1989). *Willie's summer dream.* San Diego: Harcourt Brace Jovanovich (132 pages).

Byars, B. (1970). *The summer of the swans.* New York: Viking (142 pages; award, audio, Braille, Chinese, French, large print, Spanish, teacher's guide, and video).

Foley, J. (1986). *Falling in love is no snap.* New York: Dell (139 pages).

Hall, L. (1986). *Just one friend.* New York: Collier (118 pages).

Morton, J. (1979). *Running scared.* New York: Elsevier (118 pages).

Nelson, T. (1989). *And one for all.* New York: Orchard (182 pages).

Key Points to Remember

Students with learning disabilities represent the largest group of pupils with disabilities in American schools. They often struggle with issues of low self-esteem, low social skills, or both. Direct and indirect interventions are effective in resolving both of these issues. The best approach is to take a person-in-environment perspective by aiming interventions at both the students with LDs and their educational environment.

It is important for practitioners to remember that evidence-based practice (EBP) is a process rather than a product. Among the steps of EBP is the necessity of filtering findings through one's own education, experience, and expertise. Thus, none of the programs discussed should simply be adopted, but *adapted* to meet the unique needs of students with LD in your state, your district, and your school. EBP should never lead to a "cookbook" practice (Raines, 2008).

References

Adelizzi, J. U., & Goss, D. B. (Eds.) (2001). The helping hand & Appendix. In *Parenting children with learning disabilities* (pp. 79–96; 221–229). Westport, CT: Bergin & Garvey.

Agard, J. A., Veldman, D. J., Kaufman, M. J., & Semmel, M. I. (1978). *How I feel toward others: An instrument of the PRIME instrument battery.* Baltimore, MD: University Park.

Albert, L. (1976). *But I'm ready to go.* Scarsdale, NY: Bradbury.

Armstrong, T. (2000). *Multiple intelligences in the classroom* (2nd ed.). Alexandria, VA: Association for Supervision and Curriculum Development.

Bear, G. G., Minke, K. M., & Manning, M. A. (2002). Self-concept of students with learning disabilities: A meta-analysis. *School Psychology Review, 31*(3), 405–427.

Bouman, S. H. (2011). *Response to intervention in California public schools: Has it helped address disproportional placement rates for students with learning disabilities?* (Doctoral dissertation). The Claremont Graduate University, United States–California. Retrieved June 1, 2011, from Dissertations & Theses: Full Text. (Publication No. AAT 3414045).

Bryan, T., Burstein, K., & Bryan, J. (2001). Students with learning disabilities: Homework problems and promising practices. *Educational Psychologist, 36*(3), 167–180.

Buhrmester, D., Furman, W., Wittenberg, M., & Reis, H. (1988). Five domains of interpersonal competence in peer relationships. *Journal of Personality and Social Psychology, 6*, 991–1008.

Cohen, J. (1988). *Statistical power analysis for the behavioral sciences* (2nd ed.). Hillsdale, NJ: Erlbaum.

Cooper, H., & Nye, B. (1994). Homework for students with learning disabilities: The implications of research for policy and practice. *Journal of Learning Disabilities, 27*(8), 470–479.

Dane, E. (Ed.) (1990). Families of children with learning disabilities. In *Painful passages: Working with children with learning disabilities* (pp. 120–156). Silver Spring, MD: NASW.

Elbaum, B., & Vaughn, S. (2001). School-based interventions to enhance the self-concept of students with learning disabilities: A meta-analysis. *Elementary School Journal, 101(3)*, 303–329.

Elbaum, B., & Vaughn, S. (2003). For which students with learning disabilities are self-concept interventions effective? *Journal of Learning Disabilities, 36*(2), 101–108.

Elksnin, L. K., & Elksnin, N. (2000). Teaching parents to teach their children to be prosocial. *Intervention in School and Clinic, 36*(1), 27–35.

Forness, S. R., & Kavale, K. A. (1996). Treating social skill deficits in children with learning disabilities: A meta-analysis of the research. *Learning Disability Quarterly, 19*(1), 2–13.

Fuchs, D., Fuchs, L. S., & Burish, P. (2000). Peer-assisted learning strategies: An evidence-based practice to promote reading achievement. *Learning Disabilities Research & Practice, 15*(2), 85–91.

Fuchs, D., Fuchs, L. S., Mathes, P. G., & Martinez, E. A. (2002). Preliminary evidence on the social standing of students with learning disabilities in PALS and no-PALS classrooms. *Learning Disabilities Research & Practice, 17*(4), 205–215.

Fuchs, D., Mock, D., Morgan, P. L., & Young, C. L. (2003). Responsiveness-to-Intervention: Definitions, evidence, and implications for the learning disabilities construct. *Learning Disabilities: Research & Practice, 18*, 157–171.

Gammon, E. A., & Rose, S. D. (1991). The Coping Skills Program for parents of children with developmental disabilities: An experimental evaluation. *Research on Social Work Practice, 1*(3), 244–256.

Gardner, H. (1999). *Intelligence reframed: Multiple intelligences for the 21st century.* New York: Basic Books.

Gerber, P. J. (2001). Learning disabilities: A life-span approach. In D. P. Hallahan & B. K. Keogh (Eds.), *Research and global perspectives in learning disabilities: Essays in honor of William M. Cruickshank* (pp. 167–180). Mahwah, NJ: Erlbaum.

Harter, S. (1985). *Manual for the Self Perception Profile for Children.* Denver, CO: University of Denver.

Harter, S. (1999). *The construction of the self.* New York: Guilford.

Hepworth, D. H., Rooney, R. H., & Larsen, J. A. (2002). *Direct social work practice: Theory and skills* (6th ed.). Pacific Grove, CA: Brooks/Cole-Thomson Learning.

Higgins, E. L., Raskind, M. H., Goldberg, R. J., & Herman, K. L. (2002). Stages of acceptance of a learning disability: The impact of labeling. *Learning Disability Quarterly, 25*(1), 3–18.

Kavale, K. A., & Forness, S. (1995). *The nature of learning disabilities: Critical elements of diagnosis and classification.* Mahwah, NJ: Erlbaum.

Kavale, K. A., & Forness, S. R. (1996). Social skill deficits and learning disabilities: A meta-analysis. *Journal of Learning Disabilities, 29*(3), 226–237.

Kavale, K. A. & Mostert, M. P. (2004). Social skills interventions for individuals with learning disabilities. *Learning Disability Quarterly, 27*(1), 31–43.

Keith, L. K., & Bracken, B. A. (1996). Self-concept instrumentation: A historical and evaluative review. In B. A. Bracken (Ed.), *Handbook of self-concept: Developmental, social, and clinical considerations* (pp. 91–170). New York: Wiley.

Kirk, S. (1962). *Educating exceptional children.* Boston: Houghton-Mifflin.

Kuzell, N., & Brassington, J. (1985). *Parenting the learning disabled child* (2 vols.). Ottawa, ON: Adlerian Centre for Counselling and Education.

Kuzell, N. D., Brassington, J., & Mahoney, W. J. (1988). Parenting the learning disabled child: Research, development and implementation of an effective course. *The Social Worker/Le Travailleur Social, 56*(3), 127–130.

Learning Disabilities Council. (2002). *Understanding learning disabilities: A parent guide and workbook* (3rd ed., revised and expanded). Timonium, MD :York.

Lenkowsky, R. S., Barowsky, E. I., Dayboch, M. P., Puccio, L., & Lenkowsky, B. E. (1987). Effects of bibliotherapy on the self-concept of learning disabled, emotionally handicapped adolescents in a classroom setting. *Psychological Reports, 61*, 483–488.

Lynn, C. J., McKay, M. M., & Atkins, M. S. (2003). School social work: Meeting the mental health needs of students through collaboration with teachers. *Children & Schools, 25*(4), 197–209.

Marsh, H. W. (1990). *Self-description Questionnaire-II.* Cambelltown, Australia: University of Western Sydney, Macarthur.

Mastropieri, M. A., Spencer, V., Scruggs, T. E., & Talbot, E. (2000). Students with disabilities as tutors: An updated research synthesis. In T. E. Scruggs & M. A. Mastropieri (Series & Vol. Eds.), *Advances in learning and behavioral disabilities: Vol. 14. Educational interventions* (pp. 247–279). Stamford, CT: Jai.

Mishna, F., Muskat, B., & Wiener, J. (2010). "I'm not lazy; it's just that I learn differently": Development and implementation of a manualized school-based group for students with learning disabilities. *Social Work with Groups, 33*(2–3), 139–159.

Mondel, S. (1980). *Psycho-social competence incomplete stories test.* Boston, MA: Tufts-New England Medical Center.

Nowicki, E. A. (2003). A meta-analysis of the social competence of children with learning disabilities compared to classmates of low and average to high achievement. *Learning Disability Quarterly, 26*(3), 171–188.

Ochoa, S. H., & Olivarez, A. (1995). A meta-analysis of peer rating sociometric studies of pupils with learning disabilities. *Journal of Special Education, 29*(1), 1–19.

Pardeck, J. T. (1998). *Using books in clinical social work practice: A guide to bibliotherapy.* New York: Haworth.

Piers, E., & Harris, D. (1969). *The Piers-Harris Children's Self-concept Scale.* Nashville, TN: Counselor Recordings & Tests.

Polacco, P. (1998). *Thank you, Mr. Falker.* New York: Scholastic Books.

Prout, H. T., Marcal, S. D., & Marcal, D. C. (1992). A meta-analysis of self-reported personality characteristics of children and adolescents with learning disabilities. *Journal of Psychoeducational Assessment, 10,* 59–64.

Raines, J. C. (2002). Brainstorming hypotheses for functional behavioral assessment: The link to effective behavioral intervention plans. *School Social Work Journal, 26*(2), 30–45.

Raines, J. C. (2003). Multiple intelligences and social work practice for students with learning disabilities. *School Social Work Journal, 28(1),* 1–20

Raines, J. C. (2006). The new IDEA: Reflections on the reauthorization. *School Social Work Journal, 31*(1), 1–18.

Raines, J. C. (2008). *Evidence-based practice in school mental health: A primer for school social workers, psychologists, and counselors.* New York, NY: Oxford University Press.

Roans, M., & Hoagwood, K. (2000). School-based mental health services: A research review. *Clinical Child and Family Psychology Review, 3*(4), 223–241.

Samuels, C. A. (2010). Boom in learning-disabled enrollments ends. *Education Week, 30*(3), 1, 14–15.

Sklare, G. B. (1997). *Brief counseling that works: A solution-focused approach for school counselors.* Thousand Oaks, CA: Corwin Press.

Sridhar, D., & Vaughn, S. (2002). Bibliotherapy: Practices for improving self-concept and reading comprehension. In B.Y.L. Wong & M. L. Donahue (Eds.), *The social dimensions of learning disabilities: Essays in honor of Tanis Bryan* (pp. 161–188). Mahwah, NJ: Erlbaum.

Sternberg, R. J., & Grigorenko, E. L. (1999). *Our labeled children: What every parent and teacher needs to know about learning disabilities.* Reading, MA: Perseus.

Swanson, H. L. (1996). Meta-analysis, replication, social skills, and learning disabilities. *Journal of Special Education, 30*(2), 213–221.

Swanson, H. L., & Malone, S. (1992). Social skills and learning disabilities: A meta-analysis of the literature. *School Psychology Review, 21* (3), 427–442.

Swanson, H. L., & Hoskyn, M. (1998). Experimental intervention research on students with learning disabilities: A meta-analysis of treatment outcomes. *Review of Educational Research, 68*(3), 277–321.

Swanson, H. L. (2001). Research on interventions for adolescents with learning disabilities: A meta-analysis of outcomes related to higher-order processing. *Elementary School Journal, 101* (3), 331–348.

Swarthout, G., & Swarthout, K. (1975). *Whales to see the.* Garden City, NY: Doubleday.

U.S. Department of Education. (2002). *Twenty-fourth annual report to Congress on the implementation of the Individuals with Disabilities Education Act.* Washington, DC: Author.

Utay, J. M., & Lampe, R. E. (1995). Use of a group counseling game to enhance social skills of children with learning disabilities. *Journal for Specialists in Group Work, 20*(2), 114–120.

Van der Heyden, A. M. (2006). Implementing RTI. RTI myths and misrepresentations: Looking at data and experience. *Communiqué, 34*(6). Retrieved from http://www.nasponline.org/publications/cq/cq346rtimyths.aspx

Walker, H. M., & McConnell, S. R. (1988). *The Walker-McConnell Scale of Social Competence and School Adjustment.* Austin, TX: Pro-Ed.

Zeleke, S. (2004). Self-concepts of students with learning disabilities and their normally achieving peers: A review. *European Journal of Special Education, 19*(2), 145–170.

CHAPTER 18

Effective Classroom Interventions for Students with Physical Disabilities

Anna G. Escamilla

Getting Started

Students with physical disabilities can be excellent pupils and individuals. Sometimes the lack of resources and information about how to facilitate education for these students makes daily classroom activities burdensome to all involved. In this chapter we will cover some practical ideas and exercises for the classroom. Resources will be offered to assist with the ongoing challenges. In addition the reader is encouraged to explore the topic of students with physical disabilities by using the many articles and other reading materials that are listed. This chapter is primarily an introduction to a very complex issue.

Physical disabilities can be defined as temporary or chronic conditions that affect functioning in walking, strength, coordination, fine motor and sensory abilities, and communication. These limitations may or may not affect activity in the classroom or school setting. The causes for physical disability include but are not limited to asthma, convulsive disorders, hemophilia, heart disease, cancer, AIDS, cystic fibrosis, cerebral palsy, birth defects, epilepsy, rheumatoid arthritis, brain injury, traumatic spinal cord injury, and amputations. Some students with physical disabilities use adaptive devices such as wheelchairs, crutches, white canes, special seating, or adaptive technology. Students with chronic illness may require medical attention during the school day. Students may be served both in special education classrooms as well as regular classrooms.

The philosophy of self-determination will guide you through the rest of this chapter in understanding adaptation, modifications, and other methods of inclusion for the student with physical disabilities. Self-determination is the ability to make daily decisions and life plans without the interference or influence of others unless requested. These are essential skills for lifelong success that must be developed early (Wehmeyer, Agran, & Hughes, 1998). The language you use to describe disability can be empowering and support self-determination. A simple method for communicating respect for students with disabilities is the use of person-first language. Identifying a student by their name, regardless of their disability, supports self-respect. To say the "handicapped child," or the "wheelchair student" identifies the disability and focuses on the student's lack of ability, above all personal identity. If it is necessary to refer to the disability, say "(Name) _____ who uses a wheelchair" or "(Name) _____ who has cerebral palsy." It is important to avoid pitying language to describe disability such as "suffers" and "afflicted." Pity does not help a student with a disability. Compassionate support should be the goal of any intervention. Other students model the language and attitude of the teachers, counselors, and social workers around the student with the disability. It is essential to live what you intend to teach about disability.

What We Know

Students with physical disabilities are not a homogeneous group. However, the attitudes toward these students by peers, teachers, and others in a school setting can have many commonalities. For this chapter meta-analyses and extensive literature reviews were compared in order to arrive at the best practices for working with students with disabilities in the classroom. Citations from identified studies current as of 1990 and reviews were checked for possible resources. In addition

Medline, Psyclit, and Eric databases were searched for any meta-analyses or comprehensive literature reviews done on children with physical disabilities and children with physical disabilities in the classroom. Table 18.1 summarizes the results of these searches. Since 2005, several small studies (i.e., Cosbey & Johnston, 2006; Egilson & Traustadottir, 2009) have started to examine issues such as teacher assistant support and its impact on student independence and the use of adaptive equipment to improve social interactions. While the results are not generalizable due to a small sample size, the topic selection may imply a tendency to explore conclusions in depth about what works in a classroom, particularly the improvement and increased development of adaptive equipment for use in classroom settings. A voice output activation aid (VOCA) can be used by programming phrases that allow a child to initiate social interactions with others, thus increasing the likelihood of social acceptance by other students. Another example of more in-depth examination includes studies dealing with teacher and student attitudes toward students with disabilities (i.e., Gal & Engel-Yeger, 2010; Diamond & Tu, 2009). While both studies are done outside the United States, the issues are universal.

Assimilating all this information leads us to conclude that the current research does not reliably support a particular intervention. However, there is evidence that guiding principles such as integrated settings, workshops for teachers and staff, peer programs, school personnel and peer educational presentations, consultation and team building, therapeutic strategies for families, and school and hospital collaboration can be beneficial in supporting children with physical disabilities (Mulvihill, Cotton, & Gyaben, 2004). In addition, the collaboration between regular and special education teachers allows for collective creativity in designing individualized interventions in the classroom. The following section provides examples to use in the classroom based on these conclusions.

What We Can Do

School settings can be very nurturing and supportive of students. This is also true as it relates to students with physical disabilities. The following section will provide information, activities, and resources about students with disabilities, their peers, teachers, and parents.

Integrated Settings

Children with physical disabilities can participate to varying degrees in the activities of children without disabilities, including social activities. For example, the student with a wheelchair needs to have access to all or most areas of the classroom. Most deaf students included in regular classrooms will have sign language communication skills, lip readings skills, or other communication methods. Sometimes the use of adaptive equipment can help facilitate participation and inclusion. Adaptive technology is a specialized practical modification of an existing device, instrument, or apparatus used in performing a variety of daily life skills including learning. Some adaptive technology is "low tech," practical, and inexpensive. Other adaptive technology is "high tech" and includes switch devices to activate a computer, screen readers, or electronic equipment for speech (see Resources section).

There are many resources and opportunities available to students with disabilities and their teachers (see "Resources" section). For example, a student with a physical disability who uses a wheelchair may work on a desk that is elevated by wooden blocks or a student with low vision may use a lamp on his or her desk. Avoid isolating the child with a disability in the back of a classroom. Encourage them to participate with their peers in activities outside of the classroom.

- Include the child with a disability in all activities (i.e., science activities, field trips, and physical education).
- Allow space to maneuver a wheelchair.
- Change seating to make it possible for all students to see and hear better, such as circular seating in small groups (Nabors & Larson, 2002).
- Encourage the students with disabilities to interact with nondisabled peers and avoid social isolation (Blum, Resnick, Nelson, & St. Germaine, 1991).
- Offer the same instruction to students with disabilities as is offered to the nondisabled student.

Table 18.1 Comparison of Meta-Analyses and Comprehensive Literature Reviews

Study	*Target Problem*	*Sample*	*Results*
Buysee & Bailey (1993). Behavioral and developmental outcomes in young children with disabilities in integrated and segregated settings: A review of comparative studies.	1. Strengths and limitations of existing research 2. Integrate findings relative to behavior and development 3. Identify needs for further research on integrated vs. segregated settings for young children with disabilities	22 studies reviewed of children with disabilities ages 0–6 in early intervention programs	1. Integrated environments facilitate social interactions for young children with disabilities 2. These settings are not detrimental to developmental outcomes in these children
LeBovidge, Lavigne, Donenberg, & Miller (2003). Psychological adjustment of children and adolescents with chronic arthritis: A meta-analytic review.	Determine whether children and adolescents with chronic arthritis are at more risk for development of adjustment problems than controls	21 studies that report overall adjustment problems, internalizing symptoms, externalizing symptoms, or self-concept of youth with arthritis	Important to assess children & adolescents with chronic arthritis for internalizing problems. These youth were not found to be at greater risk for poor self-concept or self-esteem problems than controls. Used Child Behavior Checklist (CBCL).
McGregor & Vogelsberg (1998). Inclusive schooling practices: Pedagogical and Research Foundation: A synthesis of the literature that informs best practices about inclusive schooling	Summarizes the literature base that informs our current understanding of the best approaches to support students with disabilities in inclusive settings	54 research studies on inclusion	Practices associated with inclusive schooling practices continue to evolve as experience increases. Collective resources, strategies, and creativity of both general and special education teachers are necessary and sufficient to achieve inclusion.
Mulvihill, Cotton, & Gyaben (2004). Best practices for inclusive child and adolescent out-of-school care: A review of the literature.	What are the issues and best practices in inclusive education?	Reviewed 53 sources on inclusive practices for school-age children and adolescents	There is not a single set of criteria, recommendations, or guidelines for inclusion; however, there are guiding principles. Recommend systematic, programmatic, multidisciplinary research.

(continued)

Table 18.1 *(Continued)*

Study	*Target Problem*	*Sample*	*Results*
Prevatt, Heffer, & Lowe (2000). A review of school reintegration programs for children with cancer.	Review of literature that summarizes suggestions for successful reintegration	15 programs from journal articles on school reintegration programs for children with cancer specifically compared	No empirical evidence, but evidence that normalcy beneficial in facilitating adjustment of ill child's return to school. Best practices include school staff workshops, peer programs, school personnel & peer educational presentations, consultation & team building, strategies for families, school & hospital collaboration.
Ward & Barrett (2002). A review of behavior analysis research in physical education.	Overview of behavior analysis and how it contributes to physical education	5 journals focusing on behavior analysis studies in PE. 6 single-subject studies on participants with disabilities	Lack of treatment integrity in the studies. Peers as mediators main type of intervention. Lack of evidence that behaviors were maintained or generalized. The focus of most studies was interventions designed to improve teaching behaviors.

- Encourage and assist young children to include the student with the disability in activities whenever possible.
- Offer information to the student with the disability about available student activities and clubs.
- If overheads, handouts, or the blackboard is used, read them aloud.
- Present any handouts or readings in an accessible format.
- Give students with speech difficulties time to respond to a question.
- Younger children sometimes will ask direct questions about a peer's disability. This should be encouraged if at all possible.
- Encourage students to challenge attitudes and stereotyping through direct contact and reality-based interaction.
- Remember that difficulty in communicating does not mean that a person also has a cognitive deficit.

Educational Workshops for Teachers, Staff, and Peers

Teachers are including students with physical disabilities in regular classrooms. Most teachers welcome the opportunity to provide an enriched learning environment for all of their students. Other teachers have strong reactions to this task. Frustration may be felt or even anger at what they perceive as an extra workload. It is difficult for a teacher to provide a positive inclusive classroom if they are having strong negative emotional reactions. Some teachers feel a blow to their self-efficacy as a professional for not being able to provide a perceived quality education to all students (Forlin, 1998). Support for teachers, staff, and peers in the form of educational workshops and smaller educational groups is an excellent method of making inclusion a positive experience for all. Here are some steps toward success.

- Provide teachers and other staff with information about their students' disabilities prior to their entry into the classroom.
- Obtain information from parents, previous teachers, medical resources, and the student him- or herself.
- Provide a private, small-group environment for teachers, staff, and peers where they feel they can vent emotions constructively without hurting the student or being criticized for having a less than correct attitude.
- Attempt to utilize social work and other school-based practitioners as experts in the areas of disability to assist with these support groups.
- Arrange sensitivity training on site from professionals in the field of disabilities (see Resources section).

Peer Programs

It is likely that a student with a physical disability will be absent from classes frequently (Nabors & Lehmkuhl, 2004). The student may feel frustrated by an inability to keep up with assignments (Lightfoot, Wright, & Sloper, 1998). Here are some suggested steps to take to support the student with the physical disability.

- Assign a peer or peers who are willing to take the responsibility for getting class work to the student.
- Involve the student with the disability and their volunteer peers (buddy) in selecting who will be given this task.
- Check periodically to make sure the relationship is working for both parties.
- Make every effort to ensure a mutual, reciprocal, and empowering relationship for the child with a disability.

Consultation and Team Building

It is very helpful to assemble a team of support persons and consultants for the process of including students with physical disabilities in the classroom. The most effective team is comprised of the student, their parents, teachers (both regular and special education), school medical staff, and any current medical providers. The student with the disability should be involved in all decision making regarding what to tell other students about the disability. The student's need for confidentiality should be considered first even above the needs of their parents to openly discuss these issues. The following are some suggestions:

- Sometimes students with disabilities would like to limit their disclosure to the school nurse and/or specific teachers.
- If the student decides to share information with his or her classmates, make plans to use these as teaching opportunities.
- Include professionals that can provide accurate information (Lightfoot et al., 1998).
- Get assistance from the teachers of the visually impaired in making accommodations for students.
- Consult with the speech therapists if they are involved with the student.
- Speak to parents, as well as the student, about what methods of communication they use.

Therapeutic Strategies for Families

Have compassion and understanding of the difficulties parents face when raising a child with a disability. Adolescence poses a challenge in the case of students with disabilities as much as those students without disabilities. Students may not agree with their parents' choices regarding their activities at school. Sometimes the student with the disability feels more vulnerable to taking an opposing view against their parents because they are totally dependent on them for daily support. The use of self-determination to support the development of mature judgment and preparation for life after graduation in students with disabilities can become a very effective tool to use (Wehmeyer, 1997). Teachers and social workers need to work toward developing independence in these students just as they would with students without disabilities. These steps may assist families in dealing with the stresses of having a child with a disability in a regular classroom.

- Support students in learning skills to express their opinions, desires, and needs appropriately.
- Help parents see the importance of allowing children with disabilities to take calculated risks.
- Encourage the student to express their desires.
- Develop a transition plan for when the child leaves school.
- Assist and encourage the adolescent student and parents to investigate adult services and explore options for meaningful employment or postsecondary education.
- When appropriate encourage family and individual psychotherapy services with professionals in the community.

School and Hospital Collaboration

Some differences in teacher involvement will occur when dealing with children with physical disabilities in the classroom. Among these differences is the need for interaction with external medical professionals. This becomes important not only for education about a particular disability but also because medical professionals may need information in order to provide appropriate treatment to the student.

- Obtain written consent from the parents and student to interact with their medical team.
- Set up informative meetings with the medical team associated with the individual student if possible.
- Ask the members of the medical team to send information in the form of brochures or resources to the school staff involved with the student.
- Basic planning for emergencies and daily activity should be in place prior to the student's entering the classroom.
- Include the student and the parents in all these activities.

Collaboration Between Regular and Special Education Teachers

Collaboration between teachers is probably the most important part of successful inclusion of students with physical disabilities. Both professionals must be able to have a mutually supportive attitude that in turn carries over to the inclusive classroom. The following are some suggested ideas for making this experience successful.

- Develop a climate of mutual trust.
- Involve your principal in obtaining scheduled preparation time.
- Teachers should visit and observe the classes of teachers who have experience with successful inclusion.
- Special education teachers can work with the regular teachers to determine their need for information about the medical conditions of his or her students.
- Use problem-solving skills and good communication skills.
- Work with specific task-related issues.
- Allow time for the receiving teacher to observe the student and discuss the student's needs with the current teacher and parents (Perner & Porter, 1998; McGregor & Vogelsberg, 1998).

Self-Determination Activity

Invite a panel of adults with disabilities to come to the classroom and talk about what they are doing in their lives. Ensure that these adults are willing to answer questions candidly. Ask them to explain what self-determination means to them.

Applying Interventions within a Response to Intervention Framework

The Individuals with Disabilities Education Improvement Act of 2004 allowed use of a practice for identifying students with learning disabilities called Response to Intervention (RTI). This practice applies scientific research-based interventions that are aligned with the individual needs of the student. Included in this is "frequent monitoring of student progress, and the application of the monitoring results to assist with making educational decisions including intervention, curriculum, instructional goals and methodologies" (http://www.tea.state.tx.us). Brown & Doolittle (2008) conclude that this approach will eliminate the avoidance of student need by requiring collaboration among the various professionals working with the student. This three-tiered process starts with every student receiving the same general curriculum that all students receive. Students are assessed for what they can do, non-categorically, which results in a second-tier approach of small group intervention focused on supports for enhancing a student's learning. Applying this to students with physical disabilities would allow a student to receive universal accommodations sooner in the educational process, thus avoiding delays. At Tier 3 the student with physical disabilities will have the benefit of years of accumulated data on RTI, including successful methods of education (Smith, Peters, Sanders, & Witz, 2010; Mellard, Stern, and Woods, 2011).

A criticism of the way that students are identified as needing special education has been how ethnic minority children are identified with more frequency. However, the overrepresentation of ethnic minority children in special education classes (National Council on Disability, 2002) will receive support from the appropriate application of the RTI framework in that rather than relying on racially insensitive psychometric instruments, information on student needs will come from classroom data (Brown & Doolittle, 2008).

Tools and Practice Examples

Case Example

Mary is a 10-year-old female student in the fourth grade with cerebral palsy. Cerebral palsy is a motor impairment resulting from brain damage usually during fetal development or infancy. It affects body movements and muscle coordination. She has and uses an electric wheelchair, which she operates with a joystick control. She needs assistance with eating and self-care. Mary's teacher has met with the special education consultant prior to starting the school year. They were able to assemble a team that included the student, the parents, teacher, teacher assistant, school counselor/social worker, her physical therapist, and an occupational therapist. The team worked on several parts of the needed accommodations for Mary in the classroom. Among the suggested accommodations were computer hardware and software, which allows her to use the computer by herself. Her teacher has designed class work for all students so that using the computer is routine, thereby not singling Mary out. The classroom is arranged so that all the computers face three walls and the students' backs are toward the middle of the room. In the center of the room there is a round table with chairs around it. When the students discuss parts of their lessons they come to the center of the room and sit at the table. One area of the table is cut out so that Mary's wheelchair can fit closer in with the other students. Mary agreed to let her teacher talk to the class about cerebral palsy. Her teacher, the special education consultant, and Mary prepared the lesson. Although Mary cannot speak clearly, she presented information to her classmates with support from the teacher. Mary asked for volunteers to be her buddy so that if she missed classes, she would be able to get class work to her and help her stay up with the class. Mary's teacher has informed her of the many clubs and organizations at the school and encouraged Mary to join the school Newsletter Club because Mary enjoys writing.

Resources

Here is a list of resources that are helpful to school social workers and other school counselors working with students with physical disabilities.

http://www.aucd.org: The Association of University Centers on Disabilities can provide valuable resources for training available to teachers and the public in every state.

Texas Technology Access Program: http://techaccess.edb.utexas.edu (offers information and resources with assistive technology in English and Spanish; includes a section specific to assistive technology in education)

Disability Social History Project: http://www.disabilityhistory.org (Web site by Stephen Dias, longtime disability activist, that offers facts and ideas for students about the history, including the people, involved in disability)

http://www.inclusive.co.uk (Web site with information on information technology and special needs)

http://snow.utoronto.ca (resources on best practices including online modules)

Key Points to Remember

- Although research does not yet support any particular interventions, there is substantial evidence that certain ideas and guiding principles work in the successful classroom.
- Include the student with the disability in as much decision making as possible about his or her own needs and shared information.
- Inclusive settings provide good education for students with physical disabilities.
- Peer support helps the student with the physical disability to stay up with the class when medical appointments and illness take them out of the classroom.
- Teachers who use teams of the student, professionals, and family members to help plan accommodations have more success in dealing with students with physical disabilities.
- Medical professionals need to be utilized as resources for the teachers in understanding their student's physical needs.
- The special education consultant can be very valuable to teachers in preparing their class work and classroom.
- Teachers need to have compassion and understanding toward parents and help make them part of the team for their son or daughter.

It is important when dealing with children with physical disabilities to remember that the goal to be achieved is inclusion. The research is beginning to provide the guidelines; however, it is the individual teacher, counselor, social worker, and teaching assistant who will truly change everyday lives for children with physical disabilities.

References

Blum, R., Resnick, M., Nelson, R., & St. Germaine, A. (1991). Family and peer issues among adolescents with spina bifida and cerebral palsy. *Pediatrics, 88*(2), 280–285.

Brown, J., & Doolittle, J. (2008). A cultural, linguistic, and ecological for response to intervention with English language learners. *Teaching Exceptional Children, 40*(5), 66–72.

Buysee, V., & Bailey, Jr., D., (1993). Behavioral and developmental outcomes in young children with disabilities in integrated and segregated settings: A review of comparative studies. *Journal of Special Education, 26*(4), 434–462.

Cosbey, J., & Johnston, S. (2006). Using a single-switch voice output communication aid to increase social access for children with severe disabilities in inclusive classrooms. *Research and Practice for Persons with Severe Disabilities, 31*(2), 144–156.

Diamond, K., & Tu, H. (2009). Relations between classroom context, physical disability and pre-school children's inclusion decisions. *Journal of Applied Developmental Psychology, 30*, 75–81.

Division of IDEA Coordination. (2011). *Response to Intervention (RTI). General overview of RTI.* Retrieved from http://www.tea.state.tx.us

Egilson, S., & Traustadottir, R. (2009). Assistance to pupils with physical disabilities in regular schools: Promoting inclusion or creating dependency? *European Journal of Special Needs Education, 24*(1), 21–36.

Forlin, C. (1998). Teachers' personal concerns about including children with a disability in regular classrooms. *Journal of Developmental and Physical Disabilities, 10*(1), 87–106.

Gal, E., & Engel-Yeger, B. (2010). Inclusion of children with disabilities: Teachers' attitudes and requirements for environmental accommodations. *International Journal of Special Education, 25*(2), 89–99.

LeBovidge, J., Lavigne, J., Donenberg, G., & Miller, M. (2003). Psychological adjustment of children and adolescents with chronic arthritis: A meta-analytic review. *Journal of Pediatric Psychology, 28*(1), 29–39.

Lightfoot, J., Wright, S., & Sloper, P. (1998). Supporting pupils in mainstream school with an illness or disability: Young people's views. *Child: Care, Health and Development, 25*(4), 267–283.

McGregor, G., & Vogelsberg, R. (1998). *Inclusive schooling practices: Pedagogical and research foundation: A synthesis of the literature that informs best practices about inclusive schooling.* Allegheny University of the Health Sciences, Consortium on Inclusive Schooling Practices: Brookes Publishing Co.

Mellard, D., Stern, A., & Woods, K. (2011). RTI school-based practices and evidence-based models. *Focus on Exceptional Children, 43*(6), 1–16.

Mulvihill, B., Cotton, J., & Gyaben, S. (2004). Best practices for inclusive child and adolescent out-of-school care: A review of the literature. *Family and Community Health, 27*, 52–65.

Nabors, L., & Larson, E. (2002). The effects of brief interventions on children's playmate preferences for a child sitting in a wheelchair. *Journal of Developmental and Physical Disabilities, 14*(4), 403–413.

Nabors, L., & Lehmkuhl, H. (2004). Children with chronic medical conditions: Recommendations for school mental health clinicians. *Journal of Developmental and Physical Disabilities, 16*(1), 1–15.

National Council on Disability Staff. (2002, July). *Individuals with Disability ED Act reauthorization: Where do we really stand?* Retrieved from http://www.ncd.gov/policy/education

Perner, D., & Porter, G. (1998). Creating inclusive schools: Changing roles and strategies. In A. Hilton & R. Ringlaben (Eds.), *Best and promising practices in developmental disabilities* (pp. 317–330). Austin, TX: PRO-ED.

Prevatt, F., Heffer, R., & Lowe, P. (2000). A review of school reintegration programs for children with cancer. *Journal of School Psychology 38*(5), 447–454.

Smith, S., Peters, M., Sanders, M., & Witz, K. (2010). Applying a Response to Intervention framework for noncategorical special education. *National Asssociation of School Psychologists, 38*, 8.

Ward, P., & Barrett, T. (2002). A review of behavior analysis research in physical education. *Journal of Teaching in Physical Education, 21*(3), 242–267.

Wehmeyer, M. (1997). Self determination as an educational outcome: A definitional framework and implications for intervention. *Journal of Developmental and Physical Disabilities, 9*(3), 175–209.

Wehmeyer, M., Agran, M., & Hughes, C. (1998). *Teaching self-determination to students with disabilities: Basic skills for successful transition*. Baltimore, MD: Brookes Publishing Co.

CHAPTER
19

Suicide and Suicidal Ideation among` Individuals Diagnosed with an Autism Spectrum Disorder

Oren Shtayermman

Getting Started

According to the Centers for Disease Control and Prevention (2011), among individuals ages 15 to 24 years old, there are approximately 100–200 attempts of suicide for every completed suicide. In 2009, 13.8% of U.S. high school students reported that they had seriously considered attempting suicide during the 12 months preceding the survey; 6.3% of students reported that they had actually attempted suicide one or more times during the same period. According to Berman (2009), 86% of school psychologists have counseled a student who has threatened to commit suicide, and 35% have reported that a student in their school has died of suicide.

According to Shtayermman (2008), about 50% of individuals diagnosed with an autism spectrum disorder (ASD) present with clinically significant levels of suicidal ideation. To date, only one published study exploring suicide among adolescents diagnosed with ASD has been done (Shtayermman, 2008). Therefore, there is very limited information concerning the phenomena of suicide among individuals diagnosed with ASD. However, studies that investigated mental health issues and comorbid issues among these individuals have indicated the high risk and likelihood of developing mood disorders, anxiety disorders, and other psychiatric conditions (Tantam, 2000a). All of the previously mentioned disorders have been highly linked to suicidal behavior. Individuals diagnosed with ASD are at higher risk for committing suicide than the neurotypical peer due to their difficulty with social communication and the social demands of adolescence (Green, Gilchrist, Burton & Cox, 2000; Tantam, 2000a). Some of the social demands during adolescence include dealing with increasing autonomy, finding peer groups to identify with, and forming intimate relationship with peers for the first time. Individuals diagnosed with ASD may find the social demands and transitions of adolescence more challenging because of their lack of ability to attain social reciprocity in addition to their awareness that their peers thrive from the new social opportunities.

Approximately one-third of adolescents who have attempted suicide reported experiencing isolation from peers, a breakup with a boyfriend or girlfriend, and recent peer conflicts (Prinstein, Boergers, Spirito, Little, & Grapentine, 2000). Peer conflicts and isolation from peers may increase emotional problems and serve as risk factors for suicide. Developmental scholars have consistently indicated the importance of social relationships to an adolescent's growth. Impaired social skills place individuals with ASD at a higher risk for social dysfunction. This may include trouble in attachment and peer interactions, which in turn may increase their risk for internalizing psychopathology such as depression, anxiety disorder, and suicide. According to Vanbergeijk and Shtayermman (2005), there is a need for collaboration among social workers and other mental health professionals, as well as family members and other service providers, to develop a treatment plan specific to the individual, as no two individuals with ASD are alike. Clinicians should take special consideration to the implication the syndrome has on the individual's day-to-day living.

What We Know about Individuals Diagnosed with Autism Spectrum Disorders and Suicide

In the past decade, the increase in the prevalence of ASD, and the suspected causes of this increase, have become a matter of concern for mental health professionals, researchers, educators, and parents (Newschaffer, Falb, & Gurney, 2005; Prior, 2003). Autism spectrum disorders include a group of lifelong developmental disabilities caused by an abnormality of the brain (Rutter, 2005). They are also known as neurodevelopmental disorders or neurobehavioral disorders (Bertrand et al., 2001; Croen, Grether, Hoogstrate, & Selvin, 2002). Autism was first introduced to the DSM-III in 1980 as part of the pervasive developmental disorders to convey that individuals with these conditions suffered from impairment in development and in multiple areas of functioning (Volkmar & Klin, 2005). Pervasive developmental disorder is synonymous with autism spectrum disorder.

Asperger's syndrome (AS) is considered a severe and chronic developmental disorder and it is part of the disorders on the autism spectrum (Klin, McPartland, & Volkmar, 2005). What distinguishes AS from other autism spectrum disorders is the higher linguistic and cognitive capacity. There is still confusion over and controversy around the nosological status of AS as a separate condition from autism and whether AS is a distinct diagnosis from autism or a subtype of autism (Lord & Corsello, 2005). The term is also used to describe individuals with ASD with higher verbal abilities yet who are socially disabled. The relationship between ADS and developmental disability or learning disability can be found in Table 19.1.

It has been suggested that there is considerable overlap between the clinical manifestations of ASD and a nonverbal learning disability (Rourke & Tsatsanis, 2000). The overlap is seen in the limited appreciation of humor, limited ability to understand or use the rules governing social behavior, and poor apprehension and application of nonverbal aspects of communication (Rourke & Tsatsanis, 2000). Individuals with a nonverbal learning disability are especially at risk for development of an internalized socioemotional pathology, including withdrawal, anxiety, and depression. It was also noted by Bender, Rosenkrans, and Crane (1999) that individuals with a nonverbal learning disability are also at higher risk for depression and suicide than individuals with verbal disability. Because ASD is considered to be part of the continuance of developmental disability, studies involving individuals diagnosed with developmental disabilities could be used to extract information about individuals diagnosed with ASD. According to Wachter and Bouck (2008), about 50% of individuals who are eligible for special education are also diagnosed with depression. Individuals diagnosed with ASD may be at risk for depression and suicide because of the considerable overlap between the clinical manifestations of ASD and a nonverbal learning disability. Individuals diagnosed with ASD may find the social demands and transitions of adolescence more challenging because of their lack of social reciprocity, in addition to their awareness that their peers thrive from the new social opportunities (Tantam, 2000, 2003).

Risk factors for suicide may be organized within a framework that distinguishes between proximal and distal exposures. Researchers believe this combination of factors constitutes sufficient conditions leading to suicide (Lubin, Glasser, Boyko, & Barell, 2001). Proximal risk factors are more closely related temporally to the suicidal event and may act as precipitators. Proximal risk factors may include stressful life events, such as sudden illness or bereavement, and the availability of a method for committing suicide (Lubin et al., 2001). Distal risk factors increase vulnerability to proximal risk factors and include psychopathology, personal characteristics, substance abuse, and familial risk factors. Individuals diagnosed with ASD may be at higher risk for suicide because of the potential accumulation of the abovementioned risk factors and the likelihood of struggles from a developmental perspective as well as an environmental perspective.

The prevalence of suicide attempts among adolescents tripled between the 1950s and the 1990s, and suicide is the third leading cause of death among adolescents ages 13 to 24 in the United States (CDC, 2011). Suicidal ideation is considered to be a risk factor for attempted suicide (Rudd, Joiner, & Rajab, 1996). The key role of suicidal ideation in predicting suicide attempts and completion make it a legitimate target for treatment (Shaffer & Greenberg, 2002).

Approximately one-third of adolescents who have attempted suicide reported experiencing isolation from peers, a breakup with a boyfriend or girlfriend, and recent peer conflicts (Prinstein et al., 2000). Peer conflicts and isolation from peers may increase emotional problems (Sourander et al., 2001; Sourander, Helstela, Helenius, & Piha, 2000) and serve as risk factors for suicide (Bond, Carlin, Thomas, Rubin, & Patton, 2001). Adolescents with ASD may also experience academic and social deficits as a result of their disability. Success at school, academically and/or socially, may then become a more challenging and stressful task, and they may feel isolated from their peers (Bender et al., 1999). The stigma associated with having a

Table 19.1 Terminology and Definitions

Term	*Definition*
Asperger's Syndrome	Asperger syndrome (sometimes called Asperger's syndrome, AS, or the more common shorthand Asperger's) is characterized as one of the five pervasive developmental disorders and is commonly referred to as a form of high-functioning autism. In very broad terms, individuals with AS have normal or above-average intellectual capacity and atypical or less well developed social skills, often with emotional/social development or integration happening later than usual as a result. The term "Asperger's syndrome" was coined by Lorna Wing in a 1981 medical paper. She named the syndrome after Hans Asperger, an Austrian psychiatrist and pediatrician who himself had used the term "autistic psychopathy."
Autism Spectrum Disorders	The autistic spectrum (sometimes referred to as the autism spectrum) is the idea that autism is a developmental and behavioral syndrome that results from certain combinations of traits. Although these traits may be normally distributed in the population, some individuals inherit or otherwise manifest more autistic traits. The spectrum ranges from the severe end, low-functioning autism, which has profound impairments in many areas, to Asperger's syndrome and high-functioning autism, to "normal" behavior and perhaps hypersocialization on the high end of the spectrum. In the *Diagnostic and Statistical Manual of Mental Disorders* (DSM-IV-TR) and the *International Statistical Classification of Diseases and Related Health Problems* (ICD-10), autism spectrum disorders (ASD) are classified as pervasive developmental disorders (PDD), as opposed to specific developmental disorders like dyslexia or dyspraxia.
Developmental Disability	Developmental disability is a term used to describe severe, lifelong disabilities attributable to mental and/or physical impairments, manifested before the age of 22. The term is used most commonly in the United States to refer to disabilities affecting daily functioning in three or more of the following areas: capacity for independent living • economic self-sufficiency • learning • mobility • receptive and expressive language • self-care • self-direction Usually people with mental retardation, cerebral palsy, autism spectrum disorder, various genetic and chromosomal disorders such as Down syndrome and Fragile X syndrome, and fetal alcohol syndrome are described as having developmental disabilities. This use of the term is synonymous with the use of the term "learning disability" in the United Kingdom and "intellectual disability" in Australia, Europe, Canada, and elsewhere. "Cognitive disability" is also used synonymously in some jurisdictions.
Learning Disability	In the United States, the term "learning disability" is used to refer to socio-biological conditions that affect a persons communicative capacities and potential to learn. The term includes conditions such as perceptual disability, brain injury, minimal brain dysfunction, autism, dyslexia, and developmental aphasia. In the United Kingdom, the term "learning disability" is used more generally to refer to developmental disability. Someone with a learning disability does not necessarily have low or high intelligence; it just means that this individual is working far below his or her ability due to a processing disorder, such as auditory processing or visual processing.

developmental disability may also contribute to the victimization or bullying of children with disabilities by their peers (Mishna, 2003).

Peer victimization, a form of peer conflict, may result in negative self-evaluation, which in turn may lead to internalizing problems such as depression, dissociation, or suicidal behavior (Stroch & Masia-Warner, 2004). According to Volkmar and Klin (2000), individuals diagnosed with ASD are more likely to be victims rather than victimizers, although the magnitude of this effect is not reported. Some signs of suicidal dangers are listed below.

Signs of Danger and Imminent Risk

Signs of Danger

- engaging in dangerous risk-taking behaviors
- sudden changes in peer friendships or relationships or unhealthy peer relationships
- withdrawing or isolating from friends and/or family
- self-mutilation (e.g., cutting or burning that is uncharacteristic of the student's identified disability)
- sudden mood changes or personality shifts
- challenges with sexual or gender identity (e.g., students who identify as gay, lesbian, bisexual, or transgender or who are questioning their sexuality or gender identity)
- being a bully or a victim of a bully
- depression
- sudden decline in academic performance or achievement
- uncharacteristic difficulty concentrating or thinking
- changes in eating patterns or sleeping patterns (either exceptionally more or less than typical)
- substance use or abuse (including alcohol and illegal substances, or abuse of prescription medication)
- preoccupation with the feelings of others
- unusual interest in morbid themes, death, or dying
- atypical promiscuous or sexual behavior

Signs of Imminent Risk

- preoccupation with suicide and/or death in writing, poetry, or artwork
- direct statements about suicide (e.g., "I'm going to kill myself")
- indirect statements about suicide (e.g., "Don't bother grading my test; I won't be here to pick it up," "It won't matter anymore," "Sometimes I just don't want to wake up")
- isolating behaviors
- expressing helplessness, hopelessness, or that life is meaningless
- giving away belongings or "setting affairs in order"
- a rapid change in mood from depression to contentment or happiness (may indicate that the student has made a decision and regards suicide as a way to escape pain)
- dropping out of activities that had been important
- seeking or gaining access to a weapon or other means of harming oneself

The **SAD PERSON** mnemonic is a tool that Patterson and colleagues (1983) developed to facilitate an easily remembered approach for conducting a thorough suicide risk assessment. Patterson (1983) indicated that a social worker or mental health professional should assign a score of 1 for each positive item below and apply the following way to assess for risk (see Table 19.2).

Sex—Males kill themselves four times more often than females. This is an important factor, as the ratio of males to females among individuals diagnosed with autism is 4:1.

Age—Certain age groups are more at risk, with adolescence as a higher risk group.

Depression—Depressed persons are significantly more at risk. Isolation from peers can increase depressive symptoms.

Previous attempt—Those who have previously attempted suicide are more likely to attempt it in the future.

Ethanol—Alcohol abuse is very often implicated in suicide.

Table 19.2

Score	*Risk*
0–2	No real problem, keep watching
3–4	Send home, but check frequently
5–6	Consider hospitalization
7–10	Definitely hospitalize

Rational thought—Individuals are more prone to suicide if psychotic.
Social network—The less social network, the greater the risk.
Organized plan—There is a greater risk if suicide plans are organized.
No partner—There is a greater risk of suicide if there is no partner or spouse.
Sickness—Chronic physical sickness makes suicide more likely.

What We Can Do

Attitudes toward suicidal behavior vary considerably from culture to culture. While some cultures may view suicide as appropriate under certain circumstances, others have strong sanctions against all such behavior. These cultural attitudes have important implications for both the assessment and treatment aspects of suicide.

In general, assessment and treatment of individuals with ASD and suicidal ideation should include family members, teachers, and other mental health professionals, including social workers (VanBergeijk & Shtayermman, 2005). The success of school-based suicide prevention efforts requires both the development of effective programs and the successful implementation and dissemination of such programs (Stein et al., 2010). One of the most familiar programs, available nationwide, to assist in the event of a crisis is the crisis hotline. Screening-based suicide prevention programs are designed to enhance the identification of youths suffering from mental illness and/or contemplating suicide and to refer these identified youths for appropriate care. Screening programs require a more time-intensive second stage to address false positives, and screening may not identify students who may become at risk for suicide subsequent to the screening.

A gatekeeper suicide prevention program is one of the most acceptable by school personnel. Prevention programs train teachers and school staff to improve their abilities to detect students who may be at risk for suicide and to enhance their follow-up with appropriate services through engaging the student's social support networks and facilitating referrals for treatment and counseling. Gatekeeper programs have been found to increase school staff awareness of suicide warning signs in at-risk students and knowledge of resources to treat suicidal students. The key components of a gatekeeper training program are preparing—an introduction to the tone, norms, and expectations of the learning experience; connecting—discussing one's own attitudes toward suicide and their impact on the intervention process; and understanding—an overview of the intervention needs for someone at risk. This includes knowledge and skills in identifying risk factors and developing a plan to help; assisting—presentation of a model for effective suicide prevention; and networking—information on local community resources and how to network. Individuals diagnosed with ASD may present a different kind of challenge in the identification, assessment, and treatment of suicide. Individuals who were categorized as having low emotional competence (the ability to identify, describe, and understand emotions), such as individuals diagnosed with ASD, had the lowest intentions of seeking help from both informal and formal sources (Ciarrochi, Wilson, Deane, & Rickwood, 2003). Such individuals should alert social workers and other mental health professionals to the importance of assessing suicidal ideation.

Applying Interventions within a Response to Intervention Framework

Much of the RTI process is grounded in evidence-based practice. Evidence-based practice encourages a systematic approach for integrating practical, ethical, and evidentiary issues. It involves a systematic approach to improving quality of services, including efforts to educate professionals who are lifelong learners, involving clients as informed participants, attending to the management of practices and policies that influence practice, and attending to the application challenges, including the implications of scarce resources. According to Sailor (2009), Response to Intervention (RTI) and Response to Instruction, which by and large imply the same logic model, have five practices in common: universal screening, intervention, progress monitoring, use of data to make decisions, and at least three increasingly intense tiers of support. These five practices are the defining features of Response to Intervention.

Key to the RTI model is the concept that different students require differing levels of support according to their need, and that schools should use a multi-tiered approach to providing these differing levels of support. The first tier of instruction is referred to as core or universal, which indicates that all students within the school are supported by this tier. The goal of universal supports is to provide the highest-quality instruction and curriculum while screening all students to identify those at risk of failure. As the tiers increase—from one to two and from two to three—the level of specialized support and instructional attention increases as well. These tiers exist to provide a framework for preventing student failure and for appropriately supporting students so that all can benefit maximally from the instruction they receive.

In relation to individuals diagnosed with ASD who may present with suicidal ideation, both conditions (autism and suicide) are on a spectrum, and no two individuals will present with the same level of functioning or the same intensity of suicidal thoughts or acts. Individuals diagnosed with ASD may present with different abilities and strengths. Treatment interventions such as problem-solving skills groups or organizational skills groups may not be applicable to all individuals diagnosed with AS. The need for an individualized treatment plan for each person diagnosed with ASD is well known (Schreibman & Ingersoll, 2005).

One of the main challenges in finding successful treatment interventions for individuals diagnosed with ASD has to do with the ability to generalize the treatment across different environments of the individual and over time (Schreibman & Ingersoll, 2005). Suicidal activities are considered on a continuum of progressive seriousness, which includes thoughts, contemplation, threats, attempts, and completions (Foreman, 1990). Suicidal ideation, which is defined as thoughts or wishes to take one's life, may be a precursor to suicidal behavior. The relationship between suicidal ideation, suicidal attempt, and completed suicide is complex. Because it seems reasonable to argue that suicidal ideation precedes any act of self-harm, both suicidal attempt and completed suicide represent subsets of suicidal ideation. Concrete planning of suicide and availability of means serve as potential risk factors for elevated levels of suicidal ideation. Because of the abovementioned and the fact that key to the RTI model is the concept that different students require differing levels of support according to their needs, using the quick assessment of SAD PERSON as well as incorporating suicidal intervention in schools in the form of preventive services is consistent with all the aspects of the RTI model: universal screening, intervention, progress monitoring, use of data to make decisions, and at least three increasingly intense tiers of support. If we would like to draw a comparison between the gatekeeper program and the RTI model, in RTI the three intervention tiers are on a continuum that is fluid; a student may receive services within Tier 2, then move forward to receive more intensive Tier 3 services or backward to receive less intensive Tier 1 services. Essentially, we see that the designated group of people who are trained and designated as helping professionals (from the fields of medicine, social work, nursing, psychology, etc.) could be part of any tier in the RTI model. The emergent group that could serve as potential gatekeepers could be part of any tier in the model. These could be community members who may not have been formally trained to intervene with someone who is at risk for suicide but emerge as potential gatekeepers as recognized by those with suicidal intent (for example, clergy, police, coaches, etc.) and could also be part of any tier in the model. The parallel that exists between the diagnoses, the gatekeeper program, the assessment method (SAD PERSON), and the RTI makes both the assessment of and the intervention with individuals diagnosed with ASD and suicide comprehensive and solid.

Tools and Practice Examples

Below is a case study. How would the social worker or the mental health professional assess the situation and respond in relation to suicide and the ASD of the adolescent?

Synopsis: James

James is a 15-year-old boy, the second of three children, with a long history of unusual and delayed development. His parents bring him for evaluation because of a worsening in his behavioral functioning. Over the two years before this evaluation, James has become progressively more rigid and inflexible, and his insistence on elaborate routines causes much difficulty. *He has no real friends* and displays a number of idiosyncrasies. He repeats certain phrases from television over and over and displays a fascination with bits of string and lint. He has collected considerable quantities of these items, which he insists on carrying with him. Any attempt to divert him from this unusual interest leads to agitation with periods of body rocking or head banging. Upon examination, James exhibits an unusual pattern of social relatedness—making eye contact infrequently and seeming relatively *uninterested in social interaction.* He does not use facial expressions, gestures, or body posture to regulate the interaction and lacks emotional reciprocity. His parents report that he has great trouble sustaining a conversation and is interested in discussing only certain television programs and his string collection. His language is stereotyped and repetitive with a monotonic quality. His parents also report that he exhibits some stereotyped behaviors when excited and tends to adhere to various nonfunctional routines (e.g., he always walks around a chair three times before sitting in it, a practice observed by the clinician during the evaluation). His affective range is highly constricted and *his insight and judgment are poor.* No evidence of delusions, hallucinations, or other psychotic phenomena is observed.

On examination, James was unable to follow simple requests and had marked difficulties with tasks that involved imitation. James was particularly *intolerant of change.* For example, he insisted that his parents follow exactly the same complicated routine at bedtime each night and became extremely agitated if any change in the usual pattern occurred. He was also very sensitive to the inanimate environment so that, although he often seemed almost completely oblivious to his mother's voice, he would panic when he heard the vacuum cleaner. His play involved simple object manipulation with considerable perseveration. By the time James was 12, his usual interests and his difficulty dealing with change had diminished somewhat, and he was mainstreamed for a few class periods a day in public school. With the onset of adolescence, however, James's behavior deteriorated, particularly after the onset of seizure disorder at age 14. He became more behaviorally rigid, his childhood interest in collecting unusual materials returned, and it was difficult for him to focus on educational or vocational activities.

Application of the SAD PERSON Mnemonic

Assessing an individual diagnosed with an ASD for suicide is a greater challenge for social workers and other mental health practitioners because of the complexity of the diagnosis of autism. Just as suicide is on a spectrum of continuation between thoughts and attempts, ASD has its continuation between a mild form of autism to severe. According to Sullivan, Barron, Bezmen, Rivera, and Zapata-Vega (2005), the ability to predict that a specific individual will imminently commit suicide is still elusive. In the abovementioned case, we can use the SAD PERSON mnemonic to try and determine the level of risk for suicide for James. The variables of age and gender for James immediately place him in a higher risk category. As mentioned before, there is a strong likelihood that because of the diagnosis of autism, which is considered a developmental disability, James may experience and present with depressive symptoms or diagnosis. The lack of a social support system during adolescence as well as having no significant other brings the score count to 4–5 (see Table 19.2 above).

There is wide and strong evidence of the effectiveness of gatekeeper programs at schools (Stein et al., 2010). Gatekeepers are individuals who have primary contact with those at risk for suicide and go about identifying them by recognizing suicidal risk factors. Traditionally, gatekeepers have been divided into two main groups, defined as either designated or emergent. The designated group consists of people who are trained and designated as helping professionals (from the fields of medicine, social work, nursing, psychology, etc.). The emergent group consists of community members who may not have been formally trained to intervene with someone who is at risk for suicide but emerge as potential gatekeepers as recognized by those with suicidal intent (for example, clergy, police, coaches, etc.) (Isaac et al., 2009). Gatekeeper programs are based on the premise that there are recognizable risk factors for suicide; however, individuals at risk for suicide often do not seek help (Swanke & Buila, 2010). Individuals who were categorized as having low emotional competence (the ability to identify, describe, and understand emotions) had the lowest intentions of seeking help from both informal and formal sources (Ciarrochi et al., 2003). Practitioners, social workers and other mental health professionals should be alert to the importance of assessing suicidal ideation among individuals who may be at higher risk for suicidal ideation than the neurotypical individual.

Key Points to Remember

- In the past decade, the increase in the prevalence of autism spectrum disorders, including AS, and the suspected causes of this increase, have become a matter of concern for mental health professionals, researchers, educators, and parents (Newschaffer et al., 2005; Prior, 2003).
- According to the Centers for Disease Control and Prevention (2011), among individuals age 15 to 24 years old, there are approximately 100–200 attempts of suicide for every completed suicide.
- About 86% of school psychologists have counseled a student who had threatened to commit suicide, and 35% have reported that a student in their school died of suicide.
- Individuals diagnosed with ASD are at higher risk for committing suicide than the neurotypical peer due to their difficulty with social communication and the social demands of adolescence.
- One of the ways to remember how to assess for suicide risk is using the **SAD PERSON** mnemonic.
- Gatekeeper programs have been found to increase school staff awareness of suicide warning signs in at-risk students and knowledge of resources to treat suicidal students.

Further Learning

NIMH: http://www.nimh.nih.gov/health/publications/autism/complete-index.shtml

Autism Research Institute: http://www.autism.com/index_b.asp

US Autism & Asperger Association: http://www.usautism.org

Autism Society of America (ASA): http://www.autism-society.org

The following is a list of web sites and resources for further learning provided by the American Foundation for Suicidal Prevention (AFSP).

Online Support Groups

www.suicidegrief.com

www.groww.org/Branches/sos.htm

Web Sites

www.beforetheirtime.org

Before Their Time is a three-volume, six-CD compilation of memorial songs for survivors. From Joan Baez to Cheryl Wheeler, 80 artists contributed songs they wrote after the death of someone they loved. A perfect condolence gift that provides comfort through all the stages of grief that survivors encounter.

www.thegiftofkeith.org/info/main_navigation.html

Created by a survivor family and contains information and resources about surviving suicide loss.

www.siblingsurvivors.com

Created by a survivor after she lost her sister to suicide.

www.suicidememorialwall.com

Created to remember some of the names of those who died by suicide and to encourage survivors to better understand the causes of suicide.

www.survivorsofsuicide.com

General information about surviving suicide loss.

Other Organizations

American Association of Suicidology: www.suicidology.org

Promotes public awareness, education, and training for professionals, and sponsors an annual "Healing After Suicide" conference for survivors.

Canadian Association for Suicide Prevention: www.casp-acps.ca

Online list of Canadian survivor support groups. Promotes public awareness, training, education, and advocacy.

The Compassionate Friends: www.compassionatefriends.org

For all parents, siblings, and grandparents who have experienced the death of a child, brother, sister, or grandchild. Sponsors support groups, newsletters, and online support groups throughout the country, as well as an annual national conference for bereaved families.

The Dougy Center/The National Center for Grieving Children & Families: www.dougy.org

Publishes extensive resources for helping children and teens who are grieving the death of a parent, sibling, or friend, including, "After Suicide: A Workbook for Grieving Kids."

International Association for Suicide Prevention: http://www.iasp.info/postvention.php

An international organization with a task force and newsletter dedicated specifically to postvention. The Web site lists organizations and support groups for survivors of suicide loss around the world.

National Organization for People of Color Against Suicide: www.nopcas.com

Provides resources to minority communities in the areas of survivor support and suicide prevention and education, including sponsoring an annual conference.

National Suicide Prevention Lifeline: www.suicidepreventionlifeline.org

A 24-hour, toll-free suicide prevention service available to anyone in suicidal crisis. You will be routed to the closest possible crisis center in your area. With crisis centers across the country, their mission is to provide immediate assistance to anyone seeking mental health services. Call for yourself, or someone you care about. Your call is free and confidential.

Suicide Awareness Voices of Education: www.save.org

Grassroots nonprofit organization that educates about depression and provides resources on suicide and depression, newsletter, and survivor conference.

Suicide Information and Education Centre: www.suicideinfo.ca

Computer-assisted resource library with extensive collection of materials on suicide, including information kits, pamphlets, literature searches, and clipping services.

Suicide Prevention Resource Center: www.sprc.org

Features an extensive online library of information on suicide prevention and surviving suicide loss, a nationwide calendar of events, and customized Web pages for survivors, teachers, teens, clergy, and more.

Autism Speaks: http://www.autismspeaks.org/about-us

Autism Speaks was founded in February 2005 by Bob and Suzanne Wright, grandparents of a child with autism. Their longtime friend Bernie Marcus donated $25 million to help financially launch the organization. Since then, Autism Speaks has grown into the nation's largest autism science and advocacy organization, dedicated to funding research into the causes, prevention, treatments, and a cure for autism; increasing awareness of autism spectrum disorders; and advocating for the needs of individuals with autism and their families. We are proud of what we've been able to accomplish and look forward to continued successes in the years ahead.

The Autism Internet Modules: http://www.ocali.org/project/aim

The Autism Internet Modules were developed with one aim in mind: to make comprehensive, up-to-date, and usable information on autism accessible and applicable to educators, other professionals, and families who support individuals with autism spectrum disorders (ASD). Written by experts from across the United States, all online modules are free and are designed to promote understanding of, respect for, and equality of persons with ASD

Autism Research Institute: http://www.autism.com/

For more than 40 years, the Autism Research Institute (ARI) has devoted its work to conducting research and to disseminating the results of research on individuals with ASD.

Autism Society: http://www.autism-society.org/about-us/

The Autism Society, the nation's leading grassroots autism organization, exists to improve the lives of all affected by autism. We do this by increasing public awareness about the day-to-day issues faced by people on the spectrum, advocating for appropriate services for individuals across the lifespan, and providing the latest information regarding treatment, education, research, and advocacy.

References

American Psychiatric Association. (2000). *DSM-IV-TR*. Washington, DC: Author.

Bender, W. N., Rosenkrans, C. B., & Crane, M. K. (1999). Stress, depression, and suicide among students with learning disabilities. *Learning Disability Quarterly*, *22*(2), 143–156.

Berman, A. L. (2009). School-based suicide prevention: Research advances and practice implications. *School Psychology Review*, *38*(2), 233–238.

Bertrand, J., Boyle, C., Yeargin- Allsopp, M., Decoufle, P., Mars, A., & Bove, F. (2001). Prevalence of autism in a United States population. *Pediatrics*, *108*(5), 1155–1162.

Bond, L., Carlin, J. B., Thomas, L., Rubin, K., & Patton, G. (2001). Does bullying cause emotional problems? *British Medical Journal*, *323*(7311), 480–485.

Ciarrochi, J., Wilson, C. J., Deane, F. P., & Rickwood, D. (2003). Do difficulties with emotions inhibit help-seeking in adolescence? *Counseling Psychology Quarterly*, *16*(2), 103–120.

Croen, L. A., Grether, J. K., Hoogstrate, J., & Selvin, S. (2002). The changing prevalence of autism in California. *Journal of Autism and Developmental Disorders*, *32*(3), 207–215.

Foreman, M. E. (1990). The counselor's assessment and intervention with the suicidal student. In L. C. Whitaker & R. E. Slimak (Eds.), *College student suicide* (pp. 125–140). New York: The Haworth Press.

Green, J., Gilchrist, A., Burton, D., & Cox, A. (2000). Social and psychiatric functioning in adolescents with Asperger syndrome compared with conduct disorder. *Journal of Autism and Developmental Disorders*, *30*(4), 279–293.

Isaac, M., Elias, B., Katz, Y. L., Belik, S. H., Deane, F. P., Enns, M. W., & Sareen, J. (2009). Gatekeeper training as a preventative intervention for suicide: A systematic review. *The Canadian Journal of Psychiatry*, *54*(4), 260–268.

Klin, A., McPartland, J., & Volkmar, F. R. (2005). Asperger syndrome. In F. Volkmar, R. Paul, A. Klin, & D. Cohen (Eds.), *Handbook of autism and pervasive developmental disorders* (pp. 88–125). Hoboken, NJ: John Wiley and Sons.

Lord, C., & Corsello, C. (2005). Diagnostic instrument in autistic spectrum disorders. In F. Volkmar, R. Paul, A. Klin, & D. Cohen (Eds.), *Handbook of autism and pervasive developmental disorders* (pp. 730–771). Hoboken, NJ: John Wiley and Sons.

Lubin, G., Glasser, S., Boyko, V., & Barell, V. (2001). Epidemiology of suicide in Israel. *Social Psychiatry and Psychiatric Epidemiology*, *36*, 123–127.

Mishna, F. (2003). Learning disabilities and bullying. *Journal of Learning Disabilities*, *36*(4), 336–347.

Newschaffer, C. J., Falb, M. D., & Gurney, J. G. (2005). National autism prevalence trends from United States special education data. *Pediatrics*, *115*(3), 277–282.

Patterson, W., Dohn, H., Bird, J., & Patterson, G. (1983). Assessing suicidality in adults: Integrating childhood trauma as a major risk factor. *Psychsomatics*, *24*, 343–349.

Prinstein, M. J., Boergers, J., Spirito, A., Little, T. D., & Grapentine, W. (2000). Peer functioning, family dysfunction, and psychological symptoms in a risk factor model adolescent inpatients' suicidal ideation severity. *Journal of Clinical Child Psychology*, *29*(3), 392–405.

Prior, M. (2003). Is there an increase in the prevalence of autism spectrum disorders? *Journal of Pediatric. Child Health*, *39*, 81–82.

Rourke, B. P., & Tsatsanis, K. D. (2000). Nonverbal learning disabilities and Asperger syndrome. In A. Klin, F. R. Volkmar, & S. S. Sparrow (Eds.), *Asperger syndrome* (pp. 231–253). New York, NY: Guilford Press.

Rudd, M. D., Rajab, M. H., Orman, D. T., Stulman, D. A., Joiner, T., & Dixon, W. (1996). Effectiveness of an outpatient intervention targeting suicidal young adults: Preliminary results. *Journal of Consulting and Clinical Psychology*, *64*, 179–190

Rutter, M. (2005). Genetic influences and autism. In F. Volkmar, R. Paul, A. Klin, & D. Cohen (Eds.), *Handbook of autism and pervasive developmental disorders* (pp. 425–452). Hoboken, NJ: John Wiley and Sons.

Sailor, W. (2009). *Making RTI work: How smart schools are reforming education through schoolwide response-to-intervention*. New York, NY: Jossey-Bass.

Schreibman, L., & Ingersoll, B. (2005). Behavioral interventions to promote learning in individuals with autism. In F. Volkmar, R. Paul, A. Klin, & D. Cohen (Eds.), *Handbook of autism and pervasive developmental disorders* (pp. 882–896). Hoboken, NJ: John Wiley and Sons.

Shaffer, D., & Greenberg, T. (2002). Suicide and suicidal behavior in children and adolescents. In D. Shaffer & B. D. Waslick (Eds.), *The many faces of depression in children and adolescents* (pp. 129–178). Arlington, VA: American Psychiatric Publishing.

Shtayermman, O., (2008). Suicidal ideation and comorbid disorders in adolescents and young adults diagnosed with Asperger's syndrome: A population at risk. *Journal of Human Behavior in the Social Environment*, *18*(3), 301–328.

Sourander, A., Helstela, L., & Helenius, H., & Piha, J. (2000). Persistence of bullying from childhood to adolescence—A longitudinal 8-year follow-up study. *Child Abuse and Neglect*, *24*(7), 873–881.

Lyndal, B., Carlin, J. B., Thomas, L., Rubin, K., & Patton, G. (2001). Does bullying cause emotional problems? *British Medical Journal*, *323*, 480–484.

Stein, D., Kataoka, S. H., Hamilton, A. B., Schultz, D., Ryan, G., Vona, P., & Wong, M. (2010). School personnel perspectives on their school's implementation of a school-based suicide prevention program. *The Journal of Behavioral Health Services & Research*, *37*(3), 338–349.

Stroch, E. A., & Masia-Warner, C. (2004). The relationship of peer victimization to social anxiety and loneliness in adolescent females. *Journal of Adolescence*, *27*(3), 351–362.

Suicide and Attempted Suicide. (June 11, 2011). In *Morbidity and mortality weekly report*. Retrieved from Centers for Disease Control and Prevention: http://www.cdc.gov/mmwr

Sullivan, A. M., Barron, C. T., Bezmen, J., Rivera, J., & Zapata-Vega, M. (2005). The safe treatment of the suicidal patient in an adult inpatient setting: A proactive preventive approach. *Psychiatric Quarterly*, *76*(1), 67–83.

Swanke, J. R., & Buila, S. M. D. (2010). Gatekeeper training for caregivers and professionals: A variation on suicide prevention. *Advances in Mental Health*, *9*, 98–104.

Tantam, D. (2000a). Adolescence and adulthood of individuals with Asperger syndrome. In A. Klin, F. R. Volkmar, & S. S. Sparrow (Eds.), *Asperger syndrome* (pp. 367–399). New York, NY: Guilford Press.

Tantam, D. (2000b). Psychological disorder in adolescents and adults with Asperger syndrome. *Autism*, *4*(1), 47–62.

Tantam, D. (2003). The challenge of adolescents and adults with Asperger syndrome. *Child and Adolescent Psychiatric Clinics of North America, 12,* 143–163.

VanBergeijk, E. O., & Shtayermman, O. (2005). Asperger syndrome: An enigma for social work. *Journal of Human Behavior in the Social Environment, 12*(1), 23–37.

Volkmar, F. R., & Klin, A. (2000). Diagnostic issues in Asperger syndrome. In A. Klin, F. R. Volkmar, & S. S. Sparrow (Eds.), *Asperger syndrome* (pp. 25–71). New York, NY: Guilford Press.

Volkmar, F. R., & Klin, A. (2005). Issues in the classification of autism and related conditions. In F. Volkmar, R. Paul, A. Klin, & D. Cohen (Eds.), *Handbook of autism and pervasive developmental disorders* (pp. 5–41). Hoboken, NJ: John Wiley and Sons.

Wachter, C. A., & Bouck, E. C. (2008). Suicide and students with high incidence disabilities: What special educators need to know? *Teaching Exceptional Children, 41*(1), 66–72.

PART III

Resources for Students with Substance Abuse, Health, and Interpersonal and Social Problems

SECTION IV

Effective Ways to Help Students with Substance Abuse, STDs, and Obesity

Substance abuse and sexually transmitted diseases are among the most prevalent health challenges facing today's schools. The rapid increase of obesity among children and adolescents is also a prevalent issue that has been voiced as a national concern. This section offers chapters that provide effective practices and resources for both preventing and intervening with these issues.

CHAPTER 20

Substance Abuse at Elementary Age

Effective Interventions

Lori K. Holleran Steiker ▪ Soyon Jung ▪ Kristy Gillispie

Getting Started

Substance use/abuse is usually perceived as a problem of the adult and adolescent population and seldom seriously examined with regard to elementary school children. According to the Parents' Resource Institute for Drug Education (PRIDE; 2008; 2009), however, it is not uncommon among elementary school children to experiment with various substances. The PRIDE survey (2008–2009) analyzing data collected from close to 20,000 4th–6th graders found that 1.4% of fourth graders, 2.0% of fifth graders, and 2.8% of sixth graders said they had smoked cigarettes within the past year. The proportion of the elementary school students who had consumed alcohol in the previous year ranges from 3.7% of fourth graders to 7.6% of sixth graders. Substance use by elementary school children is not limited to tobacco or alcoholic beverages—2.5% of fourth graders, 2% of fifth graders, and 2.7% of sixth graders reported inhalant use in the prior year. The percentage of the students using marijuana in the past year ranges from 0.8% for fourth graders to 1.5% for sixth graders.

In addition to the prevalence of substance use/abuse among elementary school children, it should be noted that the age of first substance use is getting younger (American Academy of Pediatrics, 1998). For example, the proportion of students who drank alcohol before age 13 years was about 16% for 11th and 12th grade males, but it was 33.3% for 10th grade males (Center for Disease Control and Prevention, 2004). It should be taken seriously because earlier onset of substance use is significantly related to heavier use and more addictive symptoms in later years, as well as more difficult rehabilitation if a problem emerges (Jenson & Howard, 1991; Knowles, 2001; Sarvela, Monge, Shannon, & Newrot, 1999; Hingson, Heeren, & Edwards, 2008). The risk of early use of substances also exists physiologically. A child's brain is different from an adult's and the deleterious effects of alcohol on a developing brain are profound (Kuhn, Swartzwelder, & Wilson, 1998).

These statistics and trends of experimentation with substances might suggest that substance use/abuse prevention programs be provided to elementary school students. There is also empirical evidence that well-designed prevention programs for elementary school children significantly reduce various problem behaviors, including substance use/abuse in their later lives (e.g., Hawkins, Catalano, Kosterman, Abbott, & Hill, 1999). The elementary school is often regarded as the ideal setting for substance use/abuse prevention programs (Gibson, Mitchell, & Basile, 1993). The reasons can be summarized as follows: First, the school environment has a powerful influence on children, given time spent, learning process, and social interaction (St. Pierre, Mark, Kaltreider, & Campbell, 2001). Second, schools are the major provider of mental health services for children (Rones & Hoagwood, 2000), and a number of school-based prevention programs have been found effective (Gibson et al., 1993). Thus, many schools already have valuable resources and accumulated know-how regarding mental health services. Finally, students are more likely to obtain information about substances and talk about drugs with their schoolteachers rather than their parents (Alcoholism & Drug Abuse Weekly, 1999, April 19).

In this chapter, the authors present an overview of selective prevention interventions, a risk and protective factor paradigm, and two examples of evidence-based programs, the Strengthening Families Program (SFP) and Positive Action (PA). The two programs are particularly worth noting because they illustrate how preventive intervention can address risk, enhance protective factors, and be effectively implemented at school settings. Lastly, practical guidelines are then presented for school social workers and other school mental health professionals who envision substance use/abuse prevention targeting elementary school children.

What We Know

Understanding Selective Prevention Programs

Preventive interventions are often classified into three categories, universal, selective, and indicated prevention, based on the target populations. This is the same public health framework upon which Response to Intervention (RTI) is based. Universal preventions address the entire population of a community or an organization such as an elementary school. Indicated preventions are directed toward specific individuals who are showing serious precursors or are already involved in problem behavior(s) such as substance use/abuse. On the other hand, selective prevention targets "subsets of the total population that are deemed to be at risk for substance abuse by virtue of their membership in a particular population segment—for example, children of adult alcoholics, dropouts, or students who are failing academically" (National Institute on Drug Abuse [NIDA], 1997b, p. 11). Selective prevention interventions are recommendable in elementary school settings, given that a majority of elementary school students do not exhibit substance use/abuse problem but a significant number of them are exposed to multiple risk factors. Although many children are at risk of substance use from an early age, relatively few substance use prevention programs target elementary-aged children (Finke et al., 2002; Marsiglia, Kulis, Yabiku, Nieri, & Coleman, 2011). This chapter will suggest important considerations for substance abuse prevention at the primary school level.

Program Goal and Theoretical Background of Selective Prevention

The ultimate goal of selective prevention is to deter the onset of substance abuse among at-risk groups and to help them be equipped with proper skills and information so that they can reduce their vulnerability (NIDA, 1997a). Based on a risk and protective factor model, selective prevention approaches usually pursue such goals by minimizing the impacts of risk factors and maximizing the effects of protective factors. Initially risk factors for substance use/abuse were limited to a narrow range of factors such as biological or psychological variables only (Jenson, 1997). Recently, however, the risk factor model is usually grounded in

Table 20.1 Risk Factors from Multidimensionals Perspectives

	Study Number (see below for reference)				
	1	*2*	*3*	*4*[a]	*5*[a]
Individual					
Problematic health status (physical and mental)		O	O	O	
Constitutional factors/Sensation-seeking orientation/(genetic predisposition to chemical dependency)	O	O	O		O
Poor impulse control			O		O
Greater levels of rebelliousness					
Attention deficits			O		
Early and persistent antisocial behavior/rebellious attitudes	O	O			O
Early initiation of the problem behavior	O				O
Favorable attitudes toward the problem behavior					
Delinquency (e.g., history of trouble w/the police)					
Decreased perception of risk					O
Lack of social bonding/alienation		O			O
Family					
Family conflict/marital discord	O	O	O		O
Family stress				O	
Family disruption and/or dysfunction due to death, divorce, and parental incarceration				O	
Poor parent–child bonding			O		
Poor parental supervision					O
Poor family management practices/discipline	O	O	O		O
Family communication			O		
Family history of mental health problem				O	
Family present use or history of substance use/abuse			O	O	O
Family history of problem behavior	O	O			
Favorable parental attitudes/parental permissiveness toward the problem behavior/substance use	O	O			O
Incidence of child abuse, neglect, and trauma		O			O
Lack of support for positive school values and attitudes				O	
Economic deprivation					O
Differential family acculturation					O
Peers					
Rejection by conforming peer group/alienation and rebelliousness	O		O		
Alienation and rebelliousness	O	O			
Peer pressure					
Peer approval of drug use					

(continued)

Table 20.1 *(Continued)*

	Study Number (see below for reference)				
	1	*2*	*3*	*4*[a]	*5*[a]
School					
School failure/academic failure/beginning in late elementary school	O		O		O
Low commitment to school	O	O	O		
Absenteeism and dropout		O			O
Lack of cultural grounding and resources, language difficulties, or both		O			
Dysfunction within the school environment such as high rates of substance abuse or unsafe school environment				O	O
School climate that provides little encouragement and support to students				O	
Lack of clear school policies regarding drug use					O
Low teacher expectations of student achievement					O
Low teacher and student morale				O	
Community/macro-level environment					
Neighborhood disorganization	O	O	O		O
Low neighborhood attachment	O	O	O		O
Residential mobility/transitions and mobility/instability: transition and mobility	O	O	O		
High population density			O	O	
Availability of alcohol and drugs	O	O			
Low community safety/high violence/high adult crime rates/ high rates of drug abuse		O	O	O	O
Community regulation/laws favorable toward drug use, firearms, or crime	O	O	O		O
Pro-use messages specifically in advertising					O
Negative community attitudes toward youth		O			
Cultural norms about alcohol and drug use/community values and attitudes that are tolerant of substance abuse			O	O	O
Hyperactivity			O		
Lack of youth recreation opportunities/lack of cultural resources/lack of active community institutions		O	O	O	
Poverty and economic deprivation	O	O	O		O
Cultural disenfranchisement					O
Situational/cultural factors					
Stressful events, multiple stressors, or both		O			
High incidence of drug and alcohol use		O			
Tension around cultural identity, acculturative stress, or both		O			

(continued)

Table 20.1 *(Continued)*

	Study Number (see below for reference)				
	1	*2*	*3*	*4*[a]	*5*[a]
Societal Factors					
National economic and employment conditions					O
Discrimination					O
Marginalization of groups					O

[a] The authors also include several other demographic risk factors such as age, gender, race/ethnicity, socioeconomic status, employment, and education. Since these factors are not specified in a useful way, however, these factors are not presented here. For example, with this information only, which gender, male or female, is risk factor is uncertain.

Studies Introduced

1. Hawkins, J. D., Catalano, R. F, & Miller, J.Y. (1992). Risk and protective factors for alcohol and other drug problems in adolescence and early adulthood: Implications for substance abuse prevention. *Psychological Bulletin, 112*(1), 64–105.
2. Developmental Research and Programs. (1997). *Communities that care: Risk assessment for preventing adolescent problem behaviors.* Seattle, WA: Developmental Research and Programs.
3. Holleran, L. K., Kim, Y., & Dixon, K. (2004). Innovative approaches to risk assessment within alcohol prevention programming. In A. R. Roberts & K. R. Yeager (Eds.), *Evidence-based practice manual: Research and outcome measures in health and human services* (pp. 677–684). New York: Oxford University Press.
4. Jenson, J. M. (1997). Risk and protective factors for alcohol and other drug use in childhood and adolescence. In M. W. Fraser (Ed.), *Risk and resilience in childhood* (pp. 117–139). Washington, DC: NASW Press.
5. National Institute on Drug Abuse. (1997). *Drug abuse prevention for at-risk groups* (NIH No. 97–4114). Rockville, MD: U. S. Department of Health and Human Services, National Institutes of Health.
6. Brounstein, P J., & Zweig, J. M. (1999). *Toward the 21st century: A primer on effective programs* (DHHS Publication No. [SMA]99–3301): Substance Abuse and Mental Health Services Administration.

comprehensive ecological frameworks. Table 20.1 shows some examples of studies that present risk factors for substance use/abuse, which range from individual attributes to macro-social environmental characteristics.

While risk factors increase the likelihood of problem incidence, protective factors reduce the likelihood because they buffer the impact of risk factors by augmenting strength. Complementing the risk factor model, prevention efforts based on a protective factor model focus on the positive and also modifiable factors rather than less mutable risks such as temperament, genetic heritage, or low socioeconomic status. A major contribution of protective factor models to the prevention approach is that they shift the prevention paradigm from a psychopathological perspective to a healthy human development perspective (Holleran, Kim, & Dixon, 2004). According to 40 Developmental Assets of Search Institute (accessible at http://www.search-institute.org), one of the most widely used and effective protective factor models, protective factors can be classified into two categories, external assets and internal assets, and each category is composed of 20 factors. The external and internal assets for elementary-age children are exhibited in the Table 20.2.

Other Characteristics of Selective Prevention

Targeting at-risk groups, selective prevention usually requires more intensive care, more professional skills, more varied treatment strategies, and a longer program duration compared to universal prevention (Kumpfer, 2003). The greatest merit of selective prevention lies in program efficiency and effectiveness. Despite larger program expenditure per capita, selective prevention is often considered more efficient than universal programs because it can cut down the total program cost by targeting individuals in need (NIDA, 1997a). In addition, a selective prevention approach can increase program efficiency by choosing optimum strategies that are well matched with identified risk factors of the program participants (Sullivan & Farrell, 2002). A particularly impressive facet of selective prevention is that its effect size is in general greater than that of universal prevention (Wilson, Gottfredson, & Najaka, 2001; Gottfredson & Wilson, 2003).

Selective prevention also has some limitations and practical difficulties. The biggest challenge in selective prevention is to identify and recruit at-risk group members. Even when a valid,

Table 20.2 Forty Developmental Assets for Elementary-Age Children

External Assets		*Internal Assets*	
Support	1. Family support	Commitment to learning	21. Achievement expectation and motivation
	2. Positive family communication		22. Children are engaged in learning
	3. Other adult relationships		
	4. Caring neighborhood		23. Stimulating activity
	5. Caring out-of-home climate		24. Enjoyment of learning and bonding with school
Empowerment	6. Parent involvement in out-of-home situation		25. Reading for pleasure
		Positive values	26. Caring
	7. Community values children		27. Equality and social justice
	8. Children are given useful roles		28. Integrity
	9. Service to others		29. Honesty
	10. Safety		30. Responsibility
Boundaries and expectations	11. Family boundaries		31. Healthy lifestyle and sexual attitudes
	12. Out-of-home boundaries		
	13. Neighborhood boundaries	Social competencies	32. Planning and decision-making practice
			33. Interpersonal skills
	14. Adult role models		34. Cultural competence
	15. Positive peer observation		35. Resistance skills
	16. Appropriate expectations for growth		36. Peaceful conflict resolution
Constructive use of time	17. Creative activities	Positive identity	37. Personal power
	18. Out-of-home activities		38. Self-esteem
	19. Religious community		39. Sense of purpose
	20. Positive, supervised time at home		40. Positive view of personal future

Source: www.search-institute.org/systems/files/40AssetsList.pdf. Reprinted with permission.

precise, and reliable scale or screening instrument is available, serious weakness still remains. As selective prevention is directed toward at-risk subgroups of the general population, selective prevention inherently has a high possibility of stigmatization. Another limitation or difficulty of selective prevention approaches is that parents or family involvement, the core part of selective prevention, is not a simple job in practice, although a growing body of research notes that the parent component is essential for program success. At-risk populations often include poor families and single-parent families, and many of these families do not have enough time or resources to ensure the parents participate in and concentrate on the program.

What We Can Do

What Works? Effective Selective Prevention Programs for Elementary School Children

Although risk and protective models enhance prevention approaches, there are also some important warnings. Above all, it should be noticed that risk factors are not always causes of the problem (Fisher & Harrison, 2004). Rather, risks are correlates or covariates, which could be simple indicators or moderators of the problem (Pandina, 1996). This means that sometimes reducing the impact of risk factors does not necessarily decrease a student's substance use/abuse. This logic also applies to protective factors. Therefore, it is recommended for school social workers and other school-based practitioners to examine successful programs, refer to research on program evaluation, and develop prevention strategies based on programs whose effectiveness is empirically proven. While there is scant research that evaluates the effectiveness of selective prevention programs with rigorous scientific methods, there are some effective selective programs that can be considered model programs. Among those, selective prevention programs particularly appropriate for elementary school children are summarized in the Table 20.3.

Although all of these programs attempt to reduce the impact of risk factors and augment the effects of protective factors, they are different in terms of strength, limitations, program focus, and central strategies. Thus, it is suggested that professionals who envision substance use/abuse prevention programs scrutinize the primary resources and program strategies to select a best model program to utilize. If a model program is selected, a visit to the program Web site is recommended to glean useful information including program effectiveness, practitioner training, and economic costs of the program. Here, detailed information about the two selective prevention programs, Strengthen Families Program and Positive Action Program, are presented because these programs are considered particularly effective and applicable for elementary school settings.

The Strengthening Families Program (SFP)

The Strengthening Families Program (SFP: http://www.strengtheningfamiliesprogram.org) is a family skills training program designed to improve family life skills, parenting skills, and children's social skills (Kumpfer, Alvarado, & Whiteside, 2003; Kumpfer, Whiteside, Greene, & Allen, 2010). This program was developed by Karol Kumpfer and her associates in 1983, targeting elementary school age children who are at high risk for substance abuse and other problem behaviors. Over the last two decades, SFP has been revised and modified for different target populations such as junior high school students, preschool children, African Americans, and Hispanics/Latinos. SFP has shown significant effectiveness consistently in replications and various ethnic groups. For school social workers and other professionals who primarily work with elementary school children and their families, the original version of SFP program is introduced in this chapter.

Program Goal and Objectives

The ultimate goal of SFP is to enhance the resiliency of at-risk children. For this goal, SFP put primary focus on reduction of risk factors in family environment and enhancement of protective factors. Under this goal, SFP has three specified objectives and relevant strategies as follows (NIDA, 1997a, pp. 20–21).

- To increase parenting skills by
    - Increasing positive attention and praise
    - Increasing parents' levels of empathy for their children
    - Increasing parents' use of effective discipline
    - Decreasing parents' use of physical punishment
    - Decreasing parents' use of demonstrating use of substances
    - To increase children's skills by
    - Increasing their communication skills
    - Increasing their skills to resist peer pressure to use substances or engage in other inappropriate behaviors
    - Increasing recognition of feelings
    - Increasing knowledge about alcohol and drugs
    - Increasing skills for coping with anger and criticism
    - Increasing compliance with parental requests
    - Increasing their self-esteem
    - Decreasing aggressive and other problem behaviors
    - Reducing intention to use in the future and the actual use of substances

Table 20.3 Effective Selective Preventions

Program	IOM: Universal	IOM: Selective	IOM: Indicative	Target population	Duration	*Program Structure*	*Reported Effectiveness*	*Personal/social competency*	*Academic support*	*In-/after-school curricula*	*ATOD info. dissemination*	*Peer resistance skill*	*Peer involvement*	*Intensive case management*	*Alternative activity*	*Family social/communi. skills*	*Parenting/parent discipline*	*Family AOD Education*	*Parent–child interaction*	*School reform*	*Teacher involvement*	*Parent–school relation*	*Community service*	*Mentoring*	*Community involvement*	*Incentives for partici. or compl.*	*Prob. identification/referral*
Across Ages http://acrossages.org/		O		9–13 yr. old	1–3 yr.	Intergenerational mentoring • Mentoring from qualified and trained elders • Life skills curriculum led by classroom teachers • Performing community service • Life/problem-solving curriculum • Workshop for parent & family members, which is designed to help them practice better parenting and participate in school activities	Quasi-experimental design research, the program showed desirable outcome in the following areas: • Reactions to stress & anxiety • Self-perception • Attitudes toward school, elders, & future • Problem-solving skills/ self-efficacy • Knowledge about substance use • Frequency of substance use	O		O	O	O			O	O	O		O		O		●	●	●	O	
CASASTART (Striving Together to Achieve Rewarding Tomorrows) http://www.casacolumbia.org/absolutenm/templates/article.asp?articleid= 287&zoneid=32		O	O	8–13 yr. old	1–3 yr.	• Case management that involves a home interview and monthly home visit • Academic support for children through tutoring and homework assistance • Social and emotional support for children through adult mentoring program • After-school curricular activities that includes recreational programs and trips • Community involvement that intends increased police presence and enhanced relationship among youth, families, and the police	Comparison of experimental subjects & control group at 1-year follow-up • Lower rate of past month use of any drugs, gateway drugs, & stronger drugs • Lower rate of past year use of any drugs & gateway drugs • Lower rate of lifetime use of any drugs or gateway drugs • Lower levels of violent crimes in the past year • Lower rate of involvement in drug sales during the past month • Lower rate of lifetime drug sales		O	O	O		O	●	O	●	●		O			O	O	O	O	O	O

FAST (Families and Schools Together) http://www.wcer.wisc.edu/projects/projects.php?project_num=64	O	O	O	5–14 yr old	1–2 yr.	• Teacher identification of at-risk student • Outreach for program participants • Multifamily group sessions including parent–child play therapy (for 8 weeks) • Ongoing monthly reunions of the multifamily group (for 21 months)	• Decrease in anxiety-withdrawal of children • Increase in parent social support • Declines in attention problem and conduct disorder • Improved family cohesion • Long-term effect has been has been reported at 2–4 yr. follow-up • Program effectiveness appears consistent in more than 53 replication sites across the nation and Canada	O		O	O	O	O		O	●	●		●		O	O			O	O	
Positive Action http://www.positiveaction.net	O	O	O	5–18 yr. old	0–12 yr.	• Daily classroom curriculum where teachers present 15- to 20-minute lessons (a total of 140 lessons) with various activities • School-climate program, which promotes the practice and reinforcement of schoolwide positive actions • Parent program that focuses on 42 weekly lessons for parents and encourages parent participation in school activities • Community program that is provided to community leaders so that a wide range of community service practices and cultivate positive actions within the community	• Program effectiveness has been observed in the following areas: academic achievement, absenteeism, discipline problem, violence and drug use, and criminal booking • Program effectiveness sustained in middle and high school years of the subjects • These outcome results have been replicated repeatedly	O		O	O	O	O					O		●	●	●			O		

(continued)

Table 20.3 *(Countinued)*

Projective Achieve http://projectachieve.us/stop-think/stop-and-think.html	O	O		3–14 yr. old	Over 3 yr.	• Stop & Think Social Skills program, in-school curricula that teach students desirable social and self-management skills • Parent training, tutoring, and support, which emphasizes ongoing parent–school collaboration • Effective classroom teacher/staff development, which is designed to increase their skills in strategic planning, organizational analysis, effective instructional and behavioral intervention • School reform, which intends more effective supports for social and academic development of students	• Decreased discipline referrals to the principal/the office • Improved in academic achievement • Decreased suspension & expulsion • Decreased grade retentions • Decreased special education referrals & placements	O			O	O				O	O			•	•	O			O		
Strengthening Families http://www.strengtheningfamiliesprogram.org	O	O		6–12 yr. old	14-week courses	• Parent skills training that employs basic behavioral parent training techniques • Children's skills training designed to develop and enhance children's social and problem-solving skills • Family life skills training that utilizes family communication exercises • Two booster sessions at 6 and 12 months after the program, which encourage positive social networking	• Decreased use and intention to use ATOD among parents as well as children • Improved parent–child bonding, family relations, & communication • Improved children's academic achievement • Improved parents' discipline skills and parenting self-efficacy • Improved children's pro-social behaviors • Reduced children's problem behaviors including substance use • Reduced children's emotional problems including depression	O	O		O	O				•	•	O	•							O	

• indicates primary strategy while O refers to one of the strategies utilized in the program

- To improve family relationships by
- Decreasing family conflicts
- Improving family communications
- Increasing parent—child time together
- Increasing planning and organization skills

Target Population

The original SFP targets at-risk children 6 to 10 years of age whose parents are substance users or abusers. Since the original version of SPF demonstrated its effectiveness in the general child population as well as at-risk children, it can also be utilized as a universal prevention program.

Program Structure and Implementation

SFP program is composed of three primary components: parent skills training, children's skills training, and family skills training. The program participants have weekly sessions, each of which lasts 2 to 3 hours. The entire program continues for 14 consecutive weeks. For the first part of a weekly session, parents and children attend their own sessions separately. This is followed by a break, when snacks and announcements are provided. Then, the family skills training session starts, and the parents and children practice the skills together, which they learned in their own session. This format provides the participants with opportunities to learn their respective skills in their own sessions and then to practice the skills within the context of parent—child interaction. The entire program curricula for parent, children, and family skills training component are presented in the Table 20.4. As shown in the table, the topics of weekly sessions are coherent across groups so that family and children learn relevant skills at the same time and practice together.

Usually each parent skills training session starts with a review of homework and the concepts taught in the previous session. Then parents learn new concepts and skills. Finally, new homework relevant to the new concept and skills is assigned. The optimum group number for the parents' training session ranges from 8 to 12 with two skilled trainers. The basic format of the children's group session is similar to the parents'. The ideal group number is six to seven with two trainers. For smooth group work process and reinforcement of desirable behavior, children who follow group rules need to be rewarded with small prizes such as school supplies. The family training session is delivered in a format similar to that of the parents' or children's training session. Depending on the number of participants and accommodating capacity of the meeting place, family groups can be divided into several small groups or remain in one large group.

How to Implement SFP

Once a school chooses to use the Strengthening Families Program (SFP), a 2- to 3-day implementer training is conducted. A 415-page instructor manual contains a teaching outline, a script for the videotapes, and detailed instructions for all activities. Each lesson has an "overview" section providing practical considerations for successful implementation of SFP, such as a detailed timeline, list of equipment, master copies of worksheets, and homework assignments. A separate manual contains four booster sessions. There must be a teacher/facilitator for the parent session and the youth session, held concurrently. Co-facilitators are recommended where feasible. It is suggested that meals or snacks be included as incentives, and whenever possible, childcare and transportation should be provided.

Each child and parent session contains parallel content. They spend the first hour separately in separate skill-building sessions and then come together in supervised family activities. For example, while the children are learning about the importance of following rules, parents are working on enhancing their use of consequences when rules are broken; when the two groups combine in the family session, the children and family members practice problem solving with role plays when a rule is followed or broken. The parent component has the following general goals: increase positive attention/praise, enhance empathy, teach supervision skills, decrease parents' drug use, increase positive modeling, and support the child's developmental stage. The family component provides a venue for children and families to practice and enhance listening, communication, respect, recognizing family strengths, cultural values, and effective problem-solving skills.

The groups utilize the following techniques: discussions, games, role plays, activities, videotapes, and modeling of positive relationships and behaviors. The facilitator uses the videotapes, which include time countdowns for group

Table 20.4 Strengthen Families Program Curriculum

Week	*Parent Skills Curriculum*	*Children's Skills Curriculum*	*Family Skills Curriculum*
1	Introduction and group building	Hello and rules	Introduction and group building
2	Developmental expectancies and stress management	Social skills I	Child's game I
3	Rewards	Social skills II	Child's game II:Rewards
4	Goals and objectives	Creating good behavior, secret rules of success	Child's game III: Goals and objectives
5	Differential attention/ Charts and spinners	How to say "NO" to stay out of trouble	Child's game IV: Differential attention/charts and spinners
6	Communication I	Communication I: Speaking and listening	Communication I: Speaking, listening, and coaching
7	Communication II	Communication II: Preparation for family meetings	Communication II: Family meetings
8	Alcohol, drugs, and families	Alcohol and drugs	Communication III: Learning from parents—parents' discussion
9	Problem-solving, giving directions	Problem-solving	Parents' game I: Problem-solving, giving directions
10	Limit setting I	Introduction to parents' game	Parents' game II: Consequences for noncompliance
11	Limit setting II	Coping skills I: Recognizing feelings	Parents' game III: Commands and time-out
12	Limit setting III	Coping skills II: Dealing with criticism	Parent's game IV: Parent and child interaction on commands and consequences
13	Development/ implementation of behavior programs	Coping skills III: Coping with anger	Development/ implementation of family meetings and behavior change programs
14	Generalization and maintenance	Graduation, resources for help, and review	Graduation party

Source: From National Institute on Drug Abuse (1997a).

discussions and activities. In fact, the facilitator starts the video as the session begins and lets it run for the full session to guide the curriculum and ensure staying on task and accomplishment of session goals. Multiethnic video narrators conduct didactic presentations and are followed by family vignettes. Once the video is completed, the remaining time can be utilized for skill practice, discussions, and mutual support within the group.

Outcomes

Through extensive evaluation, the SFP has produced desirable outcomes and proved its effectiveness in various areas, including reduced use or intentions to use substances among children; reduced child problem behaviors, aggressiveness, and emotional problems; decreased substance use among parents; improved parenting skills; and enhanced family communication skills. In a study that compared 71 SFP participating families with 47 nonparticipating families, for example, children of the SFP families were less likely to show behavioral, academic, social, and emotional problems than those of the non-SFP families (DeMarsh & Kumpfer, 1986). In addition, previously substance-using children as well as such parents showed significantly decreased use of tobacco and alcohol in pre- and post-test results (DeMarsh & Kumpfer, 1986).

Cultural Aspects

Issues involving the cultural adaptation of youth prevention programs have emerged as important (Castro, Barrera, & Holleran Steiker, 2010). The Strengthening Families Program has been adapted for a variety of unique cultures (over 17 countries have adaptations in effect), including effectiveness trials with diverse populations (African, Hispanic, Asian, Pacific Islander, and Native American) in countries including the United States, Sweden, Portugal, and Thailand.

Positive Action (PA)

Outlines

Positive Action (PA: http://www.positiveaction.net/) is a multifaceted program integrating classroom curriculum, schoolwide program, family component, and community involvement components. Its primary goals include improvement of students' academic achievement, reduction of problem behaviors, and reinforcement of positive behaviors/attitudes. Primarily based on self-concept theories that emphasize actions rather than thoughts or feelings, PA attempts to teach students "what actions are positive, that they feel good when they do positive actions, and that they then have more positive thoughts and future actions" (Flay & Allred, 2003, p. S7). A major difference between PA and other selective prevention programs is that PA intends to affect more distal factors on student behavior in a holistic approach including school reorganization. The current PA program is the result of extensive pilot work and repeated evaluation that has been conducted since its first development by Carol Gerber Allread in 1977.

Program Goal and Objectives

PA has specified goals and objectives for the school and community as well as for the individual student and family (Flay, Allred, & Ordway, 2001, p. 76).

- Individual goals
  - To give everyone the opportunity to learn and practice physical, intellectual, and emotional and social positive actions
  - To understand that success and happiness means feeling good about who you are and what you are doing (being the best you can be)
  - To develop good character, morals, and ethics
- Family goals
  - To create a positive learning environment in the home
  - To contribute to adult literacy and to develop life skills in adult family members
  - To prepare children to be effective learners prior to entering school
- School goals
  - To bring about comprehensive school reform
  - To develop lifelong skills that lead to success and happiness in school and society
  - To create a positive environment conducive to teaching and learning
  - To create a safe, drug-free school environment
  - To promote the personal and professional development of teachers, staff members, and administrators
  - To completely unite the efforts of the school, home, and community organization in promoting the social, academic, and emotional growth of children
  - To teach the leadership skills that will promote high achievement and expert performance in the global marketplace
- Community goals
  - To involve the whole community in learning and practicing the positive actions necessary for a good self-concept and a successful life
  - To contribute to a community environment

Target Population

PA targets children and adolescents 5 through 18 years of age. It can be implemented for the general student population as universal prevention, for at-risk students as selective prevention, and also for students with problem behaviors or mental health problems as indicated prevention.

Program Structure and Implementation

The PA program consists of a detailed classroom curriculum, a schoolwide climate program, and family-and community-involvement components. The classroom curriculum is composed of over 140 lessons. Guided by the teacher's kit, which includes a program manual for teachers and necessary materials, a classroom teacher presents a lesson for about 15–20 minutes almost every school day. This teacher-led classroom curriculum is delivered in various activities including stories, games, music, questions and answers, role playing, posters, and manipulative activities. The classroom curriculum is organized in six units, which are presented in Table 20.5.

The school-climate program is designed to reinforce the practice of positive actions schoolwide. For this purpose, school administrators are encouraged to utilize various activities such as assemblies, celebrations, school newspaper, community service group for students, tutoring, and diversity initiatives. There is also a guiding manual for principals, the principal's kits. This principal's manual suggests utilizing stickers, tokens, and positive notes to reinforce positive actions of elementary school students. The parents' program has two major strategies, coordinated weekly lessons and strengthened connections between parent and school. With the purpose to help parents improve their communication skills and parenting style, the family kit introduces to parents 42 weekly lessons, which are in coordination with the PA school curriculum and school-climate activities. In addition, parents are strongly encouraged to participate in various school activities, such as the decision-making team for the PA program, the development of the mission statement, and program evaluation procedures. The PA program also intends to create a better community environment that has a positive influence on child development. For this purpose, the community kit was developed. It provides community leaders, social service workers, public servants, and other stakeholders in the community with proper tools to promote positive actions, playing their roles.

Outcomes

More than 7000 schools have used the PA program nationally or internationally. The program has consistently showed desirable outcomes in substance use, absenteeism, disciplinary problems, violence, disruptive and disrespectful behaviors, school suspension, school dropout, and academic achievement including SAT scores, reading scores, and math scores. A recent study (Flay & Allred, 2003) evaluated the long-term effects of Positive Action based on matched-school design. Below are the primary findings that show significant effects of the Positive Action program on elementary school children:

- Students in PA schools performed 45% better, on average, in the Florida Reading Test than their counterparts in matched control schools.
- PA schools have 68% less violent incidents per 100 students compared to matched schools.
- The percentage of students who received out-of-school suspensions was 33.5% lower in PA schools in comparison with matched schools.

Applying Interventions within a Response to Intervention Framework

The acknowledgement of students' academic and behavioral difficulties in the school setting is imperative for effective and successful intervention and prevention strategies with regards to drugs and alcohol. The RTI model provides an alternative way to examine students related to substance abuse risk, evidence of early warning signs, and relevance in public education with respect to evaluations and referrals. The lack of understanding of children and adolescents' development, cultural background, and proper assessments to learn more about these individuals has always been a challenge for school officials. Due to the complexity of students and families with substance-related risks and problems, it is especially critical to identify such "red flags" early, to communicate concern and support in a culturally relevant fashion, and to follow up and maintain continued support beyond one-time interventions. Drug and alcohol abuse in families and

Table 20.5 The Components of Positive Action Program

Unit/Number and Topic	*Content*
Unit 1. Self-concept: What it is, how it's formed, and why it's important	The relationship of thoughts, feelings, and actions (behavior). Units 2–6 teach children what actions are positive in various domains of life, that they feel good when they do positive actions, and that they then have more positive thoughts and future actions
Unit 2. Positive actions for body (physical) and mind (intellectual)	*Physical:* exercise, hygiene, nutrition, avoiding harmful substances, sleeping and resting enough, safety *Intellectual:* creative thinking, learning/studying, decision making, problem solving
Unit 3. Social/emotional positive actions for managing yourself responsibly Unit 4. Social/emotional positive actions for getting along with others	Manage human resources of time, energy, thoughts, actions, feelings (anger, fear, loneliness, others), talents, money, and possessions. Includes self-control Treat others the way you like to be treated, code of conduct (respect, fairness, kindness, honesty, courtesy, empathy, caring, responsible, reliable), conflict resolution, communication positively (communication skills), forming relationships, working cooperatively, community service. [These are the essence of character education]
Unit 5. Social/emotional positive actions for being honest with yourself & others	Self-honesty, doing what you will say you will do (integrity), not blaming others, not making excuses, not rationalizing; self-appraisal (look at strengths and weaknesses); and being in touch with reality. [These are the essence of mental health]
Unit 6. Social/emotional positive actions for improving yourself continually	Goal setting (physical, intellectual, and social/emotional), problem solving, decision making, believe in potential, have courage to try, turn problems into opportunities, persistence
Unit 7. Review	Review of all of above

Source: From Flay & Allred (2003, p. S8). Reproduced with permission.

early childhood abuse both are risk factors that correlate with academic performance (Jeynes, 2002). Therefore, school officials, researchers, and clinical practitioners should be challenged to draw more parallels to academic and behavioral progress and those cultural barriers faced in the educational system for children and adolescents with low school performance.

When educators, school counselors, and/or administrators are creating individualized education plans (IEPs) at the individual assessment level, it is critical to consider "person in environment" as well as evidence of potential drug/alcohol use or abuse by students or by parents impacting students' readiness to learn. On a more universal level, substance abuse prevention programs should be integral with academic considerations, with outcome measures including academic performance and school retention.

Tools and Practice Examples

Through the several decades of experiences to prevent substance use/abuse, a substantial body of knowledge and skills has been accumulated. In the following sections, some of the critical information is summarized to guide school social workers and other professionals who are interested in at-risk children and preventive intervention programs.

What Needs to Be Done?

To be effective, school prevention programs should:

- *Be based on the needs of students, families, school, and community.* The needs assessment will shed light on program focus by specifying the strengths and weaknesses of program participants and environment. Although assessment instruments should be chosen, the list of risk and protective factors can be utilized for a brief needs assessment.

- *Have clear objectives.* Only when the goals and objectives are properly stated, the evaluation may produce reliable results. In addition, clear goals and objectives help practitioners keep the program focus and timelines (Knowles, 2001).
- *Be based on comprehensive multidimensional perspective.* As seen earlier, risk and protective factors are situated at multisystem levels, indicating the necessity of a multidimensional approach in prevention efforts. This guideline has been supported by many empirical studies (e.g., St. Pierre et al., 2001; Tatchell, Waite, Tatchell, Durrant, & Bond, 2004).
- *Focus on parent component.* Family involvement is the key for effective prevention (Gibson et al., 1993). Programs focusing on family relationships and parenting skills are usually effective in changing negative behaviors among parents as well as children (Gonet, 1994).
- *Include competency skills.* Social competency models, such as life skills training, have shown desirable outcomes in various studies (Gonet, 1994), and the effectiveness has been validated for elementary school students (St. Pierre et al., 2001). A social competency component is considered appropriate for universal and selected prevention programs (Griffin, Botvin, Nichols, & Doyle, 2003).
- *Utilize internal resources.* For young school children, as opposed to high school students, it is recommended that internal resources be utilized (e.g., teachers as implementers) rather than external resources (i.e., programs brought to the school by outside agencies) (Marsiglia, Holleran, & Jackson, 2000). Youth implementers, such as Peer Assistance and Leader (PAL) students, may be a great resource in elementary schools. Some of the assumptions about peer-led models, such as the fear of control and discipline difficulties, are unfounded (Erhard, 1999). It is also important to note that, in the sensitive area of substance use and abuse, peer-led programs yielded twice as much participants' self-disclosure (Erhard, 1999). All in all, there are strong indications that peer-led models may possess great potential for prevention efforts.
- *Be delivered in interactive method.* Compared to a noninteractive method, an interactive method produces greater effect size (Tobler, 1992). In some cases, a program showed effectiveness only when delivered in an interaction method (Sussman, Rohrbach, Ratel, & Holiday, 2003).
- *Be implemented in an intended way.* Well-developed and empirically proven prevention models usually have specified program manuals. To achieve program effectiveness, high fidelity is a must (Hogan et al., 2003).
- *Be followed by a booster program.* It is always recommended to provide booster sessions after program completion as the booster programs are vital for long-lasting program effectiveness (Gottfredson & Wilson, 2003; Lilja, Wilhelmsen, Larsson, & Hamilton, 2003).
- *Be culturally competent.* Just as we noted in the previous chapter, culturally appropriate prevention and intervention approaches are critical for youth (Holleran Steiker, Goldbach, Hopson, & Powell, 2011). Curricula and programs grounded in the real lives of participants are much more effective than those created by professionals outside the systems being served (Hecht, Marsiglia, & Kayo, 2004).

What Should Be Avoided?

To be effective, school prevention programs should:

- *Not target individuals with a substance abuse problem.* Only qualified specialists on drug use should provide intervention programs to identified substance users or abusers. If school social workers and counselors (given that they are not drug abuse specialists) find a student who needs intervention, they must refer the student to a proper clinical setting (Gibson et al., 1993).
- *Not provide information only.* Information or knowledge on substance use/abuse does not necessarily reduce substance use (Holleran et al., 2004; Petosa, 1992; Stoil & Hill, 1996). In the worst cases, it could increase substance use among children or adolescents (Gonet, 1994).
- *Not threaten students.* Persuading children not to use a substance in a threatening way is not effective. Rather, it could cause mistrust toward mental health professions (Gonet, 1994).
- *Not be completed in a one-shot program.* A one-shot program, such as a guest speaker or film-watching, is usually least effective (Gonet, 1994).

- *Not use a self-esteem component as a primary strategy.* Programs that put the focus on self-esteem have not been the most effective. Program results in such models are not consistent and too often disappointing (Stoil & Hill, 1996).

Key Points to Remember

In this chapter, the authors presented an overview of selective prevention interventions, explained a risk and protective factor paradigm, and provided two examples of evidence-based model programs, the Strengthening Families Program (SFP) and Positive Action (PA). It closes with critical recommendations and practical guidelines for utilizing such interventions. As with any program, and especially with elementary school students, practitioners must be very careful to protect the confidentiality of students and families. In addition, when doing prevention interventions with children, it is vital that clinicians avoid labeling and stereotyping. It is helpful to recognize that interventions that address substance abuse prevention, as noted previously, also prevent other problematic outcomes, such as rebelliousness, aggression, and absenteeism. It is also recommended that teachers and program implementers watch students carefully for potential negative responses to the intervention (e.g., emotional overload, anxiety, depression), which might give clues that other concurrent issues or more serious problems exist. In such cases, referral to a specialist or a proper clinical setting may be necessary.

References

Alcoholism & Drug Abuse Weekly. (April 19, 1999). Survey pinpoints substance use among elementary school students. *Alcoholism & Drug Abuse Weekly*.

American Academy of Pediatrics. (1998). *Caring for your adolescent: Ages 12 to 21 (pamphlet)*.

Castro, F. G., Barrera, M., & Holleran Steiker, L. (2010). Issues and challenges in the design of culturally-adapted evidence-based interventions. *Annual Review of Clinical Psychology, 6*, 213–239.

Centers for Disease Control and Prevention. (2004). *Youth risk behavior surveillance: United States, 2003 (MMWR No. SS-2)*. Atlanta: U.S. Department of Health and Human Services.

DeMarsh, J. P., & Kumpfer, K. L. (1986). Family oriented interventions for the prevention of chemical dependency in children and adolescents. In S. Ezekoye, K. Kumpfer, & W. Bukoski (Eds.), *Childhood and chemical abuse: Prevention and early intervention* (pp. 117–152). New York: Haworth.

Erhard, R. (1999). Peer-led and adult-led programs—student perceptions. *Journal of Drug Education, 29*(4), 295–308.

Finke, L., Williams, J., Ritter, M., Kemper, D., Kersey, S., Nightenhauser, J., et al. (2002). Survival against drugs: Education for school-aged children. *Journal of Child and Adolescent Psychiatric Nursing, 15*, 163–169.

Fisher, G. L., & Harrison, T. C. (2004). *Substance abuse: Information for school counselors, social workers, therapists, and counselors*. Boston: Pearson Education.

Flay, B. R., Allred, C. G., & Ordway, N. (2001). Effects of the Positive Action program on achievement and discipline: Two matched-control comparisons. *Prevention Science, 2*(2), 71–89.

Flay, B. R., & Allred, C. G. (2003). Long-term effects of the Positive Action program. *American Journal of Health Behavior, 27*(Supp. 1), S6–S21.

Gibson, R. L., Mitchell, M. H., & Basile, S. K. (1993). *Counseling in the elementary school: A comprehensive approach*. Boston: Allyn and Bacon.

Gonet, M. M. (1994). *Counseling the adolescent substance abuser: School-based intervention and prevention*. Thousand Oaks, CA: Sage.

Gottfredson, D. C., & Wilson, D. B. (2003). Characteristics of effective school-based substance abuse prevention. *Prevention Science, 4*(1), 27–38.

Griffin, K. W., Botvin, G. J., Nichols, T. R., & Doyle, M. M. (2003). Effectiveness of a universal drug abuse prevention approach for youth at high risk for substance use initiation. *Preventive Medicine, 36*, 1–7.

Hawkins, J. D., Catalano, R. F., Kosterman, R., Abbott, R., & Hill, K. G. (1999). Preventing adolescent health-risk behaviors by strengthening protection during childhood. *Archives of Pediatric and Adolescent Medicine, 153*, 226–234.

Hecht, M. L., Marsiglia, F. F., & Kayo, R. (2004). Cultural factors in adolescent prevention. *Addiction Professional, 2*(3), 21–25.

Hingson, R. W., Heeren, T., & Edwards, E. M. (2008). Age at drinking onset, alcohol dependence, and their relation to drug use and dependence, driving under the influence of drugs, and motor-vehicle crash involvement because of drugs. *Journal of Studies on Alcohol and Drugs, 69*(2), 192–201.

Hogan, J. A., Gabrielsen, K. R., Luna, N., & Grothaus, D. (2003). *Substance abuse prevention: The intersection of science and practice*. Boston: Allyn & Bacon.

Holleran, L. K., Kim, Y., & Dixon, K. (2004). Innovative approaches to risk assessment within alcohol prevention programming. In A. R. Roberts & K. R. Yeager (Eds.), *Evidence-based practice manual: Research and outcome measures in health and human services* (pp. 677–684). New York: Oxford University Press.

Holleran Steiker, L. K., Goldbach, J., Hopson, L. M., & Powell, T. (2011). The value of cultural adaptation processes: Older youth participants as substance abuse preventionists. *Child and Adolescent Social Work Journal*. doi:10.1007/s10560–011–0246–9.

Jenson, J. M., & Howard, M. O. (1991). Risk-focused drug and alcohol prevention: Implications for school-based prevention programs. *Social Work in Education, 13*(4), 246–256.

Jenson, J. M. (1997). Risk and protective factors for alcohol and other drug use in childhood and adolescence. In M. W. Fraser (Ed.), *Risk and resilience in childhood* (pp. 117–139). Washington, DC: NASW Press.

Jeynes, W. H. (2002). The relationship between the consumption of various drugs by adolescents and their academic achievement. *American Journal of Drug and Alcohol Abuse, 28*(1), 15–35.

Knowles, C. R. (2001). *Prevention that works: A guide for developing school-based drug and violence prevention programs*. Thousand Oaks, CA: Corwin Press.

Kuhn, C., Swartzwelder, S., & Wilson, W. (1998). *Buzzed: The straight facts about the most used and abused drugs (from alcohol to ecstasy)*. New York: W. W. Norton & Company.

Kumpfer, K. L. (2003). *Identification of drug abuse prevention programs: Literature review*. Retrieved July 13, 2004, from http://archives.drugabuse.gov/about/organization/despr/hsr/da-pre/KumpferLitReview.html

Kumpfer, K. L., Alvarado, R., & Whiteside, H. O. (2003). Family-based interventions for substance use and misuse prevention. *Substance Use & Misuse, 38*(11–13), 1759–1787.

Kumpfer, K. L., Pinyuchon, M., Melo, A. T., & Whiteside, H. O. (2008). Cultural adaptation process for international dissemination of the Strengthening Families Program. *Evaluation & the Health Professions, 31*, 226–239.

Kumpfer, K. L., Whiteside, H. O., Greene, J. A., & Allen, K. C. (2010). Effectiveness outcomes of four age versions of the Strengthening Families Program in statewide field sites. *Group Dynamics: Theory, Research, and Practice, 14*(3), 211–229.

Lilja, J., Wilhelmsen, B. U., Larsson, S., & Hamilton, D. (2003). Evaluation of drug use prevention programs directed at adolescents. *Substance Use & Misuse, 38*(11–13), 1831–1863.

Marsiglia, F. F., Holleran, L., & Jackson, K. M. (2000). The impact of internal and external resources on school-based substance abuse prevention. *Social Work in Education, 22*(3), 145–161.

Marsiglia, F., Kulis, S., Yabiku, S., Nieri, T., & Coleman, E. (2011). When to intervene: Elementary school, middle school or both? Effects of keepin' it REAL on substance use trajectories of Mexican heritage youth. *Prevention Science, 12*(1), 48–62.

National Institute on Drug Abuse. (1997a). *Drug abuse prevention for at-risk groups* (NIH No. 97–4114). Rockville, MD: U.S. Department of Health and Human Services, National Institutes of Health.

National Institute on Drug Abuse. (1997b). *Drug abuse prevention: What works*. Rockville, MD: U.S. Department of Health and Human Services.

Pandina, R. J. (September 19–20, 1996). *Risk and protective factor models in adolescent drug use: Putting them to work for prevention*. Paper presented at the National Conference on Drug Abuse Prevention Research: Presentations, papers, and recommendations, Washington, DC.

Parents' Resource Institute for Drug Education. (2003). *2002–03 PRIDE Surveys national summary for grades 4 thru 6*. Bowling Green, KY: Author.

Parents' Resource Institute for Drug Education. (2003). 2008–09 *PRIDE Surveys national summary for grades 4 thru 6*. Bowling Green, KY: Author.

Petosa, R. (1992). Developing a comprehensive health promotion program to prevent adolescent drug abuse. In G. W. Lawson & A. W. Lawson (Eds.), *Adolescent substance abuse: Etiology, treatment, and prevention* (pp. 431–450). Gaithersburg, MD: Aspen.

Rones, M., & Hoagwood, K. (2000). School-based mental health services: A research review. *Clinical Child and Family Psychology Review, 3*(4), 223–241.

Sarvela, P. D., Monge, E. A., Shannon, D.V., & Newrot, R. (1999). Age of first use of cigarettes among rural and small town elementary school children in Illinois. *Journal of School Health, 69*(10), 398–402.

St. Pierre, T. S., Mark, M. M., Kaltreider, D. L., & Campbell, B. (2001). Boys & girls clubs and school collaborations: A longitudinal study of a multicomponent substance abuse prevention program for high-risk elementary school children. *Journal of Community Psychology, 29*(2), 87–106.

Stoil, M. J., & Hill, G. (1996). *Preventing substance abuse: Interventions that work*. New York: Plenum.

Sullivan, T. N., & Farrell, A. D. (2002). Risk factors. In C. A. Essau (Ed.), *Substance abuse and dependence in adolescence: Epidemiology, risk factors and treatment* (pp. 87–118). New York: Taylor & Francis.

Sussman, S., Rohrbach, L. A., Ratel, R., & Holiday, K. (2003). A look at an interactive classroom-based drug abuse prevention program: Interactive contents and suggestions for research. *Journal of Drug Education, 33*(4), 355–368.

Tatchell, T. W., Waite, P. J., Tatchell, R. H., Durrant, L. H., & Bond, D. S. (2004). Substance abuse prevention in sixth grade: The effect of a prevention program on adolescents' risk and protective factors. *American Journal of Health Studies, 19*(1), 54–61.

Tobler, N. S. (1992). Drug prevention programs can work: Research findings. *Journal of Addictive Diseases, 11*(3), 1–28.

Wilson, D. B., Gottfredson, D. C., & Najaka, S. S. (2001). School-based prevention problem behaviors: A meta-analysis. *Journal of Quantitative Criminology, 17*(3), 247–272.

CHAPTER 21

Screening Substance Use/Abuse of Middle and High School Students

Lori K. Holleran Steiker · Soyon Jung · Kristy Gillispie

Getting Started

Adolescent substance use has been a major concern in this country. According to the Monitoring the Future (MTF) study conducted by the University of Michigan (University of Michigan Institute for Social Research, 2003) and supported by the National Institute on Drug Abuse (NIDA), high rates of American youth have tried or currently use various illicit drugs, alcohol, and tobacco. Among the 8th, 10th, and 12th graders surveyed in 2003, for example, one third currently use alcohol and one out of six smoke cigarettes. In addition, many adolescents use illegal drugs including marijuana, ecstasy, and LSD. Approximately 17% reported illicit drug use during the past month prior to the survey and 37% reported that they had tried it at least once during their lifetime.

The consequences of substance use are serious, costly, and extensive. Most substances have immediate physiological influences. They interfere with correct perception and rational judgment (McWhirter, McWhirter, McWhirter, & McWhirter, 2004). There is some evidence for intervening at the elementary level, but equal effectiveness when implementing in middle schools (Marsiglia, Kulis, Yabiku, Nieri, & Coleman, 2011). It is well established that adolescents are more likely to be involved in risk taking behaviors under the influence of substance(s). Not surprisingly, substance use often leads to fatal accidents and crime. Alcohol consumption, for instance, is a major cause of death among youth via motor vehicle accidents, homicides, suicides, and drowning (U.S. Department of Health and Human Services [DHHS], 2000). Furthermore, heavy drinking and smoking often contribute to various diseases: cancer, heart disease, many liver-related diseases (DHHS, 2000), and sexually transmitted diseases, including HIV/AIDS (Center for Disease Control and Prevention, 2004). The economic costs of substance abuse and drug abuse in the United States were estimated to be $167 and $110 billion, respectively, in 1995 (DHHS, 2000). Substance use has detrimental impacts on the mental health of adolescents as well. Newcomb and Bentler (1989) found that serious drug users are vulnerable to experience loneliness, depression, and suicide ideations. Moreover, substance use hinders youth from accomplishing important developmental tasks, performing expected duties, and building healthy relationships with others. Previous studies have consistently indicated that substance use is significantly associated with poor educational outcomes and academic failure (Jeynes, 2002; NCCDPHP, 2012; National Commission on Drug-Free Schools, 1990), physical fights and criminal behavior (NCCDPHP, 2012), substance abuse, violence, suicidal thoughts, competence (Burrows-Sanchez & Lopez, 2009; Gunter & Bakken, 2010), aggression, delinquency (Lynne-Landsman, Graber, Nichols, & Botvin, 2011), gender and juvenile justice system (Tarter, Kirisci, Mezzich, & Patton, 2011), and inadequate positive social connection (Havighurst, 1972). Also, distinctions are being made among adolescents from urban and rural communities (Lynne-Landsman et al., 2011; Dunn, Goodrow, Givens, & Austin, 2008) as well as the examination of substance use behavior and suicide indicators among rural middle school students (Dunn et al, 2008).

Although the detrimental consequences of adolescent substance use are immense, appropriate treatment can significantly reduce the harmful effects (Winters, Latimer, & Stinchfield, 1999). Early intervention is considered especially desirable in terms of effectiveness and efficiency. The Consensus Panel for the Center for Substance Abuse Treatment (CSAT) recommends that all adolescents showing any sign of substance use be properly screened (Winters, 2001b). Thus, professionals who work with at-risk youth must have screening resources and expertise so that the adolescents can receive more comprehensive assessment and intervention services (Winters, 2001b). Since adolescents spend a large amount of time at school, the role of school mental health professionals in identifying substance users at earlier stages and providing them with intervention opportunities cannot be overemphasized.

This chapter discusses the substance use/abuse screening methods that school mental health professionals can easily utilize. A summary table of screening tools developed particularly for the adolescent population is presented. Somewhat detailed information about two screening instruments, POSIT and RAPI, which are considered most efficient at school settings, follows. This information covers how to administer the instruments and how to interpret the results. Finally, a case example is provided to demonstrate the techniques described in the chapter.

Substance users need to be aware of their problems and motivated for change with regard to substances during each screening procedure (Winters, 2001b). School mental health professionals should remember to utilize their most astute clinical techniques to make successful initial contacts with potential substance users and refer them to suitable intervention programs.

One approach to addressing this problem is utilizing the stage of change model. The stage of change model has become an influential perspective in the area of substance abuse (Conners, Donovan, & DiClemente, 2001). Most of the research on stage of change and substances has been done on smoking. Stage of change is reportedly related to current smoking patterns, with individuals in the preparation stage smoking fewer cigarettes, reporting less dependence, and making more quit attempts. Individuals at later stages of change also express more self-efficacy to abstain, and stage of change has been found to predict success at follow-up (Prochaska & DiClemente, 1992). Pallonen (1998) broadened the model to adolescents, finding that adolescents and adults were remarkably similar in the transtheoretical measures, and, except for the processes of change, both groups exhibited similar behavior at different stages of the smoking cessation process. The research also found that adolescent smokers were generally less prepared to quit than adults were. Stage of change was related to quit attempts, although adolescents used behavioral methods, as well as cognitive-experiential processes, in the transition from contemplation to preparation.

Historically, professionals believed intervention was possible with adolescent substance abusers only if they had sufficient awareness and willingness to consider and pursue abstinence. However, with the stage of change model predomination the field, interventions have shifted toward targeting "where the client is" and working with the adolescent at whatever stage of readiness he or she presents (i.e., precontemplation, contemplation, preparation, and action) (Prochaska & DiClemente, 2005).

What We Know and Can Do

Screening Adolescent Substance Use/ Abuse

Before examining specific screening methods and procedures, it is necessary to understand the differences between screening, assessment, and diagnosis of substance use/abuse. The primary purpose of screening is to identify potential substance users who need a through assessment (Winters, 2001b). On the other hand, comprehensive assessment aims to verify substance use/abuse of an adolescent and reveal other relevant problems and service needs (Winters, 2001b). Diagnosis is carried out based on the most comprehensive measures or highly structured criteria such as those presented in the fourth edition of the *Diagnostic and Statistical Manual of Mental Disorders* (*DSM-IV*). Diagnosis is considered a more decisive conclusion compared to assessment. While *assessment* refers to "the process of gathering information," *diagnosis* is defined as the "the conclusion that is reached on the basis of the assessment" (Fisher & Harrison, 2004, p. 84).

One important point that school mental health professionals should keep in mind is that a comprehensive substance use/abuse assessment or diagnosis is best conducted by alcohol, tobacco, and other drug (commonly referred to as ATOD) specialists in general, and those involved in the intervention plan or treatment service in particular. Thus, it is recommended for school mental health professionals to provide screening services only, unless they have adequate qualification for substance use/abuse assessment and diagnosis (Fisher & Harrison, 2004). The science of drug testing has advanced over the years, and parents and schools are more often considering random drug testing to support positive student decision making and not just for punitive purpose (Russell, Jennings, & Classey, 2005). Another major shift in the field is from a medical model, problem-focused stance to a strengths-based model. For example, instead of focusing on diagnosis, scare tactics, and problem identification, school interventionists work to create honest dialogues with students, noting decisional balance as a factor and promoting healthy lifestyles and choices. In line with this is a movement toward educating about recovery as well as substance abuse and addiction (Hutchinson, Ashcraft, & Anthony, 2006; Salm, Sevigny, Mulholland, & Greenberg, 2011).

Who Needs to Be Screened?

As substance use is quite prevalent among American youth and many of them are diverge from the stereotypes of ATOD users, school social workers and school counselors need to be always aware that the possibility of a substance use problem exists when they are providing any kind of service to students. Ideally, screenings for substance use/abuse would be done universally with all students. However, given limited resources and inadequate numbers of mental health professionals at school, it would be more desirable to focus on screening students at risk for substance use/abuse or showing some indication of possible substance use.

In response to the lack of understanding and/or viable school-based intervention options for parents, school staff, and counselors, adolescents who have already started abusing substances in the United States are often prematurely admitted to addiction treatment before they are at a stage of readiness to respond to the intensive programs (Holleran Steiker, Powell, Hopson, & Goldbach, 2011). Some youth encounter significant "motivational barriers" when coerced into treatment (Winters, 1999). Approximately half of the youth in treatment relapse in the first 3 months following discharge (Brown, Mott, & Myers, 1990), and 65–80% relapse after 6 months (Brown, 2001; Cornelius et al., 2003). The cost of this revolving door to American society is dramatic; research has shown that every dollar invested in prevention achieves a savings of up to $7 USD in areas such as substance abuse treatment, not to mention their wider impact on the trajectory of young lives and their families (NIDA, 2003).

The U.S. government has emphasized that research around drug and alcohol use and abuse during late adolescence and emerging adulthood is a particularly important area because late adolescence is a significant transition point in human development, this transition often marks addictive use of substances for at-risk individuals (NIDA, 2003), and the initiation of use of so-called "hard drugs" often takes place during this period (NIDA, 2003). Regardless of this imperative, there is a dearth of programs specifically designed to intervene with high school students around drug and alcohol issues (Dent, Sussman, McCullar, & Stacy, 2001). Most U.S. prevention interventions focus on middle school students (ages 11–14) and are designed for family and traditional school settings (Kumpfer, Molgaard, & Spoth, 1996; Eggert, Nicholas, & Owen, 1995; Sussman, et al., 1997). Drug abuse prevention programs that have been effective with general populations of younger adolescents in junior high and middle school are less likely to be as effective with older, at-risk high school students between the ages of 14 and 17 (Sussman, 1996). Outcomes do tend to improve when tailored for age (White, Taylor, & Moss, 1992). School counselors in the United States often use programs developed for other youth populations or invent their own interventions out of necessity (Ringwalt et al., 2003). The few programs for high-risk high school youth (i.e., Project Toward No Drug Abuse [Sussman, 1996] and Reconnecting Youth [Eggert, Nicholas, & Owen, 1995]) note that alternative school youth receiving a tailored intervention experience greater reductions in substance use (Dent et al, 2001). In short, more research is needed to address (a) the gap between prevention and treatment; (b) the need for developmentally appropriate, engaging interventions for older youth; and (c) the specific needs of high-risk substance-abusing alternative school youth. Interventions that acknowledge the reality of substance use choices (i.e., weighing the decisional balance of payoffs and downsides) are recommended (Holleran Steiker, Powell, Hopson, & Goldbach, 2011).

An effective way to identify potential substance users for screening is to utilize a multidisciplinary team including classroom teachers. Because classroom teachers spend much time with students and have many opportunities to observe student behaviors directly, they can make a significant contribution to problem identification (Gonet, 1994). School social workers and drug counselors can encourage participation of teachers in case identification procedures and enhance the quality of information reported by the teachers, using a form specially designed to easily detect substance use among students.

Self-Report Screening Instruments for Adolescents

Although there are various approaches available, self-report screening instruments are commonly used to identify ATOD problem among adolescents (Martin & Winters, 1998). Using standardized instruments has some advantages: it reduces potential bias (Winters, 2001a); it is less likely to threaten students than other methods (Winters, 2001a); and it makes mental health professionals look trustworthy (Orenstein, Davis, & Wolfe, 1995). If school mental health professionals plan to use self-report screening instruments, the biggest challenge is selecting the best instrument in a given situation. Fortunately, many screening instruments for the adolescent population have been developed in recent years and now there is a wide range of appropriate instruments. Table 21.1 briefly introduces nine screening instruments for adolescents suitable for school settings. Since the characteristics of the instruments are very diverse, school mental health professions are advised to check the qualities, cost, and required conditions of the instruments thoroughly before choosing one. Among the nine instruments, Problem Oriented Screening Instruments for Teenagers (POSIT) and Rutgers Alcohol Problem Index (RAPI) are especially recommendable for school mental health professionals considering low cost, copyright, easy access, and psychometric traits of the instruments. Thus, these instruments are presented as exemplars.

Problem-Oriented Screening Instrument for Teenagers (POSIT)

Brief Description

POSIT is one of the most widely used instruments for adolescent substance use/abuse.[1] It was developed by National Institute on Drug Abuse (NIDA) to identify potential problems and service needs of adolescents aged 12 to 19 years. It is composed of 139 Yes/No questions under the following 10 subscales: Substance Use and Abuse; Physical Health Status; Mental Health Status; Family Relations; Peer Relations; Educational Status; Vocational Status; Social Skills; Leisure and Recreation; and Aggressive Behavior and Delinquency.

Format and Administration

The original POSIT is a paper-and-pencil questionnaire. Recently, a CD-ROM version became available. It can be self-administered or administered during an interview in a variety of settings including schools. No specific qualification is necessary for administration.

Scoring and Interpretation

POSIT can be scored and interpreted in two different ways, using either the original or the new scoring system. In the original scoring system, the questions are classified as general, age-related, or red-flag items. While every point-earning answer to general items adds one risk score in each subscale, the answer to age-related items does only for the teenagers in a specified age range. Either any point earning in red-flag items or expert-based cutoff score in a subscale is interpreted as indication of needs for further assessment or service in the problem area. In a new scoring system, however, red-flag items are not taken into account and the total score of each subscale is used to determine the level of risks in the area.

Psychometric Properties

The internal consistency of POSIT varies across the subscales and different studies. Some subscales, such as Substance Use/Abuse, Mental Health, and Aggressive Behavior/Delinquency exhibit high levels of internal consistency while others, such as Leisure/Recreation, Vocational Status, and Physical Health, show lower levels of internal consistency than conventionally acceptable ranges. However, it should be noticed that the Cronbach's alpha for the Substance Use/Abuse subscale has been identified as high ranging from .77 (Knight, Goodman, Pulerwitz, & DuRant, 2001) to .93 (Melchior, Rahdert, & Huba, 1994). Acceptable levels of test–retest reliability have been also reported (Dembo, Schmeidler, & Henly, 1996; McLaney & Boca, 1994). All the subscales of POSIT have successfully differentiated heavy substance users from nonusers, showing good concurrent differential validity

Table 21.1 Screening Instruments for Adolescent Substance or Alcohol Use/Abuse

Name of Screening Tool and Contact Info for Access	*Brief Description*	*Number of Q (time)*	*Reading Level*	*Cosf and Copyright*	*Key Reference*
Adolescent Alcohol Involvement Scale (AAIS) http://www.niaaa.nih.gov/publications/aais.htm	• *Problems measured:* alcohol use and psychosocial consequences • *Administration:* self-report • *Required qualification for use:* no specific requirement • *Reliability:* test—retest & internal consistency • *Validity:* construct & criterion (predictive, concurrent, postdictive)	14 (5 m)	No info	Cost information is not available Copyright status is unknown	Mayer & Filstead (1979)
Adolescent Drinking Index (ADI) Psychological Assessment Resources, Inc. PO Box 998, Odessa, FL 33556 (800) 331–8378 http://www.parinc.com/index.cfm	• *Problems measured:* severity of drinking problems • *Administration:* self-report or interview • *Qualification for administration:* (1) a bachelor's degree or higher in psychology or a related field; or (2) adequate training for interpreting psychological test results • *Reliability:* internal consistency • *Validity:* criterion (concurrent validity)	24 (5 m)	5th grade	Introductory kit: $82 Professional manual: $35 Test booklets (pkg/25):$53	*Mental Measurements Yearbook* (12th ed.)
Adolescent Drug Involvement Scale (ADIS) D. Paul Moberg, Ph.D. Center for Health Policy & Program Evaluation Univ. of Wisconsin at Madison 2710 Marshall Ct, Madison, WI 53705 (608) 263–1304	• *Problems measured:* levels of drug use other than alcohol • *Administration:* self-report • *Qualification for administration:* no specific requirement • *Reliability:* internal consistency • *Validity:* criterion (concurrent)	12 (4–5 m)	No info	No cost ADIS is in public domain	Moberg & Hahn (1991)
CRAFFT[b] American Medical Association Licensing and Permission 515 N. State Street Chicago, IL 60610	• *Problems measured:* substance use problem • *Administration:* self-report • *Required qualification for use:* no information available • *Reliability:* internal consistency • *Validity:* criterion	6	No info	No cost Copyrighted	Knight et al. (1999)

(continued)

Table21.1 *(Continued)*

Name of Screening Tool and Contact Info for Access	*Brief Description*	*Number of Q (time)*	*Reading Level*	*Cosf and Copyright*	*Key Reference*
Drug and Alcohol Problem (DAP) Quick Screen Richard H. Schwartz, M.D. 410 Maple Avenue West Vienna, VA 22180 (703) 338–2244	• *Problems measured:* overall problem of alcohol and other drug use • *Administration:* self-report or interview • *Qualification for administration:* no specific requirement • *Reliability & validity:* this scale has been tested in a pediatric practice setting. However, reliability and validity of the DAP Quick Screen have not been evaluated	30 (10m)	6th grade	No cost DAP is in public domain	Schwartz &Wirtz (1990)
Drug Use Screening Inventory Revised (DUSI-R)[C] The Gordian Group P.O. Box 1587 Hartsville, SC 29950 (843) 383–2201 www.dusi.com	• *Problems measured:* severity of disturbance in 10 domains including drug & alcohol use, substance use, behavior patterns, and health status. • *Administration:* self-report • *Qualification for administration:* drug counselors and other qualified users • *Reliability & Validity:* good levels of reliability and validity of DUSI-R have been reported	159 (20–40 m)	5th grade	A copy of paper DUSI-R: $2 DUSI-R software for computer administration: $199 Copyrighted	Kirisci, Mezzich, & Tarter (1995)
Personal Experience Screening Questionnaire (PESQ) Western Psychological Services 12031 Wilshire Blvd. Los Angeles, CA 90025 (310) 478–2061 http://www.wpspublish.com/Inetpub4/index.htm	• *Problems measured:* problem severity, psychosocial items, & drug use history • *Administration:* self-report or interview • *Qualification for administration:* no specific requirement • *Reliability:* internal consistency • *Validity:* content, construct, & criterion (postdictive & concurrent)	40 (10 m)	No info	$79.50 per kit (each kit includes 25 Autoscore Test Forms & 1 Manual) Copyrighted	Winters (1991) Winters (1992)

(continued)

Problem Oriented Screening Instrument for Teenagers (POSIT)[b] Elizabeth Rahdert, Ph.D. National Institute on Drug Abuse, NIH 5600 Fishers Lane, Room 10A-10 Rockville, MD 20857 (301) 443–0107	• *Goal:* to identify substance abuse and related problems and to estimate potential service needs in 10 system areas • *Type:* paper-and-pencil questionnaire CD-ROM version is also available • *Administration:* self-report or interview • *Qualification for administration:* no specific requirement • *Reliability:* test—retest & internal consistency • *Validity:* content, criterion (concurrent & predictive), construct validity (convergent & discriminant)	139 (20–30 m)	5th grade (12–19 yrs old)	No cost POSIT is in public domain	Rahdert (1991)
Rutgers Alcohol Problem Index (RAPI) Helene Raskin White, Ph.D. Center of Alcohol Studies Rutgers University P.O. Box 969 Piscataway, NJ 08855–0969 (732) 445–3579	• *Problems assessed:* problem drinking of adolescents • *Administration:* self-report or interview • *Qualification for administration:* no training required • *Reliability:* split-half, internal consistency • *Validity:* content and criterion • RAPI is appropriate for use in clinical and nonclinical samples of adolescents and young adults	23 (10 m)	7th grade	No cost Copyrighted	White & Labouvie (1989)

[a]Cost as of July, 2004

[b]CRAFFT questions can be obtained from http://www.slp3d2.com/rwj_1027/webcast/docs/screentest.html

[c]Indicates that Spanish version is available.

(Melchior et al., 1994). In a study (McLaney & Boca, 1994) in which POSIT was compared with Personal Experience Inventory (PEI), Diagnostic Interview for Children and Adolescents (DICA), and the Adolescent Diagnostic Interview (ADI), POSIT also showed both convergent and divergent validity.

Brief Evaluation of the Instrument

Based on prior empirical studies, POSIT is a recommendable screening instrument especially for substance use/abuse problems among adolescents. One of the advantages of POSIT lies in its comprehensiveness. The screening results with POSIT can identify potential problems in various areas rather than assessing substance use problems only. Such comprehensiveness might help mental health professionals make better referrals for further assessment or necessary services based on various needs of the adolescents. Easy administration and cost-effectiveness are also considerable benefits of POSIT. In addition, POSIT is in the public domain and can be easily obtained at no cost by contacting NIDA or the National Clearinghouse for Alcohol and Drug Information, or by visiting the Web site of the National Institute on Alcohol Abuse and Alcoholism.

Rutgers Alcohol Problem Index (RAPI)

Brief Description

RAPI is a simple, unidimensional screening tool for problem drinking. Its target populations are adolescents and young adults aged 12 to 21 years. The researchers at the Center of Alcohol Studies, Rutgers University, developed RAPI in 1989 to create an efficient and conceptually sound instrument to assess problem drinking among adolescents (Table 21.2). This instrument has been validated on nonclinical as well as clinical samples.

Format and Administration

RAPI is composed of 23 items describing alcohol-related problems or symptoms. The original version of RAPI asks respondents how many times they experienced each problem during the last 3 years, and provides five answer categories for each question: none; 1–2 times; 3–4 times; 6–10 times; and more than 10 times. A later version of RAPI[2] asks respondents the same questions, but the time frame was reduced to the previous year for greater specificity, as shown below. The number of answer categories was also reduced to four, ranging from "none" to "more than five times." Basically RAPI is a self-administered paper-and pencil type instrument, but it can be easily administered also in an interview format if preferable or necessary. No special training is required for administration.

Scoring and Interpretation

Scoring of RAPI is simple. If the number assigned to each answer category is added, it forms a total scale score. It should be noted, however, that the last two answer categories of the original version of RAPI need to be combined and three be assigned. Therefore, the total scores of both the original and later version of RAPI range from 0 to 69. The total score is considered to indicate the level of problem drinking. The necessity for a further assessment can be made based on the norms available. According to the most recent data provided by the RAPI developers, the mean scores for clinical sample range from 21 to 26, while those for nonclinical sample from 5.9 to 8.2, depending on gender and age. Specific information about RAPI mean score is exhibited in Table 21.3.

Psychometric Properties

The 23-item RAPI resulted from factor analyses conducted on a nonclinical sample of 1,308 adolescents (White & Labouvie, 1989). Its internal consistency measured was .92 and test–retest with a 3-year period marked .40 (White & Labouvie, 1989). RAPI has showed high correlation levels with Adolescent Alcohol Involvement Scale (AAIS), Alcohol Dependence Scale (ADS), DSM-III, and DSM-III-R (greater than .70), indicating good convergent validity. In addition, RAPI can differentiate seriously problematic drinkers from non- or less problematic drinkers in adolescence.

Brief Evaluation of the Instrument

As a screening instrument for adolescents, RAPI has several merits. First, it is efficient. Its

Table 21.2 Rutgers Alcohol Problem Index (RAPI)

Different things happen to people while they are drinking ALCOHOL or because *of ALCOHOL* drinking. Several of these things are listed below. Indicate how many times each of these things happened to you WITHIN THE LAST YEAR.

Use the following code:

0 = None
1 = 1–2 times
2 = 3–5 times
3 = More than 5 times

None	*1–2 Times*	*3–5 Times*	*More Than 5 Times*	*HOW MANY TIMES HAS THIS HAPPENED TO YOU WHILE YOU WERE DRINKING OR BECAUSE OF YOUR DRINKING DURING THE LAST YEAR?*
0	1	2	3	Not able to do your homework or study for a test
0	1	2	3	Got into fights with other people (friends, relatives, strangers)
0	1	2	3	Missed out on other things because you spent too much money on alcohol
0	1	2	3	Went to work or school high or drunk
0	1	2	3	Caused shame or embarrassment to someone
0	1	2	3	Neglected your responsibilities
0	1	2	3	Relatives avoided you
0	1	2	3	Felt that you needed *more* alcohol than you used to in order to get the same effect
0	1	2	3	Tried to control your drinking (tried to drink only at certain times of the day or in certain places, that is, tried to change your pattern of drinking)
0	1	2	3	Had withdrawal symptoms, that is, felt sick because you stopped or cut down on drinking
0	1	2	3	Noticed a change in your responsibility
0	1	2	3	Felt that you had a problem with alcohol
0	1	2	3	Missed a day (or part of a day) of school or work
0	1	2	3	Wanted to stop drinking but couldn't
0	1	2	3	Suddenly found yourself in a place that you could not remember getting to
0	1	2	3	Passed out or fainted suddenly
0	1	2	3	Had a fight, argument, or bad feeling with a friend
0	1	2	3	Had a fight, argument, or bad feeling with a family member
0	1	2	3	Kept drinking when you promised yourself not to
0	1	2	3	Felt you were going crazy
0	1	2	3	Had a bad time
0	1	2	3	Felt physically or psychologically dependent on alcohol
0	1	2	3	Was told by a friend, neighbor, or relative to stop or cut down drinking

Table 21.3 Currently Available Mean Scores of RAPI

Clinical Sample	*N*	*Mean*	*Nonclinical Sample*	*N*	*Mean*
14–16 years old males	42	23.3	14–16 years old males	151	7.5
14–16 years old females	19	22.2	14–16 years old females	147	5.9
17–18 years old males	43	21.1	17–18 years old males	211	8.2
17–18 years old females	15	26.0	17–18 years old females	208	7.4

administration and scoring procedures are simple and require only 15 minutes or less (10 minutes for administration and 3 to 5 minutes for scoring). It is in the public domain, and no cost is necessary. Second, RAPI has high utility. It can be used for nonclinical as well as clinical samples. Third, all the RAPI items are worded appropriately for teenage students and are easy to understand. Fourth, it can be used for various purposes. Based on RAPI scores, for example, service referral can be done properly and the effectiveness of the intervention program for adolescent drinkers can be evaluated. Furthermore, according to the scale developers, it is possible to use RAPI to assess all types of substance use problems. The only thing necessary is to use proper words for the substance instead of "alcohol" or "drinking." RAPI has also some limitations. Most notably, there is no clear cutoff point based on which adolescents with a drinking problem and adolescents without a problem can be classified. Another limitation is that RAPI measures only one problem area (e.g., alcohol use/abuse). Considering previous studies that have consistently found that substance use/abuse problems are complicated and related to many other areas, it would be more desirable to use RAPI with other instruments for more accurate screening or comprehensive assessment.

Applying Interventions within a Response to Intervention Framework

Academic and behavioral difficulties in the school setting often go hand in hand with middle school and high school student drug and alcohol use and abuse. It is important that school educators, administrators, counselors, and stakeholders consider the nexus of academic performance and substance behaviors for a holistic and complete picture of the students' risk, protective factors, areas of concern, and action plans. For effective and successful intervention and prevention strategies with regards to drugs and alcohol, one can utilize Tier 1 of the Response to Intervention (RTI) model, which provides guidance for proper screening and assessment to examine students' substance abuse risk, evidence of early warning signs, and relevance in public education with respect to evaluations and referrals. As alluded to in the rest of this chapter, the most successful substance abuse prevention methods and interventions are tailored to individual student needs (as noted in Tier 2 of the RTI model). Due to the complexity of students and families with substance-related risks and problems, it is especially critical to identify culturally relevant aspects of the interventions; to communicate concern and support, including family in Tier 3; and to follow up and maintain continued support beyond one-time interventions. Drug and alcohol abuse in families and early childhood abuse both are risk factors that correlate with academic performance (Jeynes, 2002). Therefore, school officials, researchers, and clinical practitioners should be challenged to draw more parallels to academic and behavioral progress and those cultural barriers faced in the educational system for children and adolescents with low school performance. IEPs should be comprehensive, building on strengths and the biopsychosocial-spiritual aspects of the individual/family (Graybeal, 2001), as these realms have all been shown to be relevant to substance abuse behaviors and choices to address problems as they arise.

Tools and Practice Examples

Tools

The student behavior checklist, which is composed of the indicative signs of substance use/

abuse and relevant problem behaviors as shown in Figure 21.1, is a good example of a tool used to screen for substance use. School mental health professionals can ask teachers to fill out this form and submit it to the interdisciplinary team or the professionals whenever the teachers find a potential substance user.

Culturally Grounded Interventions

Research supports the importance of culturally appropriate prevention and intervention approaches for youth (Holleran Steiker, Goldbach, Hopson, & Powell, 2011). When screening and intervening, it is critical to consider cultural

Teacher name: ________ Date: ______

________ (student name) has been referred to the "CARE"team.Please help us by sharing

Check those behaviors you have witnessed.Use the bottom of this form if you have any further information that you think may be of help to the CARE team.Thank you.

— Tardy: No. —
— Absent: No. —
Frequent requests to go to:
— Lav. — Phone
— Clinic — Counselor
Other (specify) ________
— Falling asleep
— Slurred speech
— Incoherent
— Stumbles
Smells of:
— Alcohol — Mouthwash
— Cigarette Smoke — Marijuan
— Talk freely of drug/alcohol use
— Brown-stained fingertips
— Bad hygine
— Unusual/frequent bruises or sores
— Declining grade(s)
From ________ To: ________

— Nonresponsiveness
— Lack of motivation
— Change of dress (negative)
— Defensiveness
— Withdrawn; loner
— Erratic behavi or from day to day
— Cheating
— Consulting in "Wrong" area
(specify) ________
— Obsence language or gestures
— Dramatic attention-getting behavior
— Sudden outbrusts
— Verbal abuse
— Fighting
Change of friends (negative)
— Class interruptions for this student
— Change of friends (negative)
— Frequent requests for schedule changes
— Poor work performance

— Other unacceptable out-of-class behavior — Other inacceptable out-of-class behavior
Example: ________ Example: ________

Use this space for any other pertinent comments: ________

Please deposit this form in an envelope in the CARE Mailbox in the Main Office.

Figure 21.1 A Sample Behavioral Checklist

Source: From *Counseling the Adolescent Substance Abuser: School-Based Intervention and Prevention* (p. 93), by M. M. Gonet, 1994. Thousand Oaks, CA: Sage. Reprinted with permission.

aspects, including age appropriateness, linguistic differences, comprehensive and critical thinking abilities, and client ethnicity. Facilitators of prevention programs often argue that evidence-based prevention programs are culturally inappropriate for their youth and agencies in their prescribed form (Botvin, 2004). Schools, agencies, and community settings describe programs as difficult to implement due to time and resource constraints (Hopson & Holleran, 2008). As a result, they spontaneously adapt the curricula, or develop "homegrown" programs to prevent substance use (Backer, 2001; Hopson & Holleran, 2008). This research suggests the need for procedures that can be used to make evidence-based curricula culturally relevant for a particular group of participants without reducing the effectiveness of the curriculum.

Many prevention curricula target family and school settings (Kumpfer, Molgaard, & Spoth, 1996; Eggert, Nicholas, & Owen, 1995; Sussman et al., 1997). One strategy for developing culturally grounded prevention programs is to engage youth in program design. Presently, youth are rarely involved in designing prevention programs (Marsiglia et al., 2004; Warren et al., 2006; Holleran Steiker, 2008). When they are involved in the creation of interventions for their peers, the culture and life experiences of participants are better captured (Marsiglia et al., 2004). Youth are able to infuse their own language, perceptions, and culture in the presentation of drug resistance strategies. They are also able to portray drug use by their peers and contexts in which they would be likely to receive a drug offer. The most successful programs are those with attention to cultural groundedness (Hansen, Miller, & Leukefeld, 1995; Palinkas et. al., 1996). Adaptation is the process of tailoring a screening tool or curriculum to the specific needs, characteristics, and culture of the target population. More attention has recently been given to culturally adapted interventions (Castro, Barrera, & Martinez, 2004; Castro, Barrera, & Holleran Steiker, 2010). Adaptation is especially critical in situations where the culture of the audience is unique—ethnically, socially, organizationally, or economically.

Due to the complex nature of implementation in real-world settings, programs that are designed as "one size fits all" are not as effective (Kreuter, Strecher, & Glassman, 1999), and, ultimately, some amount of curriculum adaptation is unavoidable (Ringwalt et al., 2003). Some curriculum developers have employed a top-down approach to adapting curricula, relying on the cultural knowledge of researchers and curriculum developers, while others engage key stakeholders from targeted communities to make changes (Marsiglia, Kulis, Hecht, & Sills, 2004). It is recommended that school helping professionals enlist youth in curricula design, adaptation, and implementation. For example, the Keepin' It REAL program is a drug prevention curriculum especially designed to engage Latino/a youth (Marsiglia et al., 2011) Much of the literature on culturally grounded prevention and intervention focuses on the students' race and ethnicity. However, the culture of the school is important to consider as well. Because of the great variation among schools and communities, it is especially important to examine and integrate school culture into the programs implemented in these settings (Hopson & Holleran, 2010).

Also, school workers are advised to consider the age and developmental stage of students who are being screened or assisted. Drug prevention programs for younger adolescents in middle school and junior high are unlikely to be as effective with older, high school students, especially those at higher risk (Sussman, 1996). Although an array of research has been conducted on school-based prevention programs with middle school and early high school students, little exists for older youth and those in alternative school settings. In an effort to prevent substance use among older youth, some high schools have applied drug testing, but research suggests that it does not deter drug use (Yamaguchi, Johnston, & O'Malley, 2003). Positive youth development or afterschool programs have also been implemented in urban schools. These programs have been shown to reduce substance use, but only when tailored to the cultural characteristics and development of the participants (Tebes et al., 2007).

Case Example

Phil is 15-year-old male whose behavior has recently changed dramatically. He has a history of being a strong student with aspirations to attend college and write creatively. He had always been somewhat eccentric, dressing uniquely, with unusual hairdos, but recently appeared disheveled and unkempt. Upon noticing an undeniable drop in his grades and motivation, his English teacher utilized the student behavior checklist, particularly noting the following behaviors: excessive tardiness, frequent requests to go to the restroom, cell phone buzzing throughout class, moments of apparent disorientation, noticeable chewing of breath mints in succession, occasionally nodding off in class. When the teacher requested a meeting with Phil, she noticed that his breath smelled of alcohol. Having a strong relationship with Phil in the past, she expressed concern and requested that he meet with her to talk. She kept her comments to factual observations rather than emotional and speculative responses. She framed her interactions in empathy and supportively suggested that they invite the school social worker to talk. Phil refused initially, but with warm encouragement and strength-based, positive persuasion, he agreed to meet with the worker.

Prior to the screening, a multidisciplinary team consisting of the school social worker, classroom teachers, specialty teachers (e.g., P.E. and art), the school nurse, and principal were made aware of concerns about Phil by his English teacher. The teacher had suggested that Phil's recent change in attention span would make in-depth screening difficult, and the team and social worker decided to begin with the RAPI.

The social worker began by noting very specific strengths of the student (i.e., has aptitude for writing, his history of good grades, his bold sense of style, his sense of humor) and then gently noted the shifts that the teacher had recognized. She cleverly described that alcohol use and experimentation are common in his age group. Further, she persuaded Phil to understand that she needed to learn more about his drinking since the teacher's concerns included awareness that he drank occasionally. She also started by asking if he had any friend that drank because association is a good clue. He openly noted that a few of his friends liked to drink, but that he only did it "once in a while." Sensing his hesitancy, she clearly described that their discussion would remain confidential, except for if the information denoted danger to self or others. She stated that she would start by conducting a brief questionnaire to get a general sense of the issues. She encouraged him to be open and honest and to ask questions if he had any. She added that she would do her best to help and advocate for the student, and that she could be most effective if he was as honest as possible. This gave him the sense that she was trying to help rather than to trap or punish him. She handed him the RAPI, and he scored on the items shown in Table 21.4.

Phil's answers clearly showed a lack of concern about his own alcohol use and a belief that he could stop at any time. However, he had admitted that alcohol had played a role in his academic work, family relationships, and peer relationships (he specifically commented that his girlfriend didn't drink or smoke "pot" and was thinking of breaking up with him if he did). The social worker reviewed his responses and shared his score of 23, noting that this indicates enough concern to warrant a more in-depth screening or assessment. When he protested, she showed him the means chart for his age group, noting that "clinical samples" are the individuals who needed further intervention. She assured him that she would work with him and that the school would not try to punish him. He expressed anger and fear. The social worker calmly and firmly explained the next steps and gave him some choices so that he could feel empowered. Due to the reference to marijuana, the worker noted that the follow-up should include a more extensive substance abuse history and assessment. This worker was familiar with several students in the school who were young people in 12-Step recovery. She was aware that students at this age talk more freely with peers than authorities. Thus, she offered that Phil could talk to someone who had been "in the same boat" if he would like. The social worker had already done "her homework" and had a list of referrals to be considered for Phil to participate in a substance abuse assessment. She also made another appointment with him to explore social supports and see if and who he would be willing to have involved, such as family or friends.

Key Points to Remember

This chapter aims to provide awareness of the scope and repercussions of adolescent substance abuse, directions for choosing and utilizing a screening tool in school settings, and an example of a screening scenario. Tools including the teacher's behavioral checklist, the POSIT, and the RAPI are evidence-supported, reliable, simple instruments for gathering information that can help school mental health professionals determine if an adolescent is in need of more intensive substance related referral and triage. It is important to note, however, that screening tools, no matter how comprehensive, cannot elicit definitive diagnoses and will not be likely to fully capture the nature of an adolescent's relationship to substances. Due to the fact that adolescents almost always hide their

Table 21.4 Phil's RAPI Test Result

None	*1–2 Times*	*3–5 Times*	*More Than 5 Times*	*HOW MANY TIMES HAS THIS HAPPENED TO YOU WHILE YOU WERE DRINKING OR BECAUSE OF YOUR DRINKING DURING THE LAST YEAR?*
0	1	**X**	3	Not able to do your homework or study for a test
0	**X**	2	3	Got into fights with other people (friends, relatives, strangers)
X	1	2	3	Missed out on other things because you spent too much money on alcohol
0	**X**	2	3	Went to work or school high or drunk
X	1	2	3	Caused shame or embarrassment to someone
0	**X**	2	3	Neglected your responsibilities
0	1	**X**	3	Relatives avoided you
X	1	2	3	Felt that you needed *more* alcohol than you used to in order to get the same effect
X	1	2	3	Tried to control your drinking (tried to drink only at certain times of the day or in certain places, that is, tried to change your pattern of drinking)
X	1	2	3	Had withdrawal symptoms, that is, felt sick because you stopped or cut down on drinking
0	1	**X**	3	Noticed a change in your responsibility
X	1	2	3	Felt that you had a problem with alcohol
0	1	2	**X**	Missed a day (or part of a day) of school or work
X	1	2	3	Wanted to stop drinking but couldn't
X	1	2	3	Suddenly found yourself in a place that you could not remember getting to
X	1	2	3	Passed out or fainted suddenly
0	**X**	2	3	Had a fight, argument or bad feeling with a friend
0	**X**	2	3	Had a fight, argument or bad feeling with a family member
X	1	2	3	Kept drinking when you promised yourself not to
0	1	2	**X**	Felt you were going crazy
0	1	2	**X**	Had a bad time
X	1	2	3	Felt physically or psychologically dependent on alcohol
0	1	2	**X**	Was told by a friend, neighbor or relative to stop or cut down drinking

use due to fear, shame, and a desire to maintain the option to use substances, workers must be gentle, creative, and tenacious. The critical data lie in the rapport built between worker and student. In order to do the effective "detective work" of drawing out the facts, building connection with the individual, and putting the pieces together, a worker can utilize motivational interviewing techniques described in other areas of this book (for information, trainings, and publications, see the MI Web site, http://www.motivationalinterview.org).

It is important to remember that adolescent substance use/abuse can be profoundly injurious mentally, emotionally, socially, and physically. In fact, it can be potentially fatal and should not be minimized as a "passing phase." Workers do best to err on the conservative side and, if concerns arise, to consult with and/or refer the student to a substance abuse expert.

Notes

1. The POSIT questionnaire and brief explanation are available at http://www.niaaa.nih.gov/publications/insposit.htm and http://www.niaaa.nih.gov/publications/posit.htm, respectively.
2. Recently, the RAPI authors developed a new version of the scale (18-item) and are testing its psychometric properties.

References

Backer, T. E. (2001). *Finding the balance: Program fidelity and adaptation in substance abuse prevention: A state-of-the-art review.* Rockville, MD: Center for Substance Abuse Prevention.

Brown, J. H. (2001). Youth, drugs and resilience education. *Journal of Drug Education, 31*(1), 83–122.

Brown, S. A., Mott, M. A., & Myers, M. G. (1990). Adolescent alcohol and drug treatment outcome. In E. R. R. Watson (Ed.), *Drug and alcohol abuse prevention: Drug and alcohol abuse reviews* (pp. 373–403). Clifton, NJ: Humana.

Burrow-Sanchez, J. J., & Lopez, A. L. (2009). Identifying substance abuse issues in high schools: A national survey of high school counselors. *Journal of Counseling & Development, 87*(1), 72–79.

Castro, F. G., Barrera, M., & Holleran Steiker, L. (2010). Issues and challenges in the design of culturally-adapted evidence-based interventions. *Annual Review of Clinical Psychology, 6*, 213–239.

Castro, F. G., Barrera, M., & Martinez, C. R. (2004). The cultural adaptation of prevention interventions: resolving tensions between fidelity and fit. *Prevention Science, 5*(1), 41–45.

Centers for Disease Control and Prevention. (2004). *Youth risk behavior surveillance: United States, 2003* (MMWR No. SS-2). Atlanta: U.S. Department of Health and Human Services.

Connors, G. J., Donovan, D. M., & DiClemente, C. C. (2001). *Substance abuse treatment and the stages of change: Selecting and planning interventions.* New York: Guilford Press.

Cornelius, J. R., Maisto, S. A., Pollock, N. K., Martin, C. S., Salloum, I. M., Lynch, K. G., et al. (2003). Rapid relapse generally follows treatment for substance use disorders among adolescents. *Addictive Behaviors, 28*(2), 381–386.

Dembo, R., Schmeidler, J., & Henly, G. (1996). Examination of the reliability of the Problem Oriented Screening Instrument for Teenagers (POSIT) among arrested youth entering a juvenile assessment center. *Substance Use and Misuse, 31*, 785–824.

Dent, C. W., Sussman, S., McCullar, W. J., & Stacy, A. W. (2001). Drug abuse prevention among youth at comprehensive high schools. *Preventive Medicine, 32*, 514–520.

Dunn, M. S., Goodrow, B., Givens, C., & Austin, S. (2008). Substance use behavior and suicide indicators among rural middle school students. *Journal of School Health, 78*(1), 26–31.

Eggert, L. L., Nicholas, L. J., & Owen, L. M. (1995). *Reconnecting youth: A peer group approach to building life skills.* Bloomington, IN: National Educational Service.

Fisher, G. L., & Harrison, T. C. (2004). *Substance abuse: Information for school counselors, social workers, therapists, and counselors.* Boston: Pearson Education.

Gonet, M. M. (1994). *Counseling the adolescent substance abuser: School-based intervention and prevention.* Thousand Oaks, CA: Sage.

Graybeal, C. (2001). Strengths-based social work assessment: Transforming the dominant paradigm. *Families in Society: The Journal of Contemporary Human Services, 82*(3), 233–242.

Gunter, W. D., & Bakken, N. W. (2010). Transitioning to middle school in the sixth grade: a hierarchical linear modeling (HLM) analysis of substance use, violence, and suicidal thoughts. *The Journal of Early Adolescence 30,* 895–915.

Havighurst, R. J. (1972). *Developmental tasks and education.* New York: David McKay.

Holleran Steiker, L. K., Goldbach, J., Hopson, L. M., & Powell, T. (2011). the value of cultural adaptation processes: Older youth participants as substance abuse preventionists. *Child and Adolescent Social Work Journal.* doi: *10*.1007/s10560-011-0246-9

Holleran Steiker, L. K., Powell, T., Hopson, L. M., & Goldbach, J. (2011) Dissonance-based interventions for substance using alternative high-school youth. *Practice (Special Edition on Social Work in Action), 23*(4), 235–252.

Hopson, L. M., & Holleran Steiker, L. K. (2008). Methodology for evaluating an adaptation of evidence-based drug abuse prevention in alternative schools. *Children in Schools, 30*(2), 116–127.

Hopson, L. M., & Holleran Steiker, L. K. (2010). The effectiveness of adapted versions of an evidence-based substance abuse prevention program for alternative school students. *Children and Schools, 32*(2), 81–92.

Hutchinson, D. S., Ashcraft, L., & Anthony, W. A. (2006). The role of recovery education. *Behavioral Healthcare, 26*(6), 12–14.

Jeynes, W. (2002). The relationship between the consumption of various drugs by adolescents and their academic achievement. *American Journal of Drug Alcohol Abuse, 28*, 15–35.

Kirisci, L., Mezzich, A., & Tarter, R. (1995). Norms and sensitivity of the adolescent version of the Drug Use Screening Inventory. *Addictive Behaviors, 20*(2), 149–157.

Knight, J. R., Goodman, E., Pulerwitz, T., & DuRant, R. H. (2001). Reliability of the Problem Oriented Screening Instrument for Teenagers (POSIT) in adolescent medical practice. *Journal of Adolescent Health, 29*, 125–130.

Knight, J. R., Shrier, L.A., Bravender, T. D., Farrell, M., Bilt, J. V., & Shaffer, H. J. (1999). A new brief screen for adolescent substanceabuse. *Archives Pediatrics & Adolescent Medicine, 153*, 591–596.

Kreuter, M. W., Strecher, V. J., & Glassman, B. (1999). One size does not fit all: The case for tailoring print materials. *Annals of Behavioral Medicine, 21*(4), 276–283. Special Section on Tailored Print Communication.

Kumpfer, K. L., Molgaard, V., & Spoth, R. (1996). The Strengthening Families Program for prevention of delinquency and drug use in special populations. In R. Peters & R. J. McMahon (Eds.), *Childhood disorders, substance abuse, and delinquency: Prevention and early intervention approaches.* Newbury Park, CA: Sage.

Lynne-Landsman, S. D., Graber, J. A., Nichols, T. R., & Botvin, G. J. (2011). Trajectories of aggression, delinquency, and substance use across middle school among urban, minority adolescents. *Aggressive Behaviors, 37*(2), 161–176.

Marsiglia, F. F., Kulis, S., Hecht, M. L., & Sills, S. (2004). Ethnicity and ethnic identity as predictors of drug norms and drug use among preadolescents in the US Southwest. *Substance Use & Misuse, 39*(7), 1061–1094.

Marsiglia, F., Kulis, S., Yabiku, S., Nieri, T., & Coleman, E. (2011). When to intervene: Elementary school, middle school or both? Effects of Keepin' It REAL on substance use trajectories of Mexican heritage youth. *Prevention Science, 12*(1), 48–62.

Martin, C. S., & Winters, K. C. (1998). Diagnosis and assessment of alcohol use disorders among adolescents. *Alcohol Health & Research World, 22*(2), 95–105.

Mayer, J., & Filstead, W. J. (1979). The Adolescent Alcohol Involvement Scale: An instrument for measuring adolescents' use and misuse of alcohol. *Journal of Studies on Alcohol, 40*, 291–300.

McLaney, M. A., & Boca, F. D. (1994). A validation of the Problem-Oriented Screening Instrument for Teenagers (POSIT). *Journal of Mental Health, 3*(3), 363–376.

McWhirter, J. J., McWhirter, B.T., McWhirter, E. H., & McWhirter, R. J. (2004). *At-risk youth: A comprehensive response.* Toronto, Canada: Brooks Cole.

Melchior, L. A., Rahdert, E., & Huba, G. J. (1994). *Reliability and validity evidence for the Problem Oriented Screening Instruments for Teenagers (POSIT).* Washington, DC: American Public Health Association.

Moberg, D. P., & Hahn, L. (1991). The Adolescent Drug Involvement Scale. *Journal of Adolescent Chemical Dependency, 2*(1), 75–88.

National Center for Chronic Disease Prevention and Health Promotion (2012). CDC Chronic Disease Prevention and Health Promotion Overview. http://www.cdc.gov/chronicdisease/index.htm. Accessed 9/30/2012.

National Commission on Drug-Free Schools. (1990). *Toward a drug-free generation: A nation's responsibility.* Washington, DC: U.S. Government Printing Office.

Newcomb, M. D., & Bentler, P. M. (1989). Substance use and abuse among children and teenagers. *American Psychologist, 44*(2), 242–248.

NIDA. (2003). *Preventing drug abuse among children and adolescents: A research-based guide for parents, educators, and community leaders.* Baltimore, MD: National Institute of Drug Abuse.

Orenstein, A., Davis, R. B., & Wolfe, H. (1995). Comparing screening instruments. *Journal of Alcohol & Drug Education, 40*(3), 119–131.

Pallonen, U. E. (1998). Transtheoretical measures for adolescent and adult smokers: similarities and differences. *Preventive Medicine, 27*(5), A29–A38.

Prochaska, J. Q., & DiClemente, C.C. (1992). Stages of change in the modification of problem behaviors. In Hersen, M., Eisler, R. M., & Miller, P. M. (Eds), *Progress in behavior modification* (pp. 184–214). Sycamore, IL: Sycamore Press.

Prochaska, J. O., & DiClemente, C. C. (2005). The transtheoretical approach. In J. C. Norcross & M. R. Goldfried (Eds.), *Handbook of psychotherapy integration* (2nd ed., pp. 147–171). New York, NY: Oxford University Press. ISBN 0195165799

Rahdert, E. R. (1991). *The adolescent assessment/referral system manual. Rockville, MD:U.S.* Department of Health and Human Services, Alcohol, Drug Abuse, and Mental Health Administration.

Ringwalt, C. L., Ennett, S., Johnson, R., Rohrbach, L. A., Simons-Rudolph, A., Vincus, A., & Thorne, J. (2003). Factors associated with fidelity to substance use prevention curriculum guides in the nation's middle schools. *Health Education & Behavior, 30*(3), 375–391.

Russell, B. L., Jennings, B., & Classey, S. (2005). Adolescent attitudes toward random drug testing in schools. *Journal of Drug Education, 35*(3), 167–184.

Salm, T., Sevigny, P., Mulholland, V., & Greenberg, H. (2011). Prevalence and pedagogy: Understanding substance abuse in schools. *Journal of Alcohol & Drug Education, 55*(1), 70–92.

Schwartz, R. H., & Wirtz, P.W. (1990). Potential substance abuse detection among adolescent patients: Using the Drug and Alcohol Problem (DAP) Quick

Screen, a 30-item questionnaire. *Clinical Pediatrics, 29*, 38–43.

Sussman, S. (1996). Development of a school-based drug abuse prevention curriculum for high-risk youths. *Journal of Psychoactive Drugs, 28*(2), 169–182.

Sussman, S., Simon, T. R., Dent, C.W., Stacy, A.W., Galaif, E. R., Moss, M. A., et al. (1997). Immediate impact of thirty-two drug abuse prevention activities among students at continuation high schools. *Substance Use and Misuse, 32*(3), 265–281.

Tarter, R. E., Kirisci, L., Mezzich, A., & Patton, D. (2011). Multivariate comparison of male and female adolescent substance abusers with accompanying legal problems. *Journal of Criminal Justice, 39*(3), 207–211.

Tebes, J. K., Feinn, R., Vanderploeg, J. J., Chinman, M. J., Shepard, J. Brabham, T., Genovese, M., & Connell, C. (2007). Impact of a positive youth development program in urban after-school settings on the prevention of adolescent substance use. *Journal of Adolescent Health, 41*(3), 239–247.

University of Michigan Institute for Social Research. (2003). Results from the 2003 Monitoring the Future Study. Retrieved July 25, 2004, from http://www.nida.nih.gov/Newsroom/03/2003MTFFact-Sheet.pdf

U.S. Department of Health and Human Services. (2000). *Healthy people 2010: Understanding and improving health* (2nd ed.). Washington, DC: U.S. Government Printing Office.

White, H. R., & Labouvie, E. W. (1989). Towards the assessment of adolescent problem drinking. *Journal of Studies on Alcohol, 50*(1), 30–37.

White, K., Taylor, M., & Moss, V. (1992). Does research support claims about the benefits of involving parents in early intervention programs? *Review of Educational Research, 62*(1), 91–125.

Winters, K. (1991). *Manual for the Personal Experience Screening Questionnaire (PESQ)*. Los Angeles: Western Psychological Services.

Winters, K. (1999). Treating adolescents with substance use disorders: An overview of practice issues and treatment outcome. *Substance Abuse, 20*(4), 203–225.

Winters, K. C. (1992). Development of an adolescent alcohol and other drug abuse screening scale: Personal Experience Screening Questionnaire. *Addictive Behaviors, 17*, 479–490.

Winters, K. C., Latimer, W. W., & Stinchfield, R. D. (1999). DSM-IV criteria for adolescent alcohol and cannabis use disorders. *Journal of Studies on Alcohol, 60*, 337–344.

Winters, K. C. (2001a). Assessing adolescent substance use problems and other areas of functioning: State of the art. In P. M. Monti, S. M. Colby, & T. A. O'Leary (Eds.), *Adolescents, alcohol, and substance abuse: Reaching teens through brief interventions* (pp. 80–108). New York: Guilford.

Winters, K. C. (2001b). Screening and assessing adolescents for substance use disorders (DHHS Publication No. SMA 01–3493). Rockwall, MD: Center for Substance Abuse Treatment, U.S. Department of Health and Human Services.

Yamaguchi, R., Johnston, L., & O'Malley, P. (2003). Relationship between student illicit drug use and school drug-testing policies. *Journal of School Health, 73*(4), 159–164.

Best Practices for Prevention of STDs and HIV in Schools

CHAPTER 22

Laura M. Hopson

Getting Started

Sexual risk behavior among adolescents continues to endanger their health and quality of life. Although the last decade has seen some improvement in sexual health statistics, sexually transmitted diseases (STDs) and Human Immunodeficiency Virus (HIV) continue to plague American youth, especially those from economically disadvantaged communities (Centers for Disease Control and Prevention [CDC], 2010). School-based prevention programs are potentially effective means of reaching large numbers of adolescents, although they will need to be part of broader community-wide strategies for improving sexual health in order to have a meaningful impact on behavior. This chapter discusses current research on the prevalence of HIV and STDs and programs that aim to reduce risk.

What We Know

According to the Youth Risk Behavior Surveillance conducted by the Centers for Disease Control and Prevention (CDC), almost half of American high school students have had sex in their lifetime, and one in three are currently sexually active. Only 6 out of 10 sexually active students used a condom during their last sexual intercourse (Eaton et al., 2010). In addition, about 14% of these sexually active teens reported having sex with four or more partners during their lifetime (Eaton et al., 2010). The high rates of sexual activity and failure to use condoms in many cases help to explain the large number of American adolescents infected with sexually transmitted diseases and HIV.

Adolescents and young adults between the ages of 13 and 24 accounted for about 17% of those living with a diagnosis of HIV/AIDS in 2008 (CDC, 2010), and they account for almost 19 million new cases of sexually transmitted infections each year (Weinstock et al., 2004). Chlamydia infection is widespread and especially problematic among economically disadvantaged women. The CDC reported that rates of Chlamydia infection increased almost 3% between 2008 and 2009, and the number of reported infections is now higher than that for any other condition (CDC, 2010). Although rates of gonorrhea infection have generally declined among American youth, women between the ages of 15 and 19 represent the largest proportion of women diagnosed with gonorrhea, at a rate of about 569 cases per every 100,000 women in this age group. Infection rates for gonorrhea among male adolescents are about 260 per every 100,000. Adolescent girls may be at higher risk than adult women for becoming infected with STDs because of their immature cervix (CDC, 2010).

Reasons for the higher prevalence of STDs among adolescents include lack of insurance and transportation, as well as discomfort with services designed for adults (CDC, 2010). In addition, prevention programs for adolescents face many challenges because adolescents often do not perceive themselves to be at risk. They may hold negative beliefs about condom use and have few skills to negotiate safer sex practices with a partner. Programs may face additional barriers because those that discuss condom use are controversial in many communities. Effective prevention may require addressing political barriers and misinformation, including the idea that sex education results in increased sexual activity among teens (CDC, 2003a).

School-based programs can reach a large number of youth before they become sexually active.

Many states now require schools to offer sex education, and most require that schools teach STD/HIV education (Kirby, 2002). The most helpful programs are comprehensive, emphasizing the importance of delaying sexual activity, as well as providing information about protection, such as condoms, for sexually active youth (Kirby & Laris, 2009).

The school setting also presents challenges for providing effective prevention programs. Some schools may not allow condom distribution, for example, which is a component of many effective HIV prevention strategies (Stryker, Samuels, & Smith, 1994). Many schools will support only abstinence-based curriculums, especially for younger teens (Lohrmann et al., 2001), which eliminates the majority of research-based prevention programs (Kirby & Laris, 2009). Empirical evaluations of abstinence-only curricula have not demonstrated effectiveness in delaying sexual activity (Kirby & Laris, 2009).

What We Can Do

Many research-based prevention programs are appropriate for school settings and have demonstrated a range of positive outcomes for adolescents. Programs have been most successful in improving condom use, knowledge about HIV, and communication skills; they have been less successful with reducing overall sexual activity (Collins et al., 2002; Johnson et al., 2003).

Evidence-based prevention programs employ a range of strategies including instruction, use of video and other media, demonstration of correct condom use, role-plays, and group discussion. The programs described in this chapter are defined as evidence based because they have been evaluated in experimental design studies that employ random assignment to treatment conditions or quasi-experimental designs that use matching or are statistically corrected for any difference in experimental and comparison groups to compensate for using nonrandom assignment. The evidence-based programs have also demonstrated statistically significant reductions in sexual risk behaviors. See Table 22.1 for a list of evidence-based programs and their supporting studies.

Evidence-based prevention programs have resulted in increased condom use (Coyle et al., 2006; Fisher et al., 2002; Kirby et al., 2004; Main et al., 1994; Rotheram-Borus et al., 2003; St. Lawrence et al., 1995), less frequent sexual intercourse, and fewer sexual partners (Jemmott,

Table 22.1 Evidence-based Programs and Supporting Studies

Evidence-Based Interventions	*Supporting Studies*	*Contact Information*
All4You!	Coyle, K. K., Kirby, D. B., Robin, L. E., Banspach, S. W., Baumler, E., & Glassman, J. R. (2006). All4You! A randomized trial of an HIV, other STDs and pregnancy prevention intervention for alternative school students. *AIDS Education and Prevention, 18*, 187–203.	Karin K. Coyle, Ph.D.; available from www.etr.org
Be Proud! Be Responsible!	Jemmott, J., III, Jemmott, L., Braverman, P., & Fong, G. T. (2005). HIV/STD risk reduction interventions for African American and Latino adolescent girls at an adolescent medicine clinic. *Archives of Pediatric Adolescent Medicine, 159*, 440–449.	John Jemmott, Ph.D., jjemmott@asc.upenn.edu; available from www.selectmedia.org.
Becoming a Responsible Teen	St. Lawrence, J., Crosby, R., Brasfield, T., & O'Bannon, R., III. (2002). Reducing STD and HIV risk behavior of substance dependent adolescents: A randomized controlled trial. *Journal of Consulting and Clinical Psychology, 70*, 1010–1021.	Available from www.etr.org

Table 22.1 *(Continued)*

Evidence-Based Interventions	*Supporting Studies*	*Contact Information*
Cognitive-Behavioral Group Intervention for Young Women	Boyer, C., Shafer, M., Shaffer, R., Brodine, S., Pollack, L., Betsinger, K., et al. (2005). Evaluation of a cognitive-behavioral, group, randomized controlled intervention trial to prevent sexually transmitted infections and unintended pregnancies in young women. *Preventive Medicine, 40*, 420–431.	Cherrie B. Boyer, Ph.D., boyer@itsa.ucsf.edu
HIV/AIDS Among Gay and Bisexual Adolescents	Remafedi, G. (1994). Cognitive and behavioral adaptations to HIV/AIDS among gay and bisexual adolescents. *HIV/AIDS Journal of Adolescent Health, 15*, 142–148.	Gary Remafedi, M.D., Box 721 UMHC 420 Delaware St. SE Minneapolis, MN 55455–0392
Focus on Kids	Stanton, B., Li, X., Ricardo, I., Galbraith, J., Feigelman, S., & Kaljee, L. (1996). A randomized, controlled effectiveness trial of an AIDS prevention program for low-income African-American youths. *Archives of Pediatric and Adolescent Medicine, 151*(4), 398–406.	Bonita Stanton, M.D., bstanton@umabnet. ab.umd; available from www.etr.org
Get Real About AIDS	Main, D., Iverson, D., McGloin, J., Banspach, S.W., Collins, J. L., Rugg, D. L., & Kolbe, L. J. (1994). Preventing HIV infection among adolescents: Evaluation of a school-based education at program. *Preventive Medicine, 23*(4), 409–417.	Deborah S. Main, Ph.D.; available from AGC Educational Media at agcmedia@starnetinc.com
Information-Motivation-Behavioral Skills Model	Fisher, J., Fisher, W., Bryan, A., & Misovich, S. (2002). Information-motivation-behavioral skills model-based HIV risk behavior change intervention for inner-city high school youth. *Health Psychology, 21*, 177–186.	Jeffrey Fisher, Ph.D., jeffrey.fisher@uconn.edu; available from www.films. org
Making a Difference	Jemmott, J. B., Jemmott, L. S., III, & Fong, G. (1998). Abstinence and safer sex HIV risk-reduction interventions for African-American adolescents: A randomized control trial. *Journal of American Medical Association (JAMA), 279*, 1529–1536.	John Jemmott, Ph.D., jjemmott@asc.upenn. edu; available from www. selectmedia.org
Making Proud Choices	Jemmott, J. B., III, & Jemmott, L. S. (2001). HIV risk-reduction behavioral interventions with heterosexual adolescents. *AIDS, 14*(Suppl. 2), S40–S52.	John Jemmott, Ph.D., jjemmott@asc.upenn. edu; available from www. selectmedia.org
Reducing the Risk	Kirby, D., Barth, R. P., Leland, N., & Fetro, J.V. (1991). Reducing the risk: Impact of a new curriculum on sexual risk-taking. *Family Planning Perspectives 23*(6), 253–263.	Available from www.etr. org

(continued)

Table 22.1 (*Continued*)

Evidence-Based Interventions	*Supporting Studies*	*Contact Information*
Safer Choices	Kirby, D., Baumler, E., Coyle, K., Basen-Enquist, K., Parcel, G., Harrist, R., & Banspach, S.W. (2004). The "Safer Choices" intervention: Its impact on the sexual behaviors of different subgroups of high school students. *Journal of Adolescent Health, 35*, 442–452.	Karin Coyle, Ph.D.; available from www.etr.org
Street Smart	Rotheram-Borus, M., Song, J., Gwadz, M., Lee, M., Van Rossem, R., & Koopman, C. (2003). Reductions in HIV risk among runaway youth. *Prevention Science, 4*, 173–187.	Mary Jane Rotheram-Borus, Ph.D.; available fromhttp://chipts.ucla.edu/interventions/manuals/intervstreetsmart.html

Jemmott, Braverman, & Fong, 2005; Main et al., 1994), as well as delayed initiation of sexual intercourse (Kirby et al., 2004). Because of the need for culturally appropriate HIV prevention, some effective programs have been tailored to meet the needs of students from particular cultural and ethnic backgrounds (Jemmott et al., 1992; Jemmott et al., 1998; Kipke, Boyer, & Hein, 1993; St. Lawrence et al., 1995). Others have been tailored for use with gay and bisexual adolescents (Remafedi, 1994; Rotheram-Borus, Reid, & Rosario, 1994) and runaway youth (Rotheram-Borus et al., 1997).

Most evidence-based HIV prevention programs share common core components. Box 22.1 displays a list of characteristics identified by Kirby and Laris (2009) that are found in effective programs.

Applying Interventions within a Response to Intervention Framework

Data-informed decision making is key for the success of any prevention strategy. A Response to Intervention (RTI) framework begins with an assessment to determine the strengths and needs of students (Hawken, Vincent, & Schumann, 2008). RTI uses data to determine the level of intervention that is likely to be most effective for a targeted group of adolescents. Primary-level interventions aim to reduce risk for academic and behavioral problems in the general population. Secondary interventions are designed for youths who are at elevated risk for adverse outcomes due to risk factors identified in an assessment. Youths who do not respond to primary- or secondary-level interventions are provided with individualized tertiary-level interventions. For all interventions, ongoing evaluation is used to monitor the progress of students and determine whether the interventions are appropriate and effective (National Center on Response to Intervention, 2010).

Although RTI is primarily used for tracking academic progress and improving classroom behavior, its principals can inform a data driven strategy for improving health behaviors, as well. Applying an RTI framework to prevention of STD's might call for conducting a baseline assessment of risk behavior within a particular school. Based on this assessment, school personnel could determine whether students are at minimal or elevated risk and could select and appropriate prevention program. Administering surveys to participating students every two to three weeks would allow for tracking progress toward improved knowledge of HIV and STDs, improved skills in refusing sexual activity or negotiating condom use, and fewer students reporting unprotected sexual activity. RTI calls for adjusting the intensity of the intervention, or changing strategies, if the ongoing evaluation indicates that participants are not making progress (National Center on Response to Intervention, 2010).

RTI employs interventions at the individual, classroom, and school levels to create the conditions

Box 22.1 The 17 Characteristics of Effective Curriculum-Based Sex and STD/HIV Education Programs

The Process of Developing the Curriculum

1. Involved multiple people with different backgrounds in theory, research, and sex and STD/HIV education to develop the curriculum
2. Assessed relevant needs and assets of target group
3. Used a logic model approach to develop the curriculum that specified the health goals, the behaviors affecting those health goals, the risk and protective factors affecting those behaviors, and the activities addressing those risk and protective factors
4. Designed activities consistent with community values and available resources (e.g., staff time, staff skills, facility space, supplies)
5. Pilot tested the program

The Contents of the Curriculum Itself

Curriculum goals and objectives:

1. Focused on clear health goals—the prevention of STD/HIV and/or pregnancy
2. Focused narrowly on specific behaviors leading to these health goals (e.g., abstaining from sex or using condoms or other contraceptives), gave clear messages about these behaviors, and addressed situations that might lead to them and how to avoid them
3. Addressed multiple sexual psychosocial risk and protective factors affecting sexual behavior (e.g., knowledge, perceived risks, values, attitudes, perceived norms, and self-efficacy)

Activities and teaching methodologies:

1. Created a safe social environment for youth to participate
2. Included multiple activities to change each of the targeted risk and protective factors
3. Employed instructionally sound teaching methods that actively involved the participants, that helped participants personalize the information, and that were designed to change each group of risk and protective factors

Box 22.1 (*Continued*)

4. Employed activities, instructional methods, and behavioral messages that were appropriate to the youths' culture, developmental age, and sexual experience
5. Covered topics in a logical sequence

The Process of Implementing the Curriculum

1. Secured at least minimal support from appropriate authorities such as departments of health or education, school districts, or community organizations
2. Selected educators with desired characteristics (whenever possible), trained them, and provided monitoring, supervision, and support
3. If needed, implemented activities to recruit and retain youth and overcome barriers to their involvement (e.g., publicized the program, offered food, or obtained consent)
4. Implemented virtually all activities with reasonable fidelity

Source: From "Effective Curriculum-Based Sex and STD/HIV Education Programs for Adolescents" by Douglas Kirby and B. A. Laris (2009), published in *Child Development Perspectives*, Volume 3, Number 1, pages 21–29.

for meaningful improvement in student success (National Center on Response to Intervention, 2010). Even when implementing an intervention that has considerable research support, school-level interventions are important for the intervention's success and sustainability. This includes ensuring that the prevention program is consistent with the values and culture of the school (Kirby & Laris, 2009). Efforts to create cultural norms around healthy behavior, including abstaining from sexual activity and condom use, also enhance the effectiveness of school-based interventions.

Tools and Practice Examples

Case Example: Jenson High School

Ms. Davis is a social worker at Jenson High School, an alternative school for students who have experienced behavioral or academic difficulties that made it difficult for them to thrive at a traditional high school. Students often come to Ms. Davis to ask her questions about sexual health, and a number of Jenson students are pregnant or parenting teens. Because Ms. Davis suspects that many of the students engage in a number of risk behaviors, such as unprotected sexual activity and drug use, she administers an anonymous survey to the student body. The results of the survey suggest that 60% of the students at Jenson are sexually active, and 40% use alcohol or drugs on a regular basis. Other results that concern Ms. Davis include a large number of sexually active students who indicated that they do not use condoms when they have sex or that they consume alcohol or drugs prior to having sex.

Ms. Davis takes the results to the principal and asks permission to implement a program designed to reduce sexual risk taking. The principal agrees that she should work to find a program that will reduce sexual risk-taking among Jenson students. Ms. Davis decides on the Street Smart program because it provides information about STDs and HIV, condom use, and the risks of combining alcohol or drug use with sexual activity. With the approval of the principal, she sends parents permission letters that describe the curriculum. She gives students who have parental permission to participate the opportunity to join the group, which will take place after school.

Street Smart

Rotheram-Borus and associates (1991, 1998) developed Street Smart to reduce sexual risk behavior among runaway youth, although the program can be adapted for use with other adolescents. In adapting the curriculum, however, it is important to maintain the critical, core components of the intervention displayed in Box 22.2 (Southwestern, n.d.). Without including all of these core components, the intervention may lose some of its effectiveness. The curriculum consists of eight 2-hour group sessions, one individual session, and a session in which the group visits a community agency. Each session of the Street Smart curriculum includes the key techniques displayed in Box 22.3.

In a study evaluating the effects of Street Smart with runaway youth, teens who received the intervention reduced the number of unprotected sexual acts and reduced their substance use in comparison with teens who did not receive

Box 22.2 Core Elements of the Street Smart Program

Core elements are components that must be included in order for an intervention to be effective. For Street Smart, these elements are:

- Opportunities to practice controlling and expressing emotions and cognitive awareness
- Teaching HIV/AIDS risks and allowing participants opportunities to apply the ideas to their own lives
- Identifying personal triggers for HIV risk behaviors
- Using peer support and skill-building in small groups
- Building skills in problem solving, assertiveness, and skills for reducing HIV/AIDS risk behaviors

Source: From HIV prevention toolbox: Street Smart, by Southwestern, The University of Texas Southwestern Medical Center at Dallas, n.d., Retrieved from http://www.utsouthwestern.edu/education/school-of-health-professions/programs/outreach-programs/CPIU/cpiu-toolbox.html

Box 22.3 Key Components of Every Street Smart Session

1. A stack of tokens, which are 1-inch × 1-inch pieces of colored paper, are given to each participant. When participants hear or see another group member doing something that they like, they give that group member a token.
2. A feeling thermometer is a scale that ranges from 0 to 100, with 100 representing the most discomfort and 0 representing a complete absence of discomfort. Facilitators use the thermometer to help participants recognize, assess, and discuss their feelings.
3. Role-playing in each session gives participants the opportunity to practice new behaviors and act out situations in a supportive environment. Role-plays in Street Smart sessions consist of two actors playing out a scene, a coach assigned to each actor to provide suggestions, one director who determines who plays each part, and other

Box 22.3 (*Continued*)

participants assigned to observe interactions, such as eye contact and body language, during the role-play.

4. The sessions are videotaped so that students can observe themselves interacting in the role-play situations.
5. Participants use the SMART model to apply the following problem-solving steps:
   a. State the problem
   b. Make a goal
   c. Actions—list the possible actions that could be taken
   d. Reach a decision about which action to use
   e. Try doing the action and review it
6. A large flipchart on a stand is used to save written material and goals set by participants so they can be reviewed later.
7. The curriculum provides choices so that facilitators have different options they can use with their participants for each session.

Source: From Street Smart, by M. Rotheram-Borus, R. Van Rossem, M. Gwadz, C. Koopman, & M. Lee, 1997. Retrieved from http://chipts.ucla.edu/wp-content/uploads/downloads/2012/01/Introduction.pdf

the intervention. The following description of sessions is based on information provided in the treatment manual for Street Smart, which can be downloaded from the following Web site: http://chipts.ucla.edu/projects/street-smart-us-2/ (Rotheram-Borus et al., 1997). Information about implementation of the intervention and training can be retrieved from the Centers for Disease Control Web site: http://www.effectiveinterventions.org/en/Interventions/StreetSmart.aspx.

Session 1: Getting the Language of HIV and STDs

The first day of Street Smart is dedicated to learning facts about HIV and STDs as well as learning about situations that present great risks for transmission of HIV and STDs. This session begins with introductions and the "Be Smart about HIV/AIDS and STDs" game in which participants form teams and answer questions about HIV/AIDS and STDs. Following the game, participants engage in role-playing and discuss situations in which they would feel high, moderate, low, and no discomfort, using the feeling thermometer to illustrate. See Box 22.3 for a description of the feeling thermometer. Another activity included in this session involves giving students nametags, some of which display a small star or square indicating that the person is HIV-positive or has an STD. This activity helps students to see how easily and quickly HIV and STDs can be spread to uninfected people. The session concludes with a discussion about participants' strengths and resources that can help them achieve their goals.

Nametag activity with Jenson High School students

Ms. Davis provides nametags to all of the participants. Two of the nametags have a small square in the corner, and two others have a small star. The students put on the nametags, and Ms. Davis asks them to pretend they are at a party, mingling with the other group members. Ms. Davis asks the students to identify at least two situations that would be triggers for risky sexual behavior and discuss them with others. She also tells them to identify someone as a potential romantic partner. After a few minutes of mingling, Ms. Davis asks the students to talk about the triggers for engaging in risky behavior. She then explains that two people in the group have a small star on their nametag and that these two group members represent people who are HIV positive. Two other people, she explains, have small squares on their nametags, representing people who have an STD. After a few minutes, the group members have discovered which group members are wearing the nametags in question. Ms. Davis explains that, if anyone in the group had engaged in risky sexual behavior with those people, they may have contracted and STD or HIV and passed it on to others. Ms. Davis encourages group members to discuss the exercise.

Session 2: Personalized Risk

In this session, participants begin by discussing how old they were when they had their first serious relationship. They role-play a situation in which they define a risk behavior and the triggers associated with the behavior. For example, two students enact a script in which a girl tells her friend that she had sex without using protection, and the friend questions her behavior. The role-play is followed by questions about the girl's triggers for unsafe sex and skills that might have helped her avoid unsafe sex. Students divide into two groups and create a list of possible triggers for having unsafe sex, and participants write down a personal trigger that puts them at risk for unsafe sex. In another role-play, participants practice setting their own limits. The facilitator also encourages group members to express appreciation for the contributions of other members.

Session 3: How to Use Condoms

The session begins with a discussion about the best color for a box of condoms. Each participant receives several condoms to handle in order to reduce discomfort with condoms. In order to encourage the students, the facilitator may say, "Open up the condoms and do whatever you want with them—stretch them, chew on them, whatever." Participants practice putting male condoms on a penis model and female condoms in the female model. The facilitator can ask the participants to use the feeling thermometer to monitor any feelings of discomfort during these activities.

Session 4: Drugs and Alcohol

This session begins with a discussion about any successes students have had in practicing behavior related to previous sessions. Through a role-playing activity, participants explore the relationship between drug and alcohol use and sexual risk behavior. The students also make a list of the advantages and disadvantages of substance use. Another role-play is used to help participants understand how substance use affects their ability to practice safer sex. The facilitator presents information about the effect of substance use on the brain and asks participants to identify triggers that put them at risk for using substances, along with ways to deal with those triggers. A third role-play helps students deal with risky situations.

Discussing beliefs about alcohol and drug use with Jenson High School students

Ms. Davis distributes cards to each of the group members. Each card displays a substance use belief, such as "Using is the only way to increase my creativity and productivity." She then tells the students to imagine that someone has told them that they believe the statement printed on the card and asks them to argue against the belief. In order to model this activity, Ms. Davis asks one of the students to pick a card and hand it to her. She reads the card out loud: "The only way to deal with my anger is by using." In response to the statement, Ms. Davis adds, "Actually, using does not help you deal with the anger at all. It's just a way to keep you from dealing with the thing that's really making you angry." Ms. Davis asks one of the students, Jamie, to practice the activity. Jamie reads her card: "My life won't get better, even if I stop using." Jamie then states her response, "Drug use can cause so many problems—conflicts with your parents, problems with money, failing in school. At least if you weren't using drugs you wouldn't have those problems to deal with." Ms. Davis tells Jamie that she did a wonderful job answering the question and proceeds to ask the next student to read his card and think of a response.

Session 5: Recognizing and Coping with Feelings

Participants begin this session by describing something about themselves that makes them proud. Using the feeling thermometer, participants rate sexually risky situations according to the amount of discomfort they cause. The facilitator may ask students to think of a situation that put them at risk for acquiring an STD and caused a great deal of discomfort, a behavior that they would rate close to 100 on the feeling thermometer. The group thinks about the emotions they feel and any physical stress responses they experience when confronted with the uncomfortable situation, as well as identifying what might have triggered it. A role-playing activity is used to help participants understand how to cope with risky situations, and a second role-play helps them learn effective problem definition as a strategy for learning to focus on manageable problems. The role-playing continues in this session with a situation in which participants have to get tested for HIV.

Session 6: Negotiating Effectively

Participants begin by reviewing any successes they have had relevant to the previous session. This session includes an opportunity for each group member to consider his or her own values regarding sexual behavior. In order to learn how to deal with peer pressure to engage in substance abuse and risky sexual behavior, participants practice using interpersonal problem-solving skills. They also participate in a role-play in which they ask potential sexual partners questions about their risk for having HIV or STDs. The facilitator asks students to generate a list of questions that would be helpful in this situation and ensures that questions such as "Do you usually use a condom?", "Do you take drugs?", and "Have you had many sexual partners?" are included on the list.

Session 7: Self-Talk

The facilitator begins this session by asking participants to tell the group things that they say to themselves to make them feel good. The facilitator explains that we have thoughts that help us practice healthier behaviors and other thoughts that are barriers to practicing those behaviors. Through participating in a game, group members learn to distinguish between harmful and helpful thoughts related to sexual risk behavior. Group members are given the opportunity to practice moving from harmful thoughts to helpful thoughts through a role-play. The facilitator helps by giving several examples of self-talk statements.

Practicing self-talk with Jenson High School students

Ms. Davis explains to the group that self-talk is something we do all the time, but we do not always realize it. She goes on to say that we can make self-talk helpful for reducing our chances of engaging in risky behavior. In explaining how to use self-talk, Ms. Davis breaks it down into parts. First, she says, you make a plan to confront a situation. Then you act on the situation. If you feel that you are getting overwhelmed, use self-talk to help yourself cope. Finally, you evaluate the situation and how you handled it. Ms. Davis distributes a handout that provides examples of self-talk for each part of the process. For the planning step, examples of self-talk include "This is going to be tough, but I can handle it" and "I'll take a few deep breaths beforehand." For acting on the situation, an example of self-talk would be "Don't let him rattle me" and "I have a right to my point of view." When feeling overwhelmed, helpful self-talk includes statements such as "He wants me to get angry" and "There's no shame in leaving and coming back later." Ms. Davis asks the class if there are statements they would like to add to the list of self-talk suggestions.

Session 8: Safer Sex

In this session, the participants learn why people sometimes take sexual risks even though they know the behavior is risky. Using the feeling thermometer, participants can assess their own level of discomfort in discussing safer sex. They learn about the kinds of rationalizations that increase risk for unsafe sex and how to deal with those rationalizations. Included in this part of the curriculum is a goal-setting activity to help group members define what they want for themselves. Students make a list of their goals and rate the goals on a scale from 1 to 10, with 1 meaning that the goal is not very important and 10 meaning that the goal is very important. The facilitator personalizes the curriculum by asking group members why they and their friends might engage in risky behaviors. Students can use their creativity in an activity that involves creating a music video, commercial, or other media to create a message promoting safer sex. Since this is the final interactive group session, the participants discuss the ending of the group.

Session 9: Personal Counseling

In the personal counseling session, the facilitator assesses whether the participants are sexually active and asks them to identify priorities and goals related to safer sex. The session is also used to help the teens identify triggers that might prevent them from practicing safer sex behaviors and develop a plan for coping with these triggers. The students are then given the opportunity to ask any questions about HIV/AIDS, STDs, testing, community resources, and anything else that they would like to know.

Session 10: Looking Over a Community Resource

For this session, the facilitator takes a group of participants to visit a relevant community resource so that the group can learn more about the services available in their community and can form links with the community agency that provides those services. Before the visit, the facilitator helps the participants develop questions for the staff at the community agency. The staff and consumers at the community agency describe the resources provided by the agency and allow participants to ask questions. To allow more time for discussion, the group may also share a meal with the agency staff and consumers. The facilitator encourages the group to make specific plans to return for another visit and to thank the staff and consumers for the visit.

There is a great need for interventions that reduce risk for STDs. Fortunately, many programs have solid research support and include treatment manuals that simplify implementation. The challenge for the future will be to work with schools and other organizations to help them overcome barriers to implementation. Because the curricula include information about condom use as well as abstinence from sexual intercourse, school staff may face opposition when trying to implement these programs, and successful implementation may require advocating for changes in state and local school policies. Because of such barriers, it is important that prevention strategies include community intervention and planning, public information campaigns, and policy-level interventions as well as effective school-based programs (CDC, 2003b).

Key Points to Remember

There is a great need for interventions that reduce risk for STDs. Fortunately, many programs have solid research support and include treatment manuals that simplify implementation. The challenge for the future will be to work with schools and other organizations to help them overcome barriers to implementation. Because the curricula include information about condom use as well as abstinence from sexual intercourse, school staff may face opposition when trying to implement these programs, and successful implementation may require advocating for changes in state and local school policies. Because of such barriers, it is important that prevention strategies include community intervention and planning, public information campaigns, and policy-level interventions as well as effective school-based programs (CDC, 2003b).

Some of the key points discussed in this chapter were:

- The prevalence of STDs and HIV among adolescents and young adults indicates a great need to reduce sexual risk behaviors among American youth.
- A number of evidence-based HIV prevention programs are appropriate for use in schools, and school-based curricula have the potential to reach many teens before they become sexually active as well as those who are who are already sexually active.
- Most of the effective HIV prevention curricula include educational and skill-building components.
- One challenge to evidence-based STD prevention is opposition to curricula that discuss safer sax practices, such as condom use.
- The Street Smart program is a 10-session program that has demonstrated reductions in sexual risk taking among runaway youth and can be adapted for use with other adolescents at risk for STDs and HIV.

Further Learning

Advocates for Youth: www.advocatesforyouth.org

The Centers for Disease Control and Prevention Division of Sexually Transmitted Diseases: http://www.cdc.gov/std/

The Centers for Disease Control and Prevention Division of HIV/AIDS Prevention: http://www.cdc.gov/hiv/dhap.htm

The Centers for Disease Control and Prevention's compendium of HIV prevention interventions with evidence of effectiveness: http://www.cdc.gov/hiv/resources/reports/hiv_compendium/index.htm

The Center for HIV Identification, Prevention, and Treatment Services (CHIPTS): http://chipts.cch.ucla.edu/

Sociometrics HIV/AIDS Prevention Program Archive (HAPPA): http://www.socio.com/happa.php

University of Texas Southwestern Medical Centers's HIV Prevention Toolbox: http://www.utsouthwestern.edu/utsw/cda/dept156726/files/181124.html

References

Boyer, C., Shafer, M., Shaffer, R., Brodine, S., Pollack, L., Betsinger, K., ... Schachter, J. (2005). Evaluation of a cognitive-behavioral, group, randomized controlled intervention trial to prevent sexually transmitted infections and unintended pregnancies in young women. *Preventive Medicine, 40*, 420–431.

Centers for Disease Control and Prevention. (2003a). *HIV/AIDS surveillance report: Cases of HIV infection and AIDS in the United States, 2003*. Atlanta, GA: U.S. Department of Health and Human Services Centers for Disease Control and Prevention (pp. 1–9). Retrieved from http://www.cdc.gov/hiv/stats/hasrlink.htm

Centers for Disease Control and Prevention. (2003b). *HIV strategic plan through 2005*. Atlanta, GA: U.S. Department of Health and Human Services, Centers for Disease Control and Prevention. Retrieved from http://www.cdc.gov/nchstp/od/hiv_plan/Table%20of%20Contents.htm

Centers for Disease Control and Prevention. (2010). *Sexually transmitted disease surveillance 2009*. Atlanta: U.S. Department of Health and Human Services.

Collins, J., Robin, L., Wooley, S., Fenley, D., Hunt, P., Taylor, J., ... Kolbe, L. (2002). Programs-that-work: CDC's guide to effective programs that reduce health-risk behavior of youth. *Journal of School Health, 72*(3), 93–99.

Coyle, K. K., Kirby, D. B., Robin, L. E., Banspach, S. W., Baumler, E., & Glassman, J. R. (2006). All4You! A randomized trial of an HIV, other STDs and pregnancy prevention intervention for alternative school students. *AIDS Education and Prevention, 18*, 187–203.

Eaton, D. K., Kann, L., Kinchen, S., Shanklin, S., Ross, J., Hawkins, J., ... Wechsler, H. (2010). *Youth risk behavior surveillance—United States, 2009 Surveillance Summaries*. Retrieved from http://www.cdc.gov/hiv/topics/surveillance/resources/reports/

Fisher, J., Fisher, W., Bryan, A., & Misovich, S. (2002). In formation-motivation-behavioral skills model-based HIV risk behavior change intervention for inner-city high school youth. *Health Psychology, 21*, 177–186.

Hawken, L. S., Vincent, C. G., & Schumann, J. (2008). Response to intervention for social behavior: Challenges and opportunities. *Journal of Emotional and Behavioral Disorders, 16*, 213–225.

Jemmott, J., III, Jemmott, L., Braverman, P., & Fong, G. T. (2005). HIV/STD risk reduction interventions for African American and Latino adolescent girls at an adolescent medicine clinic. *Archives of Pediatric Adolescent Medicine, 159*, 440–449.

Jemmott, J., Jemmott, L., & Fong, G. (1992). Reductions in HIV risk associated sexual behaviors among black male adolescents: Effects of an AIDS prevention program. *American Journal of Public Health, 82*(3), 372–377.

Jemmott, J. B., Jemmott, L. S., Fong, G. T., & McCaffree, K. (1998). Abstinence and safer sex: HIV risk reduction interventions for African American adolescents. *Journal of the American Medical Association, 279*(19), 1529–1536.

Johnson, B. T., Carey, M. P., Marsh, K. L., Levin, K. D., & Scott-Sheldon, J. (2003). Interventions to reduce sexual risk for the Human Immunodeficiency Virus in adolescents, 1985–2000. *Archives of Pediatric and Adolescent Medicine, 157*, 381–388.

Kipke, M. D., Boyer, C., & Hein, K. (1993). An evaluation of an AIDS risk reduction education and skills training (ARREST) program. *Journal of Adolescent Health, 14*(7), 533–539.

Kirby, D. (2002). The impact of schools and school programs upon adolescent sexual behavior. *Journal of Sex Research, 39*(1), 27–33.

Kirby, D., Barth, R. P., Leland, N., & Fetro, J. V. (1991). Reducing the risk: Impact of a new curriculum on sexual risk-taking. *Family Planning Perspectives, 23*(6), 253–263.

Kirby, D., Baumler, E., Coyle, K., Basen-Enquist, K., Parcel, G., Harrist, R., & Banspach, S. W. (2004). The "Safer Choices" intervention: Its impact on the sexual behaviors of different subgroups of high school students. *Journal of Adolescent Health, 35*, 442–452.

Kirby, D., & Laris, B. A. (2009). Effective curriculum-based sex and STD/HIV education programs for adolescents. *Child Development Perspectives, 3*(1), 21–29.

Lohrmann, D. K., Blake, S., Collins, T., Windsor, R., & Parrillo, A. V. (2001). Evaluation of school-based HIV prevention education programs in New Jersey. *Journal of School Health, 71*(6), 207–211.

Main, D., Iverson, D., McGloin, J., Banspach, S. W., Collins, J. L., Rugg, D. L., & Kolbe, L. J. (1994). Preventing HIV infection among adolescents: Evaluation of a school-based education program. *Preventive Medicine, 23*(4), 409–417.

National Center on Response to Intervention. (2010). *Essential components of RTI—A closer look at Response to Intervention*. Washington, DC: U.S. Department of Education, Office of Special Education Programs, National Center on Response to Intervention.

Remafedi, G. (1994). Cognitive and behavioral adaptations to HIV/AIDS among gay and bisexual adolescents. *Journal of Adolescent Health, 15*, 142–148.

Rotheram-Borus, M., Van Rossem, R., Gwadz, M., Koopman, C., & Lee, M. (1997). Street smart. Retrieved from http://www.effectiveinterventions.org/en/Interventions/StreetSmart.aspx.

Rotheram-Borus, M. J., Gwadz, M., Fernandez, M. I., & Srinivasan, S. (1998). Timing of HIV interventions on reductions in sexual risk among adolescents. *American Journal of Community Psychology, 26*, 73–96.

Rotheram-Borus, M. J., Kooperman, C., Haignere, C., & Davies, M. (1991). Reducing HIV sexual risk behaviors among runaway adolescents. *JAMA: Journal of the American Medical Association, 266*, 1237–1241.

Rotheram-Borus, M. J., Reid, H., & Rosario, M. (1994). Factors mediating changes in sexual HIV risk behaviors among gay and bisexual male adolescents. *American Journal of Public Health, 84*(12), 1938–1946.

Rotheram-Borus, M. J., Song, J., Gwadz, M., Lee, M., Van Rossem, R., & Koopman, C. (2003). Reductions in HIV risk among runaway youth. *Prevention Science, 4*(3), 173–187.

St. Lawrence, J., Brasfield, T., Jefferson, K., Alleyne, E., O'Brannon, R., & Shirley, A. (1995). A cognitive behavioral intervention to reduce African-American adolescents' risk for HIV infection. *Journal of Consulting and Clinical Psychology, 63*(2), 221–237.

St. Lawrence, J., Crosby, R., Brasfield, T., & O'Bannon, R., III . (2002). Reducing STD and HIV risk behavior of substance dependent adolescents: A randomized controlled trial. *Journal of Consulting and Clinical Psychology, 70*, 1010–1021.

Stanton, B., Li, X., Ricardo, I., Galbraith, J., Feigelman, S., & Kaljee, L. A. (1996). A randomized, controlled effectiveness trial of an AIDS prevention program for low-income African-American youths. *Archives of Pediatric and Adolescent Medicine, 151*(4), 398–406.

Stryker, J., Samuels, S. E., & Smith, M. D. (1994). Condom availability in schools: The need for improved program evaluations. *American Journal of Public Health, 84*(12), 1901–1906.

Weinstock, H., Berman, S., & Cates, W. (2004). Sexually transmitted diseases among American youth: Incidence and prevalence estimates, 2000. *Perspectives on Sexual and Reproductive Health, 36*(1), 6–10.

Effective Management of Obesity for School Children

CHAPTER 23

Reshma B. Naidoo

Getting Started

The incidence and prevalence of obesity among children and teens in the United States indicate a leveling off since 2000. Adults, on the other hand, continue to demonstrate an increase in the prevalence of obesity from 2000 to 2009 (Blank, Galuska, Pan, & Deitz, 2009) and have approximately twice the obesity rates (34%) of children (Ogden & Carroll, 2010), with preschoolers being the least likely to be obese (Ogden, Carroll, Curtin, Lamb, & Flegal, 2010). There was a dramatic spike in obesity in children, with rates tripling from 1960s through 1990 (Ogden et al., 2010). The prevalence of pediatric obesity from 1976 to 2008 increased across all age groups from 5% to 10.4% amongst the 2–5 years age group, 6.5% to 19.6% in the 6–11 years age group, and 5% to 18.1% in the 12–19 years age group (Ogden et al., 2010). Current estimates indicate that 17% of school-aged children are obese (Ogden & Carroll, 2010). Ethnic and racial disparities in the prevalence of obesity indicate that Mexican-American adolescent boys and non-Hispanic black girls are more likely to be obese (Ogden et al., 2010). This increase in obesity has been attributed to a lack of physical activity combined with unhealthy eating patterns.

Overweight children are more likely to become overweight adolescents, who in turn are more likely to become overweight adults (Biro & Wien, 2010; Dietz, 1991; Serdula et al., 1993). Overweight and obese individuals are at increased risk for several significant health and psychosocial problems (see Table 23.1) (Epstein, Wisniewski, & Weng, 1994; Freedman et al., 2007; Whitlock, Williams, Gold, Smith, & Shipman, 2005). Given the range of problems experienced by obese individuals, effective management of obesity in a school-aged population has to be addressed across multiple environments that include the home and school.

Body mass index (BMI) is a commonly used indicator of obesity in which weight (in kilograms) is divided by height (in meters) squared. A BMI at or above the 85th percentile and lower than the 95th percentile of same-age and same-gender children is defined as overweight, and a BMI at or above the 95th percentile is defined as obese (Barlow & the Expert Committee, 2007).

What We Know

Almost all children are enrolled in schools, giving us the best opportunity to introduce obesity management and prevention programs that can affect the long-term health and well-being of children. Teaching children effective ways to control their weight provides them with a foundation that they can use to maintain healthy body weights into adulthood. Furthermore, school-based programs have the potential to affect behaviors that track into adulthood (Lytle, Kelder, Perry, & Klepp, 1995).

Most school-based programs have focused on obesity prevention and weight control (Gortmaker et al., 1999; CATCH, 2003; Cheung, Gortmaker, & Dart, 2001; Carter, Wiecha, Peterson, & Gortmaker, 2001). There is a paucity of evidence-based obesity management programs or guidelines for children (Barlow & Dietz, 1998). Consequently, a consensual agreement between experts in the field resulted in the development of a list of guidelines for obesity management programs at schools (Barlow & Dietz, 1998). The major emphases of these guidelines are presented in Table 23.2.

Table 23.1 Health and Psychosocial Problems Associated with Obesity

Psychosocial Problems	*Neurocognitive Problems*	*Health Problems*	
Victims of bullying	Abnormalities in memory and higher-order language function	Coronary heart disease	Cancers
Lower social status	Visual-spatial relations	High blood pressure	Gallbladder disease
Poorer self-esteem	Executive function	Angina pectoris	Stroke
Young adult eating disorders	Poor school performance	Congestive heart failure	
	Engagement in risky behaviors	High blood cholesterol	
Reduced quality of life	Inappropriate dieting habits		Gout
Distorted body image		Type II diabetes	Eye disorders
		Hyperinsulinemia	Osteoarthritis
Depression		Insulin resistance	Sleep apnea or sleep disorders
Psychosocial ailments		Hepatic steatosis	
Loneliness		Glucose intolerance	Asthma
Social rejection		Poor reproductive health problems (stress incontinence)	

Source: Table 23.1 was compiled by synthesizing information from several sources that included Epstein, L. H., Wisniewski, L., & Weng, R. (1994). Child and parent psychological problems influence child weight control. *Obesity Research, 2*, 509–515. National Institutes of Health (1998). *Clinical guidelines on the identification, evaluation, and treatment of overweight and obesity in adults.* Bethesda, MD: Department of Health and Human Services, National Institutes of Health, National Heart, Lung, and Blood Institute. Stunkard, A. J., & Wadden, T. A. (Eds.). (1993). *Obesity: Theory and therapy* (2nd ed.). New York: Raven Press. Shaya, F. T, Flores, D., Gbrarayor, C. M., & Wang, J. (2008). School-based obesity interventions: A literature review. *Journal of School Health, 78,* 189–196.

There has been considerable research into obesity treatment programs since the 1970s; the development of structured school-based obesity management interventions have gained momentum since 2000. Current consensus espouses a multipronged, systemic approach. This intervention is based on the best practices driven by research in the field. Major research findings used to develop this program are summarized in Table 23.3.

Table 23.2 Goals for Treating Childhood Obesity

- Dietary modifications
  - Reduce intake of dietary fat
  - Increase the intake of fruits and vegetables
  - Decrease soda consumption
- Increase physical activity
- Increase nutrition knowledge
- Decrease television, computer, and video game time

Source: Information extracted from Barlow, S. E., & Dietz, W. H. (1998). Obesity evaluation and treatment: Expert committee recommendations. *Pediatrics, 102,* 29. Retrieved November 2004 from http://www.pediatrics.org/cgi/content/full/102/3/e29

There are several good school-based interventions that focus on decreasing the major identified risk factors for obesity and fostering a healthy lifestyle, such as *CATCH* (CATCH, 2011), *Eat Well and Keep Moving* (Cheung, Gortmaker, & Dart, 2001; Eat Well and Keep Moving, 2011), *Planet Health* (Carter, Wiecha, Peterson, & Gortmaker, 2001; Plant Health, 2011), and *Shape Down* (Shape Down, 2011). The goal of these programs is to teach children healthy lifestyle habits. They focus on reducing obesity, increasing physical activity, and fostering positive dietary habits and nutrition knowledge. Programs range from 4 weeks to several school years in duration. However, there is a paucity of school-based individual and/or small group programs that address the treatment and interventions of obesity management. Significant gains in nutrition knowledge, healthy behaviors, and psychosocial and academic performance with a decrease in adiposity were found following the institution of a school-wide, multilevel intervention (Hollar et al., 2010) or instructor-led interventions (Johnston et al., 2009)—for example, multilevel interventions that may fit into a Response to Intervention (RTI) framework and may be implemented within the school's current health classes and programs. Interventions requiring parental monitoring and weigh-ins and other factors may require additional resources to be implemented in a way that can achieve the desired results. Thus, a structured school-based weight loss program would help the child to decrease his/her percentage overweight by increasing health knowledge and fostering a

Table 23.3 Well-Established Treatments and Supporting Studies

Established Treatment Modality	*Supporting Studies*
Children-centered programs have long-term benefits	Epstein, Valoski, Kalarchian, et al., 1995; Epstein, Valoski, Wing, & McCurley, 1994; Epstein, Valoski, Kalarchian, & McCurley, 1995; Knip & Nuutinen, 1993; Lytle, Kelder, Perry, & Klepp, 1995
Increased lifestyle activity is more efficacious and enduring than structured exercise programs	Epstein, Wing, Koeske, Ossip, & Beck, 1982; Epstein, Valoski, Wing, & McCurley, 1994; Daniels et al., 2005
Gradually scheduled programs provide more support for behavior modification programs	Ebbeling et al., 2007; Rees, 1990; Senediak & Spence, 1985
Rewards for increasing desired or decreasing undesired behaviors are more effective reinforcers than punishment or disincentives	Coates, Jeffery, Slinkard, Killen, & Danaher, 1982; Epstein, Valoski, et al., 1995
Multimodal treatment strategies that include the family and school are more effective than unitary programs	Brownell, Kelman, & Stunkard, 1983; Carter, Wiecha, Peterson, & Gortmaker, 2001; CATCH, 2011; Cheung, Gortmaker, & Dart, 2001; Craig et al., 2007; Epstein, Wing, Koeske, Andrasik, & Ossip, 1981; Epstein et al., 1980; Epstein, Valoski, Wing, & McCurley, 1990; Gortmaker et al., 1999; Kitzmann et al., 2011; Lytle, Kelder, Perry & Klepp, 1995; Planet Health, 2011; Shape Down, 2011
Systemic approach to behavior modification	Epstein, Myers, Rayno, Saelens, 1998; Epstein, Paluch, Roemmich, Beecher, 2007; Goetz & Caron, 1999; Raue, Castonguay, & Goldfried, 1993; Golan, Weizman, Apter, & Fainaru, 1998 Wilfley et al., 2007; Johnston et al., 2007
Mentoring and support	Buckley & Zimmermann, 2003; Golan, 2006
24-hour recall records	Baxter & Thompson, 2002; Armstrong et al., 2000

healthy lifestyle. The premise of a school-based program is that (a) childhood adiposity tracks into adulthood (Freedman et al., 2005), (b) that children are able to lose weight, and (c) that children are able to maintain their weight loss into adulthood (Knip & Nuutinen, 1993). Children who have been placed on weight loss programs are better at keeping the weight off compared to adults, even 10 years after the completion of the weight loss program (Epstein, Valoski, Wing, & McCurley, 1994; Epstein, Valoski, Kalarchian, & McCurley, 1995; Wadden, Butryn, & Byrne, 2004). Furthermore, intensive, long-term school-based weight loss programs are more effective than shorter programs (Gonzalez-Suarez, Worley, Grimmer-Somers, & Dones, 2009).

What We Can Do

The Obesity Management Program (OMP) is a school-based weight loss and behavioral modification program for overweight and obese individuals. The OMP is an individual therapy, and the school-based segment can be modified for groups. This multipronged program focuses on developing a healthy lifestyle that facilitates weight loss. Skills are introduced gradually over a 14-week period (see Table 23.4) and are reinforced at home and school until the child/adolescent is able to practice them without assistance. The success of the program depends upon a home–school collaboration and requires active involvement of the family. Homework is assigned at the end of each weekly session to reinforce and practice new skills. Practicing skills and the completion of homework is essential for the success of the program.

Tools and Practice Examples

Practice Examples

Lisa had entered the sixth grade at middle school. After the first 6 weeks, Ms. Halferty, her homeroom teacher, noticed that although Lisa was making adequate academic progress, maintaining an A/B average, she had difficulty adjusting to middle school. Lisa had low self-esteem, was very self-conscious, and often sat by herself. Ms. Halferty was concerned about Lisa's isolation from her peers and attributed Lisa's social difficulties to her obesity. Lisa had always been on the heavy side, but her weight gain had accelerated in the fourth grade. She weighed 160 pounds and was 5 feet 1 inch tall at the time of this referral.

Lisa lived with her parents and her 10-year-old brother in a suburban neighborhood. Both of her parents had full-time jobs. Since Lisa and her brother were not allowed to play outside for safety reasons, they completed their homework and then watched television until their parents' return.

Establishing a Working Alliance

The focus of the initial sessions was to establish a working alliance with Lisa, her family, and the school. The problem of Lisa's obesity is viewed from a family-systemic model (Goetz & Caron, 1999), and a working alliance among the family, therapist, and child is fundamental for the success of this model (Raue, Castonguay, & Goldfried, 1993). The family, particularly parents, as the proponent of change is one of the most effective modalities of treating pediatric obesity (Epstein, Paluch, Roemmich, & Beecher, 2007; Golan, 2006; Golan, Weizman, Apter, & Fainaru, 1998).

Baseline psychosocial, anthropometric, and lifestyle data were collected in this phase. At the initial meeting with Lisa, the counselor discussed the referral, explored Lisa's perception of the problem and enlisted her participation in the obesity management program (OMP). Given the lack of empirically based short-term individualized obesity management programs, the counselor chose to use the multipronged OMP, in view of the fact that Lisa needed behavioral and dietary modifications with family and school support to ensure her adherence to the program.

The American Academy of Pediatricians describes childhood obesity as the most frustrating childhood condition to treat (Barlow & Dietz, 1998). There is no unitary cause for obesity. However, there is consensual data to indicate that the combination of excess caloric intake combined with low levels of physical activity result in obesity (Bray, 1987). The focus of the program is to make conscious small changes in lifestyle behaviors directed at diet and physical activity modifications, given that they produce the greatest long-term efficacy (Hill, 2009). Although large

Table 23.4

Week	*Objective*
Week 1 *Town meeting*	1. Establishing a family–child–school collaboration in weight management a. Rationale for program b. The role of the family–school collaboration c. Overview of the program, duration, and procedure d. Cost of the program. Family commitment and contract • U.S. obesity trends 1985 to 2010 are available at http://www.cdc.gov/nccdphp/dnpa/obesity/trend/maps/index.htm • Information on the obesity epidemic, what causes obesity and the focus of treatment can be found at: http://www.cdc.gov/obesity/childhood/problem.html • Multimedia and tools on obesity can be obtained at • http://www.cdc.gov/obesity/resources/multimedia.html • Parent handout: Obesity in children and teens: A parent information sheet is available at http://www.aacap.org/publications/factsfam/79.htm
Week 2 *Getting started*	1. Outlining the program with the child 2. Establishing baselines 3. Completing forms 4. Homework—completion of daily record sheets for the week • BMI calculators are available at http://www.cdc.gov/healthyweight/assessing/bmi/
Week 3 *On your marks …*	1. Introduction of the weekly weigh-in 2. Understanding baselines and plotting charts a. BMI b. Screen time (TV, computer, and video games) patterns c. Physical activity patterns d. Foods chart—what I am eating 3. Television and advertising—how it affects our eating patterns 4. Introduce the "Choose My Plate" program 5. Homework—completion of daily record sheets for the week. • Copies of the "Choose My Plate" program can be obtained at http://www.choosemyplate.gov/specificaudiences.html • A Web site with dietary information, facts of the day, and interesting recipes can be obtained at http://www.www.fruitsandveggiesmatter.gov
Week 4 *Get set …*	1. Weekly weigh-in 2. Checking in: diet, television/screen time, and physical activity logs. Plot your progress 3. What do I do when I watch TV or play computer/video games? 4. Reading food labels 5. Homework • A Web site with information to help children learn how to read food labels is available at http://kidshealth.org/kid/stay_healthy/food/labels.html
Week 5 *Go!*	1. Weekly weigh-in 2. Checking in: diet, television/screen time behaviors, and physical activity logs. Plot your progress 3. The "Choose My Plate " program and what that means 4. How to increase my physical activity 5. Homework • A Web site with information to help children learn about the Choose My Plate program and healthy food choices is http://www.letsmove.gov/eat-healthy • A good resource for increasing physical activity is http://www.letsmove.gov/kids

(*continued*)

Table 23.4 *(Continued)*

Week	*Objective*
Week 6 *Pacing*	1. Weekly weigh-in 2. Checking in: diet, television/screen time, and physical activity logs. Plot your progress 3. Good foods versus bad foods—a review 4. Stoplight diet 5. Homework • Peer support, food logs, and weigh-ins help to keep the child on track • *The Stoplight Diet for Children: An Eight-Week Program for Parents and Children* (1988) by Leonard Epstein and Sally Squires, published by Little Brown & Company, is a comprehensive guide. **The Stoplight Diet: A brief primer** This is a parent–child team effort developed by Dr. Leonard Epstein. * Foods are linked to the three signals on a traffic light: • High-calorie foods that contain fats, oils, and simple sugars, like soda and cookies, are "red" and should rarely be eaten. • Moderate-calorie foods, like cereal, dairy products, and meat are "yellow" and should be eaten with caution. • "Green" foods, which include most vegetables, fruits, breads, and grains, get the go-ahead. * This diet is aimed at changing what different foods mean and changing the meaning of snacks from red to healthy "green foods." • Useful parent resources for dietary changes include http://www.livestrong.com/article/339769-weight-loss-programs-with-parental-involvement-for-children http://diabetes.about.com/cs/kidsanddiabetes http://www.healthysiouxfalls.org/eatingHealthy/321diet.cfm http://www.livestrong.com/article/367159-stoplight-diet-for-kids/
Week 8 *Looking good!*	1. Weekly weigh-in 2. Checking in: diet, television/screen time, and physical activity logs. Plot your progress 3. Reviewing the stoplight diet 4. Progress: Calculating my BMI 5. How time am I spending on television/screen time? 6. Planning a "screen-free week" 7. Homework • Good resource for parents: Obesity and television facts and research can be obtained at http://caloriecount.about.com/article/television_and_obesity • Reducing TV time: Guidelines for running the "screen-free week" program as well as important dates and activities: http://www.commercialfreechildhood.org/screenfreeweek/index.html
Week 9 *Keep on moving!*	1. Weekly weigh-in 2. Checking in: diet, television/screen time, and physical activity logs. Plot your progress 3. Brainstorm ways to increase your activity when you are sitting 4. Review how the "screen-free week" will be run 5. Homework—"Screen Free Week" • A Web site for alternative activities to do with the "extra" time: http://www.commercialfreechildhood.org/screenfreeweek/index.html

(continued)

Table 23.4 (*Continued*)

Week	*Objective*
Week 10 *Paying off!*	1. Weekly weigh-in 2. Checking in: diet, television/screen time, and physical activity logs. Plot your progress 3. Re-evaluation of program a. How much of progress have I made? b. What is the worst part? c. What is the best part? d. How can it be improved? e. Resetting goals
Week 11 *Yeah!*	1. Weekly weigh-in 2. Checking in: diet, television/screen time, and physical activity logs. Plot your progress 3. How do I continue when I am no longer doing this program? 4. Homework
Week 12 *Nearly there*	1. Weekly weigh-in 2. Checking in: diet, television/screen time, and physical activity logs. Plot your progress 3. Planning termination: supervise but do not assist in the weigh-in and checking in stages 4. Homework
Week 13 *On my way!*	1. Weekly weigh-in 2. Checking in: diet, television/screen time, and physical activity logs. Plot your progress 3. Working on termination: student-run session to discuss the importance of continued adherence to the program 4. Homework
Week 14 *I'm off!*	1. Weekly weigh-in 2. Checking in for the last time 3. Termination 4. Award

weight losses have been associated with dramatic diet and lifestyle modifications, these programs have poor longevity, and participants typically regain lost weight after the cessation of the program (Tsai & Wadden, 2005; Foreyt & Goodrick, 1995). Thus, interventions for children should be aimed at dietary and behavior modifications with increased physical activity (see Table 23.2). Higher rates of success in weight management programs were associated with supportive, interactive families demonstrating parental skills aimed at the child's development of responsibility and self-image (Craig et al., 2007; Epstein, 1996; Epstein, Koeske, Wing, & Valoski, 1986; Epstein, Myers, Raynor, & Saelens, 1998; Kitzmann et al., 2011).

The Home–School Collaboration

A home–school collaboration was pivotal for the success of this intervention. A "town meeting" with Lisa's parents (see Week 1 in Table 23.4), Lisa, and the counselor was the next step. Lisa chose Ms. Halferty, her homeroom teacher, as her in school support person. Ms. Halferty was also included in the planning and execution of this program. At this meeting, the psychosocial and health consequences of Lisa's body weight were explored. Educational materials on obesity management were presented to her parents. The importance of the home–school collaboration for the success of the program was expounded.

The Longs agreed to participate in the OMP and signed a contract indicating their willingness to actively assist Lisa with this program. Lisa's mother agreed to be Lisa's "sponsor." The role of the sponsor was to provide supervision, helping Lisa to complete homework assignments, stay on task, and to provide supportive nurturance at home. The structure of the 14-week OMP was outlined, and the responsibilities of the parent sponsor were explained.

Baseline psychosocial and anthropometric data were collected at the second meeting. Psychosocial baseline data was collected on Lisa to assess her psychosocial health. There is substantive evidence to indicate that the psychosocial cost of obesity increases with the severity (Erermis et al., 2004; Wadden, Foster, Brownell, & Finley, 1984). Anxiety-depression, aggressiveness, social problems, social withdrawal, and internalizing and externalizing behavior are some of the problems that have been reported by caregivers of obese individuals (Erermis et al., 2004).

The focus of this phase of the intervention was to assess Lisa's caloric intake and expenditure and to determine her eating and activity patterns. Collecting baseline data (Figure 23.1) allows both the practitioner and the family to review the family's diet and activity patterns to identify the areas of over- and underconsumption, ascertaining problem behaviors (Barlow and Dietz, 1998).

Use of information technology such as television (Dietz & Gortmaker, 1985; Gortmaker et al., 1996) and computer/video games are purported to be a major cause of sedentary living among children (DuRant, Baranowski, Johnson, & Thompson, 1994; Marshall, Biddle, Gorely, Cameron, & Murdey, 2004). Weight gains have been associated with the lower energy expenditure on more sedentary use of information and communication technology (Kautiainen, Koivusilta, Lintonen, Virtanen, & Rimpela, 2005). These trends do not appear to exist in relation to more active use of information technology (exergames such as the WII Sports, Xbox, and Kinect) that have a higher energy expenditure (Daley, 2009; Graves, Stratton, Ridgers & Cable, 2007; Kautiainen et al., 2005). Recent data indicate that in addition to the sedentary lifestyle, watching television increases overall calorie consumption (Kelder, Perry, Klepp, & Lytle, 1994; Kotz & Story, 1994; Kraak & Pelletier, 1998; Jeffery & French, 1998; Coon & Tucker, 2002; Rey-Lopez, Vicente-Rodriquez, Biosca, & Moreno, 2008) through both the systematic advertising and consumption of calorie-dense snacks during these activities.

Lisa's task for the week was to complete daily (1) physical activity, (2) food, and (3) television and computer/video game logs for the next week (see Figure 23.2). The accuracy of recall records is affected by the frequency at which the record is completed. Accuracy is higher if the recording occurs close to the event (Baxter & Thompson, 2002). There is a rapid decay in memory, with poor reliability in recall after 24 hours (Armstrong et al., 2000). To facilitate Lisa's recall, both her parent sponsor and teacher provided her with reminders to complete her record. A note was sent home to Mr. and Mrs. Long (see Figure 23.3) outlining the program for the week. As the sponsor, Mrs. Long's role was to ensure that Lisa filled in her daily logs (Figure 23.4). In addition to being reminded at home, her classroom teacher was asked to remind Lisa to complete the log at the beginning and the end of the day.

Treatment and Intervention Strategy

After baseline data had been collated, the counselor and Lisa set up both short-term and intermediate goals (see Table 23.5). The treatment and intervention phase of the OMP focused on:

1. Providing nutrition and physical activity education (weeks 3 to 10)
2. Developing mastery over diet and activity patterns
3. Establishing a working collaborative relationship between the home and school

The treatment and intervention phase was comprised of education and behavior modification components. Nutrition education was directed at making Lisa and her family more astute in their dietary choices. Reading and understanding food labels, serving sizes, and nutrient content of foods were part of the nutrition education program. The aim was to increase the consumption of high-fiber foods and fruits and vegetables and decrease simple sugar and fat consumption. This behavioral modification program was aimed at making good food choices rather than caloric restriction. This type of intervention focuses on small behavior modifications that include eating at the same place, limiting food eaten to one or two helpings, and

Lisa Long's Goal Chart Date: July 10, 2011

Date of Birth: 7–21–2000 Age: 11 years and 11 months

Height: 5 feet 1 inch (61 inches) Weight: 160 pounds

BMI (kg/m 2)

= weight in pounds*0.455/height in inches*0.025*height in inches*0.025

= (160 lbs)*0.455/(61 inches*0.025)*(61 inches*0.025)

= 31.30 kg/m^2

Goals:

1. Diet:

    Improve my eating habits so that I lose weight

    Stop snacking on cookies and candy

    Stop eating doughnuts, Stop drinking soda and juices

2. Physical Activity:

    Start walking to school

    Walk around more when I am doing nothing.

3. Television:

    Watch only one hour of TV each day

My ideal BMI is 24.

Figure 23.1. Example of Lisa Long's Baseline Data and Goal Chart

learning to substitute low-fat and no-fat products for full-fat products. Similarly, changes in physical activity are aimed at increasing lifestyle physical activity rather than implementing a structured physical activity program. Given the low maintenance costs, lifestyle physical activity changes (e.g., walking, playing games, household chores) are more likely to have enduring results (Kohl & Hobbs, 1998) compared to structured physical activity programs. Parental encouragement and support was espoused, and rewarding goal attainment was advocated. Recommended rewards included earning things that Lisa really wanted (e.g., providing her with the opportunity to gradually earn a new pair of shoes), choosing the family activity on family game night,

Name: Data: Day:

Information Technology	*Time*		
	started	*ended*	

	Time
Breakfast:	
Lunch:	
Dinner (e.g.,2 slices of pizza and Coke):	
Snacks (e.g.,a bag of potato chips):	

Physical Activity	*Time of day*	*How long*

Figure 23.2. Individual Food, Television, and Activity Logs

or planning a family outing. Using food as an incentive was strongly discouraged. During this phase, both Lisa and her family learned alternative ways to eat without sacrificing palatability of foods. The decreased emphasis on television viewing had also given the family an opportunity to have more meaningful interactions with each other.

Termination

The final phase (weeks 12 to 14) of the intervention was to provide both Lisa and her family with the tools to continue with the OMP after the termination of the program. By this stage Lisa and her family had begun to employ behavioral modifications that resulted in better nutrition and

Dear parent/guardian/sponsor, we are finally on our way.

This week Lisa will be collecting baseline data on

* The types of food that she eats,
* her physical activity patterns, and
* the television programs she watches and computer and video games that she plays each day.

Lisa has been advised to complete the logs over the course of the day. Please remind her to complete the log at least once a day.

After we have collected this information, we will be better equipped to help Lisa attain her goal.

Thank you so much for helping Lisa with this program.

Sincerely,

Counselor

Figure 23.3. Example of Note to Parents

physical activity choices. The increased involvement of the family in this program resulted in a renewed closeness, and the Long family was spending more time on family activities and outings. The termination process was directed toward empowering Lisa and her family to continue with positive physical activity and nutrition behaviors after the removal of active school support. By the end of the 14 weeks, Lisa had become more physically active and felt empowered to control her weight. This new confidence was also seen in her relationships with her peers. Lisa had not attained her goal BMI by the end of the program and decided that checking in with the counselor once a month for the rest of the academic year would provide adequate guidance for her to remain on the program.

Tools

Useful Web Sites and Additional Resources

Carter, J., Wiecha, J., Peterson, K., & Gortmaker, S. (2001). *Planet health: An interdisciplinary curriculum for teaching middle school nutrition and physical activity.* Champaign, IL: Human Kinetics.

CATCH. (2003). *Coordinated approach to child health.* Retrieved July 13, 2004.

Cheung, L., Gortmaker, S., & Dart, H. (2001). *Eat well & keep moving: An interdisciplinary curriculum for teaching upper elementary school nutrition and physical activity.* Champaign, IL: Human Kinetics.

Epstein, L. H., & Squires, S. (1988). *The stoplight diet for children: An eight-week program for parents and children.* Boston: Little Brown and Company.

Facts on the risks of child and teen obesity (2011). Explore Weight Management for Children at http://www.livestrong.com/child-and-teen-obesity-risks

Information on Screen Free Week (2011) can be obtained at Screenfree.org, or http://commercial-freechildhood.org/screenfreeweek/

National Center for Disease Control and Prevention (May 18, 2011). *Division of Nutrition, Physical Activity, and Obesity.* Retrieved July 21, 2011, from http://www.cdc.gov/nccdphp/dnpao/

National Centers for Disease Control and Prevention. (July 21, 2011). *US obesity trends 1985 to 2010.* Retrieved July 21, 2011, from http://www.cdc.gov/obesity/data/trends.html

National Agricultural Library. (2010, December 3). *Weight and obesity. Treatment and prevention guidelines.* Retrieved July 11, 2011 from http://fnic.nal.usda.gov/nal_display/index.php?info_center=4&tax_level=2&tax_subject=271&topic_id=1309

Rimm, S. (2004). *Rescuing the emotional lives of overweight children: What our kids go though—and how we can help.* Emmaus, PA: Rodale.

Baseline—Week 1:TV Viewing Log
Name: Lisa   Date: 15 July   Day: Thursday

Program	Time		
	Started	Ended	
WildKratts	4:30 pm	5 pm	**(30 minutes)*
WordGirl	5 pm	5:28 pm	**(28 minutes)*
Simpsons	6 pm	6:30 pm	**(30 minutes)*
Wii Sport Resort	7 pm	7:30 pm	**(30 minutes)*
Internet, Facebook	7:30 pm	9 pm	**(90 minutes)*

**Total amount of time spent watching television per day:208 minutes (3 hours and 28 minutes)*

Food Log
Name: Lisa   Date: 15 July   Day: Thursday

	Tim e	Snacks	Time
Breakfast: 1 cup of dry Frosted Flakes with a cup of 2% milk, banana, small glass of orange juice, Pop Tart, a glass of milk	8 am	Cheetos, soda	10:00 am
Lunch: 2 slices of pepperoni pizza, soda, 1 brownie	12:30 pm	Ice cream sandwich, potato chips	3 pm
Dinner: Quarter-pound burger, large fries, large soda	7 pm	Chocolate cake and chocolate milk	9 pm

Physical Activity Log
Name: Lisa   Date: 15 July   Day: Thursday

Activity	Time of day	How long
Played basketball in PE	12 pm	40 minutes
Walked home from the bus stop	4:15 pm	10 minutes

**Total time spent on moderate to vigorous physical activity per day:50 minutes*
**All italicized information was completed by the counselor*
**Time spent on light physical activity per day: 30 minutes*

Figure 23.4. Example of Television, Food, and Activity Logs

Table 23.5 Short-Term and Intermediate Goals

	Goal	*Objectives*
Television	Decrease fat- and sugar-dense snacks	Increase the consumption of good foods (green and yellow from the stoplight diet) and using the Choose My Plate Program as a guide.
		Stop eating while watching TV
		Measuring portions of food before eating them.
	Increase activity level during television viewing	Decrease the amount of time spent just sitting during a television program.
		Increase physical activity during commercial breaks.
		Increase the intensity of the physical activity so that metabolism is elevated.
	Limit the total time spent watching TV and playing computer and video games to 2 hours a day with the optimal goal being 1 hour a day	Plan television and computer time at the beginning of the week.
		Plan and have a list of alternate activities to fill in the "free" time.
		Plan and carry out a "turn your television off week."
Physical activity	Increase lifestyle physical activity and just keep on moving	Increase daily walking.
		Schedule a "walk to school" or "walk back from school day."
		Start walking with training buddy (mom).
		Find a physical activity or sport that I enjoy and increase participation in this activity.
		Join a club at school.
Diet	Increase good foods	Adopt and follow the 5-a-day plan.
		Decrease simple-carbohydrate consumption.
		Follow the Choose My Plate diet.
	Decrease soda consumption	Increase water intake; reduce or eliminate soda consumption.

Weight Control Groups for Children

Childobesity.com

Shapedown.com/page2.htm slimkids.com thepathway.org

http://www.livestrong.com/weight-management-for-children/

Nutrition

http://www.choosemyplate.gov/
http://www.fruitsandveggiesmatter.gov/
http://www.letsmove.gov/eat-healthy
http://www.livestrong.com/weight-management/

Exercise

http://www.letsmove.gov/get-active
http://www.livestrong.com/article/382338-weight-loss-games-for-groups/
http://www.nutriweb.org.my/nutriteen/main/default.shtml
http://www.shapedown.com/SD_Family.html
http://www.shapeup.org/children/tips_index.html

Key Points to Remember

Some of the key points from this chapter are:

- Changing the dietary patterns of an obese child or adolescent requires a family-based initiative.
- A healthy diet can be fostered by
  - Reducing the intake of dietary fat
  - Reducing soda consumption
  - Increasing dietary fiber
  - Increasing fruit and vegetable consumption to 5 a day
- Changes in lifestyle physical activity are more enduring than a structured physical activity program.
- Limiting television and computer viewing time increases the amount of time that is available for more meaningful engagement in lifestyle physical activities.
- Children are better able to lose weight and maintain their weight loss compared to adults.
- The key to a successful program is making enduring lifestyle changes.
- A paced program that spans a longer period of time is more effective in establishing enduring lifestyle changes.
- A collaborative family and school approach is more effective than either a family or school program.

References

Armstrong, A. M., MacDonald, A., Booth, I.W., Platts, R.G., Knibb, R.C., & Booth, D. A. (2000). Errors in memory for dietary intake and their reduction. *Applied Cognitive Psychology, 14*(2), 183–192.

Barlow, S. E., & Dietz, W. H. (1998). Obesity evaluation and treatment: Expert committee recommendations. *Pediatrics, 102*(3), e29. Retrieved November 2004 from: http://www.pediatrics.org/cgi/content/full/102/3/e29

Barlow, S. E., & the Expert Committee. (2007). Expert committee recommendations regarding the prevention, assessment, and treatment of child and adolescent overweight and obesity: Summary report. *Pediatrics, 120* (Suppl.), S164–S192.

Baxter, S. D., & Thompson, W. O. (2002). Accuracy by meal component of fourth-graders' school lunch recalls is less when obtained during a 24-hour recall than as a single meal. *Nutrition Research, 22*(6), 679–684.

Bellizzi, M. C., & Dietz, W. H. (1999). Workshop on childhood obesity: Summary of the discussion. *American Journal of Clinical Nutrition, 70*(1), 173S-5.

Biro, F. M., & Wien, M. (2010). Childhood obesity and adult morbidities. *American Journal of Clinical Nutrition, 91*(5), 1499S–1505S.

Bray, G. A. (1987). Obesity—a disease of nutrient or energy imbalance? *Nutrition Reviews, 45*, 33–43.

Brownell, K. D., Kelman, J. H., & Stunkard, A. J. (1983). Treatment of obese children with and without their mothers: Changes in weight and blood pressure. *Pediatrics, 71*(4), 515–523.

Buckley, M. A., & Zimmermann, S. H. (2003). *Mentoring children and adolescents: A guide to the issues.* Westport, CT: Praeger Publishers.

Carter, J., Wiecha, J., Peterson, K., & Gortmaker, S. (2001). *Planet health: An interdisciplinary curriculum for teaching middle school nutrition and physical activity.* Champaign, IL: Human Kinetics.

Cheung, L., Gortmaker, S., & Dart, H. (2001). *Eat well & keep moving: An interdisciplinary curriculum for teaching upper elementary school nutrition and physical activity.* Champaign, IL: Human Kinetics.

Coates, T. J., Jeffery, R. W., Slinkard, L. A., Killen, J. D., & Danaher, B. G. (1982). Frequency of contact and monetary reward in weight loss, lipid change and blood pressure reduction with adolescents. *Behavior Therapy, 13*, 175–185.

Coon, K. A., & Tucker, K. L. (2002). Television and children's consumption patterns: A review of the literature. *Minerva Pediatrics, 54*, 423–436.

Daley, A. J. (2009). Can exergaming contribute to improving physical activity levels and health outcomes in children? *Pediatrics, 124*(2), 763.

Daniels, S. R., Arnett, D. K., Eckel, R. H., Gidding, S. S., Hayman, L.L., Kumanyika, S., et al. (2005). Overweight in children and adolescents: Pathophysiology, consequences, prevention, and treatment. *Circulation, 111*, 1999–2012.

Dietz, W. (1991). Physical activity and childhood obesity. *Nutrition*, 7(4), 295–296.

Dietz, W. H., Jr., & Gortmaker, S. L. (1985). Do we fatten our children at the television set? Obesity and television viewing in children and adolescents. *Pediatrics, 75*(5), 807–812.

DuRant, R. H., Baranowski, T., Johnson, M., & Thompson, W.O. (1994). The relationship among television watching, physical activity and body composition of young children. *Pediatrics, 94*, 449–455.

Eat Well and Keep Moving. (2011). *An interdisciplinary curriculum for teaching upper elementary school nutrition and physical activity*. Retrieved July 21, 2011, from http://www.eatwellandkeepmoving.org/

Epstein, L. H., Wing, R. R., Steranchak, L., Dickson, B., & Michelson, J. (1980). Comparison of family based behavior modification and nutrition education for childhood obesity. *Journal of Pediatric Psychology, 5*, 25–36.

Epstein, L. H., Wing, R. R., Koeske, R., Andrasik, F., & Ossip, D. J. (1981). Child and parent weight loss in family-based behavior modification programs. *Journal of Consultation and Clinical Psychology, 49*, 674–685.

Epstein, L. H., Wing, R. R., Koeske, R., Ossip, D. J., & Beck, S. (1982). A comparison of lifestyle change and programmed aerobic exercise on weight and fitness changes in obese children. *Behavior Therapy, 13*, 651–665.

Epstein, L. H., Koeske, R., Wing, R. R., & Valoski, A. (1986). The effects of family variables on child weight change. *Health Psychology, 5*, 1–11.

Epstein, L. H., & Squires, S. (1988). *The stoplight diet for children: An eight-week program for parents and children*. Boston: Little Brown and Company.

Epstein, L. H., Valoski, A., Wing, R. R., & McCurley, J. (1990). Ten-year follow-up of behavioral family based treatment for obese children. *JAMA, 264*, 2519–2523.

Epstein, L. H., Valoski, A., Wing, R. R., & McCurley, J. (1994). Ten-year outcomes of behavioral familybased treatment for childhood obesity. *Health Psychology, 13*(5), 373–383.

Epstein, L. H., Wisniewski, L., & Weng, R. (1994). Child and parent psychological problems influence child weight control. *Obesity Research, 2*, 509–515.

Epstein, L. H., Valoski, A. M., Kalarchian, M. A., & McCurley, J. (1995). Do children lose and maintain weight easier than adults: A comparison of child and parent weight changes from six months to ten years. *Obesity Research, 3*, 411–417.

Epstein, L. H., Valoski, A. M., Vara, L. S., McCurley, J., Wisniewski, L., Kalarchian, M. A., Klein, K. R., & Shrager, L. R. (1995). Effects of decreasing sedentary behavior and increasing activity on weight change in obese children. *Health Psychology, 14*(2), 109–115.

Epstein, L. H. (1996). Family based behavioral intervention for obese children. *International Journal of Obesity, 20*, S14–S21.

Epstein, L. H., Myers. M. D., Raynor, H. A., & Saelens, B. E. (1998). Treatment of pediatric obesity. *Pediatrics, 101*, 554–570.

Epstein. L. H., Paluch, R. A., Roemmich, J. N., & Beecher, M. D. (2007). Family-based obesity treatment, then and now: Twenty-five years of pediatric obesity treatment. *Health Psychology, 26*, 381–391.

Erermis, S., Cetin, N., Tamar, M., Bukusoglu, N., Akdeniz, F., & Goksen, D. (2004). Is obesity a risk factor for psychopathology among adolescents? *Pediatrics International, 46*(3), 296–302.

Flegal, K. M., Carroll, M. D., Ogden, C. L., & Johnson, C. L. (2002). Prevalence and trends in obesity among U.S. adults. *JAMA, 288*, 1723–1727.

Flegal, K. M., Carroll, M. D., Ogden, C. L., et al. (2010). Prevalence and trends in obesity among US adults, 1999–2008. *JAMA, 303*, 235–241.

Foreyt, J., Goodrick, K. (1995). The ultimate triumph of obesity. *Lancet, 346*, 134–135.

Freedman, D. S., Khan, L. K., Serdula, M. K., Dietz, W. H., Srinivasan, S. R., & Berenson, G. S. (2005). The relation of childhood BMI to adult adiposity: The Bogalusa Heart Study. *Pediatrics, 115*(1), 22–27.

Freedman, D. S., Mei, Z., Srinivasan, S. R., Berenson, G. S., & Dietz, W.H. (2007). Cardiovascular risk factors and excess adiposity among overweight children and adolescents: the Bogalusa Heart Study. *Journal of Pediatrics, 150*(1), 12–17.

Goetz, D. R., & Caron, W. (1999). A biopsychosocial model for youth obesity: Consideration of an ecosystemic collaboration. *International Journal of Obesity, 23*(S2), S58–S64.

Golan, M., Weizman, A., Apter, A., & Fainaru, M. (1998). Parents as exclusive agents of change in the treatment of childhood obesity. *American Journal of Clinical Nutrition, 67*, 1130–1135.

Golan. M. (2006). Parents as agents of change in childhood obesity–from research to practice. *International Journal of Pediatric Obesity, 1*, 66–76.

Gonzalez-Suarez, C., Worley, A., Grimmer-Somers, K., & Dones, V. (2009). School-based interventions on childhood obesity: A meta-analysis. *American Journal of Preventive Medicine, 37*(5), 418–427.

Gortmaker, S., Must, A., Sobol, A., Peterson, K., Colditz, G., & Dietz, W. (1996). Television viewing as a cause of increasing obesity among children in the United States 1986–1990. *Journal of the American Medical Association, 150*(4), 356–362.

Gortmaker, S. L., Cheung, L. W. Y., Peterson, K. E., Chomitz, G., Cradle, J. H., Dart, H., et al. (1999). Impact of a school-based interdisciplinary intervention on diet and activity among urban primary school children: Eat well and keep moving. *Archives of Pediatrics and Adolescent Medicine, 123*(9), 975–983.

Graves, L., Stratton, G., Ridgers, N. D., & Cable, N. T. (2008). Energy expenditure in adolescents playing new generation computer games. *British Journal of Sports Medicine, 42*, 592–594

Hill, J. O. (2009). *Can a small-changes approach help address the obesity epidemic?* A report of the Joint Task Force of the American Society for Nutrition, Institute of Food Technologists, and International Food Information Council. *American Journal of Clinical Nutrition, 89,* 477–484.

Hollar, D., Lombardo, M., Lopez-Mitnik, G., Hollar, L., Almon, M. Agatston, A. S., et al., (2010). Elective multi-level, multi-sector, school-based obesity prevention programming improves weight, blood pressure, and academic performance, especially among low-income, minority children. *Journal of Health Care for the Poor and Underserved, 21*, 93–108.

Jeffery, R. W., & French, S. A. (1998). Epidemic obesity in the US: Are fast foods and television viewing contributing? *American Journal of Public Health, 88*, 277–280.

Johnston, C. A., Tyler, C., McFarlin, B. K., Poston, W. S. C., Haddock, C. K., Reeves, R. S., et al. (2007). Weight loss in overweight Mexican American children: A randomized, controlled trial. *Pediatrics, 120*, e1450–e1457.

Johnston, C. A., Tyler, C., McFarlin, B. K., Poston, W. S. C., Haddock, C. K., Reeves, R. S., et al. (2010). Effects of a school-based weight maintenance program for Mexican-American children: Results at 2 years. *Obesity, 18*(3), 542–547

Katz, D. L. (2009). School-based interventions for health promotion and weight control: Not just waiting on the world to change. *Annual Review of Public Health, 30*, 253–272.

Kautiainen, S., Koivusilta, L., Lintonen, T., Virtanen, S. M., & Rimpela, A. (2005). Use of information and communication technology and prevalence of overweight and obesity among adolescents. *International Journal of Obesity, 29*, 925–933.

Kelder, R. W., Perry, C. L., Klepp, K. I., & Lytle L. L. (1994). Longitudinal tracking of adolescent smoking, physical activity, and food choice behaviors. *American Journal of Public Health, 84*, 1121–1126.

Kitzmann, K. M., Dalton, W.T., Stanley, C. M., Beech, B. M., Reeves, T. P., Buscemi, J. et al. (2010). Lifestyle interventions for youth who are overweight: A meta-analytic review. *Health Psychology, 29*(1), 91–101.

Knip, M., & Nuutinen, O. (1993). Long-term effects of weight reduction on serum lipids and plasma insulin in obese children. *American Journal of Clinical Nutrition, 54*, 490–493.

Kohl, H. W., & Hobbs, K. E. (1998). Development of physical activity behaviors among children and adolescents. *Pediatrics, 101*, 549–554.

Kotz, K., & Story, M. (1994). Food advertisements during children's Saturday morning television programming: Are they consistent with dietary recommendations? *Journal of American Dietetic Association, 94*, 1296–1300.

Kraak, V., & Pelletier, D. L. (1998). The influence of commercialism on the food purchasing behavior of children and teenage youth. *Family Economy Nutrition Review, 11*, 15–24.

Lytle, L. A., Kelder, S. H., Perry, C. L., & Klepp, K. I. (1995). Covariance of adolescent health behaviors—The class of 1989 study. *Health Education Research Theory and Practice, 10*, 133–146.

Marshall, S. J., Biddle, S. J. H., Gorely, T., Cameron, N. ,& Murdey, I. (2004). Relationship between media use and body fatness and physical activity in children and youth: A meta-analysis. *International Journal of Obesity, 28*(10), 1238–1246.

National Agricultural Library. (2010, December 3). *Weight and obesity. Treatment and prevention guidelines.* Retrieved July 11, 2011, from http://fnic.nal.usda.gov/nal_display/index.php?info_center=4&tax_level=2&tax_subject=271&topic_id=1309

National Centers for Disease Control and Prevention (2011, July 21). *US obesity trends 1985 to 2010.* Retrieved July 21, 2011, from http://www.cdc.gov/obesity/data/trends.html

Ogden, C., & Carroll, M. (2010). *Prevalence of obesity among children and adolescents: United States, trends 1963–1965 through 2007–2008.* NHANES, Health E-Stat. Retrieved July 21, 2011, from http://www.cdc.gov/nchs/data/hestat/obesity_child_07_08/obesity_child_07_08.htm

Ogden, C. L., Carroll, M. D., Curtin, L. R., Lamb, M. M., & Flegal, K. M. (2010). Prevalence of high body mass index in US children and adolescents, 2007–2008. *JAMA, 303*, 242–249.

Ogden, C. L., Flegal, K. M., Carroll, M. D., & Johnson, C. L. (2002). Prevalence and trends in overweight among US children and adolescents, 1999–2000. *JAMA, 288*, 1728–1732.

Planet Health. (2011). *An interdisciplinary curriculum for teaching middle school nutrition and physical activity.* Retrieved July 21, 2011, from http://www.planet-health.org/

Raue, P. J., Castonguay, L. G., & Goldfried, M. R. (1993). The working alliance: A comparison of two therapies. *Psychotherapy Research, 3*, 197–207.

Rey-Lopez, J. P., Vicente-Rodrlguez, G., Biosca, M., Moreno, L. A. (2008). Sedentary behaviour and obesity development in children and adolescents. *Nutrition, Metabolism & Cardiovascular Diseases, 18*, 242–251.

Rimm, S. (2004). *Rescuing the emotional lives of overweight children: What our kids go though—and how we can help.* Emmaus, PA: Rodale.

Screen-Free Week. (2011). *Screen-free week.* Retrieved July 21, from http://commercialfreechildhood.org/screenfreeweek

Senediak, C., & Spence, S. H. (1985). Rapid versus gradual scheduling of therapeutic contact in a family based behavioural weight control programme for children. *Behavioral Psychotherapy, 13*, 265–287.

Serdula, M. K., Ivery, D., Coates, R. J., Freedman, D. S., Williamson, D. F., & Byers, T. (1993). Do obese children become obese adults? A review of the literature. *Preventive Medicine, 22*, 167–177.

Sherry, B., Blank, H. M., Galuska, D. A, Pan, L., & Dietz, W. H. (2009). *State-specific obesity prevalence among adults—United States, 2009.* CDC. Retrieved from http://www.cdc.gov/mmwr/preview/mmwrhtml/mm5930a4.htm?s_cid=mm5930a4_w.

Tsai, A. G., & Wadden, T. A. (2005). Systematic review: An evaluation of major commercial weight loss programs in the United States. *Annals of Internal Medicine, 142*, 56–66.

Wadden, T.A., Butryn, M. L., & Byrne, K. J. (2004). Efficacy of lifestyle modification for long-term weight control. *Obesity Research, 2004* (Suppl.), 151S-162S.

Wadden, T. A., Foster, G. D., Brownell, K. D., & Finley, E. (1984). Self-concept in obese and normal-weight children. *Journal of Consulting and Clinical Psychology, 52*, 1104–1105.

Whitlock, E. P., Williams, S. B., Gold, R., Smith, P. R., & Shipman, S. A. (2005). Screening and interventions for childhood overweight: A summary of evidence for the US Preventive Services Task Force. *Pediatrics, 116*(1), 125–144.

Wilfley, D. E., Tibbs, T. L., Van Buren, D. J., Reach, K. P., Walker, M. S., & Epstein, L.H. (2007). Lifestyle interventions in the treatment of childhood overweight: A meta-analytic review of randomized controlled trials. *Health Psychology, 26*, 521–532.

SECTION V

Effective Approaches for Students Experiencing Abuse, Foster Care, and Juvenile Justice Issues

Many students face severe social problems or horrific experiences, such as physical, emotional, and sexual abuse, legal issues, and out-of-home placements that interfere with their education. The chapters in this section provide best practices for how to respond to students who may be impacted by child abuse, foster care placement, or juvenile justice involvement.

CHAPTER 24

Identifying Child Abuse or Neglect Strategies in a School Setting

Ernst O. VanBergeijk

Getting Started

Why Is the Identification of Child Abuse and Neglect an Important Topic for Schools?

Schools are the single most important institution in a child's life, after his or her own family. By the nature of their relationships with a child, both in terms of proximity and duration of contact, school personnel can make a crucial difference in a child's life by detecting maltreatment. Although most school personnel likely would agree that the identification of child abuse is important, the accurate identification and reporting of child abuse (i.e., reports made based on evidence) are multifaceted and often complicated tasks. This chapter will discuss what we know about the problems associated with the identification of child maltreatment in schools and provide guidance around the identification process. The identification of child abuse and neglect is also an important topic because of the magnitude of the problem and the long-term health and behavioral sequelae for its victims. The National Incidence Studies (NIS) have been conducted once a decade since 1974. The most recently completed National Incidence Study (NIS-4) reveals some encouraging data indicating an overall decrease in the rates of child maltreatment across a number of different types of abuse and neglect since the completion of NIS-3 (Sedlak et al., 2010). This reduction appears to be real and supported by other indicators associated with child maltreatment (Finkelhor, Turner, Ormrod, & Hamby, 2010; Finkelhor, Turner, Ormrod, & Hamby, 2011).

An estimated 1.25 million children experienced maltreatment during the 2005–2006 study year in which the NIS-4 was conducted. The definitional standard used to compute this figure was the more stringent Harm Standard as opposed to the Endangerment Standard. Under the Endangerment Standard, there is a risk of harm rather than the actual occurrence of harm, as is the case under the Harm Standard. Under the Harm Standard, is one child out of every 58 children was a victim. If one were to use the less stringent Endangerment Standard, then one child out of every nearly 3 million children met the standard for maltreatment, meaning that nearly 1 out of every 25 children experienced abuse or neglect during the study period. The implication for school-based personnel is that virtually every school with a sufficiently large student body has at least one victim of maltreatment among its population. Neglect represents the largest category of child maltreatment, with 61% of the sample suffering from this type of maltreatment under the Harm Standard and 77% under the Endangerment Standard. (Neglect, in fact, also leads to more fatalities than abuse). Of the children who experienced maltreatment during NIS-4, 44% experienced abuse under the Harm Standard, which represents an estimated 553,300 children. Often maltreatment involves multiple forms of abuse and neglect. Consequently, the percentages reported in NIS-4 exceed 100% (Sedlak et. al., 2010).

Under the Harm Standard there was a 19% decrease in the total number of children maltreated during NIS-4 as compared to the number of children maltreated during NIS-3. Sedlak et al. (2010) quickly point out that this reduction is equivalent to a 26% decline in the rate of overall harm per 1000 children in the population when one factors in the fact that the overall number of children in the United States has increased. More specifically, the incidence of sexual abuse decreased at a statistically significant rate between the two National Incidence Studies. The actual number of sexually abused children decreased by 38%, and the incidence rate or number of children who were victims of sexual abuse per 1000 decreased by 44%. The declines in both physical and emotional abuse approached statistical significance. Under the Harm Standard, there was a 15% decline in the number and a 23% decrease in the rate of physical abuse between the two studies. Emotional abuse showed slightly larger declines than physical abuse, with a 27% decrease in the number of children emotionally abused and a 33% decline in the rate of emotional abuse between NIS-3 and NIS-4 (Sedlak et. al., 2010).

Early identification of children who are at risk of abuse and neglect, and subsequent reporting and intervention, is essential to ameliorating the long-term health and behavioral sequelae facing these survivors. Enumerating all the consequences associated with abuse and neglect is beyond the scope of this chapter. However, school personnel, because of their proximity to children and the close nature of their relationships with their students, can intervene in a profoundly positive manner in these families in crisis.

Defining Child Maltreatment

Child abuse and neglect are defined by both state and federal statutes. In 1974 Congress enacted the Child Abuse Prevention and Treatment Act, more commonly referred to as CAPTA, in which the federal government provided seed money to the states to establish 24-hour-a-day child-abuse reporting hotlines and investigatory agencies (U.S. Department of Health and Human Services, 2004). This federal statute also provided states with minimum statutory guidelines for the identification of child maltreatment. Currently, six broad categories are used typically to define child maltreatment, although only 25 of the 50 states use all six categories in their state-specific definition. These categories are physical abuse, neglect, sexual abuse, sexual exploitation, emotional maltreatment, and abandonment.

Physical abuse is defined as the nonaccidental injury of a child. This can be either through inflicting an injury or allowing a child to be injured. Neglect, in contrast, is a more abstract concept. It occurs either through the omission or commission of acts that impair or threaten to impair a child's physical, mental, or emotional condition. Sexual abuse is defined as committing or allowing the commission of a sexual offense against a child as defined by penal law. A sexual offense committed against a child is not limited to rape and sodomy. It includes fondling of the child's genitalia, oral, anal, and genital intercourse, the use of an instrument to penetrate a child's vagina or rectum, and incest (New York Society for the Prevention of Cruelty to Children, 1996). Sexual exploitation is a more specific form of sexual abuse, which includes "allowing, permitting, or encouraging a child to engage in prostitution; and allowing, permitting, encouraging, or engaging in the obscene or pornographic photographing, filming, or depicting of a child for commercial purposes" (National Center on Child Abuse and Neglect Clearinghouse, 2003). Emotional abuse may be referred to as psychological abuse or maltreatment. Like neglect, it too is an abstract concept that is difficult to operationalize. According to the National Center on Child Abuse and Neglect, emotional abuse "is a pattern of behavior that impairs a child's emotional development or sense of self-worth. This may include constant criticism, threats, or rejection, as well as withholding love, support, or guidance" (National Center on Child Abuse and Neglect Clearinghouse, 2003). Finally, abandonment has been defined as "willful intent by words, actions, or omissions not to return for a child or failure to maintain a significant parental relationship with a child through visitation or communication, in which incidental or token visits or communication are not considered significant" (National Abandoned Infants Assistance Resource Center, 2002, p. iv).

Rarely are cases of child maltreatment clear cut, and rarely do they involve only one type of maltreatment. According to Ney, Fung, and Wickett (1994), less than 5% of instances of child maltreatment occur in isolation. Neglect is often a precursor to physical abuse in many cases, and it is the combination of physical abuse, physical neglect, and verbal abuse that has the greatest impact on children (Ney, Fung, & Wickett, 1994). Further, the younger the child when the verbal abuse and emotional neglect commence, the more severe and frequent the maltreatment tends to be (Ney et al., 1994).

In addition to knowing what constitutes the various types of maltreatment within the state, school personnel must also know what kinds of behaviors are exempt from mandatory reporting laws. All but 12 states articulate anywhere from one to four exemptions from the definition of child maltreatment. An exempted behavior is one that might otherwise fit the definition of child maltreatment but that is allowable under the state statute. The most common exemptions to mandatory reporting laws typically involve with holding medical treatment on religious grounds. Twenty eight states and the District of Columbia have this exception. Corporal punishment is another common exemption. Fourteen states and the District of Columbia do not consider minor injuries inflicted as a result of corporal punishment to be abuse. Cultural practices (Minnesota) and poverty (six states and the District of Columbia) are other examples of exemptions. Of note, Minnesota exempts reasonable force by principal, teacher, or school employee from its definition of maltreatment. West Virginia allows an exemption to state compulsory education. The foundation of accurate identification of child maltreatment is a firm knowledge of what constitutes reportable maltreatment in one's state of practice.

What We Know

There are five primary methods of identifying child maltreatment: direct disclosure, observation, structured interview, projective tests, and screening tools. A direct disclosure is a direct verbal report by a child to an adult that he or she has been maltreated; this is the least ambiguous method of identification. The remaining methods of identification typically are used in the absence of a direct disclosure. They rest on the adult's knowledge of child maltreatment warning signs, risk and protective factors, and the use of critical thinking to evaluate the available evidence.

Observations can range from viewing an injury (e.g., a bruise), interacting with the parent or the child alone, or viewing interactions between the parent and the child or the child and his or her peers. Often in school settings, these observations are unplanned and unstructured, and they occur without the intent of assessing abuse. In clinical settings, observations may be conducted for the explicit purpose of making a child maltreatment determination. Even under clinical conditions, observational methods do not always have adequate reliability and validity (Milner & Murphy, 1995) because there are a number of biasing factors to which the observer may be responding (e.g., race, socioeconomic status, gender of the parent, dislike of the parent).

Interviews as an identification method use a question-and-answer format to gain information about characteristics of the family, parent(s), and interaction patterns. To be most useful, the interview should be planned and structured with clear objectives with regard to the types of information that the interviewer is seeking (e.g., a parent's mental health, substance abuse, and parental expectations of the child). Specific interview protocols have been designed to aid identification. For example, the Early Trauma Inventory (Bremner, Vermetten, & Mazure, 2000) is a 56-question clinician-administered interview that assesses physical, emotional, and sexual abuse as well as general trauma that results from experiences such as loss of a parent.

There are a number of specific strategies that may enhance the interview process. For example, Faller (1997) recommends that interview questions should be ordered on a continuum ranging from more general questions to focused open ended questions (e.g., who, what, where, and when), and finally to more specific follow-up questions (e.g. "What happened after?"). In her work with sexually abused children, she has found that direct questions should be placed toward the end of the continuum and should be used when open-ended questions are not productive (e.g.,"Was it your dad who hurt you?"). Multiple choice, leading, and/or coercive questions should be avoided (e.g.,"If you don't tell the truth, you're not leaving this room"). Using interview protocols requires some training, as it is important to adhere to the predetermined protocol. Interviews that become too conversational may fail to produce sufficient information to make a determination and are likely to omit pertinent areas of inquiry.

Projective tests rest on the assumption that the child is either not able or not willing to\disclose maltreatment and/or discuss resulting psychological symptoms but that proxy indicators of this information may be interpreted from his or her play or art. Information garnered from these types of tests should be considered supplemental; it should not be the sole basis of an identification (Kayser & Lyon, 2000). The research in this area is equivocal as to the reliability and validity of these techniques. Administering and/or interpreting projective tests requires advanced training.

Finally, a range of standardized screening tools have been used in the identification process. These tools for the most part are issue specific (i.e., sexual abuse, psychological maltreatment) or are focused on psychological symptoms of distress associated with maltreatment (e.g., trauma symptoms). Most have been developed for either adult or adolescent populations and tested on substance abusing and/or psychiatric samples rather than on the general population of school age children. However, there are several that are specific to child maltreatment behavior. Some are parent-focused self-report scales such as the Child Abuse Potential Inventory (CAPI) (Haz & Ramirez, 2002). For example, the CAPI has both long and short versions and aims to assess a parent's potential to maltreat his or her child. This instrument has multiple subscales, which allow the user to assess characteristics of the parent along dimensions such as social indicators, self control, loneliness, and rigidity. Measures such as this have been empirically tested and shown to be able to distinguish at-risk parents from non abusing parents. Other tools are child focused, such as the Gully 2000 Expectations Test (Gully, 2003). This instrument was designed for children 4–17 years of age and evaluates children in terms of sexual abuse, physical abuse, exposure to family violence, and symptoms of posttraumatic stress disorder. Since the publication of the first edition of this book, progress has been made toward operationally defining various forms of familial violence. Heyman & Slip (2006, 2009) modeled the development of their Diagnostic System for Family Maltreatment after the development of the diagnostic criteria for the *Diagnostic Statistical Manual of Mental Disorders* (DSM). In the development of the DSM, researchers used a four-stage process to refine the diagnostic criteria. At the heart of the research was the Scheduled Clinical Interview for the DSM (SCID). The goal was to develop diagnostic criteria that were reliable across different clinicians. Heyman & Slip (2006, 2009) created a scheduled clinical interview to identify and diagnose child and partner physical, sexual, or emotional abuse, as well as child neglect. Their study involved 41 agency and clinical sites using 549 cases of partner maltreatment and 342 cases of child maltreatment. Raters were individuals both with and without mental health training.

The Diagnostic System for Family Maltreatment is an important development for a number of reasons. First, child maltreatment is highly correlated with domestic partner abuse. Second, school personnel need definitions they can agree upon concerning what child maltreatment or partner abuse is. Third, both school personnel and other professionals need tools that are systematic, valid, and reliable in the identification of child maltreatment and other forms of family violence. The inter-rater reliability for partner physical, sexual, and emotional abuse was good. Likewise, various raters had levels of agreement for child physical, sexual, and emotional abuse, meaning that the statistical tests used to measure the agreement between raters ranged from k = .73–.89 (Heyman & Slip, 2009). However, raters had a much more difficult time agreeing upon whether or not a situation or diagnostic criterion constituted child neglect. Despite the lack of agreement upon the diagnostic criteria of child neglect, the results of the research from the development of the Diagnostic System for Family Maltreatment are encouraging.

What We Can Do

Though there are many empirically tested tools that can help with the identification process, it is not wise to employ them before one has a firm grasp of four core areas of relevant knowledge: (a) state laws defining child maltreatment, (b) warning signs of child maltreatment, (c) recent research on risk and protective factors, and (d) critical decision-making processes. Without this foundation and a reliance on these tools, there is a risk of failing to detect all but the most severe incidents of maltreatment. The individual will not be able to intelligently interpret screening tool results with other observable evidence. This section of the chapter is devoted to the warning signs and risk factors of child maltreatment and to procedures that may be helpful in heading off errors in critical decision making.

Warning Signs

The National Center on Child Abuse and Neglect Clearinghouse (2003) offers a complete description of the warning signs of child maltreatment in its publication *Recognizing Child Abuse: What Parents Should Know*. In this booklet, physical and behavioral indicators within the categories of maltreatment are listed for both the child victim and the potential abuser. What is particularly useful are the indicators that may be seen in the school setting. In addition to "hard" indicators such as visible injuries or poor hygiene are "soft" indicators that include abrupt changes in behavior or school performance, frequent absences from school, sudden refusals to change for physical education classes, learning problems (or difficulty concentrating) that cannot be attributed to specific physical or psychological causes, and early arrival at school or other activities and a reluctance to go home. In terms of parental behavioral indicators, the authors identify harsh or indifferent behavior; abuse of drugs or alcohol; requests for teachers to use harsh physical discipline if the child misbehaves; offers explanations for injuries that are developmentally unlikely or implausible given the nature of the injury; and/or severely limits the child's social contacts, especially with other children of the opposite sex. School based practitioners should familiarize themselves with the complete set of warning signs at the national clearinghouse's Web site.

Risk Factors

The national clearinghouse also offers a concise list of empirically identified factors that increase the risk of child maltreatment and those that protect from abuse. Risk factors are organized into three categories: the child factors, parental and/or family factors, and social and environmental factors. It is important to note that although there are several child factors that increase the risk for maltreatment (e.g., premature birth, physical or cognitive disability, age), the majority of risk factors are parental/family or social/environmental. Families that are socially isolated, financially stressed, living in communities with high violence and high unemployment rates with substance abuse problems and/or problems with domestic violence are more likely to maltreat their children than are their more socially integrated, less stressed counterparts.

In recent decades researchers have focused their attention on protective factors associated with lower probabilities of maltreatment. Children with engaging, easygoing personalities and good social skills are less likely to experience maltreatment. Lowered rates are also associated with families with supportive relationships who are socially integrated into their neighborhoods, and with parents who are consistently gainfully employed.

Critical Decision Making

Critical thinking is a process of reasoned decision making that requires the use of rationality, self awareness, and open-mindedness. It involves the use of evidence rather than emotion to evaluate information and guide decision making. It is an important part of the identification process because the school-based practitioner will be required to engage with complex and often emotionally charged family situations. An essential skill for practitioners is to be able to discern pertinent data from extraneous data. Training in critical thinking skills is an important tool in this process. Gambrill (1990) offers a number of rules of thumb for critical thinking that are useful in avoiding errors in causal assumptions that can be applied in the identification of child maltreatment. Among those rules of thumb are: (a) Look for alternative explanations, (b) pay attention to sources of uncertainty, (c) attend to negative information, and (d) attend to environmental causes. Using critical thinking requires one to reflect on the quality of information available, logical flaws in reasoning, awareness of one's biases, and a willingness to consider alternatives.

Approaching the Parents

Once there is sufficient cause to suspect child maltreatment, it is often advisable to discuss these concerns with the parent. Talking with the parent is not only a matter of ethical treatment; it also can provide important information to clarify the situation. It is imperative that the parent understand that school personnel are mandated reporters. This should be communicated in writing and verbally to ensure that the parent is clear about his or her rights. Meeting with the parent or parents can be uncomfortable and at times adversarial. The school-based practitioner must keep the focus of the interview, interact in an informed and professional manner, and avoid arguing and blaming language. It is best when the social worker speaks openly, professionally, and honestly about his or her concerns and legal obligations. If the school has decided to document the child's behavior and/or hygiene record in an effort to collect information more systematically, the parent should be advised of this. Approaching the parent is contraindicated if (a) it is likely to result in immediate harm to the child or others, (b) the parent appears to be under the influence of alcohol or drugs or to be psychologically unstable, (c) it interferes with an ongoing police investigation, or (d) there is a risk of flight out of the country.

Applying Interventions within a Response to Intervention Framework

Response to Intervention (RTI) is a method used to help identify students who are having difficulty academically. The method used to identify these students is a discrepancy-based model where the student's intellectual ability (often measured by I.Q. tests) differs substantially from his or her academic achievement. The student's academic achievement is often measured by his or her grades and standardized test scores. Students with this discrepancy are often labeled as having a specific learning disability (SLD, or simply LD). With this label, students can qualify for special education services under the Individuals with Disabilities Education Act (IDEA). Critics contend that the RTI method is simply a bureaucratic approach to delay the provision of special education services, thereby saving school districts money.

Shores (2009) provides a comprehensive discussion of the RTI model in addressing behavioral and academic issues of students in general. However, Shores addresses the topic of child abuse and neglect only in the context of what she describes as Tier 3 services or "delivering intensive individualized supports" within the special education system. One approach she advocates for addressing problematic behavior is to use functional behavioral analysis (FBA) as a part of the RTI approach. FBA and other behavioral techniques have strong empirical support regarding their efficacy. The RTI approach, on the other hand, does not seem to address child abuse and neglect, nor does it have research supporting its use in intervening with maltreated children.

Children who are the victims of child maltreatment are more likely to be labeled as having a learning disability and be a part of the special education system. The learning disability could be organic or endogenous as a result of the maltreatment. Poor nutrition and medical care can lead to declines in academic performance that could be permanent. Physical abuse can result in traumatic brain injury (TBI). TBI can result in a loss of I.Q. and, consequently, the student's academic achievement suffers. It can also lead to personality changes and aggression. These changes can also be permanent. School-based personnel can help families avoid long-term consequences of neglect by knowing and connecting families with sources of financial support such as WIC, Medicaid, and SSI. Prompt reporting of suspected abuse to the proper authorities may help prevent TBI.

School personnel can also help the parents through education. Parenting classes can be extremely helpful in not only preventing future abuse but also intervening in current situations where maltreatment may be occurring and is undetected by school personnel. Topics in the parent classes or workshops can include (1) developmental milestones and what to if your child is not reaching them; (2) reasons children misbehave and the antecedents, behaviors, and consequences (ABC) model for rewarding positive behavior (similar to the FBA described by Shores, 2009); (3) stress management for parents and children; (4) supporting your child academically; (5) good nutrition; (6) active listening skills; and (7) anger management. Not only can interventions of this type prevent abuse and neglect by helping the family to create a stable, consistent, and predictable environment for their children, but they may also help ameliorate the low academic achievement of the student that is more situational or transient in nature.

Tools and Practice Examples

James is a bright, verbal 5-year-old in a kindergarten program. He has been identified as disruptive because he hits, kicks, bites, and scratches other children. At the first parent conference held at the school, the social worker meets James's parents, Mr. and Mrs. Smith. When the social worker tries to discuss James's behavior with the parents, Mr. Smith dominates the conversation and responds defensively to questions about the family. Mrs. Smith looks away from her husband and at the ground. Her arm is in a sling. The social worker notices that when Mrs. Smith does speak, she chooses her words very carefully and seems afraid she will upset Mr. Smith. At one point during this meeting, Mr. Smith mocks James for wetting the bed at night. Toward the end of the meeting, James throws water at his toddler sister, Ann, from a water play table located in the classroom. Mr. Smith explodes in anger. He splashes James, saying, "See how you like it!" At the conclusion of this parent conference, the social worker feels intimidated by Mr. Smith and is concerned about the children. The social worker decides to conduct observations of the children's behavior and speak to their teachers.

The social worker learns that James's sister Ann is in the school's day-care program in the toddler room. She is 21⁄2 years old and does not speak. Ann will not make eye contact with men. The social worker observes that when a man comes into the room, she hides behind the day-care worker's legs. If a man speaks in a normal tone of voice in the classroom, she often hides in a corner. The day-care worker often remarks that she is dirty "again" and that she has to clean Ann when she first comes to the day-care room. At times her buttocks and vagina are red and smell of urine. Staff members have found sticks, stones, dirt, and leaves in her diaper.

Mrs. Smith appears depressed and over-whelmed by the children and her arm injury. After several conversations with her, the staff remained unclear about how she was injured. Unemployed, Mr. Smith spends a great deal of time at home watching TV and drinking beer.

This case is an example of how complex a presenting situation can be. There are several soft warning signs of child maltreatment that James exhibits, including physically assaultive behavior toward his peers and functional enuresis. Ann also exhibits warning signs that are both soft and hard in nature. Ann's soft warning signs of maltreatment include her lack of language skills, which may indicate a developmental delay, and her fear of men. The hard warning signs have to do with her lack of adequate hygiene, an indicator of neglect.

There are a number of risk factors exhibited by this family. First are the belittling behavior and harsh treatment of James by his father. A second risk factor is the various behaviors consistent with partner violence exhibited by Mr. and Mrs. Smith. A third risk factor was Mr. Smith's potential substance abuse problem. A fourth risk factor was Mrs. Smith's depression. A final risk factor was Mr. Smith's unemployment.

In the state in which this case took place, emotional injury was not defined by state statute, so many of the behavioral indicators of potential harm were moot. The negative effects of witnessing partner violence were not considered an emotional injury. The willful or threatened harm that Ann faced through neglect was not immediately reported because of an exemption to the reporting mandates for cases in which poverty is potentially a contributing factor. Although Mr. Smith's behavior was belligerent, there were no hard indicators of physical abuse that necessitated reporting at that time.

James's and Ann's teachers, the principal, and school social worker met to discuss their concerns for these children based on the children's behavior and presentation and on their own knowledge of the risk factors for child maltreatment. They began a critical thinking process by articulating some of the biases (e.g., their dislike of Mr. Smith) that might be influencing their perceptions. They spent a few minutes brainstorming alternative explanations for James's behavior with awareness that there were many sources of uncertainty. They agreed that they needed much more substantive information. They created a form for the teacher and the child-care workers to document the children's well-being and begin a case record. The social worker agreed to contact Mrs. Smith (a) to express the school's concerns, (b) to ensure that Mrs. Smith understood that the school personnel were mandated reporters of child maltreatment, and, if required, (c) to inform Mrs. Smith of her options should it become clear that a report to child protective services would be forthcoming. They decided against asking Mr. Smith to come to the meeting, given their suspicions of domestic violence. They were concerned about provoking him. The social worker met with Mrs. Smith the next week. After reviewing the laws of mandated reporting, the social worker followed Faller's recommendations by asking Mrs. Smith some general questions about the children's care (e.g., "How often do you bathe Ann?") moving to more specific and focused questions after Mrs. Smith indicated that she felt that her husband was "hard on the kids" (e.g., "What do you mean, 'hard on the kids'?" "What does Mr. Smith do when he is hard on the kids?"). Mrs. Smith did not immediately disclose abusive behavior on her husband's part and appeared nervous. The social worker told Mrs. Smith that the school personnel were so concerned that they had decided to keep track of James's and Ann's behavior and hygiene. Although uncomfortable, the social worker continued to speak openly and professionally about her concerns. Because this was done in a nonjudgmental manner, Mrs. Smith eventually conceded that Mr. Smith was physically abusive to both her and her children. A subsequent report was made to the proper authorities.

Rapid Assessment Instruments and Interview Protocols

Listed below are a number of instruments that may be helpful in identifying potential abuse. Please refer to the reference provided or to the Buros Center for Testing at http://www.unl.edu/buros/for psychometric properties of the scale (i.e., the reliability and validity of the instrument) and for the number of items and the length of time it takes to administer the questionnaire or interview protocol.

Rapid Assessment Instruments

Child Abuse Potential Inventory (CAPI) (Haz & Ramirez, 2002)

Conflict Tactics Scales Parent to Child version (CTSPC) (Straus, Hamby, Finkelhor, Moore, & Runyun, 1998)

Gully's 2000 Expectations Test (Gully, 2003)

Colorado Adolescent Rearing Inventory (CARI) (Crowley, Mikulich, Ehlers, Hall, & Whitmore, 2003). Available free of charge at: http://ibgwww.colorado.edu/cadd/a_drug/links/carI_home.html

Interviews

Early Trauma Inventory (ETI) (Bremner, Vermetten, & Mazure, 2000)

Diagnostic System for Family Maltreatment (Heyman & Slip, 2006).

Resources

Books

Board of Education of the City of New York. (2000). *Identifying and reporting suspected child abuse and neglect: A practical guide for school staff.* New York: Author.

Briere, J., Berliner, L., & Bulckley, J. (2000). *The APSAC handbook on child maltreatment.* Newbury Park, CA: Sage.

Lowenthal, B. (2001). *Abuse and neglect: The educator's guide to the identification and prevention of child maltreatment.* Baltimore, MD: Paul H. Brookes.

Shores, C. (2009). *A comprehensive RTI model: Integrating behavioral and academic approaches.* Corwin: Thousand Oaks, CA.

U.S. Department of Justice, Office of Juvenile Justice and Delinquency Prevention. (1997). *Recognizing when a child's injury or illness is caused by abuse.* Washington, DC: Author.

Web Sites

Child Welfare Information Gateway: http://www.childwelfare.gov

The Children's Bureau: http://www.acf.hhs.gov/programs/cb/

NIS-4: http://www.nis4.org

National Data Archive on Child Abuse and Neglect: http://www.ndacan.cornell.edu

Organizations and Government Agencies

National Center for Missing and Exploited Children
Charles B. Wang International Children's Building
699 Prince Street
Alexandria, VA 22314–3175
Web site: http://missingkids.com
Voice 703–274–3900/274–2220
Hot line: 800–THE LOST (843–5678)

National Clearinghouse on Child Abuse and Neglect Information
330 C Street, SW
Washington, DC 20447
E-mail: nccanch@calib.com
Web site: http://nccanch.acf.hhs.gov/
Voice 703–385–7565/800–394–3366
FAX 703–385–3206

Key Points to Remember

- The identification of child maltreatment is often a complex task. Rarely does child maltreatment involve a single episode and a sole form of maltreatment.
- Competent identification of child maltreatment means that school-based professionals must have a solid foundation in the four key areas of knowledge: (1) state laws defining each type of maltreatment, (2) warning signs of maltreatment, (3) recent research findings on risk and protective factors for child abuse and neglect, and (4) critical thinking and decision-making skills.
- The five methods of identification are direct disclosure from the child, observations, interviews, projective tests, and screening tools.
- As a part of ethical practice, concerns of child maltreatment should be discussed with the parent.

References

Bremner, J., Vermetten, E., & Mazure, C. (2000). Development and preliminary psychometric properties of an instrument for the measurement of childhood trauma: The Early Childhood Trauma Inventory. *Depression and Anxiety, 12*(1), 1–12.

Crowley, T., Mikulich, S., Ehlers, K., Hall, S., & Whitmore, E. (2003). Discriminative validity and clinical utility of an abuse-neglect interview for adolescents with conduct and substance use problems. *American Journal of Psychiatry, 160*(8), 1461–1469.

Faller, K. C. (1997). *Understanding and assessing child sexual maltreatment.* Thousand Oaks, CA: Sage.

Finkelhor, D., Turner, H., Ormrod, R., & Hamby, S. (2010). Trends in childhood violence and abuse exposure: Evidence from 2 national surveys. *Archives of Pediatrics and Adolescent Medicine, 164*(3), 238–242.

Finkelhor, D., Turner, H., Ormrod, R., and Hamby, S. (2011). School, police, and medical authority involvement with children who have experienced victimization. *Archives of Pediatrics and Adolescent Medicine, 165*(1), 9–15.

Gambrill, E. (1990). *Critical thinking in clinical practice.* San Francisco: Jossey-Bass.

Gully K. (2003). Expectations test: Trauma scales for sexual abuse, physical abuse, exposure to family violence, and post-traumatic stress. *Child Maltreatment, 8*(3), 218–229.

Haz, A., & Ramirez, V. (2002). Adaptation of Child Abuse Potential Inventory in Chile: Analysis of difficulties and challenges in the application in Chilean studies. *Child Abuse and Neglect 26*(5), 481–495.

Heyman, R. E., & Slip, A. M. S. (2006). Creating and field-testing diagnostic criteria for partner and child maltreatment. *Journal of Family Psychology, 20,* 397–408.

Heyman, R. E., & Slip, A. M. (2009). Reliability of Family Maltreatment Diagnostic Criteria: 41 site dissemination field trial. *Journal of Family Psychology, 23*(6), 205–210.

Kayser, J. A., & Lyon, M. A. (2000). Teaching social workers to use psychological assessment data. *Child Welfare, 79*(2), 197–223.

Milner, J. S., & Murphy, W. D. (1995). Assessment of child physical and sexual abuse offenders. *Family Relations, 44*(4), 478–488.

National Abandoned Infants Assistance Resource Center, School of Social Welfare, University of California at Berkeley. (2002). *Expediting permanency for abandoned infants: Guidelines for state policies and procedures.* Berkeley, CA: Author.

National Center on Child Abuse and Neglect Clearinghouse. (2003). *2003 Child abuse and neglect. State Statues Series at a glance: Definitions of child abuse and neglect.* Retrieved August 2, 2004, from http://nccanch.acf.hhs.gov

New York Society for the Prevention of Cruelty to Children. (1996). *NYSPCC professionals handbook: Identifying and reporting child abuse and neglect.* New York: Author.

Ney, P., Fung, T., & Wickett, A. (1994). The worst combinations of child abuse and neglect. *Child Abuse and Neglect, 18*(9), 705–714.

Sedlak, A. J., Mettenburg, J., Basen, M., Petta, I., McPherson, K., Greene, A., and Li, S. (2010). *Fourth National Study of Child Abuse and Neglect (NIS-4) Report to Congress.* Washington, DC: U.S. Department of Health and Human Services, Administration for Children and Families.

Shores, C. (2009). *A comprehensive RTI model: Integrating behavioral and academic approaches.* Thousand Oaks, CA: Corwin.

Straus, M., Hamby, S., Finkelhor, D., Moore, D., & Runyun, D. (1998). Identification of child maltreatment with the Parent-Child Conflict Tactics Scales: Development and psychometric data for a national sample of American parents. *Child Abuse and Neglect 22*(4), 249–270.

U.S. Department of Health and Human Services, National Center on Child Abuse and Neglect . (2004). *Child maltreatment 2002: Reports from the states to the national child abuse and neglect data system.* Washington, DC: U.S. Government Printing Office.

CHAPTER 25

Helping Students Who Have Been Physically or Sexually Abused

Strategies and Interventions

Kathleen Coulborn Faller

Getting Started

Most children go to school, and they are in school for several hours 5 days a week about 10 months of the year. Thus, school is where children have the greatest exposure to professionals who can identify, report, and ameliorate sexual and physical abuse. These professionals—teachers, counselors, school social workers, and school administrators—are all mandated reporters of child abuse and neglect. It is not accidental that of all the mandated reporters, school personnel make the largest proportion of professional reports (U.S. Department of Health and Human Services [USDHHS], 2010). Similarly, the National Incidence Studies, which examine the relationship between cases of child maltreatment that are investigated by child protective services and those identified by "sentinels," such as school staff, have found that schools accounted for reporting approximately half of the almost 3 million cases of child abuse and neglect that came to professional attention (Sedlak et al., 2010).

Because of their centrality in the lives of school-age children, school personnel have the potential to play an instrumental role in ameliorating the effects of child physical and sexual abuse

What We Know

Despite the pivotal role of school personnel in intervention with children who have been physically and sexually abused, child maltreatment literature focuses primarily on the role of schools in identifying, reporting, and preventing child abuse and neglect (e.g., Broadhurst, 1984; Crosson-Tower, 2002; USDHHS, 2003). This literature consists of numerous manuals and a modest number of books. In addition, the school social work literature describes abused and neglected children as a special population to be addressed by social workers and mental health professionals in the schools, but it provides very little information about specific strategies and interventions that might support maltreated children (Allen-Meares, Washington, & Welsh, 2000; Constable, McDonald, & Flynn, 2002). There is also an emerging literature on evidence-based school interventions with children who have been maltreated (Brassard, Rivelis, & Diaz, 2009; Hanson et al., 2008; U.S/D.H.H.S., 2003). Finally, in addition to interventions that have been implemented in schools, there are other school-compatible, evidence-based practices from the child welfare literature that professionals consider to be best practice for school personnel addressing the needs of physically and sexually abused children. Topics covered are (1) the consequences of physical and sexual abuse, (2) evidence-based interventions that have been implemented with children in schools, and (3) practices derived from the child welfare literature, such as (a) the importance of support, belief, and role modeling for victims of abuse; (b) using multidisciplinary teams with abused children; and (c) abuse-specific, cognitive-behavioral treatment.

Multiple Consequences of Sexual and Physical Abuse

The research on the effects of child sexual and physical abuse indicates that abuse impairs the functioning of its victims, but not in a single, definable way (Berliner, 2011; Kolko, 2002).

The most common sequelae in sexually abused children are fears or phobias and sexualized behaviors (Chaffin, Letourneau, & Silovsky, 2002; Kendall-Tackett, Williams, & Finkelhor, 1993). The most common sequelae of physical abuse are aggression and health problems (Kolko, 2002). Both physically and sexually abused children are likely to blame themselves for their abuse and the aftermath of discovery, to have academic difficulties, and to have symptoms of posttraumatic stress disorder or other trauma symptoms (Berliner, 2011; Kolko, 2002). The effect of sexual and physical abuse is compounded by co-morbid conditions (Allen-Meares et al., 2000; Berliner, 2011). Children may be *both* sexually and physically abused and exposed to other traumatizing situations such as neglect, domestic violence, and substance abuse (http://www.ssw.umich.edu/icwtp/). Moreover, special needs children are at greater risk for physical and sexual abuse (Davies & Faller, 2007; Gorman-Smith & Matson, 1992).

School-Based Interventions to Help Maltreated Children

In 1997, the Children's Bureau funded 11 three-year demonstration projects on child maltreatment and the schools. Although most of these projects focused on teacher awareness, mandatory reporting of child maltreatment, and primary prevention with parents rather than on intervention with maltreated children, they also included some direct services for children. Direct services for children included support groups, social events, and treatment. These demonstration projects have played an important role in the development of school-based interventions to address child maltreatment, although the projects generally served fewer people than intended. Lessons learned included being mindful of scheduling when there might be competing events, such as school activities, and advice to label programs so as not to stigmatize participants. (U.S/D.H.H.S., 2003).

Following this federal initiative, Brassard et al. (2009) conducted a systematic review of evidence-based, school-based programs to address child maltreatment. As with the Children's Bureau demonstration projects, many school-based strategies target teachers and parents (U.S/D.H.H.S), but there are some that address behavioral and affective symptoms that can be the sequelae of child maltreatment (Brassard et al., 2009). Because such symptoms are nonspecific, they can also derive from other traumatic experiences. These evidence-based interventions are characterized by Brassard and colleagues as either geared for the entire classroom or "pull-out," that is, designated for children with the targeted behavioral or emotional problems (Brassard et al., 2009). Such programs may be aimed at preschool, elementary, middle, or high school populations. Most of the programs cited are structured, manualized, and actually have been studied in school settings. These programs can be delivered by school psychologists or social workers, and some even by classroom teachers. They are based upon cognitive-behavioral and/or psychoeducational principles. Among the promising programs for aggressive behaviors and conduct problems are The Incredible Years (Webster-Stratton, 2001), Dina Dinosaur (Webster-Stratton et al., 1991), Promoting Alternative Thinking Strategies (PATHS; Kunsche & Greenberg, 1994), and Second Step (Frey, Hirschstein, & Guzzo, 2000).

There are fewer school-based programs for children who exhibit trauma responses because of physical abuse, sexual abuse, domestic violence, or exposure to natural disasters. One program rated exemplary by the Office of Juvenile Justice and Delinquency Prevention (Brassard et al., 2009, p. 212) is Cognitive Behavioral Intervention for Trauma in Schools (CBITS, Jaycox, 2004). This program focuses on middle school children who have been traumatized, including children who have been physically and/or sexually abused. Brassard and colleagues have done an admirable job finding and describing these programs and providing references so that school professionals can access materials to deliver these interventions.

Although this chapter focuses on interventions for schools that specifically address the impact of maltreatment on children, for genuine change in child well-being, there must also be interventions that address parental and environmental problems that led to maltreatment and trauma.

Evidence-based Intervention Applicable to School Settings

In addition to school-specific programs, there are proven principles from other domains that can guide school personnel in their responses to child maltreatment.

Support, Belief, and Modeling Appropriate Adult Responses

According to a respectable body of research, a child's recovery from sexual abuse is more likely if the child has caretakers who support him or her and believe that the abuse in fact occurred (Bolen & Lamb, 2007a,b; Everson, Hunter, Runyon, & Edelsohn, 1989; Heriot, 1996; Hunter, Coulter, Runyan, & Everson, 1990). By extension, support and belief provided by other important people, such as teachers, school social workers, and school counselors, can ameliorate the effects of both sexual and physical abuse. For many abused children, school is their refuge from a painful home environment.

A related finding is the importance of a mentor or role model to a child's survival of adverse home circumstances. Thus, school personnel can be central to children's recovery from abuse and can provide an alternative adult response and a different model for adult behavior for children who have been physically and sexually abused.

Multidisciplinary Response

School systems and child welfare systems have a long history of a common appreciation of the importance of a multidisciplinary response to children's problems. In the 1970s, federal legislation in both education (P.L. 94–142, Education for All Handicapped Children Act) and child welfare (P.L. 93–247, Child Abuse Prevention and Treatment Act [CAPTA]) provided for multidisciplinary services to aid abused children. More recently, a multidisciplinary approach to children and adults has been applied more broadly under a series of Systems of Care (SOC) initiatives at the federal level. The USDHHS Substance Abuse and Mental Health Services Administration (CCISC MODEL 2011; SAMHSA, 2009) has been the primary federal agency advocating an SOC model, but the language has also been adopted by the child welfare system. SOC acknowledges that persons, including children, with mental health problems are identified and receiving services from a variety of systems and the importance of these systems working together on behalf of clients. School personnel can use existing skills in working as part of a multidisciplinary team, or SOC, to use the newer terminology, to intervene with abused children. Team members include not only school staff, but also child welfare staff, mental health systems, and sometimes law enforcement personnel, foster parents, court workers, and judges.

What We Can Do

Efficacy of Abuse-Specific, Cognitive-B ehavioral Treatment

In 2000, Congress established the National Child Traumatic Stress Network (NCTSN), which comprises about 60 university and community-based programs that are dedicated to developing evidence-based responses to child trauma, including child sexual and physical abuse. Evidence-based and promising practices reviewed by NCTSN form the basis of many community-based developed treatment programs for sexually abused children, and a smaller number have programs for physically abused children. Those programs that have been demonstrated to be effective take a trauma-focused cognitive-behavioral approach (e.g., Berliner, 2011; Cohen, Berliner, & Mannarino, 2003; NCTSN, 2011). Although group treatment may be more efficient, it has not been shown to be more effective (Berliner, 2011).

Instructions on Intervention

The findings described in the previous section can guide school professionals as they intervene with children who have a history of physical and sexual abuse.

Addressing the Consequences of Physical and Sexual Abuse

When children not identified as physically or sexually abused display known symptoms of abuse, school personnel need to ensure that someone will inquire about the cause of the child's symptoms. School practice, local child welfare policy, and the specifics of the case determine whether school personnel talk to the child or whether it is reported to child protective services, which will then conduct an interview.

When children identified as physically or sexually abused display known symptoms, school personnel must ensure that the symptoms are understood and addressed by other staff. Many times sequelae of physical and sexual abuse are treated simply as bad behavior, which is then punished rather than understood in terms of etiology.

All relevant school staff should understand the source of the child's problems and have sensitive, consistent, and coordinated responses to these problems. Such responses may be accomplished by having a school-based team meeting or series of meetings.

School is the natural environment for dealing with academic deficits that may result from physical and sexual abuse and/or school disruption because of foster care placement. Schools can provide tutoring and other academic support services and can ensure that the child's school record follows him or her (Ayasse, 1998).

Supporting and Believing the Child

Adults often doubt children's accounts of abuse or deny its effects, especially when the allegation is sexual abuse. Research indicates that false allegations of abuse are rare (Faller, 2003). Nevertheless, adults may spend more time agonizing about the truth of the child's allegation than about the consequences of abuse to the child. School personnel must support and believe children in order to help them heal. The determination of the likelihood of child abuse is the responsibility of other professionals (child protection workers, physicians, and judges). If these professionals have determined that the child has been abused, school personnel should assume that is true, and they should provide the child with role models of concerned and fair-minded adults.

Working as Part of the Multidisciplinary Team

When children who are victims of physical and sexual abuse attend school, school personnel must appreciate that there are other professionals involved and, within the bounds of confidentiality, reach out to them. School personnel should insist that services to the child be coordinated and that they be part of the service delivery process.

Although school personnel may act *in loco parentis* and may spend more time with abused children than the other professionals on the team, child welfare staff and court staff have final say about how a child's abuse case will be handled. The preeminent role of child welfare and court professionals can be challenging when there is disagreement about how a particular child's situation should be handled (Bross, Krugman, Lenherr, Rosenberg, & Schmitt, 1988).

Many communities now have programs and community-based teams to assure coordination of services to abused and neglected children and their families or other caretakers. An example is Wraparound Services, which draws on school, child welfare, mental health programs, and other community services to prevent children from going into foster or residential care.

Assuring the Child Receives Appropriate Treatment

School personnel should assure that victims of physical and sexual abuse receive abuse-specific, state-of-the-art treatment with a cognitive behavioral component. Child welfare staff often focus on a child's safety and may fail to follow through on treatment once the child is protected. Moreover, they may not be aware of the type of treatment that is effective.

In some full-service schools, treatment programs for physically and sexually abused children may actually be provided in the school setting, but in most communities, treatment is provided by community-based social services agencies. However, the SAMHSA SOC initiative is supporting school-based mental health services (SAMHSA, 2009).

Application of the RTI Model to Helping Children Who Have Been Physically or Sexually Abused

The RTI three-tiered approach can be applied to intervention in sexual and physical abuse. The model integrates well with the systematic review of evidence-supported, school-based interventions undertaken by Brassard and colleagues (2009). Tier 1, the universal interventions, fit into what Brassard and colleagues describe as class-based programs, that is, programs that are delivered to entire classrooms. Illustrative is the Promoting Alternative Thinking Strategies (PATHS), which emphasizes readiness, self-control, feelings, relationships, and problem-solving (Brassard et al., 2009). In addition, schools have traditionally been the venue of sexual abuse prevention and personal safety programs, which are universal. Although the stated goal of these programs is prevention of sexual abuse and other interpersonal violence, they also serve as a screening mechanism for victims, because children may report maltreatment after attending such a program. In the latter instances, they may serve a Tier 2 or even Tier 3 function.

Tier 2 interventions are equivalent to Brassard and colleagues "pull-out" programs, interventions with children who manifest behavioral indicators of maltreatment (Brassard et al., 2009). Because most school-based programs identify children in need of Tier 2 interventions based upon their behavior problems, useful screening mechanisms are office discipline referrals (ODRs). The major shortcoming of ODRs is that they are likely to identify children with externalizing behaviors, but not internalizing behaviors. However, a widely employed behavior problems scale, the Child Behavior Checklist (CBCL), for children 6–18 (Achenbach, 2007) is an appropriate screener for school social workers and counselors to employ. The CBCL is the name for the caretaker-completed form, but the CBCL has a Teacher Report Form (TFR) and a Youth Self-Report Survey (YSR). The CBCL measures internalizing behaviors (symptoms of anxiety), externalizing behaviors (e.g., aggression), and total behavior problems. It also has Sexual Problems and Post-traumatic Stress Problems subscales, which can be used as an initial screener for sexual abuse.

Tier 3 in RTI is for physically and sexually abused children—those children who need to be referred out for additional services. Children already identified as abused, but who are in safe living situations, might need referrals for treatment. Brassard and colleagues provide a decision tree for referrals to treatment outside the school setting (Brassard et al., 2009). Children whose allegations have not yet been investigated will usually need to be reported to child protective services. Teachers, indeed all school personnel, are mandated reporters.

Tools and Practice Examples

Case Example of How to Do the Intervention

Cindy is a biracial, 15-year-old girl whose Caucasian mother died of cancer when she was 8. The cancer was diagnosed when Cindy was born. Her African American father, a very accomplished electrical engineer, was overwhelmed by the loss of his wife and blamed his daughter for the mother's death. He targeted Cindy for physical, emotional, and sexual abuse. She told her school counselor about her abuse when she was 13. Cindy was very bright and sweet, but she also overate and had a problem wetting herself, problems later determined to be related to her abuse.

The school counselor never doubted Cindy's account and immediately reported the abuse to child protective services. The school stood by Cindy when her father vehemently denied the abuse. The school also advocated for Cindy when her father tried to get her declared mentally ill (because she overate, wet herself, and accused him of abuse) and committed to a day treatment center.

As a consequence of the school counselor's report, Cindy was placed in foster care with a single African American woman living in another town in the same county. The woman had three other foster children, all African American teenage girls. But they were very different from Cindy. She had played the violin in the school orchestra until her father had sold her violin because he thought her grades should be better. She was very interested in going to college.

Cindy's school was the place where she formed close relationships, both with peers and adults. She wanted to continue in her school, even though it was in a different town, and she asked her school social worker to intervene with the child welfare worker in charge of Cindy's case. Cindy's teacher, counselor, and the school social worker all attended an initial meeting with child welfare staff and were able to get her child welfare worker to agree that it was in Cindy's interest to continue at her current school.

Initially school staff assisted in arranging Cindy's transportation to and from school. Three months later, Cindy wanted to move in with the family of a close friend and schoolmate, and the school staff intervened with the child welfare worker to support Cindy's request. In addition, the school social worker persuaded the music teacher to lend Cindy a violin so she could continue to play in the orchestra.

Cindy's enuresis caused her much embarrassment, and she had a great deal of difficulty dealing with her father's utter rejection and refusal to acknowledge any wrongdoing. The school social worker and her new foster parents convinced the child welfare worker that Cindy needed therapy, and

Table 25.1 Intervention Checklist

Child identifying information	*Name*		*Age*	*Grade in school*
Types of sexual & physical abuse	1.	2.	3.	4.
Sequelae/symptoms/problems	1.	2.	3.	4.
School-based plan for managing the problems	Behavior management		Services (e.g., tutoring, school social work services)	
School personnel involved with the child (e.g., teacher, counselor, school social worker, teacher aide)	1. 2. 3.			
Is there someone in the school the child trusts/talks to?	Yes/No	Who?		
Community professionals involved with the child's case	Child welfare	Treatment provider	Other	
Team meetings	Frequency		Location	
	Who will attend?		Who convenes?	
Intervention	Therapy		Other intervention	
Other case management issues (e.g., custody, termination of parental rights)				

they worked together to select a female therapist who was well-versed in behavioral (for the enuresis) and cognitive-behavioral (for abuse aftereffects) approaches. Cindy formed an excellent therapeutic alliance with her therapist. In addition, school personnel developed a program to get Cindy to ask when she needed to go to the toilet and for school staff to immediately grant her permission so she would not have an accident at school.

Cindy was fortunate, despite her misfortune, because she had strong and consistent advocates on her behalf in her school, an excellent child welfare caseworker, and a good therapist who was aware of effective treatment for physically and sexually abused children.

Forms and Exercises

The intervention checklist in Table 25.1 is designed to assist school personnel in developing and tracking interventions and strategies to help children who have been physically and sexually abused.

Resources

Books

Freeman, E., Franklin C., Fong, R., Schaffer, G. ,& Timberlake, E. (Eds.). (1998). *Multisystem skills and interventions in school social work practice.* Washington, DC: NASW Press.

Kluger, M., Alexander, G., & Curtis, P. (Eds.). (2001). *What works in child welfare.* Washington, DC: Child Welfare League of America.

Myers, J. E. B. (Ed.). (2011). *APSAC handbook on child maltreatment* (3rd ed.). Thousand Oaks, CA: Sage.

Web Sites

American Professional Society on the Abuse of Children:www.apsac.org.

Child Welfare Information Gateway: http://www.childwelfare.gov/

http://www.childwelfare.gov/supporting/support_services/school.cfm

National Child Traumatic Stress Network: http://nctsn.org/NCTSN.org

University of South Florida School-based Mental Health Resources: http://rtckids.fmhi.usf.edu/sbmh/default.cfm

Key Points to Remember

Grade school and high school education are the only universal social programs in the United States. School personnel thereby are the most consistent professionals in the lives of physically and sexually abused children. Research suggests that there are several important interventions school staff can make on behalf of abused children. These include (1) recognizing and responding to sequelae or problems that result from having been physically or sexually abused; (2) believing, supporting, and mentoring abused children; (3) collaborating with other professionals who are involved in service delivery to abused children; and (4) ensuring that children who have been abused will receive abuse-specific therapy. In addition, recent research supports the efficacy of school-based interventions for behaviors and affects that may result from physical and/or sexual abuse, which can be delivered to the class as a whole or to targeted children with these behaviors and affects (Brassard et al., 2009).

References

Achenbach, T. (2007). *Achenbach System of Empirically Based Assessment (ASEBA)*. Retrieved July 30, 2011, from http://www.aseba.org/schoolage.html

Akande, A. A. (2001). Child abuse: Focus on team approach for school teachers and counselors. *Early Child Development and Care, 169*, 69–84.

Allen- Meares, P., Washington, R., & Welsh, B. (2000). *Social work in the schools* (3rd ed.). Needham Heights, MA: Allyn & Bacon.

Ayasse, R. (1998). Addressing the needs of foster children: The Foster Youth Services Program. In E. Freeman, C. Franklin, R. Fong, Gary Schaffer, & E. Timberlake (Eds.), *Multisystem skills and interventions in school social work practice* (pp. 52–61). Washington, DC: NASW Press.

Berliner, L. (2011). Child sexual abuse: Definitions, prevalence, and consequences. In J. E. B. Myers, (Ed.) *The ASPAC handbook on child maltreatment* (3rd ed., pp. 215–232). Thousand Oaks, CA: Sage.

Bolen, R. M., & Lamb, J. (2007a). Can nonoffending mothers of sexually abused children be both ambivalent and supportive? *Child Maltreatment, 12*(2), 191–197.

Bolen, R. M., & Lamb, J. (2007b). Parental support and outcome in sexually abused children. *Journal of Child Sexual Abuse, 16*(2), 33–54.

Brassard, M., Rivelis, E., & Diaz, V. (2009). School-based counseling of abused children. *Psychology in the Schools, 46*(3), 206–217.

Bross, D., Krugman, R., Lenherr, M., Rosenberg, D. A., & Schmitt, B. (Eds.). (1988). *The new child protection team handbook*. New York: Garland.

CCISC Model: A comprehensive, continuous, integrated system of care model. Retrieved June 21, 2011, from http://www.hss.state.ak.us/dbh/resources/print/CCISC%20MODEL%20(by%20ken%20minkoff).pdf

Chaffin, M., Letourneau, E., & Silovsky, J. (2002). Adults, adolescents, and children who sexually abuse children: A developmental perspective. In J.E.B. Myers, L. Berliner, J. Briere, C.T. Hendrix, C. Jenny, & T. Reid (Eds.), *The APSAC handbook on child maltreatment* (2nd ed., pp. 205–232). Thousand Oaks, CA: Sage.

Child Welfare Information Gateway. (2003). *School-based maltreatment programs: Synthesis of lessons learned*. Washington, DC: USDHHS.

Cohen, J., Berliner, L., & Mannarino, A. (2003). Psychosocial and pharmacological interventions for child crime victims. *Journal of Traumatic Stress, 16*(2), 175–186.

Constable, R., McDonald, S., & Flynn, J. (2002). *School social work: Practice, policy, and research perspectives* (5th ed.). Chicago: Lyceum.

Crosson-Tower, C. (2002). *When children are abused: An educator's guide*. Needham Heights, MA: Allyn & Bacon.

Davies, D., & Faller, K.C. (2007). Chapter 11: Interviewing children with special needs. In K. C. Faller, *Interviewing children about sexual abuse: controversies and best practice*. New York, NY: Oxford University Press.

Everson, M., Hunter, W., Runyon, D., & Edelsohn, G. (1989). Maternal support following discovery of incest. *American Journal of Orthopsychiatry, 59*(2), 197–207.

Faller, K. C. (2003). *Understanding and assessing child sexual maltreatment* (2nd ed.). Thousand Oaks, CA: Sage.

Frey, K. S., Hirschstein, M., & Guzzo, B. (2000). Second Step: Preventing aggression by promoting social competence. *Journal of Emotional and Behavioral Disorders, 8*(2), 102–112.

Gorman-Smith, D., & Matson, J. (1992). Sexual abuse and persons with mental retardation. In W. O'Donohue & J. Greer (Eds.), *The sexual abuse of children: Theory and research* (Vol. 1, pp. 285–306). Hillsdale, NJ: Erlbaum.

Hanson, R., Ralston, E., Self- Brown, S., Ruggiero, K., Saunders, B., Love, A., Sosnowski, P., & Williams, R. (2008). Description and preliminary evaluation of the Child Abuse School Liaison Program: A secondary prevention program for school personnel. *Journal of Psychological Trauma*, 7(2), 91–103.

Heriot, J. (1996). Maternal protectiveness following the disclosure of intrafamilial child sexual abuse. *Journal of Interpersonal Violence, 11*(2), 181–194.

Hunter, W., Coulter, M., Runyan, D., & Everson, M. (1990). Determinants of placement for sexually abused children. *Child Abuse & Neglect, 14,* 407–417.

Jaycox, L. (2004). *Cognitive-behavioral intervention for trauma in schools.* Longmost, CO: Sopris West.

Kendall-Tackett, K. A., Williams, L. M., & Finkelhor, D. (1993). Impact of sexual abuse on children: A review and synthesis of recent empirical studies. *Psychological Bulletin, 113,* 164–180.

Kolko, David (2002). Child physical abuse. In J. E. B. Myers, L. Berliner, J. Briere, C. T. Hendrix, C. Jenny, & T. Reid (Eds.), *The APSAC handbook on child maltreatment* (2nd ed., pp. 21–54). Thousand Oaks, CA: Sage.

Myers, J. E. B. (2011). *The ASPAC handbook on child maltreatment* (3rd ed.) Thousand Oaks, CA: Sage.

National Child Traumatic Stress Network. (2011). NCTSN.org. Accessed June 23, 2011.

Sas, L., & Cunningham, A. (1995). *Tipping the balance to tell the secret: The public discovery of child sexual abuse.* (Available from the London Court Clinic, 254 Pall Mall St., London, Ont. N6A 5P6 [519–679–7250])

Sedlak, A., & Broadhurst, D. (1996). *The third National Incidence Study on child abuse and neglect (NIS-3).* Washington, DC: U.S. Department of Health and Human Services.

Sedlak, A.J., Mettenburg, J., Basena, M., Petta, I., McPherson, K., Greene, A., & Li, S. (2010). *Fourth National Incidence Study of Child Abuse and Neglect (NIS–4): Report to Congress.* Washington, DC: U.S. Department of Health and Human Services, Administration for Children and Families.

Smith, C. (1998). The link between childhood maltreatment and teenage pregnancy. In E. Freeman, C. Franklin, R. Fong, G. Schaffer, & E. Timberlake (Eds.), *Multisystem skills and interventions in school social work practice* (pp. 190–205). Washington, DC: NASW Press.

Substance Abuse and Mental Health Services Administration (SAMHSA). (2009). *Working together to help youth thrive in schools and communities.* Retrieved June 23, 2011, from http://www.samhsa.gov/children/docs/shortReport.pdf

U.S. Department of Health and Human Services. (2003). *School-based child maltreatment programs: Synthesis of lessons learned.* Washington, DC: Government Printing Office.

U.S. Department of Health and Human Services, National Center on Child Abuse and Neglect. (2004). *Child maltreatment 2002: Reports from the states to the national child abuse and neglect data system.* Washington, DC: U.S. Government Printing Office.

Webster-Stratton, C. (1991). *Dinosaur social skills and problem-solving training manual.* Seattle, WA: Incredible Years.

Webster-Stratton, C., Reid, J., & Hammond, M. (2001). *The Incredible Years: Parents, teachers, and children training series.* Seattle, WA: Incredible Years.

CHAPTER 26

Helping Children in Foster Care and Other Residential Placements Succeed in School

Dorian E. Traube   Mary M. McKay

Getting Started

Many children in out-of-home placements experience emotional or behavioral difficulties. Even children who do not exhibit overt symptoms are at risk for the development of mental health difficulties as a result of histories of child abuse and neglect, poverty, adult caregiver mental health concerns, stress related to removal from their families, or placement disruption (Cox, Orme, & Rhodes, 2003). Each year, billons of dollars are spent responding to the legal, correctional, educational, and psychological needs of children in out-of-home placements (USDHHSACYF, 2007). Yet despite this, children residing in out-of-home placements are also seriously affected by deteriorating supportive resources, including a shortage of mental health service providers.

Schools are one of the few existing resources consistently available within communities, and they offer a unique opportunity to provide mental health care for children in the child protective system. Among the advantages schools provide is the opportunity to intervene with a child and foster family or group home coordinator in a community setting, to enhance children's academic progress and affect children's peer relations, to increase access to underserved children via their availability in schools, and to lessen the stigma of mental health services (Cappella, Frazier, Atkins, Schoenwald, & Glisson, 2008). Given the shortages of mental health resources in many communities, there is increasing awareness that schools are de facto mental health service providers for a majority of children, including those in out-of-home placements (Capella, et al., 2008).

What We Know About the Existing School-Based Mental Health Consultation Model

The predominant model for school-based mental health services is the consultation model. In this model, mental health providers, generally social workers, consult with teachers to develop services targeting the needs of the referred student. These consultations are important elements of providing child mental health care and are supported by numerous studies identifying the effectiveness of mental health-focused interventions in schools (Weisz, Sandler, Durlak, & Anton, 2005).

Though there is not sufficient space to detail all empirically driven models of best practice with children in out-of-home placement, the authors refer the readers to the following school-based mental health interventions.

To Treat Emotional and Behavioral Disorders

August, G. J., Lee, S. S., Bloomquist, M. L., Realmuto, G. M., & Hektner, J. M. (2004). Maintenance effects of an evidence-based preventive innovation for aggressive children living in culturally diverse, urban neighborhoods: The Early Risers effectiveness study. *Journal of Emotional and Behavioral Disorders, 12*(4), 194–204.

Webster-Stratton, C., & Reid, M. J. (2010). Adapting The Incredible Years, an evidence-based parenting programme, for families involved in the child welfare system. *Journal of Children's Services, 5*(1), 25–42.

To Treat Depression

Lynch, F. L., Hornbrook, M., Clarke, G. N., Perrin, N., Polen, M. R., O'Connor, E., & Dickerson, J.

(2005). Cost-effectiveness of an intervention to prevent depression in at-risk teens. *Archives of General Psychiatry, 62*(11), 1241–1248.

To Treat Conduct Disorders

Conduct Problems Prevention Research Group. (2002). Evaluation of the first three years of the Fast Track Prevention Trial with children at high risk for adolescent conduct problems. *Journal of Abnormal Child Psychology, 30,* 19–35.

Table 26.1 describes some of the recent, innovative, empirically driven, direct intervention school mental health models that extend the reach of schools to provide for the social and emotional needs of children.

Although these school mental health models are considered advances and have substantial empirical support, many of these models and related interventions are rejected by teachers as being either too complex to manage independently or too distinct from standard educational practices for teachers and school administrators to embrace. Further, necessary financial or innovative staff resources are often not available to sustain innovative mental health service models for children. Yet, an important advantage of each of these models is that they do not specifically identify children in out-of-home placements as being in need. Since these models promote the mental health and well-being of *all* children in a school, the child in out-of-home placement is part of a supportive, stable school environment instead of being further stigmatized for needs that developed as a result of a history of abuse or neglect.

What We Can Do—Parents and Peers as Leaders in School (PALS) Approach

Another example of an innovation in the field of school-based practice has grown out of an increasing realization that childhood mental health disorders are affected by numerous factors beyond the level of the child. However, few school-based models have considered the specific, complex interactions of the multiple factors affecting children being reared in out-of-home

Table 26.1 Innovative School-Based Mental Health Services

Program	*Author*	*Description*	*Obtaining More Information*
Project Achieve	Howard Knoff	**Elements:** Strategic planning and organizational analysis and development Problem solving, teaming, and consultation processes Effective school, schooling, and professional development Academic instruction linked to academic assessment, intervention, and achievement Behavioral instruction linked to behavioral assessment, intervention, and self-management Parent and community training, support, and outreach Data management, evaluation, and accountability **Goal:** To design and implement effective school and schooling processes that maximize the academic and social/emotional/behavioral progress and achievement of all students.	http://www.projectachieve.info/home.html

(continued)

Table 26.1 *(Continued)*

Program	*Author*	*Description*	*Obtaining More Information*
Linking the Interests of Families and Teachers (LIFT)	J. Mark Eddy, Charles R. Martinez, John Reid	**Elements:** An intervention designed to prevent problem behaviors from developing or progressing by simultaneously influencing parents, teachers, and children to enhance family interactions, increase prosocial and reduce negative peer interactions, and improve the coordination between home and school. **Goal:** To prevent conduct problems such as antisocial behavior, involvement with delinquent peers, and drug/alcohol use among elementary school children ages 6 to 11.	Eddy, J. M., Reid, J. B., & Fetrow, R. A. (2000). An elementary school based prevention program targeting modifiable antecedents of youth delinquency and violence: Linking the interests of families and teachers (LIFT). *Journal of Emotional and Behavioral Disorders, 8*, 165–176.
PENN Prevention Program	Clare Roberts, Robert Kane, Helen Thomson, Brian Bishop, Bret Hart	**Elements:** A cognitive behavioral intervention delivered in group settings that meet after school for one-and-a-half-hour sessions over a 12-week period. Groups consist of in-session instruction and weekly homework assignments. Topics include a cognitive component and a problem-solving/coping component. **Goal:** To reduce depression and anxiety in school-aged youth.	Kane, R., Thomson, T., Roberts, C., Bishop, B. (2003). The prevention of depressive symptoms in rural school children: A randomized controlled trial. *Journal of Consulting and Clinical Psychology, 71*(3). 622–628.
CASASTART	Joseph A. Califano	**Elements:** Offers children a safe place and support outside regular school hours to get the tools they need to succeed. All programs are composed of eight core services: social support, family services, education services (such as tutoring/homework assistance), out-of-school/summer activities, mentoring, morale-building incentives, community policing, and juvenile justice intervention. **Goal:** To develop partnerships among social and health service agencies, schools, and law enforcement to meet the needs of the youth and their families; prevent substance abuse and violence; reduce drug sales and related crime; improve grades and attendance; improve relationships between youth and their families; cultivate family involvement with schools and social service agencies..	http://casastart.org/

placements. The Parents and Peers as Leaders in School (PALS) approach offers an innovative, ecological model guiding school-based mental health care, and it is a potential resource for youth in out-of-home placements. PALS, developed by Atkins, McKay, Abdul-Adil, et al. at the University of Illinois at Chicago, is intended to provide individualized, flexible, and coordinated mental health services for ethnically diverse youth within their school settings. It targets children and adolescents who might not be successfully involved in care because of a shortage of providers, stigma associated with receipt of care, or lack of access to culturally relevant interventions or mobility. For children in out-of-home placements, these barriers to mental health care abound. Therefore, there is an excellent opportunity for goodness-of-fit between the PALS school-based service delivery model and the needs of children in out-of-home placement.

Premises of the PALS Service Delivery Model

The PALS model proposes that empirically based strategies, including multi systemic therapy, are available to reduce child mental health difficulties across the multiple ecologies of schools: at the school level (e.g., providing appropriate and engaging classroom activities), at the peer level (e.g., providing appropriate teacher and peer models for classroom activities), at the adult caregiver level (e.g., involving adult caregivers in the child's educational and behavioral goals at school), and at the child level (e.g., social skills). For more information on these empirically based strategies, see Atkins et al. (2003a, 2003b, 2006). The PALS model is flexible and individualized by acknowledging that contexts for child mental health will differ across children and by providing services specific to those contexts. This flexibility is particularly relevant to children in out-of-home placements because their needs will vary according to their history and current placement status.

Goals of PALS

PALS seeks to improve all children's learning experiences by:

1. helping children manage their behavior at school and at home,
2. supporting children in the classroom,
3. supporting schools in planning for children's long-term needs,
4. supporting teachers in promoting positive classroom behavior and improving learning within their classroom,
5. increasing adult caregiver involvement in the child's education,
6. assisting adult caregivers in developing necessary resources for children to succeed at school,
7. offering practical ideas to adult caregivers on how to manage the child's needs,
8. supporting adult caregivers in linking to community resources, and
9. supporting adult caregiver and teacher collaboration to improve classroom behavior and learning.

Because children spend the vast majority of their time in school, coordination between schools and care providers boost the chances that the needs of children in out-of-home placements will be attended to in a systematic and synchronized way.

PALS Systematic Assessment

A key feature of the PALS model is to identify settings in which mental health issues emerge for the child throughout the school day. Once these settings have been identified, they are targeted using a social learning theory perspective. Social learning theory guides social works to focus on:

- the degree to which students are supervised or *monitored,*
- the extent to which students are *motivated* to behave appropriately, and
- the extent to which culturally relevant prosocial alternatives and social support are *modeled* by peers and adults.

The goal of PALS is to identify the level at which social learning principles are applicable and the degree to which factors within the school environment can be modified. For children in out-of-home placements, social learning theory provides a platform for transferable skills that they can apply within and outside the school environment.

Establishing Collaborative Working Relationships

The PALS model emphasizes the need for systematic assessment of child mental health difficulties and identifies factors that contribute to these at school and in the after-school environment. The model also specifies the need to involve teachers and adult caregivers in the systematic assessment of intervention needs. As previously noted, the goal of this assessment is to target problems and potential solutions using a social learning model approach (modeling, motivation, and monitoring). The PALS social worker brings to this collaboration a range of empirically validated interventions. Teachers and adult caregivers bring the practical realities of schools and foster families and/or residential treatment environments. It is this collaborative group that develops a menu of options specific to each child and his or her classroom's needs with the goal of intervening at multiple levels of the school ecology simultaneously (e.g., increasing student motivation, increasing teacher monitoring) and at the family/residential context (e.g., availability of homework help after school, increasing foster adult caregiver involvement in school supportive activities). However, the single most important theme in PALS is that instead of targeting individual children, PALS offers services that affect the *whole* classroom and extend to contexts after school. PALS aims to increase positive attitudes and behaviors among *all* children in a classroom and give all children the opportunity for academic and social success. It is the premise of the PALS model that every teacher, classroom, and out-of-home placement has unique strengths and needs that could be overlooked by focusing on individual children. Potentially, focusing on the entire classroom creates a supportive environment for the foster child rather than further stigmatizing him or her via removal from class for individual sessions.

Steps in Conducting PALS Assessments

Foster Family Assessments

Once a child has been referred to PALS, it is necessary to complete two levels of assessments. The first level is a culturally based family/environmental assessment. Because the child is currently in foster care, it is necessary to speak directly to the foster care agency representing the child. The agency should be able to offer information about the child's social, emotional, and family history, including any auxiliary services the child may be receiving from the agency (e.g., supervised visits with the birth family, tutoring, medical care). The foster care agency will have to supply the worker with written consent to interview the child because it serves as the child's legal guardian.

After the worker receives consent to assess the child, he or she should proceed by contacting the foster family or residential facility staff to explain the PALS program and to request a meeting with them. Additionally, we advise that the worker make a visit to the foster or group home to assess the environment in which the child currently lives. Because children who have been removed from their biological family have had major disruptions in their lives, the PALS social worker should pay attention to elements of the environment that may contribute to further life disruptions, including poor supervision, chaotic daily schedules, and adult caregivers unable to know what is occurring while the child is out of the home. The environmental assessment allows the PALS team to identify and address situations in the foster child's life that may contribute to academic and social difficulties.

Classroom Assessment

The next step in implementing PALS involves assessing the classroom of the foster child. Because PALS will be implemented for the entire class, it is important to determine how that class is currently operating. Below are some key assumptions to remember when visiting classrooms.

- Every classroom has strengths and needs; identification of needs without considering strengths provides a distorted view of the classroom.
- The team will always demonstrate respect for the teachers' roles and responsibilities and appreciation for the teachers' knowledge and ability to manage the classroom.
- Assessment is ongoing and continuous; it starts from the moment the team begins to meet and continues throughout the team's time together.

Initially, the assessment can be "informal," which involves the PALS social worker or counselor acting as a *participant observer* in the classroom. Formal assessment does not differ from the steps outlined above, but more specific information is gathered:

- times of day that are especially difficult and times of day when things tend to run smoothly
- activities of the day that are especially difficult and those that run smoothly
- student's activities during these times/activities
- teacher's activities and responsibilities during these times/activities
- other adults who may be present during these times/activities
- whether or not things ever run differently, and if they do, what is happening during those atypical times

A comprehensive assessment creates the basis for developing an intervention plan that best addresses the multiple needs of the child in out-of-home placement. The assessment of the classroom allows the PALS team to determine times and situations where intervention can occur on behalf of the foster child to create a supportive environment. This supportive environment is thought to serve as a corrective experience for children who may have rarely experienced such support.

PALS Intervention

Once the assessments have been completed and appropriate goals have been established for the child, intervention can begin. At this stage there will be two levels of intervention—one with the adult caregivers and one within the classroom.

Intervention With the Adult Caregiver

PALS adult caregiver goals are hierarchical. In other words, PALS focuses first on the primary goal, adult caregiver involvement in the child's education, then the second goal, increasing adult caregivers' social support. Finally, the third goal is to assist adult caregivers in building and developing their skills to care for children. These adult caregiver goals were developed with the belief that if adult caregivers are more involved in their child's education, feel supported, and have skills, they will be better able to support the child's learning and mental health. Below are two lists, one for foster parents and one for group home workers, that can be provided to help them develop their involvement skills.

Ways Foster Parents Can Support a Positive Learning Environment

- Ask the child what happened at school that day, and listen to the response.
- Always be respectful of the child's teacher in the child's presence.
- Meet with the teacher if the child is having behavior problems to discuss appropriate consequences at home and in school.
- Respond promptly to notes and phone calls from school.
- Attend adult caregiver/teacher conferences, report card pickup day, and as many other school events as possible.
- Request meetings with teachers to discuss the child's progress, especially when problems are not occurring.

Ways for Group Home Workers to Support a Child's Education at the Residential Placement

- Supervise homework. Provide a quiet place for the child to work. Turn off the TV, do not talk on the phone unless absolutely necessary, and ask visitors to return another time, if possible.
- Check child's school bag daily for necessary school supplies and homework.
- Give reasonable rewards for good work and good behavior.
- Establish a school–home report.
- Build a positive relationship with the foster child: engage in fun activities with him or her.

This support is vital to ensuring academic and mental health success because the adult caregiver will be a stabilizing force for a child who has experienced major instability throughout his or her life.

Intervention at the Classroom Level

As mentioned previously, the PALS classroom goals are interconnected. PALS goals were developed with the assumption that if the classroom is organized and the students are academically engaged and feel supported, then behavioral problems will decrease, and academic success will increase. Below are some proposed strategies to achieve the PALS classroom goals.

Strategies for Increasing Academic Engagement

- Discuss with the teacher the assumption that students who are engaged academically learn more and have fewer behavioral problems. Teachers are all different, and the goal is not to tell the teacher how to teach. On the other hand, research has demonstrated that children are more academically engaged when lessons are interesting and the teacher's presentation is animated. Encourage teachers to be creative when presenting new information.
- Encourage teachers to give clear instructions (e.g., write them on the board or repeat them several times) and examples to illustrate what should be learned.

Strategies for Improving Classroom Organization

- Review with teachers that a well-organized class can lead to a well-behaved class.
- Encourage teachers to establish rules for in-class and out-of-class behavior and to communicate clear, well-defined consequences for breaking the rules.
- Emphasize to teachers that they need to enforce the rules and stick to the consequences.
- Encourage teachers to review the rules with the class on a regular basis, especially after a violation has occurred.
- Encourage teachers to keep an organized desk and clean classroom. They can provide an example for the children to follow regarding their own desk and books.

Applying Interventions within a Response to Intervention Framework

PALS falls within an RTI approach framework, having common components that support a multistep approach to providing services to struggling students: (1) tiers of intervention for struggling students, (2) a reliance on research-based instruction and interventions, (3) use of problem solving to determine interventions for students, and (4) monitoring of students regularly to determine if they are progressing as they should academically and behaviorally.

Deciding on a classroom intervention is based on the information gathered during the PALS practitioner's classroom observations and the teacher's needs assessment. The PALS school-based professional generates a list of possible interventions that address the classroom needs identified during the assessment phase. Once identified, the interventions are reviewed with the classroom teacher. Thus, each PALS classroom will have its own unique treatment plan. These elements of high-quality instruction, balanced assessment, and collaboration systematically interact within a multilevel system of support to provide the structures to increase success for all students.

Applying Interventions Within Response to Intervention Framework

The RTI network's definition of RTI identifies three tiers that are hallmarks of the approach: (1) high-quality, scientifically based classroom instruction, (2) ongoing student assessment, and (3) intensive interventions and comprehensive evaluation. These three tiers form the basis by which school-based practitioners can adopt best professional practice, insist upon doing what is best and necessary for all students in schools, and rise to the challenge of doing that which is socially just (RTI Action Network, 2011). Table 26.2 details the ways in which PALS facilitates an RTI approach to the early identification and support of students with learning and behavior needs.

Tools and Practice Examples

David is a 10-year-old foster child residing in a low-income urban neighborhood. His mother lost custody of him when he was 5 years old because of her drug addiction. Last year she passed away from a drug overdose. David was placed for a year and a half with a foster family in his neighborhood. However, his mother's sister requested custody of him, and the courts decided kinship foster care was the more appropriate living arrangement. David's aunt decided 6 months later that David was too difficult to control and asked that he be removed from her custody. Over the last 3 years,

Table 26.2

	RTI Tier Definition	*PALS Strategy*	*PALS Example*
Tier I	All students receive high-quality, research-based instruction in the general education classroom.	Evidence-based strategies for increasing academic engagement	Research has demonstrated that children are more academically engaged when lessons are interesting and the teacher's presentation is animated. Encourage teachers to give clear instructions and examples to illustrate what should be learned.
		Evidence-based strategies for improving classroom organization	Support classroom organization Help teachers establish well-defined rules with clear consequences
Tier II	Universal screening and progress monitoring provide information about a student's learning rate and level of achievement, both individually and in comparison with the peer group. These data are then used when determining which students need closer monitoring or intervention.	Foster family assessment	Case assessment from foster agency Assessment from foster family Assessment via direct observation through foster family home visit
		Classroom assessment	Assessment of times of day that are especially difficult and times of day when things tend to run smoothly Assessment of activities of the day that are especially difficult and those that run smoothly Assessment of student's activities during these times/activities Assessment of teacher's activities and responsibilities during these times/activities Assessment of other adults who may be present during these times/activities Assessment of whether or not things ever run differently, and if they do, what is happening during those atypical times
Tier III	Individualized, intensive interventions target the students' skill deficits.	Interventions with the foster family	Foster parent involvement with teacher and daily learning activities Integration of classroom strategies at home Foster parent involvement in ongoing monitoring of student progress
		Interventions in the classroom	Using PALS to choose and implement targeted interventions that are based on the best current evidence to meet the needs of the student Monthly classroom evaluation by PALS team

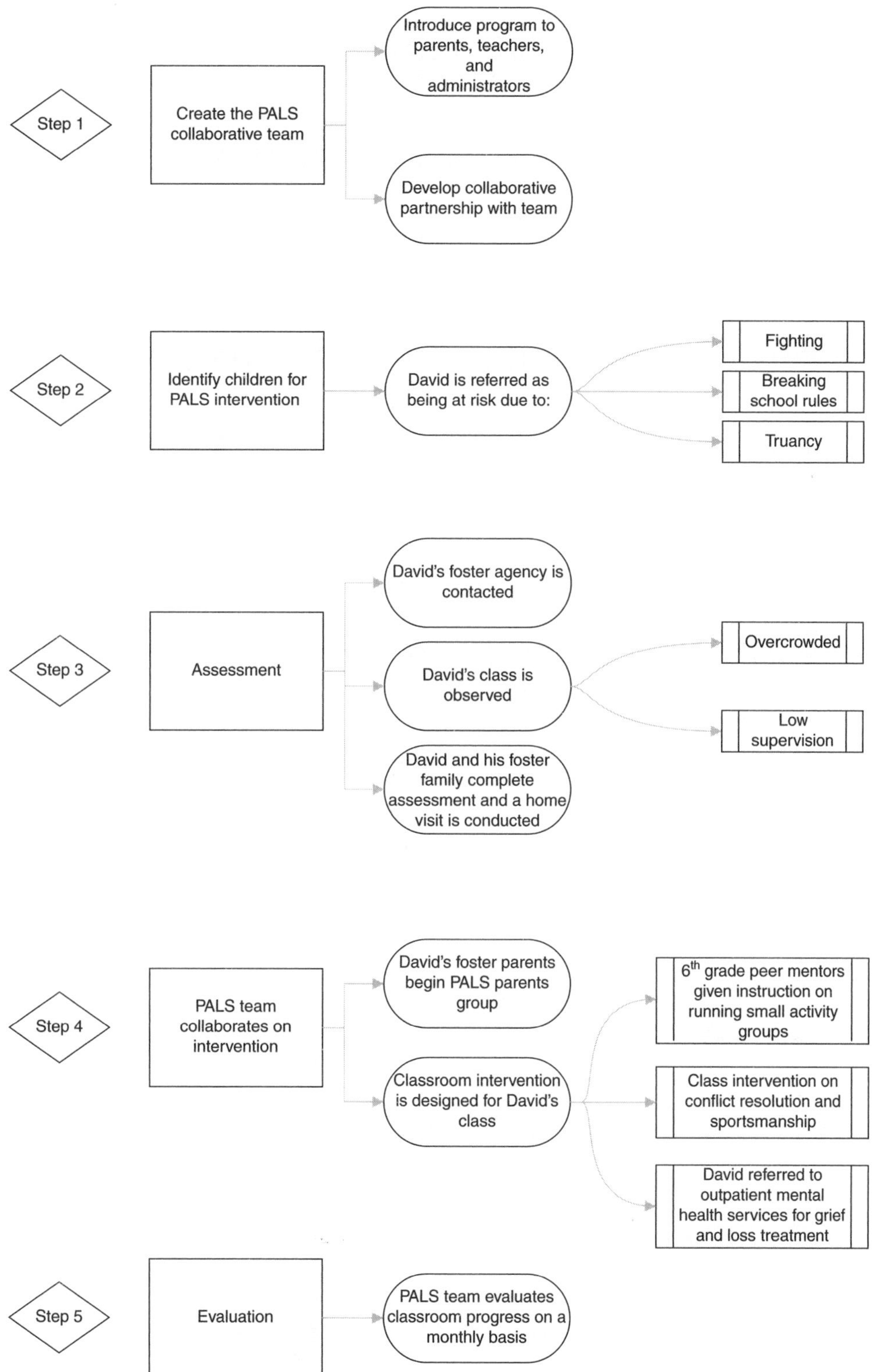

Figure 26.1 PALS Flow Chart

David has been in five different kinship foster homes and lived in four different neighborhoods. He currently lives with his mother's cousin and her three children. He has been skipping school, picking fights in his fifth-grade class, and disobeying school rules.

Figure 26.1 shows the steps for implementing the PALS model.

Key Points to Remember

- Children living in out-of-home placements have historically been affected by high rates of community violence, poverty, and substance abuse; deteriorating support resources; and a serious shortage of mental health services.
- It is important to develop effective mental health services for urban children that attend to these environmental influences.
- To this end, schools offer a unique environment for helping children and families in low income communities.
- Through schools, service providers are able to reach large numbers of traditionally underserved children and to interact with children and adult caregivers.
- The PALS program was developed as an alternative to existing service delivery models in clinics and in schools.
- PALS addresses the limitations of clinic-based consultation and school-based health clinics by (a) working directly with teachers to establish interventions that are tailored to the needs of individual teachers and classrooms and (b) involving adult caregivers in their child's education in an effort to enhance children's learning.
- It is the belief of the PALS program that classrooms have unique strengths to offer support and continued growth for children in out-of-home placements.

Further Learning

Child Welfare League of America: http://www.cwla.org/

Promising Practices Network on Children, Youth, and Families: http://www.promisingpractices.net/

Research Training Center for Children's Mental Health: http://rtckids.fmhi.usf.edu/sbmh/default.cfm

SAMHSA's National Registry of Evidence Based Programs and Practices: http://nrepp.samhsa.gov/Search.aspx

U.S. Department of Health and Human Services, Administration for Children & Families, Children's Bureau: http://www.acf.hhs.gov/programs/cb/

References

Atkins, M. S., Frazier, S. L., Birman, D., Adil, J. A., Jackson, M., Graczyk, P. A. ... McKay, M. M. (2006). School-based mental health services for children living in high poverty urban communities. *Administration and Policy in Mental Health and Mental Health Services Research, 33*(2), 146–159.

Atkins, M. S., Graczyk, P., Frazier, S., & Adil, J. (2003a). School mental health in urban communities. In M. Weist, S. Evans, & N. Lever (Eds.), *School mental health handbook* (pp. 165–178). New York, NY: Kluwer.

Atkins, M., Graczyk, P., Frazier, S., & Adil, J. (2003b). Toward a new model for school-based mental health: Accessible, effective, and sustainable services in urban communities. *School Psychology Review, 12*, 503–514.

August, G. J., Lee, S. S., Bloomquist, M. L., Realmuto, G. M. & Hektner, J. M. (2004). Maintenance effects of an evidence-based preventive innovation for aggressive children living in culturally diverse, urban neighborhoods: The Early Risers effectiveness study. *Journal of Emotional and Behavioral Disorders, 12*(4), 194–205.

Cappella, E., Frazier, S. L., Atkins, M. S., Schoenwald, S. K., & Glisson, C. (2008). Enhancing schools' capacity to support children in poverty: an ecological model of school-based mental health services. *Administration and Policy in Mental Health and Mental Health Services Research, 35*(5), 395–409.

Conduct Problems Prevention Research Group. (2002). Evaluation of the first three years of the Fast Track Prevention Trial with children at high risk for adolescent conduct problems. *Journal of Abnormal Child Psychology, 30*, 19–35.

Cox, M. E., Orme, J. G., & Rhodes, K. W. (2003). Willingness to foster children with emotional or behavioral problems. *Journal of Social Service Research, 29*(4), 23–51.

Eddy, J. M., Reid, J. B., & Fetrow, R. A. (2000). An elementary school based prevention program targeting modifiable antecedents of youth delinquency and violence: Linking the interests of families and teachers (LIFT). *Journal of Emotional and Behavioral Disorders, 8*, 165–176.

Kane, R., Thomson, T., Roberts, C., & Bishop, B. (2003). The prevention of depressive symptoms in rural school children: A randomized controlled trial. *Journal of Consulting and Clinical Psychology, 71*(3), 622–628.

Lynch, F. L., Hornbrook, M., Clarke, G. N., Perrin, N., Polen, M. R., O'Connor, E., & Dickerson, J. (2005). Cost-effectiveness of an intervention to prevent depression in at-risk teens. *Archives of General Psychiatry, 62*(11), 1241–1248.

RTI Action Network. (n.d.). *What is RTI?* Retrieved July 5, 2010, from http://www.rtinetwork.org/learn/what/whatisrti

U.S. Department of Health and Human Services, Administration on Children, Youth, and Families [USDHHSACYF]. (2007). *Child Maltreatment 2005.* Washington, DC: U.S. Government Printing Office.

Webster-Stratton, C., & Reid, M. J. (2010). Adapting The Incredible Years, an evidence-based parenting programme, for families involved in the child welfare system. *Journal of Children's Services, 5*(1), 25–42.

Weisz, J., Sandler, I., Durlak, J., & Anton, B. (2005). Promoting and protecting youth mental health through evidence-based prevention and treatment. *American Psychologist, 60*(6), 628–648.

CHAPTER 27

Connecting School-Based Practices and Juvenile Justice

Katherine L. Montgomery · Karen S. Knox · Albert R. Roberts

Getting Started

School social workers, counselors, and other mental health professionals are involved with many types of early intervention and prevention programs for at-risk children and adolescents, such as programs targeting school retention and truancy problems, drug and alcohol use, teen parenting, gangs, bullying, child abuse, sexual abuse/date rape, and family violence. The most recent report of the National Study of Delinquency Prevention in Schools reports an increase in school-based prevention programs in recent years, particularly in programs emphasizing direct services to students, family, and/or staff; organizational and environmental arrangements; and discipline or safety management activities (National Institute of Justice, 2004). Continued growth and funding for these programs come from national educational funding, juvenile justice mandates, private foundations, and corporate initiatives.

Professionals in the juvenile justice system deal with the same issues these programs address and have seen an increase in the numbers of juveniles who are placed on probation. Data from the Office of Juvenile Justice and Delinquency Prevention (OJJDP) indicate that from 1985 to 2000, there was a 108% increase of adjudicated delinquency cases ordered to formal probation, as compared with a 49% increase in adjudicated delinquency cases ordered to residential placement (OJJDP, 2011). Of the 1.1 million court cases in 2000, 58% received probation, and 14% were placed in an out-of-home placement (OJJDP, 2011). The reality is that these youth on probation are living in their family homes, attending schools, and are likely receiving services from multiple community sources.

The majority of probation cases are property crimes, but from 1985 to 2000, an increase proportionally of crimes against persons (193%), drug/alcohol-related offenses (267%), and violations of public order (214%) were ordered to formal probation (OJJDP, 2011). Even youth who have committed sexual offenses and other serious crimes may be placed on probation; some are monitored by electronic means or are subject to intensive supervision services, and others live in halfway houses or other supervised settings and attend public schools.

Schools are a key locus for prevention and intervention services, not only because children and adolescents spend so much of their time there, but also because it is the primary institution that influences their socialization in behavior, roles, and developmental tasks (Gottfredson et al., 2000). Although there are diverse views and values on schools' roles and activities in socializing our children beyond the educational boundaries, the reality is that schools fill a vital niche in addressing many of the problems faced by children and youth today.

What We Know

Poor academic performance is identified as a significant risk factor for delinquency. An early meta-analysis of longitudinal and experimental studies by Maguin and Loeber (1996) found that poor academic performance is related to the prevalence and onset of delinquency, as well as the escalation in frequency and seriousness of offense. More specifically, the poorer the academic performance, the higher the delinquency, with the odds of delinquency involvement being twice as high for students with poor academic performance than for students with high academic performance (Howell, 2009). The studies in the meta-analysis also show some evidence that poor academic performance is related to early onset of offending (Maguin & Loeber, 1996). More recent research indicates that students in high-poverty, urban schools are more at risk for being involved in the juvenile justice system and having problems with school failure and dropping out (Balfanz, Spiridakis, Neild, & Legters, 2003). The school-to-prison-to-dropout pipeline results in less than 15% of students who graduate from high school once they have re-entered public schools post incarceration (Balfanz, et al., 2003). This study also found that in the year prior to their incarceration, most of these students, who are 80% minority males, fail half or more of their classes and attend school infrequently. This study recommends that schools and juvenile probation work more closely together to identify and offer preventive services to youth involved with both systems to improve academic skills and engagement in schools (Balfanz et al., 2003).

School failure is a stronger predictor of delinquency than other variables such as economic class, racial or ethnic background, or peer group relationships (Siegel, Welsh, & Senna, 2012). Poor academic performance can stem from a variety of factors, such as learning disabilities, below-average IQ, attention-deficit hyperactivity disorder (ADHD), and other cognitive functioning problems. In a study comparing 10 evidence-based model juvenile programs, more than half included data documenting these types of cognitive deficits with their clients (Roberts, 2004). Data from the Texas Youth Commission reveals that 75% of juvenile offenders in the system's programs have IQs below the mean score of 100, and the median reading and math achievement level is fifth or sixth grade, which is 4–5 years behind their peers for the average 16-year-old (Roberts, 2004). Another study showed that youth with learning disabilities who are also involved with the juvenile justice system were not receiving alternative education services prior to probation involvement, and that youth who participated in alternative education programs after involvement with probation did not move further into the juvenile justice system (Atkins, Bullis, & Todis, 2005). Similar findings of high percentages of youthful offenders having learning disabilities have been found in international studies (Chitsabesan et al., 2007). This link between learning disabilities and academic underachievement amongst juvenile offenders appears to be substantiated by research, but there are other factors impacting on school success.

Having to repeat grades and being older than the other students in one's class also has a negative effect and puts students at risk for dropping out, being truant, and bonding weakly to school (Franklin, Kim, & Tripodi, 2006). Other factors such as a lack of family involvement, low motivation for success in school, low educational aspirations, and poor study habits are common (Montgomery, Barczyk, & Thompson, 2011). It is also typical for juvenile offenders to have a history of other school problems and antisocial behaviors, such as poor peer relations, authority problems with teachers and administrators, not following school rules, being suspended and expelled for school infractions, gang affiliation, and drug/alcohol use. The relationship between school discipline and racial disproportion in juvenile justice has been explored in several recent studies (Nicholson-Crotty, Birchmeirer, & Valentine, 2009; Roque & Paternoster, 2011). Both of these studies found that African-American youth receive more disciplinary infractions and out-of-school suspensions that cannot be explained by differences in disruptive or delinquent behaviors. Nicholson-Crotty et al. (2009) found that the association between disproportionate patterns of school discipline and court referrals persists after controlling for other factors such as poverty and urbanization. The results of disproportionate school discipline are disengagement with schools, lack of school achievement, and high dropout rates, which in turn impact on employment options and further involvement with the justice system and incarceration (Roque & Paternoster, 2011).

What We Can Do

Evidence-Based School Prevention and Intervention Programs

Research indicates that early intervention is most effective when the needs of children (early education) and parents (parental training, family strengthening, and parental support) are addressed simultaneously and when programs target persistently disruptive and delinquent children (Loeber & Farrington, 2001). Preschool programs such as Head Start, Nurturing Programs, the Perry

Preschool Project, and Home Instruction for Parents of Preschool Youth are examples of early intervention programs that address multiple needs and problems of at-risk children and families. High-quality, intensive preschool programs show strong support for preventing delinquency by preparing children for elementary school and reducing the chances of early school failure (Siegel et al., 2012; Zieglar & Styfco, 2001).

The school's role in preventing delinquency may involve programs that target the general student body or only certain at-risk students. However, school-based prevention programs usually include the following types of interventions (Ascroft et al., 2004; Gottfredson et al., 2000):

- social competency skills
- behavioral management interventions
- environmental change to increase school and behavior management
- increased bonding and socialization
- recreation or productive activities
- information and psycho education

Behavior management programs target youth who are impulsive, aggressive, or disorderly in conduct and are directed at tardiness, inadequate class preparation and performance, bad behavior, and poor attendance (Gottfredson et al., 2000). Environmental changes address school norms, clarify rules, improve school discipline, decrease classroom disruptions, and improve classroom management and organization. The Program Development Evaluation (PDE) method is a multi-component middle school organizational intervention by school teams composed of teachers, parents, and administrators. PDE demonstrated effectiveness in increasing the clarity and consistency of school rules, student success, school attachment, and staff morale, and in reducing problem behavior (Gottfredson et al., 2000; Howell, 2009).

Bonding can be achieved by increasing rewarding school learning experiences through school mentors, positive role models, field trips, team projects, special interest and support groups, extracurricular activities, culture-specific activities, and programs that, along with other recreation and youth employment programs, provide supervision of youth in after-school hours and promote attachment and a sense of school culture. Information and psychoeducational interventions usually address drug/alcohol/tobacco use, sexual abuse/date rape, family violence, teen parenting, and other criminal or risky behaviors.

Some programs attempt to prevent or reduce delinquency by manipulating factors in the learning environment. The Seattle Social Development Project (SSDP), which began in 1981, is a longitudinal study of youth to evaluate strategies that reduce or prevent delinquency. The study's 800-plus participants, who are now young adults, have been interviewed annually since elementary school.

The results of the SSDP showed effectiveness at promoting school and social functioning for elementary students, and it also indicated effectiveness as an adolescent violence prevention strategy in a follow-up study (Howell, 2009). This project involved multiple components and provided social competence training for children and training for teachers and parents on how to encourage interest in school. The program started in the first grade and continued until the sixth grade with small-group skills training for the children on problem solving, communication, and conflict resolution.

The parent and teacher training focused on how to consistently reward and encourage desirable behavior and appropriately apply negative consequences for undesirable behavior. Other parent training addressed strategies to improve academic performance and information on risk factors for delinquency (Siegel et al., 2012). Six years later, a study of the long-term effects of the SSDP found improved academic achievement and commitment to school, along with reduced misbehavior and violence at school, heavy drinking, and sexual activity among the participants (Hawkins, Catalano, Kosterman, Abbott, & Hill, 1999; Howell, 2009). The Good Behavior Game (GBG) is a unique early school-based intervention that has been studied for approximately half of a century. Its simplistic implementation, flexibility in application, and long history of scientific support make this intervention significant in juvenile delinquency prevention literature. The GBG was originally developed to address disruptive classroom behavior in first-grade students (Tingstrom, Sterling-Turner, & Wilczynski, 2006). Students receiving the intervention within their classroom were divided into two groups, and every time a student did not display the identified behavior, their entire group would receive one mark. The group with the fewest amount of marks (or both groups, if they had fewer than five marks) at the end of the school day received some type of small reward (Barrish, Saunders, & Wolf, 1969). The typical duration of the GBG intervention is approximately one academic year.

Over the past several decades, researchers have reported on the positive impact of the GBG. The GBG has been shown to reduce undesirable classroom behavior as an immediate outcome (e.g., see Barrish, Saunders, & Wolf, 1969; Bostow & Geiger, 1976; Kellam & Anthony, 1998; Salend, Reynolds, & Coyle, 1986). However, several longitudinal studies have indicated a significant impact in risk factors associated with delinquency. Academically, students who received the GBG intervention were more likely to graduate high school, go to college, and have higher scores in math and reading (Bradshaw, Zmuda, Kellam, & Ialongo, 2009). Additionally, the GBG has been found to positively impact externalizing behavior problems, peer relationships (Witvliet, van Lier, Cuijpers, & Koot, 2009), substance use problems, anti-social personality behaviors (Kellam et al., 2008), violent and criminal behavior (Petras et al., 2008), suicidal ideation and attempts (Wilcox et al., 2008), and reduced aggressive behavior (Kellam et al., 1998; Kellam et al., 1999). This fairly simple elementary-age intervention has revealed a substantial impact on subsequent behaviors that place adolescents at risk of becoming delinquent.

In addition to the GBG, there are several effective school-based prevention programs that target change in delinquency risk factor outcomes. Specifically, programs like the Coping Power Program, Families and Schools Together (F.A.S.T.), Keepin' It R.E.A.L., LifeSkills Training, Positive Action, Project Towards No Drug Abuse, Promoting Alternative Thinking Strategies (PAThS), Safe Dates, and Second Step have been shown to impact factors such as substance use, aggression, and anti-social behaviors in rigorous randomized controlled trials. These programs have been identified by the Office of Juvenile Justice and Delinquency Prevention (OJJDP) and National Registry of Evidence-based Programs and Practices (NREPP) as model programs for juvenile delinquency prevention interventions. Some of these programs are discussed further in Chapter 6. For additional information on these interventions, go to http://nrepp.samhsa.gov/and http://www.ojjdp.gov/mpg/.

Evidence-Based Juvenile Justice Treatment Programs

During the past three decades, the federal and state governments have allocated billions of dollars toward addressing juvenile delinquency. A recent change for funding sources has been toward accountability in planning and implementing outcome studies to determine program efficacy and effectiveness. A meta-analysis of 117 studies on treatment programs for noninstitutionalized juvenile offenders reports a 40% reduction on recidivism rates, with recidivism being defined as police contact or arrest. The studies evaluated programs that included counseling services (individual, family, and group), interpersonal skills training, and behavioral modification (Lipsey, Wilson, & Cothern, 2000).

A recent national survey of nine model programs that conducted systematic research with outcome measures including recidivism rates demonstrated more success than traditional institutional programs (Roberts, 2004). The similarities between these and successful school-based programs include the multisystemic focus of intervention, family/parent involvement, and an emphasis on academic achievement, vocational training, core values, behavior modification, positive socialization, family counseling, drug/alcohol counseling, group therapy, and community service. Most of the programs' populations were below grade level and/or below average IQ level and had other school problems such as truancy and disruptive behaviors.

There are three multisystemic interventions that provide a strong evidence-based foundation for intervening in the lives of delinquent youth: Multidimensional Treatment Foster Care (MTFC), Multisystemic Therapy (MST), and Multisystemic Therapy for Youth with Problem Sexual Behaviors (MST-PSB). All of these interventions have been identified as model programs by both NREPP and OJJDP and have been shown to be efficacious with juvenile offenders under the most rigorous research design and randomized controlled trials (RCT). Although these programs are not specifically designed to be school-based interventions, each of them encourages collaboration and change at the school level, so it is important that school practitioners seeking to be involved in change for the student offender be aware of these programs. Additionally, becoming aware of these programs is important because greater amounts of government organizations are mandating the use of evidence-based practices within the school system to target change for the at-risk adolescent.

MTFC is an intensive 6- to 9-month program that involves multiple levels of intervention including work with highly trained foster parents, with the youth's biological parents or aftercare family, and with the youth (SAMHSA, 2009a). Designed to serve youth ages 12–17, MTFC was developed as an alternative to residential treatment for serious and chronic juvenile offenders. A program supervisor carries a small caseload of 10 or fewer youth and oversees the implementation of the intervention through daily phone calls and weekly foster parent group sessions. The program supervisor is also responsible for coordinating skills training, individual therapy, and family therapy with identified therapists. In recent RCTs, youth receiving MTFC have displayed several significantly positive effects: lower levels of delinquency (Chamberlain, Leve, & DeGarmo, 2007; Leve, Chamberlain, & Reid, 2005), criminal referrals (Leve, Chamberlain, & Reid, 2005), and substance use (Smith, Chamberlain, & Eddy, 2010); fewer days in locked settings (Chamberlain et al., 2007; Leve et al., 2005; Leve & Chamberlain, 2007); fewer associations with delinquent peers (Leve & Chamberlain, 2005); higher school attendance and homework completion (Leve & Chamberlain, 2007); and females had fewer pregnancies (Kerr, Leve, & Chamberlain, 2009). For more information on MTFC, visit http://www.mtfc.com/.

MST is another intensive multisystemic program delivered in the natural environment and targets intervention in the juvenile offenders' home, school, and/or community as deemed clinically necessary. Juvenile offenders deemed appropriate for services have had long histories of arrests and are between the ages of 12 and 17. The trained MST therapist carries a small caseload, offers multiple weekly therapy sessions, and is available to the adolescent and family 24 hours a day over the course of four months. Recent RCTs have demonstrated several significant positive effects: lower recidivism rates (Glisson et al., 2010; Schaeffer & Borduin, 2005; Timmons-Mitchell, Bender, Kishna, & Mitchell, 2006), fewer out-of-home placements (Glisson et al., 2010), lower subsequent incarceration rates as adults (Schaeffer & Borduin, 2005), and fewer internalizing and externalizing problems (Timmons-Mitchell et al., 2006). For additional information on MST, see http://mst-services.com.

MST-PSB was developed as a clinical adaptation of MST specifically designed to serve juvenile offenders who committed sexual offenses (SAMHSA, 2009b). Similar to MST, MST-PSB is delivered in the offender's natural environment; however, this program is slightly more intensive. Master's-level trained MST-PSB therapists provide approximately 5 to 7 months of treatment to 3 to 5 adolescents and their families. During the most intense part of the program, youth typically require between 2 to 4 weekly sessions. Although most research has been conducted with adolescent male offenders, this program is designed to be implemented with both males and females. Recent RCTs have reported on the efficacy of this program with statistically significant results: lower rates of recidivism and sexually related problems, fewer externalizing problems (Borduin, Schaeffer, & Heiblum, 2009; Letourneau et al., 2009), lower parent and youth mental health problems, improved family functioning, improved emotional bonding to peers, higher grades (Borduin et al., 2009), lower levels of substance use and fewer out-of-home placements (Letourneau et al., 2009). For more information on MST-PSB, see http://mstpsb.com.

Juvenile Justice Alternative Education Programs

Youth who are expelled or placed on probation attend alternative schools until they are returned to the regular public school system. Typically, an assessment is done after 90 days to determine whether the student will remain in the alternative school. Juvenile Justice Alternative Education Programs (JJAEP) are for juvenile offenders on probation or parole who are unable to attend public school. These programs are funded by the Office of Juvenile Justice and Delinquency Prevention through block grants to states and discretionary grants to local governments and private organizations.

In Florida, the Polk County Public Schools' Juvenile Justice Education Department has programs that target school dropouts, while the juvenile justice programs are only for adjudicated, court-ordered offenders. Both programs work with students who have the following problems: learning disabilities, drug addiction, teen pregnancy, mental health disorders, family crisis, juvenile delinquency, and socialization conduct disorders. Some are dropouts, 30–40% are special education students, and 40–45% are 2 years behind grade level (Polk County Public Schools, 2012). Students are evaluated using the Florida Comprehensive Aptitude Test, student exit tests, and computer gains reports that indicate student improvement of up to two or more grade levels within the length of time in their programs. More than 70% of students who are 16 years of age or older who take the GED pass on their first try (Polk County Public Schools, 2012). Early program evaluations that were reported in the OJJDP's Model Programs Guide found that alternative schools have a positive effect on school performance, attitudes about school, and dropout rates (Cox, 1999; Cox, Davidson, & Bynum, 1995; Kemple & Snipes, 2000).

In Texas, alternative education programs for juvenile offenders were first implemented in 1997, with 26 counties currently mandated to operate JJAEPs, and the majority are managed jointly by juvenile probation and local school districts (Brooke, 2009). Data from the latest program evaluation of the JJAEPs indicates that 76% of JJAEP students are ethnic minority youth (26% African-American and 49% Hispanic, compared to the general public school student percentages of 14% African-American and 43% Hispanic), and 26% of JJAEP students are identified with special education needs (Texas Juvenile Probation Commission, 2004). These percentages reflect the disproportionality issues with minority youth in the juvenile justice system. Students are evaluated using the Texas Assessment of Knowledge and Skills (TAKS) passing rate. These scores have indicated that Hispanic (52%) and African-American (50%) youth are passing at a lower rate in reading than Anglo youth (71%) (Texas Juvenile Probation Commission, 2004).

The JJAEPs have three main models: military-style, therapeutic, and traditional school. Half of the JJAEPs are the traditional school model (51%), with only 11% using the therapeutic model and 35% using the military style. Performance measures indicate that military-style models have a higher TAKS passing rate in reading of 64% than therapeutic models (56%) and traditional school models (52%; Texas Juvenile Probation Commission, 2004). In addition to providing the required educational services, all of the programs provide a variety of other services, including life skills training, substance abuse prevention/intervention, counseling, anger management programs, tutoring, mentoring, parent programs, vocational training, and community service.

Southwest Key is a nonprofit organization that operates four JJAEP programs across Texas. The therapeutic model programs offer counseling, supervision, and transitional services to supplement traditional educational services for the youth. A strengths-based focus is used to engage students in the learning process and promote positive relationships with adult role models. The Denton County Juvenile Probation Department's JJAEP is a military-style model that offers comparable educational and support services as the traditional school and therapeutic models, but also has a behavioral management system that includes drill instructors, military uniforms, physical training, and military-style discipline and level systems cadet, private, private first class, and corporal).

In Texas, the effectiveness of JJAEPs are also assessed on school disciplinary referrals and re-contact rates (subsequent referral to juvenile probation). During the 2006–2007 school year, disciplinary referrals declined by 48% for JJAEP students returning to their regular public schools, and re-contact rates indicate that 71% of JJAEP students did not have a re-contact after 6 months and 56% did not have a re-contact within 1 year (Brooke, 2009).

School-Based Juvenile Probation Officers

Under this model, probation officers are housed in schools rather than the probation department. In addition to working with juveniles on probation, school-based probation officers also intervene with youths who are at risk for delinquency (Howell, 2009). One of the benefits of this model is increased contact between the probation officer and the youth with almost daily contact, rather than once a week or less in more traditional models. Contact can be either formal meetings or more informal interactions, with the goal of developing more substantial relationships and improving communication. Another benefit is access to administrators and teachers for referrals and feedback, and access to school documents such as attendance, grades, and discipline records. School-based probation officers can also

- intervene in crisis situations involving juvenile probation students
- assist schools in handling disruptive behaviors
- coordinate services between schools and other agencies
- coordinate reentry efforts for youth returning from a juvenile justice facility (Stephens & Arnette, 2000)

School-based probation officers perform a variety of functions:

- notifying the school of a student's conditions of probation or parole and any special educational

or therapeutic needs that should be addressed through school programming
- monitoring the attendance, school performance, and behavior of youth on probation or parole or undergoing informal behavioral adjustment
- conducting home visits and coordinating intervention services that must be obtained for students and families from sources outside the school system
- coordinating reentry conferences for students returning to school following placement in a juvenile justice facility
- providing services to minors who are not wards of the state but were referred to probation for a variety of reasons (including minor offenses, school discipline and behavior problems, and family difficulties)
- counseling young people in danger of being expelled due to truancy problems (Stephens & Arnette, 2000)

The Jackson County School-Based Probation Officer Program in Illinois was implemented in 2000 with a federal grant. The program's goals included:

- improved relationships between probation and schools
- improved relationships between probation officers and parents
- more immediate attention to potential violations
- decrease in juvenile offenses (Ashley, 2006)

The program results illustrated that school-based probation officers provided more intensive supervision, helped improve school performance of probationers, and increased collaboration between probation and the schools (Ashley, 2006).

Other benefits of school-based probation officers may be a reduction of school crime and a more positive perspective among youth about probation officers through activities such as mentoring, classroom speaking, and role modeling (Safe and Responsive Schools, n.d.).

Concerns about confidentiality of juvenile justice and student school records are an issue with this type of model, and it can be addressed through appropriate guidelines available through the OJJDP. Office space needs to be arranged to ensure privacy and confidentiality for the juvenile on probation (Safe and Responsive Schools, n.d.). Privacy and confidentiality are difficult to ensure in a school, and efforts to maximize them and minimize potential stigma and negative peer interactions with non-offending youth should be priorities.

Previous research studies suggested that school-based probation officer programs have a positive effect on academic performance, school attendance, school conduct, and recidivism (Metzger, 1997; Griffin, 1999). Torbett, Ricci, Brooks, and Zawacki (2001) conducted a process evaluation in Pennsylvania, where Allentown implemented the first school-based probation officer program. The study involved probation officers, probation chiefs/ supervisors, and school administrators with all three groups reporting high levels of satisfaction with the school-based probation program, including the services the program provides, the effect the program has on the school climate, and the communication that the program facilitates between the schools and the juvenile courts (Torbett et al., 2001). Also, 90% of the probation officers and 79% of the school administrators believed the program is effective in reducing recidivism among probationers. The school-based probation officers' most important duties were setting limits and expectations for probationers and helping them improve school attendance and conduct, as rated by school administrators and school-based probation officers (Torbett et al, 2001).

These results suggest that school-based probation should be considered a promising alternative to increase school and probation success for juvenile offenders. However, a more recent study on a rural school-based probation program found mixed results because of barriers at the micro- and macro-levels (Henderson, Mathias-Humphrey, & McDermott, 2008). At the micro-level, the school-based officers were new to the position and unfamiliar with community resources. Role confusion and turnover were also barriers. At the macro-level, barriers included the lack of a strategic planning model, coordination problems for service delivery, and a weak partnership with the schools. Location was also a barrier, as the probation officers were not housed in the schools due to the distance between schools in the rural area and lack of adequate workforce coverage (Henderson et al., 2008). One recommendation to address this problem would be for programs to develop strategic plans that target the highest-risk schools for locations for school-based officers, rather than trying to cover all of the middle and high schools in the area from an out-of-school location. While some of the early research indicates that these programs show promise, the lack of current empirical research on school-based probation officer programs reflects the need for more program evaluation to determine the effectiveness of and best practices for these programs.

Applying Interventions within a Response to Intervention Framework

If you currently provide services in American public schools, you have probably heard of Response to Intervention (RTI). You also probably have experienced the shortcomings of well-intentioned individualized education plans (IEPs), as many students in your school have been left still needing services. It was out of the necessity to most adequately provide students with effective prevention and intervention services that RTI was created (Brown-Chidsey & Steege, 2010). If you are unfamiliar with RTI, there are two good resources available:

1. Visit the National Center on Response to Intervention at following link: http://www.rti4success.org/.
2. Purchase the *Response to Intervention: Principles and Strategies for Effective Practice (2nd Edition)*, by Rachel Brown-Chidsey and Mark W. Steege.

Delinquency prevention interventions described in this chapter may be helpful resources for school clinicians and social workers who are working within an RTI framework. For example, programs like the Good Behavior Game, LifeSkills Training, Promoting Alternative Thinking Strategies, Positive Action, Safe Dates, and Second Step are all universal programs that can be delivered as a Tier 1 intervention to aid the school in preventing conduct disorder, among other problems. More intense programs, like Coping Cat, Families and Schools Together (F.A.S.T.), and the Project Towards No Drug Abuse (TND), might be relevant evidence-based alternatives for the student in need of Tier 2 or Tier 3 services.

Tools and Practice Examples

John, 14, is on probation for molesting two of his younger cousins. He is an outpatient at a counseling program for adolescent sex offenders. He lives at home with his mother and his 18-year-old sister. His father is in prison for family violence, but his mother continues to have contact with him, and the family visits him at the prison. He is scheduled to be released from prison in 3 months. John has been expelled from five schools and is currently attending a Juvenile Justice Alternative Education Program. He will not be allowed back in the public school system because he has a record of expulsions.

John has a fourth-grade reading level and is behind two grade levels in his other subjects. He has had problems since elementary school with acting out in class and being disruptive. He frequently got suspended or expelled for cursing and talking back to teachers and administrators, being tardy or truant, and fighting with his peers. He consistently receives failing grades, and while he does some of his homework, he also fails to turn in his completed assignments. He has low motivation for school success, and his home environment does not support academic achievement.

John and his family are receiving MTFC family counseling services through the local community mental health center, which has a contract with the county probation office to provide the intensive treatment necessary for John, including in-home visits and counseling services. His mother must participate and attend parent counseling with the adolescent sex offender program. His probation officer meets with John frequently and coordinates his treatment services. He does not have a history of substance abuse, but he must comply with probation rules about random urinalysis tests for drug screening. Treatment outcome evaluations are provided monthly from his sex offender treatment providers and the family counselor, and case staffings are done with the probation officer and the treatment providers on a regular basis.

John is currently having problems at home with his sister as they bicker and fight frequently. He is upset with his mother for visiting his father, and he is worried that she will let him move back home when he gets out of prison. The family is working on these issues in counseling, and he says that things are getting better at home between him and his sister because she got a job and is out of the house more often. Her absence has created a supervision problem, though, because John is not allowed to be unsupervised at home under his sex offender probation guidelines. His probation officer is looking into community service and restitution programs to address this issue.

Since starting at the JJAEP, John's grades and attendance have improved, and he completes his homework assignments and turns them in regularly. He says that the smaller class size and individual attention he receives from his teacher helps him understand the subjects better. He has a mentor from the local college, a student volunteer, helping him with his reading and math assignments. The mentor is one of the few positive male role models with whom John has had continuing contact. This relationship has opened John up to future opportunities, as he and the mentor share many life circumstances, and John sees what successes his mentor has achieved.

John has also been making progress in his sex offender treatment. Being in the group has helped him to be more responsible and to work on his relationships with peers and his family. His communication skills are improving, and he makes better eye contact when speaking to others. He has learned how to be assertive rather than aggressive, and his peers and therapists help give him feedback on how to handle his anger management problems. Though John has made much progress, he will need intensive case services to maintain the improvements he and his family have achieved. Fortunately, he is on probation for at least 2 years, and his probation officer can request extensions every 6 months to ensure continuity of treatment. However, should John commit more offenses or not comply with his probation and treatment guidelines, he can also be reevaluated and placed in a more restrictive setting, such as residential treatment or a correctional facility.

John's case is an example of multiple community-based agencies working with juvenile probation to attempt a less restrictive, rehabilitation-focused case plan for an at-risk youthful offender. Coordination of services, along with strict supervision and probation guidelines, ensures that John is receiving the needed interventions for being successful in school, at home, and on probation. Though he and his family face many issues currently and in the future, it is hoped that he will be able to maintain his progress and ultimately graduate from both probation and high school.

Resources

The following Web sites can be useful resources for information and program referral:

Communities in Schools—Helping Kids Stay in School & Prepare for Life: www.cisnet.org

Center on Juvenile and Criminal Justice: www.cjcj.org

Seattle Social Development Project: http://depts.washington.edu/ssdp/

OJJDP Model Programs Guide: http://www.ojjdp.gov/mpg/

Office of Juvenile Justice and Delinquency Prevention: http://www.ojjdp.gov/

SAMHSA National Registry of Evidence-Based Programs and Practices (NREPP): http://nrepp.samhsa.gov/

Texas Juvenile Probation Commission: www.tjpc.state.tx.us

Key Points to Remember

- *Evidence-based delinquency treatments* are the most effective interventions with delinquents that are not typically delivered in the school setting: MTFC, MST, and MST-PSB.
- *Juvenile Justice Alternative Education Programs* are for juvenile offenders who are on probation or have been paroled and are unable to attend public schools.
- *School-based juvenile probation officers* are housed in schools rather than the probation department. In addition to working with juveniles on probation, school-based probation officers intervene with youths who are at risk for delinquency.
- *School-based prevention programs* are interventions delivered in the classroom that target change with specific risk and protective factors associated with delinquency.

References

Ashley, J. (2006). Jackson County school-based probation program: Lessons learned. *Illinois Criminal Justice Information Authority, Program Evaluation Summary, 4*(1), 1–4. Retrieved from www.icjia.state.il.us/public/index.cfmmetaSection=Forms&metaPage=search

Atkins, T., Bullis, M, & Todis, B. (2005). Converging and diverging service delivery systems in alternative education programs for disabled and non-disabled youth involved in the juvenile justice system. *The Journal of Correctional Education, 56,* 253–285.

Balfanz, R., Spiridakis, K., Neild, R. C, & Legters, N. (2003). High-poverty schools and the juvenile justice system: How neither helps the other and how that could change. *New Directions, 99,* 71–89.

Barrish, H. H., Saunders, M., & Wolf, M. W. (1969). Good behavior game: Effects of individual contingencies for group consequences on disruptive behavior in a classroom. *Journal of Applied Behavior Analysis, 2,* 119–124.

Borduin, C. M., Schaeffer, C. M., & Heiblum, N. (2009). A randomized clinical trial of multisystemic therapy with juvenile sexual offenders: Effects on youth social ecology and criminal activity. *Journal of Consulting and Clinical Psychology,* 77(1), 26–37. doi:10.1037/a0013035

Bostow, D., & Geiger, O. G. (1976). Good Behavior Game: A replication and systematic analysis with a second grade class. *School Applications of Learning Theory, 8,* 18–27.

Bradshaw, C., Zmuda, J., Kellam, S., & Ialongo, N. (2009). Longitudinal impact of two universal preventive interventions in first grade on educational outcomes in high school. Journal of Educational Psychology, *101*(4), 926–937. doi:10.1037/a0016586

Brooke, L. (2009). *Juvenile justice alternative education programs.* Texas Juvenile Probation Commission. Retrieved on June 30, 2011, from www.judiciary.house.gov/hearings/pdf/Brooke090312.pdf

Brown-Chidsey, R., & Steege, M.W. (2010). *Response to intervention: Principles and strategies for effective practice* (2nd ed.). New York: Guilford.

Chamberlain, P., Leve, L. D., & DeGarmo, D. S. (2007). Multidimensional treatment foster care for girls in the juvenile justice system: 2-year follow-up of a randomized clinical trial. *Journal of Consulting and Clinical Psychology, 75*(1), 187–193. doi:10.1037/0022–006X.75.1.187

Chitsabesan, P., Bailey, S., Williams, R., Kroll, L., Kenning, C., & Talbot, L. (2007). Learning disabilities and educational needs of juvenile offenders. *Journal of Children's Services, 2,* 4–17.

Cox, S. (1999). An assessment of an alternative education programs for at-risk delinquent youth. *Journal of Research in Crime and Delinquency, 36,* 323–336.

Cox, S., Davison, W., & Bynum, T. (1995). A meta-analytic assessment of delinquency-related outcomes of alternative education programs. *Crime and Delinquency, 41,* 19–34.

Franklin, C., Kim, J. S., & Tripodi, S. J. (2006). Solution focused, brief therapy interventions for students at-risk to dropout. In C. Franklin, M. B. Harris, & P. Allen-Meares (Eds.), *School services sourcebook.* London, England: Oxford University Press.

Glisson, C., Schoenwald, S. K., Hemmelgarn, A., Green, P., Dukes, D., Armstrong, K. S., & Chapman, J. E. (**2010**). Randomized trial of MST and ARC in a two-level evidence-based treatment implementation strategy. *Journal of Consulting and Clinical Psychology, 78,* **537**–550. doi:10.1037/a0019160.

Gottfredson, G. D., Gottfredson, D. C., Czeh, E. R., Cantor, D., Crosse, S., & Hantman, I. (**2000**). *The national study of delinquency prevention in schools: Final report.* Ellicott City, MD: Gottfredson Associates.

Griffin, P. (1999). *Developing and administering accountability-based sanctions for juveniles* (OJJDP Publication No. 177612). Retrieved from https://www.ncjrs.gov/pdffiles1/ojjdp/177612.pdf.

Hawkins, J. D., Catalano, R. F., Kosterman, R., Abbott, R. D., & Hill, K. G. (1999). Preventing adolescent health-risk behavior by strengthening protection during childhood. *Archives of Pediatrics and Adolescent Medicine, 153,* 226–234.

Henderson, M. L., Mathias-Humphrey, A., & McDermott, M. J. (2008). Barriers to effective program implementation: Rural school-based probation. *Federal Probation, 72,* 28–36.

Howell, J. C. (2009). *Preventing and reducing juvenile delinquency: A comprehensive framework* (2nd ed.) Thousand Oaks, CA: Sage.

Kellam, S., Brown, C., Poduska, J., Ialongo, N., Wang, W., ... & Wilcox, H. C. (2008). Effects of a universal classroom behavior management program in first and second grades on young adult behavioral, psychiatric, and social outcomes. *Drug & Alcohol Dependence, 95,* S5–S28.

Kellam, S., Ling, X., Merisca, R., Brown, C., & Ialongo, N. (1998). The effect of the level of aggression in the first grade classroom on the course and malleability of aggressive behavior into middle school. *Development and Psychopathology, 10*(2), 165–185. doi:10.1017/S0954579498001564

Kellam, S., Ling, X., Merisca, R., Brown, C., & Ialongo, N. (2000). "The effect of the level of aggression in the first grade classroom on the course and malleability of aggressive behavior into middle school": Erratum. *Development and Psychopathology, 12,* 107.

Kemple, J., &. Snipes, J. (2000). *Career academies: Impacts on students' engagement and performance in high school.* San Francisco, CA: Manpower Demonstration Research Corporation.

Kerr, D. R., Leve, L. D., & Chamberlain, P. (2009). Pregnancy rates among juvenile justice girls in two randomized controlled trials of multidimensional treatment foster care. *Journal of Consulting and Clinical Psychology,* 77(3), 588–593. doi: 10.1037/a0015289

Letourneau, E. J., Henggeler, S. W., Borduin, C. M., Schewe, P. A., McCart, M. R., Chapman, J. E., & Saldana, L. (2009). Multisystemic therapy for juvenile sexual offenders: 1-year results from a randomized effectiveness trial. *Journal of Family Psychology, 23,* 89–102. doi:10.1037/a0014352

Leve, L. D., & Chamberlain, P. (2005). Association with delinquent peers: Intervention effects for youth in the juvenile justice system. *Journal of Abnormal Child Psychology, 33,* 339–347. doi:10.1007/s10802–005–3571–7

Leve, L. D., & Chamberlain, P. (2007). A randomized evaluation of multidimensional treatment foster care: Effects on school attendance and homework completion in juvenile justice girls. *Research on Social Work Practice, 17*, 657–663. doi:10.1177/1049731506293971

Leve, L. D., Chamberlain, P., & Reid, J. B. (2005). Intervention outcomes for girls referred from juvenile justice: Effects on delinquency. *Journal of Consulting and Clinical Psychology, 73*(6), 1181–1185. doi:10.1037/0022–006X.73.6.1181

Lipsey, M. W., Wilson, D. B., & Cothern, L. (2000). *Effective interventions for serious and violent juvenile offenders.* Juvenile Justice Bulletin. Washington, DC: Office of Juvenile Justice and Delinquency Prevention.

Loeber, R., & Farrington, D. P. (2001). Executive summary. In R. Loeber & D. P. Farrington (Eds.), *Child delinquents: Development, intervention, and service needs* (pp. xix–xxxi). Thousand Oaks, CA: Sage.

Maguin, E., & Loeber, R. (1996). Academic performance and delinquency. *Crime and Justice, 20*, 145–164.

Metzger, D. (1997). *School-based probation in Pennsylvania.* Philadelphia, PA: University of Pennsylvania, Center for Studies of Addiction.

Montgomery, K. L., Barczyk, A. N., & Thompson, S. J. (2011). Evidence-based practices for juvenile delinquency: Risk and protective factors in treatment implementation. In F. Columbus (Ed.), *Youth violence and juvenile justice: Causes, intervention, and treatment programs* (pp. 35–63). Hauppauge, NY: Nova Publishers.

National Institute of Justice (2003). *Toward safe and orderly schools – The national study of delinquency prevention in schools* (NCJ Publication No. 205005). Retrieved from https://www.ncjrs.gov/pdffiles1/nij/205005.pdf.

Nicholson-Crotty, S., Birchmeirer, Z., & Valentine, D. (2009). Exploring the impact of school discipline on racial disproportion in the juvenile justice system. *Social Science Quarterly, 90*(4), 1003–1018.

Office of Juvenile Justice and Delinquency Prevention. (2009). *In focus: Disproportionate minority contact.* Retrieved on June 30, 2011, from http//ojjdp.ncjrs.gov/dmc/about.html

Office of Juvenile Justice and Delinquency Prevention. (2011). *Model programs guide.* Retrieved from www.ojjdp.gov/mpg/progTypesProbation.aspx

Office of Juvenile Justice and Delinquency Prevention. (2011). *Statistical briefing book.* Retrieved from http://ojjdp.ncjrs.org/ojstatbb/

Petras, H., Kellam, S. G., Brown, C. H., Muthen, B. O., Ialongo, N. S., Poduska, J. M. (2008). Developmental epidemiological courses leading to antisocial personality disorder and violent and criminal behavior: Effects of young adulthood of a universal preventive intervention in first- and second-grade classrooms. *Drug and Alcohol Dependence, 95*, 45–59.

Polk County Public Schools. (n.d.) Alternative education: Department of juvenile justice programs. Retrieved from www.polkfl.net/districtinfo/departments/schoolbased/juvenilejustice/juvenilejustice-programs.htm

Roberts, A. R. (2004). Epilogue: National survey of juvenile offender treatment programs that work. In A. R. Roberts (Ed.), *Juvenile justice sourcebook: Past, present and future* (pp. 537–561). New York, NY: Oxford University Press.

Roque, M., & Paternoster, R. (2011). Understanding the 'school-to-jail-link': The relationship between race and school discipline. *Journal of Criminal Law and Criminology, 101*, 633–666.

Safe and Responsive Schools. (n.d.). *School-based probation officers.* Retrieved from http://www.indiana.edu/~safeschl/school-based_probation_officers.pdf.

Salend, S. J., & Lamb, E. A. (1986). Effectiveness of a group-managed interdependent contingency system. *Learning Disability Quarterly, 9*, 268–273.

SAMHSA. (2009a). *Multidimensional treatment foster care.* Retrieved from http://nrepp.samhsa.gov/ViewIntervention.aspx?id=48

SAMHSA. (2009b). *Multisystemic therapy for youth with problem sexual behaviors.* Retrieved from http://nrepp.samhsa.gov/ViewIntervention.aspx?id=46

Schaeffer, C. M., & Borduin, C. M. (2005). Long-term follow-up to a randomized clinical trial of multisystemic therapy with serious and violent juvenile offenders. *Journal of Consulting and Clinical Psychology, 73*(3), 445–453. doi:10.1037/0022–006X.73.3.445

Siegel, L. J., Welsh, B. C., & Senna, J. J. (2012). *Juvenile delinquency: Theory, practice, and law.* Belmont, CA: Thompson/Wadsworth.

Smith, D. K., Chamberlain, P., & Eddy, J. (2010). Preliminary support for multidimensional treatment foster care in reducing substance use in delinquent boys. *Journal of Child & Adolescent Substance Abuse, 19*(4), 343–358. doi:10.1080/1067828X.2010.511986.

Southwest Key. (2011). *Schools overview.* Retrieved on July 2, 2011, from http://www.swkey.org/schools/

Stephens, R. D., & Arnette, J. L. (2000). *From the courthouse to the schoolhouse: Making successful transitions* (NCJ Publication No. 178900). Retrieved from http://www.ncjrs.gov/html/ojjdp/jjbul2000_02_1/contents.html.

Texas Juvenile Probation Commission. (2004). *Juvenile justice alternative education programs: Performance assessment report.* TJPC Publication Number RPT-OTH-2004–05. Retrieved from www.tjpc.state.tx.us/publications/

Timmons-Mitchell, J., Bender, M. B., Kishna, M. A., & Mitchell, C. C. (2006). An independent effectiveness trial of multisystemic therapy with juvenile justice youth. *Journal of Clinical Child and Adolescent Psychology, 35*, 227–236. doi:10.1207/s15374424jccp3502_6

Tingstrom, D., Sterling-Turner, H., & Wilczynski, S. (2006). The Good Behavior Game: 1969–2002. *Behavior Modification, 30*, 225–253.

Torbett, P., Ricci, R., Brooks, C., & Zawacki, S. (2001). *Evaluation of Pennsylvania's school-based probation program*. Pittsburgh, PA: National Center for Juvenile Justice.

Wilcox, H., Kellam, S., Brown, C., Poduska, J., Ialongo, N., Wang, W., et al. (2008). The impact of two universal randomized first- and second-grade classroom interventions on young adult suicide ideation and attempts. *Drug & Alcohol Dependence, 95*, 60–73.

Witvliet, M., van Lier, P., Cuijpers, P., & Koot, H. (2009). Testing links between childhood positive peer relations and externalizing outcomes through a randomized controlled intervention study. *Journal of Consulting and Clinical Psychology*, 77, 905–915. doi:10.1037/a0014597

Zieglar, E., & Styfco, S. J. (2001). Extended childhood intervention prepares children for school and beyond. *Journal of the American Medical Association, 285*, 2378–2380.

SECTION VI

Improving School Engagement, Attendance, and Dropout Prevention

Dropping out of school is at a national crisis level and students' lack of attendance and engagement are important predictors of this problem. Programs and practices such as alternative schools that are designed to prevent dropout may not all be equally effective. Some students are also more at risk to dropout than others, such as those who demonstrate high risk indicators such as having to parent a child. The chapters in this section provide best practices for increasing student engagement and consequently, preventing school dropout.

CHAPTER 28

Effective Approaches to Increase Student Engagement

Jade Wexler Nicole Pyle

Getting Started

Few would disagree that we have a national crisis on our hands in the area of student disengagement and, ultimately, school dropout. As many as 25% of the nation's students do not graduate high school in four years (Chapman, Laird, & Kewal-Ramani, 2010), and as few as 55% of students with disabilities graduate high school with a standard diploma (Data Accountability Center, 2008). It is also concerning that recent estimates, based on the National Education Longitudinal Study (NELS), suggest that only 75% of African-American and 75% of Hispanic students graduate from high school when progress is tracked longitudinally (Mishel & Roy, 2006). In addition, particular groups of students are at higher risk for dropping out, including males who are of low socioeconomic status, as well as students who are Hispanic, African-American, or Native American (Jimerson, Reschly, & Hess, 2008).

Students who are disengaged are at a heightened risk of dropping out, and students who drop out face extreme consequences, both for the individual and for society (Alliance for Excellent Education, 2007; Belfield & Levin, 2007). Individually, a student who drops out of school may earn approximately \$6,000 to \$9,000 less per year than a high school graduate and approximately \$22,000 to \$33,000 less per year than a college graduate (National Assessment for Educational Progress, 2007). High rates of school dropout can also lead to an economic drain on society due to limited tax revenues for unemployment, as well as criminal activity (Dynarski, Gleason, Rangarajan, & Wood, 1998).

Fortunately, school dropout has become a national focus as recent federal laws, such as the No Child Left Behind Act of 2001, have posed accountability pressure on states by requiring them to incorporate graduation rates in their accountability systems. Because there has been a national emphasis on decreasing dropout rates, many federal, state, and local programs have been adopted to address this pressing issue (Rumberger, 2004). Adopting programs that utilize research-based intervention efforts and provide rigorously evaluated evidence of effectiveness is critical.

What We Know About Student Engagement

Central to the epidemic of school dropout is *student engagement,* which can be examined to understand student behavior and can be addressed by providing targeted, individualized intervention to increase engagement and, ultimately, decrease rates of dropout (Alexander, Entwisle, & Horsey, 1997; Appleton, Christenson, & Furlong, 2008; Finn, 1989). Student engagement, a complex concept that has been defined in various ways over the past 22 years (Appleton et al., 2008), can be thought of as "a concept that requires psychological connections within the academic environment (e.g., positive relationships between adults and students and among peers) in addition to active student behavior (e.g., attendance, participation, effort, pro-social behavior)" (Christenson et al., 2008, p. 1099).

A common misconception is that student engagement is a characteristic inherent only to the student. Instead, we can conceptualize it as a malleable "state of being" that can be influenced by contextual factors such as school, peers, and/or family members (Christenson, Sinclair, Lehr, & Godber, 2001). Therefore, while contextual factors such as a student's home life and socioeconomic status can play a large role in student engagement, a substantial piece of the responsibility of student disengagement and school dropout can be placed on the school and its practices (or lack of practices) that ultimately effect student engagement.

The Four Subtypes of Engagement

We, unfortunately, have a dearth of research in the area of student engagement and dropout prevention due to the fact that the field has conducted relatively few rigorous evaluations, and those that do exist do not necessarily report results of program effectiveness (Rumberger, 2004). We can, however, learn from some recent evaluations of particular programs or elements of programs and case studies. One such program that has been cited on the What Works Clearinghouse (WWC), a Web site developed by the Institute of Education Sciences to report on best practices in education according to rigorous scientific evidence, is *Check and Connect* (Sinclair, Christenson, Evelo, & Hurley, 1998; Sinclair, Christenson, & Thurlow, 2005). *Check and Connect*, originally developed as an intervention model to promote student engagement at school, is cited for positive effects for staying in school and potentially positive effects for progressing in school.

Student engagement is touted as the most critical variable in dropout prevention interventions like *Check and Connect*, and we therefore must take a closer look at the subtypes that help us understand the concept of student engagement. One of the most influential theories of student engagement, Finn's (1989) participation-identification model, describes engagement using subtypes that encompass behavioral and psychological components that focus on students' involvement and participation in the classroom and school and the students' feelings of identification with the school (Reschly & Christenson, 2006). Christenson and Anderson (2002) built on the *Check and Connect* intervention and extended Finn's work to conceptualize engagement as a taxonomy including four engagement subtypes: (1) academic, (2) behavioral, (3) cognitive, and (4) psychological (Appleton et al., 2008; Reschly & Christenson, 2006). Academic (i.e., time spent on homework or involved in class) and behavioral (i.e., following the rules and absence of disruptive behavior) indicators of engagement include observable behaviors, while cognitive (i.e., students' perceptions of the relevance of school as indicated by interest in learning) and psychological (i.e., feelings of identification and belonging) engagement indicators include more internal traits within a student (Reschly & Christenson, 2006; Sinclair, Christenson, Lehr, & Anderson, 2003). Further explanations of each subtype of engagement are defined below:

- academic—the extent to which students are motivated to learn and do well in school, indicated by the amount of time spent on homework, studying, and being attentive and involved during class
- behavioral—entails positive conduct, such as following the rules and adhering to classroom norms, as well as the absence of disruptive behaviors such as skipping school and getting in trouble
- cognitive—reflects students' perceptions of the relevance of schoolwork to future endeavors. It is indicated by their interest in learning, their valuing of school-related goals, and their ability to regulate their performance in the pursuit of those goals
- psychological—refers to feelings of identification or belonging, connection to and support by parents, teachers, and peers

Recognizing Risk Signs

Research has demonstrated that overall student engagement is one of the best predictors of dropping out, and by using the four engagement subtypes listed above, we can identify several risk indicators that can help us identify who may decide to drop out of school. Recognizing risk indicators, however, is complicated due to the fact that dropping out is related to several individual factors inherent to the student, as well as contextual factors such as the family, school, and community (Rumberger, 2004). Although complicated, it is promising that these risk indicators are malleable and, therefore, possible to intervene on. Two of the most powerful indicators (which are also two of the most malleable subtypes of engagement as previously mentioned) on which to intervene are students' *academic* and *behavioral* engagement in school (Allensworth & Easton, 2005; Balfanz, Herzog, & MacIver, 2007; Gleason & Dynarski, 2002).

Academically Disengaged Students

Students who are academically disengaged may demonstrate the following risk indicators:

- Academically, students who demonstrate high rates of *course failures* (specifically in English and math) have a higher chance of being disengaged and ultimately dropping out (Allensworth & Easton, 2005; Balfanz & Herzog, 2005; Balfanz et al., 2007; Neild & Balfanz, 2006; Rumberger, 1995).
- In addition, students who have been *retained* (specifically in grades 1 to 8), even when controlling for demographic backgrounds, are at high risk of dropping out (Goldschmidt & Wang, 1999; Roderick, 1994; Roderick, Nagaoka, Bacon, & Easton, 2000; Rumberger, 1995; Rumberger & Larson, 1998). As more states continue to institute state exit exams, retention continues to become one of the strongest indicators of dropping out.
- Finally, students whose *grades drop significantly at major transition times* (e.g., between eighth and ninth grade) are at a greater risk of dropping out (Roderick, 1993).

Behaviorally Disengaged Students

At-risk indicators of behaviorally disengaged students include the following:

- Behaviorally, students who have high rates of *absenteeism* are at high risk of dropping out. For example, attending school less than 80% of the time, which equates to missing approximately 36 days or more in the year, results in 75% of high school dropout rates (Balfanz et al., 2007).
- *Tardiness* is also a strong indicator of behaviorally disengaged students. Just being tardy more than 10% of the time increases a student's chance for dropping out (Neild & Balfanz, 2006).
- Finally, students with high rates of *behavioral infractions* (i.e., five or more) are at high risk of dropping out (Allensworth & Easton, 2005; Finn, 1989; Gleason & Dynarski, 2002; Goldschmidt & Wang, 1999; Neild & Balfanz, 2006; Rumberger, 2001).

What We Can Do

To prevent school dropout, once students are identified as disengaged and at risk for dropping out, we must intervene based on their individual needs according to the four subtypes of engagement: academic, behavioral, cognitive, and psychological engagement. Increasing student engagement, a malleable factor, will require multicomponent interventions targeting individual (values and attitudes) and/or contextual (school, family, community) factors. Although no small task and often dependent on costly, available resources, there is evidence to suggest that the cost-benefit ratio indicates that interventions designed to enhance engagement are worthy investments (Alliance for Excellent Education, 2007). In addition, because dropping out of school results from a gradual process of disengagement (Balfanz et al., 2007; Finn, 1989), it is possible for educators to intervene in this process to prevent dropout. Focusing most of our resources on the most malleable subtypes of engagement, academic and behavioral, may give educators the "biggest bang for their buck" and is therefore the focus of this chapter. We focus on ways that social workers and educators can implement school-wide and individualized, timely, and effective practices to increase student academic and behavioral engagement.

Linking Engagement to Intervention

Approaching student engagement as a framework composed of four subtypes, with academic and behavioral engagement as the two most malleable factors, provides educators a focus so that they can link engagement to intervention. Before intervening, educators must recognize the risk indicators stated above. Determining the area(s) of disengagement provides the educator with more direction regarding which subtype(s) is most appropriate to target for intervention. Each subtype necessitates a set of practices that can be implemented at the school site level in a school-wide approach or by an individual such as a social worker, teacher, or dropout advisor for a particular student or set of students identified as in need of more individualized intervention.

Although it remains a challenge to be absolutely confident about which interventions are the most effective to implement because many current practices have not been rigorously evaluated and associated with significantly improved outcomes for students at risk of disengaging and dropping out, we have some evidence to suggest promising practices to link students' academic and behavioral disengagement needs to interventions that can be implemented to target the identified risk and ultimately increase student engagement.

Promising dropout prevention practices have recently been summarized in a U.S. Department of Education Institute of Education Sciences (IES) Dropout Prevention Practice Guide (Dynarski et al., 2008). This guide summarizes the evidence we have thus far and provides six recommendations for enhancing school engagement and decreasing rates of dropout. The recommendations are divided into three categories: (a) *diagnostic* processes for identifying student-level and school-wide dropout problems (Recommendation 1); (b) *targeted interventions* for a subset of middle and high school students who are identified as at risk of dropping out (Recommendations 2, 3, and 4); and (c) *school-wide interventions* designed to enhance engagement for all students and prevent dropout more generally (Recommendations 5 and 6).

The following section provides examples of practices that social workers, educators, teachers, counselors, mentors, and dropout prevention advisors can use to respond and intervene when students demonstrate low engagement in school and are ultimately at risk for dropping out. The practices presented are aligned with the IES Practice Guide recommendations (Dynarski et al., 2008) and are also drawn from a dropout prevention program, Project GOAL (Graduation = Opportunities for Advancement and Leadership) (The Meadows Center for Preventing Educational Risk, 2011), which has been rigorously evaluated in one previously conducted two-year randomized controlled trial with eighth- and ninth-grade students in a low-income area in the Southwest and another large-scale, federally funded, randomized controlled trial with 9th and 10th grade students currently being implemented in the same area. For a more thorough explanation of these studies, please visit the Meadows Center for Preventing Educational Risk Dropout Institute Web site (see Table 28.11 in the Further Learning section at the end of this chapter).

Project GOAL is a multiple-component dropout prevention intervention for secondary students at risk of dropping out of school. The program model includes three core elements: (1) checking student data, (2) individual interventions, and (3) group interventions. Project GOAL uses the framework from the evidence-based student engagement program *Check and Connect* (Christenson et al., 2008). Project GOAL advisors routinely *check* student data on dropout risk indicators and *connect* with identified at-risk students, engaging them in school so that they make progress toward graduation. Next, we (1) outline practices that can be implemented as school-wide prevention practices, and then (2) provide guidance on more extensive individualized academic and behavioral intervention practices.

Intervention Practices to Engage Students Academically and Behaviorally

The practices included in this chapter are specific to interventions developed and implemented by the Project GOAL advisor and research team in response to students who became academically or behaviorally disengaged during the course of the Project GOAL implementation. *Please note that a more extensive review of intervention practices with downloadable resources available to assist in the implementation of the practices can be found in the Project GOAL Advisor Response Tool and the Dropout Intervention Implementation Guide (DOPIIG) on the Meadows Center for Preventing Educational Risk Web site; see Table 28.11 in the Further Learning section below.* As outlined in this chapter and in the Response Tool, the intervention practices, focusing on academic and behavioral engagement for the purpose of this chapter, present educators with authentic responses to students who are demonstrating academic and behavioral risk indicators.

School-wide Intervention Practices

There are school-wide prevention and intervention practices that can be embedded in the school culture to encourage student engagement. The following school-wide student engagement intervention practices (see Table 28.1) are actions that school leaders can adopt on a school level in an effort to increase student engagement and prevent student disengagement.

Academic Intervention Practices

An indicator of academic disengagement is low academic achievement; therefore, when a student is academically disengaging, targeting the student's poor academic achievement is a primary intervention practice. Table 28.2 below outlines intervention practices that can be implemented to academically engage students who are in danger of failing.

Students may also academically disengage because they are behind in credits as a result of retention or failed courses. Table 28.3 below outlines intervention practices that can be implemented to academically engage students who are behind in credits.

Behavioral Intervention Practices

There are several ways to link engagement to intervention when considering a student's behavior, as there are numerous applicable practices that can be implemented to target a student's risk-indicator data, such as participation in class, attendance, behavioral infractions, disengagement, and conflicts. When a student is consistently off task or demonstrating poor participation in class or in school in general, interventions must target the reason(s) for the avoidance behavior. Table 28.4 outlines intervention practices that can be implemented to behaviorally engage students and encourage participation in school and classes.

Interventions must focus on a student's pattern of attendance (or lack thereof), including when a student is tardy, skipping, or absent, to address the reason why the student is irregularly attending school. Table 28.5 below provides behavioral student engagement intervention practices for students who are tardy to school or class.

Table 28.1 School-wide Student Engagement Intervention Practices

- Set clear expectations for student conduct, as well as discipline and suspension policies; make sure they are understood by the students and parents and that consequences are clear.
- Inform all parents and students of attendance policies, tardy policies, and consequences at the beginning of each school year. Be sure policies are understood in advance to prevent attendance problems.
- Be consistent with enforcing rules and policies.
- All school personnel should model appropriate behaviors for the student. (Example: Respond to students thoughtfully and calmly. Do not yell or threaten.)

Table 28.2 Academic Student Engagement Intervention Practices for Students in Danger of Failing

- Check the student's grades to determine the reason for low/failing grades. Does the student have missing assignments, low test scores, frequent absences, or difficulty with the content?
- Check with the student's teacher to determine why the student is failing or in danger of failing, or work with the student on ways he/she can appropriately speak with a teacher to determine why the grade is low, thereby teaching the student to advocate for himself/herself directly. Share and/or discuss this information with the student to aid in making plans for improvement.
- Consider observing the student in the problem class to ascertain what behaviors may be affecting the student's academic success. Share the observations with the student and develop interventions (i.e., a time for students to attend academic tutoring or having the student move to the front of the classroom) to ensure appropriate behavior.
- Explicitly discuss with the student the reasons why it is important to pass classes and earn credits. Make connections between earning good grades and credits toward graduation and the student's current goals and success in the future.
- Help the student set monthly goals to improve grades and determine immediate steps to take so that he can be successful in meeting goals.
- Provide the necessary supplies and assist with the organization of the student's work to set up a method of keeping track of assignments.
- Encourage the student to connect with a peer who can provide help with class assignments.
- Teach the student strategies of how and when to ask for help.
- Connect the student with tutoring and/or homework help services available from the school.
- If the student receives special education services, work with the support staff to ensure that the student is receiving necessary accommodations.
- Check the student's grades frequently, giving positive reinforcement for improvements and providing ongoing support.

Table 28.3 Academic Student Engagement Intervention Practices for Students Behind in Credits

- If possible, check with teachers of failed classes and/or the school counselor to determine the reason for the lack of credits (i.e., absences, low test scores, not turning in work). This information can help to support the student in his or her current classes.
- Monitor the student's grades and check with teachers to ensure they are current. Problems in current classes will be a good indicator of why the student is behind in credits.
- Discuss with the student the reasons why it is important to pass classes and earn credits. Make connections between earning good grades and credits toward graduation and the student's current goals and success in the future.
  Support the student in talking with her or his school counselor regarding steps that could be taken to recover credits.
- Discuss with the student the options for credit recovery. Help the student set monthly goals to recover credits and determine immediate steps to meet goals. Does the school offer before- or after-school classes? Is summer school an option? Are there accelerated credit recovery programs available?
- If it is the decision of the student and parent, help the student enroll in an alternative program in order to recover credits and graduate at an accelerated pace.
- If current grades demonstrate a danger of failing, use preventive measures early, as reviewed in Table 28.2.

Table 28.4 Behavioral Student Engagement Intervention Practices for Students Who Demonstrate Poor Participation

- Check with teachers to determine if the student is off task in all classes or just specific classes. Determining the pattern of the behavior will help determine the root of the issue.
- Conduct class observations and report back to the student on behaviors observed, including positive actions and areas of improvement. Determine if the student refuses to accept fault or personal responsibility for low participation/off-task behavior.
- Speak with the student to determine why he or she is off task. Is it due to being distracted by peers, having difficulty with course content, or boredom?
- Meet with the student to remind him or her of the consequences of off-task behavior such as low grades, behavior referrals, or possible retention. Note that consequences of off-task behavior should have been explicitly taught at the beginning of the year in a school-wide and classroom prevention effort.
- Model appropriate behavior by role-playing and thinking aloud to demonstrate how to problem-solve through a given situation. See the Tools and Practice Examples section below. Also, work with teachers to sit the student next to peers who can model appropriate classroom behavior.
- Work with teachers to minimize distractions from peers and consider changing the seating arrangement if the off-task behavior is motivated by distractions from peers.
- Work with the student and his or her teachers to agree on a signal or cue for the teacher to use to remind the student when he/she begins engaging in the inappropriate behavior.
- Teach the student strategies for focusing and staying on task if the off-task behavior is motivated by distractions from peers. (Example: Teach the student self-talk strategies. See the Tools and Practice Examples section below.)
- Discuss off-task behavior with a student's parents. Enlist the parents' help in motivating the student to meet expectations.
- Connect positive behavior in class to something motivating, such as tangible incentives, special privileges, positive phone calls home, etc.
- Model for the student how he or she should seek help from the teacher rather than giving up on class assignments if the off-task behavior is caused by difficulty with course content.
- Work with the teacher to connect the student with tutorials if the off-task behavior is caused by difficulty with course content.
- Work with teachers to connect course content to a student's interest or skill level, particularly if the off-task behavior is caused by boredom. (Example: Assign special essay topics or more challenging assignments.)
- Encourage teachers to give the student a special job to do in the classroom to keep him/her busy during extra time or after completing the daily assignment.
- Consider having the student write notes during class to keep him/her active in learning. Have the student submit class notes for incentive points.
- Conduct progress monitoring by continually observing the student to record off-task or improved behavior and report the observations to the student.
- Provide frequent reinforcement for positive behavior. Set up incentives that encourage students to work toward goals together.
- Implement a self-monitoring strategy to assist the student with tracking his/her behavior in short intervals on a data sheet.
- Inform students of events, clubs, and sports on campus. Encourage attendance and offer incentives for participation.
- Inform parents of events on campus with a newsletter, personal invitation, or phone call and ask for the parents' help in getting the student positively involved in school.
- If the student's low engagement/lack of participation in school is leading to low grades or course failures, see Table 28.2.
- If the student's low engagement/lack of participation in school is leading to absenteeism, see Table 28.7.

Table 28.5 Behavioral Student Engagement Intervention Practices for Students Who Are Tardy

- Examine the student's attendance data to determine if there is a pattern of the tardy problem. Consider observing the student during transition time or walking with the student to class to determine what is distracting the student from getting to class on time.
- Discuss with the student the reasons why it is important to be on time for school and/or class. Make connections between being on time and the student's current goals and success in the future.
- Remind the student and parents of the school's tardy policy and the consequences for excessive tardies. Ask for the parents' input on how you can help the student arrive to school on time.
- After discovering the root of the problem, guide the student through problem-solving steps. Have the student brainstorm potential solutions and decide how he or she will take action to get to school on time. See the Tools and Practice Examples section below.
- Meet with the student to develop a morning schedule if the student is having trouble catching the bus in the morning. What time does the student need to wake up? How long does he/she need to get ready, get belongings together, eat breakfast? Have the student set the schedule with the advisor's and possibly the parents' help.
- Consider developing a plan with the student and parents to set a reasonable bedtime if the student is having trouble waking up in the morning.
- Help the student come up with a plan to limit time spent on distractions and get to class on time.
- Set up a reward system for the student to encourage arriving to school on time.
- Continue progress monitoring by checking student data and checking with teachers regularly to monitor tardies.
- If the student's tardiness to school is leading to low grades or failing classes, see Table 28.2.
- If the student's tardiness to school is leading to behavioral referrals and/or detention, see Table 28.9.

Absences in the form of unexcused class period absences or skipped classes demand interventions that target the reasons for the student missing that particular course. Table 28.6 below provides behavioral student engagement intervention practices for students who behaviorally disengage by skipping class.

A critical indicator that requires immediate and attentive intervention is chronic absenteeism. Students who do not attend school for part of or the entire day are severely disengaging and are at high risk for dropping out. For these behaviorally disengaged students, intervention practices must intensively address the issue of school attendance (see Table 28.7).

Conflicts, both with peers and teachers, can contribute to a student's behavioral disengagement. These disruptive social relationships may be interrelated to a student's poor participation (see Table 28.4) or may result in behavioral infractions (see Table 28.9) or even suspensions (see Table 28.10). For these behaviorally disengaged students, intervention practices may address a wide range of issues to remediate conflicts with peers or teachers (see Table 28.8).

Inappropriate student behavior that results in a behavioral infraction, such as a referral, detention, or suspension, warrants investigation and consideration about why the student is engaging in the identified behavior. Typical consequences for behavioral infractions often remove students from class and possibly from school, which only contributes to absenteeism and may positively reinforce the inappropriate behavior. Targeted intervention practices should be implemented to behaviorally engage students who have behavioral infractions (see Table 28.9).

When a student disengages by displaying inappropriate behavior and is reprimanded by receiving a behavioral infraction, such as an in- or out-of-school suspension, interventions must target the issue of the behavioral disengagement that resulted in the consequence of a suspension, as outlined in Table 28.10. Suspensions are generally the result of a behavior that could have been avoided if preventative measures were in place or targeted interventions were implemented to specifically address the risk indicator. Many ideas in other tables may be applicable to

Table 28.6 Behavioral Student Engagement Intervention Practices for Students Who Are Skipping

While reviewing student data, check which class(es) the student skips and determine if there is a pattern. Consider observing the student during transition time and/or walking the student from the previous class to the one he/she is skipping. Consider approaching the student in the location where he/she skips class (if possible and if known). Work with school administrators to secure the area and remove this option as a place for the student to go when skipping.
Discuss with the student the reasons why it is important to attend each class daily. Make connections between class attendance and the student's current goals and success in the future.
Remind the student and parents of the school's attendance policy and the consequences for skipping class.
After discovering the root of the problem, guide the student through problem-solving steps. Have the student brainstorm potential solutions and decide how he/she will take action to solve the problem. See the Tools and Practice Examples section below. Develop a contract with the student for daily class attendance. Consider if the student lacks motivation or interest in attending class. Make the consequences and rewards for following the contract clear. See the Tools and Practice Examples section below.
Work with the student and others involved if the student is skipping a class due to a conflict with a teacher or peer. Review practices in Table 28.8.
If the student is skipping because of difficulty in course content, seek tutoring for the student and contact the teacher to discuss other ways to get academic help.
Work with the teacher of the class the student is skipping to increase the student's engagement in that class. Review practices in Table 28.4.
If the student's skipping issue is leading to low grades or failing classes, see Table 28.2.
If the student's skipping issue is leading to behavioral referrals and/or detention, see Table 28.9.

prevent suspensions as a consequence of behavioral disengagement.

Applying Interventions within a Response to Intervention Framework

Using a Response to Intervention (RTI) framework as a model to implement intervention practices that target students' academic and behavioral disengagement risk-indicator data has the potential to improve the allocation of resources to the students exhibiting a variety of needs. The same essential components of an RTI framework (i.e., screening, progress monitoring, multi-tiered level of intervention, and data-based decision making) can be applied to interventions targeting student engagement. In fact, there is extensive evidence to support a multi-tiered, intensified intervention model when targeting students' behavior (www.rtinetwork.org), and these same essential components and principles can be implemented in an RTI framework to engage at-risk students.

Accurately screening student data to determine which students are most at risk for dropping out should be a priority for schools. Using student risk-indicator data (i.e., attendance, grades, behavior infractions), schools can target students who may be in need of additional intervention beyond the school-wide Tier 1 interventions being employed (see Table 28.1). Once students have been identified as in need of supplemental intervention based on screening risk-indicator data, we can use this data to determine who may need a targeted level of supplemental intervention (Tier 2) and who may need an even more intensive, individualized level of intervention (Tier 3). A Tier 2 intervention may include a social worker or dropout advisor connecting often with a student and/or having the student participate in group sessions where supplemental support is given regarding student goals and problem-solving issues. A Tier 3 intervention may include the delivery of a similar

Table 28.7 Behavioral Student Engagement Intervention Practices for Students Who Are Chronically Absent

- Discuss with the student the reasons why it is important to attend school daily. Make connections between daily attendance and the student's current goals and success in the future.
- Remind the student and parents of the school's attendance policy, the attendance rules for the school district or state, and the consequences for excessive absences.
- After discovering the root of the problem, guide the student through problem-solving steps. Have the student brainstorm potential solutions and decide how he/she will take action to solve the problem. See the Tools and Practice Examples section below.
- Meet with the student to develop a morning schedule. What time does the student need to wake up? How long does he/she need to get ready, get belongings together, eat breakfast? What time does the student need to leave the house/catch the bus? Have the student set the schedule with the advisor's (and possibly the parents') help. If the student has trouble waking in the morning, consider developing a plan with the student and parents to set a reasonable bedtime.
- Make a plan with parents to eliminate the reinforcer for staying at home (i.e., being able to watch television all day).
- Encourage the student to get involved with extracurricular programs to encourage engagement in school. Review practices in Table 28.4.
- If attendance is an ongoing problem, check the student's attendance daily in the morning and, when absent, call home immediately to determine the reason why the student is not in school that day.
- If the student's absences lead to low grades or failing classes, see Table 28.2.
- If the student's absences lead to behavioral referrals and/or detention, see Table 28.9.

intervention, although students in need of Tier 3 will require more frequent intervention than Tier 2, and should target students' specific needs. Progress-monitoring student data is also essential to identify which students continue to qualify for intervention. Progress-monitoring data can also be used by social workers, dropout advisors, or whoever is implementing the intervention to make intervention-specific diagnostic decisions based on student need.

Tools and Practice Examples

We have referenced several resources that are available for free download as part of the following two documents: the Project GOAL Advisor Response Tool (http://meadowscenter.org/projects/goal/art/) and the Dropout Prevention Intervention Implementation Guide (http://www.meadowscenter.org/institutes/dropout/resources.asp).

We encourage you to refer to these documents for examples of these resources, as well as a multitude of other ideas. Resources that have been referred to in this chapter and can be found on these Web sites include:

- teaching students a sequence of effective problem-solving steps: (1) recognize a problem exists, (2) stop and get ready to think, (3) state the problem clearly, (4) get the facts, (5) brainstorm possible solutions, and (6) pick one and take action
- demonstrating how to use self-talk to de-escalate the situation and problem solve
- implementing academic or behavioral student contracts
- modeling a think-aloud strategy to show a responsible, expected response

Key Points to Remember

- Dropping out of school is the result of a gradual process of disengaging or disconnecting from school both physically and mentally (Balfanz et al., 2007).

Table 28.8 Behavioral Student Engagement Intervention Practices for Students Who Have Conflicts with Peers and Teachers

- Meet one on one with the student to discuss the situation and determine the cause of the conflict.
- Discuss with the student how failure to solve the conflict will affect the student's path in meeting his or her goals.
- Guide the student through problem-solving steps in order to have the student come up with possible solutions. See the Tools and Practice Examples section below.
- Role-play with the student to practice appropriate responses to the situation.
- Arrange for a meeting between the student and teacher or the student and peer to discuss the situation and the plan of action.
- Remove the student from the situation to problem-solve with the student. Guide the student through problem-solving steps. See the Tools and Practice Examples section below.
- For a serious or ongoing conflict, consider setting up a mediation meeting with the help of a school counselor or other support personnel.
- If necessary, see the school counselor about a possible change in the student's schedule if it's in the best interest of the teacher and student.
- Contact parents to explain the conflict and to enlist the parents' support in the student's plan of action.
- For an ongoing conflict, consider developing a behavior-monitoring sheet for the student with help from the teacher or, when appropriate, with input from the student.
- Connect positive behavior in class to something motivating, such as tangible incentives, special privileges, positive phone calls home, etc.
- Develop a social contract to determine the agreed-upon relationship between the student and peer.
- If the conflict with the teacher or peer is leading to behavioral referrals and/or suspensions, see Table 28.10.

- Student engagement, a complex process, is central to the epidemic of school dropout and is a malleable "state of being" that can be influenced by contextual factors such as school, peers, and/or family members. (Alexander et al., 1997; Appleton et al., 2008; Christenson et al., 2001; Finn, 1989).
- Student engagement can be examined to understand student behavior and can be addressed by providing targeted, individualized intervention to increase engagement and, ultimately, decrease rates of dropout (Alexander et al., 1997; Appleton et al., 2008; Finn, 1989).
- Student engagement includes four engagement subtypes: (1) academic, (2) behavioral, (3) cognitive, and (4) psychological (Appleton et al., 2008; Reschly & Christenson, 2006).
- Academic and behavioral indicators of engagement include observable behaviors, while cognitive and psychological engagement indicators include more internal traits within a student (Reschly & Christenson, 2006; Sinclair et al., 2003).
- Social workers and educators can implement individualized, timely, and effective practices to increase student academic and behavioral engagement, the two most malleable factors of engagement.

Further Learning

There are a number of student engagement and dropout prevention Web resources (see Table 28.11) that indicate practices that have shown to be effective with at-risk students with and without disabilities.

Table 28.9 Behavioral Student Engagement Intervention Practices for Students Who Have Infractions

- Check with the teacher, administrator, or staff member involved to determine what incident(s) occurred that led to the behavioral referral or detention.
- Intervene as early as possible after discovering the violation. If possible, speak with the student right after the violation occurs (e.g., as the student is waiting in the discipline office) to help the student calm down or process the event, if necessary, before speaking with an administrator.
- Discuss with the student the reason(s) for the behavioral referral. Listen to the student's point of view and ask questions to ascertain the root cause of the student's action.
- Discuss with the student the reasons why it is important to demonstrate appropriate behavior at school. Make connections between maintaining appropriate behavior and the student's current goals and success in the future.
- Remind the student of the school's rules and be sure the student understands what rule was violated.
- After discovering the root of the problem, guide the student through problem-solving steps. (Example: Have the student practice "self-talk" strategies to calm down when angry, frustrated, or upset.) See the Tools and Practice Examples section below.
- Model and role-play with the student the appropriate way to respond when in the situation in question in the future.
- Continuously model appropriate behaviors for the student. Model the use of the problem-solving steps and expose responsible and appropriate reactions with a think-aloud strategy. See the Tools and Practice Examples section below.
- Teach students to recognize the initial signs of when a problem exists so they can respond thoughtfully before the problem escalates.
- Consider establishing a cue or signal to give the student when he/she starts engaging in inappropriate behavior. Encourage teachers to use the cue or signal to make it consistent among all class periods.
- Provide frequent positive reinforcement for students who demonstrate appropriate behavior.
- Connect with the teacher to make sure he/she is aware of the problem and to ask for specific skills the student may need help with, particularly if the inappropriate behavior is caused by difficulty with course content.
- Model for the student how to seek help from a teacher so he has an alternative to acting inappropriately when seeking attention or help.
- Work with the teacher to connect the student with tutorials.
- If the student is in need of anger-management support, consider working with teachers to allow the student to take a break when he/she gets frustrated, upset, or angry.
- Work with teachers to minimize distractions in class. (Example: Relocate the student's seat to the front row.)
- Work with teachers to provide frequent checks for understanding to keep the student focused and engaged in class.
- Conduct progress monitoring by continuing to observe the student in class and report back to the student on behaviors observed, including positive actions and areas of improvement. If the student refuses to accept personal responsibility for inappropriate behavior, address self-control behavior.
- Ask for frequent updates from teachers and school staff regarding the student's progress. Check in with the student frequently to reinforce progress and to provide support.
- Reinforce an established contract by monitoring progress and allowing the student to monitor his/her own progress.
- If the student's infraction is leading to in- or out-of-school suspensions, review Table 28.10.

Table 28.10 Behavioral Student Engagement Intervention Practices for Students Who Are Suspended

- Check with the teacher, administrator, or staff member involved to determine what happened.
- Remind the student of the school's rules and be sure the student understands what he/she did wrong. Discuss the importance of following the school rules and the consequences for continued violations.
- Work with parents to structure the suspension so that the student has a plan to do something constructive (e.g., complete late or missed assignments) while out of school.
- Check with the teacher or others involved about the student's progress. If the student is making progress, acknowledge the student with verbal praise and/or incentives.
- If the in-school suspension is the result of inappropriate behavior, see Table 28.9.
- If the in-school suspension is a result of a conflict between a peer and teacher, see Table 28.8.

Table 28.11 Student Engagement and Dropout Prevention Web Site Resources

- Center for Research on the Education of Students Placed At Risk (CRESPAR): www.csos.jhu.edu/crespar
- Check and Connect: http://checkandconnect.org/
- Institute of Education Sciences (IES), Dropout Prevention Practice Guide: http://ies.ed.gov/ncee/wwc/pdf/practiceguides/dp_pg_090308.pdf
- National Center for School Engagement: http://www.schoolengagement.org/
- National Center on Secondary Education and Transition (NCSET): www.ncset.org
- National Dropout Prevention Center: www.dropoutprevention.org
- National Dropout Prevention Center for Students with Disabilities: http://www.ndpc-sd.org
- National High School Center: http://www.betterhighschools.org/
- National Secondary Transition Technical Assistance Center: www.nsttac.org
- The Meadows Center for Preventing Educational Risk, Dropout Prevention Intervention Implementation Guide: http://www.meadowscenter.org/institutes/dropout/resources.asp
- The Meadows Center for Preventing Educational Risk, Project GOAL Advisor Response Tool: http://meadowscenter.org/projects/goal/art/
- The Meadows Center for Preventing Educational Risk, The Dropout Institute: http://www.meadowscenter.org/institutes/dropout
- What Works Clearinghouse: http://ies.ed.gov/ncee/wwc/

References

Alexander, K. K., Entwisle, D. R., & Horsey, C. (1997). From first grade forward: Early foundations of high school dropout. *Sociology of Education, 70*, 87–107.

Allensworth, E., & Easton, J. (2005). *The on-track indicator as a predictor of high school graduation*. Chicago, IL: Consortium on Chicago School Research.

Alliance for Excellent Education. (2007). *The high cost of high school dropouts: What the nation pays for inadequate high schools*. Washington, DC: Author.

Appleton, J. J., Christenson, S. L., & Furlong, M. J. (2008). Student engagement with school: Critical conceptual and methodological issues of the construct. *Psychology in the Schools, 45*(5), 369–386. doi:10.1002/pits.20303

Balfanz, R., & Herzog, L. (March, 2005). *Keeping middle grades students on track to graduation: Initial analysis and implications*. Presentation to the second Regional Middle Grades Symposium, Philadelphia, PA.

Balfanz, R., Herzog, L., & MacIver, D. J. (2007). Preventing student disengagement and keeping students on the graduation path in urban middle-grades schools: Early identification and effective interventions. *Educational Psychologist, 42*(4), 223–235.

Belfield, C. R., & Levin, H. M. (Eds.). (2007). *The price we pay: Economic and social consequences of inadequate education*. Washington, DC: Brookings Institution.

Chapman, C., Laird, J., & Kewal-Ramani, A. (2010). *Trends in high school dropout and completion rates in the United States: 1972–2008* (NCES 2011–012). Washington, DC: National Center for Education Statistics, Institute of Education Sciences, U.S.

Department of Education. Retrieved from http://nces.ed.gov/pubsearch

Christenson, S. L., & Anderson, A. R. (2002). Commentary: The centrality of the learning context for students' academic enabler skills. *School Psychology Review, 31*(3), 378–393.

Christenson, S. L., Reschly, A. L., Appleton, J. J., Bernam-Young, S., Spanjers, D. M., & Varro, P. (2008). Best practices in fostering student engagement. In A. Thomas & J. Grimes (Eds.), *Best practices in school psychology V* (pp. 1099–1119). Bethesda, MD: National Association of School Psychologists.

Christenson, S. L., Sinclair, M. F., Lehr, C. A., & Godber, Y. (2001). Promoting successful school completion: Critical conceptual and methodological guidelines. *School Psychology Quarterly, 16*, 468–484.

Data Accountability Center. (2008). *Exiting special education with a diploma during the 2002–2003 through 2006–2007 school years.* Retrieved from www.ideadata.org/docs%5CRankOrderedTables%5Cartbl1_6cs.xls

Dynarski, M., Clarke, L., Cobb, B., Finn, J., Rumberger, R., & Smink, J. (2008). *Dropout prevention: A practice guide* (NCEE 2008–4025). Washington, DC: National Center for Education Evaluation and Regional Assistance, Institute of Education Sciences, U.S. Department of Education. Retrieved from http://ies.ed.gov/ncee/wwc

Dynarski, M., Gleason, P., Rangarajan, A., & Wood, R. (1998). *Impacts of dropout prevention programs.* Princeton, NJ: Mathematica Policy Research.

Finn, J. D. (1989). Withdrawing from school. *Review of Educational Research, 59*, 117– 142.

Gleason, P., & Dynarski, M. (2002). Do we know whom to serve? Issues in using risk factors to identify dropouts. *Journal of Education for Students Placed At Risk,* 7(1), 25–41.

Goldschmidt, P., & Wang, J. (1999). When can schools affect dropout behavior? A longitudinal multilevel analysis. *American Educational Research Journal, 36,* 715–738.

Jimerson, S. R., Reschly, A. L., & Hess, R. S. (2008). Best practices in fostering student engagement. In A. Thomas & J. Grimes (Eds.), *Best practices in school psychology V* (pp. 1099–1119). New York, NY: National Association of School Psychologists.

The Meadows Center for Preventing Educational Risk. (2011). *Dropout prevention intervention implementation guide.* Retrieved from http://www.meadowscenter.org/institutes/dropout/resources.asp

Mishel, L. R., & Roy, J. (2006). *Rethinking high school graduation rates and trends.* Washington, DC: Economic Policy Institute.

National Assessment of Educational Progress. (2007). *The nation's report card: Trial urban district assessment reading 2007* (NCES 2008–455). National Center for Education Statistics, Institute of Education Sciences, U.S. Department of Education, Washington, DC.

Neild, R. C., & Balfanz, R. (2006). An extreme degree of difficulty: The educational demographics of urban neighborhood high schools. *Journal of Education for Students Placed at Risk, 11,* 123–141.

No Child Left Behind Act of 2001, Pub. L. No. 107–110 (2001).

Reschly, A. L., & Christenson, S. L. (2006). Prediction of dropout among students with mild disabilities: A case for the inclusion of student engagement variables. *Remedial and Special Education, 17*, 276–292.

Roderick, M. (1993). *The path to dropping out.* Westport, CT: Auburn House.

Roderick, M. (1994). Grade retention and school dropout: Investigating the association. *American Educational Research Journal, 31*, 729–759.

Roderick, M., Nagaoka, J., Bacon, J., & Easton, J. Q. (2000). *Update: Ending social promotion.* Chicago, IL: Consortium of Chicago School Research.

RTI Network. *Behavior Supports.* Retrieved September 11, 2012, from http://www.rtinetwork.org/

Rumberger, R. W. (1995). Dropping out of middle school: A multilevel analysis of students and schools. *American Educational Research Journal, 32*, 583–625.

Rumberger, R. W. (2001, January). *Why students drop out of school and what can be done.* Paper prepared for the conference, "Dropouts in America: How Severe is the Problem? What Do We Know about Intervention and Prevention?" Harvard University.

Rumberger, R. W. (2004). Why students drop out of school. In G. Orfield (Ed.), *Dropouts in America: Confronting the graduation rate crisis* (pp. 131–155). Cambridge, MA: Harvard Education Press.

Rumberger, R. W., & Larson, K. A. (1998). Student mobility and the increased risk of high school dropout. *American Journal of Education, 107*, 1–35.

Sinclair, M. F., Christenson, S. L., Evelo, D. L., & Hurley, C. M. (1998). Dropout prevention for youth with disabilities: Efficacy of a sustained school engagement procedure. *Exceptional Children, 65*(1), 7–21.

Sinclair, M. F., Christenson, S. L., Lehr, C. A., & Anderson, A. R. (2003). Facilitating student engagement: Lessons learned from Check & Connect longitudinal studies. *California School Psychologist, 8*, 29–41.

Sinclair, M. F., Christenson, S. L., & Thurlow, M. L. (2005). Promoting school completion of urban secondary youth with emotional or behavioral disabilities. *Exceptional Children, 71*(4), 465–482.

CHAPTER 29

Increasing School Attendance

Effective Strategies and Interventions

Johnny S. Kim ■ Calvin L. Streeter

Getting Started

Improving School Attendance Through Multilevel Interventions

Improving student attendance is a major preoccupation for many schools across the country. Though little educational research has focused on the relationship between attendance and student performance, some studies suggest that school attendance and student academic performance are closely associated (Borland & Howsen, 1998). The assumption is that when students are not in school, they cannot learn (Gottfried, 2010). Though this assumption seems plausible, the implied causal ordering of the relationship is not always clear. For example, does school attendance improve academic performance or does academic performance serve as an incentive for successful students to regularly attend school? Whatever the association, it has led many school districts, school administrators, and state governments to spend tremendous resources to carefully monitor, document, and report school attendance data.

Epstein and Sheldon (2002) suggest that improving school attendance is as important as any issue that schools face today. Concern about school attendance may focus on truancy and chronic absenteeism, as when students fail to come to school on any given day. But class cutting, where students come to school to be counted but then selectively skip one or more classes each day, is seen by some a symptom of alienation and disengagement from schools and a serious issue for many urban school districts today (see Fallis & Opotow, 2003; also see chap. 38 for a discussion of dropout prevention using alternative schools and solution-focused therapy). Either way, school attendance is a serious issue and one that requires multilevel strategies to effectively address.

Truancy has been identified as a significant early warning sign that students are headed for potential delinquent activity, social isolation, and educational failure (Baker, Sigmon, & Nugent, 2001; Loeber & Farrington, 2000). Poor attendance means that students are not developing the knowledge and skills needed for later success. In addition, when not in school, many students become involved in risky behaviors such as substance abuse, sexual activity, and other activities that can lead to serious trouble within the legal system (Bell, Rosen, & Dynlacht, 1994); Dryfoos, 1990; Huizinga, Loeber, & Thornberry, 1995; Rohrman, 1993). For many youths, chronic absenteeism is a significant predictor of dropping out of school (Dynarski & Gleason, 1999). Beyond its immediate consequences for students, truancy can have significant long-term implications for youths in terms of their becoming productive members of the community. For decades, research has shown a correlation between poor school attendance and problems later in life, such as criminal activity, incarceration, marital and family problems, trouble securing and maintaining stable employment, and violent behavior (Catalano, Arthur, Hawkins, Berglund, & Olson, 1998; Dryfoos, 1990; Dube & Orpinas, 2009; Robins & Ratcliff, 1978; Snyder & Sickmund, 1995).

Though individual students are often blamed for truancy, school attendance may be seen as an important indicator of how well the school is functioning and the kind of educational environment created within the school. For example, large schools where students are more anonymous often have more attendance problems than small schools where a missing student is more likely to be noticed (Finn & Voelkl, 1993). In addition, students are more likely to skip school when the school environment is perceived to be boring or chaotic, when students don't feel they are being intellectually challenged, or when there are no consequences for being truant.

For schools, the consequences of truancy can be significant as well. Not only is student attendance seen as one indicator of school performance, in most states money is tied directly to student attendance. Because funding formularies often include student attendance, fewer students in the classroom mean fewer resources for academic programs. School administrators and all those involved with schools have a vested interest in getting children to school and keeping them there all day (Sutphen, Ford, & Flaherty, 2010).

Truancy has important consequences for the community, too (Baker et al., 2001). These include a workforce that lacks the basic knowledge and job skills needed to fully participate in the labor market and contribute to the economy. This can result in increased costs of social services and higher rates of poverty. Local businesses are often concerned about direct losses incurred from truants' shoplifting and indirect losses from their hanging out near their businesses and fighting, using drugs and alcohol, and intimidating customers.

Thus truancy has both immediate and far reaching consequences for individual students, families, schools, and communities. Effective interventions must understand the problem from multiple perspectives and address the problem at multiple levels. This is especially the case for poor, minority students in urban neighborhoods (Spencer, 2009).

What We Know

Most of the research literature on low school attendance has focused either on its causes or its relationship to academic performance (Corville-Smith, Ryan, Adams, & Dalicandro, 1998; Lamdin, 2001). Despite the fact that absenteeism is a concern for schools, parents, social workers, and counselors, very little research has been done to examine ways to improve school attendance (Epstein & Sheldon, 2002; Lamdin, 2001). This is especially the case when looking for evidence-based research on absenteeism and school attendance. Recently Sutphen, Ford, and Flaherty (2010) reviewed the research literature on truancy interventions. The authors found only 16 studies to review between the years 1990 and 2007, with only half the studies using group comparison designs. Their review only found 6 studies that produced promising interventions, which highlights the lack of evidence-based truancy programs currently available.

Some research studied schools that offer rewards or monetary incentives to improve school attendance. Sturgeon and Beer (1990) examined 14 years of data from a rural high school in the Midwest to see if an attendance reward of exemption from taking semester tests had decreased absenteeism. They examined the school's student attendance records from 1976 to 1979, when there was no attendance reward policy, and compared them with student attendance records from 1980 to 1989, when the attendance reward policy was in effect. Results showed a statistically significant decrease in the number of absences after the attendance reward was adopted. During the years 1976–1979, the average total absent days was 1750.5, which decreased to 912.5 during the years 1980–1989.

Reid and Bailey-Dempsey (1995) randomly assigned junior high and high school girls with academic or attendance problems to either a program that offered financial incentives for improving school and attendance performance, a program that offered social and educational services to the girls and their families, or to a control group. Both the financial incentive program and case management program modestly improved school attendance over the control group, but similar results were not seen the next year. Though there was no statistically significant difference between the financial and case management programs in terms of school attendance, academic improvements were better for students receiving case management services than for students receiving only financial incentives.

Recently Miller (2002) conducted a study to see if participation in a therapeutic discipline program would improve students' attitudes on attendance, increase attendance, and provide greater insight into solving attendance problems among students at a large suburban high school. Students who were truant were randomly assigned to either the therapeutic discipline program or to a control group. The therapeutic program required students to work through a bibliotherapeutic learning packet and attend a follow-up exit conference with the dean to go over the packet. Traditional methods were used on the control group: threatening students with further disciplinary measures and in-school suspension in which students were required to do schoolwork. Both programs required students to participate in a written exercise to measure insight into ways they could help solve their truancy problems. Results from this study showed students in the therapeutic program increased class attendance, had fewer absences from classes, and listed a greater number of insights into resolving their attendance problems.

What We Can Do

A Multilevel Approach to School Attendance

Across the country, hundreds of thousands of students are absent from schools each day. In order to effectively address attendance problems, school administrators, teachers, and staff must understand the problem from a multilevel perspective. For more detailed description on Response to Intervention (RTI) and the three tiers of interventions, please see below section on applying interventions within an RTI framework. Tier 3 targeted interventions that focus only on individual students may improve attendance in the short term for that one student. But it is unlikely that such interventions will have a widespread effect on attendance across the school. In addition, school attendance must be viewed as everyone's responsibility, not just that of the school's attendance officer. Figure 29.1 emphasizes the fact that although the individual student is at the center of our concern about truancy, an effective response must involve the school, the family, and the community.

School attendance can be influenced by a number of factors specific to the student. These might include drug and alcohol abuse, mental health problems, poor physical health, teen pregnancy and family responsibilities, student employment, and a lack of understanding of the long-term consequences of school failure. Incorporating Tier 2 or 3 interventions such as cognitive behavioral therapy (Ginsburg & Drake, 2002; Harris & Franklin, 2003) for these at-risk groups of students can help to address these influential factors.

Sometimes the school itself is largely responsible for truancy. School factors often include the school climate, such as school size and attitudes of teachers and administrators, lack of flexibility in meeting the needs of students with diverse learning styles and different cultural experiences, inconsistent policies and procedures for dealing with chronic truancy, inconsistent application of those policies, lack of meaningful consequences, a chaotic school culture and/or unsafe school environment, and a curriculum that is perceived as boring, irrelevant, or unchallenging. In these instances, Tier 1 interventions that target the whole school environment, such as the Positive Action Program (Flay, Allred, & Ordway, 2001), are necessary to address school-level factors that influence school attendance.

Family factors that can affect student attendance include domestic violence, alcohol and drug abuse, inadequate parental supervision, poverty and low-wage jobs that require the parents to work long hours, lack of awareness of attendance laws, and parental attitudes toward education and the school. Therefore, school-based family interventions such as Project SAFE (Kumpfer, Alvarado, Tait, & Turner, 2002) are necessary to address family factors that affect attendance.

Communities, too, can influence school attendance. They can hurt attendance when they present few opportunities for young people or lack affordable child care or accessible transportation systems. Communities with high mobility rates and large numbers of single-parent households tend to have high truancy rates. Too, differing cultural attitudes toward education can make a difference in whether a child wants to attend school.

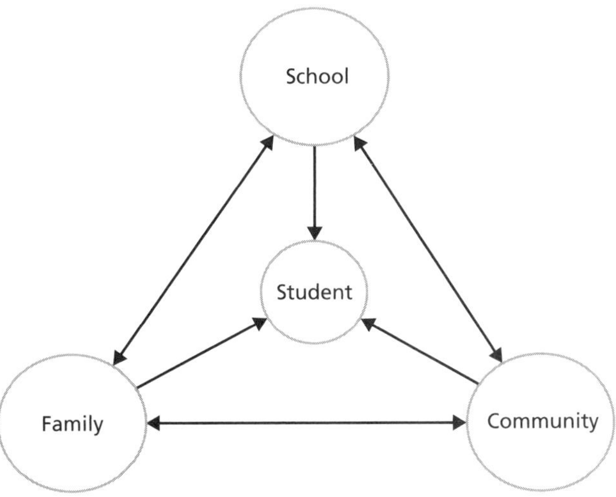

Figure 29.1 Student-Centered Multilevel Approach to School Attendance

Applying Interventions within a Response to Intervention Framework

Individual Student Strategies

Tier 2 or 3 intervention strategies that focus on the individual student tend to focus on psychoeducational interventions and cognitive restructuring (Kearney, 2003). School social workers and other counselors assess reasons a student is absent, focusing on school- and family-related issues. Cognitive and behavioral strategies can help such a student deal with anxiety, stress, and frustrations. Behavioral strategies include relaxation, imagination, and breathing exercises the student can do in class to reduce worry and nervousness (Kearney, 2003). Cognitive strategies include the use of solution-focused and cognitive-behavioral therapy techniques. School social workers and mental health professionals should also focus on increasing students' self-esteem and social skills, since most students who frequently cut school have little self-confidence academically or socially (Corville-Smith et al., 1998). After-school tutoring programs and mentoring programs can be effective strategies for students who avoid coming to school because of academic problems.

Tier 3 targeted intervention strategies that focus on students who don't like school or don't get along with a teacher or with other students are more complex and require a multilevel approach. Perhaps the strategy should focus on the student or family; are, for example, mental health services or drug/alcohol treatment services needed? Or perhaps the focus should be on academics: would these students gain more from school if it incorporated technology into the learning process and integrated vocational and school-to-work materials into the curriculum? Career internships might provide valuable hands-on experience that also further stresses the importance of attending classes. Or perhaps the focus should be on the social aspect of school: is the school one that makes students feel safe, respected, and welcomed? This can be accomplished by knowing students by name and recognizing their successes—no matter how small they may seem (Colorado Foundation for Families and Children, 2004).

This sort of multidisciplinary strategy—addressing truancy from three different sides: student, family, and school—is the only way to make long-term strides in improved school attendance. Though traditional approaches such as punishments and forcing attendance through parental involvement and truancy officers may be effective in the short run, the gains don't last.

Family Strategies

Family involvement is an integral part of reducing school absenteeism, and schools need to collaborate with families in order to improve student attendance (Epstein & Sheldon, 2002). Family problems spill over into the classrooms and can affect student attendance and academic performance. A study by Corville-Smith et al. (1998) found that absentee students, when compared with students who attended school regularly, perceived their families as being less accepting of them, less cohesive, less consistent and effective in discipline, and more conflicted and controlling.

School social workers and other school-based practitioners are in a unique position to help families deal with their child's attendance problem. One way practitioners can assist families is by providing resources for families and students. Family problems such as unsteady employment, lack of reliable transportation, divorce, and family conflict all affect student attendance and performance. Providing resources and connecting families with appropriate social services will help reduce family problems and improve the student's attendance.

Epstein and Sheldon (2002) provides a list of three effective family strategies available to school-based practitioners:

1. *Communicate with families when students are absent.* Collaboration between the school and the family begins with frequent and open talks about the student's attendance problem. An increased effort needs to be made by practitioners to provide parents with information and resources from the school. This can be done by including the parents in school meetings with teachers, administrators, school social workers, and others either at the school or via conference call. Bowen (1999) recommends that practitioners solicit the parents' perceptions of and insights into their child's attendance problem. Bowen also recommends that school staff give parents ideas about activities and techniques they can use at home to improve their child's academic and behavioral problems. Having a specific school contact person for attendance problems can also help increase communication between the school and families if the families have that person's name and phone number (Epstein & Sheldon, 2002). This designated school employee should have resources and strategies available to help parents deal with the attendance problem.

2. *Hold workshops for parents.* School-based practitioners should conduct workshops that deal specifically with attendance problems. These workshops can provide parents with new strategies and tools to improve school attendance. Workshop topics might include reasons for absenteeism, strategies for improving attendance, advice on getting students up and ready for school on time, information on transportation resources, and tips for dealing with resistance. Workshops should include specific information about attendance policies, procedures, and penalties to better inform families.
3. *Visit the home.* Some school social workers, nurses, and others use home visits and phone calls to parents as part of their family-based intervention to increase parental involvement in their child's schooling (Ford & Sutphen, 1996). Making home visits is an effective strategy for reducing rates of chronic absenteeism and is usually used when students have severe attendance problems. Home visits allow school personnel to gain a more ecological perspective on the student and her or his home environment; they can see if family problems may be contributing to the attendance problem. Based on the home visit assessment, practitioners can develop a contract with the family detailing specific goals that need to be met in order to avoid legal sanctions.

School Strategies

Changes in schools' organizational structure, curricula, and culture are needed if attendance problems are to be effectively addressed (Epstein & Sheldon, 2002). Schools should promote an environment where students feel connected to the school and invested in their learning. One way to accomplish this is to improve teacher–student relationships and engage students as active members of the school community. Reducing class sizes, if possible, will increase the interactions between student and teacher and give students the attention they need. Schools can involve students in coming up with Tier 1 universal intervention strategies and programs aimed at reducing absenteeism. By involving students and seeking their perspectives, schools help students feel important and allow their voices to be heard (Fallis & Opotow, 2003).

Some of the more common approaches schools take to address attendance problems involve referring students to school social workers and/or truant officers. This strategy can help improve attendance rates but may not be effective with chronic absenteeism. Providing attendance awards can also be helpful, but they should be given as incentives for improved attendance and not just for perfect attendance. Another strategy is to provide after-school programs that motivate students to attend school in order to participate. These after-school programs can also be educational, covering topics on improving student self-esteem and building social skills because, as we said above, absentee students more often suffer from these deficits.

Model Truancy Prevention Program

Reimer and Dimock (2005) identified several critical components for effective truancy prevention programs:

- Broad-based multidisciplinary collaboration of community agencies such as schools, social services, juvenile courts, and law enforcement.
- Family involvement that values parents "for their advice, experience, and expertise in the community, as clients of our public systems of care, and as experts in the lives of their children."
- Comprehensive approach that addresses all of the factors that affect truancy, including transportation, mental health issues, academic issues, and school climate.
- combine meaningful sanctions for truancy and appropriate incentives for attendance to promote pro-school attitudes and change the behavior of student
- create a supportive context for learning that includes organizations, community cultures, and policies
- rigorous evaluation and assessment

The National Center for School Engagement (2007) produced a report of model programs that address truancy, school attendance, and student achievement concerns. Eighteen programs were identified as "Blueprint" Model Programs based on a set of standards of program effectiveness developed by the Center for the Study of the Prevention of Violence at the University of Colorado at Boulder. Table 29.1 provides an overview of 10 of these programs. A detailed description of all programs can be found in the NCSE report (NCSE, 2007). More information on the Blueprint Model Programs is available at the Center for the Study of the Prevention of Violence Web site at http://www.colorado.edu/cspv/blueprints/index.html.

Tools and Practice Examples

Table 29.1 Blueprint Model Programs

Program Name	*Program Summary*	*RTI Level & Minority Sample*	*Effectiveness Ratings*
Behavioral Monitoring and Reinforcement Program	A school-based program targeting middle school students designed to prevent school failure among high-risk adolescents. It strives to reduce school and community delinquency, including school-based problems, unemployment, criminal behavior, and drug and alcohol abuse. The two-year program consists of four components: (1) collecting information about students' actions; (2) providing systematic feedback to students and/or parents; (3) rewarding positive student behaviors; and (4) helping students determine strategies to modify their behavior and thus earn more rewards.	Indicated 42% African-American sample	Promising Rating by CSAP
Career Academy	A school-based program designed to reduce dropout rates as well as improve school performance and career readiness among at-risk high school youth. Organized as a school within a school, students work in small learning communities to integrate academic and vocational curricula to build connections between school and work and provide students with a range of career development and work-based learning opportunities.	Indicated & Targeted Sample info unavailable	Effectiveness Rating by OJJDP Title V
Comer School Development Program	Addresses various aspects of school climate related to the prevention and reduction of violence in the school setting. Three program components include (1) a school planning team involving parents and school staff; (2) a student and staff support team including mental health and child development experts; and (3) a parent involvement program that engages parents in meaningful ways in the life of the school.	Universal 66%–94% African-American sample across 3 studies; one study also had 4% Asian-American & 6% Other ethnic background	Unrated
Positive Action through Holistic Education (PATHE)	Seeks to increase bonding to the school, reduce school disorder, and increase student educational and occupational attainment through broad-based structural changes. Changes might include adopting different disciplinary procedures, management practices, or school activities.	Indicated & Targeted 68%–100% African-American sample	Promising Rating by OJJDP Blueprints & Title V

School Transitional Environment Program (STEP)	Seeks to ease major adolescent life transitions, especially the transition from junior high school to high school. The program focuses on increasing the availability of social support to adolescents experiencing this transition and reducing the complexities involved in making the transition.	Universal 17% non-Caucasian sample	Promising Rating by OJJDP Blueprints & Effective Rating by OJJDP Title V
Taking Charge	A task-centered, cognitive-behavioral, school-based group intervention developed specifically for helping adolescent Mexican-American mothers improve problem-focused coping behavior, social problem-solving skills, and school achievement. The main objective of this 8-week program is to teach skills critical to long-term self-sufficiency of pregnant and parenting teenagers.	Indicated 96% Mexican/ Mexican-American sample	Unrated
Big Brothers Big Sisters of America (BBBSA)	Provides adult support and friendship to youth (aged 6 to 18) from single parent homes. Services are delivered by volunteers who interact regularly with a youth in a one-on-one relationship. Agencies use a case management approach to screen applicants, make and supervise the matches, and close the matches when eligibility requirements are no longer met or either party decides they can no longer participate fully in the relationship.	Indicated 71% African-American, 18% Hispanic, 3% Native American, & 3% other ethnic background sample	Model Rating by OJJDP Blueprints & Exemplary Rating by OJJDP Title V; Effective Rating by CSAP
Girl Power!	Seeks to reduce the incidence of substance abuse and related risk factors while increasing the resiliency skills of girls. The program also aims to increase school bonding and achievement through school-based activities. The program includes prevention efforts and activities at the individual, community, and policy levels.	Universal Sample info unavailable	Unrated
LA's BEST	A comprehensive, community-based after-school program designed to foster a safe environment in which interpersonal skills and self-esteem can be developed. Provides an educational support structure to enhance children's opportunities and supplement and enrich regular educational programming with new educational and recreational activities.	Indicated 74% Hispanic	Unrated

* OJJDP = Office of Juvenile Justice & Delinquency; CSAP = Center for Substance Abuse Prevention

Key Points to Remember

This chapter recognizes the challenges that school administrators, teachers, and families face in trying to improve school attendance. Overall, the highlights of this chapter include:

- Research has shown a correlation between poor school attendance and problems later in life, such as criminal activity, incarceration, marital and family problems, trouble securing and maintaining stable employment, and violent behavior.
- Though the individual student is at the center of our concern about truancy, an effective response must involve the school, the family, and the community.
- Strategies that focus on the individual student include psychoeducational interventions, cognitive restructuring, after-school tutoring programs, and mentoring programs.
- School social workers and others may also need to encourage the use of mental health and drug/alcohol treatment services for either the student or a family member of the student.
- Family interventions include providing resources and connecting families with appropriate social services to help reduce family problems, increasing communication with families when students are absent, holding workshops for parents, and visiting parents at their home.
- Changes in schools' organizational structure, curricula, and culture are needed to address serious attendance problems.

Improving school attendance is a social problem that needs to be addressed from a multilevel approach involving not only the student and the school but also the family and community. It is also not enough just to get students to show up at school by using punitive measures such as truant officers and suspensions. Schools must work to engage the student by creating a school environment that is welcoming and by addressing academic difficulties that may deter the student from attending school.

References

Baker, M. L., Sigmon, J. N. ,& Nugent, M. E. (2001). *Truancy reduction: Keeping students in school*. Washington, DC: U.S. Department of Justice, Office of Justice Programs, Office of Juvenile Justice and Delinquency Prevention.

Bell, A. J., Rosen, L. A., & Dynlacht, D. (1994). Truancy intervention. *Journal of Research and Development in Education, 57*, 203–211.

Borland, M.V., & Howsen, R. M. (1998). Effect of student attendance on performance: Comment on Lamdin. *Journal of Educational Research, 91*, 195–197.

Bowen, N. K. (1999). A role for school social workers in promoting student success through school–family partnerships. *Social Work in Education, 21*, 34–47.

Catalano, F. R., Arthur, M. W., Hawkins, J. D., Berglund, L., & Olson, J. J. (1998). Comprehensive community-and school-based interventions to prevent antisocial behavior. In R. Loeber & D. Farrington (Eds.), *Serious and violent juvenile offenders: Risk factors and successful interventions* (pp. 248–283). Thousand Oaks, CA: Sage.

Colorado Foundation for Families and Children (2004). Ten things a school can do to improve attendance. Retrieved on October 9, 2004, from http://www.truancyprevention.org/pdf/10_ImproveAttendance.pdf

Corville-Smith, J., Ryan, B. A., Adams, G. R., & Dalicandro, T. (1998). Distinguishing absentee students from regular attenders: The combined influence of personal, family, and school factors. *Journal of Youth and Adolescence, 27*(5), 629–637.

Dryfoos, J. G. (1990). *Adolescents at risk: Prevalence and prevention*. New York: Oxford University Press.

Dube, S. R., & Orpinas, P. (2009). Understanding excessive school absenteeism as school refusal behavior. *Children & Schools, 31*, 87–95.

Dynarski, M., & Gleason, P. (1999). *How can we help? Lessons from federal dropout prevention programs*. Princeton, NJ: Mathematica Policy Research.

Epstein, J. L., & Sheldon, S. B. (2002). Present and accounted for: Improving student attendance through family and community involvement. *Journal of Educational Research, 95*(5), 308–318.

Fallis, R. K., & Opotow, S. (2003). Are students failing school or are schools failing students? Class cutting in high school. *Journal of Social Issues, 59*(1), 103–119.

Finn, J. D., & Voelkl, K. E. (1993). School characteristics related to school engagement. *Journal of Negro Education, 62*, 249–268.

Flay, B. R., Allred, C. G., & Ordway, N. (2001). Effects of the Positive Action Program on achievement and discipline: Two matched-control comparisons. *Prevention Science, 2*, 71–89.

Ford, J., & Sutphen, R. D. (1996). Early intervention to improve attendance in elementary school at-risk children: A pilot program. *Social Work in Education, 18*(2), 95–102.

Ginsburg, G. S., & Drake, K. L. (2002). School-based treatment for anxious African-American adolescents: *A controlled pilot study. Journal of the American Academy of Child and Adolescent Psychiatry, 41*, 768–775.

Gottfried, M. A. (2010). Evaluating the relationship between student attendance and achievement in urban elementary and middle schools: An instrumental variables approach. *American Educational Research Journal, 47*, 434–465.

Harris, M. B., & Franklin, C. G. (2003). Effects of a cognitive-behavioral school-based, group intervention with Mexican American pregnant and parenting adolescents. *Social Work Research, 27*, 71–83.

Huizinga, D., Loeber, R., & Thornberry, T. (1995). *Urban delinquency and substance abuse: Initial findings*. Washington, DC:U.S. Department of Justice,Office of Justice Programs, Office of Juvenile Justice and Delinquency Prevention.

Kearney, C. A. (2003). Bridging the gap among professionals who address youths with school absenteeism: Overview and suggestions for consensus. *Professional Psychology: Research and Practice, 34*(1), 57–65.

Kumpfer, K. L., Alvarado, R., Tait, C., & Turner, C. (2002). Effectiveness of school-based family and children's skills training for substance abuse prevention among 6–8-year-old rural children. *Psychology of Addictive Behaviors, 16*, S65–S71.

Lamdin, D. J. (2001). Evidence of student attendance as an independent variable in education production functions. *Journal of Educational Research, 89*(3), 155–162.

Loeber, R., & Farrington, D. (2000). Young children who commit crime: Epidemiology, developmental origins, risk factors, early interventions, and policy implications. *Development and Psychopathology, 12*(4), 737–762.

Miller, D. (2002). Effect of a program of therapeutic discipline on the attitude, attendance, and insight of truant adolescents. *Journal of Experimental Education, 55*(1), 49–53.

National Center for School Engagement. (2007). *Blueprints for violence prevention programs that reduce truancy and/or improve school attendance*. National Center for School Engagement. Retrieved from www.schoolengagement.org.

Reid, W. J., & Bailey-Dempsey, C. (1995). The effects of monetary incentives on school performance. *Families in Society, 76*(6), 331–340.

Reimer, M., & Dimock, K. (2005). *Best practices and model truancy programs*. Clemson, SC: National Dropout Prevention Center/Network, Clemson University.

Robins, L. N., & Ratcliff, K. S. (1978). *Long-range outcomes associated with school truancy*. Washington, DC: Public Health Service.

Rohrman, D. (1993). Combating truancy in our schools—a community effort. *NASSP (National Association of Secondary School Principals) Bulletin, 76*(77), 40–45.

Snyder, H. N., & Sickmund, M. (1995). *Juvenile offenders and victims: A national report*. Washington, DC: U.S. Department of Justice, Office of Justice Programs, Office of Juvenile Justice and Delinquency Prevention.

Spencer, A. M. (2009). School attendance patterns, unmet educational needs, and truancy. *Remedial and Special Education, 30*, 309–319.

Sturgeon, R., & Beer, J. (1990). Attendance reward and absenteeism in high school. *Psychological Reports, 66*(3), 759–762.

Sutphen, R.D., Ford, J.P., & Flaherty, C. (2010). Truancy interventions: A review of the research literature. *Research on Social Work Practice, 20*, 161–171.

CHAPTER 30

Guides for Designing and Establishing Alternative School Programs for Dropout Prevention

Cynthia Franklin Laura Hopson David R. Dupper

Getting Started

This chapter describes the best practices in designing and establishing alternative schools and programs for students who are at risk of dropping out of school as a result of truancy, poor grades, disruptive behavior, pregnancy, repeated suspensions, or expulsions. Following a brief overview of the history of alternative education in the United States and types of alternative education, this chapter discusses those best practices that are common across successful alternative education programs. It also discusses several challenges that may arise in implementing these best practices and provides a series of steps to build a broad base of support for alternative education programs. This is followed by a case illustration that shows how a number of the best practices discussed in this chapter have been used in an alternative school.

Alternative Education in the United States

The modern alternative school movement began in earnest in the 1960s as a response to the failure of traditional schools to address the needs of large groups of students (Kershaw & Blank, 1993; Raywid, 1990, 1994). The mission of these early alternative schools was to reach students who were unsuccessful in traditional school settings or disaffected with schooling and provide them with an opportunity to learn in a different academic setting (Ascher, 1982; Atkins, Allen, & Meredith, n.d.; Gregg, 1998).

Alternative schools in urban areas were primarily focused on engaging students, especially minority youth, who were not succeeding in traditional schools. Suburban alternative schools tended to place an emphasis on introducing innovative methods of instruction. Both of these approaches shared a mission for designing and improving schools and making them more effective for diverse students. Alternative schools continued to evolve to meet needs left unaddressed by traditional public schools. By the 1970s, alternative school programs were large in number and diverse in their missions, and the populations they served included many different types of students. Today's alternative schools may be structured in different ways, such as charter schools, private schools, home schools, or district-run alternative educational programs. Despite the diversity of structures and entities offering alternative schools, most school districts run some type of alternative school program, and many of these programs are developed to handle at-risk student groups, including those students that may be on a trajectory for school dropout (Carver & Tice, 2010).

According to a national survey conducted by the National Center for Education Statistics in 2007–2008, 40% of districts reported having at least one district-administered alternative school. In addition to stand-alone alternative schools, these district-administered alternative education programs include programs housed within a traditional school (37%), programs located within juvenile detention centers (4%), and charter school programs (3%). From a policy perspective, one of the most compelling reasons for alternative education is prevention of academic failure and dropout (Henrich, 2005). Over 645,000 students attend some form of alternative education program for students identified as at risk for academic failure and dropout. Most of these students attend programs administered by school districts. In many cases, students are referred to these alternative education programs because of high-risk behaviors, including possession of weapons or drugs, fighting and disruptive verbal behaviors, academic failure, pregnancy, or mental health needs. Most districts reported that referrals for alternative education programs were based, to a great extent, on referrals from school personnel or teachers. Fewer than half of the school districts reported that referrals were predominantly based on a student's request (41%) or a parent's request (48%). In most cases, students are allowed to return to their regular school.

A Framework for Classifying Alternative Schools

Raywid (1994) discussed three primary types of alternative schools, providing a framework for understanding the range of schools available. It is noted that many schools may include characteristics of different types and may not follow the pure classifications suggested by Raywid; nevertheless, this framework is instructive in understanding different approaches to alternative education. The first type, labeled *Popular Innovations,* aims to use innovative and effective educational practices to create a school that is more conducive to learning. The second type, described as *Last-Chance Programs,* are disciplinary programs that students attend for a brief period of time as an alternative to suspension or expulsion. As a result, these schools may emphasize behavior modification strategies rather than effective educational practices. The third type of schools, labeled *Remedial Focus*, aims to improve the social, emotional, or educational functioning of students, with the intention of returning them to traditional educational settings (Raywid, 1994).

Raywid (1998) further classified alternative education programs by their emphasis on changing the student, the school, or the educational system. The *Last-Chance* and *Remedial Focus* schools aim to change the student. The *Last-Chance* programs may emphasize discipline and have a highly structure environment focused on improving behavior. *Remedial Focus* schools may function more as a sort of therapeutic community that offers intensive academic and social supports to students. Both programs tend to be temporary placements for students, aiming to send students back to their home schools with more of the skills necessary to succeed there. However, research suggests that these schools that seemingly aim to "repair and return" students to their home school typically do not achieve lasting behavior change among students (Henrich, 2005).

In contrast, schools more characteristic of the *Popular Innovations* type reinvent the school environment to promote a positive school climate. They may use a nontraditional curriculum and innovative approaches to evaluation that feature student portfolios, for example. The organizational structure may be less hierarchical than that of a traditional school, with teachers and students playing an active role in decision making. Some communities also use alternative education programs to introduce system-wide change. Initiatives that aim to create small learning communities within schools, or schools-within-schools, are examples that are currently being used to transform larger schools (Raywid, 1998).

As is suggested by Raywid's typology, alternative schools can have both progressive and punitive, disciplinary components, but in recent years these schools increasingly define their mission as intervening with students who have been expelled from their home school and are considered in some way disruptive in their regular home school environment (Franklin & Kelly, 2012). The disciplinary philosophy differs from the original philosophy of the alternative schools movement that was present in the 1960s and 1970s because this movement focused more toward school reform and improving the educational system (Franklin, 1992). This chapter suggests that more progressive schools that focus on improvements in the school environment may be more effective for helping students that are at risk to dropout than the disciplinary approaches.

Educational verses Disciplinary Schools

Over the past decade, public concerns with violence, weapons, and drugs have led to a dramatic shift from an educational purpose to a disciplinary or correctional purpose in alternative education (Gregg, 1998). For example, alternative schools today are often viewed as places where disruptive, deviant, and dysfunctional students are sent "in order to protect and benefit the students who remain in traditional schools" (McGee, 2001, p. 589). Rather than focusing on fixing the educational environment, the focus of today's alternative educational program is often on fixing the student and keeping "problem kids" out of our regular schools and off the street. See Table 30.1 for a comparison of these two opposing models of alternative education in relation to school climate and culture, staffing issues, curriculum and instruction, and entrance and exit criteria.

As seen in Table 30.1, alternative schools with an educational focus ("fix the environment") are student-centered, caring, humane learning environments where personal relationships are emphasized and the curriculum is delivered experientially. These alternative schools are more long-term in nature because they focus on the transition from school to work through vocational training (Atkins et al., n.d.). On the other hand, alternative schools with a disciplinary focus ("fix the child") are highly structured, punitive environments where student compliance is emphasized and behavior modification rather than academics is emphasized. Disciplinary alternative schools and programs are more short-term in nature, and they focus on improving students' behavior and returning them to their home schools (Atkins et al., n.d.). It is important to note that researchers have found that alternative schools that are correctional in nature, focusing on punitive disciplinary policies and practices, "reap no positive long-term gains and may even increase negative outcomes" (Gregg, 1998, p. 3). On the other hand, alternative schools that focus on education rather than punishment work best in improving student behavior and student achievement, and may work better in preventing high school dropout (Kershaw & Blank, 1993; Morley, 1991; Raywid, 1994). Relatedly, research also shows that alternative schools and programs that focus primarily on therapeutic interventions may "temporarily improve student behavior and achievement[,] but results tend to fade if and when students return to home schools" (Gregg, 1998, p. 5). Effective transition services are needed to help students return to their home high schools and continue to progress academically.

What We Know

Rigorous research on alternative schools is small, and only a few RCTs or methodologically strong quasi-experiments exist that examine these programs. One recent review following rigorous criteria, for example, found only 22 studies out of 200 that met criteria for a meta-analysis (Klima, Miller, & Nunlist, (2009). Based on the studies examined, this review concluded that alternative schools are effective approaches that can meet the educational needs of at-risk students. Studies that meet criteria for experimental designs, however, often find that alternative school programs have mixed but positive results for students depending on the outcomes measured and the length of the follow-up investigations (Cox, Davidson, & Bynum, 1995; Dynarski & Wood, 1997; Franklin, Streeter, Kim, & Tripodi, 2007; Kemple & Snipes, 2000). A meta-analysis of 57 alternative school programs found, for example, that alternative schools revealed positive results on a student's school outcomes, views toward school, and self-esteem, but these results tend to diminish after one year (Cox et al., 1995). In another study, Franklin et al. (2007) found that an alternative school for dropout prevention based on the solution-focused brief therapy model had mixed outcomes, demonstrating that students could re-engage with school and earn credits much faster than a public school comparison group of at-risk students, but at the same time, due to multiple challenges and being further behind in credits earned, the students in the alternative school did not graduate as quickly as those in the comparison group.

A follow-up study on the students participating in the alternative school, however, showed that over time the numbers of graduates from the alternative school increased to the point that there were no differences between the alternative school and the public school program. It was also found that over 50% of the alternative school graduates entered post-graduate education. These findings suggest that the alternative school was successful with many high-risk youths who were not progressing toward high school graduation. Additionally, over an extended time the alternative school was able to help youths to accrue the credits they needed to graduate and, further, helped several students go on to post secondary education. It is also important to note that the at-risk students attending the traditional high school programs (who were not as

Table 30.1 Educational Versus Disciplinary Models of Alternative Education

	Educational (fix the educational environment)	*Disciplinary (fix the child)*
Climate	• Challenging, caring, nurturing, supportive • Collaborative • Student-centered • Personal relationships, bonding to faculty and other students • Focus on whole child • High expectations for student achievement, behavior • Student behavior guided by norms	• Controlling • Highly structured, regulated • Student compliance • Student behavior controlled by rules • Focus on behavior • Punitive
Staffing	• Teacher chooses, not assigned • Hiring, seniority waivers may be needed • May be contracted on part-time or as-needed basis to meet graduation, IEP requirements • Teacher assumes multiple roles (teacher, mentor, counselor) • Repertoire of teaching skills, strategies • Caring, humane • Accountable for student success • Collegiality, teamwork • Professional community	• Controlling • Highly structured, regulated • Student compliance • Student behavior controlled by rules • Focus on behavior • Punitive
Curriculum and instruction	• Full instructional program • Integrated curriculum, interdisciplinary projects • Individualized (for learning styles, needs, current achievement levels) • Clear program goals • Experiential, hands-on learning • Vocational, career, community service components • Challenging, engaging, relevant • Structured for early, frequent success • Continuous progress model • Student responsibility for learning • Multidisciplinary: academic, behavioral, social contexts	• Academics not the focus • Provides only basics, no electives • Skill and drill • Lessons may be provided by home school • Behavior modification • Remediation
Entrance, exit criteria	• Students attend by choice • Long-term; students may graduate from program	• Student assigned or given limited options (e.g., alternative school or jail) • Short-term (1 day, rest of semester, rest of year); student returns to host school when time or behavior requirements met • By contract with parent, child • Transition services critical • Collaboration with home school, support system for returning students important

Source: Adapted from Appalachia Educational Laboratory. (1998). *Schools for disruptive students: A questionable alternative?* Policy Briefs Series. Charleston, WV: Author. Reprinted with permission.

far behind in credits needed to gain their diploma) were also able to successfully graduate in less time than those in the alternative school.

Two alternative school programs that have been more extensively researched and examined for their evidence are the Office of Juvenile Justice and Delinquency Prevention (OJJDP) alternative school program knows as *Career Academies* (Kemple & Snipes, 2000; Kemple & Willner, 2008) and the dropout prevention program *High School Redirection* (Dynarski & Wood, 1997). Both of these programs serve as exemplars for the types of outcomes found in alternative schools considering the limitations and current state of the research evidence. The OJJDP reports, for example, that in a "5-year evaluation of the career academy concept (the OJJDP alternative school model) covering nine schools and 1,900 students found that, compared with their counterparts who did not attend, at-risk students enrolled in career academies were 1) one third less likely to drop out of school, 2) more likely to attend school, complete academic and vocational courses, and apply to college, and 3) provided with more opportunities to set goals and reach academic and professional objectives" (Kemple & Snipes, 2000, cited in OJJDP Model Program Review, http://www.ojjdp.gov/mpg/progTypesAlternative.aspx). In a more recent, longer-term, follow-up study on the Career Academies, Kemple and Willner (2008) found positive results as students transitioned to adulthood, including favorable labor market outcomes The Institute of Education Sciences has further reviewed three studies that met criteria for more rigorous experimental designs for the dropout prevention, alternative school program High School Redirection. High School Redirection showed positive results on staying in school, potentially positive results on progressing in school, and no results on completing school (What Works Clearinghouse, http://ies.ed.gov/ncee/wwc/reports/dropout/hs_redirect/).

When considering all of these studies, the evidence appears to suggest that alternative schools may be an effective way to help at-risk students to progress in high school; however, they may not serve as a panacea for the successful graduation of every student. Even though the research has some limitations and the studies are small in number, the current evidence concludes that alternative schools may be worth the investment when it comes to improving student achievement and matriculation toward high school graduation. Some studies also suggest that these schools will improve rates of high school graduation and future work force outcomes.

Empirically Supported Characteristics of Successful Alternative Education Programs

Reimer and Cash (2003) have analyzed a number of empirical studies by researchers in alternative education (Kadel, 1994; Kellmayer, 1995; Public Schools of North Carolina, 2000; Raywid, 1994; Schargel & Smink, 2001; Wehlage, 1983) and contributed to the knowledge base by identifying a number of characteristics and best practices of successful alternative schools. A number of other researchers (Ascher, 1982; Barr & Parrett, 2001; Chavkin, 1993; Cox et al., 1995; Dollar, 1983; Franklin & Streeter, 1991; Ingersoll & LeBoeuf, 1997; Kraemer & Ruzzi, 2001; Morley, 1991; Northwest Regional Educational Laboratory, 2001; U.S. Department of Education, 1996; Young, 1990) have also contributed to our understanding of characteristics that distinguish successful alternative programs from unsuccessful programs.

Table 30.2 contains a comprehensive list of characteristics and best practices common to successful alternative programs based on the empirical research. Perhaps the single most important characteristic in developing an alternative school or program is employing teachers and staff who have chosen to work with and are committed to these youth. The selection of committed and caring staff is of paramount importance because "students can overcome bad teaching but they may never recover from a bad teacher who fails to project a true sense of caring and concern" (Reimer & Cash, 2003, p. 19). Successful alternative programs provide ongoing staff development in the areas of classroom management techniques, diversity training, and alternative instructional methods because most teachers did not receive this training in their formal teacher education program (Reimer & Cash, 2003). It also appears that successful alternative programs target a specific population of at-risk students and develop a holistic, humane, flexible educational program that is individualized and responsive to the social, emotional, and academic needs of these youth. Meeting the academic needs of these youth requires a hands-on, experiential curriculum that is tailored to the unique learning style of each student.

Table 30.2 Characteristics and Best Practices Common to Successful Alternative Education Programs

- a student-to-staff ratio that is lower than in mainstream schools (i.e., maximum teacher/student ratio of 1:10) (Ingersoll & LeBoeuf, 1997; Northwest Regional Educational Laboratory, 2001; Schargel & Smink, 2001)
- small student base not exceeding 250 students (Schargel & Smink, 2001)
- a clear stated mission shared by all staff and clear rules that are enforced fairly and consistently (Ingersoll & LeBoeuf, 1997; Northwest Regional Educational Laboratory, 2001; Cox et al., 1995; Schargel & Smink, 2001)
- a caring faculty who have chosen to teach in alternative schools and programs and who are committed to counseling, mentoring, and tutoring students in these programs (Barr & Parrett, 2001; Northwest Regional Educational Laboratory, 2001; Schargel & Smink, 2001)
- continual staff development opportunities (Schargel & Smink, 2001)
- school staff having high academic standards and high expectations for student achievement (Schargel & Smink, 2001)
- focus is on individualized learning that takes into account student's expectations and learning style within a *flexible schedule* that allows students to work at their own pace (Ascher, 1982; Chavkin, 1993; Dollar, 1983; Franklin & Streeter, 1991; Northwest Regional Educational Laboratory, 2001; Schargel & Smink, 2001)
- one-on-one interaction between teachers and students with a total commitment to have each student be successful (Morley, 1991;Young 1990; Schargel & Smink, 2001)
- a career-oriented curriculum (Martin & Halperin, 2006)
- a school or program that targets specific populations (i.e., primarily low school achievers or delinquents) (Chavkin, 1993; Cox et al., 1995; Franklin & Streeter, 1991)
- strong stable, and dynamic leadership (Reimer & Cash, 2003)
- provide a supportive, informal setting where personal relationships between students and teachers and a "family-like atmosphere" of respect can flourish (Morley, 1991;Young 1990; Northwest Regional Educational Laboratory, 2001; Schargel & Smink, 2001)
- provide a curriculum that can be described as "applied,""experiential,""hands-on," or "integrated"; a curriculum that emphasizes "real life learning" and that makes connections between the school and the community or "work world" (Young, 1990; Kraemer & Ruzzi, 2001; Ingersoll & LeBoeuf, 1997; Northwest Regional Educational Laboratory, 2001; Reimer & Cash, 2003)
- holistic services are provided to meet the emotional, physical, and academic needs of students (Reimer & Cash, 2003)
- clear codes of conduct (Martin & Halperin, 2006)
- student voices in decision-making and school operations is emphasized (Morley, 1991;Young 1990;Ascher, 1982; Northwest Regional Educational Laboratory, 2001)
- broad participation of the family and community is emphasized (Ascher, 1982; Ingersoll & LeBoeuf, 1997; Chavkin, 1993; Franklin & Streeter, 1991; Reimer & Cash, 2003)
- strong working relations with all parts of the school system and with other collaborating agencies that provide critical services to youth (Northwest Regional Educational Laboratory, 2001)

Many of the characteristics of effective alternative schools are consistent with school climate research, which demonstrates the influence of supportive and respectful relationships among students and adults within the school (Cohen & Geier, 2010). Quinn, Poirier, Faller, Gable, and Tonelson (2006) conducted a study of school climate in effective alternative schools by collecting data from students and teachers in programs that were designated as exemplary alternative education programs by a panel of experts. They found that students and teachers in these schools reported the following school climate characteristics:

- Rules are fair and equitably enforced.
- School personnel treat students with respect.
- Students are involved in decision making.
- School personnel are open to change.

What We Can Do

In order to show educators the importance and the potential effectiveness of alternative schools for preventing high school dropout, it is important for school social workers and counselors to work with a team of educators that are willing to help develop and sustain one or more programs. It may also be possible to target and improve an existing program since so many school districts already operate some type of alternative education program. This team can use the knowledge about the effective components of alternative schools that has been shared in this chapter to create a carefully thought out plan for developing a school that will meet the needs of students in their district. A central challenge awaiting school social workers and others is to convince the general public, as well as some teachers and administrators, that effective and humane alternative programs must offer students opportunities to learn from their mistakes and move forward positively with their lives, rather than focusing exclusively on punishment.

Steps in Designing and Establishing Effective Alternative Education Schools and Programs

The following series of sequential steps are based on the work of Reimer and Cash (2003), DeBlois (1994), Dugger and DesMoulin-Kherat (1996), and Harrington-Lueker (1994). They are designed to build a broad base of support in the initial phases of program development, to help overcome potential barriers and obstacles throughout the process, and to ensure that programs are built upon those characteristics and best practices outlined in Table 30.2.

1. *Establish a planning team or task force.* To ensure a broad base of support, it is recommended that this planning team or task force include representatives of local social service agencies, local businesses, law enforcement, and schools. It will work best if it has 6 to 15 members. Reimer and Cash (2003) state that teams with more than 15 members "become cumbersome to work with and may become splintered as time goes on. Conversely, a subgroup or powerful leader who wants to push through his/her own vision and agenda may sway a small group" (p. 17). It is advisable to start putting the team together at least 1 year ahead of the start-up date of a school or program. See Dupper (1993) for a detailed discussion of a community task force that was an integral part of an alternative program for potential dropouts in a middle school setting.
2. *Develop a philosophy and mission for the school or program.* A group consensus on the philosophical foundation is absolutely essential since this will guide the development of program policies and procedures (Reimer & Cash, 2003). A central question is whether the school or program is envisioned as educational (focused on providing an alternative learning experience) or disciplinary (focused on "fixing the child"). These two opposing philosophies are described and contrasted in Table 30.1. In determining which of these philosophies will be chosen, it is essential that school social workers and counselors make the planning team or task force aware of current research on characteristics and best practices of alternative programs (see Table 30.2).
3. *Develop the design and operation of the school or program.* This is the point at which a building principal or program director should be hired to decide upon the nuts and bolts of the school or program with advice from school district staff. At this stage of the process it is important to consider how the school or program will receive funding (per-student costs for alternative education are higher because of the lower teacher—student ratio), where it will be located (i.e., settings for alternative schools and programs range from space in a large department store to an empty office building to a portable structure), how large it will be, whom it will serve, how transportation will be provided, and how it will be staffed. Again, it is essential that the school social worker and counselors share best practices related to each of these issues.

At this point, it is also important to remember that applying for grants and holding annual fund-raising events is time consuming and tiresome (DeBlois, 1994). If the school district is too small or lacks the financial resources to support an alternative school, look into participating in a regional program run by an education service district (Northwest Regional Educational Laboratory, 2001). However, if one of the goals of the program is for students to reenter their traditional high school, then it may be helpful to be located in or near that school. It is essential that good two-way communication between the alternative and students' home schools be maintained, particularly as students are preparing to transition back to their home schools (Reimer & Cash, 2003).

4. *Select staff members.* Because of the deep suspicion and distrust that many students feel toward a school system that they believe has failed them, it is extremely important that a fragile bond of two-way trust between students and staff be established (Kraemer & Ruzzi, 2001). This is particularly true if students will be assigned to the alternative school or program rather than attend by choice. Since many of these youth have difficulty following traditional school rules, it is important that the principal or administrator in charge of student discipline also be flexible in dealing with discipline issues (Reimer & Cash, 2003).
5. *Design the alternative curriculum.* In this step, the planning team or task force must decide upon the teacher—student ratio, what curriculum will be offered, how the curriculum will be delivered, how technology will be integrated, how social services and counseling services will be delivered, and how to provide opportunities for teachers to collaborate and plan together. It should be emphasized that the most important role of each and every staff member is to be an *informal counselor and support person to students* (Kellmayer, 1995).
6. *Build community support.* One of the most effective ways of changing the public's negative perception of alternative education is by "inviting community members, including the local press, to visit your alternative school as well as to be able to document the ways in which students have grown while attending the alternative school" (McGee, 2001, p. 589). It is important to connect with surrounding businesses and community groups for ways that they can become involved (e.g., providing money and career-related opportunities). When possible, involve parents and family, particularly at the middle school level, by, for example, sending letters to them and holding parenting classes and student-led parent conferences.
7. *Establish specific enrollment and exit criteria.* Enrollment criteria must be established to prevent the alternative school or program from becoming a place where the school district dumps students who don't seem to fit anywhere else. "If the school or program becomes a dumping ground for students it was not intended to serve, it is likely that the once-enthusiastic staff will become frustrated and begin to leave the school. These teachers may be replaced with others who do not share the original vision of the school, thus causing the program's reputation to suffer and enrollment to decline" (Northwest Regional Educational Laboratory, 2001).
8. *Document and publicize program results.* To avoid closure because of school board changes, opposition from teacher's unions (Amenta, 1997), or an economic downturn (DeBlois, 1994), alternative school administrators and staff must constantly sell their program by showing that it works and that it is cost effective (e.g., it is cheaper to educate now than to build prisons later). This can be accomplished through statistics, anecdotes, and personal testimony from students and parents. To assess improvements in learning, data on changes in GPA, attendance rates, graduation rates, and dropout rates should be collected and analyzed over several years (Gregg, 1998). To assess improvements in student behavior, data on changes in the number of disciplinary referrals, suspension or expulsion rates, and in-school suspension rates should be collected and analyzed over several years (Gregg, 1998).

Applying Interventions within a Response to Intervention Framework

Response to Intervention (RTI) is a process that aims to match effective interventions to students based on need. School personnel closely monitor student progress in order to make decisions about whether goals or interventions need to be changed to improve student outcomes. When a school gives attention to effective interventions for students at risk to dropout, they may learn from the research on alternative schools and purposefully redesign their school climate and classroom instruction so that they can better serve at-risk students. Some of the strategies used by alternative schools to create a school environment that is supportive and student-driven could offer methods to improve the school climate of regular school programs, for example, such as the ones that are aimed at implementing school success variables such as reducing student-teacher ratios, establishing student advisory boards, and implementing individualized education and more flexible options in academic programs.

RTI was intended to provide a more proactive and accurate means of identifying students in need of additional services and supports as early as possible. Students are provided with increasingly intensive and individualized instruction until their performance improves. Ideally, RTI would reduce or eliminate the need for alternative schools because the services and supports that students need would be provided in a regular school setting. In actuality, alternative schools for dropout prevention may be a more intensive, Tier 3 intervention and will be applied after other approaches to keeping students in schools have failed. Alternative school students, for example, are usually students who have not been successfully served by the traditional school structure and are perceived to be in need of additional services and interventions. Thus, many of these students would meet the RTI criteria for additional services and individualized instruction, and many may already be chronically truant, be failing, or even have left the school for a time.

One problem with using alternative schools as a part of the RTI continuum of services, however, is the longer-term consequences of removing students from regular instruction in a classroom into an alternative program. For example, as has been discussed in this chapter, students in alternative schools may not successfully be referred back to their original classrooms or campuses, resulting in more permanent use of alternative school programs to manage at-risk students. In addition, current research suggests that not all students are successful in alternative schools, so if the school district wishes to improve its overall outcomes with at-risk students, an alternative school cannot be used as a "last resort" effort for all struggling students. New services may have to be designed, and a careful examination of which students will succeed in an alternative school verses which will need other services will need to be examined.

Finally, if alternative schools would follow the RTI process, they could also possibly improve their service delivery. Closely monitoring student progress and ongoing evaluation of interventions, for example, could enable alternative school teachers and staff to further individualize and use existing data to plan their services and curriculum. Since effective alternative schools prioritize individualized instruction, the RTI framework is also likely to fit well with existing structures and supports. Being brought more into a continuum of services model may also reduce the stigma that some alternative schools experience and improve their resource allocations.

Tools and Practice Examples

A School Example

Gonzalo Garza Independence High School (Garza) is an urban, public alternative school in Austin, Texas. Students enroll by choice, although they must have completed 10 credits at another school and must submit a written application. The school opened with the purpose of removing barriers to academic success and graduation. According to the state of Texas, 98% of Garza students are designated as "at risk." The school's code of honor, which is posted in every classroom and throughout the building, stipulates that everyone within the school will:

1. Demonstrate personal honor and integrity at all times.
2. Choose peace over conflict.
3. Respect themselves and others (Kelly, Kim, & Franklin, 2008).

Garza employs strategies grounded in Solution-Focused Brief Therapy (SFBT) to create a positive school climate. SFBT is a brief intervention that was originally conceptualized as a strengths-based approach to facilitating positive behavioral change in families dealing with complex problems, such as poverty and involvement with the child welfare system. Garza adopted the principles to create a Solution-Building School. All teachers and staff within the school are trained in strengths-based, future-focused dialogue with students that encourages students to articulate their own improvement goals. Because all personnel in the school are trained in the model, it promotes a school environment in which individuals share the same vision and a consistent approach to working with students. SFBT helps students define small, measurable goals and the specific steps that lead to an individual solution (Franklin, Montgomery, Baldwin, & Webb, 2012; Martin & Halperin, 2006). Practitioners, for example, help students imagine realistic solution about their educational and personal problems and articulate the ways in which the solution is already occurring in their lives. Students are also encouraged to discover and enact new solutions that will lead to the achievement of goals. Goal setting and envisioning new behaviors that are different from typical responses are important to the solution-building process, as well as an increasing confidence that one can take actions that lead to goal attainment.

Garza employs many innovative practices that are consistent with the research on promoting student engagement and a positive school climate. Some of these practices include

- a student advisory board that consults with the principal on a regular basis
- a school-to-career specialist who provides students with the chance to explore opportunities in various careers and higher education
- an emphasis on mastery of information technology
- a community-based organization, Communities In Schools, co-located at the school to provide mental health services, crisis intervention, health referrals, case management, tutoring, and mentoring (Franklin et al., 2012; Franklin, Streeter, Kim, & Tripodi, 2007; Martin & Halperin, 2006)

Consistent with many other alternative schools, Garza has a smaller student-to-teacher ratio than other schools in the district and state, with about one student for every 10 teachers. Although the majority of Garza students are designated as "at risk" by the school district, a larger percentage of Garza students meet state standards on standardized tests. Garza has continuously used research and data to develop its programs and monitor its success. When attendance of students was lower than expected, for example, the leadership team worked with students and the student advisory board, faculty, and counselors to enact new methods to improve the attendance. The school also constantly tracks and improves its standardized test scores. A testimony to the school's success is the fact that students who take the ACT and SAT exams at Garza High School also score higher on average than other students in the district and state (Austin Independent School District, n.d.). An evaluation of the school's effectiveness that employed a quasi-experimental research design revealed that Garza students, in comparison to similar students at a traditional school, earned significantly more credits over time, and more than half of Garza students in the sample entered a postgraduate education program after graduating (Franklin, Streeter, Kim, & Tripodi, 2007).

A qualitative case study also revealed that students attending Garza believed that the solution-focused school was more effective in helping them engage with school, progress academically, and graduate from high school than their previous schools (Lagana-Riordan et al., 2011). Some of the key components of Garza identified by the students within the case study were the relationship with their teachers, self-paced goal orientation, attention to social problems, and the overall positive and caring emotional climate of the school. These components are consistent with other research that has looked at how alternative schools work effectively with at-risk students, and this research demonstrates further what is important to at-risk students and how necessary relational and school climate factors may be to the success of these students. For a more detailed explanation of Garza High School's programs and practices, see Kelly, Kim and Franklin (2008).

Key Points to Remember

- A major challenge that school social workers and others face in designing and establishing effective and humane alternative schools for dropout prevention and programs is to create schools and programs that are creative outlets for students whose needs are not being met by traditional schools. It is important to create places where students will have exemplary education and opportunities to learn from their mistakes.

- The ultimate outcome for the majority of students in an alternative school or program is a successful reentry into their traditional high school. Therefore, ongoing communication with the base school is essential, and adequate supports (e.g., transition specialists) must be provided to the students as they reenter. Evidence suggests that providing follow-up and transition services to students as they return to their home schools may enhance long-term outcomes.
- Target specific populations of at-risk students (e.g., low achievers or delinquents). Targeted programs have been shown to be more effective than programs that do not target specific types of students. So, target specific groups of at-risk students (e.g., low achievers or delinquents).
- Plan for the maximum level of voluntary participation by both students and teachers. Hire teachers with both the skills and the passion to teach material in an experiential, creative, and noncompetitive manner. Develop an organizational structure that will support talented staff characterized by flexibility and autonomy, one in which students, teachers, and parents can work together to make program decisions.
- Follow the eight steps described in this chapter focusing on the design and creation of effective alternative schools. Include as many of the characteristics contained in Table 30.2 as possible, as these are, according to a number of researchers in the field, components that represent the best practices in alternative education.

Further Learning and Resources

- Dupper, D. R. (1993). School—community collaboration: A description of a model program designed to prevent school dropouts. *School Social Work Journal,* 18, 32–39. (This article provides a detailed discussion of a community task force and its importance in the overall operation of an alternative program.)
- Northwest Regional Educational Laboratory, Alternative schools: Caring for kids on the edge, *Northwest Education Magazine* (summer 1998). This organization can be reached at 101 S. W. Main Street, Suite 500, Portland, OR 97204, Telephone (503) 275–9500, e-mail: webmaster@nwrel.org, NWREL Web Site: http://www.nwrel.org
- The Center for Effective Collaboration and Practice. *Alternative schools: Information for families.* Available at http://cecp.air.org/family-briefs/docs/AltSch.pdf
- The National Dropout Prevention Center (NDPC) at Clemson University has become a well-established national resource for sharing solutions for student success. The center can be reached at 209 Martin Street, Clemson, SC 29631–1555, (864) 656–2599, e-mail: ndpc@clemson.edu; http://www.dropoutprevention.org/
- National Coalition of Advocates for Students is a private nonprofit coalition of advocacy organizations that work on behalf of students who are traditionally underserved (e.g., students of color, immigrants, students from low-income families, and special needs students). E-mail: ncasmfe@aol.com; Web site: http://www.ncas1.org/
- *Quality alternative placements for suspended or expelled students: "Lessons learned" from the Center for the Prevention of School Violence's Youth Out of the Education Mainstream Initiative* can be downloaded at http://www.ncdjjdp.org/cpsv/alt_learning/yoem/qareplace.htm
- Kennedy, R. L. & Morton, J. H. (1999). *A school for healing: Alternative strategies for teaching at-risk students.* New York: Peter Lang.
- For state-by-state information on alternative schools for disruptive students, see http://www.ecs.org/clearinghouse/15/05/1505.htm. Successful alternative education programs for troubled youth can be downloaded from http://www.ncsl.org/programs/educ/AlterEdSN.htm.

References

Amenta, R. (1997). Horizon alternative school: Why promising reforms disappear. *Education Week, 16*(22), 36, 38.

Ascher, C. (1982). ERIC/CUE: Alternative schools: Some answers and questions. *Urban Review, 14,* 65–69.

Atkins, T., Allen, J., & Meredith, M. (n.d.). *Alternative schools: Information for families.* Eugene: Center for Effective Collaboration and Practice, University of Oregon. Retrieved April 6, 2004, from http://cecp.air.org/familybriefs/docs/AltSch.pdf

Austin Independent School District. (n.d.). *1009–10 school report card.* Retrieved October 6, 2011, from http://archive.austinisd.org/schools/details.phtml?id=024&opt=ratings.

Barr, R. D., & Parrett, W. H. (2001). *Hope fulfilled for at-risk and violent youth*. Needham Heights, MA: Allyn & Bacon.

Carver, P. R., & Lewis, L. (2010). *Alternative schools and programs for public school students at risk of educational failure: 2007–08.* Washington DC: US Department of Education, National Center for Education Statistics.

Chavkin, N. F. (1993). School social workers helping multiethnic families: Schools and communities join forces. In N. F. Chavkin (Ed.), *Families and schools in a pluralistic society* (pp. 217–228). Albany: State University of New York Press.

Cohen, J., & Geier, V. K. (2010). *School climate research summary: January 2010*. Retrieved from www.schoolclimate.org/climate/research/php.

Cox, S. M., Davidson, W. S., & Bynum, T. S. (1995). A meta-analytic assessment of delinquency-related outcomes of alternative education programs. *Crime and Delinquency*, *41*, 219–234.

DeBlois, R. (1994). Keeping alternatives alive. *American School Board Journal*, *181*, 33–34.

Dollar, R. (1983). What is really going on in schools? *Social Policy*, *13*, 7–19.

Dugger, C., & Desmoulin-Kherat, S. (1996). Helping younger dropouts get back into school. *Middle School Journal*, *28*, 29–33.

Dupper, D. R. (1993). School-community collaboration: A description of a model program designed to prevent school dropouts. *School Social Work Journal*, *18*, 32–39.

Dynarski, M., & Wood, R. (1997). *Helping high-risk youth: Results from the Alternative Schools Demonstration Program*. Princeton, NJ: Mathematica Policy Research.

Franklin, C., & Streeter, C. L. (1991). Evidence for the effectiveness of social work with high school drop-out youths. *Social Work in Education*, *13*, 307–327.

Franklin, C. (1992). Alternative school programs for at-risk youth. *Social Work in Education*, *14*, 239–251.

Franklin, C., Streeter, C. L., Kim, J. S., & Tripodi, S. J. (2007). The effectiveness of a solution-focused public alternative school for dropout prevention and retrieval. *Children & Schools*, *29*(3), 133–144.

Franklin, C., & Kelly, M. K. (2012). *Alternative schools. Encyclopedia of Adolescence*. New York, NY: Springer.

Franklin, C., Montgomery, K. L., Baldwin, V., & Webb, L. (2012). Research and development of a solution-focused high school. In C. Franklin, T. Trepper, W. J. Gingerich, & E. McCollum (Eds.), *Solution-focused brief therapy: A handbook of evidence-based practice* (pp. 371–389). New York, NY: Oxford University Press.

Glass, R. (1995). Alternative schools help kids succeed. *Education Digest*, *60*, 21–24.

Gregg, S. (1998). *Schools for disruptive students: A questionable alternative?* Policy Briefs series. Charleston, WV: Appalachia Educational Laboratory.

Harrington-Lueker, D. (1994). Hanging on to hope. *American School Board Journal*, *181*, 16–21.

Henrich, R. S. (2005). Expansion of an alternative school typology. *The Journal of At-Risk Issues*, *11*(1), 25–37.

Ingersoll, S., & LeBoeuf, D. (1997). *Reaching out to youth out of the education mainstream*. U.S. Department of Justice, Office of Justice Programs, Office of Juvenile Justice and Delinquency Prevention.

Kadel, S. (1994). *Reengineering high schools for student access. Hot topics: Usable research*. Palatha, FL: Southeastern Regional Vision for Education. (ERIC Document Reproduction Service No. ED366076)

Kellmayer, J. (1995). *How to establish an alternative school*. Thousand Oaks, CA: Corwin.

Kelly, M., Kim, J. S., & Franklin, C. (2008). *Solution-focused brief therapy in schools*. New York, NY: Oxford University Press.

Kemple, J. J., & Snipes, J. C. (2000). *Career Academies: Impacts on students' engagement and performance in high school*. New York, NY: Manpower Demonstration Research Corporation.

Kemple, J. J., & Willner, C. J. (2008). *Career Academies: Long-term impacts on labor market outcomes, educational attainment, and transitions to adulthood*. New York, NY: Manpower Demonstration Research Corp.

Kershaw, C., & Blank, M. (1993, April). *Student and educator perceptions of the impact of an alternative school structure*. Paper presented at the annual meeting of the American Educational Research Association, Atlanta, GA.

Klima, T., Miller, M., & Nunlist, C. (2009). *What works? Targeted truancy and dropout programs in middle and high school* (Document No. 09–06–2201). Olympia, WA: Washington State Institute for Public Policy.

Kraemer, J., & Ruzzi, B. B. (2001). Alternative education cannot be left behind. *Education Week*. Retrieved January 23, 2004, from http://www.edweek.org/ew/newstory.cfm?slug=06kraemer.h21

Lagana-Riordan, C., Aguilar, J. P., Franklin, C., Streeter, C. L., Kim., J. S., Tripodi, S. J., & Hopson, L. (2011). At-risk students' perceptions of traditional schools and a solution-focused public alternative school. *Preventing School Failure*, *55*, 105–114.

Martin, N., & Halperin, S. (2006). *Whatever it takes: How twelve communities are reconnecting out-of-school youth*. Washington, DC: American Youth Policy Forum.

McGee, J. (2001). Reflections of an alternative school administrator. *Phi Delta Kappan*, *82*, 588–591.

Morley, R. (1991). *Alternative education* (ED349652). Clemson, SC: National Dropout Prevention Center.

North Carolina Education and Law Project. (1997). *Alternative schools: Short-term solutions with long-term consequences* (2nd ed.). Raleigh, NC: Author.

Northwest Regional Educational Laboratory. (2001). *Alternative schools: Approaches for students at risk*. Retrieved May 1, 2004, from http://www.nwrel.org/request/sept97/article2.html

Public Schools of North Carolina. (2000, March). *Case studies of best practices. Alternative schools and programs:*

1998–99. Raleigh, NC: Author. Retrieved May 5, 2004, from http://www.ncpublicschool.org/accountability/alternative/case9899.pdf

Quinn, M. M., Poirier, J. M., Faller, S. E., Gable, R. A., & Tonelson, S. W. (2006). An examination of school climate in effective alternative programs. *Preventing School Failure*, *51*(1), 11–17.

Raywid, M. (1990). Alternative education: The definition problem. *Changing Schools*, *18*, 4–5, 10.

Raywid, M. (1994). Synthesis of research: Alternative schools: The state of the art. *Educational Leadership*, *52*, 26–31.

Raywid, M. A. (1998). The journey of the alternative schools movement: Where it's been and where it's going. *High School Magazine*, *6*(2), 10–14.

Reimer, M. S., & Cash, T. (2003). *Alternative schools: Best practices for development and evaluation*. Clemson, SC: National Dropout Prevention Center/Network.

Schargel, F. P., & Smink, J. (2001). *Strategies to help solve our school dropout problem*. Larchmont, NY: Eye on Education.

U.S. Department of Education (1996). *Safe and drug-free schools. Alternative education programs for expelled students.* Retrieved May 1, 2004, from http://www.ed.gov/offices/OESE/SDFS/actguid/altersc.html

Wehlage, G. (1983). *Effective programs for the marginal high school student. Fastback 197*. Bloomington, IN: Phi Delta Kappa.

Young, T. (1990). *Public alternative education: Options and choices for today's schools*. New York: Teachers College Press.

CHAPTER 31

Solution-Focused, Brief Therapy Interventions for Students at Risk to Drop Out

Cynthia Franklin ■ Johnny S. Kim ■ Stephen J. Tripodi

Getting Started

Risk of high school dropout is one of the critical challenges that today's schools face. Recent research from the Center for Educational Statistics suggests that the current status dropout rate is 25%, but this rate quickly escalates to 50–75% when we examine the four-year graduation rates of students who live in urban settings and are ethnic minorities (Chapman, Laird, & Kewal-Ramani, 2010; Swanson, 2008). These exorbitant statistics cause some researchers to suggest that high school dropout is creating a national crisis that may threaten the United States' economic stability and challenge the very fabric of our communities (Balfanz, 2007; Swanson, 2008). High schools currently have to cope with the high accountability issues surrounding the dropout problems and are increasingly being evaluated for their abilities to reduce their dropouts and find ways to retain and graduate all of their students, including those students who are most at risk for school failure and dropout.

In order to help schools reduce the current rates of high school dropout, school social workers and other student support services professionals need effective interventions that can engage students and that can develop quick changes in student behaviors and attitudes. Since the 1990s, school social workers and counselors have been using solution-focused brief therapy (SFBT) to help at-risk students. SFBT is a strengths-based therapeutic approach that developed out of brief family therapy and has been shown in research studies to be an effective approach in helping at-risk students in school settings (Kim & Franklin, 2009).

This chapter explains the change techniques used in SFBT and demonstrates how to use this approach to help at-risk students. Information on the complexities of the dropout problem are first summarized, followed by explanations for why SFBT is a helpful approach for school settings. Finally, descriptions and case examples on how to use SFBT to change the behaviors of at-risk students are presented.

What We Know

Reasons for dropping out of high school are extremely complex, and this makes it difficult to develop a singular method for assisting students at risk to dropout. Reviews of this topic indicate that there are both institutional and individual reasons for dropouts (Rumberger, 2004). Table 31.1 provides a summary of individual, family, and school-related reasons for dropping out based on empirical studies.

It is easy to see when examining the reasons for dropping out of high school that, in order to prevent dropout, school social workers and other professionals need to be prepared to work with students across multiple problem issues and systems (e.g., school, family, and community). Yet, for all that has been written on preventing dropout, past reviews of research studies indicate that the research in this area is limited for the scope and importance of the problem (e.g., Franklin & Kelly, 2009; Prevatt & Kelly, 2003; Rumberger, 2004; Slavin & Fashola, 1998). Franklin and Kelly (2009), for example reviewed the literature on effective dropout prevention programs using five online databases: the National Registry of Evidence-based Programs and Practices (located at http://nrepp.samhsa.gov/find.asp), the U.S. Department of Education What Works Clearinghouse (located

Table 31.1 Reasons for Dropping Out

Individual	*Family*	*School-Related*
• Low grades • Poor daily attendance • Misbehavior • Alcohol and drug use • Feeling alienated from other students	• Parents not engaged in child's schooling • Teen pregnancy • Student getting married • Financial and work reasons • Permissive parenting style • Negative emotional reactions and sanctions for bad grades	• Student/teacher ratio • Quality of teachers • Seeking smaller school size • School safety concerns • Not feeling welcomed at the school

Sources: Based on studies by Aloise-Young & Chavez, 2002; Jordan, Lara, & McPartland, 1996; Rumberger, 1987; Rumberger, Ghatak, Poulos, Ritter, & Dornbusch, 1990; Rumberger & Thomas, 2000.

at http://ies.ed.gov/ncee/wwc/topic.aspx?sid=3), the National Dropout prevention Center (http://www.dropoutprevention.org/ndpcdefault.htm), the OJJDP Web site (www.ojjdp.gov/mpg), and the Campbell Collaboration (www.campbellcollaboration.org), as well as additional books and resources. They could identify only 12 dropout prevention approaches that met a rigorous criteria for evidence-based practice. See the What Works Clearinghouse (http://ies.ed.gov/ncee/wwc/topic.aspx?sid=3, n.d.), a research arm of the Department of Education's Institute for Education, for additional reviews of potentially effective dropout prevention programs.

The National Dropout Prevention Center (2012) lists 15 strategies for dropout prevention that have been found to have some degree of effectiveness (http://www.dropoutprevention.org/effective-strategies). Alternative school programs are one of the promising practices that are mentioned among the 15 strategies, but the use of alternative schools includes many different methods from individualized teaching to counseling and social approaches.

Regardless of what reviews you read, most research-based dropout interventions are multicomponent and involve using academic support, mentoring, behavioral interventions, case management, job training, and family support to try and help students that are at risk to dropout. Typical school approaches may involve more elaborate programs and the use of Response to Intervention (RTI) methods to identify and support students in need of additional help. The intervention being described in this chapter, SFBT, differs in that it is a brief intervention geared toward helping students to solve behavioral, social, and academic problems that may become barriers to their engagement and success in schools. SFBT may be applied to individuals, or in any kind of relationship context such as parent-child relationships, teacher-child relationship, or in modifying interactions of school personnel in order to improve the school climate (Franklin, Montgomery, Baldwin, & Webb, 2012). Over the past 10 years, as will be discussed below, SFBT has increasingly been applied in schools with favorable results.

Solution-Focused Brief Therapy in Schools

The development of SFBT originated in the early 1980s at the Brief Family Therapy Center in Milwaukee. This approach to counseling became very popular and widely used in the 1990s, mostly due to the demands for briefer counseling interventions. Practitioners also began to use the SFBT techniques in schools (Berg & Shilts, 2005; Franklin, Biever, Moore, Clemons, & Scamardo, 2001; Kral, 1995; Metcalf, 2008; Murphy & Duncan, 2007; Sklare, 1997; Webb, 1999). As a result, quasi-experimental design studies began to examine the success of SFBT with students who have behavioral and academic problems. Research evidence is emerging that shows SFBT is an effective intervention that gets good results in school settings. In a recent meta-analysis on solution-focused brief therapy, for example, Kim, (2008) reported that the outcome studies completed on SFBT in school settings had medium effect sizes (e.g. Franklin, Streeter, Kim, & Tripodi, 2007; Franklin, Moore, & Hopson, 2008; Springer, Lynch, & Rubin, 2000), meaning that when SFBT is applied in schools, it gets better outcomes. More recently, Kim and Franklin (2009) completed a systematic review on the effectiveness of SFBT interventions in schools and found that SFBT is a useful approach with at-risk students with a variety of emotional, behavioral, and academic problems. There are several reasons that SFBT may be an effective approach with at-risk students. First, many at-risk students may be dropout prone due to academic failure and missed days of school because of severe social problems, such being homeless, immigrants, or teen parents; family problems; and substance abuse, for example. SFBT focuses on the resolution of presenting issues using strengths, positive behaviors that already exist, goal setting, and client-selected behavior plans known as solutions. SFBT also facilitates collaboration with others involved in the student's life. This type of therapeutic approach is very flexible to situations and works well with the other team approaches used in the schools, such as RTI and the individualized education plans (IEPs) used in special education, because each perspective has a practical, behavioral, and goal-oriented approach.

Second, schools often face students with very challenging issues but have little time or money for elaborate dropout interventions. The brevity and solution-building focus of SFBT, however, complements the needs of the school without compromising potential outcomes with selected students that may receive the SFBT intervention. What school social workers and school support personnel often require in their work are brief, practical solutions to the day-to-day issues that may prevent the educational achievement of a student, and SFBT offers a change process and specific techniques for addressing the challenging issues that students present to school personnel.

Finally, SFBT is very flexible toward different ways of helping and can be used by teachers and other professionals within the school (Franklin, Montgomery, Baldwin, & Webb, 2012). The fact that SFBT is flexible to the school situation and can be used by diverse personnel points to its applicability to working in a team within a school. It is possible, for example, for school support teams to teach the approach to teachers and to support them as they apply SFBT to help at-risk students. When SFBT is applied as a team approach and used by diverse personnel to support at-risk students, it is referred to not as a therapeutic approach but as a solution-building process (Franklin et al., 2012). The techniques and change processes embedded in SFBT support solution-building and the resolution of practical problems that become barriers to progress in schools.

What Is Solution-Building?

Solution-building is a process where school support teams and other school personnel engage students in a purposeful conversation, resulting in changes in perceptions and social interactions. The solution-building process or conversation is often contrasted to the problem-solving process. Problem-solving focuses on the resolution of presenting problems through understanding the problems, enumerating alternatives that can solve the problems, and choosing an alternative. In contrast, solution-building changes the way people think about presenting problems and identifies future behaviors and tasks that have the potential to accomplish desired goals and outcomes (De Jong & Berg, 2012). Solution-building conversations result in the student discovering goals, tasks, and behaviors that change future outcomes. The SFBT practitioner acts as a catalyst or facilitator and creates an interpersonal context where the solutions emerge from the students and their ideas during the process of the conversation. In this way, solutions are co-constructed in collaborative conversation.

Change in SFBT comes from finding what already works and doing more of it (Miller & de Shazer, 2000) or creating new interactions and behaviors that have not been tried before. Doing more of what works or something different that leads to a desired outcome is the beginning of solution-building. Change also occurs by helping students to visualize a future outcome that they desire and helping them to think and talk through the steps to achieve it. The steps are further broken down into small tasks or solutions that are identified by the students. The reason that SFBT practitioners focus on small steps is to get students moving forward toward their goals and to help them be able to experience some success. Success builds confidence in students and has the potential to change their view of the situation (e.g., I was able to come back to school for one class with the teacher I like, so maybe

I do not have to drop out). Small steps are also viewed as being capable of serving as catalysts for bigger changes.

SFBT Counseling Techniques

Exception Questions

- When does the problem not occur?
- What was different about those times when things were better between you and your teacher?
- Even though this is a very bad time, in my experience, people's lives do not always stay the same. I will bet that there have been times when the problem of being sent to the principal's office was not happening, or at least was happening less. Please describe those times. What was different? How did you get that to happen?

SFBT practitioners start solution-building by exploring exceptions (Lee, 1997). Exceptions are situations when the stated complaint does not occur, occurs less often, or occurs with less intensity. Exception questions were designed to encourage students to notice evidence that not only is change possible but also that they have already had some successful attempts (Lathem, 2002). SFBT theorizes that it is more beneficial for students to increase their current successes instead of trying to eliminate the problem altogether, no matter how small the current successes appear to be (Murphy & Duncan, 2007).

The school social worker and counselor must understand the students' perception of what has worked and what they think will work to achieve their goals, in addition to trusting the students in regard to seeing solutions in exceptions (Pichot & Dolan, 2003). It is important for the social worker and counselor to emphasize the exceptions and question how the student brought about these changes. Furthermore, the social worker must believe that it was not the right solution if the student walked away from it.

Relationship Questions

- What would your teacher say about your grades?
- What would your mother say?
- If you were to do something that made your teacher very happy, what would that be?
- Who would be the most surprised if you did well on that test?

Relationship questions allow students to discuss their problems from a third-person point of view, which makes the problem less threatening and allows the social worker, counselor, or teacher to assess the students' viewpoint and the students to practice thinking about the problem from the viewpoint of others. The procedure is to ask the students what their family members and teachers think about their problem and progress, as more indicators of change helping the students to develop a vision of a future appropriate to their social context. Furthermore, students develop empathy because of relationship questions as they are able to see how the severity of their problem has affected their family and significant others. Subsequently, motivation may increase as they become cognizant of the impact their problem has had on other people in their lives.

Scaling Questions

- On a scale of 1–10, with 1 being the lowest and 10 being the highest, where would you rate yourself in terms of reaching your goals that you identified last week?
- On a scale of 1–10, with 1 being that you never go to class and 10 being that you have perfect attendance, where would you put yourself on that scale? What would it take to increase two numbers on the scale?
- On a scale of 1–10, with 1 being that you are getting in trouble every day in class and 10 being that you are doing your school work and your teacher says something nice to you, where would you be on that scale?

The school social worker and other school professionals have the option to use scaling questions to quantify and measure the intensity of internal thoughts and feelings, along with helping the students to anchor reality and move forward from their problem (Franklin & Nurius, 1998; Pichot & Dolan, 2003). Many different variations of this technique can be used, such as asking for percentages of progress, holding up a ruler or string, or drawing a line on a sidewalk. Scaling questions are a technique used to determine where students are in terms of achieving their goals. Scaling is a subjective process, but it helps students to measure and assess how much progress they may or may not have made toward goals. Typically, scaling questions have students rate where they are on a scale from 1 to 10 with 1 being the worst/lowest and 10 being the best/highest. Scaling is a technique that is familiar to most students and a helpful tool for the therapist when students are having a difficult time seeing their progress.

Franklin, Corcoran, Nowicki, and Streeter (1997) describe three different uses of scaling in SFBT. First is to determine where the students are on the scale in terms of solving their own problems; second is to look for exceptions to the problem; and third is to construct a miracle or identify solution behaviors. The highest point on the scale should always represent the desired outcome. Furthermore, the scaling sequence must end with the social worker asking the students how they will move forward to another point on the scale.

The Miracle Question

> Now, I want to ask you a strange question. This is probably a question no one has asked you before. Suppose that while you are sleeping tonight, a miracle happens, and the problem that brought you here is solved. However, because you are sleeping, you don't know that the miracle has happened. So, when you wake up tomorrow morning, what will be the first thing that you notice that is different that will tell you a miracle has happened and that the problem, which brought you here, is solved?

The miracle question strengthens students' goals by allowing them to reconstruct their story, showing a future without the students' perceived problems (Berg & De Jong, 1996; De Jong & Berg, 2001). Moreover, the social worker uses the miracle question to help students to identify ways that the solution may already be occurring in their lives. According to Pichot and Dolan (2003), the miracle question came into being by chance. One of Berg's clients suggested, "Only a miracle will help," which enabled Berg and associates to realize the power of the client imagining how the future would be without the problem.

Pichot and Dolan (2003) describe five elements that are crucial to the miracle question. The first crucial element is saying the words "suppose a miracle happens." This tells the student that a desired change is possible. Second, the student must have a basic understanding of what the miracle is, which the statement "The problem that brought you here is solved" often defines. The third crucial element to the miracle question is immediacy. The miracle must be described as happening tonight and in an environment that is realistic for students, such as in their homes. Fourth, in the hypothetical situation, the student must be unaware that the miracle has occurred. Without this, there is nothing for the student to discover, which is a vital component of the miracle question. Fifth, students must recognize the signs that indicate to them that the miracle happened.

The miracle question provides students with a vision of a problem-free future and empowers them to learn new ways of behaving. Asking this question, very gently and thoughtfully, is believed to allow a shift in the students' usual thought processes (Pichot & Dolan, 2003).

Goaling

Goaling is used as a verb in SFBT. An important distinction to make between goal setting in SFBT and other approaches to behavior change is that attaining the goal does not represent the end of counseling in SFBT; goals are considered the beginning of behavior change, not the end. The social worker and the student negotiate small, observable goals, set within a brief time frame, that lead to a new story for the student. The negotiation of goals should start immediately between the social worker and student (Franklin & Nurius, 1998). If a student is unable to think of a concrete goal, the school social worker may opt to provide multiple-choice answers. Additionally, scaling questions are beneficial to measure the student's progress toward goal attainment. Three advantages of using scales in this context are that they make goals and actions that lead to goals, they place responsibility for change on students, and students can take credit for the changes they make (Corcoran, 1998).

Walter and Peller (1996) say that goaling is the evolution of meaning about what students want to experience or what their lives may be like after the alleviation of the problem. Goaling is talking about what the student wants to do; it is not problem solving, but creative and conversational (Walter & Peller, 1996). Furthermore, goaling allows the conversation to lead to areas in students' lives that are free of the problems and where students want their lives to be.

According to Sklare (1997), the two most common types of goals that students identify are positive and negative goals. **Positive goals** are stated in terms of what the client wants and are measurable. Typical examples are "I want to get better grades" or "I want to have more friends." Most positive goals lack specific behavioral details. Asking specific details about what students will be doing when they are moving toward that goal will help students to identify specific behavioral details. So, the practitioner would say, "Let's just suppose your teacher was nicer to you. How would that help? What would you be doing differently?"

Negative goals are expressed as the absence of something. Clients will usually want themselves to stop doing something or usually want someone else to stop doing something to them. Typical examples are "I want my parents to stop bothering me" or "I want to stop getting into fights at school." When faced with negative goals, social workers must help students to reframe their goals in a way that gives students the responsibility. This can be accomplished by asking questions to help determine the students' motivation for wanting to stop doing something or wanting others to stop doing something to them. Some examples might be, "So when your parents aren't bothering you, what would that do for you?" or "When you're not getting into fights at school, what are you doing?"

The Break for Reflection

The **break** is another integral part of SFBT. It helps to transition the interview toward the final stage of the session, where the school social worker or counselor develops a set of compliments for the student and a homework task. Most social workers will simply go to their desk and write down notes or just inform students that they need a minute to reflect on the discussion and make notes on their notepad. In schools, when interviews are informal and meeting places may be in classrooms or other areas, the social worker might go to the bathroom or just take some psychological space for a moment. What is important about the break is to create a strong psychological space so that when the social worker returns, the student is paying close attention to what the practitioner is going to say next (de Shazer, 1985). The social worker finishes the solution-focused session by giving the student a set of meaningful compliments, reviewing strengths and goals identified by the student, and developing a homework task to further encourage behavioral change.

Case Example Illustrating Solution-Building Conversation

Box 31.1 provides an example of a solution-building conversation between a school-based practitioner and a 16-year-old student. A teacher has sent the student for help because he is sleeping during class, and she wants him to be taken out of her class because he will not participate.

Box 31.1 Case Example Illustrating Solution-Building Conversation

Student: I hate that teacher. She makes a big deal out of everything. I was not sleeping. I was just resting my eyes for a second. What a liar she is. Nobody likes her.

Social Worker: So, you think the teacher does not understand what you were doing in her class.

S: Yeah, that's right. She is just trying to get rid of me.

SW: Trying to get rid of you?

S: Yeah, she does not like me at all.

SW: How is it that the teacher came to not like you?

S: I do not know. You'd have to ask her.

SW: What if I did ask her, what might she say?

S: I don't know. What kind of question is that?

SW: It is an imagination question. So, let's just imagine for a moment that you did know what she might say, what might it be?

S: That's dumb.

SW: You think so?

S: Yeah!

SW: Well, sometimes I might ask dumb questions, but it is okay to answer me anyway. So, what would the teacher say about not liking you? [waits in silence, does not give up on answer, smiles, remains pleasant with student]

(continued)

Box 31.1 *(Continued)*

S: Hmm. I guess she might say that I skip the beginning or end of her class. It is **boring!** But, this sleeping thing is stupid!

SW: Of course, I know the sleeping thing you do not agree with. You were just resting your eyes. Let me see if I have this right. She would say that she does not like you because you do not come on time and stay throughout the whole class?

S: Yeah, that is it.

SW: So, I guess she might also say she wants you to keep your eyes open in her class even if you want to rest them?

S: That is hard to do because she is a terrible teacher and I just can't listen. I think she should have to take her own class to see how terrible she is.

SW: Maybe that would help?

S: I do not know.

SW: So, tell me, which is more important to your teacher right now: keeping your eyes open or coming on time and staying to the end of her class?

S: I guess keeping my eyes open because she says she is going to put me in in-school suspension.

SW: How do you feel about going to in-school suspension? I have met students who prefer that to a class.

S: No! I am going to be in worse trouble if I have to go back there again. I might have to go to the alternative learning center, and my mom is going to be mad.

SW: So, you want to stay in the teacher's class?

S: Really, I want to be moved to another class but Mr. Jones [the principal] said that was not going to happen.

SW: So, your choices are to stay in the teacher's class by finding a way to keep your eyes open or to go to the alternative learning center and face your mom?

S: It sucks!

SW: Yeah, it is a tough situation. I can see how you would feel frustrated. So, have there been times that you have somehow managed to keep your eyes open in the teacher's class?

S: Yeah.

SW: Tell me about those times.

S: Well, sometimes when it was interesting or she was reviewing for a test.

SW: You mean, sometimes the class is actually interesting? When would those times be?

S: Like when she is not lecturing and we are working on a group project.

SW: So, those times your eyes are wide open and you are participating too?

S: Yeah, I guess so.

SW: You said before that you did not close your eyes for too long. I bet sometimes in the past you managed to keep your eyes open even when she was lecturing and super-boring.

S: Yeah, I did.

SW: So, what percent of the time are you able to keep your eyes open? 5%? 10%? 25%?

S: 80% of the time!

SW: Wow! Even when she is boring.

S: Yeah, I think so.

SW: So, tell me, what percent do you think your teacher would give you?

S: Not as high because she blows everything up.

SW: Yes, of course. Well, just suppose she improved a little and gave you more of a fair rating. What might she say?

S: Maybe about 50 or 60%.

SW: That is pretty good. How do you think you can get to 90%?

S: Get more sleep so I can stand her boring lectures.

SW: Let's just suppose you did get some more sleep. How might that help?

S: I think it would just make me more alert and patient.

SW: Are there any other things that keep you from being alert and patient? Like, for example, a lot of students I know smoke a joint or take medications before class and that makes them sleepy. Or they might have fights with their parents or girlfriend that make them distracted.

S: No, I don't smoke before class. My mom makes me take my ADHD medicine but that does not make me sleepy.

SW: For my information, how much sleep do you usually get per night?

S: About 3–4 hours.

SW: What do you do instead of sleeping?

S: Listen to the stereo and watch TV. Sometimes talk to my friends in the chat room if I can sneak into my mom's computer room.

SW: So, how much extra sleep do you think you would need to keep your eyes open in this class?

S: I do not know. Maybe 2–3 hours more.

(continued)

Box 31.1 *(Continued)*

SW: So, maybe 5–6 hours?

S: Yeah.

SW: What about the teacher's percentage? What would she say you could do to get to 60 or 70%?

S: I think she likes it when I stay in the class and ask questions.

SW: You have done that before?

S: Yeah, sometimes.

SW: If you did that, would that get you to 70% with the teacher?

S: Maybe.

[At this point, the social worker tells the student that she is going to take a few moments to think about what has been said and write down some notes.]

SW: Well, you know, I am really impressed that you are able to keep your eyes open in a class that you feel is boring and that you find ways to stay in the class and ask questions in the class. How do you manage to do that?

S: I just do it. I am not always a bad student.

SW: No, I am hearing that you know how to be a good student and that you do not want to go to the alternative learning center. I wonder if you can try an experiment for just this week? Get 5–6 hours of sleep so you can have the patience and alertness to keep your eyes open all the time during the class. Also, do what you suggested. Stay in the class from the beginning to the end. Ask questions during class. See if that will keep the teacher from kicking you out of her class.

S: Okay, I could try that.

SW: So, you could try that?

S: Yeah.

SW: So, just so I am clear about your plan for staying in the class, tell me again what you plan to do. I want to write it down here in my notes. I will talk to you at the end of the week to see how it is working.

[Student rehearses plan and social worker asks about details of the suggested approach.]

The importance of this solution-building conversation is that the practitioner's dialog with the student results in the student becoming more cooperative and selecting his own solution for the problem at hand. Notice also that the practitioner continually builds the relationship with the student, forming a desired goal to work on, and asking the student to commit to the steps to accomplish the goal. This is an example of a solution-building process. The SFBT practitioner knows that this is only a small step but will seek to build on this cooperative beginning to help the student find ways to improve his behavior in the class. At the same time, the practitioner will work with the teacher to find out in detail what the teacher wants to see different in the student's behaviors. The practitioner might give an assignment to the teacher, like noticing when the student is doing what the teacher wants in the class.

Soliciting Cooperation and Motivation in Students Who Resist

Staff in the school view most students at risk of dropping out as unmotivated, uncooperative, or resistant. SFBT practitioners believe that everyone has motivation and people are in particular motivated toward personal goals. Every student has positive aspirations, and the solution-focused practitioner will tune into what those are with individual students. The focus is always on how the goal serves to motivate socially effective behaviors or positive interactions with others. SFBT views resistance as a normal human behavior. There are two types of resistance, active and passive. Every person has the ability to be resistant and uncooperative. At the same time, every person can be cooperative. Cooperation is something that can be facilitated when people have a relationship and are working together toward a win-win outcome. Facilitating cooperative behaviors increases the student's self-esteem and enables a true partnership between the practitioner and the student to emerge (Hawkes, Marsh, & Wilgosh, 1998).

SFBT practitioners take a curious position, or "not knowing approach," when working with students who are actively resisting. They find ways to agree with the students' points of view and do not actively confront the students on points of greatest resistance. This serves to disarm students. For example, if you are playing tug-of-war with someone and stop tugging back, they often lose their balance and stop pulling against you. SFBT practitioners use the same principle in managing passive resistance. When a student gives passive responses to questions, such as "I don't know," it is important for the practitioner to rephrase the question. These types of conversational tactics are meant to keep the conversation and relationship moving forward in the face of resistance.

Using Emotions to Engage and Motivate Students

Sometimes SFBT practitioners will construct positive engagement by prefacing their questions about what students are doing or might do to change, coupled with acknowledging their expressions of emotions and using those emotions as a catalyst for change (Miller & de Shazer, 2000). The emotional states that SFBT practitioners are most likely to use are those associated with positive aspirations, goals, wants, and desires. They will also juxtapose positive feelings and desires against feelings and outcomes that the student wishes to avoid. This is illustrated in the solution-focused conversation. In the example, the student wanted to remain in the class to avoid the consequences of going to the alternative learning center and facing the anger of his mom. The fears about the consequences of his behavior were used as a way to focus the student on a more positive outcome.

In another example, a student may say that she hates the school and does not like to attend but at the same time say that she really wants to graduate so she can get a better job. The SFBT practitioner would focus on the positive feeling and desire to graduate and ask questions about how that became an important goal in her life. They would be curious about how the student came to feel a desire to graduate, for example. How strong is that feeling? Who else in her social network or family shares that feeling? Are there any people who do not share that feeling about the importance of graduation? How does the student keep the positive desire when others are negative? The practitioner might also assess the strength and importance of the desire to graduate through a scaling question: "On a scale of 0–10, with 0 meaning you do not care that much whether you graduate or not and 10 being that you care a great deal and are ready to do about anything to make that happen, where would you say you are?" Additionally, practitioners might make statements like "Some students do not feel like they want to graduate or just give up. What makes you feel differently?" Such statements are aimed at complimenting and encouraging the student and increasing her positive feelings and desires toward graduation.

SFBT and RTI

The three-tier model, developed originally in public health, known as RTI focuses attention on identifying students that need additional assistance and on applying positive behavioral supports (PBS) across school programs with the goal of helping all students to succeed in school. By its very nature, RTI is designed to both prevent and help at-risk students. Interventions are often conceptualized as being implemented across all students at Tier 1 (prevention); with a select group of students that need more help at Tier 2 (selective interventions); and with a smaller, more exclusive high-risk group of about 5% of students that have special needs at Tier 3 (indicative interventions). As the school field has shifted to using RTI, a greater emphasis has been put on applying evidence-based practices, and this can be seen over the past decade as school-based mental health providers have begun to advocate for RTI and positive behavioral supports (Kelly, Kim, & Franklin, 2008; Franklin & Kelly, 2009).

The literature on school-based interventions clearly demonstrates that—regardless of the level of intervention chosen for a specific client problem—effective strategies employ a comprehensive approach that targets multiple intervention agents (e.g., teachers, parents, peers) and intervenes at multiple levels (e.g., classroom, school, home, and community) (Franklin & Kelly, 2009). RTI practices take into consideration the complexity of problems. For example, similar to the dropout problem described in this chapter, many three-tier interventions assume multiple "causes" to school problems and conceptualize clients more broadly, encompassing students, teachers, parents, and school faculty (Franklin & Kelly, 2009).

SFBT works well with RTI because it is a flexible approach that can be used at all three levels of intervention. It has been demonstrated in research and through school-based practice that SFBT has applicability to the different levels of intervention. SFBT has been successfully implemented at different levels of school programs and with diverse groups within the school environment.

For example, the techniques of SFBT have been used to:

- coach teachers in using solution-building talk in special education classrooms (see the WWOW program; Kelly, Kim, & Franklin, 2008)
- change interactions between parents, teachers, and students—such as parent/teacher meetings (Metcalf, 1995)
- help at-risk students in individual, group, and family interventions (Franklin, Biever, Moore, Clemons, & Scamardo, 2001; Murphy & Duncan, 2007)
- change school outcomes with students at risk to dropout such as Hispanic, pregnant, and parenting mothers (Harris & Franklin, 2008)
- target and change outcomes with adolescent substance abuse (Froeschle, Smith, & Ricard, 2007)
- change the school culture—such as when an entire school adopts the solution-focused change philosophy and trains all staff (including teachers and principals) in SFBT techniques (Franklin, Streeter, Kim, & Tripodi, 2007)

Diverse applications of SFBT illustrate the potential for different levels of interventions, from classroom prevention and school climate approaches to selective and indicative approaches that work with students that need more help in schools. SFBT has been used as a unique method for solving problems applied by diverse personnel, as well as a therapeutic intervention that helps students and families solve emotional and behavioral problems. When used within an RTI framework, it is possible to craft solution-focused interventions in ways that can meet different needs. At this time, we do not yet know in which level of intervention (i.e., preventive, selective, or indicative) that SFBT might be most helpful, but we do know that because of its flexibility as a solution-building process, SFBT has tremendous transportability and potential for being used in different ways to help at-risk students.

Tools and Practice Examples

Franklin et al. (2001) suggest that, in order to conduct SFBT, the school social workers and other mental health practitioners must follow a solution-focused process and, at a minimum, implement the miracle question, ask scaling questions, and provide compliments. An SFBT session format is flexible enough to adapt to the individual needs of each student but also structured enough to provide guidance to practitioners. Following, we describe the structure of an SFBT counseling session and illustrate several of the counseling techniques.

A typical session follows the structure discussed by Franklin and Moore (1999):

1. warm-up conversation to establish rapport and create relaxed environment
2. identifying problem and tracking new exceptions to the problem
3. using relationship questions to examine student's perception of how others view student's problem or problem resolution
4. asking scaling questions and coping questions
5. building goals and discovering solutions by asking the miracle question
6. taking a break to formulate compliments and homework
7. giving compliments and homework tasks

Structure of the Interview and Case Example

Most solution-focused interviews occur during traditional 50-minute sessions. In schools, however, these interviews may last for shorter periods of time. Interviews may last 20–30 minutes, for example. The structure of the interview is divided into three parts. The first part usually is spent making small talk with the student to find out a little bit about the student's life. During this first part, the social worker should be looking to understand the student's interests, motivations, competencies, and belief systems.

Social Worker: Hello, Charles. I understand your teacher, Mrs. Park, sent you here to see me because you're at risk of failing out of school. But I'd like to hear from you the reason you are here to see me and how this can help you. [allows student to state what the problem is]

Student: I don't know. I hate this school, and I just want to drop out so that people will leave me alone.

SW: So, if I'm understanding you correctly, you're here to see me because you hate the school and a lot of people—your teachers and maybe your parents—have been bugging you about your grades and doing homework?

S: Yeah.

SW: So what sorts of things do you like to do when you're not in school?

S: Ummm, I like to hang out with my friends.

SW: What do you and your friends talk about when you're hanging out?

S: I don't know. We talk about basketball and music and stuff. [social worker will continue to develop rapport and try to find out student's interests and belief systems]

The second part of the session, which takes up the bulk of the time—around 40 minutes in traditional sessions but maybe less time in school interviews—is spent discussing the problem, looking for exceptions, and formulating goals. One of the key components to SFBT that has been emphasized in this chapter is working with the student to identify the problem, to look for times when the problem is absent, to look for ways the solution is already occurring, and to develop attainable goals to help resolve the problem. The second part is usually initiated with questions like "How can I help you?" or "What is the reason you have come to see me?" or "How will you know when counseling is no longer necessary?" (Sklare, 1997).

SW: Okay, so how can I help you, or what can you get out of our meeting today so that you know it's been worth your time to see me?

S: I want my teachers and my parents to stop bugging me about my grades and doing homework. This school is just a waste of my time and my classes are stupid.

SW: Have you had a class that you didn't think was stupid or a waste of time? [example of looking for exceptions]

S: My English class last year was cool because we got to read some interesting books and have good discussions about them.

SW: What made the books interesting and the discussions good?

S: Well, they were books that I could understand and relate to. My teacher also made the time and effort to explain things to us and made sure we all got a turn to speak our thoughts.

SW: You said you hated this school, but yet you haven't dropped out yet. How have you managed to do that? [allows student to identify possible solutions and possible successes in what they've already been doing]

S: Well, I'm still going to some of my classes, but at this point I just don't care any more.

SW: Charles, for those classes that you do attend, what would your teachers say about your academic work? [example of relationship question]

S: I guess they might say that I don't pay attention in class, that I don't do my homework, and that I'm not trying.

SW: Do you agree with that?

S: I guess, but it's just that the classes are so stupid and boring.

SW: Charles, I'd like to ask you an unusual question. It's probably something no one has ever asked you before. Suppose, after we're done and you leave my office, you go to bed tonight and a miracle happens. This miracle solves all of your problems that brought you here today, but because you were sleeping, you didn't know it occurred. So, the next morning you wake up and you sense something is different. What will you notice that is different that lets you know this miracle occurred and your problems are solved? [example of the miracle question]

S: I guess I wouldn't be cutting class and maybe getting better grades.

SW: What will you be doing differently to get better grades?

S: I would probably be better prepared for class.

SW: What does being better prepared for class look like? [continue to probe and elicit more details and examples]

S: I'd pay attention in class and take some notes.

SW: What else would you be doing differently when you're getting better grades?

S: Probably doing my homework and not causing trouble in class with the teacher.

SW: So, what will you be doing instead of causing trouble in class?

S: Listen and sit there and take notes, I guess.

SW: So, on a scale from 1 to 10, with 1 being I'm dropping out of school no matter what and 10 being the miracle solved my problems and I'm going to graduate, where would you say you are right now? [example of a scaling question]

S: Three.

SW: What sorts of things prevent you from giving it a 2 or a 1?

S: Well, I know I need to get my high school diploma because I always thought I might go study how to be a med tech at college. I like the TV show "CSI" and want to work in forensics.

SW: Wow! You want to study forensics. So, you need to finish school for that. So, what would need to happen for you to be a 4 or a 5?

S: I'd need to start coming to classes and doing my work. [examples of student identifying goals and solutions. Social worker would continue looking for solutions that are already occurring in Charles's life and collaborate on identifying and setting small, attainable goals]

The final part of the session lasts around 5–10 minutes. This last part involves giving the student a set of compliments, homework, and determining whether to continue discussing this topic at another time. In school settings, practitioners such as teachers and social workers have separated this last part from the rest of the conversation. The break, for example, might be extended, and the conversation might pick up in a different class period or at a different time of the day (e.g., before and after lunch).

SW: I'd like to take a minute to write down some notes based on what we've talked about. Is there anything else you feel I should know before I take this quick break?

S: No.

SW: [after taking a break] Well, Charles, I'd like to compliment you on your commitment to staying in school despite your frustrations. You seem like a bright student and understand the importance of finishing high school. I'd like to meet with you again to continue our work together. Would that be all right with you?

S: Sure.

SW: So, for next week, I'd like you to try and notice when things are going a little bit better in your classes and what you're doing differently during those times.

Internet Resources for Solution-Focused Schools

Brief Family Therapy Center: www.brief-therapy.org

Cynthia Franklin: www.utexas.edu/ssw/faculty/franklin

Garza High School: A Solution-Focused High School: http://www.austinschools.org/garza

Key Points to Remember

Dropping out of school is a serious problem that is in epidemic proportions in urban areas and among high risk populations.

SFBT is one intervention that can help school social workers and other school professionals engage with and help at-risk youths to create solutions that may remove barriers to their school achievement. SFBT is grounded in research, and the studies have increasingly shown that this approach is helpful in changing the emotions, behaviors, and academic problems of at-risk students. SFBT is also a flexible approach that is very adaptable to the school setting and works well with the RTI approaches.

Specifically, SFBT builds on student strengths, and that may change the way students think about and approach their problems. SFBT offers conversational, questioning techniques that help practitioners to engage students in a solution-building process. A solution-building process helps students to discover goals, tasks, and behaviors that can change future outcomes.

The SFBT practitioner acts as a catalyst or facilitator and creates an interpersonal context where the solutions emerge from students and their ideas.

SFBT also provides specific skills for engaging, motivating, and eliciting cooperation in resistant students. Techniques include going with resistance, focusing on personal goals, taking a curious, not-knowing approach, playing dumb, and reinforcing positive emotions.

The structure of the SFBT counseling session has three parts. Case examples have given an overview of the parts and how SFBT can be used to help students at risk of dropping out.

References

Aloise-Young, P. A., & Chavez, E. L. (2002). Not all school dropouts are the same: Ethnic differences in the relation between reason for leaving school and adolescent substance use. *Psychology in the Schools, 39*(5), 539–547.

Balfanz, R. (2007). *What your community can do to end its dropout crisis: Learning from research and practice.* Baltimore, MD: Center for Social Organization of Schools, John Hopkins University.

Berg, I. K., & De Jong, P. (1996). Solution-building conversation: Co-constructing a sense of competence with clients. *Families in Society: The Journal of Contemporary Human Services*, 77, 376–391.

Berg, I. K., & Shilts, L. (2005). *Classroom solutions: WOWW approach.* Milwaukee, WI: Brief Family Therapy Center.

Chapman, C., Laird, J., & Kewal-Ramani, A. (2010). *Trends in high school dropout and completion rates in the United States: 1972–2008 (NCES 2011–012).* Washington, DC: National Center for Education Statistics, Institute of Education Sciences, U.S. Department of Education. Retrieved from http://nces.ed.gov/pubs2012/2012006.pdf

Corcoran, J. (1998). Solution-focused practice with middle and high school at-risk youths. *Social Work in Education, 20*(4), 232–244.

De Jong, P., & Berg, I. K. (2001). Co-constructing cooperation with mandated clients. *Social Work, 46*(4), 361–381.

De Jong, P., & Berg, I. K. (2012). *Interviewing for solutions (2nd ed.).* Pacific Grove, CA: Brooks/Cole.

de Shazer, S. (1985). *Keys to solution in brief therapy.* New York: Norton.

Franklin, C., Biever, J., Moore, K., Clemons, D., & Scamardo, M. (2001). The effectiveness of solution-focused therapy with children in a school setting. *Research on Social Work Practice, 11*(4), 411–434.

Franklin, C., Corcoran, J., Nowicki, J., & Streeter, C. (1997). Using client self-anchored scales to measure outcomes in solution-focused therapy. *Journal of Systemic Therapies, 10*(3), 246–265.

Franklin, C., & Nurius, P. (1998). Distinction between social constructionism and cognitive constructivism: Practice applications. In C. Franklin & P. Nurius (Eds.), *Constructivism in practice: Methods and challenges (pp. 57–94).* Milwaukee, WI: Families International.

Franklin, C., & Kelly, M. S. (2009). Becoming evidenced informed in the real world of school social work practice, *Children & Schools, 31*, 46–58.

Franklin, C., Kim, J., & Stewart, K. S. (2012). Solution-focused brief therapy in school settings. In C. Franklin, T. Trepper, W. Gingerich, & E. McCollum (Eds.), *Solution-focused brief therapy: A handbook of evidence-based practice* (pp. 231–246). New York, NY: Oxford University Press.

Franklin, C., Montgomery, K. L., Baldwin, V., & Webb, L. (2012). Research and development of a solution-focused high school. In C. Franklin, T. Trepper, W. Gingerich, & E. McCollum, (Eds.), *Solution-focused brief therapy: A handbook of evidence-based practice (pp. 371–389).* New York, NY: Oxford University Press.

Franklin, C., & Moore, K. C. (1999). Solution-focused brief family therapy. In C. Franklin & C. Jordan, *Family practice: Brief systems methods for social work* (pp. 143–174). Pacific Grove, CA: Brooks/Cole.

Franklin, C., Moore, K., & Hopson, L. (2008). Effectiveness of solution-focused brief therapy in a school setting. *Children & Schools, 30*, 15–26.

Franklin, C., Streeter, C. L., Kim, J. S., & Tripodi, S. J. (2007). The effectiveness of a solution-focused, public alternative school for dropout prevention and retrieval. *Children & Schools, 29*, 133–144.

Froeschle, J. G., Smith, R. L., & Ricard, R. (2007). The efficacy of a systematic substance abuse program for adolescent females. *Professional School Counseling, 10*, 498–505.

Harris, M. B., & Franklin, C. (2008). *Taking charge: A school based life skills program for adolescent mothers.* New York, NY: Oxford University Press.

Hawkes, D., Marsh, T., & Wilgosh, R. (Eds.) (1998). How to begin: The concepts of solution-focused therapy. In *Solution focused therapy: A handbook for health care professionals (pp. 5–15).* Woburn, MA: Reed.

Jordan, W. L., Lara, J., & McPartland, J. M. (1996). Exploring the causes of early dropout among race-ethnic and gender groups. *Youth & Society, 28*(1), 62–94.

Kelly, M. S., Kim, J. S., & Franklin, C. (2008). *Solution-Focused Brief Therapy in schools: A 360-degree view of the research and practice principles.* New York, NY: Oxford University Press.

Kim, J. S. (2008). Examining the effectiveness of solution-focused brief therapy: A meta-analysis. *Research on Social Work Practice, 18*, 107–116.

Kim, J. S., & Franklin, C. (2009). Solution-focused brief therapy in schools: A review of the literature. *Children and Youth Services Review, 31*(4), 464–470.

Kral, R. (1995). *Strategies that work: Techniques for solutions in schools.* Milwaukee, WI: Brief Family Therapy Press.

Lathem, J. (2002). Brief solution-focused therapy. *Child and Adolescent Mental Health*, 7(4), 189–192.

Lee, M. Y. (Ed.). (1997). A study of solution-focused brief family therapy: Outcomes and issues. *American Journal of Family Therapy, 25*, 3–17.

Metcalf, L. (1995). *Counseling toward solutions: A practical solution-focused program for working with students, teachers, and parents.* San Francisco: Jossey-Bass.

Metcalf, L. (2008). *A field guide to counseling toward solutions.* San Francisco, CA: Jossey-Bass.

Miller, G., & de Shazer, S. (2000). Emotions in solution-focused therapy: A re-examination. *Family Process, 39*(1), 5.

Murphy, J. J., & Duncan, B. S. (2007). *Brief interventions for school problems (2nd ed.).* New York, NY: Guilford Press.

National Dropout Prevention Center. (2012). National Dropout Prevention Center/Network: Effective strategies. Available: http://www.dropoutprevention.org/effstrat/effstrat.htm.

Pichot, T., & Dolan, Y. (2003). *Solution-focused brief therapy: Its effective use in agency settings.* Binghamton, NY: Hawthorne.

Prevatt, F., & Kelly, F. D. (2003). Dropping out of school: A review of intervention programs. *Journal of School Psychology, 5*, 377–395.

Rumberger, R. W. (1987). High school dropouts: A review of issues and evidence. *Review of Educational Research, 57*(2), 101–121.

Rumberger, R. W., Ghatak, R., Poulos, G., Ritter, P. L., & Dornbusch, S. M. (1990). Family influences on dropout behavior in one California high school. *Sociology of Education, 63*, 283–299.

Rumberger, R. W., & Thomas, S. L. (2000). The distribution of dropout and turnover rates among urban and suburban high school. *Sociology of Education, 73*(1), 39–67.

Rumberger, R. W. (2004). Why students drop out of school. In G. Orfied (Ed.), *Dropouts in America: Confronting the graduation rate crisis* (pp. 131–155). Cambridge, MA: Harvard Education Press.

Sklare, G. (1997). *Brief counseling that works: A solution-focused approach for school counselors.* Thousand Oaks, CA: Corwin Press/Sage.

Slavin, R. E., & Fashola, O. S. (1998). *Show me the evidence: Proven and promising programs for America's schools.* New York: Corwin Press.

Springer, D., Lynch, C., & Rubin, A. (2000). Effects of a solution-focused mutual aid group for Hispanic children of incarcerated parents. *Child & Adolescent Social Work Journal, 17*(6), 431–442.

Swanson, C. B. (2008). *Cities in crisis: A special analytic report on high school graduation.* Bethesda MD: Editorial Projects in Education.

Walter, J. L., & Peller, J. E. (1996). Rethinking our assumptions: Assuming anew in a postmodern world. In S. Miller, M. Hubble, & B. Duncan (Eds.), *Handbook of solution-focused brief therapy (pp. 9–26).* San Francisco: Jossey-Bass.

Webb, W. H. (1999). *Solutioning: Solution-focused interventions for counselors.* Philadelphia, PA: Accelerated Press.

What Works Clearinghouse. (n.d.). *Interventions for preventing high school dropout.* Retrieved from http://ies.ed.gov/ncee/wwc/topic.aspx?sid=3

Primary Prevention of Pregnancy

Effective School-Based Programs

Mary Beth Harris

CHAPTER 32

Getting Started

For decades the educational, social, and economic consequences of adolescent pregnancy and childbirth have presented a compelling challenge to schools. High schools and middle schools were coping with the growing presence of teen pregnancy for more than 15 years before it caught the country's attention in the 1980s. Between 1972 and 1990 births to teenage mothers increased by 23% to an all-time high (National Campaign to Prevent Teen Pregnancy, 2002).

These numbers alone were alarming to educators and health care professionals, but it was the continuing rise in nonmarital births and welfare dependency among adolescent mothers that placed teen pregnancy at the center of legislative debate and national program initiatives. Thus began a national focus on preventing adolescent pregnancy, fueled early on with relatively small grants and more recently with $250 million for abstinence education programs provided by the 1996 Welfare Reform Law. By 2001 more than 700 public-funded pregnancy prevention programs have been established in over 47% of urban communities across the United States, in community agencies and churches, medical facilities, and schools (Jindal, 2001).

The overall teen birth rate in the general population reduced from 59.9 per thousand in 1990 to 39.1 per thousand in 2009. Most experts agree that this reduction in the national adolescent birthrate is likely the result of several factors, including not only more sex education and pregnancy prevention programs but also growing concern about HIV and STD, and a decade of widespread financial well-being that provided youth with more life opportunities. Statistics cited in a recent report from the Alan Guttmacher Institute (2010) showed that in 2006 the birthrate for adolescent women ages 15 to 17 was 32% lower than in 1991. This report also indicates that the birthrate for younger adolescents, who are believed to be the most at risk for negative consequences, has reduced from 9.2 per 1000 in 2001 to 7.1 per thousand in 2006. Even among adolescents aged 15–19, birth rates declined for African-American women by 45% between 1991 and 2006, for non-Hispanic white women by 50%, and for Hispanic youth by 26%. With these indications of progress, however, there are 820,000 teen pregnancies each year, and over 400,000 teen births (National Campaign to Prevent Teen Pregnancy, 2006). Nearly 4 out of 10 girls in this country get pregnant at least once while they are still in adolescence. This is a higher adolescent pregnancy rate, by far, than in any other industrialized nation (Bennett & Assefi, 2005).

With teen pregnancy still an issue of deep concern, schools often depend on their mental health staff to provide pregnancy prevention services. Programs numbering in the hundreds can be overwhelming to school-based practitioners with the responsibility to select a program that is effective and that fits with the school and the local community. Teen pregnancy and sex education remain controversial "hot topics," and programs vary in emphasis and content. When social workers and mental health services are competing for school and community resources, a priority is to select or develop a pregnancy prevention program that demonstrates visible results.

This chapter explores school-based pregnancy prevention practices and three broad categories of programs currently in use in schools across the nation. It identifies programs and program components that have been evaluated and demonstrated effective in modifying adolescent sexual behavior and preventing adolescent pregnancy. It provides guidance for assessing program goodness-of-fit to the needs and values of the local school and community, and for planning and carrying out programs demonstrated effective in school settings. A bibliography of resources provides program specifics and contact information for locating programs that have been demonstrated to be effective.

What We Know

On a daily basis school-based mental health professionals witness the discouraging consequences of adolescent pregnancy for teenage parents and their children. Even though the national rate of adolescent pregnancy has diminished in the United States, the problem is still very real and present in American schools. At the forefront of concerns is the phenomenally high rate of school dropout among adolescent mothers. Across the nation, more than 60% of teen mothers who have a child before age 18 drop out of high school (Shuger, 2012).

Not completing high school or a GED by the age of 20 is a decisive indicator of future poverty. Women who become mothers in adolescence, along with their children, are far more likely to live in poverty than women who postpone childbearing until their twenties. According to Sawhill (1998), virtually all of the increase in child poverty over the past decades was related to the increase in non-marital childbearing, half of which was to mothers who had their first child in their teens. Some 51% of all mothers on welfare had their first child as a teenager. The majority of teen births occur outside of marriage (Martin et al., 2006), and about one-fourth of teen mothers have a second child within 24 months of the first birth. Both of these factors further contribute to economic dependency and poverty (National Campaign to Prevent Teen Pregnancy, 2010).

The penalties for children born to teenage mothers are numerous and serious. They are more likely to be born prematurely and at low birth weight (Martin et al., 2006), leading to a number of chronic medical and developmental problems. They are more likely to fall behind academically and less likely to graduate from high school (Levine, Emery, & Pollack, 2007; Terry-Humen, Manlove, & Moore, 2005). Sons are more likely to become involved with the law and to be incarcerated (Scher & Hoffman, 2008). Daughters and sons are 22% more likely to become teen mothers themselves (Hoffman, 2008). They are more likely to be poor. These children are more restricted by developmental, economic, and social factors that limit their resources and life options than children born to mothers age 20 and older.

What We Can Do

Over the past two decades the number of adolescent pregnancy prevention programs has mushroomed into the hundreds. These programs essentially aim to delay the initiation of sex, increase abstinence, and increase use of contraception. More than 100 pregnancy prevention programs have been evaluated (Bennett & Assefi, 2005; Franklin & Corcoran, 2000; Kirby, Rolleri, & Wilson, 2007). In this chapter we review programs in which the main goal is to prevent first-time pregnancies.

Program Categories and Emphasis

Pregnancy prevention programs can be categorized according to their distinctive features and special emphases. This chapter is concerned with school-based and school-linked programs where the school system assumes primary responsibility. It is also helpful for school-based practitioners to be familiar with local community programs offered at social service agencies or in hospitals or clinics. The format and focus of programs that have been evaluated and demonstrated effective in changing sexual behavior and preventing pregnancy fall into three broad categories: (1) sex education with or without contraception, (2) youth development or life options programs, and (3) service learning programs (Manlove et al., 2004). Abstinence program goals can be found in all of these categories, as well as program goals for reducing sexual behavior or risks related to sexual behavior. Kirby (2007) distinguish programs with abstinence goals into abstinence-only or abstinence-plus, noting that these two types actually fall along a continuum rather than neatly into separate types.

While two-thirds of 48 abstinence-plus programs that have been rigorously evaluated show effectiveness, numerous credible evaluations provide strong evidence that abstinence-only programs have no impact on sexual behavior (Kirby, 2007). For example, a 10-year evaluation of abstinence-only education programs by Mathmatica (Trenholm et al., 2007) concluded that abstinence-only programs are no more effective in preventing adolescent pregnancy and sexual activity than having no sex education program.

Sex Education Programs

These programs focus on delaying (abstinence) or reducing sexual activity. They range from short courses of fewer than 10 hours to comprehensive courses of more than 40 hours. The focus of sex education prevention programs varies. Some programs include contraceptive information and distribution, while others exclude this content. Although a survey in 2000 showed that 78% of parents of teenagers believed that their children should receive information about birth control and safe sex in school (Hoff & Greene, 2000), this remains a controversial issue and should be researched in the local district before selecting a program. Regardless of contraception as a program feature, most sex education prevention programs contain these components:

1. Skills building, including decision making, interpersonal, and assertiveness
2. Values clarification
3. Relevant information provision
4. Peer education where teens can educate other teens
5. Youth theater projects where dramatic scenarios serve as catalysts for discussion
6. Computer-assisted instruction for parents and adolescents
7. Day-long conferences and training

Life Options/Youth Development Programs

Life options programs focus on changing sexual behaviors and reducing pregnancies through enhancing life skills and increasing options for disadvantaged youths (Philliber & Allen, 1992). The core assumption, based on research evidence (Afexentiou & Hawley, 1997; Allen, Philliber, Herrling, & Kuperminc, 1997), is that youths who have higher educational aspirations and greater opportunities are more likely to delay sexual intercourse and childbearing. Life options programs target teenagers' educational and earnings opportunities, such as postsecondary education, job training programs, and guaranteed student loans.

Youth development programs with a number of components that target both sexuality and youth development are demonstrated in a number of program evaluation studies to be the most effective interventions for pregnancy prevention (Kirby, 2001). For example, the Carrera Program, a multi-component program offered by the Children's Aid Society, was demonstrated to prevent pregnancies for as long as 3 years. This program includes interventions common to many youth development/life options programs that focus on sexuality as well as youth development, offered in combination over time. Core components of the Carrera program are (1) family life and sex education, (2) individual academic assessment and preparation for standardized tests and college prep exams, (3) tutoring, (4) self-expression activities through use of the arts, and (5) comprehensive health and mental health care (Manlove et al., 2004).

Most effective life options programs, such as the Carrera Program (Philliber, Williams Kaye, Herrling, & West, 2002) and the Quantum Opportunities Program (Taggart & Lattimore, 2001), include sexuality and sexual behavior as a focus. Skills building in all life domains, however, is the primary curricular theme. Here are some of the personal and social skills included in the developmental curriculum of the Quantum Opportunities Program (Manlove et al., 2004):

- Awareness skills focusing on building self-esteem, including strategies for coping with peer pressure, stereotyping, and prejudice
- Community skills, including how to use available resources such as public transportation, libraries, and clinics
- Decision-making skills focusing on issues such as dropping out of school, marriage, parenting, and attending college
- Health skills, including first aid and preventive care

- Relationship skills that help with communication abilities
- Safety skills, including discussions of risky behaviors related to alcohol, drugs, and sex

Target populations for youth development programs are male and female multiracial junior high and high school students, similar to target populations for other pregnancy prevention programs. A number of studies have examined the effectiveness of life options/youth development programs in preventing pregnancy (e.g., Allen et al., 1997; Philliber et al., 2002), and the results are promising.

Service Learning Programs

Service learning is generally defined as curriculum-based community service that integrates classroom learning with community service activities (Denner, Coyle, Robin, & Banspach, 2005). As prevention programs that focus on positive decision making and enhanced self-awareness and self-worth rather than directly on sexuality, service learning programs show promise in both pregnancy prevention and STD/HIV prevention. Programs that have been evaluated, such as the Teen Outreach Program (Kirby, 2007; Philliber & Allen, 1992) and the Reach for Health Community Youth Service Learning program (O'Donnell et al., 2002), were found effective in preventing pregnancy as well as other positive effects such as educational achievement and social attitudes and behavior. These programs require youth to volunteer in the community and to participate in journaling, group reflections, and classroom activities and discussions. Usually service learning is differentiated from community service alone in that service learning is organized in relation to a class with clearly stated objectives and classroom goals (Franklin & Corcoran, 2000). Across school districts service learning is the central intervention with a number of youth populations and prevention programs, such as dropout prevention and gang intervention and prevention.

These are the primary program components of the Teen Outreach Program:

- Supervised volunteering. Students research agencies and services and select a volunteer opportunity in the community, such as peer tutoring or volunteering in a nursing home or hospital. Throughout the year they meet regularly with their volunteer supervisor and/or classroom facilitator around their experiences.
- Weekly classroom discussions and activities. Students share their volunteer experiences with one another, and lessons from the accompanying curriculum *Changing Scenes* are used to focus the discussion.

A classroom curriculum, *Changing Scenes,* is used throughout the program. These are some of the topics and lessons:

- A chapter on values includes a discussion in which students explore how they learn values and an activity that engages participants in exploring their beliefs about gender roles
- A chapter on relationships includes exercises and activities on making friends, romantic relationships, the difference between love and infatuation, and dealing with pressure in relationships
- A chapter on short-term and long-term personal goals includes activities on setting and achieving goals and looking at teen parenthood and some of the barriers it poses to achieving one's life goals

Characteristics of Effective Curriculum-Based Programs

We now recognize that effective programs exist in all three of the approaches and categories just discussed. Researcher-author Douglas Kirby (2001) identified characteristics of effective curriculum-based programs across all categories. These are in-common characteristics in programs that have been rigorously evaluated and found to increase the age of first sex, improve the use of contraception among sexually active teens, and/or actually reduce teen pregnancy. The following is a summary:

- They have a specific, narrow focus on *behavior,* such as delaying first sex or using contraception or condoms.
- They have theoretical approaches, such as cognitive behavior and planned behavior, that have been effective with other high-risk health-related behavior. These seek to impact the beliefs, attitudes, confidence, and skills that relate to sexual behavior, which may lead to voluntary change in sexual or contraceptive behavior.

- They give the clear message about sex and protection against STD that not having sex or using condoms or other contraception is the *right* thing to do, more than simply laying out the pros and cons of sexual choices.
- They provide basic, not detailed, information about contraception and unprotected sex.
- They address peer pressure related to sex and discuss misperceptions and "lines."
- They teach communication, negotiation, and refusal skills. Some provide clear scripts for role-playing situations on these issues.
- They occur in a safe social environment that encourages participation. They include games, role playing, written exercises, videos, and small group discussions, all to help participants personalize the material. Some use peer facilitators and videos of people the students can identify with.
- They reflect the age, sexual experience, and culture of the youth participating. For example, curriculum for middle school adolescents focuses on postponing sexual intercourse, while for high schoolers, programs usually emphasize avoiding unprotected sex with abstinence or the use of contraception.
- The most effective programs last at least 14 hours or longer and have a greater number of different activities for participants.
- They are strident in carefully selecting leaders who believe in the program, and they provide leaders with training sessions that last from 6 hours to 3 days and include both information and practice in using the strategies and exercises in the curriculum.

Applying Pregnancy Prevention Programs within a Response to Intervention Framework

Response to Intervention (RTI) is a widely used three-tier model for program planning, intervention, and evaluation in education. More recently adapted and effectively utilized with mental health and social service interventions in schools (Kelly et al., 2010), it can be a viable frame for implementing teen pregnancy prevention programs. It is based on the assumption that when risk factors continue to put a student at greater risk than the general student population after primary preventive intervention, then stronger, more focused intervention is required (Elliott, Witt, Kratochwill, & Stoiber, 2002).

As a three-tier model, RTI prescribes a primary prevention intervention for the entire student body at the first level. For students who do not respond to the Tier 1 intervention or who are assessed at greater risk than the general student body, stronger, more focused intervention is prescribed at Tier 2. For the smaller percentage of students, usually 5% to 8% (National Center on Response to Intervention, 2011), who are most at risk, still more intense Tier 3 intervention is prescribed.

For pregnancy or STD/HIV prevention, Tier 1 intervention may be, for example, general sex education curriculum included in health classes required by all ninth-grade students. Students who are assessed to be at higher risk for pregnancy or STD than the general ninth-grade population may be referred to participate in one of the programs noted in this chapter. One of the most critical processes in identifying these students is assessment based on research-informed indicators of high-risk sexual behavior and teen pregnancy. Tier 3 intervention, which may include individual counseling and focus on other individually identified needs, is prescribed for adolescents whose response to the Tier 2 program is not adequate, based on changes in behavioral and other measured outcomes. In following an RTI model for presenting a pregnancy prevention program at three levels, careful attention to the use of objective measures and scrupulous assessment data is critical.

Tools and Practice Examples

Effective Programs Lists

Research determining the effectiveness of pregnancy prevention programs continues to accumulate. This section focuses on lists of programs that have been rigorously evaluated and found to be effective, compiled by four recognized groups associated with adolescent pregnancy and other youth-related issues (Solomon & Card, 2004). The programs included in these lists are believed to be credible because they are based on actual behavior changes among teens in a program compared to a group of similar youth who were not in the program. Because the groups used slightly different criteria for selecting effective programs, the lists are somewhat diverse. Some programs, however, were selected for inclusion in three or all four lists. This section includes a brief discussion of criteria considered in selecting programs for each list, as well as a list of nine programs

(Table 32.1) that were included in at least three of the four lists (Solomon & Card, 2004).

- *The Kirby List* (Kirby, 2007). The programs included in this list met six key criteria: (1) The program outcome was the reduction of primary pregnancy and/or STD/HIV infection, (2) the primary target population was middle school or high school age, 18 years and younger, (3) the evaluation study used an experimental or quasi-experimental design with pretest and posttest, (4) the evaluation study had a sample of at least 100 in the combined treatment and comparison groups, (5) the evaluation study used outcome measures of actual behavior or health status (in addition or instead of attitude/knowledge outcome measures), and (6) appropriate statistical analysis was used in the evaluation study.
- *The Child Trends List* (Manlove et al., 2001, 2002). Studies were reviewed that focused on primary pregnancy, secondary pregnancy, initiation of sexual intercourse, frequency of sexual activity, number of partners, and/or STD/HIV prevention. Criteria included (1) a sample of youth of any age (no sample size restriction identified) and (2) evaluations with experimental design and reproductive health outcomes. Selected studies were required to measure outcomes during adolescence,

Table 32.1 Programs Included in at Least Three Effective Program Lists

Name of Program	*Kirby (2007)*	*Child Trends (2001, 2002)*	*PASHA (2007)*	*Advocates (2003)*
Sex Education Approach				
Be Proud! Be Responsible!		*	*	*
Becoming a Responsible Teen	*	*	*	*
Making a Difference:	*		*	*
An Abstinence Approach				
to STD, Teen Pregnancy,				
and HIV/AIDS Prevention				
Making Proud Choices	*	*	*	*
Reducing the Risk	*	*		*
Safer Choices	*	*	*	*
Service Learning Approach				
Reach for Health				
Community Youth Sources				
Teen Outreach Program	*	*	*	*
Sex Education + Youth Development Approach	*	*		*
Aba Aya	*	*	*	*
Children's Aid Society—				
Carrera Program	*	*	*	*

Source: Adapted and updated from Solomon & Card, 2004.

regardless of whether the sample included adolescents or younger children.

- *The PASHA List* (Card, Lessard, & Benner, 2007). The PASHA (Program Archive on Sexuality, Health & Adolescence) list is updated periodically, most recently in 2006. Replication kits containing materials needed to operate and evaluate more than 35 programs on the list are available to practitioners through PASHA (see Card, Lessard, & Benner, 2007). To be considered for this list, a program must target youth ages 10–19, although STD/HIV prevention programs targeting college students are also eligible. Evaluation criteria include an experimental or quasi-experimental design and pretest and posttest assessments. A follow-up period of at least 6 months is required for pregnancy prevention programs. Program outcomes criteria include delay of initiation of intercourse, frequency of intercourse, number of sexual partners, contraceptive use, refusal or negotiation skills, values, and attitudes toward risk-taking behavior.
- *The Advocates List* (Advocates for Youth, 2011). This list of 19 programs is part of a report published by Advocates for Youth, entitled *Science and Success: Sex Education and Other Programs That Work to Prevent Teen Pregnancy.* The list includes only programs that focus on primary pregnancies and STD/HIV infection. Programs included for consideration meet these criteria: (1) target youth ranging from infancy to the teen years, (2) evaluation criteria include an experimental or quasi-experimental design with treatment and control/comparison conditions, (3) have a sample of at least 100 combined in treatment and control/comparison groups, (4) evaluation results must have been published in a peer-reviewed journal as a proxy for high-quality design and analysis, (5) programs must have had follow-up measures at least 3 months after completion of the intervention, and (6) must have had results in which two risky sexual behaviors showed significant positive change or demonstrated a significant reduction in pregnancy and/or STD/HIV rates.

Selecting a Program and Getting Started

School practitioners know that simply having been demonstrated effective is not enough if a program does not fit the school, the community, and the target population of students. At the same time, altering the goals or content of an established and effective program in order to make it fit the needs of the local school is likely to diminish the program's effectiveness. These tips can help guide the search for the best program for your particular school and community (Solomon and Card, 2004):

1. Talk with community members such as teachers, parents, local clergy and politicians, health care providers, and students, who have an investment in the program. Inquire about their preferences and values around teen pregnancy prevention, including their views on sex education and contraception. Use what you learn from these stakeholders to aim for programs that have been found effective in achieving *goals and objectives that are relevant and acceptable* to your school and community.
2. Engage with your school's administrators and interdisciplinary mental health team about initiating a prevention program, so that all of you have investment in its operation and success. Of prime consideration is the availability of resources such as space, staff, and especially funding.
3. Look for programs that were effective with youth who are as similar to your target group of students as possible. Some important characteristics are age, gender, ethnicity, acculturation, language, incarceration status, drug and alcohol use, and literacy level. All of these can influence participants' interest in the program and ability to benefit from it.
4. Once you have narrowed your program selections to two or three, determine which of these has replication kits or treatment manuals. It is far more difficult to present a program if the original program materials are not available in a user-friendly format. PASHA (http://www.socio.com/pasha.htm), for example, offers replication kits for 35 to 40 different programs and provides sources for nine additional programs that it identifies as effective.

Bibliography of Resources

Aban Aya Youth Project
The Aban Aya Team, Sociometrics
Los Altos, CA

Becoming a Responsible Teen

Curriculum & materials contact: Doug Kirby, Ph.D., Senior Research Scientist
4 Carbonero Way
Scotts Valley, CA 95066
Phone: 800–435–8433
FAX: 800–435–8433
E-mail: dougk@etr.org
http://www.etr.org

Be Proud! Be Responsible!

Curriculum & materials contact: Select Media Film Library, 22-D
Hollywood Avenue
Hohokus, NJ 07423
Phone: 800–343–3540
FAX: 201–652–1973
http://www.selectmedia.org

Making a Difference! An Abstinence-Based Approach to HIV/STD and Teen Pregnancy Prevention

Curriculum and materials contact: Select Media Film Library, 22-D
Hollywood Avenue
Hohokus, NJ 07423
Phone: 800–343–5540
FAX: 201–652–1973
http://www.selectmedia.org

Making Proud Choices

Curriculum and materials contact: Select Media Film Library, 22-D
Hollywood Avenue
Hohokus, NJ 07423
Phone: 800–343–5540
FAX: 201–652–1973
http://www.selectmedia.org

Children's Aid Society—Carrera Program

Curriculum and materials contact: Michael Carrera, Ed.D., Program Designer
The Children's Aid Society
105 East 22nd Street
New York, NY 10010
Phone: 212–876–9716
http://www.stopteenpregnancy.com

Teen Outreach Program

Program contact: Gayle Waden, TOP National Coordinator
One Greenway Plaza, Suite 550
Houston, TX 77046–0103
Phone: 713–627–2322
FAX: 713–627–3006
E-mail: gwaden@cornerstone.to
www.cornerstone.to

Note: Profiles of these and other programs, including goals, population, program size and duration, and curriculum, can be accessed on the Web site of the National Campaign to Prevent Teen and Unplanned Pregnancy (http://www.thenational-campagin.org).

Key Points to Remember

Although the United States has achieved a large reduction over the past two decades, adolescent pregnancy and childbirth still looms large as a complex challenge for schools dealing with young parents. Teen pregnancy prevention programs are available in nearly half of all American urban communities, with a large number in public schools. School-based mental health practitioners are often responsible for originating and managing teen pregnancy prevention programs and services for students at risk in their schools. Fortunately, a substantial number of diverse programs have now been rigorously evaluated and found to be effective in postponing or diminishing adolescent sexual activity and pregnancy. Practitioners with the responsibility of selecting and establishing pregnancy prevention services in the school have many choices of effective programs that fit the needs and resources of their school and community. This chapter has explained three approaches to teen pregnancy prevention programs, including (1) curriculum-based sex education, (2) the youth development/life options approach, and (3) the service learning approach, with program examples and program availability within each approach.

References

Advocates for Youth. (2003). *Science and success: Sex education and other programs that work to prevent teen pregnancy, HIV, and sexually transmitted infections.* Washington, DC: Author. Accessed online November 12, 2004, at http://www.advocatesforyouth.org/publications/ScienceSuccess.pdf

Afexentiou, D., & Hawley, C. B. (1997). Explaining female teenagers' sexual behavior and outcomes: A bivariate probit analysis with selectivity correction. *Journal of Family and Economic Issues,* 18(1), 91–106.

Alan Guttmacher Institute. (2010). *U.S. teenage pregnancy statistics: National and state trends and trends by race and ethnicity.* Retrieved July 16, 2011, from www.guttmacher.org/pus/state_pregnancy_trends.pdf

Allen, J. P., Philliber, S., Herrling, S., & Kuperminc, G. P. (1997). Preventing teen pregnancy and academic failure: Experimental evaluation of a developmentally-based approach. *Child Development,* 64(4), 729–742.

Bennett, S. E., & Assefi, N.P. (2005). School-based teenage pregnancy prevention programs: A systematic review of randomized controlled trials. *Journal of Adolescent Health, 36,* 72–81.

Card, J. J., Lessard, L., & Benner, T. (2007). *PASHA: Facilitating the replication and use of effective adolescent pregnancy and STI/HIV prevention programs.* Los Altos, CA: Sociometrics Corporation.

Child Trends. (2001). Retrieved on November 24, 2004, from http://www.childtrends.org/PDF/KnightReports/KRepro.pdf

ChildTrends. (2002). Retrieved on November 27, 2004, from http://www.childtrends.org/PDF/KnightReports/KRepro.pdf

Denner, J., Coyle, K., Robin, L., & Banspach, S. (2005). Integrating service learning into a curriculum to reduce health risks at alternative high schools. *Journal of School Health,* 75(5), 151–157.

Elliott, S. N., Witt, J. C., Kratochwill, T. R., & Stoiber, K. C. (2002). Selecting and evaluating classroom interventions. In M. Shinn, H. Walker, & G. Stoner (Eds.), *Interventions for academic and behavior problems II: Preventive and remedial approaches* (pp. 243–294). Bethesda, MD: National Association of School Psychologists.

Franklin, C., & Corcoran, J. (2000). Preventing adolescent pregnancy: A review of programs and practices. *Social Work,* 45(1), 40–52.

Hoffman, S. D. (2008). Consequences of teen childbearing for mothers: Updated estimates of the consequences of teen childbearing for mothers. In S. D. Hoffman, & R. A. Maynard (Eds.), *Kids having kids: Economic costs & social consequences of teen pregnancy* (2nd ed., pp. 74–92). Washington, DC: The Urban Institute Press.

Hoff. T., & Greene L. (2000). Sex education in America, a series ofnational surveys of students, parents, teachers and principals. TheKaiser Family Foundation.

Jindal, B. P. (2001). *Report to House Committee on Ways and Means Subcommittee on Human Resources November 15.* Washington, DC: U.S. Government.

Kelly, M., Frey, A., Alvarez, M., Berzin, S., Shaffer, G., & O'Brien, K. (2010). School social work practice and response to intervention. *Children & Schools, 32*(4), 201–209.

Kirby, D. (2001). *Emerging answers: Research findings on programs to reduce teen pregnancy.* Washington, DC: National Campaign to Prevent Teen Pregnancy.

Kirby, D. (2007). Emerging Answers 2007: Research Findings on Programsto Reduce Teen Pregnancy and Sexually Transmitted Diseases. Washington, DC: National Campaign to Prevent Teen and UnplannedPregnancy.

Kirby, D., Rolleri, L., & Wilson, M. M. (2007). *Tool to assess the characteristics of effective sex and STD/HIV education programs.* Washington, DC: Healthy Teen Network.

Manlove, J., Terry-Humen, E., Papillo, A. R., Franzetta, K., Williams, S., & Ryan, S. (2001). *Background for community-level work on positive reproductive health in adolescence: Reviewing the literature on contributing factors.* Washington, DC: Child Trends. Retrieved online November 23, 2004, at www.childtrends.org/PDF/KnightReports/KRepro.pdf

Manlove, J., Terry-Humen, E., Papillo, A. R., Franzetta, K., Williams, S., & Ryan, S. (2002). *Preventing teenage pregnancy, childbearing, and sexually transmitted diseases: What the research shows.* Washington, DC: Child Trends. Retrieved November 22, 2004, at www.childtrends.org/PDF/Knightreports/K1Brief.pdf

Manlove, J., Franzetta, K., McKinney, K., Papillo, A. R., & Terry-Humen, E. (2004). *A good time: After-school programs to reduce teen pregnancy.* National Campaign to Prevent Teen Pregnancy. Washington, DC: Author.

Martin, J. A., Hamilton, B. E., Sutton, P. D., Ventura, S. J., Menacker, F., Kirmeyer, S. Final data for 2006. *National Vital Statistics Reports, 57*(7). Hyattsville, MD: National Center for Health Statistics.

National Campaign to Prevent Teen Pregnancy. (2002). *Teen pregnancy: Not just another single issue.* Washington, DC: Author.

National Campaign to Prevent Teen Pregnancy. (2006). *How is the 3 in 10 statistic calculated?* Washington, DC: Author.

National Center on Response to Intervention. (2011). *What is RTI?* Washington, DC: American Institutes for Research. Retrieved from http://www.rti4success.org

O'Donnell, L., Stueve, A., O'Donnell, C., Duran, R., San Doval, A., …& Pleck, J. H. (2002). Long-term reductions in sexual initiation andsexual activity among urban middle schoolers in the Reach for Healthservice learning program. *Journal of Adolescent Health, 31,* 93-100.

PASHA Programs Table. (2002). Accessed online at http://www.socio.com/newpasha/pashatablebox1.htm

Philliber, S., & Allen, J. P. (1992). Life options and community service: Teen outreach program. In B. C. Miller, J. J. Card, R. L. Paikoff, & J. L. Peterson (Eds.), *Preventing adolescent pregnancy: Model programs and evaluations* (pp. 139–155). Newbury Park, CA: Sage.

Philliber, S., Williams Kaye, J., & Herrling, S. (2001). *The national evaluation of the Children's Aid Society*

Carrera-model program to prevent teen pregnancy. Accord, NY: Philliber Research Associates.

Philliber, S., Williams Kaye, J., Herrling, S., & West, E. (2002). Preventing pregnancy and improving health care access among teenagers: An evaluation of the Children's Aid Society—Carrera program. *Perspectives on Sexual and Reproductive Health,* 34(5), 244–252.

Sawhill, I.V (1998). Teen pregnancy prevention: Welfare reform'smissing component. Brookings Policy Brief, 38.

Scher, L. S., & Hoffman, S. D. (2008). Consequences of teen childbearing for incarceration among adult children: Updated estimates through 2002. In S. D. Hoffman & R. Maynard (Eds.), *Kids having kids: Economic costs and social consequences of teen pregnancy* (2nd ed., pp. 311–321). Washington, DC: The Urban Institute Press.

Shuger, L. (2012). Teen Pregnancy and High School Dropout: WhatCommunities are Doing to Address These Issues. Washington, DC: TheNational Campaign to Prevent Teen and Unplanned Pregnancy andAmerica's Promise Alliance.

Singh, S., & Darroch, J. E. (2000). Adolescent pregnancy and childbearing: Levels and trends in developed countries. *Family Planning Perspectives,* 32(1), 14–23.

Solomon, J., & Card, J. J. (2004). *Making the list: Understanding, selecting, and replicating effective teen pregnancy prevention programs.* Retrieved from Association of School Psychologists Web site on November 23, 2004: http://www.teenpregnancy.org

Taggart, R., & Lattimore, B. C. (2001). *Quantum opportunities program: A youth development program.* Los Altos, CA: Sociometrics.

The National Campaign to Prevent Teen Pregnancy (2010). Teenpregnancy, Poverty, and Income Disparity. Retrieved from:http://www.thenational-campaign.org/why-it-matters/pdf/poverty.pdf.

Trenholm, C., Devaney, B., Fortson, K., Quay, L., Wheeler, J, & Clark,M. (2007). Impacts of Title V, Section 510 Abstinence EducationPrograms: Final Report. Retrieved from:http://www.mathematica-mpr.com/publications/pdfs/impactabstinence.pdf.

CHAPTER 33

Best School-Based Practices with Adolescent Parents

Mary Beth Harris

Getting Started

Despite the good news that teen pregnancy declined steadily during the 1990s, it remains that 34% of girls, about 400,000, in the United States become pregnant and 18% give birth before they reach age 20 (National Campaign to Prevent Teen Pregnancy, 2004; Perper & Manlove, 2009). Of these adolescents, more than 400,000 give birth every year (Henshaw, 2004). At some point, most of these young women are students in public schools, where school-based professionals face the daunting challenge of keeping them in school and helping them to navigate the heavy responsibilities of premature parenthood. These are some of the factors that make teen parents one of the most at-risk populations among American youth:

- They are significantly at risk for school dropout, with a dropout rate of 60% (National Campaign to Prevent Teen Pregnancy, 2007).
- They are twice as likely to become isolated and to be clinically depressed (Barnet, Liu, & Devoe, 2008; Cox et al., 2008).
- They are more likely than older mothers to have complications during pregnancy and less likely to receive prenatal care (Partington, Stever, Blair, & Cisler, 2009; Roth, Hendrickson Schilling, & Stowell, 1998).
- Their children are at risk for low birth weight, prematurity, developmental problems, insufficient health care, and school failure (Magill & Wilcox, 2007; Partington, Stever, Blair, & Cisler, 2009).
- They are likely to have family conflicts that limit support from their parents and the father or mother of their baby (Cooksey, Mott, & Neubauer, 2002; East, 1999; Meade, Kershaw, & Ickovics, 2008).
- As adults, they are more likely to live in poverty (Campolieti, Fang, & Gunderson, 2010; Paquette, 1999).

Public policies such as TANF have restricted economic subsidies and services for mothers and children, creating further difficulties for this vulnerable population. Young mothers who formerly depended on public assistance and social services to help them transition into adulthood and secure postsecondary education or career training are now likely to have exhausted these benefits before they leave high school. Thus, preparing young parents for immediate and long-term economic self-sufficiency has become a critical task for school-based programs.

This chapter reviews methods and interventions that are demonstrated to be effective in school settings with teen parents. We concentrate on an intervention approach that targets decision-making and behavioral skills to help young parents mitigate many of the associated risks, graduate from high school, and ultimately become self-sufficient adults.

What We Know

Predictors of Life Outcomes for Adolescent Parents

Adolescent parents face challenges in four domains that predict their immediate and long-term life outcomes: (1) education, (2) employment, (3) personal relationships, and (4) parenting (Harris & Franklin, 2003, 2008). Studies suggest a high degree of interaction among these four for determining life quality and well-being. For example, the more supportive a teen mother's relationships with friends and family, the more likely she is to achieve in school and to develop a career (Stramenga, 2003; Zupicich, 2003). In turn, the more education an adolescent parent achieves, the higher her employment income is likely to be as an adult (Campolieti, Fang, & Gunderson, 2010). Although studies show the importance of each domain, *education* is the most immediate and well-researched predictor of long-term adjustment and economic status.

School Achievement

High school graduation or achieving a GED before age 20 may be the single strongest asset any youth can have to protect against poverty and other negative outcomes in later life (Haveman & Sneeding, 2006; Orfield, Losen, Wald, & Swanson, 2004; Sandfort & Hill, 1996). Thus, school dropout for teen parents may contribute to their at-risk status more than any other factor. Regular attendance and a reasonably age-appropriate grade level, which are major school-related issues for teen parents, are recognized as the most important predictors of whether a student will graduate from high school (Burdell, 1998; DeBolt, Pasley, & Kreutzer, 1990; Haveman & Sneeding, 2006). Numerous studies (Arnold & Rotheram-Borus, 2009; Harris & Franklin, 2002, 2009; Olah, 1995) indicate that programs focusing on decision-making, problem-solving, and behavioral skills that lead to improvement in attendance and grades, personal relationships, and general social competence are the most protective interventions that schools can offer for adolescents who become pregnant.

What We Can Do

Teen Parent Programs

Programs and services for pregnant and parenting students (as well as other at-risk groups) in many urban school districts are located primarily in alternative schools. In 2000–2001, 39% of public school districts had at least one alternative school (Kleiner, Porch, & Westat, 2002). These programs are structured academically and provide such additional special courses as sex education, health, life planning, parenting, and job training (Griffin, 1998; Kleiner, Porch, & Westat, 2002). Alternative schools use a variety of models, and one that appears to be effective for dropout prevention and retrieval with teen parents and other at-risk populations, often referred to as a *school of choice* (Franklin, 1992), offers flexible schedules and individualized, self-paced learning, both compatible with the needs of adolescent parents. Additionally, nearly 90% of the nation's 10,900 alternative schools provide smaller classes, remedial instruction, crisis intervention, and career counseling (Kleiner, Porch, & Westat, 2002). Coupled with student support, these are critical services and environmental supports for learning and academic achievement among pregnant and parenting students. Although effective interventions specifically for adolescent parents may be more easily established and integrated in an alternative school setting than in a traditional school, interventions with this population are now demonstrated to be effective in both traditional and alternative school settings (Griffin, 1998; Harris & Franklin, 2008; Sadler et al., 2007).

A Cognitive-Behavioral Approach

Both as a single intervention and as a component within larger school-based programs, skills-building interventions with a cognitive-behavioral foundation have gained strong support for a number of problems. Curriculums that engage youth in processing logical consequences of behavior and mastering general and specific life skills are reported to be effective with adolescent issues such as school dropout, pregnancy prevention, adolescent parenting, drug and alcohol addiction, problem school behavior, childhood sexual abuse, and depression (Coren, Barlow, & Stewart-Brown, 2003; Dupper, 1998; Franklin & Corcoran, 1999; Harris & Franklin, 2008; Hogue & Liddle, 1999). Evidence continues to grow showing that this approach is effective in a number of areas with pregnant and parenting adolescents (e.g., Codega, Pasley, & Kreutzer, 1990; Harris & Franklin, 2008) and endorses the use of such skills-building intervention in school programs.

Conditions and Goals of Skills-Based Programs

Programs that are effective in helping participants actually master new skills have four essential conditions in common (Harris & Franklin, 2008; Hogue & Liddle, 1999):

1. The practitioner models the skill in session.
2. The adolescent role-plays and practices the skill in session.
3. The adolescent continues to practice the skill between sessions as assigned homework or a self-identified task.
4. The practitioner debriefs the adolescents about their success in practicing the skill and adjusts skills training to accommodate learning differences.

These interventions appear to be most effective with adolescents when they promote a sense of social support, competence, and self-efficacy. Enhancing internal *locus of control*—the youth's sense that he, rather than forces outside himself, determines the conditions of his life—is often a goal, as well (e.g., McWhirter & Page, 1999; Rice & Meyer, 1994). Specific, *task-related* homework assignments that give the adolescent a chance to practice identified skills, as well as *peer support and feedback*, appear to be effective in reinforcing these personal assets.

A cognitive-behavioral approach seeks to strengthen individual skills such as *coping with stress, problem solving*, and *goal setting* (e.g., Dupper, 1998; Rice & Meyer, 1994). Some interventions target skills specifically related to school achievement, personal relationships, health, and employment (e.g., Griffin, 1998; Harris & Franklin, 2002; Jemmont, Jemmont, Fong, & McCaffree, 1999), which are recognized protectors against the risks associated with teen pregnancy.

Coping Skills

Adolescents cope with stress in a variety of ways: (1) active, problem-focused strategies; (2) emotional adjustment and acceptance; and (3) avoidance and other passive responses (Chagnon, 2007; Davey, Eaker, & Walters, 2003; Erickson, Feldman, Shirley, & Steiner, 1997). The type of coping they use may be more important to resolving stressful situations than the severity or frequency of the stressor. Active, problem-focused coping, found to be more effective in achieving positive outcomes than emotion-focused coping and avoidance (Aspinwall & Taylor, 1992; Griffith, Dubow, & Ippolito, 2000; Wadsworth & Berger, 2006), is often a skill targeted with at-risk adolescents (e.g., Harris & Franklin, 2008). For example, young parents with a tendency to use active, problem-solving coping behaviors are shown repeatedly to experience less stress and to show greater acceptance, warmth, and helpfulness and less disapproval with their children (Colletta & Gregg, 1981; Passino et al., 1993). Even so, studies comparing pregnant to nonpregnant teens show that pregnant teens generally use less active coping than nonpregnant teens and identify avoidance or emotion-focused coping as their most frequent strategies (Passino et al., 1993; Codega, Pasley, & Kreutzer, 1990). Thus, increasing problem-focused coping is an important goal for a skills-based intervention with teen parents.

Social Problem-Solving Skills

Social problem-solving skills are defined as a set of specific attitudes, behaviors, and skills directed toward solving a particular real-life problem in a social context (D'Zurilla, Chang, & Sanna, 2003). They include these tasks:

1. Defining and formulating the problem
2. Generating a list of possible solutions
3. Selecting the solution with the best chance to succeed
4. Carrying out the solution strategies
5. Evaluating the outcome

Social problem-solving skills are recognized to strengthen a person's sense of self-efficacy and mastery over one's environment (Bandura, 2003). Although these assets are vital for pregnant and parenting adolescents, research suggests that these youths are less skilled in problem-solving than their nonpregnant peers (Passino et al., 1993). We conclude that problem-solving skills are a vital target for intervention with teen parents.

Task-Centered Group Modality

With few exceptions, effective skills-based interventions with adolescents are conducted in a group (Glodich & Allen, 1998; Harris & Franklin, 2002; Dellbridge & Lubbe, 2009; Dupper, 1998; Reid & Fortune, 2006). The isolation and need for peer contact and support that often accompany adolescent pregnancy make a group context especially relevant for these youth. Participant focus groups in our outcome studies with young mothers have consistently emphasized that being in a group with other pregnant and parenting students was one of the most important aspects of the intervention (Harris & Franklin, 2008).

We recommend a *task-centered group model* for skills-based intervention with teen parents. This is a form of short-term, goal-oriented treatment in which the client carries out actions or tasks between sessions to alleviate their problems (Reid, 1996; Reid & Fortune, 2006). A task-centered group is relatively structured and provides a ready format for skills-based interventions. Over 30 studies have evaluated the effectiveness of task-centered modality, including studies of children with academic problems and adolescents in academic and residential treatment settings (Reid, 1996).

Six to eight members is thought to be the ideal size for a task-centered group, although there is evidence that groups with up to 12 members can also be effective (e.g., Harris & Franklin, 2002). Characteristics such as participants' ages and literacy skills should be considered in determining group size. Two group leaders are considered ideal with this model, although a group can be led by one facilitator when necessary.

Applying Interventions within a Response to Intervention Framework

As a three-tier prevention/intervention framework, RTI in its purest form may fit more easily with pregnancy prevention than with pregnancy and parenting. However, when programs use an RTI framework to target the primary needs associated with teen pregnancy and parenting, such as school retention, parenting competence, and career planning, RTI provides an organized frame for planning and delivering program services.

The Tier 1 level, for example, should focus on the supports and interventions that most youth in this population need in order to maintain and achieve in school. They should be available to all the school's pregnant and parenting students and may include flexible schedules, school-based healthcare, and childcare.

Tier 2 level interventions target those assessed to be more at risk for academic failure or school dropout. At this level interventions may include tutoring, academic counseling, and skills-based intervention such as the Taking Charge group.

At the Tier 3 level, where intervention is focused on students assessed to be most at risk for dropout and other negative outcomes, individual case management may be provided, to include connecting to community resources such as family counseling, financial resources, or housing.

Tools and Practice Examples

Taking Charge: A Skills-Building Group for Pregnant and Parenting Adolescents

Taking Charge is a task-centered group curriculum for adolescent parents that incorporates the skills-building components and goals discussed in this chapter. Outcome studies in alternative and traditional high schools (Harris & Franklin, 2002, 2008) have demonstrated the Taking Charge curriculum to be effective in achieving these benefits with pregnant and parenting adolescent mothers:

1. School attendance and grades significantly improved.
2. Problem-solving skills significantly improved.
3. Active, problem-focused coping increased significantly.

Using the Social Problem-Solving Process in Four Life Domains

The Taking Charge program is presented in eight sessions, during which participants learn and apply the social problem-solving process (D'Zurilla & Nezu, 1982) to four important areas of their lives: school achievement, personal relationships, parenting, and career. After learning and practicing the steps, participants use this process during the next sessions to identify and set goals for resolving or mastering problems in each of these areas of their own lives.

These are the steps of the social problem-solving process:

1. Identify a problem that is a real barrier in this part of my life.
2. Identify the smaller problems that support this big problem.
3. Describe my goal for resolving this problem.

Box 33.1 Ways That Task-Centered Groups Fit the Needs of Adolescent Parents

- *Targets client's abilities.* More than some therapeutic models, task-centered intervention stresses the adolescent's abilities to identify goals and carry through with actions to obtain what she wants. The adolescent parent is assumed to have a mind and a will that are not bound by her age, past experiences, or environment.
- *Focuses on the present.* Task-centered intervention does not attempt to deal with historical origins of the client's problem but rather supports her in achieving its resolution.
- *Short-term.* Most task-centered groups are presented in 6 to 12 weeks. Short-term interventions are more likely than longer ones to meet program goals within the limited window of access to young parents.
- *Similarity of group members on target problems.* Task-centered groups are best processed when all group members are familiar with the kind of problems others are experiencing and can engage in and benefit from one another's process.

4. Identify barriers that keep me from reaching my goal.
5. Name the resources I have that can help me reach my goal.
6. List as many possible strategies as I can to help me reach my goal.
7. Pick a strategy from these that I believe has the best chance to succeed.
8. Decide on two tasks I can do immediately to carry out my strategy.
9. Now ... JUST DO IT!

Brenda: An Example of the Problem-Solving Process

Brenda, age 16, was a high school junior and the mother of a 3-month-old son. She lived with her 19-year-old boyfriend and his parents. She had lived with the family for 5 months, since before the birth of her baby. Brenda's problem-solving process is set out in Box 33.2.

Box 33.2 My Personal Relationship Goal

1. MY PROBLEM: My mother-in-law and I don't get along. She's cold to me and criticizes the way I look and dress, how I cook, and especially the way I take care of my baby.
2. SMALLER PROBLEMS: My boyfriend won't stand up to her. I think he's afraid of her. Neither does my father-in-law, even though I get along fine with him. She takes care of my baby while I'm at school, so she's with him as much as I am. My boyfriend is in welding school and only makes minimum wage 20 hours a week at his job, so we're (financially) dependent on his parents for another year. I don't have a car, so she has to take me to appointments for the baby.
3. MY GOAL: For my mother-in-law to like me better and stop criticizing me so much.
4. POSSIBLE BARRIERS: If I try to change anything between us, it may make things worse. I'm scared of her and try to stay away from her. I don't know how to talk to her. I don't like her at all.
5. MY RESOURCES: My boyfriend loves me and wants me to stay. Another resource is my cousin, who's a probation officer. She tries to help me understand my mother-in- law better. Another is my boyfriend's sister, who is cool with me when she drops by, and tells me to ignore my mother-in-law.
6. POSSIBLE STRATEGIES: (1) Confront my mother-in-law and threaten to move out if she doesn't change. (2) Go out of my way to please her without talking about it. (3) Get to know her better. (4) Clear the air with her to find out what I can do to make things better between us. (5) Take my baby and move back to my mother's house.
7. I CHOOSE: The strategy of clearing the air with my mother-in-law and finding out how I can make things better between us.
8. MY FIRST TASK: To talk to my boyfriend's sister about my goal and get her advice on how to talk to her mother. MY SECOND TASK: To tell my mother-in-law that I want to have a good relationship with her and ask her what I can do to help that happen.

Tasks Provide Practice for New Behavior

For each goal they set, group members identify two tasks that are achievable in the week between group sessions. They work with a *"this is my task"* form that guides them through identifying the task and planning how they will carry it out. Some examples of tasks that commonly appear in Taking Charge groups are these:

- Meet with my guidance counselor about my (credits, schedule, career plan, etc.).
- Talk to my (math, science, etc.) teacher about my (grade, exam, attitude, etc.).
- Talk to my boyfriend about (help with baby costs, more time together, etc.).
- Spend at least (1 hour, etc.) on homework every day this week.
- Make an appointment to (take baby for shots, apply for food stamps, etc.).

Leaders guide participants in identifying tasks by asking questions and referring to the participants' goal and strategies. They may also help participants rehearse or role-play the task in session.

Incentives Reinforce New Behavior

To ensure that members receive the greatest benefit from Taking Charge, incentives are built into the group. For example, since food is an important incentive for adolescents and Taking Charge groups often meet during the lunch period, serving lunch during group meetings is one incentive. A snack is served in groups that meet at other times. The lunch or snack is ready to eat immediately when participants arrive.

A points system is an incentive that allows group members to earn an award at the end of Taking Charge. Points are given for group and school attendance, homework, extra credit assignments, and tasks. Awards are items of particular value to participants, such as gift certificates from a favorite store. Leaders inform the group about the points system at the first session and document points each week.

At two of the eight group sessions participants receive small gifts such as personal grooming items or pizza coupons as they are about to leave the session. In order to maintain this as an incentive for group attendance, the gift is given only to those who attend the sessions at which the gifts are presented.

Implementing Taking Charge

Even though school-based clinical trials tell us that the Taking Charge curriculum is an effective intervention with adolescent mothers, the ultimate question for school professionals is how easily such a curriculum might be implemented in their school. Anyone working in a school setting knows that there are many things to consider when selecting and implementing social service and mental health programs—How will it impact budget and staff resources? Is it controversial? Is it compatible with the school's educational goals? Will the school staff support it?

Here are some important aspects of this group curriculum to consider when deciding on interventions with pregnant and parenting students.

- In the largest clinical study of the group, the group of young women who participated in the Taking Charge curriculum gained an *eight-point advantage in their GPA* during the semester over an equivalent group who did not participate in the group. The Taking Charge participant group also *increased in school attendance from 79% to 91%*, while the nonparticipants made no gains in attendance.
- A curriculum treatment manual makes it feasible for Taking Charge to be facilitated by volunteers or student interns. The curriculum is compatible with the professional training of school mental health staff, who need only minimal training to supervise volunteer leaders or to facilitate the group.
- The average cost to present the Taking Charge group is $15 to $20 per participant for incentives, in addition to minimal supplies such as paper and folders. In previous Taking Charge studies, lunch or snacks were provided by the school and occasionally donated by local restaurants and businesses.
- In some schools, awards were created using the resources of the school or community that did not involve an outlay of cash. At one school, participants who earned the highest award, and their babies, were treated to a field trip to the city zoo, with school bus transportation and picnic lunches provided by the school cafeteria. At another school, leaders arranged for award

recipients to receive manicures and hair styles at a school of cosmetology. In both instances, the alternative award was received enthusiastically by group participants.

- Although the Taking Charge curriculum is not gender-specific for adolescent parents, it has only been studied with young mothers. We cannot assume that it would be as effective with young fathers as with young mothers, although similar developmental needs and societal expectations for young mothers and young fathers suggest that the curriculum may be effective for skills building with young fathers.
- To gain sufficient mastery of the Taking Charge curriculum, we recommend that leaders spend a few hours reviewing and discussing the treatment manual, perhaps with an experienced practitioner or supervisor. Leaders report that they needed to work through the problem-solving process several times with real problems of their own before they felt prepared to help group participants with that process. The extent of training should be determined by the previous training and experience of the leaders.
- The Taking Charge treatment manual is available from Oxford University Press (Harris & Franklin, 2008).

Key Points to Remember

Pregnant and parenting adolescents continue to be an at-risk population in schools. With a 60% dropout rate, they are far less likely than their peers to graduate from high school, and they and their children are more likely to live in poverty than parents who delay pregnancy beyond adolescence.

Skills-based interventions that include problem-solving and coping skills are found to be effective in school programs with other adolescent problems, such as drugs and alcohol, school dropout, and antisocial behavior. Such interventions are gaining support as effective with teen parents. In this chapter we have examined the foundations of a cognitive-behavioral skills-based approach, as well as the compatibility of using a task-centered group for skills-building interventions. We explored the Taking Charge curriculum, a group intervention for helping adolescent mothers to achieve coping and problem-solving skills toward graduating from high school and becoming more competent parents and self-sufficient adults.

References

Arnold, E. M., & Rotheram-Borus, M. J. (2009). Comparisons of prevention programs for homeless youth. *Prevention Science, 10*(1), 76–86.

Aspinwall, L. G., & Taylor, S. E. (1992). Modeling cognitive adaptation: A longitudinal investigation of the impact of individual differences and coping on college adjustment and performance. *Journal of Personality and Social Psychology, 63*, 989–1003.

Bandura, A. (1999). A social cognitive theory of personality. In L. Pervin & O. John (Eds.), *Handbook of personality* (2nd ed., pp. 154–196). New York: Guilford Press.

Bandura, A. (2003). Role of affective self-regulatory efficacy in diverse spheres of psychosocial functioning. *Child Development, 74*(3), 769–782.

Barnet, B., Liu, J., & Devoe, M. (2008). Double jeopardy: Depressive symptoms and rapid subsequent pregnancy in adolescent mothers. *Archives of Pediatrics & Adolescent Medicine, 162*, 246–252.

Barth, R. P. (1989). *Reducing the risk: Building skills to prevent pregnancy*. Santa Cruz, CA: ETR Associates/Network Publications.

Beck, M. S. (1991). *Increasing school completion: Strategies that work* (Monographs in Education No. 13). Athens, GA: University of Georgia College of Education.

Brooks-Gunn, J., & Furstenberg, F. F., Jr. (1986). The children of adolescent mothers: Physical, academic, and psychological outcomes. *Developmental Review, 6*, 224–251.

Burdell, P. (1998). Young mothers as high school students: Moving toward a new century. *Education and Urban Society, 30*(2), 202–223.

Campolieti, M., Fang, T., & Gunderson, M. (2010). *Journal of Labor Research, 31*(1), 39–52.

Chagnon, F. (2007). Coping mechanisms, stressful events, and suicidal behavior among youth admitted to juvenile justice and child welfare services. *Suicide and Life-Threatening Behavior, 37*(4), 439–452.

Clarke, G. (1992). Cognitive-behavioral group treatment of adolescent depression: Prediction of outcome. *Behavior Therapy, 23*, 341–354.

Codega, S. A., Pasley, B. K., & Kreutzer, J. (1990). Coping behaviors of adolescent mothers: An exploratory study and comparison of Mexican-Americans and Anglos. *Journal of Adolescent Research, 5*(1), 34–53.

Colletta, N. D., & Gregg, C. H. (1981). Adolescent mothers' vulnerability to stress. *Journal of Nervous and Mental Disorders, 169*, 50–54.

Cooksey, E. C., Mott, F. L., & Neubauer, S. A. (2002). Friendships and early relationships: Links to sexual initiation among American adolescents born to young mothers. *Perspectives on Sexual and Reproductive Health, 34*(3), 118–126.

Coren, E., Barlow, J., & Stewart-Brown, S. (2003). The effectiveness of individual and group-based parenting programmes in improving outcomes for teenage mothers and their children: A systematic review. *Journal of Adolescence, 26*(1), 79–103.

Cox, J. E., Buman, M., Valenzuela, J., Joseph, N. P., Mitchell, A., & Woods, E. R. (2008). Depression, parenting, attributes, and social support among adolescent mothers attending a teen tot program. *Journal of Pediatric and Adolescent Gynecology, 21*, 275–281.

Davey, M., Eaker, D. G., & Walters, L. H. (2003). Resilience processes in adolescents: Personality profiles, self-worth, and coping. *Journal of Adolescent Research, 18*(4), 347–362.

DeBolt, M. E., Pasley, B. K., & Kreutzer, J. (1990). Factors affecting the probability of school dropout: A study of pregnant and parenting adolescent females. *Journal of Adolescent Research, 5*(3), 190–205.

Dellbridge, C., & Lubbe, C. (2009). An adolescent's subjective experiences of mindfulness. *Journal of Child and Adolescent Mental Health, 21*(2), 167–180.

Dupper, D. R. (1998). An alternative to suspension for middle school youths with behavior problems: Findings from a "school survival" group. *Research on Social Work Practice, 8*(3), 354–366.

D'Zurilla, T., Chang, E. C., & Sanna, L. J. (2003). Self-esteem and social problem-solving as predictors of aggression in college students. *Journal of Social and Clinical Psychology, 22*(4), 424–440.

D'Zurilla, T. J., & Nezu, A. (1982). Social problem-solving in adults. In P. C. Kendall (Ed.), *Advances in cognitive-behavioral research and therapy* (pp. 202–269). New York: Academic Press.

East, P. L. (1999). The first teenage pregnancy in the family: Does it affect mothers' parenting, attitudes, or mother-daughter communication? *Journal of Marriage and Family, 61*(2), 306–319.

Erickson, S., Feldman, S., & Steiner, H. (1997). *Child Psychiatry & Human Development, 28*(1), 45–56.

Fine, M. (1986). Why urban adolescents drop into and out of public high school. *Teachers College Record, 87*, 392–409.

Fischer, R. L. (1997). Evaluating the delivery of a teen pregnancy and parenting program across two settings. *Research on Social Work Practice,* 7(3), 350–369.

Franklin, C. (1992). Alternative school programs for at-risk youth. *Social Work in Education, 14*(4), 239–251.

Franklin, C., & Corcoran, J. (1999). Preventing adolescent pregnancy: A review of programs and practices. *Social Work in Health Care, 45*(1), 40–52.

Glodich, A., & Allen, J. G. (1998). Adolescents exposed to violence and abuse: A review of the group therapy literature with an emphasis on preventing trauma reenactment. *Journal of Child and Adolescent Group Therapy, 8*(3), 135–153.

Griffin, N. C. (1998). Cultivating self-efficacy in adolescent mothers: A collaborative approach. *Professional School Counseling, 1*(4), 53–58.

Harris, M. B., & Franklin, C. (2002). Effectiveness of a cognitive-behavioral group intervention with Mexican American adolescent mothers. *Social Work Research, 17*(2), 71–83.

Harris, M. B., & Franklin, C. (2008). *Taking charge: A school-based life skills program for adolescent mothers.* New York, NY: Oxford University Press.

Henshaw, S. K. (2004). *U.S. teenage pregnancy statistics with comparative statistics for women aged 20–24.* New York: Alan Guttmacher Institute.

Hogue, A., & Liddle, H. A. (1999). Family-based preventive intervention: An approach to preventing substance abuse and antisocial behavior. *American Journal of Orthopsychiatry, 69*, 275–293.

Jemmont, J. B., Jemmont, L. S., Fong, G. T., & McCaffree, K. (1999). Reducing HIV risk-associated sexual behavior among African American adolescents: Testing the generality of intervention effects. *American Journal of Community Psychology, 27*(2), 161–187.

Kalil, A., Spencer, M. S., Spieker, S. J., & Gilchrist, L. D. (1998). Effects of grandmother coresidence and quality of family relationships on depressive symptoms in adolescent mothers. *Family Relations: Interdisciplinary Journal of Applied Family Studies, 47*(4), 433–441.

Kleiner, B., Porch, R., & Westat, E. F. (2002). *Public alternative schools and programs for students at risk of education failure: 2000–01.* Washington, DC: Center for Education Statistics, U.S. Department of Education.

Larrivee, B., & Bourque, M. L. (1991). The impact of several dropout prevention intervention strategies on at-risk students. *Education, 112*, 48–63.

Magill, M. K., & Wilcox, R. (2007). Adolescent pregnancy and associated risks: Not just a result of maternal age. *American Family Physician, 75*(9), 1310–1311.

Maynard, R. A. (Ed.). (1997). Kids having kids: Economic costs and social consequences of teen pregnancy. Washington, DC: Urban Institute Press.

McWhirter, B. T., & Page, G. L. (1999). Effects of anger management and goal setting group interventions on state-trait anger and self-efficacy beliefs among high risk adolescents. *Current Psychology: Developmental, Learning, Personality, Social, 18*(2), 223–237.

Meade, C. S., Kershaw, T. S., & Ickovics, J. R. (2008). The intergenerational cycle of teenage motherhood: An ecological approach. *Health Psychology, 27*(4), 419–429.

Moore, K. A., Myers, D. E., Morrison, D. R., Nord, C. W., Brown, B. V., & Edmonston, B. (1993). The age of child birth and later poverty. *Journal of Research on Adolescence, 3*(4), 393–422.

National Campaign to Prevent Teen Pregnancy. (2004). *Fact sheet: How is the 34% statistic calculated?* Washington, DC: Author.

National Campaign to Prevent Teen Pregnancy. (2007). *Teen pregnancy: Not just another single issue.* Washington, DC: Author.

Olah, A. (1995). Coping strategies among adolescents: A cross-cultural study. *Journal of Adolescence, 18*(4), 491–512.

Orfield, G., Losen, D., Wald, J., & Swanson, C. B. (2004). *Losing our future: How minority youth are being left behind by the graduation rate crisis.* MA: Civil Rights Project at Harvard University.

Osofsky, J. D., Osofsky, H. J., & Diamond, M. O. (1988). The transition to parenthood: Special tasks and risk factors for adolescent parents. In G. Y. Michaels & W. A. Goldberg (Eds.), *The transition to parenthood: Current theory and research* (pp. 209–232). New York: Cambridge University Press.

Paquette, J. (1999). Educational attainment and employment income: Incentives and disincentives for staying in school. *Canadian Journal of Education, 24*(2), 151.

Partington, S. N., Steber, D. L., Blair, K. A., & Cisler, R. A. (2009). Second births to teenage mothers: Risk factors for low birth weight and preterm birth. *Perspectives on Sexual and Reproductive Health, 41*(2), 101–109.

Passino, A. W., Whitman, T. L., Borkowski, J. G., Schellenbach, C. J., Maxwell, S. E., & Keogh, D. R. (1993). Personal adjustment during pregnancy and adolescent parenting. *Adolescence, 28*(109), 97–123.

Pearson, L. C., & Banerji, M. (1993). Effects of a ninth-grade dropout prevention program on student academic achievement, school attendance, and dropout rate. *Journal of Experimental Education, 61*(Spring), 247–256.

Perper, K., & Manlove, J. (2009). *Estimated percentage of females who will become teen mothers: Differences across states.* Child Trends, 2009. Retrieved July 14, 2011, from http://www.issuelab.org/research/estimated-percentage-of-females-who-will-become-teen-mothers-differences-across-states

Reid, W. J. (1996). Task-centered social work. In Francis J. Turner (Ed.), *Social work treatment: Interlocking theoretical approaches* (4th ed., pp. 617–640). New York: Free Press.

Reid, W. J., & Fortune, A. E. (2006). Task-centered practice: An exemplar of evidence-based practice. In A. R. Roberts and K. R. Yeager (Eds.), *Foundations of evidence-based social work practice* (pp. 194–203). New York, NY: Oxford University Press.

Rice, K. G. & Meyer, A. L. (1994). Preventing depression among young adolescents: Preliminary process results of a psycho-educational intervention program. *Journal of Counseling and Development, 73*, 145–152.

Rodriguez, R. (1995). Latino educators devise sure-fire K–12 dropout prevention programs. *Black Issues of Higher Education, 12*, 35–37.

Sadler, L. S., Swartz, M. K., Ryan-Krause, P., Seitz, V., Meadows-Oliver, M., Grey, M., & Clemmens, D. A. (2007). Promising outcomes in teen mothers enrolled in a school-based parent support program and child care center. *Journal of School Health, 77*(3), 121–129.

Sandfort, J. R., & Hill, M. S. (1996). Assisting young unmarried mothers to become self-sufficient: The effects of different types of early economic support. *Journal of Marriage and the Family, 58*(2), 311–326.

Stern, M., & Zevon, M. A. (1990). Stress, coping, and family environment: The adolescent's response to naturally occurring stressors. *Journal of Adolescent Research, 7*(4), 290–305.

Stern, M., & Alvarez, A. (1992). Pregnant and parenting adolescents: A comparative analysis of coping response and psychosocial adjustment. *Journal of Adolescent Research, 7*(4), 469–493.

Stramenga, M. S. (2003). The role of developmental and relational factors in the career decision-making process of adolescent mothers. *Dissertation Abstracts International: Section B: The Sciences and Engineering, 64*(6-B), 2962.

Vallarand, R. J., Fortier, M. S., & Guay, F. (1997). Psychosocial mechanisms underlying quality of parenting among Mexican-American and White adolescent mothers. *Journal of Personality and Social Psychology, 72*(5), 1161–1176.

Whiston, S., & Quinby, R. F. (2009). Review of school counseling outcome research. *Psychology in the Schools, 46*(3), 267–272.

Zeidner, M., & Hammer, A. L. (1990). Life events and coping resources as predictors of stress symptoms in adolescents. *Personality and Individual Differences, 11*, 693–703.

Zellman, G. L. (1981). *The response of the schools to teenage pregnancy and parenthood.* Santa Monica, CA: Rand.

Zupicich, S. (2003). Understanding social supportive processes among adolescent mothers. *Dissertation Abstracts International Section A: Humanities and Social* Sciences, *63*(11-A), 3869.

SECTION VII

Effective Approaches for Violence, Bullying and Conflict Resolution, Sexual Assault, and Gangs

The prevention of all kinds of violence—including bullying, sexual assault, dating violence, gang violence, and interpersonal conflict between students, their peers, and teachers—is of high concern to schools. This section discusses best practices for violence prevention and conflict resolution, helping school practitioners to learn what the most effective practices and resources are for both prevention and intervention into different types of violence and conflict situations.

CHAPTER 34

Evidence-Based Violence Prevention Programs and Best Implementation Practices

Roxana Marachi   Ron Avi Astor   Rami Benbenishty

Getting Started

Social work as a profession has contributed to the national and international dialogue concerning violence prevention programs in schools. School social workers play an increasingly important role in shaping and implementing policy, interventions, and procedures that make U.S. schools safer. The chapters in this section provide a comprehensive guide to best practices in nearly all aspects of school conflict and violence, from organizational and procedural modifications, to diminishing interpersonal conflict between individuals and groups on school grounds and in the classroom. The dynamics of such serious problems as bullying, physical aggressiveness, date rape, sexual harassment, and physical violence among adolescent couples are explained in tandem with full and detailed guidance to practice responses and interventions.

In order to use resources to the best advantage and to maximize program effectiveness, it is helpful for school mental health professionals to not only know the dynamics and best approaches for assessing and intervening in school violence but also be familiar with available model programs already studied and found to be effective. As an overview leading into this section of the manual, this chapter will review several examples of effective violence prevention programs as well as model school safety programs. It should be noted that large-scale reviews of evidence-based programs have not yielded notable changes to the "model" programs described in previous years. Many of the programs of focus here have undergone years of planning and development and are still refining and increasing their processes of implementation and effectiveness. One great weakness in establishing evidence-based violence prevention programs is that they are often introduced to schools with a "top-down" approach, ignoring variations in local school contexts. Even model programs that have been demonstrated to be effective in large-scale research studies have a better chance for success at any given school if the program matches the needs and values of the community, the school, and the school staff. To assist readers in achieving such a match, we offer monitoring and mapping approaches as a guide to develop a bottom-up program and in tracking program interventions.

What We Know

In this section of the chapter we present examples of the most widely researched model school safety programs available to schools and practitioners. Table 34.1 includes the names of the programs, web sites where the programs can be explored, program components, outcome measures, and results from studies. We also include a more extensive list of web sites and resources for each program at the end of the chapter. The programs listed in Table 34.1 have been rated as "effective" by multiple national organizations. Our designation of effective is a composite of ratings from nine independent scientific organizations that evaluated the most popular school violence prevention programs. Criteria considered in designating a program as effective include (1) evidence of effectiveness based on rigorous evaluations with experimental or quasi-experimental designs; (2) the clarity of the program's goals and rationale; (3) the fit between the program content and the characteristics of the intended population and setting; (4) the integration of the program into schools' educational mission; (5) the availability of necessary information and guidance for replication in other settings; and (6) the incorporation of post treatment and follow-up data collection as part of the program. We describe in detail four programs listed in Table 34.1.

What We Can Do

Olweus Bullying Prevention Program

The Olweus Bullying Prevention Program (OBPP) is a comprehensive multi-component bullying reduction and prevention program designed for students in grades 1–9. It was developed during the 1970s by Dan Olweus to reduce bully and victim problems in Norwegian schools. Since then, it has been translated into more than 12 languages and successfully established in schools in more than 15 countries.

Content

As seen in Table 34.1 under Program Components, the OBPP is implemented at three levels of the school environment—the total school, classroom, and the individual student. At the school-wide level, the program establishes anti-bullying policy in the school system. To raise awareness and quantify the prevalence of bullying in the school, administrators distribute an anonymous 29-item student questionnaire to all students. A school conference day about bullying is established to talk about the results of the assessment and discuss interventions. Additionally, schools create an OBPP coordination team in which a representative administrator, teacher, counselor, parent, and student come together to lead the program implementation. The school adopts rules against bullying and explains to students the negative consequences for bullying behavior. All staff receive training to learn about the harmful consequences of bullying, to increase supervision in areas on campus that are prone to violence, and to provide systematic reinforcement of rules applied to all students.

At the classroom level, students have regular workshops about the harmful consequences of bullying. Students have discussions about bullying and violent behaviors, watch video presentations of bullying situations, write about ways to combat the problem, and engage in role play. Students are encouraged to increase their knowledge and empathy regarding bullying.

The individual student level involves direct consequences for bullying behaviors. There are focused interventions with those identified as bullies and victims, as well as the bystanders. The parents of involved students are given help and support to reinforce non-violence at home. School mental health workers play an essential role in more serious cases of bullying.

The goal of using interventions through all three levels is to ensure that students are given a consistent, coordinated, and strong message that bullying will not be tolerated. The OBPP teaches students that everyone has a responsibility to prevent bullying, either by refusing to support

Table 34.1. Select Evidence-Based Violence Prevention Programs and Evaluating Sources

Program	*Grade*	*Participants*	*Program components*	*Outcome measures*	*Results*
Olweus Bullying Prevention Program *(OBPP)* (Olweus, 1993) www.clemson.edu/olweus	Program target audience ages 6–15; initial large-scale evaluation on grades 4–7	Original intervention/evaluation involved 2,500 students in 42 primary and secondary schools in Norway (The program is now international and being applied in 15 countries. The materials are translated in over 12 languages.)	Core components of the program are implemented at the school level, the class level, and the individual level. Includes: • Distribution of anonymous student questionnaire assessing the nature and prevalence of bullying • Development of positive and negative consequences for students' behavior • Establishing a supervisory system • Reinforcement of school-wide rules against bullying • Classroom workshops with video and discussions to increase knowledge and empathy • Interventions with children and victims of bullying • Discussions with parents	Quasi-experimental research design with student self-report measures collected at introduction of the program, 4 months after introduction, 1-year follow-up, and 2-year follow-up • Reports of incidents of bullying and victimization • Scale of general youth antisocial behavior • Assessment of school climate—order and discipline • Measure of social relationships and attitude toward school	• Substantial reductions (50% or more for most comparisons by students' age and grade) in self-reported bullying and bully victimization • Significant reductions in self-reported vandalism, fighting, theft, alcohol use, and truancy • Significant improvements in the social climate of the classroom (as reflected in students' reports of increased satisfaction with school life and school work, improved order and discipline at school, and more positive social relationships) • Classrooms that implemented essential components of the program saw greater reductions in bully/victim problems. Result summary from http://sshs.promoteprevent.org/publications/ebi-factsheets/olweus-bullying-prevention-program citing Kallestad & Olweus, 2003; Olweus, 1991, 2005; Olweus, Limber, & Mihalic, 1999. * Evaluating Sources 1, 2, 3, 7, 8, 9

(continued)

Table 34.1 *(Continued)*

Program	*Grade*	*Participants*	*Program components*	*Outcome measures*	*Results*
Caring School Community Program (formerly Child Development Project) http://devstu.org/caring-school-community (Battistich, Schaps, Watson, & Solomon, 1996)	K-6th Grades	Evaluation studies are based on 4500+ students ages 6–12 in 24 elementary schools from 6 diverse districts throughout the U.S.	This is a comprehensive model focused on creating a cooperative and supportive school environment. Components include: 1) Class meeting lessons, which provide teachers and students with a forum to get to know one another and make decisions that affect classroom climate 2) Implementation of a model that fosters cross-grade "buddying" activities 3) Home-side activities, which foster communication at home and link school learning with home experiences and perspectives 4) School-wide community-building activities used to promote school bonding and parent involvement activities, such as interactive homework assignments that reinforce the family-school partnership	Data were collected after 1 year and 2 years of intervention. Teachers were assessed through four 90-minute observations and annual teacher questionnaires. Student assessments were self-report surveys of drug use and delinquent behavior.	Results showed that students experienced a stronger "sense of community" and more motivation to be helpful, better conflict-resolution skills, greater acceptance of people who are different, higher self-esteem, stronger feelings of social competence, less loneliness in school and fewer delinquent acts. Over a 2-year period, a significant 24% decline was found in student discipline referrals in 20 program schools, while referrals increased 42% in 4 control schools (Marshall & Caldwell, 2007). http://nrepp.samhsa.gov/ViewIntervention.aspx?id=152 * Evaluating Sources 3,4,5,7

Fast Track Project *(Conduct Problems Prevention Research Group, 1992)* www. fasttrackproject.org	Initial evaluation participants were at-risk kindergartners identified based on combined teacher and parent ratings of behavior (CBCL). Highest 10% recruited for study. N = 445 intervention children N = 446 control group children	Multiple program components. Weekly enrichment program for high-risk children and their parents. Students placed in "friendship groups" of 5–6 students each. Discussions, modeling stories and films, role-plays. Sessions focused on reviewing and practicing skills in emotional understanding and communication, friendship building, self-control, and social problem solving. Parents met in groups led by Family Coordinators to discuss parenting strategies, then 30-minute parent-child cooperative activity time, bi-weekly home visits. Academic tutoring provided by trained tutors in 30-min. sessions 3X/ week.	• Externalizing Scale of CBCL—*oppositional, aggressive, and delinquent behaviors*—. • *Parent Daily Report*—degree to which child engaged in aggressive and oppositional behaviors during previous 24 hrs (given 3x) • Child Behavior Change • Teacher assessment of acting out behaviors in school (Teacher Report Form, Achenbach, 1991) • Scale from the TOCA-R (Teacher Observation of Classroom Adaptation- Revised) • Authority Acceptance Scale • Peer rating of aggressive and hyperactive-disruptive behaviors.	Intervention group had higher scores on emotion recognition, emotion coping, and social problem solving compared to control group. They also found lower rates of aggressive retaliation compared to control group. Direct observation results: • Intervention group spent more time in positive peer interaction than did the control group. • Intervention group received higher peer social preference scores than control group. Long-term studies indicate variable findings depending on outcomes. 10-year longitudinal study examined psychiatric diagnoses for conduct disorder, oppositional defiant disorder, ADHD, and externalizing disorders. Findings suggest that the intervention could be effective in preventing externalizing disorders from developing among youth. (Conduct Problems Prevention Research Group, 1999, 2002, 2010, 2011). http://www. fasttrackproject.org/publications.php * Evaluating Sources 2, 3, 5, 6, 7, 8, 9

(continued)

Table 34.1 *(Continued)*

Program	*Grade*	*Participants*	*Program components*	*Outcome measures*	*Results*
PATHS Curriculum (Greenberg, Kusché, & Mihalic, 1998) http://www.prevention.psu.edu/projects/PATHS.html	1st–5th grades over three cohorts	198 intervention classrooms 180 control classrooms matched by school size, achievement levels, poverty and ethnic diversity 7,560 total students 845 students were in high-risk intervention or control conditions (6,715 students non-high risk children)	PATHS (Promoting Alternative Thinking Strategies). Administered to classrooms. 57 lessons (1/2 hr sessions, 2–3X/week) • Skills related to under-standing & communicating emotions • Skills related to increase of positive social behavior • Self-control and social problem solving Presented through direct instruction, discussion, modelling stories, or video Teachers attended 2.5 days training & received weekly consultation from PATHS staff. Quality of implementation was assessed by observer rating of teacher's • skill in teaching PATHS concepts" • Managing the classroom • Modeling and generalizing PATHS throughout day • Openness to consultation	1) Teachers were interviewed about behavior of each child in class (Fall/Spring of 1st year) 2) Socio-metric assessments (peer nominations made by students) collected to assess • Peer aggression • Peer hyperactivity/disruptiveness • Peer social status 3) Quality of classroom atmosphere was assessed by Observer ratings assessing the following: • Level of disruption • Ability to handle transitions • Ability to follow rules • Level of cooperation • Use of problem-solving skills • Ability to express feelings • Ability to stay focused on task • Criticism vs. supportiveness	Hierarchical Linear Modeling (Accounting for gender, site, cohort & intervention) Intervention classrooms had lower ratings of hyperactivity/disruptive behavior and aggression, and more favorable observer ratings of classroom atmosphere. Three cohorts of intervention, so teachers administered curriculum 1, 2, or 3 times. When "teacher experience" was included in analyses, teachers who taught more cohorts had higher classroom atmosphere ratings (by neutral observer). Quality of implementation Teacher skill in program implementation was also related to positive outcomes (Kam, Greenberg, & Walls, 2003). Four clinical trials conducted since 1995 revealed 32% reduction in teachers' reports of aggressive student behavior, 36% increase in teachers' reports of student self-control, 68% increase in students' vocabulary for emotions, and 20% increase in students' cognitive skills test scores. http://www.promoteprevent.org/publications/ebi-factsheets/promoting-alternative-thinking-strategies-paths * Evaluating Sources 2, 3, 4, 5, 6,8, 9

(continued)

* Evaluating sources:

1) American Youth Policy Forum: *Less Hype, More Help: Reducing Juvenile Crime, What Works-and What Doesn't* by Richard A. Mendel. Washington, DC, 2000 (http://www.aypf.org/publications/mendel/index.html).

2) Blueprints for Violence Prevention Center for the Study and Prevention of Violence (http://www.colorado.edu/cspv/blueprints).

3) Prevention Research Center for the Promotion of Human Development: http://www.prevention.psu.edu—Reducing Youth Violence and Delinquency in Pennsylvania: PCCD's Research-Based Programs Initiative Report http://www.prevention.psu.edu/pubs/docs/PCCD_ReducingYouthViolence.pdf.

4) U.S. Department of Health and Human Services—Substance Abuse and Mental Health Services Administration—National Registry of Evidence-Based Programs and Practices—http://nrepp.samhsa.gov.

5) U.S. Department of Education, Institute of Education Sciences "What Works Clearinghouse" (http://ies.ed.gov/ncee/wwc/reports/advancedss.aspx). Reducing Behavior Problems in the Elementary School Classroom—National Center for Education Evaluation and Regional Assistance. http://ies.ed.gov/ncee/wwc/pdf/practiceguides/behavior_pg_092308.pdf

6) U.S. Department of Education—Office of Safe & Drug-Free Schools www.ed.gov/about/offices/list/osdfs/index.html?src=mr.

7) U.S. Department of Justice: Office of Juvenile Justice and Delinquency Prevention's Model Programs Guide MPG: http://ojjdp.gov/mpg.

8) U. S. Department of Justice: National Criminal Justice Reference Service Report—Preventing crime: What Works, What Doesn't, What's Promising. University of Maryland Department of Criminology and Criminal Justice. NCJ 165366: https://www.ncjrs.gov/works. Main website: http://www.ncjrs.gov.

9) Youth Violence: A Report of the Surgeon General: http://www.surgeongeneral.gov/library/youthviolence/chapter5/sec3.html.

bullying behavior or by alerting an adult to the problem.

Theoretical Rationale and Conceptual Framework

The Olweus Bullying Prevention Program is based on a systematic restructuring of the school environment that redirects bullying behavior and provides rewards for more prosocial behavior. The conceptual framework is based on research on the development and modification of aggressive behavior, as well as positive childrearing dimensions (Olweus, Limber, & Mihalic, 1999). The goal is to create a school environment that (1) is characterized by adults who are engaged and caring, (2) has firm limits to unacceptable behavior, (3) has consistent responses of no rewards and negative consequences for violent behavior, and (4) has adults who act as authorities and positive role models (Olweus et al., 1999).

Much of the success of the BPP can be attributed to its being a school wide program, so that it becomes an integral part of the school environment. Students and adults participate in most of the universal components of the program. Indeed, teachers, parents, and administrators play an important role in the success of the program. School staff and parents are expected to (1) become aware of the extent of the bullying problem in their school through assessments, (2) gain an understanding of the significance and harmful effects of bullying, and (3) take an active role in enforcing rules against bullying behavior (Olweus et al., 1999).

Evaluation

As seen in Table 34.1, the first and most comprehensive evaluation study of this program was conducted with 2,500 students in Norway (also see Olweus et al., 1999). However, since then, this program has been implemented and positively evaluated in many countries. Evaluation of this program has demonstrated significant reductions in bully/victim reports across many cultures. General antisocial behaviors such as vandalism, fighting, theft, and truancy have been reduced in the program schools Improvements also have been found in classroom cultures in that students reported improved order and discipline at school, more positive social relationships, and more positive attitudes toward school and schoolwork.

It is also important to keep in mind that the historical success of a program does not necessarily guarantee its effectiveness. While international data are strong and consistent in documenting reductions of bullying and victimization, evaluations for U.S. schools have not been as consistent. In a 2011 review of the most recent OBPP studies, The Center for Schools and Communities describes challenges in implementation processes and emphasizes the need for careful attention to program fidelity in order to effectively implement the OBPP model.

"Caring School Community" Program (Formerly Called "Child Development Project")

The Caring School Community Program (formerly called the Child Development Project, or CDP) is an ecological approach to intervention that collaboratively involves teachers, parents, and students working to influence all aspects of the school community (Developmental Studies Center, 1995). Its main objective is to create a cooperative and supportive school environment for children in grades K–6. Established in 1981, the program strives to foster shared commitment to prosocial, democratic values in two specific ways: through adult guidance and through direct participation by children (Developmental Studies Center, 1995). Throughout this process, children are able to develop a sense that the school community cares for them, and they, in turn, begin to care about the school community. Over the years of program refinement, the Child Development Project has separated out into two distinct yet complementary modules: one entitled "Making Meaning" for the reading comprehension emphasis, and the current program of focus, "Caring School Community," for classroom climate and school community building. Our review of the research focuses on the Caring School Community component of the original Child Development Project.

Teachers are trained to implement most components of the intervention, and ongoing consultation and support are provided by the Developmental Studies Center. Research indicates that schools should make a minimum of a three-year commitment to the Caring School Community Program if it is to be effective (Northwest Regional Educational Laboratory, 1998). The program has been shown to be effective in both ethnically and socioeconomically diverse settings (Battistich, Solomon, Watson, & Schaps, 1997; Battistich, Schaps, Watson, & Solomon, 1996; Chang & Munoz, 2006; Marshall & Caldwell, 2007; Northwest Regional Educational Laboratory, 1998; Solomon, Watson, Battistich, Schaps, & Delucchi, 1996).

Theoretical Rationale and Conceptual Framework

The theoretical framework behind the Caring School Community program is guided by research on socialization, learning and motivation, and prosocial development (Battistich, Schaps, Watson, Solomon, & Lewis, 2000). Its overall objective is for schools to be transformed into caring and supportive communities in which everyone works collaboratively in the learning process. Such a focus is expected to foster children's intellectual and socio-moral development, self-direction, competence, and belonging (Battistich, Schaps, Watson, Solomon, & Lewis, 2000). And where these qualities are fostered, children become attached to and invested in the school community, which in turn leads them to internalize the school norms. School norms typically promote prosocial activity (e.g., concern for others) and proscribe antisocial activity (e.g., drug use or gang activity). The program is based on the idea that children's internalization of school norms will solidify their commitment to the school's community values.

Content

There are four interrelated goals on which the components of the CDP are based: (1) building warm, stable, supportive relationships; (2) attending to social and ethical dimensions of learning; (3) honoring intrinsic motivations; and (4) teaching in ways that support students' active construction of meaning (Battistich et al., 2000). These goals are interwoven into the five major components of the original CDP (Table 34.2), which were literature-based reading and language arts, collaborative classroom learning, developmental discipline, parent involvement, and school-wide activities, and are presented in Table 34.2.

The first three components are all designed for the classroom. The literature-based readings component is most directly focused on teaching for understanding. Thus, the selection of books is designed to help teachers foster a deeper and more empathic understanding of the readings among the students. The component that involves collaborative learning emphasizes the importance of working with others in a fair and cooperative manner. The final classroom component involves building care and respect for everyone in the classroom community (Northwest Regional Educational Laboratory, 1998).The two other components' foci go beyond the classroom. Parent involvement is designed to develop meaningful conversations between adults and their children; school-wide activities are focused on allowing participation by all and avoiding hierarchies and competition (Northwest Regional Education Laboratory, 1998).

Implementation

At least 80% of the school faculty must support their school's adoption of the CDP for it to be established there. Training is conducted by Developmental Studies Center's staff and involves initial consultation and planning to identify needs and goals; a 3-day summer institute to orient teachers on the CDP components and materials; three half-day follow-up workshops conducted during the school year; three on-site sessions, each lasting 2.5 days, which include consultation, in-class demonstrations, co-teaching, planning; and professional development support kits that can be used to train new staff (Developmental Studies Center, 2004).

Evaluation

As seen in Table 34.1, the Caring School Community strengthens students' sense of their school as a community, their ethical and social resources (e.g., conflict resolution skills, social problem-solving skills, commitment to democratic values, concern for others), their academic motivation (e.g., liking for school), and their abstention from drug use and other problem behaviors (e.g., gang-related activity) (Battistich et. al., 1996; Battistich et al., 1997; 2000; Battistich, Schaps, & Wilson, 2004; Northwest Regional Education Laboratory, 1998). Moreover, positive effects were reported 2 years after students left elementary school with regard to those students' conflict resolution skills, self-esteem, and involvement in

Table 34.2 Components of the Original Child Development Project

Components	*What Is Done*
1. Literature-based reading and language arts	1. *Reading aloud* allows students to have shared experience of hearing stories told aloud. 2. *Partner reads* help students build automaticity through the support of their partner. * In each of these scenarios, the teacher asks open-ended discussion questions about issues evoked by books and gives students an opportunity to discuss these issues with one another.
2. Collaborative classroom learning	1. *Peer collaboration* involves equal-status peers working in pairs or small groups on challenging projects that require collaboration. 2. *Adult guidance* involves the teacher monitoring peer groups. The teacher discusses the specific learning goals and behaviors required for successful cooperation at the beginning of each activity. The teacher also assists students in reflecting on group interaction at the conclusion of each task.
3. Developmental discipline	1. The teacher involves children in a. shaping norms of classroom; b. developing collaborative approaches to resolving conflict; c. practicing skills of nonviolent problem solving; d. helping them to anticipate problems so that they might be avoided; e. determining source of problems, thinking about solutions, and trying its effects on others. 2. Playground disputes become opportunities for children to engage in many of the above activities. 3. The teacher avoids extrinsic incentives in order to foster personal commitment to justice.
4. Parent involvement	1. *A school "coordinating team"* of parents and teachers collectively plans school-wide activities. 2. *Family participation* includes *"homeside activities"* that are designed to connect the home and school life. There are 18 activities per grade level, and each requires interaction between the parent and the student. For example, parents may discuss their culture and heritage with their child. The child then presents this information to the class.
5. School-wide activities	1. *Buddies Program* brings older and younger students together in activities, such as playing a game or going on a field trip. 2. *Grandperson's Day* draws older family members to the school to discuss their experiences. 3. *Family Read-Aloud* or *Family Film* nights bring parents and children together to engage in a learning activity.

* *Component 1 listed above is now separated out into the "Making Meaning" program, a distinct yet complementary module, whereas the other remaining components have been renamed as the Caring School Community Program. Source for original table:* Battistich, Schaps, Watson, Solomon, & Lewis, 2000 (Adapted with permission of Springer Science and Business Media); Developmental Studies Center, 1998.

extracurricular activity (Developmental Studies Center, 1995). Recent evaluations have also demonstrated improvements in student behavior with the Caring School Community Program. In a single school district evaluation, program schools demonstrated significant reductions in student discipline referrals (Chang & Munoz, 2006). Marshall and Caldwell (2007) also found a significant 24% decline in student discipline referrals over a two-year period in 20 program schools, while referrals increased 42% in four control schools.

FAST Track

The FAST Track Project is a long-term comprehensive intervention that encompasses multiple facets of children's social contexts. The intervention is comprehensive in that it has both universal (school-wide) components and targeted components that attempt to provide focused assistance to both children at high risk of antisocial behaviors and to their social systems. One of the great strengths of this program is its detailed attention to the intersection of the multiple contexts that contribute to children's developmental outcomes. The FAST Track prevention program aims to improve child competences, parent effectiveness, the school context, and school–home communications with the intention of preventing antisocial behavior across the developmental trajectory.

Theoretical Rationale and Conceptual Framework

The developmental theory guiding this intervention addresses the interaction of multiple influences on the development of antisocial behavior. These various elements include socioeconomic factors, family dynamics, peer influences, school factors, and the child's temperament.

Content

There were are four FAST Track sites in the United States, with a total of 891 children (and their families) participating (with near-equal numbers of at-risk children in both intervention and control groups). The initial sample consisted of children identified as "at risk" by a combination of teacher and parent ratings of their behavior. Children in the intervention group were provided with a host of services, including weekly enrichment programs, involvement in "friendship groups," and sessions in which they were taught and had opportunities to practice social skills. The parents of the intervention children were also provided with family coordinators who conducted biweekly home visits in efforts to enhance their parenting behavior management skills, specifically in the areas of praise, time-outs, and self-restraint. Children in the intervention group were also provided with three 30-minute academic tutoring sessions each week.

When the children in the intervention group reached adolescence (grades 6–10), the group-based interventions were de-emphasized. However, the intervention retained its curriculum-based parent and youth group meetings to support children in their transition into middle school (grades 5–7). In continuation of the earlier targeted model, individual support was provided for participants and their families in order to strengthen protective factors and reduce risk factors. The targeted intervention at the adolescent phase focused on academic tutoring, mentoring, home visiting and family problem solving, and supporting positive peer-group involvement. To address the multiple contexts in the adolescents' lives, the school tried to establish relations with the community agencies that served the participants.

FAST Track also included an important universal component for children in the first through the fifth grades in the target schools. This school-based intervention consisted of teacher-led curricula called "PATHS" (Promoting Alternative Thinking Strategies), designed to provide children with strategies in understanding the development of emotional concepts, social understanding, and self control. Since PATHS has been evaluated separately and shown to have independent positive effects, we will present PATHS separately in the next section. Some schools may choose to adopt only sections of the overall program, such as PATHS.

Evaluation

FAST Track is one of the more rigorously evaluated comprehensive violence prevention programs and has become widely known as one of the leading models of an effective approach to prevention of antisocial behaviors in youth. As shown in Table 34.1, evaluation studies of FAST Track have revealed positive outcomes for program participants. The evaluations on the initial cohort of youth selected for the study have spanned over 10 years and have continued to yield positive findings, with over 80% of the original sample remaining (Conduct Problems Prevention Research Group, 2011, 2010). In addition to those differences between treatment and control students highlighted in the table, the prevention revealed statistically significant improvements in the targeted children's social-cognitive and academic skills, as well as reductions in their parents' use of harsh discipline. The intervention children also demonstrated considerable behavioral improvements at home, in the classroom, and on the playground during and following their elementary school years. In addition to these behavioral improvements, the intervention children were at a reduced risk of being placed in special education classes than children in the control conditions. The findings generalized across ethnicity, gender, and a host of child and family characteristics.

Promoting Alternative Thinking Strategies (PATHS) Program

PATHS is the classroom curriculum component of the FAST Track intervention program. We present it separately because PATHS has been adopted and studied independently of FAST Track. PATHS was designed to promote emotional and social competence and to reduce aggression and other behavior problems in children in grades K–5 (Greenberg, Kusché, Cook, & Quamma, 1995). PATHS focuses on four domains related to school success: (1) prosocial behavior and friendship skills, (2) emotional understanding and self-control, (3) communication and conflict resolution, and (4) problem-solving skills (Conduct Problems Prevention Research Group, 2002). PATHS provides teachers and counselors with training, lesson modules, and ongoing consultation and support. Additionally, parents receive information and activities to complete with their children.

PATHS can be used with all elementary school–age children, and ideally it should be ongoing, beginning in kindergarten and continuing through fifth grade. It has been field-tested and researched in regular education classroom settings and in settings that serve special needs students such as the deaf, hearing-impaired, learning disabled, emotionally disturbed, mildly mentally delayed, and gifted (see Greenberg et al., 1995; Greenberg & Kusché, 1998).

Theoretical Rationale and Conceptual Framework

PATHS is based on five conceptual models (Greenberg, Kusché, & Mihalic, 1998). First, the ABCD (Affective-Behavioral-Cognitive-Dynamic) model of development promotes skills that are developmentally appropriate. The second model is an eco-behavioral system orientation that focuses on helping the teacher use these skills to build a healthy classroom atmosphere. The third model involves neurobiology and brain organization for cognitive development. The fourth is psychodynamic education that was derived from developmental psychodynamic theory. Finally, the fifth model includes psychological issues related to emotional awareness or emotional intelligence. These conceptual models come together in this curriculum to provide a comprehensive and developmentally based program that addresses students' cognitive processes, emotions, and behaviors.

Content

The PATHS curriculum (Greenberg et al., 1998) is taught three times a week for a minimum of 20–30 minutes a day. The curriculum contains four units with a total of 119 lessons in each unit. They consist of the following: (1) a "Turtle Unit" focusing on classroom behavior, emotional literacy, and self-control; (2) a "Feeling and Relationship Unit" focusing on building self-esteem and social competence; (3) a "Problem-Solving Unit" with instruction on the 11-step model of social problem solving and positive peer relations; and (4) a "Supplementary Lessons Unit" containing 30 lessons that delve more in depth into PATHS concepts. The lessons are age appropriate, and as we can see in Table 34.3, the lessons for third-grade students match developmental stages and cover the conceptual domains of self-control, emotional understanding, self-esteem, peer relations, and problem solving. (Lesson 93, presented in detail in Table 34.4, covers self-control and problem solving.)

The PATHS curriculum includes comprehensive materials, and the basic PATHS kit (grades 1–5) includes an instructor's manual, five curriculum manuals, feelings photographs, feelings face cards, two wall charts, and four full color posters. The Turtle Unit (for kindergarten classrooms) includes an instructor's manual, curriculum manual, turtle puppet with pad, turtle stamp, and poster. Teachers receive on-site training and technical assistance to ensure effective implementation of the program.

Table 34.3 PATHS Lessons for Grade 3

		Conceptual Domains				
Lesson Topic	*Volume & Lesson #*	*Self-Control*	*Emotional Understanding*	*Self-Esteem*	*Peer Relations*	*Problem Solving*
PATHS Rules	Vol. 1, L 1	X		X	X	X
PATHS Kid/Complimenting/Self-esteem	Vol. 1, L 2	X		X	X	X
Anger Intensity	Vol. 1, L 10		X		X	
Anger Management/Control Signals	Vol. 1, L 11–12	X		X	X	X
Fear Intensity/Sad Intensity	Vol. 1, L 15–17		X		X	
Disgusted, Delighted	Vol. 1, L 21		X		X	
Frustrated, Disappointed/Hopeful, Proud/Ashamed, Guilty, Curious/Interested/Bored, Confused/Worried/Sure, Anxious/Calm, Shy/Lonely	Vol. 2, L 23–32,37		X		X	
Embarrassed/Humiliated	Vol. 2, L 33–34		X		X	
Intentionality (Accident/Purpose), Manners	Vol. 3, L 38–44		X		X	
Jealous/Content, Greedy/Selfish/Generous, Malicious/Kind, Rejected/Included, Excluded, Forgiving/Resentful	Vol. 3,48–56		X		X	
Informal Problem Solving	Vol. 5, 90–92	X				X
Self-Control and Problem Prevention	Vol. 5, L 93–94	X				X
Friendship	Vol. 5, L 95–97.	X	X	X	X	X
Teasing	Vol. 5, L 98–101.	X	X	X	X	X
Apply Problem-Solving Steps	Vol. 4, L 89.					X

Table 34.4 PATHS Learning Self-Control, Volume 5, Lesson 93

Introduction	"Today I'm going to tell you a story about a boy who had problems, but he learned a new way to help himself."
Story: "Thomas in Control"	This is a story about a boy who did not like to go to school. Thomas felt very upset about going to school. He wanted to run outside and play with his toys or ride his bike or watch television or play a game. Thomas did not like to sit quietly. It was hard for him to pay attention when the teacher or the other kids were talking in class. Instead, Thomas would tease whoever was sitting beside him, by grabbing their pencils and books, by making faces at them, or by whispering to them. The other kids would get angry at Thomas when he bothered them and would yell at him or would do some of the same things back. Then everyone would get caught and would get into trouble. That's why some of the kids thought that Thomas was troublemaker. Sometimes when they went out to the playground at recess, the other kids would still be mad at Thomas, and they would get into a fight. All of this hate and resentment made Thomas feel very uncomfortable inside. One day when he was feeling his worst, the playground teacher told Thomas that he had to go to the principal's office because he hadn't been following the playground rules. "You know," said the principal in a very calm voice, "you have a very big problem, but I'll share a secret with you. You already have the answer to your problem with you. You carry it with you everywhere you go. It's your ability to think. Whenever you feel upset, when you are angry or frustrated, you can use your mind and think. You can stop, take a long, deep breath, and say the problem and how you feel. When you remind yourself to stop and calm down, it's like taking a rest for a minute. You can rest until you feel calm. That is how you can control yourself. And when you can control yourself, then people will say, 'Thomas has good self-control. He thinks before he does something that will cause problems.'" The principal showed Thomas the three steps for calming down. Then the principal reminded Thomas that the next time he felt upset or angry, he could think about the control signals and could calm himself down. Thomas liked the idea and wanted to try it himself. He wanted to do well in school, he wanted his teacher to like him, and he especially wanted to make friends....
On board	Begin drawing on the chalk board Feelings: comfortable and uncomfortable/ Behavior OK and not OK.
Discussion	Ask students to name the different feelings and behavior that Thomas felt and list them under the appropriate categories. Ask them to discuss the relationships between these feelings and behaviors if they are able to do so. Ask students to name the kinds of things that bug them in the classroom, playground, lunchroom, and so on, and list them in the categories. This will help students become aware of what they do that bothers others. Ask student if using the three steps to calm down would help with any of the things they listed.

Source: Story excerpt reduced for space reasons from Kusché & Greenberg (1994), available for review on www.channing-bete.com

Evaluation

PATHS was evaluated between 1994 and 2003 in various research studies using randomized control groups and was found to be effective. As seen in Table 34.1, PATHS has been found to be a model or effective program by at least six groups that review violence prevention programs nationwide for effectiveness. An overview of results from all trials reveals a reduction in aggressive behavior, conduct disorder, and violent solutions to social problems. In addition, results found an increase in self-control, vocabulary for emotions, cognitive skills, ability to tolerate frustration, and to effectively use conflict-resolution strategies (SAMHSA Model Programs, 2003). The findings have been consistent across teacher reports, self-reports, and child assessments and interviews. PATHS remains among the highest-rated social-emotional learning programs and is nationally and internationally recognized for its strong evidence base, theoretical design, and clarity of implementation. It received a perfect score for program materials and a nearly perfect score for dissemination according to the SAMHSA's National Registry of Evidence-based Programs and Practices and had the highest possible rating according to the Center for the Study and Prevention ofViolence.

The PATHS program has also been recognized for its effectiveness by the National Institute on Drug Abuse (NIDA) and the Office of Juvenile Justice and Delinquency Prevention (OJJDP).

Tools and Practice Examples

Learning Self-Control, Volume 5—Supplementary Lesson 93, Grade3

In the PATHS curriculum, each unit builds on the preceding units. Table 34.4 consists of an excerpt from supplementary lesson 93 and is intended for third graders.

The objective of this lesson is to discuss the idea of self-control as an internalized process. It emphasizes the concept of using thinking to control one's behavior and to distinguish between feelings and behaviors. The teacher reads a story about a boy named Thomas who had problems with self-control, was angry, and would get into fights with other children. Throughout the story, students learn the three steps for calming down to gain control of their behavior. The lesson is followed by the teacher drawing a hierarchy of feelings and behaviors on the board and asking questions to encourage classroom discussion. Students are encouraged to talk about how they felt when they acted without thinking first, and to say whether things got out of control and how they felt about the outcome. This lesson teaches students anger management and problem-solving skills through a developmentally appropriate story that is easy to relate to and that facilitates discussion.

Monitoring and Evaluating Violence Prevention Programs

A review of the school safety literature strongly suggests that model school safety programs should be developed and implemented in a process that ensures their relevance and applicability to each specific site. These are important assumptions of the programs described in this chapter:

- Fitting a program to a school involves grass-roots participation.
- Students and teachers in the school need to be empowered to deal with the problem.
- Democracy is the core of a good school safety program.
- Schools should demonstrate a proactive vision surrounding the violence problem in their school.

Implementing interventions or components of any model program is likely to be slightly different for every school. An eye toward the overall assumptions and flexibility should enable each school to adapt the program or general principles to its unique demographic, philosophical, and organizational needs. Several resources are provided at the end of the chapter to support implementation efforts of programs. It is critically important not only to pay attention to the outcome evaluations but also to keep in mind the importance of program fidelity, advocacy, and support from administration, and commitment to the program adoption process. Cissner and Farole (2009) highlight lessons learned from process evaluations of program implementation in the field of juvenile justice that can apply just as readily for schools as well.

Data and Program Evaluation

There are numerous new programs and systems designed to create data-driven decision-making processes within districts and schools. One of the more popular programs to address academic learning is Response to Intervention (RTI), whereby students are identified early, provided with intervention, measured for improvement, and referred to special services if there is not adequate "response" to the intervention. While the programs highlighted in this section were not designed with specific reference to RTI, they do align with the same philosophy of providing early, effective assistance to children who are struggling. Further, each of the programs supports data-driven processes to continually improve the effectiveness of intervention efforts.

A critical element of successful school safety programs is the ongoing and interactive use of data. This perspective proposes that the continuous and ongoing analysis and interpretation of data is an essential part of the intervention process. Data are used to create awareness, mobilize different school constituencies, assess the extent of the problem, plan and implement interventions, and conduct evaluations. Information is provided on a continuous basis to different groups in each step of the intervention process. Unfortunately, many U.S. schools purchase evidence-based programs but do not collect any data about their own district or school.

The process of building and implementing school safety programs is continual and cyclical, always changing to respond to new circumstances and emerging needs. Hence, the evaluation of the program's progress becomes a reassessment of the situation, leading to a new cycle of awareness building, planning, modifying, and evaluating. A school's failure to gather site-specific and comparative data could be a significant obstacle in (a) assessing whether that specific school has a violence problem, (b) adapting a school safety program, and (c) evaluating the implementation process and outcomes of the program.

Monitoring and school mapping can help create a "whole-school response" and help the school to identify, create, and/or adapt programs to the site. Monitoring is the ongoing process of collecting and using data to shape, fit, match, and evaluate the intervention. The value of monitoring comes from the two levels of information processing involved: description and comparison. The description of the basic frequency of certain behaviors may be quite instructive. For example, it is helpful to know how many weapon-related events or sexual assaults occur at a specific school.

Using Comparisons

In general, comparisons enhance the value of information by putting it in context. In order to adapt a program, it is imperative to ascertain (a) which acts are more problematic than others, (b) which grade levels are victimized more, and (c) how violence levels in a specific school compare over time and for different ethnic, age, and gender groups. For example, if bullying is not a major problem in the school, it does not make sense to adopt an anti-bullying program. Perhaps bullying is a problem only in one grade level within a large school, whereas other forms of violence are problems in other grades. Though these concerns may sound like common sense, very few schools actually collect systemic information to ascertain the extent of the school safety problem. Currently, many districts and schools across the United States are purchasing expensive violence prevention programs targeting a specific form of violence (e.g., sexual harassment, bullying, weapon use) without data about the extent of the problem in their schools. This creates a chain of difficulties through the implementation process and later in the evaluation of the program. If the problem was never established, it is difficult to know if the program ever worked. Hence, it is important to examine levels of violence over time.

Using Mapping as a Monitoring Tool

Mapping is a qualitative tool that can help monitor and generate the kind of comparisons discussed above. Mapping does not require extensive training and can provide valuable information that helps implement, monitor, and assess the ongoing health of a program. This procedure is designed to involve school constituents by revealing how forms of violence within a school building interact with locations, patterns of the school day, and social organizational variables (e.g., teacher–student relationships, teachers' professional roles, and the school's organizational response to violence; for more detail see Astor, Benbenishty, & Meyer, 2004; Astor, Guerra, & Van Acker, 2010; Astor, Meyer, & Behre, 1999; Astor & Meyer, 1999; Astor, Meyer, & Pitner, 2001; Benbenishty & Astor, 2012). An important goal of this procedure is to allow students and teachers to convey their personal theories about why specific locations and times in their schools are more dangerous. This process greatly facilitates the implementation and evaluation of the model programs reviewed in the first sections of this chapter.

Step-by-Step Instructions

Mapping, Interviews, and Interventions

The first step in this assessment procedure is obtaining a map of the school. Ideally, the map should contain all internal school territory, including the areas surrounding the school and playground. In communities where the routes to and from school are dangerous, a simple map of the surrounding neighborhood may be added to the assessment process. The focus groups should begin with the facilitator distributing two sets of identical school maps to each individual.

Map A and B: Two photocopied maps of the school are needed for each student and teacher. One map should be used to determine where students and teachers think the most events involving violence occur. Participants should also be asked to identify the locations (on the maps) of up to three of the most violent events that have occurred within the past academic year. Next to each marked event on the map, participants should be asked to write the following information: (1) the general time frame of the event (e.g., before school, after school, morning period, afternoon period, evening sports event, between classes, etc.); (2) the grade and gender of those involved in the violence; and (3) their knowledge of any organizational response to the event (e.g., someone was sent to principal's office, suspended, sent to peer counselor, nothing done, etc.). On the second map, members should be asked to circle areas or territories that they perceive to be unsafe or potentially dangerous. This second map provides information about areas within the school that participants avoid or fear even though they may not possess knowledge of a particular event.

Discussion of Violent Events and Areas

The first part of the group discussion should center on the specific events and the areas marked as unsafe or dangerous on their personal maps. We have asked questions such as "Are there times when those places you've marked on the maps are less safe?" "Is there a particular group of students that is more likely to get hurt there?" and "Why do you think that area has so many incidents?" The overall purpose of the group interviews is to explore why bullying or victimization occurs at those specific times and in those specific spaces. Consequently, the interviews should also focus on gathering information regarding the organizational response to the event (e.g., "What happened to the two students after the event?" or "Did the hall monitors intervene when they saw what happened?"), procedures (e.g., "What happens when the students are sent to the office after a fight?" "Did anyone call the parents of the bully or victim?"), follow-up (e.g., "Do the teachers, hall monitors, and/or administrators follow up on any consequences given to the students?" or "Did anyone check on the welfare of the victim?"), and clarity of procedures (e.g., "Does it matter who stops the bullying?" such as a volunteer, security guard, teacher, or principal).

Interviewers should also explore participants' ideas for solutions to the specific violence problems (e.g., "Can you think of ways to avoid bullying or victimization in that place?" or "If you were the principal, what would you do to make that place safer?"). In addition, the interviewer should explore any obstacles that participants foresee with implementation (e.g., "Do you think that type of plan is realistic?" "Has that been tried before? What happened?" or "Do you think that plan would work?"). Such obstacles could range from issues related to roles (e.g., "It's not my job to monitor students during lunch") to discipline policy and issues of personal safety (e.g., "I don't want to intervene because I may get hurt").

In schools that already have started model programs designed to address school violence, specific questions should be asked about the effectiveness of those interventions, why they work or do not work, and what could be done to make the current measures more effective. We recommend that the interviewer ask both subjective questions (e.g., "Do you think the antiviolence program is working? Why do you think it works, or why does it not work?") as well as specific questions related to the reduction of victimization (e.g., "Do you believe the antiviolence program has reduced the number of fights/name calling [or any other type of violence the school is interested in preventing] on the playground? Why or why not?").

Transferring all of the reported events onto one large map of the school enables students and staff to locate specific "hot spots" for violence and dangerous time periods within each individual school. The combined data are presented to all school constituencies, and they are asked to once again discuss and interpret the maps. Teachers and students use the maps and interviews to suggest ways to improve the settings and what aspects of the program are working or not working. For example, in one school, events were clustered by time, age, gender, and location. In the case of older students (11th and 12th graders), events were clustered in the parking lot outside of the auxiliary gym immediately after school, whereas for younger students (9th and 10th graders), events were reported in the lunchroom and hallways during transition periods. For this school, the map suggested that interventions be geared specifically toward older students, directly after school, by the main entrance, and in the school parking lot. Students and teachers agreed that increasing the visible presence of school staff in and around the parking lot for the 20 minutes after school had great potential for reducing the number of violent events. Younger students were experiencing violence mainly before, during, and after lunch, near the cafeteria. Many students expressed feelings of being unsafe between classes in the hallways. This school already had an anti-bullying program, and it was able to incorporate this specific type of intervention into existing activities designed to stem school violence.

Compiling all the interview suggestions into themes is an important second step in adapting context-relevant interventions. Students, teachers, and administrators may have differing viewpoints regarding the organizational response of the school to a violent incident. Relaying the diversity of responses to students, teachers, and administrators can provide an opportunity for reflection and may generate ways to remedy the violence problem in certain situations. When the data are presented to students, teachers, and administrators, they can center their discussions on why those areas are dangerous and what kinds of interventions could make the location safer. Mapping methods provide data-based approaches to gathering information about bullying/victimization in schools. Moreover, they provide site-specific information, which makes it easier for schools to address these problems.

Identifying specific target groups for interventions is another way data can/should be used. A school could use this monitoring system to identify particular problem areas in their school. They could then track progress in reducing violence in these locations over time and by different groups.

Key Points to Remember

Based on our review of programs, it appears that successful school-wide intervention programs have the following core underlying implementation characteristics:

They are comprehensive, intensive, ecological, and require "buy-in" from school and community.

They raise the awareness and responsibility of students, teachers, and parents regarding the types of violence in their schools (e.g., sexual harassment, fighting, and weapons use).

They create clear guidelines and rules for all members of the school community.

They target the various social systems in the school and clearly communicate to the entire school community what procedures should be followed before, during, and after violent events.

They focus on getting the school staff, students, and parents involved in the program.

They often fit easily into the normal flow and mission of the school setting.

They use faculty, staff, and parents in the school setting to plan, implement, and sustain the program.

They increase monitoring and supervision in non classroom areas.

They include ongoing monitoring and mapping, which provide information that schools can use to tailor a program to their specific needs and increase its chance of success.

Resources

Web Sites on Programs

Olweus Bullying Prevention Program: http://www.clemson.edu/olweus/

Caring School Community: http://devstu.org/caring-school-community

FAST Track: http://www.fasttrackproject.org

PATHS (Promoting Alternative Thinking Strategies): http://www.promoteprevent.org/publications/ebi-factsheets/promoting-alternative-thinking-strategies-paths

Web Sites That Evaluate School Violence Prevention Programs

American Youth Policy Forum: http://www.aypf.org/resource-search/Blueprints for Violence Prevention—Center for the Study and Prevention of Violence: http://www.colorado.edu/cspv/blueprints/modelprograms.html

National Center for Mental Health Promotion and Youth Violence Prevention: http://www.promoteprevent.org

Prevention Research Center for the Promotion of Human Development: http://www.prevention.psu.edu

U.S. Department of Health and Human Services—Substance Abuse and Mental Health Services Administration (SAMHSA) National Registry of Evidence-Based Programs and Practices: http://nrepp.samhsa.gov

U.S. Department of Education: Office of Safe and Drug-Free Schools: http://www.ed.gov/about/offices/list/osdfs/index.html?src=mr

U.S. Department of Justice: Office of Justice Programs: Office of Juvenile Justice and Delinquency Prevention—Model Programs Guide: http://www.ojjdp.gov/mpg/

U. S. Department of Justice—National Criminal Justice Reference Service Report: Preventing Crime: What Works, What Doesn't, What's Promising. University of Maryland Department of Criminology and Criminal Justice (Sherman, 1998) NCJ 165366: https://www.ncjrs.gov/works Main website: http://www.ncjr.sgov

Youth Violence: A Report of the Surgeon General: http://www.ncbi.nlm.nih.gov/books/NBK44294/

Other Resources and Reports

Centers for Disease Control and Prevention: Best Practices of Youth Violence Prevention: A Sourcebook for Community Action: http://www.cdc.gov/violenceprevention/pdf/introduction-a.pdf

Centers for Disease Control and Prevention: Injury Center: Violence Prevention: Youth Violence Prevention Strategies: http://www.cdc.gov/ViolencePrevention/youthviolence/prevention.html

Development Services Group: http://www.dsgonline.com

Indicators of School Crime and Safety—2011: http://nces.ed.gov/programs/crimeindicators/crimeindicators2011/

References

Astor, R. A., & Meyer, H. (1999). Where girls and women won't go: Female students', teachers', and social workers' views of school safety. *Social Work in Education*, 21, 201–219.

Astor, R. A., Meyer, H., & Behre, W. J. (1999). Unowned places and times: Maps and interviews about violence in high schools. *American Educational Research Journal*, 36, 3–42.

Astor, R. A., Meyer, H. A., & Pitner, R. O. (2001). Elementary and middle school students' perceptions of safety: An examination of violence-prone school sub-contexts. *The Elementary School Journal*, 101, 511–528.

Astor, R. A., Benbenishty, R., & Meyer, H. A. (2004). Monitoring and mapping student victimization in schools. *Theory into Practice*, 43, 39–49.

Astor, R. A., Guerra, N., & Van Acker, R. (2010). How can we improve school safety research? *Educational Researcher*, 39, 69–78.

Battistich, V., Schaps, E., Watson, M., & Solomon, D. (1996). Prevention effects of the child development project: Early findings from an ongoing multi-site demonstration trial. *Journal of Adolescent Research*, 11, 12–35.

Battistich, V., Schaps, E., Watson, M., Solomon, D., & Lewis, C. (2000). Effects of the child development project on students' drug use and other problem behaviors. *The Journal of Primary Prevention*, 21, 75–99.

Battistich, V., Schaps, E., & Wilson, N. (2004). Effects of an elementary school intervention on students' "connectedness" to school and social adjustment during middle school. *The Journal of Primary Prevention*, 24(3), 243–262.

Battistich, V., Solomon, D., Watson, M., & Schaps, E. (1997). Caring school communities. *Educational Psychologist*, 32, 137–151.

Benbenishty, R., & Astor, R. A. (2012). Monitoring school violence in Israel, national studies and beyond: Implications for theory, practice, and policy. In S. R. Jimerson, A. B. Nickerson, M. J. Mayer, & M. J. Furlong (Eds.), *The handbook of school violence and school safety: International research and practice* (pp. 15–26). New York: Routldege.

Center for Schools and Communities (2011). *Olweus Bullying Prevention Program in High Schools: A Review of Literature, 5*. Available online at http://www.center-school.org/documents/CSC_RB5_web.pdf

Chang, F., & Munoz, M. A. (2006). School personnel educating the whole child: Impact of character education on teachers' self-assessment and student development. *Journal of Personnel Evaluation in Education*, 19(1–2), 35–49.

Cissner, A. B., & Donald J. Farole, J. (2009). *Best practices: Avoiding failures of implementation: Lessons from process evaluations*. Center for Court Innovation, Bureau of Justice Assistance, U.S. Department of Justice, Washington, DC.

Conduct Problems Prevention Research Group. (1992). A developmental and clinical model for the prevention of conduct disorders: The Fast Track program. *Development and Psychopathology*, 4, 509–527.

Conduct Problems Prevention Research Group. (1999). Initial impact of the Fast Track Prevention Trial for conduct problems: I. The high-risk sample. *Journal of Consulting and Clinical Psychology*, 67(5), 631–647.

Conduct Problems Prevention Research Group. (1999). Initial impact of the Fast Track prevention trial for conduct problems: II. Classroom effects. *Journal of Consulting and Clinical Psychology*, 67(5), 648–657.

Conduct Problems Prevention Research Group. (2002). The implementation of the Fast Track program: An example of a large-scale prevention science efficacy trial. *Journal of Abnormal Child Psychology*, 30, 1–17.

Conduct Problems Prevention Research Group. (2010). The Fast Track Project: The prevention of severe conduct problems in school-age youth. In R. C. Murrihy, A. D. Kidman, & T. H. Ollendick (Eds.), *Handbook of clinical assessment and treatment of conduct problems in youth* (pp. 407–433). New York, NY: Springer.

Conduct Problems Prevention Research Group. (2011). The effects of the Fast Track preventive intervention on the development of conduct disorder across childhood. *Child Development*, 82(1), 331–345.

Developmental Studies Center (1995). *Child Development Project*. Retrieved May 18, 2004, from http://www.ed.gov/pubs/EPTW/eptw5/eptw5a.html

Developmental Studies Center. (1998). *Some basics of the Child Development Project presented at the AERA conference, San Diego, April 1998*. Retrieved May 23, 2004, from http://waarden.goliath.nl/studie/concepten/cdp/basics.html

Developmental Studies Center. (2004). *Comprehensive program: The Child Development Project*. Retrieved May 27, 2004, from http://www.devstu.org/research-child-development-project

Greenberg, M. T., Kusché, C. A., Cook, E. T., & Quamma, J. P. (1995). Promoting emotional competence in school-aged children: The effects of the PATHS curriculum. *Development & Psychopathology. Special Issue: Emotions in developmental psychopathology*, 7(1), 117–136.

Greenberg, M. T., & Kusché, C. A. (1998). Preventive interventions for school-age deaf children: The PATHS curriculum. *Journal of Deaf Studies & Deaf Education*, 3(1), 49–63.

Greenberg, M. T., Kusché, C., & Mihalic, S. F. (1998). *Blueprints for violence prevention, book ten: Promoting Alternative Thinking Strategies (PATHS)*. Boulder, CO: Center for the Study and Prevention of Violence.

Kallestad, J. H., & Olweus, D. (2003). Predicting teachers' and schools' implementation of the Olweus Bullying Prevention program: A multilevel study. *Prevention and Treatment, 6,* Article 21. Available online at http://psycnet.apa.org/journals/pre/6/1/21a/.

Kam, C. M., Greenberg, M. T., & Walls, C. T. (2003). Examining the role of implementation quality in school based prevention using the PATHS curriculum. *Prevention Science*, 4(1), 55–63.

Kusché, C. A., & Greenberg, M. T. (1994). *The PATHS curriculum*. Seattle: Developmental Research and Programs.

Marshall, J., & Caldwell, S. (2007). *Caring School Community implementation study four-year evaluation report*. Rapid City, SD: Marshall Consulting.

Northwest Regional Educational Laboratory. (1998). *The catalog of school reform models*. Retrieved May 23, 2004, from http://www.nwrel.org/scpd/catalog/ModelDetails.asp?ModelID=6

Olweus, D., (1991). Bully/victim problems among schoolchildren: Basic facts and effects of a school-based intervention program. In D. Pepler & K. Rubin (Eds.), *The development and treatment of childhood aggression* (pp. 411–448). Hillsdale, NJ: Erlbaum.

Olweus, D. (1993). *Bullying at school: What we know and what we can do*. Cambridge, MA: Blackwell.

Olweus, D. (2005). A useful evaluation design and effects of the Olweus Bullying Prevention Program. *Psychology, Crime, & Law*, 11, 389–402.

Olweus, D., Limber, S. & Mihalic, S. F. (1999). *Blueprints for violence prevention, book nine: Bullying prevention program*. Boulder, CO: Center for the Study and Prevention ofViolence.

Solomon, D., Watson, M., Battistich, V., Schaps, E., & Delucchi, K. (1996). Creating classrooms that students experience as communities. *American Journal of Community Psychology*, 24, 719–748.

CHAPTER 35

Bullying

Best Practices for Prevention and Intervention in Schools

Esther Howe · Jessica Wright Marini · Elayne Haymes · Tanya Tenor

Getting Started

Historically, bullying in schools has been a persistent problem worldwide. In the United States, heightened awareness of school violence due to high-profile school shootings and recent suicides by victims of the new, emerging forms of cyberbullying in the past 15 years has led parents and school officials to seek solutions to this pervasive problem. The realization that two-thirds of the perpetrators of high-profile school shootings were themselves victims of bullying has added urgency to this matter (Sampson, 2009). Although bullying can and does occur in other environments, the majority of bullying takes place in and around school buildings (Smith, Ananiadou, & Cowie, 2003).

For our purposes, we use English criminologist David Farrington's widely accepted 1993 definition of *bullying*: "Bullying is the repeated oppression, psychological or physical, of a less powerful person by a more powerful person." According to Sampson (2009) bullying represents the most underreported safety problem and yet the most prevalent form of violence suffered by children (Haynie et al., 2001). Bullying takes four major forms: physical, verbal, social, and electronic. Incidence of the particular forms varies by gender, race, and socioeconomic status.

Boys are more involved in physical or verbal bullying, while girls are more involved in relational bullying. Boys are more likely to be cyberbullies, while girls are more likely to be cyber-victims. African-American adolescents are involved in more bullying but less victimization, and adolescents from more affluent families are less likely to be physical victims but more likely to be cyber-victims (Wang, Iannotti, & Nansel, 2009). In recent years, the Internet has increasingly been used for these activities, thus leaving the victims vulnerable even at home.

Bullying can include saying or writing inappropriate things about a person, deliberately excluding an individual from activities, threatening or actually hurting an individual, making a person do things against his or her own will, and teasing. The increased popularity of cell phones and computers among adolescents has led to a rising rate of electronic forms of bullying, thus leaving the victims vulnerable even at home (Wang et al., 2009).

Bullying affects not only the bullied but also the bullies, often leading to truancy and eventual school dropout. Bullied students exhibit more physical problems, are more depressed, and achieve less in school (Michaud, 2009). Both the bullies and the bullied are at greater risk for suicide attempts. In addition, bullying can affect the climate of the schools and, indirectly, the ability of all students to learn to the best of their abilities. Both the widespread nature of the problem and the potential gravity of its consequences mandate that school personnel seek and implement sound evidence-based interventions to alleviate the problem.

What We Know

Research on the effectiveness of anti-bullying programs instituted in schools is neither strong nor definitive. Problems in developing clear evidence-based interventions emerge from both the lack of consensus about what constitutes bullying and from the lack of reliable data that usually rely on single informant reporting (Swearer, Espelage, Vaillancourt, & Hymel, 2010). These authors suggest that research be conducted by a multi-informant approach (Swearer et al., 2010).

There are, however, common factors shared by most of the programs: a whole-school approach to the problem of inclusion of the subject matter in the curriculum; close contact with parents; involvement of the broader community; increased monitoring of student behavior; encouragement of students to seek help; and subsequent provision of counseling services, as well as a plan on how to deal with cases of bullying. While the research on bullying can be confounding, to date all analyses document the importance of a whole-school approach as well as of focused group and individual counseling for both victims and perpetrators. Total staff support for the school's anti-bullying policy is essential (Swearer et al., 2010). While there is not enough evidence regarding the effectiveness of one particular program over another, it is apparent that: *The specifics of the program are not as significant as the thoroughness with which it is carried out* (Rigby, 2002). Thus, staff training is crucial to the success of any school-based anti-bullying program.

What We Can Do

The following interlocking program components will be discussed in descending ecological order: (1) an approach to involve the entire school staff; (2) life skills training groups in which all students participate; and (3) specific interventions targeted at individual perpetrators and victims. Though other components, such as better staff monitoring of playgrounds, hallways, and school bathrooms, parental involvement, and curriculum inclusion, are important, the focus of this chapter is to give explicit guidelines on how to implement the three components mentioned above. By creating a whole-school approach while also providing life skills tools and psychological supports for both perpetrators and victims, this chapter intends to outline a comprehensive approach that addresses both school climate and individual needs.

Get the School Staff on Board

A significant barrier to the success of a bullying prevention program can frequently be the lack of staff understanding or compliance with the program. School social workers need to begin working with school staff as soon as a mandate has been handed down from the state or the school administration. The first step is to have the faculty and staff fill out a questionnaire (for an example, see Rigby's Bullying in the Resources section of this chapter). Subsequently, the social worker should schedule several professional development meetings with the staff to discuss the findings of the questionnaire and to lay out the goals of the bullying prevention program. Any staff resistance should be dealt with openly, and staff 's suggestions and concerns should be listened to. The school administration's policy on bullying should be clarified. Comprehensive guidelines on what is and is not considered bullying should be presented, as well as clear protocols on how to deal with incidents of bullying both in terms of the perpetrators and the victims. Assure the staff that all of you are in this together and that the school administration and your program will support them as the anti-bullying efforts progress. To that end, monthly refresher meetings in which new concerns and opportunities can be voiced should be held.

Prevention Interventions with All Students

Once staff support has been secured, work should begin with programs that affect all students. The school social worker should encourage teachers to incorporate information about the effects of bullying in their curricula, and they should have access to model curricular units and other resources. (See the Resources section for a list of anti-bullying Web sites.) School assemblies should be called to inform all students of state law regarding bullying and the school's policies and resources for dealing with bullying.

Students should be encouraged to report incidents of bullying by promising anonymity. An essential tool for helping students access help is a suggestion box in a discreet location, which enables students to leave anonymous notes about problems they have or observe. All students should know where it is.

Whatever intervention the school chooses to use, it is essential to remember the importance of simple vigilance and oversight. In some instances, closer supervision of playgrounds, hallways, and bathrooms has led to a 50% decrease in bullying behavior and physical violence (Smith et al., 2003).

Parental involvement is an essential component of an effective program. Parents should be told about the school's antiviolence/anti-bullying program and given clear descriptions of what is and is not considered bullying behavior, what the consequences are for children who engage in such conduct, and what resources parents can avail themselves of if they fear for their children's well-being. Parents should be given phone numbers of relevant staff. A brochure telling parents the behavioral indicators to look out for is a useful tool for enlisting their support. A special section should be devoted to cyberbullying, as parents are more likely than the school to observe this particular form of bullying. The school social worker should offer to speak on these topics at a meeting of the school's parent organization.

Life Skills Groups

An essential component of a whole-school approach is a prevention-focused life skills training group conducted in collaboration with each grade's scheduled health and/or social skills/life skills curriculum. Life skills training concentrates on prosocial decision making regarding anger management, conflict resolution, peer and family relations, and so on. These groups can be run by members of the school mental health team or by specially trained teachers.

All group sessions are designed to foster self awareness and behavioral change. Topics include, but are not limited to, developing methods of self discipline, identifying consequences before taking action, recognizing the effect of one's behavior on others, learning alternative ways of getting what one wants, mastering angry and aggressive impulses and thoughts, and learning peaceful methods of resolving conflicts (Coloroso, 2003).

The curriculum in these life skills groups should focus in part on bullying, besides helping children develop sound decision-making skills. (A model lesson of a 4-week curriculum on bullying is included in section IV.) Life skills groups represent an opportunity to enhance all students' prosocial decision-making skills while increasing their sense of community, strengthening their social network, and thereby improving the social climate of the school as a whole. Students in such a school are less to likely to bully, more likely to report bullying if they observe it, and more likely to seek help if they are victims. Some countries have focused on improving school climate as their major effort to reduce bullying behavior (Swearer et al., 2010).

Working with Perpetrators and Victims

Even interventions focusing on victims and perpetrators initially use a prevention paradigm. Prevention, as it is understood in primary intervention, is a model for service predicated on the identification of unique behavioral indicators that are associated with the potential for violent behavior toward self and others (Michaud, 2009). This aspect of the intervention usually proceeds according to steps outlined below.

Step 1: Identify students who have been the victims of bullying or who have been involved in a range of experiences that are high risk for aggressive acts. This goal can be realized through an annual, whole-school population survey completed at the beginning of each year as part of an assignment in an English, health, or life skills class. (Students should be allowed to refuse to fill out the survey without repercussions.)

The survey is used to assess and prioritize students for early contact and further evaluation by the staff. The survey asks questions pertaining to a range of social and emotional experiences that have been related in the literature to violent/bullying behavior as aggressor or victim. Students assessed to have a high number of risk elements or who present a significant self description indicating potential aggression or victimization behaviors are interviewed by a staff member as quickly as possible. Risk for bullying or victimization can be assessed in greater detail, and a plan can be developed that may include one or more individual and group modalities, using the prevention components described in the previous section. Staff must gain the trust of students identified as potential victims, perpetrators, and witnesses through carefully orchestrated but informal contacts—in the lunchroom, on the playground, in brief meetings, thus weaving a safety net of social support for students (Haymes Howe, & Peck, 2003).

Step 2: Implement individual and group interventions when bullying has occurred. The intervention component of the program consists of individual and/or group sessions with anti-bullying staff, perpetrators, and victims. These incidents may be identified by other students, teachers, victims, or parents. Addressing individual acts of bullying after they occur leads to continued contact with school staff and/or referrals to community social service agencies for both the perpetrators and the victims. Parents should be notified and consent obtained for the staff to meet with their children on a regular basis. Parental support and involvement are made easier by negotiating this consent.

It is at this stage that the various anti-bullying programs diverge, predicated on whether the program supports a "rules and sanctions" approach or a problem-solving one. Currently there is no compelling evidence that one method is more effective than the other. Some schools now favor a mixed approach, choosing the intervention based on the severity of the bullying and the responsiveness of the perpetrators to problem-solving methods (Rigby, 2002). For a detailed description of the most well documented rules-and-sanctions approach, see the materials on the Olweus Bullying Prevention program (Web site to be found at the end of this chapter).

For schools adopting a problem-solving approach, peer mediation can be used to address the actions of perpetrators and victims (Cowie & Sharp, 1996). A mental health worker or teacher trained in anti-bullying work, students involved in the incident, and neutral students trained in peer mediation skills are brought together for one session to hear the facts of the case from those directly involved. When possible, bystanders who saw the incident are also included. Prior to the beginning of the meeting, a school administrator outlines the consequences for not participating in the mediation to the perpetrator. Guidelines for implementing a mediation session can be found below. Swearer et al. (2010) point out that there is a risk in peer mediation that the peer norms may support bullying behaviors. Attention must be paid to the social ecology of the students' lives when choosing appropriate interventions.

Students—victim and perpetrator—develop a behavioral contract to avoid future incidents, and the perpetrator must make symbolic or actual restitution to the victim, depending on the nature of the incident. Where indicated, students will be referred for additional interventions. Parents are informed of the mediation and its outcome, and their consent to therapeutic sessions is obtained. (See Resources to refer to other interventions using the problem-solving approach.) Treatment goals and treatment techniques are developed from evidence-based practice methods for intervening with both the bullies and the bullied.

Working with the Victims of Bullying

Students who are victims of bullying are typically anxious, insecure, and cautious. They tend to have low self-esteem and rarely defend themselves or retaliate when confronted by students who bully them (Campbell, 2005). Students with disabilities or who are part of the LGBT community are frequent targets of bullying. Outcomes for the child who has been bullied can include depression, isolation, poor school attendance, and diminished grades. At the extreme, bullied children can exhibit patterns of irrational retaliation or suicide.

To reduce the social isolation often exhibited by victims of bullying, teachers should implement cooperative learning techniques in their teaching methods. In addition, victims, who often suffer from poor social functioning (Swearer et al., 2010), should be involved in social skills training groups to enhance their understanding of social cues as well as to provide them with better responses to threats of bullying.

Working with the Bullies

Recent research on the characteristics of bullies is contradictory. While some research indicates that bullies tend to exhibit poor psychosocial functioning and be unpopular—but more popular than their victims (Haynie et al., 2001)—some recent studies indicate that they are in fact popular and respected by their peer group (Swearer et al., 2010). Still, the lack of self-regulation in their behavior and their risk for future involvement in crime and delinquent behavior make focused interventions a vital part of a school's anti-bullying efforts. Available research suggests interventions with bullies similar to those suggested for their victims: cooperative learning techniques in the classroom and social skills support groups to reduce aggressive behaviors and strengthen positive social interactions. In addition, there must be consistent enforcement of nonpunitive, graduated consequences along with parental involvement to discuss behaviors of concern, consequences for conduct violations, and systems of support.

Underlying all the recommended interventions is the theme of social support. It is a key ingredient for any anti-bullying effort: helping the victims, the bullies, and the bystanders. The value of a network of social support should not be underestimated.

Family sessions are scheduled as needed to inform parents of serious aggressive behavior problems and incidents of bullying behavior or victimization. Increasing communication with parents enables them to participate more actively in the "school-family partnership" (Bowen, 2007). Parent awareness and participation are a vital component of a bullying-prevention program, essential for the support of children. Telephone communication, in-school conferences, and home visits are included among valuable outreach efforts.

All aspects of the school's organizational and curricular components should be taken into consideration when adapting the basic elements of a bullying-prevention or intervention program. The various components must be tailored to the culture of the school and the specific characteristics of the community. A coordinator's clear understanding of possible barriers to implementation will enable him or her to develop the necessary relationships within the school and in the community.

Applying Interventions within a Response to Intervention Framework

We have reviewed the most well-researched, evidence-based interventions: involvement of all stakeholders in a school, prevention through life-skills curricula, problem-solving approaches, and the need for focused group and individual counseling for affected students, both victims and perpetrators. The components outlined herein fit well into a Response to Intervention (RTI) framework. The whole-school approach represents the first tier of intervention, life skills groups the second tier, and the groups and individual counseling sessions the third tier. These best practices for dealing with bullying and the RTI framework allow the school to implement levels of intervention according to the severity of the problem being addressed, starting with a primary prevention focus. A tool that can be used to determine the level of intervention needed is the Bullying Survey below. Anti-bullying interventions will contribute to the RTI framework by improving school climate and thus the likelihood that all students can learn in a safe environment.

Tools and Practice Examples

To reinforce the value we attach to life skills groups in the prevention of and intervention with bullying behavior, we present a comprehensive lesson plan in its entirety. This module is one part of a four-module anti-bullying unit within a broader life skills curriculum in a middle school. The curriculum includes most components of the evidence-based best practices delineated in this chapter. An anticipated by-product is the strengthening of social ties throughout the school.

Bullying Lesson One: What Is Bullying?

Objective: To introduce bullying and to explore its prevalence
Grades: 6/8
Time: 25–30 minutes
Materials: Board and markers, "Why Children Bully" sheet, Bully Survey

1. Tell the class that you are starting a unit to prevent bullying. Explain that the goal of this unit is to stop bullying in the classroom, hallway, and school bus. They will learn in this lesson the steps that can prevent bullying.
2. Ask the class to define a bully. You can use one of their definitions or this one: someone who repeatedly hurts or intimidates other people.
3. Pass out the "Why Children Bully" sheet to the class. Go through sheet with class.
4. Under the "Ways students bully" question, give examples for each category. For physical: spitting, tripping, pushing, shoving, destroying another's things, hitting. Social: gossiping, spreading rumors, ethnic or racial slurs, excluding, humiliating. Verbal: name-calling, teasing, mocking, verbal threats of aggression. Intimidation: graffiti, making a public challenge, coercion. Cyberbullying: pretending to be other people, tricking people into revealing personal information, sending or forwarding mean text messages, posting pictures without consent.
5. Divide the students into groups of three to six. Ask the groups to rate 1–5 which one of the ways outlined in "Why Children Bully" happens the most at school. Ask the groups to rate 1–5 which one of the ways outlined in "Who is a bully?" is the truest. Ask the groups to rate 1–5 which one of the ways outlined in "Ways students bully" happens the most at school. Ask the groups to rate 1–5 which one of the ways outlined in "Whom do bullies most often pick on?" is the truest. Have the group talk about the things that happen to students who have been bullied. Ask reporters to share the group's

results.6. Pass out the Bully Survey. Make sure the students don't put their names on the top of the sheet. Questions 1 and 2 are optional. Explain that answers won't be disclosed.

7. Review what a bully is, and tell the class they will learn effective ways to deal with bullying in this unit. Ask students to hand in their surveys.

Why do students bully?

1. To gain power.
2. To get attention or become popular.
3. To get material things.
4. To act out problems at home.
5. To copy another person they admire.

Who is a bully?

1. A person who doesn't care if bad things happen to other people.
2. A person who doesn't feel bad when he or she hurts others.
3. A person who likes to be in charge and always gets his or her way.
4. A person who believes others deserve to get bullied.
5. A person who is bullied at school or at home by his or her peers, parents, brothers, or sisters.

Ways students bully

1. Physical aggression
2. Social alienation
3. Verbal aggression
4. Intimidation
5. Cyberbullying by cell phone or computer

Whom do bullies most often pick on?

1. Students who are smaller.
2. Students who don't have that many friends.
3. Students who don't stick up for themselves or get help from an adult.
4. Students who are "different."
5. Most anybody, if they think they can get away with it

What can happen to people who get bullied?

1. Feel scared, alone, and sad.
2. Afraid to go to school.
3. Don't like and/or skip school.
4. Get headaches and/or stomachaches.
5. Don't feel good about themselves.

Bully survey

1. How do you most often feel at school? ———

   Answer: (a) Very Sad (b) Sad (c) OK (d) Happy (e) Very Happy
2. The adults at my school are: ———
   (a) not helpful (b) sometimes helpful
   (c) always helpful
3. How do you feel in these places? (1) Unsafe (2) OK (3) Safe ———

   In the classroom ———
   On the playground ———
   In the lunchroom ———
   In the bathroom ———
   Going to and from school ———
4. How often do other students hit, kick, or push you?
5. How often do other students say mean things to you?
6. Have you been sent mean messages through Facebook, e-mails, or text messages this school year?
7. If you have been bullied this year, whom have you told?
8. If you have been bullied this year, who has helped?
9. How often do you hit, kick, or push?
10. How often do you say mean things?
11. Have you ever used a cell phone or computer to do mean things?
12. How many people do you think are lonely at school?
13. Do you feel lonely at school?
14. List three students you like to do things with:
15. List three students you don't like to be with:
16. List three students who most need friends:

Additional modules deal with how students can help prevent bullying and get help.

Resources

The following sources provide access to relevant research, tools, and materials for school-based practitioners wishing to develop bullying prevention and intervention programs in their settings.

Avoid violence: Try mediation. Provided by Youth in Action, National Youth Network: http://www.sadd.org/campaign/campaignpdfs/mediation.pdf

ERIC/CASS Virtual Library on Bullying in School. ERIC Clearinghouse on Counseling & Students Services: http://www.ericdigests.org/2002–3/bullying.htm

Dr. Rigby's Bullying Pages: http://kenrigby.net/—This site also leads to comprehensive resources for both educators and school-based mental health practitioners looking for intervention strategies specific to the needs of their school's population.

Gay, Lesbian, & Straight Education Network. Anti-Bullying Resources: http://www.glsen.org/cgi-bin/iowa/all/antibullying/index.html

A manual for schools and communities. This manual, provided by the California Department of Education, provides comprehensive coverage of bullying in schools and is highly instructive.

Method of shared concern. This is a nonpunitive approach to bullying. Has been used worldwide: http://www.readymade.com/au/method/

Mindmatters. A service aimed at promoting the mental health of high school students; it includes a program that addresses the issue of bullying and how it can be countered by schools: http://www.mindmatters.edu.au/default.asp

Olweus Bullying Prevention Program: http://www.olweus.org/public/index.page

Stop Bullying. Provides information from various government agencies on how kids, teens, young adults, parents, educators, and others in the community can prevent or stop bullying. Includes information on cyberbullying and LGBT: http://www.stopbullying.gov/

Other Suggested Resources

The no-blame approach. This is a nonpunitive approach to dealing with bully/victim problems in schools. Generally considered to be more appropriate for use in primary schools.

Method of shared concern. This is another nonpunitive approach to bullying. Has been used successfully worldwide.

Mindmatters. A service aimed at promoting the mental health of high school students; it includes a program that addresses the issue of bullying and how it can be countered by schools.

Key Points to Remember

We conclude with the caveat that the research on the effectiveness of anti-bullying interventions is not strong. Rigby (2002) points out that interventions *do* work, but not as effectively as one would hope. Nonetheless, there are several key points to remember when developing a successful anti-bullying program in a school or district:

1. All the stakeholders must be on board.
2. There needs to be a comprehensive, whole-school approach.
3. There should be specifically targeted interventions for both the bullied and the bullies.

Two other factors emerge with clarity:

1. The exact components of the program do not matter as much as the quality and thoroughness with which the interventions are implemented.
2. Given the potentially severe consequences of bullying, it is a moral imperative to continue to implement such programs and to formulate and revise programs based on solid evidence.

References

Banks, R. (1997). *Bullying in schools.* ERIC Digest. Champaign, IL: ERIC Clearinghouse on Elementary and Early Childhood Education.

Bowen, G. L. (2007). In the context of risk: Supportive adults and the school engagement of middle school students. *Family Relations, 56*(1), 92–10.

Campbell, M. A. (2005). Cyber bullying: An old problem in a new disguise? *Australian Journal of Guidance and Counseling, 15*(1), 68–76.

Coloroso, B. (2003). *The bully, the bullied, and the bystander.* New York, NY: Harper Resource.

Cowie, H., & Sharp, S. (1996). *Peer counselling in schools: A time to listen.* London: David Fulton.

Haymes, E., Howe, E., & Peck, L. (2003). Whole school violence prevention program: A university–public school collaboration. *Children and Schools, 25*, 121–127.

Haynie, D. L., Nansel, T., Eitel, P., Crump, A. D., Saylor, K., Yu, K., & Simons-Morton, B. (2001). Bullies, victims, and bully/victims: Distinct groups of at-risk youth. *Journal of Early Adolescence, 21*(1), 29–49.

Michaud, P.-A. (2009). Bullying: We need to increase our efforts and broaden our focus. *Journal of Adolescent Health, 45*(4), 323–325.

Olweus, D. (2004). The Olweus Bullying Prevention Programme: Design and implementation issues and a new national initiative in Norway. In P. K. Smith, D. Pepler, & K. Rigby (Eds.), *Bullying in schools: How successful can interventions be? (pp. 13–36)*. Cambridge, England: Cambridge University Press.

Rigby, K. (2002). *A meta-evaluation of methods and approaches to reducing bullying in pre-schools and in early primary school in Australia.* Canberra, Australia: Commonwealth Attorney General's Department.

Sampson, R. (2009). *Bullying in schools.* Center for Problem-Oriented Policing. Retrieved from www.cops.usdoj.gov

Smith, P. K., Ananiadou, K., & Cowie, H. (2003). Interventions to reduce school bullying. *Canadian Journal of Psychiatry, 48,* 591–599.

Swearer, S. M., Espelage, D. L., Vaillancourt, T., & Hymel, S. (2010). What can be done about school bullying? Linking research to educational practice. *Educational Researcher, 39,* 38–47.

Wang, J., Iannotti, R. J., Nansel, T. R., (2009). School bullying among adolescents in the United States: Physical, verbal, relational, and cyber. *Journal of Adolescent Health, 45*(4), 368–375.

Effective Peer Conflict Resolution

CHAPTER 36

Debra J. Woody

Getting Started

Extreme acts of violence in schools across the country have increased interest in school-based conflict resolution programs over the last decade. Fortunately, such horrendous violence as the acts that occurred at Columbine High School is relatively rare. However, these situations have advanced our understanding of the effects that unresolved conflicts can have on students, teachers, and the school environment and have brought to light the more common, chronic, less extreme acts of violence that occur daily at many school campuses. These chronic acts of violence occur in the form of verbal threats, cursing, name calling, insults, racial slurs, pushing, grabbing or shoving, punching or kicking, fighting, offensive sexual comments, and harassing through email and phone. School-based conflict resolution programs are crucial to reducing these types of violence (CDC, http://www.cdc.gov/violenceprevention/pdf/PreventingYV-a.pdf; Newman, Holden, & Delville, 2005; Slonje & Smith, 2008; Opotow, 1989). School-based conflict resolution programs have been developed to provide students with skills to better handle, manage, and resolve conflict and to teach and promote tolerance and acceptance among students and school personnel.

What We Know

The American School Counselor Association (2006) suggests the development of school-based conflict resolution programs that promote a safer school environment. Research reports on the effects of these programs have been positive throughout the literature of social work and other mental health professions. Results from these empirical investigations indicate that teaching conflict resolution skills to students increases their knowledge of nonviolent means to conflict resolution (Cohen et al., 2000; Jones, 2003; Woody, 2001), promotes the development of cooperative skills to use in conflict situations, and reduces maladaptive behaviors that in return contributes to the overall improvement in the school's climate (Burrell, Zirbel, & Allen, 2003); Garrard & Lipsey, 2007; Jones, 2003). In some schools, conflict resolution programs significantly reduced the need for severe disciplinary interventions, including reducing the number of student suspensions for fighting (Breunlin, Cimmarusti, Bryant-Edwards, & Hetherington, 2002). Also, conflict resolution programs were found to have a positive effect even on students on a path for future violent behavior (Aber, Brown, & Jones, 2003). Some students have transferred the skills learned in conflict resolution to non-classroom and non-school settings (Johnson, Johnson, Dudley, Ward, & Magnuson, 1995). These outcomes were true regardless of the age group targeted in the conflict resolution program.

School-based conflict resolution programs are also recognized as cost effective (Batton, 2003). In one report, a cost-benefit analysis compared the cost of a statewide conflict resolution program to the cost of school detentions, expulsions, in school suspensions, Saturday schools, and other types of disciplinary actions. The cost of the conflict resolution program was less than one fourth the cost of the disciplinary programs.

What We Can Do

In selecting a conflict resolution program, it is helpful to know the characteristics of programs that have been found most effective. Several key ingredients found in successful conflict resolution programs are summarized in Box 36.1 (Dusenbury, Falco, Lake, Brannigan, & Bosworth, 1997).

Other investigators suggest several factors characteristic of ineffective violence prevention programs

Box 36.1 Key Components of Successful Conflict Resolution Programs

1. A comprehensive approach that includes family, peers, media, and the community (including the school community)
2. Programs that begin in kindergarten or first grade and are reinforced across the school years
3. Programs that go beyond violence prevention to include conflict resolution skills
4. Programs appropriate for the developmental level of the students targeted
5. Programs that teach students how to manage conflict instead of how to eliminate all conflict
6. Program content that promotes personal and social competencies
7. Interactive techniques that use group work, cooperative learning, discussion, and role plays or behavioral rehearsal to develop personal and social skills.
8. Program content that includes materials that are culturally sensitive to groups represented in the student body
9. Programs that include teacher training and development
10. Programs designed to promote effective classroom management strategies, including good and effective discipline and positive control in the classroom
11. Programs that include activities that foster norms against violence, aggression, and bullying
12. An approach that teaches *all* students—not just a select few—how to resolve conflicts

Adapted from Johnson & Johnson (1995), "Why violence prevention programs don't work and what does." *Educational Leadership, 52*(5), 63–68. Reprinted with permission. The Association for Supervision and Curriculum Development is a worldwide community of educators advocating sound policies and sharing best practices to achieve the success of each learner. To learn more, visit ASCD policies at www.ascd.org. Also adapted from Dusenbury, Falco, Lake, Brannigan, & Bosworth (1997), "Nine critical elements of promissing violence prevention programs." *Journal of School Health, 76*(10), 409–414. With the permission of Blackwell Publishers

Box 36.2 Six Elements of Ineffective Conflict Resolution Programs

1. Using scare tactics
2. Adding a violence prevention program to a school system that is already overwhelmed
3. Segregating aggressive students into a separate group for any purpose
4. Programs that are too brief and not supported by a positive school environment
5. Programs that focus only on self-esteem enhancement
6. Programs that only provide information

Adapted from Dusenbury, Falco, Lake, Brannigan, & Bosworth (1997, pp. 413–414). With the permission of Blackwell Publishers.

(Dusenbury et al., 1997). They warn that programs with these characteristics (presented in Box 36.2) may actually increase aggressive behavior.

One last consideration about effective conflict resolution programs is that they are often based on social learning theory, attribution theory, and anger replacement therapy, with specific curriculum content related to these theories included in the program. The essential content areas that should be included are listed in Box 36.3.

In addition to the elements and specific content included in conflict resolution programs, there are several different types of conflict resolution programs identified in the literature. In one approach, for example, conflict resolution material

Box 36.3 Successful Content Areas

1. Information about the negative consequences of violence for the perpetrator as well as victims, friends, family members, and others
2. Anger management skills that teach self-control
3. Social perspective taking, which teaches students that others often have a different, equally valid, and less anger-producing perspective on the same situation
4. Decision-making and problem-solving skills
5. Active listening and effective communication skills
6. Courtesy, compassion, caring, and respect for others, with content that focuses on prejudice, sexism, and male–female relationships

is infused into regular academic teaching materials (see, for example, Stevahn, Johnson, Johnson, 2002). In another approach, conflict resolution skills are taught to a select group of students who become peer mediators (see for example, Johnson, Johnson, Dudley, Ward, & Magnuson, 1995). And in other programs, groups of students identified as "high risk" were targeted to receive conflict resolution training (see, for example, DuRant et al., 1996; Paschall & Flewelling, 1997). However, the more comprehensive the program, the more the aspects of successful programs identified above can be included in the program.

Applying Interventions within a Response to Intervention Framework

The high school where this conflict resolution model was implemented was relatively small. Infusing a model that is inclusive of all students, faculty, and staff in a large high school may prove to be more difficult, and ensuring that all participants actively use the skills learned can be even more difficult. Many students, for example, received the conflict resolution training in small groups during summer orientation. This type of structure may be unwieldy in a large setting. An alternative is to integrate conflict resolution material into the normal classroom structure. In one setting, for example, conflict resolution and peer mediation skills were infused into the social studies curriculum (see Stevahn, Johnson, & Johnson, 2002). Targeting key courses and "lead faculty" at each grade level to integrate conflict resolution training should be more manageable for a large school setting.

Findings from studies indicate that the quantity of conflict resolution materials is also important to producing meaningful outcomes (Aber, Brown, & Jones, 2003). The higher the number of lessons in conflict resolution received by students, the greater the level of gains made. This may also account for the success of the model program described in this chapter. Regardless of the method used, more infusion of conflict resolution training is preferable over less.

Some suggest, given that many risk factors for school violence originate in the home, that any conflict resolution model must include parent training (Breunlin, Bryant-Edwards, & Hetherington, 2002). This was certainly the preference of the two social workers that provided the current model in this chapter. However, due to limitations in resources, they were able to provide the training to students only in the school. Antidotal information from their students and parents suggested that aspects of the program did have a positive influence on some students' communication with family members. The provision of conflict resolution training to parents and other family members in addition to students is important to consider in future programs.

Tools and Practice Example

A Comprehensive Conflict Resolution Model

In this section I'll present an example of a comprehensive school-based conflict resolution approach, constructed and used by two social workers in an alternative high school setting. The identified school is a relatively small high school with an average enrollment of about 350 students. The school provides a nontraditional academic environment to high school students who have performed poorly in a regular high school setting. Most students are referred to the alternative school by counselors at their home school. Although the focus for referral to the alternative school is academics, for most of these students, poor school performance is symptomatic of interpersonal and psychosocial difficulties; many have problems caused by substance abuse, truancy, lack of family support, abuse, homelessness, or poverty. In addition, some of the students are pregnant or have children. After referral, most students attend the school for the remainder of their high school years. A smaller number return to their home campus after they are able to reach their identified grade level. Thus, students enter and exit the school at various points in their academic process. Many support services, including social work services, are available to students at the school.

Before the conflict resolution program was started, conflict between students and acts of violence were typical of that described in the literature. These occurred regularly, ranging from verbal threats to physical confrontation. As is also typical, when friction arose between students prior to the presence of mental health services on the campus, they were told to ignore it or to "just get over it." When social workers were initially added to the school program, most disputes between students were referred to the social workers for resolution. For more severe acts of violence, such as fighting, students were ejected from the school.

The social workers described this type of reactive referral and intervention structure as time consuming and ineffective. They spent a great portion of their day helping students resolve conflicts. This was problematic given the many other existing psychosocial needs evident in the student body. Although many students were helped in the resolution of conflicts, relatively few students were actually learning how to resolve conflicts on their own, so many repeat referrals were received. This approach did not reduce the number of conflicts occurring in the school. Thus, the social workers developed a more extensive conflict resolution program.

Structure of the Conflict Resolution Program

Unique to the conflict resolution program developed in this high school is the comprehensive approach to program structure. With the support of the principal, the plan was to create a systematic conflict resolution process. The plan included the two aspects of comprehensive programs called for in the literature. First, it was school-wide: all students, staff, administrators, and faculty were required to receive the conflict resolution training. Second, the training and intervention process continued throughout the school year.

Phase 1

The first phase was to provide training to all students currently enrolled. Twenty students were randomly pulled out of selected classes to attend a 4-hour group training session run by the social workers. The sessions continued until all students had received the training.

Phase 2

In the next phase, all school personnel, including administrators, staff members, and teachers, received the same conflict resolution training. They received the training as a group, in a 2-hour, in-service conference. In addition to the conflict resolution skills presented to the students, the school personnel received instruction on how to integrate the conflict resolution process into the school day. Teachers were instructed to remind students to use their skills when they observed a conflict between students. If the teacher needed to intervene in the situation, he or she was to use the conflict resolution model to help the students express their feelings, concerns, and so on and move toward resolution. If the conflict could not be resolved with the teacher's help, the teachers were instructed to refer students to social work services while the conflict was still in progress. Teachers were also instructed on how to use the conflict resolution and negotiation skills if they had a direct conflict with a student, another teacher, an administrator, and so on.

Phase 3

Phase 3 was the ongoing, follow-up training process. During homeroom, teachers reviewed a particular concept presented in the initial conflict resolution training and guided student discussion on it. For example, during one homeroom period, the definition of "I" messages was reviewed, and students were reminded to use this type of message when expressing feelings. These review sessions continued daily throughout the entire school year.

The following summer (and every summer thereafter), the social workers provided the conflict resolution program to new incoming students as part of a mandated half-day school orientation.

As additional new students enroll during the school year, the conflict resolution training is provided. Similarly, all new staff and faculty members are trained in the conflict resolution model. During the school year, all students receive "boosters" of the conflict resolution skills in homeroom classes. In addition, teachers continue to remind students to use their conflict resolution skills when they observe a conflict between students, and unresolved conflicts are referred to the social work staff for continued mediation and negotiation.

Curriculum Components and Content

The social workers who created this program also developed the curriculum that they used, and there is empirical support for the effectiveness of their curriculum (see Woody, 2001). However, several other established conflict resolution curricula have empirical evidence supporting their effectiveness. Some of these are listed in the Resources section of this chapter. Consistent with other conflict resolution training, the overall focus of the conflict resolution training used by the social workers in this program is enhancing communication and supplying students with a set of conflict resolution skills that they can use to successfully negotiate conflict situations. The specific content used by the social workers includes many of the areas identified in Box 36.3 as critical in effective conflict resolution curriculum. The social workers use a participatory, experiential format, which includes a significant number of role plays, exercises, and work sheets. The emphasis is on self-exploration and skill comprehension.

Phase 1: Styles and Definition of Conflict

Students are asked for a definition of conflict, and using Worksheet 36.1 below, students are instructed to think about a conflict they have had with another student and a conflict they have either observed or participated in with a teacher. Students are encouraged to talk about their answers and experiences. Next, students are asked to complete Worksheet 36.2, and these responses are also read aloud. Throughout the discussions during this phase, the social workers make several points:

1. Conflict is inevitable and is a part of life encounters and relationships.
2. The goal is to manage and negotiate conflict as opposed to avoiding conflict situations.
3. There are three basic responses to conflict: submission, aggression, and assertiveness.
4. How most individuals respond is directly and indirectly influenced by family and friends.

Phase 2: Personality Differences/ Diversity

In phase 2 of the training, the discussion of various responses to conflict is continued, including a discussion of how values and personality type influence one's response in a given situation. The True Colors portrayal of personality (available at www.truecolors.org) is used for this discussion. Through various worksheets included in the True Colors package, students learn characteristics related to their personality type, how these personality characteristics are often viewed by others, and how differences in personality and perception not only contribute to conflict but also influence how individuals often respond to conflict. For example, the students are asked about which personality color is characteristic of most teachers, and which color is characteristic of most high school students. Through this exchange, students are able to see that differences in values associated with personality (structure, rules, and organization versus fun, action, and entertainment) can result in conflict. This process often results in a revelation for many teachers as well.

Also emphasized in the training is that neither perspective is wrong or right, just different. To further illustrate this point, students participate in an exercise in which they are asked to respond to specific statements. For this exercise, signs that read either "strongly agree," "agree," "strongly disagree," or "disagree" are placed around the room. Students are instructed to place themselves in the section of the room underneath the sign that indicates their response to statements that are read aloud. Example statements include, "Females should always pay for themselves on a date," "Males should not cry or express feelings in public," "Condoms should be distributed in schools," and "Females who carry condoms are sluts." Stressed during this part of the process is acceptance and appreciation for diverse opinions and values.

Phase 3: Communication and Negotiation Skills

In the last part of the training, specific communication and negotiation skills are taught and practiced by the students. These include themes around communication blocks, nonverbal communication, active listening, and communicating with "I" messages. Many worksheets and role plays are used to illustrate these concepts. Several examples are described below.

Example 1: Zip Your Zap

The two social workers involve themselves in a dialog in front of the participants. The students are instructed to call out guesses identifying what the social workers are talking about. The social

Worksheet 36.1

Remember a conflict

Who was involved?

What was it about?

How did you respond?

When have you heard or had a conflict with another student? What was it about?

Teachers and students having conflict: What was it about?

workers continue to talk together, but they occasionally throw out candy to a student who makes a guess. This continues until someone correctly guesses that they are throwing candy to the third person who speaks, or until the set time limit is completed.

With this example, the students are able to describe their frustration and confusion as a result of not understanding what is occurring. These feelings are used by the social workers to discuss feelings about ineffective communication and times they are in an exchange with someone when the communication and intent are not clear. Also, the point is made that individuals often end up in situations that they are confused about because they are unaware of or misread the communication exchange.

Example 2

Students are paired. One participant speaks while the other listens. Participants are required to stand during this exercise and are positioned in a way that those who speak have their backs to the social workers; only the listeners can clearly see the adults. Once the dialog begins between the student pairs, the social workers hold up a series of signs with instructions for the listening partner to follow. One sign instructs the partner to continually interrupt while the other student is talking. Another sign instructs the listener to ignore the speaker.

At the conclusion of the exercise, the social workers announce that they were holding up signs for the listeners to follow and ask the speaking partners to guess what the listeners were instructed to do. They are then asked how they felt during the exchange. The social workers iterate the irritation, dissatisfaction, disappointment, and so on that the students experienced when their partners presented poor listening skills.

The social workers use this exercise as a lead-in to describing in detail a pyramid of effective communication skills (advice giving, reassuring, asking open-ended questions, summarizing and clarifying) with advice giving at the bottom of the pyramid and empathy and reflective listening at the top. Students are then provided with the opportunity to take turns practicing these skills while the other partner articulates a concern. Students are encouraged to use empathy and reflective listening as much as possible. The participants then discuss what it was like to receive empathy and reflective listening and what it was like to offer support.

Example 3: Misfire

One volunteer from the group of students acts as the source of conflict and is placed in a chair in the middle of the room. The other students are usually already seated in a circle, so they surround the volunteer. The social workers create a scenario

Worksheet 36.2

Identifying Conflict Styles in Your Family			
	AVOID	CONFRONT	PROBLEM SOLVE
GRANDFATHER			
GRANDMOTHER			
MOM			
DAD			
BROTHER			
SISTER			
GIRLFRIEND			
BOYFRIEND			
AUNT			
UNCLE			
MYSELF			

relevant to high school students. They might say, for example, that the student in the middle borrowed another student's car and returned it wrecked. Students are asked to consider what they would really say to this person if the car belonged to them. Each student is allowed to throw a crumpled piece of paper at the student in the middle of the circle and say what he or she would say to another in this type of conflict situation. After everyone has had a turn, the students are taught the skill of using "I" messages in communication. Students are then given Worksheet 36.3.

Worksheet 36.3

When using "I" messages,
try not to use the word "You"

I feel ______________________________

When ______________________________

Because ______________________________

I need or want ______________________________

Participants are asked again to respond to the scenario created under example 3, but this time to express their feelings and thoughts by completing the sentences provided in Worksheet 36.3. After students have had an opportunity to complete the sentences in writing, each participant reads his or her response to the group. Usually some participants have difficulty with this assignment and continue to use "you" statements. The social work facilitators point out the difficulty with making the transition from "you"-type blaming statements to "I" messages, and students who have difficulty with the assignment are encouraged to try again, sometimes with advice from other participants. The student volunteer is asked how each set of responses felt to him or her in an attempt to identify that the "I" messages were more tolerable than the blaming statements. Usually the student volunteer is also able to articulate that through the "I want or need" section of the sentence, they felt a resolution was possible.

A review of the concepts discussed during the training is used to wrap up the training session. Students are encouraged to use the "I"-message sentence to communicate effectively and to negotiate conflict situations.

Resources

CDC Preventing Youth Violence: Program Activities Guide: http://www.cdc.gov/violenceprevention/pdf/PreventingYV-a.pdf

Education World: www.education-world.com/a_curr/curr/71.shtm

National Service Learning Clearing House Violence Prevention: http://www.servicelearning.org/topic/area-service/ violence-prevention

PBS: It's My Life: When friends fight: http://pbskids.org/itsmylife/friends/friendsfight/article2.html

Practitioner Assessment of Conflict Resolution Programs: www.ericdigest.org/2001–4/conflict.html

Teaching Students to Be Peacemakers: www.cehd.umn.edu/carei/reports/rpractice/fall96/students.html

Violence Prevention: https://secure.edc.org/publications/prodview.asp?656

D. Prothrow-Stith (1987), *Violence prevention curriculum for adolescents*. Newton, MA: Education Development Center.

Key Points to Remember

The conflict resolution program presented in this chapter continues to be effective for several reasons:

- The program is a comprehensive, school-wide program. All students, faculty, and other school personnel receive the same conflict resolution training.
- The training continues throughout the school year.
- The conflict resolution model is used systematically throughout the school setting. When a conflict between students is observed, teachers and other school personnel prompt the students to use their conflict resolution skills.
- Teachers and administrators serve as role models to the students in that they use the conflict resolution skills in interactions with each other and with the students
- Unresolved conflicts are referred to the social workers for continued mediation and negotiation.
- Students learn that conflict is inevitable but can be resolved.
- The conflict resolution training requires active, interactive participation by the participants.
- The content of the resolution training includes effective communication and empathy skills and appreciation for diversity.

The conflict resolution program described in this chapter was developed and implemented by two school social workers, Connie Grossman and Gary Grossman at Venture High School in Arlington, Texas. For further information about the program, write to cgrossma@aisd.net and ggrossma@aisd.net.

References

Aber, J., Brown, J., & Jones, S. (2003). Developmental trajectories toward violence in middle childhood: Course, demographic differences, and response to school-based intervention. *Developmental Psychology, 39*(2), 324–348.

American School Counselor Association. (2006). *Position statement: Conflict resolution*. Retrieved July 10, 2011, from http://www.schoolcounselor.org/content

Batton, J. (2003). Cost-benefit analysis of CRE programs in Ohio. *Conflict Resolution Quarterly, 21*(1), 131–133.

Breunlin, D., Bryant-Edwards, T., & Hetherington, J. (2002). Conflict resolution training as an alternative to suspension for violent behavior. *The Journal of Educational Reserach, 95*(6), 349–357.

Burrell, N., Zirbel, C., & Allen, M. (2003). Evaluating peer mediation outcomes in educational settings: A meta-analytic review. *Conflict Resolution Quarterly, 21*(1), 7–26.

Cohen, J., Compton, R., & Diekman, C. (2000). Conflict resolution education and social and emotional learning programs: *A critical comparison of school-based efforts. Conflict Resolution Education Network: The Fourth R, 90.*

DuRant, R., Treiber, F., Getts, A., & McCloud, K. (1996). Comparison of two violence prevention curricula for middle school adolescents. *Journal of Adolescent Health, 19*(2), 111–117.

Dusenbury, L., Falco, M., Lake, A., Brannigan, R., & Bosworth, K. (1997). Nine critical elements of promising violence prevention programs. *Journal of School Health, 76*(10), 409–414.

Garrard, W. M., & Lipsey, M. W. (2007). Conflict resolution education and antisocial behavior in U.S. schools: A meta- analysis. *Conflict Resolution Quarterly, 25*(1), 9–38.

Johnson, D., Johnson, R., & Dudley, B. (1992). Effects of peer mediation training on elementary school students. *Mediation Quarterly, 10*(1), 89–99.

Johnson, D., & Johnson, R. (1995). Why violence prevention programs don't work and what does. *Educational Leadership, 52*(5), 63–68.

Jones, T. S. (2003). Editor's introduction. *Conflict Resolution Quarterly, 21,* 1–5.

Paschall, M., & Flewelling, R. (1997). Measuring intermediate outcomes of violence prevention programs targeting African-American male youth: An exploratory assessment of the psychometric properties of six psychosocial measures. *Health Education Research, 12*(1), 117–128.

Slonje, R., & Smith, P. (2008). Cyberbullying: Another main type of bullying? *Scandinavian Journal of Psychology, 49,* 147–154.

Stevahn, L., Johnson, D., & Johnson, R. (2002). Effects of conflict resolution training integrated into a high school social studies curriculum. *Journal of Social Psychology, 142*(3), 305–331.

Woody, D. (2001). A comprehensive school-based conflict resolution model. *Children and Schools, 23*(2), 115–123.

Improving Classroom Conflict Management through Positive Behavior Interventions and Supports

CHAPTER 37

Aaron M. Thompson

Getting Started

Schools and classrooms are complex and dynamic societies organized for the purposes of teaching and learning. Ultimately, teachers are the leaders of these societies, and they use their skills to organize, deliver, and manage activities to facilitate student learning. In school, students do not learn in isolation, but through numerous interactions and collaborations. Because classroom interactions and collaborations inherently involve a variety of social, emotional, and cognitive processes (Zins, Weissberg, Wang, & Walberg, 2004), conflicts will naturally occur between teachers and students and between students themselves. Therefore, the ability of a teacher to facilitate prosocial classroom interactions—with students and between students—is influenced by that teacher's ability to positively and proactively manage conflict.

When classroom conflicts are not resolved in a constructive and mutually satisfying manner, the results contribute to an increase in disruptive behavior. Disruptive behaviors negatively affect all entities in a classroom, including students engaging in such behavior, their peers, teachers, and the larger school culture. For example, students engaging in disruptive conduct evidence splintered academic skills (Gresham, Lane, & Lambros, 2000; National Association of School Psychologists, 2010; Nelson, Stage, Duppong-Hurley, Synhorst, & Epstein, 2007) and poor school relations with peers and teachers (Asher & Coie, 1990; Mann & Reynolds, 2006; Rubin, Bukowski, & Parker, 1998; Walker, Ramsey, & Gresham, 2003, 2004), and are at increased risk of school failure and dropout (Bullis & Cheney, 1999; Kaufman, 2004; Kauffman, 2001; Walker et al., 2003, 2004). The disruptive behavior of a few students negatively impacts all other students through lost instructional opportunities (Walker et al., 2004) and potential contagion effects (Agenda, 2004; Dishion, 2000). Lastly, disruptive behavior and unsettled conflicts negatively affect teachers' stress levels (Clunies-Ross, Little, & Kienhuis, 2008) and contribute to increased mobility and burnout of highly qualified teachers (Institute for Education Sciences, 2005; Grayson & Alvarez, 2005; Hastings & Bham, 2003; Joseph & Strain, 2003; Kern, Hilt-Panahon, & Sokol, 2009). All of the aforementioned consequences contribute to instability in the broader school culture (Gruenert, 2008).

To more effectively manage conflict in classrooms and address the social and academic needs of a diverse student population, over 14,000 schools have adopted a school-wide approach known as positive behavioral interventions and supports (PBIS; Office of Special Education Programs [OSEP], 2011a). The concepts underlying PBIS evolved from special education and the use of scientifically based positive behavioral strategies to teach children with challenging behaviors. The reauthorization of the Individuals with Disabilities Education Act (IDEA; 2004) brought national awareness to the use of such strategies. Subsequently, the reauthorization of IDEA led to the establishment of the National Technical Assistance Center on Positive Behavior Interventions and Supports (http://www.pbis.org/default.aspx) to collect, organize, and distribute scientifically based information to schools to be used in a multi-tiered continuum of services.

Both IDEA and No Child Left Behind (NCLB; 2001) emphasize the use of evidence-based interventions to improve academic and social outcomes for all students. Though neither piece of legislation mentions the term *Response to Intervention* (RTI), the concepts of RTI evolved from IDEA and NCLB's use of the term *scientifically based research* (Sugai & Horner, 2009). PBIS is grounded in the empirical traditions of behavioral science and evidence-based practice, but PBIS emphasizes a proactive approach to managing behavior on school-wide level. However, for schools to successfully adopt and implement a PBIS model, it is necessary to apply these concepts at the classroom level.

The aim of this chapter is to provide a guide for school practitioners, in consultation with teachers, to implement PBIS strategies in the classroom. This chapter will first present a brief history and overview of the benefits and costs of the three-tiered PBIS model (e.g., primary, secondary, and tertiary). Next, a brief discussion will cover what we know about discipline and how PBIS translates to the practice of classroom management. Using each tier as a guide, steps will be offered to detail what PBIS in the classroom looks like and what social workers, school psychologists, or counselors can do to assist classroom teachers to implement PBIS strategies. A practice example will be provided for each level of the PBIS model, including evidence-based practices and programs as tools for implementing PBIS in the classroom. Lastly, parallels between the PBIS and RTI frameworks will summarize how the tools and strategies suggested in this chapter will meet the rigorous standard of both the PBIS and RTI frameworks.

What We Know About PBIS in the Classroom

We know that a punitive approach to discipline and classroom management does not prevent or reduce misbehavior (Skiba et al., 2008). Punitive responses addressing disruptive behaviors often rely on a predetermined progression of negative consequences. At the classroom level, this progression may include (a) a reprimand, (b) loss of privilege, (c) social isolation, and (d) referral to the office (Clunies-Ross et al., 2008). Once sent to the office, a student may face a progression of negative consequences such as (a) detention, (b) suspension, or (c) expulsion (Gresham, 2004; Maag, 2001). Though national statistics reveal that the rate of punitive disciplinary responses have increased since 1974 (U.S. Department of Education, 2000), teacher-reported rates of disruptive student behavior have continued to rise (IES, 2006). In addition, schools where punitive practices are the primary discipline strategy evidence higher rates of disruptive and antisocial student behavior, lower rates of student academic performance, and coercive relations among students and between students and teachers (Skiba & Peterson, 1999, 2000). In summary, punitive and reactive measures have failed to reduce disruptive behavior, do not encourage prosocial behavior, and have been documented to disproportionately penalize minority students (Cameron & Sheppard, 2006; Clunies-Ross et. al., 2008; Colvin, Flannery, Sugai, & Monegan, 2009; Fenning & Rose, 2007; Skiba, Michael, Nardo, & Peterson, 2002).

To decrease the ineffective use of reactive disciplinary measures, schools are adopting a proactive multi-tiered service delivery model otherwise known as PBIS (Sugai & Horner, 2008). The multi-tiered framework was initially conceptualized as a public health prevention model (Commission on Chronic Illness, 1957; Gordon, 1983; Mrazek & Haggerty, 1994). PBIS models match varying levels of student risk with a continuum of evidence-based prevention and intervention strategies. Though terminology varies across disciplines (e.g., education, social work, school psychology, etc.), the majority of multi-tiered service delivery models consist of three tiers—primary, secondary, and tertiary (Sugai & Horner, 2008).

Primary or universal strategies are delivered to all students in a school or classroom (Durlak, Weissberg, Symnicki, Taylor, & Schellinger, 2011; Offord, Kraemer, Kazdin, Jensen, & Harrington, 1998). Primary strategies consist of a mission statement, a set of broad expectations, explicit behavioral guidelines underlying each expectation, procedures for teaching the guidelines, a continuum of consequences, and a plan to evaluate efforts (Sugai & Horner, 2006).

Secondary strategies can be divided into selective and indicated prevention efforts (Cicchetti & Cohen, 2006; Institute of Medicine, 1989; Mrazek & Haggerty, 1994; Offord et al., 1998). Selective prevention efforts are delivered to subgroups of students exposed to known risk factors (i.e., free and reduced lunch programs). Indicated strategies apply to students exhibiting early signs of a disorder (i.e., self-monitoring training for those with early aggressive behaviors).

Lastly, tertiary level strategies (Offord et al., 1998) are interventions for children identified with a condition (i.e., special education services). It is at the tertiary level that "prevention" effectively becomes "intervention" (Cicchetti

Table 37.1 Benefits and Drawbacks of Each Level of the PBIS Model

PBS Level	*%**	*Benefits*	*Costs*
Primary (Universal)	≈80%	• Broad application • No iatrogenic effects • No contagion effects • Focus on context • Effective for low at-risk	• Impersonal • Not individualized • May be expensive • Potentially wasteful • Low effects for high risk
Secondary (Targeted: Selective & Indicated)	≈15%	• Accurate with assessment • Moderately individualized • Efficient dissemination • Effective for moderate at-risk	• No services just above cut • Risk of iatrogenic effects • Risk of contagion effects • Less focus on context
Tertiary (Clinical)	≈5%	• Individualized • Multi-systemic approach • Multidisciplinary approach • Effective for high at-risk	• Resource intensive • No focus on context • Risk of iatrogenic effects • Risk of labeling effects

Notes: PBS = positive behavior supports; * Percentages will vary based upon local norms and expectations

& Cohen, 2006; Mrazek & Haggerty, 1994), though intervention services are applied to prevent further decline of the condition. Tertiary services in schools are intensive, individualized, and may involve special education services (Crone, Hawken, & Horner, 2010; Sugai & Horner, 2008).

As detailed in Table 37.1, there are benefits and costs to each level of prevention within the multi-tiered PBIS model. For example, primary prevention strategies broadly address contextual factors that may buffer risk (e.g., skills training for teachers to identify mental health issues in children), but these efforts are not sufficient to support an estimated 20% of students (Offord et al., 1998; Sugai & Horner, 2008). Secondary strategies use measureable indicators (i.e., early screening, disciplinary referrals) to identify approximately 15% of students needing supports beyond primary services, but the drawbacks include withholding services to students just above the indicated or selected cut points (Offord et al., 1998). Lastly, tertiary efforts are reserved for the 5% of students needing support beyond primary and secondary services. However, tertiary services are resource intensive and may expose students to labeling and contagion effects (Dishion, 2000). As there are benefits and costs to each level of the model, schools and classrooms can best serve students from different homes, cultures, and backgrounds by combining strategies from each of the tiers into a full-service model.

What We Can Do

To begin, school practitioners can assist teachers in assessing the classroom supports currently in place. Invariably, some students will need additional guidance, and practitioners can assist teachers in identifying students and services appropriate for secondary supports. Lastly, if students fail to respond to primary and secondary supports, intensive tertiary-level supports will likely involve a team-based approach to address the students' needs.

Primary Classroom Supports

Primary-level supports begin as broad concepts underlying the basic human need for social order in a classroom and narrow in scope as we define the specific behavioral rules needed to maintain order. Systematic reviews of evidence-based primary classroom management approaches reveal that the most effective practices begin with the following basic components: (a) a structured classroom mission statement; (b) clearly worded classroom expectations; (c) explicit rules for daily classroom procedures; (d) steps to teach, review, and integrate rules; (e) a range of positive and negative consequences to increase desired behaviors and reduce inappropriate behaviors; and (f) procedures to collect data to evaluate student acquisition of primary-level efforts (Simonsen, Fairbanks, Briesch, Myers, & Sugai, 2008).

Structured Classroom Mission Statement

A classroom mission statement should serve as the underlying rationale for classroom structure. Overall, an effective classroom mission statement should be clear and concise, enumerate student and teacher responsibilities, and address both academic and social expectations (Sugai & Horner, 2006).

Classroom Expectations

Classroom expectations are broad but are narrower than the mission statement they reflect. Classroom expectations should be limited in number (i.e., 3 to 5 rules) and should be expressed in positive language describing an observable behavior. For example, "Keep Body Parts to Self" is an action-oriented expectation more observable than the commonly cited expectation "Respect Others." Lastly, if your school has a set of expectations, they need to be adopted in the classroom to permit seamless expectations across the school.

Explicit Rules for Daily Classroom Procedures

Specific rules should be created using behavioral terms to operationalize each expectation for every classroom procedure. Table 37.2 shows a matrix with five school-wide expectations across the top and common classroom routines down the left vertical column. Using a matrix similar to the example in Table 37.2, teachers can use explicit language to provide students with behavioral instructions for each routine listed. For example, when describing the observable behaviors of a person following the expectation "Being Considerate of Others" for the classroom routine of "Getting Help," a teacher might expect that a student would (a) remain seated, (b) raise your right or left hand, and (c) request help when the teacher calls your name. As schools are predicated upon white, middle-class values, the more explicit the descriptions are, the more likely that students from non-white and low-income homes will be successful in meeting the expectations (Delpit, 1995). Teachers might consider seeking student input when completing the behavioral matrix. In this way, a teacher increases student autonomy, ownership, and cooperation while exposing students to the rules. The matrix should be revisited throughout the year, particularly if new routines are introduced.

Table 37.2 Translating School-wide Rules into Expected Behaviors for Classroom Routines

School-wide Expectations *Classroom Routines*	*Keep Body Parts to Self*	*Complete Assigned Work*	*Follow Teacher Directions*	*Be in Assigned Area at All Times*	*Be Considerate of Others*
Entering/Leaving Room					
Being Prepared					
Getting Help					
Getting Supplies					
Sharpening Pencil					
Whole Group Instruction					
Small Group Instruction					
Independent Seatwork					
Cooperative Learning					
Completing Work Early					

Steps to Teach, Review, and Integrate Rules

Expectations and rules need to be taught on a daily basis. School practitioners can assist teachers in translating classroom procedures into a lesson plan format. Research suggests that successful lesson plans to address classroom procedures should consist of (a) a definition of the skill (i.e., the behavioral rule being taught, the logic underlying the rule, and the corresponding classroom expectation), (b) a range of teaching examples (i.e., what the desired behaviors look like and what undesirable behaviors might look like), (c) steps to model the behavior for students, (d) an engaging activity to allow students to practice the skill, and (e) steps to follow up on the lesson (i.e., prompts, reminders, and reinforcements for students; Langland, Lewis-Palmer, & Sugai, 1998). Practitioners might prepare and teach these lessons, but evidence suggests the concepts are more effective when teachers actually teach, integrate, and reinforce the lessons for students throughout the course of the school day (Durlak et. al., 2011). To avoid replicating efforts across classrooms, teachers and practitioners should collaborate to develop lesson plans that meet common classroom procedures. This collaborative effort will also solidify expectations for students across adults and settings in a school. Many example lesson plans following the above format can be found at OSEP's PBIS Web site cited in the Further Learning section of this chapter. In addition to skills instruction in classroom rules, teachers can select from many evidence-based programs to assist students in gaining social and emotional competencies (Durlak et al., 2011).

Creating a Range of Positive and Negative Consequences

In behavioral terms, consequences follow a behavior and shape whether that behavior is repeated or extinguished. Positive consequences communicate that a behavior is valued, making the reoccurrence of the behavior more likely. Negative consequences communicate that a behavior is undesirable and make the reoccurrence of the behavior less likely. Behavior is shaped by the consistent application of effective positive and negative consequences. Effective consequences should (a) link the behavior to the consequence, (b) not humiliate, (c) elevate the craft of teaching above rewarding or punishing behaviors, and (d) exist on a continuum (Oliver, Wehby, & Reschly, 2011).

Positive Consequences for Student Compliance

A range of positive consequences is listed in Table 37.3. Small and everyday positive consequences should be brief, free, simple, and should be offered at a ratio of 4 positive reinforcements to 1 negative reprimand (Osher, Dwyer, Jimerson, 2006). Moderate and frequent positive consequences should be intermittent and random or should be connected to specific behavioral indicators (e.g., turning in all assignments for one week in exchange for lunch with the teacher). Lastly, large and infrequent positive consequences need to be accompanied by numerous prompts and reminders and should be based upon a combination of individual and group-level contingencies (i.e., all individual work for all students in the class needs to be completed; Oliver et al., 2011). When providing students with positive consequences, always look a student in the eye and pair the positive response with a brief explanation of *why* you are recognizing the behavior (Goldstein & Brooks, 2007).

Negative Consequences for Student Noncompliance

Table 37.3 also lists a range of negative consequences for student noncompliance. Negative consequences need to be clear and specific, should be delivered with a brief reminder of the expectation violated, and should teach and preserve a student's self-worth. It is imperative to teach students that they are not all the same or have the same needs, and therefore a teacher may tailor negative consequences in an equitable fashion (dependent upon frequency of the behavior, student intent, and degree of harm done). In this way, equity can be used to meet the varying needs of students rather than give each student the same (or "fair") treatment (Mendler, 2005). Next, if a teacher uses a stepwise sequence of negative consequences, it is important to acknowledge the teacher's prerogative to use a "bypass" clause for any student acts that threaten the safety of others in the classroom. Lastly, when delivering negative consequences, (a) maintain proximity and eye contact, (b) keep a calm voice and be in control, and (c) teach the expected behavior to the student (Goldstein & Brooks, 2007).

Monitoring Primary Supports

There are efficient ways to directly assess student understanding and integration of primary-level

Table 37.3 Example Range of Positive and Negative Consequences

	Small & Everyday	Moderate & Frequent	Large & Infrequent
Positive Consequences	Social praise ("Good job") Smile, high five, handshake Stickers, stamps, smiley face Positive home note Select music for seatwork Free drinking fountain pass	Weekly positive home call Lunch with teacher/principal Work "escape" ticket Student seat selection Computer time "Buddy" class recess	Large group project Community field trip Cooking in the classroom Class sporting event (kickball) Office helper or hat day Class movie day
	→	→	→
Negative Consequences	Nonverbal (proximity, glance) Class pre-correction Individual pre-correction Individual correction In-class conference After-class conference	Instructional modification Seat modification "Buddy" class timeout Student & principal conference Parent contact Student & parent conference	Office referral Reparation Loss of privilege Loss of recess Working lunch detention Working after school Detention

supports. Students may be quizzed on the behavioral rules following lesson plans. Another evidence-based strategy for assessing students' use of behavioral expectations is to use the Good Behavior Game (Barrish, Saunders, & Wolf, 1969; Lannie & McCurdy, 2007). Another way of monitoring the transfer of primary behavioral rules is to keep a log of common behavior problems by recording the number and type of reprimands given throughout the course of a day. A teacher can also use a self-monitoring strategy to count the number of positive reinforcements that are provided to students to be sure he or she is acknowledging more positives than negatives and calling on a diverse group of students (Kalis, Vannest, & Parker 2007).

Secondary Classroom Supports

Secondary strategies provide additional supports for students beyond primary strategies (OSEP, 2011b). Prior to implementing secondary classroom supports, teachers and school practitioners should assess the fidelity of all primary-level efforts (Crone et al., 2010). Secondary interventions generally involve small student groups, include direct instruction, and are accompanied by a data-keeping mechanism to gauge a student's response to the intervention. A growing body of research suggests that secondary interventions can be implemented by both teachers and paraprofessionals to improve outcomes for 67% of students (OSEP, 2011b).

The OSEP Technical Assistance Center on Positive Behavior Interventions and Supports lists the following features of secondary supports: (a) continuous availability, (b) low teacher burden, (c) consistent with primary supports, (d) faculty are aware of secondary efforts, (e) utilizes functional assessment and data to monitor student progress, (f) adequately resourced, and (g) students elect to participate (OSEP, 2011b). Examples of secondary interventions containing the above features include the Behavior Education Program (BEP; Crone et al., 2010), the Check in/Check out strategy (CICO; Filter et al., 2007), and the Self-management Training And Regulation Strategy (STARS; Thompson & Webber, 2010; Thompson, 2012).

Tertiary Classroom Supports

Tertiary classroom supports work best when both primary and secondary strategies are in place and practiced with fidelity (Crone et al., 2010). Tertiary-level supports are individualized and intensive, involve comprehensive assessment, and require a team collaborative approach involving the student's family (OSEP, 2011c). The purpose of a tertiary support plan is to design multi-element supports and may include special education services.

The OSEP Technical Assistance Center on Positive Behavior Interventions and Supports lists the following features of tertiary supports: (a) multidisciplinary team approach, (b) use of comprehensive assessment in multiple domains (i.e., functional assessment, interviews, behavior protocols), (c) examine contextual triggers, (d) result in an individualized plan with goals and objectives, (e) involve direct skills instruction, and (e) include ongoing data to monitor a student's progress (OSEP, 2011c). The difference between secondary and tertiary levels of support is defined by the individualized nature of the support plan. An individualized plan should assess and meet the needs of the student across multiple domains, provide suggestions for classroom modifications, utilize a wraparound process to integrate community-based services, and detail response procedures if the target behaviors include aggression toward others. For students with multiple problem behaviors, a direct functional behavioral assessment (FBA) should provide data to prioritize complex and competing behaviors according to the frequency, intensity, and duration of such behaviors (Goldstein & Brooks, 2007).

Applying Interventions within a Response to Intervention Framework

The RTI framework has been described as an alternative method to the discrepancy model for identifying students for special education services (Sugai & Horner, 2009). Though RTI has been more commonly used to identify students with learning deficits, it is being more widely accepted as a method for providing services to students with social, emotional, and behavioral difficulties (Gresham, 2005). Within the behavioral context, RTI and PBIS are conceptually similar frameworks with roots in IDEA (2004) and NCLB (2001). Both the RTI and PBIS frameworks promote the use of a continuum of interventions and the use of data to guide efforts and match varying levels of student need to services. Six core similarities of RTI and PBIS can be found in Box 37.2.

The steps described in this chapter address the application of PBIS at the classroom level. As such, the key features shared by RTI listed above are met within each level of the PBIS classroom management steps described here. Using data to assess and evaluate primary strategies before implementing secondary and tertiary strategies reinforces the need to review our own educational practices to gain insight into what practices we can change to better meet the needs of students.

The PBIS approach to classroom management provides accessible solutions to the daily challenges faced in schools. When we implement primary classroom strategies and evaluate those efforts and whether they are practiced with fidelity, the majority of students will have access to the explicitly defined expectations needed to succeed. Thus, students requiring more individualized secondary

Box 37.1 PBIS Tools

- Classroom management self-assessment: http://www.pbis.org/pbis_resource_detail_page.aspx?Type=4&PBIS_esourceID=174
- Classroom observation tool: http://www.pbis.org/evaluation/evaluation_tools.aspx
- Lesson plans for teaching expectations: http://www.pbis.org/training/student.aspx
- Learning inventories and multiple intelligences tests: http://www.businessballs.com/howardgardnermultipleintelligences.htm#multiple
- Good Behavior Game manual: http://www.evidencebasedprograms.org/static/pdfs/GBG%20Manual.pdf

Box 37. 2 Core Similarities Between PBIS & RtI

1. Interventions are supported by scientifically based research.
2. Interventions are organized on a continuum to support varying student needs.
3. A problem-solving approach is used to assess and allocate resources.
4. Early screening and ongoing assessment are key elements to evaluate student progress.
5. Data are used to monitor a student's response to a selected intervention.
6. Implementation fidelity should be considered when determining intervention success.

strategies, such as the BEP or STARS, will be fewer. However, secondary strategies should promote student involvement and utilize ongoing data (FBA and self-monitoring data) to assess a student's response to the intervention. Finally, for the few students who need intensive supports, a team-based effort will provide the wraparound services and access additional community supports to assist a student and his or her family in meeting needs.

Tools and Practice Examples

Implementing Primary Classroom Supports

Primary Support Tools

A brief classroom management self-assessment and peer observations by a practitioner will assist in planning and prioritizing primary supports. Teachers and practitioners can visit http://www.pbis.org/ to find the tools listed in Box 37.1.

Primary Support Practice Example

At the beginning of the school year, Ms. Peace worked to implement PBIS in her classroom. She reviewed her rules and procedures, revisited comments from three peers who observed her class, and completed a classroom management self-assessment. Ms. Peace began her PBIS plan by writing a mission statement:

> *In Ms. Peace's classroom, we will seek the knowledge, skills, and strategies to reach our goals and become lifelong learners. To do this, students are responsible for coming to class prepared, contributing to a safe classroom, setting reasonable goals, and making good choices. To help students, Ms. Peace will prepare activities to challenge all students, listen to student ideas and goals, and help students work toward their goals.*

Next, Ms. Peace created a chart with the five school-wide PBIS expectations written across the top and her daily classroom procedures down the side (see Table 37.2). On the first day of school, Ms. Peace worked with students to create a list of behaviors for each procedure and each expectation listed on the chart. Ms. Peace posted the chart and referred to the rules regularly.

Ms. Peace spent time each day—beginning with the first day of school—teaching the behavioral rules to students. Ms. Peace used lesson plans that referred to the school-wide expectations being taught, listed the behavioral rules for each expectation, stated the reason for the rules, modeled each behavior for students, and used a brief student activity to allow students to practice the behavioral rules. Observations from Mr. Trust, the school social worker, revealed that Ms. Peace prompted students on the rules, identified positive examples of students engaging in the behavioral rules more often than reprimanding students, and rewarded students using a continuum of positive consequences (see Table 37.3). When she rewarded students, Ms. Peace was mindful to look them in the eye and pair the feedback with the observed rule. Ms. Peace assessed student understanding of the rules and used contingency games like the Good Behavior Game to engage students in following the rules.

Ms. Peace was attentive to her students' learning styles. She assessed all her students' strengths by using an interest inventory and a multiple intelligences survey. Ms. Peace integrated this assessment information into her lessons to accommodate various learning styles and differentiate instruction based on her students' needs. She selected two students each Friday whose parents she called to tell them how well their child was doing, behaviorally and academically.

Secondary Classroom Supports

Secondary Support Tools

When a self-assessment and a classroom management observation reveal that all primary-level classroom strategies are in place and practiced faithfully, but that a few students still exhibit challenging behaviors, those students may require secondary supports. Per OSEP guidelines, most secondary supports will involve assistance from school-based practitioners and should begin with an FBA (OSEP, 2011c). An FBA refers to a range of procedures to assess contextual factors maintaining a behavior. An FBA should (a) seek to identify and describe target behaviors, (b) prioritize behaviors based upon the degree of the behaviors (e.g., frequency, duration, and intensity), (c) identify contextual variables that condition the behavior,

(d) develop hypotheses related to the function of the behavior, and (e) result in an individualized FBA intervention (Goldstein & Brooks, 2007). Teachers can engage in indirect functional assessment using the following tools:

- Functional Assessment Checklist for Teachers (FACTS-A): http://www.pbis.org/common/pbisresources/tools/EfficientFBA_FACTS.pdf
- Guess and Check: Teacher Guided FBA: http://www.pbis.org/common/pbisresources/tools/Guess_and_Check_version2.pdf

A direct FBA completed by an educational paraprofessional will supplement a teacher's indirect FBA and across multiple contexts (i.e., playground, cafeteria, classroom, engaged in multiple academic pursuits) using observations, interviews, and behavior protocols. For forms and procedures to complete a direct FBA, visit the OSEP Web site at http://www.pbis.org/common/pbisresources/publications/PracticalFBA_TrainingManual.pdf.

Once FBA data is available, the teacher and paraprofessional should consider relevant accommodations (e.g., academic, social, or environmental adjustments) to intervene in the behaviors. Next, a child who continues to have difficulty despite accommodations may require more intensive strategies such as the CICO (Filter et al., 2007), the BEP (Crone et al., 2010), or the STARS program (Thompson & Webber, 2010; Thompson, 2012). Each of the programs uses a daily report card to monitor the response of students on goals defined using FBA data.

The STARS program includes all aspects of the BEP and CICO, but STARS includes direct instruction to teach students how to define problems, identify solutions, weigh benefits and consequences, select the best solution, and write goals to implement the solution. Following student training, both the student and teacher monitor the student's performance on behavioral goals. Prior research and meta-analyses suggest that self-monitoring improves student behavioral performance for students from a range of cultural backgrounds and is effective with internalizing and externalizing behaviors (Briesch & Chafouleas, 2009; Fantuzzo, Rohrbeck, & Azar, 1987; Shapiro, Durnan, Post, & Levinson, 2002). Figure 37.1 presents a sample behavioral report card that a student and teacher would use to monitor the student's performance on classroom rules.

Using a report card similar to that in Figure 37.1, a student and teacher would monitor the student's behavioral performance on the same goal. After the specified period, the student and a school practitioner calculate the daily percentages (dividing the number of "yes" marks circled by the total number [13] of "yes" marks possible for each expectation). The student can also calculate the total performance percentage across all five expectations (summing all "yes" marks circled and dividing the sum by the total [65] possible across all expectations). It is helpful to visualize the performance over time using a graph similar to that in Figure 37.2 to plot the daily percentages for both the teacher and student perspectives. After the graphs are prepared, the student meets with the teacher and the practitioner to examine the graphs and identify discrepancies between the perspectives. Areas of discrepancy are noted, and new goals can be written to increase the rate of agreement between the student and teacher from the current rate (e.g., 67%) to a level just above current performance (e.g., 70%). The process is feasible and has been reported to have a low degree of teacher burden (Thompson & Webber, 2010; Thompson, 2012)

Secondary Support Practice Example

Consistent use of all primary and secondary strategies kept 80% of Ms. Peace's students on track with classroom expectations. However, a few students continued to exhibit difficult behaviors. By November, Ms. Peace had submitted six office referrals for four students in her class. In addition, Ms. Peace completed forms found on OSEP's PBIS Web site to provide indirect FBA data to guide her efforts. The school social worker, Mr. Trust, supplemented Ms. Peace's efforts with a direct FBA. Together, Ms. Peace and Mr. Trust met with the four students to train them in the STARS self-monitoring strategy.

Using the STARS process and FBA data, Ms. Peace and Mr. Trust worked with the students to write relevant behavioral goals that reflected the classroom expectations each student was struggling to meet. Ms. Peace and Mr. Trust led the small group of students in the steps of self-monitoring their behavioral performance on each expectation (see Figure 37.3) and informed the students that Ms. Peace would also be monitoring their performance. These procedures resulted in the students having access to direct instruction in the skills required to meet the expected behaviors, provided ongoing data to monitor each student's progress, and empowered students in the change process to learn the classroom expectations. As evidenced by the STARS daily report, three out of the four students improved their behavioral performance.

Tertiary Classroom Supports

Tertiary Support Tools

Tertiary supports require a team-based approach to examining all data associated with secondary efforts such as FBAs and STARS data. Due to this individualized nature, a tertiary package of strategies will likely involve a "wraparound" plan for a child. A wraparound plan should assess strengths and areas of need, and pair those needs with external community resources. A tertiary plan should address problematic behaviors using a behavior intervention plan (BIP) that is based upon existing FBA and classroom performance data. If some of the problematic behaviors include aggression, the BIP should address emergency procedures for managing such behaviors. For more tertiary-level supports, including documents to guide the wraparound process, visit http://www.pbis.org/evaluation/evaluation_tools.aspx to locate the Educational Information Assessment Tool; the Home, School, Community Tool; the Student Disposition Tool; and the Wraparound Integrity Tool (OSEP, 2011c).

Tertiary Practice Example

Donnie, one of the students in Ms. Peace's secondary support group, continued to struggle

STARS Daily Behavior Goals

Student: Date:

This student:	Completed his/her work	Kept body parts to self	Was considerate of others	Followed directions	Stayed in assigned area
8:00 - 8:30	Yes - No	Yes - No	Yes - No	Yes - No	Yes - No
8:30 - 9:00	Yes - No	Yes - No	Yes - No	Yes - No	Yes - No
9:00 - 9:30	Yes - No	Yes - No	Yes - No	Yes - No	Yes - No
9:30 - 10:00	Yes - No	Yes - No	Yes - No	Yes - No	Yes - No
10:00 - 10:30	Yes - No	Yes - No	Yes - No	Yes - No	Yes - No
10:30 - 11:00	Yes - No	Yes - No	Yes - No	Yes - No	Yes - No
11:00 - 11:30	Yes - No	Yes - No	Yes - No	Yes - No	Yes - No
11:30 - 12:00	Yes - No	Yes - No	Yes - No	Yes - No	Yes - No
12:00 - 12:30	Yes - No	Yes - No	Yes - No	Yes - No	Yes - No
12:30 - 1:00	Yes - No	Yes - No	Yes - No	Yes - No	Yes - No
1:00 - 1:30	Yes - No	Yes - No	Yes - No	Yes - No	Yes - No
1:30 - 2:00	Yes - No	Yes - No	Yes - No	Yes - No	Yes - No
2:00 - 2:30	Yes - No	Yes - No	Yes - No	Yes - No	Yes - No

Total # yes = 65 70% yes = 46 85% yes = 55 90% yes = 58

Notes & Assignments

Parent signature ______________________

Figure 37.1. STARS Behavior Goal Card

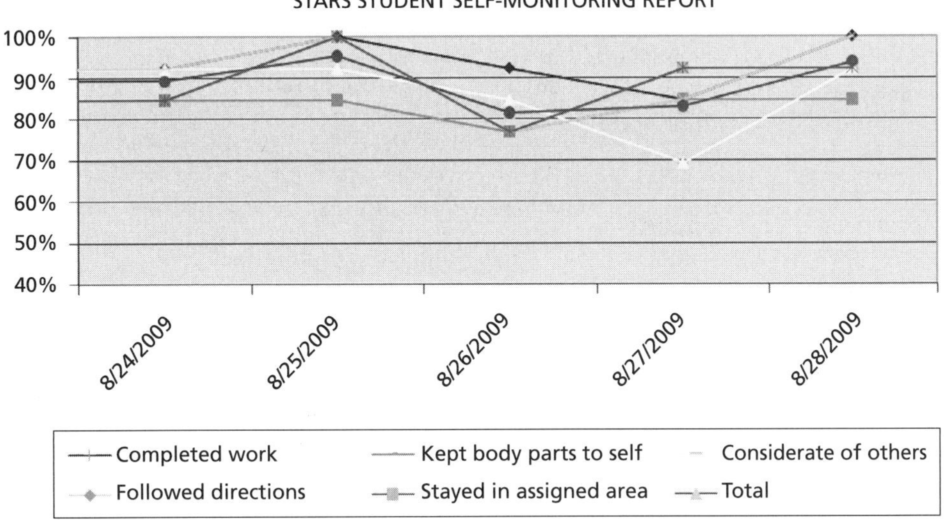

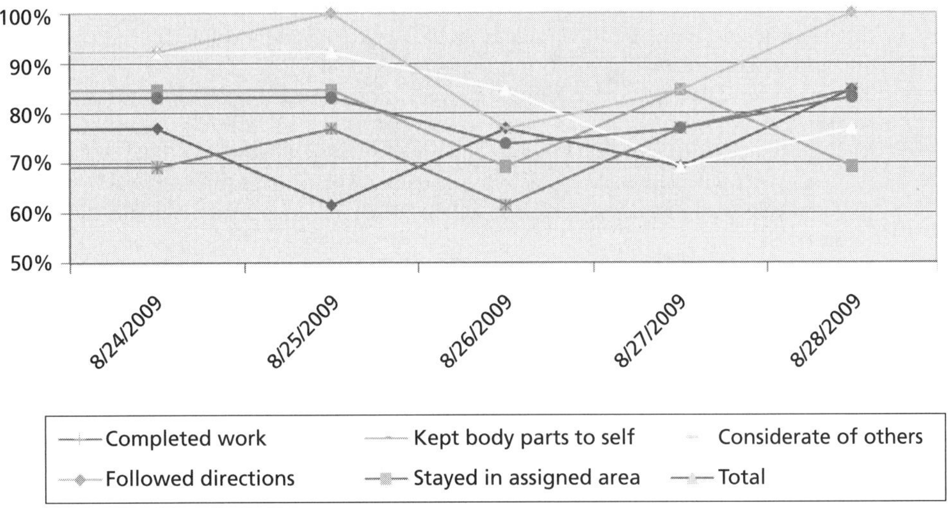

Figure 37.2. Student and Teacher Daily Behavioral Monitoring Report

and was having a difficult year. In the classroom, Donnie possessed several strengths, but he was easily frustrated and engaged in aggressive forms of problem solving. Earlier in the year, Donnie's family was referred to social services for safety concerns in the home. After considering Donnie's FBA and STARS data, Ms. Peace and Mr. Trust decided that Donnie was not responsive to the secondary efforts and needed access to the school's student support team and wraparound process.

Members of the student support team, which included Donnie's parents, asked questions to assess the family's strengths and areas of need. They learned that Donnie's mother was diagnosed with bipolar disorder but did not have medication. The lack of medication was a direct result of an injury Donnie's father experienced on the job, which left the family unable to pay for medical service. The student support team identified the appropriate community agencies to assist the family with medical services, made

Purpose: Provide initial training for students in how to accurately self monitor behavior and set goals.

1. Identify and prioritize difficult behaviors
   a. Functional Behavior Analysis (FBA)
      i. Indirect Teacher FBA
      ii. Direct School Practitioner FBA

2. Operationalize behaviors with a definition the student can understand and teach expected behaviors
   a. Example: "*Being Considerate of Others*" for the classroom routine of "*Getting Help*," a student would: (1) remain Seated, (2) raise your right or left hand, and (3) request help when the teacher calls your name.
   b. Develop lesson plans to teach expected behaviors for all procedures
   c. Check for understanding with student by asking for specific behavior examples (e.g., making noises in classroom, talking out of turn)

3. Teach Students to Observe Behavioral Performance using a Recording Tool
   a. Use FBA information to determine
      i. Priority of goals: intensity, duration, and frequency of behaviors
      ii. Interval schedule: how often the student should record self-monitoring data
   b. Define goal statement based upon FBA
      i. The goal should be stated in positive language and be specific, observable, measureable, and realistic
      ii. Make goal specific to problem behavior and suggest a replacement behavioral strategy
         1. Example: "I will increase my 'Following Directions' percentage from 75% to 79% by complying with my teacher's request within 30 seconds after I am given directions from my teacher."
      iii. Start with one to three goals; monitor progress and adjust number of goals as needed
   c. How to complete data recording
      i. Strategies for reliable ratings
         1. Watch with timer
   d. Use examples from FBA and ask students to rate themselves

4. Trial Run
   a. Observe and rate a short class session with both observer and student completing recordings
   b. Compare observer ratings with student ratings
   c. Practice determining goals and completing contract
   d. Take advantage of this opportune time to talk about the definition of classroom expectations
      i. The definition of acceptable behavior is determined by the teacher
      ii. Ask the student to role play the "teacher" and review their data

5. Teach students to calculate percentages and graph percentages. Repeat procedure.

Figure 37.3. Lesson Plan for STARS Student Training

several phone calls, and scheduled meetings for Donnie's parents to inquire about unemployment assistance. The team agreed that a BIP for Donnie would include specific skills training, the continuance of the STARS strategy, and a "free pass" to the counselor's office to be used when Donnie felt angry. The team agreed to revisit the plan in one month.

Key Points to Remember

There is a great deal of research supporting the implementation of the PBIS model at the school level. Important to the school-wide application of the PBIS model, the steps described here outline several common research-supported efforts that teachers should implement at the classroom level to reduce disruptive behavior and manage conflict. However, these efforts will be most successful in schools where investments and commitments are made to apply PBIS in a school-wide manner. Faithful implementation of a PBIS model requires administrative and financial support, full support of a school's staff, and a long-term (5–7 years; Sugai & Horner, 2008) plan to achieve full implementation of a school-wide PBIS model.

No one intervention works for all children in all settings—classrooms, schools, and communities vary. Therefore, school practitioners should be aware that dependent upon local classroom, school, and community norms, the percentages of students who may fall within each level of needs support in the common PBIS model will vary. For practitioners working with students who present complex and difficult behaviors, using the FBA process to prioritize students and difficult behaviors (i.e., based upon behavioral frequency, duration, and intensity) will untangle confounds. Indeed, the research underlying the use of FBA and self-monitoring data is the most widely evaluated and reported component of the multi-tiered PBIS model (Lewis et. al., 2010), though these studies largely consist of single-subject designs due to the individualized nature of the interventions (Thompson, 2011). Lastly, RTI and PBIS are not just avenues for identifying students for special education—they are best educational practices.

Further Learning

Social workers and school-based professionals can gather information (i.e., resources including papers, citations, tools, FBA documents, lesson plans, videos) on assisting teachers with implementing PBIS strategies at the classroom level by visiting the OSEP Technical Assistance Center on Positive Behavior Interventions and Supports at http://www.pbis.org/default.aspx.

Primary PBIS Classroom Support Resources

Langland, S., Lewis-Palmer, T., & Sugai, G. (1998). Teaching respect in the classroom: An instructional approach. *Journal of Behavioral Education, 8*, 245–262.

Sugai, G., & Horner, R. H. (2009). Response to Intervention and school-wide positive behavior supports: Integration of multi-tiered system approaches. *Exceptionality, 17*, 223–227.

Secondary PBIS Classroom Support Resources

Crone, D. S., Hawken, L. S., & Horner, R. H. (2010). *Responding to problem behavior in schools.* New York, NY: Guilford Press.

Filter, K. J., McKenna, M. K., Benedict, E. A., Horner, R. H., Todd, A. W., & Watson, J. (2007). Check in/check out: A post-hoc evaluation of an efficient, secondary-level targeted intervention for reducing problem behaviors in schools. *Education and Treatment of Children, 30*(1), 69–84.

Thompson, A. M., & Webber, K. C. (2010). Reconnecting student and teacher perceptions of school rules: A reasonable approach to managing students with difficult behaviors. *Children and Schools, 32*(3), 29–40.

Tertiary PBIS Classroom Support Resources

Goldstein, S., & Brooks, R. B. (2007). Understanding and managing children's classroom behavior: Creating sustainable, resilient classrooms. Hoboken, NJ: Wiley & Sons.

References

Agenda, P. (2004). *Teaching interrupted: Do discipline policies in today's public schools foster the common good.* Retrieved from http://www.publicagenda.org/files/pdf/teaching_interrupted.pdf

Asher, S. R., & Coie, J. D. (1990). *Peer rejection in childhood.* New York, NY: Cambridge University Press.

Barrish, H. H., Saunders, M., & Wolf, M. M. (1969). Good behavior game: Effects of individual contingencies for group consequences on disruptive behavior in the classroom. *Journal of Applied Behavioral Psychology, 2,* 119–124.

Briesch, A. M., & Chafouleas, S. M. (2009). Review and analysis of literature on self-management interventions to promote appropriate classroom behaviors (1988–2008). *School Psychology Review, 24,* 106–118. doi:10.1037/a0016159

Bullis, M., & Cheney, D. (1999). Vocational and transition interventions for adolescents and young adults with emotional and or behavioral disorders. *Focus on Exceptional Children, 31,* 1–24. Retrieved from http://www.eric.ed.gov/ERICWebPortal/search/detailmini.jsp?_nfpb=true&_&ERICExtSearch_SearchValue_0=EJ604909&ERICExtSearch_SearchType_0=no&accno=EJ604909

Cameron, M., & Sheppard, S. M. (2006). School discipline and social work practice: Application of research and theory to intervention. *Children & Schools, 28*(1), 15–22. Retrieved from http://www.redorbit.com/news/education/357611/school_discipline_and_social_work_practice_application_of_research_and/

Cicchetti, D., & Cohen, D. J. (2006). *Developmental psychopathology: Theory and method* (Vol. 1). Hoboken, NJ: John Wiley and Sons.

Clunies-Ross, P., Little, E., & Kienhuis, M. (2008). Self-reported and actual use of proactive and reactive classroom management strategies and their relationship with teacher stress and student behavior. *Educational Psychology, 28,* 693–710. doi:10.1080/01443410802206700

Colvin, G., Flannery, K. B., Sugai, G., & Monegan, J. (2009). Using observational data to provide performance feedback to teachers: A high school case study. *Preventing School Failure, 53,* 95–104. doi:10.3200/PSFL.53.2.95-104

Commission on Chronic Illness. (1957). *Chronic illness in the United States* (Vol. 1). Cambridge, MA: Harvard University Press.

Crone, D. S., Hawken, L. S., & Horner, R. H. (2010). *Responding to problem behavior in schools.* New York, NY: Guilford Press.

Delpit, L. (1995). *Other people's children: Cultural conflict in the classroom.* NY, NY: New Press.

Dishion, T. J. (2000). Cross-setting consistency in early adolescent psychopathology: Deviant friendships and problem behavior sequelae. *Journal of Personality, 68,* 1109–1126. doi:10.1111/1467-6494.00128

Durlak, J. A., Weissberg, R. P., Symnicki, A. B., Taylor, R. D., & Schellinger, K. B. (2011). The impact of enhancing students' social and emotional learning: A meta-analysis of school-based universal interventions. *Child Development, 82,* 405–432. doi:10.1111/j.1467-8624.2010.01564.x

Fantuzzo, J. W., Rohrbeck, C. A., & Azar, S. T. (1987). A component analysis of behavioral self-management interventions with elementary school students. *Child and Family Behavior Therapy. 9,* 33–43. doi:10.1300/J019v09n01_03

Fenning, P., & Rose, J. (2007). Overrepresentation of African American students in exclusionary discipline. *Education and Urban Society, 42,* 536–559. doi:10.1177/0042085907305039

Filter, K. J., McKenna, M. K., Benedict, E. A., Horner, R. H., & Todd, A. W. (2007). Check in/Check out: A post-hoc evaluation of an efficient, secondary-level targeted intervention for reducing problem behaviors in schools. *Education and Treatment of Children, 30,* 69–84. doi:10.1353/etc.2007.0000

Goldstein, S., & Brooks, R. B. (2007). *Understanding and managing children's classroom behavior: Creating sustainable resilient classrooms.* Hoboken, NJ: Wiley & Sons.

Gordon, R. S. (1983). An operational classification of disease prevention. *Public Health Reports, 98*(2), 107–109.

Grayson J. L., & Alvarez, H. K. (2005). School climate factors relating to teacher burnout: A mediator model. *Teacher Education, 24,* 1349–1363. doi:10.1016/j.tate.2007.06.005

Gresham, F. M., Lane, K. L., & Lambros, K. M. (2000). Comorbidity of conduct problems and ADHD. *Journal of Emotional and Behavioral Disorders, 8*(2), 83. doi:10.1177/106342660000800204

Gresham, F. M. (2004). Current status and future directions of school-based behavioral interventions. *School Psychology Review, 33,* 326–343. doi:10.1016/j.ridd.2003.04.003

Gresham, F. M. (2005). Response to Intervention: An alternative means for identifying students as emotionally disturbed. *Education and Treatment of Children, 28,* 328–244.

Gruenert, S. (2008). School culture and climate: They are not the same thing. *Principal, 87*(4), 56–59. Retrieved from http://www.naesp.org/resources/2/Principal/2008/M-Ap56.pdf

Hastings, R. P., & Bham, M. S. (2003). The relationship between student behavior and teacher burnout. *School Psychology International, 24,* 115–127. doi:10.1177/0143034303024001905

Individuals with Disabilities Education Improvement Act of 2004, 20 U.S.C. § 1400 *et seq.* (2004).

Institute of Medicine. (1989). *Research on children and adolescents with mental, behavioral, and developmental disorders: Mobilizing a national initiative.* Washington, DC: National Academy Press.

Joseph, G. E., & Strain, P. S. (2003). Comprehensive evidence-based emotional curricula for young children: An analysis of efficacious adoption potential. *Topics in Early Child Special Education, 23*, 62–73. doi:10.1177/02711214030230020201

Kalis, T. M., Vannest, K. J., & Parker, R. (2007). Praise counts: Using self-monitoring to increase effective teaching strategies. *Preventing School Failure, 51*(3), 20–27.

Kauffman, J. M. (2001). *Characteristics of emotional and behavioral disorders in children and youth* (7th ed.). Upper Saddle River, NJ: Merrill/Prentice Hall.

Kaufman, P. (2004). The national dropout data collection system: History and the search for consistency. In G. Orfeild (Ed.), *Dropouts in America: Confronting the graduation rate crisis* (pp. 107–130). Cambridge, MA: Harvard Education Press.

Kern, L., Hilt-Panahon, A., & Sokol, N. J. (2009). Further examining the triangle tip: Improving support for students with emotional and behavioral needs. *Psychology in the Schools, 46*, 18–32. doi:10.1002/pits.20351

Langland, S., Lewis-Palmer, T., & Sugai, G. (1998). Teaching respect in the classroom: An instructional approach. *Journal of Behavioral Education, 8*, 245–262. doi:10.1023/A:1022839708894

Lannie, A., & McCurdy, B. L. (2007). Preventing disruptive behavior in the urban classroom: Effects of the good behavior game on student and teacher behavior. *Education and Treatment of Children, 30*(1), 85–98. doi:10.1353/etc.2007.0002

Lewis, T. J., Jones, S. L., Horner, R. H., & Sugai, G. (2010). School-wide positive behavior support and students with emotional/behavioral disorders: Implications for prevention, identification, and intervention. *Exceptionality, 18*, 82–93. doi:10.1080/09362831003673168

Maag, J. W. (2001). Rewarded by punishment: Reflections on the disuse of positive reinforcement in schools. *Exceptional Children, 67*, 173–186.

Mann, E. A., & Reynolds, A. J. (2006). Early intervention and juvenile delinquency prevention: Evidence from the Chicago longitudinal study. *Social Work Research, 15*, 153–167.

Mendler, A. N. (2005). *Just in time: Powerful strategies to promote positive behavior.* Bloomington, IN: National Education Service.

Mrazek, P. G., & Haggerty, R. J. (1994). *Reducing risks for mental disorders: Frontiers for preventive intervention research.* Washington, DC: National Academy Press.

National Association of School Psychologists. (2010). *Social skills: Promoting positive behavior, academic success, and school safety.* Retrieved from http://www.nasponline.org/resources/factsheets/socialskills_fs.aspx

Nelson, J. R., Stage, S., Duppong-Hurley, K., Synhorst, L., & Epstein, M. H. (2007). Risk factors predictive of the problem behavior of children at risk for emotional and behavioral disorders. *Exceptional Children, 73*(3), 13. Retrieved from http://www.eric.ed.gov/ERICWebPortal/search/detailmini.jsp?_nfpb=true&_&ERICExtSearch_SearchValue_0=EJ757113&ERICExtSearch_SearchType_0=no&accno=EJ757113

No Child Left Behind Act of 2001, 20 U.S.C.A. § 6319 *et seq.* (2008).

Office of Special Education and Programs (OSEP) Technical Assistance Center on Positive Behavioral Interventions and Supports. (2011a). *Positive behavioral interventions and supports: Effective school-wide interventions.* Retrieved from http://www.pbis.org/default.aspx

Office of Special Education and Programs (OSEP) Technical Assistance Center on Positive Behavioral Interventions and Supports. (2011b). *Frequently asked questions: What is secondary prevention?* Retrieved from http://www.pbis.org/school/secondary_level/faqs.aspx

Office of Special Education and Programs (OSEP) Technical Assistance Center on Positive Behavioral Interventions and Supports. (2011c). *Frequently asked questions: What is tertiary prevention?* Retrieved from http://www.pbis.org/school/tertiary_level/faqs.aspx

Offord, D. R., Kraemer, H. C., Kazdin, A. E., Jensen, P. S., & Harrington, R. (1998). Lowering the burden of suffering from child psychiatric disorder: Trade-offs among clinical, targeted, and universal interventions. *Journal of American Academy of Child and Adolescent Psychiatry, 37*, 686–694. doi:10.1097/00004583–199807000–00007

Oliver, R., Wehby, J., & Reschly, D. J. (2011). Teacher classroom management practices: Effects on disruptive or aggressive student behavior. *Campbell Systematic Reviews, 4*, 1–56. doi:10.10.4073/csr.2011.4

Osher, D., Dwyer, K., & Jimerson, S. R. (2006). Safe, supportive, and effective schools: Promoting school success to reduce school violence. In S. R. Jimerson & M. J. Furlong (Eds.), *Handbook of school violence and school safety: From research to practice* (pp. 51–71). Mahwah, NJ: Erlbaum.

Rubin, K. H., Bukowski, W., & Parker, J. G. (1998). Peer interactions, relationships, and groups. In W. V. Damon & N. Eisenberg (Eds.), *Handbook of child psychology (5th edition). Volume 3. Social, emotional, and personality development* (pp. 619–700). New York, NY: John Wiley and Sons.

Shapiro, E. S., Durnan, S. L., Post, E. E., & Levinson, T. S. (2002). Self-monitoring procedures for children and adolescents. In M. R. Shinn, H. M. Walker, & G. Stoner (Eds.), *Interventions for academic and behavior problems II: Preventive and remedial approaches* (pp. 433–454). Bethesda, MD: NASP Publications.

Simonsen, B., Fairbanks, S., Briesch, A., Myers, D., & Sugai, G. (2008). Evidence-based practices in classroom management: Considerations for research to practice. *Education and Treatment of Children, 31*, 351–380.

Skiba, R. J., Michael, R. S, Nardo, A. C., & Peterson, R. L. (2002). The color of discipline: The sources of racial and gender disproportionality in school punishment. *Urban Review, 34*, 317–342. doi:10.1023/A:1021320817372

Skiba, R. J., & Peterson, R. L. (1999). The dark side of zero tolerance: Can punishment lead to safe schools? *Phi Delta Kappan, 80,* 372–382. Retrieved from http://cranepsych.edublogs.org/files/2009/07/dark_zero_tolerance.pdf

Skiba, R. J., & Peterson, R. L. (2000). School discipline at a crossroads: From zero tolerance to early response. *Exceptional Children, 66,* 335–347. doi:10.1080/10459880009599794

Skiba, R., Reynolds, C. R., Graham, S., Sheras, P., Conoley, J. C., & Garcia- Vazquez, E. (2008). Are zero tolerance polices effective in the schools? An evidentiary review and recommendations. *American Psychologist, 63,* 852–862.

Sugai, G., & Horner, R. H. (2006). The evolution of discipline practices: School-wide positive behavior supports. In J. K. Luiselli & C. Diament (Eds.), *Behavior psychology in the schools: Innovations in evaluations, support, and consultation* (pp. 23–50). London, England: Haworth Press.

Sugai, G., & Horner, R. H. (2008). What we know and need to know about preventing problem behavior in schools. *Exceptionality, 16,* 67–77. doi:10.1080/09362830801981138

Sugai, G., & Horner, R. H. (2009). Response to Intervention and school-wide positive behavior supports: Integration of multi-tiered system approaches. *Exceptionality, 17,* 223–227. doi:10.1080/09362830903235375

Thompson, A. M. (2011). A systematic review of evidence-based classroom interventions for students with challenging behaviors in school settings. *Journal of Evidence-Based Social Work, 8,* 304–322. doi:10.1080/15433714.2010.531220

Thompson, A. M. (2012). A randomized trial of the Self-management Training and Regulation Strategy (STARS): A selective intervention for students with disruptive behaviors. ProQuest: Ann Arbor, MI.

Thompson, A. M., & Webber, K. C. (2010). Reconnecting student and teacher perceptions of school rules: A reasonable approach to managing students with difficult behaviors. *Children and Schools, 32,* 29–40.

United States Department of Education, Institute for Education Sciences (IES). (2005). *Special analysis 2005—mobility in the teacher workforce.* Retrieved from http://www2.ed.gov/admins/comm/choice/onpe/statresources_pg4.html?exp=1

United States Department of Education, Institute for Education Sciences (IES). (2006) *Teacher's perceptions about teaching and school conditions, by control and level of school: 1993–94, 1999–2000, and 2003–04.* Retrieved from http://nces.ed.gov/programs/digest/d08/tables/dt08_072.asp

United States Department of Education, Office of Civil Rights . (2000). *Projected suspension rate values for the nation's public schools: Elementary and secondary school civil rights compliance reports.* Washington, DC: Author. Retrieved from http://www2.ed.gov/about/offices/list/ocr/index.html?src=oc

Walker, H. M., Ramsey, E., & Gresham, F. M. (2003). Heading off disruptive behavior: How early intervention can reduce defiant behavior and win back teaching time. *American Educator, 45,* 6–21. Retrieved from http://www.aft.org/newspubs/periodicals/ae/winter0304/walker.cfm

Walker, H. M., Ramsey, E., & Gresham, F. M. (2004). How disruptive students escalate hostility and disorder—and how teachers can avoid it. *American Educator,* 27(4), 22–27. Retrieved from http://www.aft.org/newspubs/periodicals/ae/winter0304/walker2.cfm

Zins, J. E., Weissberg, R. P., Wang, M. C., & Walberg, H. J. (2004). *Building academic success on social and emotional learning: What does the research say?* New York, NY: Teachers College Press.

CHAPTER 38

Acquaintance Sexual Assault and Sexual Harassment: Treatment and Prevention among Teens

Erin A. Casey ▪ Paula S. Nurius

Getting Started

Nearly all youth are directly or indirectly affected by peer-to-peer sexual harassment or assault. Approximately 11% of adolescent girls and 4% of adolescent boys have been raped at some point in their lives (CDC, 2006), with substantially higher percentages experiencing attempted rape or unwanted sexual touching (Maxwell, Robinson, & Post, 2003). Over 60% of all sexual violence is perpetrated against individuals under the age of 18 (Basile, Chen, Black, & Saltzman, 2007), the vast majority of which is never reported (Young, Grey, & Boyd, 2009). Up to 80% of both boys and girls experience sexual harassment at least occasionally, with the prevalence of girls harassed in school settings rivaling or exceeding that of working women (Fineran & Gruber, 2009) and online sources expanding solicitation and sexual harassment exposure (Mitchell, Wolak, & Finkelhor, 2008). Moreover, more than half of all adolescents of both sexes report perpetrating sexual harassment at some point during their time in school, according to the American Association of University Women (AAUW; 2001). Sexual harassment and assault carry both immediate and long-term emotional, psychological, and physical consequences and can cause post-assault reactions that interfere with school performance and other achievement. School personnel are uniquely positioned to recognize and respond to the signs that a young person has been hurt and are ideally situated to implement primary prevention programs that hold promise for reducing sexual violence. This chapter summarizes recent literature on effective responses to sexual victimization and on the primary prevention of sexual harassment and assault within the school context.

What We Know

Sexually harassing behaviors between teens include behavior such as unwanted sexual jokes, gestures, name calling, anti-gay put-downs, pinching, grabbing, texting or emailing sexual pictures, spreading sexual rumors in person or via social media, and unwanted sexual touching (AAUW, 2001). Sexual harassment among adolescents most often takes the form of "hostile environment" harassment in which ongoing physical, verbal, or nonverbal conduct of a sexual nature creates a school climate that is offensive, damaging, and intimidating to one or more students (Stein, 1999). Sexual coercion and assault range from unwanted touching of sexual parts of the body to attempted or completed oral, anal, or vaginal forced intercourse. Sexual contact may be obtained through coercive behaviors such as threats, false promises, attempts to intoxicate the victim, or use of physical force or weapons. Teens are most often assaulted by acquaintances, dates, or current or former partners (Basile et al., 2007).

The continuum of sexually violent behaviors from harassment to rape holds serious impacts for victims. Sexual harassment is associated with fear, school avoidance, substance use, depression, and stress-related physical complaints (AAUW, 2001; Gruber & Fineran, 2008). Survivors of rape or attempted rape can also face consequences including post-traumatic stress symptoms, suicidal ideation, disrupted relationships, and a damaged sense of safety and self-efficacy (for review, see Campbell, Dworkin, & Cabral, 2009). Victimization increases vulnerability to future physical and sexual abuse, creating the risk for compounded traumatic experiences over time (Macy, 2008). Victimized youth are at risk for a range of medical consequences including physical trauma, exposure to STIs, and unplanned pregnancy (Kevin, 2010). Among the risk factors for perpetration are alcohol and drug use involvement (Young, King, Abbey, & Boyd, 2009) and an earlier history of trauma, highlighting the connection between violence exposure and later risk (Russell, Nurius, Herting, Thompson, & Walsh, 2010).

What We Can Do

Responses to Victim Disclosures of Sexual Harassment or Assault

Although no empirical research addresses effective school-based responses to the immediate aftermath of sexual assault or harassment, substantial research has documented post-assault factors that can generally ameliorate emotional distress for victims. This section briefly reviews these findings and uses them to identify important aspects of short-term intervention with young people who have experienced harassment or assault. School personnel are also urged to connect survivors with community resources such as sexual assault service centers and mental health programs for longer-term support and attention to post-trauma issues. Recommendations in this section are consistent with the tertiary tier of the Response to Intervention (RTI) framework.

Factors that have been associated with reduced psychological distress and enhanced recovery among adult sexual assault victims include social support, a lack of self-blame, feelings of control over one's life and recovery, and a coping style that does not avoid or deny the abusive experience or its effect (Frazier, 2003; Ullman, Filipas, Townsend, & Starzynski, 2007). Survivors of sexual violence also do better when they feel believed by support systems and when they attribute the causes of their assault to factors external to themselves (Ullman et al., 2007). In responding, the role of school personnel is to address disclosures of mistreatment, to enhance emotional and physical safety at school for victims, and to initiate referrals that boost a student's support network and resources outside of school. Specific strategies for responding supportively to disclosures of sexual assault or harassment are summarized in Box 38.1 and are discussed below.

Enhancing Social Support

Positive, non-blaming responses in which survivors feel listened to and believed are associated with decreased psychological distress following a sexual assault (Ullman et al., 2007). Expanding the network of positive social support available to a student is also a critical aspect of intervention (Koss & Harvey, 1991). School personnel can assist survivors in identifying and expanding sources of constructive support and can provide information to friends and family members regarding the nature and importance of affirming responses to the survivor. Referrals to local sexual assault programs can further bolster support and provide needed information and advocacy related to medical or legal processes. School personnel need also to consider the larger school environment and the potential for blaming or inappropriate responses to the student. Steps to enhance confidentiality, limit rumors, and help victimized students cope with inappropriate responses from peers, school personnel, or the news media may be helpful.

Restoring a Sense of Control

School personnel can help victims restore a sense of control by offering information regarding expected physical, emotional, and psychological symptoms associated with the sexual victimization. Recent victims of sexual assault may experience sleep disturbances, intrusive thoughts about the event, irritability, distractibility, numbing or spacing out, fearfulness, and physical discomfort (for review, see Resnick et al., 2007). Anticipating these difficulties, knowing that these are normal responses to a traumatic event, and hearing that they subside for most people may decrease young people's anxiety and help them to restore a sense of control (Resnick et al., 2007). Practitioners should also be aware that students' cultural backgrounds and family environments will affect the meaning that they attach to assaults, the kinds of post-assault concerns they experience, and the post-assault options that they perceive as viable (Fontes, 1995). Additionally, the degree to which a sexually abusive experience traumatizes a victim, and the specific factors that compromise a victim's mental and physical health, vary from person to person (Gidycz & Koss, 1991). Thus, referral to culturally appropriate health and mental health services is critical.

Box 38.1 Responding to Disclosures of Sexual Harassment or Assault

Establish a supportive relationship.

- Express appreciation that the student came forward.
- Explicitly express belief in the student and a willingness to listen.
- Respond nonjudgmentally to the student's disclosure.
- Reaffirm that the student is not to blame for the victimization.
- Attend to the immediate and longer-term physical and emotional safety of the student.

Restore feelings of control.

- Allow the student to set the pace of the interview.
- Engage the student in collaborative problem solving about safety.
- Ask the student what kind of outcome he or she is hoping for, and tailor interventions to honor the student's wishes as much as possible.
- Be open and clear about requirements related to mandated reporting or school harassment policy.

Provide information and referral.

- Normalize feelings or symptoms described by the student as understandable, common reactions to an upsetting event. Provide information about common post-assault physical and emotional reactions.
- Offer information about sexual assault—specific resources available in the community and how to contact them.
- Assess interest in other referrals, such as counseling or health services, legal or victim advocacy services, and cultural or community support resources.

Mobilize effective social support.

- Talk with the student about how or when to disclose his or her experience to family members or friends. Provide support, problem solving, or rehearsal about disclosing to others.
- Provide family members with information about sexual harassment or assault, and about the kinds of responses that will be most helpful to teens (e.g., believing the student, being nonjudgmental, communicating support and validation).

Enhancing Safety

A primary goal of immediate post-incident response with a victim of sexual harassment or assault is to assess and enhance both immediate and longer-term physical and emotional safety (Resnick, Acierno, Holmes, Dammeyer, & Kilpatrick, 2000). This is especially critical for teens who have experienced sexual aggression and may have physical injuries and other medical concerns such as pregnancy and exposure to sexually transmitted diseases, or who may be at risk for further encounters with the perpetrator. In addition to medical attention, sexually assaulted students should be provided information about medical forensic services, typically available through local emergency rooms (particularly if the assault occurred within the prior 96 hours). Once immediate physical safety is assured, targets of harassment or assault will need help in devising a plan for staying safe inside and outside school. School personnel should watch out for the student and be alert to the possibility of additional trouble, help the student find alternatives to some routines (such as using a particular walking route), identify a safe zone in the school where the student can go when feeling threatened, notify the alleged offender that he or she must stay away from the student, connect the student with resources for obtaining a protective court order if applicable, and provide ample adult supervision in places where harassment is more likely (Stein, 1999).

Additional Considerations in Responding to Disclosures of Sexual Harassment or Assault

Reporting to Law Enforcement and Mandated Reporting

Adolescents who experience physically abusive sexual harassment or sexual assault should receive information about reporting to local law enforcement. The decision to formally report an assault is difficult, and young people may need information about the process and help in sorting out the pros and cons of making a report. Local sexual assault programs can provide information and often offer in-person advocacy during this process. Additionally, most jurisdictions mandate reporting if a minor has been assaulted or is in ongoing danger of abuse. School personnel need to be familiar with mandated reporting requirements and sexual assault statutes in their jurisdictions.

Legal Obligations Related to Sexual Harassment

Sexual harassment in schools receiving federal funds is a prohibited form of sex discrimination under Title IX of the Federal Educational Amendments (Office for Civil Rights, 1997). Schools are required by the Office for Civil Rights to develop and disseminate procedures for registering complaints related to sex discrimination, including incidents of sexual harassment. Additionally, many states have statutes requiring schools to develop and publish policies and procedures specifically addressing sexual harassment and/or bullying. Sample school policies on sexual harassment can be found in a free document distributed by the AAUW at www.aauw.org. School policies should be disseminated to students and parents, and they must be supported by prompt response to complaints or rumors of harassment. School administrators should identify a small team of trained faculty and staff who can be available to receive and investigate incident reports or rumors.

Anti-harassment policies must also describe consequences for substantiated harassing or assaultive behavior. In addition to common school sanctions (such as in-house detention or suspension, community service within the school, etc.), interventions should include a teaching component that provides a young person with clear definitions of inappropriate behavior and information about the effects of his or her behavior on the target (Stein, 1999). This may be accomplished through tailoring activities in anti-harassment curricula for use by the harasser, or asking the perpetrator to write an "empathy" letter detailing his or her behavior and the effects it has had on the target and on the school environment. Consequences for cases of serious physical harassment or assault should be determined through legal system processes.

The Primary Prevention of Sexual Assault and Harassment

Primary prevention efforts seek to eliminate harassing and assaultive behavior before it develops by targeting and changing risk factors for aggression among individuals and in the environment. Research on prevention highlights the importance of multilevel approaches that address risks at individual, peer, family, school, and community levels (for review, see Casey & Lindhorst, 2009). Sexual violence prevention is best supported by strong, enforced anti-harassment policies; staff who are trained to intervene in witnessed or reported incidents of harassment; parent education; and clear, school-wide systems for addressing inappropriate behavior (Sanchez et al., 2001; Stein, 1999). In addition to the resources listed near the end of this chapter, school district curriculum offices and local sexual assault programs are often able to provide staff with in-service training on preventing violence and intervening with perpetrators and victims. Further, prevention approaches may be strengthened by engaging youth in the process of planning and implementing antiviolence programs and complemented by efforts to actively support and reward respectful behavior among students. Three types of prevention programs are specifically addressed here: acquaintance rape prevention programs for mixed-sex or male-only audiences, vulnerability-reduction programs for female audience, and school-wide sexual harassment prevention interventions. All of these programs fit within the primary prevention tier of the RTI framework.

Sexual Assault Approaches for Mixed-Sex or Male-Only Groups

Prevention programs that target young audiences tend to consist of educational and interactive presentations in the classroom or other group settings. Although schools may invite experts from local sexual assault programs or other community agencies to provide presentations, prevention efforts are perhaps best led by school staff who can be available for follow-up discussions, handle disclosures, and integrate prevention learning objectives into ongoing lesson planning. Several curricula are available to support these efforts and are listed in the Tools section below.

Prevention efforts are most successful at impacting participants' knowledge and attitudes about sexual assault when they involve multiple sessions, later "booster" sessions, or integration into ongoing academic curricula rather than a single encounter (for review, see Vladutiu, Martin, & Macy, 2011). Effective programs also incorporate interactive elements rather than relying on didactic content delivery, and use presenters, materials, content, and activities that reflect and are relevant to the cultural diversity of the specific audience (Heppner et al., 1999). Finally, many researchers now conclude that single-sex sessions are more effective than mixed-sex groupings, although both approaches can be successful in increasing knowledge and decreasing victim-blaming or rape-supportive attitudes among participants (Anderson & Whiston, 2005). Whether designing programs for male-only or mixed-sex audiences, it is important to defuse the defensiveness that the subject matter can raise for young men. Researchers argue that approaches that address males as potential allies in ending sexual violence and as part of the "solution" are more effective in changing attitudes than approaches that focus on males as perpetrators (Berkowitz, 2002). To date, only the Safe Dates curriculum (see the Tools section below) has demonstrated an impact on sexual assault perpetrating *behavior* among adolescents (Foshee et al., 2004).

Across programs, prevention program content most associated with knowledge and attitude change includes clear definitions and concrete examples of what constitutes sexual assault, content that challenges "rape myths" (beliefs about rape that are widely held but untrue, such as "women say no when they really mean yes" or "girls who wear revealing clothing are asking for sex"), and discussion about gender role socialization (Vladutiu et al., 2011; Schewe, 2002). Finally, "bystander" components, in which participants build skills to intervene on a potential victim's behalf and to speak out about inappropriate peer behavior, have been shown to increase college students' willingness to take action in the face of disrespectful conduct or a potential sexual assault (Banyard, Moynihan, & Plante, 2007). Bystander interventions may also help to address peer and school-level norms by helping to make respectful, nonaggressive behavior a more visible expectation within friendship groups and schools.

Reducing Adolescent Girls' Vulnerability

Sexual assault prevention programs for all-female audiences typically focus on enhancing young women's ability to reduce exposure to potentially assaultive situations and to respond self-protectively when faced with the threat of rape. These programs should be delivered with an understanding that some audience members will already have been assaulted and that the content of presentations should in no way suggest that victims invite or are responsible for their assault. Factors associated with rape-avoidance for women include reducing exposure to known situational risks and using active, physical resistance to a potential assailant (Schewe, 2002; Ullman, 2002). Situational risk factors for sexual violence include settings involving alcohol or drug consumption; being in an isolated or vulnerable setting with a perpetrator; and being in the company of a male who is derogatory toward women, ignores boundaries, or attempts to assert control (Marx, Calhoun, Wilson, & Meyerson, 2001; Ullman, 2002). Additionally, passive or negotiating approaches to resisting a potential perpetrator are less effective than physical resistance or yelling in avoiding assault (Ullman, 2002). Effective preventive interventions with girls may therefore include information about recognizing the above risk factors and about self-defense techniques in the face of threat. To date, however, no tested risk reduction curricula are available for adolescent populations.

Building on the work of Nurius and Norris (1996), Rozee and Koss (2001) propose providing young women with the "AAA" (Assess, Acknowledge, Act) model of recognizing and responding to sexual threats. This approach would provide girls with tools (such as information about risk factors) to assess a situation as potentially dangerous, empowerment in acknowledging this threat, and practice with behavioral options for acting on their assessment. It is important to note that many situational risk factors occur in normative socializing environments for young people, and that women must negotiate the dissonance between simultaneously pursuing safety and social goals—for example, developing habits of vigilance and resistance in the same circumstances in which they are seeking friendship, popularity, experimentation, and intimacy (Nurius, 2000). Indeed, assertive defending against sexual assault appears to be undermined by situational appraisals such as confusion or concern about the perpetrator's judgment of her, self-blame or a sense that others would blame her, and, more distally, a developmental priority for establishing a stable, intimate relationship (Nurius, Norris, Macy, & Huang, 2004). Young women with histories of prior victimization have substantially different profiles of situational coping with sexual assault, indicating the value of tailoring preventive interventions (Macy, Nurius, & Norris, 2007). Prevention efforts can be enhanced by giving young women the opportunity to explore these complexities and to role-play and practice feasible responses to threats of sexual assault (Marx et al., 2001). Orchowski and colleagues (2008) describe an empirically tested example of a sexual assault risk reduction and self-defense program for women that incorporates the elements described above. Additionally, many communities have local self-defense programs offered through law enforcement or sexual assault agencies. These programs should be carefully scrutinized prior to referring students and should contain the elements inherent in the AAA model.

Sexual Harassment Prevention

Although awareness about sexual harassment in schools has increased dramatically over the past decade, empirically tested sexual harassment-specific prevention curricula are nearly nonexistent. SafePlace's Expect Respect curriculum (see Tools), which addresses both dating violence and sexual harassment among teens, is one of the few evaluated programs discussed in the literature (Sanchez et al., 2001). Effective principles for sexual harassment prevention programs likely mirror those described above for sexual assault. Additionally, companion chapters in this volume on bullying and school violence will provide additional guidance. In the context of sexual harassment, it is especially important to clearly define unacceptable behaviors and their impact. Because many students who engage in harassing behavior are unaware of the effects of their conduct or see such behavior as normative (AAUW, 2001), educating them about the emotional and psychological effects on the targets of harassment may support behavior change. Like sexual assault prevention, many sexual harassment and bullying curricula include "bystander" education components that aim to enhance non-targeted students' ability to speak out against harassment, intervene on behalf of a peer, or seek adult assistance. For example, the Expect Respect program produced a positive change in young people's intention to intervene in bullying (Sanchez et al., 2001), and these findings lend support to the inclusion of bystander skill building in sexual harassment prevention education. A sample outline for a sexual harassment prevention presentation is provided in Box 38.2.

Box 38.2 Sample Sexual Harassment Prevention Presentation

1. Define sexual harassment.

- Provide a sample definition from school policy.
- Brainstorm a list of behaviors that could be considered harassment.
- Discuss difference between flirting and harassment: (i.e., flirting is mutual, respectful, complimentary, fun; harassment is one-sided, repeated, demeaning).
- Address behaviors that are both anti-gay harassment and sexual harassment (such as using the word *gay* as a put-down or making threats to students who identify as sexual minorities).
- Provide information about the prevalence of harassment in schools.

2. Address myths associated with sexual harassment, such as the ones listed below, through discussion or small-group activities.

- People invite harassment through their dress or actions.
- Harassment isn't harmful if the intention is to joke around and have fun.
- People who complain about harassment have no sense of humor or are too sensitive.
- Only girls get sexually harassed.

3. Explore the effects of sexual harassment.

- The goal of the discussion is not only to enhance participants' knowledge of the effects of harassment but also to increase empathy and understanding that harassment can be very hurtful, regardless of the harassers' intent.

(continued)

Box 38.2 (*Continued*)

4. What to do?

- Brainstorm options for bystanders/witnesses of incidents. Role-play potential bystander responses
- Brainstorm options for targets of harassment. Provide information about reporting procedures.
- Brainstorm options for what people can do if they realize they have offended someone.
- Brainstorm options for what students in general can do to end harassment and mistreatment.

5. Providve resources for follow-up, reporting, and community referrals.

In designing sexual harassment prevention interventions, it is particularly critical to address overall school climate and responsiveness in addition to student behavior (Stein, 1999). Classroom interventions alone may be ineffective if the larger school atmosphere contains overt or subtle support for harassing behaviors or fails to respond to incident reports. Elements of an ecological approach to harassment prevention might include the following: conducting a school-wide survey of students' experiences of harassment and disseminating the results among staff, students, and parents as a way of highlighting the importance of prevention and of tracking progress; sponsoring a sexual harassment awareness week with anti-harassment poster contests, speakers, essay contests, or student-planned educational activities; appointing an anti-harassment advisory committee of staff, students, and parents to plan school-wide "respect" promotion campaigns; and conducting a review and revision of existing sexual harassment policy with participation of students and parents. Finally, it is critical to provide ongoing opportunities for staff to discuss approaches to addressing harassment, to collectively examine and challenge attitudes that prevent active intervention, and to receive training on responding (Stein, 1999).

Applying Interventions within a Response to Intervention Framework

RTI refers to a national educational framework aimed at identifying and responding to problems affecting K-12 students' learning through addressing these problems earlier, before the child is far behind or entangled in seriously undermining behavioral problems. The framework links to a positive behavioral interventions and supports (PBIS) infrastructure that runs parallel to RTI, addressing the roles of individual and environmental factors in a problem-solving model to prevent inappropriate behavior through teaching and reinforcing appropriate behaviors. Although literature or curriculum are not yet available that directly connect PBIS or RTI to sexual violence prevention, the structure and priorities of PBIS are consistent with future development of research-supported interventions related to sexual violence. Further, training materials related to other acts of aggression such as bullying and school violence prevention are available on the PBIS Web site (see Further Learning below). Described by the OSEP Technical Assistance Center on Positive Interventions & Supports Web site (http://pbis.org/school/default.aspx), school-wide PBIS aims for an integrated, multilevel approach to defining, teaching, and supporting appropriate behaviors, including classroom and non-classroom settings. Tiers are distinguished in terms of three levels of support that can be conceptually linked to sexual assault and harassment prevention and intervention.

The first, or primary, tier consists of school-wide, universal interventions for all students, reaching 80%–90% of the student body. Core elements include defining and modeling behavioral expectations, developing reward systems for appropriate behavior, and monitoring data for decision making. In the context of sexual aggression, this includes developing or enhancing clear school-wide policies, training staff to consistently intervene in inappropriate behavior, establishing baseline data through surveying students regarding experiences of harassment, and implementing aforementioned evidence-based prevention curricula. The secondary RTI tier consists of selective interventions with a rapid response capacity for at-risk youth, reaching approximately 5%–10% of the student body. Students most at risk for victimization and who may benefit from tailored, small-group prevention, for example, primarily include those with prior trauma histories (Macy, 2008). Second-tier response also includes improving home/school communication and harassment-related data monitoring. Finally, the tertiary tier involves individualized interventions with intensive, specialized services for high-risk students. In the context of assault and harassment, these include implementing highly tailored interventions with victimized or adjudicated students, close behavioral monitoring, and focused monitoring in specific problem contexts within the school.

Tools: Curricula Relevant to Sexual Violence Intervention and Prevention

- Expect Respect. For information about this school-based program addressing dating violence as well as sexual harassment and assault, see www.vawnet.org (search for "Expect Respect").
- Flirting or Hurting? Curriculum for students in grades 6–12 by Nan Stein and Lisa Sjostrom. Distributed by Wellesley College Center for Research on Women: www.wcwonline.org.
- Men Can Stop Rape: www.mencanstoprape.org. This organization offers strategies and tangible tools for engaging boys in sexual violence prevention and antiviolence work.
- Safe Dates. An empirically evaluated violence prevention curriculum by Vangie Foshee. Available through the Hazelden Foundation at www.hazelden.org.
- Steps to Respect. Empirically evaluated anti-bullying and harassment curriculum for grades 3–6, Distributed by Committee for Children: www.cfchildren.org.

Key Points to Remember

Risk of sexual victimization is at its lifetime highest in adolescence through early adulthood. The high incidence of sexual victimization, together with pervasive underreporting and long-term harm to both victims and perpetrators, underscores how important it is that school personnel take an active role in the identification, intervention, and prevention of sexual harassment and assault. Immediate responses to victims of assault or harassment should focus on enhancing short- and long-term safety, increasing positive social support, connecting the victim with appropriate resources, and helping the victim to regain a sense of control.

Additionally, school personnel can enhance their impressive efforts to foster safe school climates by incorporating intervention and prevention programs that both ameliorate the effects of sexual mistreatment and reduce its occurrence. Efforts should be grounded in evidence of effectiveness and, if possible, use tested curricula. It is also worth reiterating the importance of supporting classroom prevention curriculum with efforts at every level to consistently convey expectations of respectful treatment among members of the school community and to challenge inappropriate behavior. When students are embedded in a climate characterized by respect and safety, they can more easily apply the skills and knowledge gained through prevention curricula and can assist school staff in undertaking the vital task of fostering violence-free schools.

Further Learning

- American Association of University Women: www.aauw.org (search site for "sexual harassment"). Provides free resources for educators addressing sexual harassment.
- National Sexual Violence Resource Center: www.nsvrc.org. Provides resources and links to educational and local organizing programs.
- Office for Civil Rights—U.S. Department of Education: www.ed.gov (search site for "sexual harassment"). Provides information regarding schools' legal responsibilities related to addressing sexual harassment.
- OSEP Technical Assistance Center on Positive Interventions & Supports: http://pbis.org/school/default.aspx. Provides training and publications resources linking PBIS to preventing school violence.
- Prevention Institute: www.preventioninstitute.org. Provides information about an ecological

approach to prevention and links to sexual violence-related prevention resources.

- Rape, Abuse & Incest National Network: www.rainn.org. Provides comprehensive information regarding sexual violence and a national list of local sexual assault programs.

References

American Association of University Women. (2001). *Hostile hallways: Bullying, teasing, and sexual harassment in schools.* Washington, DC: Author.

Anderson, L. A., & Whiston, S. C. (2005). Sexual assault education programs: A meta-analytic examination of their effectiveness. *Psychology of Women Quarterly, 29,* 374–388.

Banyard, V. L., Moynihan, M. M., & Plante, E. (2007). Sexual violence prevention through bystander education: An experimental evaluation. *Journal of Community Psychology, 35,* 463–481.

Basile, K. C., Chen, J., Black, M. C., & Saltzman, L. E. (2007). Prevalence and characteristics of sexual violence victimization. *Violence and Victims, 22,* 437–448.

Berkowitz, A. D. (2002). Fostering men's responsibility for preventing sexual assault. In P. Schewe (Ed.), *Preventing violence in relationships: Interventions across the life span (pp. 163–196).* Washington, DC: American Psychological Association.

Campbell, R., Dworkin, E., & Cabral, G. (2009). An ecological model of the impact of sexual assault on women's mental health. *Trauma Violence and Abuse, 10,* 225–246.

Casey, E. A., & Lindhorst, T. P. (2009) Toward a multi-level, ecological approach to the primary prevention of sexual violence: Prevention in peer and community contexts. *Trauma, Violence and Abuse, 10,* 91–114.

Centers for Disease Control and Prevention. (2006). Youth risk behavior surveillance—United States, 2005. *Morbidity and Mortality Weekly Report, 55*(SS-5), 1–108.

Fineran, S., & Gruber, J. E. (2009). Youth at work: Adolescent employment and sexual harassment. *Child Abuse & Neglect, 33*(8), 550–559.

Fontes, L. A. (1995). *Sexual abuse in nine North American cultures.* Thousand Oaks, CA: Sage.

Foshee, V. A., Bauman, K. E., Ennett, S. T., Fletcher-Linder, G., Benefield, T., & Suchindran, C. (2004). Assessing the long-term effects of the Safe Dates Program and a booster in preventing and reducing adolescent dating violence victimization and perpetration. *American Journal of Public Health, 94,* 619–624.

Frazier, P. (2003). Perceived control and distress following sexual assault: A longitudinal test of a new model. *Journal of Personality and Social Psychology, 84*(6), 1257–1269.

Gidycz, C. A., & Koss, M. P. (1991). Predictors of long-term sexual assault trauma among a national sample of victimized college women. *Violence and Victims, 6,* 175–190.

Gruber, J. E., & Fineran, S. (2008). Comparing the impact of bullying and sexual harassment victimization on the mental and physical health of adolescents. *Sex Roles, 59,* 80–92.

Heppner, M. J., Neville, H. A., Smith, K., Kivlighan, D. M., & Gershuny, B. S. (1999). Examining immediate and long-term efficacy of rape prevention programming with racially diverse college men. *Journal of Counseling Psychology, 46*(1), 16–26.

Kevin, M. R. (2010). Child sexual abuse, links to later sexual exploitation/high-risk sexual behavior, and prevention/treatment programs. *Trauma, Violence, & Abuse, 11*(4), 159–177.

Koss, M. P., & Harvey, M. R. (1991). *The rape victim: Clinical and community interventions.* Thousand Oaks, CA: Sage.

Macy, R. J., Nurius, P. S., & Norris, J. (2007). Latent profiles among sexual assault victims: Highlighting implications for defensive coping and resistance. *Journal of Interpersonal Violence, 22*(5), 543–565.

Macy, R. J. (2008). A research agenda for sexual revictimization: Priority areas and innovative statistical methods. *Violence Against Women, 14,* 1128–1147.

Marx, B. P., Calhoun, K. S., Wilson, A. E., & Meyerson, L. A. (2001). Sexual revictimization prevention: An outcome evaluation. *Journal of Consulting and Clinical Psychology, 69,* 25–32.

Maxwell, C. D., Robinson, A. L., & Post, L. A. (2003). The nature and predictors of sexual victimization and offending among adolescents. *Journal of Youth and Adolescence, 32*(6), 465–477.

Mitchell, K. J., Wolak, J., & Finkelhor, D. (2008). Are blogs putting youth at risk for online sexual solicitation or harassment? *Child Abuse & Neglect, 32*(2), 277–294.

Nurius, P. S. (2000). Women's perception of risk for acquaintance sexual assault: A social cognitive assessment. *Aggression and Violent Behavior, 5,* 63–78.

Nurius, P. S., & Norris, J. (1996). A cognitive ecological model of response to sexual coercion in dating. *Journal of Psychology and Human Sexuality, 8,* 117–139.

Nurius, P. S., Norris, J., Macy, R. J., & Huang, B. (2004). Women's situational coping with acquaintance sexual assault: Applying an appraisal-based model. *Violence Against Women, 10,* 450–478.

Office for Civil Rights. (1997). *Sexual harassment guidance.* Washington, DC: Author, Department of Education.

Orchowski, L. M., Gidycz, C. A., & Raffle, H. (2008). Evaluation of a sexual assault risk reduction and self-defense program: A prospective analysis of a revised protocol. *Psychology of Women Quarterly, 32,* 204–218.

Resnick, H., Acierno, R., Holmes, M., Dammeyer, M., & Kilpatrick, D. (2000). Emergency evaluation and intervention with female victims of rape and other violence. *Journal of Clinical Psychology, 56,* 1317–1333.

Resnick, H., Acierno, R., Waldrop, A. E., King, L., King, D., Danielson, C. ... Kilpatrick, D. (2007). Randomized controlled evaluation of an early intervention to prevent post-rape psychopathology. *Behavior Research and Therapy, 45,* 2432–2447.

Rozee, P. D., & Koss, M. P. (2001). Rape: A century of resistance. *Psychology of Women Quarterly, 25,* 295–311.

Russell, P. L., Nurius, P. S., Herting, J., Thompson, E., & Walsh, E. (2010). Violent victimization and perpetration: Joint and distinctive implications for adolescent well-being. *Victims and Offenders, 5,* 329–353.

Sanchez, E., Robertson, T. R., Lewis, C. M., Rosenbluth, B., Bohman, T., & Casey, D. M. (2001). Preventing bullying and harassment in elementary schools: The Expect Respect model. In R. A. Geffner, M. Loring, & C. Young (Eds.), *Bullying behavior: Current issues, research, and interventions (pp. 157–180).* New York, NY: Hayworth.

Schewe, P. A. (2002). Guidelines for developing rape prevention and risk reduction interventions. In P. Schewe (Ed.), *Preventing violence in relationships: Interventions across the life span (pp. 163–196).* Washington, DC: American Psychological Association.

Stein, N. (1999). *Classrooms and courtrooms: Facing sexual harassment in K-12 schools.* New York, NY: Teachers College Press.

Ullman, S. E. (2002). Rape avoidance: Self-protection strategies for women. In P. Schewe (Ed.), *Preventing violence in relationships: Interventions across the life span (pp. 137–162).* Washington, DC: American Psychological Association.

Ullman, S. E., Filipas, H. H., Townsend, S. M. & Starzynski, L. L. (2007). Psychosocial correlates of PTSD symptom severity in sexual assault survivors. *Journal of Traumatic Stress, 20,* 821–831.

Vladutiu, C. J., Martin, S. L., & Macy, R. J. (2011). College or university-based sexual assault prevention programs: A review of program outcomes, characteristics and recommendations. *Trauma, Violence and Abuse, 12,* 67–86.

Young, A. M., Grey, M., & Boyd, C. J. (2009). Adolescents' experiences of sexual assault by peers: Prevalence and nature of victimization occurring within and outside of school. *Journal of Youth & Adolescence, 38,* 1072–1083.

Young, A. M., King, L., Abbey, A., & Boyd, C. J. (2009). Adolescent peer-on-peer sexual aggression: Characteristics of aggressors of alcohol and non-alcohol-related assault. *Journal of Studies on Alcohol and Drugs, 70*(5), 700–703.

CHAPTER 39

Effective Interventions with Dating Violence and Domestic Violence

Beverly M. Black ▪ Arlene N. Weisz

Getting Started

This chapter emphasizes the development of dating violence prevention programs in schools and briefly discusses interventions for victims and perpetrators. We have selected this emphasis because of the advantages of presenting prevention programs in schools. Schools present an ideal opportunity for offering prevention programs, because they offer universal education (prior to the legal dropout age) and have repeated contact with youth (Jaffe, Wolfe, Crooks, Hughes, & Baker, 2004). Presenting programs to all youth rather than those considered vulnerable or at risk decreases the stigma of attending the program (Durlak, 1997). Youth may be more receptive to messages that are received under less stigmatizing conditions. Some experts suggest that youth who are most at risk are the least likely to seek formal help (Avery-Leaf & Cascardi, 2002), so universal programs are advantageous for them. Since victims and perpetrators are unlikely to seek help about dating violence from adults (Ashley & Foshee, 2005; Black, Tolman, Callahan, Saunders, & Weisz, 2008), it is very important to reach peers with knowledge of how to help a friend who is involved in dating violence. Having contact with adults who are clearly open to discussing dating violence may also increase youths' willingness to seek help from adults when a violent incident occurs (Weisz & Black, 2009).

This chapter is written for school staff who wish to conduct prevention programs. However, readers should also consider contacting a local domestic violence program or free-standing youth prevention program for assistance. Many of these agencies present prevention programs at no charge to the schools. Collaborating with an external prevention program offers the advantage of having the program presented by specialists. Staff members from an outside agency will bring experience in presenting prevention and education programs, and they often bring ample experience in working with survivors and/or perpetrators that can enrich their educational programs. For schools that do decide to work with an agency to conduct a dating violence education program, the following material will help school staff think about how they would like the program to be conducted and will help staff engage in knowledgeable dialog with an agency's staff to prepare for the program.

What We Know

The Importance of Dating Violence Prevention

Dating violence, the perpetration or threat of violence by a person in a relationship, has emerged as a significant social problem and public health concern among American youth. Depending on the definition of teen dating violence (TDV), between 9% and 30% of high school students have been victims of teen dating violence (Eaton, Davis, Barrios, Brener, & Noonan, 2007; Howard & Wang, 2003; Molidor & Tolman, 1998). One in four teens in a relationship report that they have been harassed, put down by their partner, or called names through cell phones and texting (Liz Claiborne Inc., 2007). Dating violence occurs among youth of all racial and ethnic backgrounds (YRBS, 2007). Both girls and boys are victims and perpetrators of dating violence; perpetrating dating violence and being a victim of dating violence are often correlated with each other.

Adolescents who have experiences with dating violence are at increased risk for physical and psychological harm (Ackard & Neumark-Sztainer, 2002; Callahan, Tolman, & Saunders, 2003; Molidor & Tolman, 1998) and serious health risk behaviors (Silverman, Raj, Mucci, & Hathaway, 2001). Girls are particularly at high risk; they are more likely than boys to experience emotional or physical injury from dating violence (Bennett & Fineran, 1998; Muñoz-Rivas, Graña, O'Leary, & González, 2007). Many times girls, in particular, fail to recognize the injuries and harm being inflicted upon them (Banister & Schreiber, 2001).

While youth usually say that dating violence is unacceptable, they often accept violence as a part of jealousy and relationships (Cauffman, Feldman, Jensen, & Jensen, 2000; Lavoie & Hebert, 2000; Prospero, 2007). Adolescents' tendency to exaggerate gender-specific roles and accept mythical notions about romance makes them particularly vulnerable to violence in their relationships (Furman, Ho, & Low, 2007). Adolescent relationships may also be prone to violence because of the dependency that they place on each other for social acceptance and for social conformity (Tolman, Spencer, Rosen-Reynoso, & Porche, 2003). The majority of adolescents report approval of violence toward a dating partner under some circumstances (Sugarman & Hotaling, 1998), and the majority of those who have experienced violence in their relationship continued to date the perpetrator of the violence against them (Jackson, Cram, & Seymour, 2000; Sugarman & Hotaling, 1998). Banister, Jakubec, and Stein (2003) found that girls' desire to have a dating partner outweighed their health and safety concerns.

Empirical Support for Dating Violence Prevention Programs

Despite the fact that numerous prevention programs have been developed, empirical evaluations of prevention programs remain rare. An analysis of several studies that included comparison no-intervention groups found that the programs did improve attitudes and behaviors (Raymond-Ting, 2009), but only a handful of studies have examined behaviors in addition to attitudes and knowledge (Foshee et al., 1998; Raymond-Ting, 2009; Wolfe et al., 2003). Even fewer evaluation studies have been conducted using samples of minority youth in the inner city. In particular, we know little about the characteristics and content of prevention programs that relate to program effectiveness. Table 39.1 summarizes current empirical research on the characteristics of dating violence prevention programs related to effectiveness.

Few research projects have examined which program components contribute to effectiveness in youth dating violence prevention (Avery-Leaf & Cascardi, 2002; Schewe, 2003). Therefore, this chapter presents the decisions that developers of prevention programs must make and, where possible, presents evidence supporting particular approaches. In some cases, knowledge gained from other types of youth prevention programs, such as substance abuse and AIDS prevention (Durlak, 1997), may be logically extrapolated to dating violence prevention without specific empirical validation. Similarly, knowledge from social learning theory (Bandura, 1977) and persuasion theory (Hovland, Janis, & Kelley 1953; Insko, 1967) can be applied to youth dating violence prevention, but evidence to support these applications is rarely available.

What We Can Do

Steps and Issues to Consider When Beginning a Dating Violence Prevention Program

Prevention Educators

- Because dating violence issues are so sensitive, your school may require some orientation regarding the need for this program. Weisz and Black (2009) present suggestions from experienced prevention program presenters about how to orient administrators and faculty.
- School staff should have training to conduct prevention sessions (Avery-Leaf & Cascardi, 2002; Weisz & Black, 2009). Presenters need thorough knowledge of the issues, because youth will ask many questions. They also need to be trained to avoid the victim blaming that is so common in our society. School staff may seek training from a local domestic violence program to help them become more expert in dating violence issues.
- Many experts believe that knowledge of youth culture or willingness to learn from youth

Table 39.1 Programs That Conducted Research on Best Practices in Youth Dating Violence Prevention

Study	*Format*	*Target*	*Evaluation Design*	*Results*	*Explanation of Results*
Wolfe et al., (2003)	Community-based; 18 sessions; focus on abuse dynamics, skills, and social action	14–16 years	Cluster randomized trial; 2.5-year follow-up	Physical and emotional abuse decreased; listening skills & group involvement related to a decline in physical abusiveness.	Didactic and interactive interventions are effective in changing attitudes (at least in the short term).
Schewe (2003)	School-based programs with variations in length, format, and content	5th–12th grade	Pre-/post-test design	Effectiveness: more sessions, shorter duration; male/female co-facilitators, homework, role-plays, discussions, healthy relationship skills, warning signs. Non-effectiveness: gender role & self-defense content, videos, quizzes, anonymous question box, games, artwork.	Program length, content, format, and characteristics can positively and negatively relate to program effectiveness.
Foshee et al. (2005)	School-based; 10 sessions, with theater production, poster contest; community component	8th and 9th grade	Pretest, 3-year follow-up; control group	At follow-up, youth in prevention program reported less psychological abuse, moderate physical and sexual violence perpetration, and moderate physical dating violence victimization than control group.	Dating violence norms, gender-role norms, and awareness of community services influenced the outcomes of the program.
Jaycox et al. (2006)	School-based; 3 sessions	High school	Pre-test, post-test, 3-year follow-up; randomized control group	At post-test found improvements in knowledge, attitudes, and help-seeking intentions; at follow-up knowledge effects and perception of potential helpfulness of lawyers persisted.	Random selection of schools and classrooms with at least 80% Latino teens
Lowe, Jones, & Banks (2007)	School-based; 4 sessions provided by 4 community agencies; used lecture, group activities, and videos	9th grade	Pre-/post-test design	Improved knowledge for whole sample and improved attitudes for those with violence-tolerant attitudes at pre-test.	Some youth had little room for improvement in attitudes; knowledge building was equally effective for all youth (gender/ ethnicity)

about their culture is also necessary (Weisz & Black, 2009). The educators must be able to help youth feel comfortable talking about sensitive issues. Because youth are reluctant to tell adults about dating violence victimization, educators must overcome this obstacle by making it clear that they are approachable and nonjudgmental.

- There is no research demonstrating the superiority of using mixed-gender versus single-gender program presenters (Avery-Leaf & Cascardi, 2002). Most research on gender composition of prevention groups is about college students. Black et al. (2012) found that middle school males benefit most from participation in a same-gender program and females benefit most from a mixed-gender program. Experienced prevention practitioners often report advantages of having male presenters, but many believe females can be very successful addressing male and female youth (Weisz & Black, 2009). Similarly, expert prevention practitioners believe an ethnic match between youth and presenters is a good idea but far from essential for a successful program (Weisz & Black, 2009).

Recruitment of Youth

- Start before they date. Many educators believe middle school is an ideal time to start prevention programs because students have not yet established dating patterns (Avery-Leaf & Cascardi, 2002). Though middle school youth may not be officially "dating," they may be forming romantic attachments and developing patterns of behavior within these attached relationships.
- Determine whether your school requires parental consent for youth to participate in the program or in program evaluation.
- Target all youth, not just those particularly at risk (Avery-Leaf & Cascardi, 2002; Weisz & Black, 2009). Programs generally address all youth in particular classes, operating on the principal that making programs voluntary eliminates those most in need of the program.
- Decide whether you want to separate or combine girls and boys (Black et al., 2012; Weisz & Black, 2009). Some experts believe that youth are more open when they can talk in separate groups, while others believe that dialog between genders is essential. One option is to separate genders for some sessions or some small-group exercises and combine them for others.
- Consider the optimal group size. Most educators try to avoid addressing assemblies (Hilton, Harris, Rice, Krans, & Lavigne, 1998) because they believe smaller groups enable discussions that truly capture youths' attention and enable them to participate in active learning (Weisz & Black, 2009).

Steps to Guide Program Structure, Content, and Evaluation

Program Structure

- Plan multiple sessions. Although some programs of short duration have been found to be effective (Lavoie, Vezina, Piche, & Boivin, 1995), multiple-session programs are generally more effective (Avery-Leaf & Cascardi, 2002; Raymond-Ting, 2009; Schewe, 2000; Weisz & Black, 2001). Experts recommend presenting at least three to four sessions.
- Decide how you want the sessions to be spaced. Weekly sessions allow students time to integrate the material. However, some experienced practitioners prefer presenting one session per day for several days to increase chances of students' retaining and using information from one session to the next (Weisz & Black, 2009). Between sessions, some educators ask students to do assignments that reinforce their message.
- Make the sessions interactive. Experts recommend devoting time to discussion, role plays, and skill development (Durlak, 1997; Raymond-Ting, 2009; Schewe, 2003). Practitioners agree that discussion of issues that students raise seems to attract their attention and enables the content to be locally relevant (Weisz & Black, 2009). Empirical evaluation does not support the use of videos, games, artwork, or anonymous question boxes (Schewe, 2003). However, expert practitioners believe that judicious use of short videos attracts youths' attention and raises important issues for discussion (Weisz & Black, 2009), and urban youth in a middle school study reported high levels of satisfaction with the use of videos (Elias-Lambert, Black, & Sharma, 2010).
- Set guidelines for discussion at the beginning of the program. Examples of guidelines included in the curricula listed at the end of the chapter show that these guidelines are based on sound

principals of group leadership, such as respect for everyone's opinions and feelings.

Content

- Find out whether the prevention material must be reviewed by anyone in your school or district. Sometimes content about dating or violence is considered controversial and must be reviewed before it is presented.
- Use a curriculum developed by experts. These people will have experience presenting their material to many school groups. Box 39.1 includes a sample lesson from "Expect Respect" (Rosenbluth & Bradford-Garcia, 2002), and the reference list includes other recommended curricula.
- Choose a program that matches your audience. The curriculum and audiovisual materials should be sensitive to the primary cultural group of the youth who participate in your program. Youth are more likely to pay attention to images and stories about people who seem similar to them (Hovland, Janis, & Kelley 1953). The material should address youth in sexual minorities, because dating violence is not limited to heterosexual couples. It should also address the vulnerabilities of youth with disabilities.
- Develop wide-ranging content. Content should include: forms of violence, information about the magnitude of the problem, relationship myths, power and control versus equality, warning signs and red flags, definitions of consent, healthy and unhealthy relationships, relationship rights and responsibilities, resources for seeking help, healthy relationship skills, and how peers can help friends.
- Consider whether you want your program to address larger, societal violence issues that contribute to dating violence.
- Consider combining content. Some programs combine content on sexual violence with content on dating violence prevention, but other programs separate them.
- Train students to be educators. Incorporating peer education requires training and supervision of peer educators, but it can increase the number of students that are reached. In addition, students may pay more attention and respond better to their peers (Weisz & Black, 2010). The peer educators themselves will learn a great deal. They can be influential in changing the school's atmosphere, and they will be prepared to help friends who consult them about an incident of dating violence. One approach to peer education is to train high school students to address middle school students. Other programs recruit youth to perform in interactive theatrical presentations about dating violence.
- Select gender-neutral materials. Research suggests that these are more effective than materials that consistently describe males as perpetrators and females as victims. No program will be effective if it alienates the male students (Avery-Leaf & Cascardi, 2002; Weisz & Black, 2009).
- Include information on peer intervention. Programs using the "bystander approach" of teaching students how to intervene in peers' abusive relationships can convey a nonblaming, empowering approach to nonviolence.

Goals and Program Evaluation

- Do conduct an evaluation. This will help you to measure how effective your program is. An evaluation can also identify aspects that need improvement. It is considered optimal to test students at the outset and after the program has run its course. Conducting a 3- to 6-month follow-up on knowledge, attitudes and behaviors would be ideal. The presenters might ask classroom teachers to administer the surveys so that time is not taken away from presentation and discussion.
- Get feedback from students. Process evaluation that asks students to recommend improvements to the program can also be very helpful.

Galvanizing the School and Involving Stakeholders in Dating- and Domestic Violence Prevention

School-wide Involvement

- Give the program visibility outside the classroom. Programs that create an atmosphere in the school that supports the prevention program's norms are considered most effective (Foshee, et al., 1998). You might organize students to put up posters that are purchased or created by youth for a contest. Musical events featuring musicians who promote nonviolence can be very appealing to youth (Center for Prevention and Study of Violence, 2000).

- Offer a training session for faculty so they understand and can reinforce the information you are presenting to the students. This session can inform faculty that they might be confusing youth by expressing attitudes that are contrary to those taught in your prevention program (Weisz & Black, 2009).

Parental Involvement

- Let parents or guardians know what their children are learning. Given their influence in their children's lives (Black & Weisz, 2003), parents can be your program's most important allies and can reinforce its messages. A parent meeting can be an ideal forum in which to present information and to influence parents' own knowledge and attitudes. The information may help parents who are dealing with domestic violence and may decrease students' exposure to parental violence, which researchers think predisposes youth to violent actions (Skuja & Halford, 2004).
- Publish a newsletter. If your program is more than one or two sessions, it is helpful to send home a newsletter periodically to inform parents about the content of the program.
- We include in this chapter (Box 39.2) an exercise intended to supplement or replace a parent orientation if parents are unable to attend. This exercise asks youth to interview their parents about dating violence issues.

Preparation for Unintended Consequences of Programs

- Be prepared to help youth decide what they should and should not disclose during programs (Weisz & Black, 2009). Even though youth should be reminded about confidentiality and respect, it is important to protect survivors from revealing information that may become the source of gossip or ridicule after the program is over.
- Inform the students of your professional obligations to report child abuse or threats to harm.
- Have a plan and resources in place to respond to disclosures of child abuse or dating violence, because youth frequently approach prevention educators for help after a presentation.

Working with Survivors and Perpetrators of Dating Violence and Domestic Violence

It can be difficult to employ the best counseling and social work skills when presented with a teen survivor of dating violence, because it is upsetting to see harm inflicted on someone so young. However, it is very important for helpers to listen with empathy instead of telling survivors what to do or minimizing the seriousness of their concerns (Weisz, Tolman, Callahan, Saunders, & Black, 2007). Otherwise, the helper risks repeating the same type of controlling behavior used by the abuser. Within state legal guidelines, it is important not to force survivors to tell their parents or legal authorities about dating violence. It is better to help them explore the advantages and disadvantages of telling someone. Similarly, pressuring them to break up with an abuser is not empowering. The idea of breaking up with an abuser may seem very complicated and troubling to survivors and, furthermore, does not guarantee their safety. Again, it is better to explore the survivor's thoughts about safety and about remaining in the relationship versus leaving it (Davies, Lyon, & Monti-Catania, 1998). It is important for a helper to express concerns about a survivor's safety and to urge the survivor to develop a safety plan for use if violence occurs again or is imminent. Group work with survivors of dating violence can be very powerful in decreasing isolation and helping youth share safety planning ideas with each other (Levy, 1999).

Couples counseling is controversial for abusive intimate partner relationships (Bograd & Mederos, 2007) because the victim cannot speak freely in a joint session—the abuser may punish her later for what she said. Most domestic violence experts recommend couples counseling only after perpetrators have received ample intervention to help them accept responsibility for their decisions to use violence and have learned not to use it.

Research supports the practice of group treatment for perpetrators. Groups decrease isolation and increase youths' openness to learning new behaviors from peers rather than from an individual adult therapist (Davis, 2004). Because many regions do not have agency-based groups available for adolescent dating violence perpetrators, you may want to consider developing a group within your school (Davis, 2004). The focus of intervention should be psychoeducational with an emphasis on learning new coping strategies and on increasing accountability for one's behavior (Peacock & Rothman, 2001).

Applying Interventions within a Response to Intervention Framework

Dating and domestic violence prevention programs can easily be applied within the RTI framework. Several TDV prevention programs are evidenced-based as discussed in this chapter.Although we lack research on specific aspects of programming, we do know that prevention programs can reduce youth perpetration of dating violence.

Assessment of youth risk for TDV can also be conducted prior to participation in a TDV prevention program. TDV prevention programs generally have pre-test, post-test, and follow-up assessments. Assessment instruments provide information about each student's knowledge, attitudes, and behaviors related to dating violence. A lack of understanding about TDV, attitudes reflecting an acceptance of TDV, and continued high levels of TDV perpetration and victimization suggest that a student may need more intensive interventions.

Parental involvement is key in TDV prevention programming. Parents need to be informed about what students are learning related to TDV so they can discuss issues with their children. They need to provide messages as consistent as youth receive in school and be knowledgeable in addressing their children's questions and concerns.

Tiered Instruction. Various forms of TDV interventions are available and can be provided by school systems:

- Tier 1—All school systems should conduct a risk assessment of youth and should provide universal evidenced-based TDV prevention programming to its students. Students assessed as at risk due to factors related to TDV (i.e., child abuse and exposure to domestic violence in the home) are referred to Tier 2 interventions.
- Tier 2—Students assessed as being at risk can receive specialized programming provided during the school day, such as participation in a small support group similar to that used in Expect Respect for high-risk youth. Youth showing progress in their knowledge base, attitudes, and TDV behaviors are returned to the classroom to continue with universal TDV programming. Youth not demonstrating changes in knowledge, attitudes, or behaviors are referred to Tier 3.
- Tier 3—
- Students at this level are referred for individual counseling and work with trained workers in the area of dating violence. Students are most likely referred to local community domestic violence programs who offer specialized services for youth.

Tools and Practice Examples

Box 39.1 Sample Lesson from the Expect Respect Curriculum

Session 10: Identifying Warning Signs of Dating Violence

Healthy Partner Auctions

Instructions

- Pass out the handout **What I Need to Know about a Partner Before I Get into a Serious Relationship** and discuss what group members would like to know.
- Pass out the handout **Healthy Partner Auction.** Explain that the characteristics will be auctioned off to the highest bidder. Each group member will have $1,000 to spend during the auction. The starting bid is $100, and members can bid only in increments of $100.
- Ask group members to prioritize for themselves on the handout which characteristics they absolutely want to have in a partner. How much is each of these traits worth to them? Let the auction begin.
- Keep track of how much characteristics were sold for and who bought them by writing the highest bidder's initials and winning bid next to each item on the handout.

(continued)

Box 39.1 *(Continued)*

Discussion

- Which are the most valued characteristics?
- Why are these characteristics so important to you?
- Was there a bidding war for a certain characteristic? Why?
- Are all characteristics realistic?
- Who can support you in finding a healthy relationship?
- Are there people or situations you want to avoid?

Healthy Partner Auction

What Is Important to You?

How much would you bid for someone who ...

1. Has a lot of money
2. Loves children
3. Shares in the decision making with you
4. Knows himself/herself and is comfortable being alone
5. Drives an expensive car
6. Accepts you for who you are, not for how you look
7. Has many of the same values as you do
8. Is a good student
9. Is able to express anger without being violent or abusive
10. Doesn't expect you to be perfect
11. Is a good listener and communicates well
12. Takes responsibility for what he/she says and does
13. Comes from a powerful and well-known family
14. Doesn't rush into the relationship but slowly gets to know you better
15. Accepts when you spend time away with your friends
16. Has supportive friends other than you
17. Asks permission before touching you or being sexual
18. Will support you and your goals
19. Makes and keeps commitments
20. Is able to work through conflict by talking

What I Need to Know about a Partner Before I Get into a Serious Relationship

1. How much time does he or she spend with family?
2. How does he or she handle disagreements in the family?
3. How does he or she handle anger?
4. How does he or she act with peers?
5. How does he or she act with younger children?
6. Are his or her values compatible with mine?
7. Are his or her words consistent with his or her actions?
8. Have he or she been abusive to a previous dating partner?
9. Does he or she act controlling and possessive?
10. Is he or she extremely jealous?

(continued)

Box 39.1 *(Continued)*

11. Does he or she use alcohol or drugs?
12. Does he or she have a history of being in trouble with the law?
13. Does he or she want to spend every free moment with me?
14. Does he or she have other interests and friends?
15. How does he or she handle conflict?
16. Does he or she want to make all the decisions?
17. Does he or she want to get serious quickly?
18. Does he or she talk about his or her expectations in a relationship?
19. Does he or she want a sexual relationship that is compatible with what I want?
20. What other information would YOU want to have before getting serious with someone?

Source: From *Expect Respect: A support group curriculum for safe and healthy relationships,* by Ball, B., Rosenbluth, B., & Aoki, A. Austin, TX: Safe Place. Copyright 2008. Reprinted with permission.

Box 39.2 Exercise for Students to Interview Parents

Parent Interview: Dating Violence Prevention Program

Interview Feedback Form*

The goal of this exercise is to enhance the communication between student and parent(s) and share in a dialog about relationships. Students should read the question to their parent(s) and allow them time to give a response. The student then shares his or her response with the parent(s) and discusses similarities and differences that occur.

1. What components do you think contribute to a healthy relationship?
   Student shares response:
   Parents share response:
2. What do you understand dating violence to be? What are the warning signs of dating violence?
   Student shares response:
   Parents share response:
3. What steps can you take toward ending dating violence?
   Student shares response:
   Parents share response:

*This form is shortened to preserve space. Create a form with spaces for student to record their own and their parents' responses. You might want to offer an incentive for students to bring back completed forms. *Source:* This interview was developed by James Ebaugh and Beverly Black.

Resources

Curricula

Break the Cycle. For more information go to http://www.breakthecycle.org/how-we-help, 5777 W. Century Blvd., Suite 1150 Los Angeles, CA 90045, 310.286.3383 admin 310.286.3386 fax

Expect Respect. For more information about this curriculum, see www.austin-safeplace.org. For information about conducting the program, consult http://www.vawnet.org.

Healthy Relationships: A Violence-Prevention Curriculum: http://www.m4c.ns.ca/news.html. A French translation of the program is available from Men For Change at info@m4c.ns.ca.

Safe Dates. For more information, contact Vangie Foshee, University of North Carolina at Chapel Hill School of Public Health, Campus Box 7400, Chapel Hill, NC 27599–7400.

Videos and Other Aids

Break the Cycle: http://www.breakthecycle.org/

Causing Pain: Real Stories of Dating Abuse and Violence (CDC, 2006): Available for download at http://www.youtube.com/watch?v=F9Ctwk8R470

Dating in the Hood: http://www.intermedia-inc.com

Dating Matters: Understanding Teen Dating Violence Prevention at CDC is a free, online course available to educators, school personnel, youth leaders, and others working to prevent TDV. http://www.vetoviolence.org/datingmatters/

Dangerous Games, available at http://www.intermedia-inc.com

It Ain't Love: http://tc.clientrabbit.com/files/resources/tit_aint_love.htmlNational Teen Dating Violence Prevention Initiative: http://www.americanbar.org/groups/public_Education/initiatives_awards/national_teen_dating_violence_prevention_initiative.html

Revolving Ophelia by Lifetime: http://www.mylifetime.com/movies/reviving-ophelia

A list of videos is available at: http://www.nrcdv.org

National Dating Abuse Helpline: 1–866–331–9474/1–866–331–8453 TTY

Teen Power and Control Wheel, which describes different types of dating violence abuse, is available at http://www.ncdsv.org/images/Teen_PC_wheel_NCDSV.pdf. This Web site also includes power and control and equality wheels in Spanish.

Key Points to Remember

Dating violence—experienced in some form by about one third of all U.S. high school students—is the perpetration of violence or threats of violence upon a partner in a relationship. Although many prevention programs have been developed to confront this issue, few have been subjected to empirical evaluation. However, by comparing the multiple programs currently in use and the evaluation studies that are available, it is possible to establish a set of guidelines for implementing new dating violence prevention programs in a school setting:

- Staff should receive orientation regarding the need for and benefits of such a program. Though few may be needed to present the programs, all staff must be trained to handle questions from students.
- Current practice suggests that youths should be targeted for prevention programs as early as middle school, when romantic relationships may be beginning to form. Whether the program is being presented to all youths or just those in an at-risk population, parental consent may be needed for the child's participation.
- Experienced practitioners tend to advocate a program consisting of multiple sessions over a short period of time. These sessions may be presented weekly or daily, with support existing for both.
- The curriculum for the program should be chosen carefully to represent the school's primary cultural makeup, address minority sexual lifestyles, and be gender neutral.
- Parents should be kept involved with the program and their child's progress by means of parent sessions and/or newsletters (for longer programs).
- Program presenters should be trained and ready to deal with issues requiring immediate attention (e.g., children currently being abused) or exceptional care (e.g., children who have been abused or otherwise victimized).

References

Ackard, D. M., & Neumark-Sztainer, D. (2002). Date violence and date rape among adolescents: Associations with disordered eating behaviors and psychological health. *Child Abuse & Neglect, 26*(5), 455–473.

Ashley, O. S., & Foshee, V. A. (2005). Adolescent help-seeking for dating violence: Prevalence, sociodemographic correlates, and sources of help. *Journal of Adolescent Health, 36,* 25–31.

Avery-Leaf, S., & Cascardi, M. (2002). Dating violence education in schools: Prevention and early intervention strategies. In P. A. Schewe (Ed.), *Preventing violence in relationships: Interventions across the life span.* Washington, DC: American Psychological Association.

Bandura, A. (1977). *Social learning theory.* Englewood Cliffs, NJ: Prentice Hall.

Banister, E. M., & Schreiber, R. (2001). Young women's health concerns: Revealing paradox. *Health Care for Women International, 22*(7), 633–648.

Banister, E. M. Jakubec, S. L., & Stein, J. A. (2003). "Like, what am I supposed to do?" Adolescent girls' health concerns in their dating relationships. *Canadian Journal of Nursing Research, 35*(2), 16–33.

Bennett, L., & Fineran, S. (1998). Sexual and severe physical violence among high school students: Power beliefs, gender, and relationship. *American Journal of Orthopsychiatry, 68*(4), 645–652.

Black, B. M., & Weisz, A. N. (2003). Dating violence: Help-seeking behaviors of African American middle schoolers. *Violence Against Women, 9*(2), 187–206.

Black, B. M., Weisz, A. N. & Jayasundara, D. S., (2012). Dating violence and sexual assault prevention with middle schoolers: Does group gender composition impact dating violence attitudes? *Child & Youth Services, 33, 158–173.*

Black, B, M., Tolman, R. M., Callahan, M., Saunders, D. G., & Weisz, A. N. (2008). When will adolescents tell someone about dating violence victimization? *Violence Against Women, 14*(7), 741–758.

Bograd, M., & Mederos, F. (2007). Battering and couples therapy: Universal screening and selection of treatment modality. *Journal of Marital and Family Therapy, 25*, 291–312.

Callahan, M. R., Tolman, R. M., & Saunders, D. G. (2003). Adolescent dating violence victimization and psychological well-being. *Journal of Adolescent Research, 18*(6), 664–681.

Cauffman, E., Feldman, S., Jensen, L. A., & Jensen, J. A. (2000). The (un)acceptability of violence against peers and dates. *Journal of Adolescent Research, 15*(6), 652–673.

Center for Prevention and Study of Violence. (n.d.). *Blueprints for violence prevention: Overview of multi-systemic therapy.* Retrieved May 31, 2000, from http://www.colorado.edu/cspv/blueprints/model/ten_Multisys.htm

Davies, J., Lyon, E., & Monti-Catania, D. (1998). *Safety planning with battered women: Complex lives/difficult choices.* Thousand Oaks, CA: Sage.

Davis, D. L. (2004). Group intervention with abusive male adolescents. In P. G. Jaffe, L. L. Baker, & A. J. Cunningham (Eds.), *Protecting children from domestic violence: Strategies for community intervention (pp. 49–67).* New York: Guilford.

Durlak, J.A. (1997). *Successful prevention programs for children and adolescents.* New York: Plenum.

Eaton, D. K., Davis, K. S., Barrios, L., Brener, N. D., & Noonan, R. K. (2007). Associations of dating violence victimization with lifetime participation, co-occurrence, and early initiation of risk behaviors among U.S. high school students. *Journal of Interpersonal Violence, 22*, 585–586.

Elias-Lambert, N., Black, B. M., & Sharma, Y. (2010). Middle school youth: Satisfaction with and responses to a dating violence prevention program. *Journal of School Violence, 9*, 136–153.

Foshee, V. A., Bauman, K. E., Arriaga, X. B., Helms, R. W., Koch, G. G., Linder, G. F., & Fletcher, G. (1998). An evaluation of Safe Dates, an adolescent dating violence prevention program. *American Journal of Public Health, 88*(1), 45–50.

Foshee, V. A., Bauman, K. E., Ennett, S. T., Suchindran, C., Benefield, T., & Linder, G. F. (2005). Assessing the effects of the dating violence prevention program "Safe Dates" using random coefficient regression modeling. *Prevention Science, 6*(3), 245–258.

Furman, W., Ho, M. J., & Low, S. M. (2007). The rocky road of adolescent romantic experience: Dating and adjustment. In R. C. M. E. Engels, M. Kerr, & H. Stattin (Eds.), *Friends, lovers and groups: Key relationships in adolescence (pp. 61–80).* Chichester, England: John Wiley & Sons.

Hilton, N. Z., Harris, G.T., Rice, M. E., Krans, T S., & Lavigne, S.E. (1998). Antiviolence education in high schools: Implementation and evaluation. *Journal of Interpersonal Violence 13*, 726–742.

Hovland, C. I., Janis, I. L., & Kelley H. H. (1953). *Communication and persuasion.* New Haven, CN: Yale University Press.

Howard, D. E., & Wang, M. Q. (2003). Risk profiles of adolescent girls who were victims of dating violence. *Adolescence, 38*(149), 1–14.

Insko, CA . (1967). *Theories of attitude change.* New York: Appleton-Century-Crofts.

Jackson, S. M., Cram, F., & Seymour, F. W. (2000). Violence and sexual coercion in high school students' dating relationships. *Journal of Family Violence, 15,* 23-36.

Jaffe, P. G., Wolfe, D, Crooks, C, Hughes, R., & Baker, L. L. (2004). The fourth R: Developing healthy relationships through school-based interventions. In P. G. Jaffe, L. L. Baker, & A.J. Cunningham (Eds.), *Protecting children from domestic violence: Strategies for community intervention (pp. 200–218).* New York: Guilford.

Jaycox, L. H., McCaffrey, D., Eiseman, B., Aronoff, J., Shelley, G. A., Collins, R. L., & Marshall, G. N. (2006). Impact of a school-based dating violence prevention program among Latino Teens: Randomized controlled effectiveness trial. *Journal of Adolescent Health, 39*(5), 694–704.

Lavoie, F., Vezina, L., Piche, C., & Boivin, M. (1995). Evaluation of a prevention program for violence in teen dating relationships. *Journal of Interpersonal Violence, 10*(4), 516–524.

Levy, B. (1999). Support groups: Empowerment for young women abused in dating relationships. In B. Levy (Ed.), *Dating violence: Young women in danger (pp. 232–239).* Seattle: Seal.

Liz Claiborne Inc. (2008). *Tween and teen dating violence and abuse study.* New York, NY: Liz Claiborne. Retrieved from http://www.loveisrespect.org/wp-content/uploads/2008/07/tru-tween-teen-study-feb-081.pdf

Lowe, L. A., Jones, C. D., & Banks, L. (2007). Preventing dating violence in public schools. *Journal of School Violence, 6*(3), 69–87.

Molidor, C., & Tolman, R. M. (1998). Gender and contextual factors in adolescent dating violence. *Violence Against Women, 4*(2), 180–194.

Muñoz-Rivas, M. J., Graña, J. L., O'Leary, K. D., & González, M. P. (2007). Aggression in adolescent dating relationships: Prevalence, justification, and health consequences. *Journal of Adolescent Health, 40*(4), 298–304.

Peacock, D., & Rothman, E. (2001, November). *Working with young men who batter: Current strategies and new directions.* Harrisbrug, PA: VAWnet. a project of the National Resource Center on Domestic Violence/Pennsylvania Coalition Against Domestic Violence.. Retrieved August 28, 2012, from http://www.vawnet.org/applied-research-papers/print-document.php?doc_id=415

Prospero, M. (2007). The role of perceptions in dating violence among young adolescents. *Journal of Interpersonal Violence, 1*(4), 470–484.

Raymond-Ting, S. (2009). Meta-analysis on dating violence prevention among middle and high schools. *Journal of School Violence, 8*, 328–337.

Rosenbluth, B., & Bradford-Garcia, R. (2002). *Expect Respect: A support group curriculum for safe and healthy relationships (3rd ed.).* Austin, TX: Safe Place.

Schewe, P. A. (2000). *STAR: Southside Teens About Respect A Comprehensive Community-Based Teen Dating Violence Prevention Program.* Retrieved August 28, 2012, from http://tigger.uic.edu/~schewepa/web-content/newpages/STAR.html

Schewe, P. A. (2003). *The teen dating violence prevention project: Best practices for school-based TDV prevention programming.* Unpublished report.

Silverman, J. G., Raj, A., Mucci, L. A., & Hathaway, J. (2001). Dating violence against adolescent girls and associated substance use, unhealthy weight control, sexual risk behavior, pregnancy, and suicidality. *Journal of American Medical Association, 286*(5), 1–18.

Skuja, K., & Halford, W. K. (2004). Repeating the errors of our parents? Parental violence in men's family of origin and conflict management in dating couples. *Journal of Interpersonal Violence, 19*(6), 623–638.

Sugarman, D. B., & Hotaling, G. T. (1998). Dating violence: A review of contextual and risk factors. In B. Levy (Ed.), *Dating violence: Young women in danger* (pp. 100–118). Seattle, WA: Seal Press.

Tolman, D. L., Spencer, R., Rosen-Reynoso, M., & Porche, M.V. (2003). Sowing the seeds of violence in heterosexual relationships: Early adolescents narrate compulsory heterosexuality. *Journal of Social Issues, 59*(1), 159–178.

Weisz, A. N., & Black, B. M. (2001). Evaluating a sexual assault and dating violence prevention program for urban youth. *Social Work Research, 25*, 89–100.

Weisz, A. N., Tolman, R. M., Callahan, M., Saunders, D. G., & Black, B. M. (2007). Informal helpers' responses when adolescents tell them about dating violence or romantic relationship problems. *Journal of Adolescence, 30*, 853–868.

Weisz, A. N., & Black, B. M. (2009). *Programs to reduce teen dating violence and sexual assault: Perspectives on what works.* NY: Columbia University Press.

Weisz, A. N., & Black, B. M. (2010). Peer education and leadership in dating violence prevention: Strengths and challenges. *Journal of Aggression, Maltreatment, and Trauma, 19*(6), 641–660.

Wolfe, D. A., Wekerle, C., Scott, K., Straatman, A. L., Grasley C., & Reitzel-Jaffe, D. (2003). Dating violence prevention with at-risk youth: A controlled outcome evaluation. *Journal of Consulting and Clinical Psychology, 71*(2), 279–291.

YRBS . (2007). *Youth Risk Behavior Surveillance System.* National Center for Chronic Disease Prevention and Health Promotion, Division of Adolescent and School Health. Retrieved June 4, 2009, from http://www.cdc.gov/HealthyYouth/yrbs/index.htm

CHAPTER 40

Effective Intervention with Gangs and Gang Members

Timothea M. Elizalde Gilbert A. Ramirez

Getting Started

Gang presence in public schools continues to be an ongoing issue across the United States. As public school districts are being held more and more accountable for student performance and required to implement increased standardized measures, resources to address and support student populations that are rapidly falling behind and are less engaged in school are slowly vanishing. However, gang presence in public schools remains a constant and significant factor that requires careful attention and consideration. Data suggest that the correlation between gang presence and crime on school grounds is significant (Howell & Lynch, 2000). Research continues to grow and highlight that intervention measures can be successful in working with gang members and decreasing gang-related crime and violence in schools. This chapter expands on our previous publication and provides ongoing review of best practice measures for providing prevention and intervention measures for gang members in a school setting as well as providing a review of various tools and resources that can be utilized in assessing one's school and community for appropriate gang intervention measures. Instruments will also be reviewed to help guide practitioners in accurately assessing the needs of individual clients and gang members for support and intervention services. Studies that substantiate the ongoing need for gang intervention in schools and review of an evidence-based program that can be used in schools with middle school and high school students who are gang members or on the verge of becoming involved with gangs will be outlined. The focus of the chapter is a step-by-step guide to assessing the need for a gang intervention group. Addressing possible resistance to implementation efforts and methods for gaining support from school administration and staff, creating a successful school-based gang intervention program, and building the necessary data to substantiate and maintain an intervention program will be discussed.

What We Know

Research on gangs and gang prevalence in U.S. schools continues to grow. A study conducted by the U.S. Departments of Education and Justice (Chandler, Chapman, Rand, & Taylor, 1998) suggests that gang presence in schools extends from metropolitan urban districts to suburbia, small towns, and rural areas. Although gang involvement is associated with lower income households (less than $7,500 a year), it is increasingly noted in households with income levels of $50,000 and higher (Howell & Lynch, 2000). According to the 2009 National Gang Youth Survey, there were an estimated 28,100 gangs or 731,000 gang members identified across roughly 3,500 reporting jurisdictions nationwide. Additionally, gang prevalence and activity rates showed an increase in 2009 (34.5%) when compared to the reported 32.4% in 2008 (Egley & Howell, 2011). Student self-reports of victimization at school such as theft, theft by force or with use of weapon, and physical assault all appear to be more prevalent when gangs have been identified in a school. Although gang involvement is commonly identified in students age 13 and older, it is seen in all levels of education, including elementary through secondary levels. It is apparent that regardless of household income, residence, or school grade level, gang presence in public schools is constant.

The Importance of Collaboration

A collaborative effort can ultimately lead to more successful reduction in gang prevalence in schools and the community. For example, increasing school security and suppression alone is not typically as successful as when they are combined with intervention and prevention measures. Research suggests that gang violence can be reduced through a comprehensive gang initiative that includes a combination of suppression, prevention, and intervention (Police Executive Research Forum, 1999). School security/suppression efforts can be effective if used in conjunction with community involvement and intervention programs that take place during school hours (Gottfredson & Gottfredson, 1999). Since our last publication, the appropriate assessment of students' attitudes and beliefs systems as well as their environmental perceptions of their school and neighborhood community have been shown to be crucial. School social workers are encouraged to look at the school and neighborhood dynamics that exist and, more importantly, to work with students to examine their perceptions of these environments given that these perceptions ultimately form the realities of each student regardless of conditions reported by data and other reports.

The Social and Psychological Paradigm of Gang Involvement

Human beings have basic social and emotional need for love, protection, identity, respect, friendship, loyalty, personal power, responsibility, rewards, consequences, and rituals/rites of passage. These needs are often met for teenagers through their connections to family, schools, peers, and peer organizations. For gang members, needs such as belonging, protection, power, and family tradition are met through gang affiliation. The need to connect with others who share a common language or culture can be a strong factor, as well as the need to identify with others who share the common experience of poverty, violence, racism, and poor access to economic and educational opportunities. The primary goal of gang intervention programs is to have more of these needs met by family, school, and community, and fewer by gangs.

Through a school-based gang intervention program, youth can be helped to redefine how they use their value system and their innate social and leadership skills to get their needs met in a prosocial manner. Many gang-involved youth have such skills but are using their abilities to lead themselves and others down a dangerous path. The skills they use to participate in illegal and dangerous behaviors are the same skills they can use to complete high school, get a job, have positive relationships, participate in meaningful and positive activities, and seek postsecondary education and careers. An effective intervention program can guide them to discover better uses for these skills and shift them to activities that will provide better outcomes for their lives.

Many gang-involved youth come from disadvantaged backgrounds, and a frequent misconception is that their parents do not care about their education and are neglectful. This is not usually the case. In fact, if a parent's educational experience is from another country, culture, or religious background, this may affect the way in which they view the access to educational opportunities. Thus, if parents did not attend high school or college themselves, it is difficult for them to guide their children through experiences that they themselves have not had and advocate on their children's behalf. This is where the social worker can be crucial in engaging the family with exposing the youth to as many career and educational opportunities as possible and exploring activities that can positively channel the incredible adolescent energy.

Gang-involved populations are often completely disengaged from traditional school roles and activities such as student government, athletics, band, chorus or drama. Tables 40.1 and 40.2 are two tools that can be used to help assess a student's attitude and belief framework in regards to school importance and connection and assess a student's engagement level with regards to school. There are many opportunities within a comprehensive gang intervention program to assist youth in redefining their school experience and reengaging them in the school culture. As the intervention program expands and a greater sense of belonging and self-worth begins to manifest, opportunities build upon each other, and changes become more rapid and remarkable.

What We Can Do

A survey of school-based gang prevention and intervention programs by Gottfredson and Gottfredson (1999) offers a look at the gang prevention and intervention methods that have

Table 40.1 Commitment to School—Seattle Social Development Project

These items measure feelings about the importance of school and coursework. Students are asked to check the response that best corresponds with their beliefs.

1. How often do you feel that the schoolwork you are assigned is meaningful and important?

   ☐ Never ☐ Seldom ☐ Sometimes ☐ Often ☐ Almost always

2. How interesting are most of your courses to you?

   ☐ Very interesting and stimulating ☐ Quite interesting ☐ Fairly interesting

   ☐ Slightly dull ☐ Very dull

3. How important do you think the things you are learning in school are going to be for your later life?

   ☐ Very important ☐ Quite important ☐ Fairly important ☐ Slightly important

   ☐ Not at all important

Now, thinking back over the past year in school, how often did you ...

4. Enjoy being in school?

   ☐ Never ☐ Seldom ☐ Sometimes ☐ Often ☐ Almost always

5. Hate being in school?

   ☐ Never ☐ Seldom ☐ Sometimes ☐ Often ☐ Almost always

6. Try to do your best work in school?

   ☐ Never ☐ Seldom ☐ Sometimes ☐ Often ☐ Almost always

Scoring and Analysis: Point values are assigned as follows:

First response	=	5 (For example, in item 1, the first response is "Never." In item 2, the first response is "Very interesting and stimulating.")
Second response	=	4
Third response	=	3
Fourth response	=	2
Fifth response	=	1

Items 2, 3, and 5 should be reverse-coded. Point values are summed for each respondent and divided by the number of items. Higher scores indicate a lower commitment and involvement in school.

Source: Dahlberg, L. L., Toal, S. B., Swahn, M., Behrens, C. B. (2005). *Measuring violence-related attitudes, behaviors, and influences among youths: A compendium of assessment tools* (2nd ed.). Atlanta, GA: Centers for Disease Control and Prevention, National Center for Injury Prevention and Control.

been most successful and productive across the nation. In particular, their report outlines areas that were considered to be rated as best practice when included in a prevention or intervention program. This chapter will highlight models provided by social workers, counselors, psychologists, and other therapeutic professionals. Gottfredson and Gottfredson (1999) found that programs that include these features were more effective:

- a formal assessment or diagnosis
- written treatment goals that are agreed on by the client
- a system that monitors or tracks behavior

Table 40.3 from the report of Gottfredson and Gottfredson (p. 11) describes these and other characteristics that received higher scores in the effectiveness portion of the study.

Table 40.2 Attitudes toward School—Denver Youth Survey

These items measure attitudes toward school (e.g., homework, teachers' opinions). Youths are asked to check the response that best corresponds with their beliefs.

1. Homework is a waste of time.

☐ Strongly agree ☐ Agree ☐ Disagree ☐ Strongly disagree

2. I try hard in school.

☐ Strongly agree ☐ Agree ☐ Disagree ☐ Strongly disagree

3. Education is so important that it's worth it to put up with things about school that I don't like.

☐ Strongly agree ☐ Agree ☐ Disagree ☐ Strongly disagree

4. In general, I like school.

☐ Strongly agree ☐ Agree ☐ Disagree ☐ Strongly disagree

5. I don't care what teachers think of me.

☐ Strongly agree ☐ Agree ☐ Disagree ☐ Strongly disagree

Scoring and Analysis: Point values for items 2–4 are assigned as follows:

Strongly Agree	=	4
Agree	=	3
Disagree	=	2
Strongly Agree	=	1

Items 1 and 5 should be reverse-coded. Point values are summed for each respondent and divided by the number of items. The intended range of scores is 1–4, with a higher score indicating a more positive attitude toward education.

Source: Dahlberg, L. L., Toal, S. B., Swahn, M., Behrens, C. B. (2005). *Measuring violence-related attitudes, behaviors, and influences among youths: A compendium of assessment tools* (2nd ed.). Atlanta, GA: Centers for Disease Control and Prevention, National Center for Injury Prevention and Control.

In addition to this table, Gottfredson and Gottfredson examined program adequacy and program quality for pertinence to program effectiveness. The "overall program adequacy" of programs and models was judged on a scorecard. Those with some or all of the practice measures identified in Table 40.1, in addition to counseling or therapy services offered weekly over a period of several months, were given higher program ratings.

Regarding program quality, Gottfredson and Gottfredson identify numerous factors that should be in place for a program to meet the requirements of a quality program. These factors include the following:

- extensive training of facilitator
- adequate supervision of clients during activity
- school administrative support for the proposed activity
- integration of multiple sources of information and utilization of field experts
- structured activities that have a sense of "scriptedness"
- activities that are part of the regular school day and not scheduled as an after-school program or in addition to the regular school day

The study goes on to address curriculum-based intervention programs and the areas each curriculum should have in place to be considered a best practice method. Overall, the study is a preliminary report, and much of the research on gang prevention or intervention effectiveness examines numerous factors depending on the type of model utilized. In an article entitled

Table 40.3 Measuring Best Practice (*Methods*)—Counseling, Social Work, Psychological, or Therapeutic Activity

- *Sometimes, usually,* or *always* makes formal assessments to understand or diagnose the individual or his/her situation.
- *Always* prepares a written diagnosis or problem statement for each participant.
- *Always* develops written treatment goals for each participating student.
- Student *usually* or *always* agrees to a treatment plan contract.
- A contract to implement a treatment plan is *always* agreed to by the client.
- Specific treatment goals for individuals depend on *individual needs as indicated by assessment.*
- When referrals are made, school-based personnel *contact the provider* to verify that service was provided or to monitor progress.
- The counseling or social work plans *always* include a method for monitoring or tracking student behavior over time.

Source: Gottfredson & Gottfredson (1999), p. 11.

"Responding to Gangs in the School Setting," Arciaga, Sakamoto, and Jones highlight that the OJJDP Strategic Planning Tool, developed by the National Gang Center, provides an outline of research-based interventions that are identified as best practice methods for implementing prevention efforts with schoolchildren ages 6 to about 17. The following is a condensed snapshot of those efforts that schools should consider when looking at intervention services (http://www.nationalgangcenter.gov/SPT; Arciaga, Sakamoto, & Jones, 2010, pp. 3–4:

- provide family strengthening/effectiveness training to improve parenting skills, build life skills in youth, and strengthen family bonds
- promote emotional and social competencies in elementary school-aged children, while simultaneously enhancing the educational process in the classroom
- increase prosocial peer bonds and strengthen students' attachment and commitment to schools
- develop gender-specific programs
- steer at-risk youth from delinquent peers to prosocial groups and provide positive peer modeling
- educate youth to modify their perception that gang membership is beneficial
- provide social support for disadvantaged and at-risk youth from helping teachers, responsible adults, parents, and peers

Preparing the Ground

Conduct a Comprehensive Assessment

As the national economy grew so uncertain, public school districts across the country also began to feel the financial impact of decreased budgets and overwhelming demands to meet student's needs. Given numerous cuts in budgets and a narrowed focus of where financial assistance can be allocated, the necessity for use of instruments that assist in providing quality assessment and outcomes evaluations becomes even more crucial. Assessment and data collection is often the primary factor needed to support and maintain any intervention efforts when looking at creating or sustaining programming for students. However, the downside to creating new tools for data collection and assessment is the amount of time and background knowledge one must have to create a tool that will prove to be both reliable and valid. Nevertheless these instruments are essential. Thankfully, there are numerous tools that have been created and are continually being evaluated for consistency that practitioners can obtain and/or utilize upon gaining permission that can aid them in establishing both baseline data and outcome evaluations. These tools will range from assessment of need, to appropriate assessment of clients for interventions services, to gains and improvements of clients upon provision of services. It is essential, in assessing the school for a gang intervention program, to identify the extent of gang presence and the amount of administrative and staff support needed to move forward. Table 40.4 presents a checklist of conditions that can be used as a general assessment tool to help determine the severity of gang activity in a particular school.

The data that schools maintain on student activity can also reveal conditions leading to an environment vulnerable to aggression, violence, or gang prevalence and can assist in securing administrative support needed to initiate a gang intervention program. The more data demonstrating the need for intervention services, the more support for moving the school toward a proactive approach to reducing or eliminating the chance of gang violence on or near the school campus.

School enrollment rates and dropout rates should be examined, and staff should be alert to pockets of students detached or isolated from general school activity. Mental health staff should become familiar with the dynamics of the surrounding community by examining crime rates and incidence of drug trafficking, violent assaults, gang arrests, and domestic violence. Also significant is the number of child protective service responses to neglect or abuse calls in the area.

The Compendium of Assessment Tools published by the National Center for Injury Prevention and Control of the Centers for Disease Control (CDC) and Prevention (2005) is an excellent resource for practitioners to review for a list of tools that can be utilized for assessment of violence-related behaviors, attitudes, and influences among youth. Included in this chapter are multiple tools from this publication that relate specifically to assessing the needs of youth for gang intervention support.

Table 40.5 (a-g) is a compilation of multiple assessment tools that can assist social workers in assessing youth attitudes/beliefs; environmental conditions; and psychosocial, cognitive, and behavioral arenas to determine appropriateness and necessity for intervention services. These tools can assist the social worker in gaining a clearer understanding of a particular student's beliefs and experiences as it pertains to their home, community conditions, exposure to community violence or problems, and overall exposure and attitudes toward gangs. Lastly, there is a tool included to help social workers gain insight into a student's level of ethnic identity, given gang culture so often tends to have strong ties to ethnic culture and cater to this sense of belonging. All of these factors play a huge role in conducting individual student assessment and can be utilized to determine the level of intervention service that may be needed as well as the amount of community collaboration that may be needed to help support a student, the degree of family transition, and the ethnic composition in the local area. This knowledge will assist in gaining a clear portrait of the community and individual student. Since "zero tolerance" policies do not exist beyond the school, conflicts created in the community often spill onto campus grounds. A well-informed community portrait provides a framework for understanding issues that the school may encounter currently and in the future.

Establish a Foundation: Initiating the Group Process

Implementing a gang intervention program provides a good opportunity to do important work in the organizational systems of the school. In evaluating the effects of gangs on the climate of your school, it is important to meet the staff at their current tolerance level. If they are fed up with constant disputes and violence and believe that the current policies are not working, they may be ready to support a comprehensive intervention program. However, if they are resistant, you must advance more slowly, perhaps by starting a small support group or offering assistance with mediation after a conflict. In either case, it is important to use the assessment tools (refer to Tables 40.4 and 40.5a–g) to gather and organize baseline community and school data to use in advocating for an intervention program.

Program Components

Gang intervention and prevention programs employ multiple levels of practice, including individuals, groups, and larger family, organizational, and community systems. Gang-involved student support groups are the initial and core activity for most school-based gang intervention programs. The following additional components and activities are added as the program expands:

1. Parent involvement
    - parent support groups and/or family therapy
    - fund raising
    - award ceremonies

Table 40.4 Gang Assessment Tool

1. Do you have graffiti on or near your campus?	5 points
2. Do you have crossed-out graffiti on or near your campus?	5 points
3. Do your students wear colors, jewelry, clothing, flash hand signs, or display other behavior that may be gang related?	10 points
4. Are drugs available at or near your school?	5 points
5. Has a significant increase occurred in the number of physical confrontations/stare-downs within the past 12 months in or near your school?	5 points
6. Are weapons increasingly present in your community?	10 points
7. Are beepers, pagers, or cellular phones used by your students?	10 points
8. Have you had a drive-by shooting at or around your school?	15 points
9. Have you had a "show-by" display of weapons at or around your school?	10 points
10. Is your truancy rate increasing?	5 points
11. Are an increasing number of racial incidents occurring in your community or school?	5 points
12. Does your community have a history of gangs?	10 points
13. Is there an increasing presence of "informal social groups" with unusual (aggressive, territorial) names?	15 points

Scoring and Interpretation

15 or less	No significant gang problem exists.
20–40	An emerging gang problem; monitoring and development of a gang plan are recommended.
45–60	Gang problem exists. Establish and implement a systematic gang prevention and intervention plan.
65 or more	Acute gang problem exists, meriting a total prevention, intervention, and suppression effort.

Source: Gangs in schools: Signs, symbols, and solutions by Arnold P. Goldstein and Donald W Kodluboy 1998, pp. 31–32. Adapted from "Gangs vs. schools: Assessing the score in your community" by Ronald D. Stephens, March 1992, School Safety Update (National School Safety Center, 141 Duesenberg Dr., Suite 11, Westlake Village, CA 91362; www.nssc1.org), p. 8.

2. Case management
   - referrals to health/mental health/psychiatric services
   - referrals to income support agencies and housing
   - links to employment opportunities and job training
   - links to sports organizations, clubs, tutoring programs, mentor programs, art programs, theater programs, and so on
3. Mediation and conflict resolution training
   - conflict resolution training for youth and opportunities to use new skills
   - mediation in gang disputes
4. Culturally relevant activities and exposure to new experiences
   - sales of ethnic snack foods that students and parents jointly prepare
   - cultural events such as plays, musical productions, art exhibitions, and so on, especially those that provide strong ties to cultural traditions
   - introduction to established clubs that help students to connect to and have pride in their cultural traditions (BSU [Black Student Union], MEChA [Movimiento Estudiantíl Chicanos de Atzlán], Asian club, Native American Club and so on)

Table 40.5a Stressful Urban Life Events Scale

These items measure stressful life events. Respondents are asked to indicate if they have experienced a traumatic event (e.g., moved to a new home, been robbed, lost a family member or close friend) in the past year.

Item		
1. During the last year, did you get poor grades on your report card?	Yes	No
2. During the last year, have you gotten into trouble with a teacher or principal at school?	Yes	No
3. During the last year, did you get suspended from school?	Yes	No
4. During the last year, did your family move to a new home or apartment?	Yes	No
5. During the last year, has your family had a new baby come into the family?	Yes	No
6. During the last year, has anyone moved out of your home?	Yes	No
7. During the last year, did a family member die?	Yes	No
8. During the last year, did another close relative or friend die?	Yes	No
9. During the last year, has a family member become seriously ill, injured badly, and/or had to stay at the hospital?	Yes	No
10. During the last year, has someone else you know, other than a member of your family, gotten beaten, attacked, or really hurt by others?	Yes	No
11. During the past year, have you seen anyone beaten, shot, or really hurt by someone?	Yes	No
12. During the last year, did you change where you went to school?	Yes	No
13. During the last year, have you seen or been around people shooting guns?	Yes	No
14. During the last year, have you been afraid to go outside and play, or have your parents made you stay inside because of gangs or drugs in your neighborhood?	Yes	No
15. During the last year, have you had to hide someplace because of shootings in your neighborhood?	Yes	No

(This scale originally had 23 items, but 8 were dropped in the adaptation by Attar et al., 1994.)

Scoring and Analysis

Point values are assigned as follows: Yes = 1; No = 0. This measure has five subscales, with the score of each subscale calculated by summing the responses to the items and dividing by the total number of items. The five subscales are:

Hassles: Includes items 1, 2, 13, 14, and 15. A higher score indicates greater exposure to daily life hassles during the past year.

Life Transitions: Includes items 4, 5, 6, and 12. A higher score indicates greater exposure to life transitions during the past year.

Circumscribed Events: Includes items 3, 7, 8, 9, 10, and 11. A higher score indicates greater exposure to discrete stressful events during the past year.

Violence: Includes items 10, 11, 13, 14, and 15. A higher score indicates greater exposure to violence during the past year.

School Problems: Includes items 1, 2, and 3. A higher score indicates greater experience with school problems during the last year.

Source: Dahlberg, L. L., Toal, S. B., Swahn, M., Behrens, C. B. (2005). *Measuring violence-related attitudes, behaviors, and influences among youths: A compendium of assessment tools* (2nd ed.). Atlanta, GA: Centers for Disease Control and Prevention, National Center for Injury Prevention and Control.

Table 40.5b Children's Exposure to Community Violence

These items measure the frequency of exposure (through sight and sound) to violence in one's home and neighborhood. Respondents are asked to indicate how often they have seen or heard certain things around their home and neighborhood (not on TV or in movies).

1. I have heard guns being shot.

   ☐ Never ☐ Once or twice ☐ A few times ☐ Many times

2. I have seen somebody arrested.

   ☐ Never ☐ Once or twice ☐ A few times ☐ Many times

3. I have seen drug deals.

   ☐ Never ☐ Once or twice ☐ A few times ☐ Many times

4. I have seen someone being beaten up.

   ☐ Never ☐ Once or twice ☐ A few times ☐ Many times

5. My house has been broken into.

   ☐ Never ☐ Once or twice ☐ A few times ☐ Many times

6. I have seen somebody get stabbed.

   ☐ Never ☐ Once or twice ☐ A few times ☐ Many times

7. I have seen somebody get shot.

   ☐ Never ☐ Once or twice ☐ A few times ☐ Many times

8. I have seen a gun in my home.

   ☐ Never ☐ Once or twice ☐ A few times ☐ Many times

9. I have seen alcohol such as beer, wine, or hard liquor in my home.

   ☐ Never ☐ Once or twice ☐ A few times ☐ Many times

10. I have seen gangs in my neighborhood.

    ☐ Never ☐ Once or twice ☐ A few times ☐ Many times

11. I have seen somebody pull a gun on another person.

    ☐ Never ☐ Once or twice ☐ A few times ☐ Many times

12. I have seen someone in my home get shot or stabbed.

    ☐ Never ☐ Once or twice ☐ A few times ☐ Many times

Scoring and Analysis:

Point values are assigned as follows:

Never	=	1
Once or twice	=	2
A few times	=	3
Many times	=	4

Point values are summed and then divided by the total number of items. Intended range is 1–4, with a higher score indicating more frequent exposure to acts of crime and violence.

Source: Dahlberg, L. L., Toal, S. B., Swahn, M., Behrens, C. B. (2005). *Measuring violence-related attitudes, behaviors, and influences among youths: A compendium of assessment tools* (2nd ed.). Atlanta, GA: Centers for Disease Control and Prevention, National Center for Injury Prevention and Control.

Table 40.5c Perceived Community Problems—Chicago Youth Development Study

These items measure the extent to which youth and their caregivers feel certain negative qualities are problems in their communities (e.g., unkempt front yards, vacant lots, noise, vandalism). Youth and their caregivers are asked to indicate how strongly they agree or disagree with 14 statements about their neighborhoods.

	Strongly Agree	*Agree*	*Neither*	*Disagree*	*Strongly disagree*
1. Dirty or unkempt front yards are a problem on my block.	1	2	3	4	5
2. There is a public park near to my block.	1	2	3	4	5
3. Vacant lots are a problem on my block.	1	2	3	4	5
4. Morning noise is quite irritating on my block.	1	2	3	4	5
5. Night noise is quite irritating on my block.	1	2	3	4	5
6. Abandoned or boarded-up homes are a problem on my block.	1	2	3	4	5
7. Vandalism is a problem in my neighborhood.	1	2	3	4	5
8. Burglary is a problem in my neighborhood.	1	2	3	4	5
9. Homelessness is a problem in my neighborhood.	1	2	3	4	5
10. Crime has gotten worse in my neighborhood in the last few years.	1	2	3	4	5
	A Little	*Some*	*Pretty Much*	*A Lot*	*A Serious Problem*
11. Gangs are a problem in my neighborhood.	1	2	3	4	5
12. Graffiti is a problem in my neighborhood.	1	2	3	4	5
13. Drugs are a problem in my neighborhood.	1	2	3	4	5
14. Violent crime is a problem in my neighborhood.	1	2	3	4	5

Scoring and Analysis

Point values are assigned as indicated above. Point values are summed and then divided by the number of items. The intended range of scores is 1–5, with a higher score indicating a higher level of neighborhood crime, dilapidation, and disorganization.

Source: Dahlberg, L. L., Toal, S. B., Swahn, M., Behrens, C. B. (2005). *Measuring violence-related attitudes, behaviors, and influences among youths: A compendium of assessment tools* (2nd ed.). Atlanta, GA: Centers for Disease Control and Prevention, National Center for Injury Prevention and Control.

Table 40.5d Neighborhood/Block Conditions

These items measure residents' perceptions of the neighborhood conditions (e.g., severity of problems, sense of safety). Respondents are given a list of common urban problems and are asked to indicate the extent to which each is a problem on their block.

	No problem	*A minor problem*	*A serious problem*
1. Property damage? Is that ...	1	2	3
2. Drug dealing? Is that ...	1	2	3
3. Groups of young people hanging around? Is that ...	1	2	3
4. Physical assaults of people on the street? Is that ...	1	2	3
5. Organized gangs? Is that ...	1	2	3
6. Physical fighting? Is that ...	1	2	3
7. Gunshots? Is that ...	1	2	3
8. Lack of supervised activities for youth? Is that ...	1	2	3
9. Feeling unsafe while out alone on your block during the day? Is that ...	1	2	3
10. Feeling unsafe while out alone on your block during the night? Is that ...	1	2	3
11. Inadequate recreational facilities available for young people? Is that ...	1	2	3
12. Feeling unsafe in your home? Is that ...	1	2	3
13. Poor city services, like trash pick-up and police response? Is that ...	1	2	3

Scoring and Analysis

Point values for responses are summed and then divided by the total number of items. Blank items should not be counted in the number of responses. Higher scores indicate higher levels of perceived problems in residents' neighborhood.

Source: Dahlberg, L. L., Toal, S. B., Swahn, M., Behrens, C. B. (2005). *Measuring violence-related attitudes, behaviors, and influences among youths: A compendium of assessment tools* (2nd ed.). Atlanta, GA: Centers for Disease Control and Prevention, National Center for Injury Prevention and Control.

Table 40.5e Exposure to Gangs—Houston School Cohort Survey

These items measure exposure to gangs and gang membership.

1. Are there gangs in your neighborhood?	☐ Yes	☐ No
2. Are gang members troublemakers?	☐ Yes	☐ No
3. Do you have friends who are gang members?	☐ Yes	☐ No
4. Are there gang members in this school?	☐ Yes	☐ No
5. Would you like to be a gang member?	☐ Yes	☐ No
6. Are you a gang member?	☐ Yes	☐ No

(*continued*)

Table 40.5e *(Continued)*

Scoring and Analysis

Point values are assigned as follows:

Yes = 1

No = 0

Item 2 should be reverse-coded, and then the scale can be scored by adding all point values and dividing by the total number of responses. Blank items are not counted in the number of responses. Higher mean scores indicate higher levels of exposure to gangs and gang members. Lower mean scores indicate lower levels of exposure to or favorability of gangs and gang membership.

Source: Dahlberg, L. L., Toal, S. B., Swahn, M., Behrens, C. B. (2005). *Measuring violence-related attitudes, behaviors, and influences among youths: A compendium of assessment tools* (2nd ed.). Atlanta, GA: Centers for Disease Control and Prevention, National Center for Injury Prevention and Control. *Source:* Dahlberg, L. L., Toal, S. B., Swahn, M., Behrens, C. B. (2005). *Measuring violence-related attitudes, behaviors, and influences among youths: A compendium of assessment tools* (2nd ed.). Atlanta, GA: Centers for Disease Control and Prevention, National Center for Injury Prevention and Control.

Table 40.5f Attitudes Toward Gangs

These items measure attitudes toward gangs. Respondents are asked to indicate how true certain statements about gangs are for them.

	Not true for me	*True for me*
1. I think you are safer, and have protection, if you join a gang.	0	1
2. I will probably join a gang.	0	1
3. Some of my friends at school belong to gangs.	0	1
4. I think it's cool to be in a gang.	0	1
5. My friends would think less of me if I joined a gang.	0	1
6. I believe it is dangerous to join a gang; you will probably end up getting hurt or killed if you belong to a gang.	0	1
7. I think being in a gang makes it more likely that you will get into trouble.	0	1
8. Some people in my family belong to a gang, or used to belong to a gang.	0	1
9. I belong to a gang.	0	1

Scoring and Analysis: Point values are as indicated above. Items 5, 6 and 7 are reverse coded, then a total is derived by summing all items. Higher scores indicate a more positive (accepting) attitude toward gangs.

Source: Dahlberg, L. L., Toal, S. B., Swahn, M., Behrens, C. B. (2005). *Measuring violence-related attitudes, behaviors, and influences among youths: A compendium of assessment tools* (2nd ed.). Atlanta, GA: Centers for Disease Control and Prevention, National Center for Injury Prevention and Control.

Table 40.5g Multigroup Ethnic Identity

This assessment measures aspects of ethnic identification, ethnic practices, and belonging. Respondents are asked to indicate how they feel about or react to their ethnicity or their ethnic group.

1. I have spent time trying to find out more about my own ethnic group, such as its history, traditions, and customs.

   ☐ Strongly agree ☐ Somewhat agree ☐ Somewhat disagree ☐ Strongly disagree

2. I am active in organizations or social groups that include mostly members of my own ethnic group.

   ☐ Strongly agree ☐ Somewhat agree ☐ Somewhat disagree ☐ Strongly disagree

3. I have a clear sense of my ethnic background and what it means for me.

   ☐ Strongly agree ☐ Somewhat agree ☐ Somewhat disagree ☐ Strongly disagree

4. I like meeting and getting to know people from ethnic groups other than my own.

   ☐ Strongly agree ☐ Somewhat agree ☐ Somewhat disagree ☐ Strongly disagree

5. I think a lot about how my life will be affected by the ethnic group I belong to.

   ☐ Strongly agree ☐ Somewhat agree ☐ Somewhat disagree ☐ Strongly disagree

6. I am happy that I am a member of the group I belong to.

   ☐ Strongly agree ☐ Somewhat agree ☐ Somewhat disagree ☐ Strongly disagree

7. I sometimes feel it would be better if different ethnic groups didn't try to mix together.

   ☐ Strongly agree ☐ Somewhat agree ☐ Somewhat disagree ☐ Strongly disagree

8. I am not very clear about the role of my ethnicity in my life.

   ☐ Strongly agree ☐ Somewhat agree ☐ Somewhat disagree ☐ Strongly disagree

9. I often spend time with people from ethnic groups other than my own.

   ☐ Strongly agree ☐ Somewhat agree ☐ Somewhat disagree ☐ Strongly disagree

10. I really have not spent much time trying to learn more about the culture and history of my ethnic group.

    ☐ Strongly agree ☐ Somewhat agree ☐ Somewhat disagree ☐ Strongly disagree

11. I have a strong sense of belonging to my own ethnic group.

    ☐ Strongly agree ☐ Somewhat agree ☐ Somewhat disagree ☐ Strongly disagree

12. I understand pretty well what my ethnic group membership means to me, in terms of how to relate to my own group and other groups.

    ☐ Strongly agree ☐ Somewhat agree ☐ Somewhat disagree ☐ Strongly disagree

13. In order to learn more about my ethnic background, I have often talked to other people about my culture.

    ☐ Strongly agree ☐ Somewhat agree ☐ Somewhat disagree ☐ Strongly disagree

14. I have a lot of pride in my ethnic group and its accomplishments.

    ☐ Strongly agree ☐ Somewhat agree ☐ Somewhat disagree ☐ Strongly disagree

15. I don't try to become friends with people from other ethnic groups.

    ☐ Strongly agree ☐ Somewhat agree ☐ Somewhat disagree ☐ Strongly disagree

(*continued*)

Table 40.5g *(Continued)*

16. I participate in cultural practices of my own group, such as special food, music, or customs.

☐ Strongly agree ☐ Somewhat agree ☐ Somewhat disagree ☐ Strongly disagree

17. I am involved in activities with people from other ethnic groups.

☐ Strongly agree ☐ Somewhat agree ☐ Somewhat disagree ☐ Strongly disagree

18. I feel a strong attachment toward my own ethnic group.

☐ Strongly agree ☐ Somewhat agree ☐ Somewhat disagree ☐ Strongly disagree

19. I enjoy being around people from ethnic groups other than my own.

☐ Strongly agree ☐ Somewhat agree ☐ Somewhat disagree ☐ Strongly disagree

20. I feel good about my cultural or ethnic background.

☐ Strongly agree ☐ Somewhat agree ☐ Somewhat disagree ☐ Strongly disagree

Scoring and Analysis

Point values are assigned as follows:

Strongly agree	=	4
Somewhat agree	=	3
Somewhat disagree	=	2
Strongly disagree	=	1

The total score is derived by reversing the negative items (8 and 10), summing across items, and obtaining a mean. Subscales are as follows: *Affirmation and Belonging* (items 6, 11, 14, 18, and 20), *Ethnic Identity Achievement* (items 1, 3, 5, 8, 10, 12, and 13), and *Ethnic Behaviors* (items 2 and 16). A high score indicates a strong level of ethnic identity; a low score indicates a weak level of ethnic identity.

Source: Dahlberg, L. L., Toal, S. B., Swahn, M., Behrens, C. B. (2005). *Measuring violence-related attitudes, behaviors, and influences among youths: A compendium of assessment tools* (2nd ed.). Atlanta, GA: Centers for Disease Control and Prevention, National Center for Injury Prevention and Control.

- sporting events, car shows, and other events of interest to the youth
- visits to universities, community colleges, technical/vocational schools
- attendance at job/career or college fairs
- participation in school dances, celebrations, and theme days
- planning of an end-of-year event; use fund-raisers to help youth meet their goal
- exposure to fine dining, museums, and cultural centers
- introduction to Experimental Education, ropes courses, rock climbing, and challenging events

5. Service learning
   - volunteer drives for local programs for homeless, children, animals, and so on
   - food drives for the holidays; have the youth help deliver food to families in their neighborhoods (include their families in the giving and receiving of the food)
   - prevention presentations (As the group becomes more established and builds credibility as leaders in their community, have them make presentations to professional groups, college classes, community groups, and children advocacy groups about how to work with gang-involved youth.)
   - service on a youth advisory board for a community organization
   - preparation of a meal that the youth serve to their families at an award ceremony that celebrates their achievements both big and small
6. Community collaborations
   - media coverage for an activity that highlights the youth's strengths and service to community
   - solicitation of financial and in-kind donations from community merchants for scholarships or for entry into an event such as a baseball, basketball, or hockey game; zoo;

water park; restaurant; or cultural/musical/artistic event
- links with adult mentors in the community
- partnerships with local businesses to provide jobs or job mentor opportunities
- collaboration with all outside providers that are working with the youth to provide continuity of care and to avoid duplication of services

7. Collaboration with school staff and administration
   - maintenance of open communication with the students' teachers. If there is a problem, this is an opportunity to assist the youth in problem solving
   - maintenance of open communication with administrators so that you are included in the loop of communication when discipline issues arise; also, taking time to communicate individual and group successes
   - collaborations with school counselors, who can provide educational guidance and information about postsecondary options
   - help from staff for securing caps, gowns, graduation invitations, yearbooks, and other things students may not be able to afford

With numerous other priorities in the school competing for funding and staff resources, such a comprehensive program can be challenging to start. The list above is the ideal.

Additional Training for Practitioners

In establishing a support group and other services for gang-involved students, practitioners may consider professional training in areas specific to this kind of program. Mediation and conflict resolution, multiparty dispute resolution, and aggression replacement training are excellent tools for leaders. Cultural awareness/competency and bilingualism are also assets for staff involved in gang intervention services. Experiential education is a group model that we have found to be a good fit with our gang intervention groups.

Experiential education is a unique teaching and learning process that is applicable to many learning environments, including therapeutic groups. In experiential education, participants learn by doing rather than by being given answers to questions. Participants are asked to actively explore questions and solve problems through direct hands-on experience.

Experiential education is most often understood as a specific set of activities such as outdoor adventures, cooperative games, challenge courses, and ropes courses. The basic experiential learning cycle consists of goal setting, experiencing, processing, generalizing, and applying. The group begins by setting goals and then is given a challenge activity to meet those goals, therefore providing concrete experiences. After the activity, the group processes its observations and reflections. Participants are then able to form abstract concepts and generalize the learning to their own life experience. Once the experience is generalized, they can test it out in new situations.

Establishing a Student Support Group

Here are some guidelines for establishing a support group for gang-affiliated youth in the school:

1. Use a co-facilitation model to provide continuity and support for leaders.
2. Get referrals from an administrator familiar with the discipline history of students involved in gang behaviors on campus.
3. Limit group to 10 people. It should consist of students in the same gang or students associated with the same gang to ensure higher levels of trust. Although, if there are only small pockets of varying gangs, explore their ability to be in the same group and use your professional judgment regarding membership.
4. Meet with students individually about interest in participating in a support group.
5. Check the students' class schedules. Find a time that does not take students out of a core class.
6. Speak individually with teachers about what you are doing and gain their support.
7. Contact parents in person or by phone to tell them about the support group and activities. Send a permission form home (in parents' first language) to obtain parental consent.
8. Meet again with the student for an intake interview and assessment of needs. Talk about the short-term and long-term goals he or she would like to reach. Explain the basics of confidentiality and ask for a commitment to attend at least three group sessions before making a decision about staying or leaving the group. Give students freedom to decide about their own participation in the group.
9. Collect baseline data on behaviors you want the group to affect, such as grades, absences,

suspensions, and discipline reports. This will help you and the student to better evaluate his or her progress throughout the year.

10. Find a consistent private space where there will be no interruptions during the group process. It is important that youth in the group feel they are the priority.
11. Set a schedule. Once established, groups can meet all year, and a session should last 1.5 hours.
12. The ability to be in the support group until graduation provides more group continuity and better outcomes.

Session Format and Content

The first session should be devoted to orientation. After making introductions, defining the limits of confidentiality, and getting the group started on initial activities, allow participants to be the key players in determining the rules, topics of interest, and activities. It is essential that the group members feel a sense of ownership.

Sticking to a predictable format lends stability and consistency to the group process, though the topics and activities will vary. This provides a sense of safety among participants, and the process of following positive rituals may transfer into participants' lives.

This is the format that we have found effective in our own school-based practice:

Snack and Settle:As group members arrive, providing them with a snack and time to settle in is a good way to get things started. (Snack food often can be obtained through local donations.) This beginning provides for informal interaction and building ritual into the group session. It meets basic needs for food and safety.

Brain Gym: Once everyone is seated, begin a brain gym activity (for more information, see Brain Gym International in the Resources section) or have a couple of minutes of deep breathing or 2-minute melt (Goldstein, 1998). These activities help the youth to get focused as well as provide ritual for the beginning of the session.

Positive Peer Feedback: Have students design their own cards with their names. At the beginning of each session, have participants select a name card randomly. Ask the students to remember the name on the card and to notice something positive that the person does, says, or contributes during the session.

Check-in: Go around the room and have the youth check in by using a feeling word or two that best describes their feelings at that point in time and the reason they are feeling this way. This check-in gives facilitators an opportunity to see if there is a pressing issue that needs to be addressed immediately or if the scheduled topic or activity can proceed. It also often provides information about an impending dispute that requires intervention.

Business: Next, take a brief time to discuss coming activities, set group goals, or plan a community project. Keep this brief and schedule alternative times to go into more detail or actually participate in the activities.

Topic/Activity: Facilitators should have a menu of activities planned for the session, and this menu should draw from concerns of the youth present and the needs assessed for the group. However, be flexible and ready to change the plan if a gang conflict is arising. Use the session to help the youth understand their feelings about the conflict and identify strategies to confront the situation in a manner that will provide them with dignity, respect, and a way out. The leader can help the group explore the pros and cons of mediation versus a violent confrontation. Some topics and issues that are important to gang-involved youth:

- *Relationships:* family, friends, legal, gang conflicts
- *Social and economic issues:* sexuality, teen pregnancy, parenting, jobs, money, hobbies, youth activities
- *Academic issues:* goals, conflict with teachers, conflict with peers, tutoring, truancy, grades, achievement, post-secondary education plans
- *Self-esteem issues:* self-care, goal setting, acknowledgment
- *Grief and loss issues*
- *Communication and conflict resolution skills*
- *Substance abuse*
- *Aggression and anger management issues*

Once the group has defined goals and decided on topics, as co-facilitators you will plan your group sessions accordingly. For gang-involved participants, experiential education is a group method that tends to feel less intrusive to youth who have been guarded about their feelings and also provides many physical challenges. Leaders must be well trained in experiential education before working with this population. Given that experiential education provides fun, challenge, and opportunities for personal growth, students become quickly enthusiastic about attending group sessions.

Debrief: Use this time to go around the group and ask the participants about one thing that they learned or are taking away from the group session.

Positive feedback: Have the participants take turns giving positive feedback to the person whose name card they selected at the beginning of the session. Be prepared for resistance and insist on only positive feedback.

Check-out: At the closure of the session, have each member briefly disclose their feelings once again. This allows the practitioner to gauge the immediate effect of the group session, and it allows the participants to take note of any shift in their own attitudes or feelings.

Working within the System

In order to foster change at the micro-level for gang-involved youth, working toward systemic change is vital. For example, a youth may show a positive change in attitude toward resolving personal conflict during a group or individual session, but if other gang members are threatening him or he is subject to violence at home and these larger conflicts are not addressed or mediated, the individual may feel unable to make this change.

Collaboration with Juvenile Probation and Parole System

Since many gang-involved youth have criminal records, they often have a court-mandated probation agreement and a juvenile probation and parole officer to monitor their adherence to the agreement. Collaborating with the JPPO will help your interventions coincide with probation mandates and support the youth in reaching their set goals. The group support you are offering, along with individual and family therapy and other culturally relevant activities, may also help the youth meet mandates set forth in their probation agreement, such as counseling, community service, employment, curfew, school attendance, positive interaction with peers, and abstinence from drugs and alcohol. When youth are consistently engaged in positive activities of their choosing, there is much less free time to be involved in negative behaviors. Likewise, there is a positive connection between meaningful participation and other important protective factors for the youth. This outcome is directly linked to research by the Search Institute with regards to developmental assets. The more internal and external assets young people have, the more likely they will grow up healthy, caring, and responsible (Search Institute, 1997, 2006).

Collaboration with Other Stakeholders

Developing collaborative relationships with the school resource officer, security or police officers, school staff, parents, and administration is crucial to your ability to offer appropriate prevention and intervention strategies before, during, and after a conflict. Suppose, for example, there has been a gang altercation on campus, and students have been suspended. Because suspension deals only with immediate discipline issues and does not help resolve the original dispute, the conflict may have grown in magnitude by the time the suspended students return to campus. This is where your credibility with the youth, the police, the administration, and parents is paramount. This rapport will enable you to offer mediation to help resolve the conflict in a socially acceptable and legal manner and may help prevent a lethal altercation. Most youth who are provided with a dignified way out of the situation will want to mediate the conflict.

School social workers play an intricate function in balancing the roles of each stakeholder in the process: police, administrators, parents, and social workers. Police officers have the role of suppression and legal direction, administrators have the role of maintaining school policy, procedure, and discipline, parents have the role of advocate and caretaker of their child, and the social worker has the role of offering therapeutic intervention strategies and coordinating efforts. All these roles must be respected as separate yet equally important in ultimately serving the best interest of students and the safety of the school. Working to this end is often challenging, but the ultimate outcome is worth the collaborative effort.

When there is a peaceful agreement at the end of multiparty gang mediation, gang-involved youth, their parents, school staff and administrators, and the school community experience a sense of relief and safety. This may also demonstrate to the judge, the probation officer, and the police that the disputants are learning nonviolent ways to deal with their conflicts. These skills inevitably provide a benefit to the youth in their probation status. They learn that as they use new skills to confront their conflicts, they earn trust and freedom, something that adolescents highly value. Many of these conflict resolution skills also transfer to interactions with their families, and many experience improved relationships at home.

After the gang members have taken part in the program for a while, you'll begin to see a metamorphosis occur in them. You will be able to see the paradigm shift (Table 40.6). *Respect,* which before was gained by threats, manipulation, and fear, becomes a value that is earned, mutual, and modeled; *power,* which was acquired by guns, force, and violence, becomes an outward sign of inner strength, self-control, and personal empowerment; *friends,* once a means of the ability to provide a car, drugs, alcohol, and money, become people who are supportive, reliable, and caring.

Applying Interventions within a Response to Intervention Framework

Working within a Response to Intervention (RTI) framework, school social workers are naturally in a prime position to contribute their expertise in the areas of early identification, service planning, and service implementation for students when it relates to social, emotional, and behavioral challenges in a school environment. Ultimately, the importance of early identification of students who may be struggling with school, performing at lower-than-expected levels, and requiring more support is a natural practice for many school social workers when conducting client assessments. In fact, school systems that have undertaken the RTI framework should be encouraged to consult with their school social workers as a resource given their specialized

Table 40.6 Paradigm Shift

Gang Definition	*Individual Needs*	*Redefining Through Support Group and Intervention Program*
Jealousy, possessive, manipulative	Love	Unconditional, supportive, caring
Guns, force, violence	Power	Empowerment, inner strength, self-control
Fearless, tough guy	Identity	Unique, individual, personality
"Us" vs. "them"	Trust	Powerful, established with time, rewarding
Threats, fear based, manipulative	Respect	Earned, mutual, modeled
"No rats"	Honesty	Without judgment, safe
Conditional: car, alcohol, drugs	Friends	Supportive, reliable, caring
Conditional	Loyalty	Requires commitment and accountability
High risk, dangerous, illegal	Fun	Natural, childlike, risk taking
Earned by criminal behavior	Honor	Earned through commitment and achievement
Expectation of illegal behavior	Duty	By choice, importance of word
Obey gang rules	Responsibility	Meaningful, important, rewarding
Veterans vs. Pee Wees Older vs. younger/newer	Authority	Veterans support Pee Wees Older support younger/newer
Instant gratification	Rewards	Earned, enjoyable, worthwhile
Severe, deadly, fear based	Consequences	Just, fair, purposeful
Sex, drug use, weapons use, probation, jail, fights, suspension	Rituals/Rites of Passage	Students become teachers, mentors; they graduate, go to college, have careers

training to work with these exact student arenas. However, most of the responsibility of early identification is being placed on the shoulders of teachers and other educators with the requirement that teachers demonstrate that they have exhausted all possible teaching strategies with students and an ongoing pattern of limited student results/progress prior to looking at further referral for assessment and/or a needs assessment for support. This framework has contributed to a rather controversial approach to supporting students and ongoing debates as to the effectiveness of this methodology. Despite where one may stand in regards to this debate, school social workers should be seen as allies in building capacity to not only support early identification methods but also look at strategies for support and support resources and/or program implementation when it comes to services for students. In relation to our proposed gang intervention model, it directly follows those steps outlined in the RTI framework of looking at not only early identification but also accurate assessment for at-risk students and intervention services. Lastly, we propose a systems approach model that incorporates collaboration and outreach with all stakeholders who might play a significant role in supporting a student, from family, to community service providers, to the school itself. Regardless if one is a proponent or opponent of the RTI framework, this does not negate the fact that what has been presented in this chapter supports that if a student demonstrates early school failure, increased at-risk factors, and/or decreased protective factors, he or she is more likely to gravitate toward gangs and/or gang-related behavioral patterns. This substantiates the very basis why early intervention is so desperately needed to adequately support students in school. School social workers who have substantial gang problems within their school environment should be encouraged to speak with their administration as to how a gang intervention program follows those primary methods underlined in RTI and should advocate for implementation of supports.

One challenge that social workers may run into when working to create multidisciplinary teams on their campus to support students at a systems level is that of protecting students' personal information and working within the confines of the Family Educational Rights and Privacy Act (FERPA). However, it is important to remember that FERPA specifies that school personnel can share student information with other collaborative and multidisciplinary members so long as the information shared is related to health and safety emergencies. When addressing gang-related issues, it is rather easy to substantiate that collaborative team efforts are addressing health and safety dangers that gangs pose on campuses and make every effort to document the supporting information and gain parental consent to share all relevant information with other agencies as needed (Arciaga et al., 2010).

Tools and Practice Examples

How One High School Developed a Gang Intervention Program

The gang and racial tension had built to an all-time high in this urban high school. There were daily incidents of violence and threats of violence on the campus. The environment was disruptive, and both students and staff felt unsafe. When the administration asked for faculty advice, the initial and natural responses were suppressive: "stricter policies; more police; more campus security; suspension from school." The school's social worker understood that most of the conflict was not perpetuated by personal disputes among the individuals involved but rather by gang loyalties and activities at the school. This appeared to be an opportune time for the social worker to introduce gang mediation strategies to the administration. However, when the social worker proposed multiparty gang mediation, there was great hesitation and doubt that such an intervention would have any effect. Given the resistance, the social worker offered to use mediation to help resolve individual disputes. A week later, the assistant principal called the social worker to deal with a dispute between two students who were members of rival gangs. When the mediation was held, it became evident that there were many others involved. The immediate disputants were free to speak for themselves but, according to gang culture, were not allowed to speak for others involved. Thus, a number of other (student) members of the two gangs were called into the session as they were identified, and a mutual agreement for peace was reached. No student needed to be suspended, no probation officers had to be called, and, in the end, the session was a multiparty gang mediation process.

This success helped the school administration to consider more favorably the idea of such an intervention.

Later in the year, a huge rival gang fight occurred on the campus, and many students were suspended. Once again the social worker suggested intervening with a multiparty gang mediation, informing administrators that although the fight was over and the participants suspended, the problem had not been resolved. In fact, the suspension time only allowed for the rivals to plan revenge, and rumors were surfacing about the use of weapons. The administration was not comfortable having such an intervention take place on campus, so the social worker offered to intervene off campus. When this was agreeable to school administration, the social worker collaborated with an organization in the community, one that worked with gang-involved youth and was familiar with the disputants, and received permission to conduct the mediation at its facility.

A date and time was set with the disputing gangs, and each member was contacted individually to ask for his participation. The disputants were anxious yet eager to resolve the problem. Many had probation agreements and a lot to lose, including school credits, their freedom, family relationships, and, worst-case scenario, their lives.

The rivals met at an office where they were first searched for weapons and then invited in for a pizza dinner. After pizza, the disputants sat at a business table where they were provided with pencil, pad, and water. The mediation was conducted by co-mediators with other gang intervention specialists present for safety. The disputants agreed to follow mediation rules and mutually decided to speak in Spanish during the mediation. After nearly 3 hours, a peace agreement was reached, and all participants signed.

When the youth returned to school, they found the social worker's office. Because of the rapport built during the mediation process, the students began dropping by and disclosing information about other conflicts in their personal lives. It quickly became evident to the social worker and to her young visitors that their common bond was that they were all dealing with complex and overwhelming life circumstances. They required an outlet other than the maladaptive ways that they were using to manage their problems. The social worker suggested a support group to help the young men with future gang, personal, family, and school problems. The young men agreed, and the onetime rivals participated in a support group that was inevitably the birth of the school's gang prevention and intervention program. The program grew and is still in place at the high school today, containing all the components for a comprehensive program that are described in this chapter.

Further Learning

Brain Gym International: http://www.braingym.org

Office of Juvenile Justice and Delinquency Prevention (OJJDP), National Gang Center Strategic Planning Tool: http://www.nationalgangcenter.gov/SPT

National Youth Gang Center: http://www.iir.com/nygc/publications.htm

Centers for Disease Control and Prevention, Compendium of Assessment Tools: http://www.cdc.gov/ncipc/pub-res/measure.htm

Key Points to Remember

Given the trends in school gang activity, intervention and prevention should not be ignored. Research indicates that intervention services for gang-involved youth can be effective if they incorporate measures identified in this chapter. Initiating a comprehensive gang intervention program requires an extensive assessment of the school and community, support from administration and staff, outreach to community agencies, coordination with the juvenile justice system, and collaboration with community partners. When initiating a comprehensive program is not possible, concentrate on implementing a support group. Other components of the program can be added to this foundation. Practitioners are in a position to profoundly affect the school by redefining the way it approaches working with gang-involved youth. Youth will respond positively to the effort to support and reconnect them to the school community and culture. This outcome can perpetuate a culture in which youth are no longer viewed as gangsters but as strong individuals who can contribute to their community.

References

Arciaga, M., Skamoto, W., & Jones, E. F. (2010). *Responding to gangs in the school setting*. National Gang Center Bulletin. Washington, DC: U.S. Department of Justice, Office of Juvenile Justice and Delinquency Prevention.

Chandler, K. A., Chapman, C. D., Rand, M. R., & Taylor, B. M. (1998). *Students' reports of school crime: 1989 and 1995*. Washington, DC: U.S. Department of Education, Office of Educational Research and Improvement, National Center for Education Statistics, and U.S. Department of Justice, Office of Justice Programs, Bureau of Justice Statistics.

Dahlberg, L. L., Toal, S. B., Swahn, M., & Behrens, C. B. (2005). *Measuring violence-related attitudes, behaviors, and influences among youths: A compendium of assessment tools* (2nd ed.). Atlanta, GA: Centers for Disease Control and Prevention, National Center for Injury Prevention and Control.

Egley, A., & Howell, J. C. (2011). *Highlights of the 2009 National Youth Gang Survey*. Washington, DC: U.S. Department of Justice, Office of Justice Programs, Office of Juvenile Justice and Delinquency Prevention.

Goldstein, A. P. (1998). *The peace curriculum: Expanded aggression replacement training*. Erie, CO: Research Press, Center for Safe Schools and Communities.

Gottfredson, G. D., & Gottfredson, D. C. (1999, July 29). *Survey of school-based gang prevention and intervention programs: Preliminary findings*. Paper presented at the National Youth Gang Symposium, Las Vegas, NV.

Howell, J. C., & Lynch, J. P. (2000). *Youth gangs in schools*. Washington, DC: U.S. Department of Justice, Office of Justice Programs, Office of Juvenile Justice and Delinquency Prevention.

Police Executive Research Forum. (1999). *Addressing community gang problems: A model for problem solving*. Washington, DC: U.S. Department of Justice, Office of Justice Programs, Bureau of Justice Assistance.

Search Institute. (1997, 2006). *40 Developmental Assets for Adolescents (ages 12–18)*. Retrieved May 28, 2011, from www.search-institute.org

PART IV

Crisis Intervention, Group Work, and Parental and Family Resources

SECTION VIII

Effective Crisis Intervention Methods

Crisis intervention occupies a good amount of time of most school-based professionals. This section addresses several different types of crisis situations that schools may face, including suicidal threat of students, natural disasters, violent crises, and grief and loss situations. Each chapter provides best practices to follow and several resources for helping students and school professionals address these situations.

CHAPTER 41

School-Based, Adolescent Suicidality

Lethality Assessments and Crisis Intervention Protocols

Albert R. Roberts Karen S. Knox Miki Tesh

Getting Started

Every 15 minutes, someone in this country commits suicide. This equates to 95 suicides each and every day throughout the United States. Suicides and suicide attempts take place in every age group, ethnic and racial group, gender, socioeconomic status, and geographic area (American Association of Suicidality, 2010). Suicide is a prevalent social problem and public health problem for adults and youths. In 2007, 4320 youth aged 10–24 died by suicide (AAS, 2010). Adolescents and young adults seem to be especially vulnerable. More specifically, suicide is the third leading cause of death among young people between the ages of 10 and 24; accidents and homicides are the first and second (AAS, 2010). Suicide attempts have occurred among children as young as 7 years of age (Roberts & Yeager, 2005). Research reports that male youth die by suicide five times more frequently than females. Native American and Alaskan Native youth have the highest rate of suicide at 14.8 per 100,000, with Anglo youth the next highest at 7.3 per 100,000. Latinas report more attempts than other racial or ethnic groups (11.1%). LGBT youth are three times more likely to have attempted suicide than their straight peers (AAS, 2010). Adolescents and young adults diagnosed with Asperger's syndrome are also at risk for higher rates of suicide, with a study reporting 50% of the sample having a clinically significant level of suicidal ideation (Shtayermman, 2008). Early detection and identification of acutely suicidal adolescents have the potential to dramatically decrease the prevalence of this significant social problem throughout the United States. Most children and youth who have ideas and thoughts about suicide exhibit specific warning signs, symptoms, gestures, and behaviors, which can be recognized by school social workers, mental health consultants, and crisis counselors who are trained in suicide assessment and crisis intervention.

School social workers and mental health consultants to the schools can develop competency in evidence-based suicide risk assessments and interventions. For the most part, suicidal behaviors and impulses are temporary and transient. Evidence-based studies have indicated that most individuals who have killed themselves have given some type of prior warning (Jobes, Berman, & Martin, 2005). The school social workers and mental health counselors are therefore in pivotal life-saving positions. Effective lethality assessments and evidence-based crisis intervention can certainly save lives, especially since most suicidal youth are ambivalent.

Here are three important operational definitions:

1. *Suicide:* the deliberate, intentional, and purposeful act of killing oneself
2. *Ambivalence:* having two mixed and opposing feelings at the same time, such as the desire to live and the desire to die
3. *Lethality:* the potential for a specific method and suicide plan to actually end the individual's life

What We Know

Suicide Warning Signs and Risk Factors

It is important to be aware of precipitating factors or events, risk variables, and biological or socio-cultural factors that seem to put youths at imminent risk of deliberate self-harm and suicide attempts. Common triggering or precipitating events, also known as *the last straw,* include rejection or humiliation, such as a broken romance, being repeatedly bullied or teased, intense verbal abuse by parents, or the death of a parent. The key to whether or not a significant stressful life event leads to suicide or to a productive life is based on the internal meaning and perceptions that each person attaches to the event. For example, Dr. Viktor Frankel lost his wife and entire family in the concentration camps during World War II but instead of giving up, Frankel decided that no matter what torture the Nazis administered, they could not take away his will to live. His classic book, *Man's Search for Meaning,* has inspired hundreds of thousands of readers to never give up and to do their very best to lead productive lives devoted to helping others. A number of risk variables, or suicide warning signs, have been documented (AAS, 2010; Fergusson, Woodward, & Horwood, 2000; Krug, Dahlberg, Mercy, Zwi, & Lozano, 2002; Muehlenkamp, Cowles, & Gutierrez, 2010; Waldrop et al., 2007). These include the following:

- intense emotional pain
- extreme sense of hopelessness and helplessness about oneself
- socially isolated and cut off from other young people
- giving away important personal possessions
- prolonged feelings of emptiness, worthlessness, and/or depression
- prior suicide attempts
- mental confusion
- prior family history of suicide
- past psychiatric history
- presence of weapon
- alcohol or substance abuse
- anger, aggression, or irritability
- childhood physical or sexual abuse
- sleep disturbances
- loss of positive motivation
- loss of interest in pleasurable things
- poor personal cleanliness
- excessive focus on death and dying self-injurious behavior

Specific clues to suicide include statements such as "Life sucks and I might as well end it all," "I'd be better off dead," "I wish I was dead," "I am planning on killing myself," "I bought a new dress to be buried in," or "I borrowed my uncle's gun in order to shoot myself at midnight."

The National Mental Health Association has developed the following list of warning signs of someone considering suicide:

- verbal suicide threats, such as "you'd be better off without me around"
- expressions of hopelessness and helplessness
- personality changes
- depression
- daring or risk-taking behavior
- previous suicide attempts
- giving away prized possessions
- lack of interest in future plans

Protective factors for youth suicide are also important in assessment and include family and school connectedness, safe schools, academic achievement, self-esteem, and reduced access to firearms (AAS, 2010). Protective factors vary within different cultures, and the importance of religion/spirituality and supportive family connectedness must be considered for culturally sensitive assessment and intervention (Goldston et al., 2008). A qualitative study with African American adolescents reported on the role of religion and help-seeking within the church community for suicide interventions (Molock et al., 2007). The importance of family as a protective factor is indicated in empirical studies across ethnic groups, including Chinese, Korean, America Indian, African American, and Hispanic adolescents (Bryant & Harder, 2008; Cheng et al., 2009; Cho & Haslam, 2010; Duarte-Velez & Bernal, 2007; Goldston et al., 2008; Joe, Clarke, Ivey, Kerr, & King, 2007; Medina & Luna, 2006; Walls, Chapple, & Johnson, 2007). Supportive family relationships have been identified as protective factors for LGBT youth also.

Within the current care environment, social workers are required to determine imminent, moderate, and low suicide risk. In doing so, the individual practitioner is required to assign the patient to the most appropriate level of care. The implementation of Roberts's seven-stage model provides appropriate interventions for resolution of moderate and low suicidal ideation immediately upon the individual seeking assistance. Additionally, application of the seven-stage model can provide insight in a nonthreatening manner to assist the patient in development of cognitive stabilization when completing the initial assessment and when the appropriate intervention protocol is followed.

What We Can Do

School Social Workers and Crisis Intervention Center Collaboration

Several states, including Florida, Georgia, Illinois, Massachusetts, Minnesota, New York, Ohio, Pennsylvania, Texas, Utah, Washington, and Wisconsin, maintain several 24-hour telephone crisis intervention and suicide prevention programs. These programs usually work closely with school social workers and other mental health professionals in the community. This service provides a lifeline as well as an entry point to behavioral health care for persons with major depression or suicidal thoughts and ideation. When crisis workers answer the cry for help, their primary duty is to initiate crisis intervention, beginning with rapid lethality and triage assessment and establishing rapport. In essence, crisis intervention and suicide prevention include certain primary steps in an attempt to prevent suicide:

- Conduct a rapid lethality and biopsychosocial assessment.
- Attempt to establish rapport and at the same time communicate a willingness to help the caller in crisis.
- Help the caller in crisis to develop a plan of action which links him or her to community health care and mental health agencies. The most frequent outcome for depressed or suicidal adolescents is that they are either stabilized by the crisis social worker or transported to psychiatric screening and intake at a behavioral health care facility, hospital, or addiction treatment program.

The crisis intervention worker or mental health consultant assumes full responsibility for the case when a suicidal student arrives at school. The person cannot be rushed and handled simply by a referral to another agency. Crisis workers should follow the case until complete transfer of responsibility has been accomplished by some other agency assuming the responsibility. The crisis worker should complete the state-mandated mental health and psychiatric screening reports, which make an initial determination as to whether the person is a danger to himself or others. The ultimate goal of all crisis and suicide prevention services is to strive to relieve intense emotional pain and acute crisis episodes, while helping the person to find positive ways to cope with life (Roberts, 2000; Roberts & Yeager, 2005).

It is imperative for all crisis clinicians to establish rapport with the person in crisis by listening in a patient, hopeful, self-assured, interested, and knowledgeable manner. Skilled crisis workers try to communicate an attitude that the person has done the right thing by contacting them, and they convey willingness and an ability to help. An empathetic ear is provided to the person in crisis in order to relieve her intense stress by active listening. The crisis worker should relate to this person in a confidential, spontaneous, and noninstitutionalized manner (Yeager & Gregoire, 2000).

Suicide Assessment

The author developed a seven-stage crisis intervention protocol in 1990 (Roberts, 1991). The most critical first step in applying Roberts's seven-stage crisis intervention model is conducting a lethality and biopsychosocial risk assessment. This involves a relatively quick assessment of the number and duration of risk factors, including imminent danger and availability of lethal weapons, verbalization of suicide or homicide risk, need for immediate medical attention, positive and negative coping strategies, lack of family or social supports, poor judgment, and current drug or alcohol use (Eaton, 2005; Eaton & Roberts, 2002; Roberts, 1991, 2000).

If possible, a medical assessment should include a brief summary of the presenting problem, any ongoing medical conditions, and current medications (names, dosages, and time of last dose). The highest suicide risk is among persons who express suicidal ideation, present with agitation and impulsivity, have a suicide plan, have access to a lethal weapon, exhibit poor judgment, are delusional and/or exhibiting command hallucinations, and are intoxicated or high on illegal drugs.

After listening to the story of the person in crisis and asking several key questions, the crisis worker makes a determination as to whether or not the individual has a high suicide risk. If the youth has a lethal method (e.g., a firearm) readily available and a specific plan for suicide, or has previously attempted suicide, then he is considered as having a high suicide risk. In sharp contrast, the youths evaluated as low suicide risk still need help, but they are primarily depressed and expressing ambivalent thoughts about what it's like to be in heaven versus hell. They have not yet planned the specific details of suicide. Other youths may be seeking information on how to help a friend or family member or about problems related to a broken romance, loneliness, or a sexually transmitted disease, or they may be in need of emergency medical attention due to illicit drug abuse.

With regard to inpatient versus outpatient psychiatric treatment, the most important determinant should be imminent danger—lethal means to suicide. It is also extremely important for crisis clinicians to make a multiaxial differential diagnosis using the *DSM-IV-TR,* which determines acute or chronic psychosocial stressors, dysfunctional relationships, decreased self-esteem or hopelessness, severe or unremitting anxiety, intimate partner violence, personality disorders (particularly borderline personality disorder), major depressive disorders, bipolar disorders, and comorbidity (American Psychiatric Association, 2003). Several recent studies have found that persons with suicide ideation have comorbid substance abuse and other mental disorders 60–92% of the time (Roberts, Yeager, & Streiner, 2004). Making accurate assessments and predicting short-term risk of suicide (1 to 3 days) has been found to be much more reliable than predicting long-term risk (Simon, 1992). Other serious clues to increased suicidal risk are when a person has no social support network, poor judgment, or poor impulse control and adamantly refuses to sign a contract for safety (Rudd & Joiner, 1998). Other chapters in this volume cover the assessment and evidence-based interventions for mental disorders, intimate partner violence, and substance abuse in schools.

Crisis Intervention

Crisis intervention with children and adolescents is difficult and is difficult to do well. As the acuity of mental health consumers increases and the service delivery system buckles under the increasing pressure of those seeking services, it becomes clear that specific and efficacious interventions and guidelines are needed to keep the process flowing. Members of the National Association of School Psychologists participating in a survey reported that most were school crisis team members, but less than one half had graduate-level training in suicide risk assessment (Debski et al., 2007). There is growing evidence of the risk factors for suicide, including a precipitating event, such as multiple stressors, a traumatic event, major depression, increased substance abuse, deterioration in social or occupational functions, hopelessness, and verbal expressions of suicidal ideation (Weishaar, 2004). For some individuals, dealing with ambivalence—simultaneous thoughts of self-harm and thoughts of immediate gratification and satisfaction—is a day-to-day event. For some, the thought of suicide mistakenly appears to be an immediate fix to an emotionally painful or acutely embarrassing situation that seems insurmountable.

For the depressed, impulsive, and chemically dependent youth, suicide may seem like the easy way out of a downward spiral of emotional pain.

Therefore it may be helpful to include a working definition of crisis:

> *Crisis:* An acute disruption of psychological homeostasis in which one's usual coping mechanisms fail and there exists evidence of distress and functional impairment; the subjective reaction to a stressful life experience that compromises the individual's stability and ability to cope or function. The main cause of a crisis is an intensely stressful, traumatic, or hazardous event, but two other conditions are also necessary: (1) the individual's perception of the event as the cause of considerable upset and/or disruption; and (2) the individual's inability to resolve the disruption by previously used coping mechanisms. Crisis also refers to "an upset in the steady state." It often has five components: a hazardous or traumatic event, a vulnerable state, a precipitating factor, an active crisis state, and the resolution of the crisis. (Roberts, 2002)

The definition of a crisis stated above is particularly applicable to youths in acute suicidal crisis because these individuals usually seek help only after they have experienced a hazardous or traumatic event and are in a vulnerable state, have failed to cope and lessen the crisis through customary coping methods, lack family or community social supports, and want outside help. Acute psychological or situational crisis episodes may be viewed in various ways, but the definition we are using emphasizes that a crisis can be a turning point in a person's life (Roberts & Yeager, 2005).

Crisis intervention generally refers to a social worker, behavioral clinician, or crisis counselor entering into the life situation of an individual or family to alleviate the impact of a crisis episode in order to facilitate and mobilize the resources of those directly affected. Rapid assessment and timely intervention on the part of crisis counselors, social workers, psychologists, or child psychiatrists is of paramount importance.

Crisis interveners should be active and directive while displaying a nonjudgmental, accepting, hopeful, and positive attitude. Crisis interveners need to help crisis clients to identify protective factors, inner strengths, psychological hardiness, or resiliency factors which can be utilized for ego bolstering. Effective crisis interveners are able to gauge the seven stages of crisis intervention, while being flexible and realizing that several stages of intervention may overlap. Crisis intervention should culminate with a restoration of cognitive functioning, crisis resolution, and cognitive mastery (Roberts, 2000).

Applying Interventions within a Response to Intervention Framework

The Response to Intervention (RTI) framework is helpful in applying school-based suicide screening, prevention, and intervention plans to students, families, and school personnel. The RTI framework consists of three levels: Tier I levels target the entire school population and would consist of screening all students for suicide and associated risk factors. The Columbia Teen Screen program administers the Columbia Suicide Screen (CSS) to students to complete that has questions about risk factors such as suicidal ideation, prior suicide attempts, depression, anxiety, and substance use (Scott et al., 2010). Students who screen positive in Tier 1 are then seen by a school psychologist, counselor, or social worker for a second assessment and evaluation, which are Tier 2 services. Tier 2 service also include individual and group counseling, mental health referrals, and case management services for at-risk students. Tier 3 services target students who are in active crisis and may need inpatient treatment or hospitalization. Tier 3 services would include working with the student's parents, friends, and other students or school personnel who may be affected by the crisis or suicide attempt. The Sources of Strength Suicide Prevention Program is an example of how the RTI framework is applied. This school-based suicide prevention program's goal is to reduce individual risk factors by increasing identification and referral for students at high risk for suicide. Tier 1 involves direct screening of school populations for mood, substance abuse, and suicide problems; Tier 2 involves training school staff to increase identification and referral of suicidal students; and Tier 3 is a hybrid program combining psychoeducational curricula with screening to increase student self-referrals (Wyman et al., 2010).

Tools and Practice Examples

A description of current suicide prevention assessments and intervention tools for adolescents is provided in Table 41.1 for use as resources for school-based mental health professionals. Below is a case scenario. How would you assess the situation and how should the school social worker or mental health counselor respond?

Synopsis: Maryann

Maryann has barricaded herself in the teachers' lounge for the past 2 hours. She has called her cousin on her cell phone to offer him her favorite CDs. Her mother, Mrs. Smith, is a social studies teacher in the school. Maryann has just broken up with her boyfriend and had taken an overdose of sleeping pills 8 months ago in a similar situation.

At that previous time, Maryann had been rushed to the ER as she was distraught about the breakup with her previous boyfriend. Making matters worse, Maryann lost her father within the past year from cirrhosis of the liver. Maryann's mother usually drives her daughter home from school at 2:30 p.m. It is 4:30 and the janitor and Mrs. Smith recently found out that Maryann has barricaded herself in the teacher's lounge. Maryann has been crying. She refuses to come out, has barricaded the door with furniture, refuses to talk, and has asked her mother to put a large bottle of soda outside the lounge. Finally, Maryann said that she plans to sleep in the lounge and not come out until the morning. It is unclear whether or not Maryann has illegal drugs with her.

Application of Roberts's Seven-Stage Crisis Intervention Model

After reading the above case synopsis and reviewing the suicide risk assessment flow chart (Figure 41.1), would your preliminary rapid assessment rate Maryann as low, moderate, or high suicide risk?

It is important to keep in mind that while many persons at high risk of suicide have expressed/exhibited a specific suicide plan and availability of a lethal method (e.g., firearms or a rope or belt for hanging), there are exceptions. There is a relatively small group of individuals who do not talk to anyone before making a lethal suicide attempt but do give clear clues of imminent suicide risk, for example, the honors high school student who fails a course for the first time and can't sleep may be in imminent danger. Although he has never had a problem sleeping and has been an honor student for the past 3 years, he may magnify the inconvenience of retaking a course as the worst and most shameful thing ever. Another example would be a youth or young adult who never expressed paranoid delusions and now has expressed irrational fears that a violent gang with 100 members is after him and will try to kill him tonight. These delusions are an outgrowth of a drug-induced psychosis. *Psychiatric screeners, crisis workers, counselors, social workers, family members, and close friends should be made aware of the fact that a critical clue to suicidal ideation and/or suicide attempts includes a drastic change in behavior patterns, daily routine, or actions* (e.g., youths barricading themselves in their rooms for 24 hours and refusing to come out to eat or go to the bathroom, giving away prized possessions, having paranoid delusions or command hallucinations (e.g., hearing voices that tell them to harm themselves) for the first time, or talking about how wonderful it would be to go to heaven to be with a recently deceased and loving father) (Roberts & Yeager, 2005).

The school social worker needs to determine whether Maryann is at moderate to high risk of lethality and whether she needs to immediately call the 24-hour crisis center. The preliminary lethality assessment is based on the following six high-risk factors:

1. This is the first time that Maryann has ever barricaded herself in the teachers' lounge.
2. She seems to be depressed as shown by her not eating for 24 hours and crying for many hours.
3. She had a previous suicide attempt only 8 months ago.
4. She just gave away prized possessions—all of her favorite CDs.
5. Her father, to whom she was close, died less than 12 months ago.
6. She refuses to communicate with anyone.

You are the school social worker or crisis counselor, and you are dispatched to the school. The following application focuses on what you should say and do when you arrive. We describe this crisis situation with specific details and statements on ways in which to apply each of the seven stages

Table 41.1

Suicide Tools & Assessments	*Current Reference*	*Original and Other References*	*Description*
IS PATH WARM (Acronym)	Berman, A. L. (2009). School-based suicide prevention: Research advances and practice implications. *School Psychology Review, 38*(2), 233–238.	American Association of Suicidality: http://www.suicidology.org/web/guest/stats-and-tools/warning-signs	Risk assessment acronym, IS PATH WARM: I Ideation; S Substance abuse; P Purposelessness; A Anxiety; T Trapped; H Hopelessness; W Withdrawal A Anger; R Recklessness; M Mood changes
C-CASA: Columbia Classification Algorithm of Suicide Assessment	Bursztein, C., & Apter, A. (2009). Adolescent suicide. *Current Opinion in Psychiatry, 22*(1), 1.	Posner, K., Oquendo, M. A., Gould, M., et al. (2007). Columbia Classification Algorithm of Suicide Assessment (C-CASA): Classification of suicidal events in the FDA's pediatric suicidal risk analysis of antidepressants. *Am J Psychiatry, 164*, 1035–1043.	Rating system that looks at the suicidal risk when antidepressant medication is used.
SRA: Suicide Risk Assessment	Fallucco, E. M., Hanson, M.D., & Glowinski, A.L. (2010). Teaching pediatric residents to assess adolescent suicide risk with a standardized patient module. *Pediatrics, 125*(5), 953.		Risk assessment acronym, AFRAID: A Affective/Anxiety disorder, F Family conflict, R Revolver, A Attempt history, I Impulsive aggression, D Drugs/alcohol.
C-CARE/CAST & C-CARE (Counselor Care)	Miller, D. N., Eckert, T. L., & Mazza, J.J. (2009). Suicide prevention programs in the schools: A review and public health perspective. *School Psychology Review, 38*(2), 168–188.	Randell, B. P., Eggert, L. L., Pike, K. C. (2001). Immediate post intervention effects of two brief youth suicide prevention interventions. *Suicide and Live Threatening Behavior, 31*, 41–46. & http://www.sdsuicideprevention.org/pdf/contentmgmt/ccare_cast.pdf	School-based suicide risk intervention program that focuses on coping, problem solving, cognitive strategies, reinforcing strengths, stopping risky behaviors, and increasing support. It includes counseling and group sessions. It is a brief motivational counseling intervention, in 2 sessions.

(continued)

Table 41.1 *(Continued)*

Suicide Tools & Assessments	*Current Reference*	*Original and Other References*	*Description*
SOS: Signs of Suicide	Miller, D. N., Eckert, T. L., & Mazza, J. J. (2009). Suicide prevention programs in the schools: A review and public health perspective. *School Psychology Review, 38*(2), 168–188.	Aseltine, R. H., & DeMartino, R. (2004). An outcome evaluation of the SOS suicide prevention program. *American Journal of Public Health, 94*, 446–451. http://www.dmh.state.ms.us/pdf/SOS%20HighSchool%20overview%20for%20website.pdf	School-based suicide prevention program, which includes a self-report tool of suicide attempts and suicidal ideation.
ZLSD: Zuni Live Skills Development	Miller, D. N., Eckert, T. L., & Mazza, J. J. (2009). Suicide prevention programs in the schools: A review and public health perspective. *School Psychology Review, 38*(2), 168–188.	LaFromboise, T., & Howard-Pitney, B. (1995). The Zuni life skills development curriculum: Description and evaluation of a suicide prevention program. *Journal of Counseling Psychology, 42*, 479–486.	School curriculum that provides suicide education and interventions that address risky behaviors
CASE: Chronological Assessment of Suicide Events	Shea, S. C. (2009). Suicide assessment: Part 1: Uncovering suicidal intent, a sophisticated art. *Psychiatric Times, 26*(12), 17–19.	Shea, S. C. (1998). The chronological assessment of suicide events: A practical interviewing strategy for the elicitation of suicidal ideation. *Journal of Clinical Psychiatry, 59*(20), 58–72.	A specific approach where the clinician elicits thoughts of suicide from the person, providing a safe and comforting environment so that the person will, in the future, remember the positive experience and reach for the phone to talk to someone, instead of reaching for the gun

CAMS: Collaborative Assessment and Management of Suicidality	Shea, S. C. (2009). Suicide assessment: Part 1: Uncovering suicidal intent, a sophisticated art. *Psychiatric Times, 26*(12), 17–19.	Jobes, D. A. (2006). *Managing suicidal risk: A collaborative approach.* New York, NY: Guilford Press.	Includes gathering information on risk factors and warning signs, collecting information on a person's suicidal ideation and plan, assessing risk, and providing an intervention. It takes a multidimensional approach focused on strengthening therapeutic alliance.
Suicide Prevention Toolkit for Rural Primary Care	Taliaferro, L. A., & Borowsky, I. W. (2011). Perspective: Physician education: A promising strategy to prevent adolescent suicide. *Academic Medicine, 86*(3), 342.	Suicide Prevention Resource Center (SPRC) www.sprc.org/pctoolkit/index.asp Western Interstate Commission on Higher Education and Suicide Prevention Resource Center (2009)	The focus is on educating clinicians and office staff on suicide risks, developing mental health partnerships, managing patients, changing policies, and educating patients. It is a Web-based tool designed for a primary health care setting, focusing on resource connections with other services in rural settings.
ISO-30: Inventory of Suicide Orientation	Varghese, P., & Gray B. P. (2011). Suicide assessment of adolescents in the primary care setting. *The Journal for Nurse Practitioners,* 7(3), 186–192.	King, J., & Kowalchuk, B. (1994). Manual for ISO-30 Adolescent: Inventory of Suicide Orientation-30. Minneapolis, MN: National Computer Systems.	This is a 30-question, self-administered test for youth that determines overall suicidal ideation and hopelessness. It takes about 10 minutes to complete. It is designed for adolescents 13–18 years old.

(continued)

Table 41.1 *(Continued)*

Suicide Tools & Assessments	*Current Reference*	*Original and Other References*	*Description*
SSI: Beck Scale for Suicide Ideation	Varghese, P., & Gray B. P. (2011). Suicide assessment of adolescents in the primary care setting. *The Journal for Nurse Practitioners,* 7(3), 186–192.	Beck, A. T., & Steer, R. A. (1991). *Beck Scale for Suicide Ideation: Manual.* San Antonio, TX: The Psychological Corporation. Holi, M. M., Pelkonen, M., et al. (2005). Psychometric properties and clinical utility of the Scale for Suicidal Ideation (SSI) in adolescents. *BMC Psychiatry, 5*(1), 8.	This is a 21-question test that is self-administered. It takes about 10 minutes to complete and determines suicidal thinking. It measures intensity, pervasiveness, and future risk of suicidal thoughts in adults.
CES-DC: Center for Epidemiological Studies–Depression Scale for Children	Varghese, P., & Gray B. P. (2011). Suicide assessment of adolescents in the primary care setting. *The Journal for Nurse Practitioners,* 7(3), 186–192.	Center for Epidemiological Studies Depression Scale for Children. http://www.brightfutures.org/mentalhealth/pdf/professionals/bridges/ces_dc.pdf. Accessed May 31, 2010.	This is a 20-question test that determines depression in children and adolescents.
PHQ-2: Patient Health Questionnaire	Varghese, P., & Gray B. P. (2011). Suicide assessment of adolescents in the primary care setting. *The Journal for Nurse Practitioners,* 7(3), 186–192.	Center for Quality Assessment and Improvement in Mental Health. The Patient Health Questionnaire-2 (PHQ-2). http://www.cqaimh.org/pdf/tool_phq2.pdf. Accessed May 31, 2010.	This is two simple and short screening questions, which could be used in any setting to determine depression.

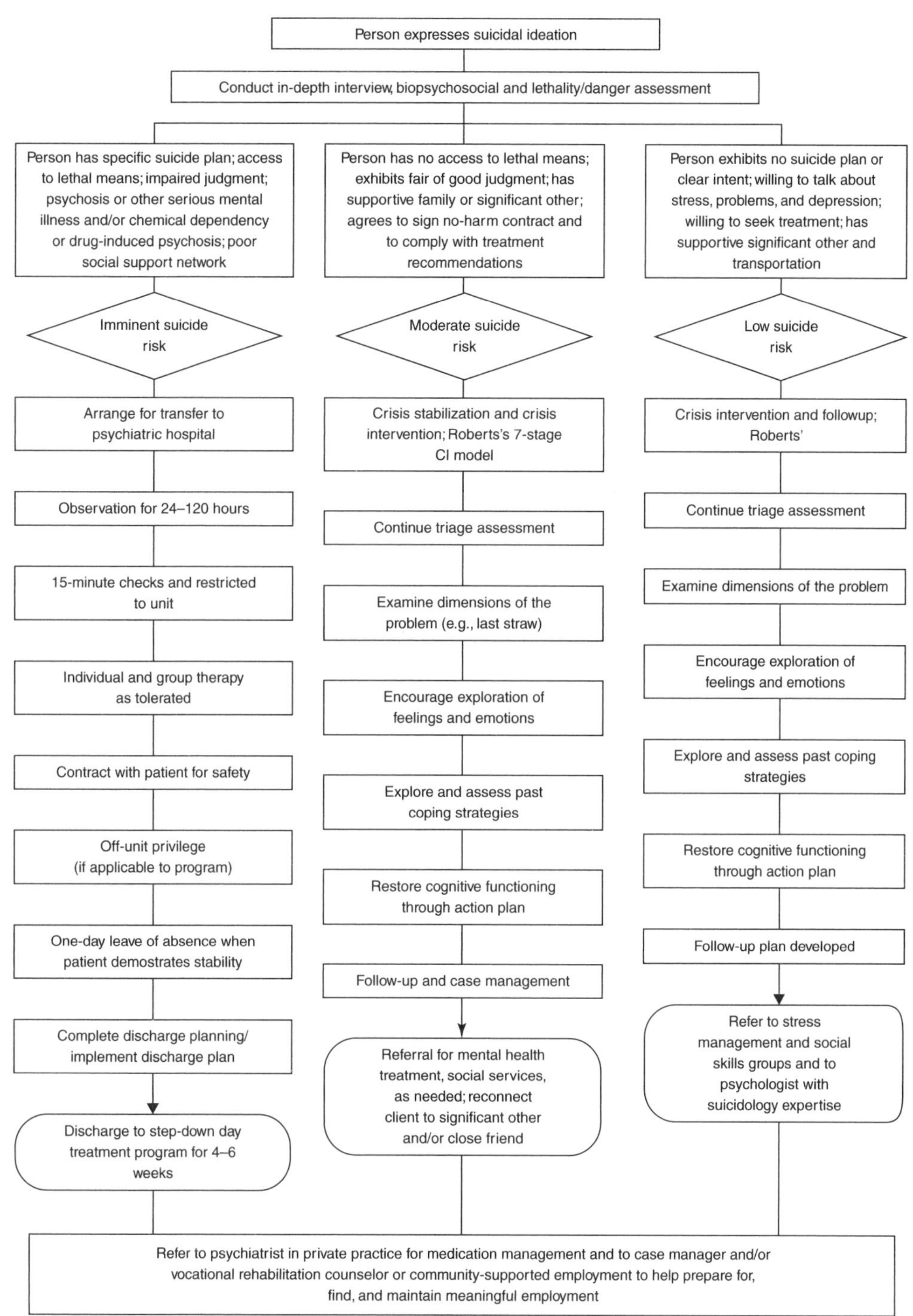

Figure 41.1. Suicide Risk Assessment and Intervention Flowchart

Source: Roberts, A. R., & Yeager, K. (2005). Lethality assessments and crisis intervention with persons presenting with suicide ideation. In A. R. Roberts (Ed.), *Crisis intervention handbook: Assessment, treatment, and research* (3rd ed.). New York: Oxford University Press. Reprinted with permission.

in Roberts's crisis intervention model. First, it is important to be aware that stages 1 and 2 often take place simultaneously. However, in the case of life-threatening and high-risk suicide ideation, child abuse, sexual assault, or domestic violence, the emphasis is on rapid crisis, lethality, and triage assessment.

Stage 1: Assess Lethality by Talking Relatively Quickly to the Mother and Then Patiently to the Teenager

- Ask the mother if the daughter has been taking Acutane for acne. Then, ask the mother if Maryann was ever prescribed any antidepressant medication.
- If yes, does she know if the daughter has been taking her medication, what is the name of it, and who prescribed it?
- Was it prescribed by a family doctor or a psychiatrist?
- Does Maryann have access to her medications or any other drugs?
- Also, upon arrival at the school or outside the teachers' lounge, ask the mother if anything has changed in the past 20–30 minutes (since they reached you) in her daughter's situation.

The crisis worker needs to obtain background information quickly from the mother: rapid collateral assessment. Next, give the mother something to do so she is not in the way (i.e., ask her to call the ex-boyfriend or Maryann's best girlfriend to obtain background data, especially whether or not Maryann has recently taken any illegal drugs).

- Assess Maryann's danger to herself and others (suicidal or homicidal thoughts), substance abuse history, and preexisting mental disorders.
- Ask questions about symptoms, traumatic events, stressful life events, future plans, suicidal ideation, previous suicide attempts, and mental illness.
- Ask about upcoming special events or birthday celebrations that Maryann may be looking forward to, or recollections of happy events or celebrations in the past that may well be repeated in the future (special events can instill hope for the future).
- Determine if Maryann needs immediate medical attention and if there are drugs, sleeping pills, or weapons in her possession.

Rapid Triage Assessment

1. The individual is a danger to herself or others and is exhibiting intense and acute psychiatric symptoms. These students generally require short-term emergency hospitalization and psychopharmacotherapy to protect them from self-harm or from harming other persons. (Priority I requires emergency medical treatment, ambulance or rescue transport, and admission to a psychiatric screening center.)
2. The individual is in a precrisis stage due to ineffective coping skills, a weak support system, or ambivalence about seeking the help of a therapist. These students may have mild or no psychiatric symptoms or suicide risk. They may need one to three sessions of crisis counseling and referral to a support group.
3. The third type of student may have called a suicide prevention program or indicated to a friend or a teacher that she is sad, anxious, lonely, and/or depressed (Roberts, 2002).

It is important to make a determination as to whether or not Maryann needs the mobile crisis intervention team to respond quickly to her home or school. In similar situations, the youth may have just attempted suicide or is planning to attempt suicide shortly or may be experiencing command hallucinations of a violent nature (Priority I). The student may be experiencing delusions and may be unable and fearful of leaving the teachers' lounge (Priority II), or she may be suffering from mood disturbances or depression and fleeting suicidal ideation, with no specific suicidal plan (Priority III: she is probably in need of an appointment with a caring social worker).

Stage 2: Establish Rapport

It is very important to introduce yourself as the school social worker or mental health counselor if Maryann has not met you before and speak in a calm and neutral manner.

- Social workers or mental health counselors should do their best to make a psychological connection to the 16-year-old in a precrisis or acute crisis situation.

- Part of establishing rapport and putting the person at ease involves being nonjudgmental, listening actively, and demonstrating empathy.
- Establish a bridge, bond, or connection by asking Maryann what CDs or posters she likes:
    - "Do you have any posters on your wall at home right now?"
    - "Do you have a favorite TV show?"
    - "Do you have a favorite recording artist?"
- Another alternative approach is brief self-disclosure. For example:
    - When I was 16 years old, my boyfriend broke up with me. I think I understand the emotional pain and sadness you are going through. I thought I loved my boyfriend very much. In fact, he was my first love. He broke up with me for another girl, and I was very sad just like you. But, about 2 months after the breakup, I met someone else and we had a very enjoyable long-term relationship.
- Ask Maryann what her favorite dessert or candy is.
- It is important to understand that many adolescents are impulsive and impatient, may have escape fantasies, and are very sensitive and temperamental. As a result, don't lecture, preach, or moralize. Make concise statements, be caring, display keen interest, and do not make disparaging or insulting statements of any kind.

Stages 3 and 4 sometimes take place simultaneously.

Stage 3: Identify the Major Problem, Including Crisis Precipitants or Triggering Incidents

- Ask questions to determine the final straw or precipitating event that led Maryann into her current situation.
- Focus on the problem or problems and prioritize and focus on the worst problem first.
- Listen carefully for symptoms and clues of suicidal thoughts and intent.
- Make a direct inquiry about suicidal plans and nonverbal gestures or other communication (e.g., diaries, poems, journals, school essays, paintings, or drawings).
- Since most adolescent suicides are impulsive and unplanned, it is important to determine whether or not Maryann has easy access to a lethal weapon or drugs (including sleeping pills, methamphetamines, or barbiturates).

Stage 4: Deal With Feelings and Emotions and Provide Support

- Deal with Maryann's immediate feelings or fears.
- Allow the client to tell her story and why she seems to be feeling so bad.
- Provide preliminary empathy to the impact of Maryann's breakup with her boyfriend.
- Use active listening skills (i.e., paraphrasing, reflection of feelings, summarizing, reassurance, compliments, advice giving, reframing, and probes).
- Normalize the client's experiences.
- Validate and identify her emotions.
- Examine her past coping methods.
- Encourage ventilation of mental and physical feelings.

Stage 5: Exploring Possible Alternatives

First, reestablish balance and homeostasis, also known as equilibrium:

a. Ask Maryann what has helped in the past; for example, what did she do to cope with the loss and grief of losing a loved family member after her father passed away?
b. Initiate solution-based therapy (e.g., use a full or partial miracle question): Let's just suppose that you made it home today and went to sleep and overnight a miracle happened, but you did not know it happened, and you changed your mind about dying. What would be the first thing you would notice that was different when you woke up?
c. Ask her about bright spots from her past (e.g., hobbies, birthday celebrations, sports successes, academic successes, vacations).
d. Mutually explore and suggest new coping options and alternatives.
e. It is important for the crisis worker to jog the client's memories so she can verbalize the last

time everything seemed to be going well and she was in a good mood. Help the client to find untapped resources. If appropriate, it may be helpful to mention that you have specialized in helping youths and have helped hundreds of other teens in crisis.

f. Provide Maryann with a specific phone number of a therapist and a plan to follow. The therapist needs to be someone who is willing and able to work with challenging and difficult adolescents in crisis.

Stage 6: Formulating an Action Plan

In this stage, an active role must be taken by the crisis worker; however, the success of any intervention plan depends on the client's level of involvement, participation, and commitment. The crisis worker must help Maryann look at both the short-term and long-range impacts in planning intervention. The main goals are to help the client achieve an appropriate level of functioning and maintain adaptive coping skills and resources. It is important to have a manageable treatment plan, so the client can follow through and be successful. Do not overwhelm the client with too many tasks or strategies, which may set the client up for failure.

Clients must also feel a sense of ownership in the action plan, so that they can increase the level of control and autonomy in their lives and to ensure that they not become dependent on other support persons or resources. Obtaining a commitment from the client to follow through with the action plan and any referrals are important activities for the crisis worker, which can be maximized by using a mutual process in intervention planning. Ongoing assessment and evaluation are essential to determine whether the intervention plan is appropriate and effective in minimizing or resolving the client's identified problems. During this stage, Maryann should be processing and reintegrating the crisis impacts to achieve homeostasis and equilibrium in her life.

Termination should begin when the client has achieved the goals of the action plan or has been referred for additional services through other treatment providers. It is important to realize that many suicide-attempt survivors may need booster sessions from time to time or longer-term therapeutic help in working toward crisis mastery.

Stage 7: Follow-Up Phone Call, In-Person Appointment for Booster Session, or Home Visit

Let Maryann know that she can call you, and give her your beeper number. Let her know that the beeper is for an emergency. In addition, depending on the crisis worker's assessment when leaving the school, it would be useful to schedule a follow-up with the therapist to whom Maryann is being referred, so that there is a team approach. Follow-up also may include a session with the school social worker or crisis worker scheduled for 2 days or one week later (Roberts & Yeager, 2005).

Further Learning

American Association of Suicidology (AAS): www.suicidology.org

American Foundation for Suicide Prevention (AFSP): www.afsp.org

Canadian Association for Suicide Prevention: www.suicideprevention.ca

International Association for Suicide Prevention (IASP): www.med/iasp

National Alliance for the Mentally Ill (NAMI): www.nami.org

National Institute of Mental Health (NIMH): www.nimh.nih.gov

National Strategy for Suicide Prevention: www.mentalhealth.org/suicideprevention

Suicide Information and Education Center: www.siec.ca

Key Points to Remember

- Suicide: the deliberate, intentional, and purposeful act of killing oneself
- Suicidal ideation: thinking, planning, visualizing, and fantasizing about committing suicide
- Lethality assessment: assessing the risk factors and potential for a specific method and suicide plan
- No suicide contract: an agreement and/or written contract stipulating that the client will not commit suicide; usually have contingency plans and action strategies detailing alternatives for the client to seek out and utilize instead of committing suicide

- Risk factors: characteristics and other variables associated with those who engage in suicidal behavior; do not establish a cause of suicidal behavior, they only describe an association.
- Protective factors: characteristics and other variables associated with those who do not engage in suicidal behavior
- Crisis intervention: brief time-limited therapy with clients in active crisis to stabilize and restore the individual to a pre-crisis level of functioning
- Suicide prevention programs: school-based services that screen and assess students at-risk for suicide and depression

References

American Association of Suicidology. (2010). *Suicidal behavior among lesbian, gay, bisexual, and transgender youth fact sheet.* Retrieved June 30, 2011, from www.suicidology.org/web/guest/stats-and-tools/fact-sheets

American Association of Suicidology. (2010). *Youth suicidal behavior fact sheet.* Retrieved June 30, 2011, from www.suicidology.org/web/guest/stats-and-tools/fact-sheets

American Psychiatric Association Steering Committee on Practice Guidelines. (2003). *Practice guideline for the assessment and treatment of patients with suicidal behavior.* Washington, DC: Author.

Berman, A. L. (2009). School-based suicide prevention: Research advances and practice implications. *School Psychology Review, 38*(2), 233–238.

Bryant, C. E., & Harder, J. (2008). Treating suicidality in AfricanAmericanadolescentswithcognitive-behavioral therapy. *Child and Adolescent Social Work Journal, 25,* 1–9. doi: 10.1007/s10560–007–04002

Bursztein, C., & Apter, A. (2009). Adolescent suicide. *Current Opinion in Psychiatry, 22*(1), 1.

Cheng, Y., Tao, M., Riley, L., Kann, L., Ye, L., Tian, X., ...Chen, D. (2009). Protective factors relating to decreased risks of adolescent suicidal behaviour. *Child: Care, Health and Development, 35*(3), 313–322. doi: 10.1111/j.1365–2214.2009.00955.x

Cho, Y. B., & Haslam, N. (2010). Suicidal ideation and distress among immigrant adolescents: The role of acculturation, life stress, and social support. *Journal of Youth and Adolescence, 39,* 370–379. doi:10.1007/s10964–009–9415-y

Debski, J., Spadafore, C. D., Jocob, S., Poole, D. A., & Hixson, M. D. (2007). Suicide intervention: Training, roles, and knowledge of school psychologists. *Psychology in the Schools, 44*(2), 157–170. doi: 10:1002/pits.20213

Duarte-Velez, Y. M., & Bernal, G. (2007). Suicide behavior among Latino and Latina adolescents: Conceptual and methodological issues. *Death Studies, 31,* 435–455. doi:10.1080/07481180701244579

Eaton, Y., & Roberts, A. R. (2002). Frontline crisis intervention: Step-by-step practice guidelines with case applications. In A. R. Roberts and G. J. Greene (Eds.), *Social workers' desk reference* (pp. 89–96). New York: Oxford University Press.

Eaton, Y. M. (2005). The comprehensive crisis intervention model of Safe Harbor Behavioral Health Crisis Services. In A. R. Roberts (Ed.), *Crisis intervention handbook: Assessment, treatment and research* (3rd ed., pp. 619–631). New York: Oxford University Press.

Fallucco, E. M., Hanson, M. D., & Glowinski, A. L. (2010). Teaching pediatric residents to assess adolescent suicide risk with a standardized patient module. *Pediatrics, 125*(5), 953.

Fergusson, D. M., Woodward, L. J., & Horwood, J. (2000). Risk factors and life processes associated with the onset of suicidal behavior during adolescence and early adulthood. *Psychological Medicine, 30,* 23–39.

Goldston, D. B., Molock, S. D., Whitbeck, L. B., Murakami, J. L, Zayas, L. H., & Nagayami Hall, G, C. (2008). Cultural considerations in adolescent suicide prevention and psychosocial treatment. *American Psychologist, 63*(1), 14–31. doi:10.1037/0003–066X.63.1.14

Jobes, D. A., Berman, A. L., & Martin, C. (2005). Adolescent suicidality and crisis intervention. In A. R. Roberts (Ed.), *Crisis intervention handbook* (3rd ed., pp. 395–415). New York: Oxford University Press.

Joe, S., Clarke, J., Ivey, A. Z., Kerr, D., & King, C. A. (2007). Impact of familial factors and psychopathology on suicidality among African American adolescents. *Journal of Human Behavior in the Social Environment, 15*(2/3), 199–218. doi:10.1300/J137v15n02_12

Krug, E. G., Dahlberg, L. L., Mercy, J. A., Zwi, A. B., & Lozano, R. (Eds.). *World report on violence and health.* Geneva: World Health Organization.

Medina, C., & Luna, G. Suicide attempts among adolescent Mexican American students enrolled in special education classes. *Adolescence, 41*(162), 299–312.

Miller, D. N., Eckert, T. L., & Mazza, J. J. (2009). Suicide prevention programs in the schools: A review and public health perspective. *School Psychology Review, 38*(2), 168–188.

Molock, S. D., Barksdale, C., Matlin, S., Puri, R., Cammack, N., & Spann, M. (2007). Qualitative study of suicidality and help-seeking behaviors in African American adolescents. *American Journal of Community Psychology, 40,* 52–63. doi:10.1007/s10464–007–9122–3

Muehlenkamp, J. J., Cowles, M. L., & Gutierrez, P. M. (2010). Validity of the self-harm behavior questionnaire with diverse adolescents. *Journal of Psychopathological Behavior Assessment, 332,* 236–245.

Roberts, A. R. (1991). *Contemporary perspectives on crisis intervention and prevention.* Englewood Cliffs, NJ: Prentice-Hall.

Roberts, A. R. (2000). Glossary. In A. R. Roberts (Ed.), *Crisis intervention handbook: Assessment, treatment and research* (2nd ed., pp. 513–529). New York, NY: Oxford University Press.

Roberts, A. R. (2002). Assessment, crisis intervention and trauma treatment: The Integrative ACT Intervention Model. *Brief Treatment and Crisis Intervention, 2*(1), 1–21.

Roberts, A. R., Yeager, K. R., & Streiner, D. L. (2004). Evidence-based practice with comorbid substance abuse, mental illness and suicidality: Can the evidence be found? *Brief Treatment and Crisis Intervention, 4*(2), 123–136.

Roberts, A. R., & Yeager, K. R. (2005). Lethality assessments and crisis intervention with persons presenting with suicidal ideation. In A. R. Roberts (Ed.), *Crisis intervention handbook: Assessment, treatment and research* (3rd ed., pp. 35–63). New York: Oxford University Press.

Rudd, M., & Joiner, T. (1998). The assessment, management, and treatment of suicidality: Toward clinically informed and balanced standards of care. *Clinical Psychology: Science and Practice, 5*, 135–150.

Scott, M., Wilcox, H., Huo, Y., Turner, J. B., Fisher, P., & Shaffer, D. (2010). School-based screening for suicide risk: Balancing costs and benefits. *American Journal of Public Health, 100*(9), 1648–1652.

Shea, S. C. (2009). Suicide assessment: Part 1: Uncovering suicidal intent, a sophisticated art. *Psychiatric Times, 26*(12), 17–19.

Shtayermman, O. (2008). Suicidal ideation and comorbid disorders in adolescents and young adults diagnosed with Asperger's syndrome: A population at risk. *Journal of Human Behavior in the Social Environment, 18*(3), 301–328.

Simon, R. I. (1992). *Psychiatry and law for clinicians.* Washington, DC: American Psychiatric Press.

Taliaferro, L. A., & Borowsky, I. W. (2011). Perspective: Physician education: A promising strategy to prevent adolescent suicide. *Academic Medicine, 86*(3), 342.

Varghese, P., & Gray B. P. (2011). Suicide assessment of adolescents in the primary care setting. *The Journal for Nurse Practitioners,* 7(3), 186–192.

Waldrop, A. E., Hanson, R. F., Resnick, H. S., Kilpatrick, D. G., Naugle, A. E., & Saunders, B. E. (2007). Risk factors for suicidal behavior among a national sample of adolescents: Implications for prevention. *Journal of Traumatic Stress, 20*(5), 869–879. doi:10.1002/jts.20291

Walls, M. L., Chapple, C. L., & Johnson, K. D. (2007). Strain, emotion, and suicide among American Indian youth. *Deviant Behavior, 28*, 219–246. doi:10.1080/01639620701233100

Weishaar, M. E. (2004). A cognitive-behavioral approach to suicide risk reduction in crisis intervention. In A. R. Roberts and K. Yeager (Eds.), *Evidence-based practice manual: Research and outcome measures in health and human services* (pp. 749–757). New York: Oxford University Press.

Wyman, P. A., Brown, C. H., LoMurray, M., Schmeelk-Cone, K., Petrova, M., Yu, Q.,...Wang, W. (2010). An outcome evaluation of the sources of strength suicide prevention program delivered by adolescent peer leaders in high schools. *American Journal of Public Health, 100*(9), 1649–1653.

Yeager, K. R., & Gregoire, T. K. (2000). Crisis intervention application of brief solution-focused therapy in addictions. In A. R. Roberts (Ed.), *Crisis intervention handbook: Assessment, treatment and research* (2nd ed., pp. 275–306). New York: Oxford University Press.

CHAPTER 42

Developing School-Wide and District-Wide Crisis Prevention/Intervention Protocols for Natural Disasters

Karen S. Knox ▪ Tara Powell ▪ Albert R. Roberts

Getting Started

While schools have historically had emergency response plans for natural disasters, the need for crisis intervention/prevention plans and teams in school settings has become more evident with increases in school violence, terrorist threats/acts, and other traumatic situations. In the past, crisis preparedness may have seemed more important to schools at high risk for natural disasters, but it is clear that being prepared for potential crisis situations and their aftermath is today's reality for all schools. Much has been learned from research and intervention with those experiencing natural disasters and other tragic school incidents, and that knowledge and experience has contributed to more comprehensive planning and development to meet the needs of the local community and school community.

This chapter provides an overview of the research studies and literature on how to develop school crisis intervention/prevention plans and teams and a discussion of the empirical evidence that supports best practices with victims and survivors of natural disasters. A crisis intervention model is presented as a guideline for planning at the regional, district, and school levels. Specific steps for crisis intervention services and debriefing in the aftermath of a natural disaster are also provided, as are resources and Web sites that aid school personnel in crisis preparedness, training, and response. A case example then illustrates how the model can be applied as a school responds to a natural disaster. This article identifies some of the typical issues and impacts of natural disasters, but one must remember that each situation is unique and even the most comprehensive plans cannot anticipate all of the possible scenarios and effects. It is also important to present crisis plans in a supportive way and to emphasize prevention, rather than expectation, to try to minimize any anxiety and fear among those involved.

What We Know

Early empirical research on children and adolescents experiencing natural disasters examines a variety of impact and treatment issues, including specific issues associated with certain types of natural disasters, that is, hurricanes, tornadoes, earthquakes, and floods (Asarnow, Glynn, Pyrnoos, Nahum, Gunthrie, Cantwell, & Franklin, 1999; Feinberg, 1999; Goenjian, Molina, Steinberg, & Fairbanks, 2001; Jones, Fray, Cunningham, & Kaiser, 2001; Shaw, Applegate, & Shorr, 1996; Zenere, 2001). For example, the warning time or advance notice associated with hurricanes can give people time to gather belongings and seek refuge but also allows more time for fear and anxiety to increase. In contrast, the sudden devastation of earthquakes and tornadoes leaves people little time to prepare and may cause more confusion and panic responses.

More recent research on survivors of Hurricane Katrina and the tsunamis focuses on treatment and intervention approaches to establish best practices (Cohen et al., 2009; Brushan & Kumar, 2007; Pfefferbaum, Houston, Wyche, & Van Horn, 2008; Rowe & Liddle, 2008; Salloum, Garside, Irwin, Anderson, & Francois, 2009; Salloum & Overstreet, 2008; Terranova, Boxer, & Morris, 2009). Literature addressing other issues, such as posttraumatic stress disorder symptoms; the impacts of relocation and displacement; coping styles; and developmental, cultural, and ethnic considerations, also contributes to the knowledge base for best practices in this field (Akinsulure-Smith, 2009; Brown, Mistry, & Akinsulure-Smith, 2009; Brown, Mistry, & Bigler, 2007; Evans & Oehler-Stinnett, 2008; Kruczek & Salsman, 2006; Rosen, Greene, Young, & Norris, 2010; Scheeringaet al., 2007; Teasley, 2007). This literature provides insights from previous personal experiences and research studies on how school-based mental health and social work professionals can plan and prepare for and intervene after natural disasters. Empirical studies indicate that trauma-based cognitive behavioral therapy, school-based group CBT, cognitive processing, and eye movement reprocessing and desensitization (EMDR) show evidence of effectiveness with children and adolescent survivors of natural disasters and other traumatic incidents (CATS Consortium, 2008; Rosner, Kruse, & Hagl, 2010; Silverman et al., 2008). Current research emphasizes collaboration among schools, communities, and state and federal organizations and programs; teaching children and adolescents effective coping strategies; fostering supportive relationships among peers and with families; and helping survivors to process their emotions and reactions (Adamson & Peacock, 2007; Brock, Sandoval, & Lewis, 2001; Brown, McQuaid, Farina, Ali, & Winnick-Gelles, 2006; Lazarus, Jimerson, & Brock, 2002; Nickerson, Brock, & Reeves, 2006).

Cultural and ethnic factors can affect how survivors of natural disasters recover. Economically disadvantaged people often live in areas that are geographical fragile or vulnerable to natural disasters with fewer economic resources and greater unmet needs for recovery (Rosen et al., 2010; Teasley, 2007). One study reports on the perception of a sample of African-American children, finding that 40% believe that most of the victims of Hurricane Katrina were "poor, black people" (Brown, Mistry, & Bigler, 2007). It is important to remember that with natural disasters, recovery efforts take place within organizational and community cultures that help people come together for support and healing. Organizations aiding in recovery and relief efforts need to ensure culturally competent personnel and services. An analysis evaluating the extent to which crisis counseling programs provide services to diverse client populations reports that 56% of the sample are at the "precompetence" stage of cultural competence, and that programs offering more culturally competent and diverse service served more members of minority groups (Rosen et al., 2010).

What We Can Do

School-Based Crisis Intervention

Drawing from personal and professional experiences with school crises, literature describing practical guides and steps in developing school crisis plans and teams became available (Allen et al., 2002; Brock, Lazarus, & Jimerson, 2002; Brock, Sandoval, & Lewis, 2001; Eaves, 2001; Newgass & Schonfeld, 2000; Rock, 2000; Sandoval, 2002; Schonfeld, Lichtenstein, Pruett, & Speese-Linehan, 2002; Wanko, 2001; Watson & Watson, 2002). These manuals and handbooks include strategies on how to plan and intervene in specific crisis situations, training curriculums, case vignettes, samples of forms, and ideas for supplies and crisis kits. School crisis planning guides are currently available from the U.S. Department of Education (see Tools section) that use a four-phase model of crisis management: (1) Mitigation/Prevention, (2) Preparedness, (3) Response, and (4) Recovery. Phase 1 requires schools to inventory potential dangers and threats to prevent and reduce injury and property damage. The second phase requires schools to have a crisis management plan and provide training to school personnel and students, and the third phase is the implementation of the crisis plan. The goal of the last phase is to restore the infrastructure and return to the learning environment of the school as soon as possible.

Another current model in use is organized by five main functions: (1) Incident Command, (2) Operations, (3) Planning and Intelligence, (4) Logistics, and (5) Finance. This model is based on Homeland Security's National Incident Management System and allows for greater coordination and collaboration with multiple disaster relief organizations, law enforcement, and first responders (Nickerson, Brock, & Reeves, 2006).

School Crisis Response Model

A school crisis response model should address the levels and types of intervention, as well as the collaboration among the school system, the local community, state resources, and federal programs. School crisis intervention models typically have three levels:

- *Primary prevention* activities, such as emergency response planning and training, crisis drills in schools, establishing a crisis team, and preparing for medical, security, communication, and media responses
- *Secondary intervention* steps during the natural disaster or crisis to minimize its effects and to keep the situation from escalating, including evacuating students to safety, notification to family members and parents, and immediate crisis intervention strategies to address the emotional impacts and physical safety needs of those involved
- *Tertiary intervention* in the aftermath, including debriefing, support groups, short-term counseling, and referral to other community-based programs and long-term services as needed

These three levels of intervention require participation and support from key personnel at different levels or divisions of the school system, from the central administration to school principals and other campus faculty and staff, and may vary depending on the needs of the community and the size and number of school districts and campuses involved. Newgrass and Schonfeld (2000) recommend a hierarchical model as follows:

- *Regional resource team* composed of a multidisciplinary team with representatives from the school administration and mental health, police, academic, and social services, which meets to develop and review programs, protocols, and policies; to provide support and training to district level teams; and to act as an information clearinghouse
- *District level teams* to provide the crisis response oversight for the school system, including central office administrators and mental health staff who oversee district policies and procedures, resource allocation, staff training and supervision, and technical assistance to the schools within the district at the time of crisis
- *School-based crisis teams* consisting of the school administrator(s), the school nurse, social workers, school counselors, teachers, and support and security staff, who provide direct crisis intervention services and ongoing counseling services

This type of crisis response model allows flexibility to meet the needs of different levels of crisis situations from incidents involving only one school campus, to those involving more than one school in a district or the entire community. A comprehensive model must incorporate all of the different levels of intervention and resources to adequately plan for and respond to the variety of school crisis situations that could be anticipated. Coordinating and implementing the many needs involved in a school crisis can be confusing and cause response delays, if previous planning has not been adequate.

The following school crisis response model provides a guide for planning and developing a region-wide plan. While this model doesn't include all of the specific tasks and activities involved at each level, it does give a framework for how to distribute and organize the various steps and procedures that need to be implemented for a timely and coordinated response. Other pertinent issues and obstacles will need to be developed for the unique needs of each school and the surrounding community. For example, larger metropolitan areas with several school districts may have more problems with coordinating services and personnel due to student body size and geographical considerations, while smaller school districts may have limitations in resources and technical assistance.

School Crisis Response Model

School-Based Crisis Teams

The purpose of the school-based crisis team is to delegate and implement the roles and duties that are needed during and after a crisis. Team size varies depending on the size of the school district and individual schools within the district, but typically ranges from four to eight members. If the team is too large, it can be unmanageable and difficult to schedule meetings and trainings. If the team is too small, then there may not be enough members to cover critical tasks. It is recommended that teams be multidisciplinary with members from the school administration, school counselors, social workers, the school nurse, teachers, security officers, and support staff. There should also be alternates or members who serve as backups or on a rotating basis to address potential problems with members being unavailable or suffering burnout. Some suggested roles and tasks for the crisis team members include:

- *team leader*: responsible for planning and presiding at team meetings; oversees the functioning of the team and its members; conducts drills and readiness checks; and reports to district level contacts

- *assistant team leader*: assists in planning and implementing tasks; coordinates training and support services for team members; and is responsible if the team leader is unavailable
- *media coordinator*: serves as the contact person for all media inquiries and as a link with the regional and district teams
- *staff notification coordinator*: establishes and initiates a telephone tree or alternate communication system to notify team members, other school staff, and people affected by the crisis, such as students, families, and staff, in an organized manner
- *in-house communications coordinator*: screens all incoming calls; maintains a phone log; assists the staff notification coordinator; and maintains a phone directory of regional and district-level teams, staff, and community resources
- *crowd management coordinator*: collaborates with the school security personnel, local law enforcement, and emergency departments to supervise evacuation and crowd control procedures and to assure the safe and organized movement of students and staff to minimize the risk of harm
- *evaluator*: designs questionnaires and structured interviews for evaluation; collects data on crisis team performance and outcomes; coordinates debriefing and demobilization procedures with the crisis team members as a part of the evaluation process (Brock, Sandoval, & Lewis, 2001)

Debriefing refers to stress-relieving activities and processing of the incident. Typically, this occurs between 24 and 72 hours after the critical incident and can be done individually and with the team as a group. Debriefing meetings should encourage the team members to support each other and not be critical. The purpose of debriefing is to evaluate whether any crisis team members need to be referred for counseling services and to begin the evaluation process. This type of debriefing is not intended to be therapeutic, as in critical incident stress debriefing or management, and is primarily evaluative in nature. Any clinical intervention services for crisis team members should be done by non-team, qualified professionals outside of the school setting (Williams, 2006).

Demobilization refers to evaluative information-gathering strategies for the purpose of improving responses and prevention planning. Information and feedback are gathered through written surveys or structured interviews with individuals or in a group setting after the crisis situation has been resolved. Information on the school crisis intervention process and procedures, problems with the implementation of the crisis response plan, and other unforeseen circumstances or factors affecting the efforts are examples of the type of information gathered during demobilization.

It is important to have a *building plan* to provide space for medical triage, safety, shelter, communication, and other emergency needs of the law enforcement and medical personnel who are dealing with the immediate crisis situation. There should also be designated support rooms that are adequately staffed by qualified counseling personnel and crisis team members to provide mental health triage, referral, and brief time-limited interventions. School crisis team members need to develop guidelines for referring students and monitoring their status, as well as procedures for getting parental permission for treatment, referrals for ongoing treatment or school-based support groups, and other follow-up services as needed (Schonfeld et al., 2002).

The school crisis team may also need to deal with issues of grief and loss, such as how to convey formally the condolences of the school or class; how to handle personal belongings; appropriate displays of memorials, such as flowers, candles, photos, and so on; attending funeral services; and school memorial or recognition services. The nature and timing of such memorializations need to be given careful thought and planning to ensure that they do not escalate the effects of the crisis situation or prematurely try to create closure (Schonfeld et al., 2002).

Training and resources for school crisis teams require time, money, and effort that many financially burdened school districts may be reluctant to fund. However, there are training curriculums, manuals, and workshops available to assist in this process. School districts may want to cross-train crisis team members at various levels or provide specialized training relevant to the team members' roles and responsibilities. In-service trainers who could conduct workshops on a regular basis as needed would be cost effective and would provide continuity in the training, which should be viewed as an ongoing need. School crisis team members who are professionally qualified to provide direct counseling and crisis intervention services would need more in-depth and specialized training on

Table 42.1 School Crisis Response Model

Level of Intervention	*Regional*	*District*	*School*
Primary Prevention	Community-level crisis response plan and team	Emergency response policies/procedures	Emergency and evacuation plans and drills
	Policies and procedures	Safety and security issues	Prevention programs
	Support and resources	Training and education	Support services
	Networking	Communication systems	Crisis intervention team
Secondary Intervention	Activate community response team and plan involving school, emergency medical personnel, police, mental health and social service providers Technical assistance Networking with community resources	Activate district-level plan and procedures Coordinate school-level crisis teams Link to regional level Communication and media Resource allocation for schools Ongoing support and resources	Activate school crisis plan and teams Emergency and evacuation procedures Notification/ communication Debriefing/demobilization Short-term crisis counseling Referrals for long-term counseling or other services
Tertiary Intervention	Policy and procedures evaluation	Program and response plan evaluation	Memorialization
	Ongoing planning and needs assessment for the region	District team meetings to improve procedures and prevention strategies	Follow up with school crisis team members Practice evaluation of interventions and programs

specific types of crises. Collaboration with community professionals who have experience and expertise in crisis intervention could be another resource for ongoing training and clinical services.

Applying Interventions within a Response to Intervention Framework

The Response to Intervention (RTI) framework is helpful in applying crisis prevention and intervention plans to provide students, families, and school personnel with effective strategies and services. The RTI framework consists of three levels: Tier 1 interventions would provide information and training about the school's crisis prevention and intervention plan and procedures to all students and school personnel to ensure that they are familiar with the emergency procedures. This level would include drills and preparedness activities for students and school personnel, as well as information and protocol procedures for parents in the event of a school emergency or disaster. Tier I interventions would also provide school-wide crisis intervention services and events in the aftermath of a natural disaster.

Tier 2 interventions target students and school personnel who may be at risk for developing PTSD and experiencing continuing problems in recovery from the disaster. This level of intervention would use screening tools or assessment instruments to identify students who need more therapeutic interventions, such as individual and group counseling that can be provided by school social workers, counselors and psychologists. EAP counseling services may be helpful for school personnel, and debriefing services for crisis team members would be included at this level. Tier 3 interventions would be focused primarily with families of students and school personnel to provide referrals for community-based supplemental services and more intensive interventions for those with continuing mental health and trauma-based counseling needs. The following school programs are excellent resources to use within the RTI framework:

www.lausd-oehs.org/docs/ModelSSP/ModelSafeSchoolPlanV2Template.pdf: The Los Angeles Unified School District's Model Safe School Plan offers planning and intervention services at all three tiers with emergency procedures for specific types of school crises.

www.nasponline.org/prepare/index.aspx: The National Association of School Psychologists PREPARE Program is a school crisis prevention and intervention training curriculum for school-based mental health and education professionals.

Tools and Practice Examples

Tools

The following assessment instruments for PTSD were developed for children and used primarily with hurricane, earthquake, and natural disasters:

- Children's PTSD Inventory (Saigh et al., 2000)
- Child Post-Traumatic Stress Disorder Reaction Index (CPTSD-RI), (Steinberg, Brymer, Decker, & Pynoos, 2004)
- Child PTSD Symptom Scale (Foa, Johnson, Feeny, & Treadwell, 2001)
- Kauai Recovery Index (Hamada, Kameoka, Yanagida, & Chemtob, 2003)
- Oklahoma State University Post-Tornado (now Traumatic) Stress Disorder Scale Child Form (OSU PTSDS-CF) (Evans & Oehler-Stinnett, 2008)

School Crisis Team Training Guides and Resources

- Brock, S. E. (2002). Crisis theory: A foundation for the comprehensive crisis prevention and intervention team. In S. E. Brock, P. J. Lazarus, & S. R. Jimerson (Eds.), *Best practices in school crisis prevention and intervention* (pp. 5–17). Bethesda, MD: National Association of School Psychologists.
- Brock, S. E., Sandoval, J., & Lewis, S. (2001). *Preparing for crises in the schools: A manual for building school crisis response teams* (2nd ed.). New York: Wiley.
- www2.ed.gov/admins/lead/safety/crisisplanning.html:
  The U.S. Department of Education's Web site has a crisis planning guide for schools and communities.
- http://crisisguide.neahin.org/crisisguide/:
  The National Education Association Web site has a School Crisis Guide.

Tip Sheets, Helpful Web Sites, and Other Resources

- www.crisisinfo.org: This link to the AAETS Web site provides national standards and resources for university and school-based crises.
- www.nasponline.org/resources/listingc.aspx: The National Association for School Psychologists' Web site has training manuals and literature on best practices for school crisis management and intervention.
- www.ptsd.va.gov: The National Center for PTSD offers a guidebook for clinicians and administrators and information on PTSD in children and adolescents.
- www.schoolcrisisresponse.com: The National Center for Crisis Management offers a practical guide for school crisis response training.

Case Example

Between September 4, 2010, and July of 2011, thousands of earthquakes have struck Christchurch, New Zealand. Although many have been small aftershocks, three large earthquakes ranging from magnitude 6.3 to 7.1 have caused extensive damage to the city, taking numerous lives and destroying much of the city center. Thousands of people have been displaced or lost their homes and jobs, and over 200 have been confirmed dead. Many of those impacted by the quake are children. Moreover, it has been calculated that over 10,000 children attend schools that are so badly damaged they will have to be shut down for safety reasons. One of the hardest hit areas from the numerous earthquakes was Mt. Pleasant, a suburb of Christchurch. Many families are still displaced from their homes or living in undamaged portions of their homes such as garages. It is estimated that 40% of the homes in this suburb will have to be demolished. Parts of the school were destroyed by the impact of the earthquake, and utilities such as water, electricity, and sewage were severely disrupted. As a result the school was closed for three and a half weeks in order to regain power, bring in a water tank, and assess the safety of the buildings.

When the school reopened, school administration noticed the immense emotional needs of the children, their parents, and the staff in the school. Almost all people in the Mt. Pleasant community had experienced some sort of loss from damaged housing, death or injury of a family member, or the diminished sense of safety felt in the wider population of Christchurch. In response to the specific emotional needs of the Mt. Pleasant community, the school swiftly reacted to re-establish a sense of normalcy and provide services to those who were experiencing emotional distress. The school's initial response was to ensure that the teachers' emotional health was intact. The administration met with the teachers to discuss how they were coping and provided release time during the day to any of the staff who were experiencing difficulties or had their own damaged houses to attend to. Class numbers were reduced due to many families moving out of the area, so many teachers were able to double up for support and security. Counselors provided services to school staff to aid in their emotional needs.

To address the emotional needs of the children, teachers were informed about what types of behaviors to expect when the school commenced. For example, the emotional strain on children affected by the earthquake can be exhibited in a variety of ways, including intrusive thoughts, re-experiencing the trauma, avoidance of similar situations around the trauma, hyperarousal, and anger. Additionally, internalizing symptoms (anxiety and depression) and externalizing symptoms (anger and acting out) may be mental health consequences for children who have experienced a disaster. In order to address all the specific needs of the children who were experiencing emotional distress, support teachers were assigned to classrooms to assist staff if there were difficulties with individual students. These support teachers would work with those students who were more adversely impacted by talking and or drawing with them.

The school also set up safety protocols to notify parents by text that their children were safe if an earthquake was to happen again and to teach emergency preparedness measures to all of the students. On the first day of reopening, teachers discussed the preparedness measures and went further to help each child identify their acts of bravery during the earthquake. These statements were read as each child received their "Medal ofValour." The administration also observed that the students were hyper-alert to re-traumatization from any emergency drills, so they used song and talk rather than acting out safety drills. With the many aftershocks, the children knew what to do. Following any aftershocks, the teachers led the children in breathing and relaxation exercises.

The deputy principal led a number of groups using the FRIENDS for Life program for the children displaying the most obvious signs of heightened anxiety from the numerous aftershocks. Many of these children were having difficulty with separation from their parents, sleep issues, and feeling secure at either at home or at school. The FRIENDS for Life program is a cognitive-behavioral program of 10 sessions that teaches children skills to cope with anxiety more effectively and builds emotional resilience, problem-solving abilities, and self-confidence (www.friendsinfo.net/).

The school remained open after the second large earthquake in February, 2011, and continuing aftershocks triggered post-trauma symptoms in some of the children. Another 6.3 quake on June 13 again saw damage to the local area and the school. The school was closed for a further two days, and many children who had made good progress faced emotional setbacks.

The school responded to the children's needs by partnering with mental health professionals from Save the Children to provide psychoeducational programming to both the students and their parents. Administration observed that some parents were suffering from continuous stress from the earthquake, which was also adversely impacting their children. Save the Children's Journey of Hope curricula, an eight-session psychoeducational program catering to the emotional and developmental needs, was then offered to the students (www.savethechildren.org.nz/see/emergencies/ChCh/). The curricula were provided after school, and within a week over 80 children were signed up for the program. The program was implemented through the June session of school. A three-hour, psychoeducational adult Journey of Hope workshop was also offered to the parents before the children's program commenced. This workshop provided stress relief tools and coping mechanisms to parents who were experiencing difficulties with the aftermath of the earthquake and the continuing aftershocks.

As of July 2011, approximately two-thirds of the children enrolled previously have returned to schools in Christchurch, and the rebuilding and recovery efforts are still ongoing. To learn more from the children about their experiences with the earthquake, please read the stories they have shared at http://whenmyhomeshook.co.nz/.

Key Points to Remember

Current literature and research indicate that collaboration and planning between schools and communities are necessary to develop intervention and prevention plans for natural disasters and other types of crisis situations. Important points to address in this effort include:

- *School crisis intervention models* usually have three levels: primary prevention planning and preparation, secondary intervention during the crisis situation, and tertiary intervention in the aftermath.
- *School crisis response levels* are typically at the regional, district, and school levels.
- *School crisis teams* delegate and implement the roles, duties, and responsibilities that are needed during and after a crisis situation and include a team leader; assistant team leader; coordinators for the media, staff notification, in-house communication, and crowd management; and an evaluator.
- *Debriefing* involves stress-relieving and processing activities within 24–72 hours to evaluate team members' need for referral for counseling services.
- *Demobilization* refers to strategies to gather information and feedback from the crisis team members to improve responses and procedures in the future.
- *Impact issues*, such as relocation, parental reactions, coping styles, grief and loss, and developmental, cultural, and ethnic considerations, are important to address in counseling the survivors of natural disasters.
- *Follow-up strategies* to provide support and long-term services from local community organizations and programs should also be included.

Further Learning

www.aaets.com: The American Academy of Experts in Traumatic Stress is a professional organization providing training and continued learning materials.

www.apapracticecentral.org/outreach/disaster/index.aspx: The American Psychological Association's Disaster Response Network Web site has literature and training materials for professionals.

www.disasterassistance.gov: This Web site offers information, resources, and links for disaster response and disaster responses organizations.

www.fema.gov: The Federal Emergency Management Agency's Web site has a section on school crisis for professional and families.

www.keepschoolssafe.org: This Web site has a link for information and resources on disasters and is sponsored by the National Association of Attorney Generals and the National School Boards Association.

www.nctsn.org/: The National Child Traumatic Stress Network—established by Congress in 2000, this organization is a collaboration between academic and community-based service centers to improve the care and services for traumatized children and their families.

www.starrtraining.org: The National Institute for Trauma and Loss in Children's Web site provides trainings and professional materials.

References

Adamson, A. D., & Peacock, G. G. (2007). Crisis response in the public schools: A survey of school psychologists' experiences and perceptions. *Psychology in the Schools, 44*(8), 749–764. doi:10.1002/pits.20263

Akinsulure-Smith, A. M. (2009). Brief psychoeducational group treatment with re-traumatized refugees and asylum seekers. *The Journal for Specialists in Group Work, 34*(2), 137–150. doi:10.1080/01933920902798007

Allen, M., Burt, K., Bryan, E., Carter, D., Orsi, R, & Durkan, L (2002). School counselors' preparation for and participation in crisis intervention. *Professional School Counseling, 6*(2), 96–102.

Asarnow, J., Glynn, S., Pyrnoos, R.S., Nahum, J., Gunthrie, D., Cantwell, D.P., & Franklin, B. (1999). When the earth stops shaking: Earthquake sequelae among children diagnosed for pre-earthquake psychopathology. *Journal of the American Academy of Child & Adolescent Psychiatry, 38,* 1016–1023.

Brock, S. E., Sandoval, J., & Lewis, S. (2001). Preparing for crises in the schools: A manual for building school crisis response teams (2nd ed.). New York: Wiley.

Brock, S. E. (2002). Crisis theory: A foundation for the comprehensive crisis prevention and intervention team. In S. E. Brock, P. J. Lazarus, & S. R. Jimerson (Eds.), *Best practices in school crisis prevention and intervention* (pp. 5–17). Bethesda, MD: National Association of School Psychologists.

Brock, S. E., Lazarus, P. J., & Jimerson, S. R. (Eds.). (2002). *Best practices in school crisis prevention and intervention.* Bethesda, MD: NASP Publications.

Brown, C. S., Mistry, R. S., & Bigler, R. S. (2007). Hurricane Katrina: African American children's perceptions of race, class, and government involvement amid a national crisis. *Analyses of Social Issues and Public Policy,* 7(1), 191–208.

Brown, E. J., McQuaid, J., Farina, L., Ali, R., & Winnick-Gelles, A. (2006). Matching interventions to children's mental health needs: Feasibility and acceptability of a pilot school-based trauma intervention program. *Education and Treatment of Children, 29*(2), 257–286.

Brushan, B. J., & Kumar, J. S. (2007). Emotional distress and posttraumatic stress in children surviving the 2004 tsunami. *Journal of Trauma and Loss, 12,* 245–257. doi:10.1080/15325020600945996

CATS Consortium. (2008). Implementing CBT in traumatized children and adolescents after September 11: Lessons learned from the child and adolescent trauma treatments and services (CATS) project. *Journal of Clinical Child and Adolescent Psychology, 36*(4), 581–592.

Cohen, J. A., Jaycox, L. H., Walker, D. W., Mannarino, A. P., Langley, A. K., & DuClos, J. L. (2009). Treating traumatized children after Hurricane Katrina: Project fleur-de-lis. *Clinical Child Family Psychology Review, 12,* 55–64. doi:10.1007/s10567–009–0039–2

Eaves, C. (2001). The development and implementation of a crisis response team in a school setting. *International Journal of Emergency Mental Health, 3*(1), 35–46.

Evans, L. G., & Oehler-Stinnett, J. (2008). Validity of the OSU post-traumatic stress disorder scale and the behavior assessment system for children self-report of personality with child tornado survivors. *Psychology in the Schools, 45*(2), 121–131. doi:10.1002/pits.20285

Feinberg, T. (1999). The Midwest floods of 1993: Observations of a natural disaster. In A. S. Canter & S. A. Carroll (Eds.), *Crisis prevention & response: A collection of nasp resources* (pp. 223–239). Bethesda, MD: National Association of School Psychologists.

Foa, E. B., Johnson, K. M., Feeny, N. C., & Treadwell, K. R. H. (2001). The child PTSD Symptom Scale (CPSS): A preliminary examination of its psychometric properties. *Journal of Clinical Child Psychology, 30,* 376–384.

Goenjian, A. K., Molina, L., Steinberg, A. M., & Fairbanks, L. A. (2001). Post traumatic stress and depressive reactions among adolescents after Hurricane Mitch. *American Journal of Psychiatry, 158,* 788–794.

Hamada, R. S., Kameoka, V., Yanagida, E., & Chemtob, C. M. (2003). Assessment of elementary school children for disaster-related posttraumatic stress disorder symptoms: The Kauai Recovery Index. *Journal of Nervous & Mental Disease, 191*(4), 268–272.

Jones, R. T., Fray, R., Cunningham, J. D., & Kaiser, L. (2001). The psychological effects of Hurricane Andrew on ethnic minority and Caucasian children and adolescents: A case study. *Cultural Diversity and Ethnic Minority Psychology,* 7, 103–108.

Kruczek, T., & Salsman, J. (2006). Prevention and treatment of posttraumatic stress disorder in the school setting, *Psychology in the Schools, 43*(4), 461–470. doi:10.1002/pits20160

Newgass, S., & Schonfeld, D. (2000). School crisis intervention, crisis prevention, and crisis response. In A. R. Roberts (Ed.), *Crisis intervention handbook: Assessment, treatment, and research* (pp. 209–228). New York, NY: Oxford University Press.

Nickerson, A. B., Brock, S. E., & Reeves, M. A. (2006). School crisis teams within an incident command system. *The California School Psychologist, 11,* 64–72.

Pfefferbaum, B., Houston, J. B., Wyche, K. F., & Van Horn, R. L. (2008). Children displaced by Hurricane Katrina: A focus group study. *Journal of Loss and Trauma, 13,* 303–318. doi:10.1080/15325020701741989

Rock, M. L. (2000). Effective crisis management planning: Creating a collaborative framework. *Education & Treatment of Children, 23*(3), 248–265.

Rosen, C. S., Greene, C. J., Young, H. E., & Norris, F. H. (2010). Tailoring disaster mental health services to diverse needs: An analysis of 36 crisis counseling programs. *Health & Social Work, 35*(3), 211–220.

Rosner, R., Kruse, J., & Hagl, M. (2010). A meta-analysis of interventions for bereaved children and adolescents. *Death Studies, 34,* 99–136. doi: 10.1080/07481180903492422.

Rowe, C. L., & Liddle, H. A. (2008). When the levee breaks: Treating adolescents and families in the aftermath of Hurricane Katrina. *Journal of Marital and Family Therapy, 34*(2), 132–146.

Saigh, P., Yaski, A. E., Oberfield, R. A., Green, B. L., Halamandaris, P. V., Rubenstein, H., ... McHugh, M. (2000). The Children's PTSD Inventory: Development and reliability. *Journal of Traumatic Stress, 30,* 369–380.

Salloum, A., & Overstreet, S. (2008). Evaluation of individual and group grief and trauma interventions for children post disaster. *Journal of Clinical*

Child & Adolescent Psychology, 37(3), 495–507. doi:10.1080/15374410802148194

Salloum, A., Garside, L. W., Irwin, C. L., Anderson, A. D., & Francois, A. H. (2009). Grief and trauma group therapy for children after Hurricane Katrina. *Social Work with Groups, 32*, 64–79. doi:10.1080/016095

Sandoval, J. (Ed.). (2002). *Handbook of crisis counseling, intervention, and prevention in the schools.* Mahwah, NJ: Erlbaum.

Scheeringa, M. S., Salloum, A., Arnberger, R. A., Weems, C. F., Amaya-Jackson, L., & Cohen, J. A. (2007). Feasibility and effectiveness of cognitive-behavioral therapy for post-traumatic stress disorder in preschool children: Two case reports. *Journal of Traumatic Stress, 20*(4), 631–636. doi:10.1002/jts

Schonfeld, D. J., Lichtenstein, R., Pruett, M. K., & Speese-Linehan, D. (2002). How to prepare for and respond to a crisis. Alexandria, VA: Association for Supervision and Curriculum Development.

Shaw, J. A., Applegate, B., & Shorr, C. (1996). Twenty-one month follow up of children to Hurricane Andrew. *Journal of the American Academy of Child & Adolescent Psychiatry, 35*, 359–366.

Silverman, W. K., Ortiz, C. D., Viswesvaran, C., Burns, B. J., Kolko, D. J., Putnam, F. W., & Amaya-Jackson, L. (2008). Evidence-based psychological treatments for children and adolescents exposed to traumatic events. *Journal of Child & Adolescent Psychology, 31*(1), 156–183. doi:10.1080/15374410701818293

Steinberg, A. M., Brymer, M. J., Decker, K. B., & Pynoos, R. S. (2004). The University of California at Los Angeles Post-traumatic Stress Disorder Reaction Index. *Current Psychiatry Reports, 6*, 96–100.

Teasley, M. L. (2007). Organizational cultural competence and disaster relief preparation: Implications for policy and practice. *Journal of Race and Policy*, May, 7–17.

Terranova, A. M., Boxer, P., & Morris, A. S. (2009). Changes in children's peer interactions following a natural disaster: How predisaster bullying and victimization rates changed following Hurricane Katrina. *Psychology in the Schools, 46*(4), 333–347. doi:10.1002/pits.20379

Wanko, M. A. (2001). *Safe schools: Crisis prevention and response.* Lanham, MD: The Scarecrow Press.

Watson, R. J., & Watson, R. S. (2002). *The school as a safe haven.* Westport, CT: Bergin & Garvey.

Williams, M. B. (2006). How schools respond to traumatic events: Debriefing interventions and beyond. *Journal of Aggression, Maltreatment & Trauma, 12*(1/2), 57–81.

Zenere, F. J. (2001). Tremors of trauma: Responding to the El Salvador earthquakes. NASP Communique, 29(7), 10–11.

CHAPTER 43

Immediate School-Based Intervention Following Violent Crises

Shane R. Jimerson · Stephen E. Brock · Jacqueline A. Brown

Getting Started

Amid a decade of shootings and other violent events on school campuses, education professionals are faced with new challenges. While the vast majority of school campuses will never experience a violent death, other forms of school violence, such as assaults, are more common (Robers, Zhang, & Truman, 2010). While there is limited research addressing schools' interventions to these crises, many lessons may be learned from those who have attended to the aftermath of school violence. The lessons learned from these events inform our crisis intervention strategies for working with students at school (Brock & Jimerson, 2012; Brock et al., 2009; Jimerson, Nickerson, Mayer, & Furlong, 2011; Reeves, Nickerson, & Brock, 2011).

This chapter provides a brief review of the practice and theory of school-based crisis intervention. To support the implementation of these activities, this chapter provides a framework for conceptualizing the elements of school crisis intervention, reviews specific school crisis interventions, and discusses relevant research. It concludes with an overview of the school crisis intervention process and provides a case illustration.

What We Know about the Mental Health or Social Problem

We define *crisis interventions* as those activities, typically directed by school-based mental health professionals that address the social and emotional consequences of a crisis event. Recognizing that the form and content of school crisis interventions will change over time (National Institute of Mental Health, 2002), our school crisis intervention framework (the prepare model) consists of a chronological system that divides crisis events into five phases (a) **P**revent and Prepare (for psychological trauma risk), (b) **R**eaffirm (physical health and safety), (c) **E**valuate (physical trauma), (d) **P**rovide Interventions **a**nd **R**espond (to psychological needs), and (e) **E**xamine Effectiveness (of crisis prevention and intervention). Table 43.1 illustrates this conceptualization of the time periods during which the different elements of school crisis intervention occur. This chapter will focus primarily on the reaffirm, evaluate, provide interventions and respond, and examine effectiveness stages of crisis intervention.

Immediate School Crisis Intervention Elements and Relevant Research

No systematic, experimental research has been conducted on violent school crises due to the low incidence rate, as well as the unpredictability of their occurrence. Therefore, the crisis intervention elements discussed below have been validated via anecdotal evidence and by a review of crisis-related literature (Brock et al., 2009).

Immediate Prevention

The classroom-based crisis intervention of the PREPaRE model recognizes that (a) school-associated crisis events can affect a significant percentage of the student body, and b) students may require concrete examples of the commonality

Table 43.1 PREPaRE Model Stages of Prevention and Intervention

Prevent and Prepare	*Reaffirm*	*Evaluate*	*Provide Interventions and Respond*	*Examine Effectiveness*
Prevent and prepare for crises Foster student resiliency Implement and maintain a school crisis team Engage in crisis planning	Reaffirm physical health (water, shelter, food, clothing) Facilitate perceptions of safety and security	Evaluate psychological trauma Assess physical proximity to crisis Assess threat perception (physical or emotional pain) Assess personal vulnerabilities Evaluate crisis reactions and coping behaviors	Re-establish social support systems Provide psychological education and empower survivors Provide immediate psychological first aid Make referrals for long-term mental health	Examine crisis response and whether plan was implemented properly Revise crisis plans Engage in planning that will facilitate efforts for future recovery

Source: Adapted from Brock et al. (2009)

of their crisis experiences and reactions to help them understand that what they are going through is not necessarily abnormal. Group counseling should be given to those students who are secondary or vicarious crisis survivors, and should be offered as a part of a comprehensive crisis program. The primary goals of the PREPaRE model are to re-establish immediate coping ability, ensure that common crisis experiences and reactions are normalized, and ensure that students feel more connected upon hearing common experiences and reactions of fellow peers. In a typical session, the format of the session is first introduced, crisis facts are provided and rumors are dispelled, students share crisis stories, crisis reactions are identified, participants are empowered, and the session is closed by beginning to place the crisis event in the past and moving forward. At the same time, it is important to keep in mind that providing group crisis intervention to a student who does not require psychological first aid may be counterproductive, and that students from different cultural groups may attribute different meanings to the crisis event and how to show respect for the deceased (Bernstein et al., 2007).

Reaffirm Physical Health and Facilitate Perceptions of Safety

Reaffirming physical health includes doing so both within the general student and special student populations. The National Child Traumatic Stress Network and the National Center for PTSD (Brymer et al., 2006) provide suggestions for reaffirming health and safety among the general student population following a crisis. These consist of identifying officials who can address issues surrounding physical safety that are beyond the control of crisis interveners (e.g., law enforcement personnel), removing objects that could cause harm from the school environment (e.g., broken glass), and being sensitive to particular subgroups that may be targets of crisis-related persecution due to their ethnic or religious background or to other affiliations. Suggestions for assisting students with special needs are also provided by Brymer and colleagues, which include ensuring that proper lighting is available to prevent individuals with physical challenges from injuring themselves, and providing students with access to mobility and sensory devices, as well as medication. It is also important that acute needs are responded to for all students and emotionally overwhelmed students are identified and properly supported.

Facilitating perceptions of safety of all students and staff is also critical following a crisis. Unless crisis team members and other caregivers are sure that students are safe and are able to provide them with food or services, it is important that they do not make promises that they are unable to keep (Brymer et al., 2006). Research has emphasized that children are affected by the reactions of their caregivers following a crisis. For example, Ostrowski, Christopher, & Delahanty (2007) found that boys' PTSD symptoms 6 weeks following an injury, and both boys' and girls' PTSD symptoms 7 months following the same injury, were predicted by maternal post-traumatic stress symptoms. Furthermore, findings have indicated that there is a positive correlation between the degree of exposure to a crisis event and subsequent stress reactions (Galea et al., 2007) and that exposure to crisis events via television viewing is also a risk factor for PTSD (Bernstein et al., 2007). Consequently, it is important to minimize exposure to the crisis event itself, its immediate aftermath, and subsequent media coverage to increase a sense of physical safety. Perceptions of safety and security can also be fostered through psychological education and intervention activities, such as providing students with factual information about the reality of the situation.

Evaluate Psychological Trauma

When it comes to crisis situations, it is important to note that individuals will respond differently and will require diverse interventions. Although those who require immediate assistance following crises may be apparent, it is equally important to identify which students do not require additional intervention, to prevent unnecessary crisis exposure and inaccurately communicating that they are unable to independently cope with the crisis. The following factors place individuals at increased risk for psychological trauma:

1. *Physical proximity*: Individuals in close physical proximity to the crisis are at greater risk for developing psychological trauma (Lawyer et al., 2006).
2. *Emotional proximity*: Knowing someone who was a crisis victim is associated with negative mental health outcomes. For example, research has shown that children who had lost a family member during an earthquake were more likely to experience depression (Eksi et al., 2007).
3. *Personal vulnerability factors:* There are both internal and external factors that may increase an individual's vulnerability to trauma. Individual factors include poor emotional regulation, pre-existing mental illness, and avoidance coping. External factors include lack of family resources and support and lack of perceived social support.
4. *Threat perceptions:* Children who perceive the event as being extremely negative are at greater risk for trauma. For example, Groome and Soureti (2004) found that subjective reports of children who reported believing that their lives were in danger after being exposed to an earthquake were associated with greater amounts of anxiety.

Professionals must also bear in mind that there are cultural variations in crisis reactions and grief. For example, in the dominant African-American culture, coping is often viewed as an act of will that is controlled by the individual, and failure to cope is associated with weakness. In the dominant Asian-American culture, feelings and problems are often not expressed so as to avoid losing respect. In both instances, crises can cause feelings of shame, which can affect crisis reactions (Sullivan, Harris, Collado, & Chen, 2006). It is important to consider cultural diversity in advance. Asking questions with sensitivity regarding student beliefs and traditions before and following an incident will provide understanding that is needed for support services.

Establishing Social Support Systems

Individuals with strong familial and social support systems are better able to cope with life stressors than those without such supports, and are at less risk of developing traumatic stress (Charuvastra & Cloitre, 2008). Given this assertion, it is not surprising that the re-establishment and use of naturally occurring supports (e.g., parents, peers, and teachers) is a frequently recommended and empirically supported crisis intervention (Brock et al., 2009).

It is also important that students are returned to familiar environments and their regular routines, and that caregivers are provided with the knowledge needed to support their children in recovering from their exposure to a crisis. Returning to community routines and natural environments is important to recovering from crises, with reduced community disruption being associated with less traumatic stress (Brymer et al., 2006). Caregivers should respond by listening and understanding when youth need to express their anger and distress about what has occurred (Heath & Sheen, 2005).

Cultural considerations should also be taken into account following a school crisis, as different groups have their own values, beliefs, and preferences surrounding social support. For example, findings have shown that social support, spirituality, and an Afrocentric perspective were protective factors for African-American children exposed to chronic violence (Jones, 2007). Findings have also suggested that Asian-American children perceive themselves as needing less social support than Caucasian children (Demaray & Malecki, 2002).

Psychological Education

Psychoeducation helps provide survivors with increased control over the recovery process, promote social support, and teach coping strategies (e.g., Phoenix, 2007), which are all related to the reduced risk of post-traumatic stress (Charuvastra & Cloitre, 2008). There are different forms of psychoeducation, which include informational documents, caregiver trainings, and student psychoeducational groups. Informational documents provided within the school setting are aimed at providing caregivers (or students at the secondary level) the information they need to help support students in coping with the crisis. Caregiver training includes helping parents identify psychopathological crisis reactions and coping behaviors and provides them with strategies to manage their own crisis reactions. Finally, student psychoeducational groups focus on providing students with crisis facts, common crisis reactions, pathological crisis reactions and coping strategies, and strategies to manage their stress in response to the crisis.

Individual Psychological First Aid

The primary goal of individual psychological first aid is to directly facilitate coping with crisis problems and reactions in a fashion that allows for a return to pre-crisis functioning levels. Individual first aid requires school crisis interveners to make psychological contact with the person in crisis, identify crisis problems, examine possible solutions, help the person to take concrete problem-solving action, and when necessary ensure connections to appropriate helping resources (Brymer et al., 2006). Very little research exists regarding the efficacy of individual psychological first aid interventions following crisis events. However, given that these interventions facilitate active or approach coping strategies (i.e., they aim at helping students to take concrete problem-solving actions), that research has suggested that such coping is associated with lower rates of mental illness (Taylor & Stanton, 2007) and that avoidant coping strategies are predictive of post-traumatic stress (Pineles et al., 2011), these interventions may be said to have some empirical support.

Group Psychological First Aid

These interventions actively explore and process crisis experiences and share individual crisis reactions. By doing so in a group setting, these interventions aim to help students feel less alone and more connected to their classmates by virtue of their common experiences and reactions (Sandoval, Scott, & Padilla, 2009).

Risk Screening and Referral

Finally, risk screening and referral (also known as psychological triage) is a dynamic process that helps school crisis intervention teams identify those individuals who *do* and *do not* need their services. All of the crisis interventions just reviewed can be considered a part of risk screening and referral. Arguably, the most important outcome that would support the effectiveness of any risk screening and referral protocol would be a low incidence of failure to identify and refer students who have significant mental health problems secondary to crisis exposure. When making referrals, it is also important to seek out treatment providers who are from diverse backgrounds and who speak a language other than English (Nickerson & Heath, 2008). With parent permission, it is also important that school-based mental health professionals collaborate with the treatment provider in the community setting to best meet the student's needs. To our knowledge, there is no research assessing the effectiveness of any school-based risk screening and referral protocol. There are, however, substantial data that can be used to validate the inclusion of specific risk factors in risk screening. These factors include physical proximity and duration of exposure to the crisis, emotional proximity to the crisis (i.e., having significant relationships with crisis victims and threat perceptions), the severity and type of crisis reactions (e.g., the diagnosis of an acute stress disorder is a powerful predictor of later PTSD), and a host of external and internal resources (Brock et al., 2009).

Examine Effectiveness of Crisis Prevention

Following a crisis, it is important to examine crisis prevention, preparedness, response, and recovery results. This examination process serves seven general purposes: (a) assessing effectiveness, (b) improving implementation and enhancing effectiveness, (c) better managing limited resources, (d) documenting accomplishments, (e) justifying required resources, (f) supporting the need for increased levels of funding, and (g) satisfying ethical responsibilities to demonstrate positive and negative effects of program participation. There are various practical reasons underlying the importance of such examination. First, the examination of prevention efforts is important to discern the effectiveness of programs and strategies implemented to promote healthy student behaviors and reduce the number and intensity of crisis events. Second, the examination of preparedness efforts is vital to the annual systematic reviews of school crisis teams and school crisis plans. Third, the examination of response and recovery efforts can offer the school crisis team valuable lessons, including reaffirming that both the immediate and longer-term needs of school community members were met.

There are different types of examination that can be conducted when examining crisis efforts. These include the following: (a) *needs assessment,* where areas to be addressed are identified so that plans and strategies can be developed to focus on these needs; (b) *process analysis,* to understand what was done and by whom and to assess whether these activities were consistent with established plans; and (c) *outcome evaluation,* to assess the effectiveness of the stated objectives of crisis prevention, preparedness, response, and recovery activities.

Overall, there is a lack of research examining the effectiveness of school efforts following a crisis. Although more research needs to examine this area, there are also some challenges that are associated with such systematic data collection. These include the unpredictable nature of crises; the naturalistic in vivo contexts of schools; the difficulty of analyses to reveal causality of specific intervention strategies given the multifaceted nature of crisis prevention, preparedness, response, and recovery; and the ethical and professional concerns raised by conducting controlled studies with students in crisis.

Professional Mental Health Interventions

Although not considered an immediate crisis intervention, the longer term mental health treatment provided by mental health professionals (e.g., clinical social workers and psychologists) to individuals who develop psychopathology (e.g., posttraumatic stress disorder) subsequent to crisis exposure deserves some mention here. While there is only limited research examining immediate crisis interventions, the literature regarding these psychotherapeutic responses is much more substantial. Cognitive-behavioral therapy (CBT) has been shown to be the most effective treatment for other disorders that may develop in individuals following a crisis, such as depression, anxiety, and behavior problems (e.g., Weisz & Kazdin, 2010). Specific treatments include in vivo exposure, eye-movement desensitization and reprocessing (EMDR), anxiety management training, group-delivered CBTs, parent training, and psychoeducation.

Multicomponent Crisis Intervention

As illustrated in the discussion of various intervention strategies, no single intervention activity will provide resolution for all individuals in the aftermath of a violent school crisis event. When it comes to crisis intervention, one size does not fit all. Considering the complexity inherent in the multitude of individual and contextual factors that affect post-crisis responses, systematic and multifaceted crisis intervention approaches are encouraged. It must also be acknowledged that changes in perceptions and reactions are likely to occur over time. By making use of a chronological framework, the intervention strategies outlined above address the unique considerations of crises that affect children in the school context. Insights based on research, practical experience, and theory should be incorporated into chronologically based school crisis management plans aimed at facilitating the coping and adjustment of students in the wake of crises.

What We Can Do

The process of school crisis intervention requires a multidisciplinary school crisis team that attempts to manage the myriad challenges generated by a crisis event. Preparation for responding to the aftermath of any crisis should include a comprehensive, yet flexible, plan that takes into account a school's diverse populations. While there are many practical considerations addressed in the development of a school-based crisis intervention plan, such plans often overlook the unique needs of those who are affected. The efficacy of intervention efforts will likely be positively influenced by taking time to address a few of these special considerations, including the developmental level of the students and the ethnic and linguistic diversity of the student population.

Before reviewing the process of school crisis intervention, it is important to acknowledge that resolution of the acute crisis situation is a prerequisite to the initiation of the school mental health response (or the immediate crisis intervention). In other words, the work of emergency response personnel (e.g., police and paramedics) takes precedence over the work of school mental health responders. The meeting of emergency medical needs and ensuring physical safety is prerequisite to the work of the school crisis intervention team. It is also important to acknowledge that prerequisite to the implementation of these guidelines is the development of a crisis team with a clear leadership structure. That is, it must be understood who is in charge of the crisis intervention. Adapted from the work of Brock et al. (2009), the process of school crisis intervention is now discussed.

Preparation

The process of school crisis intervention begins with crisis planning. A comprehensive crisis intervention plan should be designed to be flexible enough to address the full range of potential crises. In order to achieve as high a level of preparedness as possible, an intervention plan that encompasses the following key elements should be developed: (a) formation and maintenance of a school/community crisis team; (b) training of teachers and support staff on crisis intervention procedures, including important developmental and cultural considerations along with annual reviews of the crisis plan; (c) formation of guidelines for school staff facilitating student coping; (d) development of an accounting system for all students immediately following a crisis; (e) coordination with the community in the event of a crisis; (f) offering of parent education programs; and (g) preparation of a longer term follow-up plan in addition to the immediate intervention plan. Because individuals from diverse cultural backgrounds may respond differently, crisis plans should be customized according to the community and students they serve. The unique characteristics and demographics of the school and the community must be considered when planning a comprehensive crisis response plan (Annandale, Heath, Dean, Kemple, & Takino, 2011). Key considerations include the ethnic and cultural groups within the school community, preparing a plan that is culturally relevant, and preparing resources in the relevant languages.

Assess the Crisis Situation

Following the occurrence of a crisis event, the first task to be completed is for the crisis intervention team leadership to assess the crisis situation. This involves gathering crisis facts and estimating the event's impact on the school. This information is used to decide upon the level of crisis response required (e.g., school site level versus district level). Information sources include law enforcement, medical personnel, and the families of crisis victims.

Disseminate Crisis Information

Once the basic facts have been identified, the crisis intervention team leadership should hold a crisis management meeting, during which crisis facts are shared and initial intervention activities planned. In addition, crisis facts need to be shared with the broader school community. Sharing crisis information is critical to a school crisis intervention as crisis rumors are typically more frightening than crisis facts. Especially when being shared with students, these facts should be disseminated in as normal and natural an environment and manner as possible. An example includes an announcement read simultaneously by classroom teachers, rather than having an all-school assembly. It is important to note that when making decisions about what information to share with a school, it may be appropriate to avoid mentioning particularly frightening crisis details. If such facts are not publicly available or being speculated upon, then there will be no reason to discuss them. However, no matter how unpleasant the facts are, if students have questions about them, it will typically be appropriate to answer them as honestly as possible.

Begin to Identify Crisis Victims

As the facts are collected, the school crisis intervention team should also begin identifying both physical and psychological crisis victims. The most important factor in determining the degree of psychological trauma experience by a child is proximity to the crisis event. However, students' familiarity with crisis victims and severity of their crisis reactions are also predictors of psychological injury.

Crisis intervention guidelines must specify a procedure for identifying crisis victims. When there are large numbers of victims, a psychological triage will need to be conducted (Brock et al., 2009). Part of such triage is to ensure that parents, teachers, and the school community are aware of the signs and symptoms of posttraumatic stress in students and colleagues and accept the responsibility for referring those individuals for appropriate treatment.

Provide Specific Crisis Interventions

As psychological trauma victims are identified, decisions need to be made regarding the provision of crisis intervention services (the elements of which were discussed in the first part of this chapter). These services need to ensure that the acute distress or grief experienced by students is supported in a professional, empathic manner and that the psychological equilibrium of students and faculty members is restored as soon as possible. In addition, these interventions continue the process of identifying crisis victims. While it should be expected that, with the support of their natural caregiving environments, most students will recover from their crisis event exposure, some may require more direct crisis intervention assistance, such as psychological first aid or professional mental health intervention. The presence of any degree of lethality, such as suicidal or homicidal thinking, or an inability to cope with the traumatizing circumstances are reasons for making an immediate professional mental health counseling referral. Heath and colleagues (Heath, Nickerson, Annandale, Kemple, & Dean, 2009) have emphasized the importance of increasing cultural sensitivity when responding to crises and discuss strategies to overcome cultural barriers. These include addressing issues of distrust and resistance to services, language and communication barriers, and empowering social support.

Debrief and Evaluate the Crisis Response

Finally it is essential that crisis response procedural guidelines include activities designed to care for the caregivers. Following a crisis response, all crisis team members will need to be offered the opportunity to debrief. In addition, they need to evaluate the effectiveness of the response. No two crises are alike. Thus, given the proper reflective thought, all crises are potential learning experiences. These debriefings also provide an opportunity to begin to develop the long-term planning that may be required (e.g., coordinating school with community mental health interventions, planning for memorials, planning for anniversaries).

Applying Interventions within a Response to Intervention Framework

School crisis interventions have been conceptualized according to the Response to Intervention

(RTI) framework (e.g., Brock et al., 2009). Within this framework, support following school crises is provided at the "universal" (provided to all students who are at risk for psychological trauma), "selected" (individuals who are judged to be moderately to severely traumatized), and "indicated" (individuals who are judged to be severely traumatized) levels. In the previous sections, interventions that fit within this framework were already outlined, including individual psychological first aid, group psychological first aid, and the importance of providing referrals to those who would benefit from additional treatment outside of the school setting. To summarize some of this information according to the RTI framework, the previous Table 43.1 that describes the different levels of school crisis interventions is provided.

Tools and Practice Examples

To illustrate the process of a school crisis intervention, we offer the following scenario and then speculate on a school's hypothetical intervention response:

> On June 9, an 11-year-old, Robert, threatened to kill a fellow sixth grader, after his classmate had repeatedly bullied him since the beginning of the school year. The classmate thought nothing of the threat and did not report it to anyone. The following day, Robert brought his father's gun to school and shot his classmate, who died immediately.

Preparation

Ideally, the school at which this crisis took place will not have waited until this crisis event to consider how it will respond to a crisis at school. The degree to which the school was prepared will facilitate all subsequent crisis intervention activities.

Assessing the Situation

Subsequent to emergency medical personnel and law enforcement officials completing their assigned tasks, such as transporting the victim to a hospital and removing the firearm, the crisis team begins to assess the crisis situation. This may occur on the same day as the crisis or a subsequent day, depending upon whether children remain in school, given the nature of the event. In the present case, facts regarding the crisis were first obtained. Specifically, Robert's principal spoke with emergency response workers, law enforcement officials, and both Robert's mother and the mother of the victim to determine what had happened. In the meantime, after law enforcement had completed the investigation, the mental health professionals met with Robert's classroom teacher to gather facts about the events of the previous day.

Disseminating Information

The day following the shooting, the school's principal mental health professionals, including the school social worker and school psychologist, met in order to share the information they had gathered and gauge the degree of impact on the educational community. They decided that, first, a meeting would be held with teachers in order to help them learn how to talk to their classes. In an effort for the teachers to be supported while sharing information about the victim's death with their students, mental health professionals from the broader educational community made themselves available.

Identifying Crisis Victims

While visiting classrooms in support of teachers, the mental health professionals paid close attention to the behavior of students in an effort to identify students demonstrating signs of acute distress, either emotional or behavioral. Furthermore, they also offered open office hours so that students who needed additional support could be referred to them by their teachers or request to go to their offices. Parents were also asked to share with mental health professionals any significant changes in the behavior of their children.

Providing Crisis Interventions

The first crisis interventions offered were designed to minimize exposure to crisis images. Specifically, immediately after the shooting, all students were directed away from the scene of the medical emergency. Next, parents were given the crisis facts and offered psychological education regarding how they can help their children to cope with the shooting and given guidance regarding how to identify the need for mental health intervention. Especially important was the guidance offered regarding how young children look to the significant adults in their lives to gauge how threatening the event was. Given this fact, they were advised to be sure they were in control of their own emotions when they set out to comfort their children.

To facilitate the coping process, as well as to continue the process of identifying psychological trauma victims, the school social worker and school psychologist spent the first several days following the shooting in the fifth-grade classrooms. Here they offered individual and small-group psychological first aid. Group psychological first aid also was made available to all other classrooms in the school. These sessions were facilitated by the community mental health professionals (who had been brought into the school to support this crisis intervention).

In a continuing effort to prevent the development of significant trauma and loss responses, the school social worker and the school psychologist decided to visit the victim's fifth-grade classroom and offer individual counseling support daily during the next 4 weeks. They continued to provide counseling in small groups to the students in the classroom. Students who had observed the shooting were also designated for individual counseling with the mental health professionals. Voluntary counseling groups were established for other children in the school.

Throughout this time period, students continued to be monitored for signs of psychopathology that might signal the need for referral to a community mental health professional.

Debriefing and Evaluating the Crisis Response

In order to debrief, the entire crisis team met at weekly intervals during the first month following the death of the student. Each member of the school crisis intervention team reported on his or her current activities and shared updated information related to the community response to the death and Robert's status. This was also the chance for the crisis intervention team members to offer support to each other. Clearly, such crisis intervention will take its toll on the mental health of the crisis interveners.

The school social worker and school psychologist evaluated the effectiveness of the group and individual counseling and discussed the needs of the student population. Later, to get further information, personal interviews were conducted with teachers in order to gather information about their perceptions of students' reaction to the death of their schoolmate, as well as to intervention services. From these evaluative efforts, decisions were made regarding how the school's crisis intervention plan could be improved.

Key Points to Remember

Tragic crisis events, such as shootings on school campuses, affect children, families, educational professionals, schools, and communities in innumerable ways. Thus, it is imperative that schools and communities prepare for such events (Brock & Jimerson, 2012). It is clear that while the trauma from a violent school crisis can be extensive, the damage may be addressed and recovery achieved through the use of immediate and proactive school-based crisis interventions. The ongoing preparation and training of educational and mental health professionals will assist in addressing the relevant issues by their acquiring knowledge of both the issues and methods for supportive interventions in the classroom as well as in larger group settings.

Comprehensive school crisis intervention plans and advanced preparation are essential to being ready to respond to a crisis event at school (Brock & Jimerson, 2012; Brock et al., 2009). Such plans must include mental health professionals, who can assist in providing appropriate support services for diverse students, families, faculty, and staff. Thus, it is strongly recommended that educational professionals engage in professional development and prepare a comprehensive crisis intervention plan. The lessons learned by numerous educational and mental health professionals responding to school crises across the country should further inspire all educational and mental health professionals to thoroughly prepare for such devastating events so that, should the need arise, they will be well equipped to respond and assist in the school community's recovery process.

References

Annandale, N. O., Heath, M. A., Dean, B., Kemple, A., & Takino, Y. (2011). Assessing competency in school crisis plans. Journal of School Violence, 10, 16–33. d oi:10.1080/15388220.2010.519263

Bernstein, K. T., Ahern, J., Tracy, M., Boscarino, J. A., Vlahov, D., & Galea, S. (2007). Television watching and the risk of incident probable posttraumatic stress disorder. The Journal of Nervous and Mental Disease, 195, 41–47. doi:10.1097/01.nmd.0000244784.36745.a5

Brock, S. E., & Jimerson, S. R. (Eds.). (2012). *Best practices in crisis prevention and intervention in the schools.* Bethesda, MD: National Association of School Psychologists.

Brock, S. E., Nickerson, A. B., Reeves, M. A., Jimerson, S. R., Lieberman, R. A., & Feinberg, T. A. (2009). *School crisis prevention and intervention: The PREaRE model.* Bethesda, MD: National Association of School Psychologists.

Brymer, M., Jacobs, A., Layne, C., Pynoos, R., Ruzek, J., Steinberg, A., … Watson, P. (2006). *Psychological first aid: Field operations guide* (2nd ed.). Rockville, MD: National Child Traumatic Stress Network and National Center for PTSD. Retrieved June 8, 2011, from http://www.nctsnet.org/nctsn_assets/pdfs/pfa/2/PsyFirstAid.pdf

Charuvastra, A., & Cloitre, M. (2008). Social bonds and posttraumatic stress disorder. Annual Review of Psychology, 59, 301–328. doi:10.1146/annurev.psych.58.110405.085650

Demaray, M. K., & Malecki, C. K. (2002). Critical levels of perceived social support associated with student adjustment. School Psychology Quarterly, 17, 213–241. Retrieved from http://www.apa.org/pubs/journals/spq/index.aspx

Eksi, A., Braun, K. L., Ertem- Vehid, H., Peykerli, G., Saydam, R., Toparlak, D., & Behiye, A. (2007). Risk factors for the development of PTSD and depression among child and adolescent victims following a 7.4 magnitude earthquake. International Journal of Psychiatry in Clinical Practice, 11, 190–199. doi:10.1080/13651500601017548

Galea, S., Brewin, C. R., Gruber, M., Jones, R. T., King, D. W., King, L. A., … Kessler, R. C. (2007). Exposure to hurricane-related stressors and mental illness after Hurricane Katrina. Archives of General Psychiatry, 64, 1427–1434. doi:10.1001/archpsyc.64.12.1427

Groome, D., & Soureti, A. (2004). Post-traumatic stress disorder and anxiety symptoms in children exposed to the 1999 Greek earthquake. British Journal of Psychology, 95, 387–397. doi:10.1348/0007126041528149

Heath, M. A., & Sheen, D. (2005). *School-based crisis interventions: Preparing all personnel to assist.* New York, NY: Guilford Press.

Heath, M. A., Nickerson, A. B., Annandale, N., Kemple, A., & Dean, B. (2009). Strengthening cultural sensitivity in children's disaster mental health services. School Psychology International, 30, 347–373. doi:10.1177/0143034309106944

Jimerson, S. R., Nickerson, A. B., Mayer, M. J., & Furlong, M. J. (Eds). (2011). *Handbook of school violence and school safety: International research and practice* (2nd Ed.). New York, NY: Routledge.

Jones, J. M. (2007). Exposure to chronic community violence: Resilience in African American children. Journal of Black Psychology, 33, 125–149. doi:10.1177/0095798407299511

Lawyer, S. R., Resnick, H. S., Galea, S., Ahern, J., Kilpatrick, D. G., & Vlahov, D. (2006). Predictors of peritraumatic reactions and PTSD following the September 11th terrorist attacks. Psychiatry, 69, 130–141. doi:10.1521/psyc.2006.69.2.130

National Institute of Mental Health. (2002). *Mental health and mass violence: Evidence-based early psychological intervention for victims/survivors of mass violence. A workshop to reach consensus on best practices.* [NIH Publication No. 02–5138] Washington, DC: U.S. Government Printing Office.

Nickerson, A. B., & Heath, M. A. (2008). Developing and strengthening crisis response teams. School Psychology Forum, 2, 1–16. Retrieved June 9, 2011, from http://www.nasponline.org/publications/spf/issue2_2/nickerson.pdf

Ostrowski, S. A., Christopher, N. C., & Delahanty, D. L. (2007). Brief report: The impact of maternal posttraumatic stress disorder symptoms and child gender on risk for persistent posttraumatic stress disorder symptoms in child trauma victims. Journal of Pediatric Psychology, 33, 338–342. doi:10.1093/jpepsy/jsl003

Phoenix, B. J. (2007). Psychoeducation for survivors of trauma. Perspectives in Psychiatric Care, 48, 123–131. doi:10.1111/j.1744-6163.2007.00121.x

Pineles, S. L., Mostoufi, S. M., Ready, C. B., Street, A. E., Griffin, M. G., & Resick, P. A. (2011). Trauma reactivity, avoidant coping, and PTSD symptoms: A moderating relationship? Journal of Abnormal Psychology, 120, 240–246. doi: 10.1037/a0022123

Reeves, M. A., Nickerson, A. B., & Brock, S. E. (2011). Preventing and intervening in crisis situations. In T. M. Lionetti, E. P. Snyder, & Christner, R. W. (Eds.), *A practical guide to building professional competencies in school psychology.* New York, NY: Springer.

Robers, S., Zhang, J., & Truman, J. (2010). *Indicators of school crime and safety: 2010* (NCES 2011–002/NCJ 230812). Washington, DC: National Center for Education Statistics, U.S. Department of Education, and Bureau of Justice Statistics, Office of Justice Programs, U.S. Department of Justice.

Sandoval, J., Scott, A. N., & Padilla, I. (2009). Crisis counseling: An overview. Psychology in the Schools, 46, 246–256. doi:10.1002/pits.20370

Sullivan, M., Harris, E., Collado, C., & Chen, T. (2006). Noways tired: Perspectives of clinicians of color on culturally competent crisis intervention. Journal of Clinical Psychology: In Session, 62, 987–999. doi:10.1002/jclp.20284

Taylor, S. E., & Stanton, A. L. (2007). Coping resources, coping processes, and mental health. Annual Review of Clinical Psychology, 3, 377–401. doi:10.1146/annurev.clinpsy.3.022806.091520

Weisz, J. R., & Kazdin, A. E. (Eds.) (2010). *Evidence-based psychotherapies for children and adolescents* (2nd ed.). New York, NY: Guilford Press.

CHAPTER 44

Best Practice Grief Work with Students in the Schools

Linda Goldman

Getting Started

School social workers, counselors, and other mental health professionals must create an environment for grieving children that provides a safe haven for expression and release of thoughts and feelings, a respect for their grief process, and an acknowledgment of the complex levels of loss associated with the death of a loved one. Involving children in memorializing and creating the recognition that young people are an integral part of the grief community can only enhance their self-worth and dignity as they feel acknowledged by society.

Today's children live in a world affected by death, war, terrorism, violence, sexuality, abuse, and abandonment. If young people are not affected directly, they are influenced vicariously by a media that all too often acts as a surrogate parent and extended family to many of our children. From the death of a classmate to a dad's deployment, girls and boys are becoming increasingly subject to traumatic grief by prevailing social and societal issues in their home, school, community, nation, and world.

Parents and professionals must create environments where children and teens are recognized mourners. Children become recognized mourners when they are given a voice to communicate their grief, an avenue to physically commemorate a loved one, and a safe haven for expression and commemoration. Training needs to be provided for social workers, educators, and parents on the topics of grief and trauma, which so affect our young people today. The University of Maryland's School of Social Work provided such a forum in its Advanced Certification for Children and Adolescents programs, in which practical and theoretical information is presented to clinicians.

Montgomery County, Maryland, created trainings for teachers and counselors on the creation and implementation of grief support in their schools, including procedures for the development of ongoing support groups. Safe Harbor, a grief support program for children and teens, provides outreach education and information for grieving children and families.

What We Know

The Nature of Grief

Fox (1988) explained that one useful way to help bereaved children to monitor their ongoing emotional needs is to "conceptualize what they must do in order to stay psychologically healthy" (p. 8). Fox emphasized that in order to assure that children's grief will be good grief, they must accomplish four tasks: understanding, grieving, commemorating, and going on. Each child's unique nature and age-appropriate level of experience can influence how he or she works through these tasks.

Bereaved children may not process grief in a linear way (Goldman, 2000, 2013 in-press). The tasks may surface and resurface in varying order, intensity, and duration. Grief work can be messy, with children being inundated with waves of feelings when they least expect it, for example, listening to music with friends, hearing a story, or even being at a birthday party. Tommy's dad was shot and killed in front of his house. A few months later, Tommy attended a birthday party. A balloon burst, and he thought it was a bullet. He ran out of the room screaming and crying. He hadn't expected to be hit with a grief bullet that day.

Children's Developmental Understanding of Death

This section has been adapted from Goldman (2005). Children's understanding of death changes as they develop, as explained by Piaget's cognitive stages of development (Ginsberg & Opper, 1969). Gaining insight into children's developmental stages allows predictability and knowledge of age-appropriate responses.

Pre-Operational Stage (Usually 2–7 Years)

The child conceptualizes death with magical thinking, egocentricity, reversibility, and causality. Young children developmentally live in an egocentric world, filled with the notion that they have caused and are responsible for everything. Children's magical thinking causes them to feel that their words and thoughts can magically cause an event. Five-year-old Sam screamed at his older brother, "I hate you and I wish you were dead!" He was haunted with the idea that his words created his brother's murder the following day. Sam's egocentric perception placed him at the center of the universe, capable of creating and destroying at will the world around him.

Alice, at age 4, displayed her egocentricity when she explained that she felt she had killed her mother. When I asked how she did that, she responded, "My mom picked me up on the night she had her heart attack. If she hadn't picked me up, she wouldn't have died, so I killed her." Alice felt that she was the central cause of the death. Talking about the medical facts of how Mom died, her heart condition, smoking, and lack of taking proper medicine helped to reduce the common mindset of a young child that she magically caused the death to happen.

Angela, a 6-year-old first-grader, was very sad after her dad died of cancer. She age-appropriately perceived death as reversible and told her friends and family that her dad was coming back. She even wrote him a letter and waited and waited for the mailman to bring back a response. Angela's mom explained to her the following definition of death for young children: "Death is when a person's body stops working. Usually someone dies when they are very, very old, or very, very, very sick, or their bodies are so injured that the doctors and nurses can't make their bodies work again" (Goldman, 2000).

Concrete Operations (Usually 7–12 Years)

During this stage, the child is very curious, the concept of death becomes more realistic, and he or she seeks new information. Ten-year-old Mary wanted to know everything about her mother's death. She said she had heard so many stories about her mom's fatal car crash that she wanted to look up the story in the newspaper to find out the facts. Eleven-year-old Margaret wondered about her friend who got killed in a sudden plane crash: "What was she thinking before the crash, was she scared, and did she suffer?"

Tom age-appropriately wondered if there was an afterlife and exactly where his dad was. At this stage of development, children commonly express logical thoughts and fears about death, can conceptualize that all body functions stop, and begin to internalize the universality and permanence of death. They may ponder the facts about how the terrorists got the plane to crash, wanting to know every detail. When working with this age group, it is important to ask, "What are the facts that you would like to know?" and help them to find answers through family, friends, the media, and experts.

Prepositional Operations, Implications, and Logic Stage of Development (Usually Age 13 and Older)

This stage is usually characterized by the adolescent's concept of death. Many are self-absorbed at this age, seeing mortality and death as a natural process that is remote from their day-to-day lives and something they cannot control. Young people are often wrapped up with shaping their own lives and deny the possibility of their own deaths.

Sixteen-year-old Malcolm expressed the following age-appropriate thoughts when he proclaimed," I don't want to think about death now. I want to think about living my life!" Teens benefit greatly by peer support groups as it is developmentally appropriate to value feedback and support from peers.

Common Signs of Grieving Children

Social workers, educators, parents, and other mental health professionals need to familiarize themselves with the common signs of grieving children. In this way, they can educate children and caring adults who work with children about the ways that young people feel and think. Knowing these signs helps to normalize them and reduce anxiety about them for children and adults as well. Children may:

- imitate the behavior of the deceased
- want to "appear normal"
- need to tell their story over and over again
- enjoy wearing or holding something of the loved one
- speak of the loved one in the present
- tend to worry excessively about their health and the health of surviving loved ones
- become the class bully or class clown
- regress and become clingy or wet the bed
- have headaches or stomachaches
- display poor eating patterns
- appear hyperactive or impulsive or have an inability to concentrate
- begin to use drugs or alcohol or become sexually promiscuous
- show a change in grades and lack of interest in school

Grief and ADD

Sometimes children and teens are misdiagnosed with attention-deficit disorder or learning disabilities after an experience of traumatic loss. Hyperactivity, impulsivity, distractibility, and inability to concentrate are common grief symptoms that can become the behavioral criteria to diagnose learning problems. It is essential to take a loss inventory of the grieving child to become aware of any past or present loss issues and identify if the behavior signs observed are a by-product of a grief and loss situation.

Seven-year-old Sam was a second-grader whose best friend, Adam, was killed in a car crash on the day before Christmas. He came back to school after the winter holidays with extreme restlessness and frequent swings of emotional outbursts and withdrawal. This continued for several months with decrease in attention and school performance. The grief symptoms continued well into third grade, and Sam's teacher relayed to his mom that he may be exhibiting attention deficit. She suggested that Sam receive an evaluation by his pediatrician.

Sam was placed on Ritalin and given this drug for the next 3 years. He continued to have nightmares and the bed wetting that had begun with his friend's death, and these anxieties were never addressed inside or outside of the school system. He became a part of the learning disabled population, and his deep grief and its symptoms remained buried (Goldman, 2001).

Signs of Grieving Children in the Classroom

The bereaved child may display one or several of these behaviors:

- become the class clown
- become withdrawn and unsociable
- become restless and unable to stay seated
- call out of turn
- not complete schoolwork
- have problems listening and staying on task
- become overly talkative
- become disorganized
- engage in reckless physical actions
- show poor concentration around external stimuli
- show difficulty in following directions

Caring adults need to educate and become educated in learning the signs of normal and complicated grief. Gaining a respect for and acceptance of the feelings of anxiety and depression that occur with grief can normalize common characteristics and reduce anxiety for children and the adults around them. Social workers and other caring professionals must become a strong force in differentiating between grief and ADD signs.

What We Can Do

Normalize Grief

Professionals and parents can realize that children do not like to feel different, and often the grieving child does. When grieving children have experienced the death of someone close to them, they may choose not to talk about the death because they do not want to appear not normal. Not talking about the death allows some children to feel they still have some control over what has happened in their lives or hide any shame about feeling different.

Tom was playing on the school football team, and the final tournament was a major event. Most of the moms and dads of the team members came to support their children for the game. Tom scored the winning touchdown for his team. Charlie, Tom's coach, ran over to congratulate him, and all the other boys and their parents joined in the celebration. "Where's your dad?" Coach Charlie asked. "He's working today, and couldn't come," Tom replied. Coach Charlie was unaware that Tom's dad had died the year before. Tom needed to save face and avoid his dad's death in order to "appear normal."

As an advocate for the grieving child, school social workers, counselors, and other mental health professionals need to be sure that these girls and boys are identified and given strategies to help them work through their grief. A grief and loss inventory (e.g., Goldman, 2000, pp. 125–129) is a helpful tool for the school system, which not only provides a loss history but also accountability in keeping a record of recommendations, interventions, and follow-ups. This loss inventory becomes an avenue of communication for the school system. In this way, faculty members like Coach Charlie can review this tool in order to identify grieving students like Tom and create modifications and interventions to help them with their process.

Recognize Grief Feelings

Children gain a greater understanding of themselves when they can express previously hidden emotions. The awareness of unrecognized feelings also allows social workers, other mental health professionals, educators, and parents to be more in touch with what is going on in the grief process. Grief feelings and thoughts are continuous and ever-changing, inundating the children's lives like waves on the ocean. These thoughts and feelings may arrive without warning, and children feel unprepared for their enormity in a school setting.

Encourage Acknowledgment and Memory Sharing

The bereaved child needs to acknowledge a parent or sibling who died by using his or her name or sharing a memory. It can be useful to create a memory table where children can bring treasured objects or favorite pictures, reminding them of their person. They can leave them there for others to see, or join together in a memory circle and talk about what the picture or object means to them.

Applying Interventions within a Response to Intervention Framework

"Response to Intervention (RTI) is a multi-tier approach to the early identification and support of students with learning and behavior needs. The RTI process begins with high-quality instruction and universal screening of all children in the general education classroom" (VanDerHeyden, 2011, para 1).

This model is applicable to working with the grieving student in the schools. All too often, grief distracts a child from concentration and may diminish his or her capacity to learn. The common behavioral signs of grief that include impulsivity, distractibility, inability to concentrate, and hyperactivity may be used to identify a learning problem without addressing the underlying issues in the bereavement process.

The RTI approach can use the services of teachers, guidance counselors, and social workers to identify the grieving child and implement appropriate interventions to enhance learning and resilience.

Classroom instruction that supports children's concepts of death and allows for open discussion enhances overall well-being. Resources such as *Children Also Grieve* (Goldman, 2005) enhance and explore children's understanding of the grief process. Educating professionals on the common signs of grieving children and those that are at risk is crucial. Then, once identified, these children can be assessed and monitored to continually allow for accountability in the school systems for interventions that accommodate bereaved students.

Assessment of students is necessary for identifying concerns and issues of the grieving student. Crucial areas for assessment for the school mental health practitioner include the following six key areas in intervening with a child whose parent has died: "(1) strengths of the child and supports the child experiences; (2) how the child was informed about the parent's death; (3) previous losses the child has experienced and how the child coped with those losses families while carrying out their work responsibilities; (4) the child's somatic complaints, behavior, and other signals; (5) the child's cognitive distortions; and (6) reminders of the parent's death (Aisenberg, p. 581)."

Aisenberg (p. 578) presents three goals necessary for intervention in grief work. They include providing a safe place for the child, facilitating a child's telling his or her story, and an environment that promotes healing and resilience. Awareness of common questions that children ask about death can facilitate the accomplishment of these goals. By preparing words to use and a willingness to respond, the grieving child can openly travel through his or her process with adult support. "We can not protect children from life's tragedies, but we can ease their journey by responding openly to their questions (Goldman, 2009, p. 100)."

The level and intensity of intervention can be monitored by the student's response to instruction and performance level. Parent involvement is an integral piece of this program, providing partnership with the school in terms of information, progress, and interventions of the children, as well as the school staff that will implement goals and activities. It is useful for schools implementing RTI to provide parents with information about their child's progress, the instruction and interventions used, the staff who are delivering the instruction, and the academic or behavioral goals for their child.

Tools and Practice Examples

Bereaved children need to tell their story over and over again. One of the common signs of grieving children under stress is this need to repeatedly share the story of their loss. We can help them do this by listening, sharing, and providing opportunities to help them retell and reframe their experience. Giving children an open-ended opportunity for relaying a hard time and expressing difficulties, remaining worries, and a new self-view gives them permission to recreate a worrisome experience. We can ask children to "tell us about a day you will never forget," and often they choose dates associated with traumatic experiences such as September 11, 2001, or the day someone they loved died.

Interventions

Working With Young Children: Projective Play

Projective play allows many young children to work through complex issues, including their grief process, by using play. Play allows them to use their imaginations to safely express thoughts and feelings. Children have a restricted verbal ability for sharing feelings and a limited emotional capacity to tolerate the pain of loss; they communicate their feelings, wishes, fears, and attempted resolutions to their problems through play (Webb, 2002).

Providing props, such as helping figures, puppets, costumes, and building blocks, allows children to re-create their experience and role play what happened and ways to work with what happened. Children feel empowered when they can imagine alternatives and possible solutions, release feelings, and create dialog through projective play.

Many children spontaneously built towers of blocks as the Twin Towers and then knocked them down with an airplane to replay the attack. Alex explained to his nursery school teacher as the tower fell:" Airplanes make buildings go BOOM!"

Children can re-create the disaster setting with doctors, nurses, firefighters, and police officers who helped in the disaster by using props for projective play. Sally pretended to be a nurse helping those hurt at the Pentagon crash, and Jimmy put on a fire hat and gloves and said, "Don't worry, I'll save you. Run for your lives."

During a play therapy session, children who survived the death of their dad, who was a firefighter, decided to reenact the disaster. Their play illustrated their desire to become firefighters and "save as many people as possible." Kevin, age 4, watched with his family in their car as his father was murdered at a convenience store. His play presented constant replaying of the murder and "good guy/bad guy" scenarios.

Puppets and stuffed animals are a safe way for children to speak of the trauma. "I wonder what Bart the puppet would say about the trauma. Let's allow Bart to tell us about his story."

Memory Work

Memory work can be a helpful tool to safely process the events after a death. The following questions can provide a foundation for discussion:

Where were you when [the trauma] happened?
What was your first thought?
What are the facts about [the trauma]?
What sticks with you now?
Do you feel like you did anything wrong?
What is it you still want to know?
What scares you the most?
What makes you feel peaceful?
What can you do to feel better?

Memory Books

Bereaved children need to use memory work to create a physical way to remember their feelings and share them. Memory books are a collection of feelings and thoughts through drawings and writings that allow children to re-experience memories in a safe way. They serve as a useful tool to enable children to tell about their person who died and to open discussion. Children can tell about how their person died and share funny, happy, or sad memories. Melissa is a 12-year-old whose dad died of cancer. She shared her funniest memory of her dad in her memory book:

> My funniest memory of my father is when… he came home from getting his hair shaved off after being diagnosed with lung cancer. During his cancer he always kept a good attitude. That's just my Dad's personality—a good sense of humor. Why do the good people have to die?—By Melissa, Age 13. (Goldman, 2000, p. 90)

Memory Boxes

Memory boxes contain pictures and special objects that remind children of their person who died. They can be decorated with pictures and words that remind the children of their loved one or special containers meaningful to the person who died. Jane made a memory box with pictures and special objects that reminded her of her friend Zoe, who died suddenly in a plane crash. She included pictures, stuffed animals, a list of her top favorite memories, and other special items to remind her of her friend.

Writing, Poetry, and Journaling

Bereaved children need to use tools such as drawing, writing, role playing, and reenactment to safely project feelings and thoughts about their loss and present life outside of themselves. Letter and poetry writing are grief therapy techniques that give children concrete ways to commemorate the death of a loved one. Seven-year-old Ashley wrote the following Mother's Day letter to her mom the year after her mother died. She decided with her teacher to send off a balloon and an "I love you" note for her mother:

> Dear Mom,
>
> I really miss you. I am doing good in school. I can't figure out what to get you yet for Mother's day.
> I love you. Ashley

Eight-year-old Julia's best friend, Anne, and her family died in the 2001 terrorist attack. She created this poem as a tribute to her friend in her memory book:

> Julia
> Active, funny, kind
> Good Friend of Anne
> Loss, anger, grief
> Who misses her funny, caring and silly ways
> Who worries about war and our President
> Stomachaches, headaches, muscles get tense
> Who heals by reading, laying down, talking
> Remembers by memories and hearing her name
> Who wishes for peace and unity
> Strong. (Goldman, 2005)

Tools to Help Bereaved Children Feel Safe

Bereaved children often are preoccupied with their own health and the health of their loved ones. Providing a reality check, such as calling their surviving parent during the school day or allowing visits to the school nurse, is reassuring to boys and girls that they and their families are okay. Surviving parents can have a physical exam and bring a doctor's note to the child saying the exam went well. Children can also make fear boxes, safe or peaceful boxes, or a worry list.

Sandra put together a peaceful box. She found toys, stuffed animals, and pictures that made her feel safe and peaceful. Alex made a fear box. He cut out pictures from newspapers and magazines about what frightens him and pasted them around the box. He wrote down fears and put them inside. Denise created a worry list. She made a list of worries from 1 to 5. Number 1 was the biggest. Suggest that children talk about their lists with someone they trust, like a parent, sibling, teacher, or good friend.

Systems Changes and Interventions

"The goal of helping children of all ages to cope with death is to promote their competence, facilitate their ability to cope, and recognize that children are active participants in their lives" (Silverman, 2000, p. 42). Grieving children have become the norm in our educational system, with more and more children experiencing traumatic grief at earlier and earlier ages. Social workers, educators, and parents can support the concept of young people being an integral part of a family or community grief team and allow them to become recognized mourners.

Adults Can Create Interventions That Advocate for the Grieving Child

Bereaved children need interventions to accommodate their loss issues. The mental health professional, educator, or parent may serve as a liaison and advocate for the grieving child in the school. Often the suggestion and implementation of simple interventions for grieving girls and boys are useful and practical means of facilitating their process. Children should be given choices of places to which they can go within the schools, people with whom they are comfortable talking, and times that they find are best to call and be reassured about loved ones. They can choose a safe place outside the classroom when these unexpected, overwhelming feelings arise, without needing to explain why in front of fellow classmates. The following are suggestions for school interventions (adapted from Goldman, 2001):

- Allow the child to leave the room if needed.
- Allow the child to call home if necessary.
- Create a visit to the school nurse and guidance counselor periodically.
- Change some work assignments.
- Assign a class helper.
- Create some private time in the day.
- Give more academic progress reports.

Grief-Based Support Groups

Seven-year-old Tony became a member of a school-based grief therapy group, which he attended with four other children aged 6 to 9. He attended this group, led by his guidance counselor, for several months. The children made memory books, commemorated loved ones, and shared photos and stories. Tony had been diagnosed with attention-deficit disorder a year after his father's murder. After attending this group, his concentration in school became more focused, and eventually he was taken off medication. He continued going to a children's bereavement group in a neighborhood hospice program for the rest of the school year.

One of the best techniques for adolescents is peer support and discussion groups, as they are much more comfortable at this age talking with peers about death and trauma than with adults. Many teen survivors of trauma feel comforted and free to share their thoughts when they are placed in support groups only for other teens who are survivors of similar experiences. Tony's dad died in the September 11 Pentagon crash. He explained the value of his teen support group, which included other survivors of September 11 as follows:" I don't have to explain a lot of things. I already know they understand."

Adults Can Provide Activities Helpful for Bereaved Children

Several interventions that allow children safe expression of thoughts and feelings are worry lists, fear boxes, peaceful places, and reality checks. They provide safe activities for children to process their grief responses.

Thomas was the 17-year-old captain of his football team. He was killed instantly in an automobile accident the night before the first day of school. Parents and teachers provided a forum for grieving students to actively commemorate his death. The school developed a memory library shelf for Thomas where books could be donated in his name. A memory location was created on the football field where students could visit during the day and feel they were with Thomas. Friends established a memory chat room where the only prerequisite for entering was to share a memory of Thomas. The school created a memory wall with a Thomas mural that remained throughout the year. Teachers and students could write or draw a memory or note at any time during the school day.

Educators Can Benefit From a Loss and Grief Inventory

A loss and grief inventory (e.g., Goldman, 2000) is a useful tool for creating and storing history on the grieving child throughout his academic life. This history includes all losses and important dates of birthdays and deaths of loved ones that may have a great impact on the child through the years. It also provides accountability for recognizing the grieving child and accurately documenting necessary accommodations, follow-ups, and recommendations.

Educators, Parents, and Other Professionals Can Use "Teachable Moments" to Acknowledge a Loss

Teachable moments are spontaneous mini-lessons created in the moment using a life experience that is happening now. The death of Goldie, the goldfish in Mrs. Arnold's classroom, was a huge loss to her kindergarten class. Goldie's death during school provided a teachable moment when the children could express their feelings about death and commemorate the loss with a burial ritual and memorial service. The death of Rocky, Margie's dog, was very sad. Family and friends came together and participated in a ceremony for Rocky, and Margie and her sister shared a poem about how much they loved their special dog.

The shootings at Columbine High School created many teachable moments at homes and at schools across the country to dialog about the bullying, victimization, and violence that affect so many children. One school system sent a poster signed by all of its students and teachers, sharing their concern and prayers for the Columbine students. A discussion of the terrorist attack on Russian children led a group of teens to raise money for their aid.

Adults Can Actively Involve Children and Teens in Commemorating

Here are some ways:

- Create a ceremony, such as releasing a balloon with a special note or lighting a candle.
- Create a memorial wall with stories and pictures of shared events.
- Have an assembly about the person who died.
- Plant a memorial garden.
- Initiate a scholarship fund.
- Establish an ongoing fundraiser, such as a car wash or bake sale, with proceeds going toward the bereaved family's designated charity.
- Place memorial pages and pictures in the school yearbook or school newspaper.
- Bake cookies and bring to a grieving friend.
- Send flowers to the grieving family.

Key Points to Remember

What we can mention, we can manage. This idea is a useful paradigm for social workers, educators, parents, and other caring professionals to understand when establishing an oasis of safety for the grieving child. Allowing children to acknowledge and express thoughts and feelings involving grief and loss is an ongoing and integral piece of their grief process.

Children in the 21st century face losses in the form of sudden fatal accidents and deaths due to illness, suicide, homicide, and disease. There are also many social issues that have a similar effect on children. Loss of family stability from separation and divorce, violence and abuse, bullying and victimization issues, foster care and abandonment, unemployment, multiple moves, parental imprisonment or deployment, and family alcohol and drug addiction are a few of the many grief issues affecting today's young children. Societal and global issues of war, terrorism, and nuclear threat create an overlay of trauma on top of these preexisting issues for our students.

Educators can provide a grief vocabulary, resources, crisis and educational interventions, preventions, and follow-up procedures. Administrators, teachers, and parents can join in creating comfort zones for the grieving children within the school system. By opening communication about loss and grief issues, adults are able to create a bridge between the world of fear, isolation, and loneliness and the world of truth, compassion, and dignity for the grieving child.

Resources

CD-ROM for Teachers and Counselors

A Look at Children's Grief (with 2 CEU credits). Two 1-hour modules: Children's Loss and Grief and Grief Resolution Techniques. info@adec.org or 860–586–7503.

Books for Teachers and Parents

Kathleen Cassini and Jacqueline Rogers, *Death in the Classroom.* Burnsville, NC: Compassion Books, 1996. This is a teacher's resource that offers guidance for working with death in the classroom.

Linda Goldman, *Breaking the Silence: A Guide to Help Children With Complicated Grief: Suicide, Homicide, AIDS, Violence and Abuse,* 2nd Ed. New York: Taylor & Francis, 2002. A guide for adults to help children with complicated grief issues. Includes chapters on suicide, homicide, AIDS, violence, and abuse; guidelines for educators; national resources; and an annotated bibliography.

Linda Goldman, *Life and Loss: A Guide to Help Grieving Children,* 2nd Ed. Washington, DC: Taylor & Francis, 2000, 3rd Edition in-press, 2013. This is a resource for working with children and normal grief. It provides information, resources, hands-on activities, a model of a goodbye visit for children, and an annotated bibliography.

Linda Goldman, *Raising Our Children to Be Resilient: A Guide to Helping Children Cope with Trauma in Today's World.* New York: Taylor & Francis, 2005. This book deals with contemporary grief and trauma issues that affect children and interventions for healing and resiliency.

Linda Goldman, *Great Answers to Difficult Questions About Death: What Children Need to Know.* London and Philadelphia: Jessica Kingsley Publishers, 2009. This resource creates words to use for parents and professionals to dialogue with children about death.

Kathryn Markell and Marc Markell, *The Children Who Lived: Using Harry Potter and Other Fictional Characters to Help Grieving Children and Adolescents.* New York: Taylor and Francis, 2008. This book outlines activities to help grieving children and adolescents by focusing on fictional child and adolescent characters experiencing grief in 11 novels.

Robert Stevenson. *What Will We Do? Preparing a School Community to Cope With Crisis, 2002.* This clear and informative book helps prepare school personnel to help children cope with death-related topics. Amityville, NY: Baywood Publishers.

Books for Children and Teens

J. Bode, *Death Is Hard to Live With.* New York: Bantam Doubleday Dell, 1993. Teenagers talk frankly about how they cope with loss.

Linda Goldman, *Bart Speaks Out: An Interactive Storybook for Young Children About Suicide.* Los Angeles, CA: WPS, 1996 (ages 5–10). This interactive storybook provides words to use with young children in discussing the sensitive topic of suicide.

Linda Goldman, *Children Also Grieve; Talking about Death and Healing.* London and Philadelphia: Jessica Kingsley Publisher, 2005 (Ages 4–10). This is an interactive storybook told through the eyes of Henry, a Tibetan Terrier, after the death of a grandfather. A memory book is included.

Marge Heegaard, *When Someone Very Special Dies.* Minneapolis, MN: Woodland, 1996 (ages 9 and up). This is a workbook for young children, which uses artwork and journaling to allow them to understand and express their grief.

B. Mellonie and R. Ingpen, *Lifetimes: The Beautiful Way to Explain Death to Children. New* York: Bantam, 1983 (ages 4–10). Explains the life cycle of plants, animals, and people.

Marlene Lee, *The Hero In My Pocket.* Early Light Press, 2005 (ages 4–8). This book helps children honor their own thoughts, feelings, and memories while honoring the loss of a military service member.

Donna O'Toole, *Aardy Aardvark Finds Hope.* Burnsville, NC: Mt. Rainbow, 1998 (ages 5–8). This is a story about animals that presents pain, sadness, and eventual hope after death.

Doris Stickney and Robyn Nordstrom. *Water Bugs and Dragonflies: Explaining Death to Young Children.* Cleveland, Ohio: Pilgrim Press, 2010 (ages 5-10). This is a meaningful story for young children about death.

Enid Traisman, *Fire in My Heart, Ice in My Veins.* Omaha, NE: Centering, 1992. This is a book for teenagers to journal thoughts and feelings and record grief memories.

S. Varley, *Badger's Parting Gifts.* New York: HarperCollins, 1992 (for all ages). Badger was a special friend to all the animals. After his death, each friend recalls a special memory.

References

Aisenberg, E. (chapter in). Best practice methods in a school-based environment. Grief Work With Elementary and Middle-School Students Walking With Hope When a Child Grieves. Chapter 55, pp. 577–585.

Fox, S. (1988). Good grief: Helping groups of children when a friend dies. Boston: New England Association for the Education of Young Children.

Ginsberg, H., & Opper, S. (1969). *Piaget's theory of intellectual development.* Englewood, NJ: Prentice-Hall.

Goldman, L. (200 , 3rd Edition in-press 2013). *Life and loss: A guide to help grieving children, 2nd Ed.* New York: Taylor & Francis.

Goldman, L. (2001). *Breaking the silence: A guide to help children with complicated grief,* 2nd Edition. New York: Taylor & Francis.

Goldman, L. (2005). *Raising our children to be resilient: A guide to helping children cope with trauma in today's world.* New York: Taylor & Francis.

Goldman, L. (2009). *Great answers to difficult questions about death: What children need to know.* London and Philadelphia: Jessica Kingsley Publishers.

Silverman, P. (2000). *Never too young to know: Death in children's lives.* New York: Oxford University Press.

VanDerHeyden, Ph.D. RTI Action Network, Education Research and Consulting, Inc., Fairhope, AL. http://www.rtinetwork.org/learn/what/approachesrti

Webb, N. B. (Ed.). (2002). *Helping bereaved children: A handbook for practitioners (2nd ed).* New York: Guilford.

SECTION IX

Improving Group Work and Training Resources

Delivery of services in groups is a component of many evidence-based practices. Group work, training others, and professional development are some of the most effective ways that school-based professionals can increase their personal impact on school services and may also be cost-effective alternatives to more individually designed practices. The chapters in this section discuss effective group work and professional development resources.

CHAPTER 45

Designing and Facilitating Support Groups and Therapy Groups with Adolescents

Importance of the Topic for Schools

Charles D. Garvin

Getting Started

Adolescents experience concerns and problems that have manifestations related to their stage of development. Virtually all can be observed in the school environment and affect or are affected by that environment, and all of those listed below have been treated successfully with group therapy in the school setting.[1]

- Poor relationships with peers. This is of great importance to teens as they move beyond the dominant role of the family into that of the peer culture. This problem is often associated with a deficit in social skills development.
- Emotional reactions in adolescence. Two emotions that are observed in the school environment are depression and anger. Depressed adolescents may not perform well in the classroom, may appear withdrawn, and may have a large number of absences. Angry students may vent at teachers or classmates; this anger may take the form of verbal abuse, property destruction, or frequent fighting
- Substance abuse. Many adolescents experiment with drugs and alcohol. The use may be induced by peer pressures. Students can become seriously addicted, with devastating effects on social and educational activities.
- Posttraumatic stress. Some adolescents are exposed to traumatic events, such as family violence, school violence (such as a school shooting), or a natural disaster (explosion, flood, tornado). Afterward, the student may experience nightmares, phobias, or anxiety attacks that seriously impede the student's school performance.

- Delinquency. Some adolescents become involved in either individual or gang-related illegal acts and, as a result, perform poorly in school. They are often expelled, if the acts occur in school, or are sent to alternative schools for students labeled delinquent.

What We Know

A number of studies have been conducted that demonstrate the effectiveness of group work for the above problems. An issue is that the majority of the studies evaluated the use of a cognitive-behavioral group approach. Approaches that use other models portrayed in the literature on social work with groups are also likely to be used in schools (Garvin, 1997; Northen & Kurland, 2001; Shulman, 2010; Toseland & Rivas, 2012), but these have not been evaluated as rigorously as those derived from cognitive-behavioral theory.

Group practitioners assess individual change by using any of the instruments that have been developed for one-on-one work. Many instruments have also been developed for assessing changes in group conditions, and the major ones have been described by Toseland et al. (2004, pp. 25–27).

Table 45.1 summarizes studies of the evidence for the effectiveness of group work with adolescents in schools. The table also includes references to studies that derive from multicultural perspectives. As can be seen, the effectiveness of a cognitive-behavioral group approach has been demonstrated with respect to adolescent depression, substance abuse, anger and disruptive classroom behavior, anxiety disorders, and posttraumatic disorders. A psychoeducational approach was effective with reducing risky behaviors. One study (Wagner & Macgowan, 2004) used an eclectic approach derived from cognitive theory, skills training, problem solving, and motivation enhancement. Several approaches were effective with students of color, such as narrative therapy with Hispanic adolescents and an indigenous African approach to empower inner-city African American female students.

Groups are especially appropriate for adolescents because of their strong investments in peer relationships as they seek less dependence on their families. They use peer groups to help them to develop their identities, select appropriate sets of values, strengthen close relationships, and explore intimacy.

What We Can Do

This section will be an overview of the steps in conducting support and treatment groups for adolescents. A difficulty in providing such an overview is that, as shown above, groups are conducted to help adolescents with a variety of concerns, and different interventions are utilized for each concern. Some of these interventions are specific to the treatment approach, such as the use of role models or the examination of distortions in the members' thought processes. Other interventions are utilized in all approaches and relate to maintaining the group as the means and context of treatment, such as defining the group's purpose and increasing members' attraction and commitment to the group.

Another semantic issue is posed by the title of this chapter, which refers to "support" and "therapy." For purposes of this chapter, we define *support groups* as those in which members provide encouragement to each other, in addition to examples of their successful coping with problems. *Therapy* will include all of the above processes but, in addition, the social worker and mental health practitioner will help the members to explicitly seek changes in their behaviors and in the attitudes and emotions related to the behaviors in question.

The Pre-Group Phase

In order to have a successful group experience, the group must be well planned in advance. The following are the types of planning that must be accomplished:

- *Determine group purpose.* The group's purpose, once defined, guides all of the other activities that precede the first meeting of the actual group.
- *Recruitment.* The practitioner must plan a strategy for obtaining a sufficient number of members for the group; this relates to the size issue to be discussed next.

Composition and Size

A treatment group typically has about 7 members, although a support group may have as many as 10–12 members. It is important in any group to choose members who are likely to be compatible

Table 45.1 Group Programs with Empirical Support

Type of Problem and Description of Intervention
Depression
Nicolas, G., Arntz, D. L., Hirsch, B., & Schmiedigen, A. (2009)
Cultural adaptation of a group treatment for Haitian American adolescents.
Substance abuse
Chernicoff, E. R. & Fazelbhoy, S. R. (2007)
Cognitive-behavioral groups for substance-abusing adolescents.
Wagner, E. F., & Macgowan, M. J. (2004)
Explored students' beliefs and learned behaviors, enhanced coping skills to handle negative moods and engage in social interactions, managed social pressures to use, and increased students' motivation to change. Served high- and middle-school students identified on instruments as frequent users of substances.
Anger/disruptive classroom behavior
Bidgood, B. A., Wilkie, H. & Katchaluba, A. (2010)
Releasing the steam: An evaluation of the supporting tempers, emotions, and anger management (STEAM) program for elementary and adolescent age children.
Lochman, J. E., Barry, T. D., & Pardini, D. A. (2003)
Social cognitive treatment for aggressive boys in 4th–6th grades, 18 sessions.
Reactions to trauma
Layne, C. M., et al. (2008)
Effectiveness of a school-based group psychotherapy program for war-exposed adolescents: A randomized controlled trial.
Foy, D. W., & Larson, L. C. (2006)
Group therapies for trauma using cognitive-behavioral therapy.
Anxiety disorders
Bernat, D.H., Bernstein, G. A., Victor, A. M., & Layne, A. E. (2008)
School-based interventions for anxious children: 3-, 6-, and 12-month follow-ups.
Sauter, F. M., Heyne, D., & Westenberg, P. M. (2009)
Cognitive behavior therapy for anxious adolescents: Developmental influences on treatment design and delivery.
Ethnically oriented interventions related to empowerment and strengthening identity
Malgady, R. G., & Costantino, G. (2003)
Served Hispanic adolescents to reduce such behaviors as anxiety, depression, acting out; sought to enhance ethnic identity and self-esteem through narrative therapy based on heroic models.
Scott, C. C. (2001)
Sought to empower African-American females through employing a Kawaida philosophy using rituals, symbols, affirmations, African proverbs, rhythm, and song, 14 sessions.
Rossello, J., Bernal, G., & Rivera-Medina, C. (2008)
Individual and group CBT and IPT for Puerto Rican adolescents with depressive symptoms.
Shechtman, Z. (2006)
Counseling groups for Arab adolescents in intergroup conflict in Israel: Report of an outcome study.

with each other and to be able to help one another attain both individual and group goals. Members should also find several other members of the group who are similar to themselves on characteristics they view as important. Thus, a member of a specified ethnic group or gender will be most likely to benefit from the group if there are others who are similar in this way. Other characteristics that may be salient are age, social class, social skills, and academic skills. Davis and Proctor (1989) have described the research on group composition in relationship to race and gender.

Preparation

Research has shown that if members participate in a personal interview with the practitioner before the first meeting to prepare them for the group, they are more likely to benefit from the group than members who do not have this preparation (Meadow, n.d.; Yalom & Leszcz, 2005).

The preparation of members for school-based groups includes the following:

- discussion of the purpose of the group
- discussion of how the potential member's concerns relate to this group's purpose
- evidence that this type of service can benefit members
- the nature of the potential member's previous experience as a group member and how this is likely to affect her or his participation in this group
- the hopes and fears of the potential member regarding the group experience

Members during this preparation are frequently asked to sign a form indicating their understanding of the group's intent and their willingness to participate in it.

Frequency

The number of times the group will meet may be only once, for a brief period (such as six times), or for as long as a semester or an academic year. A single-session group usually has the purpose of helping members to deal with a concrete event, such as the death of a classmate. Most groups meet for a short period, such as 6–10 sessions. The advantage of this is that members are likely to be motivated to attend a group that has such short-term limits, and yet this is a sufficient length of time for members to learn a set of coping skills, solve a set of clear-cut problems, and develop the kind of trust in the practitioner and other members that will enable them to express relatively private thoughts and feelings. Meetings are usually held on a weekly basis, although some groups with highly motivated and resilient members may meet twice a week.

Meetings are typically about 1–1.5 hours in duration, although some groups may meet for 45-minute periods. Longer periods may make it difficult for members to sustain interest or to handle intense feelings that arise in longer encounters.

Group Beginnings: The Process of Group Formation

The way that the practitioner helps the group in its initial meetings to form will have a great impact on how well the group accomplishes its purposes. This process of formation may take a full session in a group meeting only a few times; a group that is likely to continue for a full semester may spend several meetings in handling the tasks of formation. These tasks consist of the following:

Review of Group Purpose

Even though the practitioner has described the group's purpose in the initial announcements about the group and in the preparatory interviews with the members, this issue should be considered again when the group meets for the first time. This is because when members actually "see" who is present, they may decide to alter the group's purpose.

During group formation, members should be helped to create individual goals that are compatible with the purposes of the group. Members may be reminded of the goals they have selected, and it is often appropriate in adolescent groups to record the goals in a personal notebook.

Norms

It is essential that members adopt a series of norms about their behavior in the group. It is inappropriate for the facilitator to simply state the "rules" and leave it at that, as the members must have enough of a discussion to indicate that they have all agreed to the norms and understand them. One of the most universal norms is confidentiality, in which members indicate that they will not repeat to anyone outside the group who else is in the group and what anyone else has said, although they are free to talk to others about what they, themselves, have said. All group workers have reported that they seldom, if ever, hear of a breach of this rule.

Emotional Reactions

Members are likely to have mixed feelings about the group, especially when the group begins. They are likely to have positive feelings about the group because they hope it will help them. On the other hand, they may fear that it will exacerbate their difficulties or that they will fail to find acceptance from the other members.

Development of Relationships

Unless members have formed relationships with at least some other members and with the practitioner, they are unlikely to wish to remain in the group or to give and receive help from other members. At the first session, the practitioner seeks to initiate this process by having members introduce themselves in ways that help them discover commonalities. Adolescents especially respond well to the numerous "ice-breakers" that are available (Barlow et al., 1999).

The Middle Phases of the Group

Once the above tasks related to group beginnings have been accomplished, the group is ready to undertake activities to attain its goals. Practitioners will draw upon procedures described below, albeit with differences related to various purposes and theories. In addition, the practitioner must consider processes found in the middle phases of group development.

Characteristics of Middle Phases

It would seem that once the group has formed, all would be smooth sailing. This is often not the case. Countless practitioners have observed a conflict phase early in a group's life, undoubtedly induced by members becoming comfortable enough to question the initial leadership, norms, and purposes of the group (Toseland & Rivas, 2012). The practitioner's role is to remain supportive during this phase and to mediate conflicts that may arise. After this period, the group is likely to return to a pursuit of its goals with renewed vigor.

Common Change Processes

Change processes in groups focus on helping members to change the way they view themselves and their world (perceptions), the way they understand themselves and their world (cognitions), the way they respond emotionally (affects), the way they behave (actions), and how they can use their reasoning to create their own approaches to change (problem solving). Let us now briefly consider how groups can help adolescents in these ways.

1. Changing perceptions. Members' difficulties may be caused by how they experience situations through what they see or hear.[2] Some of the examples of this are the student who hears from peers that there is no harm in the use of marijuana, from parents that all members of some ethnic group are bad, or from teachers that he or she is inferior. One of the powers of the group is that other members may not share these perceptions and can provide overwhelming evidence about contrary views that will lead to a valuable change in the member's perceptions.

2. Changing cognitions. We refer here to beliefs that members hold about the causes and consequences of events. Examples are member As belief that if he is rejected by a potential girlfriend, this means that he will be rejected by all future women; member B's belief that if she gets a low grade on an examination, she will always fail examinations; or member C's idea that if he fails to start a fight with a classmate, he will be viewed as a weakling. Group members can suggest cognitions that are the opposite of these, such as that member A is likely to be acceptable to other young women; B has succeeded on examinations before and, with effort, will do so again; and C will be viewed as a stronger person if he indicates that he does not wish to solve disputes physically. Another important way of approaching cognitive change through groups is through process

comments. This entails the social worker, or other members, noting interactions among members and enhancing the members' awareness of the interactions, the meaning each of the members involved attaches to the interactions, and whether the ways that the members interact further their treatment goals and, if not, what changes they would like to make in these interactions (Garvin, 1997, p. 164).

3. Changing affects. Member affects are often the source of the members' problems in any group and especially in adolescent groups. The major examples are anxiety, anger, and depression. Each of these types of feeling can be ameliorated in groups, albeit with very different procedures. Anxiety can often be lessened by any one of several group activities. Progressive relaxation can usefully be taught in almost any group because virtually all problems are accompanied by feelings of tension. This technique involves teaching members to systematically relax each muscle group. Space does not permit us to provide details on this, but excellent resources are available (Rose, 1998, pp. 296–307). Members can also be asked to visualize peaceful scenes as a means of achieving relaxation. A third approach is based in breathing exercises (Rose, 1998, pp. 304–305). Interventions in groups to reduce anger involve teaching members to express anger in safe ways, such as discussing the anger and the internal events associated with it and expressing the anger in such a manner as to acknowledge the humanity and the needs of the other persons involved (Rose, 1998, pp. 437–459).

Reducing depression requires the practitioner to help members to grieve losses and replace inactivity with productive actions. When members remain inactive or even withdrawn, they may repeatedly think of the sadness they are experiencing, thus increasing it (Curry et al., 2001).[3]

4. Changing actions. While attention to members' affects and thoughts are likely to result in their behaving differently, several approaches are used by group practitioners to help group members acquire new behaviors. These approaches make use of the opportunities afforded by the group environment. These include members using each other as role models, members practicing new behaviors in role plays, and members reinforcing the appropriate behavior of other members. Group workers will often use activities that encourage members to act in new ways. Such activities include games, drama, dance, and crafts.

5. Problem solving. All approaches to group work make use of problem solving. This process involves members defining the problem and the goal sought, seeking alternative solutions to the problem, evaluating the alternatives, choosing an alternative, and implementing the best alternative.

The Ending Phases of the Group

The way that the practitioner facilitates the group when it is about to end will have an impact on what personal changes members retain when the group ends. The amount of time allotted to this varies, depending on how long the group has been in existence. A short-term group will usually allocate all of the final session to a termination process. A group that has been in existence for a semester or longer may spend at least two sessions on termination. The following are the tasks of the ending phase:

- Members discuss the degree to which they have attained individual goals.
- Members evaluate the degree to which the group and the practitioner have been helpful.
- Members plan activities they will undertake after the group ends to maintain positive changes.
- Members discuss both positive and negative feelings about ending. Positive ones may relate to goals they have attained and pleasures the group has afforded them. Negative ones may relate to the fact that they may not see the practitioner or other members, as a group, again.

Applying Interventions within a Response to Intervention Framework

The Response to Intervention (RTI) framework seeks to integrate academic and behavioral supports into one system. This approach seeks to have these supports correlated with one another for the following reasons:

1. The same issues can be addressed by each set of supports so that solutions reinforce one another.
2. Conflicting expectations are avoided so that teachers, parents, and students are not confused by different sets of goals.

3. Professionals providing different types of services will find it easier to communicate with each other regarding their methods, approaches, and outcomes.

Group work with adolescent students is well positioned to fit with this framework in several ways.

1. The classroom can also be regarded as a group, and so-called Tier 1 services can be provided, for example, by either the teacher or a school social worker or counselor to the entire class using group work principles such as mutual aid, group problem solving, and assessment of how students participate in this group experience. The group facilitator, be it teacher or another person, can divide the class into smaller subgroups if the class is a large one. Observers can also help identify students with additional needs. Behavioral health information, coping mechanisms, and ways of dealing with stress can be provided in this way.
2. Tier 2 services can be offered through groups, such as diagnoses derived from observing students in support and other types of groups, including how the students interact with other students in their group.
3. Tier 3 services can be offered in groups such as the groups described in this chapter. Examples are groups for treatment of anxiety, depression, anger, or trauma. In some cases, other forms of therapy such as individual or family can be recommended based on the students' experiences with these group therapy experiences.

Tools and Practice Examples

Clarke and his colleagues (2003) describe a group program for depressed adolescents. They identified potential members of the group through the use of well-tested screening instruments and included teens who used drugs as long as they were not actively using during sessions. They excluded teens who had active psychotic or bipolar disorders. They also excluded teens who were major suicidal risks.

The investigators established ground rules in the first session and explained the plan for the 16 2-hour sessions to come. They also explained a social learning theory model of depression. The program utilized in this group had two components. One, primarily used in sessions 2–5, was to help the youth increase their rates of age-appropriate and pleasant activities. Group leaders helped the members to select a list of fun activities that they would like to do more often. The youths found a relationship between their moods and these activities. The youths then set small but achievable goals for increasing their activity level. They also used problem solving to remove barriers to engaging in these activities.

The second component was based on cognitive therapy and occupied most of sessions 5–10. The practitioner explained the following model: Triggering situations lead to unexamined beliefs, which contribute to feelings. The early sessions employed cartoons to illustrate common beliefs leading to frustration, anger, or depression. Members were taught how to assess whether these beliefs are rational or not. They were then coached on ways of substituting realistic, positive thoughts, after which they rated their mood changes. The members helped each other with suggestions and ideas throughout this process. The authors noted that teens are much more likely to accept this kind of analysis from each other than from adults.

The members were also taught to relax through progressive muscle relaxation and deep-breathing techniques. Final sessions were devoted to problem solving, negotiation, and communication skills. The final session focused on maintaining gains, learning how to recognize a recurrence of depression, and developing a personal depression prevention plan. Members reviewed their progress, dealt with feelings about the group ending, and discussed ways of replacing the support that the group had provided.

Key Points to Remember

- Carefully specify the purpose of the group and state this in a way that recognizes how the problem is seen in the adolescent community.
- Select members who are likely to be compatible in terms of age, culture, and personal attributes.
- Conduct a pre-group interview with each prospective member.

- In first meetings, accomplish group formation tasks, such as clarification of purpose, initiation of relationships among members, agreement on norms, and creation of individual goals.
- After formation, plan *with the members* what the activities will be to achieve the purposes of the group. These activities will encourage changes in members' perceptions, cognitions, affects, and behaviors.
- At the end of the group, engage in such termination tasks as assessment of change, evaluation of the group experience, expression of feelings about endings, and determination of how to maintain desirable changes.

Notes

1. Since this book is directed at school social workers and related mental health professionals, we shall use the term *group work* rather than *group therapy* in this chapter as this is the designation we believe is most employed by social workers.
2. There are, of course, other senses, but these are the ones on which we shall focus here.
3. Any of these emotional responses may require treatment from a psychiatrist, such as prescribing medications.

References

Barlow, C, Blythe, J., & Edmonds, M. (1999). *A handbook of interactive exercises for groups*. Boston: Allyn & Bacon.

Bernstein, G. A., Bernat, D. H. Victor, A. M., & Layne, A. E. (2008). School-based interventions for anxious children: 3–, 6–, and 12–month follow-ups. *Journal of the American Academy of Child and Adolescent Psychiatry*, *47*(9) 1039–1047.

Bidgood, B. A., Wilkie, H., & Katchaluba, A. (2010). Releasing the steam: An evaluation of the supporting tempers, emotions, and anger management (STEAM) program for elementary and adolescent-age children. *Social Work with Groups: A Journal of Community and Clinical Practice*, *33*(2–3), 160–174.

Clarke, G. N., DeBar, L. L., & Lewinsohn, P. M. (2003). Cognitive-behavioral group treatment for adolescent depression. In A. E. Kazdin & J. R. Weisz (Eds.), *Evidence-based psychotherapies for children and adolescents* (pp. 120–134). New York: Guilford.

Davis, L., & Proctor, E. (1989). *Race, gender, and class: Guidelines for practice with individuals, families, and groups*. Englewood Cliffs, NJ: Prentice-Hall.

Curry, J.F, Wells, K.C., Lochman,J.E., Craighead, W, Nagy, P.D. (2001). Group and Family cognitive behavior therapy for adolescent depression and substance abuse. *Cognitive and Behavioral Practice. 8*(4), 367-376.

Foy, D. W., & Larson, L. C. (2006). Group therapies for trauma using cognitive-behavioral therapy. In V. M. Follette & J. I. Ruzek (Eds.), *Cognitive-behavioral therapies for trauma* (2nd ed., pp. 388–404) New York, NY: Guilford Press.

Garvin, C. D. (1997). *Contemporary group work* (3rd ed.). Boston: Allyn & Bacon.

Koss-Chioino, J. D., Baca, L., & Vargas, L.A. Group therapy with Mexican American and Mexican adolescents: Focus on culture. In U. P. Gielen, J.G., J.M. Fish, & M. Jefferson (Eds.), *Principles of multicultural counseling and therapy* (pp. 231–252). New York, NY: Routledge/Taylor and Francis Group.

Layne, C.M., Saltzman, W.R., Poppleton, L.B., Pašalić, G.M., Duraković, A., Mušić, E … .Pynoos, R.S.(2008). Effectiveness of a school-based group psychotherapy program for war-exposed adolescents: A randomized controlled trial. *Journal of the American Academy of Child and Adolescent Psychiatry*, *47*(9), 1048–1062.

Lochman, J. E., Barry, T. D., & Pardini, D. A. (2003). Anger control training for aggressive youth. In A. E. Kazdin & J. R. Weisz (Eds.), *Evidence-based psychotherapies for children and adolescents* (pp. 263–278). New York: Guilford.

Malgady, R. G., & Costantino, G. (2003). Narrative therapy for Hispanic children and adolescents. In A. E. Kazdin & J. R. Weisz (Eds.), *Evidence-based psy-chotherapies for children and adolescents* (pp. 425–438). New York: Guilford.

Meadow, D. (n.d.). *Connecting theory and practice: The effect of pregroup preparation on individual and group behavior* (mimeographed).

Nicolas, G., Arntz, D. L., Hirsch, B., & Schmiedigen, A. (2009). Cultural adaptation of a group treatment for Haitian American adolescents. *Professional Psychology: Research and Practice*, *40*(4), 378–384.

Northen, H., & Kurland, R. (2001). *Social work with groups* (3rd ed.). New York: Columbia University Press.

Rose, S. D. (1998). *Group therapy with troubled youth: A cognitive-behavioral interactive approach*. Thousand Oaks, CA: Sage.

Rossello, J., Bernal, G., & Rivera- Medina, C. (2008). Individual and group CBT and IPT for Puerto Rican adolescents with depressive symptoms. *Cultural Diversity and Ethnic Minority Psychology*, *14*(3), 234–245.

Sauter, F. M., Heyne, D., & Westenberg, P. M. (2009). Cognitive behavior therapy for anxious adolescents: Developmental influences on treatment design and delivery. *Clinical Child and Family Psychological Review, 12*(4), 310–335.

Scott, C. C. (2001). The sisterhood group: A culturally focused empowerment group model for inner city African-American *youth. Journal of Child and Adolescent Group Therapy, 11*, 77–85.

Shechtman, Z. (2006). Counseling groups for Arab adolescents in an intergroup conflict in Israel: Report of an outcome study. *Peace and Conflict: Journal of Peace Psychology, 12*(2), 119–137.

Shulman, L. (2010). *The skills of helping individuals, families, and groups* (4th ed.). Itaska, IL: Peacock.

Toseland, R.W., Jones, L.V., & Gellis, Z. D. (2004). Group dynamics. In C. D. Garvin, L. M. Gutierrez, & M. J. Galinsky (Eds.), *Handbook of social work with groups* (pp. 13–31). New York: Guilford.

Toseland, R.W., & Rivas, R. F. (2012). *An introduction to group work practice* (7th ed.). Boston: Allyn & Bacon.

Wagner, E. F., & Macgowan, M. J. (2004). *School-based treatment of adolescent substance abuse problems: Student assistance program group counseling.* (unpublished manuscript)

Yalom, I. Leszcz, M. (2005). *The theory and practice of group psychotherapy* (5th ed.). New York: Basic.

CHAPTER 46

Designing and Facilitating Groups with Children

Craig Winston LeCroy

Getting Started

School is the major socializing institution for children. In school, children develop social behavior in addition to learning academic skills. There is a clear link among the social, emotional, and cognitive development of children. Although schools focus on children's educational and cognitive skills and capabilities, an important but neglected area of concern is the healthy psychosocial development of children. Indeed, most educators, parents, and the public want schools to have a broader agenda that includes health, character development, social competence, and civic engagement (Wiseman & Hunt, 2008). It is increasingly understood that schools (preschool through high school) play a critical role in fostering mental health and integrating mental health strategies throughout the curriculum (Healthy People, 2010). Our schools must begin to acknowledge the importance of instructing students in a new set of basics: responsible decision making, socially competent behavior, healthy behavior, positive mental health, and positive contributions to family, peers, and their community. Without such skills, children face numerous negative consequences later in life or fail to develop to their fullest capacity.

The purpose of this chapter is to provide some guidelines for designing and facilitating therapeutic groups for children. The primary focus is on elementary- and middle-school children between the ages of 6 and 12. Offering various small groups in schools can facilitate the socialization and academic education of children. Lela Costin (1969) argued more than 35 years ago that social workers should apply group work methods more broadly in school settings. Groups can equip children with prosocial skills to help them replace aggressive or withdrawn behaviors with appropriate coping strategies. For example, interpersonal skills can be taught to enhance communication with peers, parents, and authority figures.

Numerous opportunities exist for the implementation of various group-based programs that can help to facilitate the successful socialization of children and adolescents in our schools. Groups have been organized to serve children and adolescents with social skills deficiencies, anger control problems, substance abuse, attention-deficit/hyperactivity disorder, trauma recovery, anxiety, coping with divorce of parents, pregnancy prevention, school dropout, stress, grief and loss, obsessive-compulsive disorder, and many combinations of these themes. School social workers and other mental health practitioners can play an important role in the design and implementation of such group programs.

There are a number of advantages of working with children in groups. The peer group is a natural part of child and adolescent development, and as such the treatment more nearly simulates their real world than the client–adult dyad. Groups also represent a more efficient way of delivering interventions than do dyads. Group membership commonly ends the sense of isolation and lack of understanding that many students experience, since they are surrounded by other children who are dealing with similar issues and problems. Groups may be divided into subgroups for certain exercises and as a way of increasing the amount and breadth of interactions in the group. Certain interventions are more accessible or more effective in small groups, for example, the use of brainstorming in teaching problem-solving skills, or the use of feedback from other members following role playing, or designing extra-group tasks and goals. Games and other recreational activities help to build cohesion and motivation. Finally, groups enhance the generalization of change since each member observes and helps to solve a diversity of problems manifested by the other clients.

What We Know

Most of the empirical evidence for interventions with children and adolescents has been conducted as part of special programs that are offered in a group setting. Three well-known reviews (Catalano et al., 2002; Wilson-Simmons, 2007; National Research Council, 2002) have all concluded that promotion is successful in obtaining positive outcomes and reducing negative outcomes. Durlak and Wells (1997) conducted a meta-analysis to examine the impact of more than 150 primary prevention programs; 73% of the studies were conducted in a school setting. The overall results were that programs enhanced competencies such as assertiveness, communication skills, self-image, and school achievement. Strong benefits were realized for young children aged 2–7 with interventions using a behavioral approach. More recently, Durlak and Weissberg (2007) examined 73 after-school programs that promote personal and social skills. In a meta-analysis, they that found youth who participate in programming show significant progress in improving attitudes, behavioral adjustment, and school performance.

In a more treatment-focused review, Greenberg, Domitrovich, and Bumbarger (2001) reviewed more than 130 programs for schoolchildren ranging in age from 5 to 18. The intent of the review was to examine rigorously evaluated interventions that reduced psychological symptoms, such as aggression or depression, or reduced factors associated with child mental disorders. Overall results were favorable, and the authors concluded that longer-term programs are better; multiple domain-based programs (e.g., individual, school, and family) are more effective than an exclusive child focus; and with school-age children it is better to address school ecology and school climate.

Tobler, Roona, Ochshorn, Marshall, Streke, and Stackpole (2000) examined child and adolescent outcome studies over a span of 20 years. Programs were classified as noninteractive or interactive, with interactive programs obtaining stronger effects. In particular, high-intensity interactive programs with 16 or more hours of curriculum had greater impact than low-intensity (6 hours or less) programs. Greater benefits were also found for programs that included life skills models, refusal skills, goal setting, assertiveness, communication, and coping strategies. Using this research, Zins et al. (2002) make a compelling case for the relationship between programs that promote psychosocial functioning and improved school attitudes, behavior, and performance.

Most of these empirically supported groups range in size from 5 to 15 members, although the norm is about 6–9. They range in duration from 6 to 20 sessions, depending on the complexity of the presenting problems. Most group sessions last from 45 minutes to 1.5 hours. Most groups are closed and time limited, with a fixed beginning and ending time. Note that there are some data to support smaller groups over larger groups and to support providing group structure, which permits intense interaction by everyone in the group. The more complex the problems, the longer the length of time and the more sessions that are required. Table 46.1 presents examples of key group studies with empirical support.

What We Can Do

While there are many types of therapeutic groups from which children can benefit, the remainder of this chapter will focus on social competence–based groups as one example. Social competence training is often conducted in a group format that provides support and a reinforcing context for learning new responses and appropriate behaviors in a variety of social situations. The group is a natural context for social skills training because of the peer interactions that take place as the group members work together. Additionally, the group allows for the extensive use of modeling and feedback, which are successful components of group treatment.

The following seven basic steps delineate the process that group leaders can follow when doing social skills training (based on LeCroy, *Handbook of Evidence-based Treatment Manuals for Children and Adolescents*, 2008). These guidelines have been found to be effective in teaching social skills with middle-school students (LeCroy, 2004) and elementary-school students (King & Kirschenbaum, 1992). Table 46.2 presents these steps and outlines the process for teaching social skills. In each step, there is a request for group member involvement.

Table 46.1 Group Programs with Empirical Support

Type of Problem and Description of Intervention
Aggressive behavior/violence prevention
Feindler & Gerber, 2008 TAME: Teen Anger Management Education Program that focuses on school, home, and individual treatment; goal is to increase bonds in these domains; social, cognitive, and problem-solving skills are emphasized
Olweus, 2007 Multicomponent program; attempts to restructure the school environment to reduce opportunities and rewards for bullies
Withdrawn and isolated behavior
Painter, 2008 Program is based on a social skills training model for young children; emphasizes teaching new skills and reinforcement for new behaviors
Weiss & Harris, 2001 Program for autistic children that applies social skills training and behavior modification primarily to enhance social interaction skills
Peer mediation/positive youth development
Shinn & Yoshikawa, 2008 School-wide school climate programs for elementary schools; promotes successful participation in family, school, peer group, and community
McGinnis, 2011 Curriculum for learning general social skills
Divorce
Pedro-Carroll, 2008 10-session program that emphasizes support and skill building for children of divorce; includes content on problem solving, anger management, and coping
Social competence
Fraser, Nash, Galinsky, & Darwin, 2000 Curriculum-based program that promotes self-control, group participation, and social awareness; emphasis is on decision-making and problem-solving skills
LeCroy & Daley, 2001a Broad-based universal prevention program that focuses on preteen and early adolescent girls; uses a psychoeducational and social skills training approach

This is because it is critical that group leaders involve the participants actively in the skills training. Also, this keeps the group interesting and fun for the group members.

1. Present the social skill being taught. The first step is for the group leader to present the skill. The leader solicits an explanation of the skill, for example, "Can anyone tell me what it means to resist peer pressure?" After group members have answered this question, the leader emphasizes the rationale for using the skill. For example, "You would use this skill when you're in a situation where you don't want to do something that your friends want you to do, and you should be able to say 'no' in a way that helps your friends to be able to accept your refusal." The leader then requests additional reasons for learning the skill.

2. Discuss the social skill. The leader presents the specific skill steps that constitute the social skill. For example, the skill steps for resisting peer pressure are good nonverbal communication (includes eye contact, posture, voice volume), saying "no"

Table 46.2 A Summary of the Steps in Social Skills Training

1. Present the social skill being taught
   A. Solicit an explanation of the skill
   B. Get group members to provide rationales for the skill
2. Discuss the social skill
   A. List the skill steps
   B. Get group members to give examples of using the skill
3. Present a problem situation and model the skill
   A. Evaluate the performance
   B. Get group members to discuss the model
4. Set the stage for role playing the skill
   A. Select the group members for role playing
   B. Get group members to observe the role play
5. Group members rehearse the skill
   A. Provide coaching if necessary
   B. Get group members to provide feedback on verbal and nonverbal elements
6. Practice using complex skill situations
   A. Teach accessory skills, e.g., problem solving
   B. Get group members to discuss situations and provide feedback
7. Train for generalization and maintenance
   A. Encourage practice of skills outside the group
   B. Get group members to bring in their problem situations

early in the interaction, suggesting an alternative activity, and leaving the situation if there is continued pressure. Leaders then ask group members to share examples of when they used the skill or examples of when they could have used the skill but did not.

3. Present a problem situation and model the skill. The leader presents a problem situation. The following is an example of a problem situation for resisting peer pressure:

> You are with your friend at recess, and he suggests you both play a mean trick on another student, who is also a friend of yours.

The group leader chooses members to role play this situation and then models the skills. Group members evaluate the model's performance. Did the model follow all of the skill steps? Was his or her performance successful? The group leader may choose another group member to model if the leader believes that the student already has the requisite skills. Another alternative is to present to the group videotaped models. This has the advantage of following the recommendation by researchers that the models be similar to the trainee in age, sex, and social characteristics.

4. Set the stage for the role playing of the skill. For this step, the group leader needs to construct the social circumstances for the role play. Leaders select group members for the role play and give them their parts to play. The leader reviews how to act out their roles with them. Group members not in the role play observe the process. It is sometimes helpful if they are given specific instructions for their observations. For example, one member may observe the use of nonverbal skills; another member may be instructed to observe when "no" is said in the interaction.

5. Group members rehearse the skill. Rehearsal or guided practice of the skill is an important part of effective social skills training. Group leaders and group members provide instructions or coaching before and during the role play and provide praise and feedback for improvement. Following a role-play rehearsal, the leader will usually give instructions for improvement, model the suggested improvements, or coach the person to incorporate the feedback in the subsequent role play. Often the

group members doing the role play will practice the skills in the situation several times to refine their skills and incorporate the feedback offered by the group. The role plays continue until the trainee's behavior becomes more and more similar to that of the model. It is important that "over-learning" take place, so the group leader should encourage many examples of effective skill demonstration followed by praise. Group members should be taught how to give effective feedback before the rehearsals. Throughout the teaching process, the group leader can model desired responses. For example, after a role play, the leader can respond first and model feedback that starts with a positive statement.

6. Practice using complex skill situations. The last phase deals with more difficult and complex skill situations. Complex situations can be developed by extending the interactions and roles in the problem situations. Most social skills groups also incorporate the teaching of problem-solving abilities. Problem solving is a general approach to helping young people to gather information about a problematic situation, generate a large number of potential solutions, evaluate the consequences of various solutions, and outline plans for the implementation of a particular solution. Group leaders can identify appropriate problem situations and lead members through the above steps. The problem-solving training is important because it prepares young people to make adjustments as needed in a given situation and is a skill with large-scale application (see Fraser, Nash, Galinsky, & Darwin, 2000, for more details).

7. Train for generalization and maintenance. The success of the social skills program depends on the extent to which the skills that young people learn transfer to their day-to-day lives. Practitioners must always be planning for ways to maximize the generalization of skills learned and promote their continued use after training. There are several principles that help to facilitate the generalization and maintenance of skills. The first is the use of overlearning. The more that over-learning takes place, the greater likelihood of later transfer of skills. Therefore, it is important that group leaders insist on mastery of the skills. Another important principle of generalization is to vary the stimuli as skills are learned. To accomplish this, practitioners can use a variety of models, problem situations, role-play actors, and trainers. The different styles and behaviors of the people used produce a broader context in which to apply the skills learned. Perhaps most important is to require that young people use the skills in their real-life settings. Group leaders should assign and monitor homework to encourage transfer of learning. This may include the use of written contracts to do certain tasks outside of the group. Group members should be asked to bring to the group examples of problem situations where the social skills can be applied. Lastly, practitioners should attempt to develop external support for the skills learned. One approach to this is to set up a buddy system where group members work together to perform the skills learned outside the group.

Practical Considerations in Conducting Social Skills Training Groups

Conducting group prevention and intervention services is an efficient use of a school social worker's and mental health counselor's time, as several students can be seen at one time. However, groups must be recruited and constructed with certain key factors in mind. First, recruitment for groups will depend on the goals of the particular program. It may be necessary to limit the number of participants involved, in which case procedures must be used to help identify the students most likely to benefit from the program. This screening process can be accomplished by administering assessment devices, identifying students who meet specified risk criteria, conducting pre-group interviews, or designing a referral system for teachers and other professionals to use to refer children directly to the group. On the other hand, limiting groups only to children who meet certain risk criteria may not be best in some groups. Some research indicates that including participants who are highly socially competent can have positive implications. Given that some groups will contain children who act out antisocially, a higher degree of poor social skills modeling could initially take place. By including high-functioning children in an antisocial group, the opportunity for prosocial modeling increases. Also, it may be less difficult to maintain order (Merrell & Gueldner, 2010). Finally, group composition includes factors such as how well the group participants know one another, how heterogeneous the group is, how large the group is, the age and developmental level of the participants, and their gender. It is important that all members of a group have the time and attention they need to practice skills and receive important feedback; therefore, the group should be 6–10 members with two leaders. Merrell and Gueldner (2010) propose that the members of the group should not vary in age by more than 2 or

3 years. It is not difficult to recognize the need for language and interventions to be age- and developmentally appropriate. Presenting group material that requires a high level of cognitive ability will not be effective for group members who are either too young or who are functioning at a lower level develop-mentally than the skill requires.

Applying Interventions within a Response to Intervention Framework

Social skills training groups can fit within the Response to Intervention (RTI) framework as one level of intervention (Vaughn, Wanzek, & Fletcher (2007). In particular, if schools implement a screening process to identify children who could benefit from services, the group social skills treatment model is one level of intervention that can occur within school services. Often social workers or counselors implement social skills training with children who are either identified by teachers or identified through another assessment process such as a school-wide screen. The focus of RTI on evaluation of instruction and progress can be achieved with the use of evaluation tools (LeCroy & Okamoto, 2002), which can measure progress when in the groups.

Tools and Practice Examples

A Group Program for Early Adolescent Girls

A social skills training psychoeducational prevention program called Go Grrrls (LeCroy & Daley, 2001a) was developed specifically for preteens or early adolescent girls. This program was designed using empirical information about the developmental tasks critical for the successful transition to adolescence and adulthood. A randomized control group evaluation found empirical support for the short-term impact of the program (LeCroy, 2004; LeCroy & Daley, 2001a). In response to common problems empirically identified, a group of core developmental tasks (e.g., development of positive gender-role identification, body image, and self-image) were identified as program goals.

Building a Solid Foundation of Skills

We have already discussed the importance of overlearning in social skills training. The Go Grrrls program is designed to increase the odds of participants' overlearning by selecting key skills that girls need to learn and building participants' confidence and mastery of these skills over several sessions. For the focus area of "assertiveness," the Go Grrrls program provides three sessions that help girls to learn this skill. In one of the early group meetings, girls are introduced to the general concept of assertiveness and are given practice using this skill. In two later sessions, girls are given additional practice using assertiveness skills. To reinforce the skills learned, girls turn in journal assignments from a workbook (LeCroy & Daley, 2001b). Table 46.3 illustrates how social skills may be combined in a complementary fashion to help participants build strengths.

Key Points to Remember

As school social workers and other practitioners work toward the goal of enhancing the socialization process of children, methods for promoting social competence, such as social skills training, have much to offer. This direct approach to working with children has been applied in numerous problem areas and with many child behavior problems. It is straightforward in application and has been adapted so that social workers, counselors, teachers, and peer helpers have successfully applied the methodology. Social workers and mental health counselors can make an important contribution to children, families, and schools through preventive and remedial approaches like those described in this chapter. As we have seen, children's social behavior is a critical aspect of their successful adaptation to society. The school represents an ideal place for children to learn and practice social behavior. It provides the needed multipeer context and offers multiple opportunities for newly learned behaviors to be generalized to other situations and circumstances. Research supports the efficacy of prevention and intervention programs like these in the schools. These promising treatment approaches offer accountability, an opportunity to reduce some of the difficulties that children face, and the skills and abilities for them to realize their full potential.

Table 46.3 Go Grrrls Skill-Building Goals and Treatment Approach

Program Goal	*Related Social Skills Training*
Core skill: Assertiveness	
Goal: To teach girls to act assertively rather than passively or aggressively	1. Discuss the skill of assertiveness
Rationale: Teaching basic assertiveness skills to girls will help them speak up in classrooms and withstand peer pressure and will serve as a foundation for learning more specific refusal skills.	2. Group leaders demonstrate assertive, passive, and aggressive responses to sample situations 3. Group members practice identifying assertive behavior 4. Group members practice assertiveness skills 5. Group leaders and other members provide feedback Sample scenario: You are in science class, and the boy you are partners with tells you that he wants to mix the chemicals and you can be the secretary. What do you do?
Core skill: Making and keeping friends	
Goal: To equip girls with the tools they need to establish and maintain healthy peer relationships	1. Discuss the components of a successful conversation, including the beginning, middle, and end
Rationale: Disturbances in peer relationships are among the best predictors of psychiatric, social, and school problems. Teaching friendship skills can reduce these problems. Strong friendship skills can be an important protective factor.	2. Group leaders demonstrate both ineffective and effective conversational skills 3. Group members practice identifying effective conversational skills, such as making eye contact and asking questions of the other person 4. Group members practice conversational skills in role-play situations 5. Group leaders and other members provide feedback Sample scenario: It is your first day of junior high and you don't know anyone in your homeroom. Start a conversation with the girl who sits next to you.

References

Catalano, R. F., Berglund, M. L., Ryan, J. A. M., Lonczak, H. S., & Hawkins, J. D. (2002). Positive youth development in the United States: Research findings on evaluations of positive youth development programs. *Prevention & Treatment, 5*, Article 15. Retrieved August, 1, 2002, from http://journals.apa.org/prevention/volume5/pre0050015a.html

Costin, L. B. (1969). An analysis of the tasks of school social work. *Social Service Review, 43*, 247–285.

Durlak, J. A., & Wells, A. M. (1997). Primary prevention mental health programs for children and adolescents: A meta-analytic review. *American Journal of Community Psychology, 25*, 115–152.

Durlak, J. A., & Weissberg, R. P. (2007). *The impact of after school programs that promote personal and social skills.* Chicago, IL: Collaborative for Academic, Social and Emotional Learning.

Feindler, E. L., & Gerber, M. (2008). TAME: Teen anger management education. In C. LeCroy (Ed.), *Handbook of evidence-based treatment manuals for children and adolescents* (pp. 139–169). New York, NY: Oxford University Press.

Fraser, M. W., Nash, J. K., Galinsky, M. J., & Darwin, K. M. (2000). *Making choices: Social problem-solving skills for children*. Washington, DC: NASW Press.

Greenberg, M.T, Domitrovich, C. E., & Bumbarger, B. (2001). The prevention of mental disorders in school-aged children: Current state of the field. *Prevention & Treatment, 4*. Available: http://journals.apa.org/prevention/volume4/pre0040001a.html

Healthy People 2020. (2011). *Topics & objectives index*. Retrieved from http://www.healthypeople.gov/2020/topicsobjectives2020/

King, C. A., & Kirschenbaum, D. S. (1992). *Helping young children develop social skills.* Pacific Grove, CA: Brooks/Cole.

LeCroy, C. W., & Daley, J. (2001a). *Empowering adolescent girls: Examining the present and building skills for the future with the Go Grrrls program.* New York: Norton.

LeCroy, C. W., & Daley, J. (2001b). *Go Grrrls workbook.* New York: Norton.

LeCroy, C. W., & Okamoto, S. K. (2002). Guidelines for selecting and using assessment tools with children. In A. R. Roberts & G. J. Greene (Eds.), *Social workers' desk reference* (pp. 381–384). New York, NY: Oxford University Press.

LeCroy, C. W. (2004). Experimental evaluation of the "Go Grrrls" preventive intervention for early adolescent girls. *Journal of Primary Prevention, 25*, 457–473.

LeCroy, C. W. (2008). Social skills training. In C. LeCroy (Ed.), *Handbook of evidence-based child and adolescent treatment manuals* (pp. 99–138). New York, NY: Oxford University Press.

McGinnis, E. (2011). *Skillstreaming the elementary school child: A guide for teaching prosocial skills* (3rd ed.). Champaign, IL: Research Press.

Merrell, K. W., & Gueldner, B. A. (2010). *Social and emotional learning in the classroom: Promoting mental health and academic success.* New York, NY: Guildford Press.

National Research Council and Institute of Medicine. (2002). *Community Programs to Promote Youth Development,* Committee on Community-Level Programs for Youth. Jacquelynne Eccles, Jennifer Appleton Gootman, Editors. Board on Children, Youth and Families, Division of Behavioral and Social Sciences and Education. Washington DC: National Academy Press.

Olweus, D. (2007). *Olweus bullying prevention program: Schoolwide guide.* New York, NY: Hazelden.

Painter, K. K. (2008). *Social skills groups for children and adolescents with Asperger's syndrome: A step-by-step program.* London, England: Jessica Kingsley.

Pedro-Carroll, J. (2008). The children of divorce intervention program: Fostering children's resilience through group support and skill-building. In C. LeCroy (Ed.), *Handbook of evidence-based treatment manuals for children and adolescents* (pp. 314–359). New York, NY: Oxford University Press.

Shinn, M., & Yoshikawa, H. (2008). *Toward positive youth development: Transforming schools and community programs.* New York, NY: Oxford University Press.

Tobler, N. S., Roona, M. R., Ochshorn, P., Marshall, D. G., Streke, A.V., & Stackpole, K. M. (2000). School-based adolescent drug prevention programs: 1998 meta-analysis. *Journal of Primary Prevention, 20,* 275–337.

Vaughn, S., Wanzek, J., & Fletcher, J. M. (2007). Multiple tiers of intervention: A framework for prevention and identification of students with reading/learning disabilities. In B. M. Taylor & J. Ysseldyke (Eds.), *Educational interventions for struggling readers* (pp. 173–196). New York, NY: Teacher's College Press.

Weiss, M., & Harris, S. L. (2001). Teaching social skills to people with autism. *Behavior Modification, 25,* 785–802.

Wilson-Simmons, (2007). *Positive youth development: An examination of the field.* Princeton, NJ: Robert Wood Johnson Foundation.

Wiseman, D. G., & Hunt, G. H. (2008). *Best practice in motivation and management in the classroom.* New York, NY: Charles C. Thomas.

Zins, J. E., Weissberg, R. P., Wang, M. C., & Walberg, H. J. (2002). *Building school success through social and emotional learning.* New York, NY: Teachers College Press.

CHAPTER 47

Design and Utility of Social Skills Groups in Schools

Pam Franzwa · Louisa Triandis · Gena Truitt · David Dupper

Getting Started

This chapter discusses the use of social skills groups as a preventive or remedial intervention with children and youth. It will utilize the Response to Intervention (RTI) model as a framework for discussion and recommendation of targeted interventions for children with varying skill development goals. Tier 1 strategies are preventative in nature and appropriate for all children, either in groups or whole classroom settings. Tier 2 strategies are targeted preventions/interventions designed to address identified student social skills needs that are not being met by Tier 1 strategies. These programs and interventions can be done classroom-wide, but small groups may be more effective. Tier 3 strategies are appropriate for those children who have needs beyond those met by Tier 1 and Tier 2 programming (Hawken, Vincent, & Schumann, 2008).

Next will be a discussion of the importance of social competence for healthy social and emotional development, followed by a review of the assessment process as an essential link in identifying children and adolescents' various levels of social skills development. A review of evidenced-based programs will be provided, followed by examples of specific programs utilizing the Tier 1, 2, and 3 models. The chapter concludes with a review of evidence-based programs designed to address social skills development with identified tier recommendations, including a list of resources for both classroom teachers and student support personnel. A video demonstration of a social skills group is provided in a Web link.

What We Know

Social Competence as an Essential Aspect of Healthy Development

The development of social competence is a crucial aspect of healthy, normal development (LeCroy, 2002). Social competence is demonstrated through behaviors that parents, teachers, and peers consider important, adaptive, and functional in relation to environmental demands and age-appropriate social expectations (Gresham, Sugai, & Horner, 2001). For example, the ability to form positive and mutually satisfying relationships with peers, teachers, family, and community members is indicative of healthy social competence.

The acquisition of social skills and development of social competency are particularly important for students who demonstrate significant delays in cognitive, academic, and emotional-behavioral functioning, including students qualified for special education services or 504 plans (Gresham & MacMillan, 1997).

A very broad group of professional disciplines such as social work, education, and psychology have an interest in social skills as a construct in both research and practice. Gresham has divided the various definitions of social skills into three categories: behavioral, peer acceptance, and social validity definitions. The vast majority of studies have used behavioral definitions of social skills and define them as "situation-specific behaviors that maximize the chances of reinforcement and minimize the chances of punishment based on one's social behavior" (Merrell & Gimpel, 1998, p. 5). Gresham, Sugai, and Horner (2001) define social skills as "specific behaviors that an individual uses to perform competently or successfully on particular social tasks (e.g., starting a conversation, giving a compliment, entering an ongoing playgroup)" (p. 333).

Peer acceptance definitions of social skills depend on popularity indices, for example, a child is viewed as being socially skilled if she is accepted and liked by her peers (Merrell, Juskelis, Tran, & Buchanan, 2008).

According to Gresham (1986), the social validity definition of social skills is a hybrid of these two categories and has received increasing empirical support since the 1980s. Based upon their extensive review of more than two decades, Caldarella and Merrell (1997) have developed an empirically based taxonomy of positive child and adolescent social skills. The five most common social skill dimensions identified through their meta-analysis are (1) peer relation skills (e.g., compliments/praises/applauds peers), (2) self-management skills (e.g., remains calm when problems arise, receives criticism well), (3) academic skills (e.g., accomplishes tasks/assignments independently, listens to and carries out teacher's directions), (4) compliance skills (e.g., follows rules, shares materials), and (5) assertion skills (e.g., initiates conversations with others, questions unfair rules appropriately).

Numerous social problems such as gang membership, drug use, sexual promiscuity, suicidal and homicidal behavior, delinquency, and school dropout have all been linked to deficits in social competence. Moreover, the negative consequences of low levels of social competence in adolescence tend to persist into the adult years (Rose, 1998). Issues of employment, domestic violence, addiction, criminal activity, and mental illness in adults have all been linked to poor social skills (Beelman, 2006).

Assessment of Social Skills

The assessment and screening process is the essential foundation for the development of interventions for children and youth with social-behavioral problems (Merrell, 2001). The most direct and objective method of assessing social skills is through *direct observation*. Three assessment methods for evaluating children's social skills are naturalistic behavioral observation, behavior rating scales, and interviewing.

Naturalistic behavioral observational coding systems can be broken down into five types of procedures: event recording, interval recording, time-sampling recording, duration recording, and latency recording (Merrell, 2001). Space limitation will not allow for detailed explanations of each observation procedure. Therefore, readers seeking a detailed explanation of these coding systems should see Merrell (2001, pp. 6–9).

Behavior rating scales assess a diverse spectrum of social-emotional behavior in children and youth that ranges from general screening for clinical diagnoses of attention hyperactivity disorders to conduct disorders (Merrell, 2001). Some widely used standardized behavior rating scales are the School Social Behavior Scales, Social Skills Rating System (SSRS), and Walker-McConnell Scales of Social Competence and School Adjustment (Merrell, 2001). For more in-depth analyses of each of these scales, see Merrell (2001, pp. 10–14).

Interviewing is the most common assessment method and provides an opportunity to obtain a holistic view of the child. Interviewing techniques can adapt to a variety of situations, from highly structured to free-flowing conversations (Merrell, 2001). Interviews can be with individuals or with families that provide valuable information about environmental considerations and behavioral observations from family members (Merrell, 2001). The flexibility of interviewing can include role-play where children can act out social behaviors (Merrell, 2001). There is a lack of standardized interviewing techniques that are consistently used by practitioners that make interviewing a secondary method of social skills assessment (Merrell, 2001).

What We Can Do

It is appropriate to select a social skills program/curriculum after the completion of a student assessment. Table 47.1 below describes programs with empirical data indicating efficacy (evidence-based) and is divided using the RTI Tier 1, 2, and 3 models. Tier 1 programs can be implemented universally. They can be used in small groups, in classrooms, and/or school-wide. Tier 2 programs are more targeted and designed for children who have needs beyond those provided by

Tier 1 interventions. They can be implemented in classrooms or small groups. Tier 3 intervention programming is indicated for students whose needs exceed the preventative curriculum of Tier 1 and 2 programming. These interventions are typically done in small group or alternative settings, but can be done in a classroom. If done classroom-wide the behaviors are integrated and reinforced for students at all levels. For example, if a problem-solving lesson is incorporated into the whole school curriculum, teachers intervening in disputes on the playground can reinforce the problem-solving techniques learned in individual classrooms.

A special population to consider is students identified with autism spectrum disorders (ASDs). A meta-analysis identifies video modeling and video self-modeling (VSM) as effective in teaching social skills and meeting the criteria for designation of an evidence-based practice. Video modeling is an intervention technique that involves participants watching a video of someone modeling a desired behavior and then imitating the behavior of the person in the video (Bellini & Akulian, 2007).

Tools and Practice Example

The above table (Table 47.1) shows curriculum possibilities for use with different tier groups. When choosing a social skills program, the components in Box 47.1 have been identified as essential.

Video Example

A link to a YouTube video demonstrating a social skills group is available at www. Both the children and adults are actors, and this is not an actual group. It does, however, give a good example of how one would go about doing a check-in, reviewing the rules of a group, doing a social skills lesson with role-plays, and doing a wrap-up to determine what skills have been learned. The children are much more compliant than those you would typically have in a small social skills group designed to address Tier 2 or Tier 3 behavior. You should be prepared for more disruptive behaviors, but keep in mind that as long as the children are not disturbing other people (such as the child who keeps spinning in his or her chair), the behavior can simply be ignored. You should have some system in place to deal with more serious disruptions. Having a child "recalculate," as the children described it, while in the room works effectively, as it allows children to still absorb the material while they get themselves back on track. This video should serve as a useful tool to remember crucial pieces of a social skills group.

Key Points to Remember

- The development of social competence is an essential part of healthy, normal development.
- Many children and adolescents require assistance developing their social skills to help them be the most successful human beings they can be.
- It is important to use an accurate tool for assessment of a student's skills before and after the implementation of a social skills group.
- Individual curriculum/programs can be identified using the RTI model of Tier 1, Tier 2, and Tier 3 levels of prevention/intervention, which is a useful construct to help choose programs specific to the implementer's needs.
- Social competence promotion programs have been shown to have positive effects on children and adolescents' problem-solving skills, social relations with peers and adults, school adjustment, and reduction in high-risk behaviors.
- For social skills training to be beneficial for students with more serious social-emotional needs (for example, serious emotional disturbance), lessons should be more targeted, frequent, and intense, with the skills being reinforced more powerfully and immediately at home and in the classroom.
- Those programs that begin with young children in elementary or even preschool and continue throughout middle and high school have been found to be most effective in having a lasting impact. Ideally, the skills taught in group are reinforced school-wide on a daily basis by teachers and staff.

Table 47.1 Evidence-Based School Social Skills Development Programs

Program Description	*Target Tier*	*Class/Group/School*	*Age*	*Cross-Cultural Competency*	*Stated Goal*	*Includes Parent Curriculum*
Aggression Replacement Training (ART)—30 cognitive behavioral interventions for children and adolescents	Tier 3 Designed for aggressive and violent adolescents	Small group	12–17	Rural, urban, suburban, all socioeconomic backgrounds	Improve children and adolescents' social competence, anger management skills, and moral reasoning to reduce aggression	No
Incredible Years (IY)—Curriculum for parents, teachers, and children	Tiers 1, 2, 3	Class and small group	2–12	Adapted for use with African-American and Latino populations	Promotes social competence to prevent, reduce, and treat aggression and conduct-related problems	Yes
Project SUCCESS—School-based curriculum, outreach activities, and targeted small group sessions	Tiers 1, 2, 3	Class, small group, school-wide component	11–18	Effective with Caucasian, Latino, African-American, and Asian-American students	Reduce substance abuse by building resistance and social competency skills	Yes
Promoting Alternative Thinking Strategies (PATHS)—Violence prevention curriculum	Tier 1	Whole class	Pre-school through sixth grade	Material translated into French, Dutch, and Hebrew	Increase self-control, emotional awareness, and interpersonal problem-solving skills	No
Positive Action School—Family and community components to be used together or alone; based on the theory that positive actions result in a positive self-concept	Tier 1, 2, 3	Whole class and school-wide component	5–18	Available in Spanish; found effective with diverse ethnic groups	Improve academic achievement and multiple behaviors, including conflict resolution and decision making	No
Reconnecting Youth (RY)—Peer group approach to building life skills utilizing parents and school personnel	Tiers 2, 3	Small group, special class	14–18	Suburban and urban multicultural groups from diverse ethnic/racial populations	Dropout prevention; goals of increased academic achievement, decreased substance use, increased mood management	Yes
Second Step—Classroom-based curriculum organized by grade level designed to prevent violence	Tier 1	Class/Whole school	Pre-school to ninth grade	Used with diverse geographic, racial, ethnic, and socioeconomic groups; Spanish language supplement	Teaches social and emotional skills, including empathy, problem solving, decision making, goal setting, and risk assessment	Yes

Box 47.1 Recommended Components of Social Skills Groups

- include an affective component (e.g., stress management)
- include a cognitive component (e.g., problem solving)
- include a behavioral component (e.g., social skills training)
- include diverse and interactive teaching methods such as *modeling*, the process of learning a behavior by observing another person in the group perform that behavior; *role-playing* or *behavioral rehearsal*, in which group members are asked to "try on" new modes of verbal and nonverbal behavior; *feedback*, in which following a role-play, group members receive feedback from the group leader and group members about their performance; and *prompting* or *coaching*, when the group leader, prior to or during a role-play performance, provides verbal instructions to teach new social skills (each broad skill must be broken into its component parts so that it can be learned more easily)
- include behavioral homework assignments where group members are encouraged to practice newly acquired skills in their natural environment
- incorporate generalization from the beginning of program
- be multiyear and allow children and youth to build on previous learning programs
- emphasize a real-world application of skills to promote the generalization of skills
- be implemented as early as possible in a child's life—ideally the training should begin in pre-school and continue through high school
- focus on teaching children and youth to recognize and manage their emotions, appreciate the perspectives of others, establish positive goals, make good decisions, handle interpersonal situations and conflicts, and develop responsible and respectful attitudes and values about self, others, work, health, and community service

Sources: Caplan & Weissberg (1988); Gresham (2002); LeCroy (1983, 2002); Poland, Pitcher, & Lazarus (2002); Scott (n.d.); Weissberg, Kumpfer, & Seligman (2003)

Further Learning

National Center for Mental Health Promotion and Youth Violence Prevention: Evidence-Based Program Fact Sheets. Multiple resources on evidence-based practices can be found at http://www.promoteprevent.org/publications/ebi-factsheets. Suggested resources that can be found at the Web site include Incredible Years, Aggression Replacement Therapy (ART), Project Success, Promoting Alternative Thinking Strategies, Positive Action, Reconnecting Youth, and Second Step.

Skill Streaming the Elementary School Child: New Strategies and Perspectives for Teaching Prosocial Skills by Ellen McGinnis and Arnold P. Goldstein. Information about this program can be found at http://www.uscart.org/sselementary.htm.

The Prepare Curriculum: Teaching ProSocial Competencies, by Arnold P. Goldstein. *The Prepare Curriculum* presents a series of 10 course-length interventions grouped into three areas: reducing aggression, reducing stress, and reducing prejudice. Information about this program can be found at http://www.uscart.org/Prepare%20Curric.htm.

The *Overcoming Obstacles* program includes a comprehensive relevant life skills curriculum for middle and high school students. Information about this program can be found at http://www.overcomingobstacles.org/.

References

Beelman, A. (2006). Child social skills training in developmental crime prevention: Effects on antisocial behavior and social competence. Psicothema, 18(3), 603–610.

Bellini, S., & Akulian, J. (2007). A meta-analysis of video modeling and video self-modeling interventions for children and adolescents with autism spectrum disorders. Exceptional Children, 73(3), 264–288.

Caldarella, P., & Merrell, K. W. (1997). Common dimensions of social skills of children and adolescents: A taxonomy of positive behaviors. School Psychology Review, 26, 264–278.

Caplan, M. Z., & Weissberg, R. P. (1988). Promoting social competence in early adolescence: Developmental considerations. In G. H. Schneider, G. Attili, J. Nadel, & R. P. Weissberg (Eds.), *Social competence in developmental prospective* (pp. 371–386). Boston, MA: Kluwer Academic.

Gresham, F. M. (1986). Conceptual issues in the assessment of social competence in children. In P. S. Strain, M. J. Guralnick, & H. M. Walker (Eds.), *Children's social behavior: Development, assessment, and modification* (pp. 143–179). New York, NY: Academic Press.

Gresham, F. M. (2002). Best practices in social skills training. In A. Thomas & J. Grimes (Eds.), *Best practices in school psychology* (4th ed., Vol. 2, pp. 1029–1040). Bethesda, MD: National Association of School Psychologists.

Gresham, F. M., & MacMillan, D. L. (1997). Social competence and affective characteristics of students with mild disabilities. Review of Educational Research, 67, 377–415.

Gresham, F. M., Sugai, G., & Horner, R. H. (2001). Interpreting outcomes of social skills training for students with high-incidence disabilities. Exceptional Children, 67, 331–344.

Hawken, L. S., Vincent, C. G., & Schumann, J. (2008). Response to Intervention for social behavior: Challenges and opportunities. Journal of Emotional and Behavioral Disorders, 16(4), 213–226.

LeCroy, C. W. (Ed.). (1983). *Social skills training for children and youth.* New York, NY: Haworth.

LeCroy, C. W. (2002). Child therapy and social skills. In A. R. Roberts & G. J. Greene (Eds.), *Social workers' desk reference* (pp. 406–412). New York, NY: Oxford University Press.

Merrell, K. W. (2001). Assessment of children's social skills: Recent developments, best practices, and new directions. Exceptionality, 9(1–2), 3–18.

Merrell, K. W., & Gimpel, G. A. (1998). *Social skills of children and adolescents: Conceptualization, assessment, treatment.* Mahwah, NJ: Erlbaum.

Merrell, K. W., Juskelis, M. P., Tran, O. K., & Buchanan, R. (2008). Social and emotional learning in the classroom: Evaluation of *strong kids* and *strong teens* on students' social-emotional knowledge and symptoms. Journal of Applied School Psychology, 24(2), 209–224.

Poland, S., Pitcher, G., & Lazarus, P. M. (2002). Best practices in crisis prevention and management. In A. Thomas & J. Grimes (Eds.), *Best practices in school psychology* (4th ed., Vol. 2, pp. 1057–1079). Bethesda, MD: National Association of School Psychologists.

Rose, S. R. (1998). *Group work with children and adolescents: Prevention and intervention in school and community systems.* Thousand Oaks, CA: Sage.

Scott, D. (n.d.). *Program outcomes for youth: Social competence.* Retrieved from http://ag.arizona.edu/sfcs/cyfernet/nowg/sc_decision.html

Weissberg, R. P., Kumpfer, K. L., & Seligman, M. E. P. (2003). Prevention that works for children and youth. American Psychologist, 58, 425–432.

Video corresponding to this chapter can be found in http://www.oup.com/us/schoolsourcebook

CHAPTER 48

Conducting In-Service Training and Continuing Education for Staff and Teachers

Brenda Coble Lindsey ■ Margaret White ■ Wynne S. Korr

Getting Started

Professional development activities, including in-service training and continuing education, are one way that teachers and other school professionals acquire new information in hopes of improving the overall quality of education (Kwakman, 2003). Frequently, these types of activities are presented as full-day in-service seminars by outside experts (Sandholtz, 2002). Mandatory attendance is usually required for teachers as well as school social workers and other school service professionals. It is difficult to select a single topic that is relevant to everyone. As a result, there is significant risk that participants find these one-shot workshops irrelevant and the information presented easily forgotten (Guskey & Suk Yoon, 2009). Traditional in-service seminars, organized as discrete events, reinforce the notion that professional development is separate from daily work tasks and responsibilities (Fullan, 2010). This approach falls short in its ability to ensure that the importance of acquiring new learning is integrated into everyday routines. Moreover, the deep-rooted practice of relying solely upon one-day comprehensive workshops as the conduit to promoting school cultures that promote lifelong learning is ineffective (Fullan, 2009). Professional development must be based on evidence, thoughtfully planned, and address the needs of adult learners (Hassel, 1999).

What We Know

How do the needs for learning of adults differ from children? There are several important factors that must be in place in order for adults to consider professional development activities to be worthwhile. Adults prefer interactive educational experiences that are meaningful, practical, and can be immediately integrated into daily work routines (Joyce & Calhoun, 2010). Professional development activities are most effective in work environments or school cultures that demonstrate a commitment to lifelong learning. These activities must include *ongoing opportunities for people to learn from each other,* especially from those facing similar challenges; a strong value of *collaboration* and a high importance placed on working together to solve problems; and *encouragement of autonomy and creativity* in the selection of work tasks and responsibilities (Guskey & Suk Yoon, 2009). Learning is an energetic process in which new knowledge is constantly created, reflected upon, and integrated in such a way that the work environment itself becomes stimulating and celebrates innovativeness (Fullan, 2009).

What We Can Do

Designing Effective Professional Development Programs

Quality professional development programs place great emphasis on what is taught as well as how it is taught. Both content and delivery style are important and deserve equal consideration (Hassel, 1999). The four essential steps to establishing a comprehensive professional development program are design, implementation, evaluation, and sharing of knowledge. Specific tasks that must be accomplished during each phase are

Design. Identify stakeholders; determine the planning process; review educational goals for the state, district, and school; conduct a needs assessment; create professional development goals; identify the best available research on a chosen topic; select content and activities; pinpoint resources; develop evaluation methods; and secure sanction for the plan. (Hassel, 1999)

Implementation. Provide learning experiences that disseminate relevant content about a topic of interest; encourage a climate that values collaboration and sharing of new ideas as a way to solve problems; collect data as required for the evaluation component of the plan; remain abreast of the best available research; integrate ongoing opportunities for learning into everyday activities; offer follow-up and coaching sessions to ensure participants successfully implement new skills; provide incentives to encourage the implementation of innovative strategies; reevaluate and revise the staff development plan as needed. (Hassel, 1999)

Evaluation. Complete data collection; analyze results; disseminate findings.

Sharing. Utilize information gained from the evaluation phase to inform future professional development planning processes; circulate professional development materials to others. (Hassel, 1999)

Meaningful professional development should be an entrenched organizational practice that supports and maintains a stimulating learning environment for the school community (Hassel, 1999).

Let us consider key aspects of the implementation phase in greater depth:

1. *Encourage a climate that values collaboration and sharing to solve problems.* Collaboration promotes the development of organizational norms that value the practice of ongoing learning (Kwakman, 2003). In turn, this practice facilitates creation of a stimulating school environment where activities are designed to support and promote the pursuit and creation of learning opportunities (Joyce & Calhoun, 2010).
2. *Integrate ongoing opportunities for further learning into everyday activities.* Schools need to be a place of learning for teachers and students alike (Kwakman, 2003). When ongoing learning is a part of everyday responsibilities, professional development can lead to improvement on the part of individuals as well as the organization (Fullan, 2009).
3. *Offer follow-up and coaching sessions.* It is essential to provide ongoing learning opportunities that reinforce how to apply newly acquired knowledge and skills (Sandholtz, 2002). This practice not only increases the chances of application of new learning in daily practice but also emphasizes the value of lifelong learning.

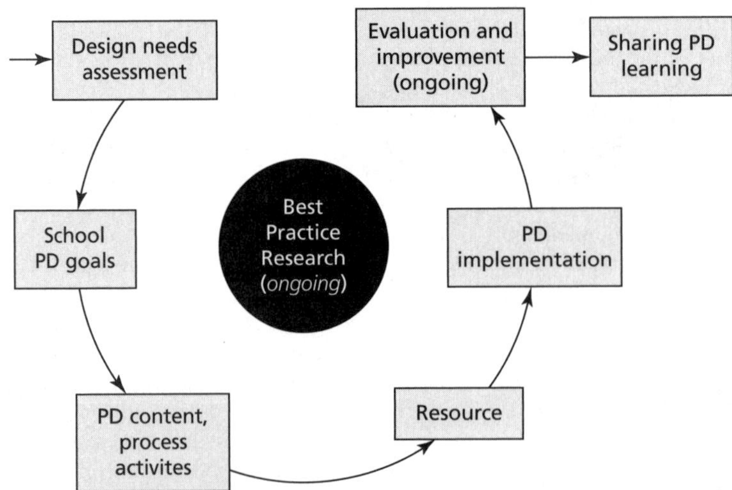

Figure 48.1. Professional Development Cycle
Source: Hassel (1999)

An Example of Best Practices for Professional Development: Positive Behavior Support and Intervention (PBIS)—A Response to Intervention Approach

To illustrate how to conduct staff training that incorporates principles of adult learning and focuses on an evidence-based program, we will use the positive behavior support and intervention (PBIS) model. PBIS is a promising Response to Intervention (RTI) approach that utilizes evidence-based practices, Tiers 1, 2, and 3, on a school-wide, individual, and classroom basis. School-wide positive intervention approaches to behavior management have received increased attention in recent years and have been validated in a number of studies (Blakeslee, Sugai, & Gruba, 1999; Brooks, Todd, Tofflemoyer, & Horner, 2003; Cushing, Horner, & Barrier, 2003; Kennedy et al., 2001; Kern et al., 1994; Lewis, Sugai, & Colvin, 1998; Luiselli, Putnam, & Sunderland, 2002; Mayer et al., 1983; McCurdy Mannella, & Eldridge, 2003; Sasso et al., 1992; Sugai, Sprague, Horner, & Walker, 2000; Horner et al., 2010; Lewis & Jones, 2010; McIntosh et al., 2010; Oswald et al., 2005; Sugai & Horner, 2009). These proactive approaches are designed to prevent and reduce behavior problems on an individual, classroom, and school-wide basis (Sugai & Horner, 2002; Sugai & Horner, 2009). Through the use of positive behavior support interventions, schools create affirmative learning environments. School-wide positive behavior support approaches include

- clear and consistent behavior expectations
- procedures for communicating expectations to staff and students, in addition to encouraging expected behaviors
- methods of preventing problem behaviors
- data collection systems used to determine decision making
- classroom behavior management practices and routines that parallel the school-wide discipline system

These approaches combine behavior analysis techniques with practices and principles of organizational behavior management (Sugai & Horner, 2002; McIntosh et al., 2010). School-wide positive behavior support approaches rely upon data-based decision making and research-validated practices in order to guide responses to behavior management issues.

Sugai and Horner (2009) reported that PBIS encompasses a number of promising practices that can also bring about improvements in school learning environments. These methods include collaborative team problem solving, ongoing professional development, ongoing evaluation and assessment, and securing support for PBIS initiatives as a means of preventing problem behaviors. Fullan (2009) identified those same types of practices to be effective in creating school environments that foster success. PBIS has the potential to prevent problem behaviors while also bringing about improvements in the atmosphere in schools.

What Is Needed to Implement PBIS

Schools interested in adopting PBIS must make a commitment to utilize a team-based approach, secure sanction from at least 80% of school staff, and possess enthusiastic administrative support (Sugai & Horner, 2002; Horner, Sugai, & Anderson, 2010; McIntosh et al., 2010). In addition, schools must provide training to school staff so that required tasks are performed accurately, use easily managed data-collection methods, provide abundant opportunities for staff development, and offer ongoing recognition and reinforcement for staff accomplishments. School-wide PBIS approaches are more likely to be effective when all of these recommended components are in place (Sugai & Horner, 2002; Horner, Sugai, & Anderson, 2010; McIntosh et al., 2010). Adequate staff training is essential to implementing PBIS.

Case Example: PBIS Implementation in Illinois PBIS Network

The Illinois PBIS Network is a component of the Illinois Statewide Technical Assistance Center (ISTAC)—an Illinois State Board of Education-funded initiative promoting effective practices to benefit all children (www.pbisillinois.org). The Illinois PBIS Network defines its mission to "build capacity of schools, families, and communities to promote social and academic success of all students, including those with emotional/behavioral and other disabilities."

Key focus areas of the Illinois PBIS Network include:

- prevention-based school-wide systems of positive behavior support
- data-based decision-making for instruction of behavior and academics
- wraparound planning for students with complex emotional and behavioral needs and their families
- community-based supports for families, youth, and schools (www.pbisillinois.org)

To accomplish these goals, the Network provides informational professional development opportunities to school districts interested in learning about PBIS and ongoing professional development to school districts that have made a 3- to 5-year commitment to school-wide positive behavioral intervention and supports. The approach to professional development follows guidelines for district commitment as delineated in the School Wide Positive Behavior and Support Implementers Blueprint and Self Assessment (www.pbis.org).

Outline of PBIS Professional Development Efforts: Initial Phase of PBIS Implementation

Introduction. Schools can learn about PBIS through Web-based information on the Illinois PBIS Network Web site "Getting Started" section, attend informational meetings on PBIS, or attend Statewide Leadership Conferences. Web-based materials at www.pbisillinois.org define PBIS and provide a 30-minute video overview from the OSEP Center on PBIS entitled: "Creating the Culture of Positive Behavior Supports" and list procedures for getting started with PBIS.

Overview training. After reviewing general information, district leaders consisting of central office administrators, including the superintendent or his/her designee, the Director of Special Education, and one or more school principals attend a half-day presentation on the systems, data, and practices of PBIS. Interactive and small group activities are an integral part of the overview presentation. These activities allow school staff to experience firsthand the benefits of using team-based collaboration methods, which are a central element of PBIS implementations.

The overview also includes a detailed discussion of the necessary District Commitment for Success documents. Signing these documents reaffirms the commitment to ongoing professional development activities and a clear understanding that system change takes 3–5 years. The documents also detail the role of the PBIS Network in offering ongoing training and technical assistance. To establish accountability for continued support, training, and evaluation, the District Commitment also includes appointing a PBIS District Administrator (.1 FTE) and identifying a PBIS External Coach (.2 FTE per five implementing schools) with adequate FTE allocation. Additional FTE allocation may be needed for larger schools and/or high school districts. In addition, each school has an internal coach.

The District External Coach coordinates overall district PBIS efforts, provides information and technical assistance, keeps teams focused, and knows and utilizes local community resources, while the Building Internal Coach leads the individual building team. Illinois PBIS Technical Assistance Coordinators based regionally throughout the state provide technical assistance, training, and support in the process.

Leadership team. A key component of the District Commitment document is a district leadership team composed of a PBIS administrator, a District External Coach, PBIS Building coaches, representation from various grade levels and departments, parent representation, and community representation (Sugai & Horner, 2002). This leadership team is necessary to lead and increase the working capacity of the PBIS system. According to the School Wide PBIS Implementer's Blueprint and Self-Assessment, the team has the primary objective of increasing the system's capacity for training, coaching, evaluation, and coordination.

Coaches' training. As previously stated, a key component of implementing PBIS in Illinois is the role of the External and Internal Coach. Prior to Tier 1 Universal Team Training, the External Coach attends trainings that teach techniques to coordinate and lead district teams through the process of establishing and maintaining PBIS in the district. Initial trainings include the nine elements of district-level implementation, reflecting and evaluating district status, and creating priority steps. Coaches are invaluable in ensuring the stability of PBIS efforts in local schools. In Coaches' training, participants learn how to support implementation efforts in order to ensure that plans are carried out as intended. The initial Coaches' Trainings, as with Coaches trainings at all tiers, include large group presentations that discuss ways to evaluate PBIS implementation efforts coupled with small group activities designed to encourage participants to evaluate PBIS initiatives at their schools. As with other PBIS trainings, interactive discussion is a built-in component, and content is designed so it can be immediately applied.

Leadership Team members and School Teams attend PBIS New Team Tier 1 Universal Trainings.

An initial two-day training is designed to help participants develop a preliminary plan for implementing PBIS on a school-wide basis. This interactive workshop utilizes a combination of large and small group discussion to teach the systems, data, and practices of PBIS. Activities are hands-on and intended to ensure that team members can immediately integrate ideas into practice. As previously stated, prior to Tier 1 Universal Trainings, External and Internal Coaches attend trainings on their role in leading teams.

A follow-up one-day Universal Training usually 3–6 months after the initial Universal team training allows teams to review their data, evaluate current implementation, and plan next steps for implementation. During this follow-up segment of training, participants continue to develop methods of teaching ongoing expectations to their students and staff, create universal classroom rules and management techniques, and continue to evaluate and design strategies based on individual school data.

Implementation Phase of PBIS

Follow-up Network meetings. Network meetings are offered monthly in various regions of the state. These sessions are intensive and provided by regional PBIS Technical Assistance Coordinators. Teaching techniques are designed to help team Internal Coaches and External Coaches apply what they have learned to real-life situations in their daily practice. Methods used include case analysis and consultation, power points with examples from numerous building teams, and dialogue regarding the application of Tier 1 Universal evidence-based practices to solve implementation issues. In addition, during these meetings, teams review data tools to strengthen implementation. One key tool utilized in these training is the Illinois PBIS Phases of Implementation (POI) tool. This tool helps teams look at RTI tiered implementation and serves as a guide for looking at quality implementation at each tier. In addition, other evidence-based tools such as the Benchmarks of Quality and the Team Implementation Checklist are reviewed. These tools and additional tools can be found on www.pbisassessment.org. PBISAssessment.org is a Web-based application designed to assist in high-fidelity, sustained implementation of school-wide positive behavioral interventions. In addition to monitoring progress, teams utilize these tools in planning additional professional development.

Tier 2 Secondary Training. A central tenet of PBIS is that data is utilized to identify target populations of students that are at risk for behavioral or academic failure (Sugai & Horner, 2002). As districts move into working with these targeted students (Tier 2 Secondary), districts add a Tier 2/Tier 3 External Coach and Tier 2/Tier 3 Building Coaches. These district and school-based consultants are typically school social workers, school psychologists, guidance counselors, and other professionals with expertise in evidence-based practices. These Coaches attend Coaches Training prior to Tier 2/Tier 3 Team Training and as trainings continue to utilize interactive discussion, small group activities, and large group presentations to ensure implementation in the schools with fidelity.

Tier 2/Secondary Training is divided into two primary days of training. In the first session, teams learn how to establish a seamless system of support from Tier 1 to Tier 2 levels of intervention. Teams learn how to identify students, set up data decision rules, and review critical features of secondary interventionsand implementation of Check in Check Out. A key element of Tier 2 interactive training, as with all PBIS trainings, is teams working continuously with their school data.

The second day of Tier 2/Secondary Training focuses on the continuum of Simple Tier 2/Secondary Interventions. Through interactive presentations, team members review their Check in Check Out System and learn how to implement Social/Academic Instructional Groups, Check in Check Out with Individualized Features and Mentoring.

Presentations at both of these trainings utilize a combination of large and small group interactive discussion-based activities. Large group discussions focus on how to identify and intervene with clusters of students who might benefit from Tier 2 interventions. Small group activities are designed to help teams develop initial plans for implementation of the process at their school (Scott, 2001). These activities are designed to reinforce the concept of using data to guide decisions through a collaborative team-based approach. During the trainings, team members develop a plan that can be implemented immediately to address issues related to specific target student populations at their school.

Follow-up for Tier 2 implementation is also available through regional network meetings.

Functional behavior assessment trainings. The Illinois PBIS Network offers a series of trainings providing a greater understanding of functional behavior assessment and how it can be applied with individual students who exhibit the most challenging and intensive behavior issues. Sugai, Lewis-Palmer, and Hagan-Burke (1999–2000) define functional behavior assessment as "a systematic process for understanding problem behavior and the factors that contribute to its occurrence and maintenance" (p. 150). This assessment is considered best practice in situations where students exhibit challenging behavior that is not easily understood or when typical intervention strategies have proven to be unsuccessful (Crone & Horner, 2003). Functional behavior assessment trainings focus on developing a system for how and when functional behavior assessments will be conducted, identifying the steps of functional behavior assessment, teaching the participants how to use data in determining function, and following through with plans for behavioral interventions based on the functional behavior assessments. A combination of large and small group instruction is used to facilitate a greater understanding of functional behavior assessment. Training activities encourage all participants to develop a system within their school for how and when functional behavior assessments will be conducted. In addition, as an action plan, participants write one behavioral pathway (setting events, antecedents, behavior consequences) and create a behavior intervention plan based on the assessment. Training activities encourage all participants to utilize data to identify potential students at their school who may benefit from a functional behavior assessment and subsequent behavioral plan. Participants also develop plans that can be used right away to implement the approach in their school.

PBIS Technical Assistance Coordinators provide follow-up for this series of training through Tier 2/Tier 3 Networking meetings and through technical assistance via the Web. These follow-up trainings allow teams to apply functional behavior assessment principles to individual student behaviors. Specifically, assistance is provided in accurately identifying the antecedents and consequences of behavior as well as developing positive replacement behaviors. Content includes sophisticated data collection and analysis methods and function behavior planning procedures that can be adopted as a part of the PBIS efforts at school.

Tier 3 school-based wraparound trainings. The Illinois PBIS Network offers a series of trainings to help participants understand the systems, data, practices, and central concepts of the wraparound process and how it can be applied to meet the needs of students with most significant academic/behavioral/emotional challenges. Wraparound is a process used to develop and implement intervention plans tailored to the unique individualized needs of students who exhibit chronic problem behavior (Scott & Eber, 2003). These trainings include large group presentations and case studies around the components of the wraparound process (Eber, 2000). The trainings detail the approach of wraparound as a defined process, comprehensive assessment of the needs the students and of the adults who support the students, strategies for organizing assistance, social supports on behalf of the child, and utilizing data in the process (Eber, Lindsey, & White, 2010). The trainings also integrate small group activities throughout designed so teams can develop action plans for their schools. To ensure the most favorable outcomes in the Tier 3 wraparound process, schools must rely on the data-based decision-making process, ongoing self-assessment of fidelity, and rigorous process monitoring (Eber, Lindsey, & White, 2010). A key to meeting this outcome is the ongoing technical assistance provided through these Tier 3 trainings.

Data management training. A key component of PBIS is data-based decision making. Many Illinois schools utilize the School-Wide Information System (SWIS), a Web-based data collection system and analysis system designed to evaluate office discipline referral information (www.swis.org). SWIS gives school personnel the ability to evaluate discipline data in a meaningful way. Results can be utilized to identify areas of concern and create easy-to-read graphs and charts that depict data. Findings are used to guide implementation of school-wide behavioral approaches as well as plans for working with individual student behavior (Lindsey & White, 2010).

Illinois PBIS Technical Assistance Coordinators serve as SWIS facilitators and train school districts how to fully integrate data-based decision making in their school. The training is computer based and interactive to ensure that participants are immediately able to apply what they have learned. Content includes sample data entry into a facilitator account, review and planning around mock data, and setting up their own school account.

All of the Illinois PBIS trainings are designed to be interactive and meaningful, and include the immediate application of training materials to routine work situations. All Illinois Network Trainings follow in a clear series, adapt with new research, and build upon a commitment to evidence-based practices. Small group training activities have a built-in collaboration and shared problem-solving component. The regional Technical Assistance Coordinators provide follow-up and training, and coaching ensures the sustainability of Illinois PBIS initiatives. These components reflect essential qualities necessary for professional development. PBIS professional development training also reflects the critical steps for professional development, including design, implementation, evaluation, and sharing segments (Hassel, 1999). The integration of evidence-based practice principles throughout the PBIS approach suggests a tremendous potential to improve the learning environment for schools.

Tools and Practice Examples

Professional Development Checklist

Design

- Identify/invite stakeholders
- Identify leaders
- Determine planning process
- Review educational goals for the state, district, and school
- Conduct a needs assessment
- Create professional development goals
- Design the professional development plan
- Identify the best available research on a chosen topic
- Select content and activities
- Pinpoint resources: financial, expertise for activity and design, future needs
- Develop evaluation methods
- Secure sanction for the plan

Implementation

- Provide learning experiences that disseminate relevant content about a topic of interest
- Encourage a climate that values collaboration
- Share ideas as a way to solve problems
- Collect data for the evaluation component
- Remain abreast of the best available research
- Integrate ongoing opportunities for learning into everyday activities
- Offer follow-up and coaching sessions to ensure that participants successfully implement skills
- Provide incentives to encourage implementation of innovative strategies

Evaluation

- Complete data collection
- Analyze results
- Disseminate findings
- Reevaluate and revise the staff development plan

Sharing

- Utilize information gained from the evaluation phase in order to plan future professional development
- Circulate professional development materials

Key Points to Remember

Effective professional development requires attention to content as well as delivery (Hassel, 1999). Four essential steps to planning in-service training are:

- *Design.* What is to be accomplished and how?
- *Implementation.* The plan in action.
- *Evaluation.* Was it effective?
- *Sharing.* Let others know what works.

These practices can be adapted to any continuing education approach for teachers and other school service personnel. Professional development efforts should reinforce the importance of lifelong learning as a way to improve the quality of education.

References

Blakeslee, T., Sugai, G., & Gruba, J. (1999). A review of functional assessment use in data-based intervention studies. *Journal of Behavioral Education, 4*, 397–414.

Brooks, A., Todd, A., Tofflemoyer, S., & Horner, R. (2003). Use of functional assessment and a self-management system to increase academic engagement and work completion. *Journal of Positive Behavior Interventions, 5*(3), 144–152.

Crone, D., & Horner, R. (2003). *Building positive behavior support systems in schools: Functional behavior assessment.* New York: Guilford.

Cushing, L., Horner, R., & Barrier, H. (2003). Validation and congruent validity of a direct observation tool to assess student social *climate. Journal of Positive Behavior Interventions, 5*(4), 225–237.

Eber, L. (2000). *Applying wraparound approaches through schools: Intensive interventions and supports for students with EBD and their families and teachers.* (Available from Emotional Behavioral Disabilities/Positive Behavior Interventions and Supports Network, Illinois State Board of Education, West 40 ISC #2, 928 Barnsdale Road #254, LaGrange Park, IL 60526, www.ebdnetwork-il.org)

Eber, L., Lindsey, B. & White, M. (2010). Tier 3 Case Example: Wraparound in Clark, J. & Alvarez, M. Response to Intervention: A Guide for School Social Workers. Oxford: New York. pp. 167-190

Fullan, M. (2009). Leadership development: The larger context. *Educational Leadership, 67*(2), 45–59.

Fullan, M. (2010). The big ideas behind whole system reform. *Education Canada, 50*(3), 24–27.

Guskey, T., & Suk Yoon, K. (2009). What works in professional development? *Phi Delta Kappan, 90*(7), 495–500.

Hassel, E. (1999). *Professional development: Learning from the best.* Retrieved July 27, 2011, from http://www.learningpt.org/pdfs/pd/lftb.pdf

Horner, R. (1994). Functional assessment: Contributions and future *directions. Journal of Applied Behavior Analysis, 27*(2), 401–404.

Horner, R., Sugai, G., & Anderson, C. (2010). Examining the evidence base for school-wide positive behavior support. *Focus on Exceptional Children, 42*(8), 1–14.

Joyce, B., & Calhoun, E. (2010). *Models of professional development.* Thousand Oaks, CA: Corwin.

Kennedy, C., Long, T., Jolivette, K., Cox, J., Tang, J., & Thompson, T (2001). Facilitating general education participation for students with behavior problems by linking positive behavior supports and person-centered planning. *Journal of Emotional and Behavioral Disorders, 9*, 161–171.

Kern, L., Childs, K., Dunlap, G., Clark, S., & Falke, G. (1994). Using assessment-based curricular intervention to improve the classroom behaviors of a student with emotional and behavioral challenges. *Journal of Applied Behavior Analysis, 27*, 7–19.

Kwakman, K. (2003). Factors affecting teachers' participation in professional learning activities. *Teaching and Teacher Education, 19*, 149–170.

Lewis, T, Sugai, G., & Colvin G., (1998). Reducing problem behavior through a school-wide system of effective behavioral support: Investigation of a school-wide social skills training program and contextual interventions. *School Psychology Review, 27*, 446–459.

Lewis, T., & Jones, S. (2010). School-wide positive behavior support and students with emotional/behavioral disorders: Implications for prevention, identification, and intervention. *Exceptionality, 18*, 82–93.

Lindsey, B. & White, M. (2010). Tier 1 case example: School-wide Information Systems (SWIS) in Clark, J. & Alvarez, M. Response to Intervention: A Guide for School Social Workers. Oxford: New York. pp. 55-69

Luiselli, J., Putnam, R., & Sunderland, M. (2002). Longitudinal evaluation of behavior support intervention in a public middle school. *Journal of Positive Behavior Interventions, 4*(3), 182–188.

Mayer, G., Buttersworth, T., Nafpaktitis, M., & Sulzer-Aaroff, B. (1983). Preventing school vandalism and improving discipline: A three year study. *Journal of Applied Behavior Analysis, 16*, 355–369.

McCurdy B., Mannella, M., & Eldridge, N. (2003). Positive behavior support in urban schools: Can we prevent the escalation of antisocial behavior? *Journal of Positive Interventions, 5*(3), 158–170.

McIntosh, K., Filter, K., Bennett, J., Ryan, C., & Sugai, G. (2010). Principles of sustainable prevention: Designing scale-up of school-wide positive behavior support to promote durable systems. *Psychology in the Schools, 47*(1), 5–21.

Oswald, K., Safran, S., & Johanson, G. (2005). Preventing trouble: Making schools safer places using positive behavior supports. *Education and Treatment of Children, 28*(3), 265–278.

Sandholtz, J. (2002). Inservice training or professional development: Contrasting opportunities in a school/university partnership. *Teaching and Teacher Education, 18*, 815–830.

Sasso, G., Reimers, T, Cooper, L., Wacker, D., Berg, W., Steege, M., Kelly L., & Allaire, A. (1992). Use of discipline and experimental analyses to identify the functional properties of aberrant behavior in school settings. *Journal of Applied Behavior Analysis, 25*(4), 809–821.

Scott, T. (2001). *Targeted interventions: Facilitating systemic interventions for students with challenging behavior.* (Available from EBD/PBIS Network, Illinois Emotional and Behavioral Disabilities/Positive Behavior Interventions and Supports Network, Illinois State Board of Education, West 40 ISC #2, 928 Barnsdale Road #254, LaGrange Park, IL 60526, www.ebd-network-il.org)

Scott, T., & Eber, L. (2003). Functional assessment and wraparound as systemic school processes: Primary, secondary and tertiary systems examples. *Journal of Positive Behavior Interventions, 5*(3), 131–143.

Sugai, G., Lewis-Palmer, T., & Hagan-Burke, S. (1999–2000). Overview of the functional behavioral assessment process. *Exceptionality, 8*(3), 149–160.

Sugai, G., Sprague, J., Horner, R., & Walker, H. (2000). Preventing school violence: The use of office discipline referrals to assess and monitor school-wide discipline interventions. *Journal of Emotional and Behavioral Disorders, 8*(2), 94–101.

Sugai, G., & Horner, R. (2002). The evolution of discipline practices: School-wide positive behavior supports. *Child & Family Behavior Therapy, 24*(1–2), 23–50.

Sugai, G., & Horner, R. (2009). Responsiveness-to-intervention and school-wide positive behavior supports: Integration of multi-tiered system approaches. *Exceptionality, 17*, 223–227.

SECTION X

Enhancing Parental Involvement and Family Resources

Parental and family involvement improves the success of students in schools, and one of the most important contributions that school services professionals can make in a school is to serve as a link between home and school. This section discusses best practices for working with different types of families and how to remove the barriers that may keep students from succeeding in schools. Effective practices and resources for engaging with diverse families and increasing parental and family involvement are covered.

CHAPTER 49

Effective Strategies for Involving Parents in Schools

Hilary Bunting ▪ Hilary Drew ▪ Amber Lasseigne ▪ Dawn Anderson-Butcher

Getting Started

Given that parent involvement creates such beneficial outcomes (Gettinger & Guetschow, 1998; Henderson & Mapp, 2002; McKay & Stone, 2000; McNeal, 1999; Shaver & Walls, 1998), it seems strange that many schools continue to struggle with actively engaging parents as partners with schools. For instance, one elementary school serving more than 240 students in Columbus, Ohio, has only 3 members in its Parent–Teacher Organization. A different school in the community serving more than 500 middle-schoolers had only 12 parents attend parent–teacher conferences. Many schools, including these two, continue to struggle with recruiting, facilitating, and sustaining parent involvement. The question then becomes not why should parents be involved in schools but rather how and what works for school and family partnerships (Christenson, 2010; Reschly & Christenson, 2009).

What We Know

If we know that parent participation is such a powerful strategy, why is it so difficult to get parents actively engaged in schools? Although this problem can be easily discarded as the parents' lack of concern for children and schooling, nothing could be further from the truth (Christenson, 2003; Henderson & Mapp, 2002; Lawson &

Briar-Lawson, 1997; Tett, 2001). Most parents want to be involved in their children's education, regardless of their race or socioeconomic status (Alameda, 2003; Cromer & Haynes, 1991; McKay & Stone, 2000; Shaver & Walls, 1998). Recruiting and retaining parents to be involved in more marginalized schools and in the education of their children, however, still proves to be an incredible challenge. Simply stated, not all parents show up at schools and request to volunteer or engage in the ways in which schools expect them to be involved.

Creative, alternative designs are needed to recruit uninvolved parents, especially where poverty and parents representing ethnic minorities are concerned (Christenson, 2003; Lawson & Briar-Lawson, 1997; McKay & Stone, 2000). This chapter explores several key strategies that have been shown to be essential for recruiting parents to be involved in schools (Alameda, 2003; Barton, Drake, Perez, St. Louis, & George, 2004; Christenson, 2003; Henderson & Mapp, 2002; Jacobi, Wittreich, & Hogue, 2003; Lawson & Briar-Lawson, 1997; Lynn & McKay, 2001; Raffaele & Knoff, 1999; Riggins-Newby, 2003). These strategies are grounded in ever-changing definitions of parent involvement.

Defining Parent Involvement

Parental involvement is a broad and diverse concept that can necessitate different approaches. Strategies around parent involvement in schools are most typically defined in relation to Epstein's work (1996, 2001). The seven types of involvement she delineates are as follows: (1) Schools help families by offering parenting classes and other supports; (2) parents establish home environments to support learning; (3) effective communication is created between home and school; (4) parents volunteer in school or classrooms; (5) parents encourage learning at home by helping children with activities related to their school work; (6) parents become involved in decision making, advocacy, and committee work; and (7) parents collaborate with the community to improve education for all children.

Of these strategies, Epstein's first type of parent involvement (i.e., schools helping families) is critical to the recruitment of parents in schools within marginalized communities. This approach is also called *family support* and is especially applicable when parents have multiple unmet needs and issues that impede their abilities to be engaged in schools and in the lives of their children. Traditional parent involvement programs initiated by schools often viewed parents as supporters of school-wide goals and student educational needs. Research identifies many limitations to this approach. Socioeconomic status, social isolation, cultural differences between parents and teachers, parents' sense of efficacy within the school, parents' educational experiences in school, parents' time commitments and family responsibilities, and race and ethnicity, if they are faced with racial discrimination, are important predictors of successful parental involvement programs (Alameda, 2003; Barton et al., 2004; Gettinger & Guetschow, 1998; Henderson & Mapp, 2002; Lynn & McKay, 2001; McNeal, 1999). Given these underlying factors that predict involvement, one of the most effective ways to recruit parents to be involved in schools is by helping them meet their basic needs first. Figure 49.1 overviews this strategy, proposing that factors influencing parent engagement must first be addressed in order to promote traditional school-and home-based parent involvement.

Expanding the Definition of Parent Involvement

If schools are truly going to recruit all parents to be involved, they must begin addressing these underlying factors and expanding their perspectives of parent involvement.

Two-way exchanges between parents and schools that take into account the cultural, emotional, and societal issues that parents face (Barton et al., 2004) are important to engaging diverse parents in schooling. Schools must begin offering assistance, referrals, resources, and social supports to parents (Anderson-Butcher, 2006; Briar-Lawson et al., 1997; Lawson & Briar-Lawson, 1997). As parent and family needs are increasingly met, parents may eventually become more engaged in schools and in their children's education. When schools are willing and able to address this aspect of the recruitment process, they send a powerful message of care and concern to parents (Briar-Lawson et al., 1997; Lawson & Briar-Lawson, 1997). By addressing these needs, schools can help to increase parents' time, flexibility, skills, motivation, and energy to become involved. In essence, parents become more "recruitable" and more likely to be involved in schools in traditional ways.

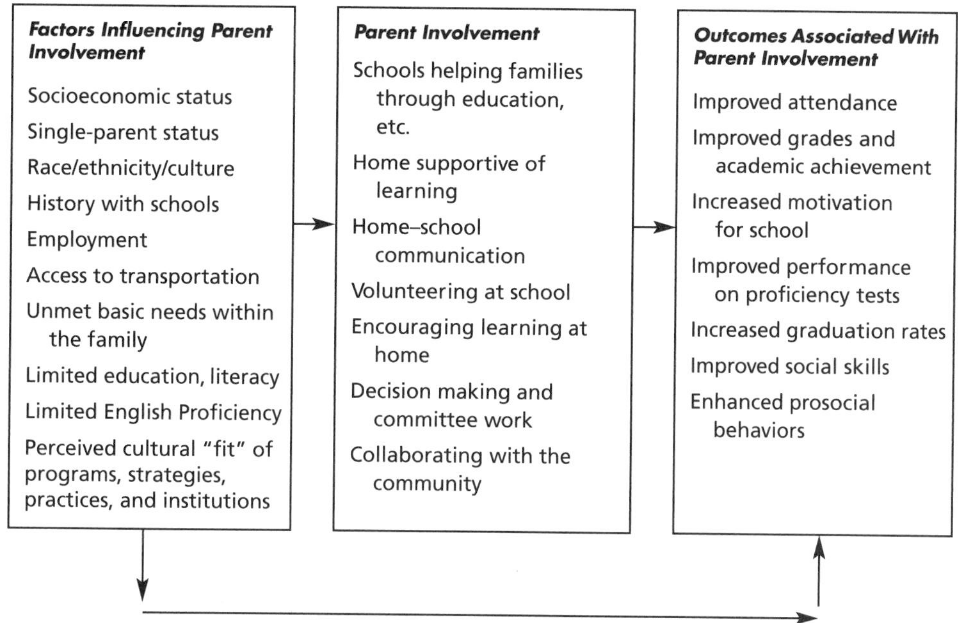

Figure 49.1 Addressing Basic Needs to Promote Parent Involvement and Positive Student Outcomes

What We Can Do

Steps to Recruiting Parents Through Addressing Basic Needs

Several strategies become critical to the recruitment of parents, including (1) assessing parent and family needs; (2) addressing identified needs through services and supports; (3) building relationships; (4) viewing parents as experts; (5) having parents as leaders; (6) creating spaces for parents; (7) creating meaningful and engaging activities; and (8) fostering culturally competent practices

1. Assessing Parent and Family Needs

Some type of needs assessment process will be helpful to parents (Briar-Lawson et al., 1997; Chavkin & Garza-Lubeck, 1990; Jacobi et al., 2003). Several different methodologies might be used, including surveying parents, conducting focus groups, or interviewing select parent representatives from schools. Sample questions might include: What services are available to families in the community? What are parental and family needs? What are the challenges that parents and families face in accessing supports? What are the barriers to parent involvement in schools? Whatever assessment strategy is chosen, parents can be involved in the needs assessment process in creative and meaningful ways. For instance, parents might help to design the survey, determining what types of questions should be asked. They also can help to frame the questions, decide how to set up the survey items so they are easily readable and user-friendly, and determine how to get the best response rates (i.e., via phone calls, send surveys home with students, go door to door, mailings, etc.). One might also consider asking parents to help with the data collection and analysis process, thus valuing their roles as parents, experts, and leaders within the school (Kondrat & Cash, 2004; Lynn & McKay, 2001).

2. Addressing Identified Needs

Schools must address these issues by providing parents with targeted services once needs have been identified (Alameda, 2003; Anderson-Butcher, 2006; Epstein, 1996, 2001; Lawson & Briar-Lawson, 1997; McKay & Stone, 2000). Parent involvement in school now also means parents' participation in these school-linked and school-based services and supports. For instance, schools might offer General Equivalency Diploma (GED) programs, English as a Second Language (ESL) classes, job training, computer classes, and literacy clubs. School-based mental health providers, health clinics, and other social service agencies might co-locate to schools, providing services on-site, where families are more likely to access them. Workshops could develop work-related competencies and life skills, allowing parents to become more employable and in turn more likely to become involved with the school (Shaver & Walls, 1998).

In addition, support service continuums within schools could be developed that link students and families to needed community resources and supports. This begins with the early identification of needs by teachers and results in referrals to school supportive service staff and other community-based services (Anderson-Butcher, 2006). Student support teams and related interagency collaborations then can effectively reach out to parents and connect families to needed supports (Anderson-Butcher & Ashton, 2004).

Clearly, a variety of methods can be used to tackle the various factors that limit parent recruitment and traditional types of parent involvement. Parents will alter their perspectives toward the school, especially once the word gets out that the school, in partnership with other community-based agencies, cares about meeting student, parent, and family needs (Alameda, 1995, 2003). They will see schools and their staff as supportive, helpful, welcoming, and caring. These school attributes in turn will greatly enhance the likelihood that parents will become involved in traditional and nontraditional services offered at school.

3. Building Relationships

Parents will be more inclined to work with the schools if the schools take the time to build positive relationships with them (Chavkin & Garza-Lubeck, 1990; Christenson, 2003; Lawson & Briar-Lawson, 1997). Schools can start developing rapport by first making positive contacts with parents. Most parents only hear from the school when their child is in trouble or is not performing well academically. Schools need to shift this paradigm so that they also communicate with parents via positive communications related to student behaviors at school (Henderson & Mapp, 2002).

This can be accomplished through a variety of methods. To name a few, teachers, administrators, and support staff can write positive newsletters related to students' achievements, provide positive phone calls to homes, encourage tours of the school, and conduct home visits to simply tell parents that they are glad their child attends the school (Henderson & Mapp, 2002; Lynn & McKay, 2001; Raffaele & Knoff, 1999). More specifically, newsletters might include stories regarding upcoming events, various classes' projects and achievements, good student reports, and how parents can support their child's learning at home (Lynn & McKay, 2001). Phone calls might describe positive student behaviors witnessed by any of the school employees (Henderson & Mapp, 2002). Teachers can also send positive progress notes home to parents, reporting good behavior and academic effort from their child.

Kumpfer and Alvarado (1998) highlight several attributes which further develop relationships and trust between school personnel and parents, including warmth, genuineness, and empathy; communication skills in presenting and listening; an openness and willingness to share; sensitivity to family and group processes; dedication to, care for, and concern about families; flexibility; humor; and credibility. These interpersonal qualities of effective service staff play a major role in building relationships between the school and parents.

4. Viewing Parents as Experts

Parents' lack of involvement in the schools can be traced back to the belief that educators and schools are the authorities on their child's education (Riggins-Newby, 2003). If schools want to recruit parents, they will have to view parents as experts in their children's education, communicating that parents' roles in the lives of their children are irreplaceable (Briar-Lawson et al., 1997; Jacobi et al., 2003; Lawson & Briar-Lawson, 1997).

One strategy that schools can employ involves holding parent–teacher conferences prior to the start of school (Jacobi et al., 2003). Here, teachers may not yet have had the opportunity to interact with the students in the classroom and hopefully have few preconceived notions regarding the students' behaviors and academic abilities. The parents will be the authority on their children and will be able to give the information they feel is pertinent regarding their children's educational needs. In this situation, parents are regarded as the experts.

An additional way to engage parents' expertise is by asking them to share their cultural traditions and skills with students at the school (Henderson & Mapp, 2002). Parents may speak to individual classes about cultural traditions and history. They might teach students how to hip-hop dance, weave baskets, or braid hair in after-school programs. Some schools take this a step further and facilitate parent-to-parent supports in the community. For instance, mothers in one community and newly immigrated refugee parents meet weekly, teaching each other about their own cultures, values, holiday traditions, and food preparation.

These and other strategies help to enhance school–family relationships and bridge the cultural gap between parents and schools (Chavkin & Garza-Lubeck, 1990). Parents have a wealth of knowledge and expertise that can be used to expand the education of students and to provide leadership and support to other families, which should be used to the fullest extent within the school.

5. Having Parents as Leaders

In addition to experts, parents also can lead efforts to recruit other parents (Briar-Lawson et al., 1997). The key is to get currently engaged parents to become actively involved in recruiting additional parents.

The first step in finding parents to be leaders involves the creation of a resource base of those parents who are already involved (Lynn & McKay, 2001; Raffaele & Knoff, 1999). The identification of some initial parents will seem obvious (i.e., the "cheerleaders"). These are the parents who are involved in the PTO, come to the parent–teacher conferences, help to run the school dances, and organize bake sales. The goal, however, is to also identify and recruit those parents who are not actively engaged in the school. Finding leaders among this group is more challenging. For this, it may be helpful to survey the school staff (teachers, coaches, aides, secretaries, etc.), asking them to list parents who have contributed to their efforts within the school. For example, school staff could name parents who have brought cookies, driven children to practices, bought gifts at holidays, made copies, or done anything else that has benefited various school efforts (e.g., Alameda, 2003). This list will give schools an idea of the parents who might be potential leaders and who can recruit other parents to be involved in the schools.

Once a list of potential parents has been created (a core of about 8–10 parents is a great start), the parents should be invited to an informational meeting related to generating parent involvement in the school (this meeting could double as a needs assessment strategy). Don't get too discouraged if only a few parents show up, as more parents will become involved as these parents recruit their friends, their children's friends' parents, and their neighbors. At this initial meeting, these parent leaders might be asked what they perceive parents want from the school, what they perceive family needs to be, what parents in the community might want to learn about, and what they might be willing to teach other parents. They also should ask parents if they would be interested in recruiting additional parents to be involved in the school.

At this point, some authors suggest that this core collection of parents receive training related to parent leadership and involvement (Alameda, 1995, 2003; Briar-Lawson et al., 1997). More specifically, parents might learn how to relate to educators, professionals, students, and other parents; might learn leadership and communication skills; and might develop problem-solving skills as they strategize about how to best reach and recruit additional parents. These skills and others will empower parents to support others in their communities, but also will empower parents to help themselves in meeting their own basic needs. Some schools have used stipends to honor parents for the work and services they provide. These stipends serve as occupational ladders into jobs as paraprofessionals, social service workers, and other helping service positions (Briar-Lawson et al., 1997).

6. Creating Spaces for Parents

While schools are creating the capacity for parent leadership and expertise, they might consider creating safe and welcoming places within the school where parents can receive communication from the school and access information about needed school and community resources. This could be set up in the form of family/parent resource centers, which send the message to parents that schools want parents involved and are willing to help families with their needs and wants (Lynn & McKay, 2001; Raffaele & Knoff, 1999; Riggins-Newby, 2003). Ideally, these centers are located within school buildings and are parent-led and parent-run. Parent liaisons (who are parents of students at the school, as opposed to professionals) staff resource centers and serve as single points of contact where other parents can go for support. These liaisons receive leadership training on how to be an advocate and support to parents. They accompany parents to meetings within the school, make home visits with school officials, and teach parents about school policies and procedures (Alameda, 2003; O'Connor, 2001). In addition, on-site services and supports from local agencies are provided at the centers; and brochures, phone numbers, and contact information for other community-based organizations are on hand for parent liaisons to distribute to interested parents (Alameda, 2003).

Resource centers also have the potential to become places where parents may give support to and receive support from other parents (Henderson & Mapp, 2002). For instance, some parents need additional supports in various personal aspects of their lives (i.e., paying bills, filling out job applications, etc.). The Parent Liaison and other parents at the center might assist parents with these issues, providing ongoing supports as needed within the schools.

7. Creating Meaningful and Engaging Activities

In addition to these other strategies, another key parent recruitment strategy involves offering meaningful activities in which parents can become involved (Halsey, 2004; Raffaele & Knoff, 1999). Realizing that parents will come from various skill levels and educational backgrounds, schools need to be creative in the opportunities they make available for parent involvement. They need to explore the parent and family assets and provide opportunities for parent and family involvement that match these skill sets and strengths.

One particular elementary school in Ohio valued this strategy, finding a creative way to engage even parents with limited educational backgrounds (Johnson, 2004). More specifically, this school had parents with limited literacy skills volunteer at the school by listening to students read stories aloud. These parents would challenge the students' ability to comprehend the story by asking them a variety of questions after the story was completed. At the end of the presentation, the parents would give the students standing ovations, congratulating them on their reading skills and effort.

This school found an alternative and highly meaningful way for often marginalized parents to engage "where they were at" within the school and the classroom. Additional examples of other possible ways in which parents can contribute are found in Table 49.1.

Once parents start to become involved in the schools, positive reinforcement and acknowledgment will ensure their continued support. These and other strategies, such as using certificates, stipends or honorariums and appreciation ceremonies for parents, will increase the retention rate of parents in the school (Alameda, 2003; Briar-Lawson et al., 1997; Christenson, 2003). Furthermore, opportunities offered by and for the parents need to be fun, interactive, social, and recreational (Anderson-Butcher, Khairallah, & Race-Bigelow, 2004; Kumpfer & Alvarado, 2003). Picnics, parties, ceremonies, and fun family and community events will also help to recruit and retain parents and families (Anderson-Butcher et al., 2004; Fischer, 2003).

8. Fostering Culturally Competent Practices

Culture notably influences parent involvement (Carlisle, Stanley, & Kemple, 2005). Culture impacts how parents express their love and commitment to their children (LaRocque, Kleiman, & Darlin, 2011) and the types of parental involvement activities in which parents are more likely to engage (Graves & Wright, 2011). For example, Graves and Wright (2011) found parental involvement differences between ethnic groups. Specifically, European-American parents were more likely to be involved in home-based parental involvement activities such as reading to their children, while African-American parents were more likely to be involved in school-related activities such as volunteering at school. As schools become more diverse, school staff members are challenged to identify and employ strategies to work effectively with diverse parents (LaRocque et al., 2011).

School staff attitudes and behaviors significantly influence how parents perceive the school interest in their families and their relation with the school (Carlisle et al., 2005; LaRocque et al., 2011). Parents of diverse cultures are at risk to be perceived as disinterested, particularly if they are unsure of their role in the school (Carlisle et al., 2005). Such perceptions may lead parents of diverse cultures to disengage from the school. Understanding families of diverse cultures by increasing cultural competence is critical to combating or preventing negative perceptions (LaRocque et al., 2011). Further, Thao (2009) outlined strategies to engage immigrant families in schools, such as building relationships (e.g., showing interest in the diverse experiences of students and their families), providing needed information and guidance (e.g., information to understand the educational system), having bilingual interpreters or family liaisons, and offering additional support (e.g., adult literacy programs) (Thao, 2009). Such strategies may be applicable to all families of diverse cultures, not exclusively immigrant families.

9. Additional Tools and Keys for Success

There are several other important factors which should be considered when recruiting parents to

Table 49.1 Other Meaningful Ways for Parents to Be Involved in Schools

Make phone calls to other parents for various events	Read to students
Help with crafts and other class project preplanning	Listen to students read
Recruit other parents to get involved	Support in-school suspension rooms
Invite neighbors to school events	Chaperone field trips
Pick up supplies for birthday parties	Speak at career days
Observe children in classrooms	Serve as an office assistant
Run errands for school events	Tutor children at school or in the neighborhood
Serve as a parent/teacher conference greeter	
Offer other parents support (e.g., baby-sitting)	Attend parent workshops
Train children or parents on computers	Instruct workshops
Help run school clubs and student council meetings	Plan career days
Teach others about different cultures	Serve as a physical education instructor
Coordinate newsletters	Coordinate the school store
Help run/facilitate boys/girls mentoring groups	Assist in the lunchroom
Help set up/break down community events	Serve as a teacher aide for a day
Decorate a classroom or bulletin board	Assist in the library
Serve as a fundraising drive coordinator	Supervise on the playground
Build relationships with local churches and other agencies	Coordinate food drives
	Organize phone trees
Organize community–school events	Facilitate family support programs
Visit neighbors and other parents	Support other parents at school conferences
Send cards to new families in the neighborhood	Help other parents with transportation
Staff the parent/family resource center	Provide birthday cards for students
Operate parent suggestion boxes	Set up car-pooling activities
Plan teacher appreciation days	Hold high expectations for the school
Network with other parents around school policies	Help other parents be better parents
Compile lists of community resources	Develop mentoring parents for parents
	Provide transition services for Limited English Proficiency families

Sources: From Briar-Lawson et al., 1997; Chavkin & Garza-Lubeck, 1990; Christenson, 2003; Raffaele & Knoff, 1999.

be involved in schools (Anderson-Butcher et al., 2004;Briar-Lawson et al., 1997;Jacobi et al., 2003; Kumpfer & Alvarado, 2003; Lawson & Briar-Lawson, 1997). These strategies target key barriers related to parent recruitment and involvement and include:

- *Time.* Schedule meetings and activities right after work because once people go home, it becomes hard to leave again. Schedule breakfast meetings.
- *Location.* Place matters. Meetings and programs can be held at schools, churches, community centers, and elsewhere. Some meetings might happen at parents' place of employment.
- *Food.* Snacks and meals are great incentives for families, especially if activities are right after work so parents don't have to worry about dinner.
- *Child care.* Have teachers, students, or local agency representatives (e.g., Boys and Girls Club employees) baby-sit. Provide structured children's social and life skills programs that run simultaneously with the parents' meetings.
- *Recruitment.* Recruit participants through local recreation centers, churches, laundromats, bowling alleys, and the like. Various entities can help recruit parents in different ways.
- *Transportation.* Offer transportation to and from the school or program. Use school buses or vans from partnering community agencies.
- *Translation.* Translate materials or have people who speak the same language make contacts with parents.
- *Messenger.* Examine the strategies used to recruit parents, particularly who is relaying the message. Ask involved parents to contact and recruit other parents. Have staff from after-school programs or pastors at churches recruit parents.
- *Fun.* Make sure that parent activities also include social and recreational aspects.

Applying Interventions within a Response to Intervention Framework

It is important to utilize parent involvement as part of the campus Response to Intervention (RTI) framework. RTI comprises assessment and intervention using a multilevel prevention system designed to maximize student achievement and reduce behavioral problems (National Center on Response to Intervention, 2010) and focuses on both academic and non-academic interventions such as parent engagement initiatives. Parent involvement is critical to improve student learning outcomes and experiences at school; therefore, engaging parents in RTI seems natural (Christenson, 2010). Further, parent involvement and support are important to the success of reform systems in schools, such as RTI; therefore, involving parents early to build support for change is critical (Mellard, 2010). Not only is parent engagement critical, it is required for any school that receives federal funds under the Elementary and Secondary Education Act (ESEA).

Mellard (2010) provided a number of ways parents could become engaged in RTI, such as asking parents for input on the strengths and weakness of the current delivery of services, eliciting parents' assistance to simplify the RTI language into understandable terms, engaging parents in monitoring their child's progress and planning the next steps of intervention, and gathering parent feedback regarding the implementation of RTI (Mellard, 2010). Ultimately, RTI has the potential to foster partnerships between parents and schools, as it allows for "establishing shared goals, contributions and accountability across home and school at the first sign of a learning or behavioral concern for students" (Christenson, 2010, p. 21).

Applying RTI to parent involvement also allows for different levels of supports to target parent identified needs and priorities in relation to children's education. Using the three levels (i.e., universal, targeted, and intensive), Christenson (2010) suggests universal interventions focus on information sharing and communication; targeted interventions respond to the unique needs of the family by providing more individualized learning supports and referrals to address specific family needs; and intensive interventions provide regular, ongoing services and monitoring to assist with more challenging academic, social, and emotional issues (for instance, through daily check-ins and wraparound supports for highly impacted families). Strategies and interventions directed to parents and families are necessary to further support students across the learning continuum. Just as students require individualized instruction as part of a complete RTI system in school, families would benefit from individualized supports from their teachers, principals, and schools.

Tools and Practice Examples

An example of a comprehensive parent recruitment plan exists in Columbus, Ohio, and revolves around a particular elementary school in a diverse, urban community. Approximately 50% of the students are African American, and 88.3% of the students are economically disadvantaged (Ohio Department of Education, 2004). Initially, this school had one active and two inactive members involved in its Parent–Teacher Organization. The school also had a Parent Liaison funded through Title I dollars. There was limited involvement in parent-teacher conferences, classrooms, and the school in general.

The Ohio State University's P-12 Project's community and youth development partnership committee was charged with working with this school, which is adjacent to the university neighborhoods, particularly focusing on increasing parent involvement in the school and its after-school program. Members of the committee included representatives from the schools, the Boys and Girls Club, the United Way, the YWCA, local faith-based organizations, Communities in Schools, the Godman Guild, parents from the community, and faculty members from the university.

In order to better understand the needs of the families, the first thing the group did was conduct a needs assessment with the parents (Kondrat & Cash, 2004). A small group of currently involved parents was recruited and offered honorariums to support the project (honorariums were $50/month). In essence, there was a discussion about the importance of parent involvement in the school and in children's lives, as well as an overview of how many barriers and challenges exist that limit parents' ability and motivation to be truly engaged. Parents were then told that the school needed their expertise in order to truly assess parent and family needs within the school and community.

Two parents and the Parent Liaison volunteered to help. These parents assisted in the creation of the needs assessment survey. They co-led efforts with the school and the Boys and Girls Club after-school program to organize a celebratory, end-of-the-year, community-wide event for families, where they recruited more than 75 parents to complete the surveys (parents were provided with $5 gift certificates to a grocery store to complete the survey; food was provided at the event; fun recreational activities were included). These parents then coanalyzed the data with members of the partnership committee.

After examining the results, the parents and committee members decided that one way to address the needs of parents and families was through the creation of a resource manual containing information about the various social and health services located in the neighborhoods. A 150-page resource guide was created with the direction of the parents. For example, a focus group (with food) was held with parents to discuss how the layout of the manual should look. If parents could not attend, committee members connected with these parents via phone or through home visits to get their expertise on the issue. These parents (along with friends of the original parents) are currently involved in the dissemination of this manual. They are providing input into how to best get the manual into the hands of the parents who need it most and are developing leadership strategies which involve parents in the distribution of manuals within the school and community.

Other ripple effects have occurred, where parents have learned new skills, participated in new roles, received new jobs, and engaged in new activities. To name a few, parents presented and facilitated sessions at a state-wide urban schools conference focused on addressing nonacademic barriers to learning. Parents have advocated for their own schools to be included in the P-12 Project target area. The Boys and Girls Club has successfully written a grant to fund four family liaisons charged with recruiting parents within each of their programs across the city. A master's of social work community development class was relocated to the school, focusing its mobilization strategies on engaging parents and families in new ways within the neighborhood. Relationships between parents and others in the community have been developing (one parent received support in resume and cover letter writing and now has a university faculty member to serve as a reference).

More parent involvement and leadership activities are continuing. For instance, plans are under way to develop a school-family-community coalition that focuses on strengthening the families within the neighborhood. Families and university faculty are advocating for the building of a state-of-the-art Boys and Girls Club facility in the university neighborhood.

Parent leaders receive honorariums and stipends in a university sport-based positive youth development program connected to local schools (Anderson-Butcher, Riley, Iachini, Wade-Mdivanian, & Davis, 2011). Both serve as examples of how parents can be involved in leadership activities within programs and institutions supporting their children. In summary, when parents were given the opportunity to become actively and meaningfully involved, the project took on a deeper meaning for parents, and they recruited other parents to join in the efforts. Many of the best practice strategies discussed in this chapter were used to recruit parent involvement. Parents continued their involvement and recruited others to be engaged because of the meaningful work in which they were involved and the appreciation they received for their efforts. Parent involvement at the school and in the community has been redefined, and parents are more involved in the school as a result.

Key Points to Remember

Involving parents in schools is challenging, especially given the many barriers that parents face today. A new expanded model of parent involvement, one in which schools ask how they can support parents as opposed to how parents can support schools, will help with parent recruitment and retention. This chapter provides several strategies that can be used within this new parent involvement framework. Several questions may also guide the thought process, including: Does the school have opportunities to involve parents? How does the school make parents feel welcomed at the school? Does the school examine how it can support families and parents? Does the school respond to identified parent and family needs? Does the school allow parents to have leadership roles? Are there chances for parents to become meaningfully involved? Have parent leadership classes been offered? Is there space in the school to allow parents to have their own area? Have parents been offered opportunities to expand their skills? Are parents valued as experts in their children's education? Has the school made a concerted effort to build relationships with parents? Are common barriers to parent involvement (e.g., transportation, child care, time) being addressed?

These questions and others may help schools to creatively think through the best ways in which they can involve parents. As new strategies are developed, and schools begin exploring how they can support families, parents will in turn be more likely to engage in their children's education and the school in general. The end result of these efforts will include better outcomes for youth, families, and schools.

References

Alameda, T. (1995). The healthy learners project: Bringing the community into the school. In K. Hooper-Briar & H. A. Lawson (Eds.), *Expanding partnerships for vulnerable children, youth and families (pp. 46–56).* Alexandria, VA: Council on Social Work Education.

Alameda, T. (2003). *Empowerment, social support, and self-esteem of parents involved in an elementary school program.* Unpublished doctoral dissertation, Florida International University, Miami.

Anderson-Butcher, D., & Ashton, D. (2004). Innovative models of collaboration to serve children, youth, families, and communities. *Children & Schools, 26*(1), 39–53.

Anderson-Butcher, D., Khairallah, A., & Race-Bigelow, J. (2004). An in-depth examination of a mutual support group for long-term Temporary Assistance for Needy Families recipients. *Social Work, 49*(1), 131–140.

Anderson-Butcher, D. (2006). Building effective family support programs and interventions. In C. Franklin, M. Harris, & P. Allen-Meares (Eds.), *The school services sourcebook.* New York: Oxford University Press.

Anderson-Butcher, D. (2006). The role of the educator in early identification, referral and linkage. In R. J. Waller (Ed.), *Child and adolescent mental health issues in the classroom.* Thousand Oaks, CA: Sage.

Anderson-Butcher, D., Riley, A., Iachini, A., Wade-Mdivanian, R., & Davis, J. (2011). Sports and youth development . In R. J. R. Levesque (Ed), *Encyclopedia of adolescence* (pp. 2846–2859). New York, NY: Springer.

Barton, A. C., Drake, C., Perez, J. G., St. Louis, K., & George, M. (2004). Ecologies of parental engagement in urban education. *Educational Researcher, 33*(4), 3–12.

Briar-Lawson, K., Lawson, H.A., Rooney B.J., Hansen, V., White, L. G., Radina, E., & Herzog, K. L. (1997). *From parent involvement to parent empowerment and family support: A resource guide for school community leaders.* Oxford, OH: Institute for Educational Renewal, Miami University.

Buerkle, K., Whitehouse, E. M., & Christenson, S.L. (2009). Partnering with families for educational success. In C. R. Reynolds & T. B. Gutkin (Eds.), *Handbook of school psychology* (4th ed., pp. 655–680). New York, NY: Wiley & Sons.

Cahn, E. (1998). *Time dollars.* Chicago: Family Resource Coalition of America.

Carlisle, E., Stanley, L., & Kemple, K. M. (2005). Opening doors: Understanding school and family influences on family involvement. *Early Childhood Education Journal, 33,* 155–162.

Chavkin, N. F, & Garza-Lubeck, M. (1990). Multicultural approaches to parent involvement: Research and practice. *Social Work in Education, 13*(1), 22–34.

Christenson, S. L. (2003). The family-school partnership: An opportunity to promote the learning competence of all students. *School Psychology Quarterly, 18*(4), 454–482.

Christenson, S. L. (2010). Engaging with parents: The power of information, responsiveness to parental need, and ongoing support for the enhanced competence of all students. *Communiqué, 39*(1), 20–24.

Cromer, J. P., & Haynes, N. M. (1991). Parent involvement in schools: An ecological approach. *Elementary School Journal, 91*(3), 271–278.

Epstein, J. L. (1996). Perspectives and preview on research and policy for school, family, and community partnerships. In T Alameda (2003). *Empowerment, social support, and self-esteem of parent involved in an elementary school program.* Unpublished doctoral dissertation, Florida International University, Miami.

Epstein, J. (2001). *School, family, and community partnerships: Preparing educators and improving schools.* Boulder, CO: Westview Press.

Fischer, R. L. (2003). School-based family support: Evidence from an exploratory field study. *Families in Society: The Journal of Contemporary Human Services, 84*(3), 339–347.

Gettinger, M., & Guetschow, K. W (1998). Parental involvement in schools: Parent and teacher perceptions of roles, efficacy, and opportunities. *Journal of Research and Development in Education, 32*(1), 38–52.

Graves, S. L., & Brown Wright, L. (2011). Parent involvement at school entry: A national examination of group differences and achievement. *School Psychology International, 32*(1), 35–48.

Halsey P. A. (2004). Nurturing parent involvement: Two middle level teachers share their secrets. *Clearing House,* 77(4), 135–137.

Henderson, A. T, & Mapp, K. L. (2002). *A new wave of evidence: The impact of school, family, and community connections on student achievement*. Austin, TX: National Center for Family and Community Connections with Schools, Southwest Education Developmental Laboratory.

Jacobi, E. F, Wittreich, Y., & Hogue, I. (2003). Parental involvement for a new century. *New England Readers Association Journal, 39(3)*, 11–16.

Johnson, J. (2004, April). *Addressing non-academic barriers within schools*. Paper presented at the New Models for Urban School Improvement: Addressing Barriers to Academic Achievement and Successful Schools, Urban Schools Conference, Columbus, OH.

Kondrat, D., & Cash, S. (2004). *Exploring community and parent involvement in the university district neighborhood*. Columbus: Ohio State University P-12 Project.

Kumpfer, K. L., & Alvarado, R. (1998, November). *Effective family strengthening interventions*. Washington, DC: U.S. Department of Justice, Office of Justice Programs, Office of Juvenile Justice and Delinquency Prevention.

Kumpfer, K. L., & Alvarado, R. (2003). Family-strengthening approaches for the prevention of youth problem behaviors. *American Psychologist, 58*(6–7), 457–465.

LaRocque, M., Kleiman, I., & Darling, S. M. (2011). Parental involvement: The missing link in school achievement. *Preventing School Failure, 55*(3), 115–122. doi:10.1080/10459880903472876

Lawson, H., & Briar-Lawson, K. (1997). *Connecting the dots: Progress toward the integration of school reform, school-linked services, parent involvement, and community schools*. Oxford, OH: Institute for Educational Renewal, Miami University.

Lynn, C.J., & McKay, M. M. (2001). Promoting parent-school involvement through collaborative practice models. *School Social Work Journal, 26*(1), 1–14.

McKay, M.M., & Stone, S. (2000). Influences on urban parent involvement: Evidence from the national education longitudinal study. *School Social Work Journal, 25*(1), 16–30.

McNeal, R. B. (1999). Parental involvement as social capital: Differential effectiveness on science achievement, truancy and dropping out. *Social Forces, 78*, 117–144.

Mellard, D. (2010, January). *What role do parents play in the RTI process, including when do they become involved, are they on the decision making team, and where can they learn more about RTI?* National Center on Response to Intervention. Retrieved June 8, 2011, from http://www.rti4success.org/subcategorycontents/ask_the_experts

National Center on Response to Intervention. (2010, March). *Essential components of RTI—A closer look at Response to Intervention*. Washington, DC: U.S. Department of Education, Office of Special Education Programs, National Center on Response to Intervention.

O'Connor, S. (2001). Voices of parents and teachers in a poor white urban school. *Journal of Education for Students Placed at Risk, 6*(3), 175–198.

Ohio Department of Education. (2004). *School report card*. Available: http://www.ode.state.oh.us/report-cardfiles/2002–2003/BUILD/024034.pdf

Raffaele, L. M., & Knoff, H. M. (1999). Improving home-school collaboration with disadvantaged families: Organizational principals, perspectives, and approaches. *School Psychology Review, 28*(3), 448–466.

Reschly, A. L., & Christenson, S. L. (2009). Parents as essential partners for fostering students' learning outcomes. In R. Gilman, E. S. Huebner, & J. M. Furlong (Eds.), *Handbook of positive psychology (pp. 257–272)*. New York, NY: Routledge

Riggins-Newby, C. G. (2003). Families as partners: Urban principals respond. *Educational Digest, 68*(8), 23–25.

Shaver, A.V., & Walls, R.T. (1998). Effects of Title I parent involvement on student reading and mathematics achievement. *Journal of Research and Development in Education, 31*(2), 90–97.

Tett, L. (2001). Parents as problems or parents as people? Parental involvement programs, schools and adult educators. *International Journal of Lifelong Education, 20*(3), 188–198.

Thao, M. (2009, December). *Parent involvement in schools: Engaging immigrant parents*. Wilder Research. Saint Paul, Minnesota. Retrieved from http://www.wilderresearch.org

Yun, M., & Kusum, S. (2008). Parents' relationships and involvement: Effects on students' school engagement and performance. *Research in Middle Level Education Online, 31*(10), 1–11.

CHAPTER 50

What Parents and Teachers Should Know

Effective Treatments for Youth with ADHD

Steven W. Evans Julie S. Owens Carey E. Reinicke
Ruth C. Brown Allen B. Grove

Getting Started

Attention-deficit/hyperactivity disorder (ADHD) is the most common mental health disorder among children and adolescents with a prevalence rate of between 3 and 5%. ADHD is both a common disorder and one with serious consequences. The results of several longitudinal studies of children with ADHD followed into adolescence led to the consensus that 50–70% of children diagnosed with ADHD continue to meet diagnostic criteria for ADHD when they are adolescents (Barkley, 1998). Although precise figures are not available, the rate of ADHD among adolescents in special education, juvenile justice, mental health, and substance abuse treatment settings is estimated to be at least 25% (Tucker, 1999).

Presenting problems for children with ADHD typically include academic difficulties, discipline problems at school and home, and conflict with peers. Adolescents with ADHD have many of these same problems but often with more serious consequences, such as dropping out of school and legal problems. Moreover, due to physical and social maturation, adolescents encounter new sets of problems, such as automobile accidents, traffic tickets, difficulty in romantic relationships, vocational problems, and substance use or abuse (Barkley, Anastopoulos, Guevremont, & Fletcher, 1992; Barkley, Murphy, & Kwasnik, 1996).

Educators are challenged by the problems experienced by students with ADHD every day. Since 1991, schools have been required to provide psychosocial and educational interventions for adolescents with ADHD who meet eligibility criteria for special education services (Davila, Williams, & MacDonald, 1991). While there has been a great deal of research on classroom-based behavioral interventions for children with ADHD (Pelham & Fabiano, 2008) and user-friendly materials to translate that research to educators and practitioners (DuPaul & Stoner, 2003), there has been very little empirical literature to guide the implementation of these interventions with adolescents.

What We Know

The support for the effectiveness of psychosocial treatments for children with ADHD is vast and has been summarized in the literature (Pelham & Fabiano, 2008). Both behavioral parent training and behavioral classroom interventions meet criteria for well-established treatments according to criteria reported by Lonigan, Elbert, and Johnson (1998). These conclusions have been translated into practice recommendations published by the American Academy of Pediatrics (2011) and the American Academy of Child and Adolescent Psychiatry (American Academy of Child and Adolescent Psychiatry, 2007). Psychosocial treatment has been reported to produce long-term benefits, including reducing the need for stimulant medication (MTA Cooperative Group, 2004) and improving some areas of functioning more effectively than medication (e.g., Langberg et al., 2010). In addition, parents report greater satisfaction when their children receive psychosocial treatment than when they receive medication alone (MTA Cooperative Group, 1999).

The literature on effective treatment for adolescents with ADHD is much smaller than the research literature on children (Wolraich et al., 2005). There are no psychosocial treatments that qualify as empirically supported for this population; however, there is growing evidence supporting some specific interventions (Sadler & Evans, 2011). Early indications are that some individual interventions, such as note taking (Evans, Pelham, & Grudberg, 1995) and family therapy (Barkley, Edwards, Laneri, Fletcher, & Metevia, 2001), appear to produce improvement, but comprehensive psychosocial programs may be what are needed to achieve meaningful overall improvement (Evans, Schultz, DeMars, & Davis, 2011; Schultz, Evans, & Serpell, 2009). A great deal of research and development is needed in this area before definitive conclusions can be reached.

What We Can Do

Daily report cards and contingency management are two empirically supported behavioral interventions for youth with ADHD that can be used at home and school. The procedures for each are reviewed later in the chapter, but there are three specific guidelines related to invervention integrity that will be reviewed first.

The first guideline is *consistent adherence.* This means that the techniques must be used in a manner that becomes expected and clearly recognized by the child. For example, if a teacher is putting a mark on the board every time a child interrupts, and the child earns classroom privileges based on the number of marks, then these conditions must be held constant for the child. Every time the teacher notices the child interrupt, a mark must go on the board. The teacher must resist the temptation to give a verbal warning that the next time he interrupts, she really will put a mark on the board. Instead, the mark needs to be placed. When an adult makes exceptions to behavioral interventions such as these, the contingencies can become personal and hurtful. For example, if a teacher frequently grants exceptions to putting a mark on the board, then the child may attribute hostility to the teacher when she really does place the mark on the board, and the consequence becomes a personal message. If the teacher is consistent, then the consequence of a mark is simply part of the system and allows the teacher to be allied with the student. This is especially true if the teacher maintains a positive approach with the child even when placing the mark. For example, she may say, "I have to put this mark here because you spoke out. This is your third mark this morning. I know you can stop before getting five. I'll remind you about raising your hand."

The second part of consistency is enforcing the *consequences* of the system. Continuing with the previous example, the child may have to eat by himself in the cafeteria if he receives five marks in the morning. Being consistent means that if the child gets five marks, he always eats by himself. As in the preceding example, the teacher should not make exceptions. Thus, both the consistency in recording the marks as well as delivering the consequences are important.

The second guideline is *persistence.* Behavior change frequently takes a long time. The behavioral interventions being used may take weeks and maybe months before achieving the desired change. A frequent mistake of parents and teachers is to implement a technique, and if it does not work in a few days (or few hours), they conclude that it does not work and abandon it. When consulting with parents and teachers, it is common to hear someone say that they have tried all those behavioral techniques and nothing works. In reality, there is a chance that they did try many of them; in fact, they may have tried many in the same day and not achieved immediate satisfaction by late afternoon, so they concluded that the techniques are ineffective! This scenario is quite common, as a frequent reaction from children immediately following the implementation of an intervention is to test the limits. This involves an escalation in the targeted behavior to see if the parent or adult is really going to follow through. It is during the initial stages of implementation that parents and teachers frequently need the most support to continue. Change in problematic behaviors takes time, and it can take 3 months or more to achieve notable progress (Owens et al., 2012). Thus, parents and teachers are encouraged to implement a given intervention for two months (making modifications along the way, as needed) before making conclusions about the child's response and/or abandoning the intervention.

The final guideline involves *closely monitoring* target behaviors. As can be seen from the descriptions of some of the specific interventions that follow, there are assessment systems that are part of some of the techniques. It is frequently useful to graph or chart these data to guide decisions regarding potential modifications to techniques. Sometimes, certain interventions may be ineffective or children may respond in an unexpected manner, and strategies need to be adjusted. Careful assessment and consultation with someone well trained in behavioral techniques can help teachers and parents to make these adjustments.

Behavioral interventions are effective techniques for children with ADHD; however, they are frequently oversimplified in everyday use. Adhering to the guidelines of consistent adherence, persistence, and close monitoring along with consulting with someone trained and experienced with behavioral techniques will increase the odds of success. When possible, start with simple interventions and learn from experience. Effective, sophisticated behavioral programs have usually evolved over time and transitioned through many iterations based on data from careful assessments. The following interventions are empirically supported treatments for children with ADHD (Pelham & Fabiano, 2008). Their application with middle and high school students will require some modifications (Evans & Youngstrom, 2006). Additional descriptions of these and other procedures are available through the sources listed in Table 50.1.

Overview of Daily Report Cards

Daily Report Cards (DRCs) are used to modify specific behaviors at school using behavior

Table 50.1 Sources for Behavioral/Psychosocial Interventions for Youth with ADHD

Source	*Description*
Bambara, L. M., & Kern, L. (2005). *Individualized supports for students with problem behaviors: Designing positive behavior plans.* New York, NY: Guilford Press.	Provides specific directions and examples for implementing classroom behavior management and prevention strategies
DuPaul, G. J., & Kern, L. (2011). *Young children with ADHD: Early identification and intervention.* Washington, DC: American Psychological Association.	Description of how to provide interventions for young children (2 to 5 years of age) with ADHD
DuPaul, G. J., & Stoner, G. (2003). *ADHD in the Schools: Assessment and Intervention Strategies.* New York, NY: Guilford Press.	Description of how to conduct school-based assessments and interventions with students diagnosed with ADHD
Evans, S. W., & Hoza, B. (Eds.). (2011). *Treating attention-deficit/hyperactivity disorder: Assessment and intervention in developmental context.* New York, NY: Civic Research Institute.	An extensive review of the literature on individuals with ADHD, including some thorough reviews of home- and school-based psychosocial interventions for children and adolescents
Evans, S. W., & Youngstrom, E. (2006). Evidence based assessment of attention-deficit hyperactivity disorder: Measuring outcomes. *Journal of the American Academy of Child and Adolescent Psychiatry, 45*(9), 1132–1137.	Describes methods for adapting the DRC to middle and high schools
Langberg, J. M. (2011). *Homework, organization, and planning skills (HOPS) interventions.* Bethesda MD: National Association of School Psychologists.	A manual for providing homework, organization, and planning interventions to middle school students
Power, T. J., Karustis, J. L., & Habboushe, D. F. (2001). *Homework success for children with ADHD: A family-school intervention program.* New York, NY: Guilford Press.	Describes a system for collaboration between parents and educators to manage homework and facilitate success at school
Raggi, V., Chronis-Tuscano, A. M., Fishbein, H., & Groomes, A. (2009). Development of a brief, behavioral homework intervention for middle school students with attention-deficit/hyperactivity disorder *School Mental Health, 1*(2), 61–77.	Describes a homework management system and reports results of a small sample trial

management techniques at school and contingent privileges at home. In order to implement a DRC, a teacher should identify and operationally define two or three specific behaviors that she would like to target for a particular child. After establishing the operational definitions, the teacher should track the frequency of the behaviors for approximately five school days to establish a baseline. The baseline data provide an indicator of the current frequency of the behavior. These data should be used to determine the goal criterion for each target behavior. A good rule of thumb is to set the goal at a level that the child could have achieved on three of the five days of baseline. This allows the child to experience success and earn some of the home-based rewards at the start of the intervention. Once the teacher has defined the behaviors and established the goals, the DRC can be created (see Figure 50.1 for an example of DRC). Wording target behaviors positively (e.g., Michael will raise his hand before speaking with five or fewer interruptions per day) instead of negatively (e.g., Michael will not interrupt more than five times in a day) can make the intervention user-friendly to the child and parents. Sometimes it is not practical to state goals positively, and clarity may sometimes take precedence over a positive orientation. We recommend the use of frequency counts on a DRC whenever possible; however, teacher ratings of a behavior may be used instead of counts (e.g., never, rarely, sometimes, frequently).

The child is responsible for taking the DRC home each day. The parents are to review it, provide feedback and support, and implement the appropriate contingencies (see Figure 50.1 for a sample privilege system). It is important to have the lowest level of home contingencies reserved for when the child fails to bring home the DRC so there is some incentive for bringing it home when the marks are poor. Home contingencies should be outlined on the DRC to facilitate communication between parents and teachers and improve consistency (see example in Figure 50.1). DRCs may be saved to serve as an assessment system to track change in the target behaviors over time.

Procedures

- Teachers and parents agree to implement DRCs consistently, persistently, and with close monitoring.
- Input from the child is solicited, but ultimate decisions are based on the parents' and teacher's priorities with some consideration of the child's suggestions.
- Teachers and parents establish operationally defined target behaviors for the child.
- Teachers monitor each target behavior for 5 school days to obtain baseline data and set the goal criterion for each target. Parents establish a set of home contingencies for the DRC.
- A parent or teacher integrates the classroom and home information into one DRC form.
- The parent and teacher review the form and make any necessary final revisions. The DRC is

Michael's Daily Report Card	**Date:** October 20, 2011	
Target Behavior	**Frequency of Behaviors**	**Goal Met?**
1. Michael will raise his hand before speaking with 5 or fewer interrptions	# of interruptions 1	(☺) ☹
2. Michael will complete 75% of morning class work.	% Complete 50	☺ (☹)
3. Michael will remain seated during class with 3 or fewer instances of out of seat.	# of times out of seat ##	(☺) ☹
	Total Smiles:	2

Michael's Home -Based Privilege System
If Michael forgets to bring home his DRC, he must go to bed 15 minute early (7:45)
If Michael earns 0 smiles, there are no rewards
If Michael earns 1 smile, he can choose 1 reward below : Popsicle after dinner, 15 minutes of computer games
If Michael earns 2 smiles, he can choose 1 reward below : Walk the dog with Mom/Dad, 30 minutes of computer games, 1 TV show, 8:15 bedtime
If Michael earns 3 smiles, he can choose 1 reward below : 1 board game with mom/Dad , 45 minutes of computer games, 2 TV show, 8:30 bedtime

Figure 50.1 Sample DRCs and Home-Based Privilege Systems

explained to the child by both the parents and the teacher, and a day is selected to initiate the intervention (see Table 50.2 for implementation steps).

- The DRC is kept in place at least 10 days before considering any significant changes to the procedures (some minor changes may be made ahead of time).
- When the child achieves consistently high performance on a target behavior, the criteria may be adjusted toward the normal range. Continuing with the example of Michael noted above, his criteria may be changed to raising his hand with three or fewer interruptions. It is important to remember that the ultimate goal is movement into the normal range for the child's age and not perfection.
- Target behaviors and home contingencies may continue to be adjusted as the child changes his behavior. Targets that are never achieved may need to be modified to include a reduced expectation with the understanding that the higher expectations will return as he progresses.
- Regular communication between parents and teachers can facilitate consistency, persistence, and close monitoring.

Limitations

The DRCs can be a very effective intervention for children with ADHD, although they do require considerable coordination between parents and teacher. If either the teacher or the parents are not consistent and persistent, the intervention is likely to fail. In addition, the contingent rewards and consequences have to be sufficiently salient to modify the behaviors and at least get the child to bring the DRC home. If getting the DRC home is a serious obstacle, the teacher may send it home using e-mail or telephone calls and leave a voice message with the information. If parents are not consistently enforcing the contingencies, teachers may provide contingencies in the last half hour of the day for the marks on the DRC so the intervention is self-contained in the classroom. Free time; the opportunity to spend time on a computer; time in the gym with an aide, teacher, or administrator; and access to art materials are classroom reinforcers that have worked for many children in this situation.

Further Information

Additional information about the use of DRCs can be found at the Center for Children and Families at Florida International University (William Pelham, director), http://casgroup.fiu.edu/CCF/pages.php?id=1358, in the book *ADHD in the Schools: Assessment and Intervention Strategies* (2nd ed.) by George DuPaul and Gary Stoner (2003), and in a book by Kelley (1990) titled *Home-School Notes: Promoting Children's Classroom Success.*

Overview of Contingency Management

According to social learning theory, people behave the way they do because they have learned to do so. They engage in a behavior because at some time that behavior was rewarded or they expect to receive a reward (e.g., verbal praise, attention, friends). Similarly, they choose not to engage in a behavior because they have been punished or expect to receive punishment (e.g., scolding, loss of friends, humiliation) if they engage in that behavior. Contingency management uses these principles to structure rewards and punishments in a way that improves the child's behavior.

The first step in changing a child's behavior is to have clearly defined expectations. These should be defined in simple terms that are age-appropriate and describe specific behaviors. These should describe behaviors in which the child should not engage, as well as behaviors in which the child should engage. For example, Billy often talks excessively, which gets him in trouble at school and is problematic at home. Billy's teachers send notes home about the problems that he causes in the classroom. In addition, Billy often interrupts his parents while they are talking to each other, talking on the phone, reading, or watching television, which leads to them being frustrated and upset with Billy rather than telling Billy to "quit talking so much" or to "quit interrupting," the behaviors that are expected of him need to be clearly labeled and defined. Billy's parents tell him that "interrupting" means talking when someone else is talking or busy doing something, such as reading or watching television. In addition, Billy's parents tell him that when he wants to say something to someone who is busy, he should ask for permission by touching the person's arm or asking politely if he may say something.

Table 50.2 Recommended Steps for Teacher to Implement a High-Quality Daily Report Card

Recommended Step	*How to Say It/Do It*
1. At the start of the day or class period, remind the child of his/her target behaviors and goals.	"Remember, Michael, if you can raise your hand with 5 or fewer interruptions, you can meet your goal. You did well yesterday, so let's have another great day"
2. At the start of the day or class period, ask the child what he/she earned the night before (if rewards were earned) or ask the child what reward he/she might be working toward that day.	"Michael, I remember you earned 2 Yeses yesterday. What treat/reward/privilege did you choose at home last night?...That's great. What are you working toward today?"
3. At the start of an activity that is particularly relevant to a child's DRC target, remind the child of the target.	"Remember, Michael, if you complete 75% or more of our worksheets this morning, you'll be on target to earn a Yes."
4. When the child exhibits a negative target behavior, the teacher should give feedback by mentioning *both* the behavior that the child exhibited AND the DRC as soon as possible after the behavior occurred.	"Michael, you just spoke without raising your hand. That's one interruption on your report card."
5. When the child exhibits a negative target behavior, track that behavior as it occurs using whatever format you prefer.	Track the behavior on the DRC, on a Post-it note, the teacher's clipboard, the chalkboard, or the child's desk.
6. When the child exhibits a negative target behavior and is getting close to earning a frown face, provide specific feedback.	"Michael, you just spoke without raising your hand. If you do that once more, you'll earn a No today. Try to work really hard to keep your Yes."
7. Praise the child when he/she exhibits a positive behavior that is incompatible with negative target behavior on the DRC.	"Michael, great job raising your hand. What would you like to say?"
8. At the end of the day, give the child the DRC and briefly review his/her success.	"Michael, you earned two out of three Yeses today. Good job raising your hand and getting your work done today. Tomorrow, let's work really hard on staying in your seat so you can earn all three Yeses. Enjoy your treats tonight."

After defining the target behaviors, parents and teachers may use contingency management to modify the behaviors. Contingency management involves applying reinforcements and punishments conditionally in relation to the child exhibiting the target behaviors. Reinforcement is used to increase the frequency, duration, or intensity of a behavior. This may be done by providing a child with something he or she wants after exhibiting a desirable behavior, such as the opportunity to play video games (i.e., positive reinforcement) or helping the child to avoid something he or she does not want, such as skipping the requirement to complete an evening chore (i.e., negative reinforcement). Punishment, on the other hand, is used to decrease the frequency, duration, or intensity of a behavior. Like reinforcement, there are two kinds of punishment. A child may be punished by providing him or her with something undesirable, like an extra evening task (i.e., positive punishment), or requiring him or her to miss something enjoyable, like skipping dessert at dinner (i.e., negative punishment). Careful and systematic manipulation of these contingencies can be effective at modifying behaviors as long as they are implemented with consistency, persistence, and close monitoring.

Procedures

The following procedures outline the steps for a token economy, which is one form of contingency management. Other forms of contingency management are described in the references in Table 50.1.

- The teacher or parent operationally defines two or three behaviors with specific criteria for earning points. For example, at home a child may earn 5 points for going to bed within 10 minutes without negative comments after being told no more than twice. At school a child may earn 7 points for completing all of assigned work in the morning work period.
- The teacher or parent identifies a set of rewards that will be used in the token economy. The rewards should be desirable (i.e., salient), and having a variety of rewards can improve saliency. Not all rewards need to be tangible. For example, tokens to be a line leader, spend time in the gym with the principal, eat lunch with the teacher, and other privileges may also be included. These rewards are often referred to as a prize box or treasure chest, and when children have earned enough points, they may go to this area and choose items that they can afford with their points. When starting a token economy, no more than two or three target behaviors should be included. Other target behaviors may be added later.
- Points may be recorded on a sheet on the refrigerator at home or on the student's desk at school. Young children frequently prefer tangible points, such as poker chips or tickets.
- It is frequently helpful to set designated times to visit the prize box. Otherwise, it is common for children to want to visit frequently "just to see what I might want."

Limitations

Token economies require that the teacher or parent maintain a "store" of rewards, including tangible items and privileges. In addition, there can be problems related to the security of earned points. Children involved in token economy systems have been known to steal tokens from other children (when they are concrete, like poker chips) or plagiarize the marking of points on recording forms. Token economies often rely exclusively on rewards, and for many children with moderate to severe impairment, punishment may also be required. Token economies may be combined with response cost systems to add punishment to the system. Response cost involves losing points for behaviors. For example, a child may lose 5 points for hitting someone. Response cost may help to increase the saliency of the system; however, response cost systems also introduce other problems. Children with frequent problems learn that they are likely to lose points so they try to spend points as soon as they get them so they have nothing to lose. Furthermore, when a child knows that he is likely to lose points, the saliency of the value of points is reduced, making the original system less effective.

Token economies can become quite complex, and parents and teachers may observe that students learn that they can get all of the points they need by concentrating on only one target behavior. The strength of token economies is their ability to address many problems at once; however, the complexity that results from this is also their major limitation.

Further Information

Further information about token economies and other forms of contingency management is available in the book *Individualized Supports for Students with Problem Behaviors: Designing Positive Behavior Plans* by Linda Bambara and Lee Kern (2005) and in a parent training manual called *Defiant Children: A Clinician's Manual for Assessment and Parent Training* (2nd ed.) by Russell Barkley (1997).

Applying a Response to Intervention Framework

The interventions described in this chapter are consistent with a Response to Intervention (RTI) approach for students with behavior problems. The DRC and contingency management align with Tier 2 interventions, although, with some modification, the DRC can be applied at Tier 1 and Tier 3 as well (see Vujnovic, Holdaway, Owens, & Fabiano, in press for review). It is likely that these two interventions will be optimally effective if the teacher already provides effective classroom behavior management to all of the students (Tier 1). Our data suggest that when behavioral interventions are provided with integrity, it can take two months or more of consistent implementation to achieve the desired behavior change (Evans et al., 2011; Owens et al., 2008). As a result, a student's response to interventions should be assessed on a monthly basis and should not be considered to have failed these Tier 2 interventions until they have been provided with integrity for at least two months. At each RTI review meeting, the child's progress, as well as the teacher's implementation integrity, should be assessed and modifications applied as necessary. When a student does not respond to these interventions, other behavioral interventions that require more attention to the child than can be provided by a classroom teacher may be warranted. These approaches are typically similar to the DRC and contingency management, but the degree of monitoring is increased, the frequency of providing contingent rewards and consequences is greater, and the amount of prompting and coaching is enhanced. These modifications may require a classroom aide and are often considered part of a Tier 3 intervention.

Tools and Practice Example

Tools

Figure 50.1 provides an example of a Daily Report Card that can be used to assist students with ADHD to modify their behavior. Table 50.2 describes the recommended steps for teachers to achieve high-quality implementation of the DRC and offers examples for how to accomplish each step.

Case Example

Brian is a 9-year-old boy with a diagnosis of ADHD in the fourth-grade class taught by Mr. O'Grady. Brian is demonstrating problems completing assignments both at home and at school and is frequently disruptive in the classroom. He speaks out during class without being called on, pesters children sitting near him, and frequently plays with items at his seat in a manner that is distracting to others. Mr. O'Grady has tried verbal reprimands and prompts and has met with Brian's parents to discuss ways to help Brian. Mr. O'Grady and Brian's parents decided to try a Daily Report Card. Mr. O'Grady developed three target behaviors to use on the card (see Figure 50.1). Mr. O'Grady defined the three target behaviors as (1) Brian will complete and turn in all assignments on time, which requires Brian to complete all items on every assignment (seatwork and homework) and turn them in to Mr. O'Grady at or before the expected time (score is total submitted complete over total expected); (2) Brian will raise his hand prior to speaking during class, which requires Brian to say things during the class time (not including transitions, PE, or lunch) only after being called on by the teacher (score is number of times Brian did not follow rule); and (3) Brian will respect the space and quiet of others, which requires Brian to not disturb others by intruding upon their space or disrupting their quiet work area (score is number of times Brian did not follow the rule).

Mr. O'Grady met with Brian's parents to describe the procedures and to help them establish some contingencies to implement at home based on the scores from the Daily Report Card. The parents wanted to use time playing video games, bedtime, and attending soccer practice as the contingencies at home. Mr. O'Grady recommended that they choose something other than soccer practices because missing practices could result in Brian being removed from the team. In addition, Brian's participation on the soccer team is one of the only prosocial, enjoyable and successful outlets for him. Brian's parents agreed to initially rely on time playing video games and bedtime.

After 2 weeks of sending home the Daily Report Cards, Mr. O'Grady called Brian's parents to find out how the procedures were working at home. They reported that things were going well. Upon further questioning, Mr. O'Grady learned that Brian had not brought home the DRC on 3 days. The parents had not implemented appropriate restrictions because Brian had told them that he had a substitute teacher on those days and she did not give him his card. Mr. O'Grady informed the parents that he had not missed any days of school in the last 2 weeks. He encouraged the parents to enforce the contingencies every day regardless of the story Brian tells them. Mr. O'Grady agreed to call the parents if he is absent.

After another 2 weeks, he called them again, and Brian's parents were discouraged. They told him that they were going to discontinue using the DRC because the marks were not getting any better, and it was a battle every evening to enforce the rules. Mr. O'Grady empathized with them, but urged them to continue. He noted that if they can continue to be consistent and persistent in their implementation, he was confident that Brian would improve. He explained that many children with ADHD require 2–3 months of a well-implemented plan before exhibiting notable improvements in behavior. The parents were skeptical but agreed to continue.

Mr. O'Grady maintained contact with Brian's parents and used encouragement, coaching, and support to facilitate their collaboration. After 6 more weeks, there was a trend toward improvement with his disruptive behavior and speaking out. Problems persisted with completing homework, and the interventions targeting task completion needed to be adjusted. A homework management system for the parents (see Power, Karustis, & Habboushe, 2001; Raggi, Chronis-Tuscano, Fishbein, & Groomes, 2009) and a set of immediately available rewards and negative consequences for use at school during seatwork time were developed. In addition to consistency and persistence, Brian was greatly aided by the communication and collaborative implementation of interventions between his parents and his teacher.

Key Points to Remember

Two examples of empirically supported treatments for children with ADHD have been described. When implemented with consistency, persistence, and close monitoring, each of these is likely to be effective in modifying the behavior of most children with ADHD. They can be applied at home and in school. Regular communication between parents and teachers can improve the success rate of these interventions. In addition, these techniques work best when coordinated by adults who take a critical-thinking and problem-solving approach to the obstacles. Finally, these techniques are most effective when delivered independent of emotional messages. For example, punishment is not a method of retaliation, and rewards should not be provided because an adult likes a child without the child having earned them. Given the frustration and tension that frequently accompany parents and teachers working with youth with ADHD (Johnston & Mash, 2001), it can be challenging to provide the consistency, persistence, and close monitoring necessary while maintaining a supportive and positive relationship.

References

American Academy of Child and Adolescent Psychiatry. (2007). Practice parameter for the assessment and treatment of children and adolescents with attention-deficit/hyperactivity disorder. *Journal of the American Academy of Child and Adolescent Psychiatry, 46*(7), 894–921.

American Academy of Pediatrics, Subcommittee on Attention-Deficit/Hyperactivity Disorder, Committee on Quality Improvement. (2011). ADHD: Clinical practice guideline for the diagnosis, evaluation, and treatment of attention-deficit/hyperactivity disorder in children and adolescents. *Pediatrics, 128*(5), 1–16.

Bambara, L. M., & Kern, L. (2005). *Individualized supports for students with problem behaviors: Designing positive behavior plans.* New York, NY: Guilford Press.

Barkley, R. A., Anastopoulos, A. D., Guevremont, D. C, & Fletcher, K. E. (1992). Adolescents with attention deficit hyperactivity disorder: Mother-adolescent interactions, family beliefs and conflicts, and maternal psychopathology. *Journal of Abnormal Child Psychology, 20,* 263–288.

Barkley, R. A., Murphy, K. R., & Kwasnik, D. (1996). Motor vehicle driving competencies and risks in teens and young adults with attention deficit hyperactivity disorder. *Pediatrics, 98,* 1089–1095.

Barkley, R. A. (1997). *Defiant children: A clinician's manual for assessment and parent training* (2nd ed.). New York: Guilford.

Barkley, R. A. (1998). *Attention deficit hyperactivity disorder: A handbook for diagnosis and treatment.* New York: Guilford.

Barkley, R. A., Edwards, G., Laneri, M., Fletcher, K., & Metevia, L. (2001). The efficacy of problem-solving communication training alone, behavior management training alone, and their combination for parent-adolescent conflict in teenagers with ADHD and ODD. *Journal of Consulting and Clinical Psychology, 69,* 926–941.

Davila, R., Williams, M., & MacDonald, J. (1991). *Clarification of policy to address the needs of children with attention deficit disorders within general and/or special education.* Washington, DC: Department of Education.

DuPaul, G. J., & Stoner, G. (2003). *ADHD in the schools: Assessment and intervention strategies* (2nd ed.). New York: Guilford.

Evans, S. W., Pelham, W., & Grudberg, M. V. (1995). The efficacy of notetaking to improve behavior and comprehension of adolescents with attention deficit hyperactivity disorder. *Exceptionality, 5*(1), 1–17.

Evans, S. W., Schultz, B. K., DeMars, C. E., & Davis, H. (2011). Effectiveness of the Challenging Horizons after-school program for young adolescents with ADHD. *Behavior Therapy, 42*, 462–474.

Evans, S. W., & Youngstrom, E. (2006). Evidence based assessment of attention-deficit hyperactivity disorder: Measuring outcomes. *Journal of the American Academy of Child and Adolescent Psychiatry, 45*(9), 1132–1137.

Johnston, C., & Mash, E. J. (2001). Families of children with attention-deficit/hyperactivity disorder: Review and recommendations for future research. *Clinical Child and Family Psychology Review, 4*(3), 183–207.

Kelley, M. L. (1990). *School-home notes: Promoting children's classroom success.* New York, NY: Guilford Press.

Langberg, J. M., Arnold, L. E., Flowers, A. M., Epstein, J. N., Altaye, M., Hinshaw, S. P.,...Hechtman, L. (2010). Parent reported homework problems in the MTA study: Evidence for sustained improvement in behavioral treatment *Journal of Clinical Child and Adolescent Psychology, 39*(2), 220–233.

Lonigan, C. J., Elbert, J. C., & Johnson, S. B. (1998). Empirically supported psychosocial interventions for children: An overview. *Journal of Clinical Child Psychology, 27,* 138–145.

MTA Cooperative Group. (1999). A 14-month randomized clinical trial of treatment strategies for attention-deficit/hyperactivity disorder. *Archives of General Psychiatry, 56,* 1073–1086.

MTA Cooperative Group. (2004). National Institute of Mental Health multimodal treatment study of ADHD follow-up: 24-month outcomes of treatment strategies for attention-deficit/hyperactivity disorder. *Pediatrics, 113,* 754–761.

Owens, J. S., Holdaway, A. S., Zoromski, A. K., Evans, S. W., Himawan, L. K., Girio-Herrera, E., & Murphy, C. (2012). Incremental benefits of a daily report card intervention over time for youth with disruptive behavior. *Behavior Therapy, 43,* 848–861.

Owens, J. S., Murphy, C. E., Richerson, L., Girio, E. L., & Himawan, L. K. (2008). Science to practice in underserved communities: The effectiveness of school mental health programming. *Journal of Clinical Child and Adolescent Psychology, 37,* 434–447.

Pelham, W. E., & Fabiano, G. A. (2008). Evidence-based psychosocial treatments for attention-deficit/hyperactivity disorder. *Journal of Clinical Child and Adolescent Psychology. 37*, 184–214.

Power, T. J., Karustis, J. L., & Habboushe, D. F. (2001). *Homework success for children with ADHD: A family-school intervention program.* New York, NY: Guilford Press.

Raggi, V., Chronis-Tuscano, A. M., Fishbein, H., & Groomes, A. (2009). Development of a brief, behavioral homework intervention for middle school students with attention-deficit/hyperactivity disorder. *School Mental Health, 1*(2), 61–77.

Sadler, J., & Evans, S. W. (2011). Psychosocial interventions for adolescents with ADHD. In S. W. Evans & B. Hoza (Eds.), *Treating attention-deficit/hyperactivity disorder: Assessment and intervention in developmental context.* New York, NY: Civic Research Institute.

Schultz, B. K., Evans, S. W., & Serpell, Z. N. (2009). Preventing failure among middle school students with ADHD: A survival analysis. *School Psychology Review, 38*, 14–27.

Tucker, P. (1999). Attention-deficit/hyperactivity disorder in the drug and alcohol clinic. *Drug and Alcohol Review, 18*, 337–344.

Vujnovic, R. K., Holdaway, A. S., Owens, J. S., & Fabiano, G. A. (in press). Response to Intervention (RTI) for Youth with ADHD: Incorporating an Evidence Based Intervention within a Multi-tiered Framework. In M. D. Weist, N. Lever, C. Bradshaw, & J. S. Owens (Eds.), *Handbook of school mental health* (2nd ed.).

Wolraich, M. L., Wibbelsman, C. J., Brown, T. E., Evans, S. W., Gotlieb, E. M., Knight, J. R.,...Wilens, T. (2005). Attention deficit hyperactivity disorder in adolescents: A review of the diagnosis, treatment and clinical implications. *Pediatrics, 115*(6), 1734–1746.

CHAPTER 51

Effective Intervening with Students from Single-Parent Families and Their Parents

Mo Yee Lee ■ Cathy Grover Ely

Getting Started

In 2008, there were 10,536,000 single-parent households in the U.S. (U.S. Census Bureau, 2011). Approximately 21.8 million children under the age of 21 were being raised by a single parent, which represented 26.3% of all children under 21 in the U.S. Mothers accounted for 82.6% of all custodial parents, and fathers represented 17.4% of all custodial parents (U.S. Census Bureau, 2009). In addition, the proportion of all U.S. children born to unmarried parents increased from about 4% in 1940 to 39.7% in 2007. One important social trend is single motherhood among young women of color between the ages of 15 and 24 (Romo & Segura, 2010). Seven out of 10 African-American newborns and 50% of Hispanic infants are born to unmarried parents (National Vital Statistics, 2009). Single parents are a diverse group and generally include single mothers, single fathers, and never-married and divorced parents. The challenges encountered by many single parents and their children are well documented and include the following:

1. Economic challenges. Single-parent families have significantly higher rates of poverty and material hardship than their married counterparts (Kalil & Ryan, 2010). Over 24% of single parents and their children had 2007 incomes below the federal poverty level, which was about twice as high as the overall poverty rate of the total population (U.S. Census Bureau, 2009). Single parents of color have higher rates of poverty. Among single-parent families, about 44% of African-Americans and 33% of Latinos live below the federal poverty level (U.S. Census Bureau, 2007).
2. School and behavioral problems in children. Studies on family structure reveal that children from single-parent homes tend to have higher rates of absenteeism and truancy than those from two-parent households (Kleine, 1994). They have significantly lower educational aspirations (Garg, Melanson, & Levin, 2007) and less favorable perceptions toward teacher-student relationships than students from intact families (Fan, Williams, & Corkin, 2011). Young persons who lived in one-parent households were more likely to participate in sexual intercourse, skip school, fight, and use alcohol or tobacco (Holmes, Jones-Sanpei, & Day, 2009; Oman et al., 2002). Empirical evidence also suggests that poverty and living in a poor neighborhood are associated with school and mental health or behavioral problems (McLanahan, Garfinkel, Mincy, & Donahue, 2010; Moore, Redd, Burkhauser, Mbwana, & Collins, 2009; Thornberry, Smith, Rivera, Huizinga, & Stouthamer-Loeber, 1999; Wandersman & Nation, 1998).
3. Overburden and lack of social support. Based on the strain perspective (Kitson & Morgan, 1990), single parents are more apt to experience multiple losses, economic challenges, and increased childcare responsibilities when compared to married parents (Kalil & Ryan, 2010). Studies also indicate that single parents are more isolated than their married counterparts because of the divergent paths that they have taken (McLanahan & Booth, 1989). These factors can contribute to boundary confusion between the parent and the child in a single-parent family. The child and parent can become "peers" as exemplified by the comment: "I lost my drinking buddy when my mom started going to AA. She's no fun any more." Another possibility is role reversal in which the child takes on the role of parenting an overwhelmed parent who is struggling with

financial problems and child-care responsibilities (Wallerstein, 2001).

4. Emotional stress in children. Children in a single-parent household often experience conflict over loyalty issues when dealing with parental divorce or separation (Maccoby, Buchanan, Mnookin, & Dornbusch, 1993). Children must also negotiate changes and new roles when courtship, dating, or marriage occurs in their families (Anderson et al., 1999; Bray, 1999). Emotional distress associated with family changes has been shown to be related to behavioral and emotional adjustment problems in children (Emery, 1999; Lee, 2002; McLanahan et al., 2010).

What We Know

While effective interventions with students from single-parent families and their parents should address the unique characteristics and challenges encountered by these families, it is imperative for school social workers and mental health counselors to recognize and respect single-parent families as a diverse and heterogeneous group. The student's idiosyncratic situation and life context is more than a simple description or label. The following trends have emerged that address prevention and remedial interventions with students from single-parent families. These trends recognize the interconnectedness of students, parents, schools, and the community (Figure 51.1). The students' school problems are systemic in nature and are not "owned" by the students or their families. Resolving students' school problems requires partnership and a focus on students' strengths and resilience.

Interventions Based on a Resilience, Strengths, and Solution-Oriented Perspective

Saleebey (1996) argued that most helping professions in the United States are saturated with practice approaches that are based upon a deficits or pathology perspective. This is likely to occur with single-parent families. For instance, studies on family structure reveal that children from single-parent homes tend to have higher rates of absenteeism and truancy and are more likely to participate in sexual intercourse, skip school, fight, and use alcohol or tobacco than those from two-parent households (Holmes, Jones-Sanpei, & Day, 2009; Kleine, 1994; Oman et al., 2002). While these findings are helpful for us to understand the challenges encountered by students from single-parent families, such negative evaluation can be stigmatizing and not helpful in working with them. In contrast to the deficits perspective is the *resilience* perspective, which views single-parent families as having the resources and coping skills for successfully handling their life situations (Emery & Forehand, 1999; Haggerty et al., 1994). A recent meta-analysis of school-based prevention and intervention programs showed that strengths-based assessment and intervention is crucial in the development of academic, social, and personal competencies for children (Reddy, Newman, De Thomas, & Chun, 2009). The role of school social workers and counselors is to work with the students and their families so that they learn to tap into the resources within them. The counselor does not change people but rather serves as a

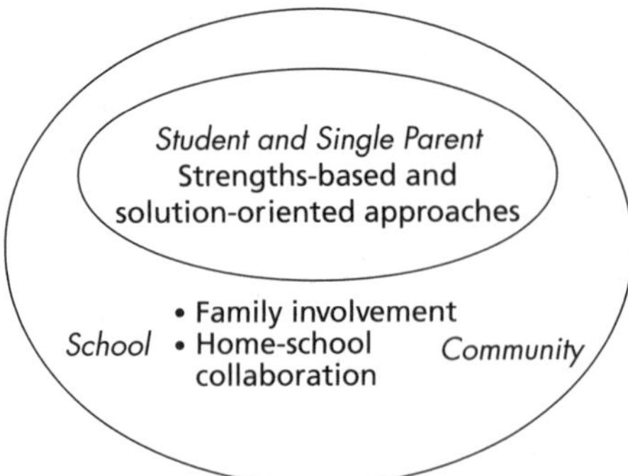

Figure 51.1 A Model of Effective Intervention with Students from Single-Parent Families

catalyst for students and parents to discover and use their resources to accomplish their goals. Solution-focused therapy provides well-defined interventions that operationalize a resilience and strengths perspective in working with students and their families (Durrant, 1995; Kelly, Kim, & Franklin, 2008; Metcalf, 2008; Murphy, 2008). The use of solution-focused interventions in a school setting showed promising evidence of effectiveness with a wide range of students' behavioral, emotional, and mental health problems on an individual basis and in groups, with students and their families, and in school-based consultations (Gingerich & Wabeke, 2001; Kim, 2008; see Table 51.1).

Interventions Focused on Family Involvement or Family-School Collaboration

As has been discussed elsewhere in this book studies consistently indicate that family involvement is a key factor in student success (Broussard, 2003; Minke & Anderson, 2005). Research has shown that family involvement predicts academic self-concept in students. In addition, parental involvement buffers the negative impact of single-parent families on students' academic self-concept and educational aspirations (Garg et al., 2007). In the Goal 2000: Educate America Act, President Bill Clinton included and signed into law the goal for increasing parent participation in education (U.S. Department of Education, 1994, P.L. 103–227). Germain (1999) noted that the school social worker "stands at the interface not only of child and school, but family and school, and community and school" (p. 36). Further, the school social worker and other mental health counselors are "in a position to help child, parents, and community develop social competence, and, at the same time, to help increase the school's responsiveness to the needs and aspirations of children, parents, and community" (p. 36). Research has shown the benefits of parental involvement on students' academic aspirations (Garg et al., 2007), student motivation to learn and competence (Gonzalez-DeHass, Willems, & Holbein, 2005), and student achievement (Pomerantz, Moorman, & Litwack, 2007). One prominent collaborative family-school initiative is the Family Builders approach that was first developed by the Catholic Archdiocese of Louisville, Kentucky, in 1994 to support children's academic and social competence (Sar

Table 51.1 Empirical Support for Solution-Focused Therapy with Single Parents

	Design	*Population*	*Outcomes*
Morrison et al., 1993	One-group pre- & post-test	30 elementary students	67% showed improvement that was maintained over a 2-year period
Durrant, 1995	Single-case design	1 fourth-grade girl with anxiety disorder	Improved anxiety symptoms
Littrell, Maila, & Vanderwood, 1995	One-group pre- & post-test	High school students in one-session SFT groups for academic and personal problems	Improved problem situation and goal attainment
LaFountain, Garner, & Eliason, 1996	One-group pre- & post-test	Elementary, middle, and high school students in 8-session SFT group	Improved self-esteem and coping
Zimmerman, Jacobsen, MacIntyre, & Watson, 1996	One-group pre- & post-test	Parents in 6-session SFT parenting groups	Improved role image, objectivity, communications, and limit setting in parents

(continued)

Table 51.1 *(Continued)*

	Design	*Population*	*Outcomes*
Murphy & Duncan, 1997	Single-case design	1 adolescent boy with oppositional behavior	Improved behavioral outcomes
Springer et al., 2000	Quasi-experimental design	10 Hispanic elementary students	Improved self-esteem for the SFBT group and not for the comparison group. However, no significant differences were found between the two groups at the end of the study.
Franklin et al., 2001	Single-case design	7 middle school students	Five of seven (71%) students improved based on teacher's report using Conners' Teacher Rating Scale
Newsome, 2004	Quasi-experimental design	52 middle school students	Significant increase in the mean grade scores of the SFBT group and decrease in the mean grade scores of the comparison group. No significant difference on attendance measure.
Corcoran, 2006	Quasi-experimental design	86 students aged 5–17	While SFBT and the comparison groups improved at post-test, no significant differences were observed between the 2 groups.
Froeschle et al., 2007	Experimental design	65 eighth-grade female students	Significant differences were found between SFBT and the comparison group on measures related to drug use and competent behavior scores based on parents' and teachers' assessments.
Franklin et al., 2008	Quasi-experimental design	59 middle school students	Improved outcomes on Externalizing scores based on teachers' assessments and youth's assessments and Internalizing scores based on teachers' assessments for SFBT group. Non-significant change in the comparison group. Non-significant differences observed between both groups on youth's self-report on Internalizing score.

Table 51.2 Empirical Support for Parental and Family Involvement in Students' Outcomes

Bempechat, 1990	Increased academic achievement in students
Bowen, 1999	Improvements in students' academic and social behavior and improved parent-teacher communications
Desimone, 1999	Raised test scores in students
Garg, Melanson, & Levin, 2007	Family involvement predicted academic self-concept and educational aspirations. In addition, there were no significant differences between adolescents from single-parent families and intact families in academic self-concept and educational aspirations when parents were highly involved.
Haynes, Comer, & Hamilton-Lee, 1989	Improved self-esteem, motivation, and behavior in students
Henderson, 1987	Improved attendance in students
Henderson & Berla, 1994	Reduced dropout rates in students
McDonald et al., 1997	Improved academic competence and behaviors in students, reduced family conflict, improved parent involvement in school, improved parent leadership, created friendship network in the community
Sar & Wulff, 2003	Positive changes in school's treatment of student problems, families felt empowered to engage in problem solving, improved children's psychological outcomes
Vaughn, White, Johnston, & Dunlap, 2005	Family-centered PBS led to positive outcomes in student's behavior and custodial parent.

& Wulff, 2003; see Table 51.2). Families and School Together (FAST; McDonald, Billingham, Conrad, Morgan, & Payton, 1997) is another collaborative model that combined clinical intervention with community development to address problems in students. It is a multifamily group intervention program designed to build protective factors for children (4–12 years old) and to empower parents to be the primary prevention agents for their own children. Positivbehavior support (PBS) is another intervention approach that incorporates research-based practices with systems change strategies to reduce or prevent problem behaviors and to improve quality of life in students (Sugai & Horner, 2006). Family participation is perceived as a critical enabler in sustaining individualized PBS (Bambara, Nonnemacher, & Kern, 2009). These programs/approaches focus on general student populations, including students from single-parent homes. Operation Positive Change is a program that adapts PBS best practices to primarily single parents in a linguistically diverse and underserved urban community (Markey, Markey, Quant, Santelli, & Turnbull, 2002). These approaches assume that the problems of children are usually systemic in nature and should be solved in the school setting in collaboration with other involved parties. Interventions or strategies for improvement are important; however, they are secondary to the collaborative partnership among families, schools, and other involved parties. In addition, students and families are viewed as legitimate partners in solving their own problems. The competence of families and schools is strengthened to handle the problem and to develop solutions as opposed to reliance on outside professionals (McDonald et al., 1997; Robbins & Carter, 1998; Sar & Wulff, 2003).

What We Can Do

A Strengths-Based, Solution-Focused Approach to Working with Students and Their Families

Originally developed at the Brief Family Therapy Center in Milwaukee by Steve de Shazer, Insoo Kim Berg, and their associates (Berg, 1994; DeJong

& Berg, 2002; de Shazer, 1991), the purpose of strengths-based, solution-focused interventions is to engage students and their parents in a solution-building process in which they find out what works for them. Such an approach involves the following assumptions (Berg, 1994; Lee, Sebold, & Uken, 2003): (1) There are exceptions to every problem pattern; (2) it is more helpful to focus on what students can do and their strengths than what is lacking and the problems in the change process; (3) language is powerful in creating and sustaining reality; therefore, the preferred language is the "language of solution and change"; (4) problems and solutions are the students' construction, and they determine the goals of treatment; and (5) because everything is connected, it is not necessary for the solutions to be directly related to the problems or vice versa. Often, these interventions are used when counseling students independently or with their single parents (e.g., Durrant, 1995; Kelly et al., 2008; Murphy, 2008), in conducting student or parent groups (Littrell et al., 1995; Zimmerman et al., 1996), and in school-based consultations (Metcalf, 2008).

Initiating Change

Defining the Problem

The students and parents are immediately encouraged to give a clear and explicit statement of their presenting complaint. In a school setting, major complaints are often initiated by teachers or parents in the form of students' inabilities to do homework, cooperate in class, or other behavioral concerns independent of or in relation to other students. Sometimes, students may also self-refer for personal problems.

1. Explore the behavioral and environmental factors maintaining the complaints.
2. Assess students' and parents' help-seeking status in terms of customers, visitors, or complainants. (DeJong & Berg, 2002)

Students and Parents as Assessors

Without focusing on the history of the problems, the school-based practitioner begins strengths-based, solution-oriented assessment that assists students and parents in identifying solutions for their problems. The school-based practitioner does not assume an expert position in conducting assessment with the purpose of determining a comprehensive treatment plan for each particular student. Students or single parents are the assessors, who constantly self-evaluate what is the problem, what may be feasible solutions to the problem, what is the desirable future, what are the goals of treatment, what strengths and resources they have, what may be helpful in the process of change, how committed or motivated they are to make change a reality, and how quickly they want to proceed with the change (Greene & Lee, 2011; Lee et al., 2003).

Building Initiative for Change

A major goal of assessment is to provide a context for students to begin noticing a different reality, which focuses on their competencies and possibilities for beneficial change. The most available starting point is what they have already been doing well and what they already possess (Lee et al., 2003). Useful questions are: What are some of your recent successes? When was the last time that you successfully broke a habit that was hard to break? What kinds of things do teachers and friends compliment you on? What things are you doing now that contribute to your life in school going better?

Searching for Exceptions

Every problem pattern includes some sort of exception to the rule (de Shazer, 1985). Despite the multideficiencies or problems that students or single parents may perceive that they have, there are always times when they handle their school problems in a more satisfying way or in a different manner. These exceptions provide the clues for solutions (Murphy, 2008) and represent students' "unnoticed" strengths and resources to address the problems they have in school. *Exception questions* and *coping questions* are useful to assist students in noticing, amplifying, sustaining, and reinforcing these exceptions regardless of how small or infrequent they may be (Durrant, 1995).

Envisioning a Desirable Future

For positive change to happen, students and parents need to be hopeful about the future and develop a clear vision of life in school either without the presenting complaint or with acceptable improvements in the school problem. A widely used format suggested by solution-focused therapy is the *miracle question* (Berg & Miller, 1992).

Setting Goals of Treatment

Building on visions of a desirable future is the process of helping students and parents to develop useful goals that provide a context of change. Lee, Sebold, and Uken (2003) have described the criteria for goals:

Useful. The goal needs to be personally meaningful and useful in improving lives in school.
Interpersonal. When students work on their goals, other persons will be able to notice the changes they have made and potentially be affected by the students' changed behavior.
New. The goal needs to be something different, a behavior that the student or parent has not generally done before.
Regular. The goal has to be a behavior that the student can practice on a regular basis.

Establishing Clear Indicators of Change

Students, parents, and teachers usually easily recognize the presence of the problem. However, in terms of change, it is more important for them to know when the student is making positive progress. *Scaling questions* provide a simple tool for students and parents to quantify and evaluate their situation and progress so that they establish a clear indicator of progress for themselves (Berg, 1994).

Giving Feedback

It is important to provide *feedback* to students and families that summarizes the essence of the session so that useful discussion is highlighted and expanded. The feedback includes three components: compliments, bridging statements, and task assignments that assist students and parents in noticing and practicing solutions in their natural life context (de Shazer & Molnar, 1984).

Task Assignments

If students and parents are customers and able to identify exception behaviors to the school problem, ask them to *do more of what works.*
If students and parents are visitors or unsure of goals, use *observing tasks:* "Between now and the next time we meet, I want you to observe, so that you can tell me next time, what happens in your [school, family, relationships with friends] that you want to continue to have happen." (Molnar & de Shazer, 1987).
If students and parents perceive no control over the problem, assign them to *do something different* or use the *prediction task* (Berg, 1994).

Consolidating Change

The primary tasks for the middle and latter phases of treatment are to expand and consolidate useful change efforts. Usually, the following responses are encountered:
Students and parents report positive experiences as a result of their change efforts.
Students and parents report not working on the goal.
Students and parents report no change or that the goal is not helpful.

When Students and Parents Report and Share Positive Changes

1. Review positive changes and stay curious about all the details so that the possibilities and meanings of the change efforts can be fully examined and explored.
2. Help students to evaluate the impact their behavior has had on others who may have directly or indirectly experienced the changes.
3. Assist students and parents to make connections between what they have done and positive outcomes. This process of discovering the details and exploring the full impact of the change behavior magnifies its importance and expands the meaning that is attributed to it. Direct and indirect compliments are critical to this process not only because they offer important feedback but also because they set expectations for change (Lee et al., 2003).

When Students and Parents Report That They Have Not Worked on the Goal

Students' and parents' response to their change effort is just a response, and there is no good or bad response.

1. Accept the statement.
2. Ask the students and parents to state their goal.

3. Look for exceptions.
4. Notice the unnoticed small events.
5. Help students and parents to evaluate their commitment to the change effort.
6. Help them to evaluate the usefulness of the goal.
7. Compliment any goal work.
8. Help students and parents detail future goal work.

When Students and Parents Report No Change or the Goal Is Not Helpful

All change efforts are helpful even when a student states that the change effort has failed to produce the desired results. Such feedback helps the student to discover what is not a solution and provides an opportunity to explore new ideas. It encourages the school-based practitioner and the student to look in other directions that will likely hold more promise.

1. Ask students and parents what their goal is.
2. Help them to be specific about their goal behavior and the responses to it.
3. Look for exceptions to "not helpful."
4. Help them to reevaluate the usefulness of their goal: Was part of the work on your goal helpful? Did you discover any clues about what would be more helpful? What do you think you will need to do differently to be more successful? Are there some adjustments that you would make?
5. Compliment any goal efforts (Lee et al., 2003).

Strengths-based, solution-oriented interventions are often used when working with students independently or with their single parents. In addition, these interventions are useful in working with teachers and school personnel individually, in team meetings, or in parent-teacher meetings (Metcalf, 2008). For instance, the school-based practitioner can suggest an observation task to the teacher: "I am working with Johnny to help him stay focused in your class. It'll be very helpful if you can work with me in the process. Between now and Friday, I would like you to observe, so that you can share with me, what's going on in the class that helps Johnny to stay focused." Similarly, the school-based practitioner can ask everyone in a parent-teacher meeting the following questions, which naturally bring a solution-oriented spirit instead of a blaming stance to the meeting: What kinds of things about Eric would you compliment? What little things is Johnny (or his parent) doing lately that may be helpful to him being able to come to school on time? What little things can each of you do to help Susanne feel safe at school?

The school-based practitioner cautiously refrains from providing/suggesting any predetermined solutions. The practitioner is responsible for creating a dialogical context in which student, teachers, and parents experience a solution-building process that is initiated from within and grounded in student strengths.

Pragmatic Guidelines: Interventions for Family Involvement or Family-School Collaboration

While strengths-based, solution-oriented strategies focus more on a microlevel of interventions, interventions that focus on family involvement and family—school collaboration happen on a mezzo-or macrolevel. They address the interface of school, family, and community. Effective facilitation of family—school collaboration has to be considered from diverse vantage points:

- Readiness of the parents and their resources and capacities for participation
- Awareness and sensitivity of the school personnel
- Effective models/procedures of family—school collaboration

Readiness of Parents and Their Resources and Capacities for Participation

Single parents have been described as "one person working two full-time jobs." They are less likely to report frequent contact with schools, volunteering, or communication with their children about school (McKay & Stone, 2000; Minke & Anderson, 2005). Bowen (1999) proposed that the school social worker and mental health counselor could be instrumental in facilitating parent—school communication regarding individual students.

Establish inclusion by inviting parents to school meetings where their children's academic and social progress is discussed.

Advocate for meetings at times that parents can attend.

Arrange for transportation or child care.

Promote an exchange of information at meetings such that parents' perceptions, insights, and suggestions are included in decisions.

Elicit from school staff specific activity ideas and resources for parents to use at home to address student academic and behavioral goals.

In situations in which parents cannot attend meetings, school social workers can model or coordinate efforts to ensure that parents are informed of meeting topics, have a chance to convey their concerns and insights, are given a summary of meeting outcomes, and receive specific activity ideas and resources to use at home.

Awareness and Sensitivity of the School Personnel

Home—school communication and collaboration is based on the premise that school personnel recognize diverse family contexts and cultures through respectful and effective communication. While teachers and administrators are primarily educated, middle-class Caucasians, student populations tend to be more diverse and heterogeneous. Home—school communication can be stifled when teachers and families are of differing backgrounds (Broussard, 2003). The following methods have been suggested for school personnel to increase their awareness and sensitivity in including families from diverse backgrounds, including single-parent families, as partners in education.

School personnel should work to expand their knowledge base of literature that addresses inequitable practices and its impact on students' academic and behavioral outcomes.

Systematically assess the school to determine teachers' and administrators' awareness and respect for family lifestyles outside of their experience and the extent of teacher-initiated family contact. Formal (e.g., survey) or informal (e.g., observation, discussion) assessments provide information for targeting interventions.

Engage in collaborative in-service training with teachers and administrators using family knowledge modules and strategies, such as case scenarios, role playing, classroom film analysis, and self-reflection, to increase awareness and respect for diverse family lifestyles and cultural backgrounds.

Establish parent groups and parent resource centers (see Lawson & Briar-Lawson, 1998) as well as conduct parent workshops that promote information sharing, mutual support, empathy, and a sense of community. Parents can be involved with the school through parent orientations, parent ombudspersons, or ad hoc parent-school teams.

Develop collaborative relationships with community members and institutions, school administrators, teachers, families, and youths who can contribute to and benefit from family information.

Effective Models/Procedures of Family-School Collaborative Initiatives

Home—school collaborative models provide interventions that combine remediation of problems with community development by merging micro and macro dimensions of practice. The following procedures and components have been empirically tested and found to be useful in facilitating family—school collaboration with respect to individual students' academic or behavioral problems (Bowen, 1999; McDonald et al., 1997; Sar & Wulff, 2003).

Assess the student's school functioning on the basis of interviews with teachers and parents and observation of the student's behavior in the school.

The community of concern is identified and invited to a meeting. The *community of concern* includes individuals affected by or concerned about the problem presented by the student. They can be parents, relatives, neighbors, or family friends.

In the meeting, the parameters of the student's problem are established by discussing the related contexts of the problem.

School staff and families examine their strengths and offer their views on how the problem may be understood. Respect and appreciation of all viewpoints is necessary during this brainstorming process. Each participant describes a strength of the student and a concern. The student is then asked if he or she knew that people felt that way about him or her (or had these concerns). The student is given an opportunity to reflect and respond.

The community of concern identifies strategies that have worked before and pieces together a solution or set of solutions. Consensus is reached on the solution(s) and roles are assigned. It is helpful to identify specific academic or behavioral goals with the student as well as accompanying strategies (i.e., home activity ideas) and materials for meeting the goals.

The treatment plan should be carefully implemented with the school social worker or counselor contacting parents and teachers on a regular basis to check and monitor progress.

When positive changes are accomplished, these changes, even subtle ones, are celebrated to affirm growth, potential, confidence, and hope (Powell, 1996).

Upon termination, the community of concern discusses how to maintain the positive changes. Follow-up meetings are scheduled and provisions for relapses are made. Participants also reflect on what they achieved and learned.

After treatment completion, parents and teachers are expected to independently maintain their partnership in addressing the student's needs.

Utilizing Parents as Resources in the Community

Schools can also support and promote programs in the community that serve to address students' problems in the school setting. One useful intervention is the development of parent support groups and programs (e.g., Markey et al., 2002). The increasing numbers of at-risk students and dropouts correspond to changes in family structure, including the growth of single-parent families (Kottman & Wilborn, 1992). Counselors can train parents to help parents, which is a way of utilizing community resources to increase efficiency in serving students. For instance, parent study groups have been utilized to provide direct assistance to parents and indirect help to children. Weekly group discussions focusing on parents and their needs are held to establish the parents as an integral component of the school (Kottman & Wilborn, 1992). In addition, school social workers and counselors can develop and coordinate psycho educational groups facilitated by parents who have experience with particular student problems and situations (Thomas & Corcoran, 2003). These paraprofessionals were found effective for parent—child interaction training in a low-income, ethnic minority sample (Strayhorn & Weidman, 1991). To successfully reach out to and engage the single-parent community, school professionals have to carefully consider the following strategies (Lochman, 2000; McKay & Stone, 2000):

Adopt an active problem-solving approach with parent communities to identify, from their perspectives, factors that facilitate participation as well as barriers to participation.

Conduct parent meetings in community settings.

Provide child care and transportation for meetings.

Facilitate cohesion building in parent groups through appropriate sharing of personal experiences, creating informal support networks within the group, and utilizing parents' own ideas rather than rigidly imposing the program's techniques.

Develop parent interventions that address family communication and that contain personally relevant topics such as parental stress.

Develop programs that incorporate the relevant cultural contexts of the parent community. Programs need to be based on an understanding of family processes and family change strategies across socioeconomic, ethnic, and community backgrounds to be relevant and effective.

Applying Solution-Focused Interventions within a Response to Intervention Framework

A strengths-based, solution-focused approach fits very well with the three-tiered Response to Intervention (RTI) and positive behavior support (PBS) frameworks. While RTI is designed to provide early, effective assistance to children who are having *learning* difficulties, PBS offers a parallel process that provides *behavioral* interventions to support academic success. PBS does not attempt to remediate a student's behavior in a clinical setting through the expertise of a clinician. Rather, PBS emphasizes a lifestyle focus in natural settings using an array of assessment and support procedures that are implemented by teachers and families (Carr et al., 1999; Turnbull & Turnbull, 1999).

Children living in poverty are more likely to be raised by single parents and to live in households where there is less parental supervision and more parental distress. Research finds that poor children are more likely to experience frequent moves and changes in family structure than more affluent children (Moore, Vandivere, & Ehrle, 2000; Moore, Vandivere, & Redd, 2006). In turn, these students are more likely to be identified in early screenings for social, emotional, and behavioral concerns than children whose lives are relatively stable. When a student is identified as struggling in school, a strengths-based, solution-focused approach assumes that there must be exceptions to any problem pattern, including patterns of learning and behavioral difficulties. Interventions focus on helping students, parents, and teachers to notice, identify, and expand the times when the child is successful in school.

RTI and PBS frameworks strive to build responsive environments that "stack the deck" in favor of appropriate student behavior and preferred quality of life outcomes (Turnbull & Turnbull, 1999). Solution-focused interventions can be utilized within these frameworks to focus on building strengths and creating a sense of competence and mastery in students and parents. Lucyshyn, Blumberg, and Kayser (2000) have offered three suggestions for improving the quality of support to families raising a child with problem behavior: offer family-centered, home-based services in which professionals recognize the expertise of the family; organize behavior support around the daily routines and demands of family life; and actively partner with parents so that wisdom and perspectives come together on behalf of the child with problem behaviors. Strengths-based, solution-focused interventions interrupt negative cycles and initiate a cycle of competence in which the attentions of teachers, parents, and students are beneficially shifted to the times when the students are successful.

Tools and Practice Example

Lewis is an 18-year-old 11th-grader who failed the 9th grade due to a lack of earned credits. When Lewis was in the 7th grade, his mother, Karen, and father divorced. Since that time, Lewis has had little contact with his father. Karen works two jobs to provide financially for her son. According to Lewis's teachers, he struggles with "staying on task" and completing his schoolwork. While Lewis is of average ability, his classroom behaviors often get in the way of his working up to his potential. Lewis was referred to the school social worker because his off-task behaviors have been escalating into loud outbursts and confrontations with other students, disrupting the educational process.

The school social worker met with the teacher to obtain a description of the problem behavior in terms of frequency and intensity as well as to discover exceptions to the problem behavior. Were there days when Lewis was on task and completing his schoolwork? What was different about those times? After gathering information from the teacher, the social worker met with Lewis.

Social Worker: Lewis, your teacher, Mrs. Jones, is concerned about your behavior in class and the way it is affecting your grades. What do you think about your work and the way you are in Mrs. Jones's class?

Lewis: I'm doing okay.

SW: What would I see if I were a fly on the wall watching you in Mrs. Jones's class?

Lewis: First, I go to my folder and get my work and do the kick-off for the day. Then, Mrs. Jones gives us our assignment and how to do it. I do it. I finish before everyone else most of the time.

SW: Then what?

Lewis: I can't believe I'm in trouble. I do my work. I just want to get my stuff done. I'm not looking to cause a problem.

SW: You aren't in trouble, Lewis. Mrs. Jones shared with me that you have days that are really good where you quietly complete your work and are respectful to others. We'd like to know how you do that so there can be more of those kinds of days. How do you make those days happen?

Lewis: She said I had good days?

SW: Yes. I'm wondering how we could work together so that you have more good days.

Lewis was originally defensive when discussing the problem identified by his teacher. After sharing with him an exception to the problem and complimenting him on his good days as supported by teacher information, Lewis changed from a visitor to a customer who was interested in doing something different. Lewis was also engaged as the expert on his behavior, holding the key to making changes in how he did his work and the way he acted in Mrs. Jones's class. Lewis shared that he had difficulty sitting still to complete his assignments, and while he frequently "finished" before his classmates, his work was not always complete. He indicated that on days when he had 8 hours of sleep, he was more focused and less irritable.

SW: You seem to have a good idea of what works for you. What else are you good at?

Lewis: My job. I bus tables at the Steak House. I'm fast.

SW: How is it that you are so good at your job?

Lewis: It's important to me. I want to make money to help my mom. Plus, I get to move around a lot, and I like being busy.

SW: You're a busy guy. It must be hard for you to slow down and focus on desk work in school. Suppose that after our meeting today, you go home, go to work, and go to bed. While you are sleeping, a miracle happens and your school problem is suddenly solved, like magic. Because you were sleeping, you don't know that a miracle happened, but when you wake up tomorrow morning, you will be different. How will you know a miracle has happened? What will be the first small sign that tells you that the problem is resolved?

Lewis described how he would get up after sleeping for 8 hours. His mom would have breakfast with him before school. He would go to school and do his work. Then, Lewis would go home, eat, go to work, and get to bed on time. In response to "How will others know that something is different about you?" Lewis replied that his mom would notice because he would not be up waiting for her to get home from work. Lewis explained that he liked to look after his mom by waiting up for her to get home from work. The social worker and Lewis discussed other ways that he could look after his mom and still get 8 hours of sleep. Lewis's goal was to get 8 hours of sleep on school nights. This goal fit with the teacher's goal of having Lewis complete his work and being respectful to others because these behaviors were contingent on Lewis getting 8 hours of sleep. When Lewis was asked about how confident he was about changing his sleep schedule (on a scale of 1–10), he was uncertain about giving up his responsibility of checking on his mom at night when she arrived home.

After collecting information about the problem and setting goals individually with Mrs. Jones and Lewis, a meeting was scheduled for the social worker, Mrs. Jones, Lewis, and Karen. Karen was initially disturbed by the prospect of having to meet about Lewis's class work and behavior, but she was immediately more responsive when the social worker complimented her on raising such a caring son who was so dedicated to his mother. When asked about others who might be invited as members of a community of concern, Karen reported that she could not think of anyone and that she had little contact with school personnel because of her "chaotic" life. Karen shared how it had been very difficult raising Lewis on her own and that she wondered if she was "doing it right." She enjoyed having Lewis meet her at the door at night to talk with her but had often felt guilty that he stayed up so late. She reported that he insisted on "being there" for her. The social worker asked Karen to think about other ways that Lewis could be there for her and to bring them to the meeting.

The first meeting was canceled due to Karen's work conflict, so a second meeting was scheduled in the break room of Karen's workplace. Karen greeted the group and was visibly impressed with the efforts of the school staff. Since the phone conversation, Karen and Lewis had discussed that he would go ahead and go to bed before she arrived home. He would leave the hall light on, and Karen would turn it off when she went to bed. Lewis would know that his mom was home by the "light signal." Also, Karen and Lewis would have breakfast together in the mornings before going to work and school. Karen wondered how other single parents managed their lives and was pleased to get a list of other single parents' phone numbers to contact from time to time for support. The phone list was provided by a single-parent support group coordinated by the school social worker in collaboration with a community mental health agency. Karen also identified the best way to reach her for updates on Lewis's progress in his schoolwork and classroom behavior.

By working together as a team, a simple yet effective solution was developed for Lewis. Lewis did improve on completing his assignments. An additional intervention was developed with input from the expert, Lewis, who requested a "busy box" of activities to work on after completing assignments at the end of class. Through increasing his sleep to 8 hours and staying busy, Lewis made great strides in completing his class work and being respectful to others. A follow-up meeting was held at the school to celebrate the success. Karen and Lewis were proud of their efforts and thought they could accomplish "whatever comes next."

Key Points to Remember

Schools increasingly become the de facto mental health service system for many children and adolescents (Burns et al., 1995), and there is an increased emphasis on developing empirically supported interventions with students and their families (Adelman & Taylor, 2000; Pomerantz et al., 2007). Traditional treatment of school problems in students from single-parent families is mostly influenced by an individual and deficits perspective. In essence, treatment has mostly focused on clinical practices with students and their families in resolving school problems that emphasize individual responsibilities for the problems. Recent advances, however, suggest that effective intervention with students from single-parent families requires multilevel skills that enable the school social worker or counselor to effectively work with students and their families and to facilitate home-school collaboration in the process. The described interventions recognize the systemic nature of students' problems and the interconnectedness of students, families, school, and community (Sar & Wulff, 2003). The focus is on utilizing student, single-parent family, and community strengths in resolving the problems. Specific interventions are directed by the idiosyncratic characteristics of particular students and their family milieu, although it echoes the wisdom that "it takes a village to raise a child."

Useful Internet Resources

Bridges4Kids: http://www.bridges4kids.org/At-Risk.html

National Coalition for Parent Involvement in Education: http://www.ncpie.org

National PTA: http://www.pta.org

RTI Action Network: http://www.rtinetwork.org/essential/family/schools-familes-and-rti

SAMHSA's National Registry of Evidence-based Programs and Practices: http://www.nrepp.samhsa.gov

School Mental Health Project, UCLA, Center for Mental Health in Schools: http://smhp.psych.ucla.edu

SEDL: Advancing Research, Improving Education: http://www.sedl.org/pubs/free_family_community.html

Single Parents Alliance of America: http://www.spaoa.org

Solution-Focused Brief Therapy Association: http://www.sfbta.org/sfbt_training.html

References

Adelman, H. S., & Taylor, L. (2000). Shaping the future of mental health in schools. *Psychology in the Schools, 37*, 49–60.

Anderson, E. R., Greene, S. M., Hetherington, E. M., et al. (1999). The dynamics of parental remarriage: Adolescent, parent, and sibling influences. In E. M. Hetherington (Ed.), *Coping with divorce, single parenting, and remarriage: A risk and resiliency perspective* (pp. 295–321). Mahwah, NJ: Erlbaum.

Bambara, L. M., Nonnemacher, S., & Kern, L. (July, 2009). Sustaining school-based individualized positive behavior support: Perceived barriers and enablers. *Journal of Positive Behavior Interventions, 11*, 161–176.

Bempechat, S. B. (1990). *The role of parent involvement in children's academic learning: A review of the literature*. New York: ERIC Clearinghouse on Urban Education.

Berg, I. K. (1994). *Family-based services: A solution-focused approach*. New York: Norton.

Berg, I. K., & Miller, S. (1992). *Working with the problem drinker: A solution-focused approach*. New York: Norton.

Bowen, N. K. (1999). A role for school social workers in promoting student success through school family partnerships. *Social Work in Education, 21*, 34–47.

Bray, J. H. (1999). From marriage to remarriage and beyond: Findings from the developmental issues in step families research project. In E. M. Hetherington (Ed.), *Coping with divorce, single parenting, and remarriage: A risk and resiliency perspective* (pp. 253–272). Mahwah, NJ: Erlbaum.

Broussard, C. A. (2003). Facilitating home-school partnerships for multi-ethnic families: School social workers collaborating for success. *Children and Schools, 25*, 211–222.

Burns, B. J., Costello, E. J., Angold, A., Tweed, D., Stangl, D., Farmer, E. M. Z., & Erkanli, A. (1995). Children's mental health service use across service sectors. *Health Affairs, 14*, 147–159.

Carr, E. G., Horner, R. H., Turnbull, A. P., Marquis, J., Magito-McLaughlin, D., McAtee, M., ... Doolabh, A. (1999). *Positive behavior support for people with developmental disabilities: A research*. Washington, DC: American Association on Mental Retardation. [ERIC Document Reproduction Service No. ED 439580]

Corcoran, J. (2006). A comparison group study of solution-focused therapy versus "treatment-as-usual" for behavior problems in children. *Journal of Social Service Research, 33*, 69–81.

DeJong, P., & Berg, I. K. (2002). *Interviewing for solutions* (2nd ed.). Pacific Grove, CA: Brooks/Cole.

de Shazer, S. (1985). *Keys to solutions in brief therapy*. New York:, NY: Norton.

de Shazer, S. (1991). *Putting difference to work.* New York: Norton.

de Shazer, S., & Molnar, A. (1984). Four useful interventions in brief family therapy. *Journal of Marital and Family Therapy, 10,* 297–304.

Desimone, L. (1999). Linking parent involvement with student achievement: Do race and income matter? *Journal of Educational Research, 93,* 11–31.

Durrant, M. (1995). *Creative strategies for school problems: Solutions for psychologists and teachers.* New York: Norton.

Emery, R. E. (1999). *Marriage, divorce, and children's adjustment.* Thousand Oaks, CA: Sage.

Emery, R. E., & Forehand, R. (1999). Parental divorce and children's well-being: A focus on resilience. In R. J. Haggerty et al. (Eds.), *Stress, risk, and resilience in children and adolescents: Processes, mechanisms, and interventions* (pp. 64–99). Cambridge: Cambridge University Press.

Fan, W., Williams, C. M., & Corkin, D. M. (2011). A multilevel analysis of student perceptions of school climate: The effect of social and academic risk factors. *Psychology in the Schools, 48,* 632–647.

Franklin, C., Biever, J. L., Moore, K. C., Clemons, D., & Scamardo, M. (2001). Effectiveness of solution-focused therapy with children in a school setting. *Research on Social Work Practice, 11,* 411–434.

Franklin, C., Moore, K., & Hopson, L. (2008). Effectiveness of solution-focused brief therapy in a school setting. *Children & Schools, 30,* 15–26.

Froeschle, J. G., Smith, R. L., & Ricard, R. (2007). The efficacy of a systematic substance abuse program for adolescent females. *Professional School Counseling, 10,* 498–505.

Garg, R., Melanson, S., & Levin, E. (2007). Educational aspirations of male and female adolescents from single-parent and two biological parent families: A comparison of influential factors. *Journal of Youth Adolescence, 36,* 1010–1023.

Germain, C. B. (1999). An ecological perspective on social work in the schools. In R. Constable, S. McDonald, & J. P. Flynn (Eds.), *School social work: Practice, policy and research perspectives* (pp. 33–44). Chicago: Lyceum.

Gingerich, W. J., & Wabeke, T. (2001). A solution-focused approach to mental health intervention in school settings. *Children and Schools, 23,* 33–47.

Gonzalez- DeHass, A. R., Willems, P. P., & Holbein, M. F. D. (2005, June). Examining the relationship between parental involvement and student motivation. *Educational Psychology Review, 17,* 99–123.

Greene, G. J., & Lee, M.Y. (2011). *Solution-oriented social work: A practice approach to working with client strengths.* New York: Oxford University Press.

Haggerty, R. J., Sherrod, L. R., Garmezy, N., & Rutter, M. (1994). Stress, risk, and resilience in children and adolescents: Processes, mechanisms, and interventions. Cambridge: Cambridge University Press.

Haynes, N., Comer, J., & Hamilton-Lee, M. (1989). School climate enhancement through parental involvement. *Journal of School Psychology, 27,* 97–100.

Henderson, A. T. (Ed.). (1987). *The evidence continues to grow: Parent involvement improves student achievement.* Columbia, MD: National Committee for Citizens in Education.

Henderson, A. T., & Berla, N. (1994). *A new generation of evidence: The family is critical to student achievement.* Columbia, MD: National Committee for Citizens in Education.

Holmes, E. K., Jones-Sanpei, H. A., & Day, R. D. (2009). Adolescent outcome measures in the NLSY97 family process data set: Variation by race and socioeconomic conditions. *Marriage and Family Review, 45,* 374–391.

Kalil, A., & Ryan, R. M. (2010, Fall). Mothers' economic conditions and sources of support in fragile families. *The Future of Children, 20,* 39–61.

Kelly, M. S., Kim, J. S., & Franklin, C. (2008). *Solution focused brief therapy in schools: A 360 degree view of research and practice.* New York: The Oxford University Press.

Kim, J. S. (2008). Examining the effectiveness of solution-focused brief therapy: A meta-analysis. *Research on Social Work Practice, 18,* 107–116.

Kitson, G. C., & Morgan, L. A. (1990). The multiple consequences of divorce. *Journal of Marriage and the Family, 52,* 913–924.

Kleine, P. A. (1994). *Chronic absenteeism: A community issue* [Report No. EA026196] East Lansing, MI: National Center for Research on Teacher Learning. [ERIC Document Reproduction Service No. ED375494]

Kottman, T., & Wilborn, B. L. (1992). Parents helping parents: Multiplying the counselor's effectiveness. *School Counselor, 40,* 10–14.

LaFountain, R. M., Garner, N. E., & Eliason, G.T. (1996). Solution-focused counseling groups: A key for school counselors. *School Counselor, 43,* 256–267.

Lawson, H., & Briar- Lawson, K. (1998). *Connecting the dots: Progress toward the integration of school reform, school-linked services, parent involvement and community schools.* Oxford, OH: Miami University, Danforth Foundation and Institute for Education Renewal.

Lee, M. Y. (2002). A model of children's post-divorce behavioral adjustment in maternal- and dual-residence arrangements. *Journal of Family Issues, 23*(5), 672–697.

Lee, M.Y., Sebold, J., & Uken, A. (2003). *Solution-focused treatment with domestic violence offenders: Accountability for change.* New York: Oxford University Press.

Littrell, J. M., Malia, J. A., & Vanderwood, M. (1995). Single-session brief counseling in a high school. *Journal of Counseling and Development, 73,* 451–458.

Lochman, J. E. (2000). Parent and family skills training in targeted prevention programs for at risk youth. *Journal of Primary Prevention, 21*(2), 253–265.

Lucyshyn, J. M., Blumberg, E. R., & Kayser, A. T. (2000). Improving the quality of support to families of children with severe behavior problems in the first decade of the new millennium. *Journal of Positive Behavior Interventions, 2*, 113–114.

Maccoby, E. E., Buchanan, C. M., Mnookin, R. H., & Dornbusch, S. M. (1993). Post divorce roles of mothers and fathers in the lives of their children. *Journal of Family Psychology, 7*, 24–38.

Markey, U., Markey, D. J., Quant, B., Santelli, B., & Turnbull, A. (2002, Fall). Operation positive change: PBS in an urban context. *Journal of Positive Behavior Interventions, 4*, 218–230.

McDonald, L., Billingham, S., Conrad, T., Morgan, A. O. N., & Payton, E. (1997). Families and Schools Together (FAST): Integrating community development with clinical strategies. *Families in Society, 78*, 140–155.

McKay, M. M., & Stone, S. (2000). Influences on urban parent involvement: Evidence from the National Education Longitude Study. *School Social Work Journal, 25*(1), 16–30.

McLanahan, S. S., & Booth, K. (1989). Mother-only families: Problems, prospects, and politics. *Journal of Marriage and the Family, 51*, 557–580.

McLanahan, S., Garfinkel, I., Mincy, R. B., & Donahue, E. (2010, Fall). Introducing the issue. *The Future of Children, 20*, 3–16.

Metcalf, L. (2008). *Counseling toward solutions: A practical solution-focused program for working with students, teachers, and parents*. San Francisco, CA: John Wiley & Sons.

Minke, K. M., & Anderson, K. J. (2005, Summer). Family-school collaboration and positive behavior support. *Journal of Positive Behavior Interventions, 7*, 181–185.

Molnar, A., & de Shazer, S. (1987). Solution focused therapy: Toward the identification of therapeutic tasks. *Journal of Marital and Family Therapy, 13*(4), 349–358.

Moore, K., Vandivere, S., & Ehrle, J. (2000). *Turbulence and child well-being. Assessing the New Federalism Report B-16*. Washington, DC: Child Trends and The Urban Institute. Retrieved from http://www.urban.org/UploadedPDF/anf_b16.pdf

Moore, K., Vandivere, S., & Redd, Z. (2006). A sociodemographic risk index. *Social Indicators Research, 75*, 48–841.

Moore, K. A., Redd, Z., Burkhauser, M., Mbwana, K., & Collins, A. (2009, April). Children in poverty: Trends, consequences, and policy options. *Child Trends Research Brief, 11*, 1–12.

Morrison, J. A., Olivios, K., Dominguez, G., Gomez, D., & Lena, D. (1993). The application of family systems approaches to school behavior problems on a school-level discipline board: An outcome study. *Elementary School Guidance & Counseling, 27*, 258–272.

Murphy, J. (2008). *Solution-focused counseling in schools*. Alexandria, VA: American Counseling Association.

Murphy, J. J., & Duncan, B. L. (1997). *Brief intervention for school problems*. New York: Guilford Press.

National Vital Statistics Reports. (2009). Births: Final data for 2006. Retrieved from http://www.cdc.gov/nchs/data/nvsr/nvsr57/nvsr57_07.pdf

Newsome, S. (2004). Solution-focused brief therapy (SFBT) groupwork with at-risk junior high school students: Enhancing the bottom-line. *Research on Social Work Practice, 14*, 336–343.

Oman, R. F., McLeroy, K. R., Versely, S., Aspy, C. B., Smith, D. W., & Penn, D. A. (2002). An adolescent age group approach to examining youth risk behaviors. *American Journal of Health Promotion, 16*, 167–176.

Pomerantz, E. M., Moorman, E. A., & Litwack, S. D. (2007, September). The how, whom, and why of parents' involvement in children's academic lives: More is not always better. *Review of Educational Research, 77*, 373–410.

Powell, J. Y. (1996). A schema for family-centered practice. *Families in Society, 77*, 446–448.

Reddy, L. A., Newman, E., De Thomas, C. A., & Chun, V. (2009). Effectiveness of school-based prevention and intervention programs for children and adolescents with emotional disturbance: A meta-analysis. *Journal of School Psychology, 47*, 77–99.

Robbins, T., & Carter, M. (1998, August–September). Family builders: Counseling families in Catholic schools. *Momentum*, 31–33.

Romo, L. F., & Segura, D. A. (2010). Enhancing the resilience of young single mothers of color: A review of programs and services. *Journal of Education for Students Placed at Risk, 15*, 173–185.

Saleebey, D. (1996). The strengths perspective in social work practice: Extensions and cautions. *Social Work, 41*, 296–304.

Sar, B. K., & Wulff, D. P. (2003). Family builders approach: Enhancing the well-being of children through family-school partnerships. *Children and Schools, 25*, 241–251.

Springer, D. W., Lynch, C., & Rubin, A. (2000). Effects of a solution-focused mutual aid group for Hispanic children of incarcerated parents. *Child & Adolescent Social Work Journal, 17*, 431–432.

Strayhorn, J., & Weidman, C. (1991). Follow-up one year after parent-child interaction training: Effects on behavior of preschool children. *Journal of American Academy of Child and Adolescent Psychiatry, 30*, 138–143.

Sugai, G., & Horner, R. (2006). A promising approach for expanding and sustaining school-wide positive behavior support. *School Psychology Review, 35*, 245–259.

Thomas, C., & Corcoran, J. (2003). Family approaches to attention deficit hyperactivity disorder: A review to guide school social work practice. *Children & Schools, 25*(1), 19–34.

Thornberry, T. P., Smith, C. A., Rivera, C., Huizinga, D., & Stouthamer-Loeber, M. (1999). *Family disruption and delinquency* [Report No. UD033207]. East Lansing, MI: National Center for Research on Teacher Learning. [ERIC Document Reproduction Service No. ED436604]

Turnbull, A. P., & Turnbull, H. R. (1999). Comprehensive lifestyle support for adults with challenging behavior: From rhetoric to reality. *Education and Training in Mental Retardation and Developmental Disabilities, 34,* 373–394.

U.S. Census Bureau. (2007). *Age and sex of all people, family members and unrelated individuals iterated by income-to-poverty ratio and race: 2007.* Washington, DC: Author. Retrieved from http://pubdb3.census.gov/macro/032008/pov/new01_100_09.htm

U.S. Census Bureau. (2009, November). *Custodial mothers and fathers and their child support, 2007.* Washington, DC: U.S. Department of Commerce, Economic and Statistics Administration, U.S. Census Bureau.

U.S. Census Bureau. (2011). *U.S. Census Bureau Statistical Abstract of the United States: 2011.* Retrieved from http://www.census.gov/compendia/statab/2011/tables/11s1336.pdf

U.S. Department of Education. (1994). *Goals 2000: National education goals.* Washington, DC: Author.

Vaughn, B. J., White, R., Johnston, S., & Dunlap, G. (2005, Winter). Positive behavior support as a family-centered endeavor. *Journal of Positive Behavior Interventions,* 7, 55–58.

Wallerstein, J. (2001). The challenges of divorce for parents and children. In J. Westman (Ed.), *Parenthood in America: Undervalued, underpaid, under siege* (pp. 127–139). Madison: University of Wisconsin Press.

Wandersman, A., & Nation, M. (1998). Urban neighborhoods and mental health: Psychological contributions to understanding toxicity, resilience, and interventions. *American Psychologist, 53,* 647–656.

Zimmerman, T. S., Jacobsen, R. B., MacIntyre, M., & Watson, C. (1996). Solution-focused parenting groups: An empirical study. *Journal of Systemic Therapies, 15,* 12–25.

Working With Families From Religious Fundamentalist Backgrounds

CHAPTER 52

Jennifer D. Yates Allan Hugh Cole, Jr.

Getting Started

Religious fundamentalism, defined below, is an influential phenomenon in the United States. It is found in various religions and faith traditions, including Christian, Jewish, Islamic, Hindu, and Buddhist movements. School social workers, psychologists, and counselors are particularly likely to encounter fundamentalist beliefs in schools because fundamentalism has significant numbers of adherents within Protestant Christianity (Almond, Appleby, & Sivan, 2003, p. 90). However, issues of religious identification blur the boundaries between fundamentalism and other conservative Protestant movements, rendering a "head count" of those adhering to a fundamentalist worldview quite complicated. Estimates of Americans who embrace a fundamentalist belief system are speculative at best, and range from 5% to 10% of the population. This estimate does not include evangelicals or other conservatively religious Christians who may embrace tenets of fundamentalism to varying degrees (Numrich, 2007).

In an increasingly pluralistic society, school social workers and mental health counselors practice with diverse religious populations, which include those who embrace fundamentalist belief systems. Moreover, school social workers, psychologists, and counselors often serve as the principal resource for educating, building, and sustaining relationships, and helping to foster ongoing communication among school personnel, students, and their families. The goal is to formulate and support interventions needed for ameliorating problems in living that impact students and families in the school environment and beyond. Practitioners thus need to be familiar with a growing and increasingly diverse number of religious traditions and spiritualities that students may embrace, including the qualities and distinctions of the religious fundamentalist worldview. Likewise, practitioners must be sensitive to particular challenges, both interpersonal and systemic, that may arise in schools with these populations. Furthermore, it is important for practitioners to identify and adopt resources for effective practice that respect and draw on what *clients* believe, value, and determine they need, on the one hand, and what practice standards, values, and ethics require, on the other. Given the prominence of Response to Intervention (RTI) as a framework for service delivery, it is critical that school-based practitioners be able to attend to these matters in a culturally competent manner within an RTI framework.

What We Know

Characteristics of Fundamentalism

Fundamentalism is difficult and even controversial to define. Coined in the early part of the 20th century, the term originally described a movement of conservative Christians who stood in opposition to attempts by Protestant evangelicals to bring traditional Christian tenets in line with modern thought (Marsden, 2006). However, toward the end of the 20th century and particularly since the events of 9/11, the term has gained a pejorative flavor in popular thought, often associated with bigotry, fanaticism, and terrorism (Munson, 2008). As such, the term "fundamentalist" should be used with care when describing religiously conservative individuals. The difficulty and controversy in defining fundamentalism may in part be derived from the intangible and emotionally charged nature of religious belief itself and the divergent viewpoints found among different religions and, not infrequently, within the same religion. In this sense, one person's fundamentalist is another's religious conservative is another's evangelical. Furthermore, the term is often misused in the media and in popular culture. Confusion arises in these areas because religious and nationalist or ethnic loyalties are often conflated with religiosity, so that what is called religious fundamentalism is more accurately described as religious nationalism or ethnonationalism (Almond, Appleby, & Sivan, 2003, p. 90). Further complicating a definition is a recent repudiation of the term by those who once identified as fundamentalist. Because the term has taken on a pejorative nuance, many religiously conservative Christians who once identified as fundamentalist are now identifying as evangelicals or conservative Christians, although their beliefs have not necessarily changed (Munson, 2008). Furthermore, while fundamentalist belief systems can be found within all major world religions and denominations (Aten, Mangis, & Campbell, 2010) the term "fundamentalist" does not appear to be embraced by conservative Muslims or Jews. Muslims with fundamentalist "impulses" tend to identify as "Islamists" (Kramer, 2003; Munson, 2008, p. 699), while Jews who embrace fundamentalist beliefs often describe themselves as "Modern Orthodox" or "Ultra-Orthodox" (Munson, 2008, p. 695).

While use of the term particularly, for labeling purposes, remains controversial, the beliefs and attitudes associated with the construct known as religious fundamentalism remain. This is in part evidenced in a recent Gallup poll indicating that 30% of Americans claim to interpret the Bible literally (Jones, 2011). Indeed, scholars of religion continue to detect fundamentalist inclinations within major religious movements. However, these scholars conceptualize the exact nature of this inclination differently. Some (Almond, Appleby, & Sivan, p. 17) emphasize the ideological and relational characteristics associated with those who fight to preserve what they consider to be traditional and "right" beliefs and practices. Others (Williamson, Hood, Ahmad, Sadiq, & Hill, 2010) argue that fundamentalism is best described by attitudes believers hold in relation to their sacred texts. Specifically, they argue that fundamentalists believe their sacred text is divinely inspired, "inerrant, privileged above all other texts, authoritative, and unchanging as the embodiment of timeless truth" (Williamson et al., 2010, p. 721). While scholars disagree on its exact nature, at its most basic level, it can be argued that fundamentalism is characterized by strict conformity to sacred scripture and to a moral code thought to be derived from it (Munson, 2008). What is important to our discussion here is to understand prevalent characteristics within fundamentalist and religiously conservative communities so that we can work successfully with adhering students and families. Before beginning that discussion, however, it is important to point out that just like issues of immigrant or ethnic-minority status, there are within-group differences, and holding to a religious belief system of any sort involves matters of degree. The school mental health practitioner should always inquire about how important religion is to a client, and not assume any particular religious background or qualities thereof.

There are nine qualities, accepted among many religion scholars, that characterize religious fundamentalism (Almond, Appleby, & Sivan, 2003, pp. 90–115). The social worker's and counselor's knowledge of these characteristics, as well as his or her awareness of the common tendency to conflate religious understandings, identity, and commitments with other facets of life, may be helpful in both assessment and ongoing practice with students and their families. These characteristics provide a heuristic structure for understanding some qualities that may comprise a conservatively religious or fundamentalist frame of reference. It is important to note that the presence of these characteristics will vary significantly across the spectrum of individuals who embrace fundamentalist or conservatively religious worldviews.

Fundamentalism's characteristics, the first five of which are ideological in nature and the last four of which are relational, are:

- Reactivity and defensiveness, especially with respect to the marginalization of one's religion and its traditions by secularism, modernization, government, and the erosion of their religion's values and influence. Often this leads to activist efforts to assuage the marginalization and gain influence.
- Selectivity, particularly with respect to what is embraced and rejected in both the religious tradition and modernity. Selectivity often highlights valued distinctions—whether religious or secular in kind—between the fundamentalist and the mainstream.
- Dualistic worldview, where sharp distinctions are drawn between light and darkness,

spiritual and material, and good and evil. This is especially evident with respect to morals and truth.

- Affirmation of inerrancy and the absolute, particularly as they concern what the fundamentalist views as divinely inspired sacred texts and religious tradition. Closely related are literal readings and understandings of texts and traditions whose instructions and truths the fundamentalist claims, applies, and advocates. This may translate into dogmatism and rigidity of beliefs, values, and behavior.
- Millennial and messianic views of history whose climax involves miraculous phenomena, including a triumph of light over darkness and good over evil. Typically inseparable from this experience is the inaugural role played by an omnipotent redeemer figure.
- Elect membership composed of divinely chosen and called persons. This often leads to a sense of superiority among the chosen and thus a devaluation of what others may have to offer.
- Sharp boundaries separating the elect and non-elect (saved and unsaved, moral and sinful, clean and unclean). This often creates an "us against them" mentality and can lead to guardedness or even distrust of those outside the religion.
- Tension between commitment to voluntary and egalitarian membership, wherein faithful insiders presumably have equal status, and yielding to the authority of a charismatic leader, who is set apart from the community.
- Strict conformity to behavioral requirements prescribed by religious commitments, so that individuality and unconventionality are devalued (if not rejected) and group norms are affirmed and maintained.

Assessment

In order to be attuned to a student or family's religiosity, the school-based mental health practitioner will want to conduct a culturally sensitive assessment exploring the degree to which a religiously conservative family's worldview may be informed by the characteristics of fundamentalism described above. Understanding the family's principal frame of reference is important, as it should inform culturally competent practice. Given the constraints of time and resources so common in a busy school setting, this assessment may likely occur at the outset of a parent meeting or phone conversation, and may be embedded within the process of joining with the family. However, exploring a family's faith tradition can become very sensitive in schools, particularly because of the policies to keep religion and education separate in public schools. Consequently, mental health practitioners working in the public schools may feel constraints upon the ways in which they are able to address the religiosity of their students and families. Recently there has been movement within various fields of mental health to expand the notion of cultural competence to include religion (Eriksen, Marston, & Korte 2002; Walton, Limb, & Hodge, 2011; Hodge & Nadir, 2008; Moore-Thomas & Day-Vines, 2008). Culturally competent practice involves the provision of services informed by an understanding of a student's values, beliefs, cultural heritage—all of which may be intertwined with a student's religion and spirituality. Understanding religion as another form of cultural diversity may provide some precedent for mental health practitioners working in schools to feel more comfortable exploring students' religious and spiritual narratives.

Given that characteristics of fundamentalism may include reactivity or defensiveness, particularly in regard to perceived religious marginalization, it is possible that interventions provided by mental health practitioners in public school systems could be viewed with a degree of suspicion. Consequently, forging a relationship based upon demonstrating value and respect for the family's religious frame of reference is critical. Approaching assessment from a strengths-based perspective holds promise for culturally competent practice with religiously conservative or fundamentalist families (Hodge & Nadir, 2008; Walton, Limb, & Hodge, 2011). Operating from a strengths-based perspective involves identifying a client's unique resources and harnessing their use to ameliorate problems (Park & Peterson, 2008). Such an approach may be particularly effective with families who may fear ridicule or rejection of their religious beliefs and practices. Emphasizing such strengths may serve to implicitly legitimize the family's beliefs and practices while communicating respect and facilitating trust (Hodge & Nadir, 2008). Additionally, tapping into unique strengths and resources derived from a family's spirituality or faith community may be used to inform religiously congruent interventions.

Because the school-based practitioner is unlikely to possess expertise in multiple religions, a strength-based assessment may involve possessing an open stance that privileges the student or family as the "expert" on the family's religious and spiritual practices. Practitioners can, therefore, inquire about the family's beliefs and practices by asking open-ended questions such as, "I'm not familiar with that form of Buddhism. Would you mind telling me a little about it and the role it plays in your life?" Assessment questions may also serve to illuminate strengths that can inform interventions, such as "It sounds like faith has been a source of strength for your family. How might the wisdom from your faith tradition speak to the issue we're discussing here today?" or "In what ways has your faith been helpful to you in the past when you have struggled with difficult challenges?" (Walton, Limb, & Hodge, 2011, p. 52). Asking strength-based assessment questions while getting to know the family can yield valuable information. For example:

School Psychologist: What outside activities does Andre have?

Parent: He is involved three nights a week with our church.

SP: That's wonderful! It sounds like church is important to him then?

P: Yes. We taught him to believe in God, and we're happy about his commitment to his faith and our church.

SP: Sounds like your church might be important to others in your family too.

P: Yes. It's very important to everyone. My husband's involved in lay ministry, and I've been teaching vacation Bible school for years.

SP: That's great! It sounds like you're all very involved. Do you mind if I ask what church?

P: The Church of Christ. (The school psychologist recognizes the church as one with fundamentalist beliefs, but if one did not recognize the church, one could say something like, "I am not familiar with that church. I am curious, do you mind, and do not feel like you have to answer this, but I am always interested in the beliefs of different churches. So, what do you believe?" Most people with fundamentalist beliefs will be happy to share their faith with you.)

SP: So, it sounds like your church is a source of support for your family.

P: Yes. It's been particularly good for Andre. He is co-leading Wednesday night Bible study, and is becoming involved with the worship band.

SP: Sounds like Andre has leadership skills then?

P: Yes he does.

While brief, this assessment may have assisted the school psychologist in accomplishing the following:

- Demonstrating respect for the family's faith tradition, and in doing so, laying a foundation for the development of a trusting relationship
- Gaining insight into the family's religious frame of reference and worldview
- Learning about Andre's support systems
- Providing insight into Andre's strengths, including leadership skills and musical talents
- Realizing that Andre's church may be a source of untapped resources for he and his family

Information derived from a strengths-based assessment can unearth culturally relevant information that may not only facilitate a trusting relationship with the family but also provide information that can inform interventions that are amenable to the family and their worldview.

Challenges

School social workers and mental health counselors face several potential challenges when working with families who possess religiously conservative and fundamentalist belief systems. Some of the challenges center principally on the school-based practitioner; others center on the client; and still others play out in the relationship between them.

One challenge is that concerted efforts to engage in nonbiased practice, surely a noble and necessary objective, may lead to the social worker and counselor neglecting to identify and utilize what is of greatest value to the client, namely, the client's religion. As a result, this may prompt neglect of what orients the client's cognitions and behaviors most profoundly. That is, in an attempt to remain open and nonjudgmental practitioners, social workers may fail to privilege the client's unique and particular frame of reference, worldview, or "meaning system"—all of which are grounded in religious commitments—and also may fail to make proper use of those in practice (Denton, 1990; Stalley, 1978). This usually plays out as the practitioner's sensitivity to remaining unbiased or "objective" results in not recognizing and working with the *client's* biases and subjective experiences: in this case, religious ones. Not only does this hinder the process of gaining information and perspective, it also diminishes the resources within the client's religious faith that may be drawn on during interventions. Denton (1990) notes that along with the "polemical" side of fundamentalism, there is a "private" side, which emphasizes love and support (p. 8). Drawing on York's (1987) discussion of religion's role in hospital neonatal care, Denton points out that "fundamentalism provided families with opportunities for socialization, belongingness, increased status and role opportunities, forgiveness, ability to relinquish responsibility for one's actions and problems, and spiritual guidance in the form of rules, values, and rituals" (Denton, 1990, p. 8). Moreover, emotional distress has been found to be assuaged through participation in a fundamentalist church (Ness & Wintrob, 1980). It is an important benefit to clients as social workers recognize and affirm the potential value and resources found within the client's religious orientation as part and parcel of honoring their own commitments to nonbiased practice.

A second challenge is that fundamentalism may be foreign, suspect, or objectionable for the practitioner, which may make remaining open to the client's experience, meaning system, and values even more problematic. Here, the practitioner may be aware of the client's religious orientation and may have been attuned to its impact on the client's life, problem, and potential resources for intervention. However, the practitioner's own distaste for the client's religious worldview and commitments, and perhaps the corresponding belief that these are unhealthy or otherwise inappropriate, prevents assigning them proper significance. The result is akin to what was mentioned previously, namely, a failure to work within the client's principal fame of reference.

This particular challenge may actually be the more typical and complicating one. One reason is that psychodynamically oriented practitioners, who still make up a large portion of social workers and other counselors, tend to have an ambivalent relationship with religion in general—professionally, if not personally—and are particularly suspicious of religious fundamentalism (Northcut, 2004). Related to that, facets of the fundamentalist worldview are in tension with, if not contradictory to, many counselors' values and ethics, which may result in a prima facie bias against what the fundamentalist client reveals, values, or requires (Denton, 1990). Hodge (2002) goes as far as to claim that social work often oppresses more conservative Christians in its widespread lack of tolerance for evangelical belief systems. He notes that whereas social work is to be commended for its tolerance with respect to gender, race, ethnicity, age, sexual orientation, and class, among other variables, religion remains the glaring omission in the field's commitment to inclusion (Hodge, 2002, p. 402). If this omission is apparent in practice with evangelicals, it is likely more so in practice with those who possess fundamentalist belief systems that are typically more pronounced and in greater tension with social work and mental health norms, values, and ethics. Practitioners must remain sensitive to these tendencies among their profession and discern whether or not any of these are inhibiting their own effective practice.

A third set of challenges relates more directly to the characteristics and inclinations of religious fundamentalism previously cited. Families from religiously fundamentalist backgrounds may fear that their beliefs and worldview will be misunderstood, ignored, or invalidated by school personnel (Miller, 1995). This fear, along with concerns about interaction with the secular world, may lead to suspicion of the school-based practitioner, the institution he or she represents, and what both may have to offer. Particularly difficult may be the client's reactionary and defensive postures toward those in the public schools, who represent the government. Tied to this may be the client's perceived marginalization by those in power, the school personnel being examples, who are often viewed as instruments of the outside, immoral world and as being complicit in its downfall. That mind-set may be joined with a corresponding suspicion of what is valued by so-called experts, who are trained by secular universities in social sciences and who represent the mainstream.

Moreover, a religiously conservative or fundamentalist frame of reference can be characterized by a dualistic, black-and-white understanding of the world. Often connected with that understanding is intolerance for ambiguity or the gray areas of life. The fundamentalist penchant for clear-cut and firm understandings, particularly with respect to morals, truth, and personal behaviors, may temper, if not prevent, the client from considering the new ideas, understandings, and behaviors that the social worker and mental health counselor offer.

Yet another difficulty may come with the primacy and authority those with fundamentalist belief systems may grant to sacred texts (Bible, Koran, or Torah) or to charismatic leaders. These attitudes too may minimize the value given to other kinds of authority and expertise, including what the social worker embodies and represents. Similarly, fundamentalism's strongly demarcated gender roles typically results in men having authority over women, which poses a particular challenge for the female social worker and other school-based practitioners. Another challenge may involve the family understanding a student's academic, behavioral, or emotional problems to be solely spiritual in nature. This can present significant challenges when a student is struggling with severe mental illness. In such instances, value may be placed on supernatural intercession in the form of miracles which may limit the client's openness to interventions the social worker and mental health counselor may provide and which may result in a measure of passivity.

Two additional challenges stem from conservatively religious clients' suspicion of those outside their own religious group. Such suspicion may prompt a feeling of having been disloyal among those who venture beyond the group for assistance. It may also mitigate efforts that the social worker makes to help the client change behaviors away from those endorsed by group and religious norms.

Any of these tendencies may challenge the practitioner's efforts to establish rapport, acquire information, and work collaboratively with the client to formulate and implement strategies for change. Note too that clients' suspicions or distrust not only dissuade them from engaging the school and its personnel. They may also eventuate in the social worker or other counselor being mistrustful of the client. That is, when we perceive the client's lack of trust, we may resent this personal reaction, and thus be less open to trusting or valuing the client's perspective. In all of these scenarios, effective practice is compromised.

What We Can Do

Cultivate Awareness of Various Religions and Their Potential Resources

Social workers and other counselors must educate themselves on a variety of religions and spiritualities, particularly those represented by the client populations they serve. While one need not become an expert, a basic understanding of, and appreciation for, various religions and spiritualities fosters rapport with clients and, presumably, reduces the number of inaccurate assumptions the practitioner may otherwise make about what the client believes, values, and desires. Moreover, increased familiarity with another's frame of reference allows the practitioner to utilize that frame more generously in practice, thus facilitating more acceptable and useful interventions. When clients perceive the practitioner's sensitivity to their way of understanding and living in the world, clients tend to be more receptive to what the practitioner may say about the clients' condition and offers of strategies for change.

The following resources provide excellent information on numerous religions and spiritualities, including fundamentalist movements. These are helpful for increasing one's knowledge and sensitivities.

Books

Ammerman, NT. (1988). *Bible believers: Fundamentalists in the modern world.* New Brunswick, NJ: Rutgers University Press.

Greeley, A. M., & Hout, M. (2006). *The truth about conservative Christians: What they think and what they believe.* Chicago, IL: University of Chicago Press.

Mead, F. S., & Hill, S. S. (2010). *Handbook of denominations in the United States* (13th ed.). Nashville, TN: Abingdon.

Web Sites

http://www.wellesley.edu/RelLife/transformation/
http://www.adherents.com
http://cmes.hmdc.harvard.edu/research/iw
http://pluralism.org
http://religionandpluralism.org/

School-based mental health professionals may benefit too from building relationships with clergy and faith-based institutions in their communities. Forging these collaborative and strength-based partnerships may serve the dual purpose of cultivating awareness of religious diversity while simultaneously providing intervention. The development of collaborative relationships with clergy has the potential to provide the school-based practitioner with insights from students' faith traditions as well as serve to clarify values and interpret beliefs. Additionally, some faith-based institutions may be able to provide resources for students who are members of the congregation. As such, broader partnerships with faith-based institutions may be particularly important for students living in low-income and inner-city communities, as neighborhood schools are often considered important institutions in communities where resources are limited (Bryan & Henry, 2008). Further, if it becomes apparent that a student from a conservative religious community requires a higher level of intervention, creative and collaborative interventions utilizing resources from the faith community can be considered. For example, clergy collaboration might be called upon in addressing issues for which religious clarification may be needed, such as a family's confusion regarding how to interpret and treat mental illness. Some conservatively religious families as well as some from non-dominant cultures may assign a strictly spiritual etiology to serious mental health concerns, and would benefit from medically informed information offering alternative explanations and treatment options. Although this alliance is not easy in public schools, ministerial resources can be helpful for persuading families to trust and cooperate. Not only does this provide educational opportunities, it may also prove helpful for collaborative work with clients whom social workers, counselors, and clergy all serve. Further areas for collaboration might include issues such as child abuse or domestic violence, for example. Building relationships with clergy and congregants who possess fundamentalist beliefs may prove more difficult than doing so with more progressive and open religious communities, but it is important to keep in mind that most religious communities have those who are more open or who might even want to enhance the community's openness. Offering an open community forum on issues of importance to the school and inviting conservatively religious leaders may be one way to identify those who are approachable. Efforts to learn from and work with leaders within fundamentalist traditions may well prove to be worthwhile, particularly as this facilitates greater understanding, sensitivity, and appreciation among all parties and thus fosters more normative working partnerships.

Cultivate Self-Awareness

Just as crucial as increasing one's awareness of various religions, spiritualities, and fundamentalist movements is developing greater awareness of oneself, both as a person and as a practitioner. Keen insights pertaining to who we are and what we bring to practice by virtue of our own experiences remain essential for effective school-based practice. It is important to commit to an ongoing process of self-discovery and understanding, so as to mitigate our making false assumptions, acting out in inappropriate ways with clients, or otherwise obstructing practice appropriately centered on *their* experiences, needs, and goals. These insights have particular import for working with those who embrace a fundamentalist worldview, especially when the practitioner does not share the same religious orientation.

As Sue and Sue (1990) have noted with respect to divergent worldviews among "culturally different" practitioners and clients, "Counselors who hold a world view different from that of their clients and are unaware of the basis for this difference are most likely to impute negative traits to clients" (p. 137). Hence, school-based practitioners must put into place a framework and method for ongoing self-assessment, wherein they seek clarity about a variety of matters. The goal is to foster practice attuned to what the client values and seeks and to prevent the practitioner's biases or preconceptions from detracting from appropriate client self-determination.

Listed below are some matters (foci) the mental health practitioner can explore, along with a set of questions designed to facilitate greater self-awareness:

- *Focus:* one's own religious or spiritual orientation. To the extent we consider, comprehend, evaluate, and utilize another's religiosity in our practice, we tend to do so by appealing first to our own internal frame of reference. We are inclined to use our own religious or spiritual history, understanding, and commitments—or perhaps our lack thereof—as the baseline for interacting with the history, understanding, and commitments of another. Though this is inevitable, an unreflective appeal to our own experience hampers our commitment to begin with the client's frame of reference and to assign priority to it. When that happens, practice is com promised. Ask yourself the following questions:
- What, if anything, do I believe about God, the spiritual realm, and the sacred in life?
- What value do I place on my own spiritual beliefs, and to what extent does this shape my own conceptions of life, death, hardships, relationships, meaning, values, goals, behaviors, and the like?
- On a scale of 1–10, with 1 representing "non-existent" and 10 representing "very central,"

what role does my religious faith or spirituality play in my daily life?

- What has been my experience with religion—my own or others'—and how has that informed my perception of religious faith, whether positively, negatively, or both?
- To what extent do my preconceptions about religion or spirituality affect my practice, particularly when religiosity plays a central role?

In addition to asking these questions, other strategies that can be used to facilitate awareness of one's worldview and spiritual beliefs include using a spiritual genogram, composing a spiritual autobiography, guided journaling, and practicing mindfulness. Wiggins (2008) offers descriptions of these strategies and provides guidelines for their use.

- *Focus:* one's preconceptions of or biases toward those who adhere to a conservatively religious or fundamentalist worldview. For most persons, social workers and other counselors included, some experiences, practices, behaviors, or values are difficult to understand, acknowledge, or accept. Such difficulties are not limited to the religious sphere. Yet, as previously mentioned, religious fundamentalism and practice with clients who embrace it may pose particular challenges to social workers and other mental health professionals because of divergent world views and commitments. Related to this, religiosity is often closely tied to racial, ethnic, class, or cultural identities and expressions. Consequently, school-based practitioners must assess their responses to a client's religiosity while considering their feelings about those factors as well. Ask yourself the following questions:

  What do I know about the type of religion my client embraces?

  Do I need to know more before making an assessment of its role, meaning, and value, both for the client and for our work together? If so, how may I acquire more knowledge and understanding?

  What do I believe and how do I feel about my client's conservatively religious or fundamentalist beliefs as I understand them? How may this either facilitate or hamper practice?

  How do I tend to react or respond to those I perceive to be substantially different from me, whether religiously or otherwise, and what informs that reactivity or response?

  What is particularly problematic for me, if anything, in what I understand to be my client's beliefs, values, and goals?

  Are there elements of my client's religious orientation that may be utilized as resources for effective practice? How open am I to working with them?

If a practitioner finds it particularly difficult to work with a client, whether due to conflicts centered on religious fundamentalism or something else, the mental health professional needs to seek the counsel of a supervisor. Consultation with the supervisor may elicit ways the practitioner can in fact work with the client after all. Or, if that is not possible, the supervisor may assist the practitioner with identifying another practitioner or additional resources (within the institution or agency or beyond) which will provide for the client's needs. Supervisory resources with clinical expertise are not always available in school settings. So, the practitioner must be creative in reaching out for assistance in such cases.

Appealing to the Code of Ethics

Cultivating both our understanding of a client's religious worldview and our awareness of ourselves as practitioners must always be correlated with an appeal to the profession's *Code of Ethics* (National Association of Social Workers, 2008). All counseling professionals have a code of ethics that they can use to help them with ethical and other sensitive matters related to values. Informed by the core values of service, social justice, the dignity and worth of the person, the importance of human relationships, integrity, and competence, for example, the *NASW Code of Ethics* for social workers provides ethical principles and standards meant to guide practice at all times, but particularly in instances where value disparity or ethical dilemmas threaten effective practice. As McGowan notes, "Practitioners' choice of values is always the primary determinant of what they actually do with clients" (1995, p. 28). That points to the fact that our own personal values, those of institutions like the schools we serve, and, perhaps, those tied to differing religious worldviews and commitments inevitably play a role in practice. This includes both how we assess the client context or need and how we intervene. As previously suggested, recognizing this and devising strategies for incorporating it in our work with integrity is a necessary first step for effective practice. When value conflicts arise, however, and lead to ethical dilemmas, the social work profession requires that practitioners appeal to the *Code of Ethics* as the definitive guide for practice decisions.

As McGowan (1995) emphasizes, however, complications arise when practitioners have to choose between two conflicting values, like the dignity and worth of the individual, on the one hand, and the obligation to promote social justice and the interests of the larger community, on the other. Similarly, the *Code of Ethics* is not overly prescriptive. Rather, it provides a more general guiding framework for applying ethical principles to ethical dilemmas. That means the social worker will need constantly to rely on practice wisdom and collaborative analysis with colleagues and supervisors, along with the norms proffered by the *Code of Ethics,* when dilemmas arise.

When faced with an ethical dilemma in respect to the social work Code of Ethics, the mental health professional might raise the question, "What does a commitment to the social work Code of Ethics allow in my practice with this client?" To explore this, the practitioner might want to ask the following questions:

- To what extent, if any, does my client's faith, its norms, and its practices violate the standards, values, and ethics of social work?
- Am I identifying a concern as being ethically suspect when it is more accurately described as stemming from my own negative opinion of the client and his or her religious orientation?
- Can I work with my client in a manner consistent with the standards and values of the social work profession and particularly the social work *Code of Ethics?*
- If I cannot work with this client, how may I make the most appropriate referral?

Becoming Culturally Capable

Augsburger (1986) puts forth a concept that social workers and mental health counselors may utilize in their practice with any client whom they perceive to be "culturally different" from themselves, including those with fundamentalist belief systems. Specifically, practitioners must become *culturally capable,* meaning they must develop frameworks and methods for practice that promote client welfare and prevent client oppression, whatever the reasons. To that end, Augsburger lists five characteristics—which can be both measured and taught—that distinguish culturally capable professionals (1986, pp. 20–21):

- A clear understanding of one's own values and basic assumptions. This means recognizing that others' values and assumptions, though perhaps different from one's own, are nonetheless legitimate and potentially useful.
- A capacity for welcoming, entering into, and prizing other worldviews without negating their legitimacy.
- Seeking sources of influence in the person and the context, the individual and the environment.
- An ability to move beyond counseling theory, orientation, or technique and be an effective human being. This means respecting not only one's professional training and insights, as important as those are, but also one's capacities for building and sustaining human connections and relationships with the client and thus fostering deep and high-quality rapport.
- Seeing others, along with oneself, as universal citizens, marked by unity amid diversity. This means the social worker must seek connections with the client that transcend differences of religion and its constituent qualities.

Developing these capacities, in conjunction with the strategies for enhancing self-awareness described previously and in other ways that the school-based practitioner finds most helpful, will enhance practice with those who embrace religiously fundamentalist worldviews. This is particularly important in cases where a practitioner, the client, or both discern significant differences between them in worldviews, commitments, or practices.

Case Example: The Roberts Family

As you read the following case scenario, consider how you would assess the situation and how you would respond on behalf of the school.

> Johnny Roberts, a fourth-grader, has been referred to you by his teacher, Ms. Jones. He is a conscientious student, pleasant with his peers and teachers, and slightly introverted.

His performance in the classroom has declined noticeably during the last month. He seems constantly tired and unable to focus and has fallen asleep during class on at least three occasions. Prior to contacting you, Ms. Jones had a phone conference with Johnny's mother in which she learned that his family's church congregation has recently moved from one location to another and that the family is spending several late nights each week involved with the activities of building this new church. Following the phone conference, Ms. Jones implemented various classroom accommodations designed to facilitate Johnny's improved focus in the classroom. Ms. Jones shares with you that her interventions have not yielded much success, and asks you, the school social worker, to intervene.

The following commentary focuses on what you, the social worker, might consider as you contact the family, how you may respond to particular issues that surface, and a few general strategies for intervention.

Precontact

- Given the information that Ms. Jones shared, what do you assume about Johnny's family's religion? How open are you to hearing more about this from Johnny and his parents?
- If your hunch that Johnny's family attends a church that espouses a Christian fundamentalist belief system proves accurate, how might you establish rapport, indicating your openness to, and desire for, learning more about the family's involvement in their congregation? How specifically might you explore this with the parents? What questions might you ask?
- What challenges do you anticipate in light of what you know about fundamentalism? If these surface, how specifically might you respond?

One need not be exhaustive. Reflections here are taking place almost exclusively in the realm of speculation. Yet, thinking about possible scenarios, far from biasing the social worker prematurely or inappropriately, actually may help to anticipate both one's own struggles and the family's before the fact. This mitigates potential breakdowns in rapport and in the forming of collaborative partnerships, which inform effective practice.

Contact

Establishing Rapport

- Telephone the parents and introduce yourself as the school social worker.
- Convey both your own and the school's affection for Johnny, and share your reason for calling as you calmly yet clearly express your concerns. Specifically, indicate that Ms. Jones and you have noticed the changes in Johnny's classroom affect and engagement, as mentioned above.
- While men in families that adhere to fundamentalist beliefs frequently "represent" the family in conversations with outsiders, women often have more authority and purview in matters involving children. So, either the father or mother may be the principal parental contact.
- Assuming you are speaking with the mother, explore with her some reasons that Johnny may be so tired at school. It may be best initially to refrain from sharing what you know about the family's involvement in the congregation. Leading with that knowledge may indicate that you view this negatively, and that may prompt a more defensive posture and response. If, after several attempts at encouraging disclosure of this information, the mother is not forthcoming, you may decide to ask her about it more directly.
- In whatever manner the information is put forth, convey a desire to know more about the congregation, its activities, and the family's involvement in both. It will be important to maintain a tone of genuine inquiry as opposed to a tone that could be interpreted as judgment. Conveying interest promotes deeper rapport and better partnerships and learning opportunities. You may also decide to try to build a connection with the parents by conveying some of your own knowledge or experiences with what you perceive to be similar religious communities. The goal here, again, is to foster rapport and gain more insight concerning the family's primary frame of reference, not to convey your own knowledge or expertise. Maintain your awareness of appropriate self-disclosure throughout this process as you look for ways to make personal connections.

Through this rapport-building phase, you learn that the family does indeed present with most of the aforementioned characteristics of fundamentalism and that the only identifiable precipitator of Johnny's changed classroom affect and behavior is the family's level of involvement in the congregation. Johnny's parents demonstrate genuine care and concern for him and indicate their desire for him to do well in school. They seem to frame his behaviors, however, in terms of disrespect for his elders (for his teacher, Ms. Jones) and laziness, which you associate with their religious understandings of authority, respect, and work ethic. From the outset you have looked for any indicators of abuse or neglect and have identified none, save the fact that Johnny is not getting enough rest. While this is unacceptable, you determine that it does not yet rise to a level such that not reporting it immediately to the appropriate authorities violates either state laws or the *Code of Ethics*. Confident that you and Johnny's parents have established enough rapport to work together, you proceed to the intervention phase in hopes that you can affect positive change.

Intervention

You identify two goals for an initial intervention. The first is to reframe the way the parents perceive Johnny's decline in the classroom. That is, you want to help them understand that Johnny is not disrespectful or lazy at all, but that he is simply not getting the rest that a boy his age requires. The second goal is to encourage the parents to recognize that Johnny may need to forgo some time spent at church in order to get to bed at an earlier hour, thus feeling more rested and ready to learn.

- You may say, "I really appreciate your sensitivity to the importance of being alert and attentive in the classroom. As you said, this promotes good learning for all students. Frankly, I have never known Johnny to be anything but respectful and energetic in class. That's a credit to your parenting! It's only been about a month now that I've noticed a big change. So, I wonder if it may just be that Johnny needs to get to bed a little earlier and get more sleep."
- The parents may be unwilling, or unable, to recognize the connection between church activities and Johnny's decline in school. If so, then you may need to help them make the connection a bit more directly. You may say something like this: "It occurs to me that Johnny being sleepy and less engaged in class started at about the same time you say that your congregation moved. I realize how exciting it can be to build a new church and also how eager churches are to get people heavily involved. And it seems like this is a good place for your family, that you're happy there. But, I'm wondering whether it may help Johnny to feel better at school, and thus perform better, if you, or at least he, were to get home a bit earlier on school nights."
- The parents may refuse this and become defensive. If so, then you have to judge whether pushing the point further at this time is appropriate. You may be confident that you have established enough rapport with the parents to facilitate ongoing work and thus decide to end this conversation for now and to call again in a week or two. Or, you may invite them to a face-to-face conference. If so, thank the parents for their time, indicate your affection for Johnny once again, and express your confidence that together you'll find a solution to your shared concern, namely, Johnny and his well-being. Also, let the parents know that you plan to be in touch with them again (by phone or in person) within the time period discussed. Make sure you follow up accordingly. Your failure to do so may convey your lack of genuineness, particularly with persons who tend to think more rigidly about responsibility, one's "word," keeping commitments, and the like.
- If the parents are open to the possibility that Johnny might be leaving church too late at night or, perhaps, that he might be spending too many nights a week there, then you will want to explore ways to help them think about alternative arrangements.
- Invite the father's participation if that has not happened, but do not insist on it.
- Underscore the value you recognize that the family places on their involvement in the congregation, so as not to diminish its importance. To do that will undermine your rapport and working relationship.
- Also remind them of the value they have already affirmed in Johnny's being alert, attentive, and participating in the classroom. You may say something like this: "I'm wondering if you could explore ways to get Johnny home and to bed earlier. Maybe he could leave early with one of you [the parents]. Or, maybe you could think about him being out fewer nights each week. Or, maybe both are good things to consider." You may also add, "I really think that if Johnny gets more sleep, he'll feel and do better not only at school, but at church too, and that's what we all want."

Follow Up

Assuming the initial conversation with Johnny's parents goes well, and that there is a basis for continued work, a follow-up conference should build on the first conversation's content and foster continued collaborative efforts to help Johnny. If challenges like those mentioned previously arise, you, the social worker, should utilize the strategies discussed as you look for ways to meet them. Remembering that a tenuous relationship is better than none at all, the school social worker must seek with zest and genuine openness to meet, understand, and work with students and families from fundamentalist backgrounds to the greatest extent possible.

Applying Interventions within a Response to Intervention Framework

Understanding RTI

RTI is a multi-tiered system of support that provides evidenced-based intervention services to students at varying levels of school performance. Schools that implement RTI organize intervention resources in a manner that facilitates individualized assistance to students as they demonstrate increasing educational needs. The provision of evidenced-based interventions and monitoring the progress of those interventions are crucial components of the model (Fuchs & Fuchs, 2006).

RTI is typically conceptualized as a three-tier structure of increasing support. Interventions at Tier 1 are often devised to enrich the educational performance of the entire school population. Such interventions may include instructional modifications implemented by the classroom teacher at the first indication a student might be struggling. As such, Tier 1 interventions strive to address the following question: "Are routine interventions accessible to all students sufficient to help this student achieve educational success?" Tier 2 interventions are more individualized and intensive in nature, and are designed to address a student's unique educational challenges. These interventions are intended to support students who did not adequately respond to Tier 1 interventions. In some cases, Tier 2 interventions are devised in a Student Success Team (SST) meeting and may be informed by input from the student (if appropriate), student's family, teachers, and other school professionals. Tier 2 interventions are intended to address the following question: "Can an individualized intervention plan implemented in a general education setting improve the student's educational performance to a level that is broadly commensurate with his or her peers?" Finally, Tier 3 supports typically comprise the most intensive educational interventions available to the school and target problems that were not resolved by assistance provided at the previous two tiers. Tier 3 supports strive to address the following question: "What ongoing interventions does the student require to facilitate educational success, and in what educational settings should these interventions be provided?" (Wright, 2007, pp. 3–5).

How Might Interventions Designed for Conservatively Religious Families Be Provided within an RTI Framework?

There is substantial variability in the way school districts throughout the country interpret and implement RTI frameworks. Given the diversity of ways RTI may be operationalized, it can certainly be implemented in a manner that works effectively with students hailing from religiously conservative and fundamentalist backgrounds. As was previously stated, strength-based approaches may be particularly effective in working with families who are religiously conservative. When this notion is combined with the awareness that family and church influences are often particularly strong with those who embrace religiously conservative or fundamentalist beliefs, it becomes evident that it will be important to implement RTI in a manner that allows for both strength-based and school-/home-/community-based interventions.

Tools and Practice Examples

Case Example: Revisiting the Roberts Family

It has now been two weeks since the school social worker has communicated with Johnny's mother. It seems as though there has been little change in

Johnny's school behaviors and performance. He continues to demonstrate difficulty attending to instruction, he periodically falls asleep in class, and now he is failing to consistently turn in homework—all of which are affecting his progress report grades. Because of his lack of response to the previously described Tier 1 interventions, the teacher has decided to bring Johnny's difficulties to the attention of the school's SST process. Before moving to Tier 2, however, it may be useful to review Johnny's Tier 1 interventions, which included:

- Parent-teacher phone conference soon after Johnny's difficulties initially became evident
- Implementation of various classroom accommodations designed to facilitate improvement in Johnny's attention and classroom participation
- Social worker-parent phone conference addressing potential causes and remedies for Johnny's difficulties
- Follow-up call from school social worker

Intervention

Our Tier 2 system of supports begins with the school counselor calling Mrs. Roberts and inviting her to the SST meeting, which he describes as an opportunity to "collaboratively come up with interventions to better support Johnny." Mrs. Roberts agrees to attend the meeting along with the Johnny's teacher, the school counselor, and the school psychologist. At the meeting, Mrs. Roberts reports that Johnny's doctor has ruled out attention deficit hyperactivity disorder (ADHD) and other health concerns. She goes on to state that she still fears Johnny is "just being rebellious," but also sees how his "tiredness" might be contributing to his difficulties. Furthermore, his teacher reports that according to curriculum-based measurements, Johnny is performing at grade level in all academic areas. Mrs. Roberts adds that although the family had made attempts to get Johnny home earlier in the evening, the demands at church have increased, and as a result he continues to get insufficient sleep. With medical concerns and academic skill deficits ruled out, the team is able to hypothesize that Johnny's schedule continues to be a significant source of his difficulties. The team agrees upon the measurable intervention goals of improving Johnny's rate of homework completion as well as his attention to task during class. It is believed that his weekly progress grades will improve once these areas are addressed. In order to meet those goals, the team puts the following strength-based and collaborative interventions in place:

- Mr. and Mrs. Roberts will consult with the pastor for advice regarding Johnny's recent educational difficulties. (This intervention serves to validate the importance of the family's faith and is congruent with the family's values, as it acknowledges the authority of the church pastor.)
- The school psychologist, who is familiar with conservative Christianity, will be available to communicate with the pastor if questions or clarifications are needed. (This intervention demonstrates a willingness to work collaboratively and has the potential to forge partnerships with resources outside of the school that are of import to the family.)
- A release of confidentiality is signed to enable the psychologist and pastor to communicate.
- Johnny will be placed on home-school contingency contract with built-in reinforcement designed to facilitate improvement in attention to task and homework completion. (This again communicates respect, as it validates the family's importance by acknowledging them as a valuable resource and including them in the intervention.)

The above interventions serve the dual purpose of validating the family and their unique resources, while placing the onus upon the family to act as agents of change. The team agrees to reconvene in six weeks to assess Johnny's progress, and decides to measure his progress by reviewing the data collected on the contingency contract, as well attending to general observations by the teacher.

Soon after the meeting, the school psychologist receives a call from the church pastor, who also expresses concern about Johnny's recent difficulties. He consulted with the school psychologist regarding whether Johnny's behavior was a form of rebellion and concluded that it was not. He then went on to maintain that he was not aware Johnny's family was getting home late, and as such he had already worked with the family to modify their scheduled time at church. The pastor also told the psychologist that he is meeting weekly with Johnny to review the contract.

Follow Up

The team reconvenes after the six weeks of intervention and finds that Johnny's attention and homework completion as measured by the contract have significantly improved. His weekly progress grades have improved as well. While the team may choose to extend the interventions beyond six weeks, due to their efficacy, Johnny will not require a higher level of intervention. However, had the interventions not proved successful, new interventions would be devised and implemented. Such interventions might be aimed at addressing authority—important in fundamentalist belief systems—in a more focused way. This might include further consultation with the pastor or inviting Johnny's father and/or pastor to future meetings; it also might involve a mental health referral or, if indicated, a call to Child Protective Services.

Because RTI is an adaptable model of service delivery, it can be utilized in ways that work effectively with families from religiously conservative and fundamentalist backgrounds. Progress monitoring is a structural feature of RTI that has the potential to serve as a home-school method of communication amenable to developing trusting relationships with families who, for religious or other reasons, may be wary of public school culture. Additionally, while the structure of RTI can accommodate variety of interventions, it is important that those interventions be informed by culturally sensitive and evidenced-based practices. And as such, when implemented with best practices and clinical wisdom, RTI can be a powerful service delivery model for families adhering to conservatively religious and fundamentalist worldviews.

Key Points to Remember

- Those adhering to a religiously fundamentalist belief system may view, comprehend, and live in the world utilizing as their primary frame of reference and meaning the ideals, teachings, and practices of their religious tradition. School-based mental health practitioners benefit the family with fundamentalist beliefs by enhancing their awareness and understanding of the family's religious orientation and considering ways that the strengths associated with it may be utilized in effective practice.
- Social workers and other mental health professionals often do not share the fundamentalist's worldview and thus may be suspicious if not rejecting of both the client's right to his or her religious understandings and commitments and the resources for effecting the appropriate changes that the social worker may offer in practice interventions. This means that the social worker and other professionals must commit to ongoing self-reflection and make use of frameworks like those put forth here to assess candidly their own biases and preconceptions and how those are figuring into practice. As is true in school-based practice with any population, ethical dilemmas may arise in practice with families embracing a fundamentalist worldview. When this happens, practitioners must appeal to their *Code of Ethics* as the principal guiding framework for decision making, consult with peers and especially with a supervisor, and seek to identify ways of working through the ethical dilemma so that both client needs and values and the social workers ethics are maintained.
- As an adaptable model of service delivery, RTI can be utilized in ways that work well with families from fundamentalist backgrounds. The model is compatible with strength-based and home-school-community interventions that have been effective in working with this population. As such, when implemented with best practices and clinical wisdom, RTI can provide an effective framework for providing intervention with families who embrace fundamentalist and conservatively religious worldviews.

References

Almond, G. A., Appleby, R. S, & Sivan, E. (2003). *Strong religion: The rise of fundamentalism around the world.* Chicago, IL: University of Chicago Press.

Aten, J. D., Mangis, M. W., & Campbell, C. (2010). Psychotherapy with rural religious fundamentalist clients. *Journal of Clinical Psychology: In Session, 66*(5), 512–523.

Augsburger, D.W. (1986). *Pastoral counseling across cultures.* Philadelphia, PA: Westminster.

Bryan, J., & Henry, L. (2008). Strength-based partnerships: A school-family-community partnership approach to empowering students. *Professional School Counseling, 12*(2), 149–156.

Denton, R. T. (1990). The religiously fundamentalist family: Training for assessment and treatment. *Journal of Social Work Education, 1,* 6–16.

Eriksen, K., Marston, G., & Korte, T. (2002). Working with god: Managing conservative Christian beliefs that may interfere with counseling. *Counseling and Values*, *47*, 48–68.

Fuchs, D., & Fuchs, L. (2006). Introduction to Response to Intervention: What, why, and how valid is it? *Reading Research Quarterly*, *41*(1), 93–99.

Hodge, D. R. (2002). Does social work oppress evangelical Christians? A "new class" analysis of society and social work. *Social Work*, *47*(4), 401–414.

Hodge, D. R., & Nadir, A. (2008). Moving toward culturally competent practice with Muslims: Modifying cognitive therapy with Islamic tenets. *Social Work*, *53*(1), 31–41.

Jones, J. (2011, July 8). *In U.S., 3 in 10 Say They Take the Bible Literally*. Retrieved July 30, 2011, from GALLUP Web site: http://www.gallup.com/poll/148427/Say-Bible-Literally.aspx

Kramer, M. (2003). Coming to terms: Fundamentalists or Islamists? *Middle East Quarterly*, spring, 65–78.

Marsden, G. M. (2006). *Fundamentalism and American culture*. New York, NY: Oxford University Press.

McGowan, B. G. (1995). Values and ethics. In C. H. Meyer & M. A. Mattaini (Eds.), *The foundations of social work practice: A graduate text* (pp. 28–41). Washington, DC: NASW Press.

Miller, D. R. (1995). The school counselor and Christian fundamentalist families. *School Counselor*, *42*(4), 317–322.

Moore-Thomas, C., & Day-Vines, N. L. (2008). Culturally competent counseling for religious and spiritual African American adolescents. *Professional School Counseling*, *11*(3), 159–165.

Munson, H. (2008). "Fundamentalisms" compared. *Religion Compass*, *2/4*, 689–707.

National Association of Social Workers. (2008). *Code of Ethics*. National Association of Social Workers. Retrieved from http://www.socialworkers.org/pubs/code/code.asp

Ness, R. C., & Wintrob, R. M. (1980). The emotional impact of fundamentalist religious practice: An empirical study of intergroup variation. *American Journal of Orthopsychiatry*, *50*, 302–315.

Northcut, T. B. (2004). Pedagogy in diversity: Teaching religion and spirituality in the clinical social work classroom. *Smith College Studies in Social Work*, *74*(2), 349–358.

Numrich, P. D. (2007). Fundamentalisms and American pluralism. *Journal of Ecumenical Studies*, *42*(1), 9–14.

Park, N., & Peterson, C. (2008). Positive psychology and character strengths: Application to strengths-based school counseling. *Professional School Counseling*, *12*(2), 85–92.

Stalley, R. F. (1978). Non-judgmental attitudes. In N. Timms & D. Watson (Eds.), *Philosophy in social work*. London, England: Routledge & Kegan.

Sue, D. W., & Sue, D. (1990). *Counseling the culturally different: Theory & practice*. New York, NY: Wiley.

Walton, E., Limb, G. E, & Hodge, D. R. (2011). Developing cultural competence with Latter-Day Saint clients: A strengths-based perspective. *Families in Society: The Journal of Contemporary Social Services*, *92*(1), 50–54.

Wiggins, M. I. (2008). Therapist self-awareness of spirituality. In J. D. Aten & M. M. Leach (Eds.), *Spirituality and the therapeutic process* (pp. 53–74). Washington, DC: American Psychological Association.

Williamson, W. P., Hood, R. W., Ahmad, A., Sadiq, M., & Hill, P. C. (2010). The intratextual fundamentalism scale: Cross-cultural application, validity evidence, and relationship with religious orientation and the Big 5 factor markers. *Mental Health, Religion & Culture*, *13*(7/8), 721–747.

Wright, J. (2007). *RTI toolkit: A practical guide for schools*. Port Chester, NY: Dude Publishing.

York, G. Y. (1987). *Religious-based denial as a coping mechanism for the rural client*. Paper presented at the Annual Conference of the National Association for Rural Mental Health, Hendersonville, NC.

CHAPTER 53

Intervening With Students and Families Who Frequently Relocate or Are Homeless

Sanna J. Thompson ▪ Tiffany N. Ryan ▪ Jihye Kim

Getting Started

Family housing instability or frequent relocation is difficult for children and adolescents and causes stress due to the loss of the central organizing structure of their lives (Rafferty, Shinn, & Weitzman, 2004). Children in these families may experience a loss of identity, disconnection from familiar surroundings, and intense sadness and loss (Aviles de Bradley, 2011). Children who frequently move are more likely to be poor, come from single-parent households, and have caregivers who are unemployed or failed to graduate from high school (Wong, Piliavin, & Wright, 1998). For families who become homeless, the loss of home is typically sudden, unexpected, and traumatic. Disruption of normal family functioning and fears concerning safety and security are heightened among the children involved (Hyman, Aubry, & Klodawsky, 2011). Children, feeling that parents cannot be depended on for stability and safety, may respond with anger and disruptive behavior. In situations where the family must live in a shelter situation, typical family functioning changes in response to the institutional setting's rules and hierarchy of authority.

Family housing instability often affects the continuity of the children's schooling. Research has shown that children who experience frequent relocation, including homelessness, also experience excessive school mobility, are at increased risk of failing a grade (Heinlein & Shinn, 2000; Walsh & Donaldson, 2010), and have poor academic performance. Students who change schools frequently are twice as likely to have nutrition, health, and hygiene problems; are four times as likely to drop out; and are 77% more likely to have multiple behavioral problems (Simpson & Fowler, 1994). Teachers have limited time and resources to address most of these problems; thus, involvement of the student, the parent(s), and the school social worker is required.

One major problem confronting highly transient students is their difficulty enrolling in school without proper documentation, such as previous school records, birth certificates, and immunization records. Delaying enrollment and missing days or weeks of school result in academic failure and increase the risk that the student will simply drop out of school. For homeless and immigrant students, the McKinney-Vento Homeless Education Assistance Improvements Act of 2001 requires that school disctricts provide a specialized liaison to help these students and families overcome barriers to enrollment. To improve the likelihood of academic success for all highly mobile students, barriers to education must be removed and helpful interventions provided that ensure accessibility to vital educational services.

What We Know

Interventions that have shown the greatest effectiveness in ameliorating youth problems encourage the inclusion of parents or caregivers. School social workers, counselors, and other school-based practitioners are indispensable in coordinating educational services to students, while providing effective interaction with parents as well. One family-oriented intervention model that has considerable empirical support and demonstrated success with high-risk and drug-using youth is multidimensional family therapy (MDFT; Liddle et al., 2001; Liddle & Hogue, 2000). MDFT is based on the integration of existing therapeutic theories in areas such as case management, school interventions, drug counseling methods, use of multimedia, and HIV/AIDS prevention (Liddle, 2002). Even though the research on this model has mostly demonstrated efficacy with youth who have substance abuse and other high-risk behavior problems, it appears to be an effective approach for ameliorating crisis situations.

MDFT has an integrative therapeutic philosophy and clinical approach that focuses on developing relationships with important individuals in the student's life (Hogue, Dauber, Stambaugh, Cecero, & Liddle, 2006;Liddle, 2009) and is something that schools can make use of with students and families. MDFT encompasses a collaborative, individualized approach that requires a high degree of engagement by families. It relies on an empirical knowledge base of risk and protective factors associated with high-risk youth behaviors to assess and intervene in students' problems. Strategies for engagement are employed to capture the interest of the family and assess risk and protective factors within the specific ecological context of the family (Liddle, Dakof, Henderson, & Rowe, 2010). Problems or crises provide critical assessment information that focuses intervention efforts.

In consultation with parents, teachers, shelter staff (if the family is homeless), and others, the school social worker or other school-based practitioners coordinate and facilitates interactions with the individuals most involved with the student. Sessions are held wherever the appropriate parties can be convened (home, school, shelter, juvenile court, etc.) and whenever the need arises. Change is multidimensional and multifaceted as it emerges from the interactions among systems, people, domains of functioning, and interpersonal processes. Working with multiple systems in a coordinated way, inside and outside the family, is fundamental to MDFT.

What We Can Do

Phase 1: Building the Foundation

Intervention begins with the process of building collaborative relationships with the student and the family. School social workers and counselors, recognizing the highly mobile family situation as a crisis, must establish an alliance and facilitate engagement for intervention. Working with students and their parent(s), they work to encourage treatment receptivity and motivation for change. Resistance is normal; resistant behaviors can provide direction for intervention implementation. School social workers and other school professionals utilizing the MDFT framework create a context in which the student and parents can deal with the hopelessness, helplessness, and despair often experienced in stressful living conditions.

Once the student has been identified, the school-based practitioner must establish an alliance with the student and parent(s). The social worker or mental health counselor connects with the parent(s) and child and assists them to understand the experiences of the other. A critical component for success is helping the student and parent(s) feel that MDFT can address their concerns, assist them to convey their personal feelings about their family life, and work to overcome problem areas. Alliance building begins with demonstrating genuine interest and concern for the family's well-being.

Sample Sentences Intended to Stimulate Discussion with the Student

- "I can and will be on your side at least some of the time." Students need to be aware of the school-based practitioner's genuine interest, respect, and support for them individually. MDFT necessitates developing strong alliances with students and the subsystems that affect them.
- "When your parents and teachers understand you more fully, they can appreciate what you are going through." Recognizing the difficulties experienced by the student due to frequent housing disruption, the social worker or counselor addresses the feelings, responses, and needs of the student.
- "Some aspects of who you are will always remain private (we can talk about these things between us if you like), but it is important for your parents and teachers to know about some of the concerns you are facing. I can help with this." School-based practitioners can provide a feeling of security by discussing issues of confidentiality. In addition, students are provided support when they agree to discuss sensitive material for the purpose of enhancing others' understanding of their life and needs.

Sample Sentences Intended to Stimulate Discussion with Parent(s)

- "I've seen how difficult this is for you. My heart goes out to you, and I will do everything I can to support you." The school-based practitioner presents as an ally who will support the caregivers' attempts to provide appropriate parenting to their child and cope with their own feelings of hopelessness concerning their living situation.
- "If I hear right, what you are saying is that you feel absolutely alone in dealing with your problems. I see what a hard time you're having trying to keep your family together after losing your home." Acknowledgment of the difficult situations that impede successful parenting and family management validates the parents' challenging role. It acknowledges that the parents have individual problems, disappointments, desires, hopes, and dreams that are separate from their role as parents.

Phase 2: Identifying Themes within Multidimensional Subsystems

An MDFT social worker's efforts focus on understanding the events, personal and family characteristics, and responses that are affected by the family's residential instability or frequent moves. Themes or problem areas are identified and assessed to determine the need for change. School-based practitioners attempt to understand the individual's functioning, as well as the mechanisms of interconnection among the multiple systems that affect the student's life.

Student Subsystem

Housing instability increases the likelihood that students may exhibit low academic achievement, disruptive classroom behaviors, or mental or physical health difficulties. Exploration of students' history and development of strategies to promote their adjustment in school are crucial.

School Attendance

Students may be frequently absent from school because of the family's relocations, students running away from home or shelter, lack of transportation to school, or low motivation or fears concerning attending a new school.

Academic Achievement

Students may exhibit poor academic performance, deficient cognitive skills, and learning disabilities. They may have had to repeat a grade. These factors often result from repeated absences or low expectations of academic success.

Classroom Behaviors

Highly mobile students may not easily conform to new classroom environments due to their chaotic home lives. They may present with a short attention span, hyperactivity, or disruptive behavior.

Basic Needs

Students may suffer from a lack of proper nutrition, appropriate clothing and shoes, and school supplies. Difficulties in transportation and lack of resources often constrain their participation in school-related activities.

Physical Health

Highly mobile students frequently are exposed to hunger and poor nutrition. They generally have more colds, diarrhea, stomach problems, skin diseases, respiratory infections, and hearing and visual impairments than students with permanent homes. They often fail to receive appropriate medical treatment due to the family's frequent moves or lack of insurance; thus, illnesses may become chronic or severe. These students also have a greater likelihood of drug or alcohol abuse, high-risk sexual behaviors, teen pregnancy, and sexually transmitted diseases.

Mental Health

Students living in highly transient situations often suffer from depression, anxiety, aggression, and suicidal ideation. They may fail to develop a sense of trust, continuity, and belongingness. Feelings of isolation, loss, and low self-esteem are increased by a sense that they are different from their peers because they do not have a stable home or fashionable clothing.

Parent Subsystem

Many parents experiencing unstable housing suffer from financial difficulties, have substance use or mental health problems, have low educational status, and have difficulties in parenting and communicating with their children. Although parents may have a positive attitude toward the education of their children, they may have limited participation in their child's academic performance due to lack of time or transportation, taking care of other children, being unfamiliar with school systems, or being reluctant to discuss their children's issues out of shame or hopelessness.

Student/Family Interaction Subsystem

Housing instability often leads to stressful situations that affect family relationships and negatively influence students' development. Students may have experienced severe conflict or violence in their family, neglect, abandonment, or physical or sexual abuse. Parents may lack the skills to provide consistent and age-appropriate limit setting. Due to their residential instability, they may be inattentive to their child's academic development and fail to monitor school attendance and performance. The communication between students and their parents should be examined. Their chaotic living conditions are likely to cause defensiveness and blame, further eroding the relationship.

Extrafamilial Subsystems

Peers

Constructing and continuing relationships with peers can be impeded by lack of stable housing, a telephone, or transportation. Students may experience stigmatization by classmates who tease them about their residential status, poor physical appearance, and lack of personal possessions. Due to feeling shame, fear, or alienation, they may respond in aggressive or hostile ways. These students also are vulnerable to association with gangs and other deviant peers who engage in antisocial behaviors.

Teachers and School Personnel

Students may not tell their teachers about their residential status due to being ashamed or afraid of differential treatment. They may feel stigmatized by school staff when enrolled with "homeless" status.

Shelters and Other Social Agencies

Students are often affiliated with shelters, the juvenile justice system, child protective services, and other social service agencies. These systems are often resources that can provide supportive connections for the student and family. Many highly mobile families living in a series of temporary homes, shelters, or hotels often experience crowded conditions and lack privacy. Finding appropriate space for the student to do homework, where noise problems are reduced, is often difficult.

Phase 3: Working With Themes

This stage of the intervention focuses on facilitating processes and fostering skills that allow the student and parent(s) to identify and work on particular problem areas that require change. MDFT involves understanding the individual's functioning, as well as the mechanisms of interconnection among the systems that affect the student's life. Social workers and other staff primarily explore risk and protective factors that affect the student's school performance directly or indirectly. They work with the many systems involved in the student's academic motivation and performance.

Identify Main Themes and Set Goals

The first step involves determining the areas of the student's life that will be most accessible for intervention. These will not be the only available areas for intervention, but are identified as those most likely to create successful change. Core themes are consistently addressed, while working minimally with other areas.

Make Plans for the Sessions

Social workers and counselors work with students inside and outside of the school setting. Sessions are provided as needed (daily or weekly), and the context of each session changes to provide maximum flexibility and opportunity to implement clinical methods. Various sessions are designed for most effective interactions, such as meeting with the family in their current residence (i.e., in the shelter and including shelter staff in the session), with the student during after-school program sessions with student peers, with the student and family while waiting to see the school principal, or with the student at a restaurant.

Work With Multiple Systems and Multiple Approaches

Utilizing multidimensional thinking, school social workers and counselors develop a variety of alliances with the student, the family (parents, siblings, other relatives), and extrafamilial systems (school, juvenile justice, shelter staff, if homeless). Facilitating the progression of interactions with these various systems must be accomplished simultaneously. Everything focuses on the students' needs, how their successful academic achievement can be facilitated, and how they can be directed to prosocial and developmentally appropriate pursuits. The school-based practitioners involved must be skilled in applying different types of interactions needed with students, parents, other family members, school staff, and juvenile justice officials. For example, addressing poor academic performance involves changing many things that currently support the behavior, such as the student's attitudes and beliefs, affiliation with and access to deviant peers, failure to bond with prosocial institutions (school), the family environment (including residential instability), and parenting practices.

Develop Successive Approximations

A step-by-step approach is utilized to encourage needed change. Small steps are identified that ultimately lead to successful outcomes. MDFT school social workers engage with the student to determine the set of circumstances, daily activities, and interpersonal and intrapersonal processes that are impeding positive change. They then identify specific steps to overcome the difficulty or improve the targeted problem area.

Provide Linking

School social workers and others may utilize *linking,* which is the process of shaping change across many areas and in a variety of environments, including school, family, and the individual. Therapeutic continuity is achieved through connecting each session to the others through a series of building blocks that generalize gains made in one problem area to another area of difficulty. Linking also involves highlighting the progress made by one family member to motivate and facilitate change in other family members.

Phase 4: Sealing the Changes

The MDFT school-based practitioner establishes meaning for the changes that have occurred by putting into words some of the successes. Specific successes and accomplishments that occurred while engaged in the intervention are discussed and used as evidence of and prompts for how new crises or problems can be managed in the future. For example, deepening the student's affiliation with school, other important social institutions, and the family can be viewed as a major accomplishment.

Applying Interventions within a Response to Intervention Framework

The Response to Intervention (RTI) framework refers to a tiered system of instruction in which each tier provides increasingly intense services to students to maximize their achievement and reduce behavioral problems (National Center on Response to Intervention, 2010). This framework addresses four essential elements for academic learning, including high-quality instruction through collaborative multilevel prevention systems, screening assessments, progress monitoring, and using evidence in making decisions. This framework is responsive to the diversity of students' culture, residential instability, and socioeconomic status. Through screening and progress monitoring, assessments guide appropriate placement of students into three basic levels or tiers.

In Tier 1, students' progress is monitored using benchmark scores for measurable goals. Tier 2 applies to students who demonstrate inadequate responsiveness, despite receiving high-quality core instruction. Supplemental interventions occur within or outside of the general education classroom. Progress is monitored to determine intervention success in addressing the student's identified difficulties. Adjustments to the intervention and intensity of services are implemented as needed upon review of outcomes data. Tier 3 is for students who require more intense, explicit, and individualized instruction. Interventions may be similar to those in Tier 2 except they are intensified in frequency and duration.

While all the components of the RTI framework function together, implementing Multidimensional Family Therapy (MDFT) is particularly appropriate when viewing this framework from the perspective of collaborative efforts aimed at addressing specific behavioral problems, such as substance abuse and delinquent behaviors. The initial step (Tier 1) in the process of implementing MDFT within a school-based system would begin with the identification of children/youth at risk for problem/challenging behaviors, especially related to substance abuse. Appropriate screening to identify students with poor academic functioning and behavioral difficulties would also include assessment of substance use issues. This screening should also take into account cultural and socioeconomic disparities associated with heightened difficulties these students might face. For students who screen positive for behavioral and substance use difficulties, MDFT is one evidence-based practice that could be considered. MDFT is clearly a Tier 2 intervention strategy, but may also be utilized in a Tier 3 strategy when even more intensive intervention is needed to produce successful outcomes.

Application of MDFT within an RTI Framework

Drawing upon the case example of Kate and her family, it is clear that MDFT can be incorporated in a school setting. However, one of the major criticisms of implementing the full MDFT intervention is its complexity and high level of intensity (therefore, high cost). The following suggestions are presented in terms of how the intervention may be practically implemented with the limited resources often found in school settings. Phases of the MDFT intervention reflect the various tiers of the RTI framework and suggest how Kate might move from Tier 1 prevention to a MDFT, Tier 2, targeted intervention.

Tier 1

Tier 1 (prevention) activities occur prior to MDFT implementation. In Kate's case, her teachers were the first to notice her withdrawal, diminishing interest, and decreasing grades. They contacted the school social worker for assessment of Kate's performance and behavioral challenges. Kate's mother, Megan, was informed of these concerns with Kate's academic progress. In discussing the problem with Kate, she described having problems with depression, feeling isolated, and not having a quiet space in which to do homework. Recognizing the importance of having active communication between Kate, her teachers, and her mother, the school social worker developed collaborative activities aimed at identifying resources to encourage Kate and formulated goals to help her succeed. These types of activities occurred before and during Phase 1 of the MDFT intervention process.

Tier 2

As Tier 2 activities are much more targeted and intensive, the activities associated with this level would take place only when Tier 1 prevention efforts were not effective. In Kate's case, these prevention efforts were not successful in improving her grades and engagement in school. In fact, she has begun hanging out with other kids that are known drug users, and her grades have plummeted. Instead of withdrawing in class, she is now acting out, and skipping class has become more problematic.

Tier 2 (intervention): Due to the intensity and increase in Kate's problems, the school social worker moves into Phase 2 of MDFT. She schedules meetings with Kate, her mother, primary teachers, and the school resource officer. This first meeting is held at the apartment where they are currently living because Megan does not have transportation to come to the school. They discuss areas where Kate is struggling and decide to focus on her negative peer affiliations, as this appears to have the most impact on her other negative behaviors and has a high potential for change. They also identify a space especially for Kate to do homework. The social worker agrees to have biweekly contact with Megan to keep her updated on Kate's progress; the social worker also agrees to have weekly sessions with Kate. She works through the four phases of MDFT, while drawing upon others in the school setting that can also assist Kate. If these activities are successful, decreasing the intensity of the intervention will occur; however, if Kate's behaviors do not improve, more intensive MDFT activities (Tier 3) may be required.

Tools and Case Examples

Kate is a 12-year-old, fifth-grade girl who is currently living in a homeless shelter with her mother and two younger brothers. She was admitted to a new school last week and was referred to the MDFT school social worker. This school is the third school she has been admitted to this year. The family has lived in multiple shelters since her mother divorced 2 years ago and her father abandoned them. Her mother, Megan, is currently unemployed.

Phase 1: Building the Foundation

- Upon Kate's admission to the school, the social worker meets with her and listens to her story, demonstrating genuine interest in her welfare and building trust.
- The social worker meets alone with Megan, Kate's mother, and explores the family's housing situation and its impact on Kate.

Phase 2: Identifying Themes

- The social worker meets with Kate and Megan together to assess various themes. Themes include:
    - academic failure due to extensive absences
    - feelings of loss and loneliness due to moving away from friends
    - lack of a supportive father
    - limited financial support to gain stable housing
    - Megan's poor parenting due to depression
- Kate and Megan agree that "Kate's frequent absences from school and falling behind her peers" is the first area to address with the MDFT social worker.

Phase 3: Working With Themes

- The social worker meets with Kate to set goals, including:
    - catch up on missed curriculum
    - attend school daily
    - complete all homework daily
- The social worker and Kate identify the subsystems needed to support her goals:
    - Parent subsystem
        - The social worker introduces Megan to Kate's teacher and other school staff. She talks to Megan about Kate's need to find space to complete homework and her engagement with the school.
    - Extrafamilial subsystems
        - School: The social worker holds meetings with Kate's teacher and principal to increase awareness of her situation and needs. They develop a special educational plan for Kate; A tutor is recruited to assist Kate after school.
        - Shelter: The social worker works with shelter staff to find a quiet place where Kate can study in the evening.
        - Transportation is made available for Kate's commute to school each day.
- The social worker continues to work extensively with multiple systems for approximately 3 months; discussions increasingly expand to other themes.

Phase 4: Sealing the Changes

The MDFT social worker monitors Kate's academic performance and continues to remain in contact with her and Megan, but in a more limited way. As the social worker supports Kate and Megan in their new skills, they will be provided crisis intervention when needed.

Resources

Aviles de Bradley, A. M. (2011). Unaccompanied homeless youth: Intersections of homelessness, school experiences and educational policy. *Child & Youth Services, 32*(2), 155–170.

Center for Treatment Research in Adolescent Drug Abuse. (2011). Available: http://www.miami.edu/ctrada.

National Association for the Education of Homeless Children and Youth. (2011). Available: http://www.naehcy.org.

Texas Homeless Education Office. (2011). Available: http://www.utdanacenter.org/theo/resources.html

Key Points to Remember

- Students' unstable or highly mobile living conditions are multidimensional phenomena.
- Treatment focuses on building multiple collaborative relationships with the student, family, and other subsystems.
- Equipped with a general understanding of the situation, the MDFT school social worker explores themes needed for change to occur.
- Themes most accessible and likely to be successful are addressed initially; additional themes are addressed as appropriate.
- School social workers and other mental health counselors work extensively with multiple systems and approaches; sessions are held where and when needed.
- Changes that occur during the intervention are praised and connected to future expectations.

References

Heinlein, L. M., & Shinn, M. (2000). School mobility and student achievement in an urban setting. *Psychology in the Schools, 37*(4), 349–357.

Hogue, A., Dauber, S., Stambaugh, L. F., Cecero, J. J., & Liddle, J. A. (2006). Early therapeutic alliance and treatment outcome in individual and family therapy for adolescent behavior problems. *Journal of Consulting and Clincial Psychology*, *74*(1), 121–129.

Hyman, S., Aubry, T., & Klodawsky, F. (2011). Resilient educational outcomes: Participation in school by youth with histories of homelessness. *Youth & Society*, *43*(1), 253–273.

Liddle, H. A., & Hogue, A. (2000). A family-based, developmental-ecological preventive intervention for high-risk adolescents. *Journal of Marital & Family Therapy*, *26*(3), 265–279.

Liddle, H. A., Dakof, G. A., Parker, K., Diamond, G. S., Barrett, K., & Tejeda, M. (2001). Multidimensional family therapy for adolescent drug abuse: Results of a randomized clinical trial. *American Journal of Drug & Alcohol Abuse*, *27*(4), 651–688.

Liddle, H. A. (2002). *Multidimensional family therapy for adolescent cannabis users* [DHHS pub. No. 02–3660]. Rockville, MD: Center for Substance Abuse Treatment, Substance Abuse and Mental Health Services Administration.

Liddle, H. A. (2009). Treating adolescent substance abuse using multidimensional family therapy. In J. Weisz & A. Kazdin (Eds.), *Evidence-based psychotherapies for children and adolescents* (Vol. 2, pp. 416–434). New York, NY: Guilford Press.

Liddle, H. A., Dakof, G. A., Henderson, C.E. & Rowe, C. (2010). Implementation outcomes of multidimensional family therapy-detention to community: A reintegration program for drug-using juvenile detainees. *International Journal of Offender Therapy and Comparative Criminology*, *55*(4), 587–604.

National Center on Response to Intervention. (2010). Available: http://www.rti4success.org/pdf/rtiessentialcomponents_042710.pdf

Rafferty, Y., Shinn, M., & Weitzman, B. C. (2004). Academic achievement among formerly homeless adolescents and their continuously housed peers. *Journal of School Psychology*, *42*, 179–199.

Simpson, G. A., & Fowler, M. G. (1994). Geographic mobility and children's emotional/behavioral adjustment and school functioning. *Pediatrics*, *93*(2), 303–309.

Walsh, S., & Donaldson, R. (2010). Invited commentary: National safe place: Meeting the immediate needs of runaway and homeless youth. *Journal of Youth and Adolescence*, *39*(5), 437–445.

Wong, Y.-L. I., Piliavin, I., & Wright, B. R. (1998). Residential transitions among homeless families and homeless single individuals: A comparison study. *Journal of Social Service Research*, *24*(1/2), 1–27.

CHAPTER 54

Children and Youth Impacted by Military Service

A School-Based Resilience Building and Behavioral Health Perspective

Eugenia L. Weiss · Jose E. Coll

Getting Started

Children of military service members face unique stressors. These stressors include frequent geographic relocations, extended and multiple parental deployments (many of which are combat deployments) and the associated separations from their parent(s), and post-deployment adjustment including the loss of a parent and crises resulting from combat posttraumatic stress disorder or other injuries incurred by the service member parent. According to the Department of Defense (DoD, 2009), there are 1.9 million children with a parent serving in the U.S. military, and of these children 1.2 million attend a public school near or on U.S. military installations. There are 194 schools that are operated by the Department of Defense Education Activity (DoDEA) that provide uniformity in curriculum and ease school transitions; however, the majority of military-impacted children are in public school systems and not in Department of Defense schools. Although children connected to military service are known as being highly resilient, many experience emotional and behavioral challenges at rates above the national average; for instance, about one-third of the children report symptoms of anxiety associated with long term parental deployments (Chandra et al., 2011). The stressors not only impact emotional and behavioral functioning but also have been shown to result in lower academic performance, especially when examining the impact of lengthy and cumulative parental deployments (Richardson et al., 2011). Schools are in a unique position to facilitate the adjustment of children faced with the current demands of the military lifestyle. Schools are optimal environments for the provision of prevention and intervention services, since these are settings that provide access to many children and are a familiar and safe context (Jaycox et al., 2006), especially since many military families may not seek community or military behavioral health services for reasons associated with stigma or for fear of negative work-related repercussions for the service member parent.

Thus it is imperative that school administrators, educators, and pupil personnel (i.e., counselors, school social workers, and psychologists) become aware of the multiple issues being faced by children from military families and become better equipped to provide the necessary support systems to promote resilience and growth in these students. This chapter will outline the strengths and stressors associated with the military lifestyle, with particular emphasis on understanding military culture from a civilian perspective, deployment-related stressors, effects of parent (i.e., service member) injury upon the child, and the challenges associated with geographic mobility. The reader may refer to Rubin, Weiss, and Coll (in press) for a more complete review of these topics. The chapter will provide examples of what school personnel, from resilience and behavioral health perspectives, can do to promote wellness in the students impacted by military service, which is especially critical in times of war.

What We Know about Military-Connected Children and Youth

Military culture comprises a distinct subset of American society governed by a separate set of laws, norms, traditions, and values (Exum, Coll, & Weiss, 2011). The authors note that key characteristics of military culture include an emphasis on "mission readiness," as well as the importance of military unit cohesion within a hierarchical or rank-based system. The tenets or virtues of military service, regardless of branch of service, include courage, honor, loyalty, commitment, integrity, and an expectation of adherence to these values (Exum, Coll, & Weiss, 2011; Coll, Weiss, & Metal, in press). The family is also held up to the same rigorous standards of conduct and thought to be a reflection of the military member. Furthermore, although the family plays a large role in the success of the military, it always comes second to the needs of the military. One important aspect of the military lifestyle is the constant mobility that families must undertake. In fact, military families move significantly more than civilian families, and the average military child will attend between six and nine schools in grades K-12, and many experience problems with school transfers (Booth, Segal, & Bell, 2007; Council of State Governments, 2008). School Liaison Officers (SLOs) representing different branches of the military will partner with military families and the schools in order to ease school transfers. The liaisons are the first point of contact for families transitioning into new schools; they are "ombudsmen" between military dependent students and schools. Their role is to help identify potential barriers stemming from the military lifestyle that impact student academic success. For a directory listing of SLOs, please refer to the Further Learning section of this chapter under Military K-12 Partners. SLOs also advise commanders and superintendents on educational issues and have played a key role in helping state officials understand and adopt the Interstate Compact on Educational Opportunity for Military Children. To date, some states (36) have adopted the Interstate Compact to eliminate barriers to "educational success" in terms of having policies and procedures in place to ease school transfers between states and school districts (Council of State Governments, 2008). The facilitation rendered by the Interstate Compact includes transfer of transcripts and credits and easing enrollment procedures, as well as providing comparable services to incoming students with disabilities and individualized education plans (IEPs). For children with disabilities, military installations offer an Exceptional Family Member Program (EFMP) liaison to work with the schools and the families to advocate for the needed special education services. As a side note, in cases where there is a "special needs" dependent family member, all branches of the military require EFMP program enrollment to help the military determine the Permanent Change of Station (PCS) assignments for service personnel and their families.

One of the consequences of the constant moving (including sometimes living abroad) is the family becoming susceptible to isolation and alienation from extended family members and from civilians (Hall, 2011). Family members often feel that their lives are transient, and so sometimes they do not readily invest in new relationships, communities, or schools. Another area of concern involves parental absence related to extended deployments and military trainings away from home and the impact of these separations on children's well-being. Combat-related deployments further exacerbate the stress of separation because children and youth worry that the deployed parent may be injured or killed in the line of duty (Burrell et al., 2006). In fact, for many, long-term parental separation can be detrimental to emotional and behavioral functioning across developmental stages (Windle, 1992).

Forty-three percent of service members have children, and almost 50% are married, 6.5% are single parents, and 2.1% are in dual-military families, where both spouses are members of the military and at times deploy simultaneously (Office of the Deputy Under Secretary of Defense, 2008). Military personnel that are deployed from the National Guard or Reserve units are civilians who are part-time military personnel who are then activated into "active-duty status." Not since World War II have Reserve components been more deployed within what has been termed as the mobilization of the "total force" (Exum, Coll, & Weiss, 2011). These families face additional stressors in relation to occupational and economic losses, since the service member parent takes a leave from his or her civilian job to be deployed and then often returns from deployment to find that the job is no longer viable (due to a poor economy) or the individual has been passed up for a promotion, as well as having less earning potential while serving his or her country. Additionally, Guard and Reserve families often live at great distances from military bases, and thus they often lack the resources that full-time or active-duty personnel have in terms of greater access to built-in military support systems.

Service member combat injury is another area that vastly affects military families and children. It is estimated that over 30,000 military children have been impacted by parental combat injuries during the current and continuous "Global War on Terror" (Cozza & Guimond, 2010). Although more service personnel are surviving combat, 15% to over 30% of all returning veterans from

Iraq (Operation Iraqi Freedom—OIF/ Operation New Dawn, OND) and Afghanistan (Operation Enduring Freedom—OEF) will meet the American Psychiatric Association's (APA) *Diagnostic and Statistical Manual of Mental Disorders* (DSM-IV-TR; APA, 2000) criteria for posttraumatic stress disorder (PTSD), mood disturbances, anxieties, and comorbid substance abuse, as well as mild traumatic brain injury (e.g., concussion) associated with blast exposure from roadside bombs or intermittent (or improvised) explosive devices (Tanielian & Jaycox, 2008; United States Army Medical Department, 2008). PTSD is typically characterized by three main clusters of symptoms: re-experiencing symptoms (e.g., intrusive memories, nightmares, flashbacks), avoidance symptoms (e.g., avoiding thoughts and activities associated with traumatic events), and hyperarousal symptoms (e.g., sleep disturbance, irritability/anger, difficulty concentrating, hypervigilance, and an exaggerated startle response) (APA, 2000). Rosenheck and Fontana (1998) found that the more severe and complex the parental exposure to combat, the greater the extent of distress among children. The effects of a combat veteran's trauma on the family has been recognized in the literature as "secondary traumatization," a phenomenon where the veteran's trauma is unwittingly transferred to his or her partner and children, who then experience similar symptoms as the traumatized veteran (Dekel & Goldblatt, 2008; Figley, 1995; Nelson & Wright, 1996). In fact, parental distress in either the returning combat veteran or in the caregiver parent (i.e., the non-deployed parent) has been demonstrated to contribute to poor emotional and behavioral adjustment in children (Chandra et al., 2011). An additional concern involves the high rates of interpersonal violence and child maltreatment in both active-duty and veteran (i.e., separated or retired from military service) populations, which are estimated to be three times higher than those rates for the U.S. civilian population (Houppert, 2005). Interestingly, poorly managed stress in the caregiver (i.e., the non-deployed parent) is a critical factor in cases of child maltreatment. A study by Gibbs et al., (2007) found that the rate of substantiated child maltreatment (i.e., neglect) among Army families was 42% greater during deployments, and incidents of physical abuse also increased when the parent service member returned home (Gibbs et al., 2007). Even in service members who do not suffer from the symptoms of depression or PTSD, a study found that family violence is mostly related to family reintegration problems upon the service member's return home from deployment (Taft, Vogt, Marshall, Panuzio, & Niles, 2007).

Finally, the children and siblings of service members must also cope with the grief and loss associated with service member injury and death. Since the inception of OEF/OIF/OND, there have been more than 5600 U.S. casualties, along with an alarming rate of service member suicides (Cohen & Mannarino, 2011). The authors note that most bereaved military children will experience adaptive grief responses, but some may develop "traumatic grief." Traumatic grief, a form of complicated grief and in this context, is understood as the child having repeated images of death scenarios, real or imagined (i.e., service member death as a result of combat or by suicide); engaging in revenge fantasies against the enemy; and lashing out at others perceived by the child as not understanding; an avoidance of the reminders associated with the deceased may complicate the natural course of the grief experience (Cohen & Marannino, 2011). Yet another type of loss faced by children is termed "ambiguous loss" (Boss, 2004), which occurs when there is uncertainty regarding the status of a family member. The author states that the lack of clarity blocks the grief process because it prevents the cognitions that are necessary for decision making, relational boundary making, and coping. Examples of ambiguous loss are paradoxical in nature—for instance, when a service member is physically present but psychologically absent, as in the case of a parent having PTSD, or when a parent is psychologically present but physically absent, as in the case of service members that are missing in action or are prisoners of war (Dekel & Monson, 2010). Ambiguous loss can produce feelings of anxiety, worry, sadness, and guilt in children and spouses of military personnel.

Deployment is the assignment of military personnel to temporary, unaccompanied duty (i.e., without family members) away from their permanent duty station (Stafford & Grady, 2003). A model for understanding the psychological phases and transitions that military families undergo as a part of the deployment process is called the "emotional cycle of deployment," where each stage is characterized by a specific time frame with particular emotional challenges that service personnel and their family members may often face (Pincus et al., 2007). For example the pre-deployment phase is the psychological and physical preparation in the months preceding the actual deployment, and it is typified by alternating feelings of anticipation and loss for both the service member and for the family (Pincus et al., 2007). During the deployment phase, when the service member has actually departed from the home, children's responses will vary depending on their age and stage of development; some may feel angry, sad, numb, or lonely (Fitzsimons & Krause-Parello, 2009). Children may feel that the deployed parent has left the home because of their misbehavior, or they may experience extreme emotions related to feelings of abandonment (Stafford & Grady, 2003). A recent large study by Mansfield et al. (2011) demonstrates that Army children with deployed parent(s) (OEF/OIF) are experiencing more incidents of mental health-related problems, such as acute stress reactions, depressive disorders, and behavioral disorders than their civilian counterparts; furthermore, the longer the deployments, the higher the rate of adjustment problems. The next phase in the cycle of deployment is the sustainment phase, which occurs from the first month of deployment through the month prior to the service member's return home. Sustainment is the time in which the family has the opportunity to create new sources of support as well as new routines without the service member (Pincus et al., 2007). Children often assume additional roles and responsibilities in the home and are thus forced to become more independent, and many will take pride in their newfound competencies (Weins & Boss, 2006). The redeployment phase occurs within the month prior to the service member's return home and involves the anticipation of homecoming and the family and service member experiencing mixed emotions often consisting of excitement and apprehension (Pincus et al., 2007). The final phase in the emotional cycle of deployment is the post-deployment or reintegration phase, when the service member is reunited with his or her loved ones. Initially, the homecoming can be a honeymoon period, but it is often followed by challenges for everyone in the family. New roles and responsibilities need to be renegotiated, and children may have undergone significant developmental changes during the service member's absence, thus creating new parenting challenges for the service member parent, including a loss of parental authority and having to emotionally attach or reattach to his or her spouse and children (Bowling & Sherman, 2008). The reintegration phase becomes even more complicated if the returning parent is physically injured or somehow changed by the war experience, either psychologically, behaviorally, or in terms of belief systems. The reader may refer to Weiss, Coll, & Metal (2011) for further exploration of the alteration of veteran worldviews following combat experience.

Very little is known about the impact of deployment or war-related stressors on student academic functioning. A recent study on the perceptions of school personnel on the effects of deployment and student academic impact found that some military-connected youth were having problems with school engagement issues, such as not following through with homework, inconsistent attendance, and poor classroom participation; furthermore, the stress that deployment caused in the youth resulted in behavioral issues, which then translated into lower academic performance (Richardson et al., 2011). Other studies have suggested that reading and math scores are lower during parental deployment (Lyle, 2006; Pisano, 1996), as well as standardized test scores (Engel, Gallagher, & Lyle, 2006).

What We Can Do

Utilizing a Response to Intervention (RTI) model (Van der Heyden & Jimerson, 2005), which is guided by the principles of data-driven practices, we will review existing models of prevention and intervention services for schools educating children from military families. One such existing prevention and intervention program being implemented with military-connected youth that is also evidence-based is the FOCUS (Families OverComing Under Stress) project. This is a family-centered resiliency-training intervention program that serves active-duty U.S. Navy and Marine Corps personnel and their children on military bases and installations (Lester et al., 2011; National Child Traumatic Stress Network, 2009). It is a program that was adapted for the OEF/OIF/OND families by the University of California, Los Angeles, and sponsored by the U.S. Bureau of Navy Medicine. FOCUS is a strengths-based model provided in a 6- to 8-week format to families with children. FOCUS teaches specific skills related to the challenges and stressors that military families face during wartime, including emotional regulation, problem solving, communication issues, and goal setting (MCCS Camp Pendleton, 2010). The goal of the FOCUS prevention and intervention program is to promote healthy development in children by increasing positive family relationships and coping skills through the use of psycho-education, strengths building, management techniques for traumatic stress, and support through the stages of deployment (Lester et al., 2011; MacDermid, Samper, Schwarz, Nishida, & Nyaronga, 2008). The model includes the use of a structured assessment protocol in order to meet the specific needs of each family and the application of a family-generated narrative timeline of events; it is also consistent with the Combat and Operational Stress Continuum Model that is used in the Navy and Marine Corps, which helps to de-stigmatize and normalize reactions to stressful events (Lester et al., 2011). The assessment protocol consists of multiple sources of reporting (child self-report; parent report on child symptoms; parent—both service member and civilian—self-report) as well as the use of standardized instruments such as the Brief Symptom Inventory, Kidscope (child coping skills), Strengths and Difficulties Questionnaire, and the McMaster Family Assessment Device. Data is also collected utilizing many of these instruments at the conclusion of the program. As recommended in the RTI principles, the utilization of ongoing data collection and analysis guides practice and should be used to make informed decisions about student needs. Although the FOCUS model is exemplary with a strong research base, there is a limitation in that (at the time of this writing), it is not being implemented military-wide. On a positive note, it is currently being adapted to be used with military dependent children in civilian school settings. The intervention protocol is based on resilience training around the stages of deployment and specific skill building in relation to meeting the challenges associated with each cycle of deployment. For example, one technique that is used with children is called the "feeling thermometer," which helps children recognize a range of feelings (i.e., from relaxed/content to anxious/angry) and provides stress management tools.

Some schools around the nation are utilizing evidence-based cognitive behavioral models to address trauma in schools. In a meta-analysis and review of effective child/adolescent interventions for trauma, Rolfsnes and Idsoe (2011) found that cognitive behavioral therapies were most effective and that the application of these models, such as the CBITS (Cognitive Behavioral Intervention for Trauma in Schools) by Stein et al. (2003), within the school setting was found to be most effective over the application of TF-CBT (Trauma-Focused Cognitive Behavioral Therapy), which is typically delivered in a clinic setting. CBITS is a school-based group intervention for children designed to address symptoms relating to PTSD, depression, anxiety, and exposure to trauma. Children are seen by a school-based clinician in a group setting (comprising six to eight children) for 10 one-hour sessions and for one to three individual sessions. Additionally, parents and teachers receive educational sessions regarding common reactions to trauma (two sessions for parents and one session for teachers). In addition to providing psycho-education, the intervention for children is composed of relaxation training (i.e., deep breathing exercises and progressive relaxation), social problem solving, challenging cognitive distortions or upsetting thoughts (i.e., cognitive therapy), and exposure-based approaches for the resolution of trauma.

From our perspective, as efficacious as the CBITS model is, there are several limitations worth mentioning. A potential drawback with the CBITS is that it is not specifically geared for military-connected children, thus it is not culturally sensitive to the lifestyle issues and demands associated with military service. Additionally, it is meant to be delivered by mental health professionals in the schools, and thus it is difficult to obtain the professional resources to apply it school-wide and within the classroom setting. However, the model has been demonstrated to be flexible in that it has been translated into different languages and has been utilized efficaciously with different cultural groups. Working off RTI guidelines, schools would need to work collaboratively with military communities around the nation and abroad as a means of meeting the diverse needs of the student body and offering effective and culturally relevant interventions.

An international model that is gaining momentum in the area of school-based programs is a teacher-delivered resilience-focused intervention program (Wolmer et al., 2011a). The program was initially developed as a systemic-ecological model helping traumatized children cope in the aftermath of mass disasters. This program has been empirically supported both in Turkey following the 1999 earthquake and in Israel following the Second Lebanon War (Laor et al., 2003; Wolmer et al., 2003; Wolmer et al., 2011a,b). The premise behind the model is that the intensive and familiar teacher-student relationship that occurs in a natural classroom setting enables immediate teacher-student feedback and follow-up and reduces the stigma associated with a student being singled out for treatment (Wolmer et al., 2003).

According to the authors, teachers are trained in a structured protocol of eight 2-hour classroom sessions. The model uses an imaginary character, named "Adam," who writes letters to the children and invites them to share and process their traumatic experiences; through psycho-education, narratives, play, and personal diaries, the children are helped to process and restructure traumatic experiences. The protocol also includes instruction on coping with intrusive thoughts and dealing with loss, anger, and guilt feelings. Follow-up studies utilizing this approach have concluded that immediate symptom relief was found in children exposed to trauma and the improvement was sustained over three years; additionally, the participating children displayed better academic, social, and behavioral adaptation than the matched control groups (Wolmer et al., 2005). A recent study by Wolmer et al. (2011b) demonstrated that an adapted version that de-emphasizes the trauma or the psychopathology aspect and emphasizes a resilience-building component in order to strengthen adaptive coping and competence in the area of social-emotional functioning has also been effective. This adapted protocol consists of fourteen 45-minute teacher-delivered and manualized modules that encompass stress management skills, relaxation exercises, affect regulation skills, and identification of negative thinking, as well as themes that promote social-emotional functioning. As expected, this model also yielded positive results in reducing children's stress and improving mood at a three-month follow-up (Wolmer et al., 2011b). The authors recommended that those children who are indeed suffering from trauma symptoms would need to be identified early on and provided with specialized clinical interventions and outside behavioral health resources in addition to the teacher-delivered protocols. The RTI guidelines also encompass teaching children the necessary skills for success beyond academic achievement, where skill-based learning regarding social, emotional, and behavioral aspects of functioning would be especially well suited for military-connected children who are under the constant stress of parental deployment, loss, and trauma. Please refer to the appendix section of Wolmer et al. (2011b) for an outline of the teacher-based resilience intervention protocol.

Finally, a trauma protocol that has been piloted for use in U.S. schools and that combines the cognitive behavioral elements of CBITS and the use of non-clinical school personnel to deliver the program is the Support for Students Exposed to Trauma (SSET). Teachers or counselors are trained over two days in the model and deliver SSET over 10 weekly group sessions during class time (in a lesson plan format) without individual or parent sessions (Jaycox et al., 2009). An adaptation of the SSET model to serve children in military families has been proposed by Wong and associates, primarily addressing the stressors associated with deployment and frequent relocations (M. Wong, personal communication, October 20, 2011). Refer to Table 54.1 for the proposed draft protocol.

In the following section under Tools and Practice Examples we will provide a case scenario of an actual therapy client, though the names and details of the case have been altered to protect client confidentiality. This case is illustrative of the kind of cultural sensitivity that schools need to adopt in order to not compound the stressors already being faced by military children.

Applying Interventions within a Response to Intervention Framework

A school intervention model that meets all of the requirements under the RTI framework is a recently DoDEA funded grant titled "Building Capacity to Create Highly Supportive Military-Connected School Districts" by the University of Southern California (2010). This project could also be an appropriate vehicle to pilot the teacher-based resilience intervention model. This four-year grant includes a consortium of eight school districts in San Diego, CA, with a focus to "ease the challenges that military students face due to transitions and deployments; support the socio- and emotional needs of military students; encourage parental involvement; create infrastructure and evidence-based materials for state and national data-driven military-connected school (MCS) systems" (http://buildingcapacity.usc.edu/). Part of the initiative is to train civilian educators and school personnel to understand and respond to the unique experiences of military children, including combat stress reactions and secondary trauma. Research in school-based interventions (rather than clinic-based) demonstrates that "supportive" schools are protective settings from post-traumatic stress reactions that shield students from serious emotional and behavioral problems as well as from academic failure (Astor, Benbenishty, &

Table 54.1 Proposed Adaptation of SSET for Children in Military Families

Module	*Rationale*	*Concept*	*Learning Objective*
1	Stress of parental deployments & frequent moves call for general coping strategies that improve mood and behavior	Thoughts, feelings, and behaviors	Understand link between thoughts, feelings, and behaviors
2	Elevated worry & concern about deployed parent call for worry- and anxiety-reduction strategies	Relaxation & other strategies to reduce anxiety and worry	Learn ways to effectively reduce anxiety; apply this to current stress experienced
3	Stress of parental deployments and frequent moves call for general coping strategies that improve mood and behavior	Challenging unrealistic negative thoughts	Learn ways to challenge unrealistic negative thoughts; apply this to current problems related to deployment
4	Disruption of positive family routines and single-parent households reduce opportunities for positive social and physical activities	Pleasant activity scheduling for self & family, including exercise and positive family rituals	Identify ways to increase positive affect through activities; apply this to daily and weekly schedule
5	Social disruptions caused by frequent moves and family changes in roles and responsibilities require social skills to navigate changes	Improving communication with parents, peers, and school personnel	Recognize the difference between assertive, aggressive, and passive speech and behavior and build assertiveness skills
6	Stress of deployment can impair academic performance, requiring planning & organizational skills	Getting organized for success	Identify ways to improve organization for homework & studying, including planning with home caregiver
7	Stress of parental deployments & frequent moves call for general coping strategies that improve mood and behavior	Problem solving: brainstorming	Learn how to generate many creative solutions for a problem; apply this to current problems related to deployment
8	Stress of parental deployments & frequent moves call for general coping strategies that improve mood and behavior	Problem solving: pros and cons	Learn how to evaluate pros and cons related to a potential solution to a problem; apply this to current problems related to deployment

Estrada, 2009). This grant initiative is examining various evidence-based models (derived from an extensive database) to be utilized in the schools as potential models of intervention like the SSET or other programs (e.g., many of which are substance abuse-specific or anti-school-violence models). We are proposing that Wolmer et al.'s teacher-delivered resilience-focused intervention with some cultural modifications would be a good option to consider for implementation. Another aspect of this grant initiative involves placing Master of Social Work students who are supervised and specialty trained in military social work in these school settings as a source of support and consultation. The grant is based on an empowerment model, where schools, families (e.g., parent involvement), stakeholders, and policymakers all come together to address the needs of military children to create public school environments that are welcoming for students and are able to appropriately address their educational and socioemotional needs. The principle behind this paradigm is in part derived from Huebner et al.'s (2009) community capacity building model, where both informal and formal support networks, the use of social capital, and shared community responsibility and competence will play a role in individual (i.e., student) and family outcomes. Part of USC's Building Capacity model is to lead educational research and school reform policies for supporting military-connected schools. The goal is to examine how all of the factors—such as military context, risk, family, community and military supports, and school climate (i.e., principal leadership, teacher awareness and support; peer awareness)—combine to affect emotional, academic, and social outcomes in schoolchildren impacted by military service. (Please see Tunac De Pedro et al. (2011) for a comprehensive review of educational research and recommendations regarding military connected youth and school reform.)

Tools & Practice Examples

Tyler is a 9-year-old Caucasian male who was attending outpatient counseling with a private practitioner (first author). The client was able to participate in counseling through his father's health insurance for military dependents (TRICARE). Tyler had a history of suffering from attention deficit disorder, hyperactive type (APA, 2000), for which he had been receiving services with this therapist. Tyler attended school on a military installation that was run by the local school district. Each week, Tyler presented as a friendly, outgoing, and active young man, but one week he appeared sad, sullen, and withdrawn. The therapist inquired if anything new or different had happened in his life, since his father is a U.S. Marine who was at the time serving in Afghanistan. Tyler stated that the only thing that had occurred was that the vice principal of his school had come into his classroom the day before and had announced that his friend Brady would not be returning to school because Brady's father had been killed in Afghanistan. Tyler then wondered if his own father would meet the same fate as Brady's father. Tyler then became very anxious, and his mother stated that he did not sleep the evening of the news.

In the above case scenario, we would recommend utilizing a teacher-based intervention where the teacher could inform the students of Brady's father's death (with the assumption that the children may hear of this casualty regardless, as the military community on base is very tight-knit). The teacher could then process the students' feelings through Wolmer et al.'s (2011a,b) revised model, which also addresses loss reactions. However, in order for this to effectively take place, the school administrators, educators, and pupil personnel would need to be trained on military culture and worldviews (e.g., rank-based system, cycle of deployment) as well as on how to cope with student stress. The teacher would also need ongoing support to be able to manage his or her own feelings of stress and loss. Following RTI guidelines, schools should develop and provide ongoing training and support for teachers and staff. Teachers would also need to identify how their own perceptions of war may differ and, therefore, would need to reflect on how they would communicate to the students, in this scenario, the fatality. Moreover, as the educator moves through the model, he or she would need to monitor the students for academic and emotional changes and ensure that if students move to others schools this information is shared with parental consent. The cornerstone of this approach entails a shift in the professional identity of the teacher. In order to gain teacher buy-in, schools would need to facilitate and support teachers in this endeavor, and teachers would need assistance in reconstructing their professional identities or "meaning making" in terms of values and beliefs regarding what education is really about (Van den Berg, 2002). In this light, education would need to encompass student learning and development beyond the current U.S. educational policies that emphasize test scores over a child's social-emotional development and growth. Parents would also play a key role in supporting what the teacher does in the classroom and reinforcing this approach at home. Therefore, what we are suggesting is truly a community-based approach.

The teacher-based resilience intervention protocols that we are proposing based on Wolmer et al.'s model would need to be further adapted to include cultural aspects of U.S. military life. Wolmer et al. based their intervention model on the Israeli population, where participation in the armed forces is mandatory for most Israeli citizens (with the exception of the religious Orthodox), in contrast to the U.S., where we have an all-volunteer force. The war dynamics are also different, wherein the U.S. wars are waged on foreign soil and American children are not typically exposed to rocket fire as the Israeli children are, nor do they live under the constant threat of attack. These culture-based variations provide a context for provision and types of services; however, these differences would need to be further investigated in order to ascertain whether or not these would impact the approach.

Key Points to Remember

- The unique stressors faced by children and youth impacted by military service and the need for providing U.S. military cultural competence, knowledge, and skills to all school personnel.
- School personnel to utilize military school liaisons and for school officials to advocate for the Interstate Compact Law to ease school transfers among other things.
- Children and youth will have different reactions to separation from their deployed parent(s) according to age, developmental level, and how the remaining spouse (parent) copes.
- The notion of a teacher-delivered model of resilience building for children to be utilized as a model to help children cope with the stressors associated with military life.
- Children and youth from National Guard and Reserve families are especially vulnerable to stress, as they are often residing in civilian communities and are not near military installations, and they do not have easy access to military supports.
- The provision of support, training, and consultation services for school personnel to be able to implement a more supportive school environment for children who are connected to military service.

Further Learning

- Interstate Compact: http://www.mic3.net
- The Military Child Education Coalition (MCEC) is a one-stop shop for resources for teachers, parents, and professionals assisting children and youth with military stressors and school transitions. Additionally, they offer workshops and training for professionals: http://www.militarychild.org.
- SchoolQuest is a Web site geared toward military families to provide information on school records and transferring school credits, provided by MCEC: http://schoolquest.org/.
- John Hopkins Military Child Initiative Training offers a Web course for school professionals on understanding military-related issues as they impact children and ways to build student resilience: http://www.jhsph.edu/mci/training_course/.
- Military K-12 Partners (DoDEA Partnership) provides information on important policies, procedures, and best practices supporting the needs of military families' education; a directory of school liaisons, teacher trainings, and grant applications are all available online at http://www.militaryk12partners.dodea.edu.
- Working with Military Children: A Primer for School Personnel is a very valuable resource for school personnel that provides general information on military culture, cycles of deployment, relocation, and crisis and provides helpful student activities. It was developed by the Virginia Joint Military Family Services Board and can be obtained at http://www.nmfa.org/site/DocServer?docID=642.
- SOAR: Student Online Achievement Resources is a student Web-based achievement resource site where students take assessments aligned to state standards and are given individualized tutorials to improve their academics: http://www.soarathome.org/.
- The National Military Family Association provides information for military families, resources, and toolkits at http://www.nmfa.org.
- Operation: Military Kids, the U.S. Army's collaborative effort with America's communities to support children and youth impacted by deployment, provides local resources for community support to enhance well-being: http://www.operationmilitarykids.org.
- The Yellow Ribbon Program is for National Guard and Reserve families and provides benefit information, youth summer camps, community referrals, and activities for children during deployments. http://www.yellowribbon.mil/theribbon/tags/tag/national-guard
- FOCUS (Families Overcoming Under Stress) is a resilience-building program led by the

University of California, Los Angeles, for Navy and Marine Corps affiliated children and families: http://www.focusproject.org/.

- Building Capacity, a partnership between the University of Southern California, DoDEA and military-connected schools and districts to improve school climate in order to address military students' needs and circumstances: http://buildingcapacity.usc.edu/.
- The U.S. Department of Education Impact Aid is a federally funded program to reimburse school districts for loss of tax revenue when schools are located on military installations: http://www2.ed.gov/about/offices/list/oese/impactaid/index.html.
- The Military Impacted Schools Association provides a variety of Web-based resources at http://www.militaryimpactedschoolsassociation.org.
- The Military Family Research Institute at Purdue University offers publications, resources, news, grant information, and events: http://www.mfri.purdue.edu/.
- The National Child Traumatic Stress Network provides childhood trauma information and treatment descriptions as well as Web-based trainings. General information on the CBITS can be found here: http://www.nctsnet.org/sites/default/files/assets/pdfs/cbits_general.pdf.
- Support for Students Exposed to Trauma: The SSET Program is available online at http://www.rand.org/pubs/technical_reports/TR675/.

References

American Psychiatric Association. (2000). *Diagnostic and statistical manual of mental disorders* (4th ed., text revision). Washington DC: Author.

Astor, R. A., Benbenishty, R., & Estrada, J. N. (2009). School violence and theoretically atypical schools: The principal's centrality in orchestrating safe schools. *American Educational Research Journal, 46*(2), 423–461.

Booth, B., Segal, M. W., & Bell, B. D. (2007). *What we know about Army families: 2007 update.* Retrieved from http://94.23.146.173/ficheros/0fa2c1b991df31e6138c0e9c4e72244b.pdf

Boss, P. (2004). Ambiguous loss research, theory, and practice: Reflections after 9/11. *Journal of Marriage and Family, 66*(3), 551–566.

Bowling, U. B., & Sherman, M. D. (2008). Welcoming them home: Supporting service members and their families in navigating the tasks of reintegration. *Professional Psychology: Research and Practice, 39*(4), 451–458.

Burrell, L. M., Adams, G. A., Durand, D. B., & Castro, D. A. (2006). The impact of military lifestyle demands on well-being, Army, and family outcomes. *Armed Forces & Society, 33,* 43–58.

Chandra, A., Lara-Cinisomo, S., Jaycox, L. H, Tanielian, T., Han, B., Burns, R. M., & Ruder, T., (2011). *Views from the homefront: The experiences of youth and spouses from military families.* Santa Monica, CA: RAND Corporation.

Cohen, J. A., & Mannarino, A. P. (2011). Trauma-focused CBT for traumatic grief in military children. *Journal of Contemporary Psychotherapy,* 41(4), 219–227.

Coll, J. E., Weiss, E. L., & Metal, M. (in press). Culture and Diversity in the Military. In A. Rubin, E. L. Weiss, & J. E. Coll (Eds.), *Handbook of military social work.* Hoboken, NJ: Wiley & Sons, Inc.

Council of State Governments. (2008). *Interstate compact on educational opportunity for military children.* Retrieved from http://csg.org/programs/ncic/EducatingMilitaryChildrenCompact.aspx

Cozza, S. J., & Guimond, J. M. (2010). Working with combat-injured families through the recovery trajectory. In S. MacDermid Wadsworth & D. Riggs (Eds.), *Risk and resilience in U.S. military families* (pp. 259–277). New York, NY: Springer.

Dekel, R., & Goldblatt, H. (2008). Is there intergenerational transmission of trauma? The case of combat veterans' children. *American Journal of Orthopsychiatry, 78*(3), 281–289.

Dekel, R., & Monson, C. M. (2010). Military-related post-traumatic stress disorder and family relations: Current knowledge and future directions. *Aggression and Violent Behavior, 15,* 303–309.

Department of Defense Demographics. (2009). *A profile of the military community.* Retrieved from http://www.militaryhomefront.dod.mil/

Engel, R. C., Gallagher, L. B., & Lyle, D. S. (2006). *Military deployments and children's academic achievement: Evidence from Department of Defense Education Activity Schools.* U.S. Military Academy. West Point, NY: Department of Social Sciences.

Exum, H., Coll, J. E., & Weiss, E. L. (2011). *A civilian counselor's primer for counseling veterans* (2nd ed.). Deerpark, NY: Linus Publications.

Figley, C. (1995). Compassion fatigue as secondary traumatic stress disorder: An overview. In C. Figley (Ed.), *Compassion fatigue: Coping with secondary traumatic stress disorder in those who treat the traumatized* (pp. 1–20). New York, NY: Brunner/Mazel.

Fitzsimons, V. M., & Krause-Parello, C. A. (2009). Military children: When parents are deployed overseas. *The Journal of School Nursing, 25*(1), 40–47.

Gibbs, D. A., Martin, S., Kupper, L., & Johnson, R. (2007). Child maltreatment in enlisted soldiers' families during combat-related deployments. *Journal of the American Medical Association, 298,* 528–535.

Hall, L. K. (2011). The importance of understanding military culture. *Social Work in Health Care, 50*(1), 4–18.

Houppert, K. (2005). *Base crimes: The military has a domestic violence problem*. Foundation for National Progress. Retrieved from http://www.motherjones.com/news/featurex/2005/07/base_crimes.html

Huebner, A. J., Mancini, J. A., Bowen, G. L., & Orthner, D. K. (2009). Shadowed by war: Building community capacity to support military families. *Family Relations, 58*, 216–228.

Jaycox, L. H., Langley, A. K., Stein, B. D., Wong, M., Sharma, P., Scott, M., & Schonlau, M. (2009). Support for students exposed to trauma: A pilot study. *School Mental Health, 1*(2), 49–60.

Jaycox, L. H., Morse, L. K., Tanielian, T., & Stein, B. D. (2006). *How schools can help students recover from traumatic experiences: A tool kit for supporting long-term recovery*. Santa Monica, CA: RAND Corporation.

Laor, N., Wolmer, L., Spirman, S., & Wiener, Z. (2003). Facing war, terrorism, and disaster. Toward a child-oriented comprehensive emergency care system. *Child & Adolescent Psychiatric Clinics of North America, 12,* 343–361.

Lester. P., Leskin, G., Woodward, K., Saltzman, W., Nash, W., Mogil, C., Paley, B., & Beardslee, W. (2011). Wartime deployment and military children: Applying prevention science to enhance family resilience. In S. MacDermid Wadsworth & D. Riggs (Eds.), *Risk & resilience in U.S. military families* (pp. 149–173). New York, NY: Springer.

Lyle, D. S. (2006). Using military deployments and job assignments to estimate the effect of parental absences and household relocations on children's academic achievement. *Journal of Labor Economics, 24*(2), 32.

Mansfield, A. J., Kaufman, J. S., Engel, C. C. & Gaynes, B. (2011). Deployment and mental health diagnoses among children of U.S. Army personnel. *Archives of Pediatric Adolescent Medicine*. Advance online publication. doi: 10.1001/archpediatrics.2011.123

MacDermid, S. M., Samper, R., Schwarz, R., Nishida, J., & Nyaronga, D. (July, 2008). *Understanding and promoting resilience in military families*. West Lafayette, IN: Military Family Research Institute at Purdue University. Retrieved from https://www.mfri.purdue.edu/resources/public/reports/Understanding%20and%20Promoting%20Resilience.pdf

MCCS Camp Pendleton. (2010). *Marine and family services: FOCUS*. Retrieved from http://register.mccscp.com/home/Family-Services/CYTP/focus.aspx

Nelson, B. S., & Wright, D. W. (1996). Understanding and treating post-traumatic stress disorder symptoms in female partners of veterans with PTSD. *Journal of Marital and Family Therapy, 22*(4), 455–467.

Office of the Deputy Under Secretary of Defense. (2008). *2008 demographics: Profile of the military community*. Washington DC: Department of Defense (Military Community and Family Policy).

Pincus, S., House, R., Christenson, J., & Adler, L. (2007). The emotional cycle of deployment: A military family perspective. *My Hooah 4 Health Deployment*. Washington, DC: U.S. Army Center of Health Promotion and Preventive Medicine.

Pisano, M.C. (1996, March). *Implications of deployed and non-deployed fathers on seventh graders' California achievement test scores during a military crisis*. Paper presented at the Annual Meeting of the National Association of School Psychologists, Atlanta, GA.

Richardson, A., Chandra, A., Martin, L. T., Setodji, C. M., Hallmark, B. W., Campbell, N. F.,...Grady, P. (2011). *Effects of soldiers' deployment on children's academic performance and behavioral health*. Santa Monica, CA: RAND Corporation.

Rolfsnes, E. S., & Idsoe, T. (2011). School-based intervention programs for PTSD symptoms: A review and meta-analysis. *Journal of Traumatic Stress, 24*(2), 155–165.

Rosenheck, R., & Fontana, A. (1998). Transgenerational effects of abusive violence on the children of Vietnam combat veterans. *Journal of Traumatic Stress, 11*(4), 731–741.

Rubin, A., & Weiss, E. L., Coll, J. E. (Eds.) (in press). *Handbook of military social work*. Hoboken, NJ: Wiley & Sons, Inc.

Stafford, E. M., & Grady, B. A. (2003). Military family support. *Pediatric Annals, 32*(2), 110–115.

Stein, B. D., Jaycox, L. H., Kataoka, S. H., Wong, M., Tu, W., Elliott, M. N., & Fink, A. (2003). A mental health intervention for schoolchildren exposed to violence: A randomized controlled trial. *Journal of the American Medical Association, 290*, 603–611.

Taft, C. T., Vogt, D. S., Marshall, A. D., Panuzio, J., & Niles, B. L. (2007). Aggression among combat veterans: Relationships with combat exposure and symptoms of posttraumatic stress disorder, dysphoria, and anxiety. *Journal of Traumatic Stress, 20*, 135–145.

Tanielian, T., & Jaycox, L. (2008). *Invisible wounds of war: Psychological and cognitive injuries, their consequences and services to assist recovery*. Santa Monica, CA: RAND.

Tunac, De Pedro, K. M., Astor, R. A., Benbenishty, R., Estrada, J., DeJoie Smith, G. R., & Esqueda, M. C. (2011). The children of military service members: Challenges, supports and future educational research. *Review of Educational Research, 81*(4), 566–618.

United States Army Medical Department, Mental Health Advisory Team (MHATV). (2008, March). *Army report on mental health of soldiers in Afghanistan and Iraq*. Retrieved from U.S. Army Medical Department Web site: www.armymedicine.army.mil/news/releases/20080306mhatv.cfm

University of Southern California. (2010). *Building capacity to create highly supportive military-connected school districts*. Retrieved from http://buildingcapacity.usc.edu

University of Southern California. (2010). *DoDEA grant proposal: Building capacity to create highly supportive military-connected school districts*. Los Angeles, CA: Author.

Van den Berg, R. (2002). Teachers' meanings regarding educational practice. *Review of Educational Research, 72*(4), 577–625.

Van der Heyden, A. M., & Jimerson, R. (2005). Using Response to Intervention to enhance outcomes for children. *The California School Psychologist, 10*, 21–33.

Weins, T. W., & Boss, P. (2006). Maintaining family resilience before, during, and after military separation. In C. A. Castro, A. B. Adler, & C. A. Britt (Eds.), *Military life: The psychology of serving in peace and combat* (Vol. 3; pp. 13–38). Bridgeport, CT: Praeger Security International.

Weiss, E. L., Coll, J. E., & Metal, M. (2011). The influence of military culture and veteran worldviews on mental health treatment: Implications for veteran help-seeking and wellness. *International Journal of Health, Wellness & Society, 1*(2), 75–86.

Windle, M. A. (1992). A longitudinal study of stress buffering for adolescent problem behaviors. *Developmental Psychology, 28*(3), 522–530.

Wolmer, L., Hamiel, D., Barchas, J. D., Slone, M., & Laor, N. (2011a). Teacher-delivered resilience-focused intervention in schools with traumatized children following the Second Lebanon War. *Journal of Traumatic Stress, 24*(3), 309–316.

Wolmer, L., Hamiel, D., & Laor, N. (2011b). Preventing children's posttraumatic stress after disaster with teacher-based intervention: A controlled study. *Journal of the American Academy of Child and Adolescent Psychiatry, 50*(4), 340–348.

Wolmer, L., Laor, N., Dedeoglu, C., Siev, J., & Yazgan, Y. (2005). Teacher-mediated intervention after disaster: A controlled three-year follow up of children's functioning. *Journal of Child Psychology & Psychiatry, 46*, 1161–1168.

Wolmer, L., Laor, N., & Yagzan, Y. (2003). School reactivation programs after disaster: Could teachers serve as clinical mediators? *Child & Adolescent Psychiatric Clinics of North America, 12*, 363–381.

Effectively Working with Latino Immigrant Families in the Schools

CHAPTER 55

Eden Hernandez Robles ▪ Alan Dettlaff ▪ Rowena Fong

Getting Started

In 2009 the U.S. Census Bureau (2011a) estimated that 20% of all elementary and high school students were classified as Hispanic. Although Hispanics (both male and female) have experienced a slight decline in the dropout rate, they have continued to drop out at over twice the rate of their white and black counterparts (U.S. Census Bureau, 2011b). In addition, Hispanic males dropped out at higher rates when compared to Hispanic females, and also have lower rates of college enrollment (4.7%) when compared to Hispanic females (6.2%) (U.S. Census Bureau, 2011c). Only 12% of all college students (both undergraduate and graduate) are Hispanic, and 14% of all Hispanics age 25 and older attain a bachelor's degree (U.S. Census Bureau 2011a).

Referred to as Hispanics in census data, the Latino population, particularly those who have migrated from other countries, represents the largest and fastest growing population in the United States. In 2010, the Latino population, consisting of persons from Mexico, Cuba, Dominican Republic, Central America, South America, and other Latin countries, represented 16.3% of the total U.S. population, an increase of 15.2 million people since 2000. Between 2000 and 2010, the Latino population increased by 43%, which was more than four times the growth of the total U.S. population (Ennis, Rios-Vargas, & Albert, 2011). Latino children represent 22% of all children under the age of 18 in the United States (Fry & Passel, 2009). Although foreign-born Latino children represent only 11% of Latino children, more than half (52%) of Latino children are U.S.-born children of Latino immigrants (Fry & Passel, 2009). While children of immigrants reside primarily in six states that have been traditional destination states for immigrants—California, Texas, New York, Florida, Illinois, and New Jersey—the number of children with immigrant parents has more than doubled in most other states, while states including North Carolina, Nevada, Georgia, Arkansas, and Nebraska have experienced growth rates of more than 300% since 1990 (Fortuny, Capps, Simms, & Chaudry, 2009).

Given the rapidly increasing Latino immigrant population, school-based professionals face increasing pressure to assist in the adjustment of children from immigrant families entering school systems. For these children, stressors related to immigration and acculturation may significantly impede the learning process. Upon migration, immigrants are faced with a number of challenges that distinguish them from their native-born counterparts. The migration experience itself can be considerably dangerous, with many immigrants experiencing violence, robbery, and sexual assault (Solis, 2003). Once in the new country, children in immigrant families continue to experience stress resulting from language differences, unfamiliar customs, loss of routine, and continuing threats of violence and discovery. Additional pressures resulting from acculturation can lead to a variety of strains and difficulties on family systems, as parents and children experience changing cultural contexts along with the loss of previously established support systems (Dettlaff & Rycraft, 2006). While some foreign-born children overcome these challenges with apparent ease, many others experience very difficult and stressful transitions to their lives in the United States (Goodman, 2004; Tazi, 2004).

Research indicates that the inability to cope or adjust to cultural stressors can result in poor or stagnated academic achievement for children in immigrant families (Moon, Kang, & An, 2009; Padilla & Perez, 2003; Shin, 2004). Thus, the increasing population of immigrant children in school systems necessitates that school-based professionals recognize and respond to the unique needs of this population to facilitate positive academic outcomes. Thomas (1992) contends that the failure to address the adjustment challenges faced by immigrant children within school systems contributes indirectly to their academic failure. Compounding the existing challenges faced by immigrant children, lack of academic achievement can then lead to increased risk of poor self-esteem and dropout (Battin-Pearson et al., 2000; Suh, Suh, & Houston, 2007).

What We Know

The cultural, psychological, and linguistic challenges that stem from experiences with immigration and acculturation make Latino immigrant students a particularly vulnerable population. Latino students in general continue to be overrepresented in special education as a result of a misinterpretation of the students' cultural and language barriers as a learning disability (Artiles, Rueda, Salazar, & Higareda, 2005; Lee, Grigg, & Donahue, 2007; Orosco, 2010; Orosco, Schonewise, de Onis, Klingner, & Hoover, 2008). However, Latinos are not overrepresented in disabilities that require biological verification (educable mental retardation) (National Resource Council, 2002).

Academic Achievement and Dropout Rates

Academic achievement and dropout rates are both areas of major concern for Latino immigrant students. Multiple barriers that the first generation faces, including low levels of cultural sensitivity in schools and inadequate academic advisement, affect the ability for subsequent generations to obtain academic success (Hill & Torres, 2010; Nevarez & Rico, 2007; Suarez-Orozco & Suarez-Orozco, 1995). Findings from Tenenbaum and Ruck's (2007) study indicated that students are often the subject of repeated discrimination as "teachers praise Latino students less, even for correct answers; behave less favorably toward them; and penalize them for lower levels of English proficiency" (Hill & Torres, 2010, p. 98). Although Latino immigrant children face many barriers that may impede their academic success, school-based professionals have the potential to foster academic achievement and completion through culturally sensitive interventions.

It is critical for the school social worker, school mental health professional, or school counselor to be both familiar with the cultural belief systems (see Table 55.1) and clear on the points about the Latino immigrant population, which are knowing the difference between immigrant children and children of immigrants and discerning that there are great variations of different subgroups coming from diverse countries. It is recommended that the school-based professional consider the Latino Dimensions of Family and Personal Identity Model, adapted from Arredondo & Glauner's (1992) Dimensions of Personality Identity Model, when working with a Latino immigrant student (Arredondo & Santiago-Rivera, 2000; see Figure 55.1). The Latino Dimensions of Family and Personal Identity Model considers A, B, and C dimensions that include age/generational status, acculturation/citizen status, and personal/familial/historical events before proceeding to work with Latinos (Santiago-Rivera et al., 2002). Using this model as an assessment would help the school-based professional in an early identification of appropriate interventions for the student.

Another consideration for the school-based professional to make when working with Latino immigrant students is the appropriate use of the Spanish language. Although the Spanish language is shared by Latino immigrants, depending on the country of origin the dialect may differ and words may change in meaning (Thorn & Contreras, 2005). Similarly, behavior and body language also differ among the subgroups of Latinos and can be a powerful form of mimesis to forge a therapeutic relationship if applied correctly (Quinones-Mayo & Dempsey, 2005). The bilingual school-based professional should be alert to these differences in dialect and prepared to adapt. For example, the term "school bus" translated from the American language would be *el autobus de transporte escolar.* However, depending on the person's country of origin, the term "school bus" can be translated differently. For persons from Mexico, a school bus is *el camion escolar,* while persons from Cuba and Puerto Rico may identify the bus as *la guagua escolar,* and persons from Uruguay or Peru may recognize the bus as *el omnibus escolar.* The variations on school bus do not end there. This example simply stresses the importance of recognizing differences in dialect and being able to adapt.

Table 55.1 Cultural Belief Systems

Principle	*Definition*	*Citation*
Los dichos	Cultural sayings that reflect cultural values or lessons. Can be used as a therapeutic tool.	Zuniga, 1992
La educación	Education in mainstream America refers to school. *La educación* is not a direct translation of education, but refers to the role of the mother for the proper social and moral upbringing of the child and can be a powerful resource.	Goldenberg & Gallimore, 1995; Valdés, 1996
El respeto	Refers to a respect for elders and authority. *Respeto* is also achieved through empathy in intimate relationships.	Santiago-Rivera et al., 2002; Simoni & Perez, 1995
Familismo	Academic term to define the observed importance of family above self; strong family ties within Latino families. However, the greater a family adapts to the U.S., the weaker *familismo* becomes.	Santiago-Rivera et al., 2002; Smokowski et al., 2008
Personalismo	Academic term to describe the importance of developing a personal relationship versus institutional relationship. A genuine interest in a person or family, not a professional distance.	Negroni-Rodriguez & Morales, 2001
La confianza	Refers to an established relationship of trust with the families.	Negroni-Rodriguez & Morales, 2001
Simpatía	Refers to the want to be social, agreeable, sharing, and empathetic, although this may differ when interacting with persons of a different culture.	Guilamo-Ramos et al., 2007; Simoni & Perez, 1995; Marin, 1993
Dignidad	Refers to a respect and honor given to a person.	Andres-Hyman et al., 2006
Obligación	Refers to a mutual expectation (responsibility) that both those in power and those that are not in power will treat each other with respect.	Padilla, 2005
Ganas	Refers to drive and ambition to achieve goals.	Auerbach, 2006
Marianismo	Academic term that refers to female gender socialization. Girls must grow up to be enduring, nurturing, spiritually strong, and pious women and mothers. This can possibly create conflict within the family.	Lopez-Baez, 1999; Santiago-Rivera et al., 2002
Machismo	Academic term that refers to male gender socialization. Boys must grow up to be responsible, loyal, and protective men and fathers. This term is often confused and used interchangeably with the term machista, which means sexist.	Morales, 1996; Santiago-Rivera et al., 2002

The non-bilingual school-based professional should be alert to these differences and cautious if employing translating services. Improper use of the language poses many ethical dilemmas and risks effectively building a therapeutic relationship with the students. Identifying possible bilingual referral sources may be the best choice for non-bilingual school-based professional, as matching the students with language-appropriate services is most important in the early stages of intervention

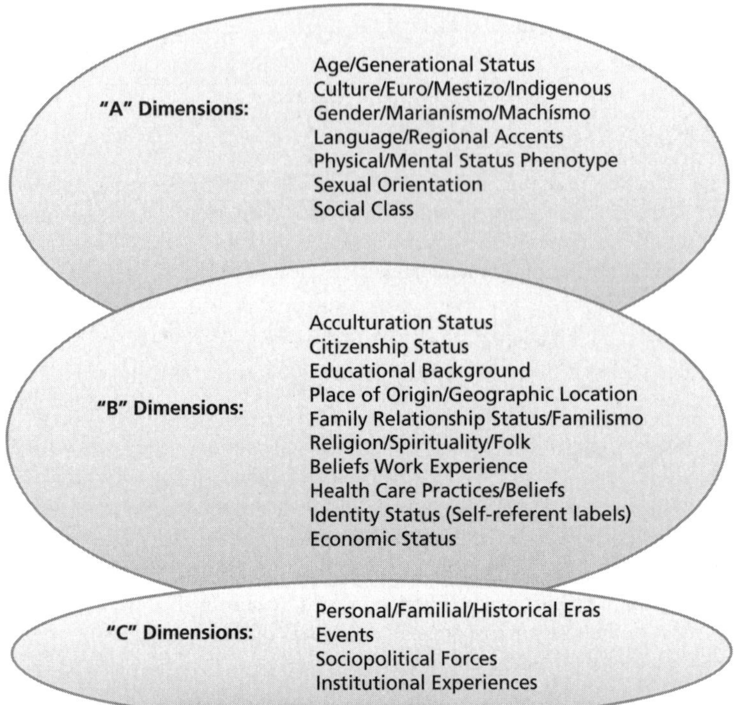

Figure 55.1 Latina/o Dimensions of Family and Personal Identity
Source: Adapted from Arredondo & Glauner, 1992

when seeking positive outcomes (Carey & Manuppelli, 2000). Nonetheless, the non-bilingual school-based professional's openness to learning these differences and key words of the language are helpful in building a relationship of trust and mutual respect.

What We Can Do

Response to Intervention (RTI) is a three-tiered model used by school systems to provide instruction and intervention or prevention to students according to their needs (RTI Action Network, 2011). Each tier is structured to both identify and then provide tailored support to students with learning or behavioral difficulties. Within the tiers, students are continually monitored for progress to determine whether further action is needed to assist the student in achieving his or her goals. The screening process to determine which tier a student will benefit from begins at the classroom level. The classroom level is considered the Tier 1 level of RTI and consists of high-quality classroom instruction using evidence-based educational practices (RTI Action Network, 2011). Students that are identified as having difficulty at this level are provided with supplemental instruction. Students that do not show adequate progress or improvement within the allotted time (generally within eight weeks) are moved into the Tier 2 level. Tier 2 supports consist of targeted interventions provided in small-group settings and are a supplement to regular classroom instruction (RTI Action Network, 2011). This level of intervention varies in duration but does not exceed past the grading level. Students who require more support are placed into the intensive Tier 3 interventions that are structured to target the student's deficits. Students that do not respond to Tier 3 interventions then become eligible for a comprehensive evaluation and are considered for special education (RTI Action Network, 2011).

Although there are few culturally sensitive evidence-based interventions available for Latino immigrant students, those that have been developed incorporate the students' traditional culture into instruction while introducing the United

States (Orosco, 2007, 2010; Klingner & Edwards, 2006; Santiago & Brown, 2004). Culturally sensitive RTI interventions facilitate the transition and adjustment of the students while supporting them in their culture as they work toward academic success (Osher et al., 2004; Osher & Osher, 2002; Lewis, 2001). The National Task Force on Early Childhood Education for Hispanics (2007) reported that schools that implement culturally relevant classroom interventions have a positive impact on the student's cognitive and social development. The following interventions are focused on academic achievement and dropout prevention for Latinos and Latino dual language learners.

Tier 1 Interventions for Latino Immigrants

Tier 1 interventions for Latino immigrants consist of English as a Second Language (ESL) courses and culturally sensitive classroom instruction. Rolstad, Mahoney, and Glass's (2005) meta-analysis of English language learner programs indicated that bilingual education yields greater results for academic achievement when compared to English-only approaches. Furthermore, transitional bilingual education programs were inferior compared to developmental bilingual education programs. These findings support previous meta-analysis findings that dual language programs have positive effects for students in all academic areas (Willig, 1985; Greene, 1998). Rolstad and colleagues (2005) acknowledged that some state policies and the federal English Acquisition Act serve as barriers to most schools seeking to improve the academic environment for Latino immigrant students. Other researchers on English language learners have indicated that bilingual educational programs coupled with culturally sensitive classroom instruction are most effective in maintaining the students at the Tier 1 level (Orosco, 2010; Klingner & Edwards, 2006).

Tier 2 Interventions for Latino Immigrants

Cheung and Slavin (2005) reviewed effective bilingual reading programs and found positive effects for students. Of the programs reviewed, many incorporated group instruction to assist students in achieving academic success. Although there is still much work to be done in developing evidence-based Tier 2 interventions (Klingner & Edwards, 2006), this review served to identify the benefits of incorporating a cultural component to classroom instruction.

Tier 3 Interventions for Latino Immigrants

Some researchers have instead focused on developing culturally sensitive school programs. For example, *Club Amigas* (Kaplan, Turner, Piotrkowski, & Silber, 2009), an evidence-based mentoring project for teenage Hispanic girls, concentrated on increasing positive attitudes toward school and motivations to go on to college by pairing them with mentors. The project further incorporated supports to assist the girls in developing their identity as Hispanics in the United States. Pretest and posttest scores revealed statistically significant improvements in how they viewed themselves as students, and qualitative results revealed that students experienced a benefit of increased learning and aspirations to continue on to college. The actual high school completion rate of the participants was not reported. However, the findings of this study support current literature that encourages schools to build culturally and linguistically sensitive intervention programs (Nesman, 2007). A similar program, *Project Wings*, an evidence-based school mental health program, was developed with an understanding that poor mental health leads to social issues such as dropping out of school and other deviant behaviors (Garcia, Pintor, Naughton, & Lindgren, 2009). The program focused on improving mental health and incorporated Zumba, sharing-circle discussions, and skill-building activities. The skill-building activities addressed such issues as acculturation, self-identity, and healthy relationships among other life aspects. This program consisted of 14 two-hour weekly sessions and was used with Latina adolescents. Pre-, mid-, and post-assessments reported improved mental health for the participants that completed the program but did not report on whether the students completed school. Achievement for Latinos through Academic Success (ALAS), although no longer in existence, was an effective evidence-based dropout prevention program for both Latino males and females that incorporated positive supports for cultural identity and encouragement for academic success for students (Fashola & Slavin, 1998). This program also incorporated the use of parent training on how to monitor and guide students in school. The high-risk non-individualized educational plan ALAS participants had a lower dropout rate when compared to non-ALAS participants.

Within an RTI framework that asserts that all children can succeed in the educational system if provided early intervention and careful monitoring of an individualized plan made up of evidence-based practices (NASDSE, 2005), Latino immigrant students have much to gain. If a culturally sensitive RTI framework is provided, careful monitoring and evaluation of the data could assist the school-based professional in determining exactly how to proceed in the best interest of the student. In addition to acquiring culturally and linguistically appropriate courses and other academic supports, the school-based professional should seek to direct the student to culturally relevant programs for all other needs. (See Appendix A for Assessment Tools.)

School-based professionals serving Latino immigrants are often faced with a difficult task that will require careful implementation of programs and services in order to assist the student. Culturally sensitive professionals or consultants could be contacted to assist school-based professionals in identifying culturally relevant programs or resources. Most culturally relevant RTI interventions have been documented as effective, but there are still many that need further evaluation. In addition, because of the complexities of the populations, school-based professionals should be prepared to meet the different sociocultural needs of the students.

Tools and Practice Examples

The RTI framework encompasses three caveats that consist of school support, progress monitoring, and diagnostics or assessment (Capone, 2011). This framework works within a three-tiered model to meet the needs of the students. A Tier 1 response for Latino immigrant students would require culturally and linguistically sensitive ESL classes and regular classroom material (Klingner & Edwards, 2006; Orosco, 2007); Tier 2 would include individualized or group supports for students that need extra academic support like peer tutoring or cooperative learning (Osher et al., 2004); and Tier 3 would provide culturally and linguistically appropriate intensive interventions for students at risk for social or behavioral problems (Capone, 2011). The third tier draws upon other supports such as after-school and in-school programs that should be monitored by the school-based professional on a behavioral action plan to track progress. The culturally sensitive RTI progress monitoring would require school-based professionals to evaluate if the overall model is working and, if not, to change it until it does (Klingner & Edwards, 2006; Orosco, 2007). By using multiple resources, the school-based professional can also effectively build a social support system for both the student and family that they otherwise do not have.

The strategies used in an RTI framework include (1) identify, (2) analyze, (3) implement, and (4) monitor and evaluate.

Identify

Identifying Latino immigrant students requires a school-based professional to be willing to employ different strategies to locate them. Sending a questionnaire home in Spanish that asks questions such as "Have you recently immigrated to the United States?" can possibly assist in locating these students. However, not all immigrants are literate in their native language, and, as pointed out before, Spanish comes in different dialects (Birman & Chan, 2008). Schools should use culturally sensitive interviewing techniques to screen incoming students for language proficiency (Valdés, 2001). Once a student has been identified and the school-based professional has assessed the unique history of the student using a model such as the Latino Dimensions of Family and Personal Identity Model, the student can be screened for other educational needs (Arredondo & Santiago-Rivera, 2000).

Analyze

Assuming that most Latino immigrant children are more fluent in Spanish, students will greatly benefit from in-school programs such as ESL. Other after-school programs that offer one-on-one tutoring or homework assistance also will serve to provide additional support to both the student and the family that may not otherwise be able to assist the child with homework. In order to identify the psychosocial needs of the child, the Center for Health and Health Care in Schools Web site offers a great list of diagnostic assessment tools available in different languages that a school-based professional can use to identify adjustment and mental health issues that may be present in the student (Birman & Chan, 2008). The consent process may prove difficult if the family is not literate, and the school-based professional should be prepared to provide alternative forms of consent beyond written consent. The National Center for Youth Law Web site is a great resource for school-based professionals looking to become familiar with the state laws and school policies regarding mental health services. Once the school-based professional has successfully dealt with these issues, resources can be located or developed, and through careful networking these same assessments can be used to monitor progress. Identifying resources for the family as well is ideal and strongly encouraged.

Implement

Once the appropriate programs and academic resources have been identified, the school-based professional should develop an individualized education plan (IEP) and an individualized family service plan. The effective school-based professional will coordinate with these programs and academic resources for the good of the student and the family. Efforts to connect the student and family to others in a similar situation will help to create an additional support system that with careful coordinating can also be evaluated for effectiveness. Team meetings with all of the student's resources will serve to open lines of communication and assist in the effective implementation of program services.

Monitor and Evaluate

The school-based professional must be diligent in monitoring the IEP. Diagnostic assessments and interviews with key resources should be conducted to ensure fidelity of treatment with the student. If any aspect of the plan is no longer working or is ineffective as demonstrated by the data collected from the assessment, then the plan should be revised and new resources should be introduced. The ultimate goal is for the student to function at his or her highest level, making a successful adjustment to life in the United States while keeping cultural strengths intact.

Case Example

The case example provided illustrates an ideal approach to working with Latino immigrant children and their families. The Montez family has recently enrolled its three children in the school district. David, age 10; Veronica, age 7; and Ruben, age 5, are enrolled at the elementary school. They are recent immigrants from Mexico and are excited to enroll their children in school for a better opportunity.

Tier 1

The school determined that the family was a Latino immigrant family at enrollment. After meeting with the family, a decision was made to place the children in an ESL program. The school-based professional also recognized the need for further supports in the classroom setting and arranged a meeting with the classroom and the ESL teacher. Both the ESL and classroom teachers had completed proper cultural sensitivity training to be able to meet the needs of children like David, Veronica, and Ruben. Regular meetings with the ESL and classroom teachers provided additional support that helped the students to adjust.

Tier 2

Veronica and Ruben were both very successful at achieving their academic milestones. David, however, had some difficulty with reading and was not making progress. The school team identified a culturally sensitive evidence-based reading program for Latino immigrant children. The necessary supports were put into place in order to provide these same services to David and other children who were also struggling to make progress. The group work and individualized lesson plans aided David in making much improvement.

Tier 3

David, Veronica, and Ruben faced new challenges when they began high school. They worked very hard to achieve good grades but didn't quite understand the college enrollment process. David wanted to drop out so he could work to help support his family, and Veronica was struggling with the idea of going on to college. In addition, the students often felt alienated by their peers and experienced a great deal of difficulty with their own cultural identity. A school-based professional that understood the difficulties unique to the students identified a culturally sensitive evidence-based academic achievement and dropout prevention program for Latino immigrant students. The students were able to gain both the academic and social support they needed in this program. All three children graduated from high school and were able to successfully enroll in college.

Resources

Web Sites

Center for Health and Health Care in Schools: http://www.healthinschools.org/~/media/Images/IssueBrief1.ashx

Familias Unidas: http://www.familias-unidas.org/index.htm

Let's Go Learn: www.letsgolearn.com/

The National Center for Youth Law: http://www.youthlaw.org/

The National Council of La Raza: www.nclr.org/

The National Task Force on Early Childhood Education for Hispanics: ecehispanic.org/

40 Developmental Assets: www.search-institute.org/Assets

National Center for Culturally Responsive Educational Systems (NCCREST): http://www.nccrest.org/

National Center on Response to Intervention (RTI for English Learners): http://www.rti4success.org/webinars/video/893

Response to Intervention Action Network: http://www.rtinetwork.org/learn/diversity

References

Andrés-Hyman, R. C., Ortiz, J., Anez, L. M., Paris, M., & Davidson, L. (2006). Culture and clinical practice: Recommendations for working with Puerto Ricans and other Latinas (os) in the United States. *Professional Psychology: Research and Practice*, *37*(6): 694–701.

Arredondo, P., & Glauner, T. (1992). *Personal dimensions of identity model.* Boston, MA: Empowerment Workshops.

Arredondo, P., & Santiago-Rivera, A. (2000). *Latino dimensions of personal identity* (adapted from Personal Dimensions of Identity Model). Unpublished manuscript.

Artiles, A. J., Rueda, R., Salazar, J., & Higareda, I. (2005). Within-group diversity in minority disproportionate representation: English language learners in urban school districts. *Exceptional Children*, *71*, 283–300.

Auerbach, S. (2006). "If the student is good, let him fly": Moral support for college among Latino immigrant parents. *Journal of Latinos & Education*, *5*(4), 275–292. doi:10.1207/s1532771xjle0504_4

Battin-Pearson, S., Abbott, R. D., Hill, K. G., Catalano, R. F., Hawkins, J. D., & Newcomb, M. D. (2000). Predictors of early high school dropout: A test of five theories. *Journal of Educational Psychology*, *92*, 568–582.

Birman, D., & Chan, W. Y. (2008, May). *Screening and assessing immigrant and refugee youth in school-based mental health program.* Retrieved from Center for Health and Health Care in Schools Web site: http://www.healthinschools.org/~/media/Images/IssueBrief1.ashx

Capone, R. (2011). *How to implement Response to Intervention (RTI) in general and with Let's Go Learn.* Retrieved from Let's Go Learn Web site: http://www.letsgolearn.com/virtual_tours/view/how_to_implement_response_to_intervention_rti_in_general_and_with_lets_go_l/

Carey, G., & Manuppelli, L. (2000). Culture class or not? In M. T. Flores & G. Carey (Eds.), *Family therapy with Hispanics: Toward appreciating diversity* (pp. 79–123). Boston, MA: Allyn & Bacon.

Cheung, A., & Slavin, R. (2005). Effective reading programs for English language learners and other language-minority students. *Bilingual Research Journal*, *29*(2), 241–267.

Cuéllar, I., Arnold, B., & Maldonado, R. (1995). Acculturation Rating Scale for Mexican Americans-II: A revision of the original ARSMA Scale. *Hispanic Journal of Behavioral Sciences*, *17*(3), 275–304. doi: 10.1177/07399863950173001

Cuellar, I., Harris, L. C., & Jasso, R. (1980). An acculturation scale for Mexican American normal and clinical populations. *Hispanic Journal Of Behavioral Sciences*, *2*(3), 199–217.

Dettlaff, A. J., & Rycraft, J. R. (2006). The impact of migration and acculturation on Latino children and families: Implications for child welfare practice. *Protecting Children*, *21*(2), 6–21.

Ennis, S. R., Rios-Vargas, M., & Albert, N. G. (2011). *The Hispanic population: 2010: 2010 Census briefs.*

Retrieved from U.S. Census Bureau Web site: www.census.gov/prod/cen2010/briefs/c2010br-04.pdf

Fashola, O., & Slavin, R. (1998). Effective dropout prevention and college attendance programs for students placed at risk. *Journal of Education for Students Placed At Risk*, *3*(2), 159–183.

Flanagan, D., Alfonso, V., Primavera, L., Povall, L., & Deirdre, H. (1996). Convergent validity of the BASC and SSRS: Implications for social skills assessment. *Psychology in the Schools*, *33*(1), 13–23.

Fortuny, K., Capps, R., Simms, M., & Chaudry, A. (2009). *Children of immigrants: National and state characteristics.* Retrieved from Urban Institute Web site: http://www.urban.org/publications/411939.html

Franco, J. N. (1983). An acculturation scale for Mexican-American children. *Journal Of General Psychology*, *108*(2), 175–181. doi: 10.1080/00221309.1983.9711491

Fry, R., & Passel, J. S. (2009). *Latino children: A majority are U.S.-born offspring of immigrants.* Retrieved from Pew Hispanic Center Web site: http://pewhispanic.org/files/reports/110.pdf

Garcia, C., Pintor, J. K., Naughton, S., & Lindgren, S. (2009, July). *Development of a coping intervention for Latina adolescents: Exploring feasibility challenges and successes.* PowerPoint lecture presented at the 20th International Nursing Research Congress on evidence-based practice, Vancouver, British Columbia.

Goldenberg, C., & Gallimore, R. (1995). Immigrant Latino parents' values and beliefs about their children's education: Continuities and discontinuities across cultures and generations. In P. R. Pintrich & M. Maehr (Eds.), *Advances in motivation and achievement: Culture, ethnicity, and motivation* (Vol. 9, pp. 183–228). Greenwich, CT: JAI Press.

Goodman, M. (2004). Balkan children and families. In R. Fong (Ed.), *Culturally competent practice with immigrant and refugee children and families* (pp. 274–288). New York, NY: Guilford Press.

Greene, J. P. (1998). *A meta-analysis of the effectiveness of bilingual education.* Claremont, CA: Thomas Rivera Policy Institute.

Guilamo-Ramos, V., Dittus, P., Jaccard, J., Johansson, M., Bouris, A., & Acosta, N. (2007). Parenting practices among Dominican and Puerto Rican mothers. *Social Work*, *52*, 17–30.

Hill, N., & Torres, K. (2010). Negotiating the American dream: The paradox of aspirations and achievement among Latino students and engagement between their families and schools. *Journal of Social Issues*, *66*(1), 95–112.

Kaplan, C., Turner, S., Piotrkowski, C., & Silber, E. (2009). *Club Amigas*: A promising response to the needs of adolescent Latinas. *Child & Family Social Work*, *14*, 213–221.

Klingner, J., & Edwards, P. (2006). New directions in research: Cultural considerations with Response to Intervention models. *Reading Research Quarterly*, *41*(1), 108–117.

Lee, J., Grigg, W., & Donahue, P. (2007). *The nation's report card: Reading 2007* (NCES 2007–496). Washington, DC: National Center for Education Statistics, Institute of Education Sciences, U.S. Department of Education.

Lewis, A. (2001). *Add it up: Using research to improve education for low-income and minority students.* Washington, DC: Poverty and Race Research Action Council.

Lopez-Baez, S. (1999). Marianismo. In J. S. Mio, J. E. Trimble, P. Arredondo, H. E. Cheatham, & D. Sue (Eds.), *Key words in multicultural interventions: A dictionary* (p. 183). Wesport, CT: Greenwood.

Marin, G. (1993). Influence of acculturation on familialism and self-identification among Hispanics. In M. E. Bernal & G. P. Knight (Eds.), *Ethnic identity: Formation and transmission among Hispanics and other minorities* (pp. 181–196). Albany, NY: SUNY Press.

Moon, S. S., Kang, S., & An, S. (2009). Predictors of immigrant children's school achievement: A comparative study. *Journal of Research in Childhood Education*, *23*, 278–289.

Morales, E. (1996). Gender roles among Latino gay and bisexual men: Implications for family and couple relationships. In J. Laird & R. J. Green (Eds.), *Lesbians and gays in couples and families: A handbook for therapists* (pp. 272–297). San Francisco: Jossey-Bass.

National Association of State Directors of Special Education. (2005). *Response to Intervention: Policy considerations and implementation.* Retrieved from NASDSE Web site: http://www.nasdse.org/Projects/ResponsetoInterventionRtIProject/tabid/411/Default.aspx

National Research Council. (2002). *Minority students in special and gifted education.* Washington, DC: National Academies Press.

National Task Force on Early Childhood Education for Hispanics. (2007). *Para nuestros ninos: Expanding and improving early education for Hispanics.* Retrieved from National Task Force on Early Childhood Education for Hispanics Web site: http://ecehispanic.org/

Nesman, T. (2007). A participatory study of school dropout and behavioral health of Latino adolescents. *The Journal of Behavioral Health Services & Research*, *34*(4), 414–430.

Negroni-Rodriguez, L., & Morales, J. 2001. Individual and families assessment skills with Latino/Hispanic Americans. In R. Fong & S. Furuto (Eds.), *Culturally competent practice: Skills, interventions, and evaluation* (pp. 132–146). Boston: Allyn & Bacon.

Nevarez, C., & Rico, T. (2007). *Latino education: A synthesis of recurring recommendations and solutions in P-16 education.* The College Board. Retrieved from http://www.collegeboard.com/prod_downloads/prof/counselors/Latino-Education-A-Synthesis.pdf

Orosco, M. (2010). A sociocultural examination of Response to Intervention with Latino English language learners. *Theory Into Practice*, *49*, 265–272.

Orosco, M. J. (2007). *Response to intervention with Latino English language learners: A school-based case study.* (Doctoral dissertation, University of Colorado at

Boulder). Retrieved from ProQuest Dissertations and Theses. (Accession Order No. CSA, LLC 072699).

Orosco, M. J., Schonewise, E. A., de Onis, C., Klingner, J. K., & Hoover, J. J. (2008). Distinguishing between language acquisition and learning disabilities among English language learners: Background information. In J. K. Klingner, J. J. Hoover, & L. Baca (Eds.), *English language learners who struggle with reading: Language acquisition or learning disabilities?* (pp. 5–16). Thousand Oaks, CA: Corwin Press.

Osher, D., Cartledge, G., Oswald, D., Sutherland, K., Artiles, A., & Coutinho, M. (2004). Cultural and linguistic competency and disproportionate representation. In R. Rutherford, M. Quinn, & S. Mathur (Eds.), *Handbook of research in emotional and behavioral disorders* (pp. 54–77). New York, NY: Guilford Press.

Osher, T. W., & Osher, D. (2002). The paradigm shift to true collaboration with families. *Journal of Child and Family Studies, 11*(1), 47–60.

Padilla, R. V. (2005). Latino/a Education in the 21st Century. In P. Pedraza & M. Rivera (Eds.), *Latino education: An agenda for community action research* (pp. 403–423). Mahwah, NJ US: Lawrence Erlbaum Associates Publishers.

Padilla, A. M., & Perez, W. (2003). Acculturation, social identity, and social cognition: A new perspective. *Hispanic Journal of Behavioral Sciences, 25*, 35–55.

Quinones-Mayo, Y., & Dempsey, P. (2005). Finding the bicultural balance: Immigrant Latino mothers raising "American" adolescents. *Child Welfare, 5*, 649–667.

Response to intervention network. (2011). Retrieved August 28, 2011, from http://www.rtinetwork.org/

Rolstad, K., Mahoney, K., & Glass, G. (2005). The big picture: A meta-analysis of program effectiveness research on English language learners. *Educational Policy, 19*(4), 572–594.

Sabogal, F., Marín, G., Otero-Sabogal, R., & Marín, B. V. (1987). Hispanic familism and acculturation: What changes and what doesn't?. *Hispanic Journal of Behavioral Sciences, 9*(4), 397–412. doi: 10.1177/07399863870094003

Santiago, D. A., & Brown, S. E. (2004). What works for Latino students. Retrieved, August, 2011, from http://www.edexcelencia.org/system/files/whatworks2Ed-new3.pdf

Santiago-Rivera, A., Arredondo, P., & Gallardo-Cooper, M. (2002). *Counseling Latinos and la familia: A practical guide.* Thousand Oaks, CA: Sage.

Shin, H. J. (2004). *Parental involvement and its influence on children's school performance: A comparative study between Asian (Chinese and Koreans) Americans and Mexican Americans* (Unpublished doctoral dissertation). Columbia University, New York.

Simoni, J. M., & Perez, L. (1995). Latinos and mutual support groups: A case for considering culture. *American Journal Of Orthopsychiatry, 65*(3), 440.

Smokowski, P. R., Rose, R., & Bacallao, M. L. (2008). Acculturation and Latino family processes: How cultural involvement, biculturalism, and acculturation gaps influence family dynamics. *Family Relations, 57*(3), 295–308. doi: 10.1111/j.1741-3729.2008. 00501.x

Solis, J. (2003). Re-thinking illegality as a violence against, not by Mexican immigrants, children, and youth. *Journal of Social Issues, 59*, 15–31.

Steidel, A., & Contreras, J. M. (2003). A new familism scale for use with Latino populations. *Hispanic Journal of Behavioral Sciences, 25*(3), 312–330. doi: 10.1177/0739986303256912

Stein, B. D., Jaycox, L. H., Kataoka, S. H., Wong, M., Tu, W., Elliott, M. N., & Fink, A. (2003). A mental health intervention for schoolchildren exposed to violence: A randomized controlled trial. *JAMA: Journal of the American Medical Association, 290*(5), 603–611. doi: 10.1001/jama.290.5.603

Steinberg, A., Brymer, M., Decker, K., & Pynoos, R. (2004). The University of California at Los Angeles post-traumatic stress disorder reaction index. *Current Psychiatry Reports, 6*(2), 96–100.

Suarez-Orozco, C., & Suarez-Orozco, M. (1995). *Transformations: Migration, family life, and achievement motivation among Latino adolescents.* Stanford, CA: Stanford University Press.

Suh, S., Suh, J., & Houston, I. (2007). Predictors of categorical at-risk high school dropouts. *Journal of Counseling and Development, 85*, 196–203.

Szapocznik, J., Scopetta, M.A., Kurtines, W., & Aranalde, M. D. (1978). Theory and measurement of acculturation. *Revista Interamericana De Psicología, 12*(2), 113–130.

Tazi, Z. (2004). Ecuadorian and Colombian children and families. In R. Fong (Ed.), *Culturally competent practice with immigrant and refugee children and families* (pp. 233–252). New York, NY: Guilford Press.

Tenenbaum, H. R., & Ruck, M. D. (2007). Are teachers' expectations different for racial minority than for European American students? A meta-analysis. *Journal of Educational Psychology, 99*, 253–273.

Thomas, T. N. (1992). Psychoeducational adjustment of English-speaking Caribbean and Central American immigrant children in the United States. *School Psychology Review, 21*, 566–576.

Thorn, A. R., & Contreras, S. (December, 2005). Counseling Latino immigrants in middle school. *Professional School Counseling, 9*(2), 167–170.

Tropp, L. R., Erkut, S., Coll, C., Alarcón, O., & García, H. (1999). Psychological acculturation development of a new measure for Puerto Ricans on the U.S. mainland. *Educational and Psychological Measurement, 59*(2), 351–367. doi: 10.1177/00131649921969794

U.S. Census Bureau. (2011a, August). *Facts for features: Hispanic heritage month 2011.* Retrieved from http://www.census.gov/newsroom/releases/archives/facts_for_features_special_editions/cb10-ff17.html

U.S. Census Bureau. (2011b, September). *Education: Elementary and secondary education: Completions and dropouts.*

Retrieved from http://www.census.gov/compendia/statab/cats/education/elementary_and_secondary_education_completions_and_dropouts.html

U.S. Census Bureau. (2011c, August). *School enrollment.* Retrieved from http://www.census.gov/hhes/school/data/cps/2009/tables.html

Valdés, G. (1996). *Con respeto: Bridging the distances between culturally diverse families and schools: An ethnographic portrait.* New York: Teachers College Press.

Valdés, G. (2001). *Learning and not learning English: Latino students in American schools.* New York, NY/London, England: Teacher College Press.

Willig, A. C. (1985). A meta-analysis of selected studies on the effectiveness of bilingual education. *Review of Educational Research*, *55*(3), 269–318.

Zuñiga, M. E. (1992). Using metaphors in therapy: Dichos and Latino clients. *Social Work*, *37*(1), 55–60.

Appendix

Assessment Tools (Available in Spanish)

Type of Measure	*Name of Scale*	*Informant/Reporter*	*Used with*
Acculturation Scale for Mexican Americans	Acculturation Scale for Mexican Americans (ARSMA)	Self-report or semi-structured interview	Mexican and Mexican-American population (Cuellar, Harris, & Jasso, 1980)
	Acculturation Scale for Mexican Americans (ARSMAII)	Self-report or semi-structured interview	Mexican and Mexican-American population (Cuellar, Arnold, & Maldonado, 1995)
	Children's Acculturation Scale	Youth self-report or semi-structured interview	Mexican children (Franco, 1983)
Acculturation Scale for Puerto Ricans	Psychological Acculturation Scale (PAS)	Self-report or semi-structured interview	Puerto Rican immigrant population (Tropp, et al., 1999)
Acculturation Scale for Cubans	Behavioral Acculturation Scale	Self-report or semi-structured interview	Cuban immigrant population (Szapcoznik, Scopetta, Kurtines, & Arnalde, 1978)
Acculturation Scale for Latinos	Acculturation Scale	Self-report or semi-structured interview	Mexicans, Cubans, Puerto Ricans and Central Americans (Sabogal, Marín, Otero-Sabogal, Perez-Stable, & Marin, 1987)
Adaptive and Maladaptive Behaviors, Thoughts, and Emotions	Behavioral Assessment System for Children (BASC)	Teacher and parent report; youth self-report	Latino kindergarten children (Flanagan et al., 1996)
Community Violence	34-Item Life Events Scale (used as a screener for cognitive-behavioral intervention for trauma in schools)	Self-report	Latino immigrants (Stein et al., 2003)
Attitudinal Familism	Familism Scale	Self-report	Less acculturated Latinos (Steidel, & Contreras, 2003)
Post-Traumatic Stress Disorder (PTSD) Symptoms	UCLA PTSD Reaction Index (PTSDRI)	Youth self-report; parent version also available	Hispanic adolescents (Steinberg et al., 2004).

CHAPTER 56

Home Visiting

Essential Guidelines for Home Visits and Engaging With Families

Barbara Hanna Wasik ■ Sheena Berry ■ Adrienne Villagomez ■ Gary L. Shaffer ■ Priya Mudholkar

Visiting with people in their homes is one of the most humane and family-centered approaches to service delivery in our society. Home visiting is uniquely supportive of family life, bringing services to families, providing services in a familiar setting, and reducing obstacles to services.

—Wasik & Bryant, 2001

Getting Started

Home visiting has a long history in education, family and child welfare, and physical and mental health services (Hancock & Pelton, 1989; Levine & Levine, 1970; Oppenheimer, 1925; Richmond, 1899). Home visits are important for serving children and youth from birth to high school and in addressing issues ranging from programs for preschool children through school-system concerns. Educational organizations rely on home visits to address a wide range of issues related to student behaviors, including attendance, discipline, physical or mental challenges, drug or alcohol abuse, depression, or antisocial activities. Home visits also focus on other student characteristics relating to school performance, such as risk for school failure among preschool children or low academic achievement among school-age children.

Why this enduring interest in and reliance on home visiting? Many believe that home visits help to break down barriers between professionals and families, reduce obstacles to services, and provide opportunities to respond to individual family needs. Minuchin and colleagues (Minuchin, Colapinto, & Minuchin, 1998) have written that, through home visiting, "the aura of authority that characterizes an official setting is muted and the reality of the family's life environment is acknowledged" (p. 204). By visiting in the home, we can gain an appreciation of the family's needs. Through our presence in the family's community, we can gain knowledge about the local culture, values, and languages. We also gain unique opportunities for engaging families. Regardless of the impetus for the home visit, home visitors need not only general knowledge and skills related to home visiting (including a repertoire of appropriate clinical/interviewing skills) but also specific knowledge and skills related to the particular focus of the visit.

Today, home visiting remains a mainstay of varied services, including early childhood intervention; nursing; protective services; and school social work. Young children and their parents are served through an extensive set of national programs, such as the Parents as Teachers, Healthy Families America, Nurse-Family Partnership, Home Instruction for Parents of Preschool Youngsters, and Early Head Start programs. In addition, hundreds of local parent support programs have included home-visiting strategies (Catalano, Berglund, Ryan, Lonczak, & Hawkins, 2002; Fraser, Day, Galinsky, Hodges, & Smokowki, 2004; Greenberg, Domitrovich, & Bumbarger, 2001). Some of these programs have been intensely researched and tested; others have been implemented with little research or empirical evidence to guide their efforts. Some programs employ professionals as home visitors while others employ paraprofessionals. Other differences among these programs include the goals of the home visit, the procedures and materials used, the duration and intensity of the visits, and whether participation is voluntary.

In this chapter, we present information relevant for school social workers and others who provide services to school-age students and their families. We begin with information on the prevalence of home visiting and a brief review of program outcomes. We then include principles for home visiting, specific information for preparing for a home visit, and a tool for guiding the actual home visit. We present information on Response to Intervention (RTI), noting how home visiting can complement a school's RTI emphasis. Updated resources are included to illustrate the various types of programs, purposes, and the outcomes of home visitation.

What We Know

Academic Success

As advocates for children's social and academic success, we recognize the need to foster close home-school relationships, helping families and students feel welcomed and appreciated at school. Research has shown a relation between parent involvement in their children's education and the child's academic outcomes. Home visitors can help families develop a closer connection with the schools and understand school expectations. During the preschool years, home visitors can promote parenting skills, especially those that relate to children's early language and literacy development. Home visitors can help families to access resources for early identification of developmental disabilities or delays. For school-age children, home visitors can help parents understand how their child is performing in school and ways the family can support the child's schoolwork. Home visitors can help coordinate interventions between the home and school. Home visiting can be instrumental in addressing low academic performance or a drop in school attendance, both of which are risk factors for poor social adjustment and mental health outcomes. During adolescence, students face additional risk factors including early pregnancy, substance abuse, and delinquency. Home visiting has demonstrated positive outcomes in addressing these risk factors, thus increasing positive mental health outcomes. Table 56.1 lists a range of home visiting programs serving children from infancy to late adolescence and their families to help improve the risk factors for poor mental health and social well-being.

Program Effectiveness

Since the 1990s, many authors have addressed the effectiveness of home visiting. They have both reviewed the existing research and conducted meta-analyses of these studies. The reviews have shown mixed results (Harding, Galano, Martin, Huntington, & Schellenbach, 2007; Greenberg, Domitrovich, & Bumbarger, 2001; Guterman, 2000; Sweet & Appelbaum, 2004). Other reviews of studies on national programs that focused on increasing parenting skills to assure children's school readiness have also obtained inconsistent findings (Gomby,2005; Astuto & Allen, 2009). The most consistently positive outcomes have come from the Nurse-Family Partnership and its earlier models (Olds, Hill, O'Brien, Racine, & Moritz, 2003), but several specific models have been identified through an extensive review process as meeting the expectations for evidenced-based interventions for young children and many of these are being implmemented by states to address a range of child and maternal concerns. (See http://homvee.acf.hhs.gov/ for a list and review of these programs.)

Two home-visiting programs are illustrative of those that have direct relevance for mental health issues. One of these is the work of Lutzker and his colleagues, who developed and researched an ecobehavioral approach to address adult and child neglect, finding strong support for reducing parental behaviors associated with abuse and neglect (Edwards & Lutzker, 2008). A second noteworthy example of an effective home-visiting program is multisystemic therapy for serious juvenile delinquents, which draws from several theories, including ecological theory, family systems theory, behavioral theory, and cognitive-behavioral theory. This home-visiting program has resulted in positive results, such as improved family functioning, less adolescent psychiatric symptoms, decrease in substance abuse and substance use, and decreased long-term rates of re-arrest (Henggeler, 2002).

Concern with the absence of positive outcome data in some experimental studies has led to detailed analyses of process and outcome data. One exemplary analysis of Hawaii's Healthy Start program questions the adequacy of the preparation and training of the home visitors (Duggan et al., 2004). In examining why child and parent outcomes were not strong, researchers found that

Table 56.1 Home-Visiting Programs

Resource	*Description*	*Selected Outcomes*	*Contact*
Parents as Teachers	Early childhood parent education and family support program. Focus: 0–5 years	Parents engage in language and literacy-promoting behaviors; children score high on kindergarten readiness tests	Parents as Teachers National Center www.patnc.org
First Step to Success	Goal is to divert antisocial behavior in kindergarteners. Three components: universal screening, school intervention, and home intervention. Being introduced to Head Start children and families. Focus: kindergarteners	Decrease in aggression; increase in adaptive behavior and academic achievement	Michelle Woodbridge, Ph.D. Study Director SRI International Ph: (650) 859–6923, Fax: (650) 859–5258 E-mail: michelle.woodbridge@sri.com
Early Risers: Skills for Success	The program is specifically aimed at children who display early aggressive, disruptive, and/or nonconformist behaviors. Focus: 6–10 years	Improvement in academic achievement and social skills; decreased behavior problems	Gerald J. August, Ph.D. University of Minnesota F256/2B West 2450 Riverside Avenue Minneapolis, MN 55454–1495 Phone: (612) 273–9711 Fax: (612) 273–9779 Email: augus001@tc.umn.edu
Multisystemic Therapy	Family-oriented family therapy, home-based. Focus: violent, substance-abusing youth 12–17 years	Cost-efficient reduction in substance use and antisocial behavior in serious, chronic, juvenile offenders	Scott W. Henggeler, Ph.D. Family Services Research Center, Medical University of South Carolina Henggesw@musc.edu
Teacher Home Visit	Raise academic achievement by increasing communication between parents and teachers. Focus: grades pre-K through 12th	Improvement in academic achievement; improvement in behavior and attitudes toward school; increase school involvement in both the child and parent	Karen Kalish Founder and Executive Director Phone: (314)-727–2727 Email: karenkalish@gmail.com Program Web site: http://www.teacherhomevisit.org/

(continued)

Table 56.1 (*Continued*)

Resource	*Description*	*Selected Outcomes*	*Contact*
Triple P	Multilevel parent and family support program. Focus: birth to age 16	Prevent child behavioral, emotional and developmental issues; encourage safe and nurturing environments; enhance parenting skills	Triple P America PO Box 12755 Columbia, SC 29211 Telephone: (803) 451.2278 Fax: (803) 451.2277 Email: contact.us@triplep.net Web site: http://www.triplep-america.com/
Family Check-Up	Provides prevention and treatment services to families at risk for low-income, child conduct problems, mental health issues, academic failure, and substance abuse. Focus: Ages 2 to 18	Enhance parenting skills and encourage parent involvement; improve maternal depression; improve child behavior, academic success, and internalizing problems	University of Oregon Child and Family Center 195 W. 12th Ave. Eugene, OR 97401 Phone: 541–346–4805 Fax: 541–346–4858

Source: U.S. Department of Health and Human Services, Substance Abuse and Mental Health Services Administration and the Administration for Children & Families; Program Web sites.

paraprofessional home visitors were not identifying or were failing to address several key predictors of abuse and neglect: partner violence, substance abuse, and parental depression.

These findings have important implications for school social workers and others who provide home-visiting services, as they provide compelling evidence of the need to assure that visitors are well trained and have the knowledge and skills essential to address the goals and objects of the program. Home visitors need to be thoroughly acquainted with the basics of visiting, equipped with strong clinical and helping skills, and knowledgeable of the skills specific to the intervention that is being implemented. Furthermore, home visitors need access to professional development and ongoing supervision in order to reflect on and improve the practice. These recommendations are consistent with an emerging literature on implementation science (Fixsen, Blasé, Duda, Naoom, & Van Dyke, 2010).

What We Can Do

Home-Visiting Principles

In this section, we present principles that help to focus the work of the home visitor, information for planning the home visit, and a framework for the home visit itself. We focus on general strategies for home visits (such as the need to engage the family in a working relationship), rather than specific interventions for particular family needs.

Principles

First, as illustrated in table 56.2, we identify principles that help to structure the home visit. These principles help home visitors to recognize that they are guests in the family's home and that they need to work with the family in a collaborative and flexible manner, provide individualized services, and help families to obtain resources that can help sustain changes over time.

Planning for the Home Visit

Preparing for a home visit may take more time than preparing to see a parent or family in an office or school setting because you must not only prepare for the content of the meeting and learn about the family but also learn about the community surrounding the home in order to gain relevant information for visiting the family. A considerable amount of preparation is essential if you have not previously visited with the family, or in

Table 56.2 Home-Visiting Principles

- Home visitors should view the family as a social system where changes in one individual in the family can influence other family members as well as the overall functioning of the family.
- Home-based interventions should be individualized, whether focused on a specific family member or the entire family.
- Home visitors can best conceptualize their helping relationship as a collaboration between the home visitor and the family members, which builds on the family's strengths.
- Home visitors must be flexible and responsive to the immediate needs of families as well as to their long-term goals.
- Home visitors need to continually evaluate the family's strengths, limitations, and progress and use this knowledge to modify interventions as necessary.
- Home visitors need to be able to encourage effective coping and problem-solving skills.
- Home visitors should remain attentive to the family's future needs and help the members consider ways that newly acquired skills or attitudes might be generalized to future situations.
- Home visitors need to link the family with natural helping systems in the community, resources that can support the family after services are terminated (e.g., extended family members, significant others, neighbors, clubs, and faith organizations).

Source: Adapted from Wasik, B. H., & Bryant, D. M. (2001). *Home visiting: Procedures for helping families* (2nd ed.). Thousand Oaks, CA: Sage.

the neighborhood. Specific preparation activities are listed next.

Learn About the Family and Its Culture

What is the composition of the family? Are supportive relatives or friends nearby? When are family members most likely to be home? Are there special considerations involved in visiting with this family? Is this a voluntary or mandated visit? If your organization or school has provided services to this family before, what knowledge can be shared with you? Such information could include which family members are most supportive for the visit or whether any difficulties have been experienced before.

As the United States is experiencing a rapid growth in its immigrant population, it is essential for home visitors to be knowledgeable and sensitive to the cultural beliefs and values of the families they serve. Communities have often changed dramatically during the past 10 to 15 years, and former expectations for schools are no longer relevant regarding the characteristics of the families they serve. Latino families, for example, have a strong cultural tradition that includes *familismo*, a Latino term referring to the value of family involvement in raising children. The Latino family also values *bien educado*, the expectations that the family will raise a child to be well-behaved and respectful. Understanding these values will help schools in their interactions with families. By contrast, the Latino family might not feel comfortable interacting with the schools, in part because they hold the teacher in high respect and will not be comfortable questioning the teacher's actions. This hesitancy is not a reflection of lack of interest; Latino families value education, but schools need to reach out with more intensity to make these parents feel welcome and their views valued. Home visitors can play a valuable role by seeking out parents, going into their homes and letting the families see that the school values the input of the parents and seeks their involvement. Similar knowledge is important for other cultural and ethnic groups, as well as families of different income levels. As the communities and schools in the United States continue to become more diverse, a focus on understanding family values and cultures will continue to be significant goals for schools.

Review the Purpose of the Visit

Reflect on the goals and purposes of the visit. Think through what you hope to accomplish on the visit and what steps you think might be necessary to accomplish the goals. Determine what materials you might need for the visit, such as school forms or records, parenting materials, or referral information. Ask yourself the following questions: If this is not the first visit, did you leave any adult or student informational materials during your last visit? Did you expect any tasks to be completed between the last visit and this one?

Remember, both general and specific knowledge and skills are essential for effective home visiting. Ask yourself what specific skills and competencies are needed for this visit. For example, does a parent need to have an interpretation of a psychological report? Should the school nurse go on this home visit with you? Do you need to address the student's low school achievement? Would it be advantageous for the student's teacher to be on this visit? Did you obtain any data (possibly data from related to the RTI assessments) at the last visit that need to be considered? Is there a specific intervention protocol to be followed for this visit?

Set the Time

Make contact with the family in advance to confirm the date and time for the visit. If this time is set up more than a few days in advance, reconfirm the day and time before the visit, if possible. This task may be difficult as families may not have phones or may be unwilling to share contact information.

Learn the Characteristics of the Neighborhood

Learn how to get to the home. If necessary, make a trial trip to the home to assure that you know the location. Have a map of the community and the neighborhood available and use an online travel direction program to assist you in your preparations.

Consider Personal Safety

In today's society, safety issues can occur in any neighborhood and, as many school social workers recognize, home visits can be potentially dangerous situations (Astor, Behre, Wallace, & Fravil, 1998). Consequently, home visitors should attend to basic personal safety issues. Having a cell phone that can be used to make quick contact with others is prudent behavior, as is letting another responsible person know when and where you will be visiting and when you are expected back. Decide if the safety concerns call for you to visit during the day or with a coworker. In some instances, you may benefit from using the school resource officer as an escort (Wasik & Coleman, 2004).

Tools for Conducting the Home Visit

The framework we present here as a tool for home visitors has relevance across home visiting for many purposes related to working with children, youth, and their families (Wasik & Sparling, 1998). Each topic presented in Table 56.3 identifies one aspect of the home visit. Reviewing each of these aspects before making a home visit will help assure that you have thoroughly thought through the overall structure of the home visit as well as made considerations for the specific visit. Reflecting on this set of items after the home visit can help you to evaluate your actions in the home and to learn from the visit. Additional detailed information appears in Wasik and Sparling (1998).

In addition to the structure provided in the table, good home visits happen when the home visitor employs strong helping skills. School social workers and other mental health counselors are introduced to these skills during their training, but it is helpful to identify list those that are especially important for home visits (see Table 56.4). In essence, you want to put the family at ease, be respectful and nonjudgmental, and use procedures that engage the family and help them to make progress toward their own goals.

The clinical skills listed in Table 56.4 are important for engaging with families and helping them to accept and address concerns. Home visitors can also benefit by using a structure, such as a problem-solving strategy, to guide their interactions related to specific concerns or issues (see Table 56.5). This strategy helps home visitors in their interactions with a family by clarifying the status or progress made in the problem-solving process and what is needed to move forward. Using a problem-solving strategy can provide greater focus to the home visit and more clarity to the concerns being addressed. A strategy such as this is especially helpful when you are not using a programmed or scripted intervention. Additional information on the use of this problem-solving strategy can be found in Wasik and Bryant (2001).

Applying Interventions within a Response to Intervention Framework

Home visiting services are supported by the Response to Intervention (RTI) model in several ways. As the reader knows, RTI provides services

Table 56.3 Aspects of Home Visits

	Visitor's Actions and Responsibilities
Greeting and engagement	Greet family members warmly and establish rapport
	Discuss purpose of home visit
Assessment of current family/child status	Ask about changes since last visit. Discuss:
	• current status of child or youth and parent/family
	• family needs and resources
Child/adolescent focus	Discuss goals/objectives for the child or adolescent Inquire about recent activities or services
	Jointly plan with family for any new activities or interventions
	Describe fully any new activities or interventions Assure that family understands
Parent–child focus	Discuss specific parent concerns regarding child/adolescent
	Help parent resolve difficulties in parent–child relationships
	Jointly plan with family for any new activities or interventions
	Assure that the family understands
Family focus	Respond appropriately to family culture, practices, and beliefs
	Encourage participation of family members as appropriate
	Discuss family social support network as needed
Health/safety	Identify/respond to health issues
	Make referrals as appropriate
Parent coping and problem solving	Use effective problem-solving strategies
	Encourage parents to clarify concerns and problems
	Help parents develop strategies and follow through
Case management and coordination	Discuss other services
	Discuss any coordination issues
	Make referrals as appropriate
Closure and planning for next steps	Recap main points of visit
	Discuss specific goals of coming weeks
	Provide
	• time for parent/family input
	• encouragement for next steps
	Arrange for next meeting

Table 56.4 Clinical Interviewing Skills

Visitor communicates warmth and caring.
Visitor conveys empathy.
Visitor puts parent/family at ease.
Visitor uses a collaborative manner.
Visitor individualizes services.
Visitor listens attentively.
Visitor is reflective and thoughtful.
Visitor is appropriately directive.
Visitor questions/probes as needed.
Visitor clarifies or restates client goals or needs.
Visitor provides support and encouragement.
Visitor compliments parents and students on strengths or positive activities.
Visitor is appropriately responsive to parent or student emotions.
Visitor uses appropriate clinical techniques.

at several levels, beginning at the universal services in Tier 1 to increased support in Tiers 2 and 3. Home visiting can also be provided universally and then become tailored to the needs of individual children and families, and can be coordinated with the school's RTI efforts. Additionally, home visiting is supported by the RTI model's ecological perspective, viewing the child as a whole by taking into consideration the many ecological systems, including the home and community, in which they interact. Finally, RTI can improve home visiting services by promoting data-informed decision making within the home visiting process. These three points are discussed next.

Tiered Services

Compared to the traditional service model in schools, RTI can facilitate a collaborative relationship between families and schools by providing universal home visiting services at the beginning and end of each academic school year from kindergarten through sixth grade, and possibly once a year from then through high school. As Tier 1 is a universal service for the school population, all families should be invited to receive home visits to help establish a strong, trusting relationship between home and school. Then, based on data collected through both home visits and school performance, home visits will increase based on need, matching Tiers 2 and 3. Though some may think home visits are not relevant for adolescents, creating stronger school-family relationships may in fact help students remain in school and perform better academically. Family involvement has been shown to correlate with better attendance, higher grades, more positive attitudes and behaviors, and higher graduation rates and enrollment in higher education for adolescents (Deslandes &

Table 56.5 Problem-Solving Strategy

1. *Problem definition:* describing a problem situation (a situation is defined as a problem when its resolution is not automatic)
2. *Goal selection:* describing what a person wants to happen
3. *Generation of solutions:* identifying a number of alternative responses that may address a problem or reach a goal
4. *Consideration of consequences:* identifying the positive and negative consequences of any solution in relation to time; money; personal, emotional, and social effects; immediate and long-term effects
5. *Decision making:* weighing the proposed solutions and consequences and appropriately determining which one is best for the individual at the time (decision making includes consideration of a person's priorities and values)
6. *Implementation:* carrying out those actions called for by the decision
7. *Evaluation:* reviewing the outcome to determine whether it met the person's goals

Bertrand, 2005; National Association of School Psychologists, 2002.)

Ecological Perspective

RTI shares the same ecological perspective as the home visiting approach to supporting children's development. Home visiting is a useful tool for viewing the child as a part of a family and gaining a better understanding of that interaction and the influence it may have on the child's academic performance. Additionally, the family's culture and surrounding community must also be taken into consideration. Home visiting can encourage parent engagement and involvement that helps foster academic achievement in children and adolescents.

In early childhood, visits may include a focus on parental support (e.g., establishing routines), implementation of specialized treatment practices, and providing information on developing communication and interaction skills (Fox, Carta, Strain, Dunlap, & Hemmeter, 2010). Throughout middle school, early adolescents experience both interpersonal and intrapersonal developmental needs that can be addressed through home visiting by providing services that foster family engagement when families are more likely to become disengaged (Davis & Lambie, 2005). Reaching out to families of older adolescents should not be minimized, because families continue to be a significant factor in the lives of these individuals.

Data-Informed Decision Making

Beginning with the universal home visiting services, a checklist or report should be completed to determine the benefits of additional visits to meet the child and family's needs throughout the school year. A school social worker or other personnel could adopt and/or tweak a measure, such as the Home Visit Report Form from the Infant Health and Development Program (Wasik & Bryant, 2001), or create one based on their school and community's individual needs. Any home visiting form should include specifics such as names of family members who participated, the visit duration, a description of the family participation, information on topics discussed, and the need for follow-up. Similar to the RTI approach, a home visiting measure can be used to set appropriate goals and objectives in line with Tier 2 and 3 services provided within the school, and detail steps toward achieving them. Lastly, a checklist or report can also facilitate the home visit and ensure that the visitor is obtaining the information needed from a visit to make an informed decision for future actions.

Practice Examples

Several publications have provided examples from home visitors, providing a look at what might take place on a home visit and how the visit can help bring about positive goals. The following situation was told to one of the authors by one of the visitors in this vignette. A school social worker and school psychologist went together on a home visit to a parent who was not responding to requests to come to the school to discuss her young son. When the visitors went to the door, the mother came partway out and stood talking with them, making it clear she wasn't too happy to see them. The social worker and school psychologist began to talk to the mother about her child, letting her know that the school was interested in providing some help to her son, and wanted some information from her that could help them with plans. As the conversation continued, the mother began to soften her stance. She said to the visitors: "I thought you came to complain about my son. I didn't know you would drive all this way out to see me just to help my son. The school must really care about him." She then agreed to come to the school where she could meet with the teacher. These two visitors made a significant contribution to this child's education, and they did it by reaching out to the family on the family's own turf.

Schools can both initiate home visiting programs and conduct visits to respond to issues. A school district could review the many ways of linking schools and families through home visiting and prioritize which ones would best help reach their goals. Goals can range from facilitating parent-school relationships to helping adolescent students remain in school. Each goal might be reached through a different professional. Teachers may conduct some, social workers others, and counselors and psychologists may take on other home visiting objectives. The National Center for Family and Community Connections with Schools (http://www.sedl.org/connections/resources/rb/rb6-readiness.pdf) identifies home visits as one way that schools can facilitate transition activities before children start kindergarten. Though home visits, schools can help establish positive relationships with the families, leading to more involvement with the schools and better student success. Teachers who make these home visits can take with them simple materials that can be left with the child, such as crayons and paper, or a child's book. They can make suggestions for ways the parents can help the child prepare for school. Schools can also use a hand-off procedure in which teachers might make initial home visits, but if there is a need for ongoing support in the home, either other school staff can take over, or the school can link with other community agencies that might be staffed for more intensive home visiting services.

Key Points to Remember

- Home visiting continues to be a significant outreach strategy for schools to make contact with families and students.
- Principles and guidelines for home visitors provide tools that can help provide more effective family-focused and culturally responsive services.
- School objectives can range from providing parenting education for families with preschool children, to helping immigrant families better understand school procedures, to helping adolescents remain engaged with school.
- Schools that have RTI programs in place will find that home visiting is a strong complement, being able to provide home visiting at different levels of intensity and for a range of social and academic concerns.

Further Learning

- Harvard Family Research Project Home Visit Forum: http://www.hfrp.org/other-research-areas/home-visit-forum
- Parent Teacher Home Visit Project: http://www.pthvp.org/
- Pew Research Center: http://pewresearch.org/
- Teacher Home Visit Program: http://www.teacherhomevisit.org/
- U.S. Department of Health and Human Services Home Visiting Evidence of Effectiveness: http://homvee.acf.hhs.gov/

References

Astor, R. A., Behre, W. J., Wallace, J. M., & Fravil, K. (1998). School social workers and school violence: Personal safety, training, and violence programs. *Social Work, 43*(3), 223–232.

Astuto, J. & Allen, L. (2009). Home visitation and young children: An approach worth investing in? *Social Policy Report, 23*, 3–23.

Catalano, R. F., Berglund, M. L., Ryan, J. A. M., Lonczak, H. S., & Hawkins, J. D. (2002). Positive youth development in the United States: Research findings on evaluations of positive youth development programs. *Prevention & Treatment,* 5, Article 15. Retrieved from http://psycnet.apa.org/journals/pre

Davis, K. M., & Lambie, G. W. (2005). Family engagement: A collaborative, systemic approach for middle school counselors. *Professional School Counseling, 9*, 144–151.

Deslandes, R., & Bertrand, R. (2005). Motivation of parent involvement in secondary-level schooling. *The Journal of Educational Research, 98*, 164–175.

Duggan, A., Fuddy L., Burrell, L., Higman, S. M., McFarlane, E., Windham, A., & Sia, C. (2004). Randomized trail of a statewide home visiting program to prevent child abuse: Impact in reducing parental risk factors. *Child Abuse and Neglect, 28,* 623–643.

Edwards, A., & Lutzker, J. R. (2008). Iterations of the SafeCare model: An evidence-based child maltreatment prevention program. *Behavior Modification, 32*, 736–756.

Fixsen, D. L., Blase, K., Duda, M., Naoom, S., & Van Dyke, M. (2010). Implementation of evidence-based treatments for children and adolescents: Research findings and their implications for the future. In J. Weisz & A. Kazdin (Eds.), *Implementation and dissemination: Extending treatments to new populations and new settings* (2nd ed., pp. 435–450). New York: Guilford Press.

Fox, L., Carta, J., Strain, P., Dunlap, G., & Hemmeter, M. L. (2010). Response to Intervention and the pyramid model. *Infants and Young Children, 23,* 3–13.

Fraser, M.W, Day, S.V., Galinsky, M.J., Hodges, V. G., & Smokowski, P. R. (2004). Conduct problems and peer rejection in childhood: A randomized trial of the Making Choices and Strong Families programs. *Research on Social Work Practice, 14*, 313–324.

Gomby, D. S. (2005). *Home visitation in 2005: Outcomes for children and parents.* Washington, DC: Committee for Economic Development: Invest in Kids Working Group.

Greenberg, M. T., Domitrovich, C, & Bumbarger, B. (2001).The prevention of mental disorders in school-aged children: Current state of the field. *Prevention & Treatment, 4,* Article 1. Available: http:// journals.apa.org/prevention.

Guterman, N. B. (2000). *Stopping child maltreatment before it starts: Emerging horizons in early home visitation services.* Thousand Oaks, CA: Sage.

Hancock, B. L., & Pelton, L. H. (1989). Home visits: History and functions. *Social Casework, 70,*21–27.

Harding, K., Galano, J., Martin, J., Huntington, L., & Schellenbach, C. J. (2007). Healthy Families America effectiveness. *Journal of Prevention and Intervention in the Community, 34,* 149–179.

Henggeler, S. W. (2002). *Serious emotional disturbance in children and adolescents: Multisystemic therapy.* New York, NY: Guilford Press.

Levine, M., & Levine, A. (1970). *A social history of the helping services: Clinic, court, school, and community.* New York: Appleton-Century-Crofts.

Minuchin, P., Colapinto, J., & Minuchin, S. (1998). *Working with families of the poor.* New York: Guilford.

National Association of School Psychologists. (2002). *Position statement on home school collaboration: Establishing partnerships to enhance educational outcomes.* Bethesda, MD: Author.

Olds, D. L., Hill, P. L., O'Brien, R., Racine, D., & Moritz, P. (2003). Taking preventive intervention to scale: The nurse-family partnership. *Cognitive and Behavioral Practice, 10,* 278–290.

Oppenheimer, J. J. (1925). *The visiting teacher movement with special reference to administrative relationships* (2nd ed.). New York: Joint Committee on Methods of Preventing Delinquency.

Richmond, M. (1899). *Friendly visiting among the poor.* New York: Macmillan.

Sweet, M. A., & Appelbaum, M. I. (2004). Is home visiting an effective strategy? A meta-analytic review of home visiting programs for families with young children. *Child Development, 75*(5), 1435–1456.

Wasik, B. H., & Sparling, J. J. (1998). *Home Visit Assessment Instrument.* Chapel Hill: Center for Home Visiting, University of North Carolina.

Wasik, B. H., & Bryant, D. M. (2001). *Home visiting: Procedures for helping families* (2nd ed.). Thousand Oaks, CA: Sage.

Wasik, B. H., & Coleman, S. (2004). *Safety issues in home visiting.* Chapel Hill: Center for Home Visiting, University of North Carolina.

PART V

Improving Multicultural and Community Relationships, School Accountability, and Resource Development

SECTION XI

Resources for Multicultural Groups and Diverse Relationships in the School

The interpersonal environment and groups that schools serve are increasingly complex and diverse. The chapters in this section address how to work effectively with children and families of color and various sexual orientations and offers further discussions about the best practices that may improve the school engagement and education of multicultural and diverse populations.

CHAPTER 57

Working with Culturally/Racially Diverse Students to Improve Connection to School and Academic Performance

Daphna Oyserman

Getting Started

About half of low-income and minority youth do not graduate from high school on time, and across income and cultural or racial-ethnic heritage, boys are more at risk than girls of underperforming in school (Elmore & Oyserman, 2011). While it is commonly assumed that most children graduate high school, in fact a careful analyses by birth cohort undertaken by Orfield and colleagues at the Harvard Civil Rights Project (Orfield et al., 2004) shows that only 76.8% of children who are Asian/Pacific Islander and 74.9% of white children graduate on time. Among American Indian (51.1%), African-American (50.2%), and Hispanic (53.2%) children, graduation rates are lower, as noted in parentheses. This analysis is important not only because it implies that all children need help graduating high school but also because it implies that children of color may face more obstacles to graduation. The impact of children of color on overall graduation rates is likely to increase in the near future since the proportion of children of color in the United States is increasing. Brookings Institute (2011) analyses of census data reveal that while currently 58.8% of all children are white, among children aged three and younger, this proportion is less than half (49.9%). This changing demographic profile of American children is due both to immigration and to differences in birth rates among various racial-ethnic groups in the United States. Generally, an increasing percentage of school-aged children are immigrants (now 18.8%), with the largest first- and second-generation immigrant population currently of Latino origin (51%).

As of 2008, Mexico was the main country of origin for immigrant children living in the United States. Thus, in immigrant families, over one-third included children born in Mexico or at least one parent born in Mexico.

While there have been some improvements in educational attainment of Latinos, they lag behind white and Asian groups in school attainment (Kohler & Lazarín, 2007). This subgroup is important because children of Hispanic heritage now make up 22% of all children in the United States (Pew Hispanic Center, Fry & Passel, 2009). Generational status, legal authorization, income, and academic attainment are related. Thus, only about 7% of Hispanic children are estimated to be unauthorized immigrants, but this percentage masks the fact that about two-thirds of foreign-born Hispanic children are unauthorized. Altogether, about a third (37%) of Hispanic children are the U.S.-born children of U.S.-born parents, more than half (52%) are the U.S.-born sons or daughters of at least one foreign-born parent, and 11% of these children are themselves foreign-born. Immigrant children are more likely to live in low-income households, to have parents with low educational attainment, and to have three or more siblings.

All of these factors interact to limit parental ability to be involved in children's schools. For social workers in schools, an important task is to help students at risk of school failure see the connection between the mundane present with its everyday behaviors and a future self—often envisioned in terms of vague yet positive hopes and dreams. Underperformance in school and school failure are an enormous waste of human potential and increase risk of negative outcomes (delinquency, depression, substance use, early risky sexual activity) in adolescence and adulthood. Low academic attainment and especially lack of a high school diploma increase risk in adulthood—it is harder to get and keep a job, harder to earn enough income, and, as a result, harder to provide for one's children. Thus, improving connection to school and academic performance is a central task for the prevention of problematic outcomes both during adolescence and in adulthood.

What We Know

Early research suggests that when asked about their hopes and dreams for themselves in adulthood—their hoped-for possible selves (PS)—youths have high hopes that do not differ across levels of risk (Oyserman & Markus, 1990a). Even very low income youth report high hopes and dreams. However, more variance is found when asking youth about their more proximal PS for the coming year (Oyserman & Markus, 1990a) and when asking youth if they are doing anything to try to attain these PS (Oyserman & Saltz, 1993). Content of more proximal positive (to-be-attained) and negative (to-be-avoided) PS (Oyserman & Markus, 1990a) and not trying to attain positive PS (or avoid negative PS) are both related to more problem behaviors (Oyserman & Saltz, 1993).

Low-income and minority status do not themselves undermine children's school-focused PS. Children living in low-income neighborhoods and growing up with parents with low educational attainment and low professional status do not differ from other children in whether they have school-focused PS. They differ from other children in whether they have strategies to attain these PS (Oyserman, Johnson, & James, 2011). Thus the question for social work interventions is how to translate already high hopes and dreams for the future into proximal PS focused on connection to school and academic attainment: that is, how to help youth link PS to current behavior (Oyserman & James, 2008).

Operationalizing PS

PS are defined as images of ourselves not as we currently are but at positive or negative end states—the self who already passed the algebra test, the self who failed to lose weight, the self who falls in with the "wrong" crowd (Oyserman & James, 2008). A central life task of adolescence and early adulthood is figuring out not simply what one is like now but also who one might become; not only what is possible for the self but also how to fit together the many available images of the future (Oyserman, 2001). PS of teens are likely to include expectations and concerns about how one will do in school, how one will fit in socially, and how to get through adolescence without becoming off track—pregnant, arrested, or hooked on drugs (Oyserman & Fryberg, 2006; Oyserman & James, 2011). Indeed, existing evidence suggests that expectations and concerns about succeeding in school or being a good student are the most common PS in adolescence, even among very low income minority teens at high risk of school failure (Oyserman & Destin, 2010; Oyserman & Fryberg, 2006). Possible selves are sometimes but not always linked to strategies for their attainment, over time, children perform best in school when their possible selves are linked with pragmatic strategies, providing them a pathway toward their possible selves (Oyserman, Bybee, Terry, & Hart-Johnson, 2004).

PS, Gender, Culture, and Racial-Ethnic Identity

For urban, low-income, and minority youths, PS and racial-ethnic identity (REI) and other social identities are likely to be interwoven (Oyserman & Destin, 2010). Moreover, gender differences are also found. Boys contrast themselves with their peers and girls assimilate the experiences of their peers into their own PS. In high-risk contexts in which many underperform, this implies that, on average, boys assume that their chances to attain their school-focused PS are higher than their peers (who on average are doing poorly). However, girls look at their low-performing peers and assume that their chances are low as well (Kemmelmeier & Oyserman, 2001a, 2001b). This may be one reason that girls in high-risk contexts perform better than boys—they are more worried that they may fail and so try harder.

In addition, findings from studies primarily focused on African-American middle and high school youths in Detroit suggest that both PS and REI play an important role in school performance and vulnerability to depression (Altschul, Oyserman, & Bybee, 2006; Oyserman, 2008; Oyserman, Bybee, & Terry, 2003; Oyserman, Gant, & Ager, 1995; Oyserman & Harrison, 1998; Oyserman, Harrison, Bybee, 2001; Oyserman, Terry, & Bybee, 2002). These studies document that academic efficacy and academic outcomes improve when academic achievement is an integral part of REI, but that having an REI that includes academic achievement is harder in segregated neighborhoods (Oyserman & Yoon, 2009; see also Altschul, Oyserman, & Bybee, 2008; Oyserman, Kemmelmeier, Fryberg, Brosh, & Hart-Johnson, 2003, for research focused on American Indian, Mexican American, and Arab youth). Simply having a positive self-image or a positive sense of connection to one's racial-ethnic group is not enough. Because PS and REI are both potential sources of academic focus, interventions that promote focus on PS as congruent with REI and on REI as congruent with school attainment are more likely to be effective (Oyserman & Destin, 2010).

How Might PS Influence Behavior?

But how do PS sustain effortful action to influence behavior? By articulating and detailing the look and feel of the future, PS may sustain effortful action by making the future come alive as a possible reality (Oyserman & James, 2008). Without an academic PS to consider, a student has no reason not to stay up late to see another TV show or video. Thus, PS may function to reduce the impact of moment-to-moment shifts in what is made salient by one's social context. They focus attention on successful attainment of self-goals and avoidance of anti-goals. Becoming like one's academic success PS could involve strategies such as "go to all my classes" and "set my alarm clock so I won't get up late." For homework to feel like an investment in one's future, rather than simply as a chore, homework has to feel like a strategy to make progress toward the future (Destin & Oyserman, 2010). PS do not develop in isolation; youth need to be able to find connections between their PS and other important identities such as REI and to feel that important others (including parents and other adults who may be role models) view their PS as plausible. Low-income youth, nonheterosexual LGBT (lesbian, gay, bi- or trans-gendered) youth and youth of color may find it difficult to create positive and believable PS focused on school as a pathway to adulthood unless these PS are fostered in a social context that creates local norms highlighting the relevance of academic achievement for being part of one's social identity (including REI, social class, and LGBT identity).

What We Can Do

There is experimental evidence that how one thinks about oneself influences school-relevant cognitive processes (perception, recall, performance; Oyserman, Sorensen, Reber, & Chen, 2009). However, research on PS generally (Oyserman & James, 2011) and on PS of minority and low-income youth specifically (Oyserman & Fryberg, 2006) is mostly correlational and necessarily leaves unanswered how to translate findings about correlations between PS, school involvement, and REI (or LGBT or social-class identity) into a framework for change. To address this gap, in our own research we have focused on experimental manipulations to capture the "active" aspects of PS and social identity (Oyserman, Bybee, & Terry, 2003; Oyserman, Bybee, Terry, & Hart-Johnson, 2004; Oyserman, Gant, & Ager, 1995; Oyserman & Markus, 1990b; Oyserman & Saltz, 1993; Oyserman, Terry, & Bybee, 2002) and used these as the basis for developing a brief intervention, outlined below. The intervention was designed, implemented, and evaluated with funding from the National Institutes of Health (Grant number MH58299, Oyserman PI). Core aims were to engage low-income youth from diverse racial-ethnic backgrounds in developing clearly articulated PS that (1) linked current school involvement with adult futures, (2) linked strategies to attain these PS to important social identities, and (3) helped students interpret difficulty in working on these PS as meaning that the PS were important, not impossible, to attain (see also Oyserman, Bybee, & Terry, 2006). Other interventions that cue connection of PS to the future, link strategies to identity, and help children interpret difficulty should also produce the same effect. For example, increasing parent involvement with school may also have this effect (Oyserman, Brickman, & Rhodes, 2007).

All too often, social work practitioners attempt to develop comprehensive interventions that require more time and resources than they are able to marshal over time. Given the need for very brief, low-budget universal interventions, we developed an intervention called School-to-Jobs with the goal of meeting the social worker's need for a brief, cheap, fun intervention that can be sustained over time in high-need schools.

The School-to-Jobs (STJ) program aims to promote development of PS pathways from middle to high school by helping youths (1) articulate PS goals and strategies to obtain their PS, (2) create a link between PS and adult identities so the future feels near, (3) create a link between PS and social identities such as REI so strategies feel identity congruent, and (4) interpret difficulties along the way as meaning that their PS is important, not impossible, to attain. The School-to-Jobs program has been successfully used with low-income children from various racial-ethnic backgrounds in a number of states. Social workers working in a school should first learn what they can about the children—their immigration, language, and acculturation situation and what other issues may be unique to the group. For example, I am currently beginning work with immigrant children from a new area, Yemen, and before proceeding I am spending time learning how children, parents, and teachers make sense of the children's identities and possibilities in America.

Thumbnail Sketch of the STJ Intervention

The goal was that the intervention would highlight and elicit the relevance of school to attaining one's PS. The intervention is small-group based (groups of about 12 students) and has been tested as both an after-school (Oyserman et al., 2002) and in-school program (Oyserman et al., 2006) for middle school students. The after-school test of the intervention followed youth to the end of the academic year and documented significantly reduced risk of being sent out of class, significantly improved attendance and time spent doing homework, as well as change in the youth's PS, comparing control and intervention youth and statistically controlling for previous academic attainment (Oyserman et al., 2006). A second randomized clinical trial of the intervention involved an in-school test with a 2-year follow-up (Oyserman et al., 2006). Here significant change was found in grades and attendance by school records, as well as reduction in grade retention (being held back a year). Again effects were mediated by change in youth PS. In terms of efficacy, a standard criteria is that a program's success should be replicated in at least two randomized trials to provide assurance that a program is probably efficacious. The STJ program meets this standard. At the next stage, the success of the STJ program needs to be replicated with a different research team to ascertain that the program is robustly efficacious. Replication to date has occurred without separate evaluation of efficacy.

STJ uses a small-group, active learning paradigm with a series of small-group activities, within which youth gain a sense of their own vision for the future and learn to develop strategies to help attain this vision; parents and community members join in developing youth's skills. The name of the program, School-to-Jobs, was chosen to emphasize the connection between current action and future goals. STJ utilizes a social cognitive approach, utilizing basic social psychological theory and research on the nature of information processing and motivation (Oyserman et al., 2002; Oyserman & Destin, 2010; Oyserman, Elmore, & Smith, 2012). This research suggests that structured activities occurring in everyday settings can have great impact on who children think they are now and what is possible for them to achieve in the future because subtle contextual shifts can powerfully change the sense made of daily experiences. The meaning made of everyday experience in turn fuels motivation.

Specifically, the goal of STJ is to develop a sequence of activities and tasks that provide youth with experiences of creating and detailing more explicit academic PS that feel congruent with REI and other social identities, feel connected to adult futures, and provide an interpretation of difficulty as meaning that school is important, not impossible, as a PS. Activities were designed to create well-explicated PS with clear, comprehensive, plausible strategies to achieve these PS.

Parents and community members are included in two final optional sessions. Adults are brought in to anchor youth in an adult worldview, to provide opportunities to practice skills needed to obtain support from adults, and to allow youth to practice obtaining support for their emerging PS from adults. Thus, adults are brought in as tools for youth rather than as teachers or authority figures. STJ sessions are interactive. Students actively engage the material. Sessions build on one another. Early sessions are easy and evoke a general sense that everyone has a future. Each subsequent session makes the future feel nearer and more connected to other identities and helps students interpret difficulty as importance by making failures and difficulties along the way normative. Below is a thumbnail sketch of the sessions, followed by an example of the "cheat sheet" summary trainers use to ensure that they are following the manual and an example of the observer checklist used to assess fidelity of delivery. The intervention, summary sheets, and fidelity assessment are collected in a manual that can be obtained from the author. As can be seen, the checklist allows for careful testing of the process, something critical for learning what is working and when.

Thumbnail Sketch of Sessions

These thumbnail sketches are taken from Oyserman, Bybee, and Terry (2006) which provides a full evaluation of the program as well.

1. *Creating a group.* (Goal: Create a positive sense of membership and set the stage for school involvement and adult PS). Activity: Trainers and participants discuss their expectations and concerns about program content; participants develop program rules. Activities include introducing one another in terms of skills and abilities to succeed this school year, human knot, and other activities that build the idea that group members have positive attributes related to school achievement and that others also want to do well in school.
2. *Adult images.* (Goal: Create a concrete experience of imagining adulthood). Activity: Participants choose from pictures portraying adults in the domains of adulthood (work, family, lifestyle, community service, health, and hobbies) and then describe how these represent their future images. (Pictures fit the racial/ethnic background of participants; making and hearing about choices gets participants to think about the future.)
3. *Time lines.* (Goal: Concretize the connection between present and future, and normalize failures and setbacks as part of progress to the future.) Activity: Participants draw personal time lines from the present as far into the future as they can. Trainers define *forks in the road* (choices that have consequences) and *roadblocks* (obstacles placed by others and situations—for example, lack of financial resources, racial and/or sexual discrimination), and participants draw at least one of each in their time line. Discussion connects current activities and future visions, and youth give each other feedback focused on sequences and ways to go around obstacles.
4. *PS and strategies boards.* (Goal: Concretize the connection between current behavior, next year, and adult attainments.) Activity: Using poster board and colored stickers, participants map out next year and adult PS and the strategies they are using now or could use. Then they map out all the school-related PS and strategies used so that participants using particular strategies can explain what they are doing and guide others through obstacles.

5. *Solving everyday problems I.* (Goal: Provide participants with concrete experience breaking down everyday school problems into more manageable parts.) Activity: In prior sessions, solo activities were the springboard to group discussion. The next sessions use group activity as springboard because participants are confident enough with one another to work together in small groups and group work reinforces positive REI. Participants solve logic problems together, developing a strategy of writing down the known to solve for the unknown. Using this success as a springboard, each group develops strategies for handling a set of school-focused problems (doing poorly in math class, tackling a big history assignment) by first listing the questions they must ask themselves or get information about prior to deciding on a course of action. The session ends with full group discussion of questions raised and decisions made.
6. *Solving everyday problems II.* (Goal: Reinforce participants' ability to make school-related plans for the future and to reach out to adults to accomplish this.) Activity: Using the same small-group format as in the previous session, participants develop a list of requirements for high school graduation and prerequisites/skills needed for entry into college and other training, then work as a large group to find out about the actual requirements for local educational institutions. This is connected back to the adult visions, time lines, and strategy board sessions—helping youth see the process by which they can attain the PS they have imagined and deal with obstacles or forks in the road.
7. *Wrapping up, moving forward.* (Goal: Organize experiences so far and set the stage for bringing parents/guardians to the group.) Activity: Participants "walk through" the program by discussing what they did in each session, what they learned in each, and what they liked and disliked about the program. Parent or other important adult involvement is discussed with a focus on how these adults from the youth's own community can help youth on their pathways to adulthood. Youth explore the similarities and differences they see between their own experiences and those they imagine their parents had.
8. *Building an alliance and developing communication skills.* (Goal: Allow youth and parents to state their concerns for the student in the coming year, see limitations of current communication skills in handling these concerns, and practice another model in a structured setting.) Activity: Parents and youth introduce one another, and youth lead a review of previous sessions. Then parents and youth separate to discuss what concerns each has about the transition to high school. These concerns form the basis for discussion of how to communicate with one another on important topics. Trainers role-play parent and youth suggestions and then operationalize communication as active listening and "taking the floor." Parents pair off with their own child to try out being an active listener and taking the floor. Both parent and child have a chance to experience the listener and the floor role, allowing both to raise and to react to a point of concern. Then participants talk about the experience and commit to practice this skill. This section focuses on REI by highlighting connections between parents and youth, the importance of school, and difficulties encountered along the way.
9. *Jobs, careers, and informational interviewing.* (Goal: Identify gaps in knowledge about how schooling links to careers and provide youth with skills to obtain this information.) Activity: Parents describe how they got their current jobs (or strategies they have tried to get jobs in the past if not currently employed), and youth describe how to find out about jobs and careers. Trainers highlight parent and youth frustration about connecting qualifications and experiences to desired careers and jobs, thus introducing the concept of informational interviewing. Parents and youth practice informational interviewing and then use this skill to do informational interviews with community members who join the group at this point. Then participants discuss ways that they can use informational interviewing at a number of junctures in the future. Youth talk about barriers to contacting people in the community who have jobs that seem of interest to them. Community members discuss ways to make contacts, responding to specific concerns raised by youth and giving youth a chance to role-play these strategies. This session focuses on REI by highlighting role models from youth's racial-ethnic community.

Applying Interventions within a Response to Intervention Framework

Education is often framed as a *universal intervention*, something provided to all children with the

Box 57.1 Detailed Outline—Session 1

- Greet/welcome participants. Check names against roster.Greet latecomers.
- Introduce one another (trainers). Also identify the trait each has that helps him or her to succeed in work or school.
- Introduce observer. Emphasize role to observe trainers to help improve program (and not to grade students).
- Ask what an introduction is. (It is a way of saying who you are and what you can contribute.) Write definition on newsprint.
- Identify goals for introductions (they differ depending on context).
- Ask about skills and abilities for succeeding in school (since this is school to jobs).
- Write tasks and examples on newsprint.
- Introduce partner skills. (Pass out marbles. Ask for questions before task begins. Circulate, check for understanding.)
- Ask youth to introduce partners. Ask them to repeat names.
- Explain concepts (expectations/concerns). Use newsprint to write group responses.
- Reinforce and repeat four basic themes that will be covered (1. setting clear goals for next year and afterward; 2. developing strategies to work on these goals; 3. thinking about a path to the future; 4. working with teachers, parents and others in the community as resources).
- Elicit group rules. Write on newsprint.
- State aim of program. Use prepared newsprint.
- State goal. Use prepared newsprint.
- Explain group naming activity. Give examples, elicit ideas.
- Explain session schedule. Provide contact information. Write on board.
- Review. Ask participant to name all names.
- Explain task, line up from youngest to oldest without talking. (Encourage. When completed, ask month of birth.)
- Congratulate. Reinforce cooperation.
- Explain task, stand in circle, cross arms in front, grab hands of two people across the circle, without letting go, uncross hands and re-form the circle. (Trainers are part of the circle.) Congratulate. Reinforce cooperation.
- Work on adult images. Ask, "What will adulthood be like for you?"
- Provide snacks. Pass out session evaluation forms. Ask for help rearranging the room.
- Pick up evaluation forms. Make sure attendance form is filled out. Say goodbyes. Rate participant participation.

This material is from the School-to-Jobs Intervention Manual, Oyserman (2006).

assumption that it benefits children and the society in which they live. However, children differ in how much of the legally mandated days and years of schooling they actually attend and in what they learn while in school. For these reasons, educational programs may also target children at risk of low attendance and performance (termed *targeted* or *selective* intervention in the 1989 Institute of Medicine framework). So that the universal intervention of education may be supplemented with additional targeted programs for children at risk of or already experiencing deficits in attendance and performance, including school dropout. The goal would be an intervention to prevent risk or ameliorate the negative consequences of problems that have already emerged in attendance and performance. Programs that are universally implemented within schools that serve at-risk children fit this framework—they can be considered targeted to the extent that they focus on schools in which risk is likely.

Within education, concern that the goal of universal education may not be met in some groups led to consideration of differences in children's "Response to Intervention" (RTI) (Shapiro, Zigmond, Wallace, & Marston, 2011). The initial question RTI was meant to address was whether specific learning disability (SLD) in children could be assessed early by carefully monitoring children's learning progress. The RTI method has now been expanded as an early intervention for those who may have SLD or a behavior disability. RTI involves screening to identify low-performing

Box 57.2 Detailed Outline—Session 2

- Greet participants by name. Take attendance.
- Say, "Today is session 2: adult images."
- Ask for what happened last session. (Elicit activities. Elicit rationale.)
- Ask students to choose pictures that represent visions of themselves as adults.
- Tell them to pick at least 10 pictures.
- Ask them to ask themselves what the pictures mean to them.
- Ask them when these pictures will be true of them.
- Tell them that all will discuss these pictures afterward.
- Make sure instructions are clear. Have participants begin. Pass out snacks.
- Mingle—check for understanding.
- Have everyone rejoin circle.
- Show pictures, explain to group, while group listens and pays attention to common themes.
- Explain task: Each participant writes on newsprint something similar about everyone's adult visions.
- Ask for questions
- Mingle, help individually as needed
- Discuss themes that are there and areas that are missing (jobs, family, friends, community involvement, lifestyle).
- Review concept of adult domains: adult images about jobs, family, friends, community involvement, lifestyle).
- Explain concept: Adult images can be goals if they are worked on, and this will be discussed in coming sessions.
- Tell them that the next session will identify role models.
- Pass out session evaluation forms. Ask for help rearranging the room.
- Pick up evaluation forms. Make sure attendance form is filled out. Say goodbyes. Rate participant participation.

This material is from the School-to-Jobs Intervention Manual, Oyserman (2006).

students, monitoring their progress while learning (rather than waiting for end-point assessments such as semester grades), implementing research-supported intervention to bolster learning, and finally intervening individually as necessary to support learning.

Thus, in addition to focusing on targeted and selected intervention for children at risk of low performance, the RTI approach highlights the need to obtain ongoing assessment to closely monitor the academic and behavioral performance of students as they are learning. Consider the School-to-Jobs intervention (Oyserman, Bybee, & Terry, 2006; Oyserman, Terry, Bybee, 2002). Rather than document that the intervention works by demonstrating differences in end-of-semester and end-of-year grades, attendance, and standardized test scores, and RTI approach would emphasize assessment at a more micro-level. This would require more sensitive measures than end-ofunit assessment. For example, changes could first occur in whether a child completes homework or participates in class or is attending to instructions. Self-reports of behavior are problematic, so what would need to be collected is process-level actual behavior (Schwarz & Oyserman, 2011). To the extent that teachers collect this information, it can be used as a more process-level assessment of child learning and of change due to intervention.

Key Points to Remember

- Motivation is identity-based; people prefer to act in identity-congruent ways.
  - Identities feel stable but are actually highly context-sensitive.
  - This means that what feels right in context may not be what had been planned outside of context.
- People do not always act to attain future identities (possible selves).
- People are more likely to act to attain their future identities when these identities:
  - come to mind in context
  - are connected to strategies

Table 57.1 School-to-Jobs Observation Form

Youth Session 1

Date ___/___/___ School Code ___

Class Code ___

Site: __________ Group __________

Trainers: __________ Observer __________

Task	*Y*	*N*	*Detailed Trainer Activity*	*Y*	*N*	*Group Behavior*	*1–5*
Start on time	—	—	*START TIME* __________				
Opening							
• Welcome			• Greet and welcome participants			• Talk with trainers	
• Introductions	—	—	• Check names against roster • Greet latecomers	—	—	• Talk with each other • Listen	—
			• Trainers introduce each other (name, University of Michigan)	—	—	• Acknowledge observer	—
			• Introduce observer				
			• Emphasize role to observe trainers to help improve program	—	—		
Introduction							
• Introduce the concept of introductions as goal oriented	—	—	• Ask what an introduction is	—	—	• Share ideas	—
			• Reinforce: is a way of saying who you are and what you can contribute	—	—		
			• Write definition on newsprint				
• Introduce school-to-jobs as success oriented			• Different goals for introductions				
			• Ask about skills and abilities for succeeding in school			• Share ideas	
			• Write tasks and examples on newsprint	—	—		
Introduction task • Group creation process—is atmosphere starting to feel like a group?	—	—	• Explain activity (partners learn of partner skills, introduce)	__	—	• Take marble	—

(continued)

Table 57.1 *(Continued)*

Task	*Y*	*N*	*Detailed Trainer Activity*	*Y*	*N*	*Group Behavior*	*1–5*
				—	—	• Separate into pairs	
	—	—	• Pass out marbles	—	—	• Share skills and abilities	
	—	—	• Ask for questions before task begins	—	—		
• Group feeling that group as a whole has skills and abilities that can be relied on.	—	—	• Circulate, check for understanding	—	—		
	—	—	• Ask youth to introduce partners	—	—	• Introduce partner	—
	—	—	• Ask for repetition of names	—	—	• Practice saying names	—
Expectations and concerns	—	—	• Introduce new task, explain concept				
	—	—	• Ask for expectations	—	—	• Participate	
• Give youth a voice	—	—	• Use newsprint to write group expectations	—	—		
	—	—	• Ask for concerns	—	—		
	—	—	• Use newsprint to write group concerns	—	—		
• Crystallize and focus group goals	—	—	• Reinforce and repeat four basic themes that will be covered.	—	—	• Listen	—
	—	—	• setting clear goals for next year and afterward				
	—	—	• developing strategies to work on these goals				
	—	—	• thinking about a path to the future				
	—	—	• working with teachers, parents, and others in the community as resources	—	—		
• Create group ownership (sense of being heard and a member of something)							
	—	—	• Elicit group rules	—	—	• Participate	
	—	—	• Write on newsprint	—	—		
Aim	—	—	• State aim (help create road map, need to think about goals, work on strategies, develop alternatives)	—	—	• Listen	—
Program aim is clarified	—	—	• Use prepared newsprint				
	—	—	• State goal (a clear, more detailed sense of what you need to do and how to do it)	—	—		
Naming group	—	—					

	—	—	• Explain activity	—	—	• Participate	—
	—	—	• Give examples, elicit ideas	—	—	• Vote	—
Schedule	—	—					
	—	—	• Explain session schedule	—	—	• Listen	—
	—	—	• Provide contact information	—	—		
	—	—	• Write on board	—	—		
Line up task	—	—	• Review: Ask participant to name all names			• Participate	
• Group creation process (is group interaction increasing? sense of collectiveness?)		—	• Explain task, line up from youngest to oldest without talking	—	—	• Move around, line up	—
	—	—	• Encourage				
	—	—	• When completed, ask to give month of birth				
	—	—	• Congratulate				
	—	—	• Reinforce cooperation	—	—		
Human knot task	—	—					
• Group creation process (is this feeling like a "group"?)	—	—	• Explain task, stand in circle, cross arms in front, and grab hands of two people across the circle; then, without letting go of hands, get them uncrossed so that we are again in a circle			• Participate	
	—	—	• Trainers are part of the circle	—	—		
	—	—	• Congratulate	—	—	• Move, re-form circle	—
	—	—	• Reinforce cooperation	—	—		
Next session and good-byes	—	—					
	—	—	• Next session will work on adult images: What will adulthood be like for you?	—	—	• Listen	—
	—	—					
	—	—	• Provide snacks	—	—	• Eat	—
	—	—	• Pass out session evaluation forms	—	—	• Complete evaluation forms	—
	—	—	• Ask for help rearranging the room				
	—	—	• Say goodbyes	—	—	• Rearrange room	
	—	—	• Rate participant participation levels	—	—		—
	—	—	• END TIME ————				

    - feel congruent with important social identities (such as racial-ethnic identity, gender identity, social class identity, and LGBT identity)
- Small shifts in context matter.
    - Who one may become (future identities) and what comes to mind when one thinks of oneself now (current identities) are dynamically created in context.
    - This means that small interventions can have large effects.

Further Learning

For more and continuously updated publications referring to each of the aspects covered in this chapter (self, identity, culture, and implications for behavior, please visit my Web site: http://sitemaker.umich.edu/daphna.oyserman

Hands-On Examples

An example of an intervention session checklist for use in rating fidelity of implementation can be found in Table 57.1.

References

Altschul, I., Oyserman, D., & Bybee, D. (2006). Racial-ethnic identity in mid-adolescence: Content and change as predictors of grades. *Child Development, 77*, 1155–1169.

Altschul, I., Oyserman, D., & Bybee, D. (2008). Racial-ethnic self-schemas and segmented assimilation: Identity and the academic achievement of Hispanic youth. *Social Psychology Quarterly, 71*, 302–320.

Destin, M., & Oyserman, D. (2010). Incentivizing education: Seeing schoolwork as an investment, not a chore. *Journal of Experimental Social Psychology, 46*, 846–849.

Elmore, K., & Oyserman, D. (2011). If "we" succeed, "I" can too: Identity-based motivation and gender in the classroom. *Contemporary Educational Psychology, 37*, 176–185. doi:10.1016/j.cedpsych.2011.05.003

Frey, R. (2011). *A demographic tipping point among America's three-year-olds.* State of Metropolitan America, No. 26, The Brookings Institution. Retrieved from http://www.brookings.edu/opinions/2011/0207_population_frey.aspx

Fry, R., & Passel, J. (2009). *Latino children: A majority are U.S.-born offspring of immigrants.* Pew Hispanic Center. Retrieved from http://pewhispanic.org/reports/report.php?ReportID=110

Institute of Medicine. (1989). *Research on children and adolescents with mental, behavioral and emotional disorders: Mobilizing a national initiative.* Washington, DC: National Academy Press.

Kemmelmeier, M., & Oyserman, D. (2001a). The ups and downs of thinking about a successful other: Self-construals and consequences of upward social comparison. *European Journal of Social Psychology, 31*, 311–320.

Kemmelmeier, M., & Oyserman, D. (2001b). Gendered influence of downward social comparisons on current and possible selves. *Journal of Social Issues, 57*, 129–148.

Kohler, A., & Lazarín, M. (2007). *Hispanic education in the United States* (Statistical Brief No 8). National Council of La Raza. Downloaded August 27, 2012, http://www.nclr.org/images/uploads/publications/file_SB8_HispEd_fnl.pdf

Orfield, G., Losen, D., Wald, J., & Swanson, C. (2004). *Losing our future: How minority youth are being left behind by the graduation rate crisis.* Cambridge, MA: The Civil Rights Project at Harvard University.

Oyserman, D. (2001). Self and identity. In A. Tessor & N. Schwarz (Eds.), *Blackwell handbook of social psychology* (pp. 499–517). Malden, MA: Blackwell.

Oyserman, D. (2008). Racial-ethnic self-schemas: Multi-dimensional identity-based motivation. *Journal of Research on Personality, 42*, 1186–1198.

Oyserman, D., Brickman, D., & Rhodes, M. (2007). School success, possible selves and parent school-involvement. *Family Relations, 56*, 279–289.

Oyserman, D., Bybee, D, & Terry, K. (2003). Gendered racial identity and involvement with school. *Self and Identity, 2*, 1–18.

Oyserman, D., Bybee, D., & Terry, K. (2006). Possible selves and academic outcomes: How and when possible selves impel action. *Journal of Personality and Social Psychology, 91*, 188–204.

Oyserman, D., Bybee, D., Terry, K., & Hart-Johnson, T. (2004). Possible selves as roadmaps. *Journal of Research in Personality, 38*, 130–149.

Oyserman, D., & Destin, M. (2010). Identity-based motivation: Implications for intervention. *The Counseling Psychologist, 38*, 1001–1043.

Oyserman, D., Elmore, K., & Smith, G. (2012). Self, self-concept and identity. In M. Leary & J. Tangney (Eds), *Handbook of self and identity* (2nd ed., pp. 69–104). New York, NY: Guilford Press.

Oyserman, D., & Fryberg, S. (2006). The possible selves of diverse adolescents: Content and function across gender, race and national origin. In C. Dunkel & J.

Kerpelmen (Eds.), *Possible selves: Theory, research, and application* (pp. 17–39). Huntington, NY: Nova.

Oyserman, D., Gant, L., & Ager, J. (1995). A socially contextualized model of African American identity: School persistence and possible *selves. Journal of Personality and Social Psychology, 69,* 1216–1232.

Oyserman, D., & Harrison, K. (1998). Implications of ethnic identity: African American identity and possible selves. In J. K. Swim & C. Stangor (Eds.), *Prejudice: The target's perspective* (pp. 281–300). San Diego, CA: Academic Press.

Oyserman, D., Harrison, K., & Bybee, D. (2001). Can racial identity be promotive of academic efficacy in adolescence? *International Journal of Behavioral Development, 25,* 379–385.

Oyserman, D. & James, L. (2008). Possible selves: From content to process. In K. Markman, W.M.P. Klein, J.A. Suhr (Eds.). *The Handbook of Imagination and Mental Stimulation.* (pp. 373–394). New York, NY: Psychology Press.

Oyserman, D., & James, L. (2011). Possible identities. In S. Schwartz, K. Luyckx, & V. Vignoles (Eds.) *Handbook of Identity Theory and Research* (pp. 117–18). New York, NY: Springer-Verlag.

Oyserman, D., Johnson, E. & James, L. (2011).Seeing the destination but not the path: Effects of socioeconomic disadvantage on school-focused possible self content and linked behavioral strategies. *Self and Identity, 10,* 474–492.

Oyserman, D., Kemmelmeier, M., Fryberg, S., Brosh, H., & Hart-Johnson, T. (2003). Racial-ethnic self-schemas. *Social Psychology Quarterly, 66,* 333–347.

Oyserman, D., & Markus, H. (1990a). Possible selves and delinquency. *Journal of Personality and Social Psychology, 59,* 112–125.

Oyserman, D., & Markus, H. (1990b). Possible selves in balance: Implications for delinquency. *Journal of Social Issues, 46,*141–157.

Oyserman, D., & Saltz, E. (1993). Competence, delinquency, and attempts to attain possible selves. *Journal of Personality and Social Psychology, 65,* 360–374.

Oyserman, D., Sorensen, N., Reber, R., & Chen, S. X. (2009). Connecting and separating mindsets: Culture as situated cognition. *Journal of Personality and Social Psychology, 97,* 217–235.

Oyserman, D., Terry, K., & Bybee, D. (2002). A possible selves intervention to enhance school involvement. *Journal of Adolescence, 24,* 313–326.

Oyserman, D., & Yoon, K.-I. (2009). Neighborhood effects on racial-ethnic identity: The undermining role of segregation. *Race & Social Problems, 1,* 67–76.

Schwarz, N., & Oyserman, D. (2011). Asking questions about behavior: Self-reports in evaluation research. In M. Mark, S. Donaldson, & B. Campbell (Eds.), *Social psychology and evaluation* (pp. 244–264). New York, NY: Guilford Press.

Shapiro, E., Zigmond, N., Wallace, T., & Marston, D. (Eds.). (2011). *Models for implementing Response to Intervention: Tools, outcomes, and implications.* New York, NY: Guilford Press.

Mental Health Interventions with Latino Students in Multicultural School Environments

A Framework for Assessing Biases and Developing Cultural Competence

Katina M. Lambros   Concepcion Barrio

CHAPTER 58

Getting Started

Why Schools Need to Assess Biases and Level of Cultural Knowledge When Working with Latino Students and Their Families

Schools are becoming increasingly culturally and ethnically diverse environments. Research shows that ethnic minority student populations are growing in the United States, and this trend is especially true for the Latino population, which increased by more than 113% from 1990 to 2010 and constitutes the largest ethnic minority group in the country, representing 16% of the population (Humes et al., 2011; U.S. Census Bureau, 2008, 2010).

The effects of culture on the academic experience and mental health functioning of Latino students are of paramount concern to families, educators, and communities alike. The *Digest of Education Statistics* (Snyder & Dillow, 2011) states that only 42% of Latino children 3 to 4 years old attended preschool in 2009, as compared to 55% of Caucasian and nearly 60% of African-American children. This suggests that for many families, exposure to early cognitive learning and cultural indoctrination occur in the home. This at-home preschool education may result in their coming to the European American K-12 educational system with a culture-specific set of knowledge, learning styles, goals, and expectations, which may make negotiating school systems difficult (Center for Mental Health in Schools at UCLA, 2001). Additionally, Latinos are at exceptionally high risk for school failure, experience considerable academic underachievement in comparison to grade-level peers (Hemphill & Vanneman, 2010), and are at significant risk for poor mental health outcomes (U.S. Department of Health and Human Services [DHHS], 2001). Furthermore, their participation in all levels of education continues to be low; they experience numerous grade retentions and have the highest school dropout rate in the nation. Regarding mental health functioning, Latino youth are also more likely to report depression and anxiety and to attempt suicide than non-Hispanic whites (Center for Mental Health in Schools at UCLA, 2008; DHHS, 2001), with female Hispanic students more likely to attempt suicide in comparison to all other youth. These statistics indeed argue for improved and more culturally relevant school-based mental health intervention for this population of children.

Unfortunately, the majority of all school-age students needing mental health services go un-served (Kataoka, Zhang, & Wells, 2002; Pihlakoski et al., 2004). Mental health intervention may be less likely for Latino youth than others in part because Latinos are underrepresented in service sectors such as schools and mental health (Yeh et al., 2004). Moreover, Latinos have less overall access to mental health care, are less likely to receive needed care, and receive a poorer quality of care (Garland et al., 2005; Howell & McFeeters, 2008; Kataoka et al., 2002; Yeh, McCabe, Hough, Dupuis, & Hazen, 2003; Slade, 2004; Wood et al., 2005). For youth who do receive mental health services, it is important to note that *schools* are considered a major mental health service provider and that a large proportion of children who received services were seen by practitioners within a school setting (AMSHA, 2009). Special education data also reflect that the mental health needs of Latino students are not being met, as they are underrepresented in the emotionally disturbed federal disability category, which serves youth having significant emotional, behavioral, and mental health problems (Yeh et al.,

2004; (U.S. Department of Education [USDE], 2009). See Section 1 for more information about working with students with mental diagnosis. Recent research indicates that disparities in school discipline practices exist for Latino students in addition to other racial and ethnic groups. More specifically, a study examined discipline referral patterns in 364 elementary and middle schools involved in School-Wide Positive Behavior Support (SWPBIS) reforms. Results revealed that Latino students were more likely than their Caucasian peers to receive expulsion or suspension as a consequence for similar problem behaviors (Skiba et al., 2011). This important research sheds additional light on previously "mixed" research findings on disciplinary overrepresentation of Latino students and also provides further support for the assessment of biases in school practices and outcomes and for the development of higher levels of cultural knowledge in working with Latino populations.

Reasons for school problems for Latino students have been attributed to inappropriate cognitive, cultural, and linguistic assessment and teaching/intervention methods (Donovan & Cross, 2002; Harry & Klingner, 2005; Treuba & Bartolome, 1997). Moreover, a lack of culturally responsive and empirically supported mental health prevention and early intervention services in schools and classrooms for this population may also contribute to disparities in referral and service use. Yet, school staff working directly with youth do not readily assume that their own teaching methods or tools may contribute to students' problems. Staff may be likely to attribute difficulties to within-child problems, and thus believe that change is required in children and families, not in the practices of schools and teachers (Harry & Klingner, 2005; Klingner et al., 2005; Means & Knapp, 1991, NCCREST, 2005). Teaching techniques are often assumed to be value-free and culturally neutral, and this assumption has prevented school providers from analyzing whether their teaching and intervention methods are equally effective with all student populations (Treuba & Bartolome, 1997). This practice is in contrast to several recent health policy reports (U.S. Department of Health and Human Services [DHHS], 1999, 2001), which have called for bringing empirically supported treatments into "real world settings," such as schools, and also stressing the need to develop, test, and modify mental health interventions with ethnic minority populations.

According to Banks (Banks, 2008; Klingner et al., 2005), in order to achieve this, the ethnic identity of every Latino student must be appreciated and respected by the teacher, other school staff, and the student's peer group. This cultural awareness, recognition, and affirmation provide a cornerstone for the learning activities taking place in the classroom and on the school campus. In addition, Latino youth must be encouraged to recognize and appreciate their own ethnic heritage and learn to appreciate the ethnic heritages of the other children. This recognition of individual ethnic identities links the teachers and students together, constituting a learning process that requires a transactional fit among child, teacher, classroom, and the academic content to be learned (Center for Mental Health in Schools at UCLA, 2001).

The purpose of this chapter is to provide a framework that promotes the development of cultural competence for practitioners working with Latino students and their families within multicultural school settings (by "practitioners," we mean any personnel, whether in the school system or in the surrounding community, who work with a school-age child). We have examined literature from the mental health and psychotherapy fields and the educational and school consultation fields, and have identified aspects of several models that can be adapted and applied to school social work practice settings with Latino students. First we address the definition of the concept of cultural competence, followed by an overview of several approaches and implications for practice.

What We Know

Cultural Competence Models and Approaches

There are numerous definitions of cultural competence in the health and mental health literature. The concept was first developed by the federally funded Child and Adolescent Service System Program in the 1980s. The definition of cultural competence developed by Cross and colleagues (1989) is comprehensive and has been frequently used in mental health services. "Cultural competence" refers to a set of congruent practice skills, knowledge, behaviors, attitudes, and policies that come together in a system, agency, or among consumer providers and professionals that enables the system, agency, or those professionals and consumer providers to work effectively in cross-cultural situations. At the provider level, cultural competence requires an examination of one's own attitudes and values, and the acquisition of the values, knowledge, skills, and attributes that will allow an individual to work appropriately in cross-cultural situations (Maternal and Child Health Bureau, 1999).

Notably, the mental health literature is replete with many approaches to cultural competence. Several models attend to the needs of specific ethnic groups, while others are applicable to diverse groups (Center for Mental Health Services [CMHS], 2000; Cross, Bazron, Dennis, & Isaacs, 1989; Sue, 1998). There are also models that address the cultural competence components related to training and staff development (Duren Green, Cook-Morales, Robinson-Zanartu, & Ingraham, 2009; Lum, 1999; Sue, Arrendondo, & McDavis, 1992). Most approaches to cultural competence emphasize the common themes of cultural awareness, knowledge, and skill that apply to the cultural competence of the organization, delivery of direct services, and training and staff development.

A model by Steven Lopez (1997) called Shifting Cultural Lenses has been received favorably by practitioners in diverse practice settings (S. R. Lopez, 2002; S. R. Lopez, Kopelowicz, & Cafiive, 2002). The model was based on three decades of psychotherapy research using both qualitative and quantitative methods. It also draws heavily from anthropological perspectives, specifically the explanatory models by Kleinman (1988, 1995). Cultural competence is viewed as an ongoing process in which the provider considers cultural factors while collecting evidence to test a given cultural hypothesis that a particular diagnosis or intervention is culturally relevant or not relevant for the client or family being served (S. R. Lopez, 1997). The model depicts two simultaneous strategies to service delivery and outreach in ethnically and culturally diverse communities. The culturally specific approach considers culture from an emic (specific or insider) perspective, which incorporates an attitude of openness in the discovery, acquisition, and interpretation of knowledge. In this approach, providers occupy the role of learner/facilitator in the process of promotion of cultural relevance and development of culturally congruent services. At the same time, the provider considers clinical evidence from an etic (general) perspective where the attitude is one of distance from the cultural group and the objective is the accumulation of universal knowledge. Through this approach, providers occupy the role of teacher/expert and evaluate culture from the vantage point of mainstream values. Culturally competent approaches balance the shift in cultural lenses in eliciting and understanding the client's cultural perspective within the provider's own framework in any given treatment domain (engagement, assessment, intervention, outreach, and collaborative work).

More specifically, the Lopez (S. R. Lopez, 1997) model of cultural competence can be applied with a variety of mental health interventions in schools and requires school staff to accurately assess their own biases and cultural knowledge and the effects they have on the type and quality of services provided to Latino students. This model requires a *shifting* of cultural lenses to consider the interface between multiple cultural perspectives in successfully understanding and addressing Latino students with school problems: (a) the student and family culture-specific framework, (b) the school provider's culture-specific and culture-general framework, (c) the school culture and climate, and (d) the culture of the surrounding community.

The operating principles of the above model can be applied in multiple settings. In order to enhance the model by Steven Lopez and align it for those who provide services in the schools, we have also included standards from a multicultural school consultation (MSC) model, which is a framework applied to various consultation models that infuse cultural considerations into the theory, research, practice, and training of consultation (Ingraham, 2000, 2003, 2004; Tarver Behring & Ingraham, 1998). In this model, the constructs of multicultural and cross-cultural consultation are central, and the primary school provider or "consultant" addresses the needs and cultural values of the "consultee(s)" and/or "clients." Within this consultation triad, one or more persons may differ culturally from the other members. This aspect of multicultural consultation is referred to as cross-cultural consultation (Ingraham, 2000, 2003, 2004; Tarver Behring & Ingraham, 1998) and has been developed for use within diverse school settings. This MSC model posits consultation through a multicultural lens and incorporates a broad consideration of diversity; it attends to all parties in the consultation process, considers the cultural context of consultation services, explores various issues related to school-based consultation across and within cultures, identifies competencies to develop in consultants and consultees, and increases attention to areas in need of further research (Ingraham, 2000, 2003, 2004, 2007). Many of the central features of the MSC model are well aligned with the Steven Lopez (1997) model of cultural competence, and as the provision of school-based mental health services requires the convergence of many service sectors/disciplines such as education, mental health, social work, counseling, and psychology, this model serves to link principles from these paradigms. The framework proposed bridges two conceptual models of cultural competence, which require additional empirical research; however, these authors wanted to present conceptual applications of it within diverse schools and more specifically with Latino students.

Research Support for Practice Method

In this section, the authors discuss school-based applications of the above mentioned models of cultural competence in hopes that school practioners will use the basic tenants across the many services that they provide (e.g., family outreach and advocacy, consultation and collaboration, referral, screening and assessment, and direct intervention). Also in this section, evidence-based mental health intervention research with Latino youth is reviewed and discussed in order to inform school social workers about a broad continuum of services and programs that may be appropriate for and enhance the mental health of Latino students.

As previously discussed, it is important that multicultural schools have culturally sensitive/responsive models of consultation to assist with implementation of *any* given intervention or school support (Booker, 2009). There are many school consultation models (Bergen & Kratochwill, 1990; Conoley & Conoley, 1992; Sheridan, Kratochwill, & Bergen, 1996) for implementing interventions within school settings; however, attention to cultural issues in these models has historically been limited (Ingraham, 2000) but is now emerging (see Booker, 2009, for a more comprehensive review of multicultural issues in school consultation models). The MSC model is one that can be applied to mental health service provision wherein cultural issues are raised and specific tailoring of the traditional consultation process is done to fit the needs and cultural values of the consultant, consultee, and client (Tarver, Behring, & Ingraham, 1998; Ingraham, 2003, 2004). Using qualitative methodology, an exploration of the relationship between culture and the consultation process within the MSC model was conducted with novice consultants and experienced teachers. Results reveal that school-based consultants were able to generate culturally grounded hypotheses of problem situations and that only through co-construction (via consultant and consultee) of case conceptualization were responsive interventions developed and applied to culturally and linguistically diverse students, including Latino youth. Additionally, the study revealed a multitude of contextual factors that may impact the MSC process (Ingraham, 2003). This model appears promising in terms of its cultural relevance; however, additional empirical research on its application with evidence-based intervention implementation within diverse school settings is needed.

Evidence-Based Mental Health Intervention Research with Latino Youth

Historically, research on mental health interventions with culturally diverse populations has been limited, and many randomized clinical trials have not included sufficient numbers of racial and ethnic minorities, thereby making it impossible to generalize efficacy of empirically supported treatments to these groups (DHHS, 2001). Research conducted in the last 10 years, however, has established evidence-based interventions that address mental health with minority youth (Ho, McCabe, Yeh, & Lau, 2010; Huey & Polo, 2008; Miranda et al., 2005). As discussed in these important reviews, determining if a treatment approach is culturally sensitive goes beyond solely examining a standard intervention's efficacy with a particular racial/ethnic group; rather, it should evaluate responsiveness on a range of cultural concerns (i.e., languages, experiences, traditions, beliefs, values). While documented interventions from both the mental health (i.e., Parent Management Training [PMT], Cognitive Behavioral Therapy [CBT], Structural Family Therapy [SFT]) and educational sectors (Incredible Years Dinosaur & Classroom Management Training, Second Step Violence Prevention, School-Wide Positive Behavioral Support & Intervention [SWPBIS], First Steps to

Success) have been found to work with Latino youth, there is less information on the cultural modification or tailoring of these interventions for this particular racial/ethnic group. Thus, the following section will briefly review research on the impact of culturally specific and culturally modified or adapted interventions for Latino youth that have potential for implementation in "real-world settings" such as multicultural schools (see Ho, McCabe, Yeh, & Lau, 2010; Huey & Polo, 2008; and Miranda et al., 2005 for a more comprehensive review of evidence-based psychosocial interventions for minority youth).

As previously discussed, mental health issues pertinent to Latino youth include internalizing problems such as depression, anxiety, and suicide ideation as well as externalizing behaviors involving conduct, delinquency, and dropout. As such, comprehensive school-based mental health programming for this group should address both dimensions. According to Miranda et al. (2005), *Cognitive Behavioral Therapy (CBT)* in small group formats has been conducted in schools (Clarke et al., 1992; Lewinsohn et al., 1996) and showed decreases in depression as well as improved cognitive performance. Furthermore, culturally sensitive adaptations (i.e., inclusion of *familism* and *respeto*) of CBT with Latino adolescents resulted in significant decreases in depression scores (Rosselló & Bernal, 1999). Another study addressing depression in a largely Latino adolescent sample compared an adapted version of *interpersonal treatments (IPT)* for depression with treatment as usual in several school-based mental health clinics. The IPT delivered in school clinics was more successful for reducing depression symptoms and improving functioning (Treatment for Adolescents with Depression Study Team, 2004). Lastly, a randomized control study of the *Cognitive Behavioral Intervention for Trauma in Schools (CBITS)* evaluated the effectiveness of a school-based mental health intervention developed for an inner-city multicultural population. This intervention targeted children's symptoms of PTSD, depression, and anxiety resulting from exposure to violence. Participants included a largely Latino low-income middle school sample in Los Angeles, and results showed that intervention students had significantly lower scores on symptoms of PTSD, depression, and psychosocial dysfunction (Kataoka et al., 2003; Stein et al., 2003).

Culturally responsive interventions for disruptive behavior problems in Latino youth have also been carefully examined (Ho, McCabe, Yeh, & Lau, 2010). A universal prevention program, *The Bridges to High School Program (Bridges/Puentes)*, targets school engagement and mental health risk in middle school Mexican-American youth. Families involved in this study reported improvements in parenting skills and decreases in youth problem behaviors. Similarly, adolescents reported improvements in parent skills, as well as increases in their own coping ability and improvements in depression (Gonzales, Dumka, Deardorff, Carter, & McCray, 2004). Barrera et al. (2002) evaluated the effectiveness of the *Schools and Homes Partnership (SHIP)* program, which was developed to address conduct problems in young elementary school students. The study participants consisted of a large number of Latino families (168 Latino and 116 Caucasian) with young children displaying behavior problems in addition to reading difficulties. This multi-component intervention showed decreases in conduct-related problems for Latino children (but not in teacher-rated internalizing problems) at the one-year follow-up point.

In this discussion of culturally responsive mental health treatments for Latino students, it seems valuable to mention relevant intervention literature from the fields of clinical psychology and mental health services research for a number of reasons. First, this body of research can and should inform the educational research, as these two important fields of study often overlap. Second, these studies are important because school social workers often connect students and families to clinical and community resources (i.e., specialty mental health, parent training programs).

A meta-analytic review of 76 studies employing cultural adaptations to mental health interventions (Griner & Smith, 2006) found a moderately strong benefit of culturally adapted mental health interventions (effect size was $d = .45$). Cultural adaptations were more efficacious when tailored to a specific racial/ethnic group in comparison to adaptations applied to groups consisting of clients from many cultural backgrounds. While this review provides support for cultural adaptations on the aggregate level, systematic examination of the *type* of cultural adaptations made to interventions seems like a critical element for future research. Unfortunately, many studies included in this meta-analysis did not provide detailed descriptions of adaptations, which are paramount to further understanding the complexity of cultural responsiveness. Additionally, this analysis included adult and adolescent samples, which make it somewhat difficult to apply the information to services provided in school settings with Latino children and adolescents.

Other findings from more recent investigations on cultural adaptations conducted specifically with Latino populations are mixed. In a study by McCabe and colleagues (2009), a randomized clinical trial of a culturally adapted version of *Parent-Child Interaction Therapy (PCIT)* was conducted with 58 Latino families. Families had children with documented behavior problems and were randomly assigned to the culturally adapted PCIT intervention (i.e., GANA), standard PCIT, or a treatment-as-usual condition. Results showed significant outcomes for GANA in comparison to treatment as usual, but not standard PCIT. Another study by Martinez and Eddy (2005) investigated a culturally adapted version of a parent management training intervention (i.e., *Nuestras Familias: Andando Entre Culturas*) with 78 Spanish-speaking Latino parents in a community setting. This intervention showed improvement in both parenting skills and aggressive and delinquent behavior for youth. *Brief Strategic Family Therapy (BSFT)*, a family systems approach to treating serious behavior problems, has also been shown to be a promising approach to reducing behavior problems as well as substance abuse in Latino youth (Szapocznik & Williams, 2000). Lastly, another study reported that cultural modifications of family interventions (i.e., *Strengthening Families Program*) did not substantially improve outcomes with diverse groups in comparison to the standard treatment protocol (Kumpfer et al., 2002). More specifically, this study indicated that cultural adaptations made by therapists that removed core components and decreased intervention dosage decreased positive treatment outcomes despite increasing family retention.

While the literature supporting cultural adaptations is emerging and promising, more research is needed to document whether cultural modifications are superior to standard evidence-based interventions and, if so, must identify the *specific* adaptive components that make them effective. Moreover, additional research on the feasibility and cost/benefit ratio of tailoring interventions to specific groups (and subsequent training of practitioners on these adapted models) may assist schools in making an informed decision about their adoption. Lastly, further study of cultural modifications and tailoring of mental health interventions for specific racial/ethnic groups that can be implemented in school settings is warranted. In summary, although new models of service delivery that promote cultural competence have been proposed in the fields of mental health and education, currently such models consist primarily of a set of guiding principles that lack empirical validation and are typically applied across all ethnic groups. No data specify the key aspects of cultural competence and what influence, if any, they have on clinical outcomes for racial/ethnic minorities (e.g., Falicov, 1998; Koss-Chioino & Vargas, 1999; S. R. Lopez, 1997; Ramirez, 1991; Ridley, Mendoza, Kanitz, Angermeier, & Zenk, 1994; Sue & Sue, 1999; Sue & Zane, 1987; Szapocznik et al., 1997).

What We Can Do

Practice Guidelines and Task Examples for Assessing Biases and Level of Cultural Knowledge

The following section begins with culturally relevant issues that must be considered and explored when working with Latino students and their families. It is important to note that these issues must not be generalized to all Latino students and families, as there is great diversity among Latino groups in the United States. Moreover, there exists substantial diversity within and between Latino subgroups related to such factors as immigration, acculturation, and socioeconomic and regional differences that may influence adherence to cultural norms. Latinos are a highly heterogeneous population comprising multiple national origins (e.g., Mexico, Cuba, Puerto Rico, and Central American and South American countries), with distinct patterns of migration or immigration and differing histories of relationships between their country of origin and the United States (Guarnaccia et al., 2007). Diversity among Latinos is also shaped by changing language use, family relationships, parenting practices, and social contexts, which have implications for health and mental health care use and outcomes (Guarnaccia et al., 2007). Nonetheless, there are also salient cultural issues that are found to characterize the Latino collective experience (Añez et al., 2008; Añez et al., 2005; Guarnaccia & Rodriguez, 1996). This diversity is reflected in variations in family patterns and traditions. The general issues listed here are highlighted for their relevance to providing school services to Latino students and families. The remainder of the section presents three case vignettes describing school-based activities in which cultural biases and knowledge were not competently assessed, and examples of how these cases could have been approached from a culturally competent perspective. Following these are more thorough discussions of each vignette within a framework of providing culturally competent (a) referral, (b) assessment, and (c) intervention for Latino students and families. Also included in this section are hands-on tips to guide school practitioners in addressing the educational and mental health needs of Latinos in a culturally relevant and competent manner.

Some cultural issues to consider in working with Latino students and families:

- Ethnic minority cultures, particularly Latino cultures, are known to be more family-centered than are Euro-American cultures (Barrio, 2000; Lin & Kleinman, 1988). The familial self or *familismo* is considered the common thread shared by Latino groups (Falicov, 1998).
- A family's cultural practices, characteristics, and coping style should be considered as cultural resources that can enhance the student's ability to meet the academic standards of the classroom. Studies have shown that acculturation to American values and behaviors can have a negative effect on the mental health of Mexican immigrants and their families, and that the retention of Mexican traditional culture can have positive effects on mental health outcomes (Vega et al., 1998).
- Due to normative role expectations that value politeness even in the face of disappointment, Latinos may avoid confrontation or direct questioning, opting for being more passive with school personnel and other professionals (Alegria et al., 2008). Moreover, Latino children may be expected to respond to adults and school staff in a cooperative, compliant, and respectful manner. Latinos' greater deference to professional authority is commonly encountered as a shared cultural value that appears to moderate response style and influence how Latinos relate to others (Marin & Marin, 1991; Miranda et al., 1996). As a result of the cultural value of respect for professionals, some Latinos may forgo openly questioning during the assessment or counseling process due to concern with disrespecting professionals or persons in positions of authority. It may lead students and their family members to participate in a process without truly understanding the nature of the clinical context (Domenech Rodriguez et al., 2006). Latino family practices need to be viewed within the given cultural context, without imposing labels (i.e., enmeshed, dysfunctional) that may pathologize familial relationships and interpersonal style.
- Latino families may show mistrust of Western medical models of mental health diagnoses and treatment and may access services from alternative sources (e.g., priests, spiritual healers, herbalists) (McCabe, 2002; Woodward, Dwinell, & Arons, 1992).
- Establishing a personal connection based on warmth and respect is particularly important in engaging Latino youth and family members into mental health services, but it should also adhere to the cultural communication style of *personalismo*, where relationship building is deeply valued (Umaña-Taylor & Bamaca, 2004).
- Latino students may be developing language skills in both English and Spanish, which may affect both academic and social performance. Therefore, the child's bilingual development and bicultural identity needs to be considered in the referral, assessment, and intervention process (Klingner, Artilles, et al., 2005)
- It is critical to carefully assess the criteria underlying mental health constructs (e.g., impulsivity, anxiety, depression) with an awareness of normative behavior within the child's cultural setting (Pitts & Wallace, 2003).

Applying Interventions within a Response to Intervention Framework

Within the school system, Response to Intervention (RTI) is a multi-tiered, problem-solving model of assessment and intervention that includes (a) systematic data collection on student performance, (b) sound implementation of evidence-based intervention (EBI) as needed, and (c) ongoing progress monitoring to adjust instruction until improved achievement and/or school behavior is demonstrated (Jimerson et al., 2007). RTI seems well positioned to enhance educational practice, address the needs of diverse learners, and potentially reduce disparities in education (i.e., achievement gap, overrepresentation in special education). Some argue, however, that in order to realize RTI's full potential, a school's RTI model must be culturally responsive to meet the needs of an increasingly diverse student body (Crockett & Esparza Brown, 2009; Klingner, Artiles, et al., 2005).

With regard to the role of culture in RTI, the National Center for Culturally Responsive Educational Systems (NCCRESt) recently issued a position statement that outlines significant challenges and considerations that must be contemplated by schools and districts in order to improve educational experiences and outcomes for culturally and linguistically diverse students (NCCRESt, 2005). Additionally, models for multicultural practices and the RTI process have been posited, and while they are not necessarily specific to mental health programming, they do address RTI, English language learners, and culturally and linguistically diverse students (Crockett & Esparza Brown, 2009).

Typically, schools do not have a myriad of mental health interventions at each RTI tier that are developed for and effective with all potential racial and ethnic groups, nor does that seem like a practical way to provide educational and/or mental health services. It does seem feasible and ultimately useful, however, to assess if a given RTI model adequately addresses Latino students and their unique needs. Using the guidelines developed by NCCRESt (2005), as well as the work of other colleagues in this area (Crockett & Brown, 2009; Klingner, Artiles, et al., 2005; Rogoff, 2003), schools might consider the following questions in regards to cultural responsiveness of their RTI model for Latino youth.

General Questions

- Does our RTI model offer tiered supports for academics as well as behavior/mental health for students, as these domains often overlap and impact one another? (Jimerson et al., 2007)
- Do our school personnel, especially the classroom teachers, interpret learning, social behavior, and development within a sociocultural context? (Klingner, Artilles, et al., 2005; Rogoff, 2003)
- Does our RTI model provide ample opportunity to examine classroom climate as well as teacher-student interactions within the learning process? (Vaughn & Fuchs, 2003)
- Does our RTI model provide opportunity to assess important dimensions of school climate (e.g., perceived multiculturalism, ethnic identity, ethnocultural empathy), as these have been found impactful for Latino youth? (Chang & Le, 2010)
- Do ongoing staff trainings focus on cultivating a deeper understanding of race, class, gender, disability status, language, culture, and educational equity? (NCCRESt, 2005)
- Does our RTI model examine data (at the school, classroom, and student level) that are disaggregated by racial/ethnic group? (Skiba et al., 2011)
- Does our RTI model employ a systems-level problem-solving approach that bridges school, home, and community? (Klingner, Artilles, et al., 2005)

Tier 1 Questions

- Does the general education curriculum offer culturally meaningful or culturally relevant materials/activities for students who are not members of the dominant or mainstream school culture? If not, are there ways to adapt some of the activities so they are more culturally inclusive for Latino learners?
- Does our school provide adequate support for teachers to become more culturally competent and to adapt given educational and discipline practices to be more culturally inclusive?
- How do our Tier 1 supports and general education curriculum address the needs of Latino students, including English language learners (newcomers and existing)?

Tier 2 Questions

- Does our RTI model employ evidence-based interventions at the secondary level? If so, do the empirical investigations on these interventions include Latino participants? (Donovan & Cross, 2002)
- Are any of the Tier 2 interventions adapted or modified for Latino students?

- Does our model offer supplemental interventions that target internalizing problems and symptoms, as these have been shown to occur more frequently in Latino youth?
- What level of data or evidence is needed to determine that a Latino student is not responding and needs more intensive intervention? Are these criteria the same for all students?

Tier 3 Questions

- Do our RTI services at this tertiary level address critical risk factors for Latino students (dropout, suicide ideation, depression, etc.)?
- How does our RTI model bridge to other important systems (parent/extended family involvement/empowerment/support, community resources) and collaborate with other service sectors (specialty mental health, primary care, juvenile justice, child welfare, substance use)?

Tools and Practice Examples

Case Vignette #1—Referral

A teacher has referred a fourth-grade Latino student, Frank, to the school social worker because he seems withdrawn, anxious, and depressed. According to the teacher, Frank doesn't participate in class discussions, makes poor eye contact with others, doesn't respond when called upon, and has few social interactions. Academically, Frank is at grade level in all subject areas. Socially, he seems quiet and well-behaved. He has one close friend, but he does not readily join established social groups or initiate conversations with unfamiliar peers. The social worker talked with Frank and his parents about the teacher's concerns. His parents shared that it is important that Frank is respectful and compliant with school staff and that he behave appropriately at home, in school, and in the community, particularly at church services. Upon interviewing Frank's teacher, the school social worker discovered that this teacher encouraged her students to assert themselves and their ideas verbally in class, required them to question and challenge academic concepts and ideas, and favored highly competitive assignments, such as class debates on course topics. She also coordinated the school plays and had a dramatic and expressive teaching style. She felt Frank was anxious during public-speaking activities, could not advocate for himself, and appeared overly sad and indifferent. As such, her evaluation of Frank in the areas of effort, citizenship, and social interaction reflected low grades. Therefore, she determined that Frank was either anxious or depressed and in need of mental health treatment.

Ideas for a more culturally competent approach: Had the classroom teacher assessed her own personal values for optimal classroom behavior (advocacy, assertion, expression) and those of Frank and his family, she would have realized that they were not congruent with the values of the child's family. Knowledge about the family's cultural orientation would have allowed her to "shift" her cultural lenses and consider the child's behavior within the context of his family culture. Frank was functioning quite well, but what the teacher perceived as signs of anxiety or depression was a behavioral style that was culturally different than her own. With this insight, the teacher could have structured social and academic activities that respected his cultural orientation while also meeting her expectations for academic performance. For example, rather then expect Frank to compete for a main character in a classroom skit, explain to him the various roles that the skit involves—including writing the storyline, building the stage, or filming—and validate his selection of any one of these tasks.

Case Vignette #2—Assessment

Mexican immigrant parents were asked by the school to attend a series of school assistance meetings (i.e., school study team, school assistance team, Response to Intervention team, problem-solving team) for their second-grade daughter, Karina. These meetings typically comprise a multidisciplinary team of school personnel who work with the teacher to design interventions for students preceding formal evaluation for special education. These meetings are often the first pathway to receiving school services. For several months, Karina has had significant academic problems in all core areas, and exhibits high levels of off-task and inattentive behavior. Her native language is Spanish, and she is designated as an English language learner. Based on observations and screenings, her expressive and receptive language abilities are delayed in both English and Spanish. Socially, she interacts well in group activities and on the playground. The team decides to implement two chosen academic and language-based interventions; however, after several weeks, Karina is not meeting grade-level standards, and her parents continue to express concerns that she "is sad and feels badly about herself." Members of the school team recommend a psychoeducational evaluation for a learning disability and explain the nature of special education services to Karina's parents. Immediately, her parents express concerns about "special education." Based on their prior experiences, they feel that these classes are for kids who are "very slow" or "crazy," and they think that attending them would bring shame on Karina and the family. They do not want her separated from her teacher, and they do not consent to the assessment process.

Ideas for a more culturally competent approach: Asking Karina's parents their thoughts about special education would have provided the school team with valuable information about realistic intervention options. Connecting them with a Spanish-speaking parent facilitator who has experience with special education services may have helped the family learn about the benefits of this plan for Karina in an incremental manner. Inviting the family to observe classroom resource services ("push-in" services) or to visit a special education classroom during reading instruction may have provided them a better sense about the children enrolled in these classes and the kinds of activities that take place. Introducing them to a bilingual special education teacher and establishing rapport may have helped them to gradually accept a continuum of service options for their daughter.

Case Vignette #3—Intervention

A sixth-grade Latino student, Juan, was diagnosed with attention-deficit/hyperactivity disorder (ADHD) by a family pediatrician. Juan has numerous problems in reading and math, and he has behavioral difficulties such as not paying attention, not remaining seated, and not joining peer groups in his school. In determining the course of intervention, school staff discussed with the family the efficacy of medication for Juan's condition. The parents expressed alarm and resisted further discussion regarding the medication intervention. Despite numerous efforts on the part of school staff to discuss a treatment plan with the family, they showed a lack of trust in school professionals, a refusal of any treatment plan involving medication, and an overall lack of engagement with the school. Further exploration by a school social worker during a home visit uncovered that the parents felt pressured by school staff to medicate the child; they regarded medication as an extreme measure and were afraid that their child could become dependent, addicted, and possibly suffer brain damage as a result of taking medication.

Ideas for a more culturally competent approach: School providers should have approached Juan's family differently by asking first about their perceptions and understanding of Juan's school and behavioral problems. This would have revealed the family's explanatory model, providing culturally specific information for shaping a culturally acceptable treatment plan that would fit with the family's values and beliefs. This would also serve to engage and build a therapeutic alliance with the family and increase their receptivity to psychoeducational information regarding ADHD. An approach founded in mutual respect and agreement between the school staff and the child's family is essential in fostering adherence to any behavioral or medication treatment plan.

Culturally Competent Referrals

There may be several referral avenues that schools use to bring students having problems to the attention of professionals, including student study or assistance teams, individual education plans, transdisciplinary teams, RTI teams, school nurses, and health service centers. These referrals may come from various sources including teachers, parents, other school staff, and outside professionals (e.g., pediatricians, social workers). Whatever referral mechanism is most frequent in schools, it is crucial to conduct assessment of the sociocultural framework of (a) the student and family being referred, (b) the referral source, and (c) the primary service provider and/or team that the student is referred to. For example, Vignette #1 describes a child who is not currently meeting the sociobehavioral expectations of his classroom. Upon further assessment, it is discovered that there is a cultural mismatch between the student and his teacher. The teacher-preferred behaviors (expressive, self-assertive, analytical) were in sharp contrast to those values and behaviors that the family held important for their son (respectful, mild-mannered). This generated a referral to a mental health provider, which was culturally biased. Had the classroom teacher shifted her cultural lenses to simultaneously consider (and assess) the cultural framework and values of Frank and his family and her own biases and values regarding the expected social norms within her classroom, perhaps a mental health referral would not have been necessary. Instead, she could have learned about Frank's cultural orientation and incorporated it into classroom activities that would promote rather than hinder the child's academic performance, self-esteem, and ethnic identity. It is also important to note that a child who is subjected to a culturally invalidating teaching environment can potentially develop symptoms of anxiety and depression that will indeed require mental health treatment. Such a situation may not be caused by inherent mental health problems but may instead represent an acculturative stress response in trying to cope with daily exposure to an insensitive teaching style. In summary, assessing the biases and cultural knowledge of all involved in the referral process is crucial.

Tips:

- When a student is referred for screening, evaluation, or service, carefully review the referral reason (academic and/or behavioral) and consider it within the cultural norms and expectations of the student, family, teacher, classroom environment, school, and any other relevant setting. Take into account cultural misinformation, racism, and cultural differences that may affect Latino learners.
- When examining the validity of a referral, remember that Latino families may differ in terms of their family composition, childrearing practices, response to disobedience, perceptions of disability/health, communication and interpersonal styles, and help-seeking behaviors. These cultural considerations should be examined in the context of how they influence students' functioning within classroom situations, schools, families, and communities (Lynch, 1992).
- As a school provider, refine the ability to recognize the limits of your own multicultural competence. Ask yourself what you know about the customs, values, and historical experiences of a particular child in your class or school with whom you are planning on working.
- Seek educational, consultative, and training experiences to improve multicultural knowledge. Identify individuals in your school who come from an ethnic or cultural heritage different than your own, who are bilingual, who have (bilingual) crosscultural, language, and academic development (CLAD/BCLAD) certifications and become familiar with departments specializing in dual-language services, English language learners, and other services or populations.

Culturally Competent Assessment

Competent assessment practices should undoubtedly be the basis for which intervention decisions are made. For schools, assessment of problems may include a psychoeducational or mental health screening/evaluation in the areas of cognition, academic achievement, learning modalities, and sociobehavioral functioning using tools that are both norm-referenced and idiographic in nature (e.g., direct observations, achievement tests, functional assessments, curriculum-based measurements, semistructured interviews). Often, information is collected from the student, as well as other individuals familiar with the child (teacher, other school staff, parents, other relatives, etc.). Information should also be collected regarding the learning environment that the child is a part of, which may include classroom instructional practices, positive behavior supports, student-teacher interactions, and peer relationships. Assessments also often involve several school staff who interact and assess the child (e.g., school social worker, psychologist, classroom teacher, speech pathologist, counselor). School staff *must* consider all assessment information within the sociocultural context of the student and his or her family. Remember that a student's cultural framework may not align with the school service provider's own cultural framework. Also consider that the student family's cultural orientation may not be in sync with the school's cultural context or those standards suggested by a particular discipline (social work, psychology, mental health). As an example, in Vignette #2 the school staff assumed that Karina's family held the same beliefs and views about special education as the school team did. Failure to assess their perspective resulted in hesitation, fear, and doubt as to whether the school could help Karina. Perhaps asking Karina's parents what they thought she needed to help with her schoolwork would have been a better place to start. Also, inviting them to visit a resource classroom prior to discussing special education may have given them a clearer picture about the children served and the types of learning activities offered in such classrooms. Having them meet a special education teacher with bilingual certification may have also eased their fears about having Karina change teachers. By shifting their cultural lenses, the school providers would have become aware of the family's perspective regarding the nature and description of the problem, their beliefs about the cause of the problem, and their expectations for treatment. It is important to seek and explore the immediate family's perspective on the problem, as not doing so may result in inappropriate treatments. Accurate assessment and an effective intervention depend on rapport and the school providers' understanding of students' cultural identity, social supports, self-esteem, and reticence about treatment because of societal stigma (S. R. Lopez, 1997). This information will guide school providers in determining a particular intervention to use with a student.

Tips:

- Mainstream, standardized, norm-referenced tests may not be valid measures for Latino students who are English language learners (ELLs), due to inappropriateness of norms, scores reflecting English proficiency, fairness of content, and differences in educational background, acculturation, and economic situation. Use a variety of assessment techniques to examine Latino students' functioning across a number of settings (e.g., school, home, community).
- Interpret assessment results by examining a Latino student's behavioral or mental health functioning in terms of (a) his or her familiarity with the majority culture's behavioral expectations and/or (b) the acculturation conflicts that may interfere with the student's ability to perform adequately within various social situations (CMHS, 2000).
- In most assessment situations, Latino students' performances are compared to a normative sample that is racially, ethnically, and culturally different. Throughout the assessment process, school providers can minimize bias by comparing the performance of an individual Latino student to other children of the same age, socioeconomic level, and linguistic and cultural background. Consider the application of more relevant norms for a better fit between the student's sociocultural background and the normative sample's sociocultural background (S.R. Lopez, 1997).
- Assessment of the Latino student's instructional and classroom environment is critical, and school providers must ask: Are the class materials appropriate for the language, academic, and sociocultural skills of the student? Can Latino students understand and relate to the content of the materials from their cultural perspective? Does the curriculum address the unique cultural and linguistic needs of the Latino student? Are teaching strategies sensitive to students' cultural differences in communication, attitudes, and values? Are cultural differences recognized and valued in the classroom? Are the rewards and incentives valued within the culture of the Latino student?
- As the primary service provider or school social worker involved in the assessment process, you should determine your own cultural biases and cultural knowledge regarding the environment, social issues, language development, second language acquisition, acculturation, educational history, quality of educational program, socioeconomic status, and experience of racism of Latino students.
- Strive to improve your diagnostic skills with Latino students by incorporating their cultural, social, and environmental reality into the assessment of behavioral and clinical symptoms.
- Assess the cultural framework of all others involved in the assessment/intervention process.
- If interpreters are necessary, choose personnel who have prior experience in schools, high proficiency in both languages, knowledge of regional dialects, and familiarity with the education and special education program in which the student is enrolled (E. C. Lopez, 1995).

Culturally Competent Intervention

Quite often, well-researched and validated treatments are not effective due to a mismatch between the treatment and the child's family's cultural values. In Vignette #3 a discussion with the parents regarding their explanatory model (Kleinman, Eisenberg, & Good 1978) about ADHD should have been conducted and would have guided the school staff on how to approach a discussion of interventions. The discussion should include open-ended questions about what they think their child's problem is, what they think causes it, if and how it has progressed in their child, what its consequences might be, and what their views are on how best to treat it. Each family's explanatory model of their child's behavioral problems is shaped by the *cultural background* of the family and their *experience* with the behavioral problems. Different beliefs about the causes of a particular disorder and the acceptability of treatment by clients of varied cultural backgrounds have been shown to alter diagnostic and treatment patterns for disorders (Sussman, Robins, & Earls, 1987; Westermeyer, 1987). Cultural factors may affect the acceptance of and adherence to treatment plans proposed by providers (Hu, Snowden, Jerrell, & Nguyen, 1991; S. Lopez, 1989).

In Vignette #3, knowledge about racial/ethnic disparities in medication use would have been helpful. More specifically, studies have documented that African American and Latino children receive less stimulant medication for ADHD, and their parents or caregivers report less use of medication for treating ADHD, than do European American children (Rowland et al., 2002; Safer & Malever, 2000). Perhaps a review of all the effective treatments for the condition, both medication *and* positive behavior supports, would have been more helpful in discussing this delicate issue with this particular family. The next step would have been to ask the family which treatments they preferred and felt would work best for their child. Intervention activities need to be framed within a school—home collaboration partnership. Empirical data are available demonstrating that Latino students achieve in programs emphasizing parent involvement in curriculum planning, school organization, classroom participation, and home activities that promote literacy in the native language (Cummins, 1989). By taking this more culturally informed approach, school providers can recognize the unique ethnocultural qualities and expectations of Latino families. The school provider can then balance culturally specific values of families with those of the intervention. This approach tests cultural and alternative hypotheses in formulating a culturally competent plan (S. R. Lopez, 1994, 1997).

For some Latino students, more direct, intensive services within the schools, such as group or individual counseling, should be considered to address mental health needs. For example, a Latino student may struggle with acculturative stress, ethnic identity confusion, and cultural reactions that can harm his or her functioning (E. C. Lopez, 1995). Latino students may also experience high levels of stress associated with learning a second language or with experiences of discrimination and racism within schools and communities. According to Lopez (1995) among the culturally sensitive techniques recommended in the literature are (a) *ethnotherapy,* whereby emphasis is placed on helping individuals develop a positive sense of ethnic identity, (b) *cuento* therapy, in which folk stories assist youth in exploring cultural identity and ego development, and (c) the use of toys and materials that reflect the students' cultural and linguistic backgrounds. Also recommended are group counseling approaches, although their utility must be evaluated for Latino children whose cultural backgrounds may not necessarily promote self-disclosure with people outside the family. Last, all implemented social skills training and counseling activities should be delivered in the students' primary or most proficient language to aid communication (CMHS, 2000; E. C. Lopez, 1995).

Tips

- Carefully consider the cultural applicability of intervention models, but do not radically modify them on the basis of limited information about the cultural congruence between their methods and the student or family belief system. Consider lower levels of modification first (S. R. Lopez, 1997).
- Incorporate Latino experiences and cultural strengths into school interventions. Incorporating activities, interaction styles, and instructional sequences that match the students' cognitive, emotional, and behavioral styles is recommended (Tharp, 1989).
- Establish school rules that reflect both the value of diversity and respect for different cultures and the importance of a climate conducive to learning.
- When using interpreters to work with Latino families to develop, refine, and evaluate interventions, provide them with time to ask parents about intervention procedures, provide feedback on implemented interventions, and explore cultural factors that may have influenced the child's or parent's behaviors (E. C. Lopez, 1995).

Key Points to Remember

- The provision of culturally competent school-based mental health services may play a role in reducing the social, cultural, and language barriers that often impede access to services and help-seeking efforts by Latino populations.
- The framework discussed here links existing models of cultural competence from the mental health field and school psychology and consultation literature.
- This framework is well aligned with public health agendas calling for cultural competence in the treatment of mental health problems in minority groups and the linkage of research models to the provision of services in schools (DHHS, 2000, 2001).
- This framework can also be applied to key activities (i.e., referral, assessment, and intervention) in working with diverse Latino children dealing with mental health issues.
- This framework is closely aligned with recent guidelines regarding culturally responsive RTI models of assessment and intervention.
- It is crucial that school practitioners and educators capitalize on the cultural strengths of the growing population of Latino students, in large part because the economic and technological future of this country depends on their educational success (Treuba & Bartolome, 1997).
- Best practices in assessing biases and cultural knowledge will guide school practitioners in addressing the educational and mental health needs of Latinos in a culturally relevant and competent manner.

References

Alegria, M., Polo, A., Gao, S., Santana, L., Rothstein, D., Jimenez, A.,... Normand, S. L. (2008, March). Evaluation of a patient activation and empowerment intervention in mental health care. *Medical Care, 46*(3), 247–256.

Añez, L. M., Paris, M., Bedregal, L. E., Davidson, L., & Grillo, C. M. (2005). Application of cultural constructs in the care of first generation Latino clients in a community mental health setting. *Journal of Psychiatric Practice, 11*(4), 221–230.

Añez, L. M, Silva, M. A., Paris, M., & Bedregal, L. E. (2008). Engaging Latinos through the integration of cultural values and motivational interviewing principles. *Professional Psychology: Research and Practice, 39*(2), 153–159.

Banks, J. (2008). *An introduction to multicultural education* (4th ed.). Boston, MA: Pearson Education.

Barrera, M., Jr., Biglan, A., Taylor, T. K., Gunn, B. K., Smolkowski, K., Black, C.,... Fowler, R.C. (2002). Early elementary school intervention to reduce conduct problems: A randomized trial with Hispanic and non-Hispanic children. *Prevention Science, 3*, 83–94.

Barrio C. (2000). The cultural relevance of community support programs. *Psychiatric Services, 51*(7), 879–884.

Bergen, J., & Kratochwill, T. (1990). *Behavioral consultation and therapy.* New York, NY: Plenum.

Booker, K. (2009). Multicultural considerations in school consultation. In J. M. Jones (Ed.), *The psychology of multiculturalism in schools: A primer for practice, training and research* (pp. 173–190). Bethesda, MD: National Association of School Psychology.

Center for Mental Health in Schools at UCLA. (2001). An introductory packet on cultural concerns in addressing barriers to learning. Los Angeles, CA: Author.

Center for Mental Health in Schools at UCLA. (2008). *Youngsters' mental health and psychosocial problems: What are the data?* Los Angeles, CA: Author.

Center for Mental Health Services. (2000). *Cultural competence standards in managed care mental health services for four underserved/underrepresented racial/ethnic groups.* Rockville, MD: Substance Abuse and Mental Health Service Administration.

Chang, J., & Le, T. N. (2010). Multiculturalism as a dimension of school climate: The impact of academic achievement of Asian American and Hispanic youth. *Cultural Diversity and Ethnic Minority Psychology, 16*(4), 485–492.

Clarke, G. N., Hops, H., Lewinsohn, P. M., Andrews, J., Seeley, J. R., & Williams, J. (1992). Cognitive behavioral group treatment of adolescent depression: prediction of outcome. *Behav. Ther., 23*, 341–54.

Conoley, J. C., & Conoley, C. W. (1992). *Consultation: A guide to practice and training* (2nd ed.). New York: Allyn and Bacon.

Crockett, D., & Brown, J., (2009). Multicultural practices and response to intervention. In J. M. Jones (Ed.), *Psychology of multiculturalism in the schools: A primer for practice, training, and research* (pp. 117–137). Bethesda, MD: National Association of School Psychologists.

Cross, T., Bazron, B., Dennis, K. & Isaacs, M. (1989). *Towards a culturally competent system of care: A monograph on effective services for minority children who are severely emotionally disturbed* (Vol. 1). Washington, DC: Georgetown University Child Development Center, CASSP Technical Assistance Center.

Cummins, J. (1989). *Empowering minority students.* Sacramento: California Association for Bilingual Education.

Cummins, J. (1984). *Bilingualism and special education: Issues in assessment and pedagogy.* San Diego, CA: College-Hill.

Domenech Rodriguez, M., Rodriguez, J., & Davis, M. (2006). Recruitment of first-generation Latinos in a rural community: The essential nature of personal contact. *Family Process, 45*(1), 87–100.

Donovan, S., & Cross, C. (2002). *Minority students in special and gifted education.* Washington, DC: National Academy Press.

Duren Green, T., Cook-Morales, V. J., Robinson-Zanartu, C., Ingraham, C. (2009). Pathways on a journey of getting it: Multicultural competence training and continuing professional development. In J. M. Jones (Ed.), *Psychology of multiculturalism in the schools: A primer for practice, training, and research* (pp. 83–113). Bethesda, MD: National Association of School Psychologists.

Falicov, C. J. (1998). *Latino families in therapy: A guide to multicultural practice.* New York, NY: Guilford Press.

Garland, A. F., Lau, A. S., Yeh, M., McCabe, K. M., Hough, R. L., & Landsverk, J. A. (2005). Racial and ethnic differences in utilization of mental health services among high-risk youths. *American Journal of Psychiatry, 162,* 1336–1343.

Gonzales, N. A., Dumka, L. E., Deardorff, J., Carter, S. J., & McCray, A. (2004). Preventing poor mental health and school dropout of Mexican American Adolescents following the transition to junior high school. *Journal of Adolescent Research, 19,* 113–131.

Griner, D., & Smith, T. B. (2006). Culturally adapted mental health interventions: A meta-analytic review. *Psychotherapy: Theory, Research, Practice, Training, 43*(6), 531–548.

Guarnaccia, P. J., Martínez Pincay, I., Alegría, M., Shrout, P. E., Lewis-Fernández, R., Canino, G. J. (2007). Assessing diversity among Latinos. *Hispanic Journal of Behavioral Sciences, 29*(4), 510–534.

Guarnaccia, P. J., & Rodriguez, O. (1996). Concepts of culture and their role in the development of culturally competent mental health services. *Hispanic Journal of Behavioral Sciences, 18*(4), 419–443.

Harry, B., & Klingner, J. K. (2005). *Why are so many minority students in special education? Understanding race and disain schools.* New York: Teachers College Press.

Hemphill, F. C., & Vanneman, A. (2010). *Achievement gaps: How Hispanic and white students in public schools perform in mathematics and reading on the National Assessment of Educational Progress* (NCES 2011–459). Washington, DC: National Center for Education Statistics, Institute of Education Sciences, U.S. Department of Education.

Ho, J., McCabe, K., Yeh, M., & Lau, A. (2010). Evidence-based treatments for conduct problems among ethnic minorities. In R. C. Murrihy, A. D. Kidman, & T. H. Ollendick (Eds.), *Clinical handbook of assessing and treating conduct problems in youth* (pp. 455–488). New York, NY: Springer.

Howell, E., & McFeeters, J. (2008). Children's mental health care: differences by race/ethnicity in urban/rural areas. *Journal of Health Care for the Poor and Underserved, 19*(1), 237–247.

Hu, T. W., Snowden, L. R., Jerrell, J. M., & Nguyen, T. D. (1991). Ethnic populations in public mental health services: Service choice and level of use. *American Journal of Public Health, 81,* 1429–1434.

Huey, S. J., Jr., & Polo, A. J. (2008). Evidence-based psychosocial treatments for ethnic minority youth. *Journal of Clinical Child & Adolescent Psychology, 37,* 1262–1301.

Humes, K. R., Jones, N. A., & Ramirez, R. R. (2011). *Overview of race and Hispanic origin: 2010 census briefs.* Washington, DC: U.S. Census Bureau.

Ingraham, C. (2000). Consultation through a multicultural lens: Multicultural and cross-cultural consultation in schools. *School Psychology Review, 29*(3), 320–343.

Ingraham, C. L. (2003). Multicultural consultee-centered consultation: When novice consultants explore cultural hypotheses with experienced teacher consultees. *Journal of Educational and Psychological Consultation, 14,* 329–362.

Ingraham, C. L. (2004). Multicultural consultee-centered consultation: Supporting consultees in the development of cultural competence. In N. M. Lambert, I. Hylander, & J. H. Sandoval (Eds.), *Consultee-centered consultation: Improving the quality of professional services in schools and community organizations.* Mahwah, NJ: Erlbaum.

Ingraham, C. L. (2007). Focusing on consultees in multicultural consultation. In G. B. Esquivel, E. C. Lopez, & S. G. Nahari (Eds.), *Handbook of multicultural school psychology: An interdisciplinary perspective* (pp. 99–118). Mahwah, NJ: Erlbaum.

Jimerson, S. R., Burns, M. K., & VanDerHeyden, A. M. (2007). *Handbook of response to intervention: The science and practice of assessment and intervention.* Berlin, Germany: Springer.

Kataoka, S., Stein, B. D., Jaycox, L. H., Wong, M., Escuerdo, P., Tu, W., ... Fink, A. (2003). A school-based mental health program for traumatized Latino immigrant children. *Journal of the American Academy of Child and Adolescent Psychiatry, 42*(3), 311–318.

Kataoka, S. H., Zhang, L., & Wells, K. B. (2002). Unmet need for mental health care among U.S. children: Variation by ethnicity and insurance status. *American Journal of Psychiatry, 159,* 1548–1555.

Kleinman, A., Eisenberg, L., & Good, B. (1978). Culture, illness, and care: Clinical lessons from anthropologic and cross-cultural research. *Annals of Internal Medicine, 88,* 251–258.

Kleinman, A. (1988). *Rethinking psychiatry: From cultural category to personal experience.* New York, NY: Free Press.

Kleinman, A. (1995). *Writing at the margin: Discourse between anthropology and medicine.* Berkeley, CA: University of California Press.

Klingner, J. K., Artiles, A. J., Kozleski, E., Harry, B., Zion, S., Tate, W., Duran, G. Z., & Riley, D. (2005). Addressing the disproportionate representation of culturally and linguistically diverse students in special education through culturally responsive educational systems. *Education Policy Analysis Archives, 13*(38), Retrieved, September 3, 2012, from http://epaa.asu.edu/v13n38/

Koss-Chioino, J. D., & Vargas, L. A. (1999). *Working with Latino youth: Culture, development, and context.* San Francisco, CA: Jossey-Bass.

Kumpfer, K. L., Alvarado, R., Smith, P., & Bellamy, N. (2002). Cultural sensitivity and adaptation in family-based prevention interventions. *Prevention Science, 3*, 241–246.

Lewinsohn, P. M., Clarke, G. N., Rohde, P., Seeley, J. R., & Hops, H. (1996). A course in coping: a cognitive-behavioral approach to the treatment of adolescent depression. In E. Hibbs & P. Jensen (Eds.). *Psychosocial treatment research of child and adolescent disorders* (pp. 109–135). Washington, DC: APA.

Lin, K. M., & Kleinman, A. M. (1988). Psychopathology and clinical course of schizophrenia: A cross-cultural perspective. *Schizophrenia Bulletin, 14*(4), 555–567.

Lopez, E. C. (1995). Best practices in working with bilingual children. In A. Thomas & J. Grimes (Eds.), *Best practices in school psychology III.* Washington, DC: National Association of School Psychologists.

Lopez, S. (1989). Patient variable biases in clinical judgment: Conceptual overview and methodological considerations. *Psychological Bulletin, 106*, 184–203.

Lopez, S. R. (1994). Latinos and the expression of psychopathology: A call for the direct assessment of cultural influences. In C. A. Telles & M. Karno (Eds.), *Mental disorders in Hispanic populations* (pp. 109–127). Los Angeles, CA: Neuropsychiatric Institute, UCLA Press Mental Health.

Lopez, S. R. (1997). Cultural competence in psychotherapy: A guide for clinicians and their supervisors. In C. Z. Watkins Jr. (Ed.), *Handbook of psychotherapy supervision* (pp. 570–588). New York, NY: John Wiley & Sons.

Lopez, S. R. (2002). Teaching culturally informed psychological assessment: Conceptual issues and demonstrations. *Journal of Personality Assessment, 79*, 226–234.

Lopez, S. R., Kopelowicz, A., & Canive, J. M. (2002). Strategies in developing culturally congruent family interventions for schizophrenia: The case of Hispanics. In H. P. Lefley & D. L. Johnson (Eds.), *Family interventions in mental illness: International perspectives* (pp. 61–90). Westport, CT: Praeger.

Lum, D. (1999). *Culturally competent practice: A framework for growth and action.* New York, NY: Brooks/Cole.

Lynch, E. W. (1992). Developing cross-cultural competence. In E. W. Lynch & M. J. Hanson (Eds.), *Developing cross-cultural competence: A guide for working with young children and their families.* Baltimore, MD: Paul H. Brooks.

Marin, G., & Marin, B.V. O. (1991). *Research with Hispanic populations.* Newbury Park, CA: Sage.

Martinez, C. R., & Eddy, J. M. (2005). Effects of culturally adapted parent management training on Latino youth behavioral health outcomes. *Journal of Consulting and Clinical Psychology, 73*, 841–851.

Maternal and Child Health Bureau. (1999). *Guidance for SPRANS grant, health resources and services administration.* Washington, DC: U.S. Department of Health and Human Services.

McCabe, K. M. (2002). Factors that predict premature termination among Mexican-American children in outpatient psychotherapy. *Journal of Child and Family Studies, 11*(3), 347–359.

McCabe, K. M., & Yeh, M. (2009). Parent-child interaction therapy for Mexican Americans: A randomized clinical trial. *Journal of Clinical Child & Adolescent Psychology, 38*, 753–759.

Means, B., & Knapp, M. S. (1991). *Teaching advanced skills to educationally disadvantaged students.* Washington, DC: U.S. Department of Education. (ED 338 722)

Miranda, J., Azocar, F., Organista, K. C., Munoz, R. F., & Lieberman, A. (1996). Recruiting and retaining low-income Latinos in psychotherapy research. *Journal of Consulting and Clinical Psychology, 64*(5), 868–874.

Miranda, J., Bernal, G., Lau, A. S., Kohn, L., Hwang, W.-C., & LaFrosmboise, T. (2005). State of the science on psychosocial interventions for ethnic minorities. *Annual Review of Clinical Psychology, 1*, 113–142.

National Center for Culturally Responsive Education Systems. (2005). *Cultural considerations and challenges in Response-to-Intervention models.* Retrieved June 1, 2008, from http://www.nccrest.org/PDFs/rti.pdf?v_document_name=Culturally%20Responsive%20RTI

Pihlakoski, L., Aromaa, M., Sourander, A., Rautava, P., Helenius, H., & Sillanpää, M. (2004). Use of and need for professional help for emotional and behavioral problems among preadolescents: A prospective cohort study of 3- to 12-year-old children. *Journal of the American Academy of Child & Adolescent Psychiatry, 43*(8), 974–983.

Pitts, G., & Wallace, P. A. (2003). Cultural awareness in the diagnosis of attention deficit/hyperactivity disorder. *Primary Psychiatry, 10*(4), 84–88.

Ramirez, M. (1991). *Psychotherapy and counseling with minorities: A cognitive approach to individual and cultural differences.* New York, NY: Pergamon.

Ridley, C. R., Mendoza, D. W., Kanitz, B. E., Angermeier, L., & Zenk, R. (1994). Cultural sensitivity in multicultural counseling: A perceptual schema model. *Journal of Counseling Psychology, 41*, 125–136.

Rogoff, B. (2003). *The cultural nature of human development.* New York, NY: Oxford University Press.

Rosselló, J., & Bernal, G. (1999). The efficacy of cognitive-behavioral and interpersonal treatments for depression in Puerto Rican adolescents. *Journal of Consulting and Clinical Psychology, 67,* 734–45.

Rowland, A. S., Umbach, D. M., Stallone, L., Naftel, A. J., Bohlig, E. M., & Sandler, D. P. (2002). Prevalence of medication treatment for attention deficit-hyperactivity disorder among elementary school children in Johnston County, North Carolina. *American Journal of Public Health, 92,* 231–234.

Safer, D. J., & Malever, M. (2000). Stimulant treatment in Maryland public schools. *Pediatrics, 106,* 533–539.

Sheridan, S., Kratochwill, T., & Bergen, J. (1996). *Conjoint behavioral consultation: A procedural manual.* New York, NY: Plenum.

Skiba, R. J., Horner, R. H. Chung, C. G., Rausch, M. K., May, S. L., & Tobin, T. (2011). Race is not neutral: A national investigation of African American and Latino disproportionality in school discipline. *School Psychology Review, 40,* 85–107.

Slade, E. P. (2004). Racial/ethnic disparities in parent perception of child need for mental health care following school disciplinary events. *Mental Health Services Research, 6*(2), 75–92.

Snyder, T. D., & Dillow, S. A. (2011). *Digest of education statistics 2010* (NCES 2011–2015). Washington, DC: National Center for Education Statistics, Institute of Education Sciences, U.S. Department of Education.

Stein, B. D., Jaycox, L. H., Kataoka, S. H., Wong, M., Tu, W., Eliot, M. N., & Fink, A. (2003). A mental health intervention for school children exposed to violence: A randomized controlled trial. *JAMA, 290*(5), 603–611.

Sue, D. W., Arrendondo, P., & McDavis, R. J. (1992). Multicultural counseling competencies and standards: A call to the profession. *Journal of Counseling and Development, 70,* 477–486.

Sue, D. W. (1998). In search of cultural competence in psychotherapy and counseling. *American Psychologist, 53,* 440–448.

Sue, D. W., & Sue, D. (1999). *Counseling the culturally different: Theory and practice* (3rd ed.). New York: Wiley.

Sue, S., & Zane, N. (1987). The role of culture and cultural techniques in psychotherapy: A critique and reformulation. *American Psychologist, 42*(1), 37–45.

Sussman, L. K., Robins, L. N., & Earls, F. (1987). Treatment-seeking for depression by black and white Americans. *Social Science and Medicine, 24,* 187–196.

Szapocznik, J., Kurtines, W., Santisteban, D. A., Pantin, H., Scopetta, M., Mancilla, Y., et al. (1997). The evolution of structural ecosystemic theory for working with Latino families. In J. G. Garcia & M. C. Zea (Eds.), *Psychological interventions and research with Latino populations* (pp. 166–190). Boston, MA: Allyn & Bacon.

Szapocznik, J., & Williams, R. A. (2000). Brief strategic family therapy: Twenty-five years of interplay among theory, research and practice in adolescent behavior problems and drug abuse. *Clinical Child Family Psychology Review, 3*(2), 117–134.

Tarver Behring, S., & Ingraham, C. (1998). Culture as a central component to consultation: A call to the field. *Journal of Educational and Psychological Consultation, 9,* 57–72.

Tharp, R. G. (1989). Psychocultural variables and constants. *American Psychologist, 44,* 349–359.

Treatment for Adolescents with Depression Study Team. (2004). Fluoxetine, cognitive-behavioral therapy, and their combination for adolescents with depression. *Journal of the American Medical Association, 292,* 807–820.

Treuba, E., & Bartolome, L. (1997). *The education of Latino students: Is school reform enough*? New York: ERIC Clearinghouse on Urban Education.

Umaña-Taylor, A. J., & Bamaca, M. Y. (2004). Conducting focus groups with Latino populations: Lessons learned from the field. *Family Relations, 53,* 261–272.

U.S. Census Bureau. (2008). *National population projections released 2008 (based on Census 2000): Summary Table 6 Percent of the projected population by race and Hispanic origin for the United States: 2010 to 2050.* Retrieved from http://www.census.gov/population/www/projections/summarytables.html

U.S. Census Bureau. (2010). *Facts for features: Hispanic Heritage Month 2010: September 15–October 15, 2010.* Retrieved from http://www.census.gov/newsroom/releases/archives/facts_for_features_special_Editions/cb10-ff17.html

U.S. Department of Education. (2009). *Twenty-nineth annual report to Congress on the implementation of the Individual with Disabilities Education Act.* Washington, DC: Author.

U.S. Department of Health and Human Services (1999). *Mental health: A report of the surgeon general.* Rockville, MD: U.S. Department of Health and Human Services, Substance Abuse and Mental Health Services Administration, Center for Mental Health Services.

U.S. Department of Health and Human Services. (2001). Mental health: Culture, race, and ethnicity—A supplement to mental health: A report of the surgeon general. Rockville, MD: U.S. Department of Health and Human Services, Substance Abuse and Mental Health Services Administration, Center for Mental Health Services.

U.S. Substance Abuse and Mental Health Administration, Office of Applied Statistics. (2009). *Results from the 2008 National Survey on Drug Use and Health: National Findings.* Retrieved February 26, 2010, from http://www.oas.samhsa.gov/NSDUH/2k8NSDUH/2k8results.cfm#8.2

Vaughn, S., & Fuchs, L. S. (2003). Redefining learning disabilities as inadequate response to instruction: The promise and potential problems. *Learning Disabilities Research & Practice, 18*(3), 137–146.

Vega, W. A., Kolody, B., Aguilar-Gaxiola, S., Alderete, E, Catalano, R., & Caraveo-Anduaga, J. (1998). Lifetime prevalence of DSM II-R psychiatric disorders among urban and rural Mexican Americans in California. *Archives of General Psychiatry, 55,* 771–778.

Westermeyer, J. (1987). Cultural factors in clinical assessment. *Journal of Consulting and Clinical Psychology, 55,* 471–478.

Wood, P.A., Yeh, M., Pan, D., Lambros, K. M., McCabe, K. M., & Hough, R. L. (2005). Exploring the relationship between race/ethnicity, age of first school-based services utilization, and age of first specialty mental health care for at-risk youth. *Mental Health Services Research,* 7(3), 185–196.

Woodward, A. M., Dwinell, A. D., & Arons, B. S. (1992). Barriers to mental health care for Latino Americans: A literature review and discussion. *Journal of Mental Health Administration, 19,* 224–236.

Yeh, M., McCabe, K., Hough, R., Dupuis, D., & Hazen, A. (2003). Racial/ethnic differences in parental endorsement of barriers to mental health services for youth. *Mental Health Services Research, 5,* 65–77.

Yeh, M., McCabe, K. M., Lambros, K., Hough, R. L., Landsverk, J., Hurlburt, M., & Culver, S. W. (2004). Racial/ethnic representation across five public sectors of care for youth with emotional and behavioral problems. In P. Garner, F. Yuen, P. Clough, & T. Pardeck (Eds.), *Handbook of emotional and behavioural difficulties in education.* London: Sage.

Yeh, M., Forness, S. R., Ho, J., McCabe, K., & Hough, R. L. (2004). Parental etiological explanations and disproportionate racial/ethnic representation in special education services for youths with emotional disturbance. *Behavioral Disorders, 29*(4), 348–358.

CHAPTER 59

Engaging with Culturally and Racially Diverse Families

Jenell S. Clarke Isok Kim Michael S. Spencer

Getting Started

The engagement process in school-based mental health services is one of the first critical junctures for successful treatment of and intervention with at-risk children from culturally and racially diverse families. If professionals are unable to engage families initially in the process, children will not be served, and problems will continue to mount or multiply. Delays in treatment may result, leading children who may have benefited from preventive school-based services to later be funneled into more punitive and rigid systems, including child welfare, juvenile justice, and foster care systems. To better engage families, culturally competent school social workers must first be conscious of the needs of diverse families and the barriers to engagement in services. Once these needs and barriers are identified, school social workers should adopt philosophies of practice that reflect cultural democracy, collaboration, critical consciousness, and social advocacy and action.

This chapter focuses on innovative and empirically based practices for engaging families of diverse backgrounds, with specific attention to immigrant and refugee families. The purpose of this chapter is twofold. First, it will provide an overview of the existing knowledge of best practices for engaging families, including addressing some of the reasons that services are underused. Second, it will provide specific recommendations and instructions for school-based practitioners that are essential for engaging culturally and racially diverse families.

What We Know

Although there is a growing body of knowledge about school-based mental health interventions, empirical research on engaging culturally diverse families doesn't exist in the practice literature. Rather, the process of engaging families is often included as part of the intervention, though not specifically tested for efficacy as a separate component. The purpose of this section is to provide a brief summary of the engagement component as it is used in empirically supported interventions, particularly with immigrant populations. However, we expect that there will be a degree of generalizability beyond immigrant groups to most communities of color.

Review of the Research

A number of studies have developed school-based mental health interventions aimed at immigrant and refugee children (e.g., Fazel, Doll, & Stein, 2009; Dillman Carpentier et al., 2007; Mitchell & Bryan, 2007).

Much of the literature provides a review of the issues and concerns of immigrant students and school mental health services, qualities of effective programs, roles of the social worker/counselor, and recommendations for intervention (Berzin, O'Brien, Frey, Kelly, Alvarez, M. E., & Shaffer, 2011; Pumariega, Rothe, & Pumariega, 2005; Stephan, Weist, Kataoka, Adelsheim, & Mills, 2007). Although none of the studies reviewed examine the engagement process specifically, together they provide insights and strategies for how to connect immigrant families with school-based mental health services. In the following section, we examine two dimensions of the engagement process for immigrant families: (1) identification of needs and barriers and (2) culturally competent practice philosophies.

Strategies for Engaging Diverse Families

Identification of Needs and Barriers

The first step to successfully engaging families is to understand their needs for services and the barriers they experience in accessing services. There are several key issues that are particularly relevant for immigrant and refugee families: (1) lack of language proficiency; (2) discrimination; (3) immigration status; (4) shortage of racially and culturally diverse providers; and (5) cultural attitudes and values.

Language Proficiency

The literature on service use among immigrant families states clearly that language is a critical barrier (e.g., Ruiz-de-Velasco, Fix, & Clewell, 2000). In conducting a needs assessment for school-based services for immigrant families, you must examine whether or not services are accessible to families who do not speak English. The checklist shown in Box 59.1 is designed to assist you in assessing your school's efforts at addressing language barriers.

In some communities, service providers will be able to identify the one or two non-English-speaking groups within their catchment area. In other communities that serve as a portal for a number of different immigrant families, the job becomes more difficult. Translators can be costly, and presenting brochures and outreach information in a multilingual format can be complex. Optimally, having a diverse staff that is representative of the community demographics is ideal. Having native speakers of different immigrant languages is also preferable.

Box 59.1

Is advertisement and outreach information provided in a multilingual format? Are intake and consent forms?

Are the languages of those immigrant groups most predominant in your community represented?

Is there a plan or strategy for those language groups not represented?

Are native speakers or translators available?

Does your school provide opportunities for ESL students to express their thoughts and feelings, especially in their native language at school?

Discrimination

Past research on discrimination has shown that exposure to discriminatory behavior is a major life stressor that has powerful adverse effects on emotional well-being (Coker et al., 2009; Kessler, Mickelson, & Williams, 1994) particularly for ethnic minorities (Araujo & Borrell, 2006; Gee, Spencer, Chen, Yip, & Takeuchi, 2007; Williams, Costa, & Leavell, 2010). Historical and contemporary experiences with discrimination, as well as documented abuses and perceived mistreatment by medical and mental health professionals, may precipitate mistrust of service providers. Studies that have examined discrimination in service use have found that higher proportions of African Americans and Latinos compared to whites felt that a health provider judged them unfairly or treated them with disrespect because of their race or ethnic background (Richardson, 2001).

This leads to underutilization of mental health services among immigrants and ethnic minority community members (e.g., Bledsoe, 2008; Burgess, Ding, Hargreaves, van Ryn, & Phelan, 2008; Spencer, Chen, Gee, Fabian, & Takeuchi, 2010).

Immigrants and their family members who encounter the mental health system are often not adequately informed about the services or their rights as clients, and they do not receive any form of advocacy throughout the process (Bledsoe, 2008; Leong & Lau, 2001).

Furthermore, they may be apprehensive about the consequences of seeking services. They may think, "Does my child really have a problem, or are they biased against my child because of his race or ethnicity? Will my child be put in a special education classroom? Will this go on my child's permanent record and haunt her throughout her academic career?" The checklist in Box 59.2 provides an assessment of discrimination as a barrier that may affect the engagement of families.

Immigration Status

Recent reports from the Urban Institute indicate that much of the growth in the children's population between 1990 and 2008 can be attributed to the rise in the population of children of immigrants (2010). According to Chaudry and Fortuny (2010), children of immigrants are disproportionately poor and less likely to use public benefits compared to their native counterparts. Furthermore, the number of U.S.-born children in mixed-status families (i.e., unauthorized immigrant parents and citizen children) increased to 4 million in 2008 (Passel & Cohn, April 2009), adding legal complexity to adequately addressing mental health issues to school children. For immigrants and refugee families, seeking outside help in this societal context, away from their comfort zone (i.e., family and ethnic community), may seem too risky or even be actively discouraged.

Despite the unease stemming from their immigrant or refugee status, schools are still well-positioned to address mental health needs of culturally and racially diverse children. According to Fazel, Doll, and Stein (2009), schools should have specialized resources already in place to coordinate help with and among families and the community. As such, the delivery of mental health services in school settings affords these children and their families the opportunity to benefit from trusting relationships already established with school staff. The school then can serve as an extension for or bridge to other services for immigrant and refugee families who are trying to acculturate and need resources to facilitate this transitional process.

Box 59.2

Do you know the history of race and ethnic relations of the target population in the United States? In your community? In your school? Is this history acknowledged?
Does your school have antibigotry policies that are understood by the community?
Are incidences of racism and bigotry documented and active steps taken?
Have staff received training in antibigotry practices, and are these trainings ongoing?

Focus: Active Antibigotry Efforts

While this list is certainly not comprehensive, it is a means to begin the process of examining ways in which discrimination exerts its influence on decisions to utilize services. A school that is actively committed to antibigotry efforts may increase the level of trust in the system. A school that has not examined or acknowledged past wrongdoings in a public way gives families no reason to trust it with their private information. Schools may be reluctant to acknowledge past discrimination because of guilt, fears of bad press, or perceived lack of importance. School social workers need to be on the forefront of these efforts in collaboration with school administration and personnel, as well as members of the community. The Southern Poverty Law Center's Teaching Tolerance program (see www.splcenter.org) is an excellent resource for those interested in implementing antibigotry education in schools.

Shortage of Racially and Culturally Diverse Providers

In *Mental Health: Culture, Race, and Ethnicity* (U.S. Department of Health and Human Services [DHHS], 2001), the supplement to the surgeon general's report on mental health, the authors point to the shortage of providers of color as one factor accounting for low utilization rates among some groups. For example, studies have found that lack of ethnic match is significantly associated with dropping out from service usage, and that clients of color engage in treatment longer when they are matched with ethnic-specific therapists or therapists who are fluent in their native language (e.g., Yeh, Eastman, & Cheung, 1994; Akutsu, Castillo, & Snowden, 2007). For example, Manderscheid and Henderson (1998) found that of mental health professionals practicing in the late 1990s, approximately 70 Asian American providers were available for every 100, 000 Asian Americans in the United States.

Bilingual and culturally diverse providers can promote an antibigotry climate in schools by providing more cultural mediators and translators for school staff, bringing diverse perspectives that can enhance problem-solving strategies, and serving families without employing translators or bilingual children or family members in the process. The checklist in Box 59.3 provides issues that may be assessed regarding diverse providers.

Focus: Lay Community Workers

Though ethnic match is not imperative to the provision of culturally competent services, providing this as an option seems reasonable. Unless the racial and ethnic profile of social workers in the United States changes radically in the near future, providers of color will continue to be in short supply. Thus, creative alternatives must be developed to utilize and empower lay community workers (i.e., paraprofessionals), who are often of diverse backgrounds and may live in the same communities as your client population. Evidence for the effectiveness of lay community workers may hold promise (DHHS, 1994). Lay workers can also provide outreach to increase the knowledge of existing school-based services. Moreover, the use of lay workers develops the capacity and skills of community members. Additionally, they provide an invaluable link to community and can serve as cultural mediators for both clients and staff.

Box 59.3

Are diverse service providers representative of the community actively recruited?
Are non-MSW staff from diverse backgrounds encouraged and supported to continue their education?
Can non-MSW community members be hired and trained to do outreach, assist, and co-facilitate sessions with MSW-level providers?

Cultural Attitudes and Values

One of the problems with establishing culturally responsive mental health services is the incongruence between the characteristics of the mental health system and the minority group, whose special needs and concerns may not be addressed by assessment instruments, agency policies, clinicians, and practices. Uba (1982) notes several cultural barriers to service use: (1) racial and cultural biases (encountering culturally inappropriate services, differential receipt of services compared); (2) conflicts between the epistemological underpinnings and characteristics of Western psychotherapy and cultural personality syndromes, values, expectations, and interpersonal styles; and (3) cultural attitudes toward seeking help and its usefulness. Unfortunately, more recent discussion of the same topic covered by Leong and Lau (2001) indicates that many of the same barriers and concerns remain unchanged.

An additional barrier to engagement is the aggregation of racial and cultural groups into a singular group, such as Asians, Latinos, immigrants, or refugees. The aggregation of diverse people into monolithic groups ignores the diversity of groups and makes generalizations across these groups misleading (Uehara, Takeuchi, & Smukler, 1994; Kim, 2006).

Differences in the myriad of national and historical backgrounds, social classes, legal statuses, migration histories, languages, religious beliefs, and other sociocultural stressors have important consequences for help seeking and service use among groups. Psychosocial factors related to immigration to the United States also pose unique risks for mental health problems. Takeuchi and colleagues (2007) reported that immigrant status is associated with a number of stressors related to adaptation to the host society and expectations of educational and economic attainment that can influence psychological adjustment. Groups that come to the United States as refugees and as a result of war, on the other hand, may experience more exposure to trauma and difficulties with adjustment than do groups who immigrated for work opportunities or schooling (e.g., Koch, 2007; Rousseau, & Guzder, 2008; Stein et al., 2002).

The checklist in Box 59.4 highlights cultural attitudes and values that may affect engagement.

Box 59.4

Do providers understand the stigma that mental health services have within the specific cultural group?
Are cultural values understood, such as those that may regulate display of emotion or family harmony?
Are there links between schools and informal service systems, such as churches, temples, healers, family supports?
Are children and families given opportunities to promote and celebrate their own cultural backgrounds?

Focus: "Loss of Face"

Among Asian cultures, Confucian philosophies may discourage open displays of emotions to maintain familial harmony. The construct "loss of face" is identified as a key and often dominant interpersonal dynamic in Asian social relations that defines an individual's social integrity and the perception of the individual as an integral member of a group. Losing face has been found to be associated with one's ability to function effectively in society in varying degrees, including assertion and self-disclosure in help-seeking situations (Zane & Yeh, 2002). Understanding the concept of loss of face can assist service providers with outreach efforts that promote services as positive.

Practice Strategies for Engaging Diverse Families

Once needs and barriers have been adequately addressed, school social workers must then adopt philosophies of practice that reflect cultural democracy, collaboration, critical consciousness, and social advocacy and action to promote engagement and appropriate service delivery. Cultural democracy is a philosophy of practice that recognizes (1) the destructive and oppressive nature of cultural domination and marginalization; (2) the importance of ensuring cultural self-determination and integrity for oppressed communities as a precondition for multicultural unity; (3) the importance of emphasizing the relationship between power, culture, and various other oppressions, including class and gender oppression; and (4) the need to invite all of the multiple voices of oppressed communities into the disclosure of liberation (Akinyela & Aldridge, 2003). There are a number of ways in which school social workers can promote the values of cultural democracy in service of engaging immigrant families in services. These approaches may include the use of community resources in collaboration with school resources, individual self-awareness and critical consciousness development, and social advocacy and action (e.g., Dillman Carpentier et al., 2007; Mitchell & Bryan, 2007).

Collaboration

Although groups of individuals who work within schools and who have a vested interest in school may have similar goals, these groups often work in opposition to one another or in isolation from one another. These groups include school social workers, school counselors, teachers, school administrators, community-based social service and mental health agencies, ethnic-specific services, researchers and academics, as well as parents and community members. Turf wars, past politics, and different professional socialization can often keep groups from working together. Distrust and cultural conflicts may keep communities isolated from those who might provide useful services.

However, if school social workers are to have any hope of engaging immigrant communities through the principles of cultural democracy, they must better use all available resources. There are a number of studies that indicate such collaborative relationships can work to improve the well-being of students (e.g., Brown, Dahlbeck, & Sparkman-Barnes, 2006; Choi, Yul, Korcuska, & Proctor, 2008; Berzin et al., 2011).

Social workers can act as facilitators of these collaborative efforts, bringing together divergent groups, bridging these differences, and highlighting commonalities, particularly in their mission to serve children. Collaboration is one important way in which social workers can bridge school and community institutions.

Focus: Ways to Develop Collaboration

- Plan and develop a coalition within your community. Identify the key stakeholders and partners within the ecological context of the target families, including parents and community members. Collectively, identify key issues around engagement, ascertain strengths and challenges that exist in the community, and develop an action plan for promoting engagement. The coalition should meet regularly. Coalitions can act as a powerful collaboration that is able to respond to complex problems, address important social policies, and seek funding for needed resources (e.g., Bryan, 2005). Coalitions keep community members involved in the decision-making process and promote empowerment.
- Understand that engaging in collaboration helps develop intergroup communication skills. People can learn and practice contact process skills and relationship protocols or cultural ways of relating to people, including respect for authority, family roles, and communication

processes (Lum & Lu, 2003). Collaboration also enhances one's knowledge about community-based resources and client support systems, both formal and informal. Participate in active community involvement and service. Involve teachers and other school personnel as well. This serves both learning about and from the community, as well as being identified within and becoming a part of the larger community you serve (Mitchell & Bryan, 2007). Too often, school staff lament the lack of parental involvement in schools, but they themselves lack involvement in their communities.

Individual Self-Awareness and Critical Consciousness Development

There are several important elements of your own self-awareness that are necessary when working with diverse families, particularly immigrant families. The first is an awareness and value of children's strengths and their daily contributions. Rather than view immigrant children as a problem or challenge, you must appreciate their physical and economic contribution to family and school. This contribution may come in the form of caring for younger siblings, providing translation skills for parents who are not literate or are not proficient in English, doing housework, mediating between the family and public institutions, and contributing to household income through wage labor (Orellana, 2001).

A second aspect of self-awareness is an understanding of your own diversity. Lum (2003) uses a framework of diversity developed by Schriver (2001) to explore understandings of diversity. He asks that social workers be able to articulate their own diversity perspective and worldview (values and beliefs, culture, family, gender, sexual orientation, socioeconomic class, spirituality, ability status, etc), the intersection between these perspectives (the implications of membership in multiple groups), and the interrelatedness and interconnectedness to other people (similarities and differences). Critical consciousness, a concept introduced by Freire (1970), takes self-awareness one step further by incorporating a greater sense of understanding of power relationships and similarities and differences among and within people. Through the examination and exploration of their own multiple identities, social workers are able to situate themselves within the world in relation to others and become better aware of their own biases and assumptions.

Social Advocacy and Action

We close this section by promoting the critical importance of social advocacy and action as an important concept and skill for school social workers to develop. Improving engagement skills requires that social workers move interpersonal practice beyond diversity and toward social justice (Reed, Newman, Suarez, & Lewis, 1997; Breton, 2004; Holcomb-McCoy & Mitchell, 2007).

Engagement with racially and culturally diverse families is certain to be a difficult task until the social, political, and historical macro forces influencing their lives are altered. But, how does one act to help effect this?

Freire (1970) states that such a project begins with a commitment to social justice. This requires a moral and ethical attitude toward equality and possibility, and a belief in the capacity of people as agents who can act to transform their world. He adds that people must first examine the contradiction between their espoused social principles and their lived experience. If they are unable to perceive and resolve social, political, and economic contradictions in their own lives, they will have great difficulty advocating for and taking action toward social justice for others. Through this commitment, people better position themselves for working with populations that have historically underused services that could potentially improve their lives.

Applying Interventions within a Response to Intervention Framework

Within an RTI framework, culturally and linguistically responsive practices involve having teachers and other supporting school staff to "purposefully consider the cultural, linguistic, and socioeconomic factors that may have an impact on students' success or failure in the classroom" (National Center on Response to Intervention, March 2010, p. 9). One of the concerns of applying RTI to culturally and racially diverse students and their families may be the focus of evidence-based practice (EBP) components within the RTI framework. A number of researchers express caution about using evidence-based practice blindly due to its positivistic methods that originated from clinical medicine. The concern is that these methods may not translate well in dealing with problems and challenges associated with the various sociocultural factors that immigrant families exhibit (Webb, 2001). Some researchers suggest using evidence-informed practice (EIP) instead of EBP (Epstein, 2009; McNeill, 2006; Nevo & Slonim-Nevo, 2011; Webb, 2001) in order to leave "ample room for clinical experience as well as the constructive and imaginative judgments of practitioners and clients who are in constant interaction and dialog with one another" (Nevo & Slonim-Nevo, 2011, p. 1).

In response to these concerns, the National Center on Response to Intervention makes available a number of resources and training modules on its Web site related to culturally responsive practice within an RTI framework (see www.rti4success.org). Additionally, the Center asked experts to address the issues regarding disproportionality (Woodruff, 2011), English-language learners (Artiles, 2011), and culturally responsive instructions (Harry, 2011), which should be incorporated seamlessly within a basic RTI framework.

Nonetheless, the responsibility of engaging immigrant families with cultural and language differences falls squarely on each school to train, implement, and evaluate the successful adaptation of RTI to their local environment. The key challenge is then to have the RTI framework be flexible enough to allow genuine, creative engagement with culturally and linguistically diverse families. As such, school staff cannot be so rigid in applying an RTI framework. To maximize the benefit to affected students and their families, each referral case should be informed by the RTI framework instead of being dictated by it.

Tools and Practice Examples

Exercise for Developing Critical Consciousness

There are a number of exercises that can be useful in various training situations (see Adams, Bell, & Griffin, 2007). Here we highlight one exercise that could be valuable in this process.

Intersectional Stand Up

Introduction: Ask participants to remain quiet throughout until the end. Participants will be asked to stand up if a statement is true for them and will be directed to sit again before the next statement is read. If participants choose not to participate or to stand, ask that they notice when they would have stood or remained seated. Read each statement twice.

Statements

Please stand if you were taken to museums, zoos, or other cultural activities as a child.
Please stand if you are an only child.
Please stand if your ancestors were slaves or indigenous peoples whose lands were colonized and taken over.
Please stand if you rarely, if ever, have to question whether a building or event will be accessible to someone of your abilities.
Please stand up if you can hold hands with your partner and not fear for your safety.
Please stand up if you do not fear to walk alone at night because of your gender.
Please stand if one or both of your parents or caretakers were not born in the United States.
Please stand if your grandparents or great-grandparents were not born in the United States.
Please stand if one or both of your parents or caretakers holds a college degree.
Please stand if your current spiritual or religious path is Christianity.
Please stand if you had to work for wages before you were 12 years old.
Please stand if you have experienced the loss of a loved one.
Please stand if you helped your parents or caregivers in caring for siblings so they could work.
Please stand if you have ever lived away from parents or caregivers for more than six months.
Please stand if you have ever been happy.
Please stand up if English is your first language.
Please stand if you speak another language in addition to English.
Please stand if you have ever been misunderstood.
Thank the participants for taking part in this exercise.

Possible Discussion Questions

What was it like for you to notice who stood when and who remained seated?

What did you learn about your own identities?
Did anything make you uncomfortable? Why or why not?
How might your learning from this activity apply to your work with diverse families?
How might your learning apply to engaging immigrant families?

Key Points to Consider

- Most people have intersecting target and agent identities.
- Oppression may be displayed in a multitude of ways on individual, systemic, and institutional levels.
- People have many differences in their backgrounds but also many similarities.
- Social workers must always practice their listening skills—not simply listening with their ears but with their hearts. Listening with one's heart entails empathy, genuineness, and sincerity. These qualities will enhance trust and promote engagement.

Key Points to Remember

In this chapter, we highlight a number of strategies for increasing our probability of successfully engaging culturally diverse families. We move away from the reliance on stereotypes and notions of better "knowing the other" and focus instead on better knowing ourselves and our service context. The strategies we have outlined would call on social workers to:

- recognize the needs of communities and barriers to service use
- address the schools' lack of proficiency with clients' languages rather than focus on clients' lack of proficiency in English
- recognize, acknowledge, and take action against discrimination, both interpersonal and institutional
- address the shortage of racially and culturally diverse providers within communities (using lay community workers may be a viable option)
- understand the diverse cultural attitudes and values of the client population to better understand how to engage them in services
- use culturally competent practice strategies incorporating the principles of cultural democracy
- collaborate with key stakeholders and community members to gain insight into how schools might address issues of engagement
- promote social advocacy and action to build the community's trust in schools and work toward addressing social, political, and historical inequalities

References

Adams, M., Bell, L. A., & Griffin, P. (2007). *Teaching for diversity and social justice* (2nd ed.). New York, NY: Routledge.

Akinyela, M. M., & Aldridge, D. P. (2003). Beyond Euro centrism, Afro centrism and multiculturalism: Toward cultural democracy in social work education. *Journal of Race, Class, and Gender, 10,* 58–70.

Akutsu, P. D., Castillo, E. D., & Snowden, L. R. (2007). Differential referral patterns to ethnic-specific and mainstream mental health programs for four Asian American. *American Journal of Orthopsychiatry,* 77(1), 95–103.

Araujo, B., & Borrell, L. (2006). Understanding the link between discrimination, mental health outcomes, and life chances among Latinos. *Hispanic Journal of Behavioral Science, 28,* 245–266.

Armbruster, P., & Lichtman, J. (1999). Are school based mental health services effective? Evidence from 36 inner city schools. *Community Mental Health Journal, 35,* 493–504.

Artiles, A. (2011). *What should educators take into consideration when instructing English language learners, particularly in an RTI framework?* Ask the Experts. Retrieved June 7, 2011, from http://www.rti4success.org/asktheexpert/video/975

Berzin, S. C., O'Brien, K. H. M., Frey, A., Kelly, M. S., Alvarez, M. E., & Shaffer, G. L. (2011). Meeting the social and behavioral health needs of students: Rethinking the relationship between teachers and school social workers. *Journal of School Health, 81*(8), 493–501.

Bryan, J. A. (2005). Fostering educational resilience and achievement in urban schools through school-family-community partnerships. *Professional School Counseling, 8*(3), 219–227.

Chaudry, A., & Fortuny, K. (2010). *Children of immigrants: Economic well-being. The Children of Immigrants Research Brief 4.* Washington, DC: The Urban Institute.

Dillman Carpentier, F. R., Mauricio, A. M., Gonzales, N. A., Millsap, R. E., Meza, C. M., Dumka, L. E., ...

Genalo, M.T. (2007). Engaging Mexican origin families in a school-based preventive intervention. *The Journal of Primary Prevention, 28*(6), 521–546.

Epstein, I. (2009). Promoting harmony where there is commonly conflict: Evidence-informed practice as an integrative strategy. *Social Work in Health Care, 48*(3), 216–231. doi:10.1080/00981380802589845

Fazel, M., Doll, H., & Stein, A. (2009). A school-based mental health intervention for refugee children: An exploratory study. *Clinical Child Psychology and Psychiatry, 14*(2), 297–309.Freire, P. (1970). Pedagogy of the oppressed. New York: Herder & Herder.

Gee, G. C., Spencer, M. S., Chen, J., Yip, T., & Takeuchi, D. T. (2007). The association between self-reported racial discrimination and 12-month DSM-IV mental disorders among Asian Americans nationwide. *Social Science & Medicine, 64*(10), 1984–1996.

Harry, B. (2011). *Why is culturally responsive instruction important within an RTI framework?* Ask the Experts. Retrieved June 7, 2011, from http://www.rti4success.org/asktheexpert/video/975

Kessler, R. C., Mickelson, K. D., & Williams, D. R. (1994). The prevalence, distribution, and mental health correlates of perceived discrimination in the United States. *Journal of Health and Social Behavior, 40*, 208–230.

Leong, F.T. L., & Lau, A. S. L. (2001). Barriers to providing effective mental health services to Asian Americans. *Mental Health Services Research, 3*(4), 201–214.

Lum, D. (2003). *Culturally competent practice: A framework for understanding diverse groups and justice issues* (2nd ed.). Pacific Grove, CA: Brooks/Cole/Thomson Learning.

Lum, D., & Lu, Y. E. (2003). Skill development. In D. Lum (Ed.), *Culturally competent practice: A framework for understanding diverse groups and justice issues* (2nd ed., pp. 128–164). Pacific Grove, CA: Brooks/Cole/Thomson Learning.

Manderscheid, R., & Henderson, M. (1998). *Mental health, United States.* Rockville, MD: U.S. Department of Health and Human Services, Center for Mental Health Services.

McNeill, T. (2006). Evidence-based practice in an age of relativism: Toward a model for practice. *Social Work, 51*(2), 147–156.

National Center on Response to Intervention. (2010, March). *Essential components of RTI—A closer look at Response to Intervention.* Washington, DC: U.S. Department of Education, Office of Special Education Programs, National Center on Response to Intervention.

Nevo, I., & Slonim-Nevo, V. (2011). The myth of evidence-based practice: Towards evidence-informed practice. *British Journal of Social Work, 41*, 1176–1197.

Mitchell, N. A., & Bryan, J. A. (2007). School-family-community partnerships: Strategies for school counselors working with Caribbean immigrant families. *Professional School Counseling, 10*(4), 399–409.

Orellana, M. F. (2001). The work kids do: Mexican and Central American immigrant children's contributions to households and schools in California. *Harvard Educational Review, 71*, 366–389.

Passel, J. S., & Cohn, D.V. (2009, April). *A portrait of unauthorized immigrants in the United States.* Washington, DC: Pew Hispanic Center.

Pumariega, A., Rothe, E. M., & Pumariega, J. (2005). Mental health of immigrants and refugees. *Community Mental Health Journal, 45*, 581–567.

Reed, B. G., Newman, P. A., Suarez, Z. E., & Lewis, E. A. (1997). Interpersonal practice beyond diversity and toward social justice: The importance of critical consciousness. In C. D. Garvin & B. A. Seabury (Eds.), *Interpersonal practice in social work: Promoting competence and social injustice* (pp. 44–77). Boston: Allyn & Bacon.

Richardson, L. A. (2001). Seeking and obtaining mental health services: What do parents expect? *Archives of Psychiatric Nursing, 15*, 223–231.

Ruiz-de-Velasco, J., Fix, M., & Clewell, B. C. (2000). *Overlooked & underserved: Immigrant students in U.S. secondary schools.* Washington, DC: The Urban Institute.

Schriver, J. M. (2001). *Human behavior and the social environment: Shifting paradigms in essential knowledge for social work practice.* Boston: Allyn & Bacon.

Spencer, M. S., Chen, J., Gee, G. C., Fabian, C. G., & Takeuchi, D. T. (2010). Discrimination and mental health-related service use in a national study of Asian Americans. *American Journal of Public Health, 100*(12), 2410–2417.

Stein, B. D., Kataoka, S. H., Jaycox, L. H., Wong, M., Fink, A., Escudero, P., & Zaragoza, C. (2002). Theoretical basis and program design of a school-based mental health intervention for traumatized immigrant children: A collaborative research partnership. *Journal of Behavioral Health Services and Research, 29*, 318–326.

Stephan, S. H., Weist, M., Kataoka, S., Adelsheim, S., & Mills, C. (2007). Transformation of children's mental health services: The role of school mental health. *Psychiatric Service, 58*(10), 1330–1338. doi: 10.1176/appi.ps.58.10.1330

Takeuchi, D. T., Alegría, M., Jackson, J. S., & Williams, D. R. (2007). Immigration and mental health: Diverse findings in Asian, Black, and Latino populations. *American Journal of Public Health, 97*(1), 11–12. doi: 10.2105/ajph.2006.103911

Uba, L. (1982). Meeting the mental health needs of Asian Americans: Mainstream or segregated services. *Professional Psychology, 13*, 215–221.

The Urban Institute. (2010, June). *Basic facts on children of immigrants.* Washington, DC: The Urban Institute.

U.S. Department of Health and Human Services. (1994). *Community health advisors: Models, research, and practice, public health services*. Atlanta, GA: Centers for Disease Control and Prevention.

U.S. Department of Health and Human Services. (2001). Mental health: Culture, race, and ethnicity—A supplement to mental health: A report of the surgeon general. Rockville, MD: U.S. Department of Health and Human Services, Substance Abuse and Mental Health Services Administration, Center for Mental Health Services.

Webb, S. A. (2001). Some considerations on the validity of evidence-based practice in social work. *British Journal of Social Work, 31*(1), 57–79. doi:10.1093/bjsw/31.1.57

Williams, D., Costa, M., & Leavell, J. (2010). Race and mental health: Patterns and challenges. In T. L. Scheid & T. N. Brown (Eds.), *A handbook for the study of mental health: Social contexts, theories, and systems* (2nd ed., pp. 268–290). New York: Cambridge University Press.

Woodruff, D. (2011). *Why is RTI an important strategy for addressing disproportionality?* Ask the Experts. Retrieved June 7, 2011, from http://www.rti4success.org/asktheexpert/video/975

Yeh, M., Eastman, K., & Cheung, M. K. (1994). Children and adolescents in community health centers: Does the ethnicity or the language of the therapist matter? *Journal of Community Psychology, 22*, 153–163.

Zane, N., & Yeh, M. (2002). The use of culturally based variables in assessment: Studies on loss of face. In K. S. Kurasaki & S. Okazaki (Eds.), *Asian American mental health: Assessment theories and methods* (pp. 123–138). New York: Kluwer Academic/Plenum.

Disclaimer

This chapter was written in my personal capacity and the views expressed in the chapter do not necessarily represent the views of the Office of Inspector General or the federal government.

Working with First Nations Students and Families

CHAPTER 60

Dorie J. Gilbert   Gail H. Sims

Getting Started

The number of U.S. persons estimated to be partly or fully of American Indian or Alaska Native heritage is approximately 4.1 million, or 1.5% of the U.S. population (Ogunwole, 2002). This group is one of the fastest growing populations because of increased birth rates, decreased infant mortality rates, and a greater willingness to report Native ancestry. Although the terms "American Indian," "Indian," and "Native American" are commonly used, they represent European-imposed, colonized names that serve to oppress indigenous, First Nations, or Native peoples, the original peoples occupying lands now called the United States (Yellow Bird, 2001). In this chapter, except when quoting or describing programs, we use the terms "First Nations" or "Native people" interchangeably to refer to the group as a whole; however, when addressing individuals, the best practice is to refer to Native people by their tribal nation or indigenous affiliation.

First Nations people represent a diverse population across the United States. Most (66%) Native people reside in metropolitan areas rather than on reservations or defined tribal areas, and nationally, there are 550 federally recognized tribes with a multitude of distinct tribal languages (Yellow Bird, 2001). As a group, they have experienced collective disenfranchisement, historical trauma, and contemporary challenges to traditional ways of life (Brave Heart, 1998, 2001a, 2001b). School social workers should be knowledgeable about how risks to the psychosocial well-being of Native people are rooted in impoverished living conditions and traumatic life events associated with oppression and loss of traditional culture and identity. Witko (2006) goes further to state that before practitioners can help Native clients achieve positive mental health, "they must first acknowledge the impact history has had on the collective experience of Indian nations" (p. 4).

Within this complex array of distressed living, a number of mental health, social, and behavioral problems as well as protective factors have been identified among Native children. In comparison to the majority culture, Native children may be at greater risk for a variety of emotional and behavioral disorders and negative psychosocial conditions. Native children enter kindergarten or first grade with relatively low levels of oral language, prereading, and premathematics skills, and less general knowledge (Farkas, 2003). Other problems often cited as affecting Native youth include suicidal behavior, substance abuse, violence, and depression; however, these problems must be considered within the context of complicated economic and social-political conditions, namely, the larger issues of past and current oppression, extreme poverty, loss of cultural identity, and historical trauma (Brave Heart, 2001a; Weaver, 2001). In discussing what Native identity means in the 21st century, Witko (2006) considers identity to be a particularly difficult challenge for Native children, especially those who do not hold a Certificate Degree of Indian Blood, an official U.S. document that certifies an individual possesses a specific degree of Native American blood of a federally recognized Indian tribe, band, nation, pueblo, village, or community. Identity is also compounded when growing up in an urban setting and for those of mixed heritage. Without multiple and clear sources for building a strong sense of identity, many Native youth turn to media and other often misguided images in their quest to define themselves.

Strengths and protective factors among Native children and adolescents include factors retained from the original culture. These include strong family bonds; emphasis on well-being of the community; wisdom and guidance of elders; cultural practices and traditions that serve to heal, empower, and increase positive ethnic identity; and sovereignty, the formalized self-determination of reservations to make choices (Weaver, 2001).

Many school social workers are in need of guidance in working with Native people; few service providers are specifically trained to work with this population. This chapter should assist school social workers and school-oriented mental health professionals in understanding how best to address the psychosocial needs of indigenous children within the school setting.

What We Know

The literature on effective interventions with First Nations people is growing. Best practices with Native students and families are culturally grounded, draw on conventional or some combination of conventional and cultural practices, and incorporate the cultural norms and values of Native people. The best practices fall into three categories: counseling and therapeutic interventions; school-based prevention programs; and family, community, and advocacy programs.

What We Can Do

Counseling and Therapeutic Interventions

Cognitive Behavioral Therapy (CBT) for Child Traumatic Stress) addresses trauma-related psychiatric symptoms in children ages 3–18. Randomized control trials showed significantly greater reductions in posttraumatic stress disorder (PTSD), depression, anxiety, problem behaviors, and parental emotional distress (Center for Substance Abuse Prevention, 2002). Given its focus on traumatic stress and reported high incidence of trauma among Native adolescents, CBT may have utility for Native populations (Yellow Horse & Brave Heart, 2004).

Family systems therapy matches well with the Native worldview of family and community collectivism. It sees family as the most important social unit and, at the same time, requires family members to explore ways in which their own behavior may be maladaptive or injurious to other family members (LaFromboise & Dizon, 2003).

Social cognitive therapy incorporates new developments, including the recognition of the impact of culture on personal agency (Bandura, 2002) and incorporation of family systems therapy and constructivist theory (Franklin & Jordan, 2003). In particular, constructivism—which emphasizes the personal realities, individual worldviews, and personal meanings of the client—strengthens the potential success of social cognitive therapy with Native people.

School-Based Prevention Programs

Most school-based programs are group-level prevention models and are recommended for use in conjunction with individual and/or family-based interventions. These programs primarily target areas such as drug or alcohol abuse, youth violence, suicide prevention, cultural identity building, and parent–child functioning (Sanchez-Way & Johnson, 2000). The following are examples of culturally congruent prevention programs that are promising best practices for Native youths:

American Indian Life Skills Development/formerly Zuni Life Skills Development is a school-based curriculum that has demonstrated increased suicide prevention skills and decreased hopelessness, among other positive outcomes, in American Indian youth. The curriculum is typically delivered over 30 weeks during the school year and includes 28–56 lesson plans covering topics such as building self-esteem, identifying emotions and stress, increasing communication and problem-solving skills, recognizing and eliminating self-destructive behavior, learning about suicide, role-playing suicide prevention, and setting personal and community goals. The program is listed in SAMHSA's National Registry of Evidence-based Programs and Practices (NREPP), and the curriculum manual is available from the University of Washington Press for a fee. Information about the program can be found at http://www.nrepp.samhsa.gov/ViewIntervention.aspx?id=81.

Storytelling for Empowerment is a SAMHSA-designated promising practice for middle school rural/reservation American Indian youth and Latino urban youth and has demonstrated effectiveness in reducing substance use, decreasing risk factors, and increasing resilience (Yellow

Horse & Brave Heart, 2004). The program was first implemented in 1995–1996 in a middle school on a rural reservation in Sells, Arizona, with 203 American Indian students participating. The curriculum is available from the WHEEL Council.

Project Venture (PV) is an outdoors experiential youth development program designed primarily for 5th–8th grade American Indian youth that aims to prevent alcohol, tobacco, and other drug use and build character and leadership using American Indian values such as family, learning from the natural world, spiritual awareness, service to others, and respect. Central program components include a minimum of 20 1-hour classroom-based activities conducted across the school year, weekly after school, weekend and summer skill-building and immersion camps, and community-oriented service learning projects throughout the year. The program has demonstrated longitudinal effectiveness based on randomized, control group study with middle-school students (Carter, Straits, & Hall, 2007), and outcome data has been reviewed by NREPP.

Native FACETS stands for Family/Friends, Active healthy choices, Cancer prevention, Eating wisely, Thankfulness, and Survival as a Native American. Designed to lower cancer risk among American Indians through youth tobacco prevention and dietary modification, the intervention teaches facts about tobacco and nutrition using films, storytelling, lectures, activities, and demonstrations, as well as media literacy exercises and problem-solving role-plays. Group leaders build the subjects' knowledge of ancestral tobacco use and its modern-day abuse, and the meaning and significance of ancestral food and traditional respect for the body. Leaders also stress the importance of family and the survival of American Indian culture as a way of combating negative peer pressures and other social influences. Youth learn and practice resistance skills, decision making, problem solving, and self-reward skills.

Family, Community and Advocacy Programs

Families and Schools Together (FAST) is a multifamily group intervention designed to build relationships between families, schools, and the communities to increase well-being among school-aged children. The groups have been adapted for use with American Indian youth in rural reservations and various other cultural groups. Part of SAMHSA's NREPP, the intervention components include outreach to parents, eight weekly multifamily group sessions, and ongoing monthly group reunions for up to 24 months to support parents in serving as primary prevention agents. Groups are facilitated by collaborative teams of parents/caregivers, professionals, and school personnel. A manualized program guide is available through the FAST Web site at http://familiesandschools.org.

Historical Trauma and Unresolved Grief Intervention (HTUG) is a psychoeducational group intervention that targets parents, with the overall goal of reducing mental health risk factors and increasing protective factors for Native children (Brave Heart, 2001a, 2001b).

American Indian Liaison Programs represent a highly promising strategy for working with Native children in school districts. A Native liaison is a person who works directly with the school district and acts a liaison between Native families and the school system. This position can be funded by the Office of Indian Education through a formula grant, available to any school district with at least 10 Indian children who are members of a state-recognized or federally recognized tribe or who have a parent or grandparent who is a member of a state-recognized or federally recognized tribe. Though the overall purpose of these grants is to assist Native children in meeting state academic standards, most programs recognize the interrelatedness of students' mental health needs and academic performance.

Steps in Implementing the Best Intervention(s)

This section includes a summary (in steps) of how to implement a promising intervention, social cognitive therapy, available for addressing the problems of Native children in the school system. A number of group-based and family- and community-based interventions have been covered. In this case study, we chose to feature social cognitive therapy because of its flexibility for school-based student and family sessions and ability to incorporate cultural constructs important to Native people, including:

- flexibility to include others, such as family members and community liaisons, in the helping process;
- flexibility to include culturally-based helping processes, specifically indigenous healing

processes where they may apply to the child/adolescent/family;

- a focus on trauma and stress, issues relevant to Native families;
- a recognition of the racial or ethnic, cultural, and socioeconomic diversity of Native families; and
- an emphasis on social construction, that is, on the personal realities, individual worldviews, and personal meanings of the child or family.

Social cognitive therapy, as presented here, involves seven major steps:

- Step 1: *Establish contact with a Native liaison.* Utilize the natural skills of a Native liaison. If your school district does not have a Native liaison, inquire about how to establish such a position at the district level.
- Step 2: *Self and Client Assessment.*
  Self-Assess. Be clear that you understand general differences between Native belief systems and dominant culture belief systems. Engage in self-assessment to be grounded in your own personal and professional values and commitment to culturally competent practice. Note how larger societal oppression affects the lives of children, families, and larger Native communities. This includes understanding the effects of historical trauma and unresolved grief (Brave Heart, 1998, 2001a, 2001b) on Native families.
  Assess cultural orientation of client. Assess the child's or family's comfort level with mainstream interventions. The comfort level of Native people with mainstream counseling practices ranges from acceptance to total rejection in favor of traditional native healing practices, with many falling in the middle of this range. Native people come from diverse backgrounds and cultural orientations; most are bicultural, meaning they are able to operate from both mainstream and Native cultural orientations.
  Assess validity of previous or current diagnoses. Eurocentric assessments can be detrimental and inappropriate for Native populations and usually stem from a practitioner's bias and/or lack of awareness of cultural differences and/or culturally biased measurement and assessment instruments (Gilbert, 2011). Ideally, assessments of Native people should use culture-specific tests, measures of cultural/ethnic identity and acculturative stress/trauma as moderators of standardized tests, thematic apperception types of tests, and, when possible, qualitative and multiple assessment strategies (Gilbert, 2011).
- Step 3: *Research the specific cultural practices and traditions of the tribe or community.* Not all families are affiliated with a tribe or Native community. However, most have some connection to a larger community, whether through other families or participation in tribal events associated with one or more Native communities. Find out the specific cultural practices and traditions of the tribe or community to which the child or family is most connected. Make note of the resources, coping abilities, and personal meanings the child or family and community bring to the situation. Be aware that with many Native communities, counseling is best accomplished within a family context. Native children tend to acquiesce to elders (including school counselors and personnel), and little will be accomplished without involving the family so that the child has permission from elders to express himself or herself.
- Step 4: *Establish credibility and trustworthiness.* Credibility begins with accomplishing the aforementioned steps. Building trust involves patience and flexibility. In the initial session, begin by engaging in nonthreatening material. Be unobtrusive, make silent observations, show humility, and allow for differences, especially with regard to time. In a traditional Native view, time is flowing and relative, which from a Eurocentric perspective may be viewed as being irresponsible with respect to time. Schedule longer sessions to account for family involvement and allow ample time for narrative expressions, keeping in mind the fluidity of time in traditional Native culture and a tendency for Native clients to "drop by" (Brave Heart, 2001b). You may also consider incorporating humor with Native people, or at least be aware that they may introduce their problem with a joke or a story. A generic suggestion is to incorporate Native themes and values (e.g., love of nature, legends, colors, animals) as a way to broach topics. In addition, the liaison can assist with building the rapport with families. Beginning with a brief, relevant self-disclosure is also helpful as a way to open communication and show relatedness. The idea is to establish a relationship and to provide a model for sharing information, especially when dealing with children.

- Step 5: *Solicit information and develop a definition of the problem from the child's or family's cultural point of view.* Avoid asking for written information. For a guide to storytelling techniques, Bigfoot and Dunlap (2006) provide clear examples of stories, a history of how stories were used, and encouragement for practitioners to incorporate storytelling, including video storytelling and journaling. Techniques for soliciting information through narratives, storytelling, and indirect communication styles are relevant for Native communication styles. Mirroring is extremely important. For one, it provides the practitioner a way of altering his or her interactions based on how the child or family interacts. For example, individual differences in Native communication styles, such as indirect or direct eye contact, should be mirrored rather than basing one's interactions on assumptions or stereotypes.
- Step 6: *Explore client's thoughts, including client's cues and reinforcements for negative behavior.* Keep in mind that the child or family may not view behavior as maladaptive. Establish an understanding of the constructs, meaning, and value associated with the behavior.
- Step 7: *Effect change in maladaptive behavior*

Provide information, models, and opportunities to master the necessary skills. Storytelling and imaginary play are recommended for use with the Native children and adolescents. It is useful to share experiences of others who have overcome similar situations. In keeping with an indirect communication style, models of behavior should be presented as suggestions.

Explore successes and failures with behavior change. Praise any successes with behavior change. Address previously failed attempts and explore individual and environmental factors that have contributed to unsuccessful attempts.

Incorporate a group experience. If possible, arrange for the child or family to meet with similar others who have experience with the behavior and endorse its effectiveness. A culturally congruent group program offers an opportunity to increase positive cultural identity and indigenous healing while promoting prosocial activities, shared responsibility, networks, and collective approaches.

Applying Interventions within a Response to Intervention Framework

Social cognitive therapy as outlined above is a particularly promising intervention within the RTI framework because it can be incorporated within this tier system and is easily adapted for use with Native American children in the school system, as illustrated above. Some of the ways that RTI and cognitive therapy are generally compatible in working with Native American students are as follows:

- RTI identifies initial and ongoing assessment as an essential component to implementation. Similarly, Step 2 of the social cognitive process as presented above illustrates how to conduct effective assessments while considering the cultural implications of working with Native children and their families. The goal is to decrease misplacement of Native students into inappropriate interventions or specialized academic settings that do not meet their needs. Steps 5 and 6 provide for a qualitative contextual assessment of the problem that is particularly important when attempting to craft a culturally responsive intervention.
- RTI emphasizes parental or family involvement as an essential component to implementation. The social cognitive intervention fosters the likelihood of support and ongoing family involvement in the student's behavioral change and academic achievement.
- RTI also emphasizes group-based intervention. It's important to incorporate culturally congruent group-based programs to increase positive cultural identity and collective values when working with Native students

Tools and Practice Examples

Eddie Snow Wolf is a 14-year-old Native ninth-grade student at Smith High School, a predominantly white and low- to middle-income public high school in the Southwest. Eddie has been at the school for 5 months, and he is struggling with the course work and having difficulty getting along with classmates. Eddie came to the attention of the school social worker, Ms. Esther Jones, after he was expelled for fighting. The vice principal referred Eddie to Ms. Jones because he felt that "some home problems" might be causing Eddie's academic and conduct problems.

Step 1: Establish Contact with a Community Liaison

Ms. Jones contacted Michael Stone, the school district's Native liaison. Ms. Jones met with Mr. Stone to brief him on what details were known about Eddie's situation, and in turn Mr. Stone briefed her on what he knew of the tribe, the Oglala Lakota, to which Eddie belonged.

Step 2: Self and Client Assessment

Self-Assessment

Ms. Jones, a 35-year-old Euro-American female, acknowledged that she had no experience working with Native populations but had read resource material with general information about Native cultural norms versus mainstream, Eurocentric norms. In addition, she understood how oppression and poverty influenced the lives of many Native families.

Assess Cultural Orientation of Client

Ms. Jones reviewed Eddie's school and transfer records and determined that just prior to entering Smith High, he had lived on a nearby reservation, and from the records, he had attended a public, nontribal school only in sixth and seventh grades. From this, she made a tentative judgment that, on a continuum, Eddie might be more aligned with traditional Native practices and somewhat uncomfortable with Eurocentric, mainstream interventions.

Assess Validity of Current and Previous Diagnoses

Ms. Jones noted that 2 years prior, when Eddie attended public school, he was identified as likely having attention deficit disorder (ADD). Knowing that Native children are often misdiagnosed, Ms. Jones decided to reevaluate the diagnosis with Mr. Stone's help.

Step 3: Research the Specific Cultural Practices and Traditions of the Tribe or Community

Mr. Stone helped Ms. Jones to research the Oglala Lakota People. Ms. Jones learned that in that tradition, communication with families is usually done along gender lines, and respect must be given to cross-gender interactions (Brave Heart, 2001b). Should both a male and female family member of Eddie's family attend the counseling session, she, as a woman, would first address the other female before addressing the male. The tribal community is very strong, with most people living in the nearby urban community but visiting the reservation frequently for cultural events. With the tribal communities, families and extended families are closely connected. A particular tribal practice is for the eldest male relative to take on the title and role of "grandfather" or "father" to younger family members. Another Lakota way of life involves a concept of *tiospaye* (a collection of related families) in which a group of blood and nonblood relatives meet as a group to discuss how to strengthen the family. Ms. Jones and Mr. Stone also recognized that Eddie's immediate family members would need to be contacted to attend the counseling, based on their understanding that many traditional Native children will not disclose personal information without the presence or permission of parents or elders.

Step 4: Establishing Credibility and Trustworthiness

At the first meeting, Ms. Jones and Mr. Stone met with Eddie and Eddie's grandfather, the only immediate family member available for the meeting. Eddie's older sister lived in a nearby city and wanted to attend but did not have transportation. The meeting was scheduled for 90 minutes rather than the usual 1 hour. Based on the Lakota practices, Ms. Jones first allowed Mr. Stone to address the grandfather. After that introduction, Ms. Jones began with a brief, informal self-disclosure. She talked about her own grandfather and how important it was for him to be involved in her life. Ms. Jones and Mr. Stone then invited Mr. Snow Wolf to discuss his role in Eddie's life. Through this they learned that Mr. Snow Wolf is Eddie's deceased father's uncle, the eldest living male. As she listened and learned about the family history, Ms. Jones discovered that Eddie's mother and father had died in a car accident 2 years earlier. She was able to connect this information to Eddie's school records and recognized that the loss of his parents coincided with teachers' identifying him as needing to be tested for ADD.

Step 5: Solicit Information

Slowly, Ms. Jones broached the topic of the fight, the reason that Eddie was expelled from school. Using indirect communication, she first talked about how school environments can be difficult at times for teens. She asked Eddie how he experienced the school as being difficult. Eddie disclosed that he felt the teachers at the school didn't care about the Native students and that teachers ignored other students' misuse of Native names. Through this conversation, it was revealed that Eddie's fight started after he had been repeatedly harassed by a white male classmate who called Eddie a "squaw boy." Eddie felt that although the teacher heard the classmate use this term repeatedly, the teacher failed to reprimand him. Eddie felt he had to take matters into his own hands to defend himself and his honor.

Step 6: Exploring Clients' Thoughts, Including Clients' Cues and Reinforcements for Negative Behavior

Ms. Jones explored what Eddie meant by "defend himself" and learned that the term "squaw boy" is a derogatory term and that by using it, the classmate was insulting Eddie and his entire family. It insulted his manhood and was especially hurtful because he came from a strong lineage of warriors. Ms. Jones learned that in Eddie's view, anyone should know that this is a derogatory slur and that the teacher should have recognized this and reprimanded the other student.

Step 7: Effecting Change in Maladaptive Behavior

Provide Information and Opportunities for the Student and Family to Master the Necessary Skills

Ms. Jones continued to meet with Eddie over the next week to discuss strategies he could use in handling conflicts with students. She asked Eddie to practice these skills and scheduled a second meeting with Eddie and his grandfather.

The next week, Ms. Jones received a phone call from Eddie's older sister. She wanted to know what was going on with Eddie. In the conversation, the sister said that Eddie and his grandfather were living in a trailer and often went without food. She wanted to know what resources were available for them but warned that they would not want anyone, not even the counselor, to know about their financial struggles. That same day, Eddie's grandfather dropped in to see Ms. Jones. Understanding that this type of "drop in" might occur, Ms. Jones made the time to see him and offered him coffee. The grandfather wanted to talk about Eddie's drinking problem. Ms. Jones thanked him for stopping in and listened carefully as he described how Eddie drinks in the evenings and doesn't complete his school-work. He wanted to know what programs were available. Ms. Jones said that she would research this. She also took the opportunity to tell him that his granddaughter, Eddie's sister, was worried that he was not eating and not staying strong enough to take care of Eddie. Mr. Snow Wolf did not respond, but when Ms. Jones handed him a piece of paper with a list of places he could go for food and other resources, he nodded and thanked her. Ms. Jones set up an appointment with the family and Mr. Stone for the following week.

Explore Successes and Failures With Behavior Change

In that session, Ms. Jones explored how Eddie was handling the dynamics of the classroom. She explored his successes and discussed more strategies. To move into the topic of substance abuse, she and Mr. Stone followed steps 5 and 6. Mr. Stone broached the topic of substance abuse by telling stories of similar students who had overcome substance abuse problems.

Incorporate a Group Experience

Ms. Jones researched and found a group-based substance abuse program for Lakota youth. Since Eddie was an enrolled member of the tribe, the program was free. Also, the program incorporated Native healing practices and included a cultural identity component that would support Eddie's sense of positive ethnic identity.

Key Points to Remember

School social workers should be knowledgeable about how risks to the psychosocial well-being of Native children, adolescents, and families are often rooted in collective disenfranchisement, historical trauma, and contemporary challenges associated with loss of traditional culture and identity.

Strong family and community bonds, wisdom and guidance of elders, and positive cultural practices, traditions, and ethnic identity are among the recognized strengths and protective factors for Native children and adolescents.

In addition to promising group-based prevention programs, this chapter highlighted social cognitive therapy for school-based intervention because of its flexibility and ability to incorporate cultural constructs important to Native children and families. A seven-step process of social cognitive therapy provides details on culturally relevant client assessment, information gathering, establishment of credibility and trustworthiness, exploration of problems and thoughts, and ultimately, methods of effecting the desired change in behavior. A case study further elucidates how these seven steps are accomplished.

The authors would like to thank Dawn Echo Romero, CACIII, LCDC, for her review and assistance with the chapter. Romero (who is part Oglala-Sincangu Lakota) has provided substance abuse counseling for youth and their families for 14 years in both Colorado and Texas.

References

Bandura, A. (2002). Social cognitive theory in cultural context. *Applied Psychology, 51,* 269–290.

Bigfoot, D. S. & Dunlap, M. (2006). Storytelling as a healing tool for American Indians. In T. M. Witko (Ed.), *Mental health care for urban Indians: Clinical insights from native practitioners* (pp. 133–153). Washington, DC: American Psychological Association.

Brave Heart, M. Y. H. (1998). The return to the sacred path: Healing historical trauma response among the Lakota. *Smith College Studies in Social Work, 68*(3), 287–305.

Brave Heart, M. Y. H. (2001a). Culturally and historically congruent clinical social work assessment with Native clients. In R. Fong & S. Furuto (Eds.), *Cultural competent social work practice: Practice skills* (pp. 163–177). Needham Heights, MA: Allyn & Bacon.

Brave Heart, M. Y. H. (2001b). Culturally and historically congruent interventions with Native clients. In R. Fong & S. Furuto (Eds.), *Cultural competent social work practice: Practice skills* (pp. 285–298). Needham Heights, MA: Allyn & Bacon.

Carter, S. L., Straits, J. E., & Hall, M. (2007). *Project Venture: An evaluation of a positive culture-based approach to substance abuse prevention with American Indian youth* (Technical Report). Gallop, NM: The National Indian Youth Leadership Project. Retrieved from http://www.niylp.org/articles/Project-Venture-manuscript-final.pdf

Center for Substance Abuse Prevention (2002). Science-based prevention programs and principles: Effective substance abuse and mental health programs for every community. A National Report by S. Schinke, P. Rounstein, & S. E Gardner. (DHHS Publication No: SMA 03–3764). Rockville, MD: US Department of Health and Human Services, Substance Abuse and Mental Health Services Administration, Center for Substance Abuse Prevention. Retrieved from http://www.preventionidaho.net/Documents/csapscience.pdf

Farkas, G. (2003). Racial disparities and discrimination in education: What do we know, how do we know it, and what do we need to know? *Teachers College Record, 105*(6), 1119–1146.

Franklin, C., & Jordan, C. (2003). An integrative skills assessment approach. In C. Jordan & C. Franklin (Eds.), *Clinical assessment for social workers: Quantitative and qualitative methods* (2nd ed.). Chicago. IL: Lyceum.

Gilbert, D. J (2011). Multicultural assessment. In C. Jordan & C. Franklin (Eds), *Clinical assessment for social workers: Quantitative and qualitative methods* (3rd ed. pp. 359–392). Chicago, IL: Lyceum.

LaFromboise, T., & Dizon, M. R. (2003). American Indian children and adolescents. In J. Taylor Gibbs, L. N. Huang, & Associates (Eds.), *Children of color: Psychological interventions with culturally diverse youth.* San Francisco, CA: Jossey-Bass.

Ogunwole, S. (2002). *The American Indian and Alaska Native population: 2000.* Washington, DC: U.S. Bureau of the Census, U.S. Department of Commerce.

Sanchez-Way, R., & Johnson, C. (2000). Cultural practices in American Indian prevention programs. *Juvenile Justice,* 7(92), 20–30.

Weaver, H. (2001). Organization and community assessment with First Nations people. In R. Fong and S. Furuto (Eds.), *Culturally competent social work practice: Practice skills* (pp. 178–195). Needham Heights, MA: Allyn & Bacon.

Witko, T. M. (2006). An introduction to First Nation's people. In T. M. Witko (Ed.), *Mental health care for urban Indians: Clinical insights from native practitioners* (pp. 3–16). Washington, DC: American Psychological Association.

Yellow Bird, M. (2001). Critical values and First Nations peoples. In R. Fong & S. Furuto (Eds.), *Culturally competent social work practice: Practice skills* (pp. 61–74). Needham Heights, MA: Allyn & Bacon.

Yellow Horse, S., & Brave Heart, M.Y. H. (2004). A review of the literature. Healing the Wakanheja: Evidence based, promising, and culturally appropriate practices for American Indian/Alaska Native children with mental health needs. In A. D. Strode (Ed.), *Mental health best practices for vulnerable populations* (pp. 35–43). Olympia, WA: Washington State Department of Social and Health Services, Mental Health Division.

CHAPTER 61

Multiple Hispanic Cultures: Considerations for Working with Students and Families

Jorge Delva Laurie M. Carpenter Cristina B. Bares

Getting Started

The Spanish-speaking Hispanic population in the United States grew from approximately 35.3 million to 50.5 million in the years between 2000 and 2010 (Ennis, Ríos-Vargas, & Albert, May 2011). In this chapter, the term "Hispanic" will be used instead of "Latino" throughout. This is done to reflect the more commonly used term employed by the U.S. Census Bureau—it does not indicate a preference over the term Latino (see Acuña, 1999, and Hayes-Bautista & Chapa, 1987, for critical analyses of these terms).

The Hispanic population currently constitutes approximately 16% of the total U.S. population, and Hispanics are expected to constitute nearly 29% of the total population by the year 2050. The term "Hispanic" refers to a widely diverse population that includes people from nearly two dozen countries. This population consists of individuals and groups who are of diverse socioeconomic, religious, sociopolitical, and racial or ethnic backgrounds, and of varying geopolitical histories. Some examples of these population groups include individuals of Mexican and Puerto Rican descent, as well as those from Central America and Caribbean countries, South America, and of multiracial/ethnic backgrounds, as is the case of people of indigenous, African, and Spanish backgrounds. Many people considered Hispanic were native to what is presently the United States; others are more recent immigrants whose religious backgrounds span Catholicism, Protestantism, Judaism, Islam, and other faiths. Many adults are highly educated, and many have not completed high school. These are just a few examples of the tremendous diversity found among Hispanics. Diversity is so broad within the Hispanic population that social workers working with this population need to pay particular attention to any stereotypes they and their school systems may hold about the particular group. This diversity suggests the need for interventions that are not only theoretically sound but also sufficiently flexible to accommodate the group's heterogeneity. Motivational Interviewing (MI) is a counseling-based intervention that has both the necessary flexibility and a strong theoretical foundation (Hettema, Steele, & Miller, 2005; Miller & Rollnick, 2002) and can thus attend to the complexities of cross-cultural counseling experiences and accommodate the needs of the individual client.

Motivational Interviewing can be applied to a range of health and mental health problems. Research has shown MI interventions to be effective at decreasing the risk of alcohol-exposed pregnancies (Ingersoll et al., 2003; Handmaker, Miller, & Manicke, 1999), promoting positive dietary change (Bowen et al., 2002; Resnicow, Jackson, Wang, & De, 2001), encouraging contraceptive use (Cowley, Farley, & Beamis, 2002), and reducing substance use (Colby et al., 1998; Stein & Lebeau-Craven, 2002; Graeber, Moyers, Griffith, Guajardo, & Tonigan, 2003; McCambridge & Strang, 2004; Baker et al., 2002). A meta-analysis of MI by Burke, Arkowitz, and Menchola (2003) established that 51% of clients in the trials who received MI interventions showed improved behaviors, while 37% of those not receiving the intervention showed improved behaviors. This effect did not appear to decrease over time. In addition, because one of the aims of MI is to build rapport in order to develop a trusting relationship between the counselor and the client, it is perfectly adaptable to the differences found among Hispanic populations.

To illustrate the use of MI with Hispanic families, this chapter includes a case study of the application of MI by a school social worker with a parent whose child is beginning to have academic problems, a risk factor for drug use initiation. The particular focus on applying MI with a parent of an academically struggling child stems from the important role that parents play in a child's development, particularly in preventing children from initiating drug use (Chilcoat, Dishion, & Anthony, 1995).

What We Know

Inadequate Access to Substance Abuse Preventive and Treatment Services in Schools

Recent research shows that access to substance use prevention and treatment services (e.g., in-school counseling and referral services) has decreased over time (Terry-McElrath, O'Malley, Johnston, & Yamaguchi, 2003). Furthermore, these services, when available, do not seem to be correlated with the prevalence level of alcohol or illicit drug use in the schools: The exception is marijuana use (Terry-McElrath et al., 2003). The same authors further found that schools with larger numbers of racial-or ethnic-minority students are less likely to offer these services than are schools with fewer racial-or ethnic-minority students.

This trend of decreasing availability of counseling services, as well as the differential rates with which they are available to minorities, is of grave concern for the Hispanic population. Research shows that the prevalence of alcohol and illicit drug use among these youth has increased considerably through the 1990s and 2000s (Delva, Wallace, O'Malley, Johnston, Bachman, & Schulenberg, 2005). It is not clear what accounts for this large increase in drug use among Hispanic youth. It is plausible that prevention programs developed and implemented during the 1980s and 1990s may not have reached a sufficiently large number of Hispanic youth, or those that did reach the populations may have been ineffective because of cultural differences. Whatever the case might be, these findings suggest there is a need to continue to identify interventions that target factors found to place Hispanic youth at risk of initiating drug use, such as academic problems (Añez, Silva, Paris, & Bedregal, 2008).

Prevention Programs

Research has shown that prevention programs that incorporate defining characteristics of culture—dialect, idioms, norms, values, worldviews, mores, group history, and societal and structural responses to the group—increase the personal relevance of the interventions and are more likely to lead to enduring behavior change than are interventions that endorse behavior change without making the change relevant to the life of the client (Cacioppo & Petty, 1981; Delva, Allen-Meares, & Momper, 2010; Marin, 1995). Research also has shown that culturally specific interventions are more likely to be effective in improving health and preventing or reducing risky behaviors than are interventions without a cultural base (Amaro, Nieves, Johannes, & Labault Cabeza, 1999; Kantor, 1997; Padilla, 1995; Szapocznik, 1995). In the case of Hispanics, research has shown that special attention needs to be paid to the cultural influences of family and gender roles, the values of *respeto* (respect) and family interdependence, and their influence on behaviors. Hispanic families share strong feelings of loyalty, reciprocity, and solidarity. These values, along with the value of hard work *(hay que trabajar duro)* and the need to endure *(hay que aguantar)* as a means of providing for one's family, serve as the core of the resiliency and motivation to succeed apparent among Hispanic families, whether it is among "old" residents of this country, recently arrived immigrants, or undocumented families.

Consequently, one crucial point of this chapter is that to maximize the effectiveness of any intervention to prevent school dropout and substance use, the school social worker must have more than tangential knowledge of the particular Hispanic population with which she works, as it is through this understanding that stereotypes can be avoided and a true rapport built. Furthermore, knowledge of the language will help the social worker acquire a greater appreciation of the behavioral and cultural norms of the families.

Motivational Interviewing

Motivational Interviewing is a counseling style that arose from the field of alcohol abuse treatment (Miller, 1983, 1999). Its goal is to reduce the natural resistance that individuals tend to experience when life circumstances call for them to make a decision to change a belief and/or a behavior (e.g., a person with a diagnosis of alcohol dependence having to make a decision to discontinue drinking). MI is a directive, client-centered counseling approach intended to help clients explore and resolve ambivalence they may experience when faced with the necessity of making lifestyle changes (Rollnick & Miller, 1995; Miller & Rollnick, 2002). Persons conducting MI are trained to communicate in an empathic, direct, and supportive manner in order to minimize normal resistance. The skills required to implement MI are directly in line with the Code of Ethics of the field of social work, as established by the National Association of Social Workers (National Association of Social Workers, 2004). As the code states that social workers must place the utmost value on promoting clients' self-determination and capacity to change, while treating each individual with respect, MI compels workers to interact with empathy and to assist clients in building their personal self-efficacy. The most conducive environment to a successful intervention using MI is one that is supportive and nonjudgmental, one that conveys to people that they are perfectly capable of making changes. A nonjudgmental attitude permits people to safely explore new behaviors.

Before further discussing some of the properties of MI, it is important to briefly note that MI has often been implemented within the context of the "stages of change" (Prochaska & DiClemente, 1984) or "transtheoretical model" (TTM) (Prochaska & DiClemente, 1985). According to TTM, a person may fall within any one of five stages, oftentimes drifting back and forth between stages. The first defined stage is the *pre-contemplation stage*, in which a person is not yet thinking in serious terms about making any changes in the next 6 months. The next stage is the *contemplation stage*, in which a person begins to seriously think about behavioral changes within the next 6 months. In the next stage, the *preparation stage*, a person is prepared to take action and intends to make a change within, for example, the next 30 days. This person may also suggest that in the past 6 months she has tried making changes. The next stage, the *action stage*, is that in which a person has made a change within the last 6 months. And finally, the *maintenance stage* is that in which a person has maintained a behavior change for longer than 6 months.[1]

Quite interestingly, when MI principles are followed, the person's readiness for change is automatically taken into consideration. This situation results from the individualized approach that MI mandates. Therefore, the MI script presented in the next section does not highlight the stages of change model, as attention to the particular stage comes naturally in the implementation of MI. As noted earlier, the MI interaction will be between a school social worker and the parent of a child who lately has begun to experience some academic problems. By using MI, the school social worker does not impose personal values and goals on the parent but helps the parent explore ways to improve the child's academic standing.

A helpful framework under which to implement MI is provided by the acronym *FRAMES,* which stands for giving *f*eedback, getting the person to take *r*esponsibility for the change that needs to take place, providing brief *a*dvice, helping the person create a *m*enu of options, using *e*mpathy throughout the interaction, and assisting the person to build his or her *s*elf-efficacy to accomplish the goals (Hester & Miller, 1995). The next section provides a step-by-step illustration of MI using the FRAMES framework.[2]

MI and the Response to Intervention Model

According to the three-tiers of the Response to Intervention (RTI) model, a Tier 3 level would apply, for example, if one were to include in the intervention the parent of the youth who is experiencing behavioral problems. That is, a Tier 3 intervention requires a more intensive individualized approach, one that MI can easily provide. On the other hand, general education about behavior and conflict management can be universally implemented in school settings (Tier 1 intervention). Informed by data that suggest a subgroup of students may need more assistance, these students can then participate in group interventions (a Tier 2 intervention). However, students who require further, more individualized, intensive, assistance would benefit from MI, which could be considered a Tier 3 intervention.

Tools and Practice Examples

MI Script: A Step-by-Step Illustration

This section consists of the first contact that the caregiver will have with the school social worker. The meeting was called by the social worker to start a discussion with Ms. Martínez, the mother of a second grader, Fernanda, who recently had begun to have academic difficulties. The meeting takes place at the school. It is important to emphasize that the dialogue presented does not capture all the different communication styles and potential topics of such a conversation between social worker and parent. Rather, it provides one particular example of how MI can be used. In a meeting of this sort, a large number of issues may surface as a result of a person's background. For example, people of some groups (mostly populations of low socioeconomic status) may expect females to take on a caregiving role with siblings and assist with chores. Or a child may have time-consuming chores if parents must work long hours. The number of possible issues is very large, and a social worker must know the population well to be prepared when meeting with parents or other family members.

The reader is encouraged to substitute his or her own style and responses according to the corresponding circumstances (e.g., the meeting includes the student's teacher, the meeting takes place at the child's home, the meeting includes a grandparent) and issues discussed. Also, details about how the script conforms to MI are kept to a minimum to avoid cutting the flow of the interaction between the social worker and parent.

MI Script

Please note that text that is italicized and in brackets or parentheses indicates comments made to highlight a point of the particular script and is not part of the script. It is highly recommended that the client (in this case, the parent) do 70% of the talking and the social worker 30% or less; otherwise, whatever interaction takes place would not be considered Motivational Interviewing (P. Weinstein, personal communication, April 13, 2004).

Introduction

Hi, Ms. Martínez, my name is Claudia González. I am the school social worker. Thank you very much for coming to meet with me today. One of the goals at our school is to meet with parents to discuss their children's progress and experiences in school. As I mentioned in our phone conversation, I wanted to meet with you to discuss how Fernanda is doing in school. Fernanda is a very bright student. You must be really proud of her. Could you tell me some of the aspirations you have for your child's future? *(The idea here is to encourage the parent discuss the aspirations she has for her child as a way to build trust and to begin building rapport.)* These are good goals to aim for, and I am getting a good sense of what is important to you. *(Begin FRAMES.)*

Feedback

This week I spoke with Fernanda's teacher, Ms. Soledad. She tells me that in the past 3 months, Fernanda has not been very focused in class, and she seems more tired than usual. For example, ... *(It would be helpful to provide a detailed example here.)* Why do you think Fernanda is feeling this way? *(You may encourage the parent to do most of the talking by paraphrasing or saying:*

- "Tell me more ..." or
- "What other things do you or Fernanda do that prepare her for school?" and/or
- "Tell me about how things are at home."
- "How difficult is it to do all the things you do?")

(Praise the parent for all the work she is doing by saying:

- "From what you tell me, despite your busy schedule, you have given a lot of thought to helping Fernanda do well in school."
- "This is very good."
- "Caring for children's schooling while managing all the family responsibilities can also be very difficult at times. Can you tell me more about how you do it?")

Responsibility and Advice

I admire your determination to help Fernanda succeed in school. I am sorry to hear about the circumstances affecting your family that may be having an effect on Fernanda's ability to concentrate in class. Do you know that despite these difficulties there are several things you can do to make sure Fernanda does not fall behind? That's right, by working together we can get Fernanda back on track, but a lot of the work will rest on what you can do at home. We at the school can also help in various ways. Let's talk about the things we can all do.

Menu

(At this point, the social worker has considerable information to help the parent develop goals that will help either further assess what might be affecting Fernanda's schoolwork or to begin taking steps to ameliorate the circumstances and to help the parent enhance her self-efficacy, her belief that she can make a big difference in helping Fernanda succeed in school.)

What are some things you are already doing to help Fernanda be focused when she comes to school?
What are some other things you could be doing, but do not currently do, that might fit in with your life and would help Fernanda?
Ms. Martínez, if you did the above things, how would they make Fernanda's school experiences even better? If you did not do these things, what would Fernanda's future look like?

Empathy

Within the FRAMES framework, empathy is listed after the menu option, but empathy is used throughout the entire process.

Self-Efficacy

(The purpose of this step is to enhance the parent's self-efficacy, the belief that she can successfully accomplish the desired goals. From the list of things the parent is already doing or wishes to be doing, identify two to three goals, potential roadblocks, and steps to overcome these and achieve the goals. The goals should be feasible, specific, and measurable. Let her take the lead in defining the goals and how to accomplish them. It is helpful to create a table that lists the goals with a rating of the likelihood they believe they can achieve the goals. Listing potential roadblocks the person may encounter in reaching these goals is also helpful. Based on work conducted with Dr. Steven Ondersma and the Detroit Center for Research on Oral Health Disparities [NIDCR Grant No. U-54 DE 14261–01], we next provide an example of a table social workers may wish to use (Table 61.1). However, social workers should feel free to use formats they already use in their day-to-day work or that may be more directly pertinent to their work settings.)

List the goals and roadblocks facing Ms. Martínez in achieving each goal.

(List the goals from the most likely to be achieved to the least likely to be achieved.)

I have enjoyed working with you today making a plan for Fernanda to have a better experience at school. You have identified a good plan to achieve this.

Key Points to Remember

This case study focuses on the interaction a social worker may have with a parent of a child who is exhibiting some difficulties at school. It is highly likely that one of the goals that may arise as a result of the conversation is that the family needs assistance with referrals to social services to receive relief from material hardships (e.g., hunger, unemployment, homelessness) or other chronic stressors (e.g., divorce, death in the family). It may also be necessary to have psychological or medical testing, as the child's difficulties may be a result of psychological (e.g., trauma, depression) or health problems (e.g., nutritional deficiency).

MI has been shown to be effective in helping people address the ambivalence of exploring

Table 61.1

GOAL	*We want to be sure you reach your goal. Could you tell me how likely are you to (state goal)? Can you tell me why you rated it this way?*	*What are the most important roadblocks you might have to overcome to reach your goal?*
1.	1 2 3 4 5 6 7 8 9 10 Less Likely — Very Likely	
2.	1 2 3 4 5 6 7 8 9 10 Less Likely — Very Likely	

Box 61.1

Goal 1: ____

____

Steps: What steps do you think you might need to take in order to be able to reach the goal by overcoming the roadblock or not letting it get in the way? ____________________

❑ *[Paraphrase wants/desires for child.* "Let me be sure I understand. You would like Fernanda to________."*]*

❑ COMMITMENT CHECK "Remember, it is important that you feel this is the right goal for you and that you feel you can accomplish it. Do you think you can achieve this goal? If you are not ready yet, you do not have to make the commitment. We can reevaluate the goal if you'd like to."

❑ GIVE COPY OF GOALS TO PARENT

I am going to give you a copy of the goals you chose, with notes about the specifics to help remind you. My name and telephone number are attached, as well.

❑ ANTICIPATE PROBLEMS

Not everything goes the way we plan. There are always challenges so please feel free to call me whenever you'd like to discuss these with me. It is important to keep working on the goals we set today even when there are problems.

❑ ENCOURAGE CONTACT

Feel free to call me if you have any problem with the goals. I would also like to call you once in a while to find out how you are doing. We can always change our goals. When is the best time to call?

Telephone number to call: ______________________________

Day and Time: ______________________________

new and healthier behaviors. In the school context, the success of this intervention results from the social worker working in partnership with the parent rather than from a top-down educational or confrontational perspective, and building rapport and trust, as these are key components of MI. Success is also linked to following the structure of the highlighted FRAMES outline, in:

- providing *f*eedback in a nonjudgmental manner,
- encouraging the parent to take *r*esponsibility to make changes,
- providing brief *a*dvice,
- creating a *m*enu of options developed jointly with the parent,
- displaying *em*pathy throughout the interaction, and
- helping the clients build their *s*elf-efficacy to change their and their children's behaviors.

As outlined previously, MI has been shown to be effective for clients facing a wide range of health issues. However, given the heterogeneity among and within these population groups, the effectiveness of MI needs to be constantly evaluated, as is the case with any other intervention. Should the evaluation or assessment indicate MI is not appropriate with a particular group, other interventions should be considered. This chapter gives the social worker an outline of one way to implement this efficacious intervention with at-risk Hispanic populations. As the intervention appears to touch on many of the inherent values and traditions of Hispanics, it is perfectly suited to work with this population, and has potential for encouraging significant behavioral change.

Acknowledgment: The information presented in this chapter on MI is informed by the work conducted by Philip Weinstein, a professor at the University of Washington, and that of the Detroit Center for Research on Oral Health Disparities, funded by the National Institute of Health [NIDCR Grant No. U-54 DE 14261–01]. Nonetheless, the implementation of MI as presented in this chapter reflects the authors' clinical and research experiences and not the views of

Dr. Weinstein and the Oral Health Center research team.

Notes

1. Readers interested in learning more about this model are encouraged to visit http://www.uri.edu/research/cprc/transtheoretical.htm. This Web site provides a series of links to important information on the stage of change model.
2. A terrific source of information on MI that can be easily obtained is available from http://www.motivationalinterview.org/.

References

Acuña, R. (1999). *Occupied America: A history of Chicanos.* Boston, MA: Addison-Wesley.

Amaro, H., Nieves, R., Johannes, S. W., & Labault Cabeza, N. M. (1999). Substance abuse treatment: Critical issues and challenges in the treatment of Latina women. *Hispanic Journal of Behavioral Sciences, 21,* 266–282.

Añez, L. M., Silva, M. A., Paris, M., & Bedregal, L. E. (2008). Engaging Latinos through the integration of cultural values and motivational interviewing principles. *Professional Psychology: Research and Practice, 39,* 153–159.

Baker, A., Lewin, T., Reichler, H., Clancy, R., Carr, V., Garrett, R., et al. (2002). *Addiction, 91,* 1329–1337.

Bowen, D., Ehret, C., Pedersen, M., Snetselaar, L., Johnson, M., Tinker, L., et al. (2002). Results of an adjunct dietary intervention program in the women's health initiative. *Journal of the American Dietetic Association, 102,* 1631–1637.

Burke, B. L., Arkowitz, H., & Menchola, M. (2003). The efficacy of motivational interviewing: A meta-analysis of controlled clinical trials. *Journal of Consulting and Clinical Psychology, 71,* 843–861.

Cacioppo, J. T., & Petty, R. E. (1981). Attitudes and persuasion: Classic and contemporary approaches. Dubuque, IA: William C. Brown.

Chilcoat, H. D., Dishion, T. J., & Anthony, J. C. (1995). Parent monitoring and the incidence of drug sampling in urban elementary school children. *American Journal of Epidemiology, 141,* 25–31.

Colby, S. M., Barnett, N. P., Monti, P. M., Rohsenow, D. J., Weissman, K., Spirito, A., et al. (1998). Brief motivational interviewing in a hospital setting for adolescent smoking: A preliminary study. *Journal of Consulting and Clinical Psychology, 66,* 574–578.

Cowley, C. B., Farley, T., & Beamis, K. (2002). "Well, maybe I'll try the pill for just a few months ..." Brief motivational and narrative-based interventions to encourage contraceptive use among adolescents at high risk for early childbearing. *Families, Systems, and Health, 20,* 183–204.

Delva, J., Allen-Meares, P., & Momper, S. L. (2010). *Cross-cultural research.* New York: Oxford University Press.

Delva, J., Wallace, J. E., O'Malley, P. M., Johnston, L. D., Bachman, J. G., & Schulenberg, J. M. (2005). The epidemiology of alcohol, marijuana, and cocaine use among Mexican American, Puerto Rican, Cuban American, and other Latin American eighth graders in the U.S.: 1991–2002. *American Journal of Public Health, 95,* 696–702.

Ennis, S. R., Ríos-Vargas, M., & Albert, N. G. (2011, May). *The Hispanic Population: 2010: 2010 Census Brief.* Available at: http://www.census.gov/prod/cen2010/briefs/c2010br-04.pdf. Accessed June 15, 2011

Graeber, D. A., Moyers, T. B., Griffith, G., Guajardo, E., & Tonigan, S. (2003). A pilot study comparing motivational interviewing and an educational intervention in patients with schizophrenia and alcohol use disorders. *Community Mental Health Journal, 39,* 189–202.

Handmaker, N. S., Miller, W. R., & Manicke, M. (1999). Findings of a pilot study of motivational interviewing with pregnant drinkers. *Journal of Studies on Alcohol, 60,* 285–287.

Hayes-Bautista, D., & Chapa, J. (1987). Latino terminology: Conceptual bases for standardized terminology. *American Journal of Public Health,* 77, 61–68.

Hester, R. K., & Miller, W. R. (1995). *Handbook of alcoholism treatment approaches: Effective alternatives* (2nd ed.). Boston, MA: Allyn & Bacon.

Hettema, J., Steele, J., & Miller, W. R. (2005). Motivational interviewing. *Annual Review of Clinical Psychology, 1,* 91–111.

Ingersoll, K., Floyd, L., Sobell, M., Velasquez, M. M., Baio, J., Carbonari, J., et al. (2003). Reducing the risk of alcohol exposed pregnancies: A study of a motivational intervention in community settings. *Pediatrics, 111,* 1131–1135.

Kantor, G. K. (1997). Alcohol and spouse abuse ethnic differences. In M. Galanter (Ed.), *Recent developments in alcoholism, Volume 13: Alcoholism and violence* (pp. 57–79). New York: Plenum.

Marin, B. (1995). *Analysis of AIDS prevention among African-Americans and Latinos in the United States.* Washington, DC: Office of Technology Assessment, U.S. Congress.

McCambridge, J., & Strang, J. (2004). The efficacy of single-session motivational interviewing in reducing drug consumption and perceptions of drug-related risk and harm among young people: Results from a multisite cluster randomized trial. *Addiction, 99,* 39–52.

Miller, W. R. (1983). Motivational interviewing with problem drinkers. *Behavioral Psychotherapy, 11,* 147–172.

Miller, W. R. (1999). Motivational interviewing: Research, practice, and puzzles. *Addictive Behaviors, 21,* 835–842.

Miller, W. R., & Rollnick, S. (2002). *Motivational interviewing: Preparing people for change* (2nd ed.). New York: Guilford.

National Association of Social Workers. (2004). *Code of Ethics of the National Association of Social Workers.* Retrieved June 22, 2004, from http://www.social-workers.org/pubs/code/code.asp

Padilla, A. M. (Ed.). (1995). *Hispanic psychology: Critical issues in theory and research.* Beverly Hills, CA: Sage.

Prochaska, J., & DiClemente, C. C. (1984). *The transtheoretical approach: Crossing traditional boundaries of therapy.* Homewood, IL: Dow Jones-Irwin.

Prochaska, J. O., & DiClemente, C. (1985). Common processes of self-change in smoking, weight control, and psychological distress. In S. Shiffman & T. Wills (Eds.), *Coping and substance abuse: A conceptual framework* (pp. 345–363). New York: Academic Press.

Resnicow, K., Jackson, A., Wang, T., & De, A. K. (2001). A motivational interviewing intervention to increase fruit and vegetable intake through black churches: Results of the eat for life trial. *American Journal of Public Health, 91,* 1686–1693.

Rollnick, S., & Miller, W. R. (1995). What is motivational interviewing? *Behavioral and Cognitive Psychology, 23,* 325–334.

Stein, L. A. R., & Lebeau-Craven, R. (2002). Motivational interviewing and relapse prevention for DWI: A pilot study. *Journal of Drug Issues, 32,* 1051–1069.

Szapocznik, J. (Ed.). (1995). *A Hispanic/Latino family approach to substance abuse prevention.* DHHS Publication No. (SMA) 95–3034. Washington, DC: SAMHSA.

Terry-McElrath, Y. M., O'Malley, P. M., Johnston, L. D., & Yamaguchi, R. (2003, November 17). *Schools as treatment access for drug-using adolescents.* Paper presented at the 131st annual meeting of the American Public Health Association, San Francisco, CA.

CHAPTER 62

Working Collaboratively with African American Students, Their Families, Cultural Networks, and School Environments

Edith M. Freeman

Getting Started

Best practices indicate that African American youths' experiences, needs, and learning styles require culturally focused interventions in addition to the psychosocial and educational strategies often used with other youths (Cherry, 1998; Harvey & Hill, 2004; Jessor, 1993). This broader focus is important for the school to accomplish its mission of educating *all* students for life (Adelman & Taylor, 1999). Hence, this chapter reviews the problem area, synthesizes best practices literature on these types of interventions with black youths, and describes a prevention program for youths and their families. A culturally relevant family example, cognitive maps, work sheets, and exercises illustrate how to apply the interventions.

What We Know

The Educational Achievement and Psychosocial-Cultural Adjustment of African American Youth

Inadequate psychosocial-cultural adjustment is influenced by a combination of individual/familial and environmental challenges that affect black children and youth in the long term. These long-term challenges include under-and unemployment; homelessness; crime and incarceration; drug use and abuse; early parenthood; little cultural pride and self-esteem; and lack of social responsibility for oneself or one's cultural group, community, or society (Banks, Hogue, Timberlake, & Liddle, 1996; Cherry et al., 1998; Freeman, 1992; Gavazzi, Alford, & McKenry, 1996; Mauer, 1999). Youths who are inadequately adjusted are more vulnerable to personal and environmental factors that contribute to their problems, because they may lack supportive social and cultural networks that aid in managing racial stress and poverty (Freeman, 2004). Enhanced psychosocial-cultural adjustment in black youths has been found to involve high cultural and self-esteem and bonding with cultural and community institutions/networks. These youths also make effective decisions to avoid or decrease their involvement in risky behaviors such as teenage parenthood, alcohol and other drug use and violence (Banks et al., 1996; Gavazzi et al., 1996).

Cultural interventions, such as teaching these youths how to apply African values to their lives, serve as protective factors and contribute to their resilience (Belgrave et al., 2004; Whaley & Davis, 2007). Thomas, Davidson, and McAdoo (2008) concluded that such interventions help African American youths to promote their cultural assets. Lack of educational achievement includes poor school performance and below-grade-level achievement, absenteeism, early dropout, behavioral disruptions, and a general lack of readiness to learn (Cherry et al., 1996). Moreover, Waller, Brown, and Whittle (1999) contend that inadequate psychosocial-cultural adjustment and educational failure among black youths are interrelated:

> The teens most likely to become pregnant are already oppressed by poverty, a lack of social support, persistent inequalities related to race and gender, and a dearth of opportunities for personal and professional fulfillment.... They are also likely to be failing in school and lacking educational or professional aspirations. (p. 468)

Other authors have documented this interrelationship through research. For example, Tolan and

McKay (1996) note that violent crimes are highest among young inner-city African American and Latino males, and Harvey and Hill (2004) conclude that African American males have the highest rates of school detentions, suspensions, expulsions, and special education placements. Higher rates of teen pregnancy and early parenthood as well as heavier use of cocaine among black youths also affect their school attendance and completion rates (Alan Guttmacher Institute, 1999; Dixon, Schoonmaker, & Philliber, 2000). Most important, Cherry et al. (1998) and Gilbert, Harvey, and Belgrave (2009) found that individual, family, and systemic factors such as discriminatory practices and oppressive policies contribute to these crime rates and to other indicators of psychosocial-cultural maladjustment and educational failure.

Research Support for Recommended Interventions: Practice Methods

This problem review led me to do a computerized search for the evidence-based, best practices research summarized in Table 62.1. In order to be included, studies had to (1) have been published in a professional journal within the past 15 years; (2) employ experimental, quasi-experimental, or naturalistic designs; (3) explore the outcomes of a school- or community-based prevention, risk reduction, or early-intervention approach; (4) focus on African American adolescents and their families in terms of academic achievement and psychosocial-cultural adjustment; and (5) use a strengths framework in the process (see Table 62.5 for these strengths frameworks) (Rones & Hoagwood, 2000).

Table 62.1 summarizes 20 studies that were included in this best practices analysis. One mixed-methods and four qualitative studies were included for comparison (Alford, 1997; Gavazzi et al., 1996; Leslie, 1998; Linnehan, 2001; Stevens, 1997), along with 15 experimental and quasi-experimental studies. Twelve, or 80%, of the latter studies had statistically significant results, with some studies reporting multiple outcomes in the three target areas for male and female African American youths from 10 to 19 years old.

Table 62.2 analyzes those studies' statistically significant outcomes, related interventions, and other contextual information. For example, it shows that moderate to long-term mentoring interventions ranging from 5 months to 1 year (activities with adult mentors, academic tutoring, and job training) led to improved academic outcomes in three studies, with better attendance rates and higher GPAs for males and females (Linnehan, 2001; Lewis, Sullivan, & Bybee, 2006; Thompson & Kelly, 2001). Six studies reported statistically significant improvements in youths' psychosocial school behavior and cultural outcomes, such as increased rule compliance, peer assertiveness skills, and awareness of Afrocentric values. Those studies targeted group training interventions for male and female youths and their parents, such as social skills or Afrocentric rite-of-passage approaches (Banks et al., 1996; Belgrave, Chase-Vaughn, Gray, Addison, & Cherry, 2000; Belgrave et al., 2004; Cherry, 1998; Johnson et al., 1998; and Thomas, Davidson, & McAdoo, 2008).

Statistically significant findings from three drug abuse prevention studies documented increased knowledge outcomes for male and female youths and their parents, based on group training sessions ranging from 7 weeks to 3 years (Brody et al., 2006; Harvey & Hill, 2004; Johnson et al., 1998). Only two studies reported less alcohol consumption as a result of culturally focused life skills training groups for male and female youths (Botvin, Schinke, Epstein, & Diaz, 1994; Botvin, Schinke, Epstein, Diaz, & Botvin, 1995). Finally, one study (Dixon et al., 2000) used a 13-week culturally focused group intervention with female youths to effect statistically significant outcomes: delayed initiation of sexual intercourse, less frequent unprotected sex, and fewer pregnancies.

In summary, long-term multiple culturally focused or Afrocentric group training interventions were effective with black male and female youths and their families in academic, psychosocial, and cultural areas. A critical gap in these studies is that few used follow-up evaluations to determine if their outcomes were maintained after interventions ended; Botvin et al. (1995) and Johnson et al. (1998) are exceptions. Moreover, none of the studies explored the efficacy of cultural interventions with individual youths and families in the three areas or the outcomes of related large systems change strategies.

What We Can Do

The Recommended Interventions: Practice Approach and Steps

Table 62.3 describes five program components for the recommended 18-month prevention approach

Table 62.1 Summary of Intervention Research on African American Families and Youths: Psychosocial-Cultural Adjustment and Educational Achievement

Study & Date	*Target Subgroup*	*Research Design and Procedures*	*Intervention Approach*	*Study Outcomes*
Brody et al. (2006) Contact Person: Gene H. Brody gbrody@uga.edu	African American females (54%) and males (46%), rural areas, mean age = 11.2, N = 332	Experimental design with control group and random assignment Procedures: Self-developed questionnaires and scales; 3-month post-intervention follow-up	SAAF prevention program had combined culturally relevant and cognitive interventions, including adaptive racial socialization, involved-vigilant parenting, expectations for alcohol use, and communication about sex. Seven separate youth and parental sessions, and seven combined youth-parental practice sessions	(a) Parents in intervention groups increased their effective communication about alcohol use, sex, and racial socialization (statistically significant). (b) Intervention group youths had lower rates of initiation of high-risk behaviors and they reported greater positive changes in parental communications (statistically significant)
Harvey & Hill, (2004) Contact person: Aminifu R. Harvey, DSW, aharvey@ssw. Umaryland.edu	African American male youths and their parents (N = 12)	Quasi-experimental comparison group design Procedures: direct observation and standardized measures	MAAT Africentric Rites of Passage Program: 3 years of weekly meetings, including an after-school component, family enhancement and empowerment activities, and individual family counseling	(a) Youths: improved self- esteem, knowledge of substance abuse & HIV, motivation for learning, racial identity, and cultural awareness (not statistically significant) (b) Parents: improved parenting skills, cultural awareness, community involvement, and racial identity (not statistically significant)
Johnson et al. (1998) Contact person: Knowlton Johnson, PhD, Kwjohn01@ulkyum. louisville.edu	Male and female youths (N = 133) and their parents (African American and white)	Randomized block comparison group design Procedures: individual interviews and written questionnaires	COPES Substance Abuse Prevention Program in youths' churches: 1-year parent training, youth training, early intervention, and follow-up case management services	(a) Youths: increased bonding with parents/siblings (statistically significant) and knowledge of and resistance to substance abuse (not statistically significant) (b) Parents: increased knowledge of substance abuse issues, use of community services, and modeling of appropriate alcohol use (statistically significant)

(continued)

Table 62.1 *(Continued)*

Study & Date	*Target Subgroup*	*Research Design and Procedures*	*Intervention Approach*	*Study Outcomes*
Cherry et al. (1998) Contact person: Valerie R. Cherry, PhD, Progressive Life Center, 1123 11th St. NW, Washington, DC 20001	African American female youths and their parents	Quasi-experimental comparison group design Procedures: a range of standardized measures	NTU Africentric Substance Abuse Prevention Program, 2 years: Rites of passage, ATOD prevention, Africentric education course, parenting and work program, in-home family therapy, annual kinship event, and training of community partners	(a) Youths: increased racial identity, happiness, and self-esteem; improved school behaviors (rule compliance and interest) (statistically significant); and enhanced antidrug attitudes, Africentric values, unity and collective responsibility, and knowledge of Africa (not statistically significant) (b) No parental outcomes reported
Thomas et al. (2008) Contact Person: Oseela Thomas University of Michigan	African American female youths ($N = 74$)	Quasi-experimental comparison group desisn Procedures: Combined self-developed and standardized measures	YES culturally relevant school-based 10-week program for 20 sessions, including Afrocentric education and libratory activism	Youths in the intervention group showed increased ethnic identity, Afrocentric values, and libratory activism (all statistically significant)
Lewis et al. (2006) Contact Person: Kelly M. Lewis, Emory University	Middle school youths: 53% and 47% females ($N = 65$)	Quasi-experimental comparison group design Procedures: Adapted standardized scales and questionnaires	Project EXCEL school-based semester-long emancipatory intervention, 3 times weekly, involving African rituals, leadership, activism, and community partnerships	Youths in the intervention group increased their achievement motivation (statistically significant), communal orientation, school connectedness, and social change activities as predicted (not statistically significant); but also increased their competitive orientation (statistically significant)

Belgrave et al. (2004) Contact Person: Faye Z. Belgrave. Virginia Commonwealth University	African American female youths in early adolescence ($N = 59$)	Quasi-experimental comparison group desisn, random assignment Procedures: Standardized inventories, questionnaires, and scales	Sisters of Nia after-school program, 30 biweekly sessions on African-descended females and Afrocentric rituals, and separate weekly tutoring	Youths in the intervention group showed increased ethnic identity and socially adaptive androgynous gender roles (statistically significant), and decreased relational aggression and violence (statistically significant)
Aktan et al. (1996) No contact person included	Inner-city African American families and youths	Quasi-experimental comparison group design Procedures: interviews, direct observations, standardized measures, and written questionnaires	Safe Haven Family Skills Program for Substance Abuse Prevention: family skills group intervention with parents and youths	(a) Youths: enhanced risk and protective factors and appropriate behaviors (not statistically significant) (b) Parents: improved parenting efficacy and behaviors toward their children, and reductions in parent or family use of substances (not statistically significant)
Royse (1998) Contact person: David Royse, PhD, College of Social Work, University of Kentucky, Lexington, Kentucky 40506	African American male youths 14–16 years old ($N = 36$)	Experimental design Procedures: standardized scales, questionnaires, and data from school records on performance and behavior	The Brothers' Mentoring Project, 15 months: organized group recreational activities once monthly between assigned volunteer mentors and youths	Slight decrease in youths' minor disciplinary infractions and increase in their major infractions (not statistically significant); and no significant changes in their self-esteem, drug and alcohol attitudes, CPAs, and school absences
Banks et al. (1996) Contact person: Reginald Banks, Temple University, Philadelphia, PA	Inner-city low-income African American male youths, 10–14 years old ($N = 33$)	Two-group comparison design Procedures: standardized measures	Adolescent Alternatives and Consequences Social Skills Training Program (AACT), 6 weeks: Africentric black history and cultural experiences, Africentric value system, African American images and themed role plays in a peer group format	Improvements in youths' trait anger, assertiveness, self-control, general anger, and experience of anger (statistically significant)

(continued)

Table 62.1 *(Continued)*

Study & Date	*Target Subgroup*	*Research Design and Procedures*	*Intervention Approach*	*Study Outcomes*
Botvin et al. (1994) Contact person: Gilbert J. Botvin Institute for Prevention Research, Dept. of Public Health, Cornell University Medical College, 411 E. 69th Street, New York 10021	African American male and female youths (N = 456)	Three-group comparison control group design Procedures: written questionnaires, standardized measures, and inventories	Culturally Focused & Generic Skills Training for Alcohol and Drug Prevention: 7½ weeks; alcohol- and drug- prevention curriculum—knowledge and attitudes; involving demonstrations, behavioral rehearsal, feedback and reinforcement, and multicultural myths/stories by peer leaders and same-race group facilitators	Youths in the two culturally relevant intervention groups had significantly higher antidrinking, antimarijuana, and anticocaine scores and lower risk-taking scores and intentions to drink beer and wine.
Botvin et al. (1995) Same contact person as above	Same participants	Same design 2-year posttreatment follow-up questionnaires, standardized measures, and inventories	Same intervention	Youths in culturally focused intervention group had statistically significant less alcohol consumption, less frequent use of alcohol, and lower risk-taking scores. Those in both intervention groups had statistically significant less drunkenness, and increased use of assertiveness skills and lower risk-taking scores
Alford (1997) Contact person: Keith Alford, Ph.D., School of Social Work, Syracuse University, Syracuse, New York	African American male youths in foster care *(N = 29)*	Naturalistic qualitative design Procedures: individual interviews and direct observations	Africentric Rites of Passage Program (AA RITES)	Themes: the importance of learning and giving back what you've learned, family solidarity and cultural inter-connectedness, condemnation of violence and unproductive behavior, spirituality
Gavazzi et al. (1996) Contact person: Stephen M. Gavazzi, Dept. of Family Relations & Human Development, Ohio State University, 171 Campbell Hall, 1787 Neil Ave., Columbia, Ohio 43210	Urban African American male youths 12–21 years (N = 37)	Naturalistic qualitative design Procedures: individual interviews	African American Culturally Specific Rites of Passage Program (AA RITES), 1-year minimum: didactic and experiential activities for three stages (separation from childhood, transformation experiences related to African heritage curriculum, and reincorporation in five core achievement areas	Themes: enhanced individual and cultural pride (interrelated); self-direction, individual responsibility and hard work, and increased knowledge of own cultural history

Dixon et al. (2000) Contact person: William W Philliber, Research Associate, 16 Main Street, Accord, NY 12404	African American female youths; program graduates (N = 33)	Quasi-experimental comparison group design Procedures: individual interviews	A Journey Toward Womanhood Africentric Pregnancy Prevention Program, 13 weeks: group intervention, 4 hours once weekly, includes self-definition, wellness, tools for survival, field trips	Statistically significant delays in initiation of sexual intercourse for Africentric group participants, who were also less likely to have had intercourse, unprotected sex (among those sexually active), and to have been pregnant
Stevens (1997) Contact person: Joyce West Stevens, DSW, Boston University School of Social Work, Boston, MA	African American adolescent girls, 11–14 years	Qualitative longitudinal design Procedures: participant observation, audiotapes of sessions, and field notes	Self Image Life Skills and Role Modeling Curriculum for Pregnancy Prevention, 10 weeks: group intervention and role model mentors	Themes: personal identity and self-efficacy, self- assertion, and intergenerational value and role conflicts
Linnehan (2001) No contact person included	African American youths, 15–18 years old (N = 202)	Time series design Procedures: data from school records	Work-based mentoring multischool program, 1 year: academic, mentoring, and behavioral interventions	Statistically significant improvements in CPAs and attendance rates for those participating in the program 6 months or more.
Leslie (1998) No contact person included	Low-income African American mothers (N = 30)	Naturalistic qualitative design Procedures: in-depth interviews	Parents' use of indigenous storytelling experiences to teach/socialize their children to Africentric values	Themes: informed values as the basis of parents' teachings: the importance of thinking ahead (having a plan), protecting the physically defenseless against the powerful, supporting altruism
Belgrave et al. (2000) No contact person included	African American girls 10–12 years old (N = 55)	Quasi-experimental comparison group design Procedures: standardized measures	Resiliency-focused Africentric group intervention, 4 months: activities and exercises for increasing self-worth	Statistically significant changes in Africentric values, ethnic identity, and self-concept in intervention group
Thompson et al (2001) No contact person included	African American at risk boys (N = 12)	Experimental design Procedures: standardized measures	Big Brothers/Big Sisters Mentoring program, 9 months: matched mentors/youths intervention	Treatment group participants made statistically significant academic gains compared to control (wait list) group

Table 62.2 Analysis of Early Intervention and Prevention Research on African American Youths and Families

Type of Research	*Categories of Outcomes*	*Effective Interventions and Practice Approaches*
Quantitative Research, Statistically Significant Outcomes	Psychosocial-Cultural School Behavior Outcomes:	
	• Improved assertiveness skills with peers, self-control, and expression of anger; and decreased anger frequency (males & females: 10–14 years)	• 6-week youth and parental social skills intervention: peer training groups with an Africentric curriculum (Banks et al., 1996)
	• Increased bonding with parents and siblings (males and females: 12 to 14 years old)	• Church-based ATOD prevention: parent-youth training groups, 1-year follow-up case management services (Johnson et al., 1998)
	• Increased rule compliance and interest in school (males and females: fifth and sixth graders)	• 2-year prevention program with youth: Africentric rites of passage and education, substance abuse prevention, and parenting and work components (Cherry et al., 1998)
	• Increased ethnic identity and socially adaptive androgynous gender roles; and decreased relational aggression at school (early adolescent females)	• 30-biweekly afterschool sessions about African descended females, Africentric rituals, and academic tutoring (Belgrave et al., 2004)
	• Increased achievement motivation and communal orientation (males and females: middle school)	• Semester-long emancipatory intervention 3-times weekly: African rituals, activism, and community partnerships (Lewis et al., 2006)
	• Increased ethnic identity, Africentric values, and libratory activism (females: mean age of 14.68)	• 10-week bi-weekly afterschool intervention: Nguzo Saba principles, holistic learning, critical pedagogy, and libratory activism (Thomas et al, 2008)
	Cultural Strengths Outcomes:	
	• Enhanced cultural identity, happiness, and self-esteem (males and females: fifth and sixth graders)	• 2-year intervention involving parents and youths: described above (research by Cherry et al., 1998)
	• Improved awareness of Africentric values, ethnic identity and physical appearance, and self-concept (females: 10–12 years old)	• 4-month group intervention: exercises and activities about self-worth, ethnic and gender identity, and Africentiric values (Belgrave et al, 2000)

Substance Abuse Resistance Skill Outcomes:	
• Improved antidrug attitudes, and decreased intention to use beer and wine, take risks, or consume alcohol (males and females: sixth and seventh graders)	• 7 ½ -week culturally focused life skills training groups for youths in substance abuse prevention program (Botvin et al., 1994, 1995)
• Increased ATOD knowledge, modeling appropriate alcohol use, and use of community services (parents of youth participants)	• Intervention involving parents and youths. described above (research by Johnson et al., 1998)
• Enhanced knowledge about drug abuse and HIV (males: 11.5 to 14.5 years old)	• 3-year Africentric groups for youths and their parents: rites of passage, family empowerment, and individual individual family counseling modules (Harvey & Hill, 2004)
• Increased positive parental communication about alcohol use and sex; and decreased initiation of related high risk behaviors by youths (rural males and females: mean age of 11.2 years old)	• 7-week culturally relevant combined and separate sessions for parents and youths, involving vigilant parenting,, clear communication about alcohol use and sex, and adaptive racial socialization (Brody et al., 2006)
Associated Pregnancy Prevention Outcomes:	
• Delayed initiation of sexual intercourse, less frequent unprotected sex, and fewer pregnancies (males and females: 14 to 19 years old)	• 13-week adolescent Africentric pregnancy prevention group services: self-definition, wellness, and survival self-sufficiency tools (Dixon et al., 2000)
Academic Achievement Outcomes:	
• Higher academic gains (male youths)	• 9-month Big Brother mentoring program (Thompson et al., 2001)
• Higher grade point averages and improved attendance rates (males and females: 11 to 14 years old)	• Year-long work-based mentoring program for at-risk youths (Linnehan, 2001)

(continued)

Table 62.2 *(Continued)*

Type of Research	*Categories of Outcomes*	*Effective Interventions and Practice Approaches*
Naturalistic Qualitative Research: Outcome Themes	Psychosocial and Cultural Strengths Outcomes: • Increased positive attitudes toward learning, awareness of cultural group's history, and interrelated cultural and self-esteem (males: 12 to 21 years old) • Increased clarity about the cultural value lessons taught by parents to their children based on cultural stories • Sense of personal-cultural identity, self efficacy, and self-assertion (females: 11 to 14 years old) Substance Abuse Resistance Skills: • Decreased parental and family use of illegal substances and increased parenting skills (parents and youths)	• 1-year Africentric rites of passage youth program: an adjunct to an independent living program (Gavazzi et al., 1996) • Parents' indigenous storytelling intervention: cultural stories used to teach their children Africentric values (Leslie, 1998) • 10-week self-image life skills and role modeling curriculum using college-age mentors (Stevens 1997), • Family skills substance abuse prevention program: group sessions for parents and youths (Aktan et al. 1996)

for youths and their parents, along with research literature that documents the approach's effectiveness. Figure 62.1 provides more program details such as the need for a start-up component of 3 or more months, which allows staff to complete the planning steps required for effective program implementation. The Afrocentric education module and the three culturally focused life skill modules for youths are sequenced to support the core rites-of-passage module over the program year. The follow-up component provides 6 months of booster and case management services to reinforce the participants' gains and to address current needs.

Although this comprehensive program is based on findings from the empirical research literature on black youths, a smaller, more compact approach is strongly suggested as a 2- to 3-year pilot. This incremental strategy can provide the necessary observational and self-report process data on the program's strengths and problem areas for implementing the post-pilot program effectively. Figure 62.1 shows the recommended comprehensive approach as well as the suggested scaled-down pilot approach (the pilot components and modules are identified by the * sign).

Social Importance of the Recommended Approach

Table 62.3 describes the program's importance based on the best practices research summarized in the previous section. In particular, the table's Program Philosophy—Social Importance and Theory/Conceptual Framework emphasize the importance of an Afrocentric, early intervention, prevention, strengths approach for helping African American youths and families to center themselves culturally. Being culturally centered—applying Afrocentric values and traditions in their daily lives—can help families to reduce risk factors and increase protective factors. Research has documented the high value African Americans place on family centeredness and extended family relationships and the amount of emotional and task support they receive from those cultural factors (Belgrade et al., 2000; Cherry et al., 1998). Therefore, including youths *with* their families and peers in group sessions is consistent with research findings and is a promising way of addressing academic, psychosocial, and cultural needs (see Expected Outcomes in Table 62.3) (Banks et al., 1996; Harvey & Hill, 2004).

Components of the Suggested Pilot Approach

To clarify how the pilot approach is connected to the total program, Tables 62.6A and 62.6B (in Appendices A and B) include steps for implementing content and experiential exercises for the pilot modules, and Tables 62.6C and 62.6D (in Appendices C and D) describe components and modules not included in the pilot program (e.g., the substance abuse prevention and social action coaching modules). The start-up and follow-up components are not included in these tables because they are not curriculum based; however, those modules are part of the discussion in this section.

The pilot components' purpose, the participants, and the number and frequency of sessions are included in this discussion. For the Afrocentric and culturally focused life skills modules, the discussion includes steps for using one of the suggested instructional tools or exercises (see examples of additional instructional tools in Tables 62.6A–62.6D).

The Initiation Component

The purpose of this 3-month component is to recruit and orient the participants, build communitywide acceptance and support for the program, and complete the planning and preparation necessary for program implementation. The best practices research analysis emphasized overcoming recruitment barriers by allowing sufficient planning time and including community stakeholders (Harvey & Hill, 2004). Therefore, the participants in this component include the potential recruit families and various community partners. Potential partners include school board members and neighborhood advisory committees. There are three modules for this component: the Engagement and Training of Community Partners, Site Selection and Preparation, and Recruitment and Orientation of Participants. Staff members for this and other components consist of a combination of professionals (program director), aides (outreach workers), and volunteers (community elders).

The Afrocentric Component

This component is designed to build the participants' character; self-esteem; cultural esteem;

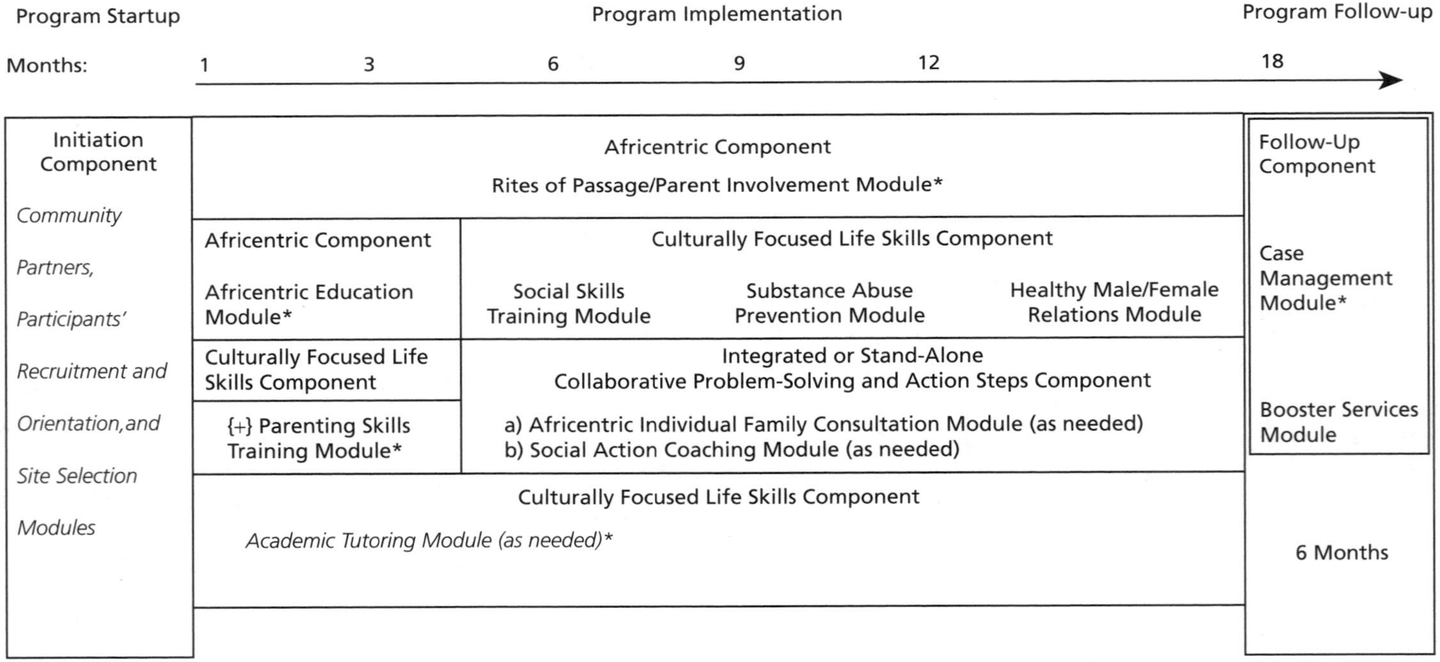

Program Startup | Program Implementation | Program Follow-up

Months: 1 | 3 | 6 | 9 | 12 | 18

Initiation Component

Community Partners, Participants' Recruitment and Orientation, and Site Selection Modules

Africentric Component

Rites of Passage/Parent Involvement Module*

Africentric Component

Africentric Education Module*

Culturally Focused Life Skills Component

Social Skills Training Module

Substance Abuse Prevention Module

Healthy Male/Female Relations Module

Culturally Focused Life Skills Component

{+} Parenting Skills Training Module*

Integrated or Stand-Alone

Collaborative Problem-Solving and Action Steps Component

a) Africentric Individual Family Consultation Module (as needed)

b) Social Action Coaching Module (as needed)

Culturally Focused Life Skills Component

*Academic Tutoring Module (as needed)**

Follow-Up Component

Case Management Module*

Booster Services Module

6 Months

*Suggested for pilot program

Figure 62.1 Program Timeline: Recommended Early Intervention Prevention Approach for Latency-Age African American Youths and Families

Table 62.3 Overview of the Recommended Early Intervention Prevention Approach for Latency-Age African American Youths and Their Families

Program Factors	*Program Description*
Program Philosophy—Social Importance	Prevention and early intervention with African American youths is critical in individual, peer group, school, immediate and extended family, cultural group, and community domains (Harvey & Hill, 2004). These youths require support to become centered in an Africentric worldview, values, and beliefs, such as harmony, balance, interconnectedness, and authenticity to reduce risk factors and increase their resilience (Cherry et al., 1998)
Theory/Conceptual Framework	A combined interacting theoretical perspective is needed, including an empowerment, capacity-building, ecological, family systems, resilience, strengths-based, psychoeducation framework
Target Population and Rationale	Male and female youths from 10 to 13 years *and* their parents: Research documents this is an optimal time for preventing risk factors and influencing gains in the identified areas (Belgrade et al., 2001; Botvin et al., 1994; Stevens, 1997; Cherry et al., 1998; Johnson et al., 1998)
Expected Outcomes	For youths: academic achievement, ATOD resistance skills, life or social skills, cultural esteem-identity-knowledge, early parenting prevention. For parents: parenting skills, modeling ATOD knowledge and non-drug use, cultural knowledge-identity-esteem, use of community services
Recruitment Strategy	The ecological/family systems aspects of the theoretical framework focus on all sources for potential recruits in youths' family, peer group, school, cultural, and community environments
Program Components	This 1-year multiple-strategy intervention/prevention program for African American youths and their families includes the first four components below, and in addition a 6-month follow-up component: • Initiation, Engagement, and Orientation Component • Africentric Component • Culturally Focused Life Skills Training Component • Problem-Solving and Action Steps Component • Case Management Follow-Up Component

and their family, community, and cultural unity. Another purpose is to help them develop a healthy Afrocentric value system and to make a positive transition from adolescence to adulthood. The participants are the target youths and their peers, who meet in separate gender-based groups for this and all components, along with same-gender facilitators and cofacilitators. Exceptions involve special occasions where all participants meet together, such as some field trips, naming ceremonies, and the graduation ritual. The best practices research literature documents the effectiveness of same-gender peer-group training for enhancing psychosocial-cultural and education outcomes through culturally focused and Afrocentric interventions in a long-term format (ranging from several months to 1 or 2 years) (Botvin et al., 1994, 1995; Cherry et al., 2000; Thompson et al., 2001).

This component consists of the Rites of Passage and Africentric Education modules. The Rites of Passage Module meets weekly in after-school sessions for a year, 3 hours per session. The module teaches participants the Seven Nguzo Saba Africentric principles and how to apply them to the rites and in their daily lives (see Table 62.4).

A goal-setting exercise can be used to address part of the component's purpose as described, because it teaches youths how to set educational and psychosocial-cultural goals for managing the transition from adolescence to adulthood. For example, the exercise worksheet (Appendix E) can be used to help participants set educational goals related to the Nguzo Saba principle of Nia (purpose). Table 62.6A describes a typical group session for this module centered on the goalsetting exercise.

First, the cofacilitators can involve the participants in brainstorming the long-term benefits of completing their education based on the youths' perspectives and aspirations. As benefits are identified, cofacilitators can list them on a flip chart and invite participants to provide more details and to discuss each benefit. Each participant can be asked to identify one or more specific goals related to the benefits, such as obtaining a college scholarship for the future benefit of having a good job. Then participants can be encouraged to identify supports (door openers), barriers (door closers), and action steps for their goals ("my" steps), with input from peers and facilitators. Future sessions can be used to review youths' goal-setting worksheets to help monitor their progress and to update and revise their supports, barriers, and action steps. Other instructional tools and exercises for this module are included in Table 62.6A.

The Africentric Education Module meets weekly for Saturday sessions over a 3-month period, 2 hours per session. The content and a description of a typical session are included in Table 62.6A, along with examples of several exercises. One example is focused on values clarification. The youths participate in a structured role play in which they express and clarify their values, and then compare them to those of a historical black figure. Instructions detail the steps the facilitator takes prior to the session (preparing brief descriptions of historical black figures selected by the youths), steps taken during the role play (brainstorming examples of challenging value conflicts with the participants before having them role-play a conflict), and post-role-play debriefings (identifying the values expressed by actors in the role plays and conflicts between their values and those of the identified historical figures). This exercise uses peers to identify and resolve common value conflicts, and cultural role models to address the conflicts and reinforce a positive cultural identity (Harvey & Hill, 2004).

The Culturally Focused Life Skills Component

This component's purpose is to improve the participants' handling and expression of feelings and to teach them the life skills of improved communication, enhanced peer/family relationships, and academic success. The Academic Tutoring and Parent Skills Training modules are the two pilot modules. The Academic Tutoring Module consists of tutoring by volunteers for those youths who need it. Tutoring sessions are scheduled on an individual basis, with a minimum of one or two sessions weekly as needed throughout the program. The modules' content, examples of exercises, and a typical session are in Table 62.6B.

One exercise is part of the orientation for all youths who receive tutoring. Tutors should discuss with each youth how he or she prepared for a recent test. The goal is to identify which of the youth's test preparation strategies worked, which were ineffective, and the connection between those strategies and the outcome (the test scores). Tutors can use the description of a typical session on Table 62.6B as a guide for helping youths to develop new study habits prior to their next exam or term paper. The study habits are culturally relevant because they address and utilize cultural values and learning styles (using the colors of African flags to highlight key areas of a book, and using rhyming words

Table 62.4 Rites of Passage: Seven Africentric Principles of the Nguzo Saba: Guidelines for Healthy Living

The Seven Principles	*Related Africentric l'allies and Goals*	*Related Program Examples of African American Youths' Africentric Action Steps*
Umoja: unity	To strive for and maintain unity in the family, community, nation, and race	Unity Rituals: Rites of passage sessions: Do unity circle, drum call, Nguzo Saba, libation
Kujichajulia: self-determination	To define ourselves, name ourselves, and speak for ourselves from a strengths perspective, instead of being defined incorrectly and spoken for by others	Great Leaders/Who Am I Exercise: Do report on great black leader, identify qualities leader attributed to his/her success, define self and qualities
Ujima: collective work and responsibility	To build and maintain our community together; to make our brothers' and sisters' problems our problems and to solve those problems together	Seniors/Youths Community Beautification Project: Learn horticulture, broker resources, work together on landscape/community tasks
Ujamaa: cooperative economics	To build and own our own stores, shops, and other businesses, and to profit together from them	Social Action Project: Develop family plan to patronize black businesses/avoid negative values
Nia: purpose	To make as our collective vocation the building and developing of our community in order to restore our people to their traditional greatness	Action Steps Goal-Setting Exercise: Brainstorm long-term benefits of completing education, define goals/motives re community benefits
Kuumba: creativity	To do always as much as we can, in the way we can, in order to leave our community more beautiful and beneficial than when we inherited it	Graduation Ceremony: Plan together the tangible products to be creatively produced representing knowledge and skills learned from participation
Imani: faith	To believe in our parents, our teachers, our leaders, our people, ourselves, and the righteousness of our struggle	Ancestral Transformation Role Play: Think, feel, and behave as historical figure: decreases negative self/group perceptions, increases pride and belief in self/cultural group

or active words to increase memory of important material) (Botvin et al., 1994, 1995).

The Parenting Skills Training Module focuses on the parents of youths in the program, and it uses a multiple-family group format. Group sessions are held weekly for a 3-month period, followed by once monthly rite-of-passage parent-involvement meetings planned by the parents. Their active involvement can lead to skills development and empowerment (Cherry et al., 1998). Individual parent training booster sessions are an important option as documented by best practices literature (Botvin et al., 1994). Content areas for this module and steps for a typical session are included in Table 62.6B, related to the family cultural maintenance process.

During discussions with parents on such topics as how to use family leisure time, manage cultural stress from discrimination, or enhance their children's cultural identity, group facilitators can introduce the strategy of incremental cultural maintenance. The action plan includes incremental steps a family can take to become more culturally centered, beginning with levels that require lesser commitment and time, such as reading a black history book or article. In addition to helping parents to select the level of cultural maintenance activities they will focus on, based on their individual needs and perspectives, facilitators can have them identify specific steps for implementing their action plan worksheet. Future sessions can be used to collectively monitor the families' progress and revise the plans as needed based on group feedback. Parents can involve youths in planning, action steps, and monitoring their cultural maintenance process.

The Follow-Up Component

The purpose of this component is to reinforce the gains that participants make during the program year and to address their current case management needs. Referrals might involve identifying and brokering academic and counseling services for youths in their schools; emergency food, clothing, and shelter for families; social supports from cultural and community resources; or medication and treatment compliance education through collaboration between school and mental health practitioners. The Case Management Module includes parents and youths who were involved in the pilot program. The frequency and number of sessions is based on each family's needs over the 6-month follow-up period. Content areas and specific action steps to be undertaken by program staff for this module include providing information and referrals, monitoring referrals, brokering existing resources, and developing new resources where significant gaps occur.

Challenges in Implementing the Pilot Approach

It is essential to acknowledge some of the challenges involved in implementing the pilot approach described in the previous sections. Recruiting participants and developing support for the program among community partners is a key challenge. This program emphasizes prevention, nonlabeling, and the importance of cultural support, which can help to address this challenge and to reinforce the parental empowerment that occurs from their active participation and successes. Early collaborative partnerships with community organizations can increase the support and involvement of community partners; research indicates that is an essential step for meeting this challenge (Cherry et al., 1998).

Maintaining youth participation is yet another challenge. The use of culturally relevant and age-relevant interventions from the best practices research literature is crucial, along with a focus on issues that are culturally meaningful to black youths. Meeting the latter challenge is a prerequisite for addressing the next one: finding user-friendly and participant-involved methods for documenting meaningful changes that occur as a result of the program (Banks et al., 1996). Cultural consultants can help to develop culturally relevant procedures for monitoring the identified issues, processes, and outcomes.

Applying Pilot Program Interventions within a Response to Intervention Framework

The recommended pilot program for African American youths and families involves the application of evidence-based school interventions from the practice research literature. Clark and Alvarez (2010) indicate that the heart of evidence-based practice in schools is the Response to Intervention (RTI) framework. Other authors suggest that field-based school social workers and school psychologists have the best opportunities to demonstrate how an evidence-based RTI framework can result in meaningful outcomes for youth and families (Ikeda, Rahn-Blakeslee, Niebling, Allison, & Stumme, 2006; nasponline, 2011; Usaj, Shine, & Mandlawitz, 2011).

Applying the RTI framework to the recommended pilot program could enhance school social workers' service delivery process with latency-age African American youths and their families. The framework could help to clarify whether the Afrocentric program's Tier 2 targeted group interventions produce meaningful outcomes in the desired psychosocial, cultural, and academic areas. Ikeda et al.'s (2006) description of the RTI's Tier 2 targeted group interventions is consistent with the pilot program's early intervention targeted group services.

Applying the RTI framework could also clarify which of the pilot program's components could be applied to a school-wide Tier 1, universal support prevention program based on the results of the pilot program. For example, such a program could involve preventive classroom sessions with youths that are facilitated by culturally diverse teams of school counselors, social workers, and psychologists. The focus could be on multiculturalism or training youth to know, understand, and value individuals from all cultures; with sessions included for parents as well (Freeman, 2004).

In addition, the RTI framework could be useful in helping school teams to review and determine to what extent meaningful outcomes are achieved from Tier 1 classroom prevention sessions and from Tier 2 early intervention targeted group services. Those teams could also determine whether youths involved in prevention and early intervention services could benefit from more intensive individualized interventions at the Tier 3 level (Clark & Alvarez, 2010). School teams could also make decisions about what the Tier 3 psychosocial, cultural, and academic interventions for youths and their families should consist of.

Tools and Case Examples

The Baker Family's Background and Recruitment to the Program

Some of these challenges are apparent in the following discussion on the experiences of an African American family in a similar early-intervention rites-of-passage program. This discussion illustrates how such programs can be effective in spite of those and other challenges. Background data and information on how the Baker family became involved in the program are described, along with outcomes from interventions that were used with different family members.

The family includes the mother, Honor Baker, and her children, Garrett, Erica, and Joleal (see the School-Community Ecomap in Appendix F for a strengths-based analysis of the family's supports and stressors). Ms. Baker agreed that the two older children could participate in the rites-of-passage program for boys and girls when the program held its orientation meeting in her church. She initially declined participation for herself because of her busy schedule (and perhaps an understandable "wait-and-see" attitude) but later decided to "sit in" on the parent-training and parent-involvement sessions.

When the program started, Mr. Baker still lived with the family, but the parents separated 3 months later because of his drug abuse. Mr. Baker took many of the family's possessions—including the children's video games, television, and bikes—and sold them for drugs. He had been a good provider and an involved parent until he started using drugs after his military service during the Gulf War.

The Family's Participation, Examples of Interventions, and Outcomes

During a discussion on giving culturally affirming messages to children, Ms. Baker mentioned that Erica was always in trouble so she seldom gave the child positive messages. When other parents agreed that acting-out children make it difficult to give positive feedback, the group facilitator gave them a group homework assignment on Catching Your Child Being Good. This assignment required them to use the Atta Girl Parents' Feedback Card in Appendix G, which Ms. Baker filled out and gave to Erica between the parent sessions. In their next session, Ms. Baker said, "This assignment was an eye opener; it gave me hope for Erica." In response to the Atta Girl Card from her mother, Erica said, "Cool." Then Erica put the card on a special area of the wall next to her bed. Ms. Baker told the project director that Erica had been suspended for fighting but that the white girl she fought with was not suspended. She thought the decision was racial. The project director suggested inviting the assistant principal and a counselor to the parent-involvement meeting later that week to talk about school discipline policies. During that session, parents discussed with the assistant principal how Erica and other students had been affected by those policies. As a result, the school suspension policy was changed to require all students involved in fights to be suspended until a hearing could be held. The assistant principal later apologized to the Baker family, a sign of respect to Ms. Baker.

Erica's Participation in the Academic Tutoring Module

Erica told her tutor during one session that she just could not learn and that her reading teacher had called her "slow" when she asked for help with a book report. The tutor told Erica that all cultural groups have their best ways of learning, and then engaged her in a discussion about African American learning styles: active learning, involving all the senses, interactive, practical in application, uses familiar cultural language and builds on cultural strengths (rhyming and movement) (see Table 62.6B). She also had Erica to complete the Youths' Affirmation Pledge in Appendix H in spite of Erica's initial reaction that she did not have any strengths. In a later tutoring session, Erica seemed especially empowered when she read from her pledge that she is more mature now than when she was as a 10-year-old, and then she said her strength is that she tries harder and "learns better when the teacher lets us ask questions or apply our class work to real life."

Garrett's Participation in the Rites of Passage Module

In one session in which the group was discussing the Nia principle (purpose) from the Nguzo Saba, the facilitators had participants complete the Action Steps Goal Setting Worksheet (Figure 62.2E). When Garrett shared his completed worksheet later during the session, he identified not having a computer as a barrier to his education goals. He acknowledged that his father had previously sold their computer for drugs. Group members gave graphic feedback about how mad that would make them feel. Garrett openly expressed his feelings for the first time in the group by admitting he was still angry about what happened. That session was a turning point for Garrett because he gradually became less withdrawn, more expressive, and more involved in the program. His completed Field Trip Critics' Review Form in Appendix I demonstrates his increased self-confidence and enhanced cultural identity and cultural pride after participating in a field trip to an African exhibit.

Additional Tools

Table 62.5 describes African American family strengths based on different frameworks from the literature.

Key Points to Remember

The Baker family continued to participate in this yearlong program until Garrett and Erica graduated, and Garrett returned the following year as a peer leader. Their participation and other positive outcomes are a testimony to the effectiveness of program components from the empirical literature for best practices with African American families:

- early intervention and prevention services for youths from 10 to 15 years of age;
- Afrocentric and other culturally focused interventions that are long term and that target academic, psychosocial, and cultural areas;
- a strengths-focused framework that builds on cultural resources and emphasizes collaboration and capacity or skill building;
- a focus on systemic risk factors that impede youths in negotiating the developmental transition from adolescence to adulthood (biased policies, violence, substance abuse, early parenthood);
- systems change coaching for lobbying to end biased policies and practices that hinder these youths' academic and psychosocial-cultural successes.

Further Learning

Afterschool Alliance. (2011). *Issue briefs*. Retrieved August 9, 2011, from http://afterschoolalliance.org/issue_br.cfm

Table 62.5 Culturally Relevant Strengths Frameworks for African American Youths and Families

Strengths Frameworks (From Color-Blind to Culture Specific)	*Personal and Social Competence Framework (CB)*	*Resilience and Risk and Protective Factors Framework (CS)*	*African Survivals Framework (CS)*	*Africentric Framework (CS)*
Assumptions about the sources of African Americans' strengths	Some individuals develop the universal life skills and competence required for survival through significant opportunities, role models, and other key experiences, while other individuals do not	The environment and the interface between individuals and environments contain both protective and risk factors that affect survival; some people develop unique coping survival capacities when faced with poverty, racial stress, and oppression (resilience)	Some African cultural institutions and traditions survived the diaspora and slavery through African Americans' creative adaptations, which circumvented culturally destructive laws, and enhanced their past survival and the maintenance of their cultural traditions	Some African cultural institutions and traditions were lost during the diaspora and slavery. They should be reclaimed and recovered to help African Americans become more centered in their culture (who they are) and to enhance their present survival
Examples of African American strengths from the literature on each framework	Universal life skills: resistance skills, decision-making skills, assertiveness, self-esteem building, anxiety management, personal relationship building (Botvin et al., 1995)	Universal resilience: family management, good communication, bonding, community help-seeking (Johnson et al., 1998)	Culture: extended family network, role flexibility, healthy enmeshment (closeness), religion and spirituality, nonverbal communication (Royse, 1996)	Culture: rituals (rites of passage, naming ceremonies, mentoring circles), African values (Nguza Saba, collectivism (Harvey & Hill, 2004), eldership (griots, healers), village community (Banks, 1996)
	Sense of personal identity, self-efficacy, assertion, self-image, life skills (Stevens, 1997)	Poverty-related risk and protective factors: isolation and community drug sales vs. bonding and peer abstinence (Aktan et al., 1996)	Kinship bonds, work orientation, flexible family roles, work orientation, religious orientation (Hill, 1999)	Collective responsibility, spirituality, help based on need (Schiele, 1997)

National Association of School Psychologists. (2011). *The role of the school psychologist in the Response to Intervention Process*. Retrieved August 13, 2011, from http://www.nasponline.org/advocacy/RTIrole.NASP/[df

National Association of State Directors of Special Education. (2011). *Response to Intervention: Policy considerations and implementation*. Retrieved August 9, 2011, from http://www.nasdse.org/Projects/ResponsetoInterventionRtlProject/tabid/411/Default.aspx

President's Commission on Excellence in Special Education. (2011). *A new era: Revitalizing special education for children and their families*. Retrieved August 13, 2011, from http://www.ed.gov/inits/commissionsboards

Rite of passage. (2011). *Improving the lives of youth*. Retrieved August 10, 2011, from http://www.rite of passage.com/

Wisconsin Department of Public Instruction. (2011). *Response to Intervention: Roles of school social workers*. Retrieved August 13, 2001, from http://www.dpl.wi.gov

References

Adelman, H. S., & Taylor, L. (1999). Mental health in schools and system restructuring. *Clinical Psychology Review, 19,* 137–163.

Alan Guttmacher Institute. (1999). *Teenage pregnancy: Overall trends and state-by-state information*. New York: Author.

Alford, K. A. (1997). *A qualitative study of an Africentric rites of passage program used with adolescent males in out of care: Looking for unexpected themes.* Unpublished doctoral dissertation, Ohio State University.

Banks, R., Hogue, A., Timberlake, T., & Liddle, H. (1996). An Afrocentric approach to group social skills training with inner-city African American adolescents. *Journal of Negro Education,* 65, 414–423.

Belgrave, F. Z., Chase-Vaughn, G., Gray, F., Addison, J. D., & Cherry, V. R. (2000). The effectiveness of a culture-and gender-specific intervention for increasing resiliency among African Americans preadolescent females. *Journal of Black Psychology, 26,* 133–147.

Belgrave, F. Z., Reed, M. C., Plybon, L. E., Butler, D. S., Allison, K. W., & Davis, T. (2004). An evaluation of Sisters of Nia: A cultural program for African American girls. *Journal of Black Psychology, 30,* 329–343.

Botvin, G. J., Schinke, S. P., Epstein, J. A., & Diaz, T. (1994). Effectiveness of culturally focused and generic skills training approaches to alcohol and drug abuse prevention among minority youths. *Psychology of Addictive Behaviors, 8,* 116–127.

Botvin, G. J., Schinke, S. P., Epstein, J. A., Diaz, T., & Botvin, E. M. (1995). Effectiveness of culturally focused and generic skills training approaches to alcohol and drug abuse prevention among minority adolescents: Two-year follow-up results. *Psychology of Addictive Behaviors, 9,* 183–194.

Brody, G. H., Murry, V. M., Gerrard, M., Gibbons, F. X., McNair, L., Brown, A. C.,...Chen, Y. (2006). The strong African American families program: Prevention of youths' high-risk behavior and a test of a model of change. *Journal of Family Psychology, 20,* 1–11.

Cherry, V. R., Belgrave, F. Z., Jones, W., Kennon, D. K., Gray, F. S., & Phillips, F. (1998). NTU: An Africentric approach to substance abuse prevention among African American youth. *Journal of Primary Prevention,* 18, 319–339.

Clark, J. P., & Alvarez, M. (2010). *Response to Intervention: A guide for school social workers.* New York, NY: Oxford University Press.

Dixon, A. C., Schoonmaker, C. T., & Philliber, W. W. (2000). A journey toward womanhood: Effects of an Afrocentric approach to pregnancy prevention among African American adolescent females. *Adolescence, 35,* 425–430.

Freeman, E. M. (1992). The use of storytelling techniques with young African-American males: Implications for substance abuse prevention. *Journal of Intergroup Relations, 29,* 53–72.

Freeman, E. M. (2004, March). *Effective narrative approaches: The intersection of narratives and culture.* Paper presented at the Annual Institute of Hospital Directors, Bruce Watkins Cultural Center, Kansas City, MO.

Gavazzi, S. M., Alford, K. A., & McKenry, P. C. (1996). Culturally specific programs for foster care youth: The sample case of an African American rites of passage program. *Family Relations, 45,* 166–174.

Gilbert, D. J., Harvey, A. R., & Belgrave, F. Z. (2009). Advancing the Africentric paradigm shift discourse: Building toward evidence-based Africentric interventions in social work practice with African Americans. *Social Work, 54,* 243–252.

Harvey, A. R., & Hill, R. B. (2004). Africentric youth and family rites of passage program: Promoting resilience among at-risk African American youths. *Social Work, 49,* 65–75.

Ikeda, M. J., Rahn-Blakeslee, A., Niebling, B. C., Allison, R., & Stumme, J. (2006). Evaluating evidence-based practice in Response-to-Intervention systems. *National Association of School Psychologists Communiqué, 34,* 2–9.

Jessor, R. (1993). Successful adolescent development among youth in high-risk settings. *American Psychologist, 48,* 117–126.

Johnson, K., Bryant, D. D., Collins, D. A., Noe, T. D., Strader, T. N., & Berbaum, M. (1998). Preventing and reducing alcohol and other drug use among high-risk youths by increasing family resilience. *Social Work, 43,* 297–309.

Leslie, A. R. (1998). What African American mothers perceive they socialize their children to value when telling them Brer Rabbit stories. *Journal of Comparative Family Studies, 29,* 173–186.

Lewis, K. M., Sullivan, C. M., & Bybee, D. (2006). An experimental evaluation of a school-based emancipatory intervention to promote African American well-being and youth leadership. *Journal of Black Psychology, 32,* 3–28.

Linnehan, F. (2001). The relation of a work-based mentoring program to the academic performance and behavior of African American students. *Jousrnal of Vocational Behavior, 59,* 310–325.

Mauer, M. (1999). *Race to incarcerate.* New York: New Press.

Stevens, J. W. (1997). African American female adolescent identity development: A three-dimensional perspective. *Child Welfare, 76,* 145–173.

Thomas, O., Davidson, W., & McAdoo, H. (2008). An evaluation study of the Young Empowered Sisters (YES!) program: Promoting cultural assets among African American adolescent girls through a culturally relevant school-based intervention. *Journal of Black Psychology, 34,* 281–308.

Thompson, L. A., & Kelly, V. L. (2001). The impact of mentoring on academic achievement of at-risk youth. *Children and Youth Services Review, 23,* 227–242.

Tolan, P. H., & McKay, M. M. (2004). Preventing serious antisocial behavior in inner-city children: An empirically based family intervention program. *Family Relations, 45,* 148–155.

Usaj, K., Shine, J. K., & Mandlawitz, M. (2011). *Response to Intervention: New roles for school social workers, 1–4.* Sumner, WA: School Social Work Association of America.

Waller, A. W., Brown, B., & Whittle, B. (1999). Mentoring as a bridge to positive outcomes for teen mothers and their children. *Child and Adolescent Social Work Journal, 16,* 467–480.

Whaley, A. L., & Davis, K. E. (2007). Cultural competence and evidence-based practice in mental health services: A complementary perspective. *American Psychologist, 62,* 563–574.

Appendix A

Table 62.6A Program Components of the Recommended Early Intervention Prevention Approach for Latency-Age African American Youths and Families (suggested modules for pilot program)

Africentric Component Content	*Examples of Main Intervention Steps*	*Examples of Experiential Activities and Exercises*	*Examples of Instructional Forms and Methods*
Rites of Passage/P.I. Module: Kwanzaa: 7 Principles 6 Principles of Ma'at Learning motivation and practical applications Physical development Creative arts Peer relations/mutual aid Family life & quality Self- & cultural esteem Natural healers, health, nutrition, and hygiene Community service	Nia Principle (purpose): 1. Discuss the meaning of purpose related to their education (future benefits, collective responsibility) 2. Describe a historical figure or ancestor who represents the Nia principle: contributions, benefits 3. Have youths write 2–4 goals that could improve their education based on the discussion, explore: • the benefits of each goal for them, the black community, and society • cultural & other barriers/supports • action steps for reaching goals	Do action steps goal-setting exercise Other examples: 1. Participate in herb gardening project with elders 2. Develop tangible products at the end of each module on learning 3. Make African crafts (ceremonial masks, jewelry) and write a brief cultural story about them	Action Steps Goal-Setting Worksheet Other examples: 1. Pictures of garden's progress and mutual work with elders 2. Audiotape of youths speaking Kiswahili about learning from family life module 3. Cultural Story Guidelines Form
Africentric Education Module: African values/rituals African/African American history Political awareness Family and community history Spirituality Importance of culture African diversity Storytelling (griots)	Values clarification: 1. Convene youth focus group to identify racial concerns/challenges 2. Briefly write their challenging situations/the underlying values 3. Discuss a list of African values—contrast with Eurocentric values 4. Have them role play a challenging situation (#2 above) 5. Group discussion, post-role-play: • African values in situation/effects • Best strategy: theirs, an elders?	Ancestral transformation role play (values clarification) Other examples: 1. Field trip to African exhibit or African American museum 2. Participate in storytelling event with elder or griot 3. Interview a first generation African American re transitions, cultural changes, and rituals	Ancestral Role Play Guidelines Form (values clarification) Other examples: 1. Field Trip Critics' Review Form 2. Draw picture of cultural lessons learned from the story and storytelling experience 3. Prepare 5-minute oral report on cultural transitions/rituals

Appendix B

Table 62.6B Program Components of the Recommended Early Intervention-Prevention Approach for Latency-Age African American Youths and Families (suggested modules for pilot program)

Culturally Focused Life Skills Component	*Examples of Main Intervention Steps*	*Examples of Experiential Activities and Exercises*	*Examples of Instructional Forms and Methods*
Optional Academic Tutoring Module: Good study habits Learning motivation and goal-setting skills Organization & planning African American learning styles Help-seeking skills Subject-specific tutorials	Building Effective Study Habits: 1. Engage youth in discussion on strengths and challenges in school 2. Help him/her identify 2 or more goals in challenged areas 3. Ask about steps taken in recent assignment; what worked or not 4. Integrate youth s analysis with review of 5 effective study habits 5. Use current assignment for youth to practice study habits in session	Apply study habit hints to steps planned for completing new class assignment Other examples: 1. Meet with high-achieving student to discuss his/her approach to learning and overcoming obstacles 2. Apply math tutorial problem lessons to program carpentry task	List of Five Effective Study Habits for African American Youths Other examples: 1. Do think sheet on good learning and overcoming obstacles 2. Use carpentry project as tangible product for math tutorial module
Parent Training Module: Quality of life/cultural maintenance process Africentric child development Parental supervision and discipline Parental rule setting and consistent consequences Parental communication, e.g., listening, culturally affirming messages, constructive feedback Nguzo Saba and values	Cultural Maintenance Process: 1. Define cultural maintenance and its effects (better family quality of life and coping with racial stress) 2. Have parents brainstorm examples of cultural activities they've done or would like to do 3. Group discussion: • cultural benefits of activities? • barriers to those activities (family or external obstacles), Q of L effects, how to overcome them? • priority activities for family based on children's development stages? • plan for doing priority activities?	In session practice: analyze family cultural maintenance priorities and do action plan Other examples: 1. Homework assignment: Catching Your Child Being Good 2. In session practice: role play parent coaching older youth on how to supervise younger sibling	Family Cultural Maintenance Action Plan Other examples: 1. "Atta Boy or Atta Gill" Parent Feedback Card 2. Facilitators' Feedback to Parents Role Play Form

Appendix C

Table 62.6C Program Components of the Recommended Early Intervention Prevention Approach for Latency-Age African American Youths and Families

Culturally Focused Life Skills Component	*Examples of Main Intervention Steps*	*Examples of Experiential Activities and Exercises*	*Examples of Instructional Forms and Methods*
Social Skills Module: Decision making Cultural stress: coping Anger management Self- and cultural esteem Resisting peer pressures Good communication Assertiveness Expressing feelings Developing friends	Decision Making in Action: 1. Review steps of skill with youths 2. Show videotape of a black youths cultural story and decision dilemma 3. Group discussion: • the youth's goal in the story? • obstacles the youth encounters? • how obstacles can be overcome by applying decision-making steps? • what obstacles exist in their community; their lessons from real life?	Watch and analyze video of cultural story—skill demonstration representing peers' real-life dilemmas Other examples: 1. Journal about and discuss the effects of using social skill in real life 2. Role-play how to use a social skill as in-session practice activity	Youths' Skill Demonstration Comment Form Other examples: 1. Guidelines for Youths' Structured Journal Entries 2. Group facilitators' Feedback-Reinforcement form: In Session Practice Activities
Substance Abuse Prevention Module: Types of drugs/effects Effects on African American community Spirituality and drugs Resistance/coping skills	Consequences of Drug Use: 1. Show pictures of drugs and explain their effects on users, the community 2. Have group write 5 questions to ask person in recovery: the speaker	Listen to speaker discuss drugs, consequences, resistance, and prevention; ask written questions	Youths' Drug Abuse Interview Worksheet (5 questions)
Male-Female Relations Module: Self-definition Developing relationships Reproductive behaviors Sexual health Gender roles Tools for success	Defining/Affirming Oneself: 1. Have youths bring picture of self & negative media photo—same gender 2. Place all picture sets on board 3. Group discussion: • self-definition process & obstacles • 2 positives and effects: self picture • 2 negatives and effects: media picture	Develop written agreement to affirm self based on discussion about racial-gender media biases	Youths' Affirmation Pledge Action Steps Form

Appendix D

Table 62.6D Program Components of the Recommended Early Intervention Prevention Approach for Latency-Age African American Youths and Families

Collaborative Problem Solving and Action Component	*Examples of Main Interventions*	*Examples of Experiential Activities and Exercises*	*Examples of Instructional Forms and Methods*
Africentric Individual Family Consultation Module: Cultural network analysis/ enhancement Solution-focused cultural questions Cultural validation Cultural value conflict analysis/ resolution Broker/link resources Solution-focused action steps and monitoring	Cultural Network Analysis Mapping Process: 1. Have family identify concerns, reason for service request/referral 2. Explain how network analysis can make clear/address concerns 3. Review use of map, entries, their role as key cultural informants 4. Use solution-focused cultural questions to elicit information from member and write in entries 5. Help family identify understanding gained from process and goals	Complete cultural network analysis map over 2 or more sessions, having members listen to and respond to each other's views Other examples: 1. Do a family cultural awareness exercise to identify sources of intergenerational value conflicts 2. In-session practice: Participate in cultural self-validation role play 3. Homework assignment: Complete checklist of action steps taken	Africentric Cultural Network Analysis Map Other examples: 1. Cultural Awareness—Hidden Value Messages Exercise Form 2. Form: Steps for Cultural Self-Validation in Oppressive Situations 3. Action Step Check list Homework Card
Social Action Coaching Module: School–community analysis/ intervention Cultural coaches' stories (overcoming/surviving) Coalition building Situations-options-consequences-solutions action planning and steps	Systems Analysis & Change: 1. Have family identify school-community concerns/make entries 2. Help them summarize supports and barriers in each domain 3. Gather detailed info on priority barrier and related support(s) 4. Brainstorm 3 or more culturally valued options and consequences 5. Identify optimal solution & plan	Do a family analysis of school- and community-related problems Other examples: 1. Share a cultural coaches' story about handling similar difficulties 2. Use the families' cultural analysis map to identify potential coalition members/collaborators	School—Community Ecomap for Analysis and Intervention Other examples: 1. Solution-focused cultural questions to elicit stories 2. Africentric Cultural Network Analysis Map

Appendix E

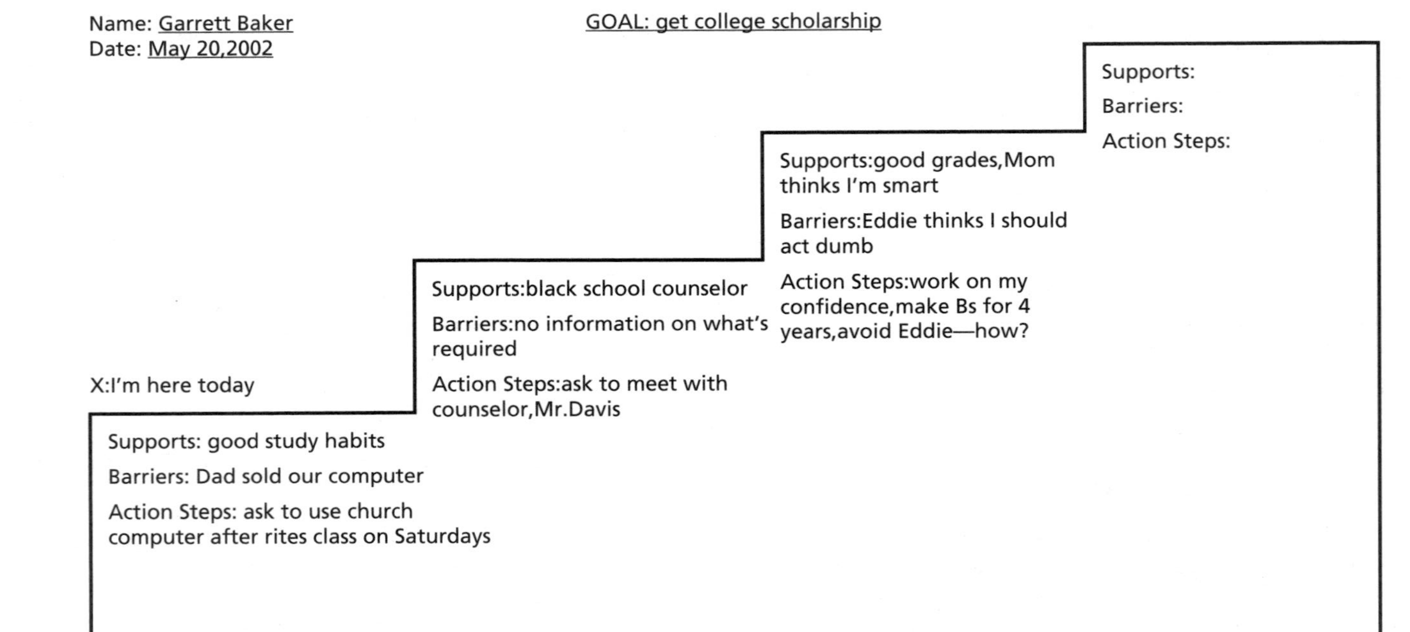

Figure 62.2. Action Steps Goal-Setting Worksheet

Appendix F

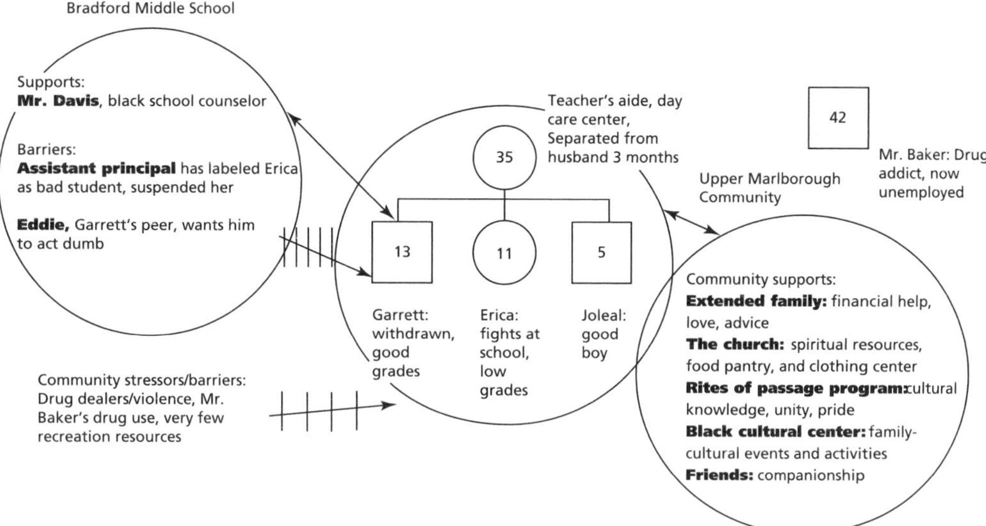

Figure 62.3. The Baker Family Example

Appendix G

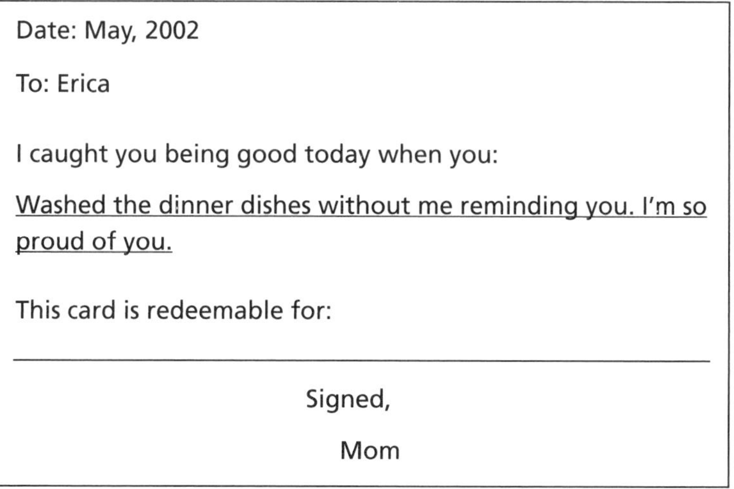

Figure 62.4. *"Atta Girl"* Parents' Feedback Card

Appendix I

The Reviewer's Name: Garrett Baker
Date of Field Trip: July 8,2002

Field Trip Event: Museum exhibit: The Lega people of Africa (the Congo)
Summary of the Review:

The Lega people were very smart. They learned hundreds of African proverbs. Then they made art to explain their proverbs. The men were strong leaders. The families had to work together to understand the art and pass tests. They could only go to the next step if the husband and wife both passed the tests. Someone kept the Lega art so it is now in the museum.The art was amazing.

Should other people see this or not see it?
It made me feel good to be a black male.All black boys and girls should see the exhibit. Parents too.

Figure 62.6. Field Trip Critics' Review Form

Appendix H

Date:May 2002

Pledge:

There are many negative cultural messages and images about African Americans in newspapers, radio, video games, television, movies, magazines, music, schools, and the community. I,Erica Baker pledge that I will examine those messages and images for their hidden effects on me and other African Americans,and reject them starting today.I know this is hard work,but I'm committed to meeting my individual responsibility and to working with peers,family,program staff,and others to continue our efforts.

Action Steps:

Starting today,I will give positive messages to myself about me as an African American every day when I wake up.For example,I will say to myself: Erica,you are a beautiful black girl and you're a good person.

I will find another time during the day when I sometimes feel bad (when I'm in school and think I can't learn, or the teacher says I'm slow), and give myself more good messages like: Erica, you're a good active learner: you're more mature and you don't give up easy.

Figure 62.5. Youths' Affirmation Pledge-Action Steps Plan

CHAPTER 63

Working with Lesbian, Gay, Bisexual, Transgender, Queer, and Questioning Students

Diane E. Elze

Getting Started

The cultural landscape for lesbian, gay, bisexual, transgender, queer, and questioning (LGBTQ) youth has shifted dramatically over the last two decades, with heightened public visibility of LGBTQ youth issues, important changes in social policies and laws, and the rise of queer youth activism (Lambda Legal Defense & Education Fund [LLDEF], 2008; Russell, Muraco, Subramaniam, & Laub, 2009). Although schools remain highly contested spaces for LGBTQ youths and their allies (Rienzo, Button, Sheu, & Li, 2006; Elia & Eliason, 2010), the well-being of sexual minority youths in schools has received considerable attention from policy advocates, educators, parents, and students (Cianciotto & Cahill, 2003; Kosciw, Greytak, Diaz, & Bartkiewicz, 2010; Russo, 2006).

Despite these gains, LGBTQ youths must still navigate family, school, and community environments marked by victimization, stigmatization, discrimination, and a lack of support from peers and adults (D'Augelli, Pilkington, & Hershberger, 2002; Elze, 2002, 2003; Himmelstein & Bruckner, 2010; Kosciw et al., 2010; Rosario, Schrimshaw, Hunter, & Gwadz, 2002; Russell, Franz, & Driscoll, 2001; Ryan, Huebner, Diaz, & Sanchez, 2009). Evidence continues to mount that such experiences are associated with psychological distress and health risk behaviors (D'Augelli et al., 2002; Elze, 2002; Hatzenbuehler, 2011; Russell & Joyner, 2001; Ryan et al., 2009) into young adulthood (Needham & Austin, 2010; Russell, Ryan, Toomey, Diaz, & Sanchez, 2011) and poorer educational outcomes and other school-related problems (Diaz & Kosciw, 2009; Greytak, Kosciw, & Diaz, 2009; Russell, Seif, & Truong, 2001), although many LGBTQ youths (lesbian, gay, and bisexual youths) do quite well (Savin-Williams, 2005).

Interventions for LGBTQ students must not only address their individual needs, but must transform the environmental contexts within which these young people function (Elze, 2002; Longres & Etnyre, 2004; Mallon, 2009). School social workers are uniquely positioned to provide counseling, information, and referrals to sexual minority adolescents and their family members and friends; to aid school-based support groups and guide students in establishing gay-straight alliances (GSAs); and to provide training and consultation on sexual orientation and gender identity diversity to students, teachers, administrators, support staff, and parents (Elze, 2003).

What We Know

Most lesbian, gay, and bisexual adolescents are functioning quite well, enjoying psychological, emotional, physical, and social well-being (Murdock & Bolch, 2005; Russell, 2005; Savin-Williams, 2005), just like the majority of adolescents (Irwin, Burg, & Cart, 2002; Moore & Zaff, 2002), and they perceive themselves to be developmentally similar to their heterosexual peers (Eccles, Sayegh, Fortenberry, & Zimet, 2004). However, sexual minority youths, like other adolescents, traverse a variety of developmental trajectories (Diamond, 2003; Rosario, Schrimshaw, & Hunter, 2011a; Russell & Consolacion, 2003; Savin-Williams & Diamond, 2000), and their lives involve complex interactions with multiple environments that expose them to continua of risk and protection (Elze, 2007). That some sexual minority youths are more at risk than others should come as no surprise given what is already known about adolescents who must negotiate social ecologies

Table 63.1 Glossary of Terms

Bisexual: A person whose sexual attraction, both physical and affectional, is directed toward persons of the same and other genders, though the degree of attraction may vary.

Coming Out: The developmental process of becoming aware of one's sexual orientation or gender identity and disclosing it to others.

Gender: Gender is an ascribed social status we are assigned at birth, based on the sex category to which we are assigned. Our society (though not all) has constructed two genders—"male" and "female."

Gender Dysphoria: Clinical symptoms of excessive discomfort, confusion, pain, and anguish from feeling an incongruity with the gender assigned to one at birth. Gender dysphoric young people often suppress and hide these feelings from others. Not all transgender youths experience gender dysphoria; some have stable identities.

Gender Expression: The communication of gender or gender identity through behaviors (e.g., mannerisms, speech patterns, dress) and appearance culturally associated with a particular gender. The ways in which people express and view gender are influenced by societal definitions of gender.

Gender Identity: A person's inner sense of being male, female, both, or something else; the gender with which one identifies, regardless of biological sex.

Gender Role: The society's prescriptions for being male and female; the pattern of attitudes, behaviors, and beliefs dictated by society that define what it means to be male and female.

Homosexual: A person whose sexual attraction, both physical and affectional, is primarily directed toward persons of the same gender. *Gay* and *lesbian* are contemporary synonyms to refer to men and women, respectively. Some young people prefer the word *queer,* finding it more inclusive. People may be involved in same-sex sexual activities and relationships but not identify themselves as gay, lesbian, or bisexual.

Heterosexism: An ideological system that devalues and stigmatizes any non-heterosexual identity, behavior, relationship, or community. Heterosexism can exist at the personal, interpersonal, institutional, or cultural levels.

Internalized Homophobia (Biphobia, Transphobia) or Heterosexism: The acceptance and internalization of negative stereotypes and images about LGBTQ people by LGBTQ people.

Sex: In this culture, sex means biologically male or biologically female. A person is assigned to a sex category at birth on the basis of what the genitalia looks like. *Intersex* refers to a person who is born with sex chromosomes, external genitalia, or an internal reproductive system that is not considered to be society's norm for either male or female.

Sexual Orientation: The direction of one's sexual attraction, or physical and affectional attraction, which can be toward the same gender (homosexuality) or other gender (heterosexuality), both genders (bisexuality), or neither. Gay, lesbian, and bisexual people are *gender variant* in that they are violating societal norms of sexual-object choice.

Transgender: An umbrella term that describes people whose gender identity and/or gender expression may be different from their biological sex or in violation of societal gender norms. They are, in other words, *gender variant.* This term may include preoperative transsexuals, postoperative transsexuals, nonoperative transsexuals, cross-dressers, gender benders, drag kings, and drag queens. (Not all transsexuals desire genital reassignment surgery.) Transgender people may be heterosexual, bisexual, gay, lesbian, or asexual. Gender variance in children may forecast a same-sex sexual orientation or transgenderism (with or without gender dysphoria), or may simply indicate variance in gender expression.

Sources: Herek, 1990; Israel & Tarver, 1997; Lambda Legal, 2010; Lev, 2004; Ryan & Futterman, 1998).

marked by environmental risks (Costa et al., 2005; Fraser, 2004).

LGBTQ youth in out-of-home care (Wilber, Ryan, & Marksamer, 2006) and homeless LGBTQ youth (Ray, 2006; Rosario et al., 2011b) are among the most at risk of sexual minority youths and may come to the attention of school social workers. Findings from a national school climate study suggest that LGBTQ youths living in rural locales, and attending schools in high-poverty areas with lower community-level educational attainment, experience greater school-based victimization than peers in other communities (Kosciw, Greytak, & Diaz, 2009). Evidence also exists that youths with romantic attractions toward both sexes may be at higher risk for psychological distress (Galliher, Rostosky, & Hughes, 2004; Russell & Consolacion, 2003), substance use (Russell, Driscoll, & Truong, 2002), and poorer school outcomes (Russell, Seif, & Truong, 2001) than youths with either same-sex or other-sex attractions. LGB youths who lack same-sex dating opportunities report higher levels of depression and anxiety than their dating peers (Russell & Consolacion, 2003), as do youths who are questioning their sexual orientation (Birkett, Espelage, & Koenig, 2009) or experiencing problems with sexual identity integration (Rosario et al., 2011a).

Less is known about transgender youths, compared to LGB youth, but emerging research shows a similar pattern of heightened risk and vulnerability within their families, schools, and communities (Greytak, Kosciw, & Diaz, 2009; Grossman & D'Augelli, 2007; Grossman, D'Augelli, & Frank, 2011; Grossman, D'Augelli, Howell, & Hubbard, 2005; McGuire, Anderson, Toomey, & Russell, 2010), particularly for transgender youth of color (Diaz & Kosciw, 2009; Garofalo et al., 2006), and poor treatment at the hands of school personnel and other service providers (Greytak, Kosciw, & Diaz, 2009; Grossman & D'Augelli, 2006; Mallon, 2009; Mallon & DeCrescenzo, 2006; Sausa, 2005).

Several studies with LGBTQ youths have identified protective factors that contribute to better health and mental health outcomes, such as family acceptance (Ryan et al., 2010), family connectedness, perceived safety in school, the presence of caring adults (Eisenberg & Resnick, 2006), moderate-to-high parental support, and a positive school climate (Espelage, Aragon, & Birkett, 2008). An evaluation of the Massachusetts Safe Schools Program (SSP) found that students rated their schools significantly higher on sexual diversity climate if at least one of the three SSP components (i.e., policies prohibiting discrimination and harassment; the presence of a GSA; and teacher training on LGBTQ issues) had been implemented (Szalacha, 2003), with the GSA being the strongest factor.

What We Can Do

Preparing Yourself for Discussing Sexual Orientation and Gender Identity Issues

Become an "askable" person who signals to students that they can safely discuss issues of sexuality, sexual orientation, and gender identity with you. Researchers and practitioners have identified strategies that practitioners can use to ready themselves for talking with youths about sexual orientation and gender identity issues (Elze, 2003; Longres & Etnyre, 2004; Mallon, 2009; Ryan & Futterman, 1998; Tully, 2000). Explore your own biases, feelings, beliefs, and attitudes toward diversity in sexual orientation, gender identity, and gender expression. Educate yourself about the psychosocial strengths and needs of LGBTQ youths (see Table 63.2) and potential foci of interventions (see Table 63.3). Familiarize yourself with local, state, and national resources for LGBTQ youths and their families. Display culturally diverse, LGBTQ-affirmative books, posters, magazines, brochures, and symbols in your office. Regularly obtain a copy of the local LGBTQ newspaper. Identify mental and physical health care professionals who specialize in serving transgender adolescents.

Demonstrating That You Are Askable

The strategies that signal to LGBTQ youths that you are a supportive person may precipitate questions from heterosexual youths and colleagues, providing opportunities for consciousness-raising. Always correct myths, stereotypes, and other misinformation that students and colleagues articulate about LGBTQ people. Normalize sexual orientation diversity and gender variant behavior, and educate others to affirm diversity in gender expressions. When explaining to students what you do in your job, include sexual orientation, gender identity, and sexuality concerns as examples of the issues that students come and talk with

Table 63.2 Psychosocial Strengths and Needs to Explore with LGBTQ Youths

Individual

- Developmental history of same-sex attractions and/or gender identity issues.
- Intersection of sexual/gender identity development with racial identity development.
- Availability and accuracy of information about sexual orientation, gender identity, and LGBTQ people (i.e., cognitive isolation, exposure to LGBTQ role models, life options for LGBTQ people).
- Feelings and beliefs about sexual orientation or gender identity.
- Degree of social isolation (e.g., disclosure to anyone) and availability of social support.
- Fears related to disclosure and its consequences and perceived benefits of disclosure.
- Chronic stress from managing stigmatization related to sexual, gender, and racial identity.
- Grief and loss issues (e.g., rejection by family and friends; perceived loss of status and dreams for their future).
- Coping strategies for dealing with stigmatization and other stressors.
- Spiritual or religious beliefs regarding sexual orientation and gender identity diversity.
- Awareness of HIV/AIDS, involvement in risky sexual behaviors, and use of risk reduction strategies.
- Mental health problems (e.g., depression, risk of suicide, anxiety, self-mutilation, substance use).
- Expressions of well-being (e.g., competence, mastery, life satisfaction, future orientation).

Family

- Cultural values, beliefs, and meanings related to sexuality, gender roles, marriage, childrearing, and parental expectations of children, adolescents, and adults.
- Awareness of the youth's sexual orientation or gender identity (e.g., Do family members know? Were they told? By whom? Did they find out another way? How long have they known?)
- Actual or anticipated risks of disclosure for family members .
- Actual or anticipated attitudes of family members.
- Presence of other LGBTQ people in the lives of family members.
- Other family stressors (e.g., substance use, mental illness, family violence, financial stress).
- History of physical, sexual, and/or emotional abuse and/or neglect.
- Nature of family's coping responses to crises and other challenges.

Peers

- Nature of peer support (e.g., How do they describe their relationships with their peers? What kind of support have they historically received from them?)
- Disclosure history (e.g., How many friends have they confided in? What was their response? How many friends could they confide in? How open can they be with their peers?)
- Actual or anticipated attitudes of peer group.
- Conflicts in or loss of peer relationships.
- Presence of other LGBTQ youths in peer group; new peer relationships and peer groups after disclosure.
- Availability of LGBTQ peers in community or on Internet.
- History of dating relationships, availability of age-appropriate dating partners.

School and Community

- The importance of attachments to ethnic community.
- Experiences with "coming out" or being perceived as LGBTQ.
- Expressions of heterosexism (e.g., antigay remarks, assumptions of heterosexuality).
- Experiences with harassment and discrimination from students, professionals, and community.
- Interactions between heterosexism and racism, sexism, ableism, and classism in school and community.
- Potential sources of support (e.g., Gay-Straight Alliance, community groups, Internet, school staff, library materials).

Sources: Elze, 2002; Hershberger & D'Augelli, 2000; Lev, 2004; Ryan et al., 2009, 2010; Ryan & Futterman, 1998; Tully, 2000.

Table 63.3 Traits of an "Askable" Practitioner

Self-awareness about personal beliefs and attitudes	+	Knowledge and appreciation of LGBTQ youth	+	Competent social work skills	+	Privilege professional over personal values	=	Ability to work with LGBTQ youth

you about. For example: "Jasmine, students come to see me for help with many different issues, like stress that is interfering with their studies; worries about alcohol or other drug use; fights with parents; problems with racism in school; concerns or questions about their sexual orientation or their gender identity; problems with homelessness; and a lot of other issues."

Use more inclusive language when exploring youths' dating interests, romantic relationships, sexual behaviors, and concerns about sexuality in assessments and intervention sessions. Use words like "partner," "special person," or "girlfriend or boyfriend." You may ask, for example, "Have you been dating anyone? A girl? A boy? Girls and boys?" "Have you been feeling attracted to girls or boys, or to both?" When discussing sexual behaviors, ask all youths, "Have you been or are you currently sexually active with males, females, or with both males and females?" This is particularly important when talking with young people about risk reduction strategies related to HIV or other sexually transmitted infections and pregnancy.

If a student responds angrily or with surprise at such a question, respond with a LGBTQ-affirmative statement, using a gentle, matter-of-fact tone of voice. Be aware that students with same-sex attractions may be testing you to see if you will agree with a homophobic statement. You also want to avoid causing young people to worry that you "saw something in them" that signaled to you that they might be LGBTQ. For example:

School Social Worker: "Jason, I can see that something is really bothering you that is hard for you to talk about. Is that right? (Jason nods.) So far, you've said that things are OK at home, and football is going well. You're having some problems in math, but you feel like you're handling that by getting some extra help. You've also said that you're not involved with any drinking or drugs, especially because football is important to you. Is that right? (Jason nods.) I know that many young people have concerns about dating relationships, or about their sexual feelings. Have you been having any concerns about your sexuality, like whether you are attracted to girls or to boys? Any concerns about your sexual feelings?"

Jason: "Why are you asking me that? Do you think I'm queer or something?"

School Social Worker: "I'm glad you're checking that out with me. I ask those questions of every student who appears distressed or troubled about something. Many students do have questions about their sexuality. Some students are attracted to people of the same sex. Some students identify as gay, lesbian, or bisexual, and some students are confused and questioning their sexuality. I believe it is important that young people, if they need to, have a chance to talk about those issues in a safe and confidential setting. Does that make sense? Do you have any other concerns about why I asked you that question? It's OK to check it out with me."

With youths who are sexually active, do not assume the gender of their sexual partners, regardless of how they self-identify. We know that youths who identify as heterosexual report same-sex sexual activities, and that self-identified gay and lesbian youths report other-sex sexual activities.

Best Practices with LGBTQ Youths

Although specific interventions with gay, lesbian, and bisexual youths have yet to be empirically tested, a compendium of best practices frequently appears in the social work, psychology, and education literatures (Hershberger & D'Augelli, 2000; Lipkin, 2004; Longres & Etnyre, 2004;Ryan & Futterman, 1998; Tully, 2000). More recently, researchers and practitioners have begun to address the needs of transgender children and adolescents (Brill & Pepper, 2008; Lev, 2004; Mallon, 2009). Treatment strategies with gender variant youths have often been grounded in theories that pathologize and aim to eliminate gender variant behaviors, despite the lack of empirical evidence supporting their effectiveness (Israel & Tarver, 1997; Lev, 2004). This chapter takes a gender variant affirmative approach to social work practice with transgender youths (see Brill & Pepper, 2008; Lev, 2004; Mallon, 2009).

When providing services to LGBTQ youths, respect the students' confidentiality. Do not disclose students' sexual orientation or gender identity to parents, other caretakers, school personnel, or students. Follow your professional code of ethics. Do not assume that LGBTQ youths' problems are related to their sexual orientation or gender identity, and do not assume that they are not. Remember that these young people are, first and foremost, adolescents, and they may bring to you such issues as clinical depression and other mental disorders, parental substance abuse or mental illness, parental unemployment and financial stress, and domestic violence.

During a session with the school social worker, Emily, a 14-year-old lesbian, said that she felt very lonely, had no friends at school, and believed that everyone was against her because of her sexual orientation. Upon further exploration, Emily disclosed that she had always been very shy and found it difficult to initiate conversations; she had only two close friends in junior high, both of whom had moved away. After realizing her sexual orientation, she felt even more self-conscious, fearing the reactions of her peers if they found out. Emily and the social worker agreed that they would work together on developing Emily's social skills and exploring her concerns around self-disclosure. Emily did not feel ready to attend a community-based LGBTQ youth group, but she thought she'd talk about that again at a later date with the social worker.

Affirm, validate, and accept youths' expressions of gender variance; same-gender attractions, desires, and behaviors; and self-identification and confusion. Even under the best of circumstances, coming out can be a confusing and difficult process, with youths experiencing feelings of loneliness, anxiety, fear, isolation, shame, loss, and guilt. Remember to start where the client is starting and proceed with gentleness and patience. With transgender youths, respect their wishes by using their preferred names and pronouns, and do not demand or enforce stereotypical gender behavior.

Avoid labeling young people, but instead help them safely explore and understand their feelings, thoughts, and behaviors related to sexuality or gender identity. Follow the youth's lead in using terminology. However, be able to say the words *gay, lesbian, bisexual,* and *transgender* comfortably and without hesitation. For example, you can reflect back the student's feelings and pose a question, as follows: "Katie, you've been having sexual feelings about your best friend, and this is worrying you. Have you been worrying that you may be gay?" When a youth discloses to you that s/he is gay, lesbian, bisexual, or transgender, respond in an affirming, supportive way; anticipate concerns about confidentiality; and give the message that you are willing to talk about any issue. For example:

"Sergio, I feel honored that you trusted me enough to share with me that you are feeling attracted to men. Please know that I will keep that confidential. I would be very interested in hearing more about your experience, if you would like to talk about it, and what it is like for you here in school and with your family. Or if there is something else that you want to talk about altogether, I'm here for that, too."

For a highly distressed youth who cries, "I don't want to be gay," encourage further expression of feelings and explore with him or her the underlying beliefs and attitudes. The distress is often grounded in myths, stereotypes, and fears of rejection and stigmatization. For example: "Joel, I can see that you are very upset at these feelings you are having. Please tell me more about what makes you say that you don't want to be gay."

Help young people build self-esteem by correcting their internalized myths and stereotypes. They may believe that they cannot enter certain occupations, will never be able to have children, or will never have a long-term relationship. Provide them with accurate and LGBTQ-affirming literature, including fiction and nonfiction written especially for LGBTQ youths. Expose students to positive and culturally diverse LGBTQ role models through literature, guest speakers, and films.

Suspect gender identity issues if you witness, or are informed by another person, that a youth frequently raises questions or concerns about gender, adopts an other-gender identity, and/or makes regular attempts to cross-dress (Israel & Tarver, 1997). If you suspect a youth may be experiencing gender identity issues, explore using such questions as "Who would you like to be in 5 years, when you think about your future?" "How would you like your life to look in 5 years?" Remember that sexual orientation and gender identity are different. Transgender youths may self-identify as gay, lesbian, bisexual, or heterosexual, or they may question their sexual orientation or not label themselves. Validate their sexual orientation as it unfolds. Transgender youths may need help in differentiating between their gender identity and sexual orientation (Israel & Tarver, 1997).

Explore with students how issues of sexuality, gender, and gender variance intersect with issues of race, class, and disabilities in their lives (McCready, 2004). LGBTQ youths are affected not only by heterosexism but by other forms of oppression, depending upon their membership in one or more social groups (e.g., racial or ethnic group memberships, religious affiliations, socioeconomic class, immigrant status, and disability status). Believe students when they share their experiences with discrimination and prejudice. Be willing to listen to their anger about mistreatment without becoming defensive or feeling that you need to stick up for the dominant social group (e.g., heterosexual, white). Be aware that the risks of "coming out" vary from person to person. Do not assume that coming out is the best choice for everyone. Immigrant youths, youths with disabilities, and youths of color, for example, may have more to lose by self-disclosure, especially if they are already marginalized within their schools.

Enhancing Youths' Problem-Solving, Decision-Making, and Adaptive Coping Skills

Help students problem-solve challenging situations, such as coming out to friends and family members; handling stigmatization and discrimination; dealing with name-calling; avoiding risky situations such as adult-oriented clubs; and finding age-appropriate dating partner(s), peers, and social and recreational activities. Use role play to help students practice new interactions, such as disclosing their identity to others, asking a same-sex person for a date, or calling a LGBTQ organization.

Assess the safety of the youths' Internet use and, if necessary, provide them with safer strategies with which to communicate with people on the Internet and guidelines for meeting people (e.g., always meet in a public place; do not disclose your home address).

Explore the youths' readiness to attend a community-based LGBTQ youth group. The thought of attending a group can be very frightening for a youth in the early stages of coming out. Do not push. Ask, "Would you be interested in hearing some information about a local group for young people who are gay, lesbian, bisexual, transgender, or questioning their sexuality?" Ease the youth's exploration of the group. Anticipate and explore the questions and concerns of your client and talk with the leaders of the group about its composition, climate, and culture (e.g., age range, racial/ethnic diversity, gender diversity, location, range of activities).

Interventions with Family Members

Emerging research from the Family Acceptance Project™ provides evidence that family reactions to youths' sexual orientation and gender identity strongly affect the well-being of LGBTQ youths and suggests specific intervention strategies. Ryan et al. (2009) found that LGB young adults that experienced high levels of family rejection during adolescence reported significantly more negative health outcomes (e.g., suicide attempts, serious depression, illegal drug use, unprotected sexual intercourse) than their peers with no or low levels of family rejection. Further, LGBT Latino and non-Latino white young adults that had experienced greater family acceptance also reported higher self-esteem, better overall health, and more social support, and less depression, suicidality, and substance abuse than their less accepted peers, although transgender young adults reported less social support and poorer general health (Ryan, Russell, Huebner, Diaz, & Sanchez, 2010).

These findings suggest that school social workers and other professionals can help families understand how rejecting behaviors significantly increase their LGBTQ children's risk for serious health problems and assist families in eliminating rejecting behaviors and expanding their repertoire of accepting behaviors. Family education booklets developed by the Family Acceptance Project™, *Supportive Families, Healthy Children*, including one that is faith-based specifically for Latter-day Saint families, list specific behaviors that increase and decrease LGBTQ youths' risk for physical and mental health problems and appear- in the resources provided at the end of this chapter.

Changing the School Climate: Creating a LGBTQ-Affirming Environment

Although most school-based interventions for LGBTQ youths have yet to be evaluated, a growing body of research points to school characteristics that matter to the well-being of LGBTQ youth. Elze (2003) found that GLB youth felt more comfortable in their schools when they were more highly integrated into heterosexual peer networks as "out" youths, and the more they perceived that administrators and teachers would act on their behalf. Several studies have found that the presence of a GSA or an LGBTQ support group was significantly associated with youths' reports of less victimization and suicidality (Goodenow, Szalacha, & Westheimer, 2006), reduced truancy (Goodenow et al., 2006; Walls, Kane, & Wisneski, 2010), greater safety in school (Kosciw et al., 2010; Walls et al., 2010), a more supportive school climate (Szalacha, 2003), and higher academic achievement (Walls et al., 2010). Further, the presence of a high school GSA was found to be associated with greater educational attainment and psychosocial well-being among young adults (Toomey, Ryan, Diaz, & Russell, 2011). Blake and colleagues (2001) found an association between GLB-sensitive HIV curricula and fewer sexual risk behaviors among LGB youths. An evaluation of the first year's implementation of the New York City Department of Education's *Respect for All* training program for secondary school educators found increased LGBTQ-affirmative knowledge, attitudes, and behaviors among the participants, with some gains maintained at the 6-month follow-up assessment (Greytak & Kosciw, 2010), suggesting the need for booster sessions to support educators' behavioral changes, such as when anti-LGBTQ remarks require interruption (Greytak & Kosciw, 2010).

Nearly 4000 school-based GSAs or LGBTQ-affirmative diversity clubs are registered with the Gay, Lesbian and Straight Education Network (GLSEN, 2010). GSAs have become the primary vehicle for LGBTQ students and their straight allies to effect LGBTQ-affirmative change within their schools (Griffin, Lee, Waugh, & Beyer, 2004; Russell et al., 2009). These clubs vary in composition, degree of adult involvement, primary purpose, trans-friendliness, and the extent to which LGBTQ youth feel comfortable being "out" within the group (Griffin et al., 2004; McGuire et al., 2010). GSAs may create safe space for LGBTQ youths and their allies; provide counseling and peer support; promote positive identity formation; raise awareness and increase visibility by educating the school community on LGBTQ issues; and build youths' self-efficacy toward advocating for LGBTQ-affirmative policies and programs (Griffin et al., 2004). LGBTQ students of color, however, may not frequent these organizations because their schools' racially defined social boundaries may influence participation in extracurricular activities, white students' experiences may be privileged within GSAs, and adult advisors may lack the knowledge and self-efficacy to effectively address the needs of LGBTQ youths of color (McCready, 2004). Collaborative strategies involving students, teachers, and administrators are required to analyze the dynamics of racial segregation within the school and its larger community context; to raise awareness about the identities, needs, and interests of queer youths of color from diverse communities; and to reflect multicultural concerns in the group's activities (McCready, 2004).

Mezzo-level interventions, as shown in Table 63.5, focus on enhancing the fit between LGBTQ students and their school environment by creating a safe and affirming milieu that supports their development as adolescents and their acquisition of a positive LGBTQ identity. School social workers, in collaboration with their colleagues, can initiate, develop, advocate for, and implement a variety of interventions that aim to change anti-LGBTQ attitudes and behaviors, promote the inclusion of LGBTQ issues in the curricula, and increase the visibility of LGBTQ students and school personnel within the school community.

Applying Interventions within a Response to Intervention Framework

A Response to Intervention Framework can be applied to multi-level school-based interventions aimed at creating supportive learning environments for LGBTQ youths. An RTI framework involves a capacity-building approach to support services; the use of evidence-based interventions organized in a multi-level prevention system (i.e., preventative, secondary and tertiary); and individual- to systems-level data collection and analysis to guide decision-making (National Center on Response to Intervention, 2011). School social workers are in an excellent position to develop, implement, and evaluate interventions to maximize all students' academic achievement and improve the educational climate in which students learn. However, school social workers spend little time on capacity-building activities, focus predominantly on individual-level interventions, and seldom engage in data analysis (Kelly et al., 2010).

Table 63.4 Foci of Interventions for LGBTQ Youths

- Clinical interventions with LGBTQ adolescents.
  - Support for issues related to sexual orientation or gender identity.
    - Help build a positive sexual and gender identity.
    - Help youths of color build a positive racial identity.
    - Enhance self-esteem.
    - Provide psychoeducational support and information (e.g., sexuality, sexual orientation, sexual/gender identity development).
    - Educate on the cultural and institutional nature of oppression.
    - Address internalized oppression.
    - Correct myths and stereotypes.
    - Help find social support, build social connections, and find allies.
    - Help build adaptive coping strategies to manage stigmatization.
    - Help envision and plan for a positive and productive future.
  - Support for other issues that may be related to or exacerbated by sexual orientation or gender identity issues.
    - Communication with parents.
    - Interpersonal and institutionalized marginalization of youths of color.
    - Intrafamilial victimization.
    - Problems with peers.
    - Academic problems.
  - Support for issues unrelated to sexual orientation or gender identity.
    - Parental stressors (e.g., substance abuse, mental illness, domestic violence).
    - Clinical depression.
    - Other stressors (e.g., death of a family member or friend, stress related to college applications.
  - Clinical interventions with family members.
    - Correct myths and stereotypes and provide psychoeducational support and information.
    - Help family members decrease highly rejecting behaviors and increase accepting behaviors.
    - Provide empathic support for feelings of grief, loss, anger, fear, shame, and guilt.
    - Refer parents to knowledgeable community professionals and LGBTQ-affirmative spiritual/religious leaders.
  - Interventions to reduce stigmatization in school and community environments.
    - Increase the capacity of school personnel to effectively interrupt oppressive behavior.
    - Support students in developing gay-straight alliances that reflect the cultural diversity of the school.
    - Intervene whenever students or school personnel use anti-LGBTQ slurs or jokes.
    - Support inclusion of LGBTQ issues in curricula.
    - Advocate for school policies that protect LGBTQ students and staff.
    - Testify in support of town ordinances granting civil rights protections and domestic partnership benefits to LGBTQ citizens.
    - Provide consultation and training to community-based youth-serving organizations.

Source: Elze, 2002; Hershberger & D'Augelli, 2000; MacGillivray, 2004; Ryan, 2001; Ryan et al., 2009;)

Applying a RTI framework to interventions with LGBTQ youths requires caution, as researchers have noted that targeting sexual minority youths for special programs may be destructive, rather than beneficial, because of the stigmatization associated with being perceived as needing an intervention (Rotheram-Borus & Langabeer, 2001; Savin-Williams, 2005). Sexual minority youths may benefit to the extent that all adolescents benefit from empirically validated interventions that promote adolescent mental and physical health, risk reduction, and overall well-being. As research identifies sexual minority youths at highest risk, targeted interventions can be developed and evaluated, such as what has occurred in HIV prevention for young men of color involved in same-sex sexual activities, although they remain at highest risk and in need of more effective prevention programs (Centers for Disease Control and Prevention, 2011).

Table 63.5 Mezzo- and Macro-Level Interventions

Physical Environment
- LGBTQ administrators, faculty, and support staff are open and visible.
- All school personnel are aware of their legal obligation to stop anti-LGBTQ harassment.
- All school personnel have been trained to effectively interrupt verbal abuse and derogatory remarks.
- School personnel respect and use transgender students' chosen names and pronouns.
- Transgender students can use bathrooms that correspond with their gender identity, or gender-neutral bathrooms (e.g., nurse's office, faculty bathroom)
- School personnel respect and use transgender students' chosen names and pronouns.
- Transgender students take physical education classes congruent with their identity and are provided with reasonable accommodations in school locker rooms.
- LGBTQ brochures, posters, and resource lists are displayed in school offices.
- LGBTQ books are in the school library.
- School dances are welcoming environments for same-sex couples and gender-variant young people. Chaperones are trained to be LGBTQ-affirmative.
- The school newspaper includes articles on LGBTQ issues.
- The school has a gay-straight alliance that is actively supported by administration, faculty, support staff, parents, and students.
- LGBTQ youth resources are included in student handbooks and resource lists.

Inclusive Curricula
- Bullying and violence prevention programs include harassment based on sexuality and gender nonconformity.
- Suicide, substance abuse, and dropout prevention programs integrate information about the unique stressors affecting the well-being of LGBTQ youths.
- Health and sexuality curricula integrate information about same-sex sexual attractions, healthy same-sex relationships, gender identity diversity, and diverse family contexts.
- Multicultural programs and community resource days should include LGBTQ issues.
- Teachers should be provided with consultants and peer mentors to help them appropriately integrate LGBTQ issues into courses.

Knowledgeable and Supportive School Personnel
- Provide administrators, teachers and support staff with ongoing training to improve their knowledge and skills for effective intervention on behalf of LGBTQ youths.
- Educate school board members on LGBTQ students' needs and rights, and on the district's legal obligations to protect all students from harm.

Policies
- Enact anti-harassment and nondiscrimination policies at the district level that include sexual orientation and gender expression.
- Educate all students and school personnel on the specific behaviors prohibited under these policies and the procedures for reporting violations.
- Apply school dress codes in a gender-neutral manner. Allow students to dress in a manner that reflects their gender identity.
- Enact state and federal legislation that prohibits discrimination and harassment on the basis of sexual orientation, gender expression and gender identity in educational institutions.

Sources: Elze, 2003; Kosciw et al., 2010; Lipkin, 2004; MacGillivray, 2004; Mallon, 2009; Thaler et al., 2009; Tully, 2000).

Intervention studies with adolescents should explore how youths' sexual minority status, and their experiences related to their status, may interact with the variables and processes under investigation, moderating, perhaps, the effects of vulnerability, risk and protective factors, or influencing youths' responses to the intervention. For example, group-based cognitive therapy is effective, both short- and long-term, in alleviating clinical depression in adolescents (Moore & Carr, 2000). There is reason to hypothesize that it would work for clinically depressed sexual minority youths. However, fears related to disclosure may prevent sexual minority youths from reaping the full benefits of a group experience.

A RTI framework applied to LGBTQ youths might include the following:

- *Primary level*
  - Train all school personnel on LGBTQ youths' needs and intervention strategies to address anti-LGBTQ and other bias-related harassment.
  - Enact anti-harassment and anti-discrimination policies, widely publicize such policies, and educate the school community, including parents, about its obligations and the procedures for reporting violations.
  - Implement anti-bullying interventions that include LGBTQ issues.
  - Provide comprehensive sexuality education which incorporates information about sexual orientation, gender identity and gender expression diversity.
  - Integrate LGBTQ issues into relevant curricular subjects (e.g., social studies, human biology).
  - Include questions on sexual orientation, gender identity and gender expression in school-wide health risk behavior surveys.
  - Conduct annual assessments of school climate with students, faculty and staff.

- *Secondary level*
  - Establish gay-straight alliances and support school-wide education and advocacy efforts.
  - Develop mutual aid support groups for LGBTQ youths.
  - Implement more intensive anti-bullying interventions with students who require more intensive programming.

- *Tertiary level*
  - Provide individual-level assessment and intervention services to all students requiring more intensive services.

Desired outcomes may include reductions in students' victimization, psychological distress and health risk behaviors; increases in safety, perceived support from personnel and peers, and comfort within the school environment.

Resources

Took-Kits, Reports, and Films

American Psychological Association. (2004). *Healthy Lesbian, Gay & Bisexual Students Project Toolbox, supplemental documents and Internet resources for Preventing Health Risks & Promoting Healthy Outcomes among LGBQ Youth, a training workshop for school personnel.* Available from APA: http://apa.org/pi/lgbt/prorams/hlgbsp/toolbox.aspx

Freker, J., & Middleton, J. (2002). (2nd ed.). *Making schools safe: Anti-harassment training program.* New York, NY: American Civil Liberties Union. Available from http://www.aclu.org/lgbt-rights_hiv-aids/making-schools-safe-training-manual

Gay, Lesbian and Straight Education Network. (2009). *Safe Space Kit: Guide to Being an Ally to LGBT Students.* Available from GLSEN: http://www.glsen.org/cgi-bin/iowa/all/library/record/1641.html?state=tools&type=educator

Gay, Lesbian and Straight Education Network. (2008). *ThinkB4YouSpeak Educator's Guide* and campaign materials. Available from GLSEN: http://www.thinkb4youspeak.com

GroundSpark and the Respect for All Project. (2007). DVD includes: *It's STILL Elementary: Talking About Gay Issues in School;* the original full-length film *It's Elementary: Talking about Gay Issues in School*; and the shorter training version of *It's Elementary*. Available from GroundSpark: http://groundspark.org/respect-for-all

Human Relations Media & GLSEN. (2003). *Dealing with difference: Opening dialogue about lesbian, gay, and straight issues.* New York: GLSEN. A 35-minute video and 82-page teacher resource book Available from Human Relations Media: http://hrmvideo.com

Just the Facts Coalition. (2008). *Just the facts about sexual orientation and youth: A primer for principals, educators, and school personnel.* Washington, DC: American Psychological Association. Available from http://www.apa.org/pi/lgbc/publications/justthefacts.html

Kim, R. (2006). *Strengthening the learning environment: A school employee's guide to gay, lesbian, bisexual, & transgender issues* (2nd ed.). Washington, DC: National Education Association. Available from http://www.nea.org/assets/docs/glbtstrengthen-learningenvirong2006.pdf

Lambda Legal Defense & Education Fund. (2010). Out, safe and respected: A guide to LGBTQ youth in schools for educators and parents. New York: Author. Available from http://www.lambdalegal.org/sites/default/files/publications/downloads/osr-admin_out-safe-respected-for-administrators_0.pdf

Lambda Legal Defense & Education Fund, National Alliance to End Homelessness, National

Center for Lesbian Rights, & National Network for Youth. (2009). *National recommended best practices for serving LGBT homeless youth.* New York, NY: Authors. Available from http://www.nclrights.org/site/DocServer/national-recommended-best-practices-for-lgbt-homeless-yo.pdf?docID=5821

National School Boards Association. (2004). *Dealing with legal matters surrounding students' sexual orientation and gender identity*. Available from http://www.nsba.org/cosa/sexualorientation

National Center for Lesbian Rights. (2011). *A place of respect: A guide for group care facilities serving transgender and gender non-conforming youth.* Available from http://www.nclrights.org/site/DocServer/A_Place_of_Respect.pdf?docID=8301

Ryan, C. (2009). *Supportive families, healthy children: Helping families with lesbian, gay, bisexual & transgender children.* San Francisco, CA: Marian Wright Edelman Institute, San Francisco State University. Available from http://familyproject.sfsu.edu

Ryan, C., & Rees, R.A. (2012). *Supportive families, healthy children: Helping Latter-day Saint families with lesbian, gay, bisexual & transgender children.* San Francisco, CA: Marian Wright Edelman Institute, San Francisco State University. Available from http://familyproject.sfsu.edu

Web Sites

These Web sites provide a wealth of resources, many of them downloadable, for educators, other professionals, parents, and LGBTQ youths.

Advocates for Youth: www.advocatesforyouth.org

Youth Resource, a Web site by and for LGBTQ youth, sponsored by Advocates for Youth. http://www.youthresource.com

American Civil Liberties Union Lesbian Gay Bisexual Transgender Project: Schools & Youth: http://www.aclu.org/lgbt-rights/youth-schools

American Psychological Association

Lesbian, Gay, Bisexual and Transgender Concerns Office

http://www.apa.org/pi/lgbt/index.aspx

Commonwealth of Massachusetts Commission on Gay, Lesbian, Bisexual & Transgender Youth: http://www.mass.gov/cgly/ (This Commission, a model for other states, is charged with ensuring the health and safety of LGBT youth in Massachusetts and makes policy recommendations to the Departments of Public Health and Elementary and Secondary Education.)

Family Acceptance Project™: http://familyproject.sfsu.edu. (This Web site provides resources for families with LGBTQ children and youth and emergent research findings on helping families support their LGBTQ children. FAP is developing culturally competent interventions for ethnically diverse families aimed at increasing family support for LGBTQ youth.)

Gay, Lesbian, and Straight Education Network (GLSEN): http://www.glsen.org

Gender Spectrum: http://www.genderspectrum.org. This Web site provides an array of resources for educators, other professionals, and families to help them sensitively address gender identity and gender expression diversity in children and adolescents and to create supportive environments for all children and teens.

Lambda Legal Defense and Education Fund: http://www.lambdalegal.org.

Lambda Legal provides information on laws, policies and legislative advocacy related to the educational rights of LGBTQ students.

Parents, Families and Friends of Lesbians and Gays (PFLAG): http://www.pflag.org.

PFLAG also sponsors Transgender and Diversity Networks accessed through its Web site. http://www.putthisonthemap.org (This Seattle-based youth development program developed an award-winning 34-minute documentary, *Reteaching Gender & Sexuality,* to place youths' voices at the forefront in educating professionals about the lives of queer/trans youth.)

The Safe Schools Coalition: http://www.safeschoolscoalition.org

Transgender Law & Policy Institute: http://www.transgenderlaw.org/index.htm. (This Web site provides updated information on existing and model policies and laws that protect the rights of transgender persons in service delivery systems, including education. "Guidelines for Creating Policies for Transgender Children in Recreational Sports" can be downloaded from the site.)

The Trevor Project: http://www.thetrevorproject.org. This project is aimed at preventing suicide among LGBTQ youth. A resource guide for educators and a comprehensive list of books and films for LGBTQ young people are among its downloadable resources.

Key Points to Remember

- School-based interventions should aim to create school environments that protect, value, and respect LGBTQ students and staff.
- School social workers can collaborate and intervene with multiple systems to help LGBTQ students establish a good fit with their school, peer, family, and community environments.
- Interventions must take into account how sexual orientation and gender identity issues intersect with issues of race, class, gender, and disability status within the social environments that youths navigate.
- LGBTQ youths' problems may or may not be related to their sexual orientation or gender identity, or they may be problems that are exacerbated by internal or external conflicts arising from their sexual orientation or gender identity.
- Much of the work done with LGBTQ youths is psychoeducational in nature, providing them with accurate and affirming information, community resources, and assistance with developing problem-solving, decision-making, and adaptive coping skills.

References

Birkett, M., Espelage, D. L., & Koenig, B. (2009). LGB and questioning students in schools: The moderating effects of homophobic bullying and school climate on negative outcomes. *Journal of Youth and Adolescence, 38*, 989–1000.

Blake, S. M., Ledsky, R., Lehman, T., Goodenow, C., Sawyer, R., & Hack, T. (2001). Preventing sexual risk behaviors among gay, lesbian, and bisexual adolescents: The benefits of gay-sensitive HIV instruction in schools. *American Journal of Public Health, 91*, 940–946.

Brill, S., & Pepper, R. (2008). *The transgender child: A handbook for families and professionals*. San Francisco, CA: Cleis Press.

Centers for Disease Control and Prevention. (2011). *HIV and young men who have sex with men*. Retrieved June 25, 2011, from http://www.cdc.gov/HealthyYouth/sexualbehaviors/pdf/hiv_factsheet_ymsm.pdf

Cianciotto, J., & Cahill, S. (2003). *Education policy: Issues affecting lesbian, gay, bisexual, and transgender youth*. New York, NY: National Lesbian and Gay Task Force. Retrieved February 5, 2004, from http://www.ngltf.org/downloads/reports/reports/EducationPolicy.pdf

Costa, F. M., Jessor, R., Turbin, M. S., Dong, Q., Zhang, H., & Wang, C. (2005). The role of social contexts in adolescence: Context protection and context risk in the United States and China. *Applied Developmental Science, 9*, 67–85.

D'Augelli, A. R., Pilkington, N. W., & Hershberger, S. L. (2002). Incidence and mental health impact of sexual orientation victimization of lesbian, gay, and bisexual youths in high school. *School Psychology Quarterly, 17*, 148–167.

Diamond, L. M. (2003). New paradigms for research on heterosexual and sexual minority development. *Journal of Clinical Child and Adolescent Psychology, 32*, 490–498.

Diaz, E. M., & Kosciw, J. G. (2009). *Shared differences: The experiences of lesbian, gay, bisexual, and transgender students of color in our nation's schools*. New York, NY: Gay, Lesbian and Straight Education Network.

Eccles, T. A., Sayegh, M. A., Fortenberry, J. D., & Zimet, G. D. (2004). More normal than not: A qualitative assessment of the developmental experiences of gay male youth. *Journal of Adolescent Health, 35*(5), 425.e11–e18.

Eisenberg, M. E., & Resnick, M. D. (2006). Suicidality among gay, lesbian and bisexual youth: The role of protective factors. *Journal of Adolescent Health, 39*, 662–668.

Elia, J. P., & Eliason, M. J. (2010). Dangerous omissions: Abstinence-only-until-marriage school based sexuality education and the betrayal of LGBTQ youth. *American Journal of Sexuality Education, 5*, 17–35.

Elze, D. (2002). Risk factors for internalizing and externalizing problems among gay, lesbian, and bisexual adolescents. *Social Work Research, 26*, 89–100.

Elze, D. (2003). Gay, lesbian, and bisexual adolescents' perceptions of their high school environments and factors associated with their comfort in school. *Children and Schools, 25*, 225–239.

Elze, D. (2007). Research with sexual minority youths: Where do we go from here? *Journal of Gay and Lesbian Social Services, 18*(2), 73–99.

Espelage, D. L., Aragon, S. R., & Birkett, M. (2008). Homophobic teasing, psychological outcomes, and sexual orientation among high school students: What influence do parents and schools have? *School Psychology Review, 37*, 202–216.

Fraser, M. W. (Ed.). (2004). *Risk and resilience in childhood: An ecological perspective* (2nd ed.). Washington, DC: NASW Press.

Galliher, R. V., Rostosky, S. S., & Hughes, H. K. (2004). School belonging, self-esteem, depressive symptoms in adolescents: An examination of sex, sexual attraction status, and urbanicity. *Journal of Youth and Adolescence, 33*, 235–245.

Garofalo, R., Deleon, J., Osmer, E., Doll, M., & Harper, G. (2006). Overlooked, misunderstood and at-risk: Exploring the lives and HIV risk of ethnic minority male-to-female transgender youth. *Journal of Adolescent Health, 38*, 230–236.

Gay, Lesbian and Straight Education Network. (2010). About Gay-Straight Alliances (GSAs). Retrieved April 29, 2010, from http://www.glsen.org/cgi-bin/iowa/all/library/record/2342.html?state=what

Goodenow, C., Szalacha, L., & Westheimer, K. (2006). School support groups, other school factors, and the safety of sexual minority adolescents. *Psychology in the Schools, 43*, 573–589.

Greytak, E. A., Kosciw, J. G., & Diaz, E. M. (2009). *Harsh realities: The experiences of transgender youth in our nation's schools.* New York, NY: Gay Lesbian and Straight Education Network.

Greytak, E. A., & Kosciw, J. A. (2010). *Year one evaluation of the New York City Department of Education Respect for All training program.* Retrieved June 15, 2011, from http://www.glsen.org/binary-data/GLSEN_ATTACHMENTS/file/000/001/1633-2.PDF

Griffin, P., Lee, C., Waugh, J., & Beyer, C. (2004). Describing roles that Gay-Straight Alliances play in schools: From individual support to school change. *Journal of Gay & Lesbian Issues in Education, 13*, 7–22.

Grossman, A. H., D'Augelli, A. R., Howell, T. J., & Hubbard, S. (2005). Parents' reactions to transgender youths' gender nonconforming expression and identity. *Journal of Gay & Lesbian Social Services, 18*, 3–16.

Grossman, A. H., & D'Augelli, A. R. (2006). Transgender youth: Invisible and vulnerable. *Journal of Homosexuality, 51*, 111–128.

Grossman, A. H., & D'Augelli, A. R. (2007). Transgender youth and life-threatening behaviors. *Suicide and Life-Threatening Behavior, 37*, 527–537.

Grossman, A. H., D'Augelli, A. R., & Frank, J. A. (2011). Aspects of psychological resilience among transgendered youth. *Journal of LGBT Youth, 8*, 103–115.

Hatzenbuehler, M. L. (2011). The social environment and suicide attempts in lesbian, gay, and bisexual youth. *Pediatrics, 127*, 896–903.

Herek, G. M. (1990). The context of anti-gay violence: Notes on cultural and psychological heterosexism. *Journal of Interpersonal Violence, 5*(3), 316–333.

Hershberger, S. L., & D'Augelli, A. R. (2000). Issues in counseling lesbian, gay, and bisexual adolescents. In R. M. Perez, K. A. DeBord, & K. J. Bieschke (Eds.), *Handbook of counseling and psychotherapy with lesbian, gay, and bisexual clients* (pp. 225–247). Washington, DC: American Psychological Association.

Himmelstein, K. E. W., & Bruckner, H. (2010). Criminal-justice and school sanctions against nonheterosexual youth: A national longitudinal study. *Pediatrics, 127*, 49–57.

Irwin, C. E., Burg, S. J., & Cart, C. U. (2002). America's adolescents: Where have we been, where are we going? *Journal of Adolescent Health, 31*, 91–121.

Israel, G. E., & Tarver, D. E. (1997). *Transgender care: Recommended guidelines, practical information, and personal accounts.* Philadelphia, PA: Temple University Press.

Kelly, M. S., Frey, A. J., Alvarez, M., Berzin, S. C., Shaffer, G., & O'Brien, K. (2010). School social work practice and response to intervention. *Children & Schools, 32*, 201–209.

Kosciw, J. G., Greytak, E. A., & Diaz, E. M (2009). Who, what, where, when, and why: Demographic and ecological factors contributing to hostile school climate for lesbian, gay, bisexual, and transgender youth. *Journal of Youth and Adolescence, 38*, 976–988.

Kosciw, J. G., Greytak, E. A., Diaz, E. M., & Bartkiewicz, M. J. (2010). *The 2009 National School Climate Survey: The experiences of lesbian, gay, bisexual and transgender youth in our nation's schools.* New York, NY: Gay, Lesbian and Straight Education Network.

Lambda Legal Defense & Education Fund. (2008). *Out, safe & respected: Your rights at school.* New York: Authors. Retrieved May 15, 2012, from http://www.lambdalegal.org/sites/default/files/publications/downloads/osr_out-safe-respected_0.pdf

Lev, A. I. (2004). *Transgender emergence: Therapeutic guidelines for working with gender variant people and their families.* New York: Haworth.

Lipkin, A. (2004). *Beyond diversity day: A Q&A on gay and lesbian issues in schools.* Lanham, MD: Rowman & Littlefield.

Longres, J. F., & Etnyre, W. S. (2004). Social work practice with gay and lesbian children and adolescents. In P. Allen-Meares & M. W. Fraser, *Intervention with children and adolescents: An interdisciplinary perspective* (pp. 80–105). Boston, MA: Allyn & Bacon.

MacGillivray, I. K. (2004). *Sexual orientation & school policy: A practical guide for teachers, administrators, and community activists.* Lanham, MD: Rowman & Littlefield.

Mallon, G. P. (2009). A call for organizational trans-formation. In G. P. Mallon (Ed.), *Social work practice with transgender and gender variant youth* (2nd ed., pp. 163–174). New York, NY: Routledge.

Mallon, G. P., & DeCrescenzo, T. (2006). Transgender children and youth: A child welfare practice perspective. *Child Welfare, 85*, 215–241.

McCready, L. (2004). Some challenges facing queer youth programs in urban high schools: Racial segregation and de-normalizing whiteness. *Journal of Gay & Lesbian Issues in Education, 1*, 37–51.

McGuire, J. K., Anderson, C. R., Toomey, R. B., & Russell, S. T. (2010). School climate for transgender youth: A mixed method investigation of student experiences and school responses. *Journal of Youth and Adolescence, 39*, 1175–1188.

Moore, K. A., & Zaff, J. F. (2002, November). *Building a better teenager: A summary of "what works" in adolescent development—Child Trends Research Brief.* Washington, DC: Child Trends. Retrieved August 25, 2005, from http://www.childtrends.org

Moore, M., & Carr, A. (2000). Depression and grief. In A. Carr (Ed.), *What works with children and adolescents? A critical review of psychological interventions with children, adolescents and their families* (pp. 203–232). Philadelphia, PA: Taylor & Francis, Inc.

Murdock, T. B., & Bolch, M. B. (2005). Risk and protective factors for poor school adjustment in lesbian, gay, and bisexual high school youth: Variable and person-centered analyses. *Psychology in the Schools, 42*, 159–172.

National Center on Response to Intervention. (2011). *The complex ecology of response to intervention*. Retrieved June 5, 2011, from http://www.rti4success.org

Needham, B. L., & Austin, E. L. (2010). Sexual orientation, parental support, and health during the transition to young adulthood. *Journal of Youth and Adolescence, 39*, 1189–1198.

Ray, N. (2006). *Lesbian, gay, bisexual and transgender youth: An epidemic of homelessness*. New York, NY: National Gay and Lesbian Task Force Policy Institute and the National Coalition for the Homeless.

Rienzo, B. A., Button. J. W., Sheu, J., & Li, Y. (2006). The politics of sexual orientation issues in American schools. *Journal of School Health, 76*, 93–97.

Rosario, M., Schrimshaw, E. W., Hunter, J., & Gwadz, M. (2002). Gay-related stress and emotional distress among gay, lesbian, and bisexual youths: A longitudinal examination. *Journal of Counseling and Clinical Psychology, 70*, 967–975.

Rosario, M., Schrimshaw, E. W., & Hunter, J. (2011a). Different patterns of sexual identity development over time: Implications for the psychological adjustment of lesbian, gay, and bisexual youths. *Journal of Sex Research, 48*, 3–15.

Rosario, M., Schrimshaw, E. W., & Hunter, J. (2011b). Homelessness among lesbian, gay, and bisexual youth: Implications for subsequent internalizing and externalizing symptoms. *Journal of Youth and Adolescence, 41*(5), 544–560. doi:10.1007/s10964-011-9681-3

Rotheram-Borus, M. J., & Langabeer, K. A. (2001). Developmental trajectories of gay, lesbian, and bisexual youths. In A. R. D'Augelli & C. J. Patterson (Eds.), *Lesbian, gay, and bisexual identities and youth: Psychological perspectives* (pp. 97–128). New York, NY: Oxford University Press.

Russell, S. T., Franz, B. T., & Driscoll, A. K. (2001). Same-sex romantic attraction and experiences of violence in adolescence. *American Journal of Public Health, 91*, 903–906.

Russell, S. T. & Joyner, K. (2001). Adolescent sexual orientation and suicide risk: Evidence from a national study. *American Journal of Public Health, 91*, 1276–1281.

Russell, S. T., Seif, H., & Truong, N. L. (2001). School outcomes of sexual minority youth in the United States: Evidence from a national study. *Journal of Adolescence, 24*, 111–127.

Russell, S. T., Driscoll, A. K., & Truong N. (2002). Adolescent same-sex romantic attractions and relationships: Implications for substance use and abuse. *American Journal of Public Health, 92*, 198–202.

Russell, S. T., & Consolacion, T. B. (2003). Adolescent romance and emotional health in the United States: Beyond binaries. *Journal of Clinical Child and Adolescent Psychology, 32*, 499–508.

Russell, S. T. (2005). Beyond risk: Resilience in the lives of sexual minority youth. *Journal of Gay and Lesbian Issues in Education, 2*, 5–18.

Russell, S. T., Muraco, A., Subramaniam, A., & Laub, C. (2009). Youth empowerment and high school gay-straight alliances. *Journal of Youth and Adolescence, 38*, 891–903.

Russell, S. T., Ryan, C., Toomey, R. B., Diaz, R. M., & Sanchez, J. (2011). Lesbian, gay, bisexual, and transgender adolescent school victimization: Implications for young adult health and adjustment. *Journal of School Health, 81*, 223–230.

Russo, R. G. (2006). The extent of public education nondiscrimination policy protections for lesbian, gay, bisexual, and transgender students: A national study. *Urban Education, 41*, 115–150.

Ryan, C. (2001). Counseling lesbian, gay, and bisexual youths. In A. R. D'Augelli & C. J. Patterson (Eds.), *Lesbian, gay, and bisexual identities and youth: Psychological perspectives* (pp. 224–250). New York: Oxford University Press.

Ryan, C., & Futterman, D. (1998). *Lesbian & gay youth: Care and counseling*. New York: Columbia University Press.

Ryan, C., Huebner, D., Diaz, R. M., & Sanchez, J. (2009). Family rejection as a predictor of negative health outcomes in White and Latino lesbian, gay, and bisexual young adults. *Pediatrics*, (123), 346–352. [Yes, that is correct]

Ryan, C., Russell, S. T., Huebner, D., Diaz, R. M., & Sanchez, J. (2010). Family acceptance in adolescence and the health of LGBT young adults. *Journal of Child and Adolescent Psychiatric Nursing, 23*, 205–213.

Sausa, L. A. (2005). Translating research into practice: Trans youth recommendations for improving school systems. *Journal of Gay and Lesbian Issues in Education, 3*, 15–28.

Savin-Williams, R. C. (2005). *The new gay teenager*. Cambridge, MA: Harvard University Press.

Savin-Williams, R. C., & Diamond, L. (2000). Sexual identity trajectories among sexual minority youths: Gender comparisons. *Archives of Sexual Behavior, 29*, 607–627.

Szalacha, L. (2003). Safer sexual diversity climates: Lessons learned from an evaluation of Massachusetts Safe Schools Program for Gay and Lesbian Students. *American Journal of Education, 110*, 58–88.

Thaler, C., Bermudez, F., & Sommer, S. (2009). Legal advocacy on behalf of transgender and gender non-conforming youth. In G. P. Mallon (Ed.), *Social work practice with transgender and gender variant youth* (2nd ed., pp. 139–162). New York, NY: Routledge. (It is a reference for one of the tables.)

Toomey, R. B., Ryan, C., Diaz, R. M., & Russell, S. (2011). High school gay-straight alliances (GSAs) and young adult well-being: An examination of GSA presence, participation, and perceived effectiveness. *Applied Developmental Science*, *15*, 175–185.

Tully, C. (2000). *Lesbians, gays, and the empowerment perspective*. New York: Columbia University Press.

Walls, N. E., Kane, S. B., & Wisneski, H. (2010). Gay-straight alliances and school experiences of sexual minority youth. *Youth & Society*, *41*, 307–332.

Wilber, S., Ryan, C., & Marksamer, J. (2006). *CWLA best practice guidelines: Serving LGBT youth in out-of-home care*. Washington DC: Child Welfare League of America.

SECTION XII

Resources for Linking the School and Community

Schools often link with the community to improve the education of their students. This section discusses best practices and resources for assessing school and community resources, integrating community services such as health care, and the development of successful transition plans for students.

CHAPTER 64

Mapping a School's Resources to Improve Their Use in Preventing and Ameliorating Problems

Howard S. Adelman Linda Taylor

Getting Started

To function well, every system must fully understand and manage its resources. Mapping is a first and essential step toward these ends, and done properly, it is a major intervention in efforts to enhance systemic effectiveness and change for addressing barriers to learning and teaching.

Schools have a variety of programs and services for students who manifest learning, behavior, and emotional problems. These range from entitlement programs for economically impoverished students, through extra help for low-performing students/schools, to special education interventions. In some places, the resources devoted to such efforts may account for as much as 30% of a school's budget. However, because school improvement initiatives continue to marginalize these "learning supports," the resources are deployed in a fragmented manner. The result is that essential resources often are deployed in redundant and wasteful ways and the overall impact is undermined. And the problem usually is compounded when efforts are made to connect community resources to schools. Given that an effective system of learning supports is fundamental to improving student achievement, greater attention must be paid to using all learning support resources effectively and efficiently (Adelman & Taylor, 1997, 2002, 2006a, 2010; Marx, Wooley, & Northrop, 1998; Rosenblum, DiCecco, Taylor, & Adelman, 1995). This means that school improvement efforts must place a high priority on mapping, analyzing, and managing these resources.

What We Know

Our particular focus here is on clarifying the mapping process. However, it should be emphasized from the outset that mapping is not an end in itself. Mapping provides a basis for resource analyses in order to make informed decisions about resource deployment. Analysis of what is needed, available, and effective provides the foundation for improving cost-efficiency and setting priorities. In a similar fashion, mapping and analyses of a complex or family of schools (e.g., a high school and its feeder middle and elementary schools) provides information for decision making that can lead to strategies for cooperation and integration to enhance intervention effectiveness and garner economies of scale.

In our work, mapping provides the basis for developing a comprehensive, multifaceted, and cohesive system of learning supports. The immediate challenges in such work are to move from piecemeal approaches by coordinating and integrating existing activity and then strengthening such activity. Then, the emphasis is on filling gaps over time. To these ends, resources must be redeployed from poorly conceived activities to enhance the potency of well-conceived programs. At the same time, resources are directed at ensuring programs are in place to reduce unnecessary referrals and to follow through more effectively with necessary referrals. Over time, the challenges are to evolve existing programs so they are more effective and then to enhance resources as needed (e.g., by working with neighboring schools, community resources, volunteers, professionals-in-training, and family engagement). As resources are enhanced, these challenges encompass solving problems related to sharing space and information, building working relationships, adjusting job descriptions, allocating time, and modifying policies (Adelman & Taylor, 2006a, 2006b).

Mapping Resources for Learning Supports

In discussing resource mapping, our concern is with those assets currently at a school or that can be accessed for use by the school to provide support for students who are manifesting learning, behavior, or emotional problems. Such assets are money, personnel, programs, services, material, equipment, facilities, social and human capital, leadership, infrastructure mechanisms, and more. The focus is on detailing first what the school currently has in terms of the resources it directly "owns" and controls and then those it has access to from other schools, the district, and the surrounding community.

Why is it important to map *both* school and community resources? Schools and communities share (a) goals and problems with respect to children, youth, and families; (b) the need to develop cost-effective systems, programs, and services; (c) accountability pressures related to improving outcomes; and (d) the opportunity to improve effectiveness by coordinating and eventually integrating resources to develop a full continuum of systemic interventions (Griffin & Farris, 2010; Houck, 2011).

What We Can Do

Appreciating the importance of resource mapping often creates a desire to accomplish the work quickly. Generally speaking, however, mapping usually is best done in stages and requires constant updating. Thus, most schools will find it convenient to do the easiest forms of mapping first and then build the capacity to do in-depth mapping over a period of months. Similarly, initial analyses and management of resources will focus mostly on detailing what exists with a view to coordinating resource use. Over time, the focus is on spreadsheet-type analyses, priority recommendations, and deploying, redeploying, and braiding resources to enhance cost-effectiveness and fill programmatic gaps. Ultimately, the work can provide the basis for evolving a comprehensive, multifaceted, and cohesive system of learning supports through systemic improvements and changes and enhancing collaborative arrangements.

Who Does It?

Resource mapping can be pursued by almost anyone. Indeed, one individual could accomplish a great deal. No matter how many are involved, the key to doing it effectively is to establish a formal mechanism for ongoing mapping and providing training and support so that it can be done well.

We recommend establishing a resource-oriented team as a prototype mechanism to do resource mapping. At the school level we designate such as a learning supports resource team; for a family of schools (e.g., a feeder pattern) the prototype is designated as a learning supports resource council.

A Resource-Oriented Mechanism for a School. Given that establishing yet another team at a school can be difficult, an existing team can divide its time to encompass the work. For example, a school could expand the role and functions of a case-oriented team (e.g., student study/assistance/success team) or a crisis team to focus on mapping and related resource-oriented functions. Of course, in doing so, care must be taken to keep agendas separate and to include additional stakeholders, such as parents, community, and student representatives, when a resource focus is the agenda. The resource-oriented agenda focuses initially on mapping as a basis for taking charge of school resources used for student and learning supports, weaving these resources into a system, and braiding in community resources to fill gaps related to addressing priority needs. All this is essential to managing and enhancing supports in ways that build a comprehensive, multifaceted, and cohesive system that is fully integrated into school improvement policy and practice.

A Resource-Oriented Mechanism for a Family of Schools. Schools in the same geographic or catchment area have a number of shared concerns, and schools in the feeder pattern often interact with students from the same family. Some school programs and personnel and community resources can be shared by several neighboring schools, thereby minimizing redundancy and reducing costs. A mechanism connecting schools can help ensure cohesive and equitable deployment of resources and also can enhance the pooling of resources to reduce costs. Such a mechanism can be particularly useful for integrating the efforts of high schools, their feeder middle and elementary schools, and community resources. This clearly is important in addressing barriers with those families who have youngsters attending more than one level of schooling in the same cluster. It is neither cost-effective nor good intervention for each school to contact a family separately in instances where several children from a family need special attention. With respect to linking with community resources, a resource-oriented mechanism is especially attractive to community agencies that often do not have the time or personnel to make independent arrangements with every school. Such a mechanism can provide leadership, facilitate communication and connection, and ensure quality improvement across sites. For example, a *Complex Learning Supports Council* might consist of representatives from the high school and its feeder middle and elementary schools. It brings together one to two representatives from each school's resource team along with community representatives.

Resource-oriented mechanisms help (a) coordinate and integrate programs at a school and for a family of schools, (b) identify and meet common needs with respect to guidelines and staff development, and (c) create linkages and collaborations among schools and with community agencies. In this last respect, it can play a special role in community outreach to both create formal working relationships and ensure equity in accessing such resources. Natural starting points for such teams and councils are the sharing of need assessments, resource mapping, analyses, and recommendations for reform and restructuring. An initial focus may be on local, high-priority concerns such as developing prevention programs and safe school plans to address community-school violence.

How to Do It

As noted previously, mapping should be done in stages, starting with a simple task and building over time.

1. A first step is to clarify people/agencies to carry out relevant roles/functions.
2. Next, clarify specific programs, activities, and services (including information on how many students/families can be accommodated).
3. Delineate the systemic mechanisms involved in processing and decision making.
4. Identify the dollars and other related resources (e.g., facilities, equipment) that are being expended from various sources.
5. Collate the various policies that are relevant to the endeavor.

At each stage, develop a set of benchmarks to guide the work. As the information is gathered, establish a computer file. In the later stages, create spreadsheet formats.

Clarify Who's Who and What They Do

One of the first mapping tasks is to develop a list that describes who provides learning supports at the school, including any representatives from community agencies who come to the school. The resulting product spells out names, titles, and general functions. Because many support staff serve several schools, it also clarifies when each individual is at the school. While it seems common sense that every school would have such a list, we find too few do.

Figure 64.1 provides a template for clarifying who's who and what they do. Once the resources are mapped, the product can be widely distributed to stakeholders as an information guide and a "social marketing" tool.

Map All Programs, Activities, and Services

After doing this, the next mapping task is to specify all existing school-based and linked learning support activities that address barriers to learning and teaching, as well as those designed to promote healthy development. This can be done initially as a "laundry list," but as soon as feasible, it needs to be organized into a logical framework. One empirically developed framework is the six areas that have been conceived as the "curriculum" of an enabling component (e.g., see Adelman & Taylor, 1997, 2002, 2006a, 2006b, 2010). These six areas are:

1. Classroom-focused enabling—helping teachers learn and develop an increasingly wide array of strategies for preventing and handling problems in the classroom.
2. Crisis response and prevention—responding to schoolwide crises, minimizing their impact, and developing prevention strategies to reduce the number of schoolwide and personal crises.
3. Support for transitions—facilitating transitions, including welcoming and providing support for new arrivals, before-and after-school activity, articulation in moving to the next level of schooling, transition to and from special education, and transition to postschool life.
4. Home involvement in schooling—facilitating comprehensive home involvement (e.g., to improve student functioning through parent education and instruction in helping with schoolwork; to meet specific parent needs through ESL classes and mutual support groups).
5. Community involvement—facilitating comprehensive volunteer and community involvement—including formal linkages with community-based health and human services, local businesses, and various sources for volunteer recruitment.
6. Student and family assistance—assisting students and families with problems that cannot be handled by the teacher alone (e.g., connecting the student and family with school and community health, human, social, psychological, and special education resources; triage; IEPs; case management).

The Center for Mental Health in Schools at UCLA has developed a set of self-study instruments that delineate many activities related to each of these areas. These provide templates to aid school personnel in mapping the status of current school site activities. Additional instruments are also available for mapping: (a) a school's systems for coordinating and monitoring student and family services and schoolwide activities and (b) school—community partnerships. All these tools are available for downloading at no cost from the centers Web site (http://smhp.psych.ucla.edu). For illustrative purposes, the school—community partnership survey is included in the Tools and Practice Examples section of this chapter.

Delineate the Systemic Mechanisms Involved in Processing and Decision Making

It is essential to clarify the "who, what, and how" of decision making related to allocating and using resources for learning support. This includes decisions about handling specific students; about establishing, maintaining, or ending programs; and about overall budget and space allocations. How many mechanisms are there? How are they connected to each other? Are the decisions made by an individual or a group? If a group, who on the group represents learning supports? Understanding mechanism deficiencies is a key to enhancing practices for specific students and their families (e.g., minimizing inappropriate referrals, providing best practice assistance) and is a critical step in taking action to end the marginalization and fragmentation of learning supports.

How Much Is Being Spent?

By this point, it should be obvious why we say mapping usually will have to be done in stages.

Each staff member is a special resource for each other.A few individuals are highlighted here to underscore some special functions.

School Psychologist:	*Resource and Special Education Teachers:*		
Times at School:	Times at School:		
Provides assessment and testing of students for special services. Counseling for students and parents. Support services for teachers. Prevention, crisis, conflict resolution, program modification for special learning and/or behavioral needs	Provides information on program modifications for students in regular classrooms as well as providing services for special education		
School Nurse:	*Other important resources:*		
Times at School:	*School-Based Crisis Team* (list by name and title)		
Provides immunizations, follow-up, communicable disease control, vision and hearing screening and follow-up, health assessments and referrals, health counseling and information for students and families			
Pupil Services & Attendance Counselor:			
Times at School:	*School Improvement Program Planners*		
Provides a liaison between school and home to maximize school attendance, transition counseling for returnees, enhancing attendance improvement activities			
Social Worker:			
Times at School:	*Community Resources*		
Assists in identifying at-risk students and provides follow-up counseling for students and parents. Refers families for additional services if needed	Providing school-linked or school-based interventions and resources		
Counselor:	Who	What They Do	When
Times at School:			
General and special counseling/guidance services. Consultation with parents and school staff			
Dropout Prevention Program Coordination:			
Times at School			
Coordinates activity designed to promote dropout prevention			
Title I and Bilingual Coordinators:			
Times at School:			
Coordinates categorical programs, provides services to identified Title I students, implements bilingual master plan (supervising the curriculum, testing, and so forth)			

Figure 64.1 Mapping Who's Who at School

After all these tasks has been accomplished, it is time to translate existing efforts into dollar expenditures and create spreadsheet formats. In some schools, the large proportion of students who are not doing well has resulted in learning supports becoming a large percentage of the budget. However, because the actual dollars spent tend to be masked in various ways, decision making and accountability related to learning supports are not a major focus of school improvement planning. Mapping the dollars is a fundamental step in changing all this. It is, of course, just one step. It provides the information for the analyses that clarify how to rethink allocations to improve resource use in preventing and ameliorating problems with the aim of enhancing student achievement.

Support for Transitions

Enhancing school capacity to handle the variety of transition concerns confronting students and their families

Current Programs/Resources

- Welcoming club
- Student peer buddy social support program
- Family peer buddy social support program
- Before school tournaments, enrichment, and recreational activities
- After-school sports, tournaments, enrichment, and recreation activities
- Student job program
- Service learning program
- End-of-year 6-week program conducted by teacher and support staff to prepare students for the next grade
- Articulation programs conducted by support staff to prepare students graduating to secondary schools
- Follow-up monitoring by teachers
- Design a transition program and support staff to identify and assist students who are having difficulty with transition into a new grade or school

Current Committee Members

(Names of those who work regularly to enhance this area of activity throughout the school)

Priorities for Future Development in This Area

- In-service for support staff related to enhancing transition programs
- Recruitment of more volunteers to aid with transition programs
- Preparation of a "Welcome to Our School" video to be shown to all newcomers and visitors—for regular use in the front office or in a special welcoming space implemented by a resource teacher and support staff for students (and their families) entering and returning from special education
- Enhance recess and lunch recreation and enrichment opportunities

Home Involvement in Schooling

Enhancing school capacity to provide those in the home with opportunities for learning, special assistance, and participation

Current Programs/Resources

- Adult education programs at the school and neighborhood
  - ESL
  - Literacy
  - Job skills
  - Child care certification program
  - Citizenship exam preparation classes
  - Parenting and helping their youngster with school work
  - Aerobics/sewing
- Parent participation and parent classes
- Some on-campus family assistance services and assistance in connecting with community services (see Student & Family Assistance)
- Family volunteers staff school welcoming club, assist in the front office, in classrooms, on the yard
- Family–staff picnic
- Training for participation in school governance
- Participation on school advisory and governance bodies
- Regular parent–teacher communications (regular phone and e-mail discussions, in-person conferences on request, monthly newsletter)
- School "beautification" program
- Planning for community involvement

Current Committee Members

(Names of those who work regularly to enhance this area of activity throughout the school)

Priorities for Future Development in this Area

- Enhance outreach programs to engage and reengage family members who are seldom in contact with the school and often are hard to reach
- Establish self-led mutual support groups for families
- Expand opportunities for families to use school facilities during nonschool hours for enrichment and recreation
- Enhance in-service for all staff to increase motivation and capability for enhancing home involvement

Figure 95.2 illustrates examples of two areas, student transitions and family–school involvement, at a school that categorizes its learning support programs based on the six aspects of an enabling component. For examples of other products, see *Resource Mapping and Management to Address Barriers to Learning: An Intervention for Systemic Change* (http://smhp.psych.ucla.edu).

Figure 64.2 Mapping Resources for Student Transitions and Family–School Involvement

Mapping Policies

With all these tasks accomplished, it is time to clarify each of the policies that determine how resources are used. The focus is on policy that positively and/or negatively affects learning support practices at a school and in the surrounding community. Such policy is found in the regulations and guidelines that direct the work. The picture that evolves usually is a set of unconnected regulations and guidelines that were developed in an ad hoc and piecemeal manner. The lack of cohesive policy tends to work against good practice and tends to produce redundancy and waste. In formulating recommendations for enhancing resource use, a policy map helps to identify what is feasible under existing policy, where waivers should be sought, and what should be pursued to enhance policy cohesion.

At this point, it should be evident that mapping resources is, in effect, an intervention for systemic change. By identifying and analyzing existing resources, awareness is heightened about their value in helping students engage and reengage in learning at school. Analyses also can lead to sophisticated recommendations for deploying and redeploying resources to improve programs, enhance cost-effectiveness, and fill programmatic gaps in keeping with priorities. And a focus on these matters often highlights the reality that the school's current infrastructure requires some revamping to ensure that necessary functions are carried out.

The products of mapping activity provide information for analyses and recommendations. They also can be invaluable for "social marketing" efforts designed to inform teachers, parents, and other community stakeholders about all that the school is doing to address barriers to learning and promote healthy development. One example is the document that emerges from mapping who's who and what they do (see Figure 64.1). Another source of such information is the school—community partnerships self-study survey.

Response to Intervention Framework and Mapping

Response to Intervention (RTI) is meant to be broad-based and preventative (Center for Mental Health in Schools, 2011a,b). However, as formulated and practiced the approach often is too limited in how it frames what needs to go on to enable learning, engage students, and keep them engaged. In particular, it pays too little attention to the need to strengthen the classroom and schoolwide context in ways that enhance the effectiveness of RTI and increase equity of opportunity for success at school.

Mapping the entire gamut of school resources encourages a broader understanding of the context for implementing RTI. In turn, this allows for analyses that clarify the limitations of the three-tier intervention pyramid and underscore the importance of moving beyond the three-tier formulation toward a comprehensive classroom and schoolwide system of student and learning supports. Our work designates such a system as an enabling or learning supports component (e.g., Adelman & Taylor, 2006b). Embedded in such a component, the classroom facets of RTI are described as a sequential approach that personalizes instruction, then, if necessary, pursues specialized interventions in a hierarchical manner. Beyond the classroom, RTI-relevant interventions are understood as embedded in the other five of the six-area framework discussed in this chapter.

Tools and Practice Examples

School–Community Partnerships Self-Study Survey

Formal efforts to create school—community partnerships to improve school and neighborhood involve building formal relationships to connect resources involved in preK—12 schooling and resources in the community (including formal and informal organizations, such as the home and agencies involved in providing health and human services, religion, policing, justice, and economic development; organizations that foster youth development, recreation, and enrichment; as well as businesses, unions, governance bodies, and institutions of higher education).

As you work toward enhancing such partnerships, it helps to clarify what you have in place as a basis for determining what needs to be done. You will want to pay special attention to:

- clarifying what resources already are available
- how the resources are organized to work together

- what procedures are in place for enhancing resource usefulness

The following survey is designed as a self-study instrument related to school—community partnerships. Stakeholders can use such surveys to map and analyze the current status of their efforts.

This type of self-study is best done by teams. For example, a group of stakeholders could use the items to discuss how well specific processes and programs are functioning and what is not being done. Members of the team initially might work separately in filling out the items, but the real payoff comes from discussing them as a group. The instrument also can be used as a form of program quality review.

In analyzing the status of their school—community partnerships, the group may decide that some existing activity is not a high priority and that the resources should be redeployed to help establish more important programs. Other activity may be seen as needing to be embellished so that it is effective. Finally, decisions may be made regarding new desired activities, and since not everything can be added at once, priorities and time lines can be established.

I. Overview: Areas for School–Community Partnership

Indicate the status of partnerships between a given school or family of schools and community with respect to each of the following areas.

II. List Current School–Community Partnerships

Make two lists: (1) those focused on improving the school and (2) those focused on improving the neighborhood (through enhancing links with the school, including use of school facilities and resources).

III. School–Community Partnerships to Improve the School

Indicate the status of partnerships between a given school or family of schools and community.

Key Points to Remember

Why Mapping Resources Is So Important

To function well, every system must fully understand and manage its resources. Mapping is a first and essential step toward these ends, and done properly, it is a major intervention in efforts to enhance systemic effectiveness and change for addressing barriers to learning and teaching.

What Are Resources?

Money, personnel, programs, services, material, equipment, real estate, facilities, social and human capital, leadership, infrastructure mechanisms, and more.

What Do We Mean by Mapping and Who Does It?

A representative group of informed stakeholders is asked to undertake the process of identifying those assets currently at a school or that can be accessed for use by the school to provide support for students who are manifesting learning, behavior, or emotional problems. The focus is on detailing first what the school currently has in terms of the resources it directly "owns" and controls and then those it has access to from other schools, the district, and the surrounding community.

Why Mapping Both School and Community Resources Is So Important

Schools and communities share (a) goals and problems with respect to children, youth, and families; (b) the need to develop cost-effective systems, programs, and services; (c) accountability pressures related to improving outcomes; and (d) the opportunity to improve effectiveness by coordinating and eventually integrating resources to develop a full continuum of systemic interventions.

Table 64.1

Please Indicate All Items That Apply	*Yes*	*Yes, but More of This Is Needed*	*No*	*If No, Is This Something You Want?*
A. Improving the school (name of school(s)):				
1. the instructional component of schooling				
2. the governance and management of schooling				
3. financial support for schooling				
4. school-based programs and services to address barriers to learning				
B. Improving the neighborhood (through enhancing linkages with the school, including use of school facilities and resources)				
1. youth development programs				
2. youth and family recreation and enrichment opportunities				
3. physical health services				
4. mental health services				
5. programs to address psychosocial problems				
6. basic living needs services				
7. work/career programs				
8. social services				
9. crime and juvenile justice programs				
10. legal assistance				
11. support for development of neighborhood organizations				
12. economic development programs				

Doing Resource Mapping

Do it in stages (start simple and build over time). Steps include (a) clarifying who's who and what they do, (b) mapping all programs, activities, and services, (c) delineating systemic mechanisms involved in processing and decision making, (d) clarifying how much is being spent, and (e) mapping policies.

What Does This Process Lead To?

Products that can be used for analyses, recommendations, and social marketing.

Resources

Here is a sample of Web sites describing processes and providing tools for mapping school and community resources.

1. *Resource mapping and management to address barriers to learning: An intervention for systemic change. Center for Mental Health in Schools.* http://smhp.psych.ucla.edu

   Discusses the processes and provides a set of self-study surveys designed to aid school staff as they map and analyze their current programs, services, and systems for purposes of developing a comprehensive, multifaceted approach to addressing barriers to learning.

Table 64.2 Overview: System Status for Enhancing School—Community Partnership

Items 1–7 ask what processes are in place. Use the following ratings in responding to these items. DK = don't know; 1 = not yet; 2 = planned; 3 = just recently initiated; 4 = has been functional for a while; 5 = well institutionalized (well established with a commitment to maintenance)						
1. Is there a stated policy for enhancing school—community partnerships (e.g., from the school, community agencies, government bodies)?	DK	1	2	3	4	5
2. Is there a designated leader or leaders for enhancing school—community partnerships?	DK	1	2	3	4	5
3. With respect to each entity involved in the school—community partnerships, have persons been designated as representatives to meet with each other?	DK	1	2	3	4	5
4. Do personnel involved in enhancing school—community partnerships meet regularly as a team to evaluate current status and plan next steps?	DK	1	2	3	4	5
5. Is there a written plan for capacity building related to enhancing the school—community partnerships?	DK	1	2	3	4	5
6. Are there written descriptions available to give all stakeholders regarding current school—community partnerships?	DK	1	2	3	4	5
7. Are there effective processes by which stakeholders learn?						
(a) what is available in the way of programs/services?	DK	1	2	3	4	5
(b) how to access programs/services they need?	DK	1	2	3	4	5
8. In general, how effective are your local efforts to enhance school—community partnerships?	DK	1	2	3	4	5
9. With respect to enhancing school—community partnerships, how effective are each of the following:						
(a) current policy?	DK	1	2	3	4	5
(b) designated leadership?	DK	1	2	3	4	5
(c) designated representatives?	DK	1	2	3	4	5
(d) team monitoring and planning of next steps?	DK	1	2	3	4	5
(e) capacity building efforts?	DK	1	2	3	4	5

2. *Building communities from the inside out.* Asset-Based Community Development Institute: http://www.abcdinstitute.org/

   Uses a "Capacity Inventory," which is an online printable questionnaire that can be presented to citizens of the community to attain their skills and use them in improving the community.

3. *Moving Through Change, Communication, Engaging People in Community, Strategic Thinking.* http://www.ael.org/rel/rural/pdf/mapping.pdf

   Determine what assets are available to help improve local education and quality of life and to help match needs and assets. Includes instructions on generating a community profile.

4. *Asset Mapping: A Powerful Tool for Communities.* Northwest Regional Educational Laboratory. http://www.nwrel.org/nwreport/dec98/article8.html

Table 64.3

Please Indicate All Items That Apply	*Yes*	*Yes, but More of This Is Needed*	*No*	*If No, Is This Something You Want?*
Partnerships to improve				
1. *The instructional component of schooling*				
a. kindergarten readiness programs				
b. tutoring				
c. mentoring				
d. school reform initiatives				
e. homework hotlines				
f. media/technology				
g. career academy programs				
h. adult education, ESL, literacy, citizenship classes				
i. other ___________________				
2. *The governance and management of schooling*				
a. PTA/PTSA				
b. shared leadership				
c. advisory bodies				
d. other ___________________				
3. *Financial support for schooling*				
a. adopt-a-school				
b. grant programs and funded projects				
c. donations/fund raising				
d. other ___________________				
4. *School-based programs and services to address barriers to learning*				
a. student and family assistance programs/services				
b. transition programs				
c. crisis response and prevention programs				
d. home involvement programs				
e. pre-and in-service staff development programs				
f. other ___________________				
Partnerships to improve				
1. *Youth development programs*				
a. home visitation programs				
b. parent education				
c. infant and toddler programs				
d. child care/children's centers/preschool programs				
e. community service programs				
f. public health and safety programs				

(*continued*)

Table 64.3 *(Continued)*

Please Indicate All Items That Apply	*Yes*	*Yes, but More of This Is Needed*	*No*	*If No, Is This Something You Want?*
g. leadership development programs				
h. other ____________________				
2. *Youth and family recreation and enrichment opportunities*				
a. art/music/cultural programs				
b. parks programs				
c. youth clubs				
d. scouts				
e. youth sports leagues				
f. community centers				
g. library programs				
h. faith community activity				
i. camping programs				
j. other ____________________				
3. *Physical health services* a. school-based/linked clinics for primary care				
b. immunization clinics				
c. communicable disease control programs				
d. EPSDT programs				
e. pro bono/volunteer programs				
f. AIDS/HIV programs				
g. asthma programs				
h. pregnant and parenting minors programs				
i. dental services				
j. vision and hearing services				
k. referral facilitation				
l. emergency care				
m. other ____________________				
4. *Mental health services*				
a. school-based/linked clinics w/ mental health component				
b. EPSDT mental health focus				
c. pro bono/volunteer programs				
d. referral facilitation				
e. counseling				
f. crisis hotlines				
e. other ____________________				

(continued)

Table 64.3 *(Continued)*

Please Indicate All Items That Apply	*Yes*	*Yes, but More of This Is Needed*	*No*	*If No, Is This Something You Want?*
5. *Programs to address psychosocial problems*				
a. conflict mediation/resolution				
b. substance abuse				
c. community/school safe havens				
d. safe passages				
e. youth violence prevention				
f. gang alternatives				
g. pregnancy prevention and counseling				
h. case management of programs for high-risk youth				
i. child abuse and domestic violence programs				
j. other ____________________				
6. *Basic living needs services*				
a. food				
b. clothing				
c. housing				
d. transportation				
e. other ____________________				
7. *Work/career program*				
a. job mentoring				
b. job programs and employment opportunities				
c. other: ____________________				
8. *Social services* a. school-based/linked family resource centers				
b. integrated services initiatives				
c. budgeting/financial management counseling				
d. family preservation and support				
e. foster care school transition programs				
f. case management				
g. immigration and cultural transition assistance				
h. language translation				
i. other ____________________				
9. *Crime and juvenile justice programs*				
a. camp returnee programs				
b. children's court liaison				
c. truancy mediation				
d. juvenile diversion programs with school				

(continued)

Table 64.3 *(Continued)*

Please Indicate All Items That Apply	*Yes*	*Yes, but More of This Is Needed*	*No*	*If No, Is This Something You Want?*
e. probation services at school				
f. police protection programs				
g. other ___________________				
10. *Legal assistance*				
a. legal aid programs				
b. other ___________________				
11. *Support for development of neighborhood organizations*				
a. neighborhood protective associations				
b. emergency response planning and implementation				
c. neighborhood coalitions and advocacy groups				
d. volunteer services				
e. welcoming clubs				
f. social support networks				
e. other ___________________				
12. *Economic development programs*				
a. empowerment zones				
b. urban village programs				
c. other ___________________				

This is part of a series of four workbooks to support community education. This workbook shows readers how to approach community development from a positive, creative perspective, one that builds on strengths and resources.

5. *Community Building Resources: Community Capacity Building & Asset Mapping©.* http://www.cbr-aimhigh.com/What_cbr_Does/philosophy.htm

   Designed as a way to animate, connect, and inform citizens and to create an environment in which relationships can build. The asset focus can be a catalyst and a spark for the people to discover, access, and mobilize their unrecognized resources, and it engages people who have not participated in the life of the community.

6. *Building Communities Through Strengths.* The Madii Institute. http://www.madii.org/amhome/amhome.html

   Identify and involve all the capabilities or capacities of a community to create community transformation or to build community self-reliance. Many communities find they have all the resources they have hoped for during the asset mapping process.

7. *A Cultural Path.* The Madii Institute. http://www.madii.org/

   Examines the importance of different aspects of culture in asset mapping. Including cultural knowledge as an asset extends the current asset mapping and other community development models and broadens the possibilities for building community.

8. *Mapping & Analyzing Learning Supports.* http://smhp.psych.ucla.edu/summit2002/tool%20mapping%20current%20status.pdf

   A tool outlining a six-step process to use in mapping resources as a basis for evaluating what is in use, doing a gap analysis, and setting priorities.

9. *Mapping Your School's Resources.* http://michigan.gov/documents/4–5_107261_7.pdf

   Designed to map resources for purposes of identifying gaps, overlaps and duplication of services, programs, and resources and to contribute to strategic planning.

10. *Aligning School & Community Resources.* http://ncset.org/topics/resources/default.asp?topic=0

    Explores how agencies and local communities can align and leverage all the resources communities offer to support young people with disabilities and their families.

11. *Funding Stream Integration to Promote Development and Sustainability of a Comprehensive System of Learning Supports.* http://smhp.psych.ucla.edu/pdfdocs/fundingstream.pdf

    Presents an example from the Louisiana State Department of how schools can integrate multiple funding streams to develop a comprehensive system of learning supports.

Following are some additional resources relevant to mapping school and community.

References

Adelman, H. S., & Taylor, L. (1997). Addressing barriers to learning: Beyond school-linked services and full service schools. *American Journal of Orthopsychiatry, 67,* 408–421.

Adelman, H. S., & Taylor. L. (2002). So you want higher achievement scores? Its time to rethink learning supports. *The State Education Standard* (pp. 52–56). Alexandria, VA: National Association of State Boards of Education.

Adelman, H. S., & Taylor, L. (2006a). *The school leader's guide to student learning supports: New directions for addressing barriers to learning.* Thousand Oaks, CA: Corwin Press.

Adelman, H. S., & Taylor, L. (2006b). *The implementation guide to student learning supports in the classroom and schoolwide: New directions for addressing barriers to learning.* Thousand Oaks, CA: Corwin Press.

Adelman, H. S. & Taylor, L. (2010). Placing prevention into the context of school improvement. In B. Doll, W. Pfohl, & J. Yoons (Eds.). *Handbook of youth prevention science* (pp. 19–44). New York, NY: Routledge.

AED . (2002). *Community youth mapping guide, tool kit, and informational video.* Washington, DC: AED Center for Youth Development and Policy Research.

Bruner, C., Bell, K., Brindis, C., Chang, H., & Scarbrough, W. (1993). *Charting a course: Assessing a community's strengths and needs.* Des Moines, IA: National Center for Service Integration.

Center for Mental Health in Schools. (1995). Addressing barriers to learning: A set of surveys to map what a school has and what it needs. Los Angeles: Author at UCLA. Available online at http://smhp.psych.ucla.edu.

Center for Mental Health in Schools. (1999). *School-community partnerships: A guide.* Los Angeles: Author at UCLA. Retrieved from http://smhp.psych.ucla.edu/pdfdocs/guides/schoolcomm.pdf

Community Building Resources. (2000). *Our book is your book—Thinking about community capacity building and asset mapping* (3rd printing). Edmonton, AB: Author.

Community Technology Center Net (1996). *Startup manual.* Chapter 2: Mapping community resources. Retrieved from http://www.ctcnet.org/what/resources/ctcnetmanual/ch2.pdf

Dedrick, A., Mitchell, G., Miyagawa, M., & Roberts, S. (1997). *From model to reality—Community capacity building and asset mapping. Listen and learn . . . the answers are with communities.* Edmonton, AB: Author.

Dedrick, A., Mitchell, G., & Roberts, S. (1994). *Community capacity building and asset mapping: Model development.* Edmonton, AB: Community Development Caritas.

Dewar, T. (1997). *A guide to evaluating asset based community development: Lessons, challenges & opportunities.* Chicago, IL: ACTA.

Fisher, R., & Kling, J. (1993). *Mobilizing the community.* Newbury Park, CA: Sage Publications.

Griffin, D., & Farris, A. (2010). School counselors and collaboration: Finding resources through community asset mapping. *Professional School Counseling, 13,* 248–256.

Houck, E. A. (2011). Intradistrict resource allocation: Key findings and policy implications. *Education and Urban Society, 43,* 271–295.

Kingsley, G. T., Coulton, C. J., Barndt, M., Sawicki, D. S., & Tatian, P. (1997). *Mapping your community: Using geographic information to strengthen community initiatives.* Washington, DC: U.S. Department of Housing and Urban Development.

Kretzmann, J. P., & McKnight, J. L. (1993). *Building communities from the inside out: A path toward finding and mobilizing a community's assets.* Evanston, IL: Center for Urban Affairs and Policy Research Neighbourhood Innovations Network.

Kretzmann, J. P., & McKnight, J. L. (1996a). *A guide to mapping and mobilizing the economic capacities of local residents.* Chicago, IL: ACTA Publications.

Kretzmann, J. P., & McKnight, J. L. (1996b). *A guide to mapping consumer expenditures and mobilizing consumer expenditure capacities.* Chicago, IL: ACTA Publications.

Kretzmann, J. P., & McKnight, J. L. (1996c). *A guide to mapping local business assets and mobilizing local business capacities.* Chicago, IL: ACTA Publications.

Kretzmann, J. P., & McKnight, J. L. (1997). *A guide to capacity inventories: Mobilizing the community skills of local residents.* Chicago, IL: ACTA Publications.

Kretzmann, J. P., McKnight, J. L., & Sheehan, G., with Green, M., & Puntenney, D. (1997). *A guide to capacity inventories: Mobilizing the community skills of local residents.* Evanston, IL: Institute for Policy Research, Northwestern University.

Marx, E., Wooley, S., & Northrop, D. (1998). *Health is academic.* New York: Teachers College Press.

McKnight, J. L. (1995). *The careless society—Community and its counterfeits.* New York: Harper Collins Publishers.

Mizrahi, T., & Morrison, J. D. (1993). *Community organization and social administration—Advances, trends and emerging principles.* Binghamton, NY: Haworth Press, Inc.

Rosenblum, L., DiCecco, M. B., Taylor, L., & Adelman, H. S. (1995). Upgrading school support programs through collaboration: Resource coordinating teams. *Social Work in Education, 17,* 117–124.

CHAPTER 65

Writing a Contract with a Community Agency for a School-Based Service

Michelle Alvarez ▪ Lynn Bye

Getting Started

This chapter provides guidance for important aspects of contracting for school social work and other mental health services. The chapter begins by highlighting the role of mental health services in schools in a Response to Intervention (RtI) framework, the benefit of supplementing existing specialized instructional personnel (SISP) with contracted mental health services, tips for hiring mental health professionals, and ideas for funding services. The chapter finishes with a discussion of funding for privately contracted services, and sample contracts are provided.

Under the pressure for students to perform at a prescribed level, school districts are now keenly aware that mental health issues impact students' academic success (Adelman & Taylor, 2004). School social work and other mental health services have long fulfilled the role of protecting the right of every child to an education (Argresta, 2004). In order to provide school-based and contracted services in an effective and efficient manner, it is important to explore what we know about the role of community services in a Response to Intervention (RTI) framework to respond to school districts' need to maximize academic outcomes for all students (Agresta, 2004).

What We Know

Benefit of Contracting for Services

As school districts grapple with challenging budget cuts that leave them with limited school-employed school social workers, contracting for services could provide an opportunity to expand the availability of services within the district. In times of financial retrenchment, school districts' shrinking budgets often result in staff cuts and fewer support staff such as school social workers. Due to the tremendous financial pressure school districts face, they may at times need to contract for essential social work services. Regardless of the funding, social workers providing services in the schools are under pressure to show results rather than simply perform services.

Many schools have become centers where families can access multiple school-linked services; however, problems with effective collaboration can arise over turf issues, differences in training/opinions, or when team members feel their expertise was not valued (Roberts, Verrnberg, Biggs, Randall, & Jacobs, 2008). Community partnerships between schools and social service agencies can be an attempt to help families access services without having to go to different agencies that may not understand the culture of the contracting institution (McCroskey, Picus, Yoo, Marsenich, & Robillard, 2004). With outside personnel entering the school, there is a potential for miscommunication (Adelman & Taylor, 2000b). An important role for a school-based school-employed social worker is to serve as a coordinator, keeping the lines of communication open between the different parties.

Hiring Mental Health Professionals

When hiring mental health professionals in schools that already employ school counselors, school social workers, and/or school psychologists, duplication of existing services and related territorial issues may be concerns. Franklin (2001) identified some of these issues and suggests strategies to capitalize on existing resources, such as collaborating with contracted mental health professionals to enhance student academic success. Specifically, Franklin's (2001) recommendations include the following:

- Involve school-employed mental health professionals in the contracting of supplemental mental health services
- Consult with school-employed mental health professionals on the scope of services that should be provided by supplemental mental health professionals so as not to duplicate services provided
- Facilitate the collaboration of services between school-employed and contracted mental health professionals
- Plan for office space and office equipment needs of contracted employees so as not to deplete resources for school-employed mental health professionals
- Ensure that contracted mental health professionals have the credentials necessary to provide the services for which they are contracted.

Funding Mental Health Services in Schools

The national trend is for most of the mental health funding to be "directed" toward "severe, pervasive and/or chronic psychosocial problems" rather than toward prevention (Adelman & Taylor, 2000a, p. 4). The "Contract with America" in the 1990s focused on tax cuts, dismantling social programs, and privatization of public service (Fisher, 2002). More recently there is a movement "toward tying significant portions of public financing for MH and psychosocial concerns to schools" (Adelman & Taylor, 2000a, p. 4). Channeling mental health funding toward schools makes sense, since schools are the major providers of mental health services for children.

The privatization of educational services is defined as "the transfer of public money or assets from the public domain to the private sector" and requires school social workers and related mental health providers to have knowledge and skills related to availability of funds for services and issues related to contracting for services (Fitz & Beers, 2002, p. 137). In privatization, billing issues present a challenge. One form of privatization is contracting services by purchasing them from individuals or businesses outside of the school. For example, school bus services are often contracted with private vendors. Like school bus companies, social workers and other related mental health professionals can contract directly with schools for the provision of specific services. In times of limited education funding, contracting for school social work services to expand services beyond the capacity of the district to employ school social workers can enable the school system to maximize resources through full access to a community agencies menu of services, such as access to mobile dental and health services and eligibility for hospital foundation funds for special projects when contracting with a hospital (personal communication, grant manager, D. Diehl, August 26, 2004). For example, a social worker in St. Cloud, Minnesota, who had a reputation as an excellent group worker, was contracted by the school district to conduct a certain number of social skills groups in specific schools. Faculty within a school often made requests to the school principal to contract with this social worker for a specific group of students.

School districts can work with local mental health agencies to pool resources to fund services. The National Assembly on School-Based Health Care as reported by the Center for Mental Health in Schools at UCLA (2008) notes that "Most SBHCs finance their operations through a diversity of funded sources from by federal, state and local public sector grants, foundations, patient revenue, private/corporate support, and in-kind contributions from school and community agency partners. According to a national survey of SBHCs, the most common sources of grant funding are state government (65%), private foundation (49%), county/city government (33%), corporate (29%), and federal government (28%). Eighty percent of SBHCs bill students" health insurance" (p. 7).

Community mental health agencies and schools are adept at leveraging their own resources to fund services for students. However, it is the collaborative funding efforts that will result in financing for school-based mental health services. Normally, a list of potential funding sources such as federal grants would be listed in this chapter. With the current drastic changes being made to grant opportunities, it is not possible to list these sources. However, it is anticipated that some level of grant funding will be made available, and information on federal grant opportunities is available at www.grants.gov.

What We Can Do

Tips for Developing Contracts

Social workers and other related health professionals interested in developing private contracts with school districts can learn some valuable tips from health providers, who have been offering privately contracted services to schools for the past 30 years. Honore, Simoes, Moonesinghe, Kirbey, and Renner (2004) make the following suggestions for developing contracts:

- Develop mutually agreed upon outcomes between the independent contractor and the hiring agency
- Write expected outcomes into the contract
- Specify when and how the outcomes will be measured
- Identify in writing how the short-term contracted services will help the school accomplish its long-term objectives
- Annually update and negotiate the contract

A sample memoranda of understanding, is available at http://smhp.psych.ucla.edu/pdfdocs/practicenotes/makingmou.pdf.htm, and additional resources provided by the University of California at Los Angeles Center for Mental Health in Schools (personal communication, L. Taylor, September 20, 2004) revealed the following content areas included in agreements between schools and school social workers or other related mental health providers.

- List parties involved in the agreement
- Describe the need for services
- Define the purpose of the agreement, the shared vision, and benefits of collaboration
- List strategies for addressing the needs
- Outline scope and boundaries of services to be provided, areas of collaboration/cooperation
- Specify compensation, work hours, funding options that are in place or will be pursued
- Clarify responsibilities, roles, and authority of all parties
- Describe methods for exchanging information and limits of confidentiality by all parties (e.g., recording, sharing, releases, reports of abuse)
- Identify how compliance with all applicable federal, state, and local laws, rules, regulations, and policies will be achieved
- Identify process for evaluating services provided under this agreement
- Outline a dispute-resolution plan
- Specify an agreement start date, life of the agreement (effective dates), and process for reviewing and updating agreement
- Obtain signatures of official from each party involved in the agreement and date of signature.

Under these general contract headings, it is important to include specifics regarding situations that may be faced during the agreement. Interviews conducted with a school administrator, a school principal, and an agency revealed the following issues that social workers and related mental health professionals who contract with schools would be wise to consider addressing in a written contract.

Contract Issues From a School Administrator's Viewpoint

The school administrators interviewed for this chapter suggest that it is important to include details on the following issues when contracting for services:

- Documentation of credentials of contracted employee (e.g., state-issued professional license, appropriate academic degree, criminal history check)
- Coordination of services provided between school and agency staff (e.g., when coordinated by the principal or a school-employed social worker, workable timeframes and times during the day can be provided for services)
- Evidence-based practices
- Terms for renewal of contract
- Congruence between goals of school and contracted services
- Space where confidential services can be provided with required equipment
- Conditions for termination of specific services
- Liability and indemnification
- Court subpoenas (i.e., who prepares the contracted worker for testimony)
- Use of dual release of information forms
- Familiarity with school district policies (e.g., schools could provide an orientation manual that includes procedures for reporting child abuse)
- Identification of responsibility for day-to-day supervision of contracted employee and handling of performance issues

- Creation of a schedule listing when contracted and volunteer personnel are expected to enter and exit the building for both organizational and security purposes (Diehl, personal communication, August 26, 2004; Johnson, personal communication, September 8, 2004)
- Ensure that the agency and the school district are aware of each other's communication policies, especially regarding media
- Create an awareness about the need for early and continuous sustainability planning to stay viable in the ever-changing funding climate (Bostick, personal communication, July 9, 2011)

Contract Issues From an Agency Staff's Viewpoint

Agency staff interviewed for this chapter identified several issues also addressed by school administrators. Additionally, agency staff identified the following items as important to include when crafting a contract:

- Scope of confidentiality (e.g., under what circumstances and with whom does the contracted school social worker or mental health provider share information?)
- Responsibility for day-to-day supervision of contracted employee and handling of performance issues
- Which party will be billing and for what specific services (Black & Wooten, personal communication, September 2, 2004; Bostick, personal communication, July 9, 2011)

Role of Mental Health Services in Schools in a Response to Intervention Framework

Barrett, Eber, and Weist (2009) note that the simultaneous adoption of parallel research-based practices is occurring in the fields of education and mental health. In schools, Response to Intervention (RTI) and positive behavior interventions and supports (PBIS) are showing good academic outcomes for students (Barrett, Eber, & Weist, 2009). At the same time, Systems of Care and family empowerment are themes in mental health. The common ground for all of these promising practices is the school setting (Barrett, Eber, & Weist, 2009).

Access to mental health services is a problem. In the United States, only 7% to 16% of children with mental health problems receive services for those problems (Maag & Katsiyannis, 2010). School-based mental health services may allow students with no insurance to access help (Amaral, Geierstanger, Soleimanpour, & Brindis, 2011). School-based mental health services have been shown to "attract students with the most serious mental health concerns and can play an important role in meeting needs that might otherwise go unmet" (Amaral, Geierstanger, Soleimanpour, & Brindis, 2011, p. 138).

As school districts implement an RTI framework to address the needs of all students in general education and special education, it is imperative to understand what role school-based mental health services can play in that process. Community mental health agencies can contribute to the success of implementing RTI through shared leadership and collaborative teamwork (Barrett, Eber, & Weist, 2009). At Tier 1 school-wide interventions, school-based mental health practitioners should be trained in the research-based strategies in order to know and participate in the school culture and climate. This provides continuity for students across settings. "School based mental health screening identified a significantly greater proportion of youth to be in clinical need of mental health services than would have likely been identified without screening, and increased rates of referral resulted in greater access to mental health services" (Husky et al., 2011, p. 505).

Tier 1 strategies can be expanded to community agency settings to ehance their effectiveness. At Tier 2, targeted group interventions, school-based mental health services can supplement group interventions provided by school-employed school social workers, school psychologist, and school counselors. As RTI teams identify students that are not responding to Tier 1 interventions, research-based group interventions are matched to the needs of students. Since school-based mental health practitioners can often bill third party insurances for group work, they could provide the team with options for a traditional 50-minute group session that might be beyond the time constraints of school personnel. It is important to coordinate the group interventions provided by school-employed and school-based mental health services to prevent duplication of services. It is also important to train school-based mental health practitioners in progress monitoring and data-based decision making to identify non-responders to the intervention, and obtain all needed consents for services and the sharing of data. If consent is not obtained, school-employed personnel will continue to provide needed services. Finally, at Tier 3, intensive individual interventions, it is consistent with previous experience with school-based mental health practitioners that they are able to provide therapy. However, they will need to be trained in progress monitoring and data collection for a Tier 3 intervention, and consent sought to integrate their findings with that of the school team.

Tools and Practice Examples

Sample Contracts

Although no contract includes all the recommended information identified in this chapter, Figures 65.1 and 65.2 show two examples of contracts that could be used as models for drafting a contract for services.

Resources

Hamilton County Family and Children First Council offer an implementation manual that includes a sample contract: http://www.hamilton-co.org/hcfcfc/Manual_Implement_School_Based.pdf

The National Center for Mental Health Promotion and Youth Violence Prevention provides a sample contract at http://sshs.promoteprevent.org/webfm_send/1083 and other tools to develop sustainable programs at http://sshs.promoteprevent.org/meetings/sessions/project-director-consortia-january-2009/day-1-planning-sustained-mental-health-ser

Sample memorandums of agreements posted by the UCLA School Mental Health Project are listed under "Relevant Documents, Resources and Tools on the Internet": http://smhp.psych.ucla.edu/qf/mou.htm

Financing school-based mental health services for school-based mental health services: http://www.healthinschools.org/Health-in-Schools/Health-Services/School-Based-Mental-Health/Financing.aspx http://rtckids.fmhi.usf.edu/rtcpubs/study04/SBMHchapter6.pdf

Key Points to Remember

This chapter provided information on important aspects of contracting school social workers and other mental health professionals (e.g., school counselors, school psychologists, community mental health professional services). Suggestions for areas that should be addressed in a contract were gleaned from the literature and interviews with school administrators and agency staff. Recommendations gleaned from the information gathered for this chapter include:

- Review existing resources before negotiating a contract (e.g., services currently provided at the school, sample contract formats)
- Coordinate contracted services with school-employed school social workers, counselors, and psychologists
- Utilize school-employed school social workers, school counselors, or school psychologists to facilitate the provision of contracted mental health services in the school
- Work closely with all parties to agree upon a common goal and a common definition of services to be provided
- Ensure that a written MOU or contract is in place to address all issues
- Orient contracted employees to all laws, regulations, and policies of a school setting

Note: Printed with permission from Evansville-Vanderburgh School Corporation.

- Orient contracted employees to all laws, regulations, and policies of a school setting

These steps should lead to a seamless delivery of mental health services in a school setting that positively enhance student learning and academic success.

Figure 65.1 Example Contract

MEMORANDUM OF UNDERSTANDING

Between the Department of Mental Health, Community Services Agency and District of Columbia Public School System

Parties
The Department of Mental Health, Community Services Agency (DMH–CSA), and the District of Columbia Public School System (DCPS), in order to provide prevention, assessment, and treatment services to children and adolescents enrolled in DCPS through a collaborative effort by both parties. A mental health clinician is defined as an employee of the DMH–CSA that is placed in a school to provide prevention, early intervention, and treatment services to students enrolled in the school.

SHARED VISION FOR MENTAL HEALTH IN SCHOOLS
To support a school environment in which all children are emotionally prepared, ready to learn, and able to progress toward productive adulthood.

SHARED MISSION FOR MENTAL HEALTH IN SCHOOLS
To create a child— and family—centered school—based mental health program to include prevention, early intervention and treatment in collaboration with schools, and community—based child and family serving organizations.

FUNCTIONS TO BE CARRIED OUT TO ACHIEVE THE VISION AND MISSION

A. Assessment for initial screening of problems, as well as for diagnosis and intervention planning (including a focus on needs and assets)
B. Referral, triage, and monitoring/management of care
C. Direct service and instruction (including primary prevention programs/activities, early intervention, individual, family, and group counseling, crisis intervention and planning)
D. Coordination, development, and leadership related to school—based programs, services, resources, and systems toward evolving a comprehensive, multifaceted, and integrated continuum of programs and services
E. Consultation, supervision, and in—service instruction with a multidisciplinary focus
F. Enhancing connections with and involvement of home and community resources

STRUCTURE FOR CARRYING OUT THE FUNCTIONS
Referral and Triage Teams. Participating schools will have or will establish an infrastructure for developing and implementing a school mental health program and for providing systemic approaches to prevention, early intervention, and treatment programs (including referral, triage, assessment, and other related interventions). The infrastructure will involve the Teacher Assistance Teams (TATs) or equivalent team with participation from the school principal or a designee, all other mental health clinicians working in the school (both school hired and DMH—CSA clinicians), the school nurse, and any other relevant staff members who would have input in the development of a school—based mental health intervention. Referrals to this team will be structured so that there is one point of entry at each school. The team then reviews the information provided in a timely manner and the most appropriate mental health clinician is assigned. All team members that have regular contact with the identified client will provide feedback on the development of an intervention plan. The clinician assigned to work with a student and his or her family, whether hired by the DMH—CSA or the school, will have responsibility for monitoring services offered and providing periodic progress reports to the TAT consistent with the provisions of the Mental Health Information Act.

Services Will Supplement Existing Programs. The school—based services provided through the DMH—CSA will supplement and not supplant services already in place. This includes mental health services already being provided by the DMH—CSA in various DC public schools. Although all students will have access to prevention activities and targeted students can be referred for early intervention activities, the school—based services provided through the DMH—CSA will not replace treatment services provided through the school for students involved in the special education process.

(continued)

Figure 65.1 *(Continued)*

SPECIFIC ROLE AND FUNCTIONS OF THE MENTAL HEALTH CLINICIAN OF THE DEPARTMENT OF MENTAL HEALTH, COMMUNITY SERVICES AGENCY

The clinician hired by the Department of Mental Health is placed in each participating school to assist in the development of a school mental health program and to provide prevention, early intervention, treatment, and assessment services to children and adolescents enrolled in the school. The clinician will also provide consultation, training, and support to teachers, administrators, and other school staff. Although functioning in a school setting, the clinician is still governed by the Department of Mental Health, Community Services Agency policies and procedures.

WORKING CONDITIONS RELATED TO THE MENTAL HEALTH CLINICIAN

The following are specific matters related to the mutual responsibilities and accountabilities of the clinician and the school in working together.

What DMH—CSA Provides. The Department of Mental Health, Community Services Agency provides supervision and support for mental health clinicians. The DMH—CSA will hire and supervise one or more clinicians who will be placed in participating schools. Each clinician is expected to attend a weekly supervisory and training meeting. The DMH—CSA policy dictates that mental health clinicians are expected to call their supervisors whenever troublesome cases or unusual incidents arise and will file unusual incident reports as required to both the DMH—CSA supervisor and to the Principal of the school to which they are assigned. Should a conflict arise with respect to DMH—CSA policies and procedures, it is the responsibility of the clinician's supervisor to work with the school in resolving the matter.

What the School Provides. For the DMH—CSA clinician to work effectively, the school must provide a private space, a locking filing cabinet, and a dedicated phone line for each clinician assigned to a school. In addition, schools are asked to provide necessary supplies, materials, and allow use of their office equipment so that mental health clinicians can conduct mental health services in ways that would enable them to complete their responsibilities at the school.

DMH—CSA Clinician as a Member of the School Team. Although not a school employee, the mental health clinician is expected to work closely with the school staff, to share nonconfidential and confidential information with the staff as appropriate under the conditions noted below, and to assist staff in responding to behavioral health concerns. Administrative aggregate information, such as the number of students seen, the number and theme of therapeutic groups, and general concerns raised, can be shared in accordance with the Mental Health Information Act, D.C.

Code Section 7—1201.01 *et seq.* Mental health clinicians can acknowledge receipt of a mental health referral and indicate whether that student has been seen. Compliance with a request to share any other information related to a student's treatment would require an appropriate release of information signed by the student. Monthly summary reports of aggregate mental health data will be provided to the principal. Efforts will be made to resolve dilemmas that arise from the legal confidentiality requirements that are in place for the DMH—CSA and the school so that all staff involved with a student can work together in the student's best interest while adhering to mandatory mental health laws.

DC Permits Students to Obtain Mental Health Services Without Parental Consent. The Mental Health Service Delivery Reform Act of 2001 indicates that a clinician may deliver outpatient mental health services and mental health supports to a minor who is voluntarily seeking such services without parental or guardian consent for a period of 90 days if the clinician determines that (1) the minor is knowingly and voluntarily seeking services and (2) the provision of services is clinically indicated for the minor's well—being. At the end of the 90-day period, the clinician will make a new determination that mental health services are voluntary and are clinically indicated. This important feature of DC law allows students to self—refer and to consent to confidential mental health services. Mental health clinicians routinely encourage students to inform and involve their parents in treatment, and concerted effort will be demonstrated in this regard. Schools must to clarify the law in meetings with parents.

(continued)

Figure 65.1 *(Continued)*

Meetings Outside of the School. Mental health clinicians may visit students' homes or community agencies as part of their job without obtaining permission from the school.

Referrals to the Mental Health Clinician. All referrals to mental health clinicians by school staff must be made in the referral format suggested by the Department of Mental Health, Community Services Agency and in a manner consistent with DCPS policy. All schools are requested to convene a team of relevant individuals that meet regularly to review and assign requests for services. The uniform referral process is critical to the Department's service delivery, record keeping, and accountability. All referrals, whether self—referral by the student or by the staff, contain confidential information and cannot be shared or copied without appropriate authorization.

Compensation for Services. According to the District Personnel Manual and the Department of Mental Health, Community Services Agency human resource policies, mental health clinicians cannot be financially compensated by the school for work completed as part of their normal duties.

Hours. The mental health clinicians are responsible for reporting their hours to the Department of Mental Health, Community Services Agency, but should sign in and out of the school if the school requires such a procedure. Mental health clinicians will report their schedules to the school on a monthly basis, and each carries a cell phone provided by the program to assure that they can be reached when out of the building.

Requests for Leave Time. Requests for leave time will be approved by supervisors at the Department of Mental Health, Community Services Agency with consideration given to school schedules and needs. Principals will be informed of this leave in writing.

Program Evaluation Responsibilities. In order to assure that we are having a positive and significant impact on children, youth, and families, the Department will collect information to assess the utilization of services and their quality as a basis for revising and improving the program at regular intervals. School staff (administrators and teachers), families, and students will be asked to participate on a regular basis in these evaluations. In addition, schools will be asked to share school—level data (e.g., attendance records, disciplinary actions, grades) so that we can assess impact on achievement and school behavior. Results will be shared with schools.

LEGAL CONSIDERATIONS

The following are legal requirements to which clinicians must adhere.

Mandatory Reporting Laws. Under D.C. Code 2–135 1, *et seq.* "the following personnel (in their professional or official capacity) must report any known (or) suspected case of child abuse (sexual or physical) or neglect: every physician, psychologist, medical examiner, dentist, chiropractor, registered nurse, licensed practical nurse, person involved in the care and treatment of consumers, law enforcement officer, school official, teacher, social service worker, day care worker, and mental health professional." The statute goes on to warn that "willful failure to make such a report by any of the above—mentioned persons may result in a fine ... and/or imprisonment." Note that school staff members, as well as mental health clinicians, are mandated reporters of child abuse and neglect. Individuals who have contact with a suspected victim of abuse or neglect should make the report within the required period of time. Mental health clinicians will comply with DC statute, Department of Mental Health, Community Services Agency policy, and DCPS policy on procedures for reporting. Clinicians, in accordance with DCPS policy, are expected to inform the school principal of a report.

Mental Health Records Are Confidential and Not Part of the School Record. All mental health clinicians must abide by the Mental Health Information Act, a statute that dictates how information should be shared and with whom. When a record is developed in response to a referral for mental health services and the DMH—CSA mental health clinician assigned to a school provides these services, that record belongs to the Department of Mental Health, Community Services Agency and is not a part of the school record. As such, only those individuals authorized by the Department of Mental Health, Community Services Agency (i.e., a direct clinical supervisor), those who have a written authorization for release of information, or those with a court order can have access to information in these records.

(continued)

Figure 65.1 *(Continued)*

Disclosure of Mental Health Information. The DC Mental Health Information Act states that "except as specifically authorized ... no mental health professional ... shall disclose or permit the disclosure of mental health information to any person" (p. 249) except "on an emergency basis ... if the mental health professional reasonably believes that such disclosure is necessary to initiate or seek emergency hospitalization of the client ... or to otherwise protect the client or another individual from a substantial risk of imminent and serious physical injury" (p. 255). (See also D.C. Code Section 7–1203.03.) A mental health clinician may disclose information with the written authorization of a parent or legal guardian to a school staff employee; however, if disclosure of mental health information is made, that school employee may not disclose said information to any one else without the written authorization of the parent or guardian as required by the Mental Health Information Act.

Release of Mental Health Records Can Be Pursuant to a Court Order. In the District of Columbia a court order *signed by a judge* is required before a mental health record can be released to the courts or court designee. A subpoena is not sufficient for the release of a mental health record. If a court order or a subpoena is served to the "custodian of the records" and they are referring to the mental health records, the mental health clinician will be responsible for following appropriate procedures outlined by the Department of Mental Health, Community Services Agency and complying with the law in regards to this request. The Department requests that the original or a copy of the court order be given to the mental health clinician in order to submit the request for an appropriate release of the record. The mental health clinician will not be allowed to turn over the mental health record immediately, but will need to contact his or her supervisor to apprise her of the situation and then call the Corporation Counsel's office to verify the court order and to discuss procedures for complying with the request.

TERMS OF THE AGREEMENT

This agreement shall be for a period of one year beginning October 1, 2001 and ending September 30, 2002.

TERMINATION CLAUSE

Violation of client's rights as outlined in the Mental Health Information Act or violation of policies or regulations of the Department of Mental Health, Community Services Agency may result in the immediate termination of this memorandum of understanding and subsequent clinical services.

I____

____

(signature of DCPS representative) have read the above and agree to follow the program procedures and expectations as defined herein as a condition of accepting the Department of Mental Health, Community Services Agency's mental health clinician in DC Public Schools. (date)

I____

____

(signature of DMH representative) have read the above and agree to follow the program procedures and expectations as defined herein as a condition of providing mental health services through the Department of Mental Health, Community Services Agency clinician in DC Public Schools.

____(date)

(11/1/01)

Note: Printed with permission from the District of Columbia Public School System. An online version of this contract can be found at http://smhp.psych.ucla.edu/pdfdocs/dcmou.pdf

Figure 65.2 Example Contract

ANCILLARY SERVICES AGREEMENT

THIS ANCILLARY SERVICES AGREEMENT ("Agreement"), made and entered into as of the _____day of __________2004, by and between the EVANSVILLE—VANDERBURGH SCHOOL CORPORATION ("EVSC") and_______________, ("Service Provider"),

WITNESSETH:

WHEREAS, the Service Provider is qualified to provide certain services, which services are more particularly described below; and

WHEREAS, the EVSC and/or students of the EVSC are in need of the Services; and

WHEREAS, the EVSC and the Service Provider wish to form a working relationship to provide the Services, as more specifically provided herein.

NOW,THEREFORE, in consideration of the mutual promises and covenants contained herein, the parties agree as follows:

1. *Services to be Provided.* Service Provider agrees to provide the following services:

____

____

____

2. *Term of Agreement; Renewal.* The term of this agreement shall be effective as of the_____day of__________, 2004, shall continue until the__________of_____, 200__, (the "Initial Term") and shall be automatically renewed for subsequent additional one (1) year terms unless terminated as provided herein.
3. *Termination of Specific Service.* EVSC may, at any time, with or without cause, terminate this Agreement as to any one or more of the Service(s) (as hereinabove defined) to be provided by Service Provider.
4. *Indemnification.* The Service Provider agrees to and shall indemnify and hold harmless the EVSC, its officers, agents, and employees, from and against any and all liability, damage, loss, cost, judgment, award, and expense, including attorney fees, which may accrue to or be incurred or sustained by the EVSC, its officers, agents, and employees, on account of any claim, suit, action, demand, or charge arising from, as a result of, or in any way related to, whether directly or indirectly, (a) the negligence or intentional conduct of the Service Provider or its employees, agents, or representatives, (b) in connection with the performance of services under this Agreement, (c) the conduct, action, or inaction of the Service Provider or its employees, agents, or representatives, or (d) any breach of this Agreement by the Service Provider.
5. *Relationship of Parties.* The parties agree that the relationship between them shall be that of an independent contractor and the agents, employees, or personnel of one party shall not be considered the agents, employees, or personnel of the other.
6. *Liability Insurance.* Service Provider shall carry in its own name, at its own cost, the following insurance or self—insurance (check those that apply):
   _____Comprehensive General Liability Insurance with limits of not less than $1,000,000.00 each occurrence, $3,000,000.00 aggregate.
   _____Workers' Compensation Insurance covering any liability incurred under the Indiana Workers Compensation Act and the Indiana Occupational Disease Act and including not less than $100,000.00 employer's liability insurance.
   _____Professional Liability Insurance with limits of not less than those prescribed for health care providers that are_____, as required by I.C. 27–12–4–1, *et seq.*

(continued)

Figure 65.2 *(Continued)*

_____Automobile Insurance with limits at least $1,000,000.00 Combined Single Liability per occurrence.

7. *Confidentiality.* The Service Provider recognizes that EVSC student records must be kept confidential pursuant to federal and state law and agrees to maintain and preserve such confidentiality at all times.
8. *EVSC Policies.* The Service Provider shall cause all of its agents, employees, or personnel providing services hereunder to observe and comply with all rules, policies, standards and guidelines of the EVSC as may be adopted and amended from time to time by EVSC, including but not limited to procedures for reporting child abuse and neglect and building security issues, in addition to those of the Service Provider.

IN WITNESS WHEREOF, the parties hereto have hereunto set their hands and seals the day and date hereinabove first written and acknowledged the effective date of this Agreement to be the_____day of__________, 2004.

EVANSVILLE-VANDERBURGH SCHOOL CORPORATION
By: ______________________________

Its: *Superintendent*

NAME OF SERVICE PROVIDER

By: ______________________________

Its: ______________________________

1997 ______________________________

Note: Printed with permission from Evansville—Vanderburgh School Corporation.

References

Adelman, H., & Taylor, L. (2000a). *A center brief and fact sheet: Financing mental health for children & adolescents.* Los Angeles: Mental Health in Schools Training and Technical Assistance Center.

Adelman, H., & Taylor, L. (2000b). Promoting mental health in schools in the midst of school reform. *Journal of School Health, 70*(5), 171–178.

Adelman, H. & Taylor, L. (2004). Mental health in schools: A shared agenda. *Emotional & Behavioral Disorders in Youth,* 59–78. Retrieved June 10, 2011 from http://smhp.psych.ucla.edu/publications/48%20Mental%20Health%20in%20Schools.pdf

Agresta, J. (2004). Professional role perceptions of school social workers, psychologists, and counselors. *Children & Schools, 26*(3), 151–163.

Amaral, G., Geierstanger, S., Soleimanpour, S., & Brindis, C. (2011). Mental health characteristics and health-seeking behaviors of adolescent school-based health center users and nonusers. *Journal of School Health, 81*(3), 138–145.

Barrett, S., Eber, L., & Weist, M. (2009). Development of an interconnected systems framework for school mental health. Retrieved June 20, 2011, from http://csmh.umaryland.edu/resources/CSMH/SMH_PBIS%20Framework.pdf

Center for Mental Health in Schools at UCLA. (2008). *A technical assistance sampler on school-based health centers.* Los Angeles, CA: Author.

Fisher, R. (2002). From Henry Street to contracted services: Financing the settlement house. *Journal of Sociology and Social Welfare, 29*(3), 25–27.

Fitz, J., & Beers, B. (2002). Education management organizations and the privatization of public education: A cross-national comparison of the USA and Britain. *Comparative Education, 38*(2), 137–154.

Franklin, C. (2001). Establishing successful relationships with expanded school mental health professionals. *Children & Schools, 23*(4), 194–197.

Honore, P., Simoes, E., Moonesinghe, R., Kirbey, H., & Renner, M. (2004). Applying principles for outcomes-based contracting in a public health program. *Journal of Public Health Management Practice, 10(5),* 451–457.

Husky, M. M., Kaplan, A., McGuire, L., Flynn, L., Chrostowski, C., & Olfson, M. (2011). Identifying adolescents at risk through voluntary school-based mental health screening. *Journal of Adolescence, 34*(3), 505–511.

Kuo, E., Stoep, A. V., McCauley, E., & Kernic, M. A. (2009). Cost-effectiveness of a school-based emotional health screening program. *Journal of School Health, 79*(6), 277–285.

Maag, J. W., & Katsiyannis, A. (2010). School-based mental health services: funding options and issues. *Journal of Disability Policy Studies, 21*(3), 173–180.

McCroskey, J., Picus, L., Yoo, J., Marsenich, L., & Robillard, E. (2004). Show me the money: Estimating public expenditures to improve outcomes for children, families, and communities. *Children & Schools, 26*(3), 165–173.

Roberts, M., Vernberg, E., Biggs, B., Randall, C., & Jacobs, A. (2008). Lessons learned from the intensive mental health program: A school-based, community oriented program for children with serious emotional disturbances. *Journal of Child & Family Studies, 17*(2), 277–289.

Rones, M., & Hoagwood, K. (2000). School-based mental health services: A research review. *Clinical Child and Family Psychology Review, 3*(4), 223–241.

Substance Abuse and Mental Health Services Administration (SAMSHA). (2004). *Comprehensive community mental health services program for children and their families*. Washington, DC: Author. Retrieved October 18, 2004, from http://www.mentalhealth.samhsa.gov/publications/allpubs/CA-0013/default.asp.

U.S. Department of Education (1999). Assistance to states for the education of children with disabilities and the early intervention program for infants and toddlers with disabilities; final regulations. *Federal Register, 64*(48), 12406–12671. Washington, DC: Author.

Walker, H., Stiller, B., Severson, H., Golly, A., & Feil, E. (1994). First step to success: Intervening at the point of school entry to prevent antisocial behavior patterns. *Psychology in the Schools, 35*(3), 259–269.

Walker, H. M., Severson H. H., Feil, E. G., Stiller, B., & Golly, A. (1998). First step to success: Intervening at the point of school entry to prevent antisocial behavior patterns. *Psychology in the Schools, 35*(3), 259–269.

Weist, M. D. (1997). Expanded school mental health services: A national movement in progress. *Advances in Clinical Child Psychology, 19*, 319–352.

CHAPTER 66

Best Practices for Designing and Developing School-Based Health Centers

Julia Graham Lear

Getting Started

Call them school-based health centers, school clinics, or expanded school health services, they represent a relatively recent development in health care at school. In the past 30 years, in almost every state, a handful or more of communities have decided that their children and youth could benefit from the delivery of basic health care at or near school, and frequently the definition of basic care includes emotional and behavioral health services. Because school social workers often have a broad net of connections inside and outside the school, community, social workers may be asked to help plan or lead efforts to create new school-based health centers. This chapter describes important factors to consider during the planning and early implementation phases of such an initiative and suggests key issues to keep in mind as the project moves forward.

What We Know

Some Background

According to the most recent survey, there were about 1909 school clinics and programs across the country in 2007–2008. The centers were found in 46 states plus the District of Columbia, Puerto Rico, and the Virgin Islands (Figure 66.1). Four states did not have school-based health centers: Hawaii, Idaho, North Dakota, and Wyoming.

The centers are located in elementary schools (9.6%), elementary-middle schools (6.8%), middle schools (7.8%), high schools (33%), middle-high schools (4.9%), K–12 schools (17.3%%), and all other schools 20.3%. While the majority of centers are located in urban areas (56.7%), 16.1% are found in suburban areas, and 27.2% in rural communities (Strozer, Juszczak, & Ammerman, 2010).

What Is a School-Based Health Center?

School-based health centers share the following characteristics:

They are located inside the school building or on the school campus. The 2007–2008 National Assembly census reported that 96% are located in the school building, while an additional 3% are located in a separate building on the school campus. As an early architect of school-based health centers, Philip J. Porter once said, "Health services need to be where students can trip over them. Adolescents do not carry appointment books, and school is the only place where they are required to spend time" (Center for Health and Health Care in Schools, 1993).

In most instances, the centers are sponsored by mainstream health organizations. Twenty-eight percent of the school-based centers are sponsored by community health centers, 25% by hospitals, and 15% by local health departments. School districts sponsor 12% of the centers, and the remaining 20% are supported by a mix of other local organizations including universities, mental health agencies, and nonprofits with a variety of purposes (Strozer et al., 2010).

The centers are staffed by licensed health professionals. Students receive care from multidisciplinary teams of professionals, each of whom can address a broad range of problems. A medical assistant supports a nurse practitioner or physician assistant. Mental health services are typically provided by a master's-level social worker. A part-time pediatrician or family practitioner

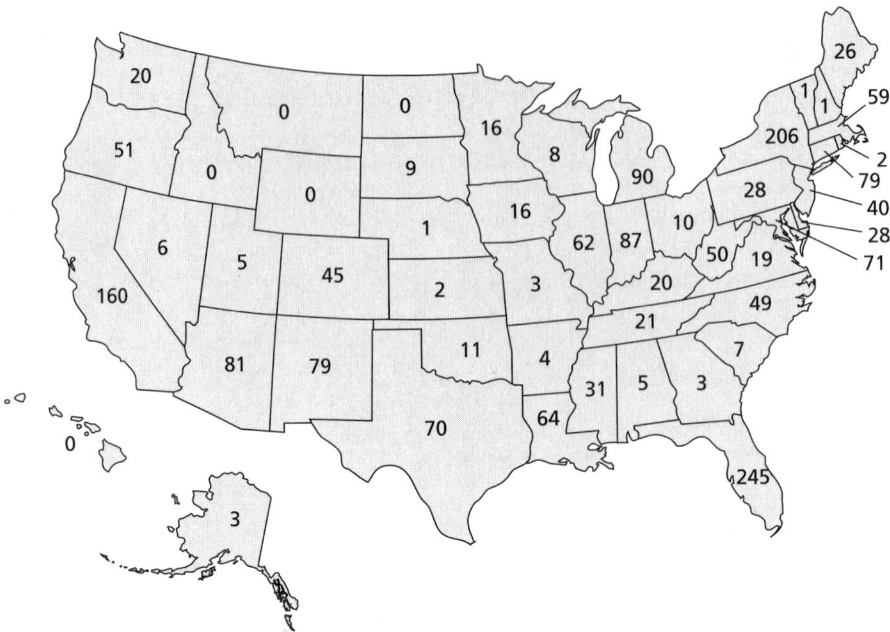

Figure 66.1 National Census School Year 2007–2008

Source: Strozer, J., Juszczak, L., & Ammerman, A. (2010). 2007 – 2008 National School-Based Health Care Census. Washington, DC: National Assembly on School-Based Health Care

and health educator may round out the core staff. Centers also may have a part-time nutritionist, dental hygienist, and substance abuse counselor, depending on the needs of students and the resources available in the community.

School-based health centers provide comprehensive services. From diagnosis and treatment of diseases to counseling for students and families, school-based health centers address a broad spectrum of health problems. The 2007–2008 NASBHC survey of 1226 centers found that leading physical health services included comprehensive health assessments (96.6%), treatment for acute illness (96.1%), prescriptions for medications (96.0%), screenings such as vision and hearing (92.7%), asthma treatment (94.6%), nutrition counseling (90.6%), and immunizations (85%). Mental health providers were employed at 74.6% of the school-based centers. Leading services included crisis intervention (96.2%), referrals (96.1%), mental health assessments (95.9%), screenings (95.4%), grief and loss therapy (94.9%), and brief therapeutic interventions (91.6%). Most centers also provide health promotion and risk reduction strategies and programs. In elementary schools these services include nutrition and fitness counseling (85.2%), injury prevention (78.9%), violence prevention (78.1%), resiliency and social skills building (71.9%), and tobacco prevention (58.6%) (Strozer et al., 2010).

School-based health centers build partnerships with parents. Typically, school-based health centers require written parental consent prior to accepting students as patients. School-based health centers also strive to get parents involved through parent newsletters, family communication seminars, and satisfaction surveys. Centers communicate with parents without compromising the confidential patient–provider relationship that teens desire and expect. Parents are immediately informed about their children's condition and treatment in life-threatening situations. While protecting teens' privacy, staff members also strongly encourage family communication.

School-based health centers build partnerships within their schools. Health centers organize open houses, attend faculty conferences, and conduct school-wide immunization campaigns. Health center staff members meet with principals, assistant principals, teachers, coaches, guidance, and other pupil support personnel, as well as front-office staff. Health center personnel, who frequently are not school district employees, team up with the school's own health staff and with the academic and administrative staff to lead staff workshops on child and adolescent health, organize health fairs, and work in multiple ways to support the school community.

School-based health centers build partnerships with the community. To organize community support, health centers establish advisory councils of parents, students, health care providers, legislators, clergy, and community and business leaders. The councils advise on local needs, help develop health center policies, educate the community about child and adolescent health concerns, and educate local and state officials about the important role health centers have in working with families and communities to support healthy children and teens.

What We Can Do

First Steps

The starting point for a school-based health center may vary considerably from place to place. In some cases, it could be a response to a school crisis; in another, an opportunity may present itself in the form of a new grant program. A center may also be identified as the right response to a long-felt need, or result from the work of a community advocate who puts together the research, political, and funding pieces essential to launch a center. The remarkable thing is that those centers that do get started have a very good chance of surviving—despite ongoing financial and other challenges.

Centers that are well designed and that succeed address the following four questions.

1. *Is there an unmet need?* Documenting unmet need is essential to assure that the center will be busy, demonstrate its use to the community, and generate the funds required to sustain the center in the future. Information about student needs also provides a critical platform on which to build the service program. Limited budgets and space will require that choices be made among the types of providers to be hired, the services to be offered, and the skills or perspectives to be reflected in the staff. A solid needs analysis provides the information necessary to determine whether to move forward with a project and, if so, how to move forward. Needs assessment tools are available for use during this process (Center for Health and Health Care in Schools, 2009).
2. *What do key stakeholders think and how will they be involved in the program?* Establishing a school-based health center is a challenging task. As with other physical and mental health programs in schools, the health center bridges two complex worlds—education and health. Key figures from both must support the initiative. Conversations with school board members, parents, the superintendent, affected principals, influential school staff, and community-based health professionals are essential for understanding their interests and involving them in the ongoing development of the program. Both during the planning phase and after the new center is launched, some of the stakeholders will serve on the health center advisory committee. The advisory committee will be the ongoing political firewall for the health center. Because members will include representatives of elected officials, parents, teachers, and recognized children's advocates, the advisory committee will reflect the community in supporting the centers.
3. *Is space available?* Finding adequate space for a school-based health center can be both a practical and political challenge. Some communities are experiencing rapid growth, and the schools are crowded. A separate facility located on the school campus may be a necessary direction. As a matter of convenience and student safety, many health center veterans argue that the center should be centrally located inside the school—across from the cafeteria or positioned off another well-traveled corridor. First floor space is generally more desirable than upper floors. If a center is to be used by community members or at times when the school is not open, ideally the center will be directly accessible from the outside. In a school with space constraints, it may be difficult to find space not already occupied by others. While principals typically determine space arrangements, health center planners will want to do what they can to assure that their new space does not generate hostility among their school colleagues. That said, securing the school principal's commitment to specific space before a final selection is announced may be a wise course of action.

4. *Are there sufficient funds to support the center, for an initial 4-year time period?* Across the country, community leaders and health professionals have launched school-based health centers with funding from a variety of sources—public funds from city or county budgets, state grant dollars, private foundation grants, and in limited instances, funding from the federal community health center grant program. It is also possible for community organizations to pool resources, blending donated dollars, staffing, and other resources to provide the components of a school-based health center. While there is variety in the sources of funding, it is generally true that it requires several years to complete program design, start up initial operations, and get the center functioning on an even keel. The initial financial plan should ideally provide for 4 years of funding (Center for Health and Health Care in Schools, 2008).

School-Based Health Center Nuts and Bolts

Whether a school-based health center is just starting up or fine-tuning a long-established program, the core components of a successful program include a memorandum of understanding (or memorandum of agreement) between the school district and sponsor of the school-based health center, alignment of health services with students' unmet health needs, staffing to provide the services, a management and training structure, and a realistic budget.

A *memorandum of understanding (MOU)* helps define the mutual responsibilities of the school-based health center and the school or school district. From the perspective of the center, it is important that the school commit to providing space, heat, light, and power as an in-kind contribution. The school may also provide the Internet connection, telephone lines, janitorial services, and/or support for some staff members. For its part, the school may want to clarify the operating hours of the center, who will use the center, and the conditions under which the center may be used. Questions the MOU could answer include: Will teachers be served at the center? Will all students be permitted to use the center? What will be the hours of service, and under what conditions may a student be excused from class to visit the center? Procedures to be used in working out day-to-day problems can also be established in an MOU.

Health services and staffing are central to the success of a school-based health center. The initial determination of student problems that have not been addressed by services in the community lays the groundwork for setting service priorities. If the primary concerns of students attending a local high school are mental health and substance abuse, then it makes sense that the initial hires or service contracts would be in those two arenas. If an elementary school serves a significant number of recent immigrant families, it would be likely that service and staffing decisions would reflect this important aspect of the community. In the main, school-based health centers are staffed with nurse practitioners who can diagnose and treat diseases and clinically trained social workers to screen, assess for, and treat mental and behavioral health problems. A mix of other full- or part-time staff completes the clinic team. They include physicians, nutritionists, nurses, health educators, and health aides. Many schools host at least some health professionals and health educators—either on staff, under contract, or available through volunteer arrangements full- or part-time. Schools, particularly those in large urban school districts, may have an array of health providers. These include school nurses, mental health professionals, substance abuse counselors, and health educators. Who these people are and whether their services are full-time or part-time will have been established during the planning process. Making certain that the school-based health center complements rather than duplicates existing services is vital.

The management and training structure for a school-based health center should take into account that the center is located off-site from its institutional home. From a management perspective, a school-based health center is generally too small to justify a full-time management position. Even if a center operates within a multisite program of four or more centers, the manager will split her or his time among the sites, often maintaining an office at the sponsoring institution. Typically this means that at any one location, day-to-day center management is handled by a senior clinician, either the nurse practitioner or the mental health professional. In addition to providing clinical services, this person assures that clinic policies and protocols are observed, that records are maintained in accord with sponsor policies, and that relationships with school staff and the center advisory committee are attended to. The school-based health center program manager, who provides the interface between the sponsoring institution and the health center, is typically responsible for preparation of annual budgets, tracking revenues and expenses, and conducting long-term planning for the financial future of the organization. This person also tends to the center's important external relationships with parents, the advisory committee, the school board, and any other community leaders with a particular interest in the center.

From a clinical practice and training perspective, there are several implications for offering health services in a location other than within the sponsoring institution. First, the persons who are selected to be the school-based health professionals, whether they are nurse practitioners, nutritionists, clinical social workers, or nurses, will preferably have several years of experience in their own fields. To practice in a satellite facility means to be distant from seasoned professionals and less likely to have easy consults close at hand. Putting inexperienced providers in a school setting deprives them of the opportunity to practice their new skills with the guidance of easily accessible senior staff. A benefit of health center sponsorship by a mainstream health care organization is that these sponsoring organizations frequently maintain a rich array of clinical training opportunities that help the health center staff keep their skills sharp as well as build relationships within the sponsoring organization. Typically these organizations will require that health center staff participate in training on a regular basis.

Persistent Issues

Two issues that are critical in the development of school-based health centers are politics and financing. They must be carefully monitored by health center leaders and advisors.

Politics

When the term *politics* is raised in connection with school-based health centers, the first words likely to occur to the reader are "teen pregnancy" or some other hot-button issue. While proposed school-based health centers may trigger a debate on teen sexuality and whether or how the centers should respond to this matter, in many communities the questions may center on cost, who is in charge, and the role of parents. Whatever the questions raised, however, developing and maintaining a school-based health center requires ongoing attention to political issues at many levels.

At the local level, within the school building, there are critical relationships to be established and maintained with other health professionals, teachers, counselors, and the administrative staff. Long-time school building staff can be a resource for understanding the school's culture and the most effective way to work with students. Outside the school building, within the superintendent's office, the school board, the county commission, the mayor's office, or in the community at large, the health center must cultivate supporters who understand the work of the center and will advocate on its behalf. When seeking support, whether from voters or from local or national elected officials, the most important advocates for the health center will be the students, their parents, and representatives of the community, in that order. Professionals who draw their paycheck from the health center cannot be as persuasive as those who use and value the service.

Strategies to build relationships with state officials and federal representatives include assuring that local representatives have visited the center, have seen firsthand the support it has within the community, and understand what must be done in the state capital or in Washington to sustain the centers. In some states, school-based health centers have benefited from partnering with child advocacy organizations in the state capital. Currently, 19 states have active school-based health center associations (see Box 66.1). The National Assembly on School-Based Health Care is also a good place to learn how to pursue these relationships. Because relationships are built over a period of time, the time to begin is when the project begins.

Financing—Making Sure There Is a Tomorrow

There is no easy road to financing school-based health centers. The very reason they fill a critical need is that they care for children and adolescents who are uninsured, are enrolled in Medicaid or CHIP programs, or need services such as early mental health interventions that are not reimbursed or are reimbursed with difficulty. Thus, the justification for a school-based health center has within it the seeds of ongoing financial struggle. In some states, such as New York, the Medicaid program treats school-based health centers equitably, and the challenge is less. In other states, where

Box 66.1 State SBHC Associations

Arizona	Massachusetts
California	Michigan
Colorado	New Mexico
Connecticut	New York
Florida	North Carolina
Illinois	Ohio
Kentucky	Oregon
Louisiana	Texas
Maine	West Virginia
Maryland	

Medicaid reimbursement rates do not cover the cost of providing care, the challenge is profound.

Studies of school-based health center funding have found that there is a wide range of costs for individual school-based health centers depending on whether the host school is located in a high, medium, or low-cost community and whether the health center offers limited or a full range of services. A report from the state of Oregon reported that SBHC costs for a 9-month year during school year 2006–2007 ranged from $41,000 to $311,250 (Nystrom & Prata, 2008). While individual centers might be primarily funded by a state grant or by city or county resources, studies have found that most centers draw support from a wide range of both public and private resources, grants, and individual insurance reimbursements.

The past 25 years of rapid growth in school-based health centers suggest the following lessons about financing school-based health centers:

- It will always be hard work. Frequently the patients are uninsured or poorly insured. Moreover, the centers often provide important services such as family counseling or teacher consultations that are not covered by health insurance.
- In close-knit, smaller communities such as Wayne County (see below), it is possible to build an extraordinary school-based program using a combination of contributed resources and volunteer professionals. However, these contributions require continued outreach to build the relationships that are the foundation for community giving.
- In complex, urban environments, school-based health center resources may be more conventional: local tax dollars, state and federal grants, as well as United Ways and other private philanthropy.
- Private philanthropy and public dollars may be available to help support SBHCs even if they do not bear the specific title "school-based health center grant program." Funds targeted on children's health services, new immigrant communities, prevention programs, health care for the uninsured, programs to prevent alcohol and substance abuse and teen pregnancy, and initiatives to build school–community partnerships are all potential resources.

Tools and Practice Examples

WISH—Wayne Initiative for School Health

Twenty years ago, Wayne County, North Carolina, had one school nurse to provide professional health services to the 20, 000 students enrolled in this rural school district some 60 miles east of Raleigh. David Tayloe, the head of the largest local pediatrics group in the county, noted that he and his colleagues rarely saw children after they entered the fourth or fifth grade. Concerned about this absence of care, as well as high rates of teen pregnancy and other problems among the community's adolescents, the pediatrician met with officials from a local hospital, the school system, and the health department to discuss how the community might organize an effective response. With the incentive of a grant program available from the Robert Wood Johnson Foundation, this group submitted an application, was successful, and opened centers in two county middle schools. Over the next 8 years, this group of community representatives became an independent non-profit collaborative named the Wayne Initiative for School Health (WISH) and began building a school-based health center network for middle and high schools in the county. By 2012, the total number of clinics had grown to 12, four middle schools and two high schools.

In 1996 when the Wayne County school health collaboration was getting started, state data identified middle school children as having the least access to health care. Parent surveys told them that parents worried about getting basic care for their children, wanted more teen pregnancy prevention, and needed greater access to children's mental health services. Barriers to care were identified as the difficulty the parents experienced in getting time off from work to take their children to the doctor and their lack of health insurance due to high cost. That parents of Wayne County truly wanted their children to have more access to health care has been demonstrated by ongoing high rates of student enrollment in the health centers. At each of the five schools, more than 85% of the children are enrolled in the centers. All students receiving services in the health centers must have a signed parental consent form on file, and parents must come to the center *in person* to enroll their child. These high enrollment rates have continued into 2011.

When the first two centers opened, they provided acute and chronic health services, mental health care, health education, nutrition education, immunizations, and physical examinations. This basic service package has been maintained. A clinic director and medical director oversee the operation of the centers. Each health center has a full-time registered nurse and aide. A group of health educators, mental health counselors, and dietitians rotate among the schools. Mental health professionals, including licensed clinical social workers, are private practice clinicians who sign MOUs with WISH and commit to a specific number of days at the health centers. These MOUs specify that the clinicians must see all students, regardless of insurance status. Clinicians are compensated by insurance payments for Medicaid and privately insured patients.

Funding for the centers remains a challenging but cooperative effort. The school system designed and built generous-sized health center offices that include a waiting room, an enclosed business and registration area, at least two exam rooms, and a room for group health education and other activities. School custodians help keep the clinic clean. The partner agencies contribute staffing and supplies. The students contribute pocket change to the "WISHing Well" and raise more than $1, 000 annually to support the center. Reimbursement for patient services is received for students enrolled in public or private health insurance plans. The four health centers that meet stringent credentialing criteria established by the state are permitted to see Medicaid-enrolled children without securing prior approval from the children's medical homes. In 2010, Blue Cross Blue Shield of North Carolina (BCBSNC) began reimbursing school-based office visits, screenings, and vaccinations for students aged 5–17 who are covered by a BCBSNC plan. The insurer intends to evaluate additional school-based health centers for inclusion in its provider network (Komives, 2010).

Program performance from a community perspective is monitored through multiple satisfaction surveys. Parents, teachers, and students are all surveyed for their views on whether the school-based health centers are meeting their needs.

Denver Health School-Based Health Center Program

Denver Health's school-based health center program celebrates its 25th anniversary in 2012. Like the Wayne Initiative for School Health, Denver's first two school-based health centers also started with a grant from the Robert Wood Johnson Foundation—but 10 years earlier, in 1987. Under the leadership of the Denver Children's Hospital, the program launched clinics in Lincoln and East high schools with full-time nurse practitioners and master's-prepared mental health professionals at all sites. In contrast to Wayne County, many of these students had community-based health providers to whom they turned for annual physical exams and routine medical services. A study conducted after 10 years of operation, however, documented that when students were concerned about confidentiality, they were more likely to use the school-based health centers. As the study report noted, the school-based health centers were the students' primary source of mental health care and reproductive health services. The centers appeared to be the *only* source for substance abuse interventions and treatment. The Denver school-based health centers on average enroll 92% of the students at their schools.

As grant funds diminished, Denver Health, the city's safety-net provider that included a 400-bed hospital, the public health department, and a network of community health centers, assumed responsibility for the school-based health centers. Because Denver Health receives substantial state funding for care to uninsured and low-income people in Colorado and because Denver Health, as a federally qualified health center, is entitled to receive cost-based reimbursement for care provided to Medicaid beneficiaries, the organization has a stronger financial base with which to support the school health centers.

With the transfer of program sponsorship, the network of centers began to expand. As of 2011, there were school-based health centers operating in four middle, two middle-high, and seven high schools. Almost 9,000 students receive services through the clinics annually. The health centers provide basic medical care, health education, and mental health care. School health center team members include advanced care providers (nurse practitioners, physician assistants, and physicians), medical assistants, mental health providers, health education specialists, insurance outreach workers, and Denver Public Schools school nurses (Denver Health, 2011).

In addition to routine clinical care, health center staffers organize a variety of programs for students, including immunization initiatives, insurance outreach and enrollment, vision and hearing screening, preventive oral health screening, asthma management, and case management of sexually active and pregnant teens.

Even with a solid financial base, Denver Health commits significant time to securing funding for its centers. Funding comes from diverse sources, including state and federal grants, patient care revenues, and key private funders such as the Colorado Health Foundation. Similarly critical in-kind contributions come from the Denver Public Schools, the Mental Health Corporation of Denver, St. Anthony's Hospital, and Arapahoe House substance abuse programs.

Key Points to Remember

The melding of primary care, mental health, and health education in one location within a school building has proven a powerful model for addressing the health needs of children but a challenging model to fund. The simplest part of starting a school-based health center will be organizing the clinical practice, arranging the staffing, and securing adequate space. The biggest job will be developing both a strong political base of support and building a network of potential donors. The first steps in that direction will include organizing stakeholders at the school building, school district, community, and state levels and making the personal connections and collaborative relationships that result in a team of people committed to the long-term success of the center.

Resources

Individuals and communities seeking to develop school-based health centers will find these organizations and Web sites of considerable help:

1. The National Assembly on School-Based Health Care (NASBHC), the national advocacy organization for school-based health centers, maintains a Web site, www.nasbhc.org, with how-to guides on starting a center. NASBHC is a critical resource for guidance in developing stakeholder networks and making the school-based health center case to local, state, and federal policymakers.
2. The 19 state school-based health center organizations (see the Box 66.1) have developed Web sites and resources that offer state-specific information.
3. The Center for Health and Health Care in Schools (CHHCS) located at the School of Public Health and Health Services at the George Washington University Medical Center also sponsors a Web site, www.healthinschools.org, with current information on funding resources, as well as extensive materials on school-based health services, school-based health centers, school-based mental health services, and school-based oral health care.

References

Center for Health and Health Care in Schools. (1993). *The answer is at school*. The George Washington University Medical Center.

Center for Health and Health Care in Schools (2008). *Financing options*. Retrieved July 15, 2011, from http://www.healthinschools.org/Consulting/Colorado-Health-Foundation-Consulting.aspx

Center for Health and Health Care in Schools. (2009). *Financing options for school-based health centers*. Retrieved July 15, 2011, from http://www.healthinschools.org/~/media/Colorado%20Health%20Foundation%20Final%20Products/TCHF_Final_Financing_Options_3_09.ashx

Center for Health and Health Care in Schools. (2009). *School-based health care initiative readiness assessment.* Retrieved July 14, 2011, from http://www.healthinschools.org/~/media/Colorado%20Health%20Foundation%20Final%20Products/Readiness_Assessment_100609_with_Appendix.ashx

Denver Health. (2011). *Denver school-based health centers annual report 2009–2010.* Retrieved July 17, 2011, from http://denverhealth.org/LinkClick.aspx?fileticket=H9a4H0jORDA%3d&tabid=178&mid=8081

Gomives, G. (2010). *Letter to the editor. N C Med J., 71,* 598.

Nystrom, R. J., & Prata, A. (2008). Planning and sustaining a school-based health center: Cost and revenue findings from Oregon. *Public Health Reports, 123*(6), 751–760.

Strozer, J., Juszczak, L., & Ammerman, A. (2010). *2007–2008 National school-based health care census.* Washington, DC: National Assembly on School-Based Health Care. Retrieved July 13, 2011, from http://www.nasbhc.org/site/c.jsJPKWPFJrH/b.2716675/k.9D3E/EQ_National_Data.htm

Video corresponding to this chapter can be found at http://www.oup.com/us/schoolsourcebook

CHAPTER 67

Transition Planning for Students with Autism and Other Intellectual Disabilities

Paul K. Cavanagh • Ernst O. VanBergeijk

Getting Started

Public education is a means by which our children are prepared to participate in our national and global economy. However, students with autism and other intellectual disabilities are ill-prepared for participating in the economy. A well-formulated transition plan can help students on the autism spectrum and students with other intellectual disabilities move from the secondary school environment to either postsecondary education, or job training, or directly to the world of work and independent living. Transition planning for students with autism and other intellectual disabilities should be based upon data concerning projected job openings, direct training using empirically based techniques, and data from the student's own individualized evaluation and assessments. Students on the autism spectrum have unique needs that extend beyond traditional education. This chapter will review the current employment rates for people with autism and other intellectual disabilities, explore the projected job openings, discuss the existing and new legislative mandates to help students with intellectual disabilities transition to life after high school, and identify models of intervention with this population. The nature of their disability profoundly affects their ability to navigate the social aspects of the world. Their transition plans will need to include social, independent living, and vocational skills goals that address their underlying social disability in order to successfully transition them into being contributing participants in our economy.

What We Know about the Mental Health or Social Problem

The United States is in the midst of the second greatest economic downturn since the Great Depression. The current national unemployment rate hovers between 9% and 10% (U.S. Department of Labor, 2011). Many parents of children with disabilities lament that their children are "The last hired: First, fired." There is actually some empirical support for this claim. The nation is considered to be at full employment when the unemployment rate is near 5%. A 2000 Harris poll (when the nation was considered to be at full employment) found that 66% of individuals with disabilities who wanted to work could not find employment (Wehman, 2001). The poll, however, did not distinguish between individuals with physical and intellectual disabilities. The rate of unemployment for individuals on the autism spectrum is thought to exceed 90% (Gerhardt, 2009). Without specific intervention, individuals with autism and other intellectual disabilities face lifetime unemployment. They will consequently need to be financially supported by their families and/or the government for their entire lives.

According to the National Center for Education Statistics (2011), the data are only slightly less daunting. In 2009, only 44% of students with an educational label of "autism" had ever been enrolled in postsecondary education in the past eight years. Currently, only 14% of students with an educational label of autism were enrolled in any postsecondary educational institution during 2009. NCES contends that 24% of students with an educational label of autism were employed in 2009 in competitive employment. Sadly, NCES found that only 7.1% of the students labeled with autism were living independently in 2009. These data have significant implications for transition planning.

Part of transition planning for individuals on the autism spectrum and those with other intellectual disabilities involves immersing oneself in data concerning employment rates and trends and synthesizing projected job openings; educational and vocational training requirements for those jobs; and the unique strengths, skill sets, interests, and deficits of an individual student. An excellent starting point for assessing the economic landscape is the U.S. Department of Labor, Bureau of Labor Statistics (BLS) Web site (http://www.bls.gov/home.htm). The BLS publishes the *Occupational Outlook Quarterly*, which analyzes the latest census and BLS data to project job openings and trends in employment.

An overarching rule of thumb to keep in mind when conducting transition planning is that "every additional level of education completed leads to increased earnings and lower rates of unemployment. And the largest earnings increase, 42%, comes with earning a high school diploma" (Liming & Wolf, 2008, p. 5). Not all students on the autism spectrum will be capable of completing an associate or bachelor's degree. For those students who are uninterested or unable to pursue a degree, postsecondary vocational training certificates should be considered and highly encouraged. However, students with disabilities who can complete a bachelor's degree are employed at a rate comparable to their nondisabled peers (Wehman, 2001).

The balancing act when writing a transition plan with a student on the autism spectrum is being able to negotiate realistic goals and outcomes with parental expectations, hopes, and dreams. They are "otherwise qualified" to attend college intellectually. The academic work of college is not the impediment to obtaining a degree. It is their impairment in the ability to decode and navigate through the social realm of college and their deficits in executive functioning that prevent them from earning a degree. Many parents and students do not understand this dilemma and are averse to considering vocational training. This is unfortunate. However, some parents and students are receptive to analyzing data in the formulation of a transition plan. For these families, directing them to the BLS Web site can be helpful in planning. According to the BLS, the occupations with largest number of total job openings (not requiring a college degree), 2006–2016, are predominantly in the service sector (see Table 67.1).

The occupations with the largest number of net job openings also mirror the occupations with largest employment growth (not requiring college degree), 2006–2016 (see Table 67.2), and the fastest growing occupations (not requiring college degree), 2006–2016 (see Table 67.3), in the sense that the occupations with the largest employment growth and fastest growing occupations are also in the service sector. Most of these jobs put students on the autism spectrum at a distinct disadvantage because many of these jobs require interacting with the public and good social skills. A student

Table 67.1 Occupations With Largest Number of Total Job Openings (not requiring college degree), 2006–2016

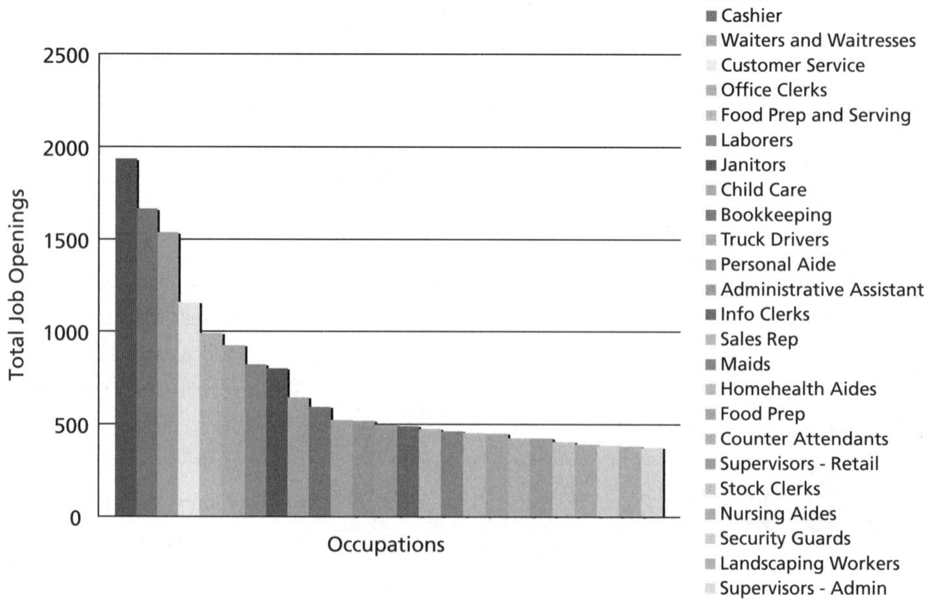

Table 67.2 Occupations With largest Employment Growth (not requiring college degree), 2006–2016

Number Change (2006-2016)

600
500
400
300
200
100
0

Occupations

- Retail
- Customer Service
- Food Prep and Serving
- Office Clerk
- Personal Aide
- Home Health Aide
- Janitor
- Nursing Aide
- Bookkeeping
- Waiters and Waitresses
- Child Care
- Administrative Assistant
- Landscaping
- Info Clerk
- Truck Driver
- Maid
- Security Guard
- Carpenters
- Medical Assistants
- Maintenance/Repair
- Food Prep
- Teacher Assistant

on the autism spectrum has a primary disability that is social in nature.

The fields of elder care and health care are the two fields where the most job growth is expected in the near future. Aside from personal aide and home health care aide positions, physical therapy and occupational therapy assistants will be in high demand. These occupations will require associate degree level training. However, physical therapy and occupational therapy aides will also be in high demand and require some vocational or on-the-job training. In addition, students with clerical skills will be in high demand in the health care and elder care fields in the medical records departments. Data entry positions are often excellent jobs for students on the spectrum because these positions do not require heavy reliance upon social skills and draw upon the strengths of a student with an autism spectrum disorder (ASD), namely his or her ability to tolerate routine tasks

Table 67.3 Fastest Growing Occupations (not requiring college degree), 2006–2016

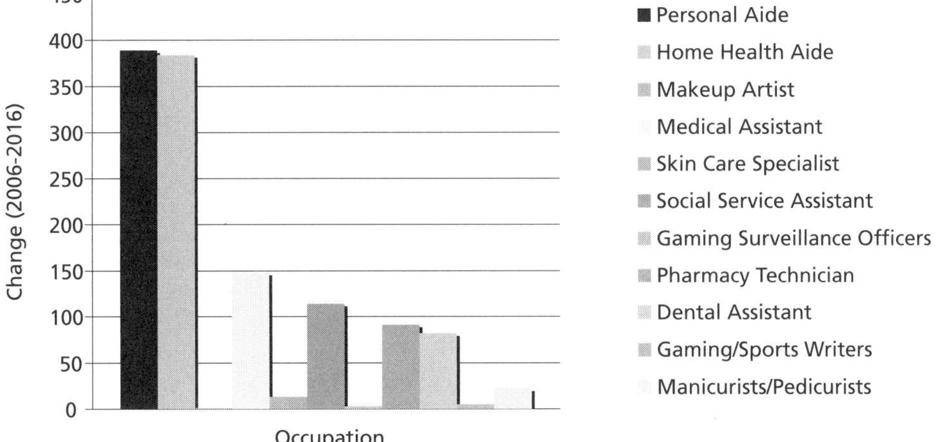

and keen attention to detail. In fact, some employers contend that their employees with ASDs who do data entry have higher degrees of accuracy and make fewer mistakes than their neurotypical peers (Bennett, 2009).

What We Can Do

School personnel who are a part of an Individualized Educational Plan (IEP) team that is responsible for writing a transition plan for a student on the autism spectrum should not only familiarize themselves with the unique qualities and deficits students with ASDs have but, as a best practice, they should also have intimate working knowledge of the relevant federal laws, policies, and programs. A complete analysis of those laws, policies, and programs is beyond the scope of this chapter. However, school personnel should have working knowledge of several laws in order to be effective (see Table 67.4). School personnel involved in transition planning should also have working knowledge their state office and local office of Vocational and Rehabilitative Services and what role they can play in a student's transition plan. This section will focus primarily upon IDEA and the Higher Education Opportunity Act of 2008.

The Education for All Handicapped Children Act (P.L. 94–142) was later reauthorized as the Individuals with Disabilities Education Act (IDEA; P.L. 101–476). Not only did IDEA change our nomenclature to person-first language, but it also introduced the concept of transition and transition services. The transition services were mandated to be a part of the student's IEP beginning at age 16 (Wright & Wright, 2000). The IEP is the blueprint or roadmap by which educators and parents help a child with a disability "prepare for employment and independent living" (Wehman, 2001, p. 9). Subsequent reauthorization of IDEA (IDEA 1997, P.L. 105–17) lowered the age at which transition goals had to be written in the IEP to age 14. From the beginning of IDEA, it is clear that special education and related services must focus upon preparing students with disabilities for employment and independent living, not solely the remediation of academic deficits and the passing of standardized tests. Beginning in 1990, IDEA also clearly established that the transition services may be provided by the educational agency OR by agencies outside of the school.

Table 67.4 Relevant Laws Related to Providing Educational Service to Students with ASD

Family Education Rights Privacy Act (FERPA) of 1974
P.L. 94–142 Education for All Handicapped Children Act of 1975
Americans with Disabilities Act (ADA) of 1990
Individuals with Disabilities Education Act (IDEA)of 1997
Individuals with Disabilities Education Improvement Act (IDEIA) of 2004
Higher Education Opportunity Act (HEOA) of 2008

When IDEA was reauthorized by Congress in 2004 it was renamed the Individuals with Disabilities Education Improvement Act of 2004 (IDEIA; P.L. 108–446) (Wright & Wright, 2006). IDEIA 2004 clarified and reiterated a number of key points. First, it defined transition services (see Table 67.5:). Second, it put to rest the debate of whether or not schools could use monies under IDEA to fund transition programs, even those on college campuses. During the public commentary period, before the passage of IDEIA, advocates asked lawmakers and the U.S. Department of Education to make explicit the ability of schools to fund transition programs, even those on college campuses. Their response makes it perfectly clear that schools can, in fact, fund transition plans that are either community based or a part of a college program (*Code of Federal Regulations Parts 300 and 301, 2006*) (see Table 67.6). Third, IDEIA 2004 reaffirmed the role of the student as a part of the IEP team and a critical constituent in the development of transition plans and postsecondary goals (see Table 67.7).

The participation of the special education student in the transition planning process is not to be taken lightly or its importance underestimated. Students with ASDs can have extreme difficulty with transitions. Once they reach a college environment they are over 18 years of age. Generally, they have also graduated from high school. Consequently, the nature of the communication with the educational organization changes drastically. Under Family Education Rights Privacy Act (FERPA), parents of the special education student who is "otherwise qualified" to attend

Table 67.5 Individuals with Disabilities Education Improvement Act (IDEIA) of 2004 (P.L. 108–446) definition of transition services

The term "transition services" means:
a coordinated set of activities for a child with a disability that—
(A) is designed to be within a results- oriented process,
- that is focused on improving the academic and functional achievement of the child with a disability to
  - facilitate the child's movement from school to post-school activities, including
    - postsecondary education,
    - vocational education,
    - integrated employment (including supported employment),
    - continuing and adult education,
    - adult services,
    - independent living, or
    - community participation.

(B) is based on the individual child's needs,
- taking into account the child's
  - strengths,
  - preferences, and
  - interests; and

(C) includes
- instruction,
- related services,
- community experiences,
- the development of employment and other post-school adult living objectives, and,
- when appropriate, acquisition of daily living skills and functional vocational evaluation.

college become "third-party entities." FERPA prohibits colleges and universities from disclosing information about a student to third-party entities. Furthermore, if a special education student has received his or her diploma, then his or her protections under IDEA have ended. While protected by IDEA, special education students' education is a right. Advocacy under IDEA is also generally parent-driven. The Americans with Disabilities Act (ADA) protects students from discrimination in colleges and universities. Under the ADA the student with disabilities must be "otherwise qualified" to attend the college. The college or university may not discriminate against an individual with a disability or deny them the privileges and benefits to which he or she is entitled solely on the basis of

Table 67.6 Ability of Schools to Fund Transition programs

Comment: A few commenters recommended that the regulations clarify that schools can use funds provided under Part B of the Act to support children in transitional programs on college campuses and in community-based settings.

Discussion: We do not believe that the clarification requested by the commenters is necessary to add to the regulations because, as with all special education and related services, it is up to each child's IEP Team to determine the special education and related services that are needed to meet each child's unique needs in order for the child to receive FAPE. Therefore, if a child's IEP Team determines that a child's needs can best be met through participation in transitional programs on college campuses or in community-based settings, and includes such services on the child's IEP, funds provided under Part B of the Act may be used for this purpose.

Source: 34 CFR Parts 300 and 301 Assistance to States for the Education of Children With Disabilities and Preschool Grants for Children With Disabilities; Final Rule (page 130)

Table 67.7 IDEIA Transition Services Participants requirements

(b) Transition services participants.

(1) In accordance with paragraph (a) (7) of this section, the public agency must invite a child with a disability to attend the child's IEP Team meeting if a purpose of the meeting will be the consideration of the postsecondary goals for the child and the transition services needed to assist the child in reaching those goals under § 300.320(b).

(2) If the child does not attend the IEP Team meeting, the public agency must take other steps to ensure that the child's preferences and interests are considered.

Source: 34 CFR Parts 300 and 301 Assistance to States for the Education of Children With Disabilities and Preschool Grants for Children With Disabilities; Final Rule (page 250)

his or her disability. Now, it is incumbent upon the student with the disability to self- identify and ask the office of disability services at the college for reasonable accommodations under the ADA. There is a perceptual shift from education being a right under IDEA to education being a privilege under ADA. There is a logistical shift during this transition from the parents being the providers of documentation of disability and chief advocates to the student with the disability being in this role.

It is a best practice for a student with an ASD to participate in the transition plans as a member of the IEP team beginning at age 14. The student with the ASD must be able to articulate his or her educational label and medical diagnosis; what the areas are in which he or she has the most difficulty; by what means he or she learns best; and what reasonable accommodations he or she will need in the postsecondary educational environment and later the employment environment. Part of the transition plan may include identifying when, where, and how to disclose the ASD and how to ask for reasonable accommodations. Role-plays with repeated practice are indicated for this population, who may have problems with social interactions. Having the student know the specifics of his or her ASD and practicing self-identification is empirically supported. Only one-half of students with disabilities who are "otherwise qualified" to attend college self-identify and receive reasonable accommodations from a college office of disabled student services. The vast majority of students, who do self-identify for accommodations under the ADA, have a physical disability. Students on the autism spectrum are at high risk of not self-identifying and, consequently, not receiving supports and dropping out of college.

Table 67.8 Key Components of CTPs & Transition Programs in General

- A curriculum & advising system specifically designed to address the needs of students with Intellectual Disabilities (ID)
- At least 51% of students' with ID time spent with neurotypical population
- Supported employment & work skills training
- Adult life skills training (e.g., financial management, grocery shopping, laundry, and home maintenance)
- Social and personal relationships counseling and training
- Encouraged social involvement in the community

The second important piece of legislation school personnel should be aware of when working with students on the autism spectrum or other intellectual disabilities is the Higher Education Opportunity Act of 2008 (P.L. 110–315). Title IV of this act governs student financial aid. Prior to 2008, only students who were enrolled in a degree-bearing program full-time at an approved institution of higher education could apply for federal student aid. Beginning in 2010, the U.S. Department of Education accepted applications from colleges and universities to have their Comprehensive Transition and Postsecondary (CTP) programs for students with Intellectual Disabilities (ID) receive approval and formal recognition. School personnel who are helping to write the transition plan should inform students and their families of this development. Now, students with an ID (broadly defined) can receive federal financial aid in the form of grants and student work-study monies as long as they are enrolled in a federally approved CTP program. As of this writing, students with ID are not eligible for federal student loan programs. Thinkcollege.net is the federal repository of the complete listing of approved

CTP programs. For more information about CTP eligibility requirements please visit http://studentaid.ed.gov/eligibility/intellectual-disabilities

When writing a transition plan, a helpful strategy is to envision the student with an ASD in the future and what his or her ultimate goals are. Planning should encompass his or her education, independent living, social skills, and employment and work backward from that point. Gerhardt (2009) provides a useful conceptualization of this process. The notion is to determine the level of community integration of the student with an ASD as a function of his or her day or employment program model (see Figure 67.1—Degree of expected community integration as a function of day or employment program model). Members of the IEP team must think of each and every step along the way to help a student reach competitive employment and full community integration if that is the goal for a higher-functioning individual on the spectrum.

An accurate assessment of the student's strengths, aptitudes, and interests as well as areas of deficits must be obtained prior to implementing the transition plan. The diagnosis and assessment of a student with a potential ASD is difficult and should be conducted by a multidisciplinary team familiar with ASDs (VanBergeijk & Shtayermman, 2005). The Vineland Adaptive Behavior Scales provide a global assessment of an individual's functioning in five different domains including communication, self-care, fine motor skills, gross motor skills, and communal living (VanBergeijk, Klin, & Volkmar, 2011). This empirically validated tool can be used to determine areas in which the IEP team must intervene prior to reaching the ultimate goals of the transition plan. Next, an assessment of prevocational and vocational skills should be conducted with an attempt to match these with the student's aptitudes and interests. A comprehensive assessment should include a travel training assessment. The lack of reliable transportation is a major barrier to employment for people with disabilities. Therefore, students with ASDs should be assessed and possibly trained to either drive a car (which is quite difficult for people with ASDs) or use public transportation. The assessment and training should not only be conducted on fixed route methods but should also involve variable route training and contingency management. Assessment and subsequent intervention should also involve independent living skills in the areas of money management, time management, laundry skills, and organization of the student's living space. Successful mastery of these skills will be essential to the student's ability to negotiate postsecondary education and training as well as independent living in the community (VanBergeijk, Klin, & Volkmar, 2008).

Once a global assessment of the student has been made, the IEP team must determine how best to proceed in fulfilling the transition plan goals. The options are (1) continue educating the student within the school district, (2) have the student pursue a postsecondary vocational certificate and work with the State Office of Vocational and Rehabilitative Services as well as potentially working with the State Office of Developmental

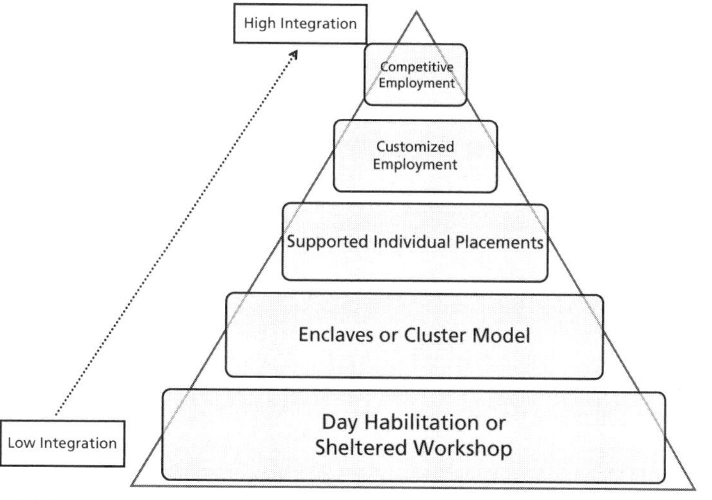

Gerhardt, P.F. (2009). The current state of services for adults with autism. Organization for Autism Research. Presented at the advancing futures for adults with autism: think tank. New York, NY.

Figure 67.1 Degree of expected community integration as a function of day or employment program model.

Disability Services, (3) allow the student to graduate from high school and attend college using the supports of the college's disability services office (a supported academic program model), or (4) enroll the student in a CTP program. Unfortunately, there is no research available to guide school personnel as to which option is the best option to choose and under what circumstances.

Enrollment in a vocational program is a suitable option if the student with an ASD has good independent living skills and his or her social skills are at a level that he or she can integrate into the community. Many students on the spectrum do not see the value of a liberal arts education and need direct hands-on training. Vocational education in the classroom is directly related to the work skills necessary to be employed successfully. In a liberal arts education, the connection between the coursework and work skills is abstract and unclear for the student with an ASD. Vocational programs offer a wide choice of career options, including computer programming, networking, and repair, which is very popular with students on the spectrum. Vocational training centers also offer certificates as a personal trainer and certificates in small animal care, and food service as well as traditional vocational training in the areas of cosmetology, plumbing, carpentry, and electrical and automotive repair. However, they generally do not provide training in independent living and social skills.

Supported academic programs (SAPs) at colleges and universities are established so that the institution ensures its compliance with the Americans with Disabilities Act (ADA). This is a viable option for a student on the spectrum who is "otherwise qualified" to attend college academically. However, the student with an ASD must have sufficient independent living and social skills to live on his or her own with limited structure and supervision. Students on the spectrum have impairments in executive functioning skills, which are meta-organizational skills. As a part of the transition plan, the student might need to be taught how to use an alarm clock and program calendar software to remind him or her when to begin researching a term paper, when to write the first draft, and when to turn in the final assignment. Unlike the high school environment, classes are taught across campus in different buildings and at variable times. The student's transition plan must include how to deal with this change in environment, including the fact there will be no bells to signal the time to go to class. SAPs are generally very good at addressing accommodations that are academic in nature. The SAPs will either change the environment (e.g., provide a quiet distraction-free alternative testing site) as an accommodation or help the student learn new skills (e.g., remedial classes to improve math skills). However, SAPs often do not understand the unique needs of students on the spectrum. They generally do not intervene where a student on the spectrum needs the most help—the social realm of college. Living in the residence hall will be the most challenging aspect of completing college for the student with an ASD. Students with autism need an interpreter of the social world much like a student with a severe hearing impairment needs an interpreter for the speaking world. Transition plans need to address social skills in the area of semantics and pragmatics of speech to help the student survive the dorm environment. Social workers and psychologists will need to help the student identify unwritten social rules that he or she is likely to encounter in college as well as role-play scenarios that he or she will face (e.g., a conflict with a roommate).

The fourth option an IEP team may consider as a part of the transition plan for a student with autism is enrollment in a CTP program. CTP programs combine aspects of vocational training programs and SAPs. However, CTP programs go one step further. They focus on job-specific social skills, independent living skills, and academic skills (see Table 67.8 for Table 67.8 and Table 67.9 for best practices of transitional programs). The goals of the CTP programs are to either transition the student to the world of work and independent living or transition the student to enroll full-time in a degree-bearing program.

When writing a transition plan involving a CTP program, IEP team members need to bear in mind that there are two types of CTP programs, each with their own strengths and weaknesses. The two types are college-based CTP programs and college-affiliated CTP programs. College-based CTP programs are programs that are a part of

Table 67.9 Best practices of transitional programs

- Using group modality
- Involving the family
- Developing community partnerships
- Taking a long term approach: the importance of follow-up
- On-going evaluation

the college or university. Students in the CTP program live in the residence halls and can avail themselves of the course selection the college has to offer and engage in its rich social life. The most important advantage for students with ASDs and their parents is that students enrolled in an U.S. DOE-approved college-based CTP programs are eligible for federal student aid under the Higher Education Opportunity Act of 2008 (P.L. 110–315; see Table 67.10).

College-affiliated CTP programs are ideal for students on the spectrum who have difficulty generalizing skills across environments. Independent living skills such as cooking, home maintenance, and laundry are taught in the student's apartment. A transfer of skills across environments is not necessary. College-affiliated CTP programs usually have a memorandum of understanding with local community colleges where students can pursue coursework and even an associate degree. Unfortunately, students enrolled in a college-affiliated CTP program do not qualify for federal student aid under HEOA 2008. It would also behoove the parents and the IEP team to determine who has oversight of the program before enrolling a student with an ASD in a college-affiliated CTP program.

There is a dearth of research involving late teens and young adults on the autism spectrum. There is no research to help IEP teams decide which option is the best option (of the four options previously discussed) for a particular student with an ASD. High-functioning students on the autism spectrum are the most challenging to IEP teams writing a transition plan because the student's intellectual abilities and achievements belie his or her profound disability, which prevents him or her from learning to be independent, engaging in the community, and gaining and retaining employment. An IEP team's work is not completed until these areas of concern are met. When designing IEP transition goals and interventions to meet those goals, teams need to keep in mind that the interventions should be practical and real world or experientially based. For example, money management skills need to be taught with real money, using bank accounts, checkbooks, and debit cards. The student needs to be held to the budget and have natural and logical consequences for not staying within his or her budget (e.g., the student cannot go to the movies that week because he spent his money on pizza). Travel training is not effective if it is conducted only in the classroom and not done in the real world with planned and unplanned interruptions in service. Social skills training should be based upon empirically supported models that use Applied Behavior Analysis as their basis, such as the Crafting Connections model (Taubman, Leaf, & McEachin, 2011). Vocational training should be conducted at a supported employment worksite for higher-functioning individuals and teach them skills they would most likely complete in a job after graduating from the program. Regardless of whether a student's transition plan involves pursuing a vocational certificate or a college degree, vocational placements are critical in teaching the student appropriate social, dress, and hygiene skills for the workplace.

Table 67.10 Types of Federal Student Aid Available to Students with Intellectual Disabilities under HEOA (P.L. 110–315)

- Pell Grants
- Federal Student Education Opportunity Grants (FSEOG)
- Student Work Study monies

Note: Under the current version of HEOA students with Intellectual Disabilities are ***NOT eligible*** for federally subsidized ***and*** unsubsidized loans

A transition plan would be incomplete if it did not involve teaching the higher-functioning student how to conduct a job search. Searching for and obtaining employment is an inherently social endeavor. Students on the autism spectrum are at a distinct disadvantage because of their disability. Only about 15%–20% of jobs are advertised through any form of media, so even using the Internet for job searches significantly limits a student's opportunities for employment (Hansen, 2010). Familial and personal connections are an underestimated and vital resource for employment. It is estimated that 80% of jobs are found through personal connections (GovCentral, 2009). Families need to be encouraged to use their personal networks to help the student with an ASD secure employment. VanBergeijk, Klin, and Volkmar (2011) advise that students with ASDs should role-play mock job interviews with videotape and specific feedback to help reduce anxiety and give general rules regarding small talk, the amount of eye contact, and the type of clothing to wear to an interview. Grandin and Duffy (2004) suggest that a student bring a portfolio of his or her work as a means of decreasing anxiety and allowing the person with an ASD to demonstrate his or her skills.

Applying Interventions within a Response to Intervention Framework

Response to Intervention (RTI) is a conceptual model and approach to intervening with students who have learning and other types of disabilities. RTI may be a helpful approach when a student's lack of educational achievement is unclear. School personnel may be unsure as to the origins of the lack of progress. This is especially true when there are potentially other factors such as poverty and/or linguistic and cultural differences that may be impacting the student's ability to learn (National Center on Response to Intervention, 2011). However, ASDs are pervasive developmental disorders that are present early in the child's growth and will remain with him or her throughout his or her life. Autistic disorder can be reliably diagnosed as early as 2 years of age (Bölte & Hallmayer, 2011). Asperger syndrome is often diagnosed at a much later age after repeated academic and social failures. The average age of diagnosis for Asperger syndrome is 8 years of age (Bölte & Hallmayer, 2011).

Implementing RTI procedures is not a best practice with the ASD population in general. Early identification and intervention with empirically based interventions such ABA and psychopharmacological treatments for the symptoms of comorbid psychiatric disorders are essential to better long-term outcomes for children on the spectrum (National Research Council, 2001). Delaying a child on the autism spectrum the ability to qualify for special education services serves no purpose for the child and lessens the probability of a favorable outcome.

Regarding the writing of transition plans, school personnel should have long ago concluded that the RTI approach is not appropriate for a student on the autism spectrum. The ASD should have been diagnosed long ago, particularly those cases that are more pronounced or severe. Then the student should have qualified for special education services long before the first transition goal is to be written at age 14. However, it is not uncommon for higher-functioning students to be diagnosed with a myriad of other disorders, such as ADHD, before eventually being correctly diagnosed with Asperger syndrome or PDD-NOS. It is also not uncommon to meet adults who struggle all their lives with employment, failed relationships, and a lack of connection to the community who are diagnosed with an ASD later in life. Early identification, classification for services, and intervention are the best bet for a child on the autism spectrum to live a life of independence. A thoughtful, well-written transition plan that addresses the unique needs of students with autism and other intellectual disabilities is critical to their successful lifelong employment and integration into the community.

Tools and Practice Examples

Case Example

Duane received a thorough neuropsychological evaluation at a well-known autism center affiliated with a university hospital. The family was referred to the center because of Duane's repeated social failures, rigidity, meltdowns, and nonstop talking about trains and other modes of transportation. Initially, he did well in school. Teachers referred to him as the "little professor" because he had such a large vocabulary and seemed to have encyclopedic knowledge about certain subjects. However, he would interrupt and correct teachers in the classroom and alienate his peers by talking over them about trains and cars. On the playground he was often seen alone. Duane was uncoordinated, frequently bumping into peers and falling down and getting hurt. His gait was awkward and when walking down stairs he took only one stair at a time. Duane was frequently bullied by other students. He appeared anxious and unaware of the impact of his behavior upon others.

At the autism center, some of the assessments that were conducted by the multidisciplinary team included (1) the Autism Diagnostic Observation Scale (ADOS), (2) the Autism Diagnostic Interview (ADI), (3) the Vineland Adaptive Behavior Scales, and (4) the Wechsler Intelligence Scale for Children-Revised (WISC-R; Bölte & Hallmayer, 2011). Results from the assessment indicated that Duane clearly fell upon the autism spectrum. Since Duane began speaking at developmentally appropriate times and his current problems with semantics and pragmatics, he was diagnosed as having Asperger syndrome at age 8. The results from the WISC-R indicated that his Verbal I.Q. fell into the very superior range. His Performance I.Q. fell into the average to low-average range.

This huge discrepancy between his Verbal I.Q. and his Performance I.Q. was typical of students with Asperger syndrome. Although Duane did not have a cognitive disability and would be considered high functioning, his processing speeds were markedly slow, and he was in need of supports in the school environment. Duane had difficulty with abstract concepts. He was very concrete and literal. The results from the Vineland indicated that Duane had difficulty with social communication, self-care, and community living.

Duane would receive special education services throughout his public education. He received physical and occupational therapy during primary school to help with his proprioception, balance, and gross and fine motor coordination issues. After the completion of PT and OT services, Duane continued to have adaptive physical education as a part of his IEP. The speech therapist and school social worker provided interventions related to his deficits in semantics and pragmatics of speech as well as understanding unwritten social rules. Over the course of his education these interventions were a combination of push-in and pull-out services. The majority of coursework was conducted in the general education classroom. However, he received resource room assistance with organizational skills and math. In high school Duane would have consumer math as a part of his IEP. The course used representational or simulated money scenarios. Duane had difficulty grasping these concepts. He had no innate sense of money and could not make change.

During Duane's senior year the IEP team, with Duane and his parents as members, developed a transition plan that decided he would not graduate from high school at age 18 along with his peers. Duane's family felt that he should attend a CTP program. The program had two concentrations—one a concentration whose students focused primarily upon social, independent living, and vocational skills, and the other a pre-degree concentration. Both the school personnel and the family liked the idea that Duane could take credit-bearing classes that could be used toward earning a degree, and he would simultaneously receive vocational training. His ultimate goal was to earn a college degree.

The three year CTP program was a good fit for both Duane and the school district. The program regularly held IEP team meetings with the school district and provided them with the documentation necessary to demonstrate his progress toward reaching his IEP and transition plan goals. With the structure and a behavior modification system in place, he made steady progress in the areas of organizational skills, hygiene, and money management. Because of his keen interest in transportation, Duane was given leadership responsibilities in his travel training class. He did very well in the credit-bearing classes he took with neurotypical college students. His professors liked him and praised him for being a good student. He struggled with his interest in the opposite sex and had many failures in his attempts to date. Duane addressed this in his advanced communications course and with his social counselors at the program. Vocationally, Duane decided he wanted to pursue clerical skills and learn a software suite of office applications. This proved to be very frustrating for him because of his fine motor coordination issues.

Despite Duane's parents' objections, the vocational team at the program found a vocational placement that truly excited Duane and held his interest. The team supported his right to self-determination and urged his parents to allow him to pursue his interest. Duane's new placement was at a transportation company that provided taxis, limousines, ambulettes, and buses to the public. His job consisted of detailing the vehicles. Duane received high praise from his supervisors for his punctuality, enthusiasm, and attention to detail. The staff at the program no longer had to hunt him down to ensure that he had gone to work. He went willingly and enthusiastically to his placement.

Although his transition plan had been for Duane to pursue a college degree, he changed his mind. Duane decided he loved to work with cars. He graduated with a certificate of completion from the vocational program and was simultaneously awarded his high school diploma. Upon graduation the vocational team at the program worked with Duane and his family to identify businesses that would hire someone on the autism spectrum and that involved cars. The team suggested they conduct an Internet search for businesses that hired people on the autism spectrum in their hometown and consult *CAREERS & the disABLED Magazine* in order to identify potential employers. (*CAREERS & the disABLE Magazine* publishes an annual list of leading corporations who hire the disabled.) Duane's father, through a friend, was able to get Duane hired at an automobile dealership detailing cars. He worked at that job for a number of years and was a valued employee.

Duane, however, was looking for a new challenge and decided to start his own business. He decided to start his own auto detailing service in what Volkmar (2012) describes as an entrepreneurial model. His business was so successful that he was able to move out of his parents' home and rent his own apartment. He moved into the apartment with his girlfriend, who he met at the CTP program he attended. As of this writing they are engaged to be married.

Key Points to Remember

- Although high-functioning individuals on the autism spectrum may not have a cognitive disability, they still can be profoundly disabled because of their social communication impairment.
- Students with ASDs will have difficulties with transitions, anxiety, and generalization of skills. Unlike students with specific learning disabilities, students with ASDs will need IEP goals that ameliorate deficits in social communication, independent living, and vocational skills. Transition plans must address these issues.
- When teaching skills to a student on the autism spectrum, the skills should be concrete, reality based, and conducted in vivo and across environments to ensure generalization of the skill. Empirically based techniques that incorporate aspects of behaviorism appear to be the most successful.
- Knowing federal laws, policies, and programs can help the student and his or her family transition to the postsecondary environment.
- Comprehensive Transition and Postsecondary (CTP) programs are an emerging model used to educate students with ASDs and other intellectual disabilities. Funding from IDEA Parts B can be used to pay for these programs if the IEP team deems it appropriate and writes it into the transition plan. Once a student with an ASD graduates from high school or reaches age 21, then the student with the Intellectual Disability may receive federal student financial aid if he or she is enrolled in an U.S. DOE-approved CTP program.

Further Learning

www.disability.gov

Equal Opportunities Publications. *CAREERS & the disABLED Magazine*: http://www.eop.com/mags-CD.php

Grandin, T. (1999). Choosing the right job for people with autism or Asperger's syndrome. Retrieved from http://www.autism.com/individuals/jobs.htm

HEATH Resource Center: Knowing Your Options: What to do and Where to Go: http://www.heath.gwu.edu/modules/awareness-of-postsecondary-options/

Vocational Rehabilitation Services: Can It Help You? http://www.heath.gwu.edu/modules/rehabilitation-services/

Opportunities in Career and Technical Education at the Postsecondary Level: http://www.heath.gwu.edu/modules/career-and-technical-education/

Non-Degree Postsecondary Options for Individuals with Disabilities: http://www.heath.gwu.edu/assets/9/non_degree_postsec_1.pdf

http://thinkcollege.net/

www.wrightslaw.com

References

Bennett, D. (2009). Thorkil Sonne: Recruit autistics. Wired Magazine, 17(10). Retrieved from http://www.wired.com/techbiz/people/magazine/17–10/ff_smartlist_sonne

Bölte, S., & Hallmayer, J. (Eds.). (2011). *Autism spectrum conditions: FAQs on autism, Asperger syndrome, and atypical autism answered by international experts.* Cambridge, MA: Hogrefe.

Code of Federal Regulations Parts 300 and 301: Assistance to States for the Education of Children With Disabilities and Preschool Grants for Children With Disabilities; Final Rule. August 14, 2006. Washington, DC: U.S. Printing Office.

Gerhardt, P. F. (2009, January). *The current state of services for adults with autism.* Presented at the Organization for Autism Research's Advancing Futures for Adults with Autism: Think Tank. New York, NY.

GovCentral. (2009). *Network to get a government job guide.* Retrieved from http://govcentral.monster.com/benefits/articles/8498-network-to-get-a-government-job-guide

Grandin, T., & Duffy, K. (2004). *Developing talents: Careers for individuals with Asperger syndrome and high functioning autism.* Shawnee Mission, MO: Autism Asperger Publishing Company.

Hansen, R. (2010). *15 myths and misconceptions about job hunting.* Retrieved from http://www.quintcareers.com/job-hunting_myths.html

Liming, D., & Wolf, M. (2008). Job outlook by education, 2006–2016. Occupational Outlook Quarterly (Fall), 1–28. Retrieved from http://www.bls.gov/opub/ooq/2008/fall/art01.pdf

National Center on Response to Intervention. (2011). *What is RTI?* Retrieved from http://www.rti4success.org/whatisrti

National Research Council. (2001). *Educating children with autism.* Washington, DC: National Academy Press.

Taubman, M., Leaf, R., & McEachin, J. (2011). *Crafting connections: Contemporary applied behavior analysis for enriching the social lives of persons with autism spectrum disorder.* New York, NY: DRL Books.

U.S. Department of Education, National Center for Education Statistics . (2011). *Digest of education statistics 2010.* Washington, DC: U.S. Printing Office. Retrieved from http://www.edpubs.gov/document/ed005216p.pdf?ck=926

U.S. Department of Labor, Bureau of Labor Statistics . (2011). *Labor force statistics from the Current Population Survey.* Retrieved from http://www.bls.gov/cps/

VanBergeijk, E. O., & Shtayermman, O. (2005) Asperger's syndrome: An enigma for social work. Journal of Human Behavior in the Social Environment, 2, 23–37.

VanBergeijk, E. O., Klin, A., & Volkmar, F. R. (2008). Supporting more able students on the autism spectrum: College and beyond. Journal of Autism and Developmental Disorders, 38,1359–1370.

VanBergeijk, E. O., Klin, A., & Volkmar, F. R. (2011). What can help people with ASC find and keep employment? In S. Bölte & J. Hallmayer (Eds.), *Autism spectrum conditions: FAQs on autism, Asperger syndrome, and atypical autism answered by international experts* (pp. 241–244). Cambridge, MA: Hogrefe.

Volkmar, F. R. (Ed). (2012). *Entrepreneurial supports. Encyclopedia of autism spectrum disorders.* New York, NY: Springer.

Wehman, P. (2001). *Life beyond the classroom: Transition strategies for young people with disabilities* (3rd ed.). Baltimore, MD: Paul H. Brookes.

Wright, P. W., & Wright, P. D. (2000). *Wrightslaw: Special education law.* Hartfield, VA: Harbor House Law Press.

Wright, P. W., & Wright, P. D. (2006). *IDEA 2004: Parts A & B.* Hartfield, VA: Harbor House Law Press.

SECTION XIII

Accountability and Resource Development

Schools function in an age of increased accountability and scrutiny about the effectiveness of their programs and practices. Cost-effectiveness and resource development are issues that present a great challenge to school systems, as well as the measurement and demonstration of effective outcomes. All of these issues greatly impact how school services are delivered. This section offers timely updates and best practices that may help to improve the accountability of school professionals. In addition, this section provides information about the funding of school-related services and how to obtain additional funds from grant writing. Chapters in this section also show how to assess and effectively report the outcomes of school-related services and emphasize the increasing important of translating evidence-based practices from research settings to the school settings.

CHAPTER 68

Using Data to Communicate with School Stakeholders

Natasha K. Bowen

Getting Started

School leaders, teachers, and school-based practitioners (such as social workers, counselors, and psychologists) are increasingly confronted with requirements to collect and make use of data. The passage of No Child Left Behind (NCLB, 2001), the 2004 reauthorization of the Individuals with Disabilities Education Act (IDEA; U.S. Department of Education, 2004), and the popularization of tiered intervention approaches such as "Response to Intervention" (RTI) have contributed to new roles and expectations for school staff with respect to data. In addition to federal mandates, myriad state and local accountability standards dictate the collection and use of data by teams of school staff, such as school improvement teams and student support teams. An important corollary of the emphasis on data collection is the requirement that data be used to guide choices about three categories of research-based strategies to improve student achievement and behavior: primary or universal prevention, secondary or selective prevention, and tertiary or indicated prevention.

The new "data-driven" climate of schools offers both opportunities and challenges for school social workers and other school-based professionals. Increasing familiarity with data may make school staff more receptive to evidence-based approaches espoused by social workers. Also, in theory, the three-tiered response to students encompassed in RTI (which primarily focuses on academic performance) and other tiered intervention responses would seem to accommodate the ecological risk and protective factor prevention approach inherent in social work training and practice. However, with inexplicable disregard for the extensive literatures of developmental psychology and psychopathology, risk and resilience, social psychology, and other fields, the models of educational practice that have emerged in response to mandates focus virtually exclusively on the assessment and targeting of risk defined as degrees of current unsatisfactory academic or behavioral performance. Many school social workers continue to work in a culture that believes the predominant variables affecting student performance are a few narrow child characteristics and instructional methods.

Social workers bring an essential ecological perspective to the discussion of how to support the success of all students in schools (Hopson & Lawson, 2011). By introducing social environmental factors (that is, characteristics of the neighborhood, school, classroom, family, and peer systems of youth) into universal assessments, social workers promote awareness of potential threats to satisfactory performance before performance declines. Awareness of social environmental risk and protective factors, in turn, promotes the use of truly preventative strategies—strategies that prevent the emergence of problems—when threats to continued adequate performance are revealed. By introducing social environmental data into assessments for youth considered for selective and indicated programming, they promote awareness of causes of poor performance that go beyond the child and instructional methods. For students who are already falling behind, staff awareness of social environmental factors promotes the targeting of influences in the environment that, without intervention, will maintain poor performance even in the context of new or intensified methods of instruction.

This chapter provides brief background on factors behind the data-driven climate in schools. Social workers and other school-based professionals must understand the rationale and terminology of these phenomena. It then explains how social environmental data are critical to the effective application of "three-tiered" approaches to improving academic performance, such as RTI. The chapter then provides practical advice on how to introduce and use social environmental data to communicate with school stakeholders so they are willing to adapt more appropriate and effective prevention strategies to improve student performance.

What We Know About Using Data to Communicate with School Stakeholders

Background on Changes in the Use of Data in Schools

The current climate of accountability and "science-based" practice in schools is rooted in federal efforts to improve educational outcomes, including inequities based on race/ethnicity and income (NCLB, 2001; U.S. Department of Education, 2004). Two central aspects of the data-driven trend in schools are more frequent and systematic assessment of performance, and the data-guided implementation of three levels or tiers of prevention to improve performance. In the past, assessment was commonly conducted by school psychologists and targeted students who were potentially eligible for special education services. Now, more students are assessed and more school personnel have data collection responsibilities. For example, as a result of NCLB, the academic performance of all students in grades 3 through 12 is now assessed annually, with data aggregated to provide "report cards" on school, district, and state academic performance and growth. Counselors, teachers, social workers, and other school staff may have roles in the collection and use of data. In North Carolina, for example, counselors have been given primary responsibility for annual standardized testing.

As currently implemented in most schools, increased assessment and tiered prevention systems are flawed from a social work perspective. First, the content of assessment in schools remains predominantly academic and behavioral. "At risk" typically means already having a low score on a particular academic or social measure. This definition of "at risk" is not consistent with the multidisciplinary developmental literature in which risk and protective factors are characteristics of the individual and environment (not outcomes), and "at risk" refers to students who have risk factors but are still performing adequately.

Second, by ignoring risk and protective factors in the social environment in their assessment of student problems, school staff limit their ability to understand sources of academic problems and therefore to *prevent* problems. Some of the literature on RTI refers to a new acknowledgment of influences on performance that are external to the child, but upon closer examination, "ecological" in school parlance appears to refer to instructional methods (Malecki & Demaray, 2007). "Ecological" intervention from this perspective is the introduction of a new teaching strategy (e.g., related to grouping, frequency, intensity) for students who have not progressed adequately with the methods used successfully with the majority of students.

Background on Approaches to Prevention

Although there are related tiered approaches used in schools, such as Positive Behavioral Intervention and Supports (PBIS), (Malecki & Demaray, 2007; Sugai & Horner, 2009), our main focus is on RTI. RTI models emerged in response to the text in one narrowly focused section of IDEA (Sugai & Horner, 2009), Section 614(b)(6)(B) (U.S. Department of Education, 2004), which states:

> In determining whether a child has a specific learning disability, a local educational agency may use a process that determines if the child responds to scientific, research-based intervention as a part of the evaluation procedures described in paragraphs (2) and (3) (p. 60).

The text refers to only one of 14 eligibility categories for special education services—"specific learning disabilities" (LDs), which can occur in reading, math, or writing. According to the *Diagnostic and Statistical Manual IV, Text Revision* (DSM, American Psychiatric Association, 1994), 5% of schoolchildren are identified as having a learning disorder (the comparable term in the DSM). In the past, LD eligibility was based on a discrepancy (often as large as two standard deviations) between the performance of a student in a subject area and his or her ability, as measured by a standardized test. School psychologists often conducted and interpreted both the performance and ability tests. Not only did Section 614(b)(6)(B) have major implications for how a small percentage of students are identified for the LD category, but the spirit of the section has affected how strategies for addressing a much broader range of academic and behavioral shortcomings in students in general are applied (Sugai & Horner, 2009).

Three-tiered approaches to prevention, such as RTI, are frameworks for decision making using assessment data. The summary of how they work presented here is derived from a number of sources on RTI and PBIS(Fuchs & Fuchs, 2005; Malecki & Demaray, 2007; National Center on Response to Intervention, 2010a; Sugai & Horner, 2009). They start with Tier 1, in which the majority of students (about 80%) receive general educational services and are screened for early deficits in the level or rate of their academic progress. Those with performance below certain cutoffs are monitored. Teachers are more likely to be involved in screening and monitoring efforts at this level, and school psychologists may be less involved. Students who do not respond to the presumably research-based instructional strategies used for the general population of students (about 15%) are then moved to Tier 2, where more intensive, instructional strategies are used. Only when students fail to make adequate progress at this stage (about 5%) do they move to Tier 3, where they can be more fully evaluated for special education eligibility. Advantages of the new system are that students do not have to be performing at a severely low level before they are identified for support, and that less-intensive supports, often in the regular classroom, are implemented before the special education process escalates. This aspect of the system is designed to prevent the deepening of problems, but not the emergence of problems to begin with.

School-based professionals should be aware of other critiques of RTI. First, three-tiered models of prevention or intervention are not new (e.g., Gordon, 1983). Almost 30 years ago, Gordon's early public health model focused on three levels of the prevention of disease and used the terms universal, selective, and indicated to replace primary, secondary, and tertiary. Nor is the notion of assessment-based, risk-appropriate prevention or intervention planning in education or mental health novel or profound (e.g., Collins, Murphy, & Bierman, 2004; Mash & Terdal, 1988; Ollendick & King, 1999; Silverman & Saavedra, 2004; Stollar, Poth, Curtis, & Cohen, 2006). The social work literature has for years promoted methods and resources for matching interventions to assessment results (G. L. Bowen, Richman, & Bowen, 2002; Gambrill, 1999; Powers, Bowen, & Bowen, 2011; Powers, Bowen, & Rose, 2005).

Second, RTI is described, defined, and even abbreviated differently across sources. It is also implemented differently across schools, districts, and states. The nature of Tier 1 varies across and sometimes within discussions of the approach (e.g., Malecki & Demaray, 2007). The educational literature (e.g., Kratochwill, Volpiansky, Clements, & Ball, 2007; Reynolds & Shaywitz, 2009) contains discussions of problems with RTI in schools, including lack of empirical evidence for the approach, measurement concerns, lack of preparation for school staff to carry out the model, definitional inconsistencies, a problematic change in the conceptualization of what constitutes a learning disorder, and the likelihood of overlooking some students in need of services. With perspective on the lack of consensus about definitions, implementation, and value of three-tiered systems, social workers and other school-based professionals will be better positioned to argue their case that a fundamental problem of the systems is the failure to incorporate *causes* of academic and social problems in assessment, decision making, and therefore prevention efforts.

In summary, an increase in the frequency and intensity of data collection in schools has resulted from federal mandates for improvement in student academic achievement. To make effective use of data, school professionals have designed three-tiered prevention frameworks, such as RTI, for academic problems. Problems with these two consequences of federal mandates highlight the importance of bringing the social work perspective to bear in efforts to support students across the country. Assessments and prevention strategies must include the social environment and the factors therein that support or threaten school success or cause unsatisfactory performance. Without social environmental assessment, problems cannot be understood, and appropriate prevention cannot occur at any level.

Background on the Current State of Educational Outcomes

The most compelling evidence of the inadequacy of current responses to federal mandates to improve academic outcomes is the status of those outcomes themselves. After approximately 10 years of NCLB mandates, the majority of students in the country are not proficient in reading or math according to the U.S. Department of Education's standards, and little progress has been made with socioeconomic and racial/ethnic achievement gaps (National Center for Education Statistics, 2011). Table 68.1 summarizes National Assessment for Educational Progress (NAEP) performance data from 2009. The data suggest that academic failure is common in American schools. They also depict a problem for three-tiered prevention approaches that is rarely, if ever, addressed in the RTI literature. As shown in Figure 68.1, based simply on the current distribution of students within categories of proficiency (less than basic, basic, proficient), support systems are starting with far fewer students in Tier 1, who need minimal supports, and far more in Tier 3, requiring intensive support, than three-tiered systems assume. After brief mention of the possibility of a small Tier 1 population, the National Center on Response to Intervention recommends that schools facing the scenario focus first on building up Tier 1 (National Center on Response to Intervention, 2010b). From the social work perspective, even with the cloudy interpretation of Tier 1 common in the RTI literature, the best first step in this process would be to assess and address risk and protective factors in the social environment of students.

To the extent that data-driven approaches have penetrated many school systems and been linked to tiered prevention strategies, they have not made the anticipated progress in improving student achievement. Although remedial strategies for students and better instructional methods for teachers will remain important for student learning, the unsatisfactory results of the last decade's efforts have likely been restricted by their failure to take into account the full range of what some social work researchers have called "eco-interactional developmental" (Richman, Bowen, & Woolley, 2004) factors that cause academic success or failure.

Background on Social Environmental Data

Findings from studies of all designs conducted by researchers in multiple disciplines converge around the fact that the functioning of an individual at any time is substantially explained by his or her past and present experiences in the social environment (e.g., Fraser, 2004; Rutter, 1985; Sameroff, 2000; Werner, 1990). Most importantly, building protection and/or reducing risk in the social environment leads to improvements in functioning for students at all levels of prevention (e.g., N. K. Bowen & Flora, 2003; Catalano, Berglund, Ryan, Lonczak, & Hawkins, 2002; Henggeler, 1991; Solomon, Battistich, Watson, Schaps, & Lewis, 2000). The cumulative findings strongly suggest that tiered efforts to prevent low school performance cannot succeed without consideration of the social environment.

Table 68.1 Math and Reading Proficiency among 4th, 8th, and 12th Graders in 2009

	Overall Percent at or Above Proficiency	*Summary of Racial/Ethnic and Socioeconomic Gaps*
Reading	32%	25–28% points
4th graders	30%	24–26% points
8th graders	37%	22–27% points
12th graders		
Math	39%	21–33% points
4th graders	34%	26–32% points
8th graders	26%	21–30% points
12th graders		

Based on information from National Center for Education Statistics (2011).

What We Know About Social Environmental Assessment and Prevention in Schools

Although current descriptions of RTI say little or nothing about the social environment, past research has indicated that teachers understand the impact of the social environment and value social environmental information on their students (N. K. Bowen & Powers, 2005). Furthermore, in the absence of data on the experiences of their students in the social environment, teachers rely on assumptions about students and families that are frequently inaccurate (N. K. Bowen & Powers, 2005). As described below, tools and models for conducting social environmental assessments and linking findings to effective school-based prevention strategies are available (N. K. Bowen & Powers, 2011; Powers et al., 2011; Powers et al., 2005), increasing the validity and utility of social environmental assessment in schools.

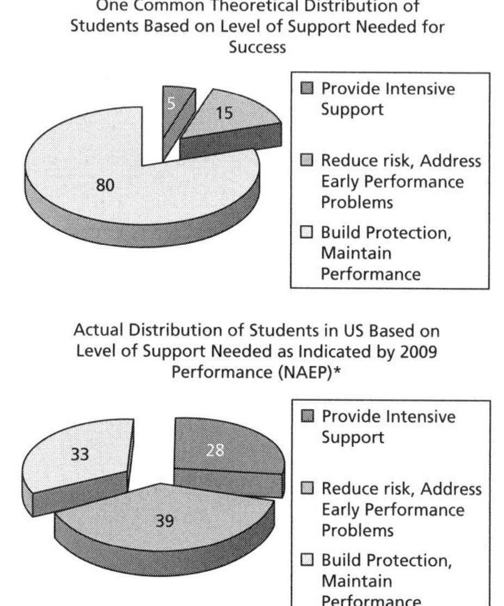

Figure 68.1. Discrepancy between Theoretical and Actual Levels of Prevention Needed for Students in an RTI Model.

* (National Center for Education Statistics, 2011) Values are based on averages across math and reading and grade levels.

Staff in many schools may justifiably feel powerless to bring about change in families and communities. Although school social workers have historically been willing to work for change outside of schools, there is plenty to do within schools. Recent and previous research, for example, has indicated the potential of strategies targeting school and classroom relationships, beliefs about ability, and norms related to stereotypes to increase students' readiness to learn and academic achievement (e.g., Durlak, Dymnicki, Taylor, Weissberg, & Schellinger, 2011; Dweck, 2006; Hopson & Lawson, 2011; Steele, 2010).

What We Can Do

To have credibility and influence in schools, social workers and other school-based professionals must be fluent in the terminology and trends around data collection and three-tiered prevention models. It is paramount that school-based professionals be familiar with the simple statistics, such as means and percentages, used to describe the academic and behavioral performance of students. Most importantly, they must introduce social environmental data into the discussion of how to improve schools and student performance.

Schools have an exceptional singularity of purpose—academic success of students. By continuously demonstrating the irrefutable links between the social environment and student academic success, school-based professionals can increase the effectiveness of efforts to improve performance. School-based professionals, such as social workers, might address this task in two steps: (a) educate school stakeholders on a theory of change that illustrates how the social environment affects the social-emotional characteristics of students that in turn make students ready to learn in the classroom (see Figure 68.2), and (b) translate the effects of social environmental interventions (including their own current work with students) into the behavioral and academic outcomes that are salient to school stakeholders. Teachers want students to behave and be engaged in the classroom; parents want school staff to like and support their children's success; principals want adequate resources and good social and academic outcomes; teachers and principals want parent educational involvement; communities want safe and highly regarded schools and well-educated graduates; and students want to feel safe, respected, and competent at school.

School-based professionals may be most successful in their early efforts to insert consideration of the social environment into achievement improvement plans if they start with characteristics of the school environment. School environmental characteristics are strong predictors of academic performance, many can be manipulated with feasible prevention strategies, and by focusing on factors that school staff have control over, common arguments against targeting social environmental risk and prevention (described below) are countered.

Specific Tactics for Using Social Environmental Data to Communicate with School Staff

After social workers and other school-based professionals have succeeded in gaining support for social environmental assessment, they may be in charge of using social environmental data to communicate the experiences and prevention needs of students to school stakeholders. Whether they advocate for within-school environmental targets or external targets, the following guidelines may be useful. The strategies are based on extensive work with principals, teachers, and district administrators in multiple schools and districts in North Carolina.

School-based professionals may collect data on one or more domain of the social environment—within the school or external to the school. Although school staff and other stakeholders are likely to be familiar with outcome data, they may be less familiar with social environmental data. Before introducing the data, it is important to explain what they are and why they matter. It is also important to indicate who provided the data. Data may have been collected from students, teachers, parents, or community members, or a combination of these sources. Preferably, data come from more than one source. School administrators, teachers, and students, for example, might provide information about school climate. Teachers and parents might provide information about parent involvement at the school. Before talking about findings, it is also important to let the audience know how many were in the sample and when the data were collected. School-based professionals will need to describe to whom exactly the findings generalize. For example, if virtually all students in a grade

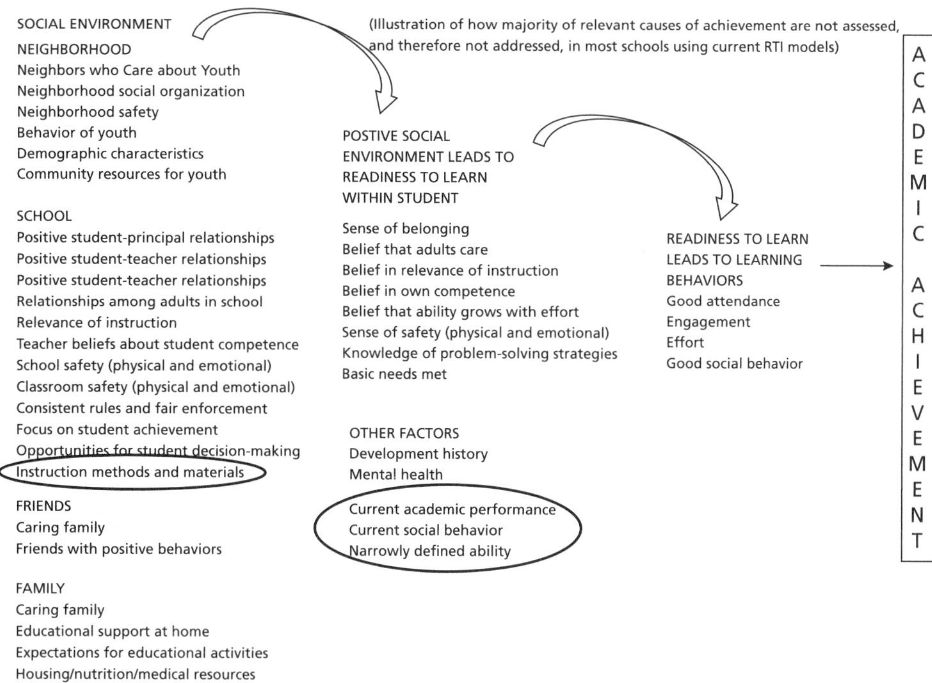

Figure 68.2. Selected Factors that Influence The Academic Achievement of Students and Factors Typically Assessed and Addressed in Schools (circled).

or a large random sample of students in the grade level were assessed, it can be asserted that the results describe the whole grade level. In contrast, if a non-random sample of students was assessed, findings generalize to a more restricted group.

Audiences differ in their familiarity or comfort level with data. All school-related audiences that school-based professionals encounter, however, will most likely respond best to the use of simple statistics, such as means and percentages, and simple graphics, such as line and bar charts. The State of North Carolina, for example, uses the two formats in Figure 68.3 to present school "report card" data. Such graphics can be created easily in a spreadsheet program.

Provide handouts with data for all audience members, if possible. If using a projected presentation, present only tables or graphs that will be large enough on screen to be seen clearly by all audience members. Audience members will not appreciate being told, "I know this is too small for all of you to see ..." To have productive, inclusive discussions of data, all audience members must have access to the findings.

Walk the audience through the parts of the data, model how to interpret specific figures in tables or graphs, and check directly with audience members to be sure they are interpreting the data correctly. When audience members misinterpret data, apologize for not better explaining what the numbers mean and re-explain in a different way and using a new example.

In spite or, or perhaps because of, the new emphasis on data collection, school stakeholders may not welcome more data. A number of common responses to the presentation of social environmental data are listed in Table 68.2. Possible ways to handle negative responses are also presented. These responses assume that the data being presented were collected with evidence-based tools from a sample representing the students being discussed. In addition to the strategies below, social workers and other school-based professionals should remember that although the most critical reactions may be voiced the most loudly, they typically do not represent the views of all audience members. Ask others to offer their perceptions of the data.

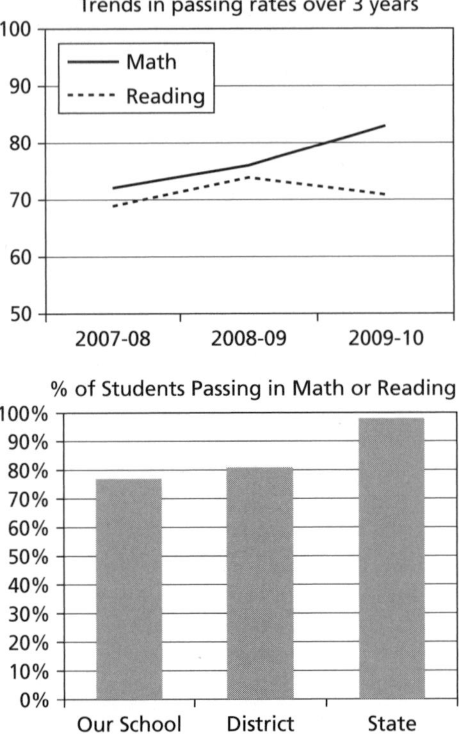

Figure 68.3. Examples of Simple Statistics and Graphics

Audiences are more receptive to negative findings in social environmental data if the presentation of findings begins with strengths in the data. It is most effective to highlight strengths of members of the audience, if applicable. For example, if speaking to parents, highlight the common finding that parents are helping their children educationally in one or more ways at home. If teachers are in the audience, note, if applicable, that students report that teachers have high expectations, or keep after them if they miss an assignment deadline. Strengths can virtually always be found in social environmental data, even if "strengths" have to be defined as some scores that are less unfavorable than others.

As members of schools and school teams, school-based professionals are part of the social environment being discussed. They can gain trust and model productive responses to negative findings by presenting themselves as both part of problems revealed in data and part of the solution. Contextual and developmental explanations for some findings can soften the impact of highly undesirable numbers. If the data indicate that students perceive little support from teachers, note that students in various situations (e.g., with difficult home lives, in middle school) may need more continuous or overt signs of support than teachers thought they needed. Girls and younger students may feel less safe at school, contributing to poor safety scores. It is important not to dismiss or excuse negative findings, but deeper discussion can start if the initial undesirable finding is introduced with some mitigating comment to reduce defensiveness.

The effective use of data to communicate with school stakeholders involves listening as well as presenting. Stakeholders will have valuable insights into positive and negative findings. Encourage audience members to express their reactions to the data. Commend their observations and thank them for their comments. Discussions among stakeholders can be more powerful for motivating action than comments of the school-based professional. If discussions veer away from understanding data or what they mean for student success, remind participants that finding ways to make students successful is the priority.

The relevance of findings to levels of prevention should be noted before ending a meeting

Table 68.2 Common Defensive Responses to Social Environmental Data

Audience Comment	*Potential Response*
1. Why should we believe these data? Students (or parents, or teachers, etc.) are not likely to provide true answers.	1. It's true that no questionnaire is perfect, but these data come from a survey that has been used with hundreds of students like those at your school. Principals, teachers, and researchers have found that the data actually do a good job showing what students think. When we follow up by talking to respondents, we find that the survey answers are actually quite accurate. But you're right—there is always some error in data.
2. We already know everything about our students (or parents, etc.).	2. It's great that at this school staff and students know each other well. That is a protective factor for your students. Still, we almost always find that there are at least a few things that the school staff learns from these questions. In addition, having these results lets you show to stakeholders outside of the school what the needs of your students are.
3. We know some of our students live in unsafe neighborhoods or in families with many problems. That is why they are low achievers.	3. It is true that schools have to work harder when students don't have family or community support. Let's just focus on the factors that we do have control over—how kids get along in our school, whether students know their teachers care, how safe they feel in our halls. We can increase achievement a lot just by working on the factors we can control.
4. Achievement starts at home. Some of "our" parents don't care about education. They don't care if their children bring home Fs. That is why their children are not succeeding.	4. Let's just focus on the factors that we do have control over—how kids get along in our school, whether students know their teachers care, how safe they feel in our halls. We can increase achievement a lot just by working on the factors we can control. Other schools have done it.

about data. The setting of goals and finding appropriate prevention strategies may require further work and meetings, but the discussion of data should be linked to those future steps. Undesirable findings presented in the absence of confidence about solutions can leave audience members overwhelmed. Aggregated data showing school-level strengths have implications for efforts to maintain current strategies related to those strengths. Risk factors that emerge at the school level suggest the need for universal prevention efforts. Risk factors that emerge for discrete subsets of the student population may indicate the need for group-level (often included in Tier 2) prevention strategies. If individual data are being reviewed, high risk combined with poor performance indicates the need for intensive individual-level strategies (Tier 3).

Finally, in addition to explaining how next steps involve reviewing strategies that have helped other schools effectively address social environmental threats to school success, remind audience members that effective strategies will lead to improvement in the areas most salient to them, whether it is funding based on average daily membership, improvement in student engagement, fewer behavioral disruptions, better math and language arts achievement, or better futures for students.

Tools and Practice Examples

This chapter has suggested that school-based professionals introduce social environmental data into schools in order to improve academic outcomes that remain unacceptable in spite of years of mandates to implement data-driven appropriate responses to students' performance deficits. In this section we refer readers to sources of information and tools for using social environmental data to communicate effectively in schools with mandates for regular data collection and tiered prevention approaches.

Social Environmental Assessment

Although assessments of specific aspects of individual domains of the social environment exist, we know of only one comprehensive social environmental assessment. The School Success Profile (SSP) for middle and high school students and the Elementary School Success Profile (ESSP) for third through fifth graders assess multiple aspects of the neighborhood, school, peer system, and family. In addition, information is gathered on aspects of students' psychological and physical well-being that mediate the effects of the social environment on outcomes. Information on the SSP and ESSP can be found at the following Web site:

http://www.schoolsuccessonline.com/

Sources on measures of individual aspects of the social environment include books that describe or present measures of relevance to schools (e.g., Fischer & Corcoran, 2000; Reynolds & Kamphaus, 2003). The following Web site includes links to additional online information on measures of the social environment:

http://www.luc.edu/sswsig/resources_practitioners.shtml

Tool for Showing Social Environmental Effects

Figure 68.2 illustrates how child traits and instruction method are only two of dozens of factors that affect the academic and behavioral performance of students. The figure can be used by social workers and school-based professionals to illustrate to school staff how unlikely schools are to see major gains in student success if they assess and target only student performance and teaching methods.

Online Database of Effective Practices for Schools

Assessing the social environment is not effective if findings cannot be linked to appropriate strategies for improvement. The Web site below lists several publicly available online databases of effective practices, some of which can be searched for interventions that have positive effects on academic achievement:

http://www.luc.edu/sswsig/resources_practitioners.shtml

The Web site schoolsuccessonline.com allows users to review school-based programs according to areas of the social environment that are in need of improvement, such as teacher support, parent-school involvement, quality of friendships, and safety at school or in the neighborhood. Evidence-based programs are described as universal or targeted.

The following articles describe how to combine social environmental assessment with goal identification and prevention selection:

Bowen, N. K., & Powers, J. D. (2011). The Elementary School Success Profile model of assessment and prevention: Balancing effective practice standards and feasibility. *School Social Work Journal, 35*, 1–15.

Powers, J. D., Bowen, N. K., & Bowen, G. L. (2011). Supporting evidence-based practice in schools with an online database of best practices. *Children & Schools, 33*, 119–123.

Powers, J. D., Bowen, G. L., & Rose, R. A. (2005). Using social environment assets to identify intervention strategies for promoting school success. *Children and Schools, 27*, 177–187.

Applying Interventions within a Response to Intervention Framework

This chapter has argued that the prevalence of the RTI framework in American public schools presents an opportunity for social workers and other school-based professionals to demonstrate convincingly how their knowledge base and expertise relate to the activities and success of other professionals in the schools. Assessment in many schools continues to focus predominantly on aspects of current performance, not on causes of or threats to performance. Strategies to improve performance focus on specifics of the students' problematic performance and the nature of instruction, not on causes of poor performance. We have argued that the failure to incorporate the multiple influences of the social environment into the most prevalent assessment and practice models used in schools has contributed to the discrepancy between theory and reality illustrated in Figure 68.1. Schools are not likely to identify appropriate prevention targets for students in need of any level of support when assessments focus only on performance. Performance problems are not likely to be resolved if their causes are not examined or addressed. This chapter has attempted to provide school-based professionals with knowledge and tools to change schools from within the prevalent framework of data-driven, three-tiered prevention efforts to accept and make use of an ecological perspective.

Key Points to Remember

1. *Talk the talk.* To be influential in school and district-level discussions about improving student academic and behavioral performance, school-based professionals must master the simple statistics used to present performance data. They must also be fluent in the terminology, purposes, and limitations of the most recent approaches used in schools to address shortcomings in student performance.
2. *Guide the talk.* Current educational mandates to improve student performance do not address the social environment. At the same time, tiered responses to differences in student performance are popular but substantially ineffective in many schools. School-based professionals, starting from a position of familiarity with data and RTI, as well as expertise in the eco-interactional developmental perspective, must steer the current discussion toward consideration of the social environment as a major contributor to performance outcomes. To gain support, they will need to explicitly link efforts to build protection and reduce risk factors in the social environment to the outcomes of interest to school stakeholders.
3. *Walk the walk.* Social workers and other school-based professionals must introduce and interpret social environmental data in school decision-making settings. They must clearly demonstrate how individual- and group-level data can guide efforts to identify students in need of levels of prevention. Resources cited in this chapter can be used to identify appropriate prevention strategies for different domains of the social environment at each level of a tiered response system. School-based professionals may need to focus first on the school environment (instead of domains outside of the school). The school environment is potent and under the control of school leaders and staff.
4. *Communicate effectively with and about social environmental data.* Lessons learned from other school-based professionals involved with schools may be helpful.
   a. Introduce audience to data:
      i. Provide overview—who provided data and when; what social environmental data are and why they are important to school outcomes.
      ii. Use simple visuals to present data.
      iii. Explain and model how to interpret data.
      iv. Check for understanding.
   b. Prepare for defenses:
      i. The data are not valid.
      ii. We know everything already.
      iii. We can't fix everything.
   c. Gain trust:
      i. Start with strengths.
      ii. Use "we," not "you."
      iii. Soften negatives—teacher support, school safety.
   d. Lead safe and interactive discussion:
      i. Listen to and respect possible explanations for undesirable scores.
      ii. Ask for overall reactions—surprises, confirmations?
      iii. Maintain a focus on how to help students, not on who to blame.
   e. Move to next steps:
      i. What do data mean for Tier 1 efforts?
      ii. What do data mean for targeted (Tier 2 and 3) efforts?
      iii. What research-based solutions are appropriate and feasible?
   f. Link data and potential solutions to outcomes of interest to audience, for example:
      i. Teachers—behavior and engagement are better when students are sure teachers care, believe they can succeed, and will help them succeed.
      ii. Leaders—achievement and funding based on attendance, safety, and special education referrals will improve when school staff increase and support safety, caring, and respect for students.
      iii. Parents—student achievement, behavior, and relationships with school staff will improve with home academic

support, communication with school, and improved parent-child relationships.

iv. Communities—school quality, neighborhood safety, and workforce quality will improve with the investment of resources and relationships with schools.

Further Learning

Federal Policies

The No Child Left Behind Act of 2001 (NCLB, 2001) increased schools' accountability for student performance and the use of annual assessments. It can be accessed at the first Web site listed below. A user-friendly summary can be found at the second Web site.

http://www2.ed.gov/policy/elsec/leg/esea02/index.html

http://www.edweek.org/ew/issues/no-child-left-behind/

A clause in the Individuals with Disabilities Act of 2004 (U.S. Department of Education, 2004) is cited as the impetus for using responsiveness to levels of general and supplemental instruction as a criterion for identifying learning disabilities in students (Sugai & Horner, 2009). RTI is a framework for using levels of prevention more broadly to support the academic and behavioral success of all students in a school. Information on IDEA and the original legislation can be found at the following government-sponsored Web site:

http://idea.edu.gov

Response to Intervention

RTI is a practice model based on the notion of using data to appropriately provide different levels of support to students. Most school-based professionals are likely to encounter some version of the model in their schools. Implementation of RTI varies across districts and states, and it may last more or less time in different districts and states. However, the core components of data-driven decision making and levels of prevention have existed for decades (albeit under different names) and are likely to continue to guide school-based practitioners and social workers in general. The need for the eco-interactional developmental (Richman et al., 2004) approach of social workers in school efforts to promote the success of all students will continue.

School-based professionals can gain a strong foundation in RTI by visiting the Web site of the National Center on Response to Intervention. The following links lead respectively to a document summarizing RTI and a 26-minute video that explain the main components of RTI:

http://www.rti4success.org/pdf/rtiessentialcomponents_042710.pdf (National Center on Response to Intervention, 2010a)

http://www.rti4success.org/webinars/video/927 (National Center on Response to Intervention, 2010b)

Research on Two Important Intervenable Classroom Characteristics

Due to their training and experience, school social workers are sensitive to the presence in many schools or classrooms of attitudes and practices that contribute to an environment in which children from nondominant economic and cultural groups do not thrive academically. Two recent and accessible summaries of research on mindsets of ability (Dweck, 2006) and stereotype threat (Steele, 2010) demonstrate how destructive fixed mindsets and stereotype threat are. They also reveal how the two phenomena can be manipulated through simple strategies. When the growth mindset is firmly established in a school or classroom and when stereotype threat is actively countered, the learning environment becomes supportive of the high achievement of all students. These two books will provide social workers and other school-based professionals with useful knowledge and strategies for improving the learning environment when social environmental data reveal problems in these areas.

Dweck, C. S. (2006). Mindset: The new psychology of success. New York, NY: Random House.

Steele, C. M. (2010). Whistling Vivaldi: And other clues to how stereotypes affect us (1st ed.). New York, NY: W. W. Norton.

References

American Psychiatric Association. (1994). *Diagnostic and statistical manual of mental disorders* (4th ed., text revision). Washington, DC: Author.

Bowen, G. L., Richman, J. M., & Bowen, N. K. (2002). The School Success Profile: A results management approach to assessment and intervention planning. In A. R. Roberts & G. J. Greene (Eds.), *Social workers' desk reference* (pp. 787–793). New York, NY: Oxford University Press.

Bowen, N. K., & Flora, D. B. (2003). When is it appropriate to focus on protection in interventions for adolescents? *American Journal of Orthopsychiatry, 72*, 526–538. doi: 10.1037/0002–9432.72.4.526

Bowen, N. K., & Powers, J. D. (2005). Knowledge gaps among school staff and the role of high quality ecological assessments in schools. *Research on Social Work Practice, 15*, 491–500. doi: 10.1177/1049731505275553

Bowen, N. K., & Powers, J. D. (2011). The Elementary School Success Profile model of assessment and prevention: Balancing effective practice standards and feasability. *School Social Work Journal, 35*, 1–15.

Catalano, R. F., Berglund, M. L., Ryan, J. A. M., Lonczak, H. S., & Hawkins, D. (2002). Positive youth development in the United States: Research findings on evaluations of positive youth development programs. *Prevention & Treatment, 5*, Article 15. Retrieved from http://www.apa.org/pubs/journals/index.aspx

Collins, L. M., Murphy, S. A., & Bierman, K. L. (2004). A conceptual framework for adaptive preventive interventions. *Prevention Science, 5*, 185–196. doi: 10.1023/B:PREV.0000037641.26017.00

Durlak, J. A., Dymnicki, A. B., Taylor, R. D., Weissberg, R. P., & Schellinger, K. B. (2011). The impact of enhancing students' social and emotional learning: A meta-analysis of school-based universal interventions. *Child Development, 82*, 405–432. doi: 10.1111/j.1467–8624.2010.01564.x

Dweck, C. S. (2006). *Mindset: The new psychology of success*. New York, NY: Random House.

Fischer, J., & Corcoran, K. (2000). *Measures for clinical practice: A sourcebook* (Vol. 1, 3rd ed.). New York, NY: Free Press.

Fraser, M. W. (Ed.). (2004). *Risk and resilience in childhood: An ecological perspective.* Washington, DC: NASW Press.

Fuchs, D., & Fuchs, L. S. (2005). Responsiveness-to-Intervention: A blueprint for practitioners, policymakers, and parents. *Teaching Exceptional Children, 38*, 57–61.

Gambrill, E. (1999). Evidence-based practice: An alternative to authority-based practice. *Families in Society: The Journal of Contemporary Human Services, 80*, 341–350.

Gordon, R. (1983). An operational classification of disease prevention. *Public Health Reports, 98*, 107–109.

Henggeler, S. W. (1991). Multidimensional causal models of delinquent behavior and their implications for treatment. In R. Cohen & A. W. Siegel (Eds.), *Context and development* (pp. 211–231). Hillsdale, NJ: Erlbaum.

Hopson, L., & Lawson, H. A. (2011). Social workers' leadership for positive school climates via data-informed planning and decision making. *Children & Schools, 33*, 106–118.

Kratochwill, T. R., Volpiansky, P., Clements, M., & Ball, C. (2007). Professional development in implementing and sustaining multitier prevention models: Implications for response to intervention. *School Psychology Review, 36*, 618–631.

Malecki, C. K., & Demaray, M. K. (2007). Social behavior assessment and Response to Intervention. In S. Jimerson, A. M. VanDerHeyden, & M. K. Murns (Eds.), *Handbook of Response to Intervention* (pp. 161–171). New York, NY: Springer Science + Business Media.

Mash, E. J., & Terdal, L. G. (1988). Behavioral assessment of child and family disturbance. In E. J. Mash & L. G. Terdal (Eds.), *Behavioral assessment of childhood disorders* (2nd ed., pp. 3–65). New York, NY: Guilford Press.

National Center for Education Statistics. (2011). *National Assessment of Educational Progress (NAEP) Data Explorer.* Washington, DC: U.S. Department of Education. Retrieved from http://nces.ed.gov/nationsreportcard/naepdata/report.aspx

National Center on Response to Intervention. (2010a). *Essential components of RTI—A closer look at Response to Intervention.* Washington, DC: U.S. Department of Education, Office of Special Education Programs, National Center on Response to Intervention. Retrieved from http://www.rti4success.org/pdf/rtiessentialcomponents_042710.pdf

National Center on Response to Intervention. (2010b). *What is RTI: The essential components* [Video]. Washington, DC: U.S. Department of Education, Office of Special Education Programs, National Center on Response to Intervention. Retrieved from http://www.rti4success.org/webinars/video/927

NCLB . (2001). *No Child Left Behind Act of 2001, P.L. 107–110, 115, Stat. 1425.* Retrieved from http://www2.ed.gov/policy/elsec/leg/esea02/index.html

Ollendick, T. H., & King, N. J. (1999). Child behavioral assessment and cognitive-behavioral interventions in schools. *Psychology in the Schools, 36*, 427–436.

Powers, J., Bowen, N. K., & Bowen, G. L. (2011). Supporting evidence-based practive in schools with an online database of best practices. *Children & Schools, 33*(2), 119–123.

Powers, J. D., Bowen, G. L., & Rose, R. A. (2005). Using social environment assets to identify intervention strategies for promoting school success. *Children and Schools, 27*, 177–187.

Reynolds, C. R ., & Kamphaus, R. W. (Eds.). (2003). *Handbook of psychological and educational assessment of children: Personality, behavior, and context* (2nd ed.). New York, NY: Guilford Press.

Reynolds, C. R., & Shaywitz, S. E. (2009). Response to Intervention: Ready or not? Or, from wait-to-fail to watch-them-fail. *School Psychology Quarterly, 24*, 130–145.

Richman, J. M., Bowen, G. L., & Woolley, M. E . (2004). School failure: An eco-interactional developmental perspective. In M. W. Fraser (Ed.), *Risk and resilience in childhood: An ecological perspective* (2nd ed., pp. 133–160). Washington, DC: NASW Press.

Rutter, M. (1985). Family and school influences on behavioural development. *Journal of Child Psychology and Psychiatry, 26*, 349–368.

Sameroff, A. J. (2000). Ecological perspectives on developmental risk. In J. D. Osofsky & H. E. Fitzgerald (Eds.), *WAIMH handbook of infant mental health: Infant mental health in groups at high risk* (Vol. 4, pp. 1–33). New York, NY: John Wiley & Sons.

Silverman, W. K., & Saavedra, L. M. (2004). Assessment and diagnosis in evidence-based practice. In P. M. Barrett & T. H. Ollendick (Eds.), *Handbook of interventions that work with children and adolescents: Prevention and treatment* (pp. 50–69). Chichester, West Sussex, England: John Wiley.

Solomon, D., Battistich, V., Watson, M., Schaps, E., & Lewis, C. (2000). A six-district study of educational change: Direct and mediated effects of the child development project. *Social Psychology of Education, 4*, 3–51.

Steele, C. M. (2010). *Whistling Vivaldi: And other clues to how stereotypes affect us* (1st ed.). New York, NY: W. W. Norton.

Stollar, S. A., Poth, R. L., Curtis, M. J., & Cohen, R. M. (2006). Collaborative strategic planning as illustration of the principles of systems change. *School Psychology Review, 35*, 181–197.

Sugai, G., & Horner, R. H. (2009). Responsiveness-to-Intervention and school-wide positive behavior supports: Integration of multi-tiered system approaches. *Exceptionality, 17*, 223–227.

U.S. Department of Education. (2004). *Individuals with Disabilities Education Improvement Act (IDEIA) of 2004. P. L. 108–446.* Federal Register.

Werner, E. E. (1990). Protective factors and individual resilience. In S. J. Meisels & J. P. Shonkoff (Eds.), *Handbook of early intervention* (pp. 97–116). Cambridge, England: Cambridge University Press.

CHAPTER 69

Constructing Data Management Systems for Tracking Accountability

Melissa Jonson-Reid

Getting Started

The call for public accountability is clear in the No Child Left Behind Act that mandates yearly accounting for school safety as well as academic achievement (www.ed.gov). To some it seems obvious that school social work services are a necessary support for academic achievement and reducing safety concerns, but as nonmandated parts of the educational system, school social workers must be cognizant of the need to communicate their importance—to be "visible" (Goren, 2002). Yet, school social workers often have large caseloads and provide a variety of services across different school settings rather than operating within a single program (Allen-Meares, 1994; Torres, 1999). This makes tracking accountability a daunting task. One means of increasing the capacity of school social workers to evaluate their services is to draw on the experience of social workers in child welfare who use computerized data management systems as a primary tool for accountability (Jonson-Reid, Kontak, & Mueller, 2001).

Child welfare agencies across the United States use computerized administrative data or management information systems (MIS) to track caseload characteristics, services, and limited outcomes. MIS make it possible to track the thousands of children served so that reports can be compiled to obtain state and federal funds, identify trends, and lobby for support. As these systems become more standardized, we are able to make comparisons across regions and support national advocacy efforts (Drake & Jonson-Reid, 1999; Jonson-Reid & Drake, 2008; U.S. DHHS, 2011).

In the past, setting up MIS programs was too costly and required too much technical expertise to be considered a viable option for the school social worker. Now, computers with sufficient storage capacity (memory) and processing speed (RAM) have become affordable. Further, computer programs have grown from basic spreadsheet applications for accounting to user-friendly database applications. Because database applications like Microsoft Access are often part of basic software packages, many districts already possess the software needed (Jonson-Reid et al., 2001; Redmond, 2003). The creation and use of MIS is no longer beyond the reach of the school social work community.

The goal of this chapter is to provide the practicing school social worker with a step-by-step approach to the creation of an MIS. It draws from the author's experiences in creating an MIS to track school social work services in a few Missouri school districts (Jonson-Reid et al., 2001; Jonson-Reid, Kontak, Citerman, Essma, & Fezzi, 2004; Jonson-Reid et al., 2007).

What We Know

Before thinking about the data elements you want to collect, it is important to consider some basic issues. Is an MIS a good idea for me? An MIS is not the answer to all evaluation needs or every practice setting. If you have a very small caseload in a well-defined program, the work involved in setting up and maintaining an MIS is probably not worth the effort. If, however, you have a large dynamic caseload, provide a wide variety of services, or work with several social work colleagues, the MIS provides some real advantages:

1. You can quickly compile reports on characteristics of the caseload or subgroups and examine their needs, services provided, and outcomes.

This information can be used for billing for Medicaid funds, grants, district reports, advocacy, or even internal monitoring.

2. You can efficiently store information over time and examine trends. For example, you can calculate how many students are carried over on your caseload each year to better predict staffing needs.
3. You will have baseline information that can be used to monitor regular services when implementing and evaluating a new project.
4. You may be able to link your database to other computerized data such as attendance to allow you to monitor the progress of students on your caseload.
5. On a larger scale, the establishment of these types of systems could provide a national look at school social work practice. It would be a tremendous advantage to have the kind of descriptive data used by child welfare to advocate for services and obtain funds.

Once you decide an MIS is the right approach for you, there are still some considerations that should be addressed before you identify variables.

Software and Hardware

Check with your district's technology person to see what software your district currently owns. In the author's experience, many districts have a program like Microsoft Access that came along with the business software purchased by the district. Another common program is Filemaker. Both have several aftermarket "how to" books available. Whatever program you choose, it is important to be able to export (move) the data easily to other programs used for data analysis. Why is this important? You are likely to reach a point at which the simple reports you can produce from the database program do not adequately answer all your questions. As long as your program can export data into a ".dbf" or an ".xls" file, you will be in good shape. You will also need either a desktop or laptop computer with sufficient memory and RAM to operate the software and store the data. Most computers come standard with over 10 gigabytes of memory, which is fine. Today an adequate desktop can be purchased for under $1,000.

Of course, if your district has funding available, another option is to purchase access to an online provider that can be used to input and track data (see example in Fitch, 2010). Even if you decide to use a prepackaged program like this, the decision-making process discussed here will help guide your selection and customization of such a service.

Confidentiality

In order to track trends in your cases or the relationship between services and outcomes, you must use individual-level data (i.e., data for each student). Of course, this means there are confidentiality concerns. The computer used should be in a secure location like your office or a secretary's office. The computer and the database you create should be password protected. If your computers are on a network, then you will want some sort of "firewall" to prevent hackers from accessing your data. Many are available, and your district information technology personnel can help you.

Data Back Up

Data loss can be a source of great anguish. Make sure you have a good virus protection package. Also, have a system in place to back up (copy) your data every so often so that if the computer hard drive should fail or your district annually wipes the network drive clean, you will not have to reenter everything. Most new computers can "burn" data onto CDs. Older computers use zip disks or tapes. These backups should be stored in a secure location.

Data Entry

Although MIS save time and increase options for accountability in the long run, the data do not enter themselves. In the author's experience, this is the largest barrier to ongoing maintenance of the MIS. Find out if your school site or district will provide clerical time for this purpose. If not, it is best to allow some time each week to enter information. This will make the task move more quickly and feel like less of a drain on your time.

Location of the database is another consideration. Tools like Microsoft Sharepoint can be used to locate an Access database in a secure online location. This would allow multiple people to input data from different locations while tracking who has access and who has added information (see sharepoint.microsoft.com for more information).

Colleagues

You can create an MIS for your own individual use. If there are several school social workers in your district, however, everyone must use the same system for tracking cases in order to create a district-wide report on school social work services. It is essential that all of you be part of the planning process. Decisions must be made about what information to input, there must be clear understanding of the meaning of the data fields, and buy-in must be obtained to ensure that the information is entered in a timely and correct fashion.

Reporting

Many school social workers lack training and/or time to address analysis of data—particularly longitudinal data. The software should allow you to create basic reports on your own. You will probably begin to ask more complex questions as you collect data and think about accountability. Your district may have a data analyst who can take the exported data and perform more complicated statistical analyses. If not, consider the formation of a partnership with a local university person (e.g., Allen-Meares & Franklin, 1998; Jonson-Reid et al., 2001).

What We Can Do

Planning

Once you decide that having an MIS is a good idea, you need to spend time planning. Kettner, Moroney, and Martin (1999) suggest seven steps to build an MIS. Five of these steps are discussed in this chapter:

1. Identify the questions to be answered.
2. Identify the data elements needed.
3. Design data collection procedures.
4. Develop data entry procedures.
5. Develop a strategy for analysis and reporting

After you start implementing the system, there are bound to be changes needed. So, after these steps are completed, you should use the first semester or so as a pilot period. Do not be surprised if the data from the initial try is less useful than hoped. After the pilot period, hold a meeting with all users to review the process and data. This will allow you to make needed modifications.

Identifying the Questions to Be Answered

You have heard the saying "garbage in, garbage out." Computers only produce information based upon what you put in them. If you try to collect too many items, users will skip data fields seen as "less important" to save time or become frustrated and stop paying attention to accuracy. Collect too little information and you will be left with useless reports. To reach a balance, it is necessary to spend time thinking about the key questions you want answered.

1. What am I accountable for? In a self-contained special education classroom, a social worker may focus on behavioral goals linked to a child's individualized educational plan. Accountability for achieving those goals can be tracked by entering scores from a pre- and post-standardized measure like the Child Behavior Checklist. Some social workers serve many students across schools for many reasons. Their outcomes may be recorded as broad categories.
2. What is my district interested in? An MIS can help communicate your value to the district, providing at least some of your outcomes are of interest to the district. Typically schools are most interested in items related to their accountability reports and funding, such as attendance, high school completion, and disciplinary referrals.
3. Am I asking if my services "caused" the outcome? MIS are not typically designed to measure cause and effect. As you have learned in coursework on research, such evaluation requires random assignment to treatment and control groups or at least some form of comparison group. This does not mean you cannot use an MIS to record this information. If you are evaluating a program and using random assignment to treatment, then you can add an indicator in the database of who is in the treatment and control groups. Then you can run the data on your outcome measure by the indicator of group membership. If you are using a comparison group (not randomly assigned), your MIS can help you track other services children in your program are receiving. Identifying other services and problems that students encounter while in your program will help you identify possible alternative explanations for the outcome.

4. What other information do you want? In addition to service outcomes, you will want to describe various aspects of what you did during the year. This will probably include describing services, case characteristics, and overall numbers for later use in reports.

Applying Interventions within a Response to Intervention Framework

The connection between data management systems and Response to Intervention (RTI) is clear, given that data-based decision making and continual assessment are core aspects of the model (Burns & Gibbons, 2008; Kelly et al., 2010). The ability to apply RTI principles on a large scale (i.e., school-wide) is dependent upon the availability of high-quality, longitudinal data in an easily accessible format so that appropriate decisions can be made. Why? Well, universal screening and then tracking of changes on empirical instruments can be done by hand for a small number of students, but if one implements such a process for hundreds or thousands of students, it seems impossible to track the data without a computerized system. While much of the RTI literature focuses on academic assessment information, the same approach can be used for behavioral issues.

So while constructing a school social work MIS certainly makes sense as a valuable tool for RTI, some decisions will need to be made. On one hand it might seem best to integrate the school social work system into a broader school system, but it's possible that some of the things you wish to track regarding services and case progress are not things that you would wish to have other educators that may be using RTI principles (i.e., teachers, administrators) to access. Therefore, it may be that you set up the reporting function for your system to easily provide components that the larger school RTI process requires while still maintaining a distinct database. Tools and Practice Examples

Tools and Practice Examples

Data Collection Procedures

Once the major questions you wish to answer have been identified, it is time to select variables and decide on a data collection method. There are two choices for data collection. Either complete hard-copy forms first and then enter the data into the computer or just enter the information directly into the computer. Even if you decide to enter data directly into the computer, you should still construct at least one hard-copy form first. It will be easier to review your variable choices and pilot the process on a few cases using a paper copy rather than constructing and then revising the data entry shell. It is also helpful to have a hardcopy option available for training or recording information when traveling. As we discuss variable selection, we will examine examples of portions of data forms. Notes in italic within the boxes provide advice about the form or categories.

Variable Selection

Identification

In order to track cases over time, you must have a consistent and unique way of identifying individuals. You can enter names into the computer or ID numbers or both. Entering only ID numbers provides additional protection against accidental disclosure, but it also means that you will have to keep a list somewhere that links the ID numbers to the names. Using the district's student ID number in your system is useful, as it is already linked to the student name and it may make it possible to link to data on the school's computer like attendance.

Demographic and Basic Case Information

Information such as gender, age or grade level, school, socioeconomic status, and some type of racial categorization are *critical*. Why? Some of the most common questions you will ask later will be related to characteristics of the students. For example, if a group of students on your caseload appears to be struggling, you will want to know what makes them different from the other cases. Or, if you wish to write a grant for elementary school girls, then these variables allow you to summarize the data for this specific group.

Dates are also key components because caseloads are dynamic. Students may come and go from your caseload during the year. One might expect different outcomes for a student who receives 3 weeks of the program compared to another who completes the program. Thus, service start or referral date and end dates are important aspects of any MIS (see Box 69.1).

Other special program indicators can be added to the case description to correspond to funding sources or other programs that may interface with your services. For example, you might want to record participation in special education or the presence of a DSM diagnosis. These allow you to easily break down your statistics by special status (see Box 69.2).

Needs or Problems

An important aspect of accountability is tracking why a student was referred to you so that you can assess change. If you use a standardized assessment tool or checklist, the score or specific categories can be entered into the computer. The advantage of using standardized instruments is that you can compare them with available research, they provide norms based on large samples, and they often can be readministered as posttests. In Box 69.3, the MIS system includes the internalizing and externalizing scores from the CBCL, as well as some subscales of interest that relate directly to the intervention.

Other social workers receive referrals for diverse issues such as health, child abuse and neglect, and homelessness. In this case, a checklist of referral reasons can be developed. If you create such a checklist, it is important to consider the following:

- Will you track the referring party's issue, the issues identified after you assess the student, or both? Recording the referring party's understanding will help you report back on initial concerns. However, your assessment may reveal other issues.
- If there is more than one person contributing data, everyone must agree on what a created category means. Otherwise, your data will not be comparable across social workers. Try to make variable labels simple and clear to minimize confusion.
- The name of the issues should be specific enough to be useful. For example, "behavior problem" is too vague. It is better to use categories like "disruptive classroom behavior" and "aggression" that can be clearly defined.
- Balance the desire for depth with the need for information and ease of data entry. Too many categories are hard to fill in and will be more difficult to summarize later. Imagine having a pie chart of problems with 50 slices—it is too confusing.
- When recording problems, do not forget funding streams or reporting requirements. Districts obtain funding through attendance, so it is a good idea to record this if you have an impact in that area. Or if funds are available

Box 69.1 Basic Demographic Information

Student ID:_______ School:______

Referral Date:______

Gender ___M ___F

Race ___ African American
___ Asian
___ Caucasian
___ Hispanic
___ Other

Grade ___ (K–12)

Note: Racial categories should describe your school's/district's population. For example, in the southwest there may be a substantial American Indian population but few Asians. There "American Indian" would be its own category, and Asian would likely be part of "Other."

Note: In this example we use grade level rather than age. You will be more likely to report information to the district that way. However, you do lack the ability to analyze whether or not the student is overage for his or her grade without capturing age or date of birth.

Eligible for Free or Reduced Lunch ____ (Yes/No)

Note: You might also choose Medicaid eligibility or Title 1 designation as an indicator of socioeconomic status depending upon the link to funding in your district.

Box 69.2 Special Case Descriptors

DSM diagnosis ___(Yes/No) Category_______________________

Note: It may be beneficial to note DSM diagnoses for students on your caseload. This will help you liaison with outside therapists and may help you obtain funding for services from organizations like the National Institutes for Mental Health. It can also aid you in choosing interventions. For example a child with ADHD may require a different approach than a child without ADHD.

Special Education ___(Yes/No)

Note: It is likely that some of your caseload will also be served under the IDEA. This may even be a funding source for you.

Disability category

___ Emotional disturbance
___ Vision/hearing
___ Learning disability: visual ___ auditory
___ Autism
___ Mental retardation
___ OHI
___ Physical (paralysis, etc.)

Note: Do not forget to record the disability type. Even if all your students are ED, there may be other disabilities present. Such combinations of issues can impact intervention. For example, an ED child with an auditory disability may have difficulty benefiting from a "talk therapy" group.

for bullying prevention, specify "bullying" as a referral reason so you can track the issue for a grant. Including categories that correspond to larger scale areas of interest also allows you to compare the prevalence of a given issue on your caseload to district, state, or national figures.

Box 69.4 illustrates a portion of a referral reason checklist.

Services or Interventions

Obviously the detail you include in case file notes is not appropriate for the MIS. Select categories or brief comments that can later be summarized with ease. If you primarily provide counseling, you may wish to specify the type of counseling such as cognitive/behavioral, rational/emotive, or a specific curriculum. This will allow you to examine trends in outcomes that are associated with various practice approaches. If you provide different services according to a wide variety of needs, you will probably have to sacrifice some specificity. If some services are rarely provided, like transportation, create a broad "other services" category with a comment area for description rather than listing them all out.

In addition to type of service, there are characteristics of services to consider. The start and end dates will tell you how long a case was served but not how often or how intensely. Detail about services can be added by recording frequency of contacts rather than checking off the type of service.

Box 69.3 Example of Standardized Assessment Scores

Pre-test Child Behavior Checklist	Internalizing score: _____
	Externalizing: _____
Subscale of interest: __________	Score: _____
Subscale of interest: __________	Score: _____

Note: You can also design your form to mimic the scale or checklist summary area for ease of data entry.

Box 69.4

Attendance ——— Rate of attendance (Start): ________
Note: It is VERY important not to just list days missed. You have to record the days missed divided by the days possible to attend. Why? Because a child referred in the beginning of October will have few possible days to miss but might miss 75% of the days. At the end of the year, a child will have more total days missed, but will hopefully be missing a smaller percentage of the possible days. If you only look at the raw numbers, your outcome will look like failure even if the child's actual attendance improved.

Bullying ___Victim? __ Perpetrator? ______
Note: Some problems should have a victim and perpetrator indicator. This is important when you consider that the perpetrator is also counted under disciplinary action while the victim is not. Further, interventions and outcomes are likely to vary along this dimension.

Child abuse and neglect suspected____ Type 1:____________________

Reported to child welfare? __ (Yes/No) Date:

If no, why not? ___ (enter number)

(1 = other reasonable explanation for injury or condition; 2 = already reported this incident; 3 = concern does not meet the definition of reportable abuse or neglect)

Type 2:_________

Reported to child welfare? ___ (Yes/No) Date:________

If no, why not? ___ (enter number)

(1 = other reasonable explanation for injury or condition; 2 = already reported this incident; 3 = concern does not meet the definition of reportable abuse or neglect)

Note: School social workers often serve maltreated children. It is important to track the form of maltreatment to tailor services, dispel myths (sometimes districts may assume sexual abuse is highly prevalent because of media reports when it is typically neglect), and design programs and interventions. Tracking the reporting of such events keeps you in compliance with the law and helps trigger the need to collaborate with child welfare.

Family Issues ___Type 1:__Type 2:__Type 3:_____
(1 = parenting; 2 = domestic violence; 3 = parental substance abuse; 4 = divorce; 5 = parental mental health; 6 = parental health; 7 = sibling conflict)

Note: There are many possible family issues. To save space, the form indicates a place to check this overall category and then leaves three spaces to indicate the specific number that corresponds to the reason. This saves data entry screen space.

Of course, five individual counseling sessions is not necessarily the same as 5 hours of counseling. You may wish to record the number of hours of each service provided to better understand intensity. These items can be recorded monthly, quarterly, or by semester. Generally it is better to keep up with entering data on smaller periods of time rather than trying to wait until the end of the year.

Boxes 69.5 and 69.6 provide examples of two service-tracking methods: one for social workers who provide only counseling and one for social workers who provide a variety of services. The social workers providing only counseling have a regular schedule and just indicate the number of sessions. In Box 69.6, the social workers track time served rather than frequency of contacts because the amount of time a service requires varies a lot from case to case. These social workers also work with outside agencies and record the name of the agency to whom they refer cases. This will allow them to identify agencies that may interact better with referred families or wish to consider joint participation in a grant.

Box 69.5 Description of Counseling Services

Individual Counseling Fall ______________ (No. of sessions) Type: ___ Cognitive Behavioral
___ Rational Emotive
___ Object Relations
___ Curriculum used: ____________________
Individual Counseling Spring ______________ (No. of sessions) Type: ___ Cognitive Behavioral
__ Rational Emotive
__ Object Relations
__ Curriculum used: ____________________

Note: Sometimes it may be easier to identify a specific counseling curriculum followed rather than the mode of therapy.

Recording Outcomes

So far, we have recorded process and assessment information. We must also be accountable for outcomes. In a district where the school social worker provides mental health services for ED children, it makes sense to enter a standardized assessment like the CBCL as the problem and then use a posttest administration for the outcome. If you are trying to improve attendance, then you will record the attendance at the close of services. The specificity of the outcome will vary by the type of services you provide. If a social worker provides a range of services for a range of issues, a case disposition coding scheme may be better. Case dispositions may include "resolved and closed" with a date, as well as other case closure reasons like expulsion or graduation (see Box 69.7). Above all, make sure your outcomes correspond logically to the services you provide! For example, it is unlikely that you will have a dramatic impact on internalizing CBCL scores if you only provide crisis intervention.

From Data Form to Computer

Once you have identified the elements you wish to record, it is time to make the data entry shell. A database program, like Microsoft Access or

Box 69.6 Examples of Broad Range of Services

Individual counseling Fall ________________ (No. of hours)
Spring ________________ (No. of hours)
Referral for services Fall ________________ (Yes/No)
Agency 1: ________________
Agency 2: ________________
Spring (Yes/No) Agency 1: ________________
Agency 2: ________________

Outside Agency Collaboration Fall hours________________
Type 1: Contact: ________________ phone: ________________
Type 2: Contact: ________________ phone: ________________
(1 = child welfare; 2 = juvenile probation; 3 = comm. mental health; 4 = regional center)
Outside Agency Collaboration Spring hours__
Type 1: _______ Contact: ________________ phone: ________________
Type 2: _______ Contact: ________________ phone: ________________
(1 = child welfare; 2 = juvenile probation; 3 = comm. mental health; 4 = regional center)

Note: Referral for services and collaboration are different. While you want to limit categories to those with meaningful numbers, you also want to be sure you are capturing information of value. In this example, a space for a contact person is added. You will not report on contact people in your evaluation report, but this can be added as a help to you so that you do not have to look up the hard copy file to remember who to call.

Box 69.7 Case Dispositions

Closing Date: ___
Total Possible Attendance Days in Service Period: ___
Days Attended During Service Period (End): ___

Note: The above combination of variables will allow you to calculate a change in the rate of attendance from the time services started to case closure. You then compare this to the attendance rate at time of referral.

Other Dispositions:
Issue resolved: ___ (1 = outside services obtained; 2 = behavior improved; 3 = entered special education)
Graduated: ___ Moved: ___ Dropped Out: ___ Expelled: ___ Deceased:

File-Maker, allows you to create an onscreen form that mimics the hard copy forms you created (see Box 69.8). Each case is presented to you as a separate screen, but the data is stored in a spreadsheet hidden from view. Most recent database programs have helpful "wizard" options that can guide you through all or part of the process. In addition to storing data, these programs can be set up to automatically produce reports. The following are some considerations you should think about regarding the data entry screen.

"Forced Entry" Items

Most programs allow "forced entry" items. This means that the person entering data cannot proceed without entering information for this item. The advantage is that such items will not have missing data. However, if you use check boxes for referral reasons there will be some boxes that are supposed to be blank. Such items should not be forced entry.

Text Versus Categories

Categories are preferable to comment boxes in computer databases. Blank spaces that require a number to represent a category (e.g., the collaboration agency types in Box 69.6) or check boxes to represent categories (e.g., racial category in Box 69.1) save space, save time in data entry, and are easier to summarize in tables and graphs. You do, however, need to allow for text responses at times. For example, what happens if a student is not referred for any of the categories listed? You will want an "Other" space with a comment area to explain "other." Sometimes these are emerging issues that you will want to add to your data screen the following year.

Pull-Downs

Most programs will allow you to create a pull-down selection for multiple-choice categories like the racial category in Box 69.1. In Box 69.4 we see that the hard-copy form offers a space for numbers to identify specific types of "family issues." On the computer, you can create a pull-down list that allows the person entering data to choose from a pre-selected list of options (like the ones in parentheses on the hard-copy forms). These prompts help remind people of the category choices, save space on the screen, and cut down data entry time.

Archiving Old Records

To track trends over time, you must set up a system to archive (save) old records. You could enter data into the same database over time by using multiple screens linked together, but this may become difficult for your computer to handle over time. An alternative is to save the old database with a new name, then copy the student information to a new database with blank values except for the names, ID numbers, race, and gender from the prior year. Bringing forward the old demographics that do not change saves you time the next year. Be sure to use the ID numbers for students only once; otherwise, you will lose the ability to link student records over time! By archiving old records, you will have the capability

Box 69.8 School Social Work Services Tracking System

Student# 0 Last First Grade 4
Ethnicity A = african amer Gender F Referral Date 1/21/2002 New reason date
School Home School ☐ EYWB ☐ ADC program ☐ VTS ☑
Referral Source #Name?

Special Programs/Services

Special Educatio ☐ Sped Type Foster Care ☐ Other DFS ☐ DFSWorke
504PLAN ☐ 504 reason Family Court ☐ DJO/other
Medication ☐ DSM Diagnosi Therapy ☐ Tx contact

Referral Reasons/Response

Abuse ☐ Family Issues ☐ Homeless ☐ Financial Issue ☐
HOTLINE 1 Hotlinel Reas famprobl
Hotline2 hotline2 Reas famprob3
Hotline3 hotline3 Reas famprob2

Academic ☐ Attendance ☐
SSD Screen: Fall ☐ SSD Screen: Spring ☐ Days Absent ○ Part Days ○ Tardies #Na
SSD IEP: Fall ☐ SSD IEP: Sprin ☐ Depression ☐ Suicidal ☐ Grief/loss ☐
Aggression ☐ Disruptive Behavior ☑ Other Emotiona ☐
OSS# ☐ISS# ☐ Emotissue
Sexual Assault ☐ Sexual Harrassment ☐ Health ☐
Victim: SA ☐ Victim: SH ☐ Healthissue
Runaway ☐ Substance Abuse ☐
Other Reason# Name? Type of Substance

Services/Time Served/Closure

Crisis Intervention: Fall ☐ Crisis Intervention: Spring ☐ Care Team: Fall ☐ Care Team: Sprin ☐
Counseling Indiv: Fall ☐ Counseling Indiv: Spring ☐ Home Liaison: Fall ☐ Home Liaison: Spring ☐
Counseling Group: Fall ☐ Group Type Case Mng/staff consult:. Fall ☐ Case Mng/staff consult: Spring ☐
Counseling Group: Spring ☐ Group Type2 Agency Liaison: Fall ☐ Agency Liaison: Spring ☐
Referral for Service: Fall ☐ Other Agency #Name? Referral for:
Referral for Service: Spring ☐ Other Agency2 #Name?Contact Hours: Fall Contact Hours: Spring
Days Absent-End of Year #Name Part days Absent #Nam TardiesEOY #Name OSS#: Fall #Name? ISS#: Fall #Name?
OSS#: Spring #Name? ISS# Spring #Name?

Close date for Fall #Name? Case Status Fall #Name?
Close date for Spring #Name? Case Status Spring #Name?
Comments

of linking records to form a longitudinal database for analysis.

Key Points to Remember

In order to continue to promote the importance of school social work, practitioners must begin to use the technology available to meet accountability standards. If the process still seems too daunting after reading this chapter, a consultant or university partner can provide help with setting up the database. It is hoped that readers will increase their use of computerization of caseload data for accountability in their own practice. As such use increases, we can also look forward to having data that can provide a better picture of practice across the nation.

References

Allen-Meares, P. (1994). Social work services in schools: A national survey of entry-level tasks. *Social Work, 39,* 560–565.

Allen-Meares, P., & Franklin, C. (1998). Partnerships for better education: Schools, universities and communities (editorial). *Social Work in Education, 20,* 147–151.

Burns, M., & Gibbons, K. (2008). *Implementing response to intervention in primary and secondary schools: Procedures to assure scientific based practices.* New York, NY: Routledge.

Drake, B., & Jonson-Reid, M. (1999). Some thoughts on the increasing use of administrative data in child maltreatment research. *Child Maltreatment, 4,* 308–315.

Fitch, D. (2010), Homeless management information system customization intervention. *Journal of Human Behavior in the Social Environment, 20*(2), 255–271.

Goren, S. (2002). The wonderland of social work in the schools or how Alice learned to cope. In R. Constable, S. McDonald, & J. Flynn (Eds.), *School social work: Practice, policy and research perspectives* (5th ed.). Chicago: Lyceum.

Jonson-Reid, M., Kontak, D., & Mueller, S. (2001). Developing a management information system for school social workers: A field-university partnership. *Children & Schools, 23*(4), 198–211.

Jonson-Reid, M., Kontak, D., Citerman, B., Essma, A., & Fezzi, N. (2004). School social work case characteristics, services and dispositions: Year one results. *Children & Schools, 26,* 5–22.

Jonson-Reid, M., Kim, J., Citerman, B., Columbini, C., Essma, A., Fezzi, N., ... Thomas, B. (2007). Maltreated children in schools: The interface of school social work and child welfare. *Children & Schools, 29*(3), 182–191.

Jonson-Reid, M., & Drake, B. (2008). Multi-sector longitudinal administrative databases: An indispensable tool for evidence-based policy for maltreated children and their families. *Child Maltreatment, 13*(4), 392–399.

Kelly, M., Frey, A., Alvarez, M., Berzin, S., Shaffer, G., & O'Brien, K. (2010). School social work practice and response to intervention. *Children & Schools, 32*(4), 201–209.

Kettner, P., Moroney, R., & Martin, L. (1999). *Designing and managing programs: An effectiveness-based approach* (2nd ed., pp. 139–166). Thousand Oaks, CA: Sage.

Redmond, M. E. (2003). School Social Work Information Systems (SSWIS): A relational database for school social workers. *Journal of Technology in Human Services, 21*(1), 161–175.

Torres, S. (1999). The status of school social workers in America. In E. Freeman, C. Franklin, R. Fong, G. Shaffer, & E. Timberlake (Eds.), *Multisystem skills and interventions in school social work practice* (pp. 461–472). Washington, DC: NASW Press.

U.S. Department of Health and Human Services, Children's Bureau. (2011). *Child maltreatment 2010.* Washington, DC: Government Printing Office.

Using the School Success Profile to Assess Outcomes

CHAPTER 70

Gary L. Bowen Danielle C. Swick

Getting Started

The United States has one of the highest high school dropout rates of any industrialized nation (OECD, 2009). A startling 25% of students do not graduate high school within four years after starting the ninth grade (Chapman, Laird, & KewalRamani, 2010). Racial and ethnic minority youths, youths from lower socioeconomic families, and males are at increased risk for dropping out of high school (Chapman et al., 2010). Other students graduate from high school but are ill prepared to continue their education or to compete for jobs capable of a living wage (Neild, Balfanz, & Herzog, 1997).

Increasing the school success for all students has become a national priority. In President Barack Obama's address to the Joint Session of Congress on February 29, 2009, he exclaimed that there is an "urgent need to expand the promise of education in America" and that long-term investments in education were vital to the nation's economic recovery. He described dropping out of high school as a "prescription for economic decline" (Obama, 2009).

The evidence-based practice planning sequence in schools to increase school success begins with a careful assessment of students' presenting situations, strengths, and needs. School mental health professionals often utilize quantitative assessment tools to gather information on students' perceptions of themselves, their performance at school, and factors that are operating in their larger environment that may be hindering or promoting their school success (G. L. Bowen & Woolley, 2007). The School Success Profile (SSP) is one such assessment tool that professionals can use to inform intervention planning and promote students' school success.

This chapter presents a brief description and history of the SSP, a strengths-based assessment tool for informing, monitoring, and evaluating social work interventions with middle and high school students. The Eco-Interactional Developmental (EID) model of school success, which provides the conceptual foundation for the SSP, is then reviewed as a perspective for understanding the interplay between students' neighborhoods, schools, families, and peers in the promotion of school success. Major findings from SSP-related research examining these domains and their effects on students' school success are also presented. The role of the SSP in the process of intervention planning is discussed, and a case example from a small, private school for low-income students with less-than-satisfactory academic achievement is presented illustrating the utility of the SSP. The chapter concludes with how the SSP can be used within a Response to Intervention (RTI) framework.

The SSP: Description and History

The SSP is a self-report survey questionnaire for middle and high school students (G. L. Bowen & Richman, 2010; Richman, Bowen, & Woolley, 2004). It consists of 263 online multiple-choice questions to assess students' perceptions of their social environment (neighborhood, school, friends, and family) and their own individual adaptation (physical health, psychological health, and school performance). The survey can either be administered in whole or users can select specific scales. The entire questionnaire takes approximately 60 to 75 minutes on average for students to complete; however, users are encouraged to construct the SSP with select scales so that it takes no more than 30 to 45 minutes to complete. The SSP yields both individual and summary group student profiles from the data, informing both micro- and macro-level practice interventions.

Since its development in 1993 in partnership with Communities In Schools, which is the largest stay-in-school network in the United States, the SSP has been utilized by more than 1000 middle and high schools and administered to approximately 100,000 students in the United States. In addition to educational settings, the SSP has also been used in numerous social services settings, including juvenile detention facilities and neighborhood youth programs. All or parts of the SSP have been translated into Spanish, Hebrew, Lithuanian, Romanian, and Portuguese. The Elementary School Success Profile (ESSP) is available for children in the third to fifth grades, and also includes assessment forms for one of their caregivers and their classroom teacher (N. K. Bowen, Bowen, & Woolley, 2004).

What We Know about School Success

Fraser and Galinsky (2010) make an important distinction between problem theory and program theory in designing and evaluating social work interventions. Problem theory attempts to explain variation in outcomes, such as school engagement and academic achievement. The product is a logic model that links antecedents or critical success variables to the desired results. Program theory specifies the link between interventions and these antecedents or critical success variables. Although the SSP works from a strengths-based perspective (i.e., working toward desired results rather than away from undesired results), the underlying process is similar. The SSP is framed and informed by an Eco-Interactional Developmental (EID) model.

The Eco-Interactional Developmental (EID) Model

The EID perspective emphasizes the reciprocal process between students and their social environments over time, including the neighborhood, the school, the family, and the peer group (Richman et al., 2004). Students' goodness of fit within these social environments frames and informs their ability to achieve desired results at school and in life (G. L. Bowen, 2009). The EID model sets forth that in order to best understand students' school success, students must be viewed in the context of not only their present realities but also their past experiences and anticipated futures—a developmental perspective.

The 30 core dimensions of the SSP are organized into a "problem theory" logic model comprising three levels of results:

- distal results (academic performance)
- intermediate results (personal beliefs and well-being, and school attitudes and behavior)
- proximal results (neighborhood, school, friends, and family dimensions)

Each dimension is labeled and defined from an asset or strength-based perspective (see Table 70.1). Distal and intermediate results are classified as student results because they are seen as the outcome of addressing the physical, psychological, and support needs of students. Proximal results are labeled as program results because they are the targets of intervention and prevention activities.

These three levels of results can be compared to hands on a clock to distinguish and represent the chain of influence among them. Distal results can be seen as the hour hand, intermediate results are the minute hand, and proximal results are the second hand. As students' social environments become increasingly supportive (second hand), students' personal beliefs and well-being improve (minute hand), which in turn fosters high academic performance and overall positive outcomes (hour hand). Distal results on the hour hand turn the slowest and are directly affected by the movement of the minute and second hands (G. L. Bowen, Woolley, Richman, & Bowen, 2001).

Research Findings from the SSP

Associated SSP-related research has focused on three major student outcomes: school engagement, trouble avoidance, and academic performance. In analyses that have looked at the effects of all of the SSP dimensions simultaneously on student outcomes, several notable findings have emerged. Three of the most consistent findings across these SSP-related studies are the positive impact of safe neighborhoods and schools, of supportive and caring adults, and of prosocial friends on student success at school (Anthony & Stone,

Table 70.1 School Success Profile Dimensions

School Environment Profile

Neighborhood

Neighborhood Safety (8 items): Youth live in a neighborhood with a low incidence of crime and violence.

Neighborhood Youth Behavior (8 items): Youth live in a neighborhood where young people engage in constructive behavior, graduate from high school, and are unlikely to break the law and get in trouble with the police.

Neighbor Support (7 items): Youth perceive their neighbors as trustworthy and supportive of young people, interested in their welfare, and willing to help them if they have a problem.

Family

Home Academic Environment (8 items): Youth report that they discuss their courses or programs at school, their school-related activities, current events and politics, and their plans for the future with the adults who live in their home.

Parent Education Support (6 items): Youth report that the adults in their home encourage and support them in their schoolwork and activities, help them get needed books or supplies, and offer help with homework or special assignments.

School Behavior Expectations (12 items): Youth perceive the adults in their home as expecting them to do their schoolwork, to attend classes, and to follow school rules.

Parent Support (5 items): Youth report that the adults in their home provide them with loving support and encouragement and spend free time with them.

Family Togetherness (7 items): Youth report that the people in their home feel a sense of emotional closeness and bonding with one another, do things together, and work together to solve problems.

School

School Safety (11 items): Youth attend a school with a low level of crime, problem behavior, and bullying behavior.

School Satisfaction (7 items): Youth enjoy going to their school, get along well with teachers and other students, and report that they are getting a good education.

Learning Climate (7 items): Youth attend a school where students get a good education, where student needs come first, where the adults at school affirm and care about students, and where every student is valued.

Academic Rigor (10 items): Youth report that their teachers have high expectations of them, assign challenging work, ask questions and give assignments that make them think, and give them feedback about their classroom performance.

Academic Relevancy (11 items): Youth report that their teachers know about different jobs and careers, help them relate classroom lessons to the real world, and encourage them to think about and discuss their future.

Teacher Support (8 items): Youth perceive teachers at their school as supportive, as caring about them and their academic success, and as expecting them to do their best.

Micro-Interactions (13 items): Youth report that they were treated respectfully and fairly by people at school and felt included at school over the past 30 days.

Friends

Friend Behavior (9 items): Youth have friends who are unlikely to break the law or get in trouble with the police, who stay out of trouble and perform well at school, and who are likely to graduate from high school.

(continued)

Table 70.1 *(Continued)*

School Environment Profile
Peer Group Acceptance (8 items): Youth feel accepted by their peers, able to be themselves, and able to resist peer pressure.
Friend Support (5 items): Youth perceive their friends as trustworthy and supportive and as responsive to their needs and feelings.
Individual Adaptation Profile
Personal Beliefs and Well-Being
Absence of Physical Impairments (3 items): Youth report that over the past week, they did not have any physical difficulties such as toothaches, trouble seeing, or difficulty hearing.
Positive Body Image (3 items): Youth do not report concerns or worry about their weight.
Physical Health (9 items): Youth evidence good health, as indicated by an absence of symptoms or physical illness over the past seven days.
Adjustment (6 items): Youth do not feel a sense of sadness, confusion, aloneness, or general despair about the future.
Self-Confidence (5 items): Youth report a sense of confidence in themselves and positive self-regard.
Spiritual Faith (4 items): Youth report that religious faith gives them strength and influences the decisions they make.
Social Support Use (8 items): Youth indicate that there are people they can turn to for various types of social support and assistance.
School Attitudes & Behavior
Success Orientation (12 items): Youth are able to picture their futures in a positive way, work hard and make choices that will guarantee a successful future, and feel confident that they will be successful in life.
School Engagement (4 items): Youth report that they find school fun and exciting, look forward to learning new things at school, look forward to going to school, and are not bored at school.
Extracurricular Participation (10 items): Youth report that they have or will have participated in school activities during the current school year that are not part of class work.
Trouble Avoidance (11 items): Youth report that they have avoided problem behaviors in the past 30 days that reflect getting into trouble at school.
Academic Performance
Grades (3 items): Youth report at least Bs or Cs or better on their most recent report card, no Ds or Fs on their most recent report card, and they describe their grades as better or much better than the grades received by other students in their classes.

2010; G. L. Bowen, Rose, Powers, & Glennie, 2008; Powers, Bowen, & Rose, 2005). Students are more likely to succeed in school (have higher school engagement, increased avoidance of school problem behaviors, and higher academic performance) when they are able to live and learn in safe places, when supportive and caring adults are present in their social environments, and when they have friends who stay out of trouble and perform well at school and who are likely to graduate from high school.

What We Can Do

The SSP is available for use by school social workers at the following Web site: http://www.schoolsuccessonline.com/. The Web site includes pricing information and administrative training materials for downloading. Both online and on-site, face-to-face administration and intervention training is offered for a fee. Schools incur additional costs

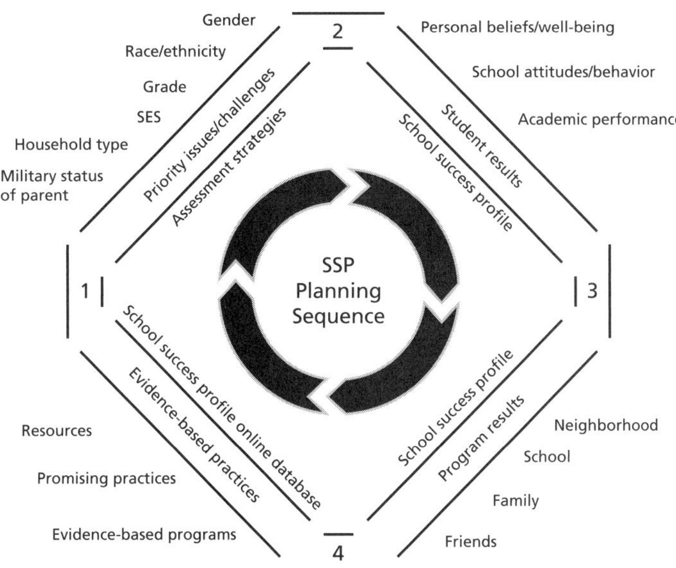

Figure 70.1 School Success Profile Planning Sequence

for on-site technical assistance and for special data analysis requests. Schools assume full responsibility for compliance with applicable institutional review requirements within their school or district for administering the SSP.

Administration

The SSP is typically administered to students in the computer lab at their school, although it can be taken from any computer with an Internet connection. A hard-copy version of the SSP is available for use, including an optical scan-scoring sheet. However, schools are encouraged to use the online version of the SSP, if at all possible. A unique serial number (student ID) and password are assigned to each student, although schools decide whether or not to link the names of students with specific IDs for tracking. Schools download individual and summary group profiles from the Web. Access to these profiles is password-protected, and sites have access only to their own data.

Summary Profiles

The SSP results in summary data in the form of individual student profiles and site-level aggregate profiles. An integrated query system allows school social workers to examine group-level results within student subgroups, both single (e.g., gender) and in combination (e.g., gender and grade). The SSP is designed to supplement and enhance practitioners' ongoing observations of and dialogue with students, not to substitute for this process. Other information, such as that from school records or observations, may either support or counter students' reports.

Individual Profile

The individual profile includes information about 30 dimensions related to the student's social environment and individual adaptation. The student's ID and the date of administration are listed at the top of the page (right-hand corner), and reference information about the student is included on the upper right-hand side of the profile form. The individual profile has attribution to a particular student only if clients have linked student names to student IDs.

Each profile dimension is a summary scale that includes multiple items. Students receive scores for only those dimensions that were included on the survey. Student scores on each dimension are coded into three colors: red, yellow, and green. The colors correspond to cutoffs that have been determined based on comparison to national norms, criterion analysis, and expert review (G. L. Bowen & Richman, 2010). Each dimension reflects a continuum of protection from red (potential risk), yellow (some caution may be warranted), and green (potential asset). SSP dimensions that were not included on the assessment are coded with a gray dot.

Summary Group Profile

A composite summary of the individual profiles at a particular site, the summary group profile helps school social workers identify areas that may represent particular strengths or concerns among students. A site may include a classroom (at least 10 students), school, district, county, or state. The summary group profile looks similar to the individual profile with the exception that information includes summary statistics for the student group. Reference information about the student group is included on the right side of the summary profile.

Summary data on the 30 SSP profile dimensions are included on the left and right sides of the page. The percentages associated with each dimension indicate the proportion of students who received one of three scores: red (potential risk), yellow (some caution may be warranted), and green (potential asset). These data reflect how students are doing as a group on the dimensions included in the social environment profile and the individual adaptation profile. Dimensions that were not included in the SSP administration are coded as not assessed.

The most positive summary group profile would include results with a high percentage of students with green (asset) codes. In reviewing the findings, school practitioners are encouraged to consider the desired performance standard for each dimension—the minimally acceptable proportion of students with asset codes. Information from the summary group profile is helpful in prioritizing interventions that address the difficulties faced by groups of students. In this way, profile data are one means by which social workers determine how to allocate their limited resources to maximize program effectiveness.

Intervention Planning

School social workers partner with students, families, teachers, other school staff, and community stakeholder groups to design appropriate intervention goals and strategies. Most often in our experience, the school improvement team or other such group within the school leads the SSP intervention process under the auspices of the school administrative team. An important starting point in the review of SSP results is the existing school improvement plan for achieving students' academic goals. The SSP intervention planning process builds upon the existing plan.

Results-focused planning (RFP), which is a program management strategy, provides an approach for using information from the SSP as a tool for intervention and prevention planning (Orthner & Bowen, 2004). A key principle of RFP is planning with the intended results in mind (Hatry, 1999). The specification of program activities receives attention only after intended results are defined. From an RFP perspective, the 18 social environment dimensions are program results that can be targeted for intervention and prevention planning as a means to influence student results associated with individual adaptation: personal beliefs and well-being, school attitudes and behavior, and academic performance.

As depicted in Figure 70.1, the SSP intervention planning sequence includes four steps:

1. Identify priority issues and challenges faced by students, including target groups that are most likely to face these issues and challenges.
2. Specify student outcomes if these priority issues and challenges are being addressed.
3. Identify social environment supports that promote the achievement of student outcomes.
4. Identify evidence-based practices that promote the promotion of social environment supports.

The transition from step 1 to step 2 shifts the focus from student problems to the specification of desired outcomes for students. Importantly, desired results are not necessarily the opposite end of the continuum from student problems. For example, the problem of fights among students at school may be redefined as the desired result of engagement by students in extracurricular activities. Steps 2 and 3 use results from the SSP, and step 4 draws upon the SSP Best Practices Database, which is free and publicly available at http://www.schoolsuccessonline.com/.

Summaries of evidence-based practice strategies/programs are provided for each of the 30 dimensions included on the SSP, including a description of the program, the objectives of the intervention, implementation requirements, the cost, evaluation research references, and contact information for further details on the program (Powers, Bowen, & Bowen, 2011). Gordon's (1983) public health typology of prevention programs informs the classification of programs and strategies as universal (programs that target all students in the school), selected/indicated (programs that target specific students who might benefit from program components), or multi-component (programs that include both universal and selective/indicated components). Promising practices (intervention ideas and strategies that have shown promise) and resources (books, articles, and Web sites that provide information about effective practices in schools) are also displayed for each dimension. The SSP research staff at UNC reviews and updates this feature of the Web site on an ongoing basis. Currently, the database includes nearly 80 Evidence-Based Practices (EBPs), about 70 promising practices, and about 130 resources.

Appling Interventions within an RTI Framework

The SSP can be used easily and effectively within an RTI framework. RTI is school-wide multi-tier prevention approach to improve student achievement and reduce behavior problems (National Center on Response to Intervention, 2010). Data-based decision making is used to inform the major components of the RTI system: screening, progress monitoring, and the multilevel prevention system (National Center on Response to Intervention). The multilevel prevention system comprises three tiers:

- Tier 1 (primary level of prevention), which includes universal screening, scientifically based classroom instruction, and monthly progress monitoring
- Tier 2 (secondary level of prevention), which consists of specialized evidence-based interventions and weekly progress monitoring
- Tier 3 (tertiary level of prevention), which comprises more intensive intervention, progress monitoring, and, if needed, special education referral (Hughes & Dexter, 2011; National Center on Response to Intervention)

The SSP can be integrated into the RTI framework in multiple ways. First, the SSP can be used as a valid and reliable universal screening tool (Tier 1) to identify students who may be at risk for poor academic and behavioral outcomes. This strengths-based assessment can be used to identify students' areas of risk, as well as protective factors that could enhance their academic and behavioral success. Second, the SSP can be used to identify evidence-based interventions at both the group (Tier 2) and individual level (Tier 3) level. As discussed earlier, summaries of evidence-based practice strategies/programs are provided in the SSP Best Practices Database for each of the 30 dimensions included on the SSP. Third, the SSP can be used as an effective tool for ongoing progress monitoring (Tiers 1, 2, and 3) to determine whether students are responding positively to small group and/or individualized interventions.

Tools and Practice Examples

The SSP was an important assessment resource in a multifaceted intervention to increase the retention of sixth-grade students and seventh-grade students attending a tuition-free, faith-based private middle school in North Carolina (NC). The school was targeted to sixth- through eighth-grade boys of low socioeconomic status with lower-than-expected performance on end-of-grade tests in math and reading, which are administered in NC. No more than 48 students attend the school (16 students in each sixth-grade entry cohort). The parent component of the intervention is described in the case example below. In the course of the intervention, the SSP was administered on six occasions to three successive cohorts of students.

Step 1: Identify Priority Issues and Challenges

The school's Board of Directors sought assistance in summer 2007 from Dr. Gary Bowen. In consultation with faculty and staff, the Board requested support in developing an intervention to increase the probability of student participation in the full three years of the program. Approximately 16 students enroll in the school in the sixth grade each year. At the point of initial contact in 2007, only about one-third of the students completed the full three years of the program. The attrition rate was highest at the end of the sixth-grade year—more than half of the students on average failed to return for the seventh grade. At more than $20,000 per year for each student to attend the school, the lost investment in students who failed to complete the program was staggering and compromised the long-range sustainability of the school.

Step 2: Define Student Outcomes

The larger goal of the intervention was to help students develop pathways from middle school to high school and then on to university and the world of work by setting both proximal and distal goals and strategies to achieve these goals. A major milestone in this pathway was completing the academic program for the full three years of study. In step 2, the priority challenge of low student retention was redefined to the desired SSP result of increasing students' school engagement, which is defined from the SSP as students finding school fun and exciting, looking forward to learning new things at school, looking forward to going to school, and not being bored at school.

Step 3: Identify Social Environment Supports

From the perspective of the Eco-Interactional Developmental model, students require support from peers, parents, community members, and teachers as resources to help them achieve their desired goals. On the basis of SSP baseline results and consultations with students, parents, teachers, and the school's Board, caregivers of the students were targeted as the primary focus of intervention. Four program results from the SSP family domain framed and informed the intervention planning process: (a) home academic environment, (b) parent education support, (c) school behavior expectations, and (d) parent support (see Table 70.1 for definitions of these dimensions). SSP-related research provides considerable support for the link between these SSP program results and the desired student result: school engagement (e.g., Powers et al., 2005).

Step 4: Specify Evidence-based Practices

Through use of a strategic visioning process, the initial intervention program was developed in full concert with parents, students, faculty and staff, and community stakeholders. A full-time school social worker was hired in 2007 to coordinate the intervention planning process and implementation. The social worker worked with the SSP project team to consult the SSP Best Practices Database for evidence-based programs and promising practices for strengthening the home and school interface, such as The Incredible Years and SOAR (Hawkins, Von Cleve, & Catalano, 1991; Webster-Stratton, Reid, & Hammond, 2001). These multi-component interventions aim to improve school climate and enhance parent-child communication. Special focus was placed on helping caregivers to effectively communicate their expectations for student performance, including their commitment to having their student complete the program. The school social worker visited caregivers in their home and worked to improve the flow of communication between teachers and caregivers. The social worker also met with students, both individually and as a group, to discuss SSP results and the implications of the results for their school engagement.

From a larger program perspective, students' retention rates have shown improvement since the initiation of the intervention, which has paralleled an overall increase in students' school engagement. As compared to 14 students who left during the 2006–2007 school year, the number of students leaving the program has been significantly lower during the last four academic years: seven students (2007–2008), two students (2008–2009), two students (2009–2010), and four students (2010–2011). Although many reasons exist for the increase in student retention, including improved student selection procedures and the hiring of a full-time social worker to work with the families of students, it is reasonable to assume that part of this success lies in using the SSP to inform and monitor the intervention process. Use of the SSP directs attention to the results to be achieved and builds accountability into the intervention process.

Key Points to Remember

- The evidence-based practice sequence begins with a detailed assessment of students' presenting situations, strengths, and needs.
- The SSP is an assessment tool for middle and high school students that assesses students'

perceptions of their social environment and their own individual adaptation.

- The 30 core dimensions of the SSP are labeled and defined from an asset- or strength-based perspective and organized into a logic model with three levels of results: distal results (academic performance), intermediate results (personal beliefs and well-being, and school attitudes and behavior), and proximal results (neighborhood, school, friends, and family dimensions).
- SSP-related studies indicate that students are more likely to succeed in school when their neighborhoods and schools are safe, when adults in their lives are supportive and caring, and when they have friends who stay out of trouble and perform well at school.
- The SSP results in profiles for each individual student respondent and a summary group profile across students. The SSP is designed to supplement and enhance practitioners' ongoing observations of and dialogue with students, not to substitute for this process.
- The SSP is administered in the context of a four-step results-focused planning process and an online best practices database of evidence-based programs, promising practices, and resources for improving student success at school.
- The SSP is available for use by school social workers via the SSP Web site: (http://www.schoolsuccessonline.com/).

Further Learning

http://www.uncssp.org/: The main Web site, which is maintained by the developers of the SSP at the University of North Carolina at Chapel Hill, provides summary information about the SSP, including an extensive list of publications and research that make use of the assessment.

http://www.schoolsuccessonline.com/: Sponsored by Flying Bridge Technologies, Inc., this Web site is used primarily for marketing the SSP and registering clients for use, although access is provided to a best practices database, a search engine for locating school-based practice resources, and a list of funders that provide grants for school-based research and practice development.

Note

Professors Gary L. Bowen and Jack M. Richman originally developed the SSP as a prototype in 1993. The SSP has undergone four major revisions (in 1997, 2001, 2005, and 2008) to increase its responsiveness as a source of information for informing student-, school-, and community-based interventions. Development of the SSP and the design and administration of the online system to administer and score it have been supported by a series of grants from the BellSouth Foundation (1992–1997), from the John S. and James L. Knight Foundation (1995–2006), from the William T. Grant Foundation (2003–2006), and from the National Institute on Drug Abuse (2005–2010).

References

Anthony, E. K., & Stone, S. I. (2010). Individual and contextual correlates of adolescent health and well-being. *Families in Society: The Journal of Contemporary Social Services*, *91*, 225–232.

Bowen, G. L. (2009). Preventing school dropout: The eco-interactional developmental model of school success. *The Prevention Researcher*, *16*(3), 3–8.

Bowen, G. L., & Richman, J. M. (2010). The School Success Profile: Assessing the social environment and the individual adaptation of middle and high school students. *Studia Universitatis Babes-Bolyai, Sociologia*, *LV*(1), 11–29.

Bowen, G. L., Rose, R. A., Powers, J. D., & Glennie, E. J. (2008). The joint effects of neighborhoods, schools, peers, and families on changes in the school success of middle school students. *Family Relations*, *57*, 504–516.

Bowen, G. L., & Woolley, M. E. (2007). Assessment tools and strategies. *Children & Schools*, *29*, 195–198.

Bowen, G. L., Woolley, M. E., Richman, J. M., & Bowen, N. K. (2001). Brief intervention in schools: The School Success Profile. *Brief Treatment and Crisis Intervention*, *1*, 43–54.

Bowen, N. K., Bowen, G. L., & Woolley, M. E. (2004). Constructing and validating assessment tools for school-based practitioners: The Elementary School Success Profile. In A. R. Roberts & K. R. Yeager (Eds.), *Evidence-based practice manual: Research and outcome measures in health and human services* (pp. 509–517). New York, NY: Oxford University Press.

Chapman, C., Laird, J., & KewalRamani, A. (2010). *Trends in high school dropout and completion rates in the United States: 1972–2008* (NCES 2011–012). Washington, DC: National Center for Education Statistics, Institute of Education Sciences, U.S. Department of Education. Retrieved from http://nces.ed.gov/pubsearch

Fraser, M. W., & Galinsky, M. J. (2010). Steps in intervention research: Designing and developing social programs. *Research on Social Work Practice, 20*, 459–466.

Gordon, R. S., Jr. (1983). An operational classification of disease prevention. *Public Health Reports, 98*, 107–109.

Hatry, H. P. (1999). *Performance measurement: Getting results.* Washington, DC: Urban Institute Press.

Hawkins, J. D., Von Cleve, E., & Catalano, R. F. (1991). Reducing early childhood aggression: Results of a primary prevention program. *Journal of the American Academy of Child & Adolescent Psychiatry, 30*, 208–217. doi:10.1097/00004583–199103000–00008

Hughes, C. A., & Dexter, D. D. (2011). Response to Intervention: A research-based summary. *Theory into Practice, 50*, 4–11.

National Center on Response to Intervention. (2010). *Essential components of RTI—A closer look at Response to Intervention.* Washington, DC: U.S. Department of Education, Office of Special Education Programs, National Center on Response to Intervention.

Neild, R. C., Balfanz, R., & Herzog, L. (2007). An early warning system. *Educational Leadership, 65*(2), 28–33.

Obama, B. (February 24, 2009). Remarks of President Barack Obama: Address to Joint Session of Congress. Retrieved July 25, 2011, from http://www.whitehouse.gov/the_press_office/Remarks-of-President-Barack-Obama-Address-to-Joint-Session-of-Congress

Organisation for Economic Co-Operation and Development. (OECD; 2009). *Education at a glance.* Retrieved July 1, 2011, from http://www.oecd.org/dataoecd/41/25/43636332.pdf

Orthner, D. K., & Bowen, G. L. (2004). Strengthening practice through results management. In A. R. Robert s & K. R. Yeager (Eds.), *Evidence-based practice manual: Research and outcome measures in health and human services (pp. 897–904).* New York, NY: Oxford University Press.

Powers, J. D., Bowen, G. L., & Rose, R. (2005). Using social environment assets to identify intervention strategies for promoting school success. *Children & Schools, 27*, 177–187.

Powers, J. D., Bowen, N. K., & Bowen, G. L. (2011). Supporting evidence-based practice in schools with an online database of best practices. *Children & Schools, 33*, 119–128.

Richman, J. M., Bowen, G. L., & Woolley, M. E. (2004). School failure: An eco-interactional developmental perspective. In M. W. Fraser (Ed.), *Risk and resilience in childhood: An ecological perspective (2nd ed., pp. 133–160).* Washington, DC: NASW Press.

Webster-Stratton, C., Reid, M. J., & Hammond, M. (2001). Preventing conduct problems, promoting social competence: A parent and teacher training partnership in Head Start. *Journal of Clinical Child Psychology, 30*(3), 283–302.

CHAPTER 71

How to Write a Successful Grant and Obtain Business and Foundation Support

Allan R. Chavkin   Nancy Feyl Chavkin

Getting Started

Mental health professionals across the nation are facing an unexpected crisis, a sea change in how their programs are being funded. They are being asked not only to write grants to fund their programs but also to fund their own positions. This is the new reality for funding mental health services in schools. No longer do schools see funding from external sources as a luxury; it is now a necessity. Increasingly, writing a grant is essential for maintaining the status quo; school social workers and mental health professionals are quickly learning that fund-raising is no longer just for add-on programs or extra services. Securing grants and developing foundation and business support are core requirements of the job.

This new reality has put major stresses on mental health professionals who have been trained primarily to provide direct services. Many professionals are at a loss about where to begin and how to proceed; some are so fearful of this new job requirement that they are leaving their positions in school settings for private agencies. The title of Kim Klein's book *Fundraising in Times of Crisis* (2003) is apt for our current quandary. The book is so popular that it is now available as an e-book.

In the long run, there must be major changes in the existing ways we fund health, education, and social services for children; however, children in this country cannot wait for the slow wheels of bureaucracy and politics to change the funding mechanisms needed for services. In the meantime, many schools and communities will need to secure grant funds for mental health positions and for programs. It is with this realistic recognition that the authors offer some practical suggestions for what is acknowledged as short-term solutions to a long-term problem for funding mental health services in the schools.

What We Know

Best practices in grant writing lead to one clear outcome—getting funded. Those who have achieved this success offer some powerful suggestions to beginners. As the list of resources at the end of this chapter indicates, there are also numerous federal and private agencies available to assist with locating resources and providing assistance for best practices in grant writing.

Deborah Kluge (2011) suggests that there are three overarching principles: conducting research, cultivating relationships, and writing an excellent proposal. She maintains that most beginners want to start writing before they have done research on the most appropriate source of funding and before they have built relationships with their collaborators or potential funders.

David Bauer (2011) also offers mental health professionals an important suggestion when he advises grant seekers to begin proactively. Too often grant seekers have their project in mind and then try to fit it to someone else's guidelines within a short period of time. There is no time to develop a relationship with the funding agency, to understand the agenda of the grantor, or to prepare a well-conceived, winning proposal. Grant seekers sometimes begin a negative process of flooding the market with their grant requests in the hope that eventually one will be accepted, but this strategy almost never works.

Drawing on the work of Festinger (1957), Bauer uses the cognitive dissonance theory to develop his "values glasses theory" of grant seeking. Understanding the thinking and values of the grantor is critical to being successful. Too many grant writers only understand their own beliefs, and they write from a very narrow perspective. Bauer is not suggesting that grant writers should pander to the grantor's values or try to disguise a project for something it is not. What Bauer is suggesting is that grant writers first try to understand the grantor so that the grant meets the needs of the grantor, the grantee, and the grant writer. He reminds us that working proactively does not necessarily mean that grant writers will spend more time writing the grant; rather, it means that grant writers will use their time well over a longer period of time instead of trying to produce, "a last minute Herculean proposal effort." It is better to begin writing the grant well before its due date rather than at the last minute, and there are ways to begin the process of writing a grant for school mental health projects before the actual application arrives. Of course, we all know that most grants are written on short notice, but those that are funded are often those that have been in the planning stages many months before the actual application arrived. Beginning proactively means knowing the audience to whom you will be writing, and accomplishing this goal requires time.

Mim Carlson (2008) stresses that a major component of being successful in grant writing is self-assessment. Drawing on her more than 25 years of experience, she advocates for first identifying what is really happening in your agency and where you want to go. Larissa and Martin Brown (2001) also stress the importance of learning about your organization and your community before you begin to think about who will fund you. You will need to be clear about your organization's purpose and how it fits within the larger scheme of your community. It is essential to be able to accurately describe your community's culture and demographics, including such factors as income, language, race, religion, age, education, or other factors. It is important to note if your community is multicultural or homogeneous.

Although there many variables involved in getting funded, grant writers who have been funded many times share similar strategies for success. The next section will present some practical steps for securing grants and other external funding.

What We Can Do

Eight Steps to Successfully Securing External Funding

Step 1: Research Sources for Funding

Box 71.1 provides a number of helpful places to begin your search for an appropriate funding source. There are many different kinds of funders, and it is important to find an appropriate funder that matches your need. Primary sources of funding information include the *Federal Register, The Catalog of Federal Domestic Assistance,* and the *Code of Federal Regulations;* all of these are now available online through an excellent Web site (http://www.grants.gov) sponsored by the federal government. This Web site contains links to every major federal grant-awarding agency. However, many beginners find the use of primary sources overwhelming; they often prefer secondary sources that summarize the major grants, requirements, and deadlines. Examples of secondary sources often available in schools include *Education Daily* and *Federal Grants and Contracts Weekly.*

It is important to note that there are critical differences between writing a grant and seeking funds from businesses and foundations. Grants usually contain a "request for proposals" (RFP), while businesses and foundations may require only a one-page letter or brief application. Despite the differences in application procedure and length, the core requirements for conceptualizing and writing the proposal are essentially the same.

Step 2: Follow the Guidelines

When a grant writer does locate a relevant source, it is imperative to read the RFP or foundation guidelines thoroughly and follow them exactly. A number of very fine proposals are eliminated at the first stage of the review process because the authors did not comply with the requirements for submission. Grant writers should make certain that they know their audience. Key questions to consider are: Who is evaluating your proposal? What kind of projects do they want to fund? What are their interests? Often it is beneficial for writers to take the time to role play what it would be like if they were receiving this request for funding. It is helpful to see examples of other recently funded proposals. These can be requested from the agencies.

Box 71.1 Resources for Grant Writing

http://www.grants.gov: This site allows organizations to electronically find and apply for competitive grant opportunities from all federal grant-making agencies. By using colored tabs and links at the top of the screen, navigation of the site is simple.

http://fdncenter.org: The mission of the Foundation Center is to strengthen the nonprofit sector by advancing knowledge about U.S. philanthropy. The website collects, organizes, and communicates information about U.S. philanthropy and offers links to many funding resources.

www.schoolgrants.org: SchoolGrants was created in 1999 as a way to share grant information with PK–12 educators. SchoolGrants provides online tips for grant writing and lists a variety of opportunities available to public and private nonprofit elementary and secondary schools and districts across the United States.

http://www.cdc.gov/: The Center for Disease Control's Procurement and Grants Office sponsors a Web site with information about funding and useful resources for grant writers. They also provide links to current statistics and data.

www.samhsa.gov/grants: SAMHSA is the federal agency charged with improving the quality and availability of prevention, treatment, and rehabilitative services in order to reduce illness, death, disability, and cost to society resulting from substance abuse and mental illnesses. They have an excellent section on current funding initiatives and guidelines for applicants.

www.grantcraft.org: The Ford Foundation provides this Web site with helpful suggestions gathered from donors and grant makers in small foundations and large, including family, corporate, and independent grant programs. These materials are meant to suggest possibilities.

www.tgci.com: The Grantsmanship Center covers all aspects of researching grants, writing grant proposals, and negotiating with funding sources. They offer a Web site, materials, and 5-day workshops on grant writing. TGCI is also active in publishing books and a magazine. TGCI's Winning Grant Proposals Online collects the best of funded federal grant proposals annually and makes them available on CD-ROM.

It is also critical that the grant writer be familiar with the criteria for review, especially the points awarded for each section of the proposal. It is only logical that if 25% of the points are awarded based on project need, then 25% of your narrative should be on project need. Box 71.2 is an example of a review criteria sheet.

Step 3: Separate the Need from the Solution

One of the biggest problems that beginning grant writers face is how to separate the need from the solution. This situation arises because we as authors have the solution in mind and we truly need the solution we are proposing. For example, school social workers might need a van to transport children to and from after-school tutoring activities. It is obvious to us how helpful that van would be. If we focus the proposal on the van, then we are focusing on the solution and not on what needs the van will meet. It would be better to document the learning needs of the students who will be transported in the van and how the van will help improve learning rather than to focus on the lack of transportation.

Perhaps the most common error with many proposals is their exclusive focus on the need for more personnel. Many times, a school principal's first response to the needs assessment question is: "I need more nurses, social workers, and aides. If I had more staff, the problems would be solved." Most likely there is an element of truth in this statement, but the statement is not a needs assessment. The statement is really the proposed solution. A better needs statement would focus on the numbers of children who are sick or without immunizations, the percentage of children who do not have adequate supervision, the low level of parental participation in school activities, or the low reading scores. Grant writers must make the connection between need and solution very early in the proposal. If you begin your proposal with the solution, you are not going to convince the reviewer why you should be funded.

The question you should always be asking is: Why should the grantor fund our project? You

Box 71.2 Sample Review Criteria

SELECTION CRITERIA	*MAXIMUM POINTS*	*POINTS*
1. National significance	30	______
2. Quality of project design	30	______
3. Quality and potential contributions of personnel	15	______
4. Adequacy of resources	15	______
5. Quality of management plan	10	______
TOTAL	100	______

Highly recommended for funding ______
Recommended for funding ______
Not recommended for funding ______

need to describe the problem and what will happen if you are not funded by considering all the possible negative ramifications. For example, you should inform the readers of the consequences of low reading or math scores. Charts, graphs, and facts provide the details that can help you be specific and persuasive about your needs. Painting a worst case scenario of your needs is often a useful tool. One or two case vignettes can highlight the human factor in your proposal (e.g., tell a brief story using first names).

Also, make certain you reference the current literature and state why your project is important. You should be sure to explain how your project will be a model for other sites. Explain how your program addresses the needs of similar schools and could also benefit them. The "upside-down pyramid approach" in Box 71.3 can be very useful here. Begin with the needs of your project and then build a relationship to how solving your needs will help not only your school, but the community, the state, and perhaps even the nation.

Box 71.3 The "Upside-Down Pyramid Approach" to Explaining a Project's Benefits

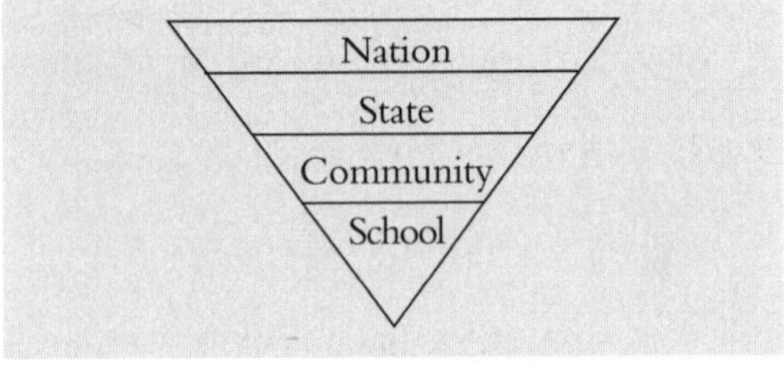

Step 4: Tell Your Story

Because school mental health projects often involve interrelated children's needs, they are sometimes difficult to describe. Because of the complexity involved in school mental health projects, telling your story well is essential for helping the funder understand exactly what your project is. Cheryl Clarke (2001) explains that storytelling is "at the core of all successful fundraising." Funders constantly report that the proposals that are easiest to understand get funded the most often.

There are many ways to tell your story, and it is often helpful to use a variety of methods to explain the needs of the project and the proposed solution. Be sure to include the demographics of your community and discuss the important multicultural implications of the project as you tell your story. Hooking the reader with a good case example is a first step and one that is usually not difficult for school social workers and mental health professionals. Sometimes what is harder for beginners and perhaps extremely difficult for professionals who work with complex social systems is to tell the story linearly and to link your goals, objectives, needs, and resources.

Boxes 71.4, 71.5, and 71.6 are useful guides that force you to link your goal and objectives to your needs and resources. As Box 71.4 suggests, begin your thinking with a statement of the problem or issue and then ask the questions: How do

Box 71.4 Project Outline

I. Concise statement of problem/issue (whom does this problem affect? how?)
II. Documentation of severity of problem (local, state, national statistics; need hard data here)
III. Beneficiaries of your project (whom will the project help? why do it?)
IV. Strengths and resources of beneficiaries
V. Strengths and resources of community
VI. Your school's strengths and resources
VII. General goal of your project (general statement of what you will do)
VIII. Specific goal statement (try to limit your project to one major goal)
IX. Specific objectives:[a]
(no more than 3–5)
Objective 1.
Objective 2.
Objective 3.

[a]Go to Objectives Worksheet (Box 71.5) before completing this section.

Box 71.5 Objectives Worksheet

OBJECTIVE 1

Who?

Does what?

When?

Under what circumstances?

To what degree?

How will you measure it?

your goal and objectives meet the needs? Are you building on the strengths of the beneficiaries? Are you using all the strengths and resources of the community and your group? Box 71.5 breaks the objective statement down into a series of questions that many grant writers find useful, and Box 71.6 presents a linear way of looking at goal, objectives, activities, and tasks.

Be clear about the distinctions among goal, objectives, activities, and tasks. You must be very careful not to get distracted by activities and lose sight of your goal. Always refer back to your goal. As you look at these worksheets, notice that there is a connection between the goal of the project, the need for the project, existing resources, and the specific objectives.

Step 5: Demonstrating Your Organizational Capability

After establishing the need for your project and telling the story of your project by describing it in detail, the next thing you need to do is write a clear plan of operation. You should make a chart of who will do what activity, when they will do it, and where they will do it. This is especially important for school mental health projects because of the complexity of the organization. It is essential that you take the time to do this. Using Box 71.6, begin with your objectives and then list each activity that must be done to complete the objective. If possible, break the activity down into tasks. Timelines and organizational charts are very helpful at this point.

You must make it clear to the reader that you are capable of carrying out the project. You can show that you can do the project in a variety of ways. If you have physical resources (office, equipment, library), describe them. If you have strong community support, list examples. You can include relevant letters of support in the appendix. Sometimes it is helpful to describe your previous track record with grants. Some grantors want to know if your organization can manage a budget and has been successful with other endeavors. It is critical to know your grantor, however, because some grantors are skeptical of applicants who already have too many grants. The grantor will want to know how this project is different from other previously funded projects. The grantor will want to make certain that this new request for funds is not a duplication of previous efforts. Make clear what is new about this request.

It is helpful to provide brief summaries (about a paragraph) for each person about the qualifications of key staff and how these qualifications relate to your proposal. There is no need to list extraneous positions or qualifications; be concise but laudatory about your personnel. If space permits, you can include one- or two-page vitae for key personnel in the appendix.

Visual aids can help you get organized and present a succinct but clear picture of your project. Box 71.7 is an example of a Gantt chart. Gantt charts were first developed by Henry L. Gantt in the 1900s, and they are still widely used today for

Box 71.6 The Linear Way of Looking at Your Proposal

Goal:

OBJECTIVE 1

Activity 1.1	how evaluated	by whom/when/what instruments/why
Task 1.11		
Task 1.12		
Task 1.13		
Task 1.14		
Activity 1.2	how evaluated	by whom/when/what instruments/why
Task 1.21		
Task 1.22		
Task 1.23		

OBJECTIVE 2

Activity 2.1	how evaluated	by whom/when/what instruments/why
Task 2.11		
Task 2.12		
Activity 2.2	how evaluated	by whom/when/what instruments/why
Task 2.21		
Task 2.22		
Task 2.23		

establishing clear time lines and responsibilities. Funders look favorably on proposals that are well thought out and include details about time lines and the person responsible for each activity.

Sometimes grant writers use other kinds of charts to explain their activities. One might see a PERT (program evaluation and review technique) chart or a project management review chart that links goals, objectives, activities, measurement, data analysis, and outcome. A well-done graphic can be much more valuable than pages of text.

Step 6: Justifying the Project Budget

James Quick and Cheryl New (2001) are correct in their statement that just about everyone has some discomfort with budgets, and fear of budgets is a major concern for first-time grant seekers. One of their first suggestions is to clarify the term by calling it your project budget. The very act of using the more specific phrase conveys what you want to do: write a budget for your proposed project.

Your project budget should be as specific as possible, and you should justify any large or unusual expenditure. Most funding agencies like to have funds go for direct services rather than equipment, but you should verify that this is the assumption of your particular funding source by contacting your funder on this issue. If at all possible, secure matching funds for your proposal. Sometimes the match can be in-kind contributions, such as time or office space/equipment. Box 71.8 is an example of a project budget outline.

Sometimes funders require matching funds according to an established ratio. Cost sharing usually refers to donated services and materials. Sometimes these in-kind contributions are personnel, facilities, or services for administering the grant. In-kind services are assigned a dollar equivalency. School project proposals should be able to describe matching funds or cost-share with community groups, state funding, or federal grants.

Box 71.7 Gantt Chart

Goal: To develop a workshop for pregnant teenagers at Green County High School to improve their life skills

Objectives and Activities	Person(s) Responsible	February	Time Frame March	April
Obj. 1: Locate appropriate curriculum				
Activity 1.1: Research topics	Jones & Luera	4–18		
Activity 1.2: Prepare presentations/ activities	Jones & Luera	18–22		
Activity 1.3: Compile all information	Jones	22–29		
Obj. 2: Collaborate with community agencies				
Activity 2.1: Meet with agency representatives	Jones & Luera	25	11	
Activity 2.2: Organize resources	Luera	22–28		
Obj. 3: Pilot the workshop				
Activity 3.1: Recruit students	Teachers	1–15		
Activity 3.2: Conduct workshop	Jones & Luera		1–22	
Activity 3.3: Evaluate Workshop	Consultant			1–15

Box 71.8 Example of Budget Summary

	Federal Portion	*School Match*	*Total*
Personnel	48,965	96,877	145,842
Supplies	2,000	6,000	8,000
Travel	1,000	1,000	2,000
Equipment	2,000	4,000	6,000
Communication	1,000	1,000	2,000
Printing	1,000	1,000	2,000
Contracted services	5,000	0	5,000
Miscellaneous	1,000	2,000	3,000
Direct costs	61,965	111,877	173,842
Indirect costs (8%)	4,957	8,950	13,907
Total costs	66,922	120,827	187,749

Two key terms you need to know are direct costs and indirect costs. Direct costs usually include personnel (wages/salaries, fringe benefits, merit, cost-of-living raises); supplies (consumable supplies, such as pens, books, videotapes, diskettes); equipment (purchase or rental); travel (in-state and out of state; broken down by destination, purpose, mileage, per diem); communication costs (telephone equipment/installation/charges, postage, fax); printing (publishing of brochures, handbooks, copying costs); contracted services (use of consultants, subcontracts); and miscellaneous (facility rental, repairs, anything not included in these categories).

Indirect costs are the overhead costs incurred in the administration of the grant. Your organization or the funder probably already has these calculated as a percentage of total direct costs. For example, some grants have an 8% indirect cost rate calculated on the basis of all direct costs; others have a 48% indirect cost rate calculated on the basis of only salaries/wages. Some foundations and a few state programs do not allow the inclusion of indirect costs in the budget. Check with the funding source and your administration to find out the specifics for your school or agency.

You should also include a section entitled "Budget Justification" or "Budget Rationale" in your proposal. It is an essential appendix to the budget and explains key budget line items. This narrative explanation can be used to make the rationale for each item immediately clear and is particularly helpful to grant reviewers.

Step 7: Demonstrating Accountability

If at all possible, projects should use an external evaluator because such an outside evaluator provides an objective look at your successes and failures. It is not the job of a mental health professional to do all of the evaluations, but it is clearly the responsibility of the mental health professional to make certain that the right questions are being asked. Your evaluation might consider questions in each of four areas: planning, implementation, outcome, and economic efficiency. You do not have to evaluate every activity or even every objective, but you must explain why you choose to evaluate specific parts of your project.

There are many kinds of evaluations (not all of them mutually exclusive). The kind of evaluation you need to conduct depends on the purpose of your evaluation. Consider which of the following evaluations are appropriate for your program: effort evaluation (person hours, visits, meetings, etc.), performance evaluation (yield, results), adequacy (change in unmet need, decreased absenteeism, increased test scores), efficiency (personnel/time/offices), process (relative success of parts of projects/aspects that could be done better), quantitative versus qualitative, formative versus summative, process versus outcome, cost-benefit versus cost-effectiveness, compliance versus quality, effectiveness versus efficiency, or inputs versus impact.

Your job is to ask the right questions. You can get assistance with the statistics, computer programs, survey design, and data collections. If you want to be successful in your project, the most important thing to remember about evaluations is to not let your project fall into the autopsy category. Many project coordinators wait until the project is over before they consider doing an evaluation. Then it is often too late to change some of the activities that could have improved the program. Cynthia Knowles (2002) reminds grant writers to build evaluation into the project from the beginning, even before the grant begins. Consider adding a process evaluation to your required evaluations of implementation and impact. You will also want to share your results and should have a plan for sharing what works in your project with others either during your program or after. Put this plan in your proposal in both the organizational plan and in the evaluation plan. Reviewers look favorably on proposals with a clear plan for dissemination of results.

Step 8: Refining Your Proposal

Writing style becomes a key factor in selecting the winning proposal when all other factors are equal. Joseph Barbato and Danielle S. Furlich (2000) make it clear that there are two parts to successful fund-raising: what you put in the proposal and how well you write it. Many grant seekers have great ideas but fall short on the second part, writing well.

Remember to always write in the active voice; avoid the unnecessarily abstract and wordy writing that often accompanies passive voice. You should avoid acronyms and jargon that are not clear to the lay reader. Use short sentences and avoid vague pronoun references. Because reviewers read many proposals in a short time, you can help them out by being as clear and precise as possible.

Include a section with appendices. This section contains supporting documents. It should not be used for essential information that needs to be in the text. It can be useful, though, for the history and background of your organization, vitae of personnel, relevant prior studies or projects, copies of support letters, evaluation instruments, or sample lesson plans.

Most important, ask outside people to read and critically review your proposal before submitting it. Do not wait until the last day to submit the proposal. It is best to have two types of readers: lay readers and experts. Lay readers are people who know nothing about your project. Have them read the proposal and see if they understand what you are saying. Expert readers know the general field and can give you feedback on missing research or a discrepancy in your organizational plans. Critique and feedback are essential to a successful proposal.

Applying Interventions within a Response to Intervention Framework

The Response to Intervention (RTI) framework is a promising approach that will appeal to government, business, and foundation funders for a number of reasons. Because RTI is data-based, the framework immediately appeals to funders who are looking for facts upon which to base funding. RTI follows in the tradition of evidence-based research, and funders are responding well to the framework. Also, since the RTI approach can be seen as a scientific practice that uses objective measures to make decisions about children, the approach can help remove subjectivity. Eliminating subjectivity can help reduce bias in identifying students for services and fits well with the mission of federal, state, and local government funders and professional codes of ethics.

In addition to being data-based and helping to reduce bias, RTI's use of the tier approach emphasizes early intervention. Tier 1 begins with universal screening for all children, Tier 2 follows with selected interventions to a smaller group of non-responsive students, and Tier 3 focuses on a very small group who exhibit chronic academic or behavioral problems. Early intervention can keep problems from escalating and can often solve difficulties early, which can save dollars for schools and funders. Being cost-effective fits well with the accountability mindset of funders and today's particularly challenging fiscal crisis in the delivery of mental health services in schools. In sum, RTI is being well received by the funding community, and there are currently many calls for further demonstration projections, evaluation efforts, and research studies.

Tools and Practice Example

Forms and Samples

The forms and samples in this section were referenced in the steps previously described. As you peruse these tools, you may find it useful to refer to the steps in which they were discussed.

A Practice Example: An Abstract Containing Successful Grant Ideas

As you are putting the finishing touches on your grant proposal, do not forget the abstract. It is often helpful to wait and write the abstract of your proposal at the end of your writing endeavor because at that point you will be clear about all the parts of the proposal, and it will be easier to write a summary at the end of this process rather than at the beginning. We next present an example to show you how an abstract can pique the readers' interest with just enough detail to get the readers to want to read more. The project is clear about its goal and objectives. It gives a specific, targeted outcome (90% of students will be taking pre-algebra classes at the end of the project). The PATH Mathematics proposal also connects its demonstration project with a plan to replicate the project in the state and nation.

PATH Math (Partnership for Access to Higher Mathematics)

The goal of PATH Mathematics is to form a partnership between Southwest Texas State University (SWT), San Marcos School District (SMCISD), and San Marcos Telephone Company to significantly improve the mathematical skills of low-income students, thereby increasing these students' readiness for postsecondary education. The project uses interactive television (ITV) to achieve three key objectives:

Objective 1: Develop and implement a new pre-algebra curriculum that will allow students tracked in lower-level classes to reach algebra I by 10th grade.

Objective 2: Develop and implement a tutoring program through which tutors from SWT will work with students at the SMCISD via ITV.

Objective 3: Develop and implement a support program through which social work interns from SWT will provide mentorship, social service, and motivational activities to strengthen SMCISD students' interest in furthering their education.

Secondary students at SMCISD will receive immediate and direct benefits from this project; by the end of 3 years 90% of ninth graders will be taking pre-algebra or above mathematics courses. We will extend the project to other rural, small schools in Texas and the nation through TI-IN Network (San Antonio, TX) and United Star Network's (national) satellite broadcast systems. This model can be replicated in virtually any American community because almost every community, regardless of size, has access to a telephone company. Schools, colleges, and universities can join forces with their telephone company and use ITV to improve the mathematical skills of their high school students.

Key Points to Remember

There are many possibilities for achieving success in grant writing. Although many times proposals are not funded on the first attempt, they are often rewritten and funded on another submission. If you are rejected, write a thank-you letter to the funding agency for considering your application and request to see reviews or a summary of reviews so that you can revise and improve your grant. Few grants are funded on the first submission; a number are funded, however, after revisions and resubmissions. Writing successful proposals is not an easy task. Most of all, it takes time and commitment. School social workers and mental health professionals who want to obtain grant funding must take the time to plan and to conceptualize what they need, what resources they already have, and how they are going to organize these resources with new funding to accomplish the tasks ahead of them.

Further Learning

Bray, I. M. (2010). *Effective fundraising for nonprofits.* Berkeley, CA: NOLO.

Browning, B. A. (2011). *Grant writing for dummies* (4th ed.). New York, NY: Wiley.

Coley, S. M. (2007). *Proposal writing: Effective grantsmanship (3rd ed).* Newbury Park, CA: Sage.

Greever, J. C. (2007). *The Foundation Center's guide to proposal writing.* New York, NY: The Foundation Center.

Grow, P. (2011). *Five days to Grants* [Kindle ed.]. Retrieved from Amazon.com.

Henson, K.T. (2012). *Successful grant writing for school leaders: 10 easy steps.* Boston, MA: Allyn & Bacon.

Karsh, E., & Fox, A. S. (2009). *The only grant-writing book you'll ever need.* New York, NY: Basic Books.

Lauffer, A. (1997). *Grants, etc.* Thousand Oaks, CA: Sage.

Ogden, T. E. (2002). *Research proposals: A guide to success* (3rd ed.). New York, NY: Raven.

Quick, J. A., & New, C. C. (2000). *Grant winner's toolkit: Project management and evaluation.* New York, NY: John Wiley & Sons.

Robbins, V. (2010). *101 Tips for aspiring grant writers.* Woodland, CA: Creative Resources & Research.

Rogers, K. (2011). *33 Funder-friendly elements no grant proposal should be without* [Kindle ed.]. Retrieved from Amazon.com

Soriano, F. I. (1999). *Conducting needs assessments: A multidisciplinary approach.* Thousand Oaks, CA: Sa

References

Barbato, J., & Furlich, D. S. (2000). *Writing for a good cause: The complete guide to crafting proposals and other persuasive pieces for nonprofits.* New York, NY: Simon & Schuster.

Bauer, D. G. (2011). *The "how to" grants manual: Successful grant seeking techniques for obtaining public and private grants* (7th ed.). Westport, CT: Praeger.

Brown, L. G., & Brown, M. J. (2001). *Demystifying grant seeking: What you really need to do to get grants.* San Francisco, CA: Jossey-Bass.

Carlson, M. (2008). *Winning grants: Step by step* (3rd ed.). San Francisco, CA: Jossey-Bass.

Clarke, C. A. (2001). *Storytelling for grant seekers.* San Francisco, CA: Jossey-Bass.

Festinger, L. (1957). *Theory of cognitive dissonance.* Stanford, CA: Stanford University Press.

Klein, K. (2003). *Fundraising in times of crisis.* San Francisco, CA: Jossey-Bass.

Kluge, D. L. (2011). Grant resources: Researching & identifying grant-making organizations. Available at: http://www.proposalwriter.com/grants.html

Knowles, C. (2002). *The first-time grant writer's guide to success.* Thousand Oaks, CA: Corwin Press, Inc.

Quick, J. A., & New, C. C. (2001). *Grant seeker's budget toolkit.* New York, NY: John Wiley & Sons.

Understanding the Current Environment of Public School Funding

How Student Support Services Are Funded

Jeffrey M. Poirier David Osher

Getting Started

Student supports, the nature and intensity of which depend on students' mental health and other needs, contribute to the development and academic success of students. School social workers and other mental health personnel have key roles in planning, coordinating, and providing this critical support (Rappaport et al., 2002). This is particularly true for universal interventions that help create positive connections between and among students and adults, help students develop social and emotional skills, and employ positive behavioral supports, all of which contribute to safe, supportive, and successful schools (Osher, Dwyer, & Jackson, 2004; Zins, Weissberg, Wang, & Walberg, 2004). This role includes linking schools and families (Osher & Keenan, 2001). Similarly, pupil service resources are necessary not only for identifying and addressing the needs of students who are at risk of academic and behavioral problems (Dwyer & Osher, 2005) but also for ensuring active family participation in this process. Finally, pupil service personnel can play a key role in intensive interventions for those students who are at the greatest level of need, including helping students access and utilize culturally appropriate community supports and working with the schools to align these supports. While we know a great deal about how to do this (Greenberg et al., 2003; Osher & Hanley, 1997; Rones & Hoagwood, 2000), funding these services can be challenging. This is an especially salient concern given current fiscal constraints and debates about how to address the federal budget deficit.

For all school social worker roles, whether as providers of specific services or members of teams that plan schoolwide initiatives, it is important to support students by providing the entitlements and services for which they are eligible. For some students this may consist of Individuals with Disabilities Education Act (IDEA) funds, while for others it may consist of Medicaid and the Children's Health Insurance Program (CHIP), child welfare services, juvenile justice services, or substance abuse services. Many schools and communities also receive grants such as safe and drug-free school monies, support for school health centers, and state and federal resources that support systems of care for children with emotional and behavioral disorders. In addition, the Affordable Care Act (Public Law 111–148) has already effected children and youth's ability to obtain health insurance coverage. Beginning in 2010, children and youth could not be denied insurance coverage because of a pre-existing condition and could remain on their parent's health insurance until their 26th birthday (Medicaid and CHIP have never been able to exclude someone because of a pre-existing condition). This provision has major implications for children and youth with behavioral health concerns. Also, in 2014, states will have the option to expand Medicaid eligibility for anyone whose income is at or below 133% of the Federal poverty level.

As discussed in this chapter, social workers can improve services for students by expanding current funding and improving the efficiency of how resources are used. Both strategies are particularly helpful as school districts face fiscal constraints and increased accountability standards, which strain school budgets. When districts experience budget cuts, schools are often affected; their ability to provide educational and other services to students may be diminished. This chapter outlines the basics of funding student support services, including the sources and types of funding streams that support these services. Strategies to expand, coordinate, and redeploy funding, which may help to minimize the effect of decreased funding and even improve services, are then discussed. This chapter is intended to be a tool that you can use to understand how services are funded and how additional funding can be tapped to create a better array of services for the students you serve. The concepts discussed are likewise useful for funding implementation of a response to intervention framework. Since financial resources are so important to school improvement, this chapter is written to enable you to be a change agent for your school and community.

What We Know

Funds for student support services largely come from public sources (i.e., federal, state, and local government grants) but also from Medicaid and CHIP, health insurance companies, including managed care, charitable groups, and foundations (SMHP, 2000). Funds may be allocated to larger units, such as schools, school districts, and children who meet certain eligibility criteria, or to smaller entities. It is important to understand funding streams and how the federal government allocates funds as well as your state and local funding formula (Osher et al., 2004).

A funding stream can be identified at its federal or state source and traced to a local end point where districts or schools access it (Osher et al., 2004). Funding streams often are redirected, however, at the state and local (county, district, municipal, community) level. For example, Medicaid is a federal–state partnership in which the U.S. Department of Health and Human Services (DHHS) Centers for Medicare and Medicaid Services (CMS) matches state expenditures for services provided to individuals who are eligible (enrolled in) Medicaid (1902(a) (10) of the Social Security Act. (i.e. Title XIX/Medicaid of the Social Security Act)) or CHIP. Title XXI of the Social Security Act. In addition, the services that are covered under the Medicaid/CHIP statutes must be delivered by licensed providers approved by states and who participate in Medicaid and (or) CHIP. States must provide certain mandated services such as the early and periodic screening, diagnosis and treatment (1905 (a) (4) (B) and 19059 (R) of the Social Security Act.) benefit for children and youth, but have discretion on reimbursing for certain optional that are important for individuals need behavioral health service. This includes targeted case management and rehabilitation services options. Thus, Medicaid and CHIP take on a state identity and are allocated through state regulations and procedures. At the local level, federal and state funds mix with local sources, creating "funding ponds" that can be accessed for student support services (Osher, McInerney, Traylor, & O'Neal, 1995; Osher et al., 2004).

Federal Funding

As of the 2008–2009 school year, approximately 9.6% of the $593 billion in public elementary and secondary school revenues came from federal sources for the 50 states and the District of Columbia (Johnson, Zhou, Nakamoto, & Cornman, 2011). This national average varies significantly between states and across school districts within states. For example, federal sources comprised 13% or more of total revenues for public schools in nine states (Alaska, California, Hawaii, Louisiana, Mississippi, New Mexico, North Dakota, Oklahoma, and South Dakota); in contrast, federal revenues comprised 6% or less of total revenues in six other states (Connecticut, Maryland, Minnesota, New Hampshire, New Jersey, and New York).

Federal funds are allocated in four ways: block grants, project grants, legislative earmarks, and direct payments. Block grants use a formula to provide a fixed amount of funding. These formulas include criteria, such as population, unemployment levels, and other demographic characteristics. Allocation of resources under block grants can be influenced by advocacy efforts, since block grants are generally distributed by states based on a plan that reflects the input of state advisory groups (SAG) for the block grant. The Community Mental Health Services Block Grants and Social Services Block Grants (Title XX of the Social Security Act) are examples of formula-based federal block grants. There is currently increased focus to direct more federal funding for mental health services into block grants.

Project, or discretionary, grants are awarded through a competitive process and have specific purposes. Applicants may be either public or private entities, and funding is provided for particular projects or services over a fixed period of time. Project grants can fund evaluations, experimental and demonstration projects, fellowships, planning, research, scholarships, surveyss, technical assistance, traineeships, training, and unsolicited contractual agreements. For example, more than 2,700 school districts received discretionary grants to fund 21st-century community learning centers in collaboration with local entities such as public agencies, businesses, postsecondary institutions, and scientific or cultural organizations (U.S. Department of Education,

Office of Elementary and Secondary Education, n.d.). These grants can be employed to fund some types of student support. A Safe School/Healthy Students grantee in Hayes, Kansas, funded the first school social workers in the county. The grant chose to employ social workers to build school—home linkages and to address the need for early interventions that provided support for families of children who were found to be at risk. Social work services included individual, family, and group interventions (Paige, Kitzis, & Wolfe, 2003). Similarly when it was a Federal Comprehensive Services for Children and Their Families grantee, Philadelphia placed school social workers in elementary schools to help the school system address the needs of children with serious emotional disturbance who were in kinship care (Woodruff et al., 1999).

Funds known as legislative earmarks are set aside for particular organizations by directives in appropriations laws. These directives specify how funding should be allocated within larger programs. Earmarks are awarded noncompetitively and occur during one fiscal year only; they do not continue over to another fiscal year. Public or private agencies are eligible for either "hard" earmarks, which are written into legislation and specify recipients and the amount of funding, or "soft" earmarks, which are awarded based on congressional committee reports.

Federal funds may also come as direct payments, which are a form of federal assistance provided directly to providers who meet state licensure and other state requirements. Medicaid is an example of such a program. Although it rarely happens, intermediate state agencies (e.g., departments of health, mental health or social services) may be delegated by the Medicaid or CHIP agency to administer programs providing direct payments.

State and Local Funding

On average, 46.7% of public elementary and secondary school revenues come from state sources, which can often support local school improvement efforts, while local funds comprise approximately 43.7% of these revenues (Johnson et al., 2011). Local funds are typically intended to support basic school components; however, these funds can sometimes be realigned at the school level to improve efficiency and meet school objectives. Local funding for education-related initiatives, much of which may originate in federal and state budgets, may come from county or city governments as well as local agencies and school districts themselves (Flynn & Hayes, 2003).

Private Funding

In addition to public sources, various types of foundations and organizations may fund local efforts. These include community, corporate, and private foundations. You should be aware of any charitable groups or foundations that may support student support services in your local area. The Foundation Center (http://www.fdncenter.org) offers access to a directory of foundations for a monthly fee. Local foundations can often be identified by word of mouth or Internet searches.

Categorical Funding

School district revenues can be either general revenue (i.e., for any educational use) or categorical revenue targeted for specific purposes. Local general revenues for education are typically *lower* in school districts with *higher* levels of poverty (U.S. Department of Education, 2003). State general revenues and categorical funding, however, are typically *higher* in districts with *higher* levels of poverty. Categorical revenues are therefore an important mechanism to bring programs and services to the nation's youth with the greatest needs.

Categorical revenues must be used to provide particular services to specific types of entities, such as children and families. Examples of categorical funding include Head Start and IDEA. Flynn and Hayes (2003) point out that categorical funding streams are difficult to coordinate or combine because of their specific eligibility requirements, program regulations (how and when services are delivered), and funding flow and administration (who administers the program and how funds flow to programs). This can lead to fragmented services (Farrow & Joe, 1992).

Categorical funding may therefore present a challenge to integrated support services. For example, children in the same program may not receive the same services if program funding comes from several categorical sources that not all children are eligible to receive. In addition, program administrators must track eligibility data, tie services to their funding sources, and follow other funding regulations (Flynn & Hayes, 2003).

Still, the easiest way to fund services may be finding a categorical program that meets your school's needs and drawing upon these funds. Categorical funds exist to support student support efforts. Examples include services for which individuals are eligible (e.g., funding for mental health services for individuals who are identified as being eligible for services under the IDEA), as well as resources for which schools are eligible. Examples of categorical school services are comprehensive school health centers, which are funded by the Federal Health Resources Services Administration, and community schools, which are funded by some districts (e.g., Chicago and Multnomah County, Oregon). Several financing strategies can add flexibility so that schools and communities can coordinate categorical funding streams; these are discussed in the following section.

What We Can Do

Funding can come from your school, district, state, the federal government, or private organizations. Beyond the general school or district funds, you must draw upon resources that originate elsewhere. These are frequently referred to as funding streams. Understanding funding streams and their limits is important, since they often fund specific people, places, or services. Public funding streams are authorized by legislation that realizes specific priorities. Therefore, you should examine funding stream requirements before you try to draw upon them to fund services related to education, child welfare, juvenile justice, mental health, and substance abuse.

As you might expect, funding streams, like school budgets, are limited—and increasingly so, given recent economic challenges and fiscal reductions at the federal, state, and local levels. Developing strategies to maximize funding are crucial, since school staff are often confronted by funding-related challenges. In addition, you should be familiar with two other strategies that may help to improve the efficiency of current funding: coordination and redeployment. Understanding these strategies, which are discussed in the following sections, will further enable you to have a proactive approach to funding student support services, potentially increasing efficiency and making funding available for additional services.

Expanding the Funding Pool

A primary financing strategy is to expand the funding pool (i.e., increase funding) by identifying previously untapped funding sources. It is important to take advantage of all available funding streams to maintain or expand services for students. Before pursuing particular funding, you should determine if:

- The district already receives funds from a particular source
- The district is eligible for such funds
- The district allocates the funds to schools
- The school is authorized to pursue additional funding independently

You should also determine the appropriate agencies (federal, state, or local) to contact and collaborate with other school staff, as well as your school district administration, to the greatest extent possible. Collaboration is discussed in greater detail later in this chapter. In addition to the references provided at the end of the chapter, you will find a list of Web-based resources that you might find useful in your efforts to enhance services for students in your school. Some of these provide information on potential grant funding, while others provide information on the financing of student support services and funding strategies. Table 72.1 lists some potential funding streams and major federal funding sources.

It is important to remember that funding sources are not static. Eligibility requirements, program regulations, and the extent and purpose of funding can change. For example, the Job Training Partnership Act is now the Workforce Investment Act. The Elementary and Secondary Education Act (ESEA), the largest federal elementary and secondary education program, was reauthorized in 2001 as the No Child Left Behind (NCLB) Act with a much greater emphasis on accountability (reauthorization of NCLB has been delayed, without a resolution in time for the beginning of the 2011–2012 school year). You should use the Web-based resources as information tools to be knowledgeable of the major agencies that provide funding.

Sometimes schools are ineligible for Medicaid and other categorical funds such as Health Resources and Services Administration (HRSA) school-based health center grants. Another approach to enlarge the funding pool is to leverage public and private resources by using available funding to qualify for additional resources, whether new or matching funds (SMHP, 2000). In this case, schools may develop relationships with other agencies (e.g., community mental health centers) or professionals (e.g., child psychiatrists), who can access these categorical funds. Medicaid is a good example of leveraging: a school that

Table 72.1 Examples of Major Funding Streams

Program	*Funding Source*	*Local Information Source*	*Purpose*
Social Security Act Title IV—Grants to states for aid and services to needy families with children and for child welfare services	Title IV-B Subparts 1 and 2 Social Security Act	Social Services	Subpart 1 promotes state flexibility in the development and expansion of coordinated child and family services programs that utilize community-based agencies and ensure all children are raised in safe, loving families. Subpart 2 enables states to develop and establish, or expand, and to operate coordinated programs of community-based family support services, family preservation services, time-limited family reunification services, and adoption promotion and support services to accomplish several objectives (e.g., prevention of child maltreatment through supportive family services).
Community Development Block Grant Programs (i.e., entitlement communities, state-administered)	Department of Housing and Urban Development, Office of Community Planning and Development	State, local government	Provides annual grants on a formula basis to entitled cities and counties to develop viable urban communities by providing decent housing and a suitable living environment.
Indian Child Welfare Act	Department of Interior, Bureau of Indian Affairs (http://www.bia.gov/WhoWeAre/BIA/OIS/HumanServices/IndianChildWelfareAct/index.htm)	Federally recognized Indian tribal government	Promotes the stability and security of American Indian tribes and families by protecting American Indian children, preventing the separation of American Indian families, and providing assistance to Indian tribes in the operation of child and family service programs.
Individuals with Disabilities Act (IDEA), Part H	Department of Education, Office of Special Education Programs (http://idea.ed.gov/explore/home)	Schools, districts, county offices of education	Supports assessment and preventive services for very young children at risk of developmental disabilities. Also transition into appropriate school setting. Requires an individualized plan.
Integration of schools and mental health systems	Department of Education, Office of Safe and Drug-Free Schools (http://www2.ed.gov/programs/mentalhealth/index.html)	State and local education agencies, Indian tribes	Supports increases in student access to quality mental health care by developing innovative programs that link school systems with local mental health systems.
Juvenile Accountability Block Grants Program	Department of Justice, Office of Juvenile Justice and Delinquency Prevention, State Relations and Assistance Division (http://ojjdp.gov/jaibg/)	State JABG Coordinator	The Juvenile Accountability Block Grants (JABG) program is administered by the State Relations and Assistance Division of the Office of Juvenile Justice and Delinquency Prevention (OJJDP), Office of Justice Programs, U.S. Department of Justice. Through the JABG program, funds are provided as block grants to states for programs promoting greater accountability in the juvenile justice system. Local and tribal governments can then apply to the states for funds to support local accountability programs. In addition, OJJDP makes grants to federally recognized tribes to strengthen tribal juvenile justice systems and to hold youth accountable. These grants are made competitively.

(continued)

Table 72.1 *(Continued)*

Program	*Funding Source*	*Local Information Source*	*Purpose*
Juvenile Mentoring Program	Department of Justice, Office of Juvenile Justice and Delinquency Prevention (http://ojjdp.ncjrs.org/jump/index.html)	Local educational agency	Targets at-risk youth to provide general guidance and support; promote personal and social responsibility; increase participation in elementary and secondary education; discourage use of illegal drugs and firearms, involvement in violence, and other delinquent activity; discourage involvement in gangs; and encourage participation in service and community activities.
Medicaid	Centers for Medicare and Medicaid Services, Department of Health and Human Services, Title XIX, Social Security Act (http://www.cms.hhs.gov/medicaid/default.asp)	State government	The federal government sets broad guidelines, but states have considerable flexibility in designing and administering the Medicaid program. Each state decides (1) who is eligible for coverage; (2) the type, amount, and scope of covered services; (3) which providers can obtain Medicaid reimbursement; and (4) how much providers get paid for the services they render.
Mentoring Grants	Department of Education, Office of Safe and Drug-Free Schools (http://www.ed.gov/programs/dvpmentoring/applicant.html)	Local educational agency	Provides assistance to promote mentoring programs for children with the greatest need. Grants are provided to programs that: (1) assist such children in receiving support and guidance from a mentor; (2) improve the academic performance of such children; (3) improve interpersonal relationships between such children and their peers, teachers, other adults, and family members; (4) reduce the dropout rate of such children; and (5) reduce juvenile delinquency and involvement in gangs by such children.
Mentoring for Safe Schools/ Healthy Students Initiatives	www.ojp.gov/programplan		As of fiscal year 2010, OJJDP sought opportunities to coordinate and collaborate with the Department of Education on school safety issues and school- and community-wide programs to reduce truancy and keep students in school. Proposed areas of collaboration may include programs to reduce truancy; prevent bullying, including cyberbullying, which is prevalent among girls; and promote conflict resolution.
No Child Left Behind Act (formerly Elementary and Secondary Education Act)	Department of Education (http://www.ed.gov/esea)	Local educational agency	Provides various supports to reduce the achievement gap (e.g., expanded local control and flexibility).

Safe Schools/Healthy Students	Department of Education, Office of Safe and Drug-Free Schools (www2.ed.gov/about/offices/list/osdfs/programs.html)	Local educational agency	Jointly funded and administered by the Departments of Education, Justice, and Health and Human Services; supports community-wide approaches to creating safe and drug-free schools and promoting healthy childhood development. Programs are intended to prevent violence and illegal use of drugs, and to promote safety and discipline. Coordination with other community-based organizations is required.
Safe Start Initiative	Department of Justice, Office of Justice Programs (www.ojp.gov/programplan)	State and local government	
Second Chance Act Adult and Juvenile Offender Reentry Demonstration Projects	Department of Justice, Office of Justice Programs (www.ojp.usdoj.gov/programplan)	State and local government, federally recognized Indian tribes	Authorizes grants for demonstration projects to promote the safe and successful reintegration of incarcerated individuals into the community. Allowable funding uses include employment services, substance abuse treatment, housing, family programming, mentoring, victim services, and methods to improve release and revocation decisions using risk assessment tools.
Social Services Block Grant	Department of Health and Human Services, Administration on Children and Families, Title XX, Subtitle A (http://www.ssa.gov/OP_Home/ssact/title20/2000.htm)	State department of social/human services	Increases state flexibility in using social service grants, and encourages states to provide services related to five goals, including preventing or remedying neglect, abuse, or exploitation of children (and adults) unable to protect their own interests, or preserving, rehabilitating or reuniting families.
Temporary Assistance for Needy Families (TANF)	Department of Health and Human Services, Administration on Children and Families, Office of Family Services, TANF Bureau (http://www.acf.hhs.gov/programs/ofa/tanf/about.html)	Social services	Direct financial income support for families with minor children; administration of program including eligibility determination.

(continued)

Table 72.1 *(Continued)*

Program	*Funding Source*	*Local Information Source*	*Purpose*
Twenty-First Century Community Learning Centers	Department of Education, No Child Left Behind Act, Title IV, Part B (http://www.ed.g0v/pr0grams/21stcclc)	State education agencies (local education agencies and nonprofit organizations may apply to states for subgrants)	Supports creation of community learning centers that provide academic enrichment opportunities during non-school hours for children, particularly students who attend high-poverty and low-performing schools. The program helps students meet state and local student standards in core academic subjects, such as reading and math; offers students a broad array of enrichment activities that can complement their regular academic programs; and offers literacy and other educational services to the families of participating children.
Vocational and Technical Education Act (Perkins Act)	Department of Education, Office of Vocational and Adult Education (http://www2.ed.gov/policy/sectech/leg/perkins/index.html)	State boards of career and technical education	Provides an increased focus on the academic achievement of career and technical education students, strengthening the connections between secondary and postsecondary education, and improving state and local accountability.
Workforce Investment Act (e.g., Youth Opportunity Grants, State and Local Formula Youth Grants)	Department of Labor (http://www.doleta.gov/usworkforce/wia/)	State and local workforce investment boards	Provides grants to assist youth ages 14–21 in high-poverty areas who have one or more of the following conditions: deficient in basic literacy skills; a school dropout; homeless, runaway, or foster child; pregnant or a parent; an offender; or requiring additional assistance to complete an educational program or to secure and hold employment. Youth are prepared for postsecondary educational opportunities or employment, and programs link academic and occupational learning.
Youth Violence Prevention Programs	Department of Justice, Office of Justice Programs (www.ojp./programplan.gov)	State and local government	Fosters innovations and advancements in youth violence prevention practices at the community level. The goal is to demonstrate the implications for policy and practice and to enhance juvenile justice, child protection, and delinquency prevention. This program focuses on supporting communities in their efforts to develop and implement effective and coordinated violence prevention and intervention initiatives by building protective factors to combat juvenile delinquency, reducing child victimization, and improving the juvenile justice system.

Box 72.1 Expanding the Funding Pool in Action

A member of a high school's student support staff is concerned about the school's high dropout rate relative to other schools in the state. She wants to identify potential funding sources for a school dropout prevention program, so she searches the CFDA database by applicant eligibility (elementary/secondary education as the functional area and local government as the organizational type) and finds almost 40 programs, one of which is dropout prevention. She learns that local education agencies are eligible to apply for dropout prevention program project grants. She then collaborates with the school and school district administration to apply for funding and creates a dropout prevention and reentry program in her high school.

is not Medicaid eligible can develop a relationship with a Medicaid-certified provider who can bill for Medicaid services provided to Medicaid-eligible students. Medicaid, which is discussed in detail in another chapter in this handbook, can be a valuable source of funding for school-based health and mental health services. As another form of leveraging, you can use federal and state entitlement funding including Medicaid and CHIP as substitutes for local expenditures, which then frees local funds for other services (SMHP, 2000).

Coordinating Funding Streams

Funding streams have specific priorities, requirements, and regulations. This may present challenges when working to coordinate funding sources (Flynn & Hayes, 2003). Increasingly, schools and communities weave together resources in seamless ways (SMHP, 2000). The U.S. Department of Education "encourages schools and districts to combine funds to more efficiently raise the achievement of the whole school community, thus increasing the capacity as a whole instead of targeting specific children" (Osher et al., 2004, p. 44). Coordination is important because fragmentation can lead to ineffective and costly interventions due to overlap across schools, social welfare, and juvenile justice; fragmentation has been blamed as the root cause of many problems associated with treating emotional and behavioral disorders (Osher & Hanley, 1996; Quinn & Poirier, 2004).

Aligning funding streams can transform traditionally separate services and programs into more integrated, comprehensive systems so that they are more responsive to children and families (Evans et al., 2003; Flynn & Hayes, 2003). Coordination also enhances collaboration for a shared goal and allows for local flexibility, a greater focus on outcomes, and greater decision making with the families of students (Bazelon, 2003; SMHP, 2000). Several coordination strategies, including braiding and blending, can enhance student support services by reducing duplication, increasing the efficient use of resources, reducing the administrative burden of multiple categorical programs, and providing more integrated supports and services (Flynn & Hayes, 2003). Further, diversifying funding sources helps to support sustainability by ensuring that budgets are mostly covered if a particular funding stream should dry up (Bazelon, 2003; Flynn & Hayes, 2003). As a school professional you should be familiar with and utilize any community or state efforts to support funding coordination.

The first strategy of resource coordination, braiding, occurs at the school, community, and program levels. It enhances flexibility in the use of funding but has distinct features that are important to note. Specifically, funding streams are combined to support particular components of integrated service plans so that funds from different agencies can be tracked for the purpose of meeting funding requirements (Osher et al., 2004). Braiding is a useful strategy if you cannot or do not want to blend funding, which is discussed shortly. Braiding "recognizes the categorical nature of existing programs and avoids some of the conflicts that can arise in blended funding pools" (Bazelon, 2003, p. 4).

Braiding "is the most common strategy for using categorical funding streams to create more integrated and comprehensive early care and education initiatives [but] ... requires a high degree of behind-the-scenes organization and record keeping" (Flynn & Hayes, 2003, p. 11). It requires a comprehensive information management system as well as a cost-accounting system to connect expenditures with their funding sources. This facilitates resource allocation and reporting (Flynn & Hayes, 2003). States or communities must also have "one point of responsibility for assessing services, as well as and the funding stream that pays for these services" (Bazelon, 2003, p.4). Examples of federal programs that are commonly braided include

Box 72.2 Braiding in Action

A bright, talented youth in foster care with a learning disability recently began taking drugs and engaging in gang behavior. In an effort to provide this student with the services she needs, school support staff could braid funding by using wraparound, IDEA, substance abuse, and gang abatement services. Under the provisions of IDEA, these otherwise discrete services can be integrated into one service plan.

Medicaid, the Child Care and Development Fund, IDEA's Grants for Infants and Families with Disabilities program, Head Start, Social Services Block Grants, Temporary Aid for Needy Families (TANF), and Title I (Flynn & Hayes, 2003).

In contrast to braiding, blended funding is a form of coordinating funding streams that state and local policy makers most often use, and it changes the structure and rules of funding streams to create flexibility in how funds are used (Flynn & Hayes, 2003). Blending funding may consist of combining flexible funding streams into a funding pond by overlapping roles and functions. Alternatively, it make take the form of decategorized funding, which is available when a state makes funding streams less categorical by modifying funding regulations and merging funds from different programs into one funding stream (Flynn & Hayes, 2003; SMHP, 2000).

Blended funding offers greater flexibility for state and local agencies, while also reducing the work required for reporting and accountability (Bazelon, 2003). It also allows systems to fund activities that specific categorical programs would not otherwise reimburse, helping to "plug funding gaps in the services continuum" (Bazelon, 2003, p. 4). Budgets and functions can also be blended (SMHP, 2000). This allows funding from several state agencies and the more flexible federal programs to be combined, with authorization, to foster collaboration for a common goal, but agencies lose control due to the inability to track funds to the service-delivery point (Bazelon, 2003; Flynn & Hayes, 2003).

Blended funding can produce more money for student support services through collaboration between service providers of different agencies (Edelman, 1998). Through this collaborative process, federal funds can be accessed that might not be available otherwise. In particular, blending allows funds to be tracked for accountability to federal program administrators while still tapping

Box 72.3 Blending in Action

Master contracting is an approach to blending that can be tailored to program or community needs. For example, in some areas agencies have replaced separate contracts from various state or county agencies with one master contract. Like other blending, this strategy depends upon state or county approval. Master contracting provides flexibility to tailor services and builds in an outcome-driven approach to accountability. Master contracting may also diminish the administrative burdens created by multiple, separate reporting requirements (Flynn & Hayes, 2003).

into other funding streams (Bazelon, 2003; Flynn & Hayes, 2003). Blended funding can:

- Expand services without additional state or local funds
- Foster increased communication and integration among agencies
- Promote coordination of care among multiple agencies, which improves efficiency by avoiding duplicative services or approaches
- Increase cooperation among agencies (Edelman, 1998)

Schools and schoolwide teams can employ blending by coordinating the use of noncategorical resources.

Coordination has been supported by federal legislation. Subpart 14, Section 5541 of the No Child Left Behind Act of 2001 creates Grants for the Integration of Schools and Mental Health Systems that can be used to enhance, improve, or develop collaborative efforts between school-based service systems and mental health service systems to provide, enhance, or improve prevention, diagnosis, and treatment of services for students. In addition, IDEA strongly promotes interagency agreements for the coordination and delivery of services from other public agencies that are responsible for paying or providing needed services (34CFR300.142).

Redeploying Resources

If funding is invested in programs and services that are ineffective or less effective than alternatives, then resources are wasted or used inefficiently at best. Redeploying existing resources requires that schools and support staff examine how funding is used and how services are provided, and consider how funds can be used more effectively (Osher et al., 2004). In some instances, funding can even be shifted from higher to comparable lower-cost programs and services (SMHP, 2000). Ineffective or redundant programs should be downsized or eliminated (Osher et al., 2004).

Resources should also be targeted at programs and services, such as prevention, that help to decrease the future demand for resources. It is likely that you will not have the resources to do a formal cost-benefit analysis or evaluation of services in your school, but these are not necessary to redeploy resources. As a member of your school support staff, it is sufficiently valuable if you identify the needs of students in your school and understand what programs and services are most effective in meeting these needs. Are there programs or services that you believe would better meet the student needs? Are there services that help to decrease demand for other services, even if marginally or over a longer period of time? You should use your understanding of what is working in your school and what is not. You should also be familiar with effective, evidenced-based programs and services.

Schools and communities must increasingly shift from a short-term mind-set of "managing" social ills to a long-term vision in which they are proactively prevented. Prevention research should be linked not only with public policy (Quinn & Poirier, 2004) but also with school practice. Significantly, investing in universal and early interventions can save communities money in the long run. In the case of youth who are delinquent, effective interventions help to deconstruct the pipeline to prison and decrease delinquency-related costs (Osher, Quinn, Poirier, & Rutherford, 2003). As prevention efforts begin to have a positive effect, it may be possible to invest funds in less costly early interventions rather than intensive interventions that have a higher per student cost.

Collaboration

Coordinating funding streams requires collaboration with agencies that provide services to students. Coordination and collaboration together help to build a comprehensive and more cost-effective support system for at-risk students and their families by reducing the fragmentation of services or "categorical drift" (agencies working in isolation), combining funds for shared purposes, and increasing service providers' awareness of the needs of students (Liontos, 1990; Osher & Keenan, 2002; Peterson, 1995). Ultimately collaboration can transform support services so that they are more responsive to children and families already receiving services from several systems (Bruner, 1991; Osher & Hanley, 1997). Children from fragile families have more complex needs that require interagency collaboration for several reasons: their families are more likely to have difficulty accessing and using all of the services they need, their families are less likely to have the skills to integrate the goals of the services they are receiving, and their families tend not to have outside resources to counteract the negative consequences when system failures occur (Bruner, 1991).

Since children are required to attend school and because schools are supposed to be concerned about the overall development of students, schools are the most accessible and appropriate place to establish collaborations with human service agencies (Ascher, 1990). As a member of your school's support staff, you can lead efforts to collaborate with other schools in your district and your school district administration to build a coalition and even to try to place a representative on one of your state's block grant state advisory group (SAG) meetings. Alternatively, you may want to work with your state school social work association to secure representation. SAGs develop priorities that determine how block grant monies will be allocated. In some cases, this can include funding for school social workers and other pupil personnel services.

Students who are at risk often receive services from a variety of agencies, and these services tend to be fragmented because there is little cross-agency communication and coordination (Peterson, 1995). In the case of students who have disabilities, "the importance of cross-system collaborations to address the needs of children with mental or emotional disorders to receive services from various child-serving agencies—most commonly, mental health and substance abuse, child welfare, education, and juvenile justice—is increasingly recognized" (Bazelon, 2003, p. 1).

To improve the effectiveness of service delivery, it is important that both school social workers and service providers are aware of both the range of services being provided to individual students and the available information that can be used to understand individual student needs (Peterson, 1995). Effective systems of care coordinate services across schools, community mental health centers, juvenile justice programs, primary health care organizations, psychiatric treatment programs, and social service organizations to most effectively address the needs of these children.

Collaboration requires planning, commitment, thoughtful action, and openness to new approaches, as well as a willingness to evaluate and reevaluate current paradigms. Time also is an important component because trust and understanding may not be immediate. Efforts to foster collaboration may present difficult challenges: some staff or representatives of agencies may resist change; agency or government regulations may limit the extent to which staff, services, and information can be coordinated; and differences in prior training among staff from different agencies may pose a difficulty (Peterson, 1995). Successful collaborations are well documented, though. Models include system of care communities, where collaboration is institutionalized.

Systems of Care

A system of care is a coordinated network of agencies and providers that makes a full range of services available to children with mental health problems (Osher et al., 2004). Systems of care are guided by three core values:

- Child-centered, youth-guided, family-focused, family-driven care
- Community-based services, management, and decision making
- Culturally and linguistically competent agencies, programs, and services that are responsive to the diverse cultural identities and experiences of the youth and families served (e.g., lesbian, gay, bisexual, or transgender youth; or immigrant families) (Stroul & Friedman, 1986; Poirier et al., 2012)

Among the principles embodied in a system of care are service coordination, prevention and early identification and intervention, smooth transitions among agencies, and a comprehensive array of services. Hence, a system of care is based on the notion of multiagency coordination and may require innovative funding models (Osher et al., 2004). This coordination and the aforementioned collaboration join education with child welfare, juvenile justice, and substance abuse services. These are each briefly discussed next, along with examples of relevant funding sources.

Child welfare services are responsible for ensuring the well-being of children and providing services if a child is not safe or has been harmed at home (McCarthy et al., 2003). Two sources of child welfare funding include the Child Welfare Services Program (Title IV-B, Subpart 1 of the Social Security Act) and Social Services Block Grants (Title XX). Title IV-B provides grants to states for a range of child welfare services and activities, without income requirements, and Title XX provides federal funds for low-income children and families (McCarthy et al., 2003). States have a large degree of discretion in determining how Title XX monies are spent, and prevention is considered a related activity.

Additional funding and programs are available for students who may be delinquent. To identify students who may be involved with the justice system, schools can ask the local juvenile court to review court records to identify the number of students under court probation. You should also contact your department of human services to determine if prevention or intervention can by funded using TANF funds. TANF funds can sometimes be used to support community programs instead of placements for youth who are delinquent. Sources of juvenile justice funding include the Neglected and Delinquent Children Program through the Department of Education, which awards formula grants to state education agencies; Juvenile Accountability Block Grants through the Department of Justice, which awards block grants to states; the Formula Grants Program as authorized under the Juvenile Justice Delinquency and Prevention Act of 2002, also through the Department of Justice and which allocates formula grants to state agencies; and Youth Opportunity Grants through the Department of Labor, which are competitive grants awarded to Local Workforce Investment Boards.

School mental health programs are intended to provide care for uninsured students as well as a comprehensive range of services for all students, so identifying funding sources is a major challenge facing these programs (Germaine, 1998). The federal government funds mental health services, for example, through Community Mental Health block grants through the Substance Abuse and Mental Health Services Administration, which also funds block grants for Prevention and Treatment of Substance Abuse and Indian Health Care Improvement Act grants through the Indian Health Service. Some state governments also fund school-based health and mental health services (Evans et al., 2003).

Unfortunately, data on mental health financing for children and youth are difficult to synthesize because of the complexity of funding sources and destinations (SMHP, 2000). Some federal funds are used to support programs at the national level, while most funds are directed to states for Medicaid, block grants, and categorical programs (SMHP). Many children actually qualify for both Medicaid and IDEA services: IDEA allows for certain health-related services included in a student's individualized Education Plan to be paid for through Medicaid (Seltzer & Parker, 2003). Common sources of funding for school mental health services are Medicaid (which enrolled 27 million children in June 2011; http://www.kff.org/medicaid/enrollmentreports.cfm Kaiser Commission on Medicaid and the Uninsured: Medicaid Enrollment: June 2011 Data Snapshot, June, 2011) which includes the Medicaid Early and Periodic Screening, Diagnosis, and Treatment (EPSDT is a benefit under Medicaid not a separate program. All children and youth are entitled to receive services under this benefit.) benefit; Title V (Maternal and Child Health Block Grant); and private non-HMO insurance (Lewin Group, 1999).

Applying Interventions within a Response to Intervention Framework

Student support and services can be coordinated and allocated in a tiered manner. This is often carried out in a three-tiered approach that includes what is done for (1) all students, (2) students at greater level of risk or need, and (3) students with the greatest level of risk or need. Multiple researchers (e.g., Dwyer & Osher, 2005; Osher et al., 2008; Walker et al., 1996) have elaborated on this approach, which has its roots in public health, and multiple federal documents have emphasized it (e.g., Dwyer, Osher, & Warger, 1998; U. S. Public Health Service, 2000). The three-tiered approach is most effective when it includes a universal foundation that promotes student success (Durlak & Weissberg, 2011; Osher, Dwyer, & Jackson, 2004). Response to Intervention (RTI) applies this logic by focusing on providing evidenced-based interventions, monitoring their effects on students who are at need, and adjusting what educators do based on the student's response to the interventions. While RTI typically has been applied to academics, schools can and should apply it to student support. RTI should be part of a school's larger strategy and efforts to fund student support services.

Key Points to Remember

This chapter provides an overview of how student support services are funded. As discussed, you can act as a change agent in your school by helping to expand, coordinate, and redeploy funding streams. Coordination can take several forms: braiding occurs more at the program or community level, and blending typically needs involvement of state and local policy makers. Redeploying resources by identifying and eliminating waste and inefficiency is an important component of expanding school services. These strategies are not mutually exclusive; they can be combined as part of a larger approach to financing school services, which, like interagency collaboration (exemplified by systems of care communities), is essential in the new environment of school funding. A better understanding of funding, funding streams and pools, financing strategies, the role of collaboration, and the resources available to you will support your efforts to build a better array of services for the youth you serve.

Web-Based Resources

Catalog of Federal Domestic Assistance: www.cfda.gov. The Catalog of Federal Domestic Assistance has a comprehensive, online database of all federal programs that provide financial assistance to state and local governments, as well as other entities, such as nonprofit organizations and individuals.

The Center for Health and Health Care in Schools: www.healthinschools.org. The Center for Health and Health Care in Schools supports the good health of children and adolescents by working with parents, teachers, health professionals, and school administrators to strengthen successful health programs at school. The Web site combines information on key school health issues with guidance on organizational and financing challenges.

The Finance Project: www.financeproject.org. The Finance Project is a research, consulting, technical assistance, and training nonprofit organization.

Free resources including working papers, resource guides, and toolkits are available on the Web site. *FindYouthInfo*: http://www.findyouthinfo.gov/funding.shtml. This Web site, created by the Interagency Working Group on Youth Programs (IWGYP), dconsists of representatives from 12 federal agencies that support programs and services focused on youth. The IWGYP promotes positive, healthy outcomes for youth. The Web site includes a Funding Information Center with a "Map My Community" tool designed to assist you in locating resources in your community that can help you build and strengthen youth programs.

The Foundation Center: http://fdncenter.org/. The Foundation Center is a leading source of information on philanthropy. It provides a subscription-based online grantmaker directory of more than 100,000 funders, including community foundations, corporations, private foundations, and public charities.

Georgetown University Child Development Center, "Funding Early Childhood Mental Health Services & Supports": http://gucchd.georgetown.edu/products/FundingECMHS.pdfhttp://gucchd.georgetown.edu/products/FundingECMHS.pdfhttp://gucchd.georgetown.edu/products/FundingECMHS.pdfhttp://gucchd.georgetown.edu/products/FundingECMHS.pdf. This provides a matrix to assist communities with developing a comprehensive financing system for early childhood mental health services.

Grants.gov: www.grants.gov. Established in 2002 as a government resource, it allows organizations to electronically find and apply for competitive grant opportunities from all federal grant-making agencies and provides access to more than 1000 grant programs and more than $500 billion in annual awards offered by federal grant-making agencies. The Web site allows automatic notification of grant announcements.

National Assembly on School-Based Health Care: http://www.nasbhc.org. A membership-based Web site, provides links to state SBHC Web sites and information on funding school-based health centers.

Schoolgrants.org: www.schoolgrants.org. Offers guidance on grant writing as well as links to federal, state, and foundation funding opportunities. State sources are listed by state, enabling easy navigation. Technical Assistance Partnership for Child and Family Mental Health: http://www.tapartnership.org/SOC/SOCfinancingResources.php Offers financing resources for sustaining systems of care.

UCLA School Mental Health Project (SMHP), Center for Mental Health in Schools: http://smhp.psych.ucla.edu. Provides technical assistance for mental health practitioners and is a significant resource for enhancing mental health in schools, including center briefs, practice guides, and resource aid packets, and also has a free newsletter with updates about relevant funding opportunities.

References

Ascher, C. (1990). *Linking schools with human service agencies* (ERIC/CUE Digest No. 62). ERIC Clearinghouse on Urban Education: http://www.ericdigests.org.

Bazelon Center for Mental Health Law. (2003). *Mix and match: Using federal programs to support interagency systems of care for children with mental health care needs.* Washington, DC: Author. http://www.bazelon.org.

Bruner, C. (1991). *Thinking collaboratively: Ten questions and answers to help policy makers improve children's services.* The Education and Human Services Consortium: http://www.cyfernet.org.

Durlak, J. A., & Weissberg, R. P. (2011). Promoting social and emotional development is an essential part of students' education. Human Development, 54, 1–3.

Dwyer, K., & Osher, D. (2005). *Safeguarding our children: An action guide revised and expanded.* Longmont, CO: Sopris West.

Dwyer, K., Osher, D., & Warger, C. (1998). *Early warning, timely response: A guide to safe schools.* Washington, DC: U. S. Department of Education.

Edelman, S. (1998). *Developing blended funding programs for children's mental health care systems.* Sacramento, CA: California Institute for Mental Health.

Evans, S. W., Glass-Siegel, M., Frank, A., Van Treuren, R., Lever, N. A., & Weist, M. D. (2003). Overcoming the challenges of funding school mental health programs. In M. D. Weist, S. W. Evans, & N. A. Lever (Eds.), *Handbook of school mental health: Advancing practice and research* (pp. 73–87). New York: Kluwer Academic/Plenum Publishers.

Farrow, F., & Joe, T. (1992, Spring). Financing school-linked integrated services. (Financing Strategy Series). The Future of Children: http://www.futureofchildren.org/.

Flynn, M., & Hayes, C. D. (2003, January). *Blending and braiding funds to support early care and education initiatives (Financing Strategy Series).* Washington, DC: www.financeproject.org.

Germaine, A. S. (1998, Spring). Funding opportunities: Promising Medicaid funding options for school mental health. On the Move with School-Based Mental Health, 3(1). UCLA School Mental Health Project: www.smhp.psych.ucla.edu.

Greenberg, M. T., Weissberg, R. P., Utne O'Brien, M., Zins, J. E., Fredericks, L., Resnick, H., & Elias, M. J. (2003). Enhancing school-based prevention and youth development through coordinated social, emotional, and academic learning. American Psychologist, 58, 466–474.

Johnson, F., Zhou, L., Nakamoto, N., & Cornman, S. Q. (2011). *Revenues and expenditures for public elementary and secondary education: School year 2008–09 (Fiscal year 2009) (NCES 2011–329).* U.S. Department of Education. Washington, DC: National Center for Education Statistics. Retrieved August 15, 2011, from http://nces.ed.gov/pubs2011/2011329.pdf

Kaiser Commission on Medicaid and and the Uninsured, *Medicaid Enrollment: June 2011 Data Snapshot.* Retrieved from http://www.kff.org/medicaid/enrollmentreports.cfm

Lewin Group. (1999). Key issues for school-based health centers providing mental health environment. Retrieved June 3, 2004, from http://smhp.psych.ucla.edu.

Liontos, L. B. (1990). *Collaboration between schools and social services (ERIC Digest Series, No. EA 48).* Eugene, OR: ERIC Clearinghouse on Educational Management.

McCarthy, J., Marshall, A., Collins, J., Arganza, G., Deserly, K., & Milon, J. (2003). *A family's guide to the child welfare system.* Washington, DC: Georgetown University Center for Child and Human Development.

Mental Health in Schools Training and Technical Assistance Center, School Mental Health Project [SMHP]. (2000, November). *Financing mental health for children & adolescents* (Center Brief). Retrieved May 21, 2004, from http://smhp.psych.ucla.edu

Mental Health in Schools Training and Technical Assistance Center, School Mental Health Project [SMHP]. (2004, February). *Financial strategies to aid in addressing barriers to learning* (Introductory Packet). Retrieved May 21, 2004, from http://smhp.psych.ucla.edu

Osher, D., McInerney, M., Traylor, K., & O'Neal, E. (1995). *Funding streams and funding ponds: An analysis of the infrastructure for financing the acquisition and use of TMM tools.* Report prepared for the Division of Innovation and Development, Office of Special Education Programs, U.S. Department of Education.

Osher, D., & Hanley, T. V. (1996). Implications of the national agenda to improve results for children and youth with or at risk of serious emotional disturbance. In R. J. Illback & C. M. Nelson (Eds.), *Emerging school-based approaches for children with emotional and behavioral problems: Research and practice in service integration* (pp. 7–36). Binghamton, NY: Haworth Press.

Osher, D., & Hanley, T. V. (1997). Building upon an emergent social service delivery paradigm. In L. M. Bullock & R. A. Gable (Eds.), *Making collaboration work for children, youth, families, schools, and communities* (pp. 10–15). Reston, VA: Council for Exceptional Children.

Osher, D., & Keenan, S. (2001). From professional bureaucracy to partner with families. Reaching Today's Youth, 5(3), 9–15.

Osher, D., & Keenan, S. (2002). *Instituting school-based links with mental health and social service agencies (Guides to Creating Safer Schools: Guide 6).* Portland, OR: Northwest Regional Educational Laboratory.

Osher, D. M., Quinn, M. M., Poirier, J. M., & Rutherford, R. B. (2003). Deconstructing the pipeline: Using efficacy and effectiveness data and cost-benefit analyses to reduce minority youth incarceration. In J. Wald & D. J. Losen (Eds.), *New direction for youth development: Deconstructing the school-to-prison pipeline* (pp. 91–120). San Francisco: Jossey-Bass.

Osher, D., Dwyer, K., & Jackson, S. (2004). *Safe, supportive and successful schools: Step by step.* Longmont, CO: Sopris West.

Osher, D., Sprague, J., Weissberg, R. P., Axelrod, J., Keenan, S., Kendziora, K., & Zins, J. E. (2008). A comprehensive approach to promoting social, emotional, and academic growth in contemporary schools. In A. Thomas & J. Grimes (Eds.) *Best practices in school psychology V* (Vol. 4, pp. 1263–1278). Bethesda, MD: National Association of School Psychologists.

Paige, L. Z., Kitzis, S. N., & Wolfe, J. (2003). Rural underpinnings for resiliency and linkages (rural): A safe schools/healthy students project. Psychology in the Schools, 40(5), 531–547.

Peterson, K. (1995). *Critical issue: Establishing collaboratives and partnerships.* North Central Regional Educational Laboratory: www.ncrel.org.

Poirier, J. M., Martinez, K., Francis, K., Denney, T., Roepke, S., & Cayce, N. (2012). Providing culturally and linguistically competent services and supports to support the needs of LGBT youth and their families. In S. K. Fisher, J. M. Poirier, & G. M. Blau (Eds.), *Improving emotional & behavioral outcomes for LGBT youth: A guide for professionals* (pp. 9–24). Baltimore, MD: Brookes Publishing Company.

Quinn, M. M., & Poirier, J. M. (2004). Linking prevention research with policy: Examining the costs and outcomes of the failure to prevent emotional and behavioral disorders. In R. B. Rutherford, M. M. Quinn, & Sarup R. Mathur (Eds.), *Handbook of research in emotional and behavioral disorders* (pp. 78–97). New York: Guilford Press.

Rappaport, N., Osher, D., Dwyer, K., Garrison, E., Hare, I., Ladd, J., & Anderson-Ketchmark, C. (2002). Enhancing collaborations within and across disciplines to advance mental health programs in schools. In M. D. Weist, S. Evans, & N. Tashman (Eds.), *School mental health handbook* (pp. 107–118). New York: Kluwer Academic Publishing Company.

Rones, M., & Hoagwood, K. (2000). School-based mental health services: A research review. Clinical Child and Family Psychology Review, 3(4), 223–241.

Seltzer, T., & Parker, R. (2003). *Teaming up: Using the IDEA and Medicaid to secure comprehensive mental health services for children and youth.* Washington, DC: Bazelon Center for Mental Health Law.

Stroul, B., & Friedman, R. (1986). *A system of care for children and youth with severe emotional disturbance (Rev. ed.).* Washington, DC: Georgetown University Child Development Center, National Technical Assistance Center for Children's Mental Health.

U.S. Department of Education, National Center for Education Statistics. (2003). *The condition of education 2003, NCES 2003–067.* Washington, DC: U.S. Government Printing Office.

U.S. Department of Education, Office of Elementary and Secondary Education. (n.d.). *21st CCLC Profile and Performance Information Collection System.* Author: http://www2.ed.gov/programs/21stcclc/awards.html

U.S. Public Health Service. (2000). *Youth violence: A report of the surgeon general.* Washington, DC: Author.

Walker, H. M., Horner, R. H., Sugai, G., Bullis, M., Sprague, J. R., Bricker, D., & Kaufman, M. J. (1996). Integrated approaches to preventing antisocial behavior patterns among school-age children and youth. Journal of Emotional and Behavioral Disorders, 4, 194–209.

Woodruff, D. W., Osher, D., Hoffman, C. C., Gruner, A., King, M., Snow, S., & McIntire, J. C. (1999). *The role of education in a system of care: Effectively serving children with emotional or behavioral disorders.* Washington, DC: Center for Effective Collaboration and Practice, American Institutes for Research.

Zins, J., Weissberg, R., Wang, M. ,& Walberg, H. J. (Eds.). (2004). *Building academic success on social and emotional learning: What does the research say?* New York: Teachers College Press.

CHAPTER 73

Where Do We Go from Here?

Mental Health Workers and the Implementation of an Evidence-Based Practice

Paula Allen-Meares

Getting Started

The primary purpose of this *School Services Sourcebook* is to provide social workers and related school-based professionals with current and diverse empirical data on interventions and approaches that address the mental health needs of various pupil groups. Between 4 million and 6 million students are thought to have serious mental health issues, which, if left untreated, can affect their futures, their lives, and society in general (Rogers, 2003). Most of these children attend school, either public or private. Therefore, the school setting becomes one of the more likely places for effective mental health services. But what is necessary to deliver these services? Where will the future of school-based intervention take us?

In this discussion, we will highlight the future of school social work, a practice that will be firmly rooted in a growing evidence base. In addition, we add a brief summary of issues specific to the selection of evidence-based interventions, methods of getting school social workers to accept and utilize evidence-based practices, and why school and communities should create partnerships for mental health services for children and adolescents.

Since the last edition of this book, much has happened in the area of evidence-based practice (EBP). Just a few years ago, the National Institutes of Health was discussing getting new evidence translated into practice/policies—better known as translational science. Today, the conversation has moved from "translational science" to "implementation science." The whole notion of translation science, implementation, and EBP is far more developed in medicine than other fields (Howard, 2011). According to Proctor and Rosen, implementation of EBP (2008) refers to the use or employment by practitioners of pretested and empirically supported treatments (ETs) to attain an outcome. Please remember that intervention research focuses on the creation of knowledge, whereas implementation research focuses on knowledge and process to achieve effective goal attainment (Niederhuber, 2010; Proctor & Rosen, 2008)

What We Know

Evidence-Based: Definitions

The future of school social work may very well rest on the emerging concept of evidence-based practices, theories, interventions, and treatments. Although there is not currently a consensus about the definition of this concept (Hoagwood, 2003), many disciplines utilize the concept, and various definitions may be found within them. In this chapter, we attempt to define *evidence-based* in a manner that can be commonly understood.

There are two different understandings of what constitutes evidence-based in use. The first comes from the medical field, where evidence-based practice has been evolving as a standard for quite some time. In medicine, evidence-based practice is described as utilizing the best available evidence to guide decisions about patient health care and choices. Furthermore, these best practices are typically combined with what the physician has experienced in the clinical setting, as well as the patient's, beliefs and experiences (Mullen, 2002).

The second understanding comes from a social work and a social science perspective, particularly, in mental health, where the evidence-based movement is starting to truly take hold (Mullen, 2002). In the mental health field, evidence-based is considered to be "any practice that has been established as effective through scientific research according to some set of explicit criteria" (Mullen, n.p.). Criteria may include treatment standardization, treatment evaluation, controlled trials, or other scientifically tested or measured outcomes. Once those criteria are selected, theories or practices that meet them are considered part of the evidence base or best practices.

"'Evidence-based practice' refers to a body of scientific knowledge about service practices ... or about the impact of clinical treatments or services on the mental health problems of children and adolescents" (Hoagwood, Burns, Kiser, Ringeisen, & Schoenwald, 2001, p. 1179). In other words, evidence-based practice stresses that the need for a scientific base in theories and methods applied to social work practice. The theoretical must be tested and proven in order to generate best practices, which ultimately support a sound knowledge base, and to ensure the very same effectiveness and efficiency in service delivery mentioned previously. According to Huang, Hepburn, and Espiritu (2003):

> Evidence-based practice is an emerging concept and reflects a nationwide effort to build quality and accountability in health and behavioral health care service delivery. Underlying this concept is (1) the fundamental belief that children with emotional and behavioral disorders should be able to count on receiving care that meets their needs and is based on the best scientific knowledge available, and (2) the fundamental concern that for many of these children, the care that is delivered is not effective care. (p. 1)

It is important to remember that utilizing any evidence-based treatment with children, regardless of its efficacy, will bring with it special challenges due to the fact that children and adolescents are not the same as adults. These differences in physical changes ("children undergo more rapid psychological, neuronal, and psychological changes over a briefer period than adults" [Hoagwood et al., 2001, p. 1181]) must be considered. In addition, practitioners must take into consideration their interactions with family, as well as their environment, whether on the playground, at school, or at home (Hoagwood et al., 2001).

The School

Given the very fact that children spend a large portion of their time in school (7 hours a day, 5 days a week, 10 months a year), it makes sense that the educational community plays a strategic role in the lives of children and their families. Indeed, the school has historically been a location in which social workers felt they could assist in children's health and welfare. "Seventy to 80% of children who receive mental health services receive them in schools; for many children the school system provides their only form of mental health treatment" (Hoagwood et al., 2001, p. 1183).

The Report of the Surgeon General's Conference on Children's Mental Health (U.S. Department of Health and Human Services, 2000) calls attention to the growing numbers of youth suffering needlessly because their emotional, behavioral, and developmental needs are not being met. It strongly suggests that it is time for the nation to treat and prevent mental illness in our youth.

Furthermore, the surgeon general's report recognizes that the responsibility for mental health care for our youth is dispersed across numerous settings and organizations: schools, primary care, the juvenile justice system, and child/family welfare systems, to name only a few. Even when evidence-based treatments are available for use by providers, utilization of those treatments, in many instances, remains low.

Unfortunately, families often cannot turn to the community anticipating relief and assistance. Rogers (2003) documents the lack of community-based services for youth with serious emotional disturbances. While appropriate and timely intervention can prevent a host of problems, such as substance abuse, juvenile delinquency, and other behavioral problems, community-based services often come up lacking.

Jessie Taft, an early leader in the functionalist movement, wrote: "The only practical and effective way to increase the mental health of a nation is through its school system. Homes are too inaccessible. The school has the time of the child and the power to do the job" (Taft, 1923, p. 398). More recently, S. Hyman, then the director of the National Institute of Mental Health, spoke to the importance of the school system as the context for the identification and treatment of school-children needing mental health treatment (Rees, 1997).

While ripe for identifying and treating children who exhibit social and mental health needs, the educational system itself is often at the mercy of institutional, local, or federal pressures or demands. As Sipple (2004) states, "The American public educational system is a beleaguered public institution fraught with relentless criticism," adding that "schools are facing ever-challenging and complex educational situations while at the same time an unprecedented inspection and expectation of practice and performance" (p. 1). Services such as special education are underfunded, and state support is either erratic or dwindling, depending on the means of each state. Schools have to involve the multiple stakeholders in its governance and decision making, reform and restructure itself to obtain excellence and relevancy, and do all of this while being cost-efficient and effective. In addition, today's educational system has numerous responsibilities on its doorstep: federal, state, and local standards, desegregation, student diversity, underachieving students, and what to do with overachievers. Add to this the expectation that physical, emotional, and behavioral problems will be addressed, and you have an environment that is overwhelmed with multiple agendas and roles (Allen-Meares, 2004). Clearly, the school and its personnel cannot achieve these multiple and important imperatives in isolation of other relevant and interested parties (e.g., community, parents).

Pertinent professional providers located in the community in collaboration with parents and school personnel will need to become a part of the solution and respond to the mental health and health issues that are going undiagnosed among pupils. We envision unusual and innovative collaborations and partnerships between the school and its community network of service providers in the decades ahead. What are currently atypical contractual arrangements between schools and their communities must become more common. Furthermore, knowledge from a cross-section of practices and empirical literatures is needed to arm these professionals with new ways to identify, treat, and prevent mental illness among children and adolescents. "No one discipline has a privileged view of either pathogenesis or treatment of mental disorders" (Rees, 1997, p. 8).

An example of a book that targets another field of social work practice, but that has relevance for this discussion, is *What Works in Child Welfare*, edited by Kluger, Alexander, and Curtis (2001). Several chapters in this book focus on interventions targeting school-age populations useful for school social workers (e.g., alcohol and drug use among adolescents, comparisons of cognitive behavioral therapy and supportive therapy, positive youth development and mentoring, what works in the treatment of delinquent youths, etc.).

What We Can Do

Criteria for the Selection of Evidence-Based Intervention

As reflected in this book, various interventions have different levels of scientific sophistication or rigor undergirding them. When considering what interventions to utilize in a school setting or a school–community provider collaboration, the following criteria should be taken into consideration (please note that this list is not exhaustive):

1. Where does the study fall on the continuum of scientific rigor? A treatment is considered to be well established if two or more studies find it superior to wait-listed control conditions, one experiment must meet criteria for a well-established treatment, or three single case studies must be conducted (Rogers, 2003). Outcome measures must be relevant and evaluation measurements must be of high quality and meet appropriate psychometric standards.
2. Was the design of the study effective? Evidence-based treatment should be supported by group design or single-subject experiments (Rogers, 2003).
3. Is the study transportable? One of the challenges of utilizing evidence-based interventions is transportability—that is to say, will the outcomes of the scientific study that validated this intervention in a laboratory or a clinical setting be consistent when applied in a school setting (Hoagwood et al., 2001)?
4. Are there contextual variables required for optimal outcomes? Services to children/youth are delivered in a variety of unique contexts—schools, child and family agencies, family, correctional systems, and community mental health centers. It is therefore urgent for the practitioner to know the context in which the research on the intervention was conducted (Hoagwood et al., 2001).
5. What were the characteristics of the experimental/treatment group in terms of important

demographics and problems in functioning? Attention to the fit with the population that is the target of the intervention is important (Hoagwood et al., 2001). In other words, there should be congruency between the experimental sample and those that are the target of application in practice.

6. Does the intervention consider co-occurring disorders? Often the intervention focuses on one specific disorder and does not adequately take into account the possibility of other disorders that are present and/or the heterogeneity of the mental health problems broadly defined within childhood and adolescence (Hoagwood, 2003).
7. Is the intervention age appropriate or developmentally sensitive? For example, an intervention found to be effective with preadolescent youth to reduce depression may well be ineffective for adolescent youths (Hoagwood et al., 2001), and similarly, effective treatments used with adults may not affect children in the same manner.
8. When should a practitioner consider a specific drug to be effective? A drug is considered efficacious if studied through random assignment and control group comparison, and with replicated results in one or more similarly well-controlled studies. Drugs can be considered efficacious following one randomized trial (Ringeisen, 2003).
9. Is the intervention culturally sensitive? Was the target group in the experiment or clinical group or single-case design comparable in terms of race, ethnicity, and so on? As the population of the United States continues to become larger and more diverse, this factor will become increasingly important (Rogers, 2003).

Implementation in Practice Setting

The National Institutes of Health (NIH) has made translational research at its institutes a priority by launching the Clinical and Translational Science Award (CTSA) in 2006 (Woolf, 2008). As a consequence, the mantra is from "bench to bedside." By 2012, the NIH expects to fund 60 such centers with a budget of $500 million per year (National Institutes of Health, 2007). The use of evidence-based knowledge is, as mentioned, gaining a foothold in social work and social science theory. How then do practitioners make the move from what they know to what science proves to be effective? Huang et al. (2003) state that "changing practice is a formidable task that occurs at a painstakingly slow pace, often requiring not only changes in practice behaviors, but restructuring programs and allocating an infusion of upfront resources" (p. 1). So how do we make this move to a more effective service delivery?

The challenges of implementing scientific evidence in practice are complex because many client and situational variables, etc., as well as practitioner's skill level, infringe on the process. In other words, implementing science takes place in the real world. Furthermore, "implementation" would need to be evaluated in order to determine goal attainment.

According to a meta-analysis, several strategies have been used to influence behavioral health care professionals to incorporate evidence-based practices into their professional behaviors (Gira, Kessler, & Poertner, 2004). These include:

1. *Dissemination.* One of the most important aspects of getting practitioners to explore and utilize new approaches and scientific data is simply ensuring they are exposed to it. A simple way to do this is through dissemination. This approach can range from the publication of guidelines, mass mailings, web sites, compiled notebooks, and so on.
2. *Continuing education.* Continuing education coursework and seminars are a part of many professions, encouraging practitioners to stay current on methods and literature after obtaining their degrees. This approach has been found to be effective in exposing practitioners to evidence-based materials and theory in randomized controlled trials, when small group activities and practice sessions are available to participants.
3. *Educational outreach.* Thomson O'Brien, et al. (2001) define an educational outreach visit as a visit paid by a trained educator with the intent of providing information to the practitioner. The educator brings the practitioner up-to-date on current practices through education, materials, and feedback.
4. *Local opinion leaders.* These individuals are defined by their colleagues as "educationally influential" (p. 73). Although it is sometimes unclear what their exact role in the professional community is, local opinion leaders typically serve as role models who assist in the

dissemination, acceptance, and implementation of evidence-based practice.

5. *Audit and feedback.* Audit and feedback is a snapshot of a practice over a period of time. Experts review a practitioner's interaction with clients and provide documentation regarding the practitioner's use of evidence-based theories and methods. Documentation may also include feedback about the "congruency between practice and best evidence" (p. 73).
6. *Continuous quality improvement (CQI).* Much like quality programs in the business world, this approach looks not at an individual's performance, but instead at the organizational level. One difference between this and other quality programs is that CQI seeks to improve both the management of administrative procedures and clinical practices.
7. *Technology.* Technology may be utilized in a variety of ways, whether tracking practice statistics, educating patients, or accessing patient data during consultation. Social workers typically use technology to keep records and collect data, not to choose or document effective treatments, although the potential to plan or choose interventions is a distinct possibility.
8. *Mass media campaigns.* Campaigns target the consumer of intervention services, working on the patient's right and ability to ask the right questions, press for different treatments, and basically manage their own care. These campaigns might include TV ads, pamphlets, and so on.

Where Do We Go From Here?

Social work practitioners, both in and out of school settings, are seeing a definite shift from traditionally accepted practices to the cutting-edge best practices. It is important to remember that whether a practitioner is quick to embrace new and better practices or moves slowly and deliberately toward the future, the ultimate goal of treatment and intervention should be concerned with the health and mental health of the children they are charged with helping.

The 2000 Surgeon General's Report (U.S. DHSS, 2000) identified several key goals that are crucial to the treatment of children with mental health issues as social work and other social sciences move from the tried and true to the tested and approved. They are as follows:

1. The development, dissemination, and implementation of best practices derived from a scientific evidence base must continue.
2. Knowledge on a variety of factors, including social and psychological development, must be researched in order "to design better screening, assessment, and treatment tools, and to develop prevention programs" (p. 5).
3. Research on contexts (e.g., school, family, community) must be supported. This research will assist us in identifying opportunities "for promoting mental health services and for providing effective prevention, treatment, and services" (p. 5).
4. Research to develop and test innovative behavioral, pharmacological, and other "mixed" interventions must also be encouraged.
5. Research on proven treatments, practices, and services developed in a lab must be increased, particularly the assessment of their effectiveness in "real-world settings" (p. 5).
6. Similarly, the effectiveness of clinical and community practices must also be studied in context.
7. Development of model programs should be encouraged, particularly those that can be sustained on a community level.
8. Private and public partnerships are key elements in facilitating the dissemination and cross-fertilization of knowledge.
9. The understanding of children's mental health care needs must increase. Additionally, training to assist practitioners to address the various mental issues among children with special health care needs and their families is necessary and urgent.
10. Research on factors that facilitate or impede the implementation of scientifically proven interventions must take place as part of the evaluation process.

Applying Interventions within a Response to Intervention Framework

Response to Intervention (RTI) has become a significant concept discussed in the evidence-based literatures. It focuses on identifying and treating children with learning disabilities (Frey, Lingo & Nelson, 2010). "Response to Intervention (RTI) is a philosophy and/or process that encompasses alternative assessment which utilizes quality interventions matched to students needs, coupled with formative evaluation to obtain data over time to make critical educational decisions. Select relevant core assumptions include:

1. that "the implementation of a multi-tiered service delivery model is necessary
2. that research-based interventions should be implemented to the extent possible
3. that progress monitoring must be implemented to inform instruction
4. that data should drive decision making ..." (http://en.wikipedia.org/wiki/Response_to_intervention)

RTI, like any other concept, has its proponents and opponents. Unfortunately, that discussion is beyond the scope of this chapter. However, RTI's reliance on evidence-based intervention is another critical step toward the integration of research in practice.

Key Points to Remember

In order for practitioners, particularly those involved in mental health services for children and adolescents, to successfully take a step toward a future practice undergirded by scientific evidence, the following must be kept in the forefront of their minds:

- Evidence-based practice is built upon a scientific foundation, meaning that it has been tested using specific criteria and proven effective. Implementation of evidenced-based theories and practices into real-world application will ensure that social workers and other mental health professionals are utilizing the best practices for the children they serve.
- The use of these evidence-based best practices may be useful in a school setting if additional criteria, such as scientific rigor and developmental appropriateness, are considered.
- School is one area where a large portion of children may be diagnosed and assisted with mental health or other social issues.
- When appropriate to do so, the creation of partnerships with family, community agencies, and other resources will help to sustain change.
- Sustainability is critical. Involving family members, other professionals, and relevant institutional providers in intervention planning, where and when appropriate, increases the likelihood that the change will be sustained.
- Training, further research, and technical support opportunities are needed to increase the likelihood that practitioners will adopt an evidenced-based practice.

May this book be a catalyst for change and effectiveness.

References

Allen-Meares, P. (2004). School social work: Historical development, influences, and practices. In P. Allen-Meares (Ed.), Social work services in schools (pp. 23–51). Boston: Pearson Education, Inc.

Frey, A., Lingo, A., & Nelson, C. M. (2010). Positive behavior support and response to intervention in elementary schools. In H. Walker, M. K. Shinn, & G. Stoner (Eds.), *Interventions for achievement and behavior problems: preventive and remedial approaches* (Vol. 3, pp.): National Association for School Psychologists.

Gira, E. C., Kessler, M. L., & Poertner, J. (2004). Influencing social workers to use research evidence in practice: Lessons from medicine and the allied health professions. *Research on Social Work Practice, 14*(2), 68–79.

Hoagwood, K., Burns, B. J., Kiser, L., Ringeisen, H., & Schoenwald, S. K. (2001). Evidence-based practice in child and adolescent mental health services. Psychiatric Services, *52*(9), 1179–1189.

Hoagwood, K. (2003). Evidence-based practice in children's mental health services: What do we know? Why aren't we putting it to use? Data Matters, 6, 4–5.

Howard, M. (2011, July). Personal communication. Email. M. Kluger, G. Alexander, & P. Curtis (2001) (Eds.), *What works in child welfare?* Washington, DC: Child Welfare League of America.

Huang, L. N., Hepburn, M. S., & Espiritu, R. C. (2003). To be or not to be ... evidence-based? *Data Matters, 6*, 1–3.

Kluger, G., Alexander, P., & Cutis (2001). *What works in child welfare.* Washington, DC: Child Welfare League of America.

Mullen, E. J. (2002, July). *Evidence-based social work-theory & practice: Historical and reflective perspective.* Minutes from the Campbell collaboration and evidence-based social work practice session at the International Conference on Evaluation for Practice, Tampere, Finland.

National Institutes of Health. (n.d). *Re-engineering the clinical research enterprise: Translational research.* Retrieved November 17, 2007, from http://nihroadmap.nih.gov/clinicalresearch/overview-translational.asp.

Niederhuber, J. E. (2010, March). Translating discovery to patient care. *JAMA, 303*(11), 1088–1089.

Proctor, E., & Rosen, A. (2008). From knowledge production to implementation: research challenges and imperatives. *Research on Social Work Practice. 18*(4), 286–191.

Rees, C. (1997). Ask the doctor: On children and mental illness. *NAMI Advocate, 8*, 10.

Ringeisen, H. (2003). Identifying efficacious interventions for children's mental health: What are the criteria and how can they be used? *Data Matters, 6*, 10–11.

Rogers, K. (2003). Evidence-based community-based interventions. In A. J. Pumariega & N. C. Winters (Eds.), *The handbook of child and adolescent systems of care* (pp. 149–170). San Francisco, CA: Jossey-Bass.

Sipple, J. (2004). Major issues in American schools. In P. Allen-Meares (Ed.), *Social work services in schools* (pp. 1–21). Boston: Pearson Education, Inc.

Taft, J. (1923). The relation of the school of mental health of the average child. *Proceedings of the National Conference of Social Work* (p. 398). Chicago: University of Chicago Press.

Thomson O'Brien, M. A., Oxman, A. D., Davis, D. A., Haynes, R. B., Freemantle, N., & Harvey, E. L. (2001). *Educational outreach visits: Effects on professional practice and health care outcomes.* Cochrane Effective Practice and Organisation of Care Group Cochrane Database of Systematic Reviews, 1. Retrieved August 22, 2005, from http://www.cochrane.org/cochrane/revabstr/AB000409.htm

U.S. Department of Health and Human Services (2000). *Report of the surgeon general's conference on children's mental health: A national action agenda.* Washington, DC: Department of Health and Human Services.

Woolf, S. H. (2008). The meaning of translational research and why it matters—Commentary. *JAMA, 299*(2), 211–213.

Index

Italicized page numbers refer to boxes, figures and tables.